End to End GUI Development with Qt5

Develop cross-platform applications with modern
UIs using the powerful Qt framework

A learning path in three sections

Pack‹t›

BIRMINGHAM - MUMBAI

End to End GUI Development with Qt5

Authors: Nicholas Sherriff, Guillaume Lazar, Robin Penea, Marco Piccolino
Reviewer: Vishnu Reddy, Sivan Greenberg, Ray Rischpater, Pierre-Yves Siret, Jürgen Bocklage-Ryannel
Content Development Editor: Priyanka Sawant
Graphics: Jason Monterio
Production Coordinator: Nilesh Mohite

Published on: September 2018

Production reference: 1240918

Published by Packt Publishing Ltd.
Livery Place
35 Livery Street
Birmingham
B3 2PB, UK.

ISBN 978-1-78953-190-9

www.packtpub.com

Mapt

Mapt is an online digital library that gives you full access to over 5,000 books and videos, as well as industry leading tools to help you plan your personal development and advance your career. For more information, please visit our website.

Why subscribe?

- Spend less time learning and more time coding with practical eBooks and Videos from over 4,000 industry professionals

- Improve your learning with Skill Plans built especially for you

- Get a free eBook or video every month

- Mapt is fully searchable

- Copy and paste, print, and bookmark content

PacktPub.com

Did you know that Packt offers eBook versions of every book published, with PDF and ePub files available? You can upgrade to the eBook version at www.PacktPub.com and as a print book customer, you are entitled to a discount on the eBook copy. Get in touch with us at service@packtpub.com for more details.

At www.PacktPub.com, you can also read a collection of free technical articles, sign up for a range of free newsletters, and receive exclusive discounts and offers on Packt books and eBooks.

Table of Contents

Section 3: Qt 5 Projects

Preface

Qt 5.9 is an application development framework that provides a great user experience and develops full-capability applications with Qt Widgets, QML, and even Qt 3D. This learning path demonstrates the power and flexibility of the Qt framework for desktop application development and shows how you can write your application once and deploy it to multiple operating systems. It will address all the challenges while developing cross-platform applications with the Qt framework.

Through this learning path, you will have a better understanding of the Qt framework and the tools to resolve serious issues such as linking, debugging, and multithreading. It will also upskill you by teaching how to create a to-do style app by going via all stages for building a successful project. You will build a suite of apps and while developing these apps you'll deepen your knowledge of Qt Quick's layout systems, and see Qt 3D and Widgets in action. The next project will be for industrial and agricultural sectors, to make sense of sensor data via a monitoring system. The apps should run seamlessly across devices and operating systems like Android, iOS, Windows, or Mac, and be cost-effective by integrating with existing web technologies. You take the role of lead developer and prototype the monitoring system. In doing so you'll get to know Qt's Bluetooth and HTTP APIs, as well as the Charts and Web Engine UI modules. These projects will help you gain a holistic view of the Qt framework.

Who this learning path is for

This book will appeal to developers and programmers who would like to build GUI-based applications. Knowledge of C++ is necessary and the basics of Qt would be helpful.

What this learning path covers

Section 1, Learn Qt 5, it demonstrates the power and flexibility of the Qt framework for desktop application development and shows how you can write your application once and deploy it to multiple operating systems.

Section 2, Mastering QT 5, you'll address all the challenges while developing cross-platform applications with the Qt framework. Through this learning path, you will have a better understanding of the Qt framework and the tools to resolve serious issues such as linking, debugging, and multithreading. It will also upskill you by teaching how to create a to-do style app by going via all stages for building a successful project.

Section 3, Qt 5 Projects, the project will be for industrial and agricultural sectors, to make sense of sensor data via a monitoring system. The apps should run seamlessly across devices and operating systems like Android, iOS, Windows, or Mac, and be cost-effective by integrating with existing web technologies. You take the role of lead developer and prototype the monitoring system. In doing so you'll get to know Qt's Bluetooth and HTTP APIs, as well as the Charts and Web Engine UI modules. These projects will help you gain a holistic view of the Qt framework.

To get the most out of this learning path

A good understanding of C++ language is highly recommended as the book is for the developers and programmers who want to build GUI-based applications. You will need any OS (Windows, Linux, or macOS) and any C++ compiler installed on your systems in order to get started.

Download the example code files

You can download the example code files for this learning path from your account at www.packtpub.com. If you purchased this learning path elsewhere, you can visit www.packtpub.com/support and register to have the files emailed directly to you.

You can download the code files by following these steps:

1. Log in or register at www.packtpub.com.
2. Select the **SUPPORT** tab.
3. Click on **Code Downloads & Errata**.
4. Enter the name of the learning path in the **Search** box and follow the onscreen instructions.

Once the file is downloaded, please make sure that you unzip or extract the folder using the latest version of:

- WinRAR/7-Zip for Windows
- Zipeg/iZip/UnRarX for Mac
- 7-Zip/PeaZip for Linux

The code bundle for the book is also hosted on GitHub at `https://github.com/PacktPublishing/Book-Name`. In case there's an update to the code, it will be updated on the existing GitHub repository.

We also have other code bundles from our rich catalog of books and videos available at `https://github.com/PacktPublishing/`. Check them out!

Conventions used

There are a number of text conventions used throughout this book.

`CodeInText`: Indicates code words in text, database table names, folder names, filenames, file extensions, pathnames, dummy URLs, user input, and Twitter handles. Here is an example: "Mount the downloaded `WebStorm-10*.dmg` disk image file as another disk in your system."

A block of code is set as follows:

```
html, body, #map {
 height: 100%;
 margin: 0;
 padding: 0
}
```

When we wish to draw your attention to a particular part of a code block, the relevant lines or items are set in bold:

```
[default]
exten => s,1,Dial(Zap/1|30)
exten => s,2,Voicemail(u100)
exten => s,102,Voicemail(b100)
exten => i,1,Voicemail(s0)
```

Any command-line input or output is written as follows:

```
$ mkdir css
$ cd css
```

Bold: Indicates a new term, an important word, or words that you see onscreen. For example, words in menus or dialog boxes appear in the text like this. Here is an example: "Select **System info** from the **Administration** panel."

Warnings or important notes appear like this.

Tips and tricks appear like this.

Get in touch

Feedback from our readers is always welcome.

General feedback: Email `feedback@packtpub.com` and mention the learning path title in the subject of your message. If you have questions about any aspect of this learning path, please email us at `questions@packtpub.com`.

Errata: Although we have taken every care to ensure the accuracy of our content, mistakes do happen. If you have found a mistake in this learning path, we would be grateful if you would report this to us. Please visit `www.packtpub.com/submit-errata`, selecting your learning path, clicking on the Errata Submission Form link, and entering the details.

Piracy: If you come across any illegal copies of our works in any form on the Internet, we would be grateful if you would provide us with the location address or website name. Please contact us at `copyright@packtpub.com` with a link to the material.

If you are interested in becoming an author: If there is a topic that you have expertise in and you are interested in either writing or contributing to a book, please visit `authors.packtpub.com`.

Reviews

Please leave a review. Once you have read and used this learning path, why not leave a review on the site that you purchased it from? Potential readers can then see and use your unbiased opinion to make purchase decisions, we at Packt can understand what you think about our products, and our authors can see your feedback on their book. Thank you!

For more information about Packt, please visit `packtpub.com`.

1
Learn Qt 5

Build modern, responsive cross-platform desktop applications with Qt, C++, and QML

1
Hello Qt

Qt is a mature and powerful framework for delivering sophisticated applications across a multitude of platforms. It is widely used in embedded devices including TVs, satellite set-top boxes, medical equipment, car dashboards, and much more. It also has a rich history in the Linux world, with KDE and Sailfish OS using it extensively and many apps in the stores being developed using Qt. It has also made great strides in the Mobile arena over the past several years. However, in the Microsoft Windows and Apple Mac OS X worlds, the dominance of C#/.NET and Objective-C/Cocoa mean that Qt is often overlooked.

This book aims to demonstrate the power and flexibility of the Qt framework and show how you can write your application once and deploy it to multiple operating system desktops. We will build a complete real-world **line of business** (**LOB**) solution from scratch, with distinct library, user interface, and unit test projects.

We will cover building a modern, responsive user interface with QML and wiring it up to rich C++ classes. We will control every aspect of our project configuration and output with QMake, including platform detection and conditional expressions. We will build "self-aware" data entities that can serialize themselves to and from JSON. We will persist those data entities in a database and learn how to find and update them. We will reach out to the internet and consume an RSS feed. Finally, we will produce an installation package so that we can deploy our application onto other machines.

In this chapter, we will install and configure the Qt framework and associated **Integrated Development Environment** (**IDE**) Qt Creator. We will create a simple scratchpad application that we will use throughout the remainder of the book to demonstrate various techniques. We will cover the following topics:

- Installing Qt
- Maintaining your installation

- Qt Creator
- Scratchpad project
- qmake

Installing Qt

Let's start things off by visiting the Qt website at `https://www.qt.io`:

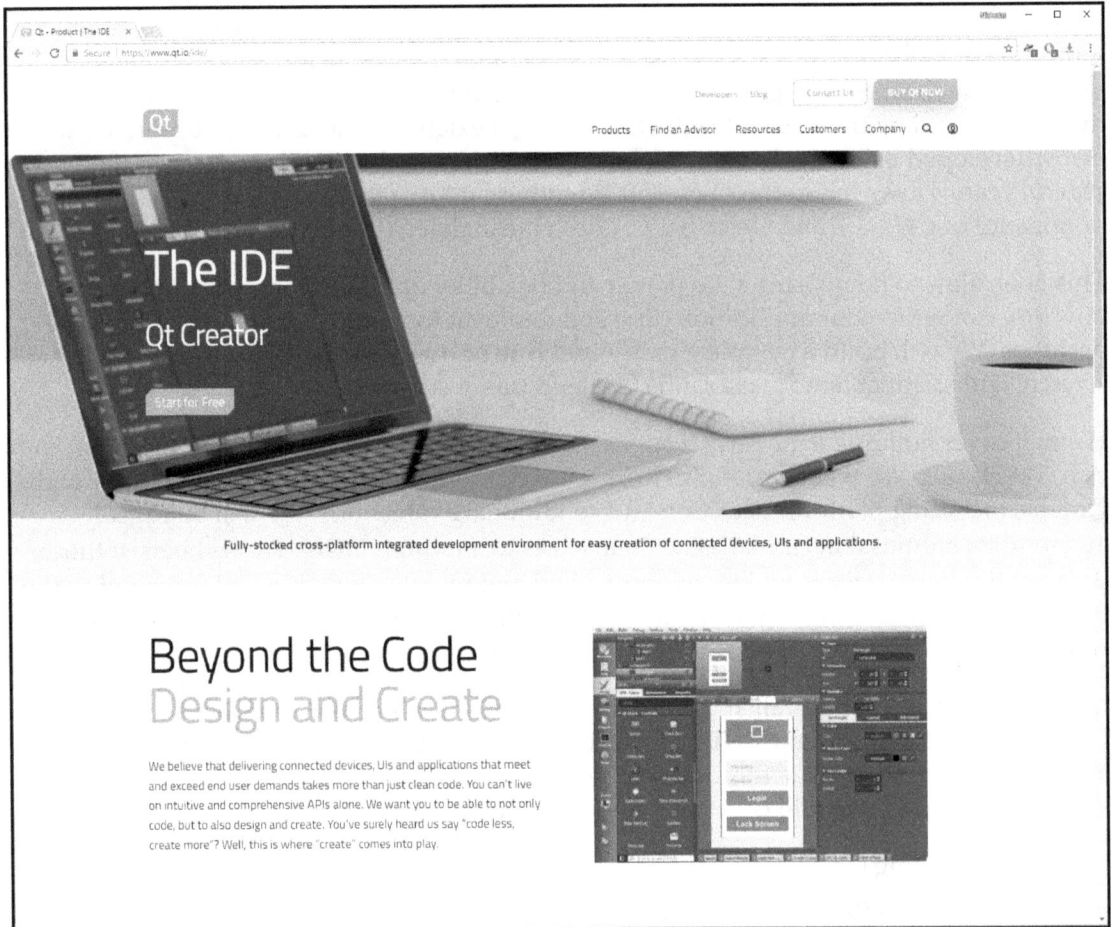

The site layout changes fairly frequently, but what you are looking for is to download Qt Open Source for **Desktop & Mobile**:

1. From the top-level menu, select **Products** and then **IDE & Tools**
2. Click on **Start for Free**
3. Select **Desktop & Mobile Applications**
4. Click on **Get your open source package**

> If you continue to use Qt beyond these personal projects, ensure that you read the licensing information available on the Qt website (`https://www.qt.io/licensing/`). Upgrade to the commercial Qt license if the scope of your projects requires it or if you want access to the official Qt support and the benefits of a close strategic relationship with the Qt company.

The site will detect your operating system and suggest a recommended download:

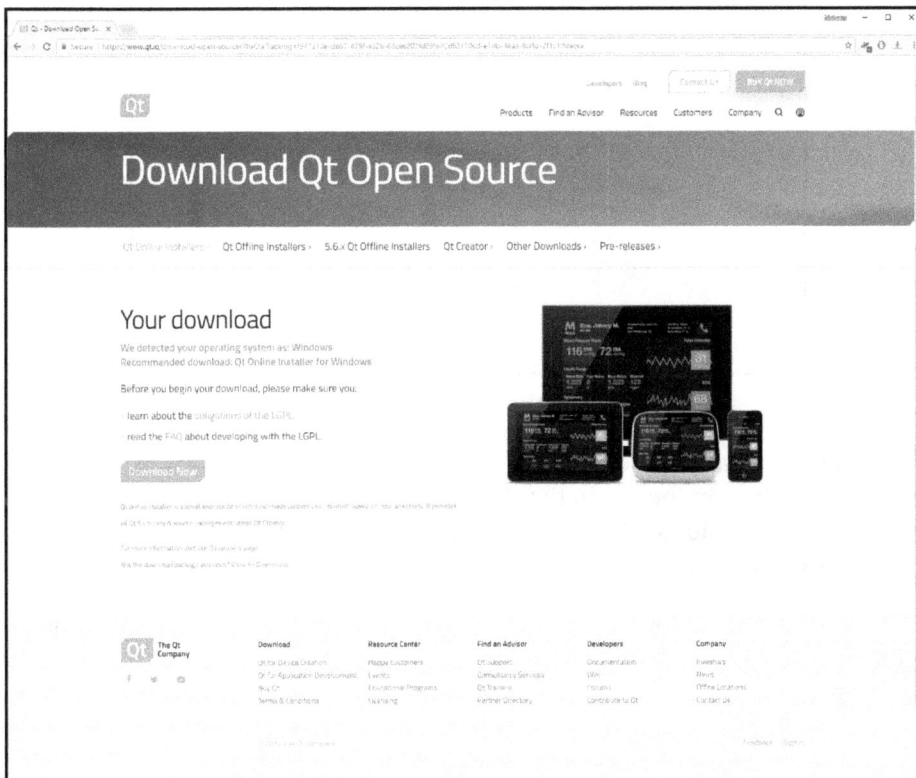

On Windows, you will be recommended the online installer * .exe file, while on Linux you will be offered a * . run file, and a .dmg file if you are running Mac OS X. In all cases, download and launch the installer:

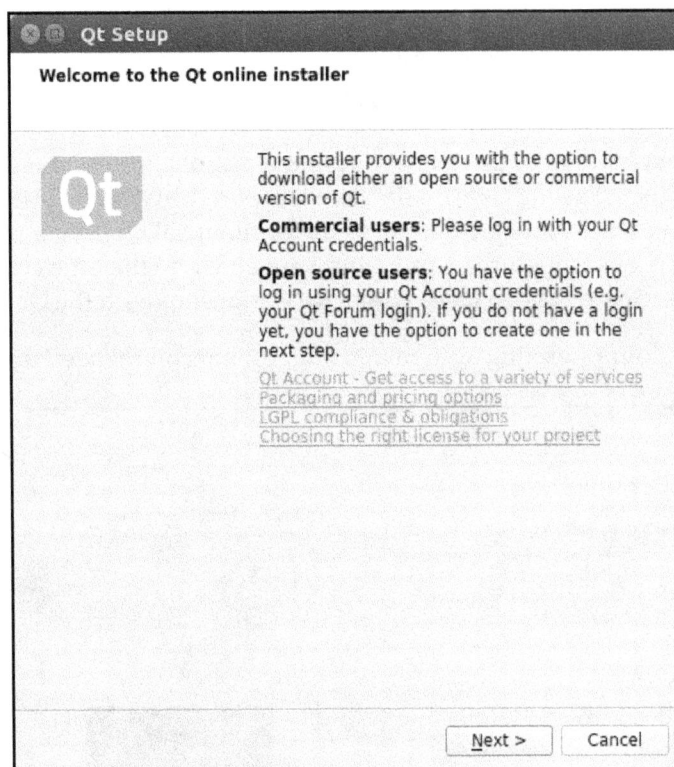

On Linux, once downloaded, you may need to first navigate to the * . run file and mark it as executable in order to be able to launch it. To do this, right-click on the file in the file manager and click on **Properties**. Click on the **Permissions** tab and tick the box that says **Allow executing file as program**.

After the initial welcome dialog, the first thing you are presented with is the option to sign up for or log in with a Qt account. Feel free to create one if you wish, but for now we'll go ahead and **Skip**:

Maintain Qt

Qt Account – Your unified login to everything Qt

Please log in to Qt Account

Login | Email

Password

Forgot password?

Need a Qt Account?

Sign-up | Valid email address

Password

Confirm Password

☐ I accept the service terms.

☐ Uninstall only

Settings   Skip   Cancel

You are then asked to select which components you wish to install.

Your first decision is which version(s) of the Qt framework you want. You can have
multiple versions installed side by side. Let's select the latest and greatest (Qt 5.10 at the
time of writing) and leave all the older versions unchecked.

Next, expand the selected version and you will see a secondary list of options. All the options where the description reads "Qt 5.9.x Prebuilt Components for ..." are what is known as a **Kit**. A Kit is essentially a toolset enabling you to build your application with a specific compiler/linker and run it on a particular target architecture. Each kit comes with Qt framework binaries compiled specifically for that particular toolset as well as necessary supporting files. Note that kits do not come with the referenced compiler; you will need to install those ahead of time. One exception to this on Windows is MinGW (which includes GCC for Windows), which you can optionally install via the Tools component list at the bottom.

On Windows, that is exactly what we'll do, so we select the **MinGW 5.3.0 32 bit** kit and also the **MinGW 5.3.0** development environment from the Tools section. On my (64-bit) machine, I already have Microsoft Visual Studio 2017 installed, so we will also select the MSVC 2017 64-bit kit to help demonstrate some techniques later in the book. On Linux, we select GCC 64-bit, while on Mac OS, we select macOS 64-bit (which uses the Clang compiler). Note that on Mac OS, you must have XCode installed, and it's a good idea to launch XCode at least once to give it an opportunity to complete its initialization and configuration.

Feel free to press pause, go and install whatever other IDEs or compilers you want to use, and then come back and pick the kits to match. It doesn't matter too much which you go for—the techniques explained throughout the book are applicable regardless of the kit, you may just get slightly different results. Note that the available kits you are presented with will differ depending on your operating system and chipset; for example, if you are on a 32 bit machine, you won't be offered any 64 bit kits.

> Below the kits are some optional Qt APIs (such as Qt Charts), which we won't need for the topics covered in this book, but feel free to add them in if you want to explore their functionality. Note that they may have different licensing agreements from the core Qt framework.

Regardless of kits and APIs, you will note in the **Tools** section that Qt Creator is installed by default and that is the IDE we will be using throughout this book:

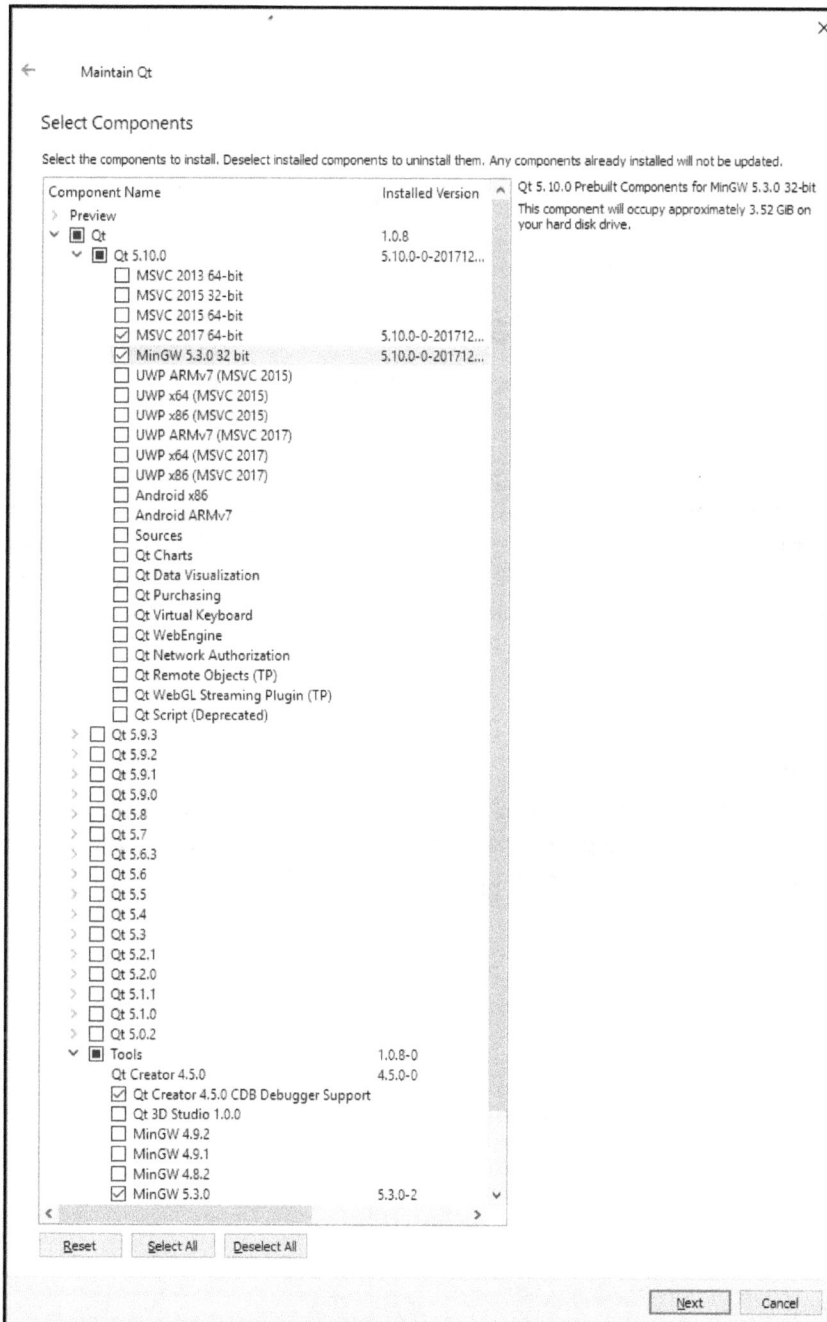

Once you are finished making your selections, click on **Next** and **Update** to kick off the installation.

> It's generally a good idea to leave the installation location as the default for consistency across machines, but feel free to install it wherever you want.

Maintaining your installation

Once installed, you can update, add, and remove components (or even the entire Qt installation) via the `Maintenance Tool` application that is located in the directory you installed Qt to.

Launching this tool provides pretty much the same experience as when we first installed Qt. The **Add or remove components** option is the one you want to add in items you may have previously not needed, including kits and even entirely new releases of the framework. Unless you actively uncheck them, components already installed on your system will not be affected.

Qt Creator

While a detailed overview of Qt Creator is beyond the scope of this book (the Qt Creator manual is accessible via the Help mode as described here), it's worth having a quick whistle stop tour before we get stuck to our first project, so launch the freshly installed application and we'll take a look:

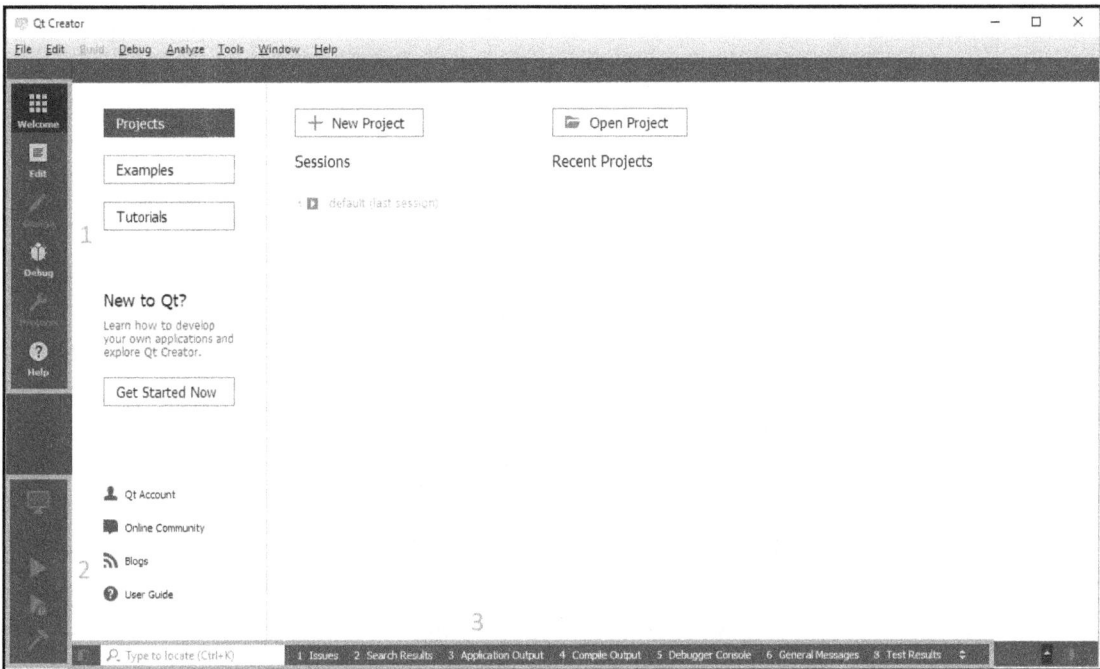

At the upper left-hand side (**1**) are the different areas or modes of the application:

- **Welcome** mode is the default when Qt Creator is launched and is the jumping off point to create or open projects. There is an extensive set of examples that help showcase the various capabilities of the framework as well as a selection of tutorial videos.
- **Edit** mode is where you will be spending the vast majority of your time and is used for editing all the various text-based files.
- **Design** is accessible only when you have a UI file open and is a WYSIWYG editor for views. Although useful for UX design and basic layout work, it can get frustrating quite quickly and we will do all of our QML work in Edit mode instead. Working this way promotes understanding of the QML (as you have to write it) and also has the advantage that the editor is not adding code that you don't want.
- **Debug** mode is used for debugging applications and is beyond the scope of this book.
- **Projects** mode is where configuration for the project is managed, including the build settings. Changes made here will be reflected in the `*.pro.user` file.
- **Help** mode takes you to the Qt Creator manual and Qt library reference.

Pressing *F1* while the cursor is on a recognized Qt symbol will automatically open context sensitive help for that symbol.

Below that, we have the build/run tools (**2**):

- **Kit/Build** lets you select your kit and set the build mode
- **Run** builds and runs the application without debugging
- **Start Debugging** builds and runs the application with a debugger (note that you must have a debugger installed and configured in your selected kit for this to work)
- **Build Project** builds the application without running it

Along the bottom (**3**), we have a search box and then several output windows:

Issues displays any warnings or errors. For compiler errors relating to your code, double-clicking on the item will navigate you to the relevant source code.

- **Search Results** lets you find occurrences of text within various scopes. *Ctrl + F* brings up a quick search, and from there selecting **Advanced...** also brings up the Search Results console.
- **Application Output** is the console window; all output from application code like `std::cout` and Qt's equivalent `qDebug()` appears here, along with certain messages from the Qt framework.
- **Compile Output** contains output from the build process, from qmake through to compilation and linking.
- **Debugger Console** contains debugging information that we won't be covering in this book.
- **General Messages** contains other miscellaneous output, the most useful of which is from qmake parsing of `*.pro` files, which we will look at later.

The search box really is a hidden gem and saves you from clicking through endless files and folders trying to find what you are looking for. You can start typing the name of a file you are looking for in the box and a filtered list appears with all matching files. Simply click on the file you want, and it opens in the editor. Not only that, there are a large number of filters you can apply too. Click your cursor in the empty search box and it displays a list of available filters. The filter m, for example, searches for C++ methods. So, say you remember writing a method called `SomeAmazingFunction()` but can't remember where it is, just head over to the search box, start typing m `Some`, and it will appear in the filtered list.

In **Edit** mode, the layout changes slightly and some new panes appear. Initially, they will be empty, but once you have a project open, they will resemble the following:

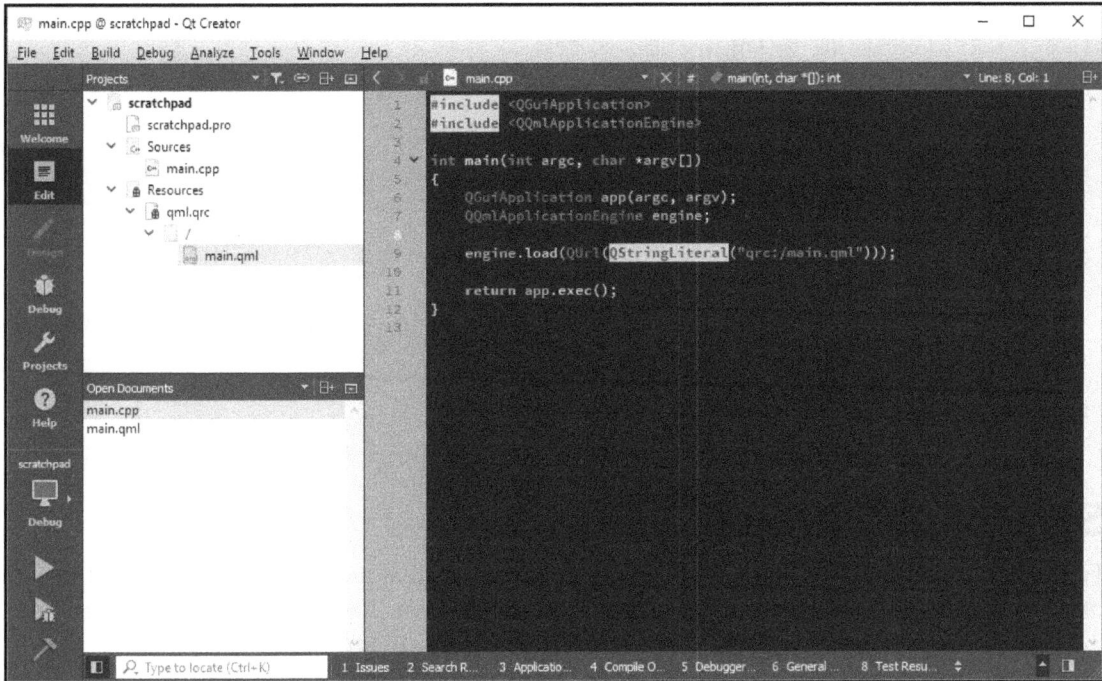

Next to the navigation bar is the project explorer, which you can use to navigate the files and folders of your solution. The lower pane is a list of all of the documents you currently have open. The larger area to the right is the editor pane where you write your code and edit documents.

Double-clicking on a file in the project explorer will generally open it in the editor pane and add it to the open documents list. Clicking on a document in the open documents list will activate it in the editor pane, while clicking on the small **x** to the right of the filename closes it.

Panes can be changed to display different information, resized, split, closed, and possibly filtered or synchronized with the editor using the buttons in the headers. Experiment to get a feel for what they can do.

As you would expect with a modern IDE, the look and feel of the chrome and the text editor is very customizable. Select **Tools > Options...** to see what is available. I generally edit the following:

- `Environment > Interface > Theme > Flat`
- `Text Editor > Fonts & Colors > Color Scheme > My own scheme`
- `Text Editor > Completion > Surround text selection with brackets > Off`
- `Text Editor > Completion > Surround text selection with quotes > Off`
- `C++ > Code Style > Current Settings > Copy... then Edit...`
- `Edit Code Style > Pointers and References > Bind to Type name > On (other options Off)`

Play around and get things how you like them.

Scratchpad project

To demonstrate how minimal a Qt project can be and to give us a programming sandpit to play around in, we'll create a simple scratchpad project. For this project, we won't even use the IDE to do it for us, so you can really see how projects are built up.

First, we need to create a root folder to store all of our Qt projects. On Windows, I use `c:projectsqt`, while I use `~/projects/qt` on Linux and Mac OS. Create this folder wherever works for you.

> Note that file syncing tools (OneDrive, DropBox, and so on) can sometimes cause problems with project folders, so keep your project files in a regular unsynchronized folder and use version control with a remote repository for backups and sharing.

For the remainder of the book, I will loosely refer to this folder as `<Qt Projects>` or similar. We will also tend toward using the Unix style / separator for file paths, rather than Windows style back slash . So, for readers using Windows, `<Qt Projects>/scratchpad/amazing/code` is equivalent to `c:projectsqtscratchpadamazingcode`. Qt tends to favor this convention too.

Equally, the majority of screenshots in the remainder of the book will be from Windows, so Linux/Mac users should interpret any references to `c:projectsqt` as `~/projects/qt`.

In our Qt projects folder, create a new folder `scratchpad` and navigate into it. Create a new plain text file called `scratchpad.pro`, remembering to remove any `.txt` extension the operating system may want to add for you.

Next, simply double-click on the file and it will open in **Qt Creator**:

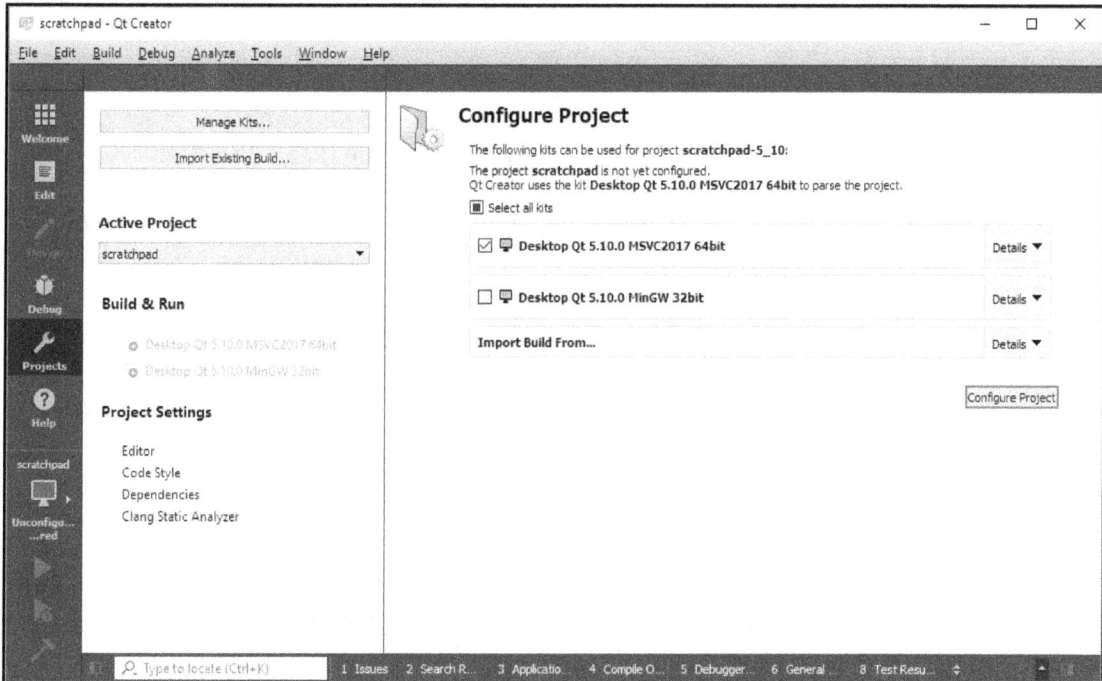

Here, Qt Creator is asking us how we want our project to be configured, namely, which kits we want to use when building and running our code. Pick one or more available kits and click on **Configure Project**. You can easily add and remove kits later, so don't worry about which ones you select.

If you switch back to the `filesystem`, you will see that Qt Creator has created a new file for us called `scratchpad.pro.user`. This is just an XML file containing configuration information. If you delete this file and open the `.pro` file again, you will be prompted to configure the project again. As its name suggests, the configuration settings are relevant to the local user, so often if you load a project created by someone else, you will need to go through the configure project step then too.

With the project successfully configured, you will see the project has been opened, even with a completely empty .pro file. That's about as minimal as a project can get!

Back in the filesystem, create the following plain text files:

- main.cpp
- main.qml
- qml.qrc

I will go through each of these files, explain their purpose, and add their content soon. In a real-world project, we would of course use the IDE to create the files for us. Indeed, that's exactly what we'll do when we create our main solution files. However, the purpose of doing it this way is to show you that when you boil it down, a project is just a bunch of text files. Never be afraid to create and edit files manually. A lot of modern IDEs can confuse and overcomplicate with menu after menu and never-ending option windows. Qt Creator may miss some of the advanced bells and whistles of other IDEs but is refreshingly lean and straightforward.

With those files created, double-click on the scratchpad.pro file in the **Projects** pane and we'll start editing our new project.

qmake

Our project (.pro) files are parsed by a utility called **qmake**, which in turn generates Makefiles that drive the building of the application. We define the type of project output we want, what source files are included as well as the dependencies and much more. Much of this is achieved by simply setting variables as we will do in our project file now.

Add the following to scratchpad.pro:

```
TEMPLATE = app

QT += qml quick

CONFIG += c++14
SOURCES += main.cpp
RESOURCES += qml.qrc
```

Let's run through each of these lines in turn:

```
TEMPLATE = app
```

`TEMPLATE` tells qmake what type of project this is. In our case, it's an executable application that is represented by `app`. Other values we are interested in are `lib` for building library binaries and `subdirs` for multi project solutions. Note that we set a variable with the = operator:

```
QT += qml quick
```

Qt is a modular framework that allows you to pull in only the parts you need. The `QT` flag specifies the Qt modules we want to use. The *core* and *gui* modules are included by default. Note that we append additional values to a variable that expects a list with +=:

```
CONFIG += c++14
```

`CONFIG` allows you to add project configuration and compiler options. In this case, we are specifying that we want to make use of C++14 features. Note that these language feature flags will have no effect if the compiler you are using does not support them:

```
SOURCES += main.cpp
```

`SOURCES` is a list of all the `*.cpp` source files we want to include in the project. Here, we add our empty `main.cpp` file, where we will implement our `main()` function. We don't have any yet, but when we do, our header files will be specified with a `HEADERS` variable:

```
RESOURCES += qml.qrc
```

`RESOURCES` is a list of all the resource collection files (`*.qrc`) included in the project. Resource collection files are used for managing application resources such as images and fonts, but most crucially for us, our QML files.

With the project file updated, save the changes.

Whenever you save a change to your `*.pro` files, qmake will parse the file. If all is well, you will get a small green bar at the bottom-right of Qt Creator. A red bar indicates some kind of issue, usually a syntax error. Any output from the process will be written out to the **General Messages** window to help you diagnose and fix the problem. White space is ignored, so don't worry about matching up the blank lines exactly.

To get qmake to take a fresh look at your project and generate new `Makefiles`, right-click on your project in the **Projects** pane and select **Run qmake**. It may be slightly tedious, but it's a good habit to manually run qmake in this way on each of your projects before building and running your application. I've found that certain types of code changes can "slip under the radar" and leave you scratching your head when you run your application and they don't seem to have had any effect. If you ever see your application ignoring the changes you've just made, run qmake on each of your projects and try again. The same applies if you get spurious linker errors.

You will see that our other files have now magically appeared in the **Projects** pane:

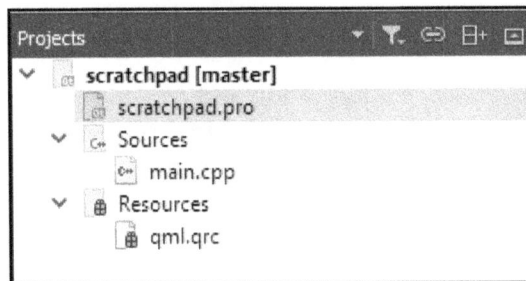

Double-click on `main.cpp` to edit it, and we'll write our first bit of code:

```cpp
#include <QGuiApplication>
#include <QQmlApplicationEngine>

int main(int argc, char *argv[])
{
    QGuiApplication app(argc, argv);
    QQmlApplicationEngine engine;

    engine.load(QUrl(QStringLiteral("qrc:/main.qml")));

    return app.exec();
}
```

All we are doing here is instantiating a Qt GUI application object and asking it to load our `main.qml` file. It's very short and simple because the Qt framework does all the complex low-level work for us. We don't have to worry about platform detection or managing window handles or OpenGL.

Possibly one of the most useful things to learn is that placing the cursor in one of the Qt objects and pressing *F1* will open the help for that type. The same is true for methods and properties on Qt objects. Poke around in the help files to see what `QGuiApplication` and `QQmlApplicationEngine` are all about.

To edit the next file in our project—`qml.qrc`—you need to right-click and select the editor you want to open it with. The default is Resource Editor:

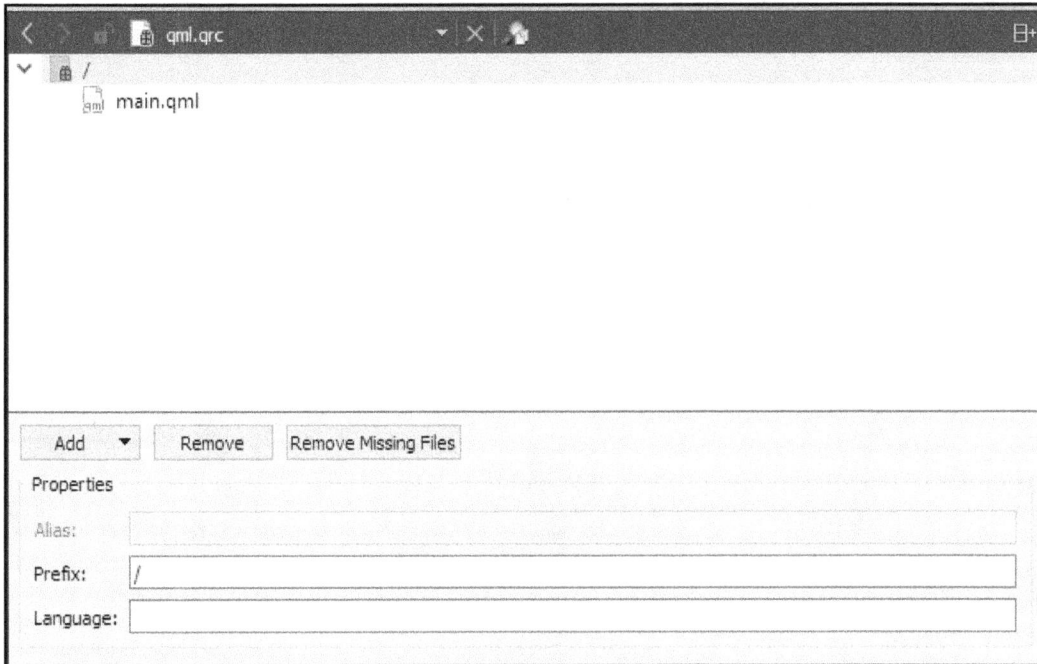

I am personally not a fan of this editor. I don't feel it makes editing any easier than just writing plain text and isn't particularly intuitive. Close this and instead choose `Open with > Plain Text Editor`.

Add the following content:

```
<RCC>
    <qresource prefix="/">
        <file>main.qml</file>
    </qresource>
</RCC>
```

Back in `main.cpp`, we asked Qt to load the `qrc:/main.qml` file. This essentially breaks down as "look for the file in a `qrc` file with a prefix of `/` and a name of `main.qml`". Now here in our `qrc` file, we have created a `qresource` element with a prefix property of `/`. Inside this element, we have a collection of resources (albeit only one of them) that has the name `main.qml`. Think of `qrc` files as a portable filesystem. Note that the resource files are located relative to the `.qrc` file that references them. In this case, our `main.qml` file is in the same folder as our `qml.qrc` file. If it was in a subfolder called `views`, for example, then the line in `qml.qrc` would read this way:

```
<file>views/main.qml</file>
```

Similarly, the string in `main.cpp` would be `qrc:/views/main.qml`.

Once those changes are saved, you will see our empty `main.qml` file appear as a child of the `qml.qrc` file in the **Projects** pane. Double-click on that file to edit it, and we will finish off our project:

```qml
import QtQuick 2.9
import QtQuick.Window 2.3

Window {
    visible: true
    width: 1024
    height: 768
    title: qsTr("Scratchpad")
    color: "#ffffff"

    Text {
        id: message
        anchors.centerIn: parent
        font.pixelSize: 44
        text: qsTr("Hello Qt Scratchpad!")
        color: "#008000"
    }
}
```

We will cover QML in detail in Chapter 2, *Project Structure*, but in brief, this file represents the screen or view presented to the user when the application launches.

The import lines are similar to `#include` statements in C++, though rather than including a single header file, they import a whole module. In this case, we want the base QtQuick module to give us access to all the core QML types and also the QtQuick window module to give us access to the `Window` component. Modules are versioned and generally, you will want to use the latest version for the release of Qt you are using. The current version numbers can be found in the Qt documentation. Note that although you get code completion when entering the version numbers, the options presented sometimes don't reflect the latest available versions.

As its name suggests, the `Window` element gives us a top-level window, inside which all of our other content will be rendered. We give it a size of 1024 x 765 pixels, a title of "scratchpad" and a background color of white represented as a hex RGB value.

Within that component (QML is a hierarchical markup language), we add a welcome message with the `Text` component. We center the text in the screen and set its font size and color, but other than that, we're not concerned with fancy formatting or anything at this stage, so that's as complicated as we'll make it. Again, we'll cover this in more detail later, so don't worry if it seems a bit alien.

That's it. To build and run our amazing new application, first select the **Kit** and **Build** configuration you want using the monitor icon at the bottom-left:

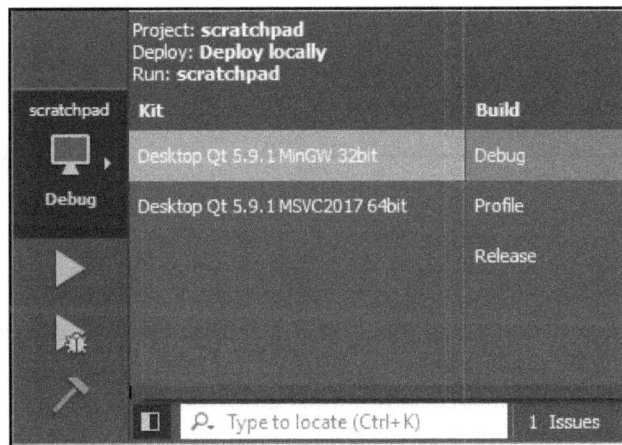

Next, right-click on the project name in the **Projects** pane and select **Run qmake**. When that has completed, **Run** the application using the green play icon:

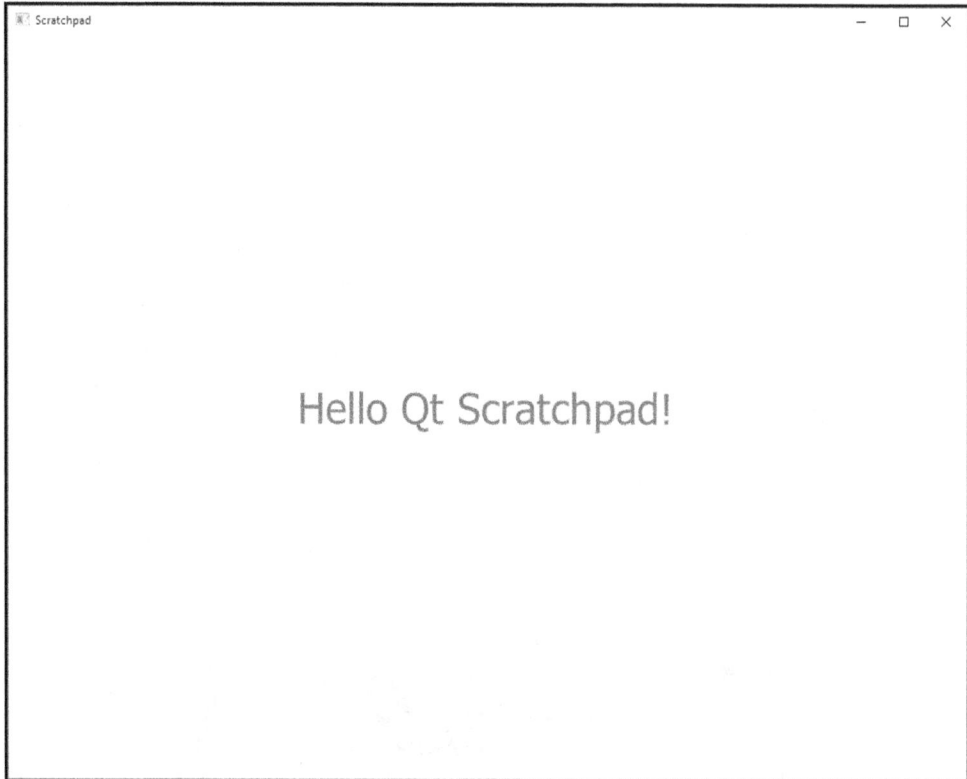

Summary

In this chapter, we downloaded, installed, and configured Qt. We've taken a whirlwind tour of the Qt Creator IDE, played with its options, and seen how to edit a variety of files with it. We've had a gentle introduction to qmake and seen how absurdly simple creating projects can be, demystifying things in the process. Finally, we built our debut project up from scratch (weak pun intended) and got the obligatory Hello World message on screen.

In Chapter 2, *Project Structure*, we will build on these basics and set up our main solution.

2
Project Structure

In this chapter, we will create a new multiproject solution that will be the foundation of our example application. We will apply a Model View Controller pattern, separating the user interface and business logic. We will also introduce Qt's unit testing framework—QtTest—and demonstrate how to integrate it into our solution. We will cover these things in this chapter:

- Projects, MVC, and unit testing
- Creating a library project
- Creating a unit tests project
- Creating a user interface project
- Mastering MVC
- The QObject base class
- QML
- Controlling project output

Projects, MVC, and unit testing

The scratchpad application we built in the previous chapter is a Qt project, represented by a `.pro` file. In a business environment, technical solutions are generally developed as part of company initiatives, and these initiatives are generally also called **projects**. To try and minimize confusion (and the number of times the word project appears!), we'll use project to mean a Qt project defined by a `.pro` file and the word initiative to refer to projects in the business sense.

The initiative we will work on will be a generic client management system. It will be something that can be tweaked and re purposed for multiple applications—for a supplier managing customers, a health service managing patients, and so on. It will perform common tasks found over and over in real-world **Line of Business (LOB)** applications, principally adding, editing, and deleting data.

Our scratchpad application is entirely encapsulated within a single project. For smaller applications, this is perfectly viable. However, with larger code bases, particularly with several developers involved, it often pays to break things up into more manageable pieces.

We will be using a super lightweight implementation of the **Model View Controller (MVC)** architectural pattern. If you haven't come across MVC before, it is primarily used to decouple business logic from the user interface. The user interface (View) relays commands to a switchboard style class (Controller) to retrieve the data and perform actions it needs. The controller in turn delegates the responsibility for the data, logic, and rules to data objects (Models):

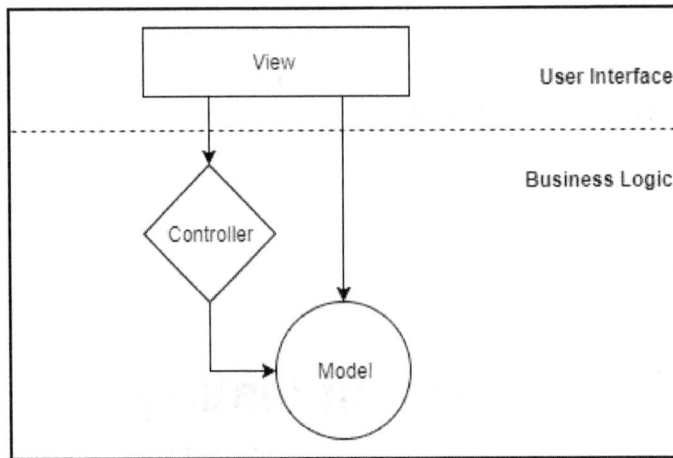

The key is that the **View** knows about the **Controller** and the **Model**, as it needs to send commands to the **Controller** and display the data held in the **Model**. The **Controller** knows about the **Model** as it needs to delegate work to it, but it doesn't know about the **View**. The **Model knows nothing about either the Controller** or the **View**.

A key benefit of designing the application this way in a business environment is that dedicated UX specialists can work on the views while programmers work on the business logic. A secondary boon is that because the business logic layer knows nothing about the UI, you add, edit, and even totally replace user interfaces without affecting the logic layer. A great use case would be to have a "full fat" UI for a desktop application and a companion "half fat" UI for a mobile device, both of which can use the same business logic. With all this in mind, we will physically segregate our UI and business logic into separate projects.

We will also look at integrating automated unit tests into our solution. Unit testing and **Test Driven Development (TDD)** has really grown in popularity in recent times and when developing applications in a business environment, you will more than likely be expected to write unit tests alongside your code. If not, you should really propose doing it as it holds a lot of value. Don't worry if you haven't done any unit testing before; it's very straightforward, and we'll discuss it in more detail later in the book.

Finally, we need a way to aggregate these subprojects together so that we don't have to open them individually. We will achieve this with an umbrella solution project that does nothing other than tying the other projects together. This is how we will lay out our projects:

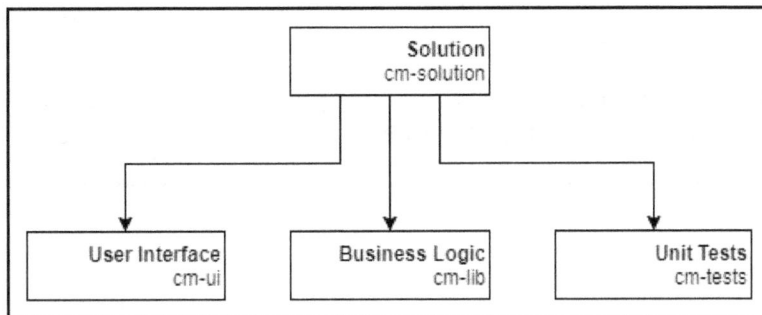

Project creation

In the previous chapter, we saw how easy it is to set up a new project just by creating a few text files. However, we'll create our new solution using Qt Creator. We will use the new project wizard to guide us through creating a top-level solution and a single subproject.

From the top menu, select **File > New File or Project and then Projects > Other Project > Subdirs Project and click on Choose…:**

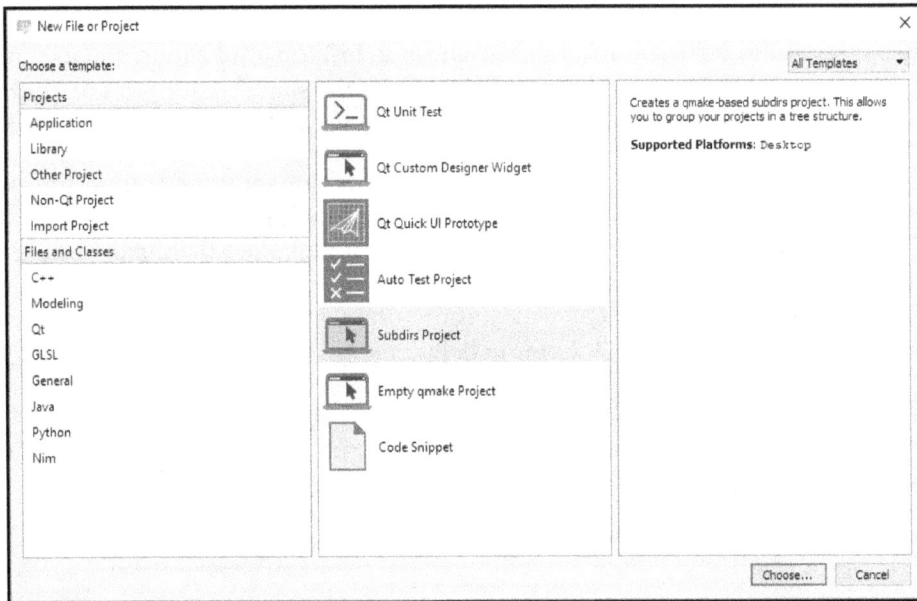

Subdirs Project is the template we need for our top-level solution project. Give it the name cm **and create it in our** qt **projects folder:**

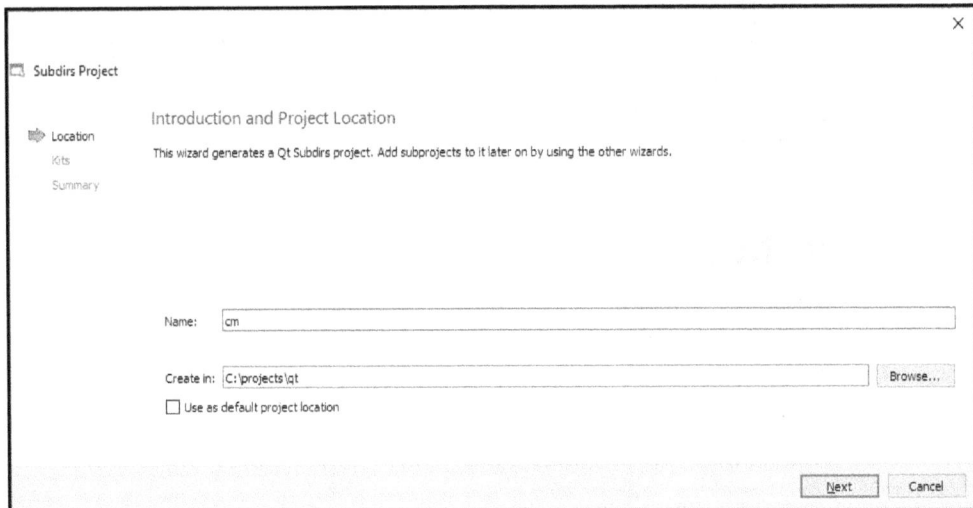

On the **Kit Selection pane, check the Desktop Qt 5.10.0 MinGW 32bit kit we installed. Feel free to select additional kits you want to try out if you have them installed, but it's not necessary. Click on Next:**

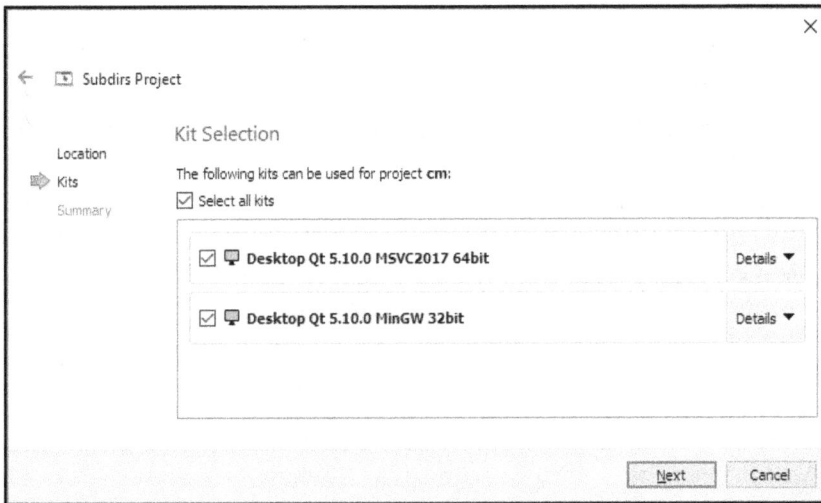

As discussed, version control is beyond the scope of this book, so in the **Project Management pane, select None from the Add to version control dropdown. Click on Finish & Add Subproject:**

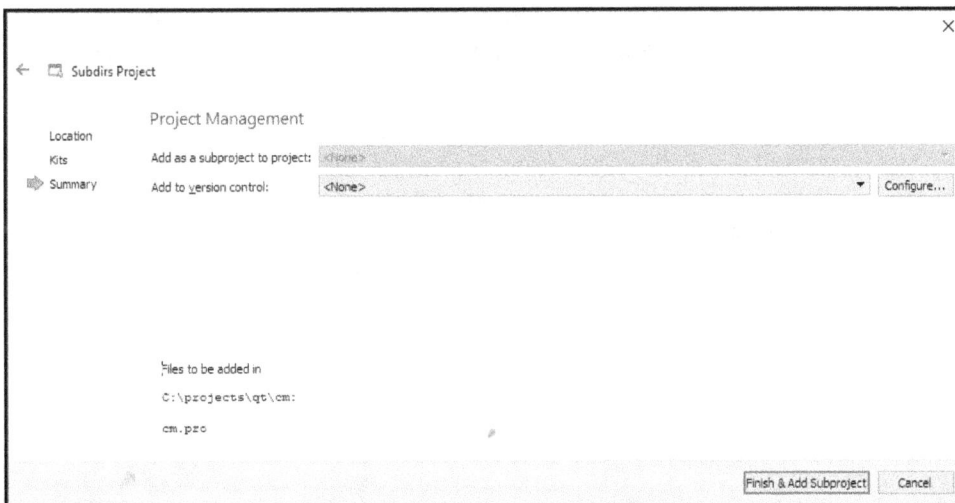

We'll add the user interface project as the first subproject. The wizard follows more or less the same pattern as the steps we've just followed, so perform the following:

1. Select **Projects > Application > Qt Quick Application - Empty and click on Choose...**
2. In the **Project Location dialog, give it the name** cm-ui **(for Client Management - User Interface), leave the location as our new** cm **folder, and click on Next.**
3. In the **Define Build System dialog, select the build system qmake and click on Next.**
4. In the **Define Project Details dialog, leave the default minimal Qt version of QT 5.9 and the Use Qt Virtual Keyboard box unchecked then click on Next.**
5. In the **Kit Selection dialog, pick the Desktop Qt 5.10.0 MinGW 32bit kit plus any other kits you wish to try and click on Next.**
6. Finally, in the **Project Management dialog, skip version control (leave it as <None>) and click on Finish.**

Our top-level solution and UI projects are now up and running, so let's add the other subprojects. Add the business logic project next, as follows:

1. In the **Projects pane, right-click on the top-level** cm **folder and select New Subproject....**
2. Select **Projects > Library > C++ Library and click on Choose....**
3. In the **Introduction and Project Location dialog, pick Shared Library as the Type, name it** cm-lib**, create it in** <Qt Projects>/cm**, and then click on Next.**
4. In the **Select Required Modules dialog, just accept the default of QtCore and click on Next.**
5. In the **Class Information** dialog, we get the opportunity to create a new class to get us started. Give the class name Client, with the client.h header file and the client.cpp source file, and then click on **Next.**
6. Finally, in the **Project Management dialog, skip version control (leave it as <None>) and click on Finish.**

Finally, we will repeat the process to create our unit testing project:

1. **New Subproject....**
2. **Projects > Other Project > Qt Unit Test.**
3. Project name cm-tests.
4. Include **QtCore and QtTest.**

5. Create the `ClientTests` test class with the `testCase1` test slot and the `client-tests.cpp` filename. Set the Type as **Test and check Generate initialization and cleanup code.**

6. Skip version control and **Finish.**

That was a lot of dialog boxes to get through, but we've now got our skeleton solution in place. Your project folders should look as follows:

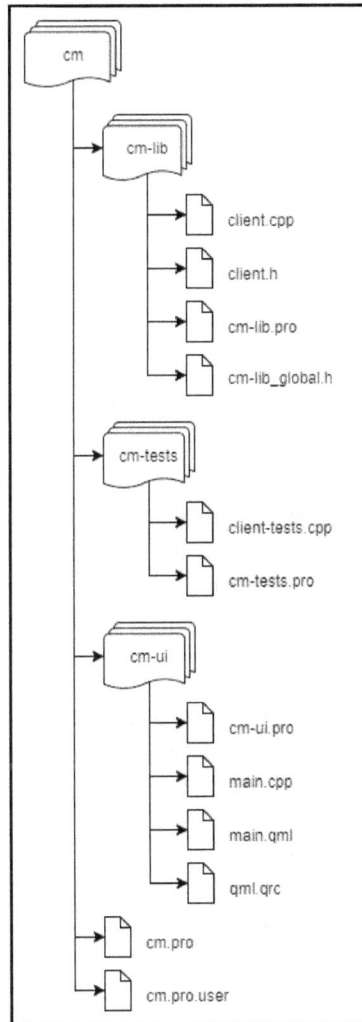

We'll now take a look at each project in turn and make some tweaks before we start adding our content.

cm-lib

First off, head to file explorer and create a new subfolder underneath cm-lib called source; move cm-lib_global.h there. Create another subfolder in source called models and move both the Client class files there.

Next, back in Qt Creator, open up cm-lib.pro and edit it as follows:

```
QT -= gui
TARGET = cm-lib
TEMPLATE = lib
CONFIG += c++14
DEFINES += CMLIB_LIBRARY
INCLUDEPATH += source

SOURCES += source/models/client.cpp

HEADERS += source/cm-lib_global.h
    source/models/client.h
```

As this is a library project, we do not need to load the default GUI module, so we exclude it using the QT variable. The TARGET variable is the name we wish to give our binary output (for example, cm-lib.dll). It is optional and will default to the project name if not provided, but we'll be explicit. Next, rather than having a TEMPLATE of app as we saw in our scratchpad application, this time we use lib to give us a library. We add c++14 features via the CONFIG variable.

The cm-lib_global.h file is a helpful little bit of preprocessor boilerplate we can use to export our shared library symbols, and you'll see that put to use soon. We use the CMLIB_LIBRARY flag in the DEFINES variable to trigger this export.

Finally, we have slightly rewritten the SOURCES and HEADERS variable lists to account for the new file locations after we moved things around a bit, and we add the source folder (which is where all of our code will live) to the INCLUDEPATH so that the path is searched when we use #include statements.

Right-click on the `cm-lib` folder in the **Projects pane and select Run qmake. When that has finished, right-click again and select Rebuild. Everything should be green and happy.**

cm-tests

Create new `source/models` subfolders and move `client-tests.cpp` there. Switch back to Qt Creator and edit `cm-tests.pro`:

```
QT += testlib
QT -= gui
TARGET = client-tests
TEMPLATE = app

CONFIG += c++14
CONFIG += console
CONFIG -= app_bundle

INCLUDEPATH += source

SOURCES += source/models/client-tests.cpp
```

This follows pretty much the same approach as with `cm-lib`, with the exception that we want a console app rather than a library. We don't need the GUI module, but we will add the `testlib` module to get access to the Qt Test features.

There really isn't much to this subproject just yet, but you should be able to run qmake and rebuild successfully.

cm-ui

Create two subfolders this time: `source` and `views`. Move `main.cpp` into `source` and `main.qml` into `views`. Rename `qml.qrc` as `views.qrc` and edit `cm-ui.pro`:

```
QT += qml quick

TEMPLATE = app

CONFIG += c++14

INCLUDEPATH += source

SOURCES += source/main.cpp
```

```
RESOURCES += views.qrc

# Additional import path used to resolve QML modules in Qt Creator's code
model
QML_IMPORT_PATH = $$PWD
```

Our UI is written in QML, which requires the `qml` and `quick` modules, so we add those. We edit the `RESOURCES` variable to pick up our renamed resource file and also edit the `QML_IMPORT_PATH` variable, which we will cover in detail when we get into custom QML modules.

Next, edit `views.qrc` to account for the fact that we have moved the `main.qml` file into the `views` folder. Remember to right-click and **Open With > Plain Text Editor:**

```
<RCC>
    <qresource prefix="/">
        <file>views/main.qml</file>
    </qresource>
</RCC>
```

Finally, we also need to edit a line in `main.cpp` to account for the file move:

```
engine.load(QUrl(QStringLiteral("qrc:/views/main.qml")));
```

You should now be able to run qmake and rebuild the `cm-ui` project. Before we run it, let's take a quick look at the build configuration button now that we have multiple projects open:

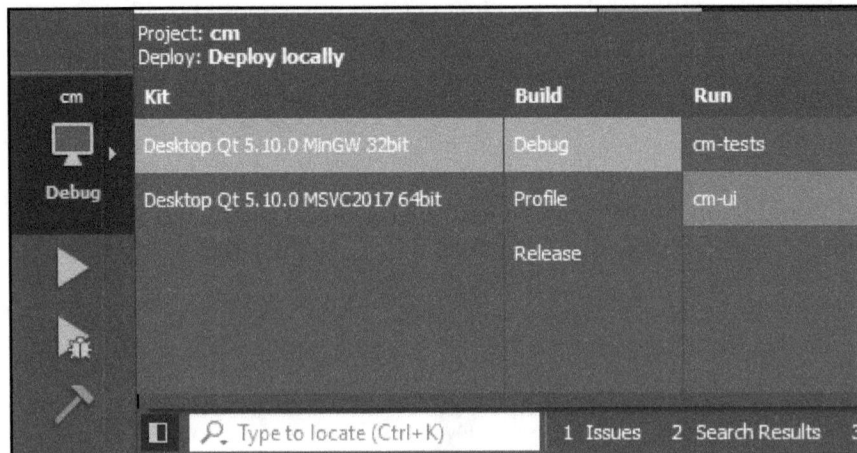

Note that now, along with the **Kit and Build options, we must also select the executable we wish to run. Ensure that** `cm-ui` **is selected and then run the application:**

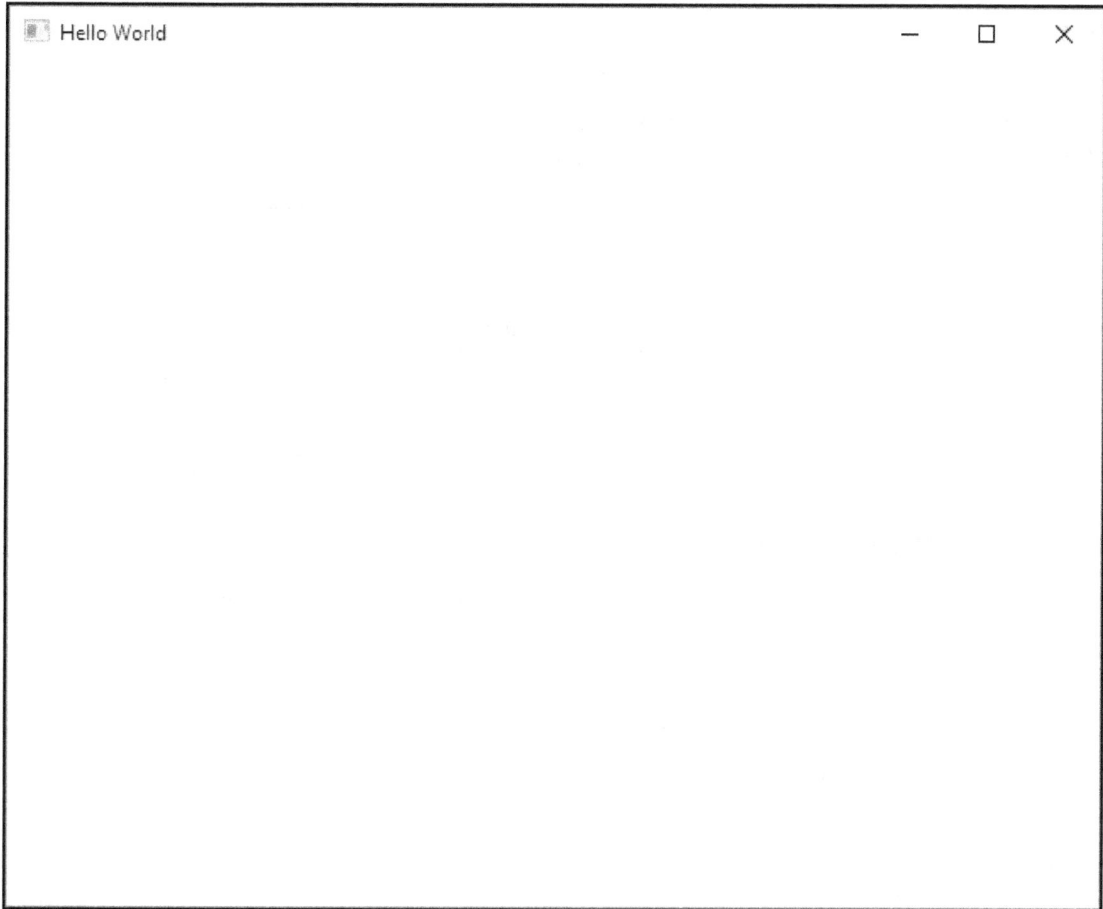

Hello World indeed. It's fairly uninspiring stuff, but we have a multiproject solution building and running happily, which is a great start. Close the application when you simply can't take any more fun!

Mastering MVC

Now that our solution structure is in place, we'll get started on the MVC implementation. As you'll see, it is very minimal and incredibly easy to set up.

First, expand `cm-ui > Resources > views.qrc > / > views`, right-click on `main.qml`, select **Rename, and rename the file as** `MasterView.qml`. **If you get a message about project editing, just select Yes to continue anyway:**

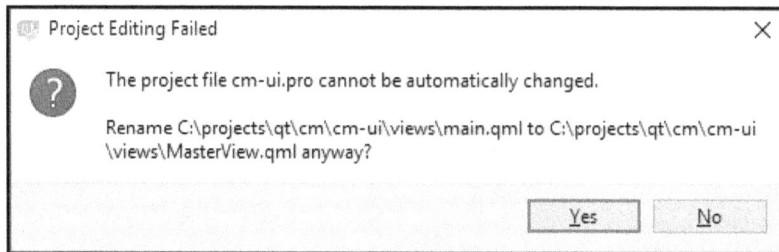

If you do get the error message, the file will still appear as `main.qml` in the **Projects pane, but the file will have been renamed in the filesystem.**

Next, edit `views.qrc` (right-click on it and select **Open With > Plain Text Editor). Replace the content as follows:**

```
<RCC>
    <qresource prefix="/views">
        <file alias="MasterView.qml">views/MasterView.qml</file>
    </qresource>
</RCC>
```

If you recall how we load this QML file in `main.cpp`, the syntax is `qrc:<prefix><filename>`. We previously had a / prefix and a `views/main.qml` relative filename. This gave us `qrc:/views/main.qml`.

A prefix of / isn't terribly descriptive. As you add more and more QML files, it's really helpful to organize them into blocks with meaningful prefixes. Having unstructured resource blocks also makes the **Projects pane ugly and more difficult to navigate, as you just saw when you had to drill down through** `views.qrc > / > views`. **So, the first step is to rename the prefix from** / **to** `/views`.

However, with a prefix of `/views` and a relative filename of `views/main.qml`, our URL is now `qrc:/views/views/main.qml`.

This is worse than it was before, and we still have a deep folder structure in `views.qrc`. Fortunately, we can add an *alias* for our file to make both of these problems go away. You can use the alias of a resource in place of the relative path, so if we assign an alias of `main.qml`, we can replace `views/main.qml` with simply `main.qml`, giving us `qrc:/views/main.qml`.

That's concise and descriptive, and our **Projects pane is neater too.**

So, going back to our updated version of `views.qrc`, we have simply updated the name of the file from `main.qml` to `MasterView.qml`, consistent with the file rename we performed, and we have also provided a shortcut alias, so we don't have to specify **views twice.**

We now need to update our code in `main.cpp` to reflect these changes:

```
engine.load(QUrl(QStringLiteral("qrc:/views/MasterView.qml")));
```

You should be able to run qmake, and build and run to verify that nothing has broken.

Next, we'll create a `MasterController` class, so right-click on the `cm-lib` project and select **Add New... > C++ > C++ Class > Choose...:**

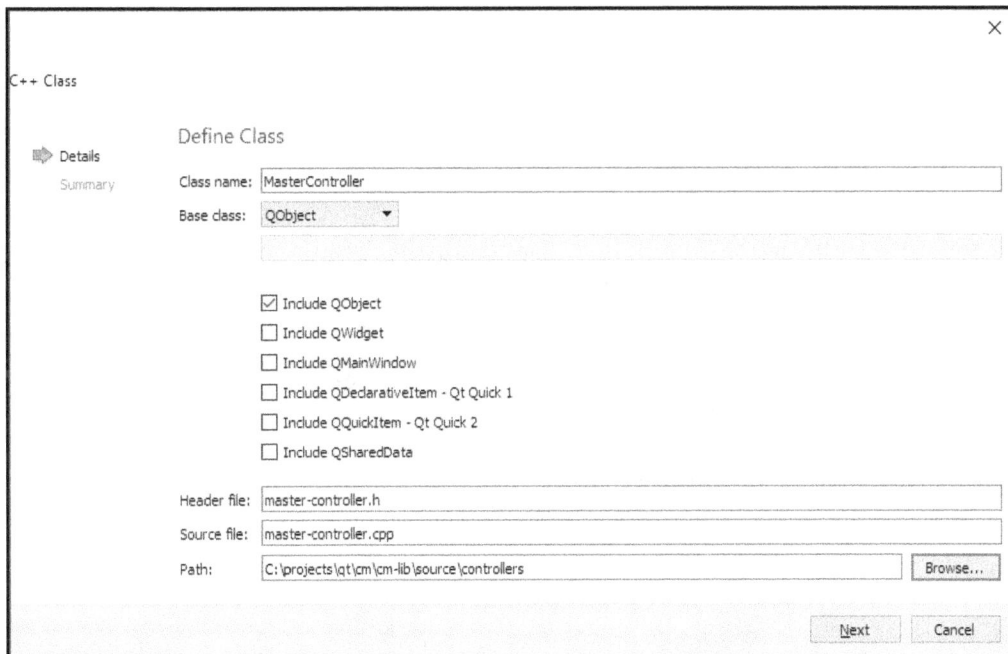

	×

C++ Class

➥ Details

   Summary

Define Class

Class name: `MasterController`

Base class: `QObject` ▼

☑ Include QObject
☐ Include QWidget
☐ Include QMainWindow
☐ Include QDeclarativeItem - Qt Quick 1
☐ Include QQuickItem - Qt Quick 2
☐ Include QSharedData

Header file: `master-controller.h`

Source file: `master-controller.cpp`

Path: `C:\projects\qt\cm\cm-lib\source\controllers`   Browse...

Next   Cancel

Use the **Browse... button to create the** source/controllers **subfolder.**

By selecting **QObject as the base class and including it, Qt Creator will write some of the boilerplate code for us. You can always add it yourself later, so don't feel like it's a necessary part of creating a new class.**

Once you've skipped version control and created the class, declare and define it as follows. Our MasterController doesn't do anything particularly exciting just yet, we're just doing the groundwork.

Here's master-controller.h:

```cpp
#ifndef MASTERCONTROLLER_H
#define MASTERCONTROLLER_H
#include <QObject>

#include <cm-lib_global.h>
namespace cm {
namespace controllers {
class CMLIBSHARED_EXPORT MasterController : public QObject
{
    Q_OBJECT
public:
    explicit MasterController(QObject* parent = nullptr);
};

}}

#endif
```

All we've really added to the default implementation Qt Creator gave us is the CMLIBSHARED_EXPORT macro Qt Creator wrote for us in cm-lib_global.h to take care of our shared library exports, and to put the class inside a namespace.

> I always have the project name as a root namespace and then additional namespaces that reflect the physical location of the class files within the source directory, so in this case, I use cm::controllers, as the class is located in the directory source/controllers.

This is `master-controller.cpp`:

```cpp
#include "master-controller.h"

namespace cm {
namespace controllers {
MasterController::MasterController(QObject* parent)
    : QObject(parent)
{
}

}}
```

> I use a slightly unorthodox style in the implementation file—most people just add `using namespace cm::controllers;` at the top of the `.cpp` file. I often like to put the code within the scope of namespaces because it becomes collapsible in the IDE. By repeating the innermost namespace scope (*controllers* in this example), you can break your code up into collapsible regions much like you can in C#, which helps with navigation in larger files, as you can collapse the sections you're not interested in. It makes no functional difference, so use whichever style you prefer.

QObject

So, what is this funky **QObject** thingy we are inheriting from which keeps popping up? Well, it's the base class for all Qt objects, and it gives us some powerful features for free.

QObjects organize themselves into object hierarchies with a *parent* object assuming ownership of their *child* objects, which means we don't have to worry (as much!) about memory management. For example, if we have an instance of a Client class derived from QObject that is the parent of an Address also derived from QObject, then the address is automatically destroyed when the client is destroyed.

QObjects carry metadata that allows a degree of type inspection and is the backbone for interaction with QML. They can also communicate with each other via an event subscription mechanism where the events are emitted as *signals* and the subscribed delegates are known as *slots*.

All you need to remember for now is that for any custom classes you write where you want to interact with it in the UI, ensure that it derives from QObject. Whenever you do derive from QObject, ensure that you always add the magical Q_OBJECT macro to your class before you do anything else. It injects a bunch of super complicated boilerplate code that you don't need to understand in order to use QObjects effectively.

We are now at the point where we need to reference code from one subproject (`MasterController` in `cm-lib`) in another (`cm-ui`). We first need to be able to access the declarations for our `#include` statements. Edit the `INCLUDEPATH` variable in `cm-ui.pro` as follows:

```
INCLUDEPATH += source
    ../cm-lib/source
```

The symbol is a "continue on to the next line" indicator, so you can set a variable to multiple values spanning several lines. Just like console commands, '..' means traverse up a level, so here we are stepping up out of the local folder (`cm-ui`) and then down into the `cm-lib` folder to get at its source code. You need to be careful that the project folders remain in the same location relative to each other, else this won't work.

Just below this, we'll tell our UI project where to find the implementation (compiled binary) of our library project. If you take a look at the filesystem alongside the top-level cm project folder, you will see one or more build folders, for example, **build-cm-Desktop_Qt_5_9_0_MinGW_32bit-Debug. Each folder is created when we run qmake for a given kit and configuration and is populated with the output when we build.**

Next, navigate to the folder relevant to the kit and configuration you are using, and you will find a **cm-lib folder with another configuration folder inside it. Copy this file path; for example, I am using the MinGW 32 bit kit in Debug configuration, so my path is** <Qt Projects>/build-cm-Desktop_Qt_5_10_0_MinGW_32bit-Debug/cm-lib/debug.

In that folder, you will find the compiled binaries relevant for your OS, for example, `cm-lib.dll` on Windows. This is the folder we want our `cm-ui` project to reference for the `cm-lib` library implementation. To set this up, add the following statement to `cm-ui.pro`:

```
LIBS += -L$$PWD/../../build-cm-Desktop_Qt_5_10_0_MinGW_32bit-Debug/cm-
lib/debug -lcm-lib
```

`LIBS` is the variable used to add referenced libraries to the project. The `-L` prefix denotes a directory, while `-l` denotes a library file. Using this syntax allows us to ignore the file extensions (`.a`, `.o`, `.lib`) and prefixes (lib...), which can vary between operating systems and let qmake figure it out. We use the special `$$` symbol to access the value of the `PWD` variable, which contains the working directory of the current project (the full path to `cm/cm-ui` in this case). From that location, we then drill up two directories with `../..` to get us to the Qt projects folder. From there, we drill back down to the location where we know the `cm-lib` binaries are built.

Now, this is painful to write, ugly as hell, and will fall over as soon as we switch kits or configurations, but we will come back and tidy up all this later. With the project references all wired up, we can head on over to `main.cpp` in `cm-ui`.

To be able to use a given class in QML, we need to register it, which we do in `main()` before we create the QML Application Engine. First, include the `MasterController`:

```
#include <controllers/master-controller.h>
```

Then, right after the `QGuiApplication` is instantiated but before the `QQmlApplicationEngine` is declared, add the following line:

```
qmlRegisterType<cm::controllers::MasterController>("CM", 1, 0,
"MasterController");
```

What we are doing here is registering the type with the QML engine. Note that the template parameter must be fully qualified with all namespaces. We will add the type's metadata into a module called **CM with a version number 1.0, and we want to refer to this type as** `MasterController` **in QML markup.**

Then, we instantiate an instance of `MasterController` and inject it into the root QML context:

```
cm::controllers::MasterController masterController;
QQmlApplicationEngine engine;
engine.rootContext()->setContextProperty("masterController",
&masterController);
engine.load(QUrl(QStringLiteral("qrc:/views/MasterView")));
```

Note that you need to set the context property before loading the QML file, and you will also need to add the following header:

```
#include <QQmlContext>
```

So, we've created a controller, registered it with the QML engine, and it's good to go. What now? Let's do our first bit of QML.

QML

Qt Modeling Language (QML) is a hierarchical declarative language for user interface layout with a syntax similar to **JavaScript Object Notation (JSON)**. It can bind to C++ objects via Qt's meta object system and also supports inline JavaScript. It's much like HTML or XAML but without the XMLness. If you are someone who likes JSON more than XML, this can only be a good thing!

Go ahead and open up `MasterView.qml`, and we'll see what's going on.

The first thing you'll see is a couple of `import` statements. They are similar to `#include` statements in C++—they bring in pieces of functionality that we want to use in the view. They can be packed and versioned modules as with QtQuick 2.9, or they can be relative paths to local content.

Next, the QML hierarchy begins with a Window object. The scope of the object is represented by the subsequent `{ }`, so everything within the braces is either a property or child of the object.

Properties follow JSON property syntax, of the form key: value. A notable difference is that speech marks are not required unless you are providing a string literal as a value. Here, we are setting the `visible` property of the **Window object to be** `true` **and the size of the window to be 640 x 480 pixels, and we are displaying Hello World in the title bar.**

Let's change the title and add a simple message. Replace the **Hello World title with Client Management and insert a Text component inside the body of the Window:**

```
Window {
    visible: true
    width: 640
    height: 480
    title: qsTr("Client Management")

    Text {
        text: "Welcome to the Client Management system!"
    }
}
```

Save your changes, and **Run qmake and Run the application:**

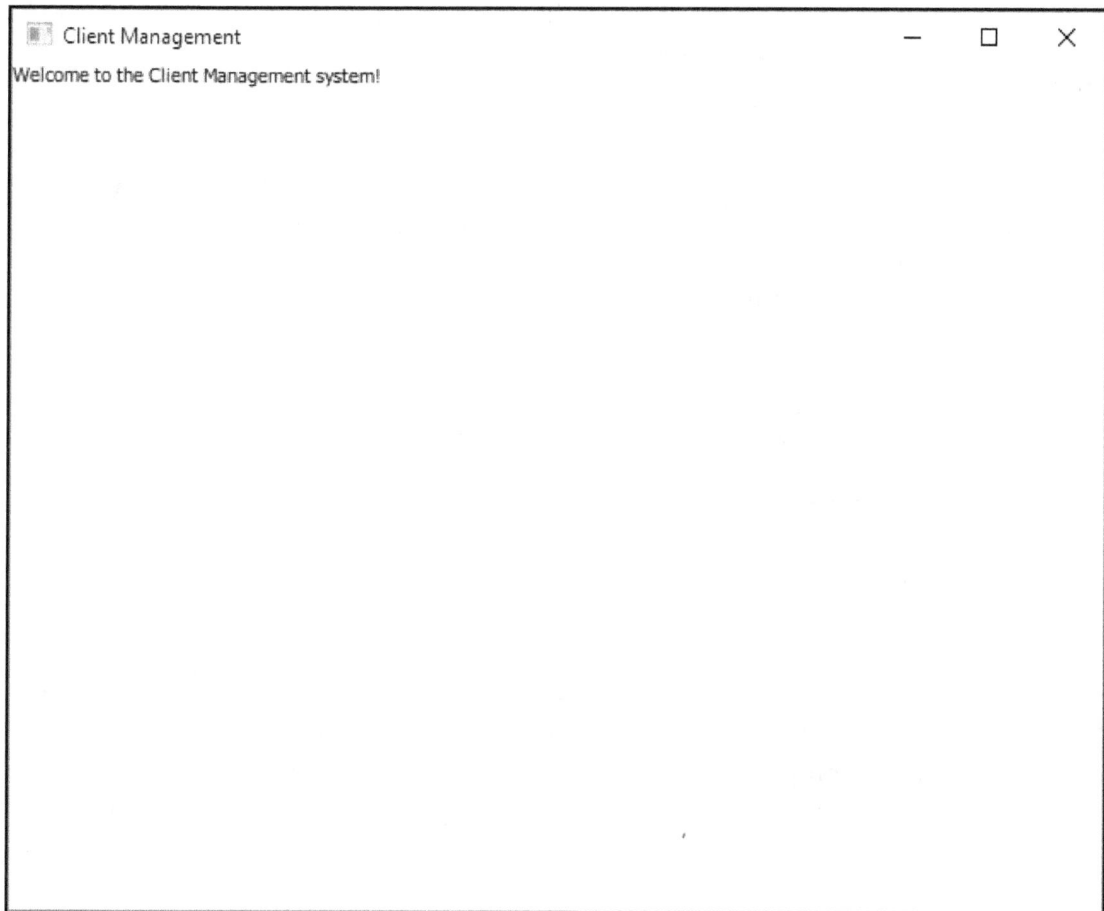

Let's make `MasterController` start earning its keep and rather than hard-coding our welcome message in the UI, we'll obtain it dynamically from our controller.

Edit `master-controller.h` and add a new public property of the `QString` type called `welcomeMessage`, setting it to an initial value:

```
QString welcomeMessage = "This is MasterController to Major Tom";
```

You will also need to #include <QString>.

In order to be able to access this member from QML, we need to configure a new property. After the **Q_OBJECT macro but before the first public access modifier, add the following:**

```
Q_PROPERTY( QString ui_welcomeMessage MEMBER welcomeMessage CONSTANT )
```

Here, we are creating a new property of the **QString type that QML can access. QML will refer to the property as** ui_welcomeMessage **and when called, will get (or set) the value in the** MEMBER **variable called** welcomeMessage. **We are explicitly setting the value of the variable up front and will not change it, so it will remain** CONSTANT.

> You can simply name the property welcomeMessage, rather than ui_welcomeMessage. My personal preference is to explicitly name things that are solely intended for UI consumption with a ui_ prefix to differentiate them from member variables and methods. Do whatever works for you.

Head back to MasterView.qml, and we will put this property to use. Change the text property of the Text component to the following:

```
text: masterController.ui_welcomeMessage
```

Note how the QML editor recognizes masterController and even offers code completion for it. Now, rather than displaying a string literal as the message, the QML will access the ui_welcomeMessage property of the instance of MasterController we injected into the root context in main(), which will, in turn, get the value of the welcomeMessage member variable.

Build and Run, and you should now see the message coming from the
`MasterController:`

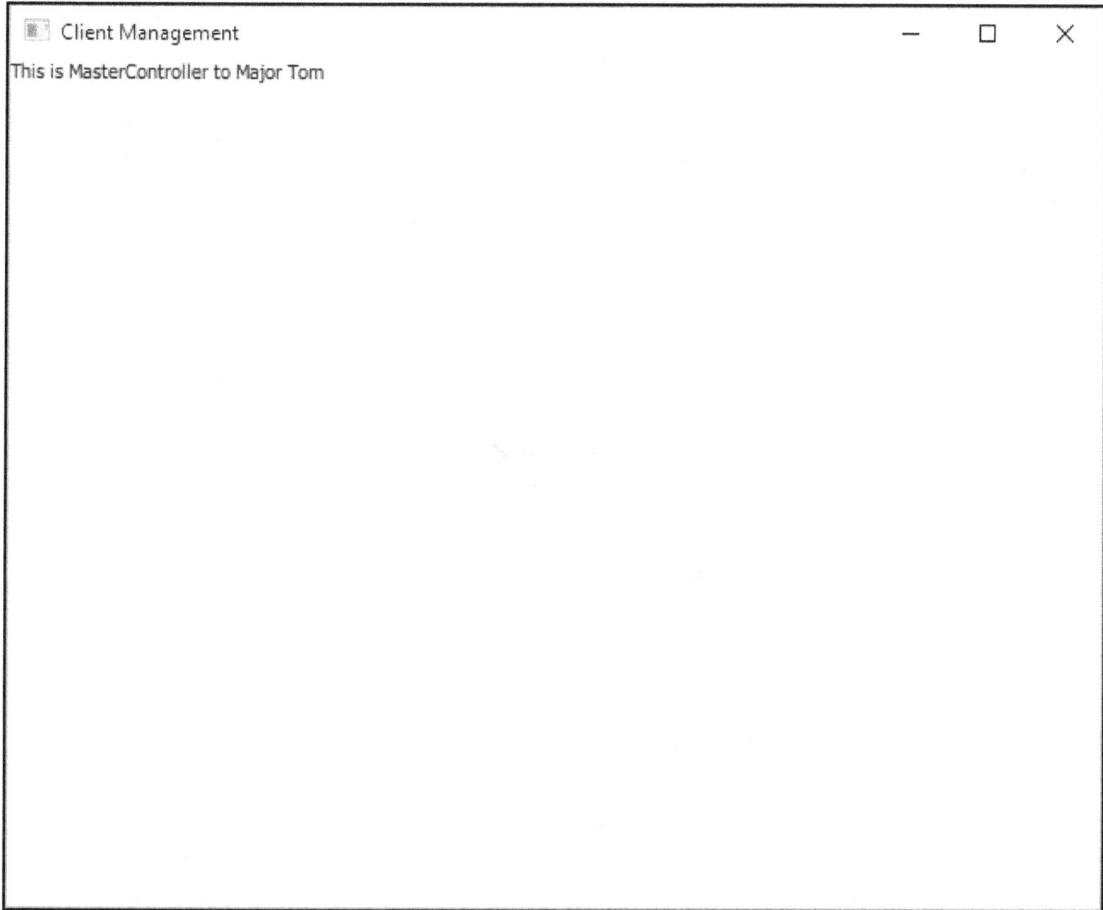

We now have a working mechanism for QML to call into C++ code and get hold of whatever data and business logic we want to provide it. Here, an important thing to note is that our `MasterController` knows nothing about the existence of `MasterView`, and this is a key part of the MVC pattern.

Project output

In order to let our `cm-ui` project know where to find the implementation of `cm-lib`, we used the `LIBS` variable in our project file. It was a pretty ugly folder name, but it's only one line and everything has worked perfectly well, so it could be tempting to leave things as they are. However, look forward to when we are ready to produce our first build for testing or even production. We've written some really clever code, and everything is building and running beautifully. We switch the configuration from **Debug to Release and...everything falls over. The problem is that we've hard-coded the library path in our project file to look in the** `Debug` **folder. Change to a different kit or another operating system and the problem is even worse, as you will have binary compatibility issues from using different compilers.**

Let's set a few goals:

- Get rid of the unwieldy `build-cm...` folders
- Aggregate all the compiled binary output into one common folder `cm/binaries`
- Hide all temporary build artifacts in their own folders `cm/<project>/build`
- Create separate build and binary folders for different compilers and architectures
- Detect those compilers and architectures automatically

So, where do these funny long folder names come from in the first place? In Qt Creator, click on the **Projects mode icon in the navigation bar. Down the left-hand side in the Build & Run section, select Desktop Qt 5.9.0 MinGW 32 bit > Build. Here, you will see the Build Settings for the MinGW kit in this solution and under the Shadow build checkbox, you will recognize the long build directory.**

We need to leave shadow builds enabled as this gives us the capability to perform builds to alternative locations for different kits. We will control the exact output of our builds in the `.pro` files, but we still need to specify a build directory here to keep Qt Creator happy. Enter **<Qt Projects>/shadow-builds. Repeat this setting for each build configuration (Debug/Release/Profile) using the dropdown at the top of the pane, and for all the kits you are using:**

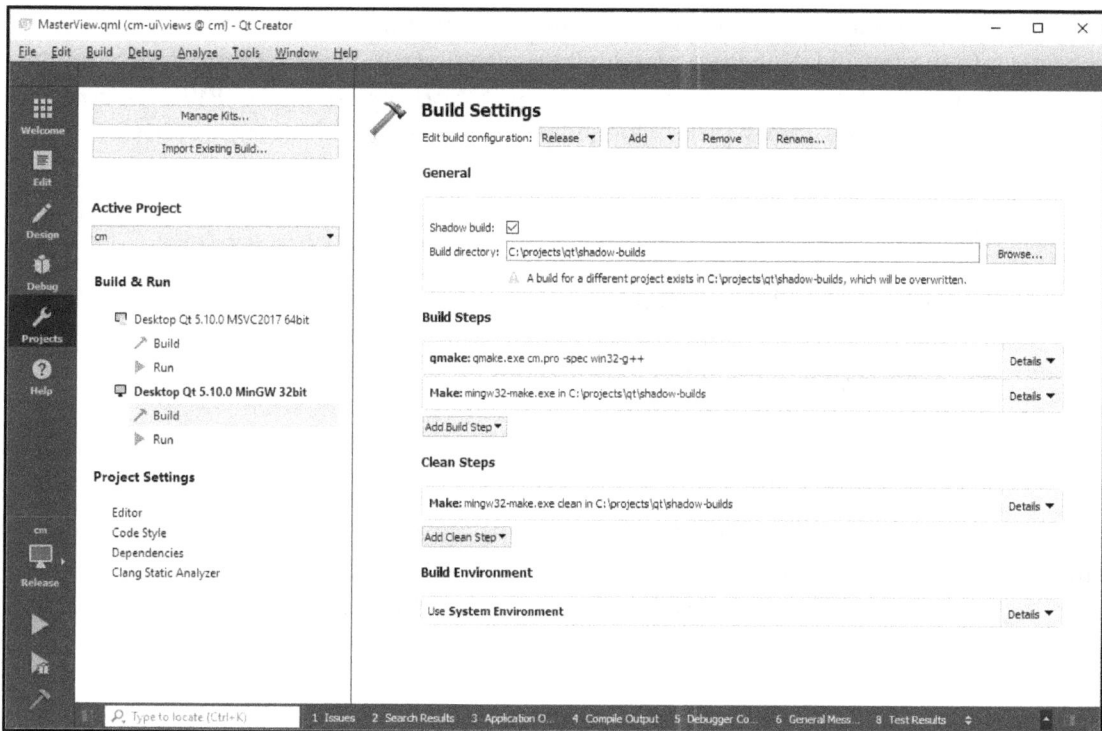

In your filesystem, delete any of the old `build-cm...` folders. Right-click on the solution folder and **Run qmake. After qmake has finished, you should see that shell** `cm-lib`, `cm-tests`, **and** `cm-ui` **folders have been created in <Qt Projects>/shadow-builds and that the long** `build-cm...` **folders have not reappeared.**

The first step for dynamically setting any relative path is to know which path you are currently on. We've already seen that in action in qmake when we used `$$PWD` to get the project working directory. To help us visualize what is going on, let's introduce our first qmake function—`message()`.

Add the following line to `cm.pro`—it doesn't matter where in the file it goes:

```
message(cm project dir: $${PWD})
```

Add the following line to `cm-lib.pro`:

```
message(cm-lib project dir: $${PWD})
```

The `message()` is a test function supported by qmake that outputs the supplied string parameter to the console. Note that you don't need to surround the text with double quotes. When you save the changes, you will see the **Project Working Directory** (**PWD**) of both the solution project and the library project logged out to the **General Messages console:**

```
Project MESSAGE: cm project dir: C:/projects/qt/cm
```

```
Project MESSAGE: cm-lib project dir: C:/projects/qt/cm/cm-lib
```

qmake actually takes multiple passes over `.pro` files, so whenever you use `message()`, you may see the same output several times over in the console. You can filter out the majority of duplicates using `message()` in conjunction with a scope—`!build_pass:message(Here is my message)`. This prevents the `message()` method from being called during the build pass.

If we look back at the default behavior of Qt Creator for shadow builds, we'll see that the aim was to allow multiple builds to sit alongside each other. This is achieved by constructing distinct folder names containing the kit, platform, and build configuration:

```
build-cm-solution-Desktop_Qt_5_10_0_MinGW_32bit-Debug
```

You can see just by looking at the folder name that the contents are from a build of the **cm** project using the **Qt 5.10.0 for Desktop MinGW 32bit kit in Debug mode. We'll now reimplement this approach in a cleaner and more flexible way.**

Rather than concatenating the information into one long folder name, we'll prefer a hierarchical structure consisting of the `Operating System > Compiler > Processor Architecture > Build Configuration` folders.

Let's first hard-code this path and then move on to automating it. Edit `cm-lib.pro` and add this:

```
DESTDIR = $$PWD/../binaries/windows/gcc/x86/debug
message(cm-lib output dir: $${DESTDIR})
```

This is to reflect that we are building with the **MinGW 32bit kit on Windows in Debug mode. Replace** *Windows* **with** *osx* **or** *Linux* **if you are on a different OS. We've added another call to** `message()` **to output this destination directory in the General Messages console. Remember that** `$$PWD` **extracts the working directory of the** `.pro` **file being processed (**`cm-lib.pro` **in this case), so this gives us** `<Qt Projects>/cm/cm-lib`.

Right-click on the `cm-lib` project, run qmake, and build. Ensure that you have the MinGW kit selected, along with Debug mode.

Navigate to `<Qt Projects>/cm/binaries/<OS>/gcc/x86/debug` in the filesystem, and you will see our library binaries without the associated clutter of build artifacts. This is a good first step, but if you now change the build configuration to Release or switch kits, the destination directory will remain the same, which is not what we want.

The technique we are about to implement will be used in all three of our projects, so rather than having to duplicate the configuration in all of our `.pro` files, let's extract the configuration to a shared file and include it instead.

In the root `cm` folder, create two new empty text files called `qmake-target-platform.pri` and `qmake-destination-path.pri`. In `cm-lib.pro`, `cm-tests.pro`, and `cm-ui.pro`, add these lines:

```
include(../qmake-target-platform.pri)
include(../qmake-destination-path.pri)
```

Add these lines somewhere near the top of the `*.pro` files. The exact order doesn't matter too much as long as they are before the `DESTDIR` variable is set.

Edit `qmake-target-platform.pri` as follows:

```
win32 {
    CONFIG += PLATFORM_WIN
    message(PLATFORM_WIN)
    win32-g++ {
        CONFIG += COMPILER_GCC
        message(COMPILER_GCC)
    }
    win32-msvc2017 {
        CONFIG += COMPILER_MSVC2017
        message(COMPILER_MSVC2017)
        win32-msvc2017:QMAKE_TARGET.arch = x86_64
    }
}

linux {
    CONFIG += PLATFORM_LINUX
    message(PLATFORM_LINUX)
    # Make QMAKE_TARGET arch available for Linux
    !contains(QT_ARCH, x86_64){
        QMAKE_TARGET.arch = x86
    } else {
        QMAKE_TARGET.arch = x86_64
```

```
        }
        linux-g++{
            CONFIG += COMPILER_GCC
            message(COMPILER_GCC)
        }
    }

    macx {
        CONFIG += PLATFORM_OSX
        message(PLATFORM_OSX)
        macx-clang {
            CONFIG += COMPILER_CLANG
            message(COMPILER_CLANG)
            QMAKE_TARGET.arch = x86_64
        }
        macx-clang-32{
            CONFIG += COMPILER_CLANG
            message(COMPILER_CLANG)
            QMAKE_TARGET.arch = x86
        }
    }

    contains(QMAKE_TARGET.arch, x86_64) {
        CONFIG += PROCESSOR_x64
        message(PROCESSOR_x64)
    } else {
        CONFIG += PROCESSOR_x86
        message(PROCESSOR_x86)
    }
    CONFIG(debug, release|debug) {
        CONFIG += BUILD_DEBUG
        message(BUILD_DEBUG)
    } else {
        CONFIG += BUILD_RELEASE
        message(BUILD_RELEASE)
    }
```

Here, we are leveraging the platform detection capabilities of qmake to inject personalized flags into the CONFIG variable. On each operating system, different platform variables become available. For example, on Windows, the win32 variable is present, Linux is represented by linux, and Mac OS X by macx. We can use these platform variables with curly braces to act like if statements:

```
win32 {
    # This block will execute on Windows only...
}
```

We can consider different combinations of platform variables to figure out what compiler and processor architecture the currently selected kit is using, and then add developer-friendly flags to the CONFIG, which we can use later in our .pro files. Remember that we are trying to construct a build path—Operating System > Compiler > Processor Architecture > Build Configuration.

When you save these changes, you should see the flags similar to the following in the **General Message console:**

```
Project MESSAGE: PLATFORM_WIN
Project MESSAGE: COMPILER_GCC
Project MESSAGE: PROCESSOR_x86
Project MESSAGE: BUILD_DEBUG
```

Try switching kits or changing the build configuration, and you should see different output. When I switch my kit to Visual Studio 2017 64 bit in Release mode, I now get this:

```
Project MESSAGE: PLATFORM_WIN
Project MESSAGE: COMPILER_MSVC2017
Project MESSAGE: PROCESSOR_x64
Project MESSAGE: BUILD_RELEASE
```

With the same project on a Linux machine with the MinGW 64 bit kit, I get this:

```
Project MESSAGE: PLATFORM_LINUX
Project MESSAGE: COMPILER_GCC
Project MESSAGE: PROCESSOR_x64
Project MESSAGE: BUILD_DEBUG
```

On a Mac using Clang 64 bit, I get the following:

```
Project MESSAGE: PLATFORM_OSX
Project MESSAGE: COMPILER_CLANG
Project MESSAGE: PROCESSOR_x64
Project MESSAGE: BUILD_DEBUG
```

> To get this to work on Windows, I had to make an assumption as QMAKE_TARGET.arch is not correctly detected for MSVC2017, so I assumed that if the compiler is MSVC2017, then it must be x64 as there was no 32 bit kit available.

Now that all the platform detection is done, we can construct the destination path dynamically. Edit `qmake-destination-path.pri`:

```
platform_path = unknown-platform
compiler_path = unknown-compiler
processor_path = unknown-processor
build_path = unknown-build

PLATFORM_WIN {
    platform_path = windows
}
PLATFORM_OSX {
    platform_path = osx
}
PLATFORM_LINUX {
    platform_path = linux
}

COMPILER_GCC {
    compiler_path = gcc
}
COMPILER_MSVC2017 {
    compiler_path = msvc2017
}
COMPILER_CLANG {
    compiler_path = clang
}

PROCESSOR_x64 {
    processor_path = x64
}
PROCESSOR_x86 {
    processor_path = x86
}

BUILD_DEBUG {
    build_path = debug
} else {
    build_path = release
}

DESTINATION_PATH =
$$platform_path/$$compiler_path/$$processor_path/$$build_path
message(Dest path: $${DESTINATION_PATH})
```

Here, we create four new variables—*platform_path, compiler_path, processor_path*, and *build_path*—and assign default values to them all. We then use the CONFIG flags we created in the previous file and construct our folder hierarchy, storing it in a variable of our own, called DESTINATION_PATH. For example, if we detect Windows as the operating system, we add the PLATFORM_WIN flag to CONFIG and as a result of that, set platform_path to windows. Switching between kits and configurations on Windows, I now get these messages:

```
Dest path: windows/gcc/x86/debug
```

Alternatively, I get this:

```
Dest path: windows/msvc2017/x64/release
```

On Linux, I get the following:

```
Dest path: linux/gcc/x64/debug
```

On Mac OS, this is what I get:

```
Dest path: osx/clang/x64/debug
```

You can just combine these platform detection and destination path creation tricks in one file, but by keeping them separate, you can use the flags elsewhere in your project files. In any case, we are now dynamically creating a path based on our build environment and storing it in a variable for later use.

The next thing to do is to plug this DESTINATION_PATH variable into our project files. While we're here, we can also structure our build artifacts using the same mechanism by adding a few more lines. Add the following to all three *.pro files, replacing the DESTDIR statement already in cm-lib.pro:

```
DESTDIR = $$PWD/../binaries/$$DESTINATION_PATH
OBJECTS_DIR = $$PWD/build/$$DESTINATION_PATH/.obj
MOC_DIR = $$PWD/build/$$DESTINATION_PATH/.moc
RCC_DIR = $$PWD/build/$$DESTINATION_PATH/.qrc
UI_DIR = $$PWD/build/$$DESTINATION_PATH/.ui
```

Temporary build artifacts will now be placed into discreet directories within the build folder.

Finally, we can fix the problem that brought us here in the first place. In `cm-tests` and `cm-ui`, we can now set the `LIBS` variable using our new dynamic destination path:

```
LIBS += -L$$PWD/../binaries/$$DESTINATION_PATH -lcm-lib
```

You can now right-click on the `cm` project, run qmake, and build to automatically build all three subprojects in one step. All the output will be sent to the correct place and the library binaries can be easily located by the other projects. You can switch kits and configurations and not have to worry about referencing the wrong libraries.

Summary

In this chapter, we took our project creation skills up to the next level, and our solution is now starting to take shape. We implemented an MVC pattern and bridged the gap between our UI and business logic projects. We dabbled with our first bit of QML and took a look at the cornerstone of the Qt framework, QObject.

We removed all those unsightly `build-cm...` folders, flexed our qmake muscles, and took control of where all of our files go. All binaries are now placed in the `cm/binaries` folder, organized by platform, compiler, processor architecture, and build configuration. All temporary build artifacts that aren't required by the end user are now hidden away. We can freely switch kits and build configurations, and have our output automatically rerouted to the correct location.

In `Chapter 3`, *User Interface*, we will design our UI and get stuck in some more QML.

User Interface 3

In this chapter, we will take a more detailed look at QML and sketch out our user interface layout. We'll create placeholder views for all of our screens and implement a framework to navigate between them. We will also discuss the content within those views, specifically how to anchor and size elements in a flexible and responsive way. We will cover these topics:

- User interface design
- Creating views
- The StackView component
- Anchoring elements
- Sizing elements
- Navigating between views

UX

If you've ever worked with other declarative UI technologies like HTML and XAML, they often take a parent/child approach to UI, that is, there is a parent or root view that is ever present and contains global functionality, such as top-level navigation. It then has dynamic content or child views, which switch in and out as needed and present context sensitive commands where necessary.

We will take the same approach, with our MasterView being the root of our UI. We will add a global navigation bar and a content pane where we can add and remove content as needed. Child views will optionally present a command bar for performing actions, for example, saving a record to a database.

Let's take a look at the basic layout we are aiming for:

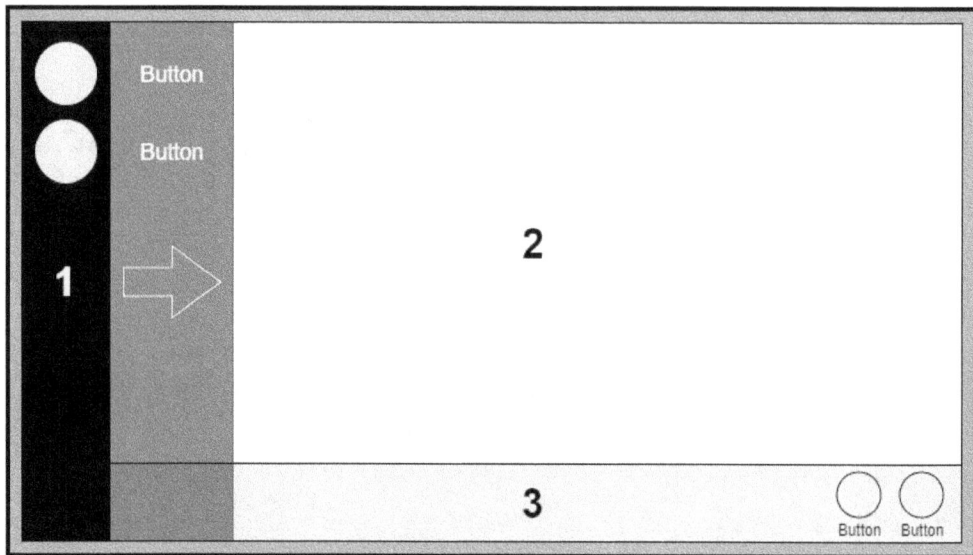

The Navigation Bar (**1**) will be ever present and contain buttons that will navigate the user to key areas within the application. By default, the bar will be narrow and the commands associated with the buttons will be represented by icons; however, pressing a toggle button will expand the bar to display accompanying descriptive text for each button.

The Content Pane (**2**) will be a stack of child views. Navigating to different areas of the application will be achieved by replacing the child view in the content pane. For example, if we add a **New Client** button on the navigation bar and press it, we will push the **New Client View** onto the content frame stack.

The Command Bar (**3**) is an optional element that will be used to present further command buttons to the user. The key difference to the navigation bar is that these commands will be context sensitive relating to the current view. For example, when creating a new client, we will need a Save button, but when we are searching for clients, a Save button makes no sense. Each child view will optionally present its own command bar. The commands will be presented by icons with a short description underneath.

Now let's plan the flow of screens, or views as we'll call them:

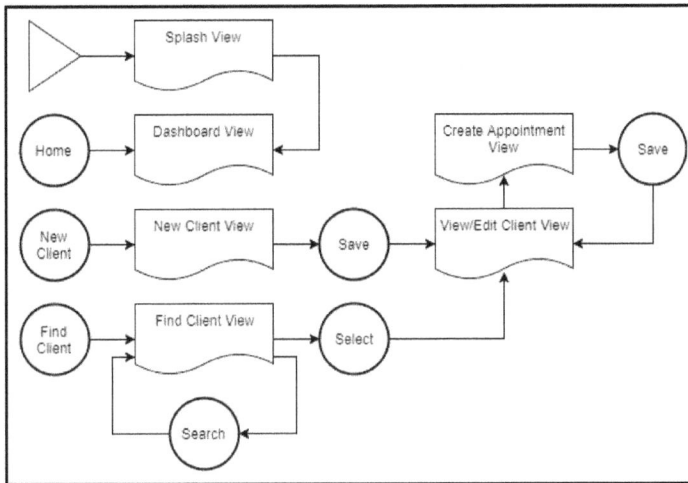

Creating views

In **cm-ui**, right-click on `views.qrc` and select **Add New...**. Select **Qt > QML File** and click on **Choose...**:

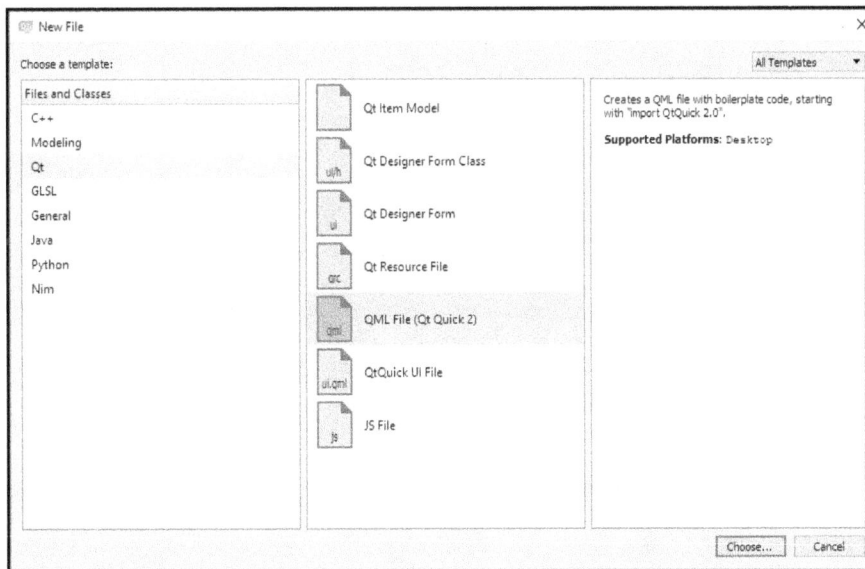

Create the `SplashView.qml` file in `cm-ui/ui/views`. Repeat this process until you've created all the following views:

File	Purpose
`SplashView.qml`	Placeholder view displayed while the UI is loading.
`DashboardView.qml`	The central "home" view.
`CreateClientView.qml`	View for entering details of a new client.
`EditClientView.qml`	View for reading/updating the existing client details.
`FindClientView.qml`	View for searching for the existing clients.

Edit `views.qrc` in the **Plain Text Editor** as we have done previously. You will see that our new views have been added to a new `qresource` block with the default prefix of the following:

```
<RCC>
    <qresource prefix="/views">
        <file alias="MasterView">views/MasterView.qml</file>
    </qresource>
    <qresource prefix="/">
        <file>views/SplashView.qml</file>
        <file>views/DashboardView.qml</file>
        <file>views/CreateClientView.qml</file>
        <file>views/EditClientView.qml</file>
        <file>views/FindClientView.qml</file>
    </qresource>
</RCC>
```

Also note that the **Projects** navigator is a bit of a mess:

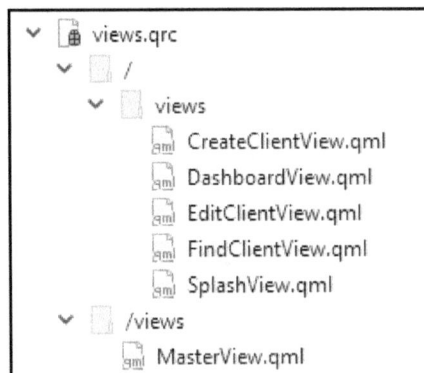

Move all the new files into the "/views" prefix block and remove the "/" block. Add an alias for each of the new files:

```
<RCC>
    <qresource prefix="/views">
        <file alias="MasterView.qml">views/MasterView.qml</file>
        <file alias="SplashView.qml">views/SplashView.qml</file>
        <file alias="DashboardView.qml">views/DashboardView.qml</file>
        <file
alias="CreateClientView.qml">views/CreateClientView.qml</file>
        <file alias="EditClientView.qml">views/EditClientView.qml</file>
        <file
alias="CreateAppointmentView.qml">views/CreateAppointmentView.qml</file>
        <file alias="FindClientView.qml">views/FindClientView.qml</file>
    </qresource>
</RCC>
```

As soon as you save these changes, you should see the navigator clean right up:

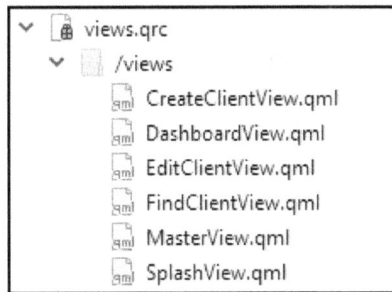

StackView

Our child views will be presented via a **StackView** component, which provides a stack-based navigation model with built-in history. New views (and views in this context means pretty much any QML) are pushed onto the stack when they are to be displayed and can be popped off the stack in order to go back to the previous view. We won't need to use the history capabilities, but they are a very useful feature.

To gain access to the component, we first need to reference the module, so add the import to **MasterView**:

```
import QtQuick.Controls 2.2
```

With that done, let's replace our **Text** element containing our welcome message with a `StackView`:

```
StackView {
    id: contentFrame
    initialItem: "qrc:/views/SplashView.qml"
}
```

We assign the component a unique identifier `contentFrame` so that we can reference it elsewhere in the QML, and we specify which child view we want to load by default—the new `SplashView`.

Next, edit `SplashView`. Update the `QtQuick` module version to 2.9 so that it matches **MasterView** (do this for all further QML files if not explicitly stated). This is not strictly necessary, but it's a good practice to avoid inconsistencies across views. There is generally not much in the way of breaking changes in minor releases of Qt, but the same code on two views referencing different versions of QtQuick may exhibit different behavior that can cause problems.

All we'll do with this view, for now, is to make a rectangle 400 pixels wide by 200 pixels high, which has a "vibrant" background color so that we can see that it has loaded:

```
import QtQuick 2.9

Rectangle {
    width: 400
    height: 200
    color: "#f4c842"
}
```

Colors can be specified using hexadecimal RGB values as we did here, or named SVG colors. I generally find hex easier as I can never remember the names of the colors!

> **TIP**
>
> If you hover your cursor over the hex string in Qt Creator, you get a really useful little pop-up color swatch.

Now run the application, and you should see that the welcome message no longer displays and instead, you are presented with a glorious orange-yellow rectangle, which is our **SplashView**.

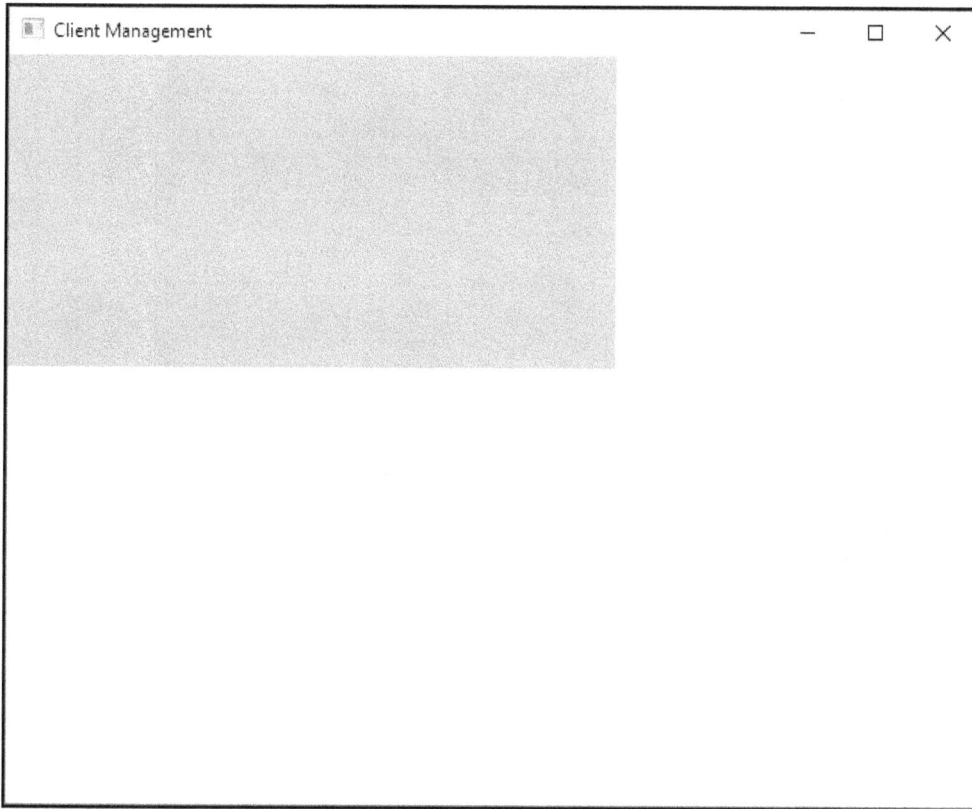

Anchors

One slight problem with our wonderful new **SplashView** is that it doesn't actually fill the window. Sure, we can change the 400 x 200 dimensions to 1024 x 768 so that it matches **MasterView**, but then what happens if the user resizes the window? Modern UI is all about responsive design—dynamic content that can adapt to the display it's being presented on, so hard-coding properties appropriate for only one platform aren't ideal. Fortunately, anchors come to our rescue.

Let's put our trusty old **scratchpad** project to use and take a look at anchors in action.

Right-click on `qml.qrc` and add a new `AnchorsDemo.qml` QML file alongside the existing `main.qml` file in the `scratchpad` folder. Don't worry about subfolders or `.qrc` prefixes, aliases, or any of that jazz.

Dip into `main.cpp` and load our new file instead of `main.qml`:

```
engine.load(QUrl(QStringLiteral("qrc:/AnchorsDemo.qml")));
```

Next, paste the following code into `AnchorsDemo`:

```
import QtQuick 2.9
import QtQuick.Window 2.2

Window {
    visible: true
    width: 1024
    height: 768
    title: qsTr("Scratchpad")
    color: "#ffffff"
    Rectangle {
        id: paleYellowBackground
        anchors.fill: parent
        color: "#cece9e"
    }
    Rectangle {
        id: blackRectangleInTheCentre
        width: 120
        height: 120
        anchors.centerIn: parent
        color: "#000000"
    }
    Rectangle {
        id: greenRectangleInTheCentre
        width: 100
        height: 100
        anchors.centerIn: parent
        anchors.verticalCenterOffset: 20
        color: "#008000"
    }
    Rectangle {
        id: redRectangleTopLeftCorner
        width: 100
        height: 100
        anchors {
            top: parent.top
            left: parent.left
```

```
        }
        color: "#800000"
    }
    Rectangle {
        id: blueRectangleTopLeftCorner
        width: 100
        height: 100
        anchors{
            top: redRectangleTopLeftCorner.bottom
            left: parent.left
        }
        color: "#000080"
    }
    Rectangle {
        id: purpleRectangleTopLeftCorner
        width: 100
        height: 100
        anchors{
            top: blueRectangleTopLeftCorner.bottom
            left: parent.left
            leftMargin: 20
        }
        color: "#800080"
    }
    Rectangle {
        id: turquoiseRectangleBottomRightCorner
        width: 100
        height: 100
        anchors{
            bottom: parent.bottom
            right: parent.right
            margins: 20
        }
        color: "#008080"
    }
}
```

Build and run the application, and you'll be presented with this rather bewildering sight:

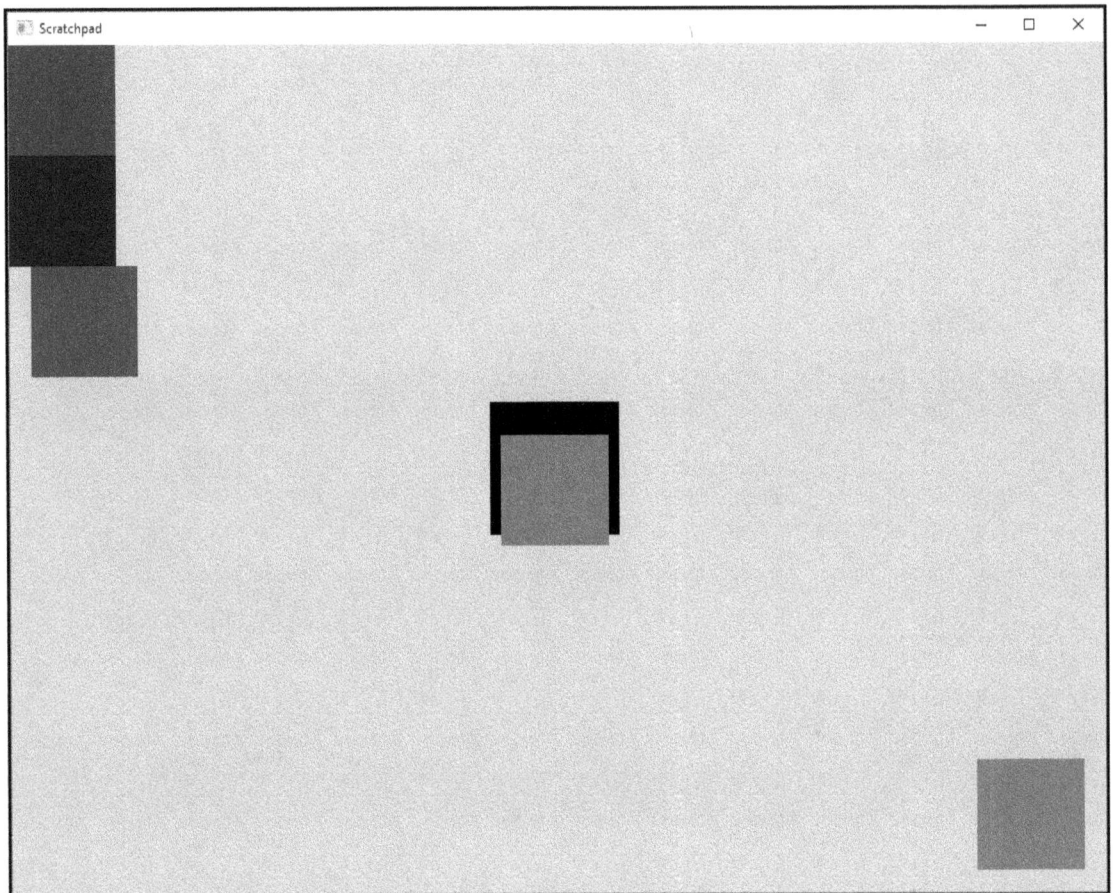

This may all look a bit confusing at first and I apologize if your color perception is suboptimal, but all we've done is draw a sequence of gaudily colored rectangles with differing anchors values. Let's walk through each rectangle one by one and see what is going on:

```
Rectangle {
    id: paleYellowBackground
    anchors.fill: parent
    color: "#cece9e"
}
```

Our first rectangle is the dull yellow brown background; `anchors.fill: parent` tells the rectangle to fill its parent, however big that may be. The parent of any given QML component is the QML component that contains it—the next level up in the hierarchy. In this case, it is the **Window** element. The **Window** element is 1024 x 768 pixels, so that's how big the rectangle is. Note that we don't need to specify width and height properties for the rectangle because they are inferred from the anchors.

This is exactly the behavior we want for our **SplashView**, but let's look at some other capabilities of anchors before we return to our main project:

```
Rectangle {
    id: blackRectangleInTheCentre
    width: 120
    height: 120
    anchors.centerIn: parent
    color: "#000000"
}
Rectangle {
    id: greenRectangleInTheCentre
    width: 100
    height: 100
    anchors.centerIn: parent
    anchors.verticalCenterOffset: 20
    color: "#008000"
}
```

We'll look at the next two rectangles together. First, we have a black rectangle that is 120 pixels square; `anchors.centerIn: parent` positions it at the center of its parent. We must specify the **width** and **height** because we are only positioning it, not sizing it.

Next, we have a slightly smaller green rectangle, also centered in its parent. We then use the `anchors.verticalCenterOffset` property to move it 20 pixels further down the screen. The *x, y* coordinate system used for positioning has its root (0, 0) at the top-left of the screen; `verticalCenterOffset` adds to the y coordinate. Positive numbers move the item down the screen, and negative numbers move the item up the screen. Its sister property—`horizontalCenterOffset`—is used for adjustments in the *x* axis.

One last thing to note here is that the rectangles overlap, and it is the green rectangle that wins out and is displayed in full. The black rectangle is pushed back and obscured. Similarly, all of our small rectangles sit in front of the large background rectangle. QML is rendered in a top-down fashion, so when the root element (**Window**) gets painted, its children are processed one by one from the top of the file to the bottom. So, items at the bottom of the file will be rendered in front of those rendered at the top of the file. The same is true if you paint a wall white and then paint it black, the wall will appear black because that's what was painted (rendered) last:

```
Rectangle {
    id: redRectangleTopLeftCorner
    width: 100
    height: 100
    anchors {
        top: parent.top
        left: parent.left
    }
    color: "#800000"
}
```

Next, we draw a red rectangle and rather than positioning or sizing the whole rectangle at once, we just anchor certain sides. We take the anchor on its **top** side and align it to the anchor on the **top** side of its parent (**Window**). We anchor its **left** side to its parent's **left** side. Hence, it becomes "attached" to the top-left corner.

We have to type the following:

```
anchors.top: parent.top
anchors.left: parent.left
```

Another helpful piece of syntactic sugar at work here is rather than doing that, we can remove the duplication and set the subproperties of the anchors group within curly braces:

```
anchors {
    top: parent.top
    left: parent.left
}
```

Next, the blue rectangle:

```
Rectangle {
    id: blueRectangleTopLeftCorner
    width: 100
    height: 100
    anchors{
```

```
        top: redRectangleTopLeftCorner.bottom
        left: parent.left
    }
    color: "#000080"
}
```

This follows the same pattern, though this time rather than attaching only to its parent, we also anchor to a sibling (the red rectangle), which we can reference though the `id` property:

```
Rectangle {
    id: purpleRectangleTopLeftCorner
    width: 100
    height: 100
    anchors{
        top: blueRectangleTopLeftCorner.bottom
        left: parent.left
        leftMargin: 20
    }
    color: "#800080"
}
```

The purple rectangle anchors to the bottom of the blue rectangle and to the left-hand side of the Window, but here we introduce our first margin. Each side has its own margin and in this case, we use `leftMargin` to give us an offset from the left anchor in exactly the same way as we saw with `verticalCenterOffset` earlier:

```
Rectangle {
    id: turquoiseRectangleBottomRightCorner
    width: 100
    height: 100
    anchors{
        bottom: parent.bottom
        right: parent.right
        margins: 20
    }
    color: "#008080"
}
```

Finally, our turquoise rectangle uses some of that empty space over on the right-hand side of the screen and demonstrates how we can set the margin on all four sides simultaneously using the `margins` property.

Note that all of these bindings are dynamic. Try resizing the window, and all the rectangles will adapt automatically. Anchors are a great tool for responsive UI design.

Let's head back to our `SplashView` in our `cm-ui` project and apply what we've just learned. Replace the fixed **width** and **height** attributes with the more dynamic `anchors.fill` property:

```
Rectangle {
    anchors.fill: parent
    color: "#f4c842"
}
```

Now, the `SplashView` will fill whatever its parent element is. Build and run, and you'll see that rather than our lovely colorful rectangle filling the screen as we expected, it has disappeared altogether. Let's take a look at why that is.

Sizing

Our rectangle will fill its parent, so the size of the rectangle depends entirely on the size of its parent. Walking up the QML hierarchy, the component that contains the rectangle is the `StackView` element back in **MasterView**:

```
StackView {
    id: contentFrame
    initialItem: Qt.resolvedUrl("qrc:/views/SplashView.qml")
}
```

Often, QML components are clever enough to size themselves based on their children. Previously, we had set our rectangle to a fixed size of 400 x 200. The `StackView` could look at that and say "I need to contain a single **Rectangle** that is 400 x 200, so I'll make myself 400 x 200 too. Easy!". We can always overrule that and set it to some other size using its **width** and **height** properties, but it can work out what size it wanted to be.

Back in `scratchpad`, create a new `SizingDemo.qml` view and edit `main.cpp` to load it on startup, just like we did with `AnchorsDemo`. Edit `SizingDemo` as follows:

```
import QtQuick 2.9
import QtQuick.Window 2.2

Window {
    visible: true
    width: 1024
    height: 768
    title: qsTr("Scratchpad")
    color: "#ffffff"
    Column {
        id: columnWithText
```

```
            Text {
                id: text1
                text: "Text 1"
            }
            Text {
                id: text2
                text: "Text 2"
                width: 300
                height: 20
            }
            Text {
                id: text3
                text: "Text 3 Text 3 Text 3 Text 3 Text 3 Text 3 Text 3 Text 3
Text 3 Text 3 Text 3 Text 3 Text 3 Text 3 Text 3 Text 3 Text 3 Text 3 Text
3 Text 3 Text 3 Text 3 Text 3 Text 3 Text 3 Text 3 Text 3 Text 3 Text 3
Text 3 Text 3 Text 3 Text 3 Text 3 Text 3 Text 3 Text 3"
            }
            Text {
                id: text4
                text: "Text 4 Text 4 Text 4 Text 4 Text 4 Text 4 Text 4 Text 4
Text 4 Text 4 Text 4 Text 4 Text 4 Text 4 Text 4 Text 4 Text 4 Text 4 Text
4 Text 4 Text 4 Text 4 Text 4 Text 4 Text 4 Text 4 Text 4 Text 4 Text 4
Text 4 Text 4 Text 4 Text 4 Text 4 Text 4 Text 4 Text 4"
                width: 300
            }
            Text {
                id: text5
                text: "Text 5 Text 5 Text 5 Text 5 Text 5 Text 5 Text 5 Text 5
Text 5 Text 5 Text 5 Text 5 Text 5 Text 5 Text 5 Text 5 Text 5 Text 5 Text
5 Text 5 Text 5 Text 5 Text 5 Text 5 Text 5 Text 5 Text 5 Text 5 Text 5
Text 5 Text 5 Text 5 Text 5 Text 5 Text 5 Text 5 Text 5"
                width: 300
                wrapMode: Text.Wrap
            }
        }
        Column {
            id: columnWithRectangle
            Rectangle {
                id: rectangle
                anchors.fill: parent
            }
        }
        Component.onCompleted: {
            console.log("Text1 - implicitWidth:" + text1.implicitWidth + "
implicitHeight:" + text1.implicitHeight + " width:" + text1.width + "
height:" + text1.height)
            console.log("Text2 - implicitWidth:" + text2.implicitWidth + "
implicitHeight:" + text2.implicitHeight + " width:" + text2.width + "
```

```
height:" + text2.height)
        console.log("Text3 - implicitWidth:" + text3.implicitWidth + "
implicitHeight:" + text3.implicitHeight + " width:" + text3.width + "
height:" + text3.height)
        console.log("Text4 - implicitWidth:" + text4.implicitWidth + "
implicitHeight:" + text4.implicitHeight + " width:" + text4.width + "
height:" + text4.height)
        console.log("Text5 - implicitWidth:" + text5.implicitWidth + "
implicitHeight:" + text5.implicitHeight + " width:" + text5.width + "
height:" + text5.height)
        console.log("ColumnWithText - implicitWidth:" +
columnWithText.implicitWidth + " implicitHeight:" +
columnWithText.implicitHeight + " width:" + columnWithText.width + "
height:" + columnWithText.height)
        console.log("Rectangle - implicitWidth:" + rectangle.implicitWidth
+ " implicitHeight:" + rectangle.implicitHeight + " width:" +
rectangle.width + " height:" + rectangle.height)
        console.log("ColumnWithRectangle - implicitWidth:" +
columnWithRectangle.implicitWidth + " implicitHeight:" +
columnWithRectangle.implicitHeight + " width:" + columnWithRectangle.width
+ " height:" + columnWithRectangle.height)
    }
}
```

Run this, and you'll get another screen full of nonsense:

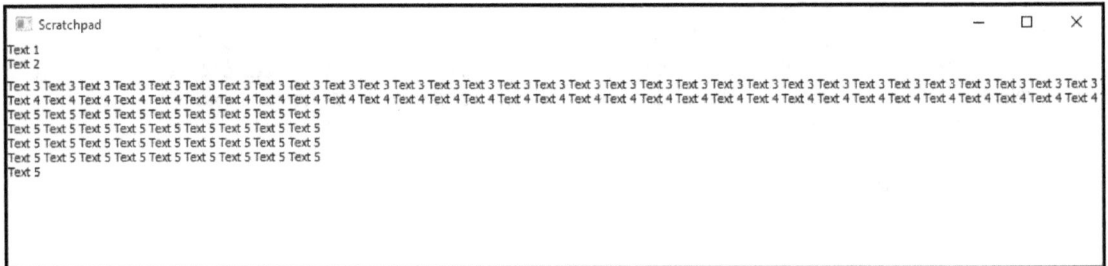

Of far more interest to us here is what is output to the console:

```
qml: Text1 - implicitWidth:30 implicitHeight:13 width:30 height:13

qml: Text2 - implicitWidth:30 implicitHeight:13 width:300 height:20

qml: Text3 - implicitWidth:1218 implicitHeight:13 width:1218 height:13

qml: Text4 - implicitWidth:1218 implicitHeight:13 width:300 height:13

qml: Text5 - implicitWidth:1218 implicitHeight:65 width:300 height:65

qml: ColumnWithText - implicitWidth:1218 implicitHeight:124 width:1218
height:124

qml: Rectangle - implicitWidth:0 implicitHeight:0 width:0 height:0

qml: ColumnWithRectangle - implicitWidth:0 implicitHeight:0 width:0
height:0
```

So, what's going on? We've created two **Column** elements, which are invisible layout components that arrange their child elements vertically. We've stuffed the first column with various **Text** elements and added a single **Rectangle** to the second. At the bottom of the view is a JavaScript function that will execute when the **Window** component has completed (that is, finished loading). All the function does is write out the implicitWidth, implicitHeight, width, and height properties of various elements on the view.

Let's walk through the elements and the corresponding console lines:

```
Text {
    id: text1
    text: "Text 1"
}
```

```
qml: Text1 - implicitWidth:30 implicitHeight:13 width:30 height:13
```

This **Text** element contains a short piece of text, and we have not specified any sizes. Its `implicitWidth` and `implicitHeight` properties are the sizes the element wants to be based on its content. Its `width` and `height` properties are the sizes the element actually is. In this case, it will size itself however it wants to, because we haven't specified otherwise, so its `width/height` are the same as its `implicitWidth/implicitHeight`:

```
Text {
    id: text2
    text: "Text 2"
    width: 300
    height: 20
}
```

```
qml: Text2 - implicitWidth:30 implicitHeight:13 width:300 height:20
```

With `text2`, the implicit sizes are the same as `text1` as the content is virtually identical. However, this time, we have explicitly told it to be 300 wide and 20 high. The console tells us that the element is doing as it's told and is indeed that size:

```
Text {
    id: text3
    text: "Text 3 Text 3 Text 3 Text 3 Text 3 Text 3 Text 3 Text 3 Text 3
    Text 3 Text 3 Text 3 Text 3 Text 3 Text 3 Text 3 Text 3 Text 3 Text
    3 Text 3 Text 3 Text 3 Text 3 Text 3 Text 3 Text 3 Text 3 Text 3
    Text 3 Text 3 Text 3 Text 3 Text 3 Text 3 Text 3"
}
```

```
qml: Text3 - implicitWidth:1218 implicitHeight:13 width:1218 height:13
```

This `text3` takes the same hands-off approach as `text1`, but with a much longer piece of text as its content. This time, `implicitWidth` is much larger as that is the amount of space it needs to fit the long text in. Note that this is actually wider than the window and the text gets cut off. Again, we haven't instructed it otherwise, so it sizes itself:

```
Text {
    id: text4
    text: "Text 4 Text 4 Text 4 Text 4 Text 4 Text 4 Text 4 Text 4 Text 4
    Text 4 Text 4 Text 4 Text 4 Text 4 Text 4 Text 4 Text 4 Text 4 Text
    4 Text 4 Text 4 Text 4 Text 4 Text 4 Text 4 Text 4 Text 4 Text 4
    Text 4 Text 4 Text 4 Text 4 Text 4 Text 4 Text 4"
    width: 300
}
```

```
qml: Text4 - implicitWidth:1218 implicitHeight:13 width:300 height:13
```

The text4 has the same lengthy block of text, but we've told it what width we want this time. You'll notice on screen that even though the element is only 300 pixels wide, the text is visible all the way across the window. The content is overflowing the bounds of its container. You can set the clip property to true to prevent this, but we're not too concerned with that here:

```
Text {
    id: text5
    text: "Text 5 Text 5 Text 5 Text 5 Text 5 Text 5 Text 5 Text 5 Text
    5 Text 5 Text 5 Text 5 Text 5 Text 5 Text 5 Text 5 Text 5
    Text 5 Text 5 Text 5 Text 5 Text 5 Text 5 Text 5 Text 5 Text
    5 Text 5 Text 5 Text 5 Text 5 Text 5 Text 5 Text 5 Text 5"
    width: 300
    wrapMode: Text.Wrap
}
```

```
qml: Text5 - implicitWidth:1218 implicitHeight:65 width:300 height:65
```

The text5 repeats the same long block of text and constrains the width to 300, but this time, we bring a bit of order to proceedings by setting the wrapMode property to Text.Wrap. With this setting, the enabled behavior is much more like what you would expect from a block of text—it fills up the available width and then wraps onto the next line. The implicitHeight and, consequently, the height of the element has increased to accommodate the contents. Note, however, that the implicitHeight is still the same as earlier; this is still the width the control wants to be in order to fit all of its content in, given the constraints we have defined, and we have defined no height constraint.

We then print out the properties of the column containing all this text:

```
qml: ColumnWithText - implicitWidth:1218 implicitHeight:124 width:1218
height:124
```

The important thing to note is that the column is able to figure out how wide and high it needs to be to accommodate all of its children.

Next, we get to the issue we encountered back in `SplashView`:

```
Column {
    id: columnWithRectangle
    Rectangle {
        id: rectangle
        anchors.fill: parent
    }
}
```

Here, we have a chicken and egg scenario. The `Column` tries to work out how large it needs to be to contain its children, so it takes a look at `Rectangle`. `Rectangle` has no explicit size information and no children of its own, it is just set to fill its parent, the `Column`. Neither element can figure out how big they are supposed to be, so they both default to 0x0, which renders them invisible.

```
qml: Rectangle - implicitWidth:0 implicitHeight:0 width:0 height:0
```

```
qml: ColumnWithRectangle - implicitWidth:0 implicitHeight:0 width:0
height:0
```

> Sizing of elements is probably the thing that has caught me out the most with QML over the years. As a general guideline, if you write some QML but then can't see it rendered on screen, it's probably a sizing issue. I usually find that giving everything an arbitrary fixed **width** and **height** is a good start when debugging, and then one by one, make the sizes dynamic until you recreate the problem.

Armed with this knowledge, let's head back to `MasterView` and fix our earlier problem.

Add `anchors.fill: parent` to the `StackView` component:

```
StackView {
    id: contentFrame
    anchors.fill: parent
    initialItem: Qt.resolvedUrl("qrc:/views/SplashView.qml")
}
```

The `StackView` will now fill its parent **Window**, which we have explicitly given a fixed size of 1024 x 768. Run the app again, and you should now have a lovely orange-yellow `SplashView` that fills the screen and happily resizes itself if you resize the window:

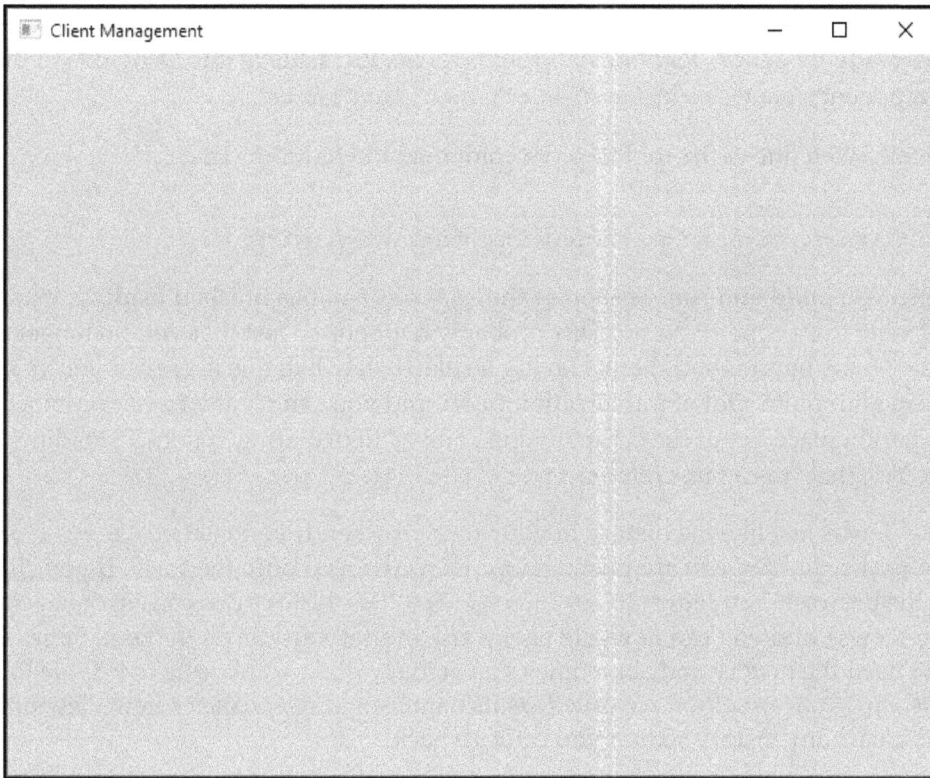

Navigation

Lets make a quick addition to our SplashView:

```
Rectangle {
    anchors.fill: parent
    color: "#f4c842"
    Text {
        anchors.centerIn: parent
        text: "Splash View"
    }
}
```

This just adds the name of the view to the screen, so when we start moving between views, we know which one we are looking at. With that done, copy the content of SplashView into all the other new views, updating the text in each to reflect the name of the view, for example, in DashboardView, the text could say "Dashboard View".

The first piece of navigation we want to do is when the `MasterView` has finished loading and we're ready for action, load the `DashboardView`. We achieve this using one of the QML component slots we've just seen—`Component.onCompleted()`.

Add the following line to the root `Window` component in `MasterView`:

```
Component.onCompleted:
contentFrame.replace("qrc:/views/DashboardView.qml");
```

Now when you build and run, as soon as the `MasterView` has finished loading, it switches the child view to `DashboardView`. This probably happens so fast that you no longer even see `SplashView`, but it is still there. Having a splash view like this is great if you've got an application with quite a lot of initialization to do, and you can't really have non-blocking UI. It's a handy place to put the company logo and a "Reticulating splines..." loading message. Yes, that was a Sims reference!

The StackView is just like the history in your web browser. If you visit `www.google.com` and then `www.packtpub.com`, you are pushing `www.packtpub.com` onto the stack. If you click on Back on the browser, you return to `www.google.com`. This history can consist of several pages (or views), and you can navigate backward and forward through them. Sometimes you don't need the history and sometimes you actively don't want users to be able to go back. The `replace()` method we called, as its name suggests, pushes a new view onto the stack and clears any history so that you can't go back.

In the `Component.onCompleted` slot, we've seen an example of how to navigate between views directly from QML. We can use this approach for all of our application navigation. For example, we can add a button for the user to create a new client and when it's clicked on, push the `CreateClientView` straight on to the stack, as follows:

```
Button {
    onClicked: contentFrame.replace("qrc:/views/CreateClientView.qml")
}
```

For UX designs or simple UI heavy applications with little business logic, this is a perfectly valid approach. The trouble is that your QML views and components become very tightly coupled, and the business logic layer has no visibility of what the user is doing. Quite often, moving to a new screen of the application isn't as simple as just displaying a new view. You may need to update a state machine, set some models up, or clear out some data from the previous view. By routing all of our navigation requests through our **MasterController** switchboard, we decouple our components and gain an intercept point for our business logic to take any actions it needs to as well as validate that the requests are appropriate.

We will request navigation to these views by emitting signals from our business logic layer and having our **MasterView** respond to them and perform the transition. Rather than cluttering up our **MasterController**, we'll delegate the responsibility for navigation to a new controller in cm-lib, so create a new header file (there is no implementation as such, so we don't need a .cpp file) called navigation-controller.h in cm/cm-lib/source/controllers and add the following code:

```
#ifndef NAVIGATIONCONTROLLER_H
#define NAVIGATIONCONTROLLER_H

#include <QObject>

#include <cm-lib_global.h>
#include <models/client.h>

namespace cm {
namespace controllers {

class CMLIBSHARED_EXPORT NavigationController : public QObject
{
    Q_OBJECT

public:
    explicit NavigationController(QObject* _parent = nullptr)
        : QObject(_parent)
    {}

signals:
    void goCreateClientView();
    void goDashboardView();
    void goEditClientView(cm::models::Client* client);
    void goFindClientView();
};

}
}
#endif
```

We have created a minimal class that inherits from QObject and implements a signal for each of our new views. Note that we don't need to navigate to the **MasterView** or the **SplashView**, so there is no corresponding signal for those. When we navigate to the EditClientView, we will need to inform the UI which **Client** we want to edit, so we will pass it through as a parameter. Calling one of these methods from anywhere within our business logic code fires a request into the ether saying "I want to go to the so-and-so view, please". It is then up to the **MasterView** over in the UI layer to monitor those requests and respond accordingly. Note that the business logic layer still knows nothing about the UI implementation. It's fine if nobody responds to the signal; it is not a two-way communication.

> Whenever you inherit from QObject, always remember the Q_OBJECT macro and also an overloaded constructor that takes a QObject parent. As we want to use this class outside of this project (in the UI project), we must also remember the **CMLIBSHARED_EXPORT** macro.

We've looked forward a little bit here and assumed that our Client class will be in the cm::models namespace, but the default Client class that Qt added for us when we created the project is not, so let's fix that before we move on:

client.h:

```
#ifndef CLIENT_H
#define CLIENT_H

#include "cm-lib_global.h"

namespace cm {
namespace models {

class CMLIBSHARED_EXPORT Client
{
public:
    Client();
};

}}

#endif
```

client.cpp:

```
#include "client.h"

namespace cm {
```

```
namespace models {

Client::Client()
{
}

}}
```

We need to be able to create an instance of a NavigationController and have our UI interact with it. For unit testing reasons, it is good practice to hide object creation behind some sort of object factory interface, but we're not concerned with that at this stage, so we'll simply create the object in **MasterController**. Let's take this opportunity to add the Private Implementation (PImpl) idiom to our **MasterController** too. If you haven't come across PImpl before, it is simply a technique to move all private implementation details out of the header file and into the definition. This helps keep the header file as short and clean as possible, with only the includes necessary for consumers of the public API. Replace the declaration and implementation as follows:

master-controller.h:

```
#ifndef MASTERCONTROLLER_H
#define MASTERCONTROLLER_H

#include <QObject>
#include <QScopedPointer>
#include <QString>

#include <cm-lib_global.h>
#include <controllers/navigation-controller.h>

namespace cm {
namespace controllers {

class CMLIBSHARED_EXPORT MasterController : public QObject
{
    Q_OBJECT
    Q_PROPERTY( QString ui_welcomeMessage READ welcomeMessage CONSTANT )
    Q_PROPERTY( cm::controllers::NavigationController*
ui_navigationController READ navigationController CONSTANT )

public:
    explicit MasterController(QObject* parent = nullptr);
    ~MasterController();
    NavigationController* navigationController();
    const QString& welcomeMessage() const;

private:
```

```
    class Implementation;
    QScopedPointer<Implementation> implementation;
};

}}
#endif
```

master-controller.cpp:

```
#include "master-controller.h"

namespace cm {
namespace controllers {

class MasterController::Implementation
{
public:
    Implementation(MasterController* _masterController)
        : masterController(_masterController)
    {
        navigationController = new NavigationController(masterController);
    }

    MasterController* masterController{nullptr};
    NavigationController* navigationController{nullptr};
    QString welcomeMessage = "This is MasterController to Major Tom";
};

MasterController::MasterController(QObject* parent)
    : QObject(parent)
{
    implementation.reset(new Implementation(this));
}

MasterController::~MasterController()
{
}

NavigationController* MasterController::navigationController()
{
    return implementation->navigationController;
}

const QString& MasterController::welcomeMessage() const
{
    return implementation->welcomeMessage;
}
```

```
}}
```

You may have noted that we don't specify the **cm::controllers** namespace for the NavigationController accessor method, but we do for the `Q_PROPERTY`. This is because the property is accessed by the UI QML, which is not executing within the scope of the `cm` namespace, so we have to explicitly specify the fullyqualified name. As a general rule of thumb, be explicit about namespaces for anything that QML interacts with directly, including parameters in signals and slots.

Next, we need to register the new `NavigationController` class with the QML system in the **cm-ui** project, so in `main.cpp`, add the following registration next to the existing one for **MasterController**:

```
qmlRegisterType<cm::controllers::NavigationController>("CM", 1, 0,
"NavigationController");
```

We're now ready to wire up **MasterView** to react to these navigation signals. Add the following element before the `StackView`:

```
Connections {
    target: masterController.ui_navigationController
    onGoCreateClientView:
contentFrame.replace("qrc:/views/CreateClientView.qml")
    onGoDashboardView: contentFrame.replace("qrc:/views/DashboardView.qml")
    onGoEditClientView:
contentFrame.replace("qrc:/views/EditClientView.qml", {selectedClient:
client})
    onGoFindClientView:
contentFrame.replace("qrc:/views/FindClientView.qml")
}
```

We are creating a connection component bound to our new instance of **NavigationController**, which reacts to each of the go signals we added and navigates to the relevant view via the contentFrame, using the same replace() method we used previously to move to the Dashboard. So whenever the goCreateClientView() signal gets fired on the **NavigationController**, the onGoCreateClientView() slot gets called on our Connections component and the CreateClientView is loaded into the **StackView** named contentFrame. In the case of onGoEditClientView where a client parameter is passed from the signal, we pass that object along to a property named selectedClient, which we will add to the view later.

> Some signals and slots in QML components are automatically generated and connected for us and are convention based. Slots are named on[CapitalisedNameOfRelatedSignal]. So, for example, if you have a signal called mySplendidSignal(), then the corresponding slot will be named onMySplendidSignal. These conventions are in play with our NavigationController and Connections components.

Next, let's add a navigation bar to **MasterView** with some placeholder buttons so that we can try these signals out.

Add a Rectangle to form the background for our bar:

```
Rectangle {
    id: navigationBar
    anchors {
        top: parent.top
        bottom: parent.bottom
        left: parent.left
    }
    width: 100
    color: "#000000"
}
```

This draws a black strip 100 pixels wide anchored to the left-hand side of the view.

We also need to adjust our `StackView` so that it allows some space for our bar. Rather than filling its parent, let's anchor three of its four sides to its parent, but attach the left-hand side to the right-hand side of our bar:

```
StackView {
    id: contentFrame
    anchors {
        top: parent.top
        bottom: parent.bottom
        right: parent.right
        left: navigationBar.right
    }
    initialItem: Qt.resolvedUrl("qrc:/views/SplashView.qml")
}
```

Now, let's add some buttons to our navigation `Rectangle`:

```
Rectangle {
    id: navigationBar
    ...

    Column {
        Button {
            text: "Dashboard"
            onClicked:
masterController.ui_navigationController.goDashboardView()
        }
        Button {
            text: "New Client"
            onClicked:
masterController.ui_navigationController.goCreateClientView()
        }
        Button {
            text: "Find Client"
            onClicked:
masterController.ui_navigationController.goFindClientView()
        }
    }

}
```

We use the `Column` component to lay out our buttons for us, rather than having to individually anchor the buttons to each other. Each button displays some text and when clicked on, calls a signal on the **NavigationController**. Our `Connection` component reacts to the signals and performs the view transition for us:

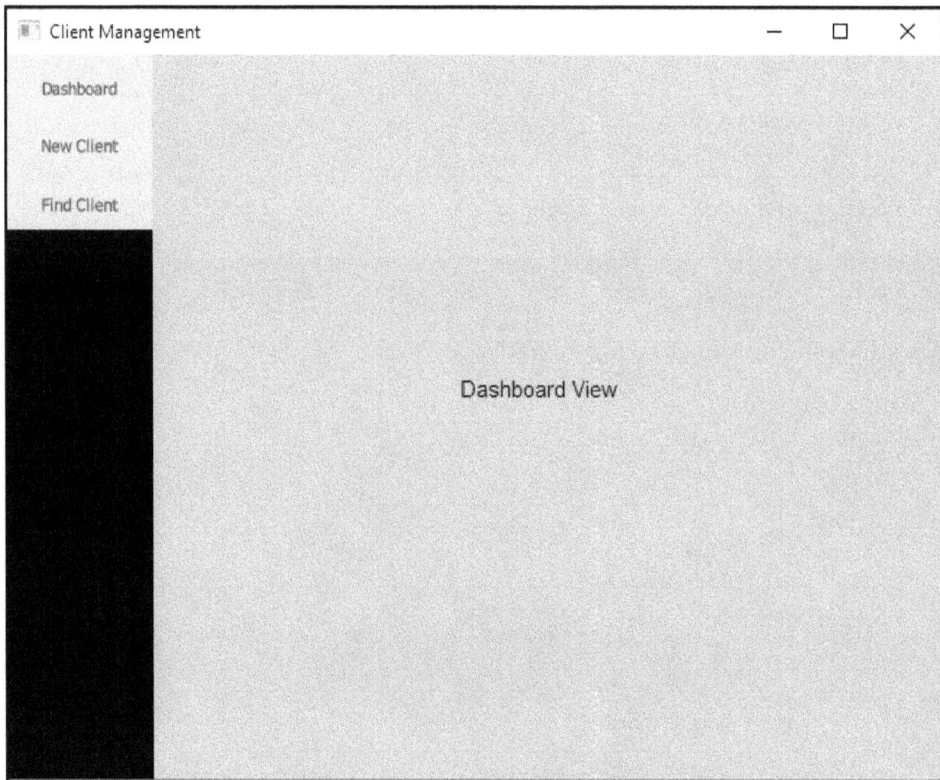

Great stuff, we have a functional navigation framework! However, when you click on one of the navigation buttons, the navigation bar disappears momentarily and comes back again. We are also getting "conflicting anchors" messages in our **Application Output** console, which suggest that we're doing something that's not quite right. Let's address those issues before we move on.

Fixing conflicts

The navigation bar problem is a simple one. As explained previously, QML is hierarchical in structure. This bears out in the way the elements are rendered—child elements that appear first are rendered first. In our case, we draw the navigation bar and then we draw the content frame. When the **StackView** component loads new content, by default it applies funky transitions to make it look nice. Those transitions can result in content moving out of bounds of the control and drawing over any content below it. There are a couple of ways to address this.

Firstly, we can rearrange the order that the components are rendered in and put the navigation bar after the content frame. This will draw the navigation bar over the top of the `StackView`, regardless of what was going on with it. The second option and the one we will implement is to simply set the `clip` property of the **StackView**:

```
clip: true
```

This clips any content that overlaps the boundary of the control and doesn't render it.

The next problem is a little more esoteric. As we've discussed, the number one cause of confused head scratching I've encountered over the past few years of QML development is the sizing of components. Some components we've used, such as **Rectangle**, are intrinsically visual elements. If their size is not defined, either directly with the `width`/`height` properties or indirectly with **anchors**, then they will not render. Other elements such as **Connections** are not visual at all and size properties are redundant. Layout elements such as **Column** may have a fixed size in one axis, but be dynamic in the other by nature.

One thing that most components have in common is that they inherit from **Item**, which in turn inherits directly from **QtObject**, which is just a plain **QObject**. In much the same way that the Qt Framework on the C++ side implements a lot of default behavior for plain old **QObject***, QML components often implement default behavior for **Item** components that we can leverage here.

In our child views, we have used **Rectangle** as our root object. This makes sense as we want to display a rectangle of a fixed size and color. However, this causes problems for the **StackView** as it doesn't know what size it should be. To provide this information, we try and anchor it to its parent (the **StackView**), but then that causes problems of its own by conflicting with the transitions the **StackView** is trying to perform when we switch views.

Our way out of this dilemma is to instead have the root of our child views be a plain old **Item**. **StackView** components have internal logic to handle **Item** components and will just size it for us. Our **Rectangle** component then becomes the child of an **Item** component that has already been sized automatically, and we can anchor to that instead:

```
Item {
    Rectangle {
        ...
    }
}
```

This is all a bit confusing and feels like Voodoo, but the takeaway here is that having **Item** as the root element in your custom QML is often a good thing. Go ahead and add a root **Item** component in this way to all the child views (but not **MasterView**).

Run the application again, and you should now have nice smooth transitions and no warning messages in the console.

Summary

We have a flexible, decoupled navigation mechanism in place and are successfully transitioning between different views. We have the basics of a navigation bar in place and a working content pane as designed at the beginning of the chapter.

Having the UI call the business logic layer to emit a signal that the UI then reacts to may seem like a bit of a roundabout way of navigating between views, but this business logic signal/UI slot design brings benefits. It keeps the UI modular as the views don't need to know about each other. It keeps the logic for navigation in the business logic layer and enables that layer to request that the UI navigate the user to a particular view without needing to know anything about the UI or the view itself. Crucially, it also gives us intercept points so that when the user requests navigation to a given view, we can handle it and perform any additional processing we need, such as state management or cleanup.

In `Chapter 4`, *Style*, we will introduce a shared style component, and QML modules and icons before we complete our UI design with a dynamic command bar.

4
Style

It's generally a good idea to aim for function before form in the development process, but the UI is the part of the application our users interact with and is a key ingredient of a successful solution. In this chapter, we will introduce a CSS-like style resource and build on the responsive design principles we introduced in the last chapter.

We will create custom QML components and modules to maximize code reuse. We will integrate Font Awesome into our solution to provide us with a suite of scalable icons and help give our UI a modern graphical look. We will tidy up the navigation bar, introduce the concept of commands, and build the framework for a dynamic, context-sensitive command bar.

We will cover the following topics in this chapter:

- Custom style resource
- Font Awesome
- Custom components
- Navigation bar styling
- Commands

Style resource

First off, let's create a new resource file to contain the non-QML visual elements we will need. In the cm-ui project, **Add New... > Qt > Qt Resource File**:

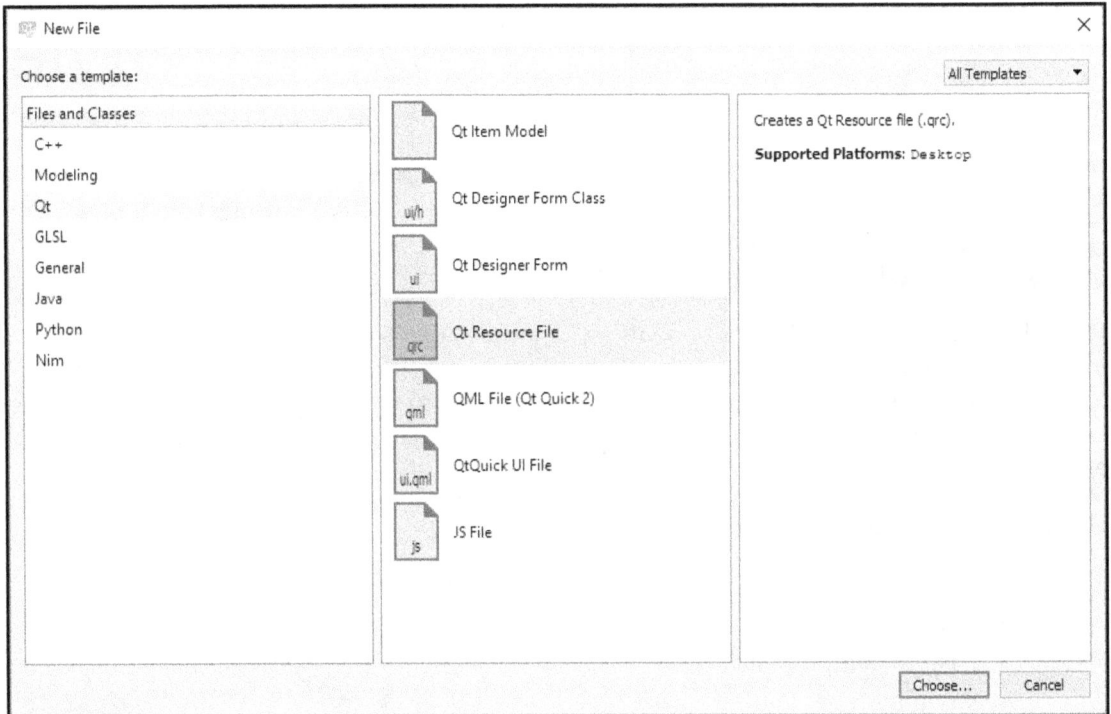

Name the file assets.qrc and place it in cm/cm-ui. Your new file will automatically open in the **Resource Editor**, which I don't find to be a particularly helpful editor, so close it. You will see that the assets.qrc file has been added to the **Resources** section of the cm-ui project. Right-click on it and select **Add New... > Qt > QML File**. Call the file Style.qml and save it to cm/cm-ui/assets.

Edit the assets.qrc file in the **Plain Text Editor** in the same way we did for the views:

```
<RCC>
    <qresource prefix="/assets">
        <file alias="Style.qml">assets/Style.qml</file>
    </qresource>
</RCC>
```

Now, edit Style.qml and we'll add a single style property to use for the background color of our views:

```
pragma Singleton
import QtQuick 2.9

Item {
    readonly property color colourBackground: "#f4c842"
}
```

What we are doing here in C++ terms is creating a singleton class with a public member variable of type const color called colourBackground with an initialized value of a hex RGB code for (very) light grey.

Now, we need to perform a little bit of a manual fudge to wire this up. We need to create a Module Definition file named qmldir (with no file extension) in the same folder as Style.qml (cm/cm-ui/assets). There is no built-in template for this type of file, so we need to create it ourselves. File Explorer in older versions of Windows used to make this a painful exercise as it always insisted on a file extension. A console command was required to forcibly rename the file. Windows 10 will happily create the file without an extension. In the Unix world, files without an extension are more common.

With the qmldir file created, edit assets.qrc and insert a new entry for it right next to Style.qml inside the /assets prefix:

```
<file alias="qmldir">assets/qmldir</file>
```

Double-click on the newly added qmldir file and enter the following lines:

```
module assets
singleton Style 1.0 Style.qml
```

We have already seen modules when we **import QtQuick 2.9**. This makes version 2.9 of the QtQuick module available for use in our views. In our qmldir file, we are defining a new module of our own called assets and telling Qt that there is a **Style** object within version **1.0** of that module, for which the implementation is in our Style.qml file.

With our new style module created and wired up, let's now put that modern off-white color to use. Start with the first child view we see, SplashView, and add the following to get access to our new module:

```
import assets 1.0
```

You'll note that we're presented with an angry red underline, suggesting that all is not well. Hover over the line with the mouse pointer, and a tooltip will tell us that we need to add the import path to our new `qmldir` definition file.

There are a couple of ways to do this. The first option is to go to the **Projects** mode and select the current kit's **Build** settings and then **Debug** mode. At the bottom in the **Build Environment** section, click on **Details**. Here, you can see a list of all the environment variables for the current kit and configuration. **Add** a new variable called **QML2_IMPORT_PATH** and set its value to the `cm-ui` folder:

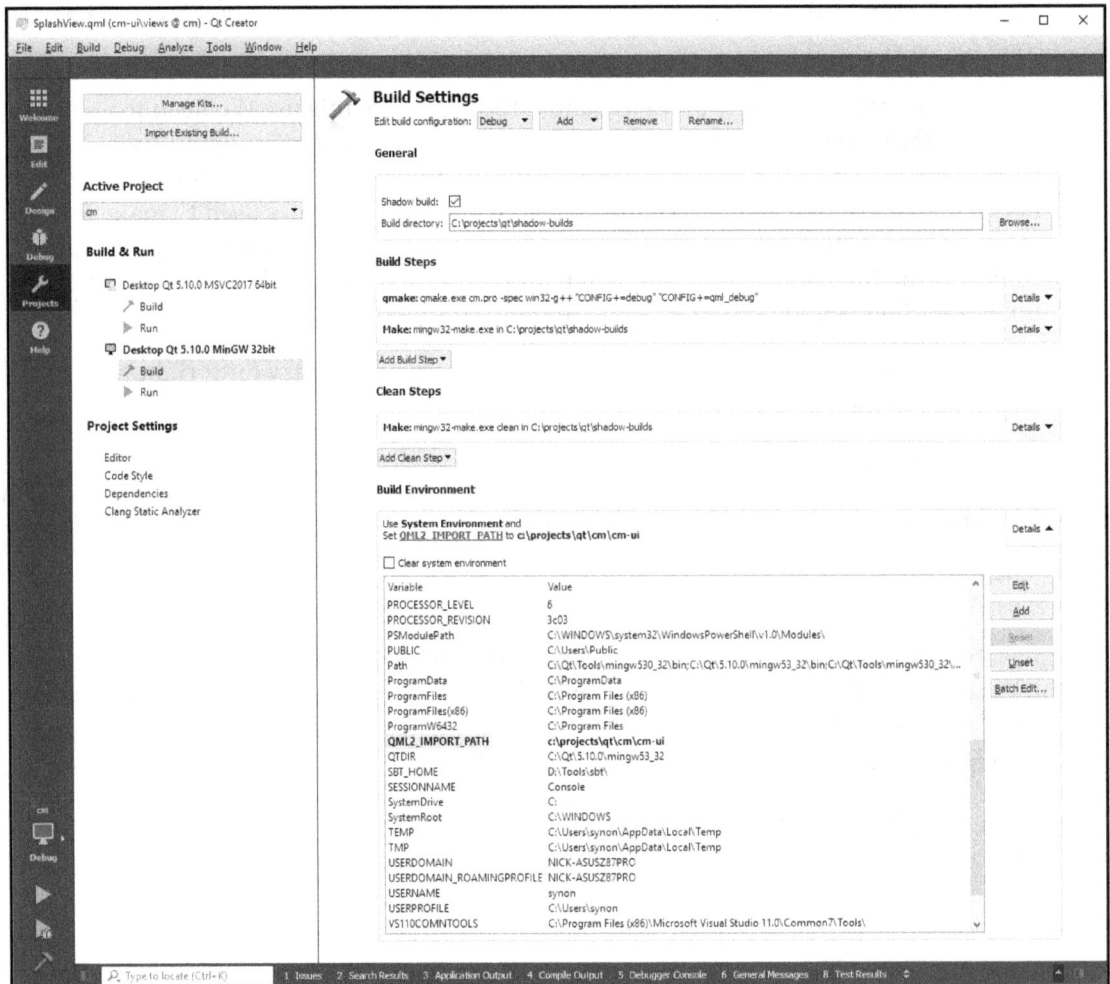

This adds the project working directory of the `cm-ui` project (`/projects/qt/cm/cm-ui`) to the QML Import Path. Note that our module name must reflect the relative path to the `qmldir` file from this import path.

The problem with this approach is that this environment variable is tied to the `cm.pro.user` file. If you share the project with other developers, they will have their own `cm.pro.user` files, and they will have to remember to add this variable too. Furthermore, it's tied to an absolute path and if you copy the project code to another machine, it may not be at that location.

The second, and preferred, option is to add the following line to `main.cpp` immediately after instantiating **QQmlApplicationEngine**:

```
engine.addImportPath("qrc:/");
```

So why `qrc:/` and not the absolute path to our `qmldir` file? You'll remember that we added our `views.qrc` resource bundle to a `RESOURCES` variable in `cm-ui.pro`. What this does is it takes all the files from `views.qrc` and compiles them into the application binary in a kind of virtual filesystem, where the prefixes act as virtual folders. The root of this virtual filesystem is referenced as `qrc:/` and by using this in the import path, we are essentially asking Qt to look inside all of our bundled resource files for any modules. Head over to `cm-ui.pro` and ensure that our new `assets.qrc` has also been added to `RESOURCES`:

```
RESOURCES += views.qrc
    assets.qrc
```

This can be a bit confusing, so to reiterate, we have added the following folder to search for new modules, either using the **QML2_IMPORT_PATH** environment variable to search our `cm-ui` project folder on our local physical filesystem, or the `addImportPath()` method to search the root of our virtual resource filesystem at runtime.

In both cases, our `qmldir` file that defines our new module is in a folder called `assets` a level below that, that is, either `<Qt Projects>/cm/cm-ui/assets` in the physical filesystem or `qrc:/assets` in the virtual.

This gives us the module name `assets`. If our folder structure was deeper, like stuff/badgers/assets, then our module would need to be called `stuff.badgers.assets`, as that is the path relative to our defined import path. Similarly, if we wanted to add another module for our existing views, we would create a `qmldir` file in `cm-ui/views` and call the module `views`.

If you see that Qt Creator is still a bit confused and the red line still persists, ensure that `cm-ui.pro` contains the `QML_IMPORT_PATH +=` `$$PWD` line.

With all this in place, we can now use our new module. Including the module means we can now access our singleton `Style` object and read properties from it. Replace the `color` property of our `SplashView`:

```
Rectangle {
    ...
    color: Style.colourBackground
    ...
}
```

Repeat this to set the background color for all of our views except `MasterView`. Remember to `include ui.assets 1.0` in each view too.

When you build and run the application, you may wonder why we've gone through all of that rigmarole when the views look exactly the same as they did before. Well, let's say that we've just had a meeting with the guys from marketing where they told us that yellowy orange is not a good fit for the brand any more, and we need to change all the views to be a clean off-white color. We would previously have had to go into every view and change the color from `#f4c842` to `#efefef`. Now, there are only seven of them, so it's not a big deal, but imagine if we had to change all the colors for all the components in 50 complex views; that would be a very painful exercise.

However, go to `Style.qml` and change the `colourBackground` property from `#f4c842` to `#efefef`. Build and run the application and bask in the glory of our rebranded app! By setting up our shared style component early, we can add the properties as we go and then restyling our app later becomes much easier. We can add properties of all types here, not just colors, so we'll be adding sizes, fonts, and other things as we progress further through our development.

Font Awesome

With our styling framework in place, let's review what our navigation bar looks like and figure out what we want to achieve:

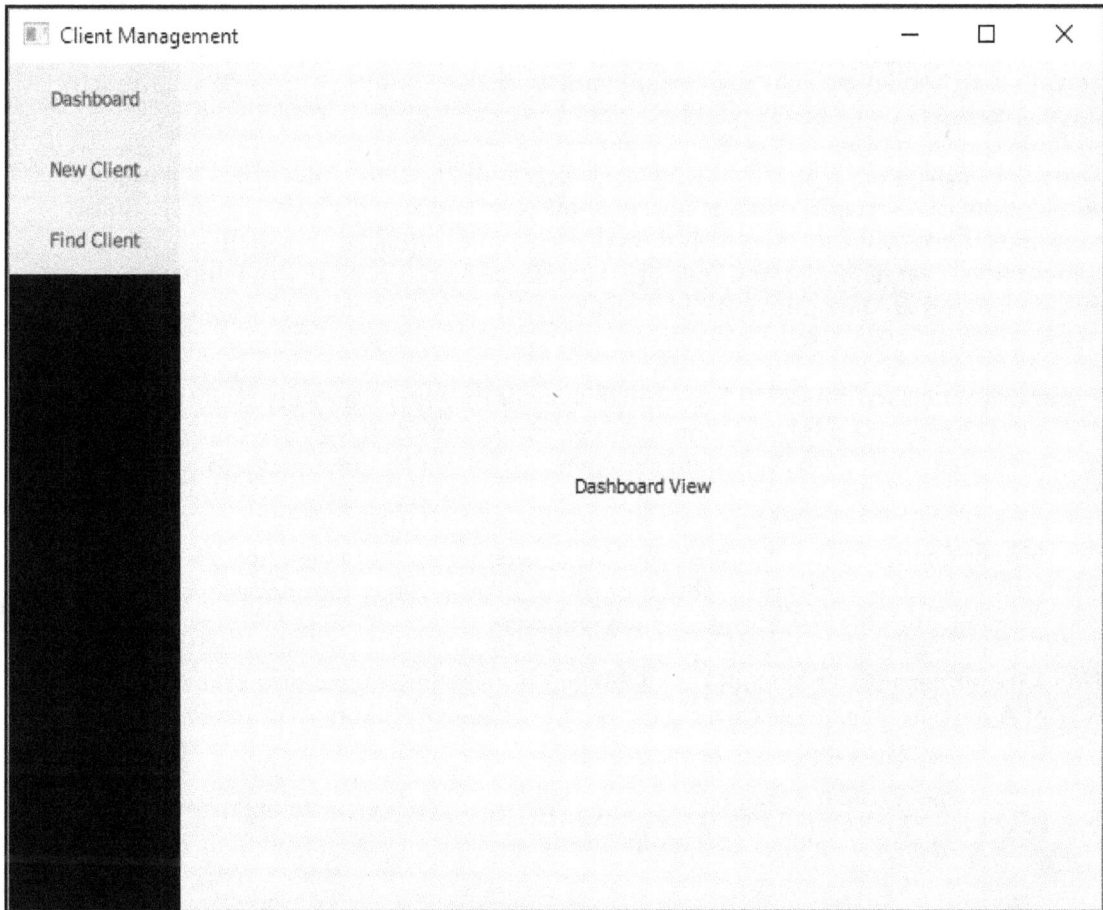

The buttons we want to display on our navigation bar are **Dashboard View** (the Home view), **New Client View**, and **Find Client View**, along with a toggle button at the top to expand and collapse the bar.

A common UI design pattern is to represent simple commands with icons. Further information about the command can be obtained by a variety of means; for example, when you hover over the button, information can be displayed in a tooltip or a status bar at the bottom of the screen. Our approach will be to have a collapsible bar. The default state of the bar will be collapsed and will display an icon representing each command. In expanded state, the bar will display both the icon and a textual description of the command. The user will be able to toggle the states with an additional button. This is a pattern particularly prevalent in mobile application development, where you want to consume as little screen space as possible by default.

There are a few options for displaying the icons for our buttons. Older desktop applications would more than likely use image files of some description. This gives you full artistic control over how your icons look, but carries several drawbacks. Image files tend to be comparatively large in size, and they are a fixed size. If you need to draw them at a different size, then they can look bad, particularly if they are scaled up or if the aspect ratio changes.

Scalable Vector Graphics (**SVG**) are much smaller files and scale very well. They are more difficult to create and can be a bit more limited artistically, but they can be very useful for the purpose of icons. However, from experience, they can be quite tricky to work with in Qt/QML.

The third option that gives you the small file size and scalability benefits of SVG but are much easier to work with are symbol font files. This is a very common solution in web development, and this is the approach we will take.

There are numerous symbol fonts available but perhaps the most popular for development is **Font Awesome**. It provides a wide range of terrific symbols and has a very helpful website; check out: `http://fontawesome.io/`.

> Check any licensing applicable for fonts you choose to use, especially if you are using them commercially.

Download the kit and open up the archive file. The file we are interested in is `fonts/fontawesome-webfont.ttf`. Copy this file into our project folder in `cm/cm-ui/assets`.

In our `cm-ui` project, edit `assets.qrc` and add the font to our resources:

```
<file alias="fontawesome.ttf">assets/fontawesome-webfont.ttf</file>
```

Remember that our alias doesn't have to be the same as the original filename, and we've taken the opportunity to shorten it a bit.

Next up, edit `Style.qml` and we'll wire the font up to our custom style for easy use. We first need the font to be loaded and made available for use, which we achieve using a `FontLoader` component. Add the following inside the root **Item** element:

```
FontLoader {
    id: fontAwesomeLoader
    source: "qrc:/assets/fontawesome.ttf"
}
```

In the `source` property, we use the `/assets` prefix (or virtual folder) we defined in our `assets.qrc` file along with the `fontawesome.ttf` alias. Now, we have loaded the font but as it stands, we won't be able to reference it from outside of `Style.qml`. This is because only properties at root component level are accessible outside of the file. Child components are deemed effectively private. The way we get around this is by creating a `property alias` for the element we want to expose:

```
Item {
    property alias fontAwesome: fontAwesomeLoader.name
    readonly property color colourBackground: "#efefef"
    FontLoader {
        id: fontAwesomeLoader
        source: "qrc:/assets/fontawesome.ttf"
    }
}
```

This creates a publicly available property called `fontAwesome`, which when called, simply redirects the caller to the `name` property of the internal `fontAwesomeLoader` element.

With the wiring done, let's find the icons we want to use. Back on the Font Awesome website, navigate to the **Icons** page. Here, you can see all the available icons. Clicking on one will display further information about it, and it is from here that we can get the key piece of information we need in order to display it, and that is the unicode character. I'll select the following icons for our menu, but feel free to choose whichever icons you want:

Command	Icon	Unicode character
Toggle Menu	bars	f0c9
Dashboard	home	f015
New Client	user-plus	f234
Find Client	search	f002

Now, let's replace the `Button` components on our `MasterView` with a `Text` component for each of our icons:

```
Column {
    Text {
        font {
            family: Style.fontAwesome
            pixelSize: 42
        }
        color: "#ffffff"
        text: "uf0c9"
    }
    Text {
        font {
            family: Style.fontAwesome
            pixelSize: 42
        }
        color: "#ffffff"
        text: "uf015"
    }
    Text {
        font {
            family: Style.fontAwesome
            pixelSize: 42
        }
        color: "#ffffff"
        text: "uf234"
    }
    Text {
        font {
            family: Style.fontAwesome
            pixelSize: 42
        }
```

```
            color: "#ffffff"
            text: "uf002"
        }
    }
```

You will also need to add the **assets 1.0** import if you haven't already:

Next, we'll add the descriptive text for the client commands. Wrap each of the Text components in a Row and add a further Text component for the description, as follows:

```
Row {
    Text {
        font {
            family: Style.fontAwesome
            pixelSize: 42
        }
        color: "#ffffff"
        text: "uf234"
```

```
    }
    Text {
        color: "#ffffff"
        text: "New Client"
    }
}
```

The Row component will lay out its children horizontally—first the icon and then the descriptive text. Repeat this for the other commands. Add the descriptions **Dashboard** and **Find Client** for the other buttons and simply an empty string for the toggle command:

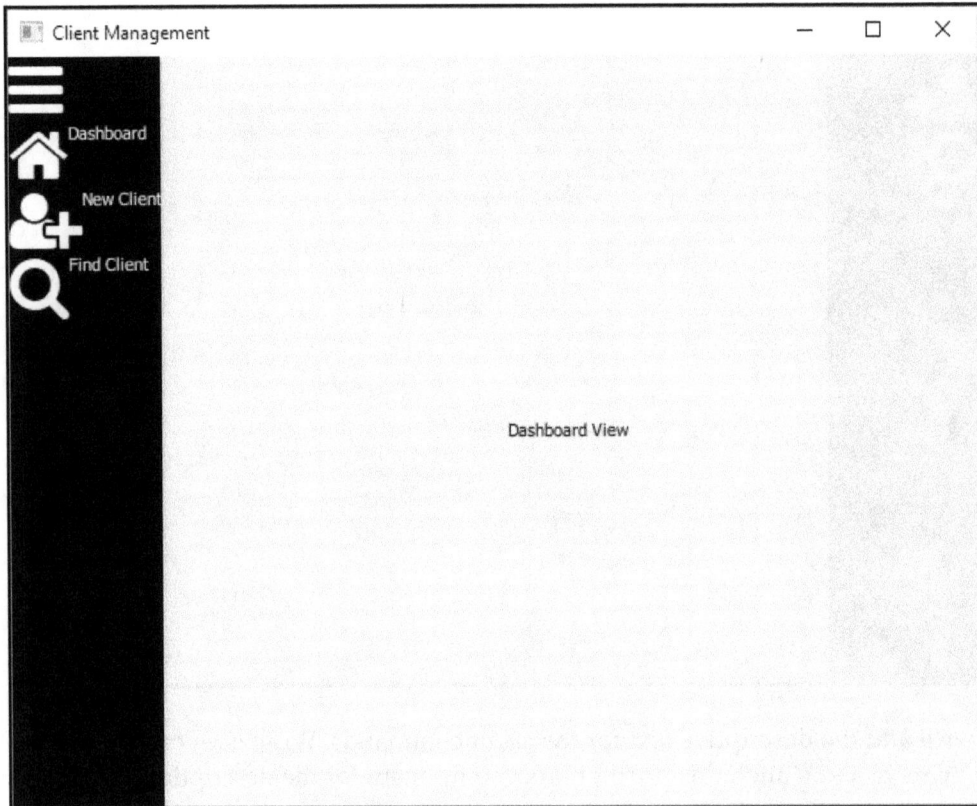

Before we get too carried away making further changes, we'll take a breath, do some refactoring, and look at introducing components.

Components

The QML, what we've just written, is functional enough, but it's already becoming difficult to maintain. Our `MasterView` is getting a little long and difficult to read. When we come to change how our command buttons look, for example, aligning the icon and text, we will have to change it in four places. If we want to add a fifth button, we have to copy, paste, and edit a whole bunch of QML to do so. This is where reusable components come into play.

Components are exactly the same as the views we have already created—just snippets of QML. The difference is purely semantic. Throughout this book, views represent screens that lay out content while components are the content.

The easiest way to create a new component is when you have already written the QML that you want to form the basis for your component, which we have done. Right-click on any of the `Row` elements we added for our commands and select **Refactoring > Move Component into Separate File**.

Name the new component `NavigationButton` and save it to a new folder—`cm/cm-ui/components`:

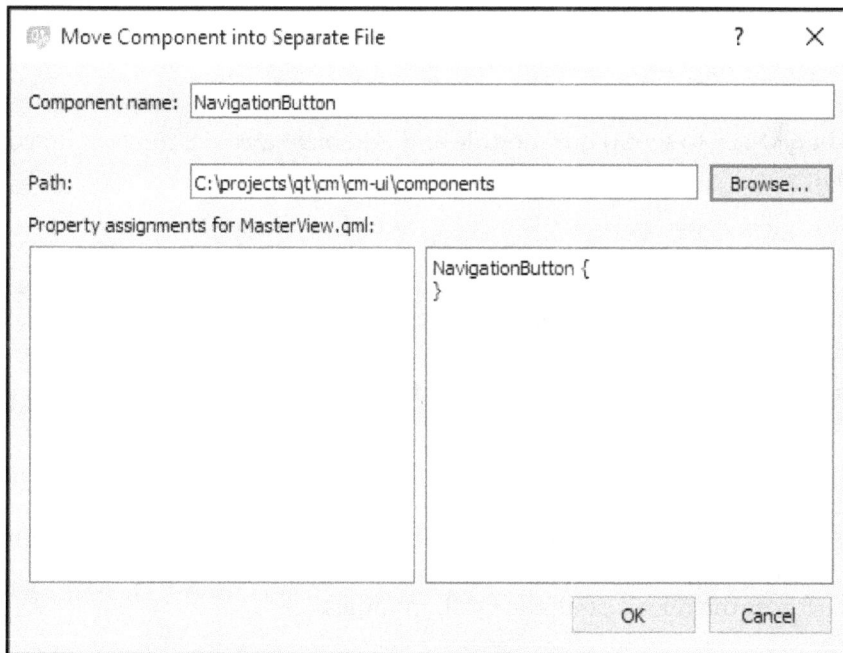

The Row element will be moved to our new file and in `MasterView`, you will be left with an empty `NavigationButton` component:

```
NavigationButton {
}
```

Unfortunately, it comes with a big red squiggly, and our app will no longer run. While the refactoring step has happily created a new `NavigationButton.qml` file for us, it's not actually included in our project anywhere, so Qt doesn't know where it is. It's easy enough to resolve though, and we just need to set up our resources bundle as we did with our views and assets:

1. Create a new `Qt Resource File` called `components.qrc` in the `cm/cm-ui` folder
2. Create an empty `qmldir` file in `cm/cm-ui/components` as we did for our assets
3. Edit `components.qrc` to include both of our new files within a `/components` prefix:

```
<RCC>
    <qresource prefix="/components">
        <file alias="qmldir">components/qmldir</file>
        <file
alias="NavigationButton.qml">components/NavigationButton.qml</file>
    </qresource>
</RCC>
```

4. Edit `qmldir` to set up our module and add our `NavigationButton` component to it:

```
module components
NavigationButton 1.0 NavigationButton.qml
```

5. Ensure that `components.qrc` has been added to the `RESOURCES` variable in `cm-ui.pro`
6. In `MasterView`, include our new components module to get access to our new component:

```
import components 1.0
```

Sometimes, getting our module to be fully recognized and banishing the red squigglies may only be accomplished by restarting Qt Creator, as that forces the reload of all the QML modules.

We now have a reusable component that hides away the implementation details, reduces code duplication, and makes it much easier to add new commands and maintain the old ones. However, there are a few changes we need to make to it before we can leverage it for our other commands.

Currently, our `NavigationButton` has hard-coded icon and description text values that will be the same whenever we use the component. We need to expose both the text properties so that we can set them to be different for each of our commands. As we saw, we can achieve this using property aliases, but we need to add unique identifiers to our `Text` elements for that to work. Let's set the default values to be something generic and also implement advice from earlier in the book to have an `Item` component as the root element:

```
import QtQuick 2.9
import assets 1.0

Item {
    property alias iconCharacter: textIcon.text
    property alias description: textDescription.text

    Row {
        Text {
            id: textIcon
            font {
                family: Style.fontAwesome
                pixelSize: 42
            }
            color: "#ffffff"
            text: "uf11a"
        }
        Text {
            id: textDescription
            color: "#ffffff"
            text: "SET ME!!"
        }
    }
}
```

Now that our component is configurable with properties, we can replace our commands in `MasterView`:

```
Column {
    NavigationButton {
        iconCharacter: "uf0c9"
        description: ""
    }
    NavigationButton {
```

```
            iconCharacter: "uf015"
            description: "Dashboard"
        }
        NavigationButton {
            iconCharacter: "uf234"
            description: "New Client"
        }
        NavigationButton {
            iconCharacter: "uf002"
            description: "Find Client"
        }
    }
}
```

This is much more concise and manageable than all of the duplicated QML we had earlier. Now, if you run the application, you'll see that while we've taken a couple of steps forward, and that we've also taken one step back:

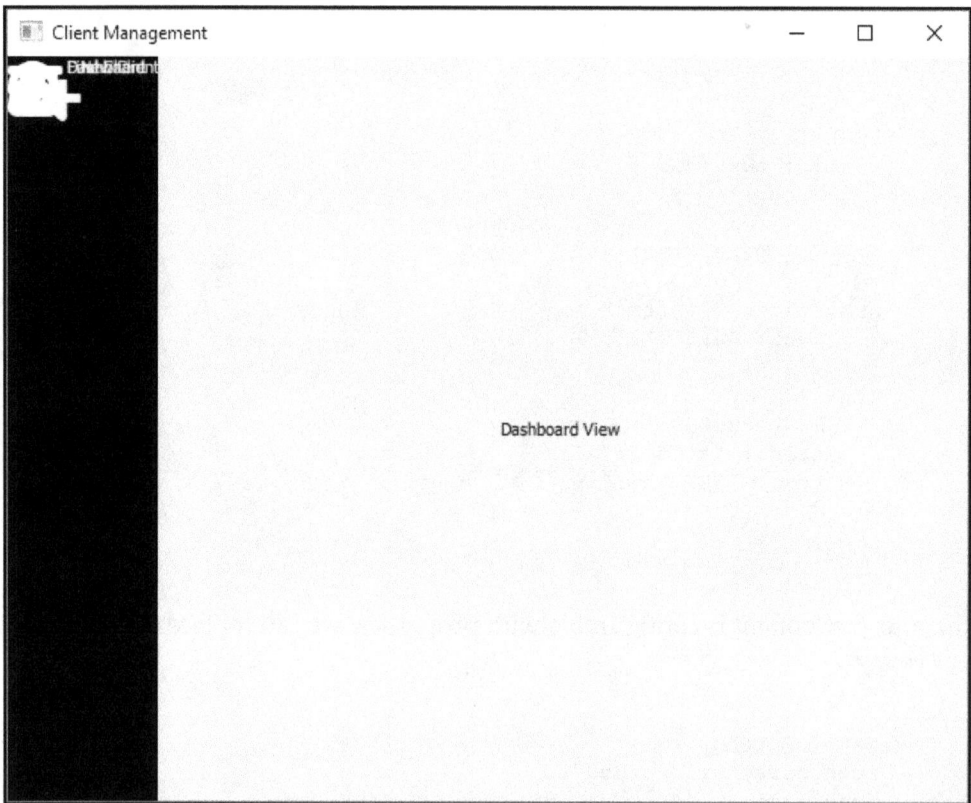

As you can see, all of our components are drawn on top of each other. The root cause of this is the issue we've touched on previously regarding sizing. We have a visual component with a root Item element, and we haven't explicitly defined its size. Another thing we are neglecting is our custom style. Let's fix those next.

Styling the navigation bar

Starting with the easy part, let's first move our hard-coded colors and icon pixel size from NavigationButton into Style.qml:

```
readonly property color colourNavigationBarBackground: "#000000"
readonly property color colourNavigationBarFont: "#ffffff"
readonly property int pixelSizeNavigationBarIcon: 42
```

We now need to think about how we want to size the elements of our button. We have an icon which we want to be square, so the width and height will be the same. Next, to that, we have a text description that will be the same height as the icon but will be wider:

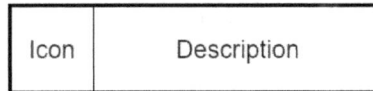

Icon	Description

The width of the entire component is the width of the icon plus the width of the description. The height of the entire component is the same as both the height of the icon and description; however, it gives us more flexibility to make the height the same as whichever is the larger of the two. That way, if we ever decide to make one item larger than the other, we know that the component will be large enough to contain them both. Let's pick starter sizes of 80 x 80 for the icon and 80 x 240 for the description and define the properties:

```
readonly property real widthNavigationButtonIcon: 80
readonly property real heightNavigationButtonIcon:
widthNavigationButtonIcon
readonly property real widthNavigationButtonDescription: 240
readonly property real heightNavigationButtonDescription:
heightNavigationButtonIcon
readonly property real widthNavigationButton: widthNavigationButtonIcon +
widthNavigationButtonDescription
readonly property real heightNavigationButton:
Math.max(heightNavigationButtonIcon, heightNavigationButtonDescription)
```

There are a couple of things to note here. Properties can be bound directly to other properties, which reduces the amount of duplication and makes the whole setup much more dynamic. We know that we want our icon to be square, so by binding the height to be the same as the width, if we want to change the total size of the icon, we just need to update the width, and the height will automatically update. QML also has strong integration with a JavaScript engine, so we can use the `Math.max()` function to help us figure out which is the larger height.

Another thing we would like the navigation buttons to do is to provide some kind of visual cue when the user hovers the mouse over a button to indicate that it is an interactive element. To do that, we need each button to have its own background rectangle.

In the `NavigationButton`, wrap the `Row` element in a new `Rectangle` and plug the sizes into our component:

```
Item {
    property alias iconCharacter: textIcon.text
    property alias description: textDescription.text

    width: Style.widthNavigationButton
    height: Style.heightNavigationButton

    Rectangle {
        id: background
        anchors.fill: parent
        color: Style.colourNavigationBarBackground

        Row {
            Text {
                id: textIcon
                width: Style.widthNavigationButtonIcon
                height: Style.heightNavigationButtonIcon
                font {
                    family: Style.fontAwesome
                    pixelSize: Style.pixelSizeNavigationBarIcon
                }
                color: Style.colourNavigationBarFont
                text: "uf11a"
            }
            Text {
                id: textDescription
                width: Style.widthNavigationButtonDescription
                height: Style.heightNavigationButtonDescription
                color: Style.colourNavigationBarFont
                text: "SET ME!!"
            }
```

```
            }
        }
    }
```

Run again, and you'll see a slight improvement:

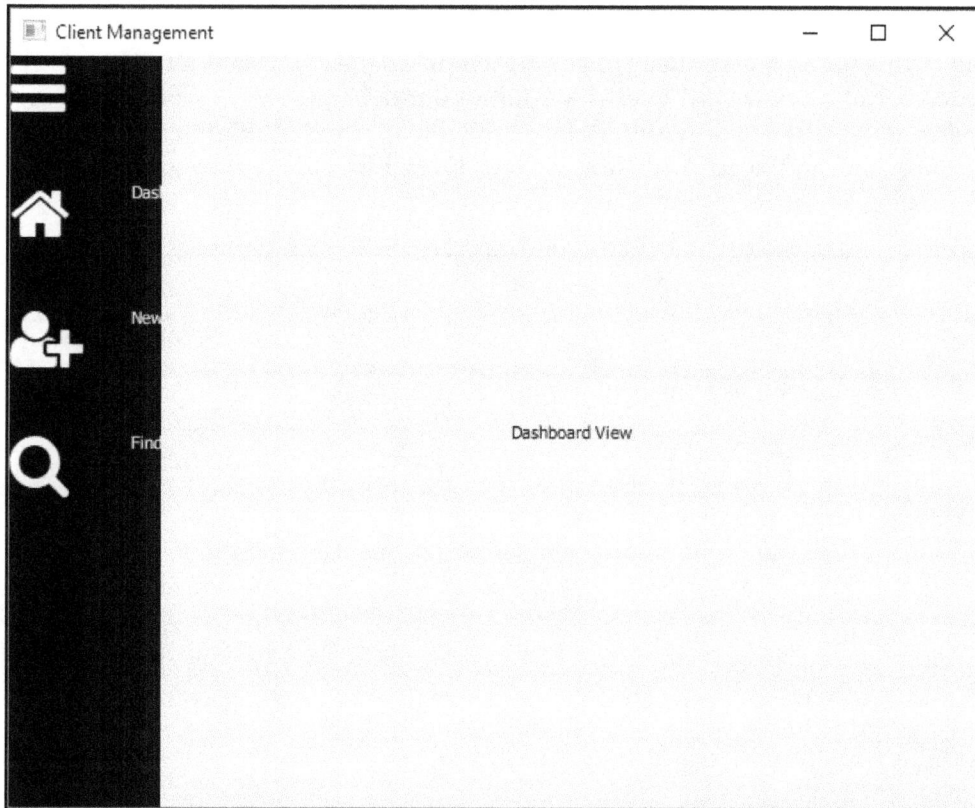

We're getting part of the description cut off because our navigation bar is hard-coded to be 100 pixels wide. We need to change this and also implement the toggle expanded/collapsed functionality. We have already calculated the sizes we need, so let's prepare by adding a couple of new properties to `Style.qml`:

```
readonly property real widthNavigationBarCollapsed:
widthNavigationButtonIcon
readonly property real heightNavigationBarExpanded: widthNavigationButton
```

The collapsed state will be just wide enough for the icon, while the expanded state will contain the entire button, including description.

Next, let's encapsulate our navigation bar in a new component. There won't be any reuse benefits in this case as there will only ever be one, but it helps keep our QML organized and makes `MasterView` more concise and easy to read.

You can right-click on the `Rectangle` component in `MasterView` and refactor our navigation bar into a new QML file, as we did for our `NavigationButton`. However, let's do it manually so that you are comfortable with both approaches. Right-click on `components.qrc` and select **Add New... > Qt > QML File**. Add `NavigationBar.qml` to `cm/cm-ui/components`:

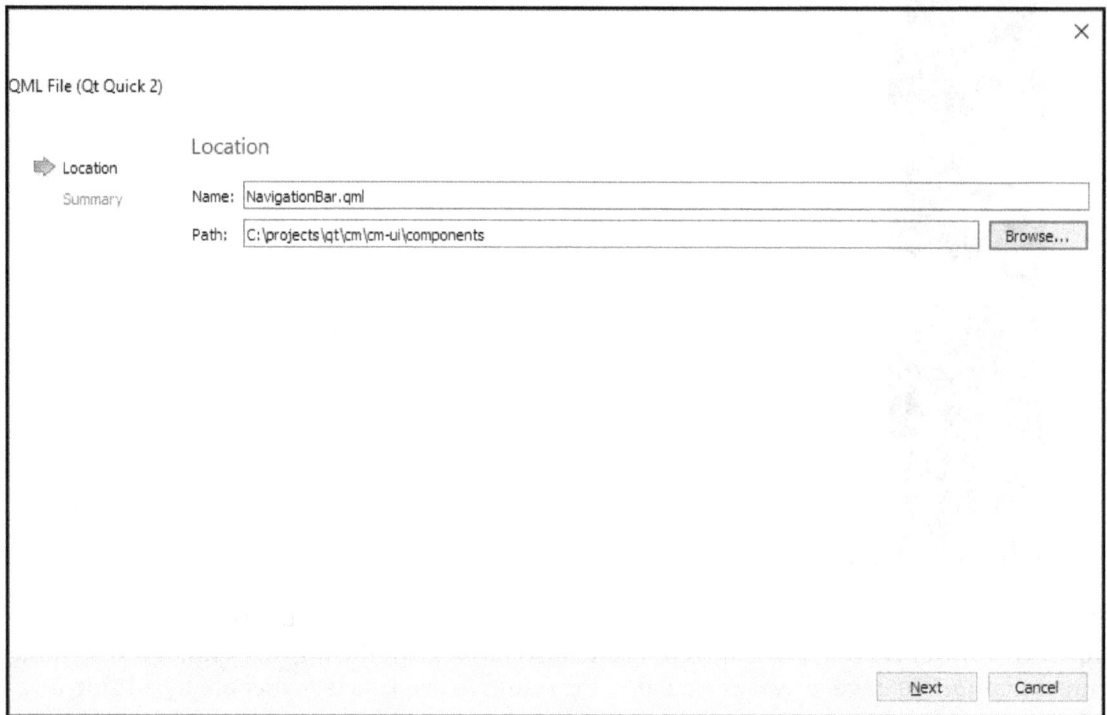

QML File (Qt Quick 2)	✕

Location

➡ Location
   Summary

Name: `NavigationBar.qml`

Path: `C:\projects\qt\cm\cm-ui\components`   Browse...

Next   Cancel

Edit `components.qrc` and move our new `NavigationBar` into the `/components` prefix section with an alias:

```
<file alias="NavigationBar.qml">components/NavigationBar.qml</file>
```

Add the component to our components module by editing `qmldir`:

```
NavigationBar 1.0 NavigationBar.qml
```

Cut the `Rectangle` and its child elements from `MasterView` and paste it into `NavigationBar.qml` inside the root `Item` element. Update the `QtQuick` module import to version 2.9 if it has been initialized to some older version. Add an import for our assets module to gain access to our Style object. Move the Rectangle's `anchors` and `width` properties to the root `Item` and set the `Rectangle` to fill its parent:

```
import QtQuick 2.9
import assets 1.0

Item {
    anchors {
        top: parent.top
        bottom: parent.bottom
        left: parent.left
    }
    width: 100

    Rectangle {
        anchors.fill: parent
        color: "#000000"

        Column {
            NavigationButton {
                iconCharacter: "uf0c9"
                description: ""
            }
            NavigationButton {
                iconCharacter: "uf015"
                description: "Dashboard"
            }
            NavigationButton {
                iconCharacter: "uf234"
                description: "New Client"
            }
            NavigationButton {
                iconCharacter: "uf002"
                description: "Find Client"
            }
```

```
        }
    }
}
```

Back in `MasterView`, you can now add the new `NavigationBar` component in where the `Rectangle` used to be:

```
NavigationBar {
    id: navigationBar
}
```

Although you get the dreaded red squigglies again, you will actually be able to run the application and verify that the refactoring hasn't broken anything.

The anchoring of our new `NavigationBar` component is fine, but the `width` is a little more complicated—how do we know whether it should be `Style.widthNavigationBarCollapsed` or `Style.heightNavigationBarExpanded`? We'll control this with a publicly accessible Boolean property that indicates whether the bar is collapsed or not. We can then use the value of this property to decide which width we want using the conditional `?` operator syntax. Set the property to be true initially, so the bar will render in its collapsed state by default:

```
property bool isCollapsed: true
```

With that in place, replace the hard-coded `width` of 100, as follows:

```
width: isCollapsed ? Style.widthNavigationBarCollapsed :
Style.heightNavigationBarExpanded
```

Next, update the `color` property of `Rectangle` to `Style.colourNavigationBarBackground`:

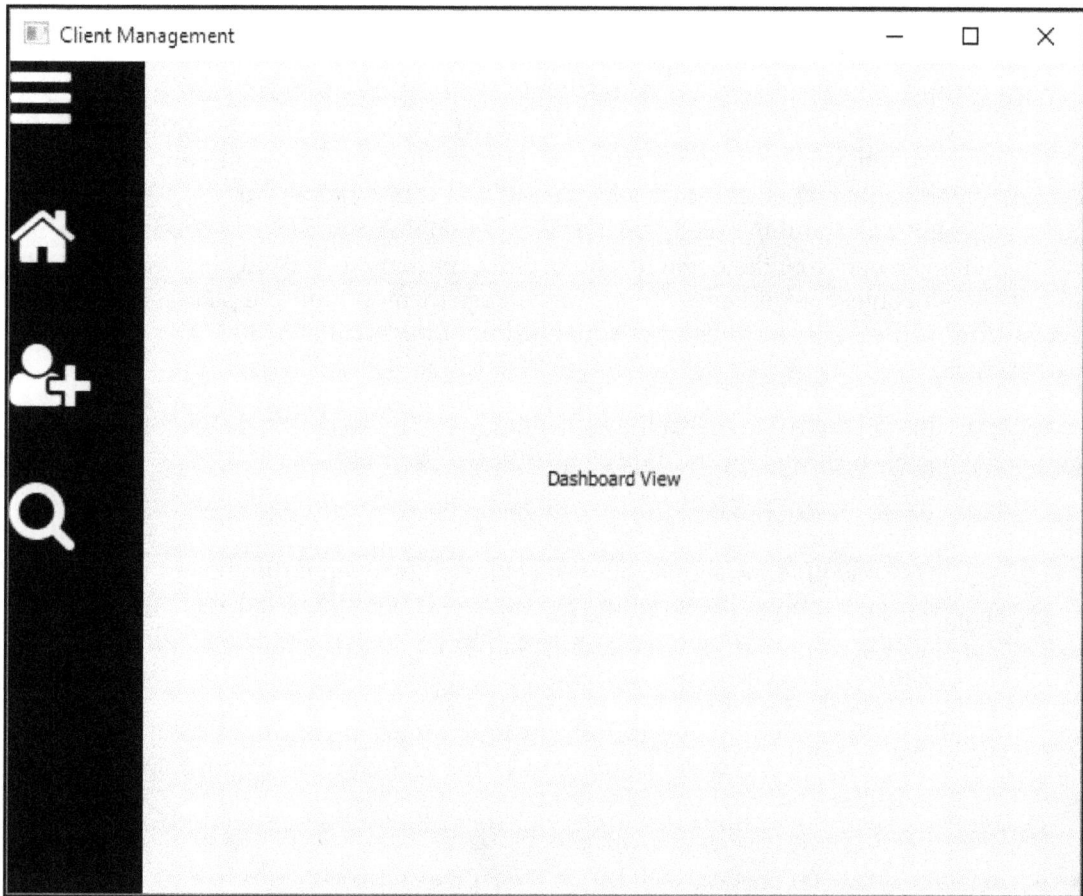

We're getting there now, but one key thing we've missed along the way is that clicking on the buttons now doesn't actually do anything anymore. Let's fix that next.

Clicking

Early on in this book, we looked at a component called `MouseArea`. This was soon superseded by our use of `Button` components, which provide the clicking functionality for us. However, now that we are rolling our own form of buttons, we need to implement the clicking functionality ourselves. Much like the `Button` components, our `NavigationButton` shouldn't really do anything when they are clicked on, other than informing their parent that the event has occurred. Components should be as generic and ignorant about context as possible so that you can use them in multiple places. What we need to do is add a `MouseArea` component and simply pass on the `onClicked` event via a custom signal.

In `NavigationButton`, we first add the signal that we want to emit whenever the component has been clicked on. Add this just after the properties:

```
signal navigationButtonClicked()
```

> **TIP**
>
> Try and give the signals quite specific names, even if they are a little long. If you simply call everything `clicked()`, then things can get a little confusing and sometimes you may find yourself referencing a different signal to the one you intended.

Next, we'll add another property to support some mouse hover magic we'll implement. This will be a `color` type, and we'll default it to be the regular background color:

```
property color hoverColour: Style.colourNavigationBarBackground
```

We'll use this color in conjunction with the `states` property of `Rectangle`:

```
states: [
    State {
        name: "hover"
        PropertyChanges {
            target: background
            color: hoverColour
        }
    }
]
```

Think of each state in the array as a named configuration. The default configuration has no name ("") and consists of the properties we have already set within the `Rectangle` element. The "hover" state applies changes to the properties specified in the `PropertyChanges` element, that is, it will change the `color` property of the element with ID `background` to be whatever the value of `hoverColour` is.

Next, inside the `Rectangle` but below the `Row`, add our `MouseArea`:

```
MouseArea {
    anchors.fill: parent
    cursorShape: Qt.PointingHandCursor
    hoverEnabled: true
    onEntered: background.state = "hover"
    onExited: background.state = ""
    onClicked: navigationButtonClicked()
}
```

We use the `anchors` property to fill the whole button background area, including icon and description. Next, we'll jazz things up a bit by changing the mouse cursor to a pointing hand when it enters the button area and enabling hovering with the `hoverEnabled` flag. When enabled, the **entered** and **exited** signals are emitted when the cursor enters and exits the area, and we can use the corresponding slots to change the appearance of our background `Rectangle` by switching between the hover state we've just implemented and the default (""). Finally, we respond to the `clicked()` signal of `MouseArea` with the `onClicked()` slot and simply emit our own signal.

We can now react to the `navigationButtonClicked()` signal in our `NavigationBar` component and add some hover colors while we're at it. Implement the toggle button first:

```
NavigationButton {
    iconCharacter: "uf0c9"
    description: ""
    hoverColour: "#993333"
    onNavigationButtonClicked: isCollapsed = !isCollapsed
}
```

We implement the `<MyCapitalisedSignalName>` convention to create a slot for our signal and when it fires, we simply toggle the value of `isCollapsed` between `true` and `false`.

You can now run the application. Click on the Toggle button to expand and collapse the navigation bar:

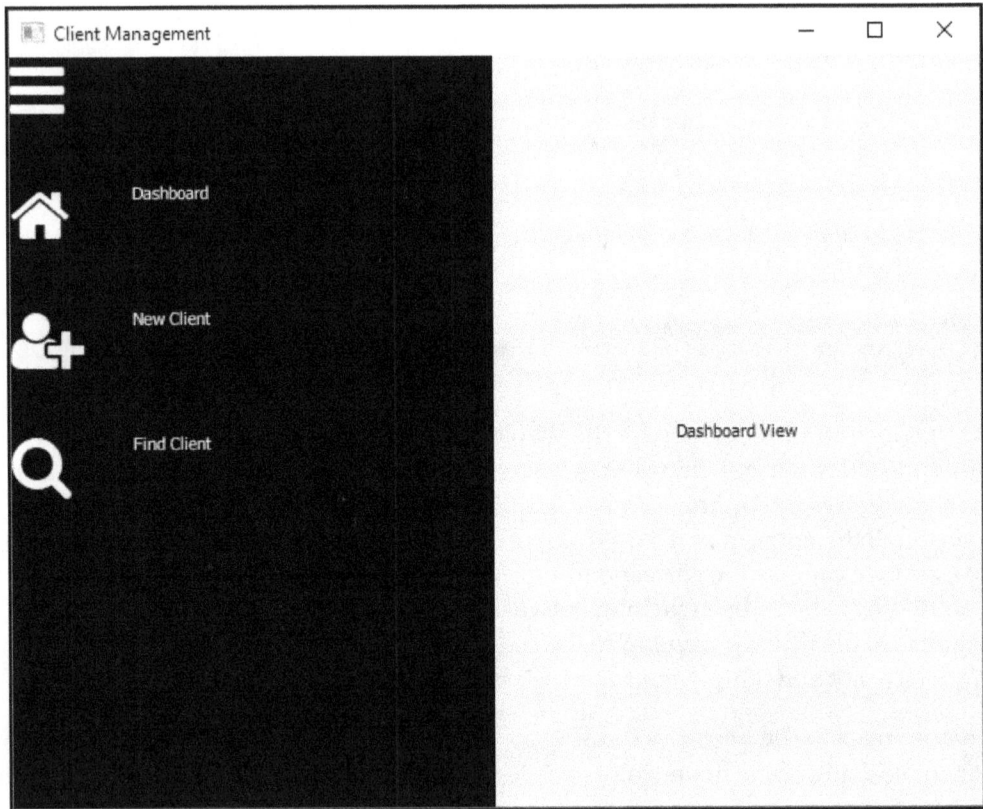

Note how because of our use of `anchors`, the child views dynamically resize themselves to accommodate the navigation bar. You will also see the pointing hand cursor and a flash of color when you hover over the button, which helps the user understand that it is an interactive element and visualizes the boundaries.

For the remaining navigation buttons, what we want to do in reaction to the clicked event is to emit the `goDashboardView()`, `goCreateClientView()`, and `goFindClientView()` signals on the `NavigationCoordinator`.

Add the `onNavigationButtonClicked` slots to the other buttons and drill down through the `masterController` object to get to the signals we want to call. Add some fancy colors of your choice too:

```
NavigationButton {
    iconCharacter: "uf015"
    description: "Dashboard"
    hoverColour: "#dc8a00"
    onNavigationButtonClicked:
masterController.ui_navigationController.goDashboardView();
}
NavigationButton {
    iconCharacter: "uf234"
    description: "New Client"
    hoverColour: "#dccd00"
    onNavigationButtonClicked:
masterController.ui_navigationController.goCreateClientView();
}
NavigationButton {
    iconCharacter: "uf002"
    description: "Find Client"
    hoverColour: "#8aef63"
    onNavigationButtonClicked:
masterController.ui_navigationController.goFindClientView();
}
```

You can now click on the buttons to navigate to the different child views.

A few last little tweaks to finish the navigation bar are to align the content of our buttons a little better and resize a few things.

The description text should align vertically with the center of the icon rather than the top, and our icons should be centered rather than pinned up against the edge of the window. The first issue is easy to solve, because we've already been consistent and explicit with our sizings. Simply add the following property to both the `Text` components in `NavigationButton`:

```
verticalAlignment: Text.AlignVCenter
```

Both the `Text` elements were sized to take up the full height of the button, so we simply need to align the text vertically within that space.

Fixing the alignment of the icons is just the same, but this time in the horizontal axis. Add the following to the `Text` component of the icon:

```
horizontalAlignment: Text.AlignHCenter
```

As for the sizings, our description text is a little small and there is a lot of empty space after the text. Add a new property to our `Style` object:

```
readonly property int pixelSizeNavigationBarText: 22
```

Use the new property in the description `Text` element:

```
font.pixelSize: Style.pixelSizeNavigationBarText
```

Next, reduce the `widthNavigationButtonDescription` property in `Style` to 160.

Run the app and we're nearly there. The sizing and alignment is much better now:

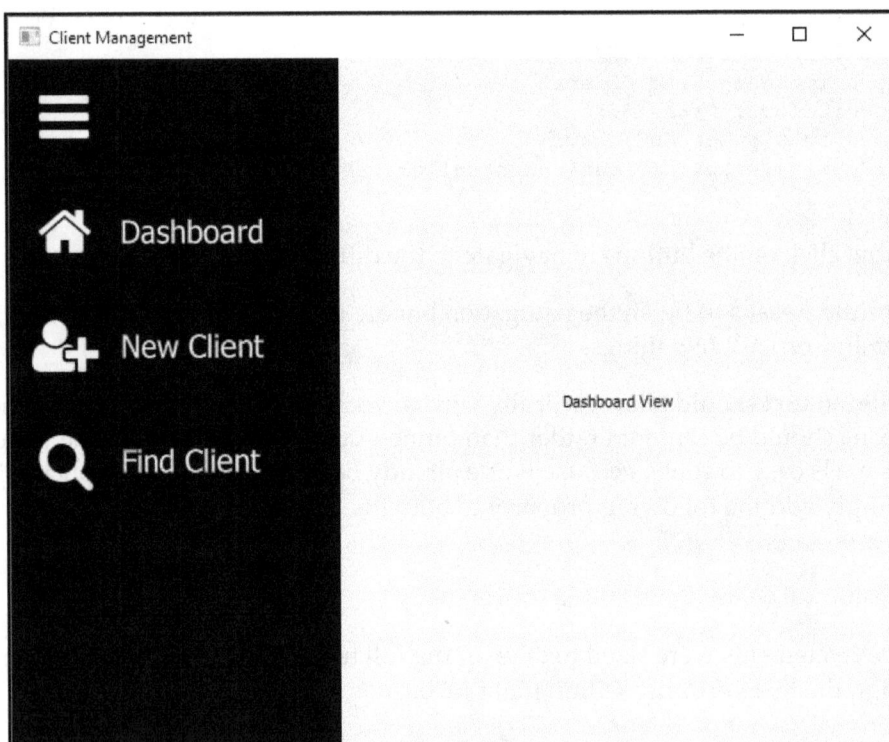

However, one thing you may not note is that when the bar is collapsed and only the icon is displayed, the `MouseArea` is still the full width of the button including the description. Try moving the mouse where the description would be, and you can see the pointing hand cursor appear. You can even click on the components and the transition happens. What we need to do to fix this is rather than the root `Item` element in `NavigationButton` being a fixed width (`Style.widthNavigationButton`), we need to make it dynamic and set it to `parent.width` instead. In order for that to work, we then need to walk up the QML hierarchy and ensure that its parent has a width too. Its parent is the `Column` element in `NavigationBar`. Set the `width` property of `Column` to be `parent.width` too.

With those changes in place, the navigation bar now behaves as expected.

Commands

The next thing on our to-do list is to implement a context-sensitive command bar. While our navigation bar is a constant presence with the same buttons regardless of what the user is doing, the command bar will come and go and will contain different buttons depending on the context. For example, if the user is adding or editing a client, we will need a **Save** button to commit any changes to the database. However, if we are searching for a client, then saving makes no sense and a **Find** button is more relevant. While the techniques for creating our command bar are broadly similar to the navigation bar, the additional flexibility required poses more of a challenge.

To help us overcome these obstacles, we will implement commands. An additional benefit of this approach is that we get to move the logic out of the UI layer and into the business logic layer. I like the UI to be as dumb and as generic as possible. This makes your application more flexible, and bugs in C++ code are easier to identify and resolve than those in QML.

A command object will encapsulate an icon, descriptive text, a function to determine whether the button is enabled or not, and finally, an `executed()` signal that will be emitted when the related button is pressed. Each button in our command bar will then be bound to a command object.

Each of our child view may have a list of commands and an associated command bar. For the views that do, we will present the list of commands to the UI via a command controller.

Create two new C++ classes in the `cm-lib` project, both of which should inherit from
QObject:

- **Command** in a new folder `cm-lib/source/framework`
- **Command Controller** in the existing folder `cm-lib/source/controllers`

command.h:

```
#ifndef COMMAND_H
#define COMMAND_H

#include <functional>

#include <QObject>
#include <QScopedPointer>
#include <QString>

#include <cm-lib_global.h>

namespace cm {
namespace framework {

class CMLIBSHARED_EXPORT Command : public QObject
{
    Q_OBJECT
    Q_PROPERTY( QString ui_iconCharacter READ iconCharacter CONSTANT )
    Q_PROPERTY( QString ui_description READ description CONSTANT )
    Q_PROPERTY( bool ui_canExecute READ canExecute NOTIFY canExecuteChanged
)

public:
    explicit Command(QObject* parent = nullptr,
                     const QString& iconCharacter = "",
                     const QString& description = "",
                     std::function<bool()> canExecute = [](){ return
                                                      true; });
    ~Command();

    const QString& iconCharacter() const;
    const QString& description() const;
    bool canExecute() const;

signals:
    void canExecuteChanged();
    void executed();

private:
```

```
    class Implementation;
    QScopedPointer<Implementation> implementation;
};

}}

#endif
```

command.cpp:

```cpp
#include "command.h"

namespace cm {
namespace framework {

class Command::Implementation
{
public:
    Implementation(const QString& _iconCharacter, const QString&
     _description, std::function<bool()> _canExecute)
        : iconCharacter(_iconCharacter)
        , description(_description)
        , canExecute(_canExecute)
    {
    }

    QString iconCharacter;
    QString description;
    std::function<bool()> canExecute;
};

Command::Command(QObject* parent, const QString& iconCharacter, const
QString& description, std::function<bool()> canExecute)
    : QObject(parent)
{
    implementation.reset(new Implementation(iconCharacter, description,
canExecute));
}

Command::~Command()
{
}

const QString& Command::iconCharacter() const
{
    return implementation->iconCharacter;
}
```

```
const QString& Command::description() const
{
    return implementation->description;
}

bool Command::canExecute() const
{
    return implementation->canExecute();
}


}
}
```

The QObject, namespaces, and dll export code should be familiar by now. We represent the icon character and description values we want to display on the UI buttons as strings. We hide the member variables away in the private implementation and provide `accessor` methods for them. We could have represented the `canExecute` member as a simple `bool` member that calling code could set to `true` or `false` as required; however, a much more elegant solution is to pass in a method that calculates the value for us on the fly. By default, we set it to a lambda that returns `true`, which means that the button will be enabled. We provide a `canExecuteChanged()` signal to go along with this, which we can fire whenever we want the UI to reassess whether the button is enabled or not. The last element is the `executed()` signal that will be fired by the UI when the corresponding button is pressed.

`command-controller.h`:

```
#ifndef COMMANDCONTROLLER_H
#define COMMANDCONTROLLER_H

#include <QObject>
#include <QtQml/QQmlListProperty>
#include <cm-lib_global.h>
#include <framework/command.h>

namespace cm {
namespace controllers {

class CMLIBSHARED_EXPORT CommandController : public QObject
{
    Q_OBJECT
    Q_PROPERTY(QQmlListProperty<cm::framework::Command>
     ui_createClientViewContextCommands READ
     ui_createClientViewContextCommands CONSTANT)

public:
    explicit CommandController(QObject* _parent = nullptr);
```

```cpp
    ~CommandController();

    QQmlListProperty<framework::Command>
    ui_createClientViewContextCommands();

public slots:
    void onCreateClientSaveExecuted();

private:
    class Implementation;
    QScopedPointer<Implementation> implementation;
};

}}

#endif
```

command-controller.cpp:

```cpp
#include "command-controller.h"

#include <QList>
#include <QDebug>

using namespace cm::framework;

namespace cm {
namespace controllers {

class CommandController::Implementation
{
public:
    Implementation(CommandController* _commandController)
        : commandController(_commandController)
    {
        Command* createClientSaveCommand = new Command(
          commandController, QChar( 0xf0c7 ), "Save" );
        QObject::connect( createClientSaveCommand, &Command::executed,
    commandController, &CommandController::onCreateClientSaveExecuted );
        createClientViewContextCommands.append( createClientSaveCommand );
    }

    CommandController* commandController{nullptr};

    QList<Command*> createClientViewContextCommands{};
};

CommandController::CommandController(QObject* parent)
```

```
    : QObject(parent)
{
    implementation.reset(new Implementation(this));
}

CommandController::~CommandController()
{
}

QQmlListProperty<Command>
CommandController::ui_createClientViewContextCommands()
{
    return QQmlListProperty<Command>(this,
implementation->createClientViewContextCommands);
}

void CommandController::onCreateClientSaveExecuted()
{
    qDebug() << "You executed the Save command!";
}

}}
```

Here, we introduce a new type—QQmlListProperty. It is essentially a wrapper that
enables QML to interact with a list of custom objects. Remember that we need to fully
qualify the templated type in the Q_PROPERTY statements. The private member that
actually holds the data is a QList, and we have implemented an accessor method that
takes the QList and converts it into a QQmlListProperty of the same templated type.

> As per the documentation for QQmlListProperty, this method of object
> construction should not be used in production code, but we'll use it to
> keep things simple.

We have created a single command list for our CreateClientView. We'll add command
lists for other views later. Again, we'll keep things simple for now; we just create a single
command to save a newly created client. When creating the command, we parent it to the
command coordinator so that we don't have to worry about memory management. We
assign it a floppy disk icon (unicode f0c7) and the **Save** label. We leave the canExecute
function as the default for now so it will always be enabled. Next, we connect the
executed() signal of the command to the onCreateClientSaveExecuted() slot of the
CommandController. With the wiring done, we then add the command to the list.

The intention is that we present the user with a command button bound to a `Command` object. When the user presses the button, we will fire the `executed()` signal from the UI. The connection we've set up will cause the slot on the command controller to be called, and we will execute our business logic. For now, we'll simply print out a line to the console when the button is pressed.

Next, let's register both of our new types in `main.cpp` (remember the `#includes`):

```
qmlRegisterType<cm::controllers::CommandController>("CM", 1, 0,
"CommandController");
qmlRegisterType<cm::framework::Command>("CM", 1, 0, "Command");
```

Finally, we need to add the `CommandCoordinator` property to `MasterController`:

```
Q_PROPERTY( cm::controllers::CommandController* ui_commandController READ
commandController CONSTANT )
```

Then, we add an `accessor` method:

```
CommandController* commandController();
```

Finally, in `master-controller.cpp`, instantiate the object in the private implementation and implement the `accessor` method in exactly the same way as we did for `NavigationController`.

We now have a (very short!) list of commands ready for our `CreateClientView` to consume.

Command bar

Let's begin by adding some more properties to Style for our command components:

```
readonly property color colourCommandBarBackground: "#cecece"
readonly property color colourCommandBarFont: "#131313"
readonly property color colourCommandBarFontDisabled: "#636363"
readonly property real heightCommandBar: heightCommandButton
readonly property int pixelSizeCommandBarIcon: 32
readonly property int pixelSizeCommandBarText: 12

readonly property real widthCommandButton: 80
readonly property real heightCommandButton: widthCommandButton
```

Next, create two new QML components in our UI project: `CommandBar.qml` and `CommandButton.qml` in `cm-ui/components`. Update `components.qrc` and move the new components into the `/components` prefix with aliases. Edit `qmldir` and append the new components:

```
CommandBar 1.0 CommandBar.qml
CommandButton 1.0 CommandButton.qml
```

For our button design, we want to lay out the description below the icon. The icon should be positioned slightly above centre. The component should be square, as follows:

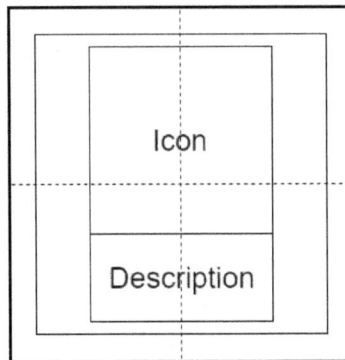

`CommandButton.qml`:

```
import QtQuick 2.9
import CM 1.0
import assets 1.0

Item {
    property Command command
    width: Style.widthCommandButton
    height: Style.heightCommandButton

    Rectangle {
        id: background
        anchors.fill: parent
        color: Style.colourCommandBarBackground

        Text {
            id: textIcon
            anchors {
                centerIn: parent
                verticalCenterOffset: -10
            }
```

```
        font {
            family: Style.fontAwesome
            pixelSize: Style.pixelSizeCommandBarIcon
        }
        color: command.ui_canExecute ? Style.colourCommandBarFont :
                                    colourCommandBarFontDisabled
        text: command.ui_iconCharacter
        horizontalAlignment: Text.AlignHCenter
    }

    Text {
        id: textDescription
        anchors {
            top: textIcon.bottom
            bottom: parent.bottom
            left: parent.left
            right: parent.right
        }
        font.pixelSize: Style.pixelSizeNavigationBarText
        color: command.ui_canExecute ? Style.colourCommandBarFont :
                                    colourCommandBarFontDisabled
        text: command.ui_description
        horizontalAlignment: Text.AlignHCenter
        verticalAlignment: Text.AlignVCenter
    }

    MouseArea {
        anchors.fill: parent
        cursorShape: Qt.PointingHandCursor
        hoverEnabled: true
        onEntered: background.state = "hover"
        onExited: background.state = ""
        onClicked: if(command.ui_canExecute) {
                    command.executed();
                }
    }

    states: [
        State {
            name: "hover"
            PropertyChanges {
                target: background
                color: Qt.darker(Style.colourCommandBarBackground)
            }
        }
    ]
    }
}
```

This is largely similar to our `NavigationButton` component. We pass in a `Command` object, which is where we will obtain the icon character and description to display in the **Text** elements as well as the signal to emit when the button is pressed, so long as the command can execute.

We use an alternative to the **Row/Column** based layout and use anchors to position our icon and description instead. We center the icon in the parent `Rectangle` and then apply a vertical offset to move it up and allow space for the description. We anchor the top of the description to the bottom of the icon.

Rather than propagating a signal when the button is pressed, we emit the `executed()` signal of the `Command` object, first verifying that the command can execute. We also use this flag to selectively color our text elements, using a paler grey font if the command is disabled.

We implement some more hover functionality with our `MouseArea`, but rather than exposing a property to pass in the hover color, we simply take the default and darken it a few shades using the built-in `Qt.darker()` method. We also only apply the state change in the `onEntered()` slot of the `MouseArea` if the command can be executed.

CommandBar.qml:

```
import QtQuick 2.9
import assets 1.0

Item {
    property alias commandList: commandRepeater.model

    anchors {
        left: parent.left
        bottom: parent.bottom
        right: parent.right
    }
    height: Style.heightCommandBar

    Rectangle {
        anchors.fill: parent
        color: Style.colourCommandBarBackground

        Row {
            anchors {
                top: parent.top
                bottom: parent.bottom
                right: parent.right
            }
```

```
Repeater {
    id: commandRepeater
    delegate: CommandButton {
        command: modelData
    }
}
            }
        }
    }
}
```

Again, this is largely the same as `NavigationBar`, but with a dynamic list of commands rather than hard-coded QML buttons. We introduce another new component—the `Repeater`. Given a list of objects via the `model` property, `Repeater` will instantiate a QML component defined in the `delegate` property for each item in the list. The object from the list is made available via the built-in `modelData` variable. Using this mechanism, we can automatically generate a `CommandButton` element for each command we have in a given list. We use another property alias so that the caller can set the command list.

Let's put this to use in `CreateClientView`. First, `import components 1.0`, and then add the following inside the root `Item` and after the `Rectangle`:

```
CommandBar {
    commandList:
masterController.ui_commandController.ui_createClientViewContextCommands
    }
```

We drill down through our property hierarchy to get the command list for the create client view and pass that list to the command bar which takes care of the rest. Don't worry if the `CommandBar` has red squiggles, Qt Creator just needs to catch up with our blistering pace.

Run the app and navigate to **Create Client View**:

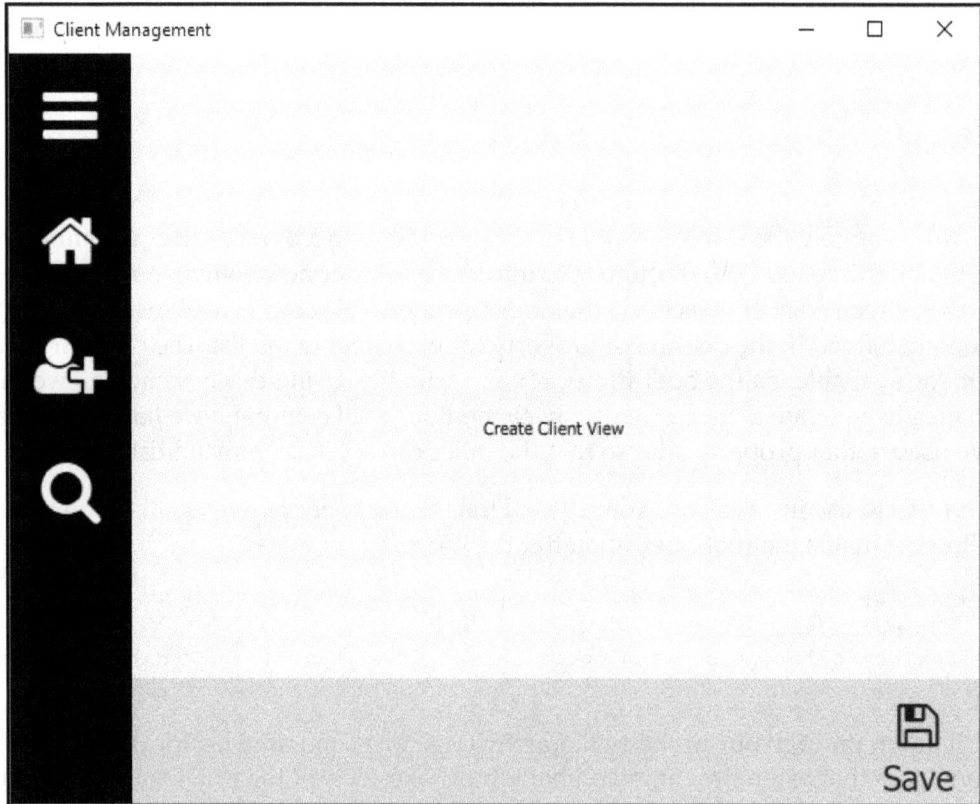

Click on the button, and you will see the message output to the console. Adding new commands is as simple as appending a new `Command` object to the QList inside `CommandController`—no UI changes needed! The command bar will automatically create a new button for every command it finds in the list. Also note that this command bar is only present on the `CreateClientView`, so it is context sensitive. We can easily add command bars to other views by simply adding extra lists and properties to the `CommandController`, as we will later.

Summary

In this chapter, we gave the navigation bar a much needed overhaul. We added our first few components and leveraged our new custom style object, with Font Awesome providing some lovely scalable graphics for us. We also introduced commands and have the framework in place to be able to add context-sensitive command buttons to our views.

In Chapter 5, *Data*, we'll get stuck into the business logic layer and flesh out our first data models.

5
Data

In this chapter, we will implement classes to handle the most critical part of any Line of Business application—the data. We will introduce self-aware data entities, which can automatically serialize to and from **JavaScript Object Notation (JSON)**, a popular serialization format used a lot in web communications. We will create the core models we need for our application and wire them up to our UI for reading and writing via custom controls. We will cover the following topics:

- JSON
- Data decorators
- Abstract data entities
- Collections of data entities
- Concrete data models
- UI controls and data binding

JSON

In case you have never come across JSON before, let's have a quick crash course. It is a simple and lightweight way to express hierarchies of objects and their properties. It is a very popular choice when sending data in HTTP requests. It is similar to XML in intent but is much less verbose.

A JSON object is encapsulated in curly braces { }, while properties are denoted in the format key: value. Strings are delimited with double quotes "". We can represent a single client object as follows:

```
{
    "reference": "CLIENT0001",
    "name": "Dale Cooper"
}
```

Note that white space and control characters such as tab and newline are ignored—the indented properties are to simply make things more readable.

> **TIP**
>
> It's usually a good idea to strip extraneous characters out of JSON when transmitting over the network (for example, in an HTTP request) in order to reduce the size of the payload; every byte counts!

Property values can be one of the following types: String, Number, JSON Object, JSON Array, and the literal values true, false, and null.

We can add the supply address and billing address to our client as child JSON objects, providing a unique key for each. While keys can be in any format as long as they are unique, it is common practice to use camel case, for example, myAwesomeJsonKey. We can express an empty address object with null:

```
{
    "reference": "CLIENT0001",
    "name": "Dale Cooper",
    "supplyAddress": {
        "number": 7,
        "name": "White Lodge",
        "street": "Lost Highway",
        "city": "Twin Peaks",
        "postcode": "WS119"
    },
    "billingAddress": null
}
```

A collection (array) of objects is enclosed in square brackets `[]` separated by commas. We can express no scheduled appointments by simply leaving the square brackets empty:

```
{
    "reference": "CLIENT0001",
    "name": "Dale Cooper",
    "supplyAddress": {
        "number": 7,
        "name": "White Lodge",
        "street": "Lost Highway",
        "city": "Twin Peaks",
        "postcode": "WS119"
    },
    "billingAddress": null,
    "contacts": [
        {
            "type": 1,
            "address": "+12345678"
        },
        {
            "type": 2,
            "address": "dale.cooper@fbi.com"
        }
    ],
    "appointments": []
}
```

Object hierarchy

Most real-world applications represent data in a hierarchical or relational manner, with the data rationalized into discrete objects. There is often a central "root" object, which parents several other child objects, either as singular objects or as a collection. Each discrete object has its own set of data items that can be any number of types. The key principles we want to cover are as listed:

- A range of data types (`string`, `integer`, `datetime`) and an enumerated value
- Object hierarchy
- Multiple single child entities of the same type
- Collections of entities

Balancing these goals with simplicity, the data diagram we will work toward is as follows:

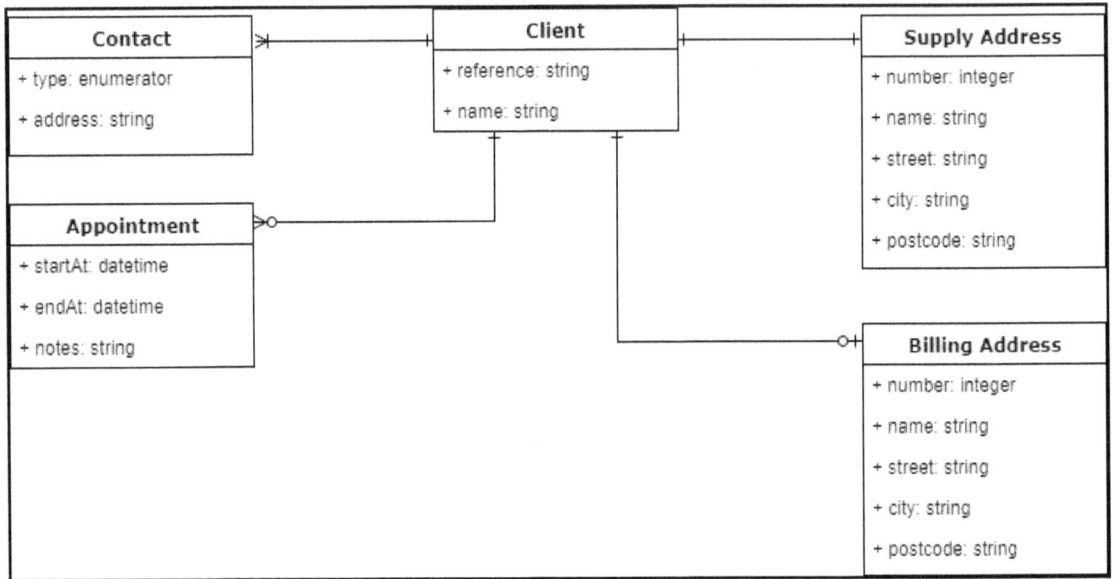

Contact	Client	Supply Address
+ type: enumerator	+ reference: string	+ number: integer
+ address: string	+ name: string	+ name: string
		+ street: string
		+ city: string

Appointment		Billing Address
+ startAt: datetime		+ number: integer
+ endAt: datetime		+ name: string
+ notes: string		+ street: string
		+ city: string
		+ postcode: string

The purpose of each of these models is described in the following table:

Model	Description
Client	This is the root of our object hierarchy and represents an individual or party our company has a relationship with, for example, a customer or a patient.
Contact	A collection of addresses that we can use to contact the client. The possible types of contact will be a telephone, email, and fax. There may be one or more contacts per client.
Appointment	A collection of scheduled appointments with the client, for example, a site visit or consultation. There may be zero or more appointments per client.
Supply address	The address central to the relationship with the client, for example, the site our company supplies energy to or the home address of a patient. There must be one supply address per client.
Billing address	An optional address different to the supply address used for invoicing, for example, the head office of a corporation. There may be zero or one billing address per client.

> **TIP**
>
> Another perfectly valid approach would be to aggregate the addresses into a collection, much like we have done with our contacts, but I want to demonstrate using the same type of object (Address) in multiple properties.

With the high-level design in place, we are now in a position to write our classes. However, before we start on our data entities, let's take a look at the data items.

DataDecorators

A simple implementation of the `name` property of our client model would be to add it as a `QString`; however, this approach has some shortcomings. Whenever we display this property in the UI, we will probably want to display an informative label next to the textbox so that the user knows what it is for, saying "Name" or something similar. Whenever we want to validate a name entered by the user, we have to manage that in the code somewhere else. Finally, if we want to serialize the value to or from JSON, again there needs to be some other component that does it for us.

To solve all of these problems we will introduce the concept of a `DataDecorator`, which will lift a given base data type and give us a label, validation capabilities, and JSON serialization out of the box. Our models will maintain a collection of `DataDecorators`, allowing them to validate and serialize themselves to JSON too by simply walking through the data items and performing the relevant action.

In our `cm-lib` project, create the following classes in a new folder `cm-lib/source/data`:

Class	Purpose
`DataDecorator`	Base class for our data items
`StringDecorator`	Derived class for string properties
`IntDecorator`	Derived class for integer properties
`DateTimeDecorator`	Derived class for date/time properties
`EnumeratorDecorator`	Derived class for enumerated properties

Our `DataDecorator` base class will house the features shared across all of our data items.

data-decorator.h:

```
#ifndef DATADECORATOR_H
#define DATADECORATOR_H

#include <QJsonObject>
#include <QJsonValue>
#include <QObject>
#include <QScopedPointer>

#include <cm-lib_global.h>

namespace cm {
namespace data {

class Entity;

class CMLIBSHARED_EXPORT DataDecorator : public QObject
{
    Q_OBJECT
    Q_PROPERTY( QString ui_label READ label CONSTANT )

public:
    DataDecorator(Entity* parent = nullptr, const QString& key =
                "SomeItemKey", const QString& label = "");
                            virtual ~DataDecorator();

    const QString& key() const;
    const QString& label() const;
    Entity* parentEntity();

    virtual QJsonValue jsonValue() const = 0;
    virtual void update(const QJsonObject& jsonObject) = 0;

private:
    class Implementation;
    QScopedPointer<Implementation> implementation;
};

}}

#endif
```

We inherit from QObject, add our `dllexport` macro and wrap the whole thing in namespaces as usual. Also, because this is an abstract base class, we ensure that we've implemented a virtual destructor.

We know that because we are inheriting from QObject, we want to receive a pointer to a parent in our constructor. We also know that all data items will be children of an **Entity** (which we will write soon and have forward declared here), which will itself be derived from QObject. We can leverage these two facts to parent our `DataDecorator` directly to an Entity.

We construct the decorator with a couple of strings. All of our data decorators must have a key that will be used when serializing to and from JSON, and they will also share a `label` property that the UI can use to display descriptive text next to the data control. We tuck these members away in the private implementation and implement some accessor methods for them.

Finally, we begin implementing our JSON serialization by declaring virtual methods to represent the value as a `QJsonValue` and to update the value from a provided `QJsonObject`. As the value is not known in the base class and will instead be implemented in the derived classes, both these methods are pure virtual functions.

data-decorator.cpp:

```
#include "data-decorator.h"

namespace cm {
namespace data {

class DataDecorator::Implementation
{
public:
    Implementation(Entity* _parent, const QString& _key, const QString&
                                                                _label)
        : parentEntity(_parent)
        , key(_key)
        , label(_label)
    {
    }
    Entity* parentEntity{nullptr};
    QString key;
    QString label;
};

DataDecorator::DataDecorator(Entity* parent, const QString& key, const
QString& label)
```

```
        : QObject((QObject*)parent)
{
    implementation.reset(new Implementation(parent, key, label));
}

DataDecorator::~DataDecorator()
{
}

const QString& DataDecorator::key() const
{
    return implementation->key;
}

const QString& DataDecorator::label() const
{
    return implementation->label;
}

Entity* DataDecorator::parentEntity()
{
    return implementation->parentEntity;
}

}}
```

The implementation is very straightforward, essentially just managing some data members.

Next, we'll implement our derived decorator class for handling strings.

string-decorator.h:

```
#ifndef STRINGDECORATOR_H
#define STRINGDECORATOR_H

#include <QJsonObject>
#include <QJsonValue>
#include <QObject>
#include <QScopedPointer>
#include <QString>

#include <cm-lib_global.h>
#include <data/data-decorator.h>

namespace cm {
namespace data {

class CMLIBSHARED_EXPORT StringDecorator : public DataDecorator
```

```
{
    Q_OBJECT
    Q_PROPERTY( QString ui_value READ value WRITE setValue NOTIFY
            valueChanged )
public:
    StringDecorator(Entity* parentEntity = nullptr, const QString& key =
"SomeItemKey", const QString& label = "", const QString& value = "");
    ~StringDecorator();

    StringDecorator& setValue(const QString& value);
    const QString& value() const;

    QJsonValue jsonValue() const override;
    void update(const QJsonObject& jsonObject) override;

signals:
    void valueChanged();

private:
    class Implementation;
    QScopedPointer<Implementation> implementation;
};

}}

#endif
```

There isn't much else going on here—we're just adding a strongly typed `QString` value property to hold our value. We also override the virtual JSON-related methods.

> When deriving from a class that inherits from QObject, you need to add the Q_OBJECT macro to the derived class as well as the base class if the derived class implements its own signals or slots.

`string-decorator.cpp`:

```
#include "string-decorator.h"

#include <QVariant>

namespace cm {
namespace data {

class StringDecorator::Implementation
{
public:
```

```cpp
    Implementation(StringDecorator* _stringDecorator, const QString&
                                                      _value)
        : stringDecorator(_stringDecorator)
        , value(_value)
    {
    }

    StringDecorator* stringDecorator{nullptr};
    QString value;
};

StringDecorator::StringDecorator(Entity* parentEntity, const QString& key,
const QString& label, const QString& value)
    : DataDecorator(parentEntity, key, label)
{
    implementation.reset(new Implementation(this, value));
}

StringDecorator::~StringDecorator()
{
}

const QString& StringDecorator::value() const
{
    return implementation->value;
}

StringDecorator& StringDecorator::setValue(const QString& value)
{
    if(value != implementation->value) {
        // ...Validation here if required...
        implementation->value = value;
        emit valueChanged();
    }
    return *this;
}

QJsonValue StringDecorator::jsonValue() const
{
    return QJsonValue::fromVariant(QVariant(implementation->value));
}

void StringDecorator::update(const QJsonObject& _jsonObject)
{
    if (_jsonObject.contains(key())) {
        setValue(_jsonObject.value(key()).toString());
    } else {
        setValue("");
```

```
        }
    }
}}
```

Again, there is nothing particularly complicated here. By using the READ and WRITE property syntax rather than the simpler MEMBER keyword, we now have a way of intercepting values being set by the UI, and we can decide whether or not we want to apply the change to the member variable. The mutator can be as complex as you need it to be, but all we're doing for now is setting the value and emitting the signal to tell the UI that it has been changed. We wrap the operation in an equality check, so we don't take any action if the new value is the same as the old one.

> Here, the mutator returns a reference to self (*this), which is helpful because it enables method chaining, for example, myName.setValue("Nick").setSomeNumber(1234).setSomeOtherProperty(true). However, this is not necessary for the property bindings, so feel free to use the more common void return type if you prefer.

We use a two-step conversion process, converting our QString value into a QVariant before converting it into our target QJsonValue type. The QJsonValue will be plugged into the parent Entity JSON object using the key from the DataDecorator base class. We will cover that in more detail when we write the **Entity** related classes.

> An alternative approach would be to simply represent the value of our various data items as a QVariant member in the DataDecorator base class, removing the need to have separate classes for QString, int, and so on. The problem with this approach is that you end up having to write lots of nasty code that says "if you have a QVariant containing a string then run this code if it contains an int then run this code...". I prefer the additional overhead of writing the extra classes in exchange for having known types and cleaner, simpler code. This will become particularly helpful when we look at data validation. Validating a string is completely different from validating a number and different again from validating a date.

`IntDecorator` and `DateTimeDecorator` are virtually identical to `StringDecorator`, simply substituting `QString` values for int or `QDateTime`. However, we can supplement `DateTimeDecorator` with a few additional properties to help us out. Add the following properties and an accessor method to go with each:

```
Q_PROPERTY( QString ui_iso8601String READ toIso8601String NOTIFY
valueChanged )
Q_PROPERTY( QString ui_prettyDateString READ toPrettyDateString NOTIFY
valueChanged )
Q_PROPERTY( QString ui_prettyTimeString READ toPrettyTimeString NOTIFY
valueChanged )
Q_PROPERTY( QString ui_prettyString READ toPrettyString NOTIFY valueChanged
)
```

The purpose of these properties is to make the UI easily access the date/time value as a `QString` preformatted to a few different styles. Let's run through the implementation for each of the accessors.

Qt has inbuilt support for ISO8601 format dates, which is a very common format when transmitting datetime values between systems, for example, in HTTP requests. It is a flexible format that supports several different representations but generally follows the format yyyy-MM-ddTHH:mm:ss.zt, where T is a string literal, z is milliseconds, and t is the timezone information:

```
QString DateTimeDecorator::toIso8601String() const
{
    if (implementation->value.isNull()) {
        return "";
    } else {
        return implementation->value.toString(Qt::ISODate);
    }
}
```

Next, we provide a method to display a full datetime in a long human readable format, for example, Sat 22 Jul 2017 @ 12:07:45:

```
QString DateTimeDecorator::toPrettyString() const
{
    if (implementation->value.isNull()) {
        return "Not set";
    } else {
        return implementation->value.toString( "ddd d MMM yyyy @ HH:mm:ss"
);
    }
}
```

The final two methods display either the date or time component, for example, 22 Jul 2017 or 12:07 pm:

```
QString DateTimeDecorator::toPrettyDateString() const
{
    if (implementation->value.isNull()) {
        return "Not set";
    } else {
        return implementation->value.toString( "d MMM yyyy" );
    }
}

QString DateTimeDecorator::toPrettyTimeString() const
{
    if (implementation->value.isNull()) {
        return "Not set";
    } else {
        return implementation->value.toString( "hh:mm ap" );
    }
}
```

Our final type, `EnumeratorDecorator`, is broadly the same as `IntDecorator`, but it also accepts a mapper. This container helps us map the stored int value to a string representation. If we consider the `Contact.type` enumerator we plan to implement, the enumerated value will be 0, 1, 2, so on; however, when it comes to the UI, that number won't mean anything to the user. We really need to present `Email`, `Telephone`, or some other string representation, and the map allows us to do just that.

`enumerator-decorator.h`:

```
#ifndef ENUMERATORDECORATOR_H
#define ENUMERATORDECORATOR_H

#include <map>

#include <QJsonObject>
#include <QJsonValue>
#include <QObject>
#include <QScopedPointer>

#include <cm-lib_global.h>
#include <data/data-decorator.h>

namespace cm {
namespace data {

class CMLIBSHARED_EXPORT EnumeratorDecorator : public DataDecorator
```

```
    {
        Q_OBJECT
        Q_PROPERTY( int ui_value READ value WRITE setValue NOTIFY
                                        valueChanged )
        Q_PROPERTY( QString ui_valueDescription READ valueDescription
                                        NOTIFY valueChanged )

    public:
        EnumeratorDecorator(Entity* parentEntity = nullptr, const QString&
        key = "SomeItemKey", const QString& label = "", int value = 0,
        const std::map<int, QString>& descriptionMapper = std::map<int,
         QString>());
        ~EnumeratorDecorator();

        EnumeratorDecorator& setValue(int value);
        int value() const;
        QString valueDescription() const;

        QJsonValue jsonValue() const override;
        void update(const QJsonObject& jsonObject) override;

    signals:
        void valueChanged();

    private:
        class Implementation;
        QScopedPointer<Implementation> implementation;
    };

    }}

    #endif
```

We store the map as another member variable in our private implementation class and then use it to provide the string representation of the enumerated value:

```
    QString EnumeratorDecorator::valueDescription() const
    {
        if (implementation->descriptionMapper.find(implementation->value)
                        != implementation->descriptionMapper.end()) {
            return implementation->descriptionMapper.at(implementation-
                                                >value);
        } else {
            return {};
        }
    }
```

Now that we have covered the data types we need for our entities, let's move on to the entities themselves.

Entities

As we have a lot of functionality we want to share across our data models, we'll implement an **Entity** base class. We need to be able to represent parent/child relationships so that a client can have supply and billing addresses. We also need to support collections of entities for our contacts and appointments. Finally, each entity hierarchy must be able to serialize itself to and from a JSON object.

Create a new class Entity in `cm-lib/source/data`.

`entity.h`:

```
#ifndef ENTITY_H
#define ENTITY_H

#include <map>

#include <QObject>
#include <QScopedPointer>

#include <cm-lib_global.h>
#include <data/data-decorator.h>

namespace cm {
namespace data {

class CMLIBSHARED_EXPORT Entity : public QObject
{
    Q_OBJECT

public:
    Entity(QObject* parent = nullptr, const QString& key =
                                            "SomeEntityKey");
    Entity(QObject* parent, const QString& key, const QJsonObject&
      jsonObject);
    virtual ~Entity();

public:
    const QString& key() const;
    void update(const QJsonObject& jsonObject);
    QJsonObject toJson() const;
```

```
    signals:
        void childEntitiesChanged();
        void dataDecoratorsChanged();

    protected:
        Entity* addChild(Entity* entity, const QString& key);
        DataDecorator* addDataItem(DataDecorator* dataDecorator);

    protected:
        class Implementation;
        QScopedPointer<Implementation> implementation;
    };

    }}

    #endif
```

entity.cpp:

```
    #include "entity.h"

    namespace cm {
    namespace data {

    class Entity::Implementation
    {
    public:
        Implementation(Entity* _entity, const QString& _key)
            : entity(_entity)
            , key(_key)
        {
        }
        Entity* entity{nullptr};
        QString key;
        std::map<QString, Entity*> childEntities;
        std::map<QString, DataDecorator*> dataDecorators;
    };

    Entity::Entity(QObject* parent, const QString& key)
        : QObject(parent)
    {
        implementation.reset(new Implementation(this, key));
    }

    Entity::Entity(QObject* parent, const QString& key, const QJsonObject&
                    jsonObject) : Entity(parent, key)
    {
        update(jsonObject);
```

```
}

Entity::~Entity()
{
}

const QString& Entity::key() const
{
    return implementation->key;
}

Entity* Entity::addChild(Entity* entity, const QString& key)
{
    if(implementation->childEntities.find(key) ==
        std::end(implementation->childEntities)) {
        implementation->childEntities[key] = entity;
        emit childEntitiesChanged();
    }
    return entity;
}

DataDecorator* Entity::addDataItem(DataDecorator* dataDecorator)
{
    if(implementation->dataDecorators.find(dataDecorator->key()) ==
        std::end(implementation->dataDecorators)) {
        implementation->dataDecorators[dataDecorator->key()] =
        dataDecorator;
        emit dataDecoratorsChanged();
    }
    return dataDecorator;
}

void Entity::update(const QJsonObject& jsonObject)
{
    // Update data decorators
    for (std::pair<QString, DataDecorator*> dataDecoratorPair :
        implementation->dataDecorators) {
        dataDecoratorPair.second->update(jsonObject);
    }
    // Update child entities
    for (std::pair<QString, Entity*> childEntityPair : implementation-
    >childEntities)
{childEntityPair.second>update(jsonObject.value(childEntityPair.first).toOb
ject());
    }
}

QJsonObject Entity::toJson() const
```

```
    {
        QJsonObject returnValue;
        // Add data decorators
        for (std::pair<QString, DataDecorator*> dataDecoratorPair :
                            implementation->dataDecorators) {
            returnValue.insert( dataDecoratorPair.first,
            dataDecoratorPair.second->jsonValue() );
        }
        // Add child entities
        for (std::pair<QString, Entity*> childEntityPair :
    implementation->childEntities) {
            returnValue.insert( childEntityPair.first,
    childEntityPair.second->toJson() );
        }
        return returnValue;
    }

    }}
```

Much like our `DataDecorator` base class, we assign all entities a unique key, which will be used in JSON serialization. We also add an overloaded constructor to which we can pass a `QJsonObject` so that we can instantiate an entity from JSON. On a related note, we also declare a pair of methods to serialize an existing instance to and from JSON.

Our entity will maintain a few collections—a map of data decorators representing the properties of the model, and a map of entities representing individual children. We map the key of each item to the instance.

We expose a couple of protected methods that are derived classes will use to add its data items and children; for example, our client model will add a name data item along with the `supplyAddress` and `billingAddress` children. To complement these methods, we also add signals to tell any interested observers that the collections have changed.

In both cases, we check that the key doesn't already exist on the map before adding it. We then return the supplied pointer so that the consumer can use it for further actions. You'll see the value of this when we come to implement the data models.

We use our populated maps for the JSON serialization methods. We've already declared an `update()` method on our `DataDecorator` base class, so we simply iterate through all the data items and pass the JSON object down to each in turn. Each derived decorator class has its own implementation to take care of the parsing. Similarly, we recursively call `Entity::update()` on each of the child entities.

Serializing to a JSON object follows the same pattern. Each data item can convert its value to a `QJsonValue` object, so we get each value in turn and append it to a root JSON object using the key of each item. We recursively call `Entity::toJson()` on each of the children, and this cascades down the hierarchy tree.

Before we can finish off our **Entity**, we need to declare a group of classes to represent an entity collection.

Entity collections

To implement entity collections, we need to leverage some more advanced C++ techniques, and we will take a brief break from our conventions so far, implementing multiple classes in a single header file.

Create `entity-collection.h` in `cm-lib/source/data`, and in it, add our namespaces as normal and forward declare Entity:

```
#ifndef ENTITYCOLLECTION_H
#define ENTITYCOLLECTION_H

namespace cm {
namespace data {
    class Entity;
}}

#endif
```

Next, we'll walk through the necessary classes in turn, each of which must be added in order inside the namespaces.

We first define the root class, which does nothing more than inheriting from `QObject` and giving us access to all the goodness that it brings, such as object ownership and signals. This is required because classes deriving directly from `QObject` cannot be templated:

```cpp
class CMLIBSHARED_EXPORT EntityCollectionObject : public QObject
{
    Q_OBJECT

public:
    EntityCollectionObject(QObject* _parent = nullptr) : QObject(_parent)
    {}
    virtual ~EntityCollectionObject() {}

signals:
    void collectionChanged();
};
```

You will need to add includes for `QObject` and our DLL export macros. Next, we need a type agnostic interface to use with our entities, much the same as we have with the `DataDecorator` and Entity maps we've implemented. However, things are a little more complicated here, as we will not derive a new class for each collection we have, so we need some way of getting typed data. We have two requirements. Firstly, the UI needs a `QList` of derived types (for example, **Client***) so that it can access all the properties specific to a client and display all the data. Secondly, our **Entity** class needs a vector of base types (**Entity***) so that it can iterate its collections without caring exactly which type it is dealing with. The way we achieve this is to declare two template methods but delay defining them until later. `derivedEntities()` will be used when the consumer wants a collection of the derived type, while `baseEntities()` will be used when the consumer just wants access to the base interface:

```cpp
class EntityCollectionBase : public EntityCollectionObject
{
public:
    EntityCollectionBase(QObject* parent = nullptr, const QString& key
                                          = "SomeCollectionKey")
        : EntityCollectionObject(parent)
        , key(key)
    {}

    virtual ~EntityCollectionBase()
    {}

    QString getKey() const
    {
        return key;
    }
```

```cpp
    virtual void clear() = 0;
    virtual void update(const QJsonArray& json) = 0;
    virtual std::vector<Entity*> baseEntities() = 0;

    template <class T>
    QList<T*>& derivedEntities();

    template <class T>
    T* addEntity(T* entity);

private:
    QString key;
};
```

Next, we declare a full template class where we store our collection of derived types and implement all of our methods, except for the two template methods we just discussed:

```cpp
template <typename T>
class EntityCollection : public EntityCollectionBase
{
public:
    EntityCollection(QObject* parent = nullptr, const QString& key =
            "SomeCollectionKey")
        : EntityCollectionBase(parent, key)
    {}

    ~EntityCollection()
    {}

    void clear() override
    {
        for(auto entity : collection) {
            entity->deleteLater();
        }
        collection.clear();
    }

    void update(const QJsonArray& jsonArray) override
    {
        clear();
        for(const QJsonValue& jsonValue : jsonArray) {
            addEntity(new T(this, jsonValue.toObject()));
        }
    }

    std::vector<Entity*> baseEntities() override
    {
        std::vector<Entity*> returnValue;
```

```
        for(T* entity : collection) {
            returnValue.push_back(entity);
        }
        return returnValue;
    }

    QList<T*>& derivedEntities()
    {
        return collection;
    }

    T* addEntity(T* entity)
    {
        if(!collection.contains(entity)) {
            collection.append(entity);
            EntityCollectionObject::collectionChanged();
        }
        return entity;
    }

private:
    QList<T*> collection;
};
```

> You will need `#include` `<QJsonValue>` and `<QJsonArray>` for these classes.

The `clear()` method simply empties the collection and tidies up the memory; `update()` is conceptually the same as the JSON methods we implemented in Entity, except that we are dealing with a collection of entities, so we take a JSON array instead of an object. `addEntity()` adds an instance of a derived class to the collection, and `derivedEntities()` returns the collection; `baseEntities()` does a little more work, creating a new vector on request and populating it with all the items in the collection. It is just implicitly casting pointers, so we're not concerned about expensive object instantiation.

Finally, we provide the implementation for our magic templated methods:

```
template <class T>
QList<T*>& EntityCollectionBase::derivedEntities()
{
    return dynamic_cast<const
EntityCollection<T>&>(*this).derivedEntities();
}

template <class T>
T* EntityCollectionBase::addEntity(T* entity)
{
    return dynamic_cast<const
EntityCollection<T>&>(*this).addEntity(entity);
}
```

What we've achieved by delaying our implementation of these methods is that we've now fully declared our templated EntityCollection class. We can now "route" any calls to the templated methods through to the implementation in the templated class. It's a tricky technique to wrap your head around, but it will hopefully make more sense when we start implementing these collections in our real-world models.

With our entity collections now ready, we can return to our Entity class and add them to the mix.

In the header, #include <data/entity-collection.h>, add the signal:

```
void childCollectionsChanged(const QString& collectionKey);
```

Also, add the protected method:

```
EntityCollectionBase* addChildCollection(EntityCollectionBase*
entityCollection);
```

In the implementation file, add the private member:

```
std::map<QString, EntityCollectionBase*> childCollections;
```

Then, add the method:

```
EntityCollectionBase* Entity::addChildCollection(EntityCollectionBase*
entityCollection)
{
    if(implementation->childCollections.find(entityCollection-
     >getKey()) == std::end(implementation->childCollections)) {
        implementation->childCollections[entityCollection->getKey()] =
                                    entityCollection;
        emit childCollectionsChanged(entityCollection->getKey());
    }
    return entityCollection;
}
```

This works in exactly the same way as the other maps, associating a key with a pointer to a base class.

Next, add the collections to the `update()` method:

```
void Entity::update(const QJsonObject& jsonObject)
{
    // Update data decorators
    for (std::pair<QString, DataDecorator*> dataDecoratorPair :
        implementation->dataDecorators) {
        dataDecoratorPair.second->update(jsonObject);
    }

    // Update child entities
    for (std::pair<QString, Entity*> childEntityPair : implementation-
        >childEntities) { childEntityPair.second-
        >update(jsonObject.value(childEntityPair.first).toObject());
    }

    // Update child collections
    for (std::pair<QString, EntityCollectionBase*> childCollectionPair
        : implementation->childCollections) {
            childCollectionPair.second-
        >update(jsonObject.value(childCollectionPair.first).toArray());
    }
}
```

Finally, add the collections to the `toJson()` method:

```
QJsonObject Entity::toJson() const
{
    QJsonObject returnValue;

    // Add data decorators
```

```
    for (std::pair<QString, DataDecorator*> dataDecoratorPair :
        implementation->dataDecorators) {
        returnValue.insert( dataDecoratorPair.first,
        dataDecoratorPair.second->jsonValue() );
    }

    // Add child entities
    for (std::pair<QString, Entity*> childEntityPair : implementation-
        >childEntities) {
        returnValue.insert( childEntityPair.first,
      childEntityPair.second->toJson() );
    }

    // Add child collections
    for (std::pair<QString, EntityCollectionBase*> childCollectionPair
        : implementation->childCollections) {
        QJsonArray entityArray;
            for (Entity* entity : childCollectionPair.second-
            >baseEntities()) {
            entityArray.append( entity->toJson() );
        }
        returnValue.insert( childCollectionPair.first, entityArray );
    }

    return returnValue;
}
```

> You will need #include <QJsonArray> for that last snippet.

We use the baseEntities() method to give us a collection of Entity*. We then append the JSON object from each entity to a JSON array and when complete, add that array to our root JSON object with the collection's key.

The past few sections have been quite long and complex and may seem like a lot of work just to implement some data models. However, it's all code that you write once, and it gives you a lot of functionality for free with every entity you go on and make, so it's worth the investment in the long run. We'll go ahead and look at how to implement these classes in our data models.

Data models

Now that we have the infrastructure in place to be able to define data objects (entities and entity collections) and properties of various types (data decorators), we can move on and build the object hierarchy we laid out earlier in the chapter. We already have a default **Client** class created by Qt Creator, so supplement that in `cm-lib/source/models` with the following new classes:

Class	Purpose
Address	Represents a supply or billing address
Appointment	Represents an appointment with a client
Contact	Represents a method of contacting a client

We'll start with the simplest of the models—the address.

`address.h`:

```
#ifndef ADDRESS_H
#define ADDRESS_H

#include <QObject>

#include <cm-lib_global.h>
#include <data/string-decorator.h>
#include <data/entity.h>

namespace cm {
namespace models {

class CMLIBSHARED_EXPORT Address : public data::Entity
{
    Q_OBJECT
    Q_PROPERTY(cm::data::StringDecorator* ui_building MEMBER building
                                          CONSTANT)
    Q_PROPERTY(cm::data::StringDecorator* ui_street MEMBER street
                                          CONSTANT)
    Q_PROPERTY(cm::data::StringDecorator* ui_city MEMBER city CONSTANT)
    Q_PROPERTY(cm::data::StringDecorator* ui_postcode MEMBER postcode
                                          CONSTANT)
    Q_PROPERTY(QString ui_fullAddress READ fullAddress CONSTANT)

public:
    explicit Address(QObject* parent = nullptr);
    Address(QObject* parent, const QJsonObject& json);
```

```
        data::StringDecorator* building{nullptr};
        data::StringDecorator* street{nullptr};
        data::StringDecorator* city{nullptr};
        data::StringDecorator* postcode{nullptr};

        QString fullAddress() const;
    };

    }}

    #endif
```

We define the properties we designed at the beginning of the chapter, but instead of using regular QString objects, we use our new StringDecorators. To protect the integrity of our data, we should really use the READ keyword and return a StringDecorator* const via an accessor method, but for simplicity, we'll use MEMBER instead. We also provide an overloaded constructor that we can use to construct an address from a QJsonObject. Finally, we add a helper fullAddress() method and property to concatenate the address elements into a single string for use in the UI.

address.cpp:

```
    #include "address.h"

    using namespace cm::data;

    namespace cm {
    namespace models {

    Address::Address(QObject* parent)
            : Entity(parent, "address")
    {
        building = static_cast<StringDecorator*>(addDataItem(new
    StringDecorator(this, "building", "Building")));
        street = static_cast<StringDecorator*>(addDataItem(new
    StringDecorator(this, "street", "Street")));
        city = static_cast<StringDecorator*>(addDataItem(new
    StringDecorator(this, "city", "City")));
        postcode = static_cast<StringDecorator*>(addDataItem(new
    StringDecorator(this, "postcode", "Post Code")));
    }

    Address::Address(QObject* parent, const QJsonObject& json)
            : Address(parent)
    {
        update(json);
    }
```

```
QString Address::fullAddress() const
{
    return building->value() + " " + street->value() + "n" + city->value()
+ "n" + postcode->value();
}

}}
```

This is where all of our hard work starts to come together. We need to do two things with each of our properties. Firstly, we need a pointer to the derived type (`StringDecorator`), which we can present to the UI in order to display and edit the value. Secondly, we need to make the base Entity class aware of the base type (`DataDecorator`) so that it can iterate the data items and perform the JSON serialization work for us. We can use the `addDataItem()` method to achieve both these goals in a one-line statement:

```
building = static_cast<StringDecorator*>(addDataItem(new
StringDecorator(this, "building", "Building")));
```

Breaking this down, we create a new `StringDecorator*` with the `building` key and `Building` UI label. This is immediately passed to `addDataItem()`, which adds it to the `dataDecorators` collection in the **Entity** and returns the data item as a `DataDecorator*`. We can then cast it back to a `StringDecorator*` before storing it in the `building` member variable.

The only other piece of implementation here is to take a JSON object, construct the address as normal by calling the default constructor, and then update the model using the `update()` method.

The `Appointment` and `Contact` models follow the same pattern, just with different properties and the appropriate variation of `DataDecorator` for each of their data types. Where `Contact` varies more significantly is in its use of an `EnumeratorDecorator` for the `contactType` property. To support this, we first define an enumerator in the header file that contains all the possible values we want:

```
enum eContactType {
    Unknown = 0,
    Telephone,
    Email,
    Fax
};
```

Note that we have a default value of `Unknown` represented by 0. This is important as it allows us to accommodate an initial unset value. Next, we define a mapper container that allows us to map each of the enumerated types to a descriptive string:

```
std::map<int, QString> Contact::contactTypeMapper = std::map<int, QString>
{
    { Contact::eContactType::Unknown, "" }
    , { Contact::eContactType::Telephone, "Telephone" }
    , { Contact::eContactType::Email, "Email" }
    , { Contact::eContactType::Fax, "Fax" }
};
```

When creating the new `EnumeratorDecorator`, we supply the default value (0 for `eContactType::Unknown`) along with the mapper:

```
contactType = static_cast<EnumeratorDecorator*>(addDataItem(new
EnumeratorDecorator(this, "contactType", "Contact Type", 0,
contactTypeMapper)));
```

Our client model is a little more complex, as it not only has data items but has child entities and collections too. However, the way we create and expose these things is very similar to what we have already seen.

`client.h:`

```
#ifndef CLIENT_H
#define CLIENT_H

#include <QObject>
#include <QtQml/QQmlListProperty>

#include <cm-lib_global.h>
#include <data/string-decorator.h>
#include <data/entity.h>
#include <data/entity-collection.h>
#include <models/address.h>
#include <models/appointment.h>
#include <models/contact.h>

namespace cm {
namespace models {

class CMLIBSHARED_EXPORT Client : public data::Entity
{
    Q_OBJECT
    Q_PROPERTY( cm::data::StringDecorator* ui_reference MEMBER
                                           reference CONSTANT )
```

```
    Q_PROPERTY( cm::data::StringDecorator* ui_name MEMBER name CONSTANT )
    Q_PROPERTY( cm::models::Address* ui_supplyAddress MEMBER
                                    supplyAddress CONSTANT )
    Q_PROPERTY( cm::models::Address* ui_billingAddress MEMBER
                                    billingAddress CONSTANT )
    Q_PROPERTY( QQmlListProperty<Appointment> ui_appointments READ
                    ui_appointments NOTIFY appointmentsChanged )
    Q_PROPERTY( QQmlListProperty<Contact> ui_contacts READ ui_contacts
                                    NOTIFY contactsChanged )

public:
    explicit Client(QObject* parent = nullptr);
    Client(QObject* parent, const QJsonObject& json);

    data::StringDecorator* reference{nullptr};
    data::StringDecorator* name{nullptr};
    Address* supplyAddress{nullptr};
    Address* billingAddress{nullptr};
    data::EntityCollection<Appointment>* appointments{nullptr};
    data::EntityCollection<Contact>* contacts{nullptr};

    QQmlListProperty<cm::models::Appointment> ui_appointments();
    QQmlListProperty<cm::models::Contact> ui_contacts();

signals:
    void appointmentsChanged();
    void contactsChanged();
};

}}

#endif
```

We expose the child entities as pointers to the derived type and the collections as pointers to a templated `EntityCollection`.

`client.cpp`:

```
#include "client.h"

using namespace cm::data;

namespace cm {
namespace models {

Client::Client(QObject* parent)
    : Entity(parent, "client")
{
```

```
        reference = static_cast<StringDecorator*>(addDataItem(new
                StringDecorator(this, "reference", "Client Ref")));
        name = static_cast<StringDecorator*>(addDataItem(new
                StringDecorator(this, "name", "Name")));
        supplyAddress = static_cast<Address*>(addChild(new Address(this),
                                        "supplyAddress"));
        billingAddress = static_cast<Address*>(addChild(new Address(this),
                                        "billingAddress"));
        appointments = static_cast<EntityCollection<Appointment>*>
        (addChildCollection(new EntityCollection<Appointment>(this,
                                        "appointments")));
        contacts =
static_cast<EntityCollection<Contact>*>(addChildCollection(new
EntityCollection<Contact>(this, "contacts")));
}

Client::Client(QObject* parent, const QJsonObject& json)
    : Client(parent)
{
    update(json);
}

QQmlListProperty<Appointment> Client::ui_appointments()
{
    return QQmlListProperty<Appointment>(this,
appointments->derivedEntities());
}

QQmlListProperty<Contact> Client::ui_contacts()
{
    return QQmlListProperty<Contact>(this, contacts->derivedEntities());
}

}}
```

Adding child entities follows the same pattern as data items, but using the addChild() method. Note that we add more than one child of the same address type, but ensure that they have different key values to avoid duplicates and invalid JSON. Entity collections are added with addChildCollection() and other than being templated, they follow the same approach.

While it was a lot of work to create our entities and data items, creating models is really quite straightforward and now they all come packed with features that we wouldn't otherwise have had.

Before we can use our fancy new models in the UI, we need to register the types in `main.cpp` in `cm-ui`, including the data decorators that represent the data items. Remember to add the relevant `#include` statements first:

```
qmlRegisterType<cm::data::DateTimeDecorator>("CM", 1, 0,
"DateTimeDecorator");
qmlRegisterType<cm::data::EnumeratorDecorator>("CM", 1, 0,
"EnumeratorDecorator");
qmlRegisterType<cm::data::IntDecorator>("CM", 1, 0, "IntDecorator");
qmlRegisterType<cm::data::StringDecorator>("CM", 1, 0, "StringDecorator");

qmlRegisterType<cm::models::Address>("CM", 1, 0, "Address");
qmlRegisterType<cm::models::Appointment>("CM", 1, 0, "Appointment");
qmlRegisterType<cm::models::Client>("CM", 1, 0, "Client");
qmlRegisterType<cm::models::Contact>("CM", 1, 0, "Contact");
```

With that done, we'll create an instance of a client in `MasterController`, which we will use to populate data for new clients. This follows exactly the same pattern that we've used for adding the other controllers.

First, add the member variable to the private implementation of `MasterController`:

```
Client* newClient{nullptr};
```

Then, initialize it in the `Implementation` constructor:

```
newClient = new Client(masterController);
```

Third, add the accessor method:

```
Client* MasterController::newClient()
{
    return implementation->newClient;
}
```

Finally, add `Q_PROPERTY`:

```
Q_PROPERTY( cm::models::Client* ui_newClient READ newClient CONSTANT )
```

We now have an empty instance of a client available for consumption by the UI, specifically `CreateClientView`, which we will edit next. Begin by adding a shortcut property for the new client instance:

```
property Client newClient: masterController.ui_newClient
```

Remember that the properties should all be defined at the root Item level and that you need to `import CM 1.0` to get access to the registered types. This just enables us to use `newClient` as shorthand to access the instance rather than having to type out `masterController.ui_newClient` every time.

At this point, everything is hooked up ready for use, and you should be able to run the application and navigate to the new client view with no problems. The view isn't doing anything with the new client instance just yet, but it's happily sitting there ready for action. Now, let's look at how we can interact with it.

Custom TextBox

We'll start with the `name` data item of our client. Back when we worked with another `QString` property in our UI with the welcome message, we displayed it with the basic text component. This component is read only, so to view and edit our property, we will need to reach for something else. There are a couple of options in the base `QtQuick` module: `TextInput` and `TextEdit`. `TextInput` is for a single line of editable plain text, while `TextEdit` handles multiline blocks of text and also supports rich text. `TextInput` is ideal for our **name**.

> Importing the `QtQuick.Controls` module makes additional text-based components like `Label`, `TextField`, and `TextArea` available. Label inherits and extends Text, `TextField` inherits and extends `TextInput` and `TextArea` inherits and extends `TextEdit`. The basic controls are enough for us at this stage, but be aware that these alternatives exist. If you find yourself trying to do something with one of the basic controls which it doesn't seem to support, then import `QtQuick.Controls` and take a look at its more powerful cousin. It may well have the functionality you are looking for.

Let's build on what we've learned and create a new reusable component. As usual, we'll begin by preparing the Style properties we'll need:

```
readonly property real sizeScreenMargin: 20

readonly property color colourDataControlsBackground: "#ffffff"
readonly property color colourDataControlsFont: "#131313"
readonly property int pixelSizeDataControls: 18
readonly property real widthDataControls: 400
readonly property real heightDataControls: 40
```

Next, create `StringEditorSingleLine.qml` in `cm/cm-ui/components`. It's not the most beautiful of names, but at least it's descriptive!

> **TIP**
> It's generally helpful to use a prefix with custom QML views and components to help distinguish them from the built-in Qt components and avoid naming conflicts. If we were using that approach with this project, we could have called this component `CMTextBox` or something equally short and simple. Use whatever approach and conventions work for you, it makes no functional difference.

Edit `components.qrc` and `qmldir` as we did previously to make the new component available in our components module.

What we're trying to achieve with this component is as follows:

- To be able to pass in any `StringDecorator` property from any data model and view/edit the value
- View a descriptive label for the control as defined in the `ui_label` property of the `StringDecorator`
- View/edit the `ui_value` property of the `StringDecorator` in a `TextBox`
- If the window is wide enough, then the label and textbox are laid out horizontally
- If the window is not wide enough, then the label and textbox are laid out vertically

With these goals in mind, implement `StringEditorSingleLine`, as follows:

```
import QtQuick 2.9
import CM 1.0
import assets 1.0

Item {
    property StringDecorator stringDecorator

    height: width > textLabel.width + textValue.width ?
    Style.heightDataControls : Style.heightDataControls * 2

    Flow {
        anchors.fill: parent

        Rectangle {
            width: Style.widthDataControls
            height: Style.heightDataControls
            color: Style.colourBackground
```

```
            Text {
                id: textLabel
                anchors {
                    fill: parent
                    margins: Style.heightDataControls / 4
                }
                text: stringDecorator.ui_label
                color: Style.colourDataControlsFont
                font.pixelSize: Style.pixelSizeDataControls
                verticalAlignment: Qt.AlignVCenter
            }
        }

        Rectangle {
            id: background
            width: Style.widthDataControls
            height: Style.heightDataControls
            color: Style.colourDataControlsBackground
            border {
                width: 1
                color: Style.colourDataControlsFont
            }
            TextInput {
                id: textValue
                anchors {
                    fill: parent
                    margins: Style.heightDataControls / 4
                }
                text: stringDecorator.ui_value
                color: Style.colourDataControlsFont
                font.pixelSize: Style.pixelSizeDataControls
                verticalAlignment: Qt.AlignVCenter
            }
        }

        Binding {
            target: stringDecorator
            property: "ui_value"
            value: textValue.text
        }
    }
}
```

We begin with a public StringDecorator property (public because it is in the root Item element), which we can set from outside of the component.

We introduce a new kind of element—Flow—to lay out our label and textbox for us. Rather than always laying out content in a single direction like row or column, the Flow item will lay out its child elements side by side until it runs out of available space and then wraps them like words on a page. We tell it how much available space it has to play with by anchoring it to the root Item.

Next comes our descriptive label in a Text control and the editable value in a `TextInput` control. We embed both controls in explicitly sized rectangles. The rectangles help us align the elements and give us the opportunity to draw backgrounds and borders.

The `Binding` component establishes a dependency between the properties of two different objects; in our case, the `TextInput` control called `textValue` and the `StringDecorator` instance called `stringDecorator`. The `target` property defines the object we want to update, the `property` is the `Q_PROPERTY` we want to set, and `value` is the value we want to set it to. This is a key element that gives us true two-way binding. Without this, we will be able to view the value from the `StringDecorator`, but any changes we make in the UI will not update the value.

Back in `CreateClientView`, replace the old Text element with our new component and pass in the `ui_name` property:

```
StringEditorSingleLine {
    stringDecorator: newClient.ui_name
}
```

Now build and run the app, navigate to the **Create Client view**, and try editing the name:

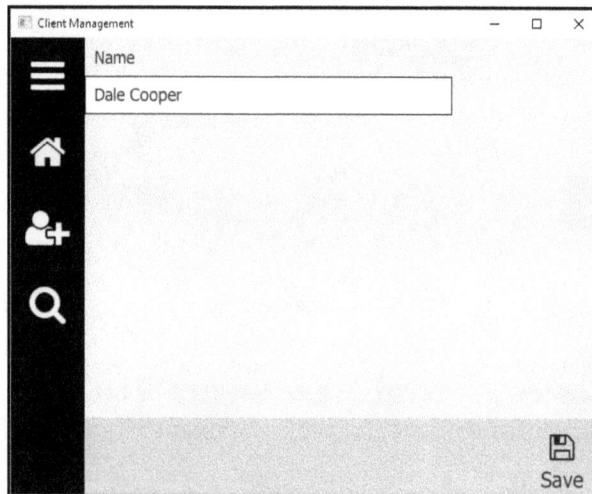

If you switch to the **Find Client view** and back again, you will see that the value is retained, demonstrating the updates are successfully being set in the string decorator.

Our newly bound view isn't exactly overflowing with data just yet, but over the coming chapters, we will add more and more to this view, so let's add a few finishing touches to prepare us.

Firstly, we only need to add another three or four properties to the view, and we'll run out of space as the default size we've set for the window is very small, so in `MasterView` bump the window size up to something comfortable for your display. I'll treat myself and go full HD at 1920 x 1080.

Even with a larger window to work with, we still need to prepare for the possibility of overflow, so we'll add our content to another new element called `ScrollView`. As its name suggests, it works in a similar way to flow and manages its content based on the space it has available to it. If the content exceeds the available space, it will present scrollbars for the user. It's also a very finger friendly control and on a touch screen, the user can just drag the content rather than having to fiddle around with a tiny scrollbar.

Although we only have one property currently, when we add more, we will need to lay them out so we'll add a column.

Finally, the controls are stuck to the bounds of the view, so we'll add a little gutter around the view and some spacing in the column.

The revised view should look as follows:

```
import QtQuick 2.9
import QtQuick.Controls 2.2
import CM 1.0
import assets 1.0
import components 1.0

Item {
    property Client newClient: masterController.ui_newClient

    Rectangle {
        anchors.fill: parent
        color: Style.colourBackground
    }

    ScrollView {
        id: scrollView
        anchors {
            left: parent.left
            right: parent.right
```

```
            top: parent.top
            bottom: commandBar. top
            margins: Style.sizeScreenMargin
        }
        clip: true
        Column {
            spacing: Style.sizeScreenMargin
            width: scrollView.width
            StringEditorSingleLine {
                stringDecorator: newClient.ui_name
                anchors {
                    left: parent.left
                    right: parent.right
                }
            }
        }
    }

    CommandBar {
        id: commandBar
        commandList:
masterController.ui_commandController.ui_createClientViewContextCommands
    }
}
```

Build and run, and you should see the nice neat screen margin. You should also be able to resize the window from wide to narrow and see the string editor automatically adjust its layout accordingly.

Summary

This was a fairly hefty chapter, but we've covered arguably the most important element of any Line of Business application, and that is the data. We've implemented a framework of self-aware entities that can serialize themselves to and from JSON and started building data bound controls. We've designed and created our data models and are now entering the homeward stretch. In Chapter 6, *Unit Testing*, we'll show some love to our so far neglected unit test project and check that our entities are behaving as expected.

6
Unit Testing

In this chapter, we will take a look at a process that has really grown in popularity in the recent years—unit testing. We'll briefly talk about what it is and why we would want to do it before covering how to integrate it into our solution using Qt's very own unit testing tool, Qt Test. We will cover the following topics:

- Unit Testing principles
- The default Qt approach
- An alternative approach
- DataDecorator tests
- Entity tests
- Mocking

Unit testing

The essence of unit testing is to break an application down into its smallest functional blocks (units) and then test each unit with real-world scenarios within the scope of the initiative. For example, take a simple method that takes two signed integers and adds them together:

```
int add(intx, int y);
```

Some example scènarios can be as listed:

- Adding two positive numbers
- Adding two negative numbers
- Adding two zeroes
- Adding one positive and one negative number
- Adding zero and a positive number
- Adding zero and a negative number

We can write a test for each of these scenarios and then every time our code base changes (any code, not just our `add()` method), these tests can be executed to ensure that the code still behaves as expected. It is a really valuable tool to give you confidence that any code changes you make aren't having a detrimental effect on the existing functionality.

Historically, these tests would have been performed manually, but tooling exists that can enable us to write code to test code automatically, which sounds like a bit of a paradox, but it really works. Qt provides a tailored framework for unit testing Qt-based applications, called Qt Test, and that is what we will use.

> **TIP**
>
> You can use other C++ testing frameworks such as Google test, which arguably offer more power and flexibility, particularly when used with Google mock, but can be a bit more fiddly to set up.

Test-driven development (**TDD**) takes unit testing to the next level and actually changes the way you write code in the first place. In essence, you write a test first. The test will initially fail (indeed, probably it won't even build) because you have no implementation. You then write the bare minimum of code it takes to make the test pass and then move on to writing the next test. You iteratively build out your implementation in this way until you have delivered the block of functionality required. Finally, you refactor the code to the required standard, using the completed unit tests to validate that the refactored code still behaves as expected. This is sometimes referred to as *Red-Green-Refactor*.

This isn't a book about unit testing, and it is certainly not about TDD, so we will be very loose with our approach, but it is a key part of modern application development, and it is important to know how it fits into your Qt projects.

We've demonstrated the mechanism for passing a simple piece of data (the welcome message) from our business logic project to our UI, so as always, starting as simply as possible, our first goal for this chapter is to write a rudimentary unit test for that behavior. Once done, we'll move on to test the data classes we implemented in the previous chapter.

The default Qt approach

When we created our `cm-tests` project, Qt Creator helpfully created a `ClientTests` class for us to use a starting point, containing a single test named `testCase1`. Let's dive straight in and execute this default test and see what happens. We'll then take a look at the code and discuss what's going on.

Switch the **Run** output to `cm-tests`, and compile and run:

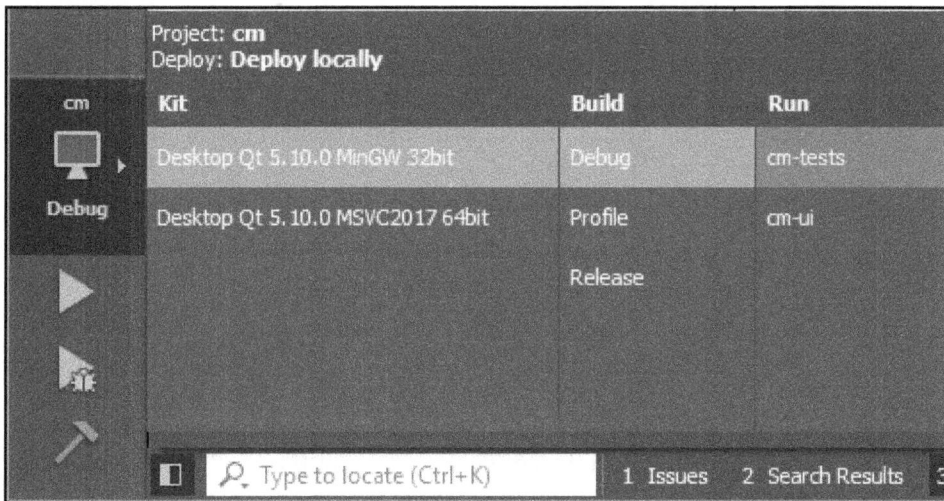

You won't see any fancy applications spring to life this time, but you will see some text in the **Application Output** pane in Qt Creator:

```
********* Start testing of ClientTests *********
Config: Using QtTest library 5.10.0, Qt 5.10.0 (i386-little_endian-ilp32
shared (dynamic) debug build; by GCC 5.3.0)
PASS   : ClientTests::initTestCase()
PASS   : ClientTests::testCase1()
PASS   : ClientTests::cleanupTestCase()
Totals: 3 passed, 0 failed, 0 skipped, 0 blacklisted, 0ms
********* Finished testing of ClientTests *********
```

We can see that three methods have been called, the second of which is our default unit test. The other two functions—`initTestCase()` and `cleanupTestCase()`—are special methods that execute before and after the suite of tests in the class, allowing you to set up any preconditions required to execute the tests and then perform any clean up afterward. All the three steps pass.

Now, in `client-tests.cpp`, add another method—`testCase2()`—which is the same as `testCase1()` but substitute the `true` condition for `false`. Note that the class declaration and method definitions are all in the same `.cpp` file, so you need to add the method in both places. Run the tests again:

```
********* Start testing of ClientTests *********
Config: Using QtTest library 5.10.0, Qt 5.10.0 (i386-little_endian-ilp32
shared (dynamic) debug build; by GCC 5.3.0)
PASS   : ClientTests::initTestCase()
PASS   : ClientTests::testCase1()
FAIL!  : ClientTests::testCase2() 'false' returned FALSE. (Failure)
....cmcm-testssourcemodelsclient-tests.cpp(37) : failure location
PASS   : ClientTests::cleanupTestCase()
Totals: 3 passed, 1 failed, 0 skipped, 0 blacklisted, 0ms
********* Finished testing of ClientTests *********
```

This time, you can see that `testCase2()` tried to verify that false was true, which of course it isn't, and our test fails, outputting our failure message in the process. `initTestCase()` and `cleanupTestCase()` are still executed at the beginning and end of the suite of tests.

Now we've seen what passing and failing tests look like, but what is actually going on?

We have a `QObject` derived class `ClientTests`, which implements an empty default constructor. We then have some methods declared as private `Q_SLOTS`. Much like `Q_OBJECT`, this is a macro that injects a bunch of clever boilerplate code for us, and much like `Q_OBJECT`, you don't need to worry about understanding its inner workings in order to use it. Each method in the class defined as one of these private slots is executed as a unit test.

The unit test methods then use the `QVERIFY2` macro to verify a given boolean condition, namely that true is, well, true. If this fails, which we have engineered in `testCase2`, the helpful message failure will be output to the console.

If there is a QVERIFY2, then presumably there must be a QVERIFY1, right? Well, nearly, there is QVERIFY, which performs the same test but does not have the failure message parameter. Other commonly used macros are QCOMPARE, which verifies that two parameters of the same type are equivalent, and QVERIFY_EXCEPTION_THROWN, which verifies that an exception is thrown when a given expression is executed. This may sound odd, as we don't ideally want our code to throw exceptions. However, things aren't always ideal, and we should always write negative tests that verify how the code behaves when something does go wrong. A common example of this is where we have a method that accepts a pointer to an object as a parameter. We should write a negative test that verifies what happens if we pass in a nullptr (which is always a possibility, regardless of how careful you are). We may expect the code to happily ignore it and take no further action or we may want some sort of null argument exception to throw, which is where QVERIFY_EXCEPTION_THROWN comes in.

After the test case definitions, another macro QTEST_APPLESS_MAIN stubs out a main() hook to execute the tests and the final #include statement pulls in the .moc file produced by the build process. Every class that inherits from QObject will have a companion .moc file generated, containing all the magic metadata code created by Q_OBJECT and other associated macros.

Now, if you're thinking "why would you test if true is true and false is true?", then you absolutely wouldn't, this is a totally pointless pair of tests. The purpose of this exercise is just to look at how the default approach that Qt Creator has pulled together for us works, and it does work, but it has a few key failings that we will need to work to fix before we write a real test.

The first issue is that QTEST_APPLESS_MAIN creates a main() method in order to run our test cases in ClientTests. What happens when we write another test class? We'll have two main() methods and things won't go well. Another issue is that our test output is just piped to the **Application Output** pane. In a business environment, it is common to have build servers that pull application code, perform a build, run the unit test suite, and flag any test failures for investigation. In order for this to work, the build tool needs to be able to access the test output and can't read the **Application Output** pane in the IDE like a human can. Let's look at an alternative approach that solves these issues.

Custom approach

The custom approach we will take still applies the same basic concepts we've just discussed. At the heart of it, we will still have a test class that contains a suite of unit test methods to be executed. All we will do is supplement this with some additional boilerplate code to allow us to easily accommodate multiple test classes and pipe the output to files rather than the console.

Let's begin by adding a new class `TestSuite` to `cm-tests` in the source folder:

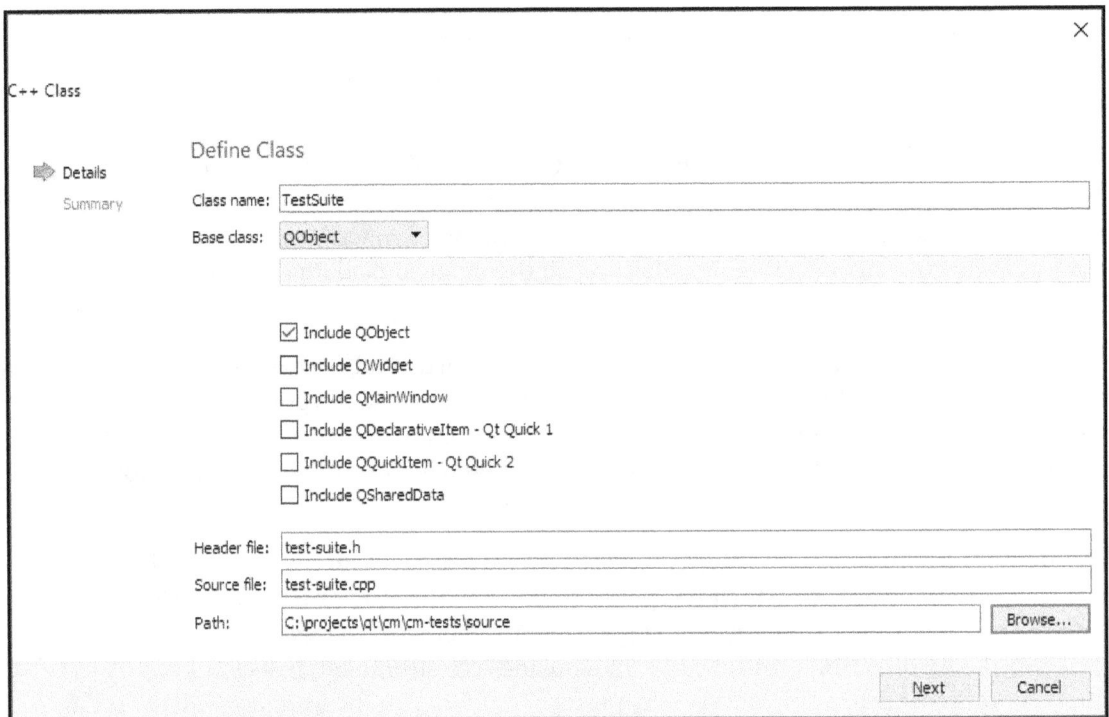

`test-suite.h`:

```cpp
#ifndef TESTSUITE_H
#define TESTSUITE_H

#include <QObject>
#include <QString>
#include <QtTest/QtTest>

#include <vector>
```

```
namespace cm {

class TestSuite : public QObject
{
    Q_OBJECT
public:
    explicit TestSuite(const QString& _testName = "");
    virtual ~TestSuite();

    QString testName;
    static std::vector<TestSuite*>& testList();
};

}

#endif
```

test-suite.cpp:

```
#include "test-suite.h"

#include <QDebug>

namespace cm {

TestSuite::TestSuite(const QString& _testName)
    : QObject()
    , testName(_testName)
{
    qDebug() << "Creating test" << testName;
    testList().push_back(this);
    qDebug() << testList().size() << " tests recorded";
}

TestSuite::~TestSuite()
{
    qDebug() << "Destroying test";
}

std::vector<TestSuite*>& TestSuite::testList()
{
    static std::vector<TestSuite*> instance = std::vector<TestSuite*>();
    return instance;
}

}
```

Here, we are creating a base class that will be used for each of our test classes. There is generally a one-to-one relationship between a regular class and a test suite class, for example, the `Client` and `ClientTests` classes. Each derived instance of `TestSuite` adds itself to a shared vector. This can be a little confusing at first glance, so we are also writing some information out to the console using `qDebug()` so that you can follow what's going on. It will make more sense when we create our first class deriving from `TestSuite`.

Next, add a new C++ Source File `main.cpp`, again to the source folder:

`main.cpp`:

```cpp
#include <QtTest/QtTest>
#include <QDebug>

#include "test-suite.h"

using namespace cm;

int main(int argc, char *argv[])
{
    Q_UNUSED(argc);
    Q_UNUSED(argv);

    qDebug() << "Starting test suite...";
    qDebug() << "Accessing tests from " << &TestSuite::testList();
    qDebug() << TestSuite::testList().size() << " tests detected";

    int failedTestsCount = 0;

    for(TestSuite* i : TestSuite::testList()) {
        qDebug() << "Executing test " << i->testName;
        QString filename(i->testName + ".xml");
        int result = QTest::qExec(i, QStringList() << " " << "-o" <<
                                  filename << "-xunitxml");
        qDebug() << "Test result " << result;
        if(result != 0) {
            failedTestsCount++;
        }
    }

    qDebug() << "Test suite complete - " <<
        QString::number(failedTestsCount) << " failures detected.";

    return failedTestsCount;
}
```

This looks more complicated than it actually is because of the qDebug() statements added for information. We iterate through each of the registered test classes and use the static QTest::qExec() method to detect and run all tests discovered within them. A key addition, however, is that we create an XML file for each class and pipe out the results to it.

This mechanism solves our two problems. We now have a single main() method that will detect and run all of our tests, and we get a separate XML file containing output for each of our test suites. However, before you can build the project, you will need to revisit client-tests.cpp and either comment out or remove the QTEST_APPLESS_MAIN line, or we'll be back to the problem of multiple main() methods. Don't worry about the rest of client-tests.cpp for now; we'll revisit it later when we start testing our data classes.

Build and run now, and you'll get a different set of text in Application Output:

```
Starting test suite...
Accessing tests from 0x40b040
0 tests detected
Test suite complete - "0" failures detected.
```

Let's go ahead and implement our first TestSuite. We have a MasterController class that presents a message string to the UI, so let's write a simple test that verifies that the message is correct. We will need to reference code from cm-lib in the cm-tests project, so ensure that the relevant INCLUDE directives are added to cm-tests.pro:

```
INCLUDEPATH += source
    ../cm-lib/source
```

Create a new companion test class called MasterControllerTests in cm-tests/source/controllers.

master-controller-tests.h:

```
#ifndef MASTERCONTROLLERTESTS_H
#define MASTERCONTROLLERTESTS_H

#include <QtTest>

#include <controllers/master-controller.h>
#include <test-suite.h>

namespace cm {
namespace controllers {

class MasterControllerTests : public TestSuite
{
```

```
    Q_OBJECT

public:
    MasterControllerTests();

private slots:
    /// @brief Called before the first test function is executed
    void initTestCase();
    /// @brief Called after the last test function was executed.
    void cleanupTestCase();
    /// @brief Called before each test function is executed.
    void init();
    /// @brief Called after every test function.
    void cleanup();

private slots:
    void welcomeMessage_returnsCorrectMessage();

private:
    MasterController masterController;
};

}}

#endif
```

We've explicitly added the `initTestCase()` and `cleanupTestCase()` scaffolding methods so that there is no mystery as to where they come from. We've also added another couple of special scaffolding methods for completeness: `init()` and `cleanup()`. The difference is that these methods are executed before and after each individual test, as opposed to before and after the entire suite of tests.

> None of these methods are doing anything for us and are there just for future reference. They can safely be removed if you want to streamline things.

`master-controller-tests.cpp`:

```
#include "master-controller-tests.h"

namespace cm {
namespace controllers { // Instance

static MasterControllerTests instance;

MasterControllerTests::MasterControllerTests()
```

```
        : TestSuite( "MasterControllerTests" )
{
}


}

namespace controllers { // Scaffolding

void MasterControllerTests::initTestCase()
{
}

void MasterControllerTests::cleanupTestCase()
{
}

void MasterControllerTests::init()
{
}

void MasterControllerTests::cleanup()
{
}


}

namespace controllers { // Tests

void MasterControllerTests::welcomeMessage_returnsCorrectMessage()
{
    QCOMPARE( masterController.welcomeMessage(), QString("Welcome to the
Client Management system!") );
}

}}
```

We again have a single test, but this time, it actually serves some meaningful purpose. We want to test that when we instantiate a `MasterController` object and access its `welcomeMessage` method, it returns the message that we want, which will be **Welcome to the Client Management system!**.

Unlike the scaffolding methods, the naming of your tests is entirely down to preference. I tend to loosely follow the `methodIAmTesting_givenSomeScenario_doesTheCorrectThing` format, for example:

```
divideTwoNumbers_givenTwoValidNumbers_returnsCorrectResult()
divideTwoNumbers_givenZeroDivisor_throwsInvalidArgumentException()
```

We construct an instance of `MasterController` as a private member variable that we will use to test against. In the implementation, we specify the name of the test suite via the constructor, and we also create a static instance of the test class. This is the trigger that adds `MasterControllerTests` to the static vector we saw in the `TestSuite` class.

Finally, for the implementation of our test, we test the value of the `welcomeMessage` of our `masterController` instance with the message we want using the `QCOMPARE` macro. Note that because `QCOMPARE` is a macro, you won't get implicit typecasting, so you need to ensure that the types of the expected and actual results are the same. Here, we've achieved that by constructing a `QString` object from the literal text.

Run `qmake`, and build and run to see the results of our test in the **Application Output** pane:

```
Creating test "MasterControllerTests"
1 tests recorded
Starting test suite...
Accessing tests from 0x40b040
1 tests detected
Executing test "MasterControllerTests"
Test result 1
Test suite complete - "1" failures detected.
Destroying test
```

This begins with the registration of the `MasterControllerTests` class via the static instance. The `main()` method iterates the collection of registered test suites and finds one, then executes all the unit tests within that suite. The test suite contains one unit test that runs and promptly fails. This may seem to be less helpful than earlier as there is no indication as to which test failed or why. However, remember that this output is simply from the `qDebug()` statements we added for extra information; it is not the true output from the test execution. In `master-controller-tests.cpp` we instantiated the `TestSuite` with a `testName` parameter of `MasterControllerTests`, so the output will have been piped to a file named `MasterControllerTests.xml`.

Navigate to the `cm/binaries` folder and drill down through the folders to where we direct our project output for the selected configuration and in there, you will see `MasterControllerTests.xml`:

```xml
<testsuite name="cm::controllers::MasterControllerTests" tests="3"
failures="1" errors="0">
    <properties>
       <property name="QTestVersion" value="5.10.0"/>
       <property name="QtVersion" value="5.10.0"/>
       <property name="QtBuild" value="Qt 5.10.0 (i386-little_endian-
              ilp32 shared (dynamic) debug build; by GCC 5.3.0)"/>
    </properties>
    <testcase name="initTestCase" result="pass"/>
    <testcase name="welcomeMessage_returnsCorrectMessage"
                    result="fail">
    <failure result="fail" message="Compared values are not the same Actual
(masterController.welcomeMessage) : "This is MasterController to Major Tom"
Expected (QString("Welcome to the Client Management system!")): "Welcome to
the Client Management system!""/>
    </testcase>
    <testcase name="cleanupTestCase" result="pass"/>
    <system-err/>
</testsuite>
```

Here, we have the full output from the tests, and you can see that the failure was because the welcome message we got from `masterController` was **This is MasterController to Major Tom**, and we expected **Welcome to the Client Management system!**.

`MasterController` is not behaving as expected, and we've found a bug, so head over to `master-controller.cpp` and fix the problem:

```cpp
QString welcomeMessage = "Welcome to the Client Management system!";
```

Rebuild both projects, execute the tests again, and bask in the glory of a 100% pass rate:

```
Creating test "MasterControllerTests"
1 tests recorded
Starting test suite...
Accessing tests from 0x40b040
1 tests detected
Executing test "MasterControllerTests"
Test result 0
Test suite complete - "0" failures detected.
Destroying test
```

Now that we have the testing framework set up, let's test something a little more complex than a simple string message and validate the work we did in the last chapter.

DataDecorator tests

In `Chapter 5`, *Data*, we created various classes deriving from `DataDecorator`. Let's create companion test classes for each of those and test the following functionalities:

- Object construction
- Setting the value
- Getting the value as JSON
- Updating the value from JSON

In `cm-tests/source/data`, create the `DateTimeDecoratorTests`, `EnumeratorDecoratorTests`, `IntDecoratorTests`, and `StringDecoratorTests` classes.

Let's begin with the simplest suite, `IntDecoratorTests`. The tests will be broadly similar across the suites, so once we've written one suite, we will be able to copy most of it across to the other suites and then supplement as necessary.

`int-decorator-tests.h`:

```
#ifndef INTDECORATORTESTS_H
#define INTDECORATORTESTS_H

#include <QtTest>

#include <data/int-decorator.h>
#include <test-suite.h>

namespace cm {
namespace data {

class IntDecoratorTests : public TestSuite
{
    Q_OBJECT

public:
    IntDecoratorTests();

private slots:
    void constructor_givenNoParameters_setsDefaultProperties();
```

```
        void constructor_givenParameters_setsProperties();
        void setValue_givenNewValue_updatesValueAndEmitsSignal();
        void setValue_givenSameValue_takesNoAction();
        void jsonValue_whenDefaultValue_returnsJson();
        void jsonValue_whenValueSet_returnsJson();
        void update_whenPresentInJson_updatesValue();
        void update_whenNotPresentInJson_updatesValueToDefault();
    };

    }}

    #endif
```

A common approach is to follow a "method as a unit" approach, where each method is the smallest testable unit in a class and then that unit is tested in multiple ways. So we begin by testing the constructor, both with and without parameters. The `setValue()` method should only do anything when we actually change the value, so we test both setting a different value and the same value. Next, we test that we can convert the decorator to a JSON value, both with a default value (0 in the case of an `int`) and with a set value. Finally, we perform a couple of tests against the `update()` method. If we pass in a JSON that contains the property, then we expect the value to be updated as per the JSON value. However, if the property is missing from the JSON, we expect the class to handle it gracefully and reset to a default value instead.

Note that we aren't explicitly testing the `value()` method. This is just a simple accessor method with no side effects, and we will be calling it in the other unit tests, so we will be indirectly testing it there. Feel free to create additional tests for it if you wish.

`int-decorator-tests.cpp`:

```
    #include "int-decorator-tests.h"

    #include <QSignalSpy>

    #include <data/entity.h>

    namespace cm {
    namespace data { // Instance

    static IntDecoratorTests instance;

    IntDecoratorTests::IntDecoratorTests()
        : TestSuite( "IntDecoratorTests" )
    {
    }
```

```
}

namespace data { // Tests

void
IntDecoratorTests::constructor_givenNoParameters_setsDefaultProperties()
{
    IntDecorator decorator;
    QCOMPARE(decorator.parentEntity(), nullptr);
    QCOMPARE(decorator.key(), QString("SomeItemKey"));
    QCOMPARE(decorator.label(), QString(""));
    QCOMPARE(decorator.value(), 0);
}

void IntDecoratorTests::constructor_givenParameters_setsProperties()
{
    Entity parentEntity;
    IntDecorator decorator(&parentEntity, "Test Key", "Test Label",
                                                        99);
    QCOMPARE(decorator.parentEntity(), &parentEntity);
    QCOMPARE(decorator.key(), QString("Test Key"));
    QCOMPARE(decorator.label(), QString("Test Label"));
    QCOMPARE(decorator.value(), 99);
}

void IntDecoratorTests::setValue_givenNewValue_updatesValueAndEmitsSignal()
{
    IntDecorator decorator;
    QSignalSpy valueChangedSpy(&decorator,
                               &IntDecorator::valueChanged);
    QCOMPARE(decorator.value(), 0);
    decorator.setValue(99);
    QCOMPARE(decorator.value(), 99);
    QCOMPARE(valueChangedSpy.count(), 1);
}

void IntDecoratorTests::setValue_givenSameValue_takesNoAction()
{
    Entity parentEntity;
    IntDecorator decorator(&parentEntity, "Test Key", "Test Label",
                                                            99);
    QSignalSpy valueChangedSpy(&decorator,
                               &IntDecorator::valueChanged);
    QCOMPARE(decorator.value(), 99);
    decorator.setValue(99);
    QCOMPARE(decorator.value(), 99);
    QCOMPARE(valueChangedSpy.count(), 0);
}
```

```
void IntDecoratorTests::jsonValue_whenDefaultValue_returnsJson()
{
    IntDecorator decorator;
    QCOMPARE(decorator.jsonValue(), QJsonValue(0));
}
void IntDecoratorTests::jsonValue_whenValueSet_returnsJson()
{
    IntDecorator decorator;
    decorator.setValue(99);
    QCOMPARE(decorator.jsonValue(), QJsonValue(99));
}


void IntDecoratorTests::update_whenPresentInJson_updatesValue()
{
    Entity parentEntity;
    IntDecorator decorator(&parentEntity, "Test Key", "Test Label", 99);
    QSignalSpy valueChangedSpy(&decorator,
                                &IntDecorator::valueChanged);
    QCOMPARE(decorator.value(), 99);
    QJsonObject jsonObject;
    jsonObject.insert("Key 1", "Value 1");
    jsonObject.insert("Test Key", 123);
    jsonObject.insert("Key 3", 3);
    decorator.update(jsonObject);
    QCOMPARE(decorator.value(), 123);
    QCOMPARE(valueChangedSpy.count(), 1);
}


void IntDecoratorTests::update_whenNotPresentInJson_updatesValueToDefault()
{
    Entity parentEntity;
    IntDecorator decorator(&parentEntity, "Test Key", "Test Label",
                                                          99);

    QSignalSpy valueChangedSpy(&decorator,
                                &IntDecorator::valueChanged);
    QCOMPARE(decorator.value(), 99);
    QJsonObject jsonObject;
    jsonObject.insert("Key 1", "Value 1");
    jsonObject.insert("Key 2", 123);
    jsonObject.insert("Key 3", 3);
    decorator.update(jsonObject);
    QCOMPARE(decorator.value(), 0);
    QCOMPARE(valueChangedSpy.count(), 1);
}


}}
```

Unit tests tend to follow an *Arrange > Act > Assert* pattern. Preconditions for the test are fulfilled first: variables are initialized, classes are configured, and so on. Then, an action is performed, generally calling the function being tested. Finally, the results of the action are checked. Sometimes one or more of these steps will not be necessary or may be merged with another, but that is the general pattern.

We begin testing the constructor by initializing a new `IntDecorator` without passing in any parameters and then test that the various properties of the object have been initialized to expected default values using QCOMPARE to match actual against expected values. We then repeat the test, but this time, we pass in values for each of the parameters and verify that they have been updated in the instance.

When testing the `setValue()` method, we need to check whether or not the `valueChanged()` signal is emitted. We can do this by connecting a lambda to the signal that sets a flag when called, as follows:

```
bool isCalled = false;
QObject::connect(&decorator, &IntDecorator::valueChanged, [&isCalled](){
    isCalled = true;
});

/*...Perform action...*/

QVERIFY(isCalled);
```

However, a much simpler solution we've used here is to use Qt's `QSignalSpy` class that keeps track of calls to a specified signal. We can then check how many times a signal has been called using the `count()` method.

The first `setValue()` test ensures that when we provide a new value that is different to the existing one, the value is updated and the `valueChanged()` signal is emitted once. The second test ensures that when we set the same value, no action is taken and the signal is not emitted. Note that we use an additional QCOMPARE call in both cases to assert that the value is what we expect it to be before the action is taken. Consider the following pseudo test:

1. Set up your class.
2. Perform an action.
3. Test that the value is `99`.

If everything works as expected, step 1 sets the value to 0, step 2 takes the correct action and updates the value to 99, and step 3 passes because the value is 99. However, step 1 could be faulty and wrongly sets the value to 99, step 2 is not even implemented and takes no action, and yet step 3 (and the test) passes because the value is 99. With a QCOMPARE precondition after step 1, this is avoided.

The jsonValue() tests are simple equality checks, both with a default value and a set value.

Finally, with the update() tests, we construct a couple of JSON objects. In one object, we add an item that has the same key as our decorator object ("Test Key"), which we expect to be matched and the associated value (123) passed through to setValue(). In the second object, the key is not present. In both cases, we also add other extraneous items to ensure that the class can correctly ignore them. The post action checks are the same as for the setValue() tests.

The StringDecoratorTests class is essentially the same as IntDecoratorTests, just with a different value data type and default values of empty string "" rather than 0.

DateTimeDecorator also follows the same pattern, but with additional tests for the string formatting helper methods toIso8601String() and so on.

EnumeratorDecoratorTests performs the same tests but requires a little more setup because of the need for an enumerator and associated mapper. In the body of the tests, whenever we test value(), we also need to test valueDescription() to ensure that the two remain aligned. For example, whenever the value is eTestEnum::Value2, the valueDescription() must be Value 2. Note that we always use the enumerated values in conjunction with the value() checks and static_cast them to an int. Consider the following example:

```
QCOMPARE(decorator.value(), static_cast<int>(eTestEnum::Value2));
```

It may be tempting to make this much shorter by just using the raw int value:

```
QCOMPARE(decorator.value(), 2);
```

The problem with this approach, other than the number 2 having much less meaning to readers of the code than the enumerated `Value2`, is that the values of `eTestEnum` can change and render the test invalid. Consider this example:

```
enum eTestEnum {
    Unknown = 0,
    MyAmazingNewTestValue,
    Value1,
    Value2,
    Value3
};
```

Due to the insertion of `MyAmazingNewTestValue`, the numeric equivalent of `Value2` is actually now 3. Any tests that used the number 2 to represent `Value2` are now wrong, whereas those that use the more long-winded `static_cast<int>(eTestEnum::Value2)` are still correct.

Rebuild and run the new test suites, and they should all happily pass and give us renewed confidence in the code we wrote earlier. With the data decorators tested, let's move on to our data models next.

Entity Tests

Now that we have some confidence that our data decorators are working as expected, let's move up a level and test our data entities. The Client class is the root of our model hierarchy and by testing that, we can test our other models in the process.

We already have `client-tests.cpp` in `cm-tests/source/models` that Qt Creator added for us when we created the project, so go ahead and add a companion header file `client-tests.h`.

`client-tests.h`:

```
#ifndef CLIENTTESTS_H
#define CLIENTTESTS_H

#include <QtTest>
#include <QJsonObject>

#include <models/client.h>
#include <test-suite.h>

namespace cm {
namespace models {
```

```cpp
class ClientTests : public TestSuite
{
    Q_OBJECT

public:
    ClientTests();

private slots:
    void constructor_givenParent_setsParentAndDefaultProperties();
    void constructor_givenParentAndJsonObject_setsParentAndProperties();
    void toJson_withDefaultProperties_constructsJson();
    void toJson_withSetProperties_constructsJson();
    void update_givenJsonObject_updatesProperties();
    void update_givenEmptyJsonObject_updatesPropertiesToDefaults();

private:
    void verifyBillingAddress(const QJsonObject& jsonObject);
    void verifyDefaultBillingAddress(const QJsonObject& jsonObject);
    void verifyBillingAddress(Address* address);
    void verifyDefaultBillingAddress(Address* address);
    void verifySupplyAddress(const QJsonObject& jsonObject);
    void verifyDefaultSupplyAddress(const QJsonObject& jsonObject);
    void verifySupplyAddress(Address* address);
    void verifyDefaultSupplyAddress(Address* address);
    void verifyAppointments(const QJsonObject& jsonObject);
    void verifyDefaultAppointments(const QJsonObject& jsonObject);
    void verifyAppointments(const QList<Appointment*>& appointments);
    void verifyDefaultAppointments(const QList<Appointment*>&
appointments);
    void verifyContacts(const QJsonObject& jsonObject);
    void verifyDefaultContacts(const QJsonObject& jsonObject);
    void verifyContacts(const QList<Contact*>& contacts);
    void verifyDefaultContacts(const QList<Contact*>& contacts);

    QByteArray jsonByteArray = R"(
    {
        "reference": "CM0001",
        "name": "Mr Test Testerson",
        "billingAddress": {
            "building": "Billing Building",
            "city": "Billing City",
            "postcode": "Billing Postcode",
            "street": "Billing Street"
        },
        "appointments": [
         {"startAt": "2017-08-20T12:45:00", "endAt": "2017-08-
                    20T13:00:00", "notes": "Test appointment 1"},
         {"startAt": "2017-08-21T10:30:00", "endAt": "2017-08-
```

```
                        21T11:30:00", "notes": "Test appointment 2"}
            ],
            "contacts": [
                {"contactType": 2, "address":"email@test.com"},
                {"contactType": 1, "address":"012345678"}
            ],
            "supplyAddress": {
                "building": "Supply Building",
                "city": "Supply City",
                "postcode": "Supply Postcode",
                "street": "Supply Street"
            }
        })";
    };


}}


#endif
```

There are three main areas we want to test here:

- Object construction
- Serialization to JSON
- Deserialization from JSON

As with previous suites, we have a couple of different flavors of test for each area—one with default data and one with specified data. In the private section, you will see numerous verify methods. They are to encapsulate the functionality required to test a particular subset of our data. The advantages of doing this are the same as with regular code: they make the unit tests much more concise and readable, and they allow easy reuse of the validation rules. Also, in the private section, we define a blob of JSON we can use to construct our Client instances. A `QByteArray`, as its name suggests, is simply an array of bytes that comes with numerous associated helpful functions:

```
void ClientTests::constructor_givenParent_setsParentAndDefaultProperties()
{
    Client testClient(this);
    QCOMPARE(testClient.parent(), this);
    QCOMPARE(testClient.reference->value(), QString(""));
    QCOMPARE(testClient.name->value(), QString(""));

    verifyDefaultBillingAddress(testClient.billingAddress);
    verifyDefaultSupplyAddress(testClient.supplyAddress);
    verifyDefaultAppointments(testClient.appointments-
                                    >derivedEntities());
    verifyDefaultContacts(testClient.contacts->derivedEntities());
```

```
}

void
ClientTests::constructor_givenParentAndJsonObject_setsParentAndProperties()
{
    Client testClient(this,
QJsonDocument::fromJson(jsonByteArray).object());
    QCOMPARE(testClient.parent(), this);
    QCOMPARE(testClient.reference->value(), QString("CM0001"));
    QCOMPARE(testClient.name->value(), QString("Mr Test Testerson"));

    verifyBillingAddress(testClient.billingAddress);
    verifySupplyAddress(testClient.supplyAddress);
    verifyAppointments(testClient.appointments->derivedEntities());
    verifyContacts(testClient.contacts->derivedEntities());
}
```

Starting with the constructor tests, we instantiate a new Client, both with and without a
JSON object. Note that in order to convert our JSON byte array to a `QJsonObject`, we need
to pass it through a `QJsonDocument`. Once we have our initialized client, we check the
name property and utilize the verify methods to test the state of the child objects for us.
Regardless of whether or not we supply any initial data via a JSON object, we expect
the `supplyAddress` and `billingAddress` objects to be created for us automatically as
well as the appointments and contacts collections. By default, the collections should be
empty:

```
void ClientTests::toJson_withDefaultProperties_constructsJson()
{
    Client testClient(this);
    QJsonDocument jsonDoc(testClient.toJson());
    QVERIFY(jsonDoc.isObject());
    QJsonObject jsonObject = jsonDoc.object();
    QVERIFY(jsonObject.contains("reference"));
    QCOMPARE(jsonObject.value("reference").toString(), QString(""));
    QVERIFY(jsonObject.contains("name"));
    QCOMPARE(jsonObject.value("name").toString(), QString(""));
    verifyDefaultBillingAddress(jsonObject);
    verifyDefaultSupplyAddress(jsonObject);
    verifyDefaultAppointments(jsonObject);
    verifyDefaultContacts(jsonObject);
}

void ClientTests::toJson_withSetProperties_constructsJson()
{
    Client testClient(this,
QJsonDocument::fromJson(jsonByteArray).object());
    QCOMPARE(testClient.reference->value(), QString("CM0001"));
```

```
    QCOMPARE(testClient.name->value(), QString("Mr Test Testerson"));

    verifyBillingAddress(testClient.billingAddress);
    verifySupplyAddress(testClient.supplyAddress);
    verifyAppointments(testClient.appointments->derivedEntities());
    verifyContacts(testClient.contacts->derivedEntities());
    QJsonDocument jsonDoc(testClient.toJson());
    QVERIFY(jsonDoc.isObject());
    QJsonObject jsonObject = jsonDoc.object();
    QVERIFY(jsonObject.contains("reference"));
    QCOMPARE(jsonObject.value("reference").toString(), QString("CM0001"));
    QVERIFY(jsonObject.contains("name"));
    QCOMPARE(jsonObject.value("name").toString(), QString("Mr Test
                                                Testerson"));
    verifyBillingAddress(jsonObject);
    verifySupplyAddress(jsonObject);
    verifyAppointments(jsonObject);
    verifyContacts(jsonObject);
}
```

The `toJson()` tests follow much the same pattern. We construct an object without a JSON object so that we get default values for all the properties and child objects. We then immediately construct a `QJsonDocument` using a call to `toJson()` in the constructor to get the serialized JSON object for us. The `name` property is tested, and then we utilize the verify methods once more. When constructing a **Client** using JSON, we add precondition checks to ensure that our properties have been set correctly before we again call `toJson()` and test the results:

```
void ClientTests::update_givenJsonObject_updatesProperties()
{
    Client testClient(this);
    testClient.update(QJsonDocument::fromJson(jsonByteArray).object());
    QCOMPARE(testClient.reference->value(), QString("CM0001"));
    QCOMPARE(testClient.name->value(), QString("Mr Test Testerson"));

    verifyBillingAddress(testClient.billingAddress);
    verifySupplyAddress(testClient.supplyAddress);
    verifyAppointments(testClient.appointments->derivedEntities());
    verifyContacts(testClient.contacts->derivedEntities());
}

void ClientTests::update_givenEmptyJsonObject_updatesPropertiesToDefaults()
{
    Client testClient(this,
QJsonDocument::fromJson(jsonByteArray).object());
    QCOMPARE(testClient.reference->value(), QString("CM0001"));
    QCOMPARE(testClient.name->value(), QString("Mr Test Testerson"));
```

```
verifyBillingAddress(testClient.billingAddress);
verifySupplyAddress(testClient.supplyAddress);
verifyAppointments(testClient.appointments->derivedEntities());
verifyContacts(testClient.contacts->derivedEntities());
testClient.update(QJsonObject());
QCOMPARE(testClient.reference->value(), QString(""));
QCOMPARE(testClient.name->value(), QString(""));

verifyDefaultBillingAddress(testClient.billingAddress);
verifyDefaultSupplyAddress(testClient.supplyAddress);
verifyDefaultAppointments(testClient.appointments-
                            >derivedEntities());
verifyDefaultContacts(testClient.contacts->derivedEntities());
}
```

The `update()` tests are the same as `toJson()`, but the other way around. This time, we construct a JSON object using our byte array and pass it in to `update()`, checking the state of the model afterward.

The various private verification methods are all simply sets of checks that save us having to repeat the same code over and over. Consider the given example:

```
void ClientTests::verifyDefaultSupplyAddress(Address* address)
{
    QVERIFY(address != nullptr);
    QCOMPARE(address->building->value(), QString(""));
    QCOMPARE(address->street->value(), QString(""));
    QCOMPARE(address->city->value(), QString(""));
    QCOMPARE(address->postcode->value(), QString(""));
}
```

Build and run the unit tests again and the new **Client** tests should all happily pass.

Mocking

The unit tests we've written so far have all been pretty straightforward. While our **Client** class isn't totally independent, its dependencies are all other data models and decorators that it can own and change at will. However, looking forward, we will want to persist client data in a database. Let's look at a few examples of how this can work and discuss how the design decisions we make impact the testability of the Client class.

Open up the `scratchpad` project and create a new header `mocking.h` file, where we'll implement a dummy Client class to play around with.

`mocking.h`:

```
#ifndef MOCKING_H
#define MOCKING_H

#include <QDebug>

class Client
{
public:
    void save()
    {
        qDebug() << "Saving Client";
    }
};

#endif
```

In `main.cpp`, `#include <mocking.h>`, update the `engine.load()` line to load the default `main.qml` if it doesn't already and add a few lines to spin up and save a dummy Client object:

```
engine.load(QUrl(QStringLiteral("qrc:/main.qml")));

Client client;
client.save();
```

Build and run the app, ignore the window, and take a look at the **Application Output** console:

```
Saving Client
```

We have a way to ask a client to save itself, but it needs a database to save itself too. Let's encapsulate our database management functionality into a `DatabaseController` class. In mocking.h, add the following implementation before the Client class. Note that you need to forward declare Client:

```
class Client;

class DatabaseController
{
public:
    DatabaseController()
    {
        qDebug() << "Creating a new database connection";
    }

    void save(Client* client)
    {
        qDebug() << "Saving a Client to the production database";
    }
};
```

Now, edit the Client class:

```
class Client
{
    DatabaseController databaseController;

public:
    void save()
    {
        qDebug() << "Saving Client";
        databaseController.save(this);
    }
};
```

Back in main.cpp, replace the Client lines with the following:

```
qDebug() << "Running the production code...";

Client client1;
client1.save();
Client client2;
client2.save();
```

Now we create and save two clients rather than just one. Build, run, and check the console again:

```
Running the production code...
Creating a new database connection
Saving Client
Saving a Client to the production database
Creating a new database connection
Saving Client
Saving a Client to the production database
```

Okay, now we're saving our clients to the production database, but we're creating a new database connection for every client, which seems a bit wasteful. The Client class needs an instance of a `DatabaseController` to function, and this is known as a dependency. However, we do not need the Client to be responsible for creating that instance; we can instead pass—or *inject*—the instance in via the constructor and manage the lifetime of the `DatabaseController` elsewhere. This technique of Dependency Injection is a form of a broader design pattern known as **Inversion of Control**. Let's pass a reference to a shared `DatabaseController` into our Client class instead:

```cpp
class Client
{
    DatabaseController& databaseController;

public:
    Client(DatabaseController& _databaseController)
        : databaseController(_databaseController)
    {
    }

    void save()
    {
        qDebug() << "Saving Client";
        databaseController.save(this);
    }
};
```

Over in main.cpp:

```
qDebug() << "Running the production code...";

DatabaseController databaseController;

Client client1(databaseController);
client1.save();
Client client2(databaseController);
client2.save();
```

Build and run the following:

```
Running the production code...
Creating a new database connection
Saving Client
Saving a Client to the production database
Saving Client
Saving a Client to the production database
```

Great, we've got a highly-efficient decoupled system architecture in place; let's test it.

In mocking.h, add a pretend test suite after the Client class:

```
class ClientTestSuite
{
public:
    void saveTests()
    {
        DatabaseController databaseController;
        Client client1(databaseController);
        client1.save();
        Client client2(databaseController);
        client2.save();

        qDebug() << "Test passed!";
    }
};
```

In `main.cpp`, after saving `client2`, add the following to run our tests:

```
qDebug() << "Running the test code...";

ClientTestSuite testSuite;
testSuite.saveTests();
```

Build and run this:

```
Running the production code...
Creating a new database connection
Saving Client
Saving a Client to the production database
Saving Client
Saving a Client to the production database
Running the test code...
Creating a new database connection
Saving Client
Saving a Client to the production database
Saving Client
Saving a Client to the production database
Test passed!
```

Our test passed, fantastic! What's not to love about that? Well, the fact that we've just saved some test data to our production database.

If you don't already implement interfaces for the majority of your classes, you soon will after you start unit testing for this precise reason. It's not used solely to avoid nasty side effects like writing test data to a production database; it allows you to simulate all kinds of behaviors that make unit testing so much easier.

So, let's move our `DatabaseController` behind an interface. Replace the plain `DatabaseController` in `mocking.h` with a supercharged interface-driven version:

```cpp
class IDatabaseController
{
public:
    virtual ~IDatabaseController(){}
    virtual void save(Client* client) = 0;
};

class DatabaseController : public IDatabaseController
{
public:
    DatabaseController()
    {
        qDebug() << "Creating a new database connection";
```

```
    }

    void save(Client* client) override
    {
        qDebug() << "Saving a Client to the production database";
    }
};
```

With the interface in place, we can now create a fake or mock implementation:

```
class MockDatabaseController : public IDatabaseController
{
public:
    MockDatabaseController()
    {
        qDebug() << "Absolutely not creating any database connections
                                                    at all";
    }

    void save(Client* client) override
    {
        qDebug() << "Just testing - not saving any Clients to any
                                                databases";
    }
};
```

Next, tweak our Client to hold a reference to the interface rather than the concrete implementation:

```
class Client
{
    IDatabaseController& databaseController;

public:
    Client(IDatabaseController& _databaseController)
        : databaseController(_databaseController)
    {
    }

    void save()
    {
        qDebug() << "Saving Client";
        databaseController.save(this);
    }
};
```

Finally, change our test suite to create a mock controller to pass into the clients:

```
void saveTests()
{
    MockDatabaseController databaseController;
    ...
}
```

Build and run this:

```
Running the production code...
Creating a new database connection
Saving Client
Saving a Client to the production database
Saving Client
Saving a Client to the production database
Running the test code...
Absolutely not creating any database connections at all
Saving Client
Just testing - not saving any Clients to any databases
Saving Client
Just testing - not saving any Clients to any databases
Test passed!
```

Perfect. By programming to interfaces and injecting dependencies, we can safely test in isolation. We can create as many mock implementations as we need and use them to simulate whatever behavior we want, enabling us to test multiple different scenarios. Once you get more involved in mocking, it really pays to use a dedicated framework like **google mock**, as they save you the hassle of having to write a bunch of boilerplate mock classes. You can easily mock the interface once using helper macros and then specify behaviors for individual methods on the fly.

Summary

In this chapter, we've taken our first proper look at the unit testing project, and you've seen how to implement unit testing using the Qt Test framework. We've also discussed the importance of programming to interfaces to enable mocking. Now we have unit tests in place for our main data classes, so if we ever accidentally change the behavior, the unit tests will fail and highlight a potential problem for us.

As we discussed, this is not a book about test driven development, and we will sometimes cut corners and go against the advice in this chapter to keep the explanation of other concepts as simple as possible, but I do urge you to implement unit testing of some kind in your projects if you can, as it is a very valuable practice that is always worth the additional time investment. Some developers like the rigor of full-blown TDD, whereas others prefer to write unit test after the fact to verify the work they have done. Find an approach that works for you and your coding style.

We will return to the test project occasionally to demonstrate certain behaviors. but we'll certainly not be achieving 100% code coverage. Now that you have the test project and scaffolding in place, it's just a case of adding further test classes for each class you want to test. As long as you inherit from `TestSuite` in the same way as we have in this chapter, they will be automatically detected and executed when you run the test project.

In `Chapter 7`, *Persistence*, we'll go ahead and implement the functionality we just discussed—persisting our data to a database.

Persistence 7

In `Chapter 5`, *Data*, we created a framework for capturing and holding data in memory. However, this is only half of the story, as without persisting the data to some external destination, it will be lost as soon as we close the application. In this chapter, we will build on our earlier work and save our data to disk in a SQLite database so that it can live on beyond the lifetime of the application. Once saved, we will also build methods for finding, editing, and deleting our data. To get all these operations for free in our various data models, we will extend our data entities so that they can load and save to our database automatically, without us having to write boilerplate code in each class. We will cover the following topics:

- SQLite
- Primary keys
- Creating clients
- Finding clients
- Editing clients
- Deleting clients

SQLite

General purpose database technology has fragmented in the recent years with the explosion of NoSQL and Graph databases. However, SQL databases are still fighting fit and absolutely an appropriate choice in a lot of applications. Qt comes with built-in support for several SQL database driver types, and can be extended with custom drivers. MySQL and PostgreSQL are very popular open source SQL database engines and are both supported by default, but are intended for use on servers and require administration, which makes them a bit unnecessarily complicated for our purposes. Instead, we will use the much more lightweight SQLite, which is commonly used as a client-side database and is very popular in mobile applications due to its small footprint.

According to the official website at `https://www.sqlite.org`, "SQLite is a self-contained, high-reliability, embedded, full-featured, public-domain, SQL database engine. SQLite is the most used database engine in the world". Paired with Qt's SQL related classes, it's a snap to create a database and store your data.

The first thing we need to do is add the SQL module to our library project to get access to all of Qt's SQL goodness. In `cm-lib.pro`, add the following:

```
QT += sql
```

Next, we'll take onboard what we discussed in the previous chapter and implement our database-related functionality behind an interface. Create a new `i-database-controller.h` header file in `cm-lib/source/controllers`:

```
#ifndef IDATABASECONTROLLER_H
#define IDATABASECONTROLLER_H

#include <QJsonArray>
#include <QJsonObject>
#include <QList>
#include <QObject>
#include <QString>

#include <cm-lib_global.h>

namespace cm {
namespace controllers {

class CMLIBSHARED_EXPORT IDatabaseController : public QObject
{
    Q_OBJECT

public:
```

```
    IDatabaseController(QObject* parent) : QObject(parent){}
    virtual ~IDatabaseController(){}

    virtual bool createRow(const QString& tableName, const QString& id,
                        const QJsonObject& jsonObject) const = 0;
    virtual bool deleteRow(const QString& tableName, const QString& id)
                                            const = 0;
    virtual QJsonArray find(const QString& tableName, const QString&
                                    searchText) const = 0;
    virtual QJsonObject readRow(const QString& tableName, const
                            QString& id) const = 0;
    virtual bool updateRow(const QString& tableName, const QString& id,
                        const QJsonObject& jsonObject) const = 0;
};

}}

#endif
```

Here, we are implementing the four basic functions of (**Create**, **Read**, **Update**, and **Delete**) **CRUD**, which are relevant to persistent storage in general, not just SQL databases. We supplement these functions with an additional `find()` method that we will use to find an array of matching clients based on supplied search text.

Now, let's create a concrete implementation of the interface. Create a new `DatabaseController` class in `cm-lib/source/controllers`.

`database-controller.h`:

```
#ifndef DATABASECONTROLLER_H
#define DATABASECONTROLLER_H

#include <QObject>
#include <QScopedPointer>

#include <controllers/i-database-controller.h>

#include <cm-lib_global.h>

namespace cm {
namespace controllers {

class CMLIBSHARED_EXPORT DatabaseController : public IDatabaseController
{
    Q_OBJECT

public:
```

```
    explicit DatabaseController(QObject* parent = nullptr);
    ~DatabaseController();

    bool createRow(const QString& tableName, const QString& id, const
                        QJsonObject& jsonObject) const override;
    bool deleteRow(const QString& tableName, const QString& id) const
                                                            override;
    QJsonArray find(const QString& tableName, const QString&
                                searchText) const override;
    QJsonObject readRow(const QString& tableName, const QString& id)
                                            const override;
    bool updateRow(const QString& tableName, const QString& id, const
                        QJsonObject& jsonObject) const override;

private:
    class Implementation;
    QScopedPointer<Implementation> implementation;
};

}}

#endif
```

Now, let's walk through each of the key implementation details in `database-controller.cpp`:

```
class DatabaseController::Implementation
{
public:
    Implementation(DatabaseController* _databaseController)
        : databaseController(_databaseController)
    {
        if (initialise()) {
            qDebug() << "Database created using Sqlite version: " +
                                                sqliteVersion();
            if (createTables()) {
                qDebug() << "Database tables created";
            } else {
                qDebug() << "ERROR: Unable to create database tables";
            }
        } else {
            qDebug() << "ERROR: Unable to open database";
        }
    }

    DatabaseController* databaseController{nullptr};
    QSqlDatabase database;
```

```
private:
    bool initialise()
    {
        database = QSqlDatabase::addDatabase("QSQLITE", "cm");
        database.setDatabaseName( "cm.sqlite" );
        return database.open();
    }

    bool createTables()
    {
        return createJsonTable( "client" );
    }

    bool createJsonTable(const QString& tableName) const
    {
        QSqlQuery query(database);
        QString sqlStatement = "CREATE TABLE IF NOT EXISTS " +
         tableName + " (id text primary key, json text not null)";

        if (!query.prepare(sqlStatement)) return false;

        return query.exec();
    }

    QString sqliteVersion() const
    {
        QSqlQuery query(database);

        query.exec("SELECT sqlite_version()");

        if (query.next()) return query.value(0).toString();

        return QString::number(-1);
    }
};
```

Starting with the private implementation, we've broken the initialization into two
operations: initialise() instantiates a connection to a SQLite database with a file named
cm.sqlite, and this operation will first create the database file for us if it doesn't already
exist. The file will be created in the same folder as the application
executable, createTables(), then creates any tables that we need which don't already
exist in the database. Initially, we only need a single table named client, but this can
be easily extended later. We delegate the actual work of creating the named table to the
createJsonTable() method so that we can reuse it for multiple tables.

A conventional normalized relational database approach would be to persist each of our data models in their own table, with fields that match the properties of the class. Recall the model diagram back in Chapter 5, *Data*, which is as follows:

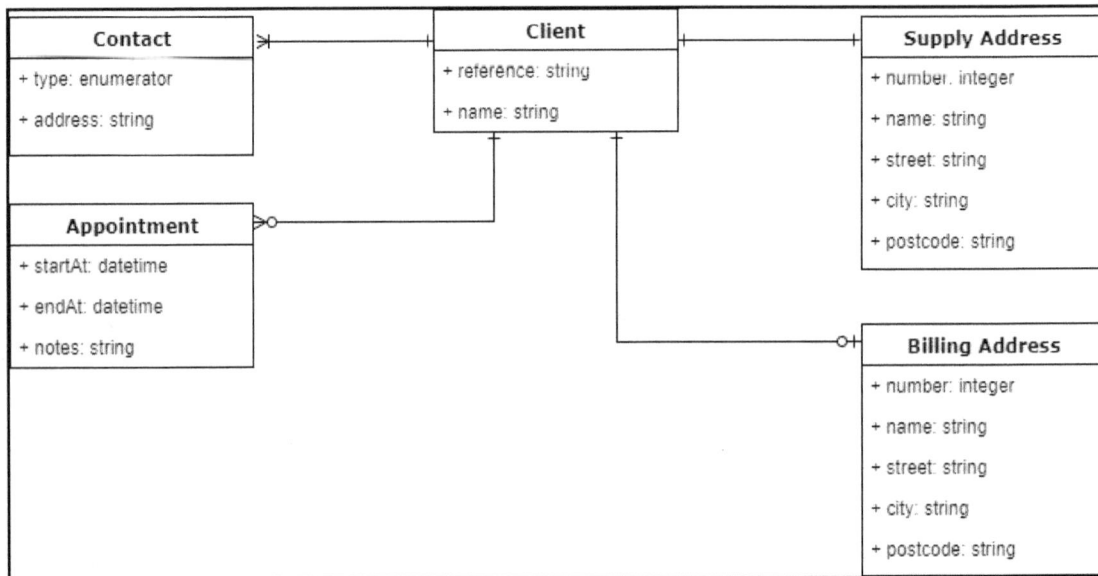

We could create a Client table with the "reference" and "name" fields, a contact table with the "type", "address", and other fields. However, we will instead leverage the JSON serialization code we've already implemented and implement a pseudo document-style database. We will utilize a single client table that will store a unique ID for the client along with the whole client object hierarchy serialized to JSON.

Finally, we've also added a `sqliteVersion()` utility method to identify which version of SQLite the database is using:

```cpp
bool DatabaseController::createRow(const QString& tableName, const QString&
id, const QJsonObject& jsonObject) const
{
    if (tableName.isEmpty()) return false;
    if (id.isEmpty()) return false;
    if (jsonObject.isEmpty()) return false;

    QSqlQuery query(implementation->database);

    QString sqlStatement = "INSERT OR REPLACE INTO " + tableName + "
                    (id, json) VALUES (:id, :json)";
```

```
    if (!query.prepare(sqlStatement)) return false;

    query.bindValue(":id", QVariant(id));
    query.bindValue(":json",
  QVariant(QJsonDocument(jsonObject).toJson(QJsonDocument::Compact)));

    if(!query.exec()) return false;

    return query.numRowsAffected() > 0;
}

bool DatabaseController::deleteRow(const QString& tableName, const QString&
id) const
{
    if (tableName.isEmpty()) return false;
    if (id.isEmpty()) return false;

    QSqlQuery query(implementation->database);

    QString sqlStatement = "DELETE FROM " + tableName + " WHERE
                            id=:id";

    if (!query.prepare(sqlStatement)) return false;

    query.bindValue(":id", QVariant(id));

    if(!query.exec()) return false;

    return query.numRowsAffected() > 0;
}

QJsonObject DatabaseController::readRow(const QString& tableName, const
QString& id) const
{
    if (tableName.isEmpty()) return {};
    if (id.isEmpty()) return {};

    QSqlQuery query(implementation->database);

    QString sqlStatement = "SELECT json FROM " + tableName + " WHERE
                            id=:id";

    if (!query.prepare(sqlStatement)) return {};

    query.bindValue(":id", QVariant(id));

    if (!query.exec()) return {};
```

```
        if (!query.first()) return {};

        auto json = query.value(0).toByteArray();
        auto jsonDocument = QJsonDocument::fromJson(json);

        if (!jsonDocument.isObject()) return {};

        return jsonDocument.object();
    }

    bool DatabaseController::updateRow(const QString& tableName, const QString&
    id, const QJsonObject& jsonObject) const
    {
        if (tableName.isEmpty()) return false;
        if (id.isEmpty()) return false;
        if (jsonObject.isEmpty()) return false;

        QSqlQuery query(implementation->database);

        QString sqlStatement = "UPDATE " + tableName + " SET json=:json
                                WHERE id=:id";

        if (!query.prepare(sqlStatement)) return false;

        query.bindValue(":id", QVariant(id));
        query.bindValue(":json",
        QVariant(QJsonDocument(jsonObject).toJson(QJsonDocument::Compact)));

        if(!query.exec()) return false;

        return query.numRowsAffected() > 0;
    }
```

The CRUD operations are all based around the QSqlQuery class and prepared sqlStatements. In all cases, we first perform some perfunctory checks on the parameters to ensure that we're not trying to do something silly. We then concatenate the table name into a SQL string, representing parameters with the :myParameter syntax. After preparing the statement, parameters are subsequently substituted in using the bindValue() method on the query object.

When creating, deleting, or updating rows, we simply return a `true`/`false` success indicator on query execution. Assuming that the query prepares and executes without error, we check that the number of rows affected by the operation is greater than 0. The read operation returns a JSON object parsed from the JSON text stored in the matching record. If no record is found or if the JSON cannot be parsed, then we return a default JSON object:

```
QJsonArray DatabaseController::find(const QString& tableName, const
QString& searchText) const
{
    if (tableName.isEmpty()) return {};
    if (searchText.isEmpty()) return {};

    QSqlQuery query(implementation->database);

    QString sqlStatement = "SELECT json FROM " + tableName + " where
                            lower(json) like :searchText";

    if (!query.prepare(sqlStatement)) return {};

    query.bindValue(":searchText", QVariant("%" + searchText.toLower()
                                                        + "%"));

    if (!query.exec()) return {};

    QJsonArray returnValue;

    while ( query.next() ) {
        auto json = query.value(0).toByteArray();
        auto jsonDocument = QJsonDocument::fromJson(json);
        if (jsonDocument.isObject()) {
            returnValue.append(jsonDocument.object());
        }
    }

    return returnValue;
}
```

Finally, the `find()` method does essentially the same thing as the CRUD operations but compiles an array of JSON objects as there may be more than one match. Note that we use the `like` keyword in the SQL statement, combined with the % wildcard character, to find any JSON that contains the search text. We also convert both sides of the comparison to lowercase to make the search effectively case-insensitive.

Primary keys

Integral to most of these operations is an ID parameter used as the primary key in our table. To support the persistence of our entities using this new database controller, we need to add a property to our `Entity` class that uniquely identifies an instance of that entity.

In `entity.cpp`, add a member variable to `Entity::Implementation`:

```
QString id;
```

Then, initialize it in the constructor:

```
Implementation(Entity* _entity, IDatabaseController* _databaseController,
const QString& _key)
    : entity(_entity)
    , databaseController(_databaseController)
    , key(_key)
    , id(QUuid::createUuid().toString())
{
}
```

When we instantiate a new `Entity`, we need to generate a new unique ID, and we use the **QUuid** class to this for us with the `createUuid()` method. A **Universally Unique Identifier (UUID)** is essentially a randomly generated number that we then convert to a string in the "{xxxxxxxx-xxxx-xxxx-xxxx-xxxxxxxxxxxx}" format, where "x" is a hex digit. You will need to `#include <QUuid>`.

Next, provide a public accessor method for it:

```
const QString& Entity::id() const
{
    return implementation->id;
}
```

The challenge now is that if we are creating an `Entity` that already has an ID (for example, loading a client from the database), we need some mechanism for overwriting the generated ID value with the known value. We'll do this in the `update()` method:

```
void Entity::update(const QJsonObject& jsonObject)
{
    if (jsonObject.contains("id")) {
        implementation->id = jsonObject.value("id").toString();
    }

    ...

}
```

Similarly, when we serialize the object to JSON, we need to include the ID too:

```
QJsonObject Entity::toJson() const
{
    QJsonObject returnValue;
    returnValue.insert("id", implementation->id);
    ...
}
```

Great! This gives us automatically generated unique IDs for all of our data models, which we can use as the primary key in our database table. However, a common usecase with database tables is that there is actually an existing field that is a great candidate for use as a primary key, for example, a National Insurance or Social Security number, an account reference, or site ID. Let's add a mechanism for specifying a data decorator to use as the ID that will override the default UUID, if set.

In our `Entity` class, add a new private member in `Implementation`:

```
class Entity::Implementation
{
    ...
    StringDecorator* primaryKey{nullptr};
    ...
}
```

You will need to `#include` the `StringDecorator` header. Add a protected mutator method to set it:

```
void Entity::setPrimaryKey(StringDecorator* primaryKey)
{
    implementation->primaryKey = primaryKey;
}
```

We can then tweak our `id()` method to return us the primary key value if appropriate, otherwise default to the generated UUID value:

```
const QString& Entity::id() const
{
    if(implementation->primaryKey != nullptr &&
!implementation->primaryKey->value().isEmpty()) {
        return implementation->primaryKey->value();
    }
    return implementation->id;
}
```

Then, in the `client.cpp` constructor, after we have instantiated all the data decorators, we can specify that we want to use the reference field as our primary key:

```
Client::Client(QObject* parent)
    : Entity(parent, "client")
{
    ...

    setPrimaryKey(reference);
}
```

Let's add a couple of tests to verify this behavior. We'll verify that if a reference value is set, the `id()` method returns that value, otherwise it returns a generated UUID loosely of the "{xxxxxxxx-xxxx-xxxx-xxxx-xxxxxxxxxxxx}" format.

In `client-tests.h` of the `cm-tests` project, add two new tests in the private slots scope:

```
void id_givenPrimaryKeyWithNoValue_returnsUuid();
void id_givenPrimaryKeyWithValue_returnsPrimaryKey();
```

Then, implement the tests in `client-tests.cpp`:

```
void ClientTests::id_givenPrimaryKeyWithNoValue_returnsUuid()
{
    Client testClient(this);

    // Using individual character checks
```

```
    QCOMPARE(testClient.id().left(1), QString("{"));
    QCOMPARE(testClient.id().mid(9, 1), QString("-"));
    QCOMPARE(testClient.id().mid(14, 1), QString("-"));
    QCOMPARE(testClient.id().mid(19, 1), QString("-"));
    QCOMPARE(testClient.id().mid(24, 1), QString("-"));
    QCOMPARE(testClient.id().right(1), QString("}"));

    // Using regular expression pattern matching
    QVERIFY(QRegularExpression("\{.{8}-(.{4})-(.{4})-(.
                       {12})\}").match(testClient.id()).hasMatch());
}

void ClientTests::id_givenPrimaryKeyWithValue_returnsPrimaryKey()
{
    Client testClient(this,
QJsonDocument::fromJson(jsonByteArray).object());
    QCOMPARE(testClient.reference->value(), QString("CM0001"));
    QCOMPARE(testClient.id(), testClient.reference->value());
}
```

Note that the checks are effectively performed twice in the first test just to demonstrate a couple of different approaches you can take. First, we check using individual character matches ('{', '-', and '}'), which is quite long-winded but easy for other developers to read and understand. Then, we perform the check again using Qt's regular expression helper class. This is much shorter but more difficult to parse for normal humans who don't speak regular expression syntax.

Build and run the tests, and they should validate the changes we have just implemented.

Creating clients

Let's put our new infrastructure to use and wire up the `CreateClientView`. If you remember, we present a save command that when clicked on, calls `onCreateClientSaveExecuted()` on `CommandController`. In order to be able to perform anything useful, `CommandController` needs visibility of the client instance to be serialized and saved, and an implementation of the `IDatabaseController` interface to perform the create operation for us.

Inject them into the constructor in `command-controller.h`, including any necessary headers:

```
explicit CommandController(QObject* _parent = nullptr, IDatabaseController*
databaseController = nullptr, models::Client* newClient = nullptr);
```

As we've seen a few times now, add the member variables to `Implementation`:

```
IDatabaseController* databaseController{nullptr};
Client* newClient{nullptr};
```

Pass them through the `CommandController` constructor to the Implementation constructor:

```
Implementation(CommandController* _commandController, IDatabaseController*
_databaseController, Client* _newClient)
    : commandController(_commandController)
    , databaseController(_databaseController)
    , newClient(_newClient)
{
    ...
}

CommandController::CommandController(QObject* parent, IDatabaseController*
databaseController, Client* newClient)
    : QObject(parent)
{
    implementation.reset(new Implementation(this, databaseController,
newClient));
}
```

Now we can update the `onCreateClientSaveExecuted()` method to create our new client:

```
void CommandController::onCreateClientSaveExecuted()
{
    qDebug() << "You executed the Save command!";

implementation->databaseController->createRow(implementation->newClient->ke
y(), implementation->newClient->id(), implementation->newClient->toJson());

    qDebug() << "New client saved.";
}
```

Our client instance provides us with all the information we need to be able to save it to the database, and the database controller performs the database interactions.

Our CommandController is now ready, but we're not actually injecting the database controller or new client in yet, so head over to master-controller.cpp and add an instance of a DatabaseController as we did with CommandController and NavigationController. Add a private member, accessor method, and Q_PROPERTY.

In the Implementation constructor, we need to ensure that we initialize the new client and DatabaseController before we initialize the CommandController, and then pass the pointers through:

```
Implementation(MasterController* _masterController)
    : masterController(_masterController)
{
    databaseController = new DatabaseController(masterController);
    navigationController = new NavigationController(masterController);
    newClient = new Client(masterController);
    commandController = new CommandController(masterController,
databaseController, newClient);
}
```

Build and run cm-ui, and you should see messages in the **Application Output** from the newly instantiated DatabaseController, telling you that it has created the database and table:

```
Database created using Sqlite version: 3.20.1
Database tables created
```

Take a look at the output folder where your binaries are, and you will see a new cm.sqlite file.

If you navigate to **Create Client View**, enter a name, and click on the **Save** button, you will see further output, confirming that the new client has been saved successfully:

```
You executed the Save command!
New client saved
```

Let's take a look inside our database and see what work has been done for us. There are several SQLite browsing applications and web browser plugins available, but the one I tend to use is found at `http://sqlitebrowser.org/`. Download and install this, or any other client of your choice for your operating system, and open the `cm.sqlite` file:

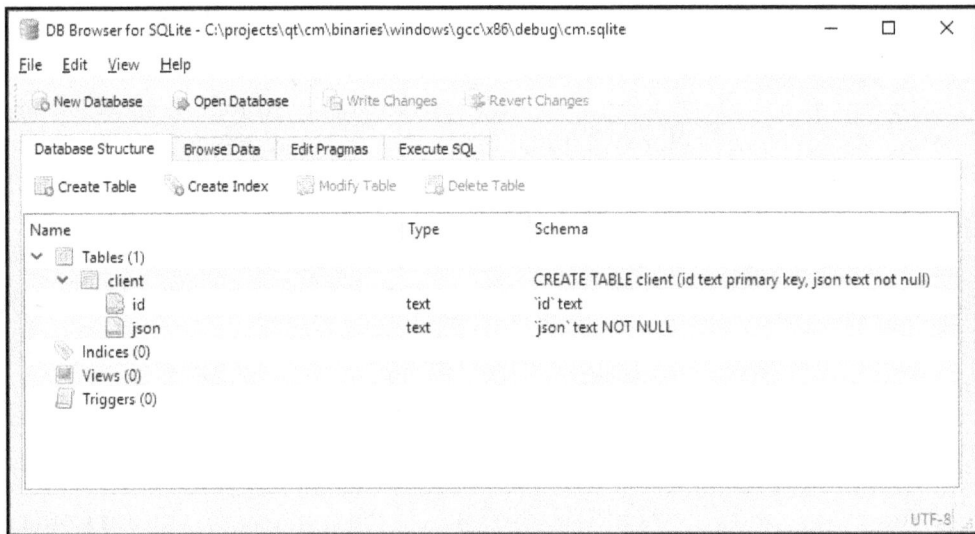

You will see that we have a **client** table, just as we asked for, with two fields: **id** and **json**. **Browse Data** for the **client** table, and you will see our newly created record with the **name** property we entered on the UI:

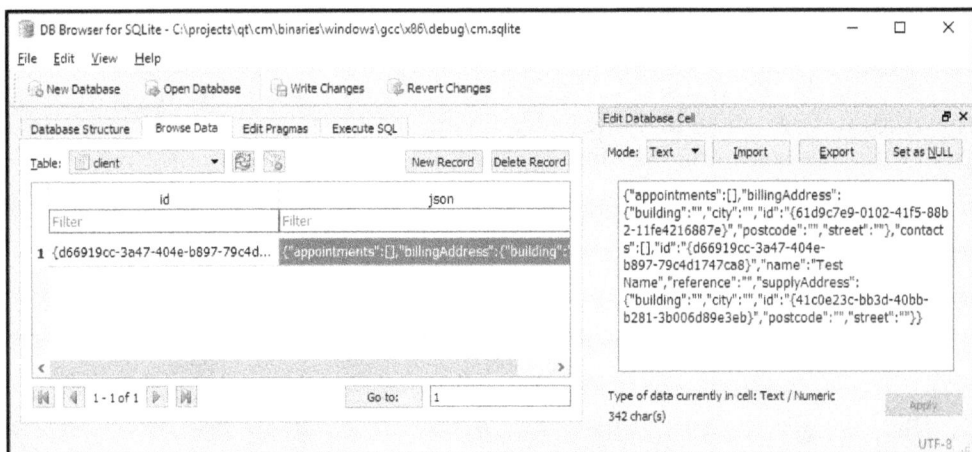

Fantastic, we have created our first client in the database. Note that the
`DatabaseController` initialization methods are idempotent, so you can launch the
application again and the existing database will not be affected. Similarly, if you manually
delete the `cm.sqlite` file, then launching the application will create a new version for you
(without the old data), which is a simple way of deleting test data.

Let's make a quick tweak to add the `reference` property of the client. In
`CreateClientView`, duplicate the `StringEditorSingleLine` component bound to
`ui_name`, and bind the new control to `ui_reference`. Build, run, and create a new client:

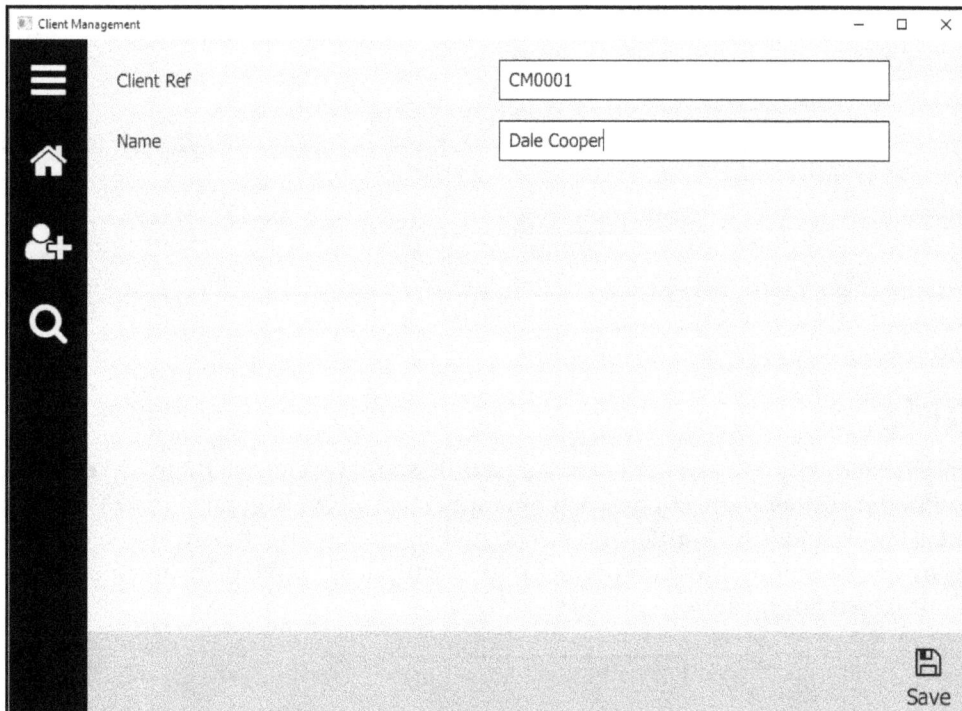

Our new client happily uses the specified client reference as the unique primary key:

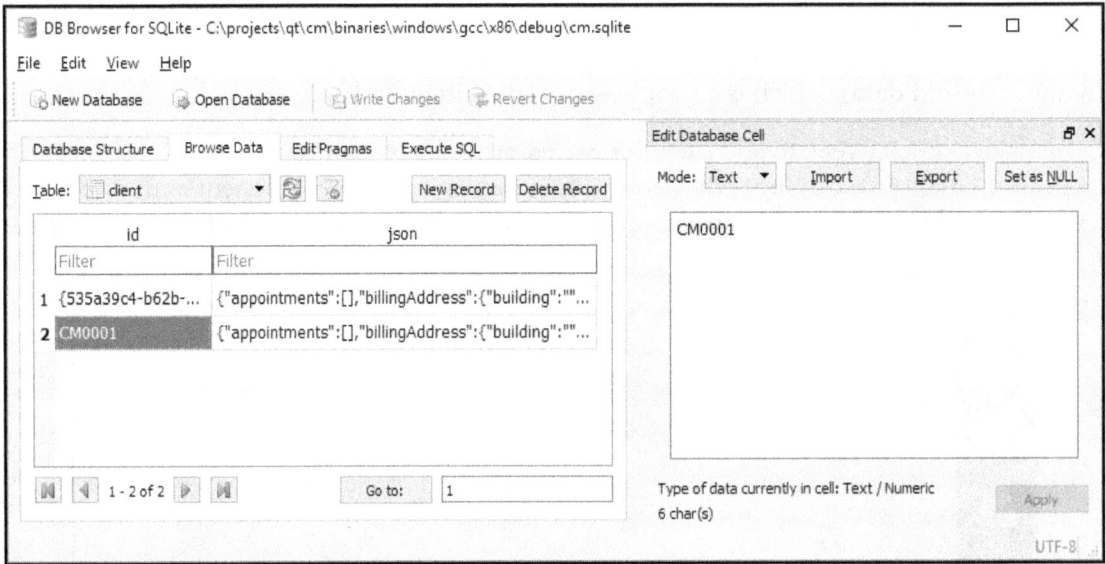

Panels

Now, let's flesh out our `CreateClientView` a little so that we can actually save some meaningful data rather than just a bunch of empty strings. We still have lots of fields to add in, so we'll break things up a little, and also visually separate the data from the different models, by encapsulating them in discreet panels with descriptive titles and a drop shadow to give our UI a bit of pizzazz:

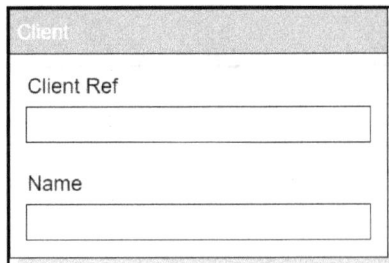

We'll begin by creating a generic panel component. Create a new QML file in `cm-ui/components` named `Panel.qml`. Update `components.qrc` and `qmldir`, as we have done for all the other components:

```
import QtQuick 2.9
import assets 1.0

Item {
    implicitWidth: parent.width
    implicitHeight: headerBackground.height +
    contentLoader.implicitHeight + (Style.sizeControlSpacing * 2)
    property alias headerText: title.text
    property alias contentComponent: contentLoader.sourceComponent

    Rectangle {
        id: shadow
        width: parent.width
        height: parent.height
        x: Style.sizeShadowOffset
        y: Style.sizeShadowOffset
        color: Style.colourShadow
    }

    Rectangle {
        id: headerBackground
        anchors {
            top: parent.top
            left: parent.left
            right: parent.right
        }
        height: Style.heightPanelHeader
        color: Style.colourPanelHeaderBackground

        Text {
            id: title
            text: "Set Me!"
            anchors {
                fill: parent
                margins: Style.heightDataControls / 4
            }
            color: Style.colourPanelHeaderFont
            font.pixelSize: Style.pixelSizePanelHeader
            verticalAlignment: Qt.AlignVCenter
        }
    }

    Rectangle {
        id: contentBackground
```

```
anchors {
    top: headerBackground.bottom
    left: parent.left
    right: parent.right
    bottom: parent.bottom
}
color: Style.colourPanelBackground

Loader {
    id: contentLoader
    anchors {
        left: parent.left
        right: parent.right
        top: parent.top
        margins: Style.sizeControlSpacing
    }
}
    }
}
```

This is an extremely dynamic component. Unlike our other components, where we pass in a string or maybe even a custom class, here we are passing in the entire contents of the panel. We achieve this using a `Loader` component, which loads a QML subtree on demand. We alias the `sourceComponent` property so that calling elements can inject their desired content at runtime.

Due to the dynamic nature of the content, we can't set the component to be a fixed size, so we leverage the `implicitWidth` and `implicitHeight` properties to tell parent elements how large the component wants to be based on the size of the title bar plus the size of the dynamic content.

To render the shadow, we draw a simple `Rectangle`, ensuring that it is rendered first by placing it near the top of the file. We then use the `x` and `y` properties to offset it from the rest of the elements, moving it slightly across and down. The remaining `Rectangle` elements for the header strip and panel background are then drawn over the top of the shadow.

To support the styling here, we need to add a collection of new `Style` properties:

```
readonly property real sizeControlSpacing: 10

readonly property color colourPanelBackground: "#ffffff"
readonly property color colourPanelBackgroundHover: "#ececec"
readonly property color colourPanelHeaderBackground: "#131313"
readonly property color colourPanelHeaderFont: "#ffffff"
readonly property color colourPanelFont: "#131313"
readonly property int pixelSizePanelHeader: 18
readonly property real heightPanelHeader: 40
readonly property real sizeShadowOffset: 5
readonly property color colourShadow: "#dedede"
```

Next, let's add a component for address editing so that we can reuse it for both the supply and billing addresses. Create a new QML file in `cm-ui/components` named `AddressEditor.qml`. Update `components.qrc` and `qmldir` as earlier.

We'll use our new `Panel` component as the root element and add an `Address` property, so that we can pass in an arbitrary data model to bind to:

```
import QtQuick 2.9
import CM 1.0
import assets 1.0

Panel {
    property Address address

    contentComponent:
        Column {
            id: column
            spacing: Style.sizeControlSpacing
            StringEditorSingleLine {
                stringDecorator: address.ui_building
                anchors {
                    left: parent.left
                    right: parent.right
                }
            }
            StringEditorSingleLine {
                stringDecorator: address.ui_street
                anchors {
                    left: parent.left
                    right: parent.right
                }
            }
            StringEditorSingleLine {
                stringDecorator: address.ui_city
```

```
                    anchors {
                        left: parent.left
                        right: parent.right
                    }
                }
                StringEditorSingleLine {
                    stringDecorator: address.ui_postcode
                    anchors {
                        left: parent.left
                        right: parent.right
                    }
                }
            }
        }
    }
```

Here, you can see the flexibility of our new `Panel` component in action, thanks to the embedded `Loader` element. We can pass in whatever QML content we want, and it will be presented in the panel.

Finally, we can update our `CreateClientView` to add our new refactored address components. We'll also move the client controls onto their own panel:

```
import QtQuick 2.9
import QtQuick.Controls 2.2
import CM 1.0
import assets 1.0
import components 1.0

Item {
    property Client newClient: masterController.ui_newClient

    Column {
        spacing: Style.sizeScreenMargin
        anchors {
            left: parent.left
            right: parent.right
            top: parent.top
            margins: Style.sizeScreenMargin
        }
        Panel {
            headerText: "Client Details"
            contentComponent:
                Column {
                    spacing: Style.sizeControlSpacing
                    StringEditorSingleLine {
                        stringDecorator: newClient.ui_reference
                        anchors {
```

```
                                        left: parent.left
                                        right: parent.right
                                    }
                                }
                                StringEditorSingleLine {
                                    stringDecorator: newClient.ui_name
                                    anchors {
                                        left: parent.left
                                        right: parent.right
                                    }
                                }
                            }
                        }
                    }
                AddressEditor {
                    address: newClient.ui_supplyAddress
                    headerText: "Supply Address"
                }
                AddressEditor {
                    address: newClient.ui_billingAddress
                    headerText: "Billing Address"
                }
            }
        CommandBar {
            commandList:
masterController.ui_commandController.ui_createClientViewContextCommands
            }
        }
```

Before we build and run, we just need to tweak the background color of our `StringEditorSingleLine textLabel` so that it matches the panels they are now displayed on:

```
Rectangle {
    width: Style.widthDataControls
    height: Style.heightDataControls
    color: Style.colourPanelBackground
    Text {
        id: textLabel
        ...
    }
}
```

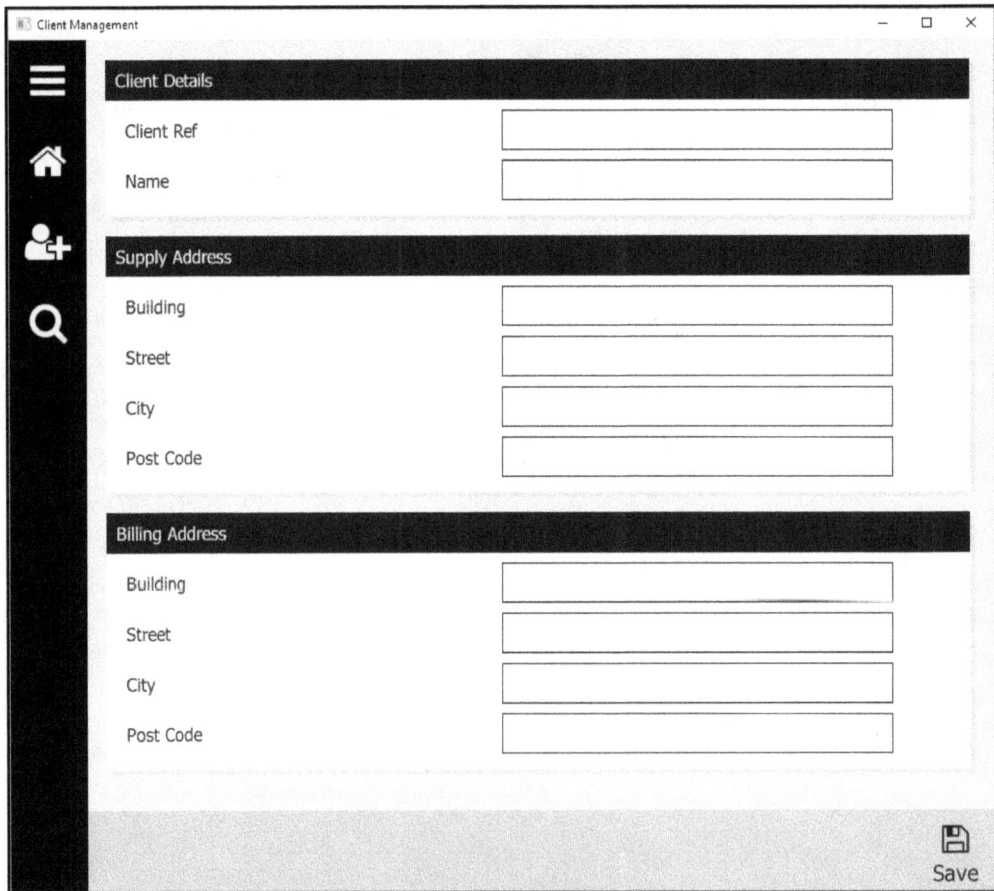

Go ahead and create a new client and check the database. You should now see the supply and billing address details successfully saved. We've now got the C in our CRUD operational, so let's move on to the 'R'.

Finding clients

We've just successfully saved our first clients to the database, so let's now look at how we can find and view that data. We'll encapsulate our searching functionality in a dedicated class in `cm-lib`, so go ahead and create a new class named `ClientSearch` in `cm-lib/source/models`.

`client-search.h`:

```
#ifndef CLIENTSEARCH_H
#define CLIENTSEARCH_H

#include <QScopedPointer>

#include <cm-lib_global.h>
#include <controllers/i-database-controller.h>
#include <data/string-decorator.h>
#include <data/entity.h>
#include <data/entity-collection.h>
#include <models/client.h>

namespace cm {
namespace models {

class CMLIBSHARED_EXPORT ClientSearch : public data::Entity
{
    Q_OBJECT
    Q_PROPERTY( cm::data::StringDecorator* ui_searchText READ
                                           searchText CONSTANT )
    Q_PROPERTY( QQmlListProperty<cm::models::Client> ui_searchResults
                READ ui_searchResults NOTIFY searchResultsChanged )

public:
    ClientSearch(QObject* parent = nullptr,
        controllers::IDatabaseController* databaseController = nullptr);
    ~ClientSearch();

    data::StringDecorator* searchText();
    QQmlListProperty<Client> ui_searchResults();
    void search();
```

```
    signals:
        void searchResultsChanged();

    private:
        class Implementation;
        QScopedPointer<Implementation> implementation;
    };

    }}

    #endif
```

client-search.cpp:

```
    #include "client-search.h"
    #include <QDebug>

    using namespace cm::controllers;
    using namespace cm::data;

    namespace cm {
    namespace models {

    class ClientSearch::Implementation
    {
    public:
        Implementation(ClientSearch* _clientSearch, IDatabaseController*
                                                    _databaseController)
            : clientSearch(_clientSearch)
            , databaseController(_databaseController)
        {
        }

        ClientSearch* clientSearch{nullptr};
        IDatabaseController* databaseController{nullptr};
        data::StringDecorator* searchText{nullptr};
        data::EntityCollection<Client>* searchResults{nullptr};
    };

    ClientSearch::ClientSearch(QObject* parent, IDatabaseController*
    databaseController)
        : Entity(parent, "ClientSearch")
    {
        implementation.reset(new Implementation(this, databaseController));
        implementation->searchText =
    static_cast<StringDecorator*>(addDataItem(new StringDecorator(this,
    "searchText", "Search Text")));
        implementation->searchResults =
```

```
static_cast<EntityCollection<Client>*>(addChildCollection(new
EntityCollection<Client>(this, "searchResults")));

    connect(implementation->searchResults,
&EntityCollection<Client>::collectionChanged, this,
&ClientSearch::searchResultsChanged);
}

ClientSearch::~ClientSearch()
{
}

StringDecorator* ClientSearch::searchText()
{
    return implementation->searchText;
}

QQmlListProperty<Client> ClientSearch::ui_searchResults()
{
    return QQmlListProperty<Client>(this,
implementation->searchResults->derivedEntities());
}

void ClientSearch::search()
{
    qDebug() << "Searching for " << implementation->searchText->value() <<
"...";
}

}}
```

We need to capture some text from the user, search the database using that text, and display the results as a list of matching clients. We accommodate the text using a StringDecorator, implement a search() method to perform the search for us, and finally, add an EntityCollection<Client> to store the results. One additional point of interest here is that we need to signal to the UI when the search results have changed so that it knows that it needs to rebind the list. To do this, we notify using the signal searchResultsChanged(), and we connect this signal directly to the collectionChanged() signal built into EntityCollection. Now, whenever the list that is hidden away in EntityCollection is updated, the UI will be automatically notified of the change and will redraw itself as needed.

Next, add an instance of `ClientSearch` to `MasterController`, just as we did for the new client model. Add a private member variable of the `ClientSearch*` type named `clientSearch`, and initialize it in the `Implementation` constructor. Remember to pass the `databaseController` dependency to the constructor. Now that we are passing more and more dependencies, we need to be careful about the initialization order. `ClientSearch` has a dependency on `DatabaseController`, and when we come to implement our search commands in `CommandController`, that will have a dependency on `ClientSearch`. So ensure that you initialize `DatabaseController` before `ClientSearch` and that `CommandController` comes after both of them. To finish off the changes to `MasterController`, add a `clientSearch()` accessor method and a `Q_PROPERTY` named `ui_clientSearch`.

As usual, we need to register the new class in the QML subsystem before we can use it in the UI. In `main.cpp`, `#include <models/client-search.h>` and register the new type:

```
qmlRegisterType<cm::models::ClientSearch>("CM", 1, 0, "ClientSearch");
```

With all that in place, we can wire up our `FindClientView`:

```
import QtQuick 2.9
import assets 1.0
import CM 1.0
import components 1.0

Item {
    property ClientSearch clientSearch: masterController.ui_clientSearch

    Rectangle {
        anchors.fill: parent
        color: Style.colourBackground

        Panel {
            id: searchPanel
            anchors {
                left: parent.left
                right: parent.right
                top: parent.top
                margins: Style.sizeScreenMargin
            }
            headerText: "Find Clients"
            contentComponent:
                StringEditorSingleLine {
                    stringDecorator: clientSearch.ui_searchText
                    anchors {
                        left: parent.left
                        right: parent.right
```

```
                }
            }
        }
    }
}
```

We access the `ClientSearch` instance via `MasterController` and create a shortcut to it with a property. We also utilize our new `Panel` component again, which gives us a nice consistent look and feel across views with very little work:

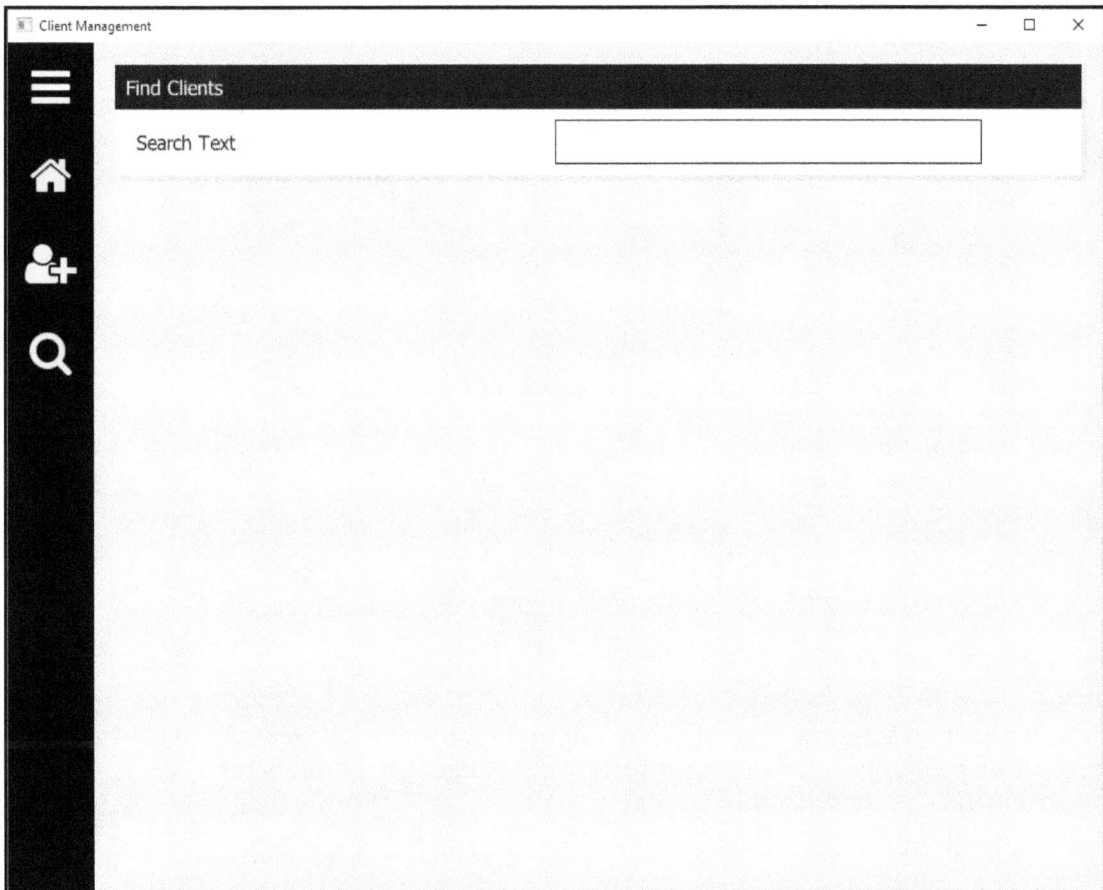

The next step is to add a command button for us to be able to instigate a search. We do this back over in `CommandController`. Before we get into the commands, we have an additional dependency on the `ClientSearch` instance, so add a parameter to the constructor:

```
CommandController::CommandController(QObject* parent, IDatabaseController*
databaseController, Client* newClient, ClientSearch* clientSearch)
    : QObject(parent)
{
    implementation.reset(new Implementation(this, databaseController,
newClient, clientSearch));
}
```

Pass the parameter through to the `Implementation` class and store it in a private member variable, just as we did with `newClient`. Hop back to `MasterController` briefly and add the `clientSearch` instance into the `CommandController` initialization:

```
commandController = new CommandController(masterController,
databaseController, newClient, clientSearch);
```

Next, in `CommandController`, duplicate and rename the private member variable, accessor, and `Q_PROPERTY` that we added for the create client view so that you end up with a `ui_findClientViewContextCommands` property for the UI to use.

Create an additional public slot, `onFindClientSearchExecuted()`, which will be called when we hit the search button:

```
void CommandController::onFindClientSearchExecuted()
{
    qDebug() << "You executed the Search command!";

    implementation->clientSearch->search();
}
```

Now we have an empty command list for our find view and a delegate to be called when we click on the button; all we need to do now is add a search button to the `Implementation` constructor:

```
Command* findClientSearchCommand = new Command( commandController, QChar(
0xf002 ), "Search" );
QObject::connect( findClientSearchCommand, &Command::executed,
commandController, &CommandController::onFindClientSearchExecuted );
findClientViewContextCommands.append( findClientSearchCommand );
```

That's it for the command plumbing; we can now easily add a command bar to
`FindClientView`. Insert the following as the last element within the root item:

```
CommandBar {
    commandList:
masterController.ui_commandController.ui_findClientViewContextCommands
}
```

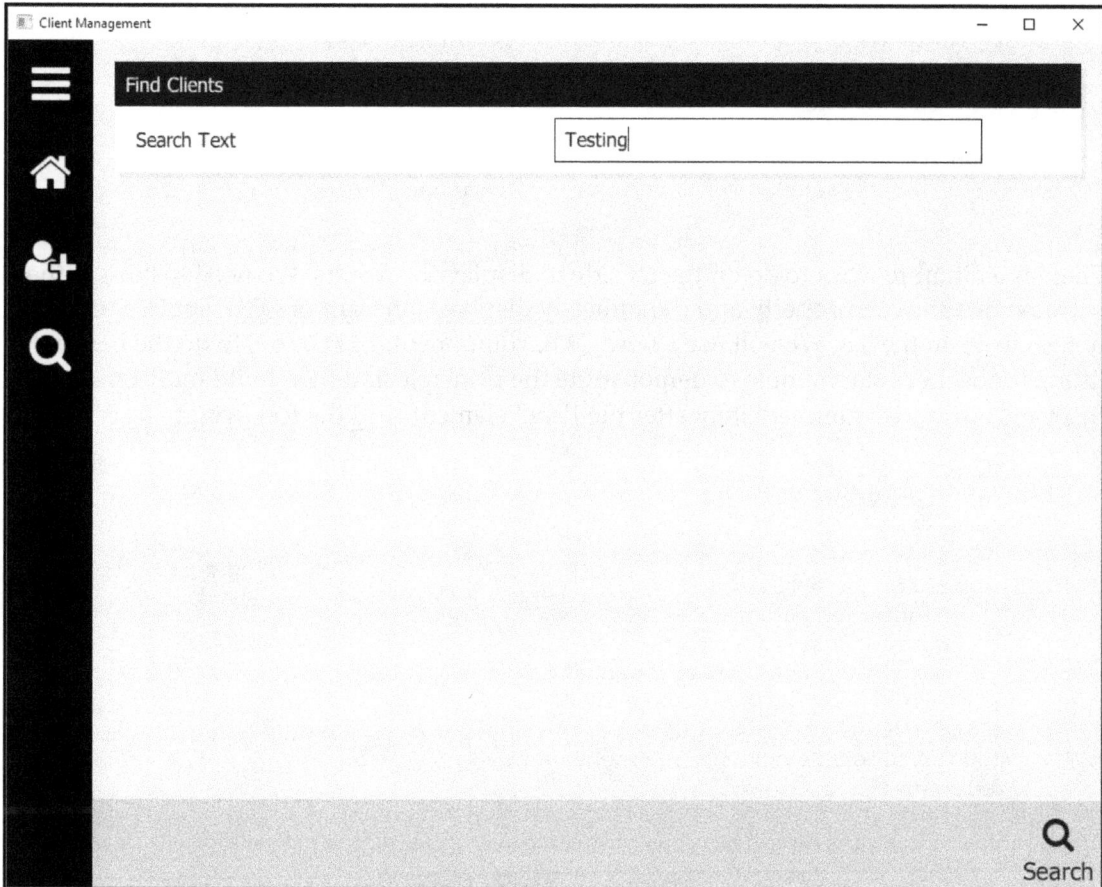

Enter some search text and click on the button, and you will see in the **Application Output**
console that everything triggers as expected:

```
You executed the Search command!
Searching for "Testing"...
```

Great, now what we need to do is take the search text, query the SQLite database for a list of results, and display those results on screen. Fortunately, we've already done the groundwork for querying the database, so we can easily implement that:

```cpp
void ClientSearch::search()
{
    qDebug() << "Searching for " << implementation->searchText->value()
                                 << "...";

    auto resultsArray = implementation->databaseController-
        >find("client", implementation->searchText->value());
    implementation->searchResults->update(resultsArray);

    qDebug() << "Found " << implementation->searchResults-
            >baseEntities().size() << " matches";
}
```

There is a bit more work to do on the UI side to display the results. We need to bind to the `ui_searchResults` property and dynamically display some sort of QML subtree for each of the clients in the list. We will use a new QML component, `ListView`, to do the heavy lifting for us. Let's start simple to demonstrate the principle and then build out from there. In `FindClientView`, immediately after the Panel element, add the following:

```qml
ListView {
    id: itemsView
    anchors {
        top: searchPanel.bottom
        left: parent.left
        right: parent.right
        bottom: parent.bottom
        margins: Style.sizeScreenMargin
    }
    clip: true
    model: clientSearch.ui_searchResults
    delegate:
        Text {
            text: modelData.ui_reference.ui_label + ": " +
                modelData.ui_reference.ui_value
            font.pixelSize: Style.pixelSizeDataControls
            color: Style.colourPanelFont
        }
}
```

The two key properties of a `ListView` are as listed:

- The `model`, which is the list of items that you want to display
- The `delegate`, which is how you want to visually represent each item

In our case, we bind the model to our `ui_searchResults` and represent each item with a simple `Text` element displaying the client reference number. Of particular importance here is the `modelData` property, which is magically injected into the delegate for us and exposes the underlying item (which is a client object, in this case).

Build, run, and perform a search for a piece of text you know exists in the JSON for one of the test clients you have created so far, and you will see that the reference number is displayed for each of the results. If you get more than one result and they lay out incorrectly, don't worry, as we will replace the delegate anyway:

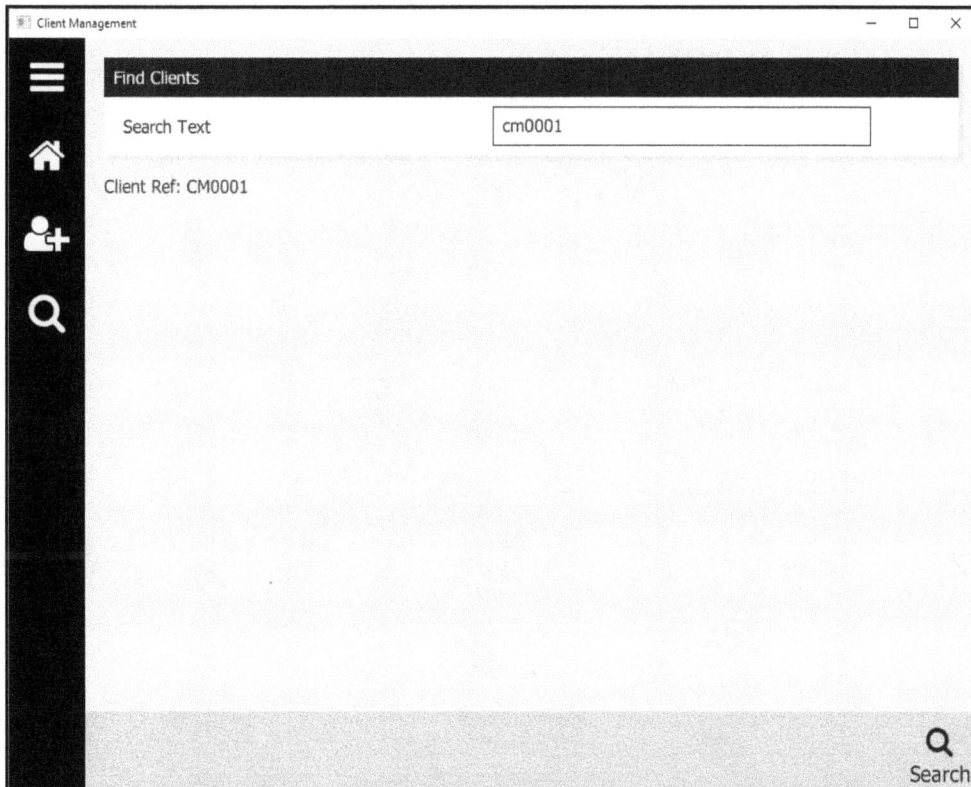

To keep things neat and tidy, we'll write a new custom component to use as the delegate. Create `SearchResultDelegate` in `cm-ui/components`, and update `components.qrc` and `qmldir` as usual:

```
import QtQuick 2.9
import assets 1.0
import CM 1.0

Item {
    property Client client

    implicitWidth: parent.width
    implicitHeight: Math.max(clientColumn.implicitHeight,
    textAddress.implicitHeight) + (Style.heightDataControls / 2)

    Rectangle {
        id: background
        width: parent.width
        height: parent.height
        color: Style.colourPanelBackground

        Column {
            id: clientColumn
            width: parent / 2
            anchors {
                left: parent.left
                top: parent.top
                margins: Style.heightDataControls / 4
            }
            spacing: Style.heightDataControls / 2

            Text {
                id: textReference
                anchors.left: parent.left
                text: client.ui_reference.ui_label + ": " +
                    client.ui_reference.ui_value
                font.pixelSize: Style.pixelSizeDataControls
                color: Style.colourPanelFont
            }
            Text {
                id: textName
                anchors.left: parent.left
                text: client.ui_name.ui_label + ": " +
                    client.ui_name.ui_value
                font.pixelSize: Style.pixelSizeDataControls
                color: Style.colourPanelFont
            }
        }
```

```
Text {
    id: textAddress
    anchors {
        top: parent.top
        right: parent.right
        margins: Style.heightDataControls / 4
    }
    text: client.ui_supplyAddress.ui_fullAddress
    font.pixelSize: Style.pixelSizeDataControls
    color: Style.colourPanelFont
    horizontalAlignment: Text.AlignRight
}

Rectangle {
    id: borderBottom
    anchors {
        bottom: parent.bottom
        left: parent.left
        right: parent.right
    }
    height: 1
    color: Style.colourPanelFont
}

MouseArea {
    anchors.fill: parent
    cursorShape: Qt.PointingHandCursor
    hoverEnabled: true
    onEntered: background.state = "hover"
    onExited: background.state = ""
    onClicked: masterController.selectClient(client)
}

states: [
    State {
        name: "hover"
        PropertyChanges {
            target: background
            color: Style.colourPanelBackgroundHover
        }
    }
]
    }
}
```

There isn't really anything new here, we've just combined techniques covered in other components. Note that the `MouseArea` element will trigger a method on `masterController` that we haven't implemented yet, so don't worry if you run this and get an error when you click on one of the clients.

Replace the old `Text` delegate in `FindClientView` with our new component using the `modelData` property to set the `client`:

```
ListView {
    id: itemsView
    ...
    delegate:
        SearchResultDelegate {
            client: modelData
        }
}
```

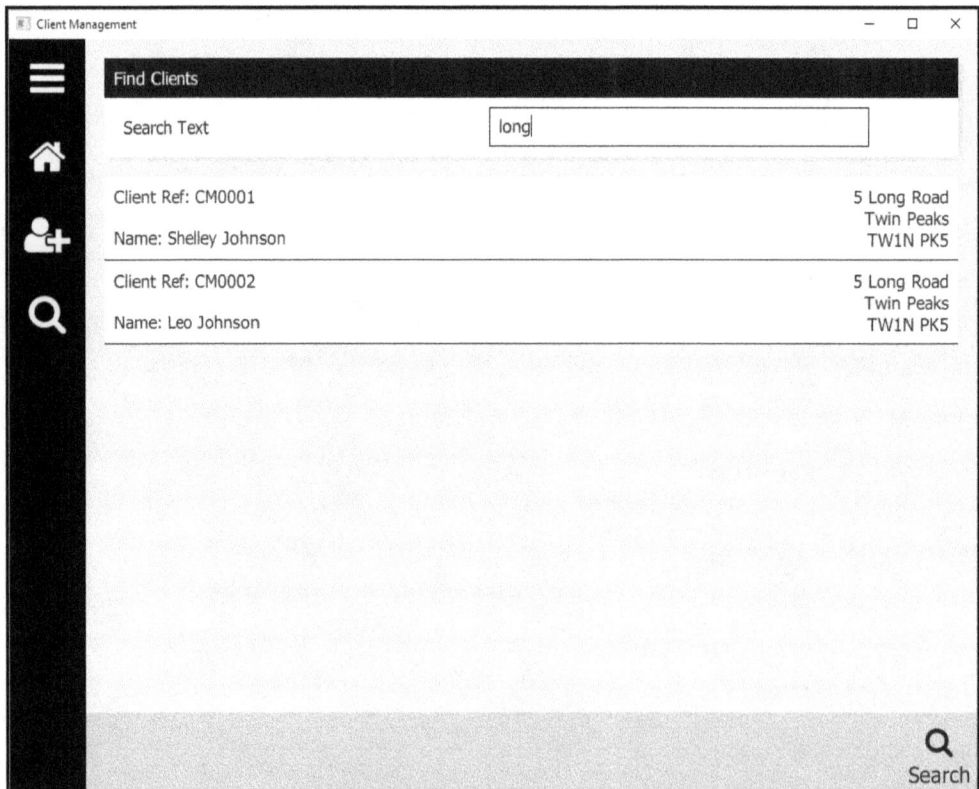

Now, let's implement the `selectClient()` method on `MasterController`:

> We can just emit the `goEditClientView()` signal directly from the `SearchResultDelegate` and bypass `MasterController` entirely. This is a perfectly valid approach and is indeed simpler; however, I prefer to route all the interactions through the business logic layer, even if all the business logic does is to emit the navigation signal. This means that if you need to add any further logic later on, everything is already wired up and you don't need to change any of the plumbing. It's also much easier to debug C++ than QML.

In `master-controller.h`, we need to add our new method as a public slot as it will be called directly from the UI, which won't have visibility of a regular public method:

```
public slots:
    void selectClient(cm::models::Client* client);
```

Provide the implementation in `master-controller.cpp`, simply calling the relevant signal on the navigation coordinator and passing through the client:

```
void MasterController::selectClient(Client* client)
{
    implementation->navigationController->goEditClientView(client);
}
```

With the searching and selection in place, we can now turn our attention to editing clients.

Editing clients

With an existing client now located and loaded from the database, we need a mechanism to be able to view and edit the data. Let's prepare by first creating the context commands we will use in the edit view. Repeat the steps we took for the Find Client View and in `CommandController`, add a new list of commands named `editClientViewContextCommands`, along with an accessor method and Q_PROPERTY.

Create a new slot to be called when the user saves their changes on the edit view:

```
void CommandController::onEditClientSaveExecuted()
{
    qDebug() << "You executed the Save command!";
}
```

Add a new save command to the list that calls the slot when executed:

```
Command* editClientSaveCommand = new Command( commandController, QChar(
0xf0c7 ), "Save" );
QObject::connect( editClientSaveCommand, &Command::executed,
commandController, &CommandController::onEditClientSaveExecuted );
editClientViewContextCommands.append( editClientSaveCommand );
```

We now have a list of commands we can present to the Edit Client View; however, a challenge that we now need to overcome is that when we execute this command, the `CommandController` has no idea which client instance it needs to work with. We can't pass in the selected client as a dependency to the constructor like we do with the new client, because we have no idea which client the user will select. One option would be to move the list of edit commands out of the `CommandController` and into the client model. Then, each client instance can present its own commands to the UI. However, this means that command functionality is fractured, and we lose the nice encapsulation that the command controller gives us. It also bloats the **client** model with functionality it shouldn't care about. Instead, we will add the currently selected client as a member within `CommandController` and set it whenever the user navigates to the `editClientView`. In `CommandController::Implementation`, add the following:

```
Client* selectedClient{nullptr};
```

Add a new public slot:

```
void CommandController::setSelectedClient(cm::models::Client* client)
{
    implementation->selectedClient = client;
}
```

Now that we have the selected client available, we can go ahead and complete the implementation of the save slot. Again, we've already done the hard work in the `DatabaseController` and client classes, so this method is really straightforward:

```
void CommandController::onEditClientSaveExecuted()
{
    qDebug() << "You executed the Save command!";

implementation->databaseController->updateRow(implementation->selectedClien
t->key(), implementation->selectedClient->id(),
implementation->selectedClient->toJson());

    qDebug() << "Updated client saved.";
}
```

From the UI point of view, editing an existing client will essentially be the same as creating a new client. So much so, in fact, that we can even probably use the same view and just pass in a different client object in each case. However, we'll keep the two functions separate and just copy and tweak the QML we've already written for creating a client. Update EditClientView:

```
import QtQuick 2.9
import QtQuick.Controls 2.2
import CM 1.0
import assets 1.0
import components 1.0

Item {
    property Client selectedClient
    Component.onCompleted:
masterController.ui_commandController.setSelectedClient(selectedClient)

    Rectangle {
        anchors.fill: parent
        color: Style.colourBackground
    }

    ScrollView {
        id: scrollView
        anchors {
            left: parent.left
            right: parent.right
            top: parent.top
            bottom: commandBar. top
            margins: Style.sizeScreenMargin
        }
        clip: true

        Column {
            spacing: Style.sizeScreenMargin
            width: scrollView.width

            Panel {
                headerText: "Client Details"
                contentComponent:
                    Column {
                        spacing: Style.sizeControlSpacing
                        StringEditorSingleLine {
                            stringDecorator:
                            selectedClient.ui_reference
                            anchors {
                                left: parent.left
```

```
                                right: parent.right
                            }
                        }
                        StringEditorSingleLine {
                            stringDecorator: selectedClient.ui_name
                            anchors {
                                left: parent.left
                                right: parent.right
                            }
                        }
                    }
                }

                AddressEditor {
                    address: selectedClient.ui_supplyAddress
                    headerText: "Supply Address"
                }

                AddressEditor {
                    address: selectedClient.ui_billingAddress
                    headerText: "Billing Address"
                }
            }
        }

    CommandBar {
        id: commandBar
        commandList:
    masterController.ui_commandController.ui_editClientViewContextCommands
    }
}
```

We change the client property to match the `selectedClient` property `MasterView` sets in the `Connections` element. We use the `Component.onCompleted` slot to call through to `CommandController` and set the currently selected client. Finally, we update `CommandBar` to reference the new context command list we just added.

Build and run, and you should now be able to make changes to a selected client and use the **Save** button to update the database.

Deleting clients

The final part of our CRUD operations is deleting an existing client. Let's trigger this via a new button on `EditClientView`. We'll begin by adding the slot that will be called when the button is pressed to `CommandController`:

```
void CommandController::onEditClientDeleteExecuted()
{
    qDebug() << "You executed the Delete command!";

implementation->databaseController->deleteRow(implementation->selectedClien
t->key(), implementation->selectedClient->id());
    implementation->selectedClient = nullptr;

    qDebug() << "Client deleted.";

    implementation->clientSearch->search();
}
```

This follows the same pattern as the other slots, except this time we also clear the `selectedClient` property as although the client instance still exists in application memory, it has been semantically deleted by the user. We also refresh the search so that the deleted client is removed from the search results. As this method stands, we've performed the correct database interaction but the user will be left on `editClientView` for a client that they have just asked to be deleted. What we want is for the user to be navigated back to the dashboard. In order to do this, we need to add `NavigationController` as an additional dependency to our `CommandController` class. Replicate what we did for the `DatabaseController` dependency so that we can inject it into the constructor. Remember to update `MasterController` and pass in the navigation controller instance.

With an instance of a database controller available, we can then send the user to the **Dashboard View**:

```
void CommandController::onEditClientDeleteExecuted()
{
    ...

    implementation->navigationController->goDashboardView();
}
```

Now that we have the navigation controller available, we can also improve the experience when creating new clients. Rather than leaving the user on the new client view, let's perform a search for the newly created client ID and navigate them to the results. They can then easily select the new client if they wish to view or edit:

```
void CommandController::onCreateClientSaveExecuted()
{
    ...

    implementation->clientSearch->searchText()-
                    >setValue(implementation->newClient->id());
    implementation->clientSearch->search();
    implementation->navigationController->goFindClientView();
}
```

With the deletion slot complete, we can now add a new delete command to the editClientContextCommands list in CommandController:

```
Command* editClientDeleteCommand = new Command( commandController, QChar(
0xf235 ), "Delete" );
QObject::connect( editClientDeleteCommand, &Command::executed,
commandController, &CommandController::onEditClientDeleteExecuted );
editClientViewContextCommands.append( editClientDeleteCommand );
```

We are now presented with the option to delete an existing client:

If you delete a client, you will see that the row is removed from the database and the user is successfully navigated back to the dashboard. However, you will also see that the **Application Output** window is full of QML warnings along the lines of `qrc:/views/EditClientView:62: TypeError: Cannot read property 'ui_billingAddress' of null.`

The reason for this is that the edit view is bound to a client instance that is part of the search results. When we refresh the search, we delete the old search results, which means that the edit view is now bound to `nullptr` and can no longer access the data. This continues to happen even if you navigate to the dashboard before refreshing the search, because of the asynchronous nature of the signals/slots used to perform the navigation. One way of fixing these warnings is to add null checks on all the bindings in the view and bind to local temporary objects if the main object is null. Consider the following example:

```
StringEditorSingleLine {
    property StringDecorator temporaryObject
    stringDecorator: selectedClient ? selectedClient.ui_reference :
    temporaryObject
    anchors {
        left: parent.left
        right: parent.right
    }
}
```

So, if `selectedClient` is not null, bind to the `ui_reference` property of that, otherwise bind to `temporaryObject`. You can even add a level of indirection to the root Client property and substitute the entire client object:

```
property Client selectedClient
property Client localTemporaryClient
property Client clientToBindTo: selectedClient ? selectedClient :
localTemporaryClient
```

Here, `selectedClient` will be set by the parent as normal; `localTemporaryClient` will not be set, so a default instance will be created locally. `clientToBindTo` will then pick the appropriate object to use and all the child controls can bind to that. As these bindings are dynamic, if `selectedClient` was deleted after loading the view (as in our case), then `clientToBindTo` will automatically switch over.

As this is just a demonstration project, it is safe for us to ignore the warnings, so we will take no action here to keep things simple.

Summary

In this chapter, we added database persistence for our client models. We made it generic and flexible so that we can easily persist other model hierarchies by simply adding a new table to our `DatabaseController` class. We covered all the core CRUD operations, including a free text search capability that matches against the entire JSON object.

In `Chapter 8`, *Web Requests*, we will continue the theme of reaching outside of our application for data and look at another extremely common Line of Business application requirement making HTTP requests to web services.

8
Web Requests

This chapter takes us worldwide as we venture even further out from our application to the internet. Beginning with writing some helper classes to manage web requests for us, we will pull data from a live RSS feed and interpret it via some XML processing. With the parsed data at hand, we can then put our QML skills to use and display the items on a new view. Clicking on one of the RSS items will launch a web browser window in order to view the related article in more detail. We will cover the following topics:

- Network access
- Web Requests
- RSS View
- RSS

Network access

The low-level networking protocol negotiation is all handled internally by Qt, and we can easily get connected to the outside world via the `QNetworkAccessManager` class. To be able to access this functionality, we need to add the `network` module to `cm-lib.pro`:

```
QT += sql network
```

One of Qt's weaknesses is the lack of interfaces, making unit testing difficult in some cases. If we just use `QNetworkAccessManager` directly, we won't be able to test our code without making real calls to the network, which is undesirable. However, a quick and easy solution to this problem is to hide the Qt implementation behind an interface of our own, and we will do that here.

For the purposes of this chapter, all we need to be able to do with the network is check that we have connectivity and send a HTTP GET request. With this in mind, create a header file `i-network-access-manager.h` in a new folder `cm-lib/source/networking` and implement the interface:

```
#ifndef INETWORKACCESSMANAGER_H
#define INETWORKACCESSMANAGER_H
#include <QNetworkReply>
#include <QNetworkRequest>

namespace cm {
namespace networking {
class INetworkAccessManager
{
public:
    INetworkAccessManager(){}
    virtual ~INetworkAccessManager(){}
    virtual QNetworkReply* get(const QNetworkRequest& request) = 0;
    virtual bool isNetworkAccessible() const = 0;
};
}}
#endif
```

`QNetworkRequest` is another Qt class that represents a request to be sent over the network, and `QNetworkReply` represents a response received over the network. We will ideally hide these implementations behind interfaces too, but let's make do with the network access interface for now. With that in place, go ahead and create a concrete implementation class `NetworkAccessManager` in the same folder:

`network-access-manager.h`:

```
#ifndef NETWORKACCESSMANAGER_H
#define NETWORKACCESSMANAGER_H
#include <QObject>
#include <QScopedPointer>
#include <networking/i-network-access-manager.h>
namespace cm {
namespace networking {
class NetworkAccessManager : public QObject, public INetworkAccessManager
{
    Q_OBJECT
public:
    explicit NetworkAccessManager(QObject* parent = nullptr);
    ~NetworkAccessManager();
    QNetworkReply* get(const QNetworkRequest& request) override;
    bool isNetworkAccessible() const override;
private:
```

```
        class Implementation;
        QScopedPointer<Implementation> implementation;
    };
    }}
    #endif
```

network-access-manager.cpp:

```
    #include "network-access-manager.h"
    #include <QNetworkAccessManager>
    namespace cm {
    namespace networking {
    class NetworkAccessManager::Implementation
    {
    public:
        Implementation()
        {}
        QNetworkAccessManager networkAccessManager;
    };
    NetworkAccessManager::NetworkAccessManager(QObject *parent)
        : QObject(parent)
        , INetworkAccessManager()
    {
        implementation.reset(new Implementation());
    }
    NetworkAccessManager::~NetworkAccessManager()
    {
    }
    QNetworkReply* NetworkAccessManager::get(const QNetworkRequest& request)
    {
        return implementation->networkAccessManager.get(request);
    }
    bool NetworkAccessManager::isNetworkAccessible() const
    {
        return implementation->networkAccessManager.networkAccessible() ==
    QNetworkAccessManager::Accessible;
    }
    }}
```

All we are doing is holding a private instance of QNetworkAccessManager and passing calls to our interface through to it. The interface can easily be extended to include additional functionality like HTTP POST requests with the same approach.

Web Requests

If you haven't worked with the HTTP protocol before, it boils down to a conversation between a client and a server consisting of requests and responses. For example, we can make a request to `www.bbc.co.uk` in our favorite web browser, and we will receive a response containing various news items and articles. In the `get()` method of our `NetworkAccessManager` wrapper, we reference a `QNetworkRequest` (our request to a server) and a `QNetworkReply` (the server's response back to us). While we won't directly hide `QNetworkRequest` and `QNetworkReply` behind their own independent interfaces, we will take the concept of a web request and corresponding response and create an interface and implementation for that interaction. Still in `cm-lib/source/networking`, create an interface header file `i-web-request.h`:

```
#ifndef IWEBREQUEST_H
#define IWEBREQUEST_H
#include <QUrl>
namespace cm {
namespace networking {
class IWebRequest
{
public:
    IWebRequest(){}
    virtual ~IWebRequest(){}
    virtual void execute() = 0;
    virtual bool isBusy() const = 0;
    virtual void setUrl(const QUrl& url) = 0;
    virtual QUrl url() const = 0;
};
}}
#endif
```

The key piece of information for an HTTP request is the URL the request is to be sent to, represented by the `QUrl` Qt class. We provide an `url()` accessor and `setUrl()` mutator for the property. The other two methods are to check whether the `isBusy()` web request object is making a request or receiving a response and also to `execute()` or send the request to the network. Again, with the interface in place, let's move on straight to the implementation with a new `WebRequest` class in the same folder.

`web-request.h`:

```
#ifndef WEBREQUEST_H
#define WEBREQUEST_H
#include <QList>
#include <QObject>
#include <QSslError>
```

```
#include <networking/i-network-access-manager.h>
#include <networking/i-web-request.h>
namespace cm {
namespace networking {
class WebRequest : public QObject, public IWebRequest
{
    Q_OBJECT
public:
    WebRequest(QObject* parent, INetworkAccessManager*
networkAccessManager, const QUrl& url);
    WebRequest(QObject* parent = nullptr) = delete;
    ~WebRequest();
public:
    void execute() override;
    bool isBusy() const override;
    void setUrl(const QUrl& url) override;
    QUrl url() const override;
signals:
    void error(QString message);
    void isBusyChanged();
    void requestComplete(int statusCode, QByteArray body);
    void urlChanged();
private slots:
    void replyDelegate();
    void sslErrorsDelegate( const QList<QSslError>& _errors );
private:
    class Implementation;
    QScopedPointer<Implementation> implementation;
};
}}
#endif
```

web-request.cpp:

```
#include "web-request.h"

#include <QMap>
#include <QNetworkReply>
#include <QNetworkRequest>
namespace cm {
namespace networking { // Private Implementation
static const QMap<QNetworkReply::NetworkError, QString> networkErrorMapper
= {
    {QNetworkReply::ConnectionRefusedError, "The remote server refused the
connection (the server is not accepting requests)."},
    /* ...section shortened in print for brevity...*/
    {QNetworkReply::UnknownServerError, "An unknown error related to the
server response was detected."}
```

```
};
class WebRequest::Implementation
{
public:
    Implementation(WebRequest* _webRequest, INetworkAccessManager*
_networkAccessManager, const QUrl& _url)
        : webRequest(_webRequest)
        , networkAccessManager(_networkAccessManager)
        , url(_url)
    {
    }
    WebRequest* webRequest{nullptr};
    INetworkAccessManager* networkAccessManager{nullptr};
    QUrl url {};
    QNetworkReply* reply {nullptr};
public:
    bool isBusy() const
    {
        return isBusy_;
    }
    void setIsBusy(bool value)
    {
        if (value != isBusy_) {
            isBusy_ = value;
            emit webRequest->isBusyChanged();
        }
    }
private:
    bool isBusy_{false};
};
}
namespace networking {  // Structors
WebRequest::WebRequest(QObject* parent, INetworkAccessManager*
networkAccessManager, const QUrl& url)
    : QObject(parent)
    , IWebRequest()
{
    implementation.reset(new WebRequest::Implementation(this,
networkAccessManager, url));
}
WebRequest::~WebRequest()
{
}
}
namespace networking { // Methods
void WebRequest::execute()
{
    if(implementation->isBusy()) {
```

```
            return;
    }

    if(!implementation->networkAccessManager->isNetworkAccessible()) {
        emit error("Network not accessible");
        return;
    }
    implementation->setIsBusy(true);
    QNetworkRequest request;
    request.setUrl(implementation->url);
    implementation->reply =
implementation->networkAccessManager->get(request);
    if(implementation->reply != nullptr) {
        connect(implementation->reply, &QNetworkReply::finished, this,
&WebRequest::replyDelegate);
        connect(implementation->reply, &QNetworkReply::sslErrors, this,
&WebRequest::sslErrorsDelegate);
    }
}
bool WebRequest::isBusy() const
{
    return implementation->isBusy();
}
void WebRequest::setUrl(const QUrl& url)
{
    if(url != implementation->url) {
        implementation->url = url;
        emit urlChanged();
    }
}
QUrl WebRequest::url() const
{
    return implementation->url;
}
}
namespace networking { // Private Slots
void WebRequest::replyDelegate()
{
    implementation->setIsBusy(false);
    if (implementation->reply == nullptr) {
        emit error("Unexpected error - reply object is null");
        return;
    }
    disconnect(implementation->reply, &QNetworkReply::finished, this,
&WebRequest::replyDelegate);
    disconnect(implementation->reply, &QNetworkReply::sslErrors, this,
&WebRequest::sslErrorsDelegate);
    auto statusCode =
```

```
implementation->reply->attribute(QNetworkRequest::HttpStatusCodeAttribute).
toInt();
    auto responseBody = implementation->reply->readAll();
    auto replyStatus = implementation->reply->error();
    implementation->reply->deleteLater();
    if (replyStatus != QNetworkReply::NoError) {
        emit error(networkErrorMapper[implementation->reply->error()]);
    }
    emit requestComplete(statusCode, responseBody);
}
void WebRequest::sslErrorsDelegate(const QList<QSslError>& errors)
{
    QString sslError;
    for (const auto& error : errors) {
        sslError += error.errorString() + "n";
    }
    emit error(sslError);
}
}}
```

The implementation looks more complicated than it is purely because of the lengthy error code map. In the event of some sort of problem, Qt will report the error using an enumerator. The purpose of the map is simply to match the enumerator to a human readable error description that we can present to the user or write to the console or a log file.

In addition to the interface methods, we also have a handful of signals that we can use to tell any interested observers about events that have happened:

- `error()` will be emitted in the event of a problem and will pass the error description as a parameter
- `isBusyChanged()` is fired when a request starts or finishes and the request becomes either busy or idle
- `requestComplete()` is emitted when the response has been received and processed and will contain the HTTP status code and an array of bytes representing the response body
- `urlChanged()` will be fired when the URL is updated

We also have a couple of private slots that will be the delegates for processing a reply and handling any SSL errors. They are connected to signals on the `QNetworkReply` object when we execute a new request and disconnected again when we receive the reply.

The meat of the implementation is really two methods—`execute()` to send the request and `replyDelegate()` to process the response.

When executing, we first ensure that we are not already busy executing another request and then check with the network access manager that we have an available connection. Assuming that we do, we then set the busy flag and construct a `QNetworkRequest` using the currently set URL. We then pass the request onto our network access manager (injected as an interface, so we can change its behavior) and finally, we connect our delegate slots and wait for a response.

When we receive the reply, we unset the busy flag and disconnect our slots before reading the response details we are interested in, principally the HTTP status code and response body. We check that the reply completed successfully (note that a "negative" HTTP response code in the ranges 4xx or 5xx still count as successfully complete requests in this context) and emit the details for any interested parties to capture and process.

RSS View

Let's add a new view to our app where we can display some information from a web service using our new classes.

There is nothing new or complicated here, so I won't show all the code, but there are a few steps to remember:

1. Create a new `RssView.qml` view in `cm-ui/views` and copy the QML from `SplashView` for now, replacing the "Splash View" text with "Rss View"
2. Add the view to `views.qrc` in the `/views` prefix block and with an alias `RssView.qml`
3. Add the `goRssView()` signal to `NavigationController`
4. In `MasterView`, add the `onGoRssView` slot to the Connections element and use it to navigate to `RssView`

5. In `NavigationBar`, add a new `NavigationButton` with `iconCharacter` `uf09e`, description `RSS Feed`, and `hoverColour` as `#8acece`, and use the `onNavigationButtonClicked` slot to call `goRssView()` on the `NavigationController`

With just a few simple steps, we've now got a brand new view wired up that we can access using the navigation bar:

Next, we'll add a context command bar to the view with the following steps:

1. In `CommandController`, add a new private member list `rssViewContextCommands`
2. Add an accessor method `ui_rssViewContextCommands()`

3. Add a Q_PROPERTY named `ui_rssViewContextCommands`

4. Add a new slot `onRssRefreshExecuted()` that simply writes a debug message to the console; for now to indicate it has been called

5. Append a new command called `rssRefreshCommand` to `rssViewContextCommands` with the `0xf021` icon character and "Refresh" label and connect it to the `onRssRefreshExecuted()` slot

6. In `RssView`, add a `CommandBar` component with the `commandList` wired up to `ui_rssViewContextCommands` on the command controller

All the hard work from earlier chapters is really paying dividends now; our new view has got its own command bar and a fully functional refresh button. When you click on it, it should write out the debug message you added to the console:

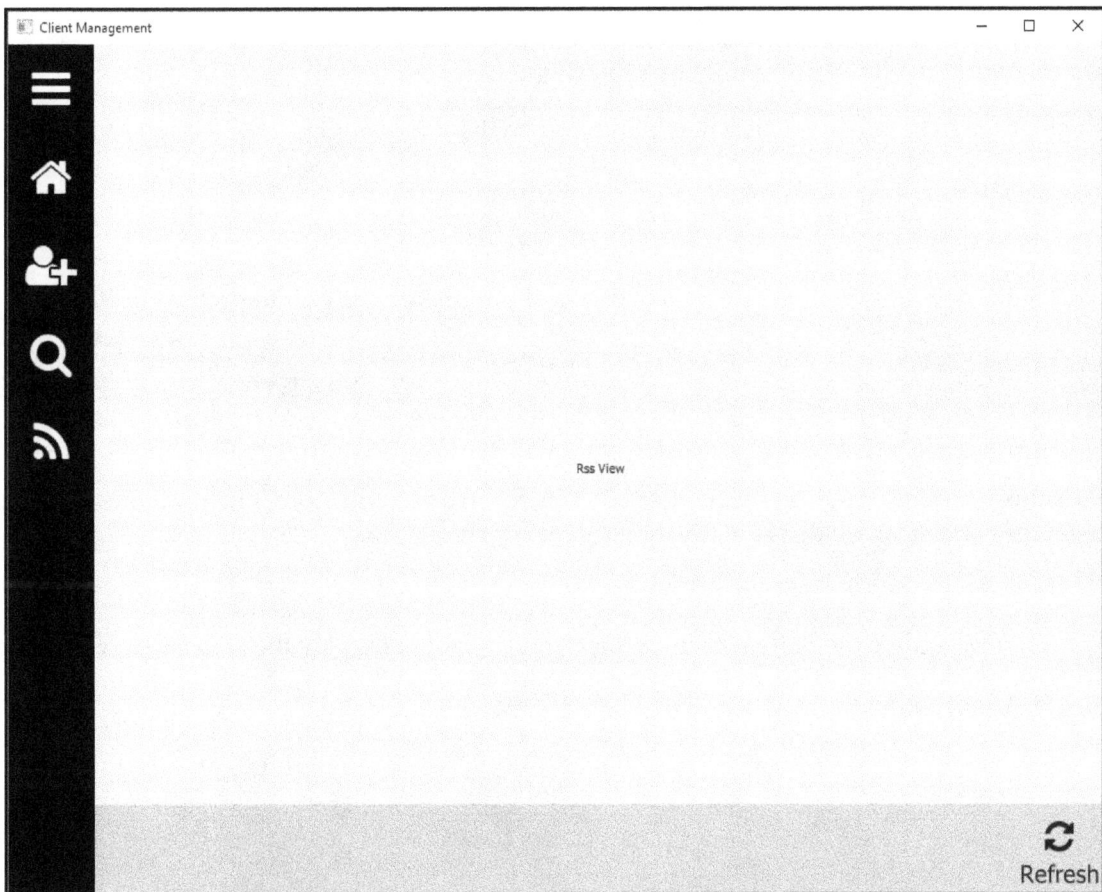

Next, we need to create instances of our `NetworkAccessManager` and `WebRequest` classes. As usual, we will add these to `MasterController` and inject a dependency to `CommandController`.

In `MasterController`, add two new private members:

```
NetworkAccessManager* networkAccessManager{nullptr};
WebRequest* rssWebRequest{nullptr};
```

Remember to include the relevant headers. Instantiate these new members in the `Implementation` constructor, ensuring that they are created before `commandController`:

```
networkAccessManager = new NetworkAccessManager(masterController);
rssWebRequest = new WebRequest(masterController, networkAccessManager,
QUrl("http://feeds.bbci.co.uk/news/rss.xml?edition=uk"));
```

Here we are using the URL for a BBC RSS feed relevant to the UK; feel free to swap this for another feed of your choice simply by replacing the hyperlink text.

Next, pass `rssWebRequest` as a new parameter to the `commandController` constructor:

```
commandController = new CommandController(masterController,
databaseController, navigationController, newClient, clientSearch,
rssWebRequest);
```

Next, edit `CommandController` to take this new parameter as a pointer to the interface:

```
explicit CommandController(QObject* _parent = nullptr, IDatabaseController*
databaseController = nullptr, NavigationController* navigationController =
nullptr, models::Client* newClient = nullptr, models::ClientSearch*
clientSearch = nullptr, networking::IWebRequest* rssWebRequest = nullptr);
```

Pass this pointer through the `Implementation` constructor and store it in a private member variable as we do for all the other dependencies:

```
IWebRequest* rssWebRequest{nullptr};
```

We can now update the `onRssRefreshExecuted()` slot to execute the web request:

```
void CommandController::onRssRefreshExecuted()
{
    qDebug() << "You executed the Rss Refresh command!";

    implementation->rssWebRequest->execute();
}
```

The command controller now reacts to the user pressing the refresh button and executes the web request. However, we don't currently do anything when we receive the response. Let's add a delegate to `MasterController` in the public slots section:

```
void MasterController::onRssReplyReceived(int statusCode, QByteArray body)
{
    qDebug() << "Received RSS request response code " << statusCode << ":";
    qDebug() << body;
}
```

Now, after we instantiate `rssWebRequest` in `Implementation`, we can wire up the `requestComplete` signal to our new delegate:

```
QObject::connect(rssWebRequest, &WebRequest::requestComplete,
masterController, &MasterController::onRssReplyReceived);
```

Now build and run the application, navigate to the RSS View, and click on **Refresh. After a brief delay, while the request is executed, you will see all sorts of nonsense printed to the Application Output console:**

```
Received RSS request response code 200 :
"<?xml version="1.0" encoding="UTF-8"?>n<?xml-stylesheet title=..."
```

Congratulations! You've got an RSS feed! Now, what is it?

RSS

Rich Site Summary (**RSS**) is a format for delivering regularly changing web content and is essentially an entire website, news broadcast, blog, or similar condensed down to bullet points. Each item consists of bare-bones information like the date and a descriptive title and is supplied with a hyperlink to the website page that contains the full article.

The data is extended from XML and must adhere to defined standards as described at `http://www.rssboard.org/rss-specification`.

Boiling it down to the basics for the purposes of this example, the XML looks as follows:

```
<rss>
    <channel>
        <title></title>
        <description></description>
        <link></link>
        <image>
            <url></url>
            <title></title>
```

```
            <link></link>
            <width></width>
            <height></height>
        </image>
        <item>
            <title></title>
            <description></description>
            <link></link>
            <pubDate></pubDate>
        </item>
        <item>
                    ...
        </item>
    </channel>
</rss>
```

Inside the root `<rss>` node, we have a `<channel>` node, which in turn contains an `<image>` node and a collection of one or more `<item>` nodes.

We'll model these nodes as classes, but first we need to pull in the XML module and write a small helper class to do some parsing for us. In `cm-lib.pro` and `cm-ui.pro`, add the `xml` module to the modules in the `QT` variable; consider this example:

```
QT += sql network xml
```

Next, create a new `XmlHelper` class in a new folder `cm-lib/source/utilities`.

`xml-helper.h`:

```
#ifndef XMLHELPER_H
#define XMLHELPER_H
#include <QDomNode>
#include <QString>
namespace cm {
namespace utilities {
class XmlHelper
{
public:
    static QString toString(const QDomNode& domNode);
private:
    XmlHelper(){}
    static void appendNode(const QDomNode& domNode, QString& output);
};
}}
#endif
```

`xml-helper.cpp`:

```
#include "xml-helper.h"

namespace cm {
namespace utilities {
QString XmlHelper::toString(const QDomNode& domNode)
{
    QString returnValue;
    for(auto i = 0; i < domNode.childNodes().size(); ++i) {
        QDomNode subNode = domNode.childNodes().at(i);
        appendNode(subNode, returnValue);
    }
    return returnValue;
}
void XmlHelper::appendNode(const QDomNode& domNode, QString& output)
{
    if(domNode.nodeType() == QDomNode::TextNode) {
        output.append(domNode.nodeValue());
        return;
    }
    if(domNode.nodeType() == QDomNode::AttributeNode) {
        output.append(" ");
        output.append(domNode.nodeName());
        output.append("=\"");
        output.append(domNode.nodeValue());
        output.append("\"");
        return;
    }
    if(domNode.nodeType() == QDomNode::ElementNode) {
        output.append("<");
        output.append(domNode.nodeName());
        // Add attributes
        for(auto i = 0; i < domNode.attributes().size(); ++i) {
            QDomNode subNode = domNode.attributes().item(i);
            appendNode(subNode, output);
        }
        output.append(">");
        for(auto i = 0; i < domNode.childNodes().size(); ++i) {
            QDomNode subNode = domNode.childNodes().at(i);
            appendNode(subNode, output);
        }
        output.append("</" + domNode.nodeName() + ">");
    }
}
}}
```

I won't go into too much detail about what this class does as it isn't the focus of the chapter, but essentially, if we receive an XML node that contains HTML markup (which is quite common in RSS), the XML parser gets a bit confused and breaks up the HTML into XML nodes too, which isn't what we want. Consider this example:

```
<xmlNode>
    Here is something from a website that has a <a href="http://www.bbc.co.
uk">hyperlink</a> in it.
</xmlNode>
```

In this case, the XML parser will see `<a>` as XML and break up the content into three child nodes similar to this:

```
<xmlNode>
    <textNode1>Here is something from a website that has a </textNode1>
    <a href="http://www.bbc.co.uk">hyperlink</a>
    <textNode2>in it.</textNode2>
</xmlNode>
```

This makes it difficult to display the contents of xmlNode to the user on the UI. Instead, we use XmlHelper to parse the contents manually and construct a single string, which is much easier to work with.

Now, let's move on to the RSS classes. In a new `cm-lib/source/rss folder`, create new `RssChannel`, `RssImage`, and `RssItem` classes.

`rss-image.h`:

```cpp
#ifndef RSSIMAGE_H
#define RSSIMAGE_H
#include <QObject>
#include <QScopedPointer>
#include <QtXml/QDomNode>
#include <cm-lib_global.h>
namespace cm {
namespace rss {
class CMLIBSHARED_EXPORT RssImage : public QObject
{
    Q_OBJECT
    Q_PROPERTY(quint16 ui_height READ height CONSTANT)
    Q_PROPERTY(QString ui_link READ link CONSTANT)
    Q_PROPERTY(QString ui_title READ title CONSTANT)
    Q_PROPERTY(QString ui_url READ url CONSTANT)
    Q_PROPERTY(quint16 ui_width READ width CONSTANT)
public:
    explicit RssImage(QObject* parent = nullptr, const QDomNode& domNode =
QDomNode());
```

```
        ~RssImage();
        quint16 height() const;
        const QString& link() const;
        const QString& title() const;
        const QString& url() const;
        quint16 width() const;
    private:
        class Implementation;
        QScopedPointer<Implementation> implementation;
    };
    }}

    #endif
```

rss-image.cpp:

```
    #include "rss-image.h"

    namespace cm {
    namespace rss {
    class RssImage::Implementation
    {
    public:
        QString url;    // Mandatory. URL of GIF, JPEG or PNG that represents
    the channel.
        QString title;  // Mandatory.  Describes the image.
        QString link;   // Mandatory.  URL of the site.
        quint16 width;  // Optional.  Width in pixels.  Max 144, default
                                                                        88.
        quint16 height; // Optional.  Height in pixels.  Max 400, default
                                                                        31

        void update(const QDomNode& domNode)
        {
            QDomElement imageUrl = domNode.firstChildElement("url");
            if(!imageUrl.isNull()) {
                url = imageUrl.text();
            }
            QDomElement imageTitle = domNode.firstChildElement("title");
            if(!imageTitle.isNull()) {
                title = imageTitle.text();
            }
            QDomElement imageLink = domNode.firstChildElement("link");
            if(!imageLink.isNull()) {
                link = imageLink.text();
            }
            QDomElement imageWidth = domNode.firstChildElement("width");
            if(!imageWidth.isNull()) {
                width = static_cast<quint16>(imageWidth.text().toShort());
```

```
        } else {
            width = 88;
        }
        QDomElement imageHeight = domNode.firstChildElement("height");
        if(!imageHeight.isNull()) {
            height = static_cast<quint16>
                                (imageHeight.text().toShort());
        } else {
            height = 31;
        }
    }
};
RssImage::RssImage(QObject* parent, const QDomNode& domNode)
    : QObject(parent)
{
    implementation.reset(new Implementation());
    implementation->update(domNode);
}
RssImage::~RssImage()
{
}
quint16 RssImage::height() const
{
    return implementation->height;
}
const QString& RssImage::link() const
{
    return implementation->link;
}
const QString& RssImage::title() const
{
    return implementation->title;
}
const QString& RssImage::url() const
{
    return implementation->url;
}
quint16 RssImage::width() const
{
    return implementation->width;
}
}}
```

This class is just a regular plain data model with the exception that it will be constructed from an XML <image> node represented by Qt's QDomNode class. We use the firstChildElement() method to locate the <url>, <title>, and <link> mandatory child nodes and then access the value of each node via the **text()** method. The <width> and <height> nodes are optional and if they are not present, we use the default image size of 88 x 31 pixels.

rss-item.h:

```
#ifndef RSSITEM_H
#define RSSITEM_H
#include <QDateTime>
#include <QObject>
#include <QscopedPointer>
#include <QtXml/QDomNode>
#include <cm-lib_global.h>
namespace cm {
namespace rss {
class CMLIBSHARED_EXPORT RssItem : public QObject
{
    Q_OBJECT
    Q_PROPERTY(QString ui_description READ description CONSTANT)
    Q_PROPERTY(QString ui_link READ link CONSTANT)
    Q_PROPERTY(QDateTime ui_pubDate READ pubDate CONSTANT)
    Q_PROPERTY(QString ui_title READ title CONSTANT)
public:
    RssItem(QObject* parent = nullptr, const QDomNode& domNode =
QDomNode());
    ~RssItem();
    const QString& description() const;
    const QString& link() const;
    const QDateTime& pubDate() const;
    const QString& title() const;
private:
    class Implementation;
    QScopedPointer<Implementation> implementation;
};
}}
#endif
```

rss-item.cpp:

```
#include "rss-item.h"
#include <QTextStream>
#include <utilities/xml-helper.h>
using namespace cm::utilities;
namespace cm {
```

```cpp
namespace rss {
class RssItem::Implementation
{
public:
    Implementation(RssItem* _rssItem)
        : rssItem(_rssItem)
    {
    }
    RssItem* rssItem{nullptr};
    QString description;    // This or Title mandatory.  Either the
                            //    synopsis or full story.  HTML is allowed.
    QString link;           // Optional. Link to full story.  Populated
                            //       if Description is only the synopsis.
    QDateTime pubDate;      // Optional. When the item was published.
                        RFC 822 format e.g. Sun, 19 May 2002 15:21:36 GMT.
    QString title;          // This or Description mandatory.
    void update(const QDomNode& domNode)
    {
        for(auto i = 0; i < domNode.childNodes().size(); ++i) {
            QDomNode childNode = domNode.childNodes().at(i);
            if(childNode.nodeName() == "description") {
                description = XmlHelper::toString(childNode);
            }
        }
        QDomElement itemLink = domNode.firstChildElement("link");
        if(!itemLink.isNull()) {
            link = itemLink.text();
        }
        QDomElement itemPubDate = domNode.firstChildElement("pubDate");
        if(!itemPubDate.isNull()) {
            pubDate = QDateTime::fromString(itemPubDate.text(),
                                                Qt::RFC2822Date);
        }
        QDomElement itemTitle = domNode.firstChildElement("title");
        if(!itemTitle.isNull()) {
            title = itemTitle.text();
        }
    }
};
RssItem::RssItem(QObject* parent, const QDomNode& domNode)
{
    implementation.reset(new Implementation(this));
    implementation->update(domNode);
}
RssItem::~RssItem()
{
}
const QString& RssItem::description() const
```

```
{
    return implementation->description;
}
const QString& RssItem::link() const
{
    return implementation->link;
}
const QDateTime& RssItem::pubDate() const
{
    return implementation->pubDate;
}
const QString& RssItem::title() const
{
    return implementation->title;
}
}}
```

This class is much the same as the last. This time we put our XMLHelper class to use when parsing the <description> node as that has a good chance of containing HTML tags. Also note that Qt also helpfully contains the Qt::RFC2822Date format specifier when converting a string to a QDateTime object using the static QDateTime::fromString() method. This is the format used in the RSS specification and saves us from having to manually parse the dates ourselves.

rss-channel.h:

```
#ifndef RSSCHANNEL_H
#define RSSCHANNEL_H
#include <QDateTime>
#include <QtXml/QDomElement>
#include <QtXml/QDomNode>
#include <QList>
#include <QObject>
#include <QtQml/QQmlListProperty>
#include <QString>
#include <cm-lib_global.h>
#include <rss/rss-image.h>
#include <rss/rss-item.h>
namespace cm {
namespace rss {
class CMLIBSHARED_EXPORT RssChannel : public QObject
{
    Q_OBJECT
    Q_PROPERTY(QString ui_description READ description CONSTANT)
    Q_PROPERTY(cm::rss::RssImage* ui_image READ image CONSTANT)
    Q_PROPERTY(QQmlListProperty<cm::rss::RssItem> ui_items READ
                                                ui_items CONSTANT)
```

```
      Q_PROPERTY(QString ui_link READ link CONSTANT)
      Q_PROPERTY(QString ui_title READ title CONSTANT)
  public:
      RssChannel(QObject* parent = nullptr, const QDomNode& domNode =
  QDomNode());
      ~RssChannel();
      void addItem(RssItem* item);
      const QString& description() const;
      RssImage* image() const;
      const QList<RssItem*>& items() const;
      const QString& link() const;
      void setImage(RssImage* image);
      const QString& title() const;
      QQmlListProperty<RssItem> ui_items();
      static RssChannel* fromXml(const QByteArray& xmlData, QObject*
                                              parent = nullptr);
  private:
      class Implementation;
      QScopedPointer<Implementation> implementation;
  };
  }}
  #endif
```

rss-channel.cpp:

```
  #include "rss-channel.h"
  #include <QtXml/QDomDocument>
  namespace cm {
  namespace rss {·
  class RssChannel::Implementation
  {
  public:
      QString description;             // Mandatory.  Phrase or sentence
  describing the channel.
      RssImage* image{nullptr};        // Optional.  Image representing the
  channel.
      QList<RssItem*> items;           // Optional.  Collection representing
  stories.
      QString link;                    // Mandatory.  URL to the corresponding
  HTML website.
      QString title;                   // Mandatory.  THe name of the Channel.
      void update(const QDomNode& domNode)
      {
          QDomElement channelDescription =
  domNode.firstChildElement("description");
          if(!channelDescription.isNull()) {
              description = channelDescription.text();
          }
```

```
            QDomElement channelLink = domNode.firstChildElement("link");
            if(!channelLink.isNull()) {
                link = channelLink.text();
            }
            QDomElement channelTitle = domNode.firstChildElement("title");
            if(!channelTitle.isNull()) {
                title = channelTitle.text();
            }
        }
};
RssChannel::RssChannel(QObject* parent, const QDomNode& domNode)
    : QObject(parent)
{
    implementation.reset(new Implementation());
    implementation->update(domNode);
}
RssChannel::~RssChannel()
{
}
void RssChannel::addItem(RssItem* item)
{
    if(!implementation->items.contains(item)) {
        item->setParent(this);
        implementation->items.push_back(item);
    }
}
const QString&  RssChannel::description() const
{
    return implementation->description;
}
RssImage* RssChannel::image() const
{
    return implementation->image;
}
const QList<RssItem*>&  RssChannel::items() const
{
    return implementation->items;
}
const QString&  RssChannel::link() const
{
    return implementation->link;
}
void RssChannel::setImage(RssImage* image)
{
    if(implementation->image) {
        implementation->image->deleteLater();
        implementation->image = nullptr;
    }
```

```
        image->setParent(this);
        implementation->image = image;
    }
    const QString& RssChannel::title() const
    {
        return implementation->title;
    }
    QQmlListProperty<RssItem> RssChannel::ui_items()
    {
        return QQmlListProperty<RssItem>(this, implementation->items);
    }
    RssChannel* RssChannel::fromXml(const QByteArray& xmlData, QObject* parent)
    {
        QDomDocument doc;
        doc.setContent(xmlData);
        auto channelNodes = doc.elementsByTagName("channel");
        // Rss must have 1 channel
        if(channelNodes.size() != 1) return nullptr;
        RssChannel* channel = new RssChannel(parent, channelNodes.at(0));
        auto imageNodes = doc.elementsByTagName("image");
        if(imageNodes.size() > 0) {
            channel->setImage(new RssImage(channel, imageNodes.at(0)));
        }
        auto itemNodes = doc.elementsByTagName("item");
        for (auto i = 0; i < itemNodes.size(); ++i) {
            channel->addItem(new RssItem(channel, itemNodes.item(i)));
        }
        return channel;
    }
}}
```

This class is broadly the same as the previous classes, but because this is the root object of our XML tree, we also have a static `fromXml()` method. The goal here is to take the byte array from the RSS web request response containing the RSS feed XML and have the method create an RSS Channel, Image, and Items hierarchy for us.

We pass the XML byte array into the Qt `QDomDocument` class, much like we have done previously with JSON and the `QJsonDocument` class. We find the `<channel>` tag using the `elementsByTagName()` method and then construct a new `RssChannel` object using that tag as the `QDomNode` parameter of the constructor. The `RssChannel` populates its own properties, thanks to the `update()` method. We then locate the `<image>` and `<item>` child nodes and create new `RssImage` and `RssItem` instances that are added to the root `RssChannel` object. Again, the classes are capable of populating their own properties from the supplied `QDomNode`.

Before we forget, let's also register the classes in `main()`:

```
qmlRegisterType<cm::rss::RssChannel>("CM", 1, 0, "RssChannel");
qmlRegisterType<cm::rss::RssImage>("CM", 1, 0, "RssImage");
qmlRegisterType<cm::rss::RssItem>("CM", 1, 0, "RssItem");
```

We can now add an `RssChannel` to our `MasterController` for the UI to bind to:

1. In `MasterController`, add a new `rssChannel` private member variable of the `RssChannel*` type
2. Add an `rssChannel()` accessor method
3. Add a `rssChannelChanged()` signal
4. Add a `Q_PROPERTY` named `ui_rssChannel` using the accessor for `READ` and signal for `NOTIFY`

Rather than creating one construction when we don't have any RSS data to feed it, we'll do it in the RSS reply delegate:

```
void MasterController::onRssReplyReceived(int statusCode, QByteArray body)
{
    qDebug() << "Received RSS request response code " << statusCode << ":";
    qDebug() << body;
    if(implementation->rssChannel) {
        implementation->rssChannel->deleteLater();
        implementation->rssChannel = nullptr;
        emit rssChannelChanged();
    }
    implementation->rssChannel = RssChannel::fromXml(body, this);
    emit rssChannelChanged();
}
```

We perform some housekeeping that checks whether we already have an old channel object in memory and if we do, it safely deletes it using the `deleteLater()` method of `QObject`. We then go ahead and construct a new channel using the XML data from the web request.

> **TIP**
>
> Always use `deleteLater()` on `QObject` derived classes rather than the standard C++ `delete` keyword as the destruction will be synchronized with the event loop and you will minimize the risk of unexpected exceptions.

We will display the RSS items in the response in a similar way to how we managed the search results, with a `ListView` and associated delegate. Add `RssItemDelegate.qml` to `cm-ui/components` and perform the usual steps of editing the `components.qrc` and `qmldir` files:

```
import QtQuick 2.9
import assets 1.0
import CM 1.0
Item {
    property RssItem rssItem
    implicitWidth: parent.width
    implicitHeight: background.height
    Rectangle {
        id: background
        width: parent.width
        height: textPubDate.implicitHeight + textTitle.implicitHeight +
                    borderBottom.height + (Style.sizeItemMargin * 3)
        color: Style.colourPanelBackground
        Text {
            id: textPubDate
            anchors {
                top: parent.top
                left: parent.left
                right: parent.right
                margins: Style.sizeItemMargin
            }
            text: Qt.formatDateTime(rssItem.ui_pubDate, "ddd, d MMM
                                                yyyy @ h:mm ap")
            font {
                pixelSize: Style.pixelSizeDataControls
                italic: true
                weight: Font.Light
            }
            color: Style.colorItemDateFont
        }
        Text {
            id: textTitle
```

```
        anchors {
            top: textPubDate.bottom
            left: parent.left
            right: parent.right
            margins: Style.sizeItemMargin
        }
        text: rssItem.ui_title
        font {
            pixelSize: Style.pixelSizeDataControls
        }
        color: Style.colorItemTitleFont
        wrapMode: Text.Wrap
    }
    Rectangle {
        id: borderBottom
        anchors {
            top: textTitle.bottom
            left: parent.left
            right: parent.right
            topMargin: Style.sizeItemMargin
        }
        height: 1
        color: Style.colorItemBorder
    }
    MouseArea {
        anchors.fill: parent
        cursorShape: Qt.PointingHandCursor
        hoverEnabled: true
        onEntered: background.state = "hover"
        onExited: background.state = ""
        onClicked: if(rssItem.ui_link !== "") {
                    Qt.openUrlExternally(rssItem.ui_link);
                }
    }
    states: [
        State {
            name: "hover"
            PropertyChanges {
                target: background
                color: Style.colourPanelBackgroundHover
            }
        }
    ]
  }
}
```

To support this component, we will need to add a few more Style properties:

```
readonly property color colourItemBackground: "#fefefe"
readonly property color colourItemBackgroundHover: "#efefef"
readonly property color colorItemBorder: "#efefef"
readonly property color colorItemDateFont: "#636363"
readonly property color colorItemTitleFont: "#131313"
readonly property real sizeItemMargin: 5
```

We can now utilize this delegate in `RssView`:

```
import QtQuick 2.9
import assets 1.0
import components 1.0
Item {
    Rectangle {
        anchors.fill: parent
        color: Style.colourBackground
    }
    ListView {
        id: itemsView
        anchors {
            top: parent.top
            left: parent.left
            right: parent.right
            bottom: commandBar.top
            margins: Style.sizeHeaderMargin
        }
        clip: true
        model: masterController.ui_rssChannel ?
masterController.ui_rssChannel.ui_items : 0
        delegate: RssItemDelegate {
            rssItem: modelData
        }
    }
    CommandBar {
        id: commandBar
        commandList:
masterController.ui_commandController.ui_rssViewContextCommands
    }
}
```

Build and run, navigate to the RSS View, and click on the **Refresh button to make the web request and display the response:**

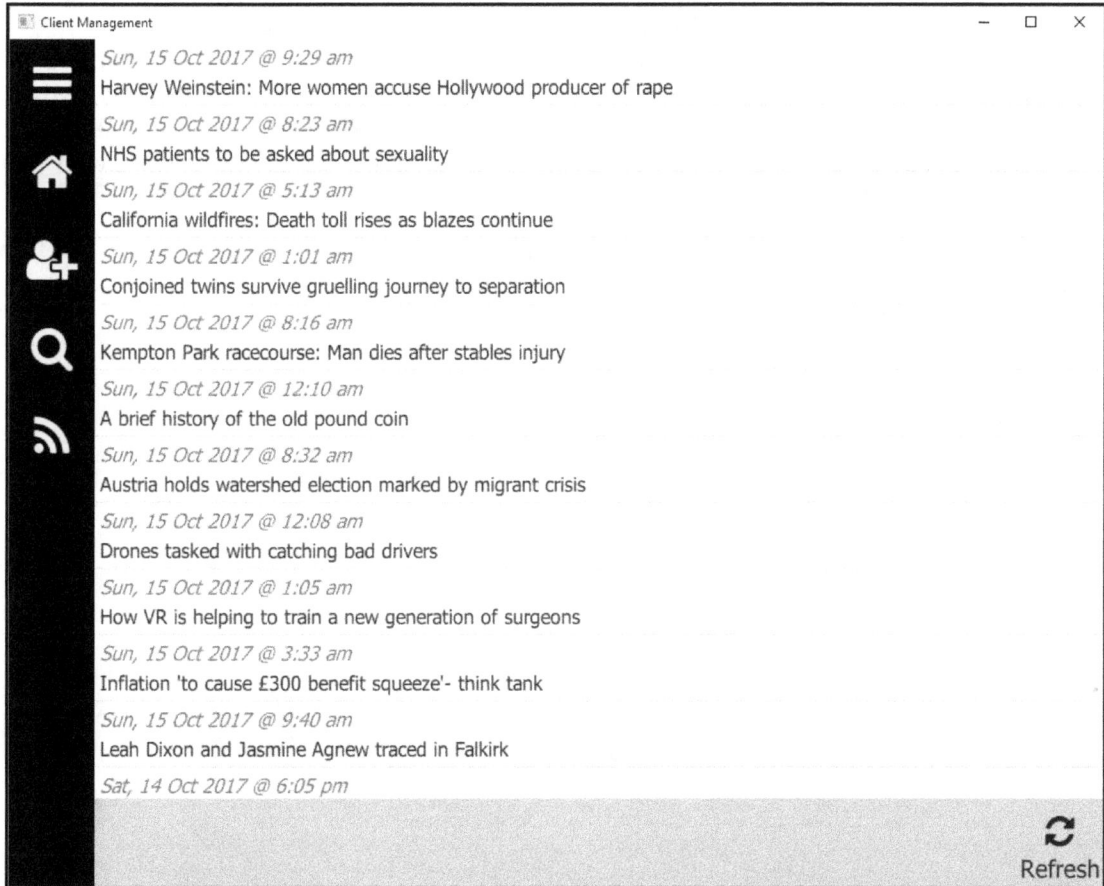

Hover over the items to see the cursor effects and click on an item to open it in your default web browser. Qt handles this action for us in the `Qt.openUrlExternally()` method, to which we pass the RSS Item `link` property.

Summary

In this chapter, we extended our reach outside of our application and began interacting with external APIs using HTTP requests over the internet. We abstracted the Qt functionality using our own interfaces to improve decoupling and make our components more test friendly. We took a quick look at RSS and its structure and how to process XML node trees using Qt's XML module. Finally, we reinforced the great UI work we've been doing and added an interactive view to display an RSS feed and launch the default web browser for a given URL.

In Chapter 9, *Wrapping Up*, we will take a look at the steps required to package our application for deployment to other computers.

9
Wrapping Up

In this chapter, we will mop up a couple of subjects that didn't quite make it into the earlier chapters. We'll make our application more testable by moving object creation into an object factory. We'll make our UI even more dynamic by adding scaling capabilities. `EnumeratorDecorator` properties get their own UI components, and we'll put them to use when we add contact management. Finally, we'll wrap everything up by packaging and deploying our application. We will cover the following topics:

- Object factories
- Dynamic UI scaling
- Adding an image to the Dashboard
- Enumerator selectors
- Managing Contacts
- Deployment and installation of our application

Object factory

In a larger system with more comprehensive `MasterController` tests in place, having all of that object creation hard-coded inside the private implementation will cause problems because of the tight coupling between the `MasterController` and its dependencies. One option will be to create all the other objects in `main()` instead and inject them into the `MasterController` constructor as we have done with the other controllers. This will mean injecting a lot of constructor parameters, and it is handy to be able to keep the `MasterController` instance as the parent of all the other objects, so we will inject a single object factory that the controller can use for all of its object creation needs instead.

The critical part of this factory pattern is to hide everything behind interfaces, so when testing `MasterController`, you can pass in a mock factory and control all the object creation. In `cm-lib`, create a new `i-object-factory.h` header file in `source/framework`:

```
#ifndef IOBJECTFACTORY_H
#define IOBJECTFACTORY_H

#include <controllers/i-command-controller.h>
#include <controllers/i-database-controller.h>
#include <controllers/i-navigation-controller.h>
#include <models/client.h>
#include <models/client-search.h>
#include <networking/i-network-access-manager.h>
#include <networking/i-web-request.h>

namespace cm {
namespace framework {

class IObjectFactory
{
public:
    virtual ~IObjectFactory(){}

    virtual models::Client* createClient(QObject* parent) const = 0;
    virtual models::ClientSearch* createClientSearch(QObject* parent,
controllers::IDatabaseController* databaseController) const = 0;
    virtual controllers::ICommandController*
createCommandController(QObject* parent, controllers::IDatabaseController*
databaseController, controllers::INavigationController*
navigationController, models::Client* newClient, models::ClientSearch*
clientSearch, networking::IWebRequest* rssWebRequest) const = 0;
    virtual controllers::IDatabaseController*
createDatabaseController(QObject* parent) const = 0;
    virtual controllers::INavigationController*
createNavigationController(QObject* parent) const = 0;
    virtual networking::INetworkAccessManager*
createNetworkAccessManager(QObject* parent) const = 0;
    virtual networking::IWebRequest* createWebRequest(QObject* parent,
networking::INetworkAccessManager* networkAccessManager, const QUrl& url)
const = 0;
};

}}

#endif
```

All the objects we will create will be moved behind interfaces apart from the models. This is because they are essentially just data containers, and we can easily create real instances in a test scenario with no side effects.

> We will skip that exercise here for brevity and leave it as an exercise for the reader. Use `IDatabaseController` as an example or refer to the code samples.

With the factory interface available, change the `MasterController` constructor to take an instance as a dependency:

```
MasterController::MasterController(QObject* parent, IObjectFactory*
objectFactory)
    : QObject(parent)
{
    implementation.reset(new Implementation(this, objectFactory));
}
```

We pass the object through to `Implementation` and store it in a private member variable as we have done numerous times before. With the factory available, we can now move all the `new` based object creation statements into a concrete implementation of the `IObjectFactory` interface (the `ObjectFactory` class) and replace those statements in `MasterController` with something more abstract and testable:

```
Implementation(MasterController* _masterController, IObjectFactory*
_objectFactory)
    : masterController(_masterController)
    , objectFactory(_objectFactory)
{
    databaseController =
objectFactory->createDatabaseController(masterController);
    clientSearch = objectFactory->createClientSearch(masterController,
databaseController);
    navigationController =
objectFactory->createNavigationController(masterController);
    networkAccessManager =
objectFactory->createNetworkAccessManager(masterController);
    rssWebRequest = objectFactory->createWebRequest(masterController,
networkAccessManager,
QUrl("http://feeds.bbci.co.uk/news/rss.xml?edition=uk"));
    QObject::connect(rssWebRequest, &IWebRequest::requestComplete,
masterController, &MasterController::onRssReplyReceived);
    newClient = objectFactory->createClient(masterController);
    commandController =
objectFactory->createCommandController(masterController,
```

```
databaseController, navigationController, newClient, clientSearch,
rssWebRequest);
}
```

Now, when testing `MasterController`, we can pass in a mock implementation of the `IObjectFactory` interface and control the creation of objects. In addition to implementing `ObjectFactory` and passing it to `MasterController` when we instantiate it, one further change is that in `main.cpp`, we now need to register the interfaces to `NavigationController` and `CommandController`, rather than the concrete implementations. We do this by simply swapping out the `qmlRegisterType` statements with the `qmlRegisterUncreatableType` companion:

```
qmlRegisterUncreatableType<cm::controllers::INavigationController>("CM", 1,
0, "INavigationController", "Interface");
qmlRegisterUncreatableType<cm::controllers::ICommandController>("CM", 1, 0,
"ICommandController", "Interface");
```

UI scaling

We've focused a lot on responsive UI in this book, using anchors and relative positioning where possible so that when the user resizes the window, the contents scale and adjust themselves appropriately. We've also pulled all the "hard-coded" properties like sizes and colors into a centralized Style object.

If we pick a property concerned with sizing, for example, `sizeScreenMargin`, it currently has a fixed value of `20`. If we decide to increase the starting size of our **Window** element in `MasterView`, this screen margin size will remain the same. Now, it's really easy to increase the screen margin too, thanks to the Style object, but it would be nice if all the hard-coded properties could scale up and down dynamically along with our **Window** element. That way, we can try out different window sizes without having to update Style each time.

As we've already seen, the flexibility of QML is extended even further with the built-in JavaScript support, and we can do just that.

First, let's create new width and height properties for the window in Style:

```
readonly property real widthWindow: 1920
readonly property real heightWindow: 1080
```

Use these new properties in `MasterView`:

```
Window {
    width: Style.widthWindow
    height: Style.heightWindow
    ....
}
```

All the size properties in Style that we've created so far are relevant to this window size of 1920 x 1080, so let's record that as new properties in Style:

```
readonly property real widthWindowReference: 1920
readonly property real heightWindowReference: 1080
```

We can then use the reference sizes and the actual sizes to calculate scaling factors in the horizontal and vertical axes. So in simple terms, if we design everything with a window width of 1,000 in mind and then we set the window to be 2,000 wide, we want everything to scale horizontally by a factor of 2. Add the following functions to Style:

```
function hscale(size) {
    return Math.round(size * (widthWindow / widthWindowReference))
}
function vscale(size) {
    return Math.round(size * (heightWindow / heightWindowReference))
}
function tscale(size) {
    return Math.round((hscale(size) + vscale(size)) / 2)
}
```

The `hscale` and `vscale` functions calculate the horizontal and vertical scaling factors respectively. For certain size properties like pixel size for fonts, there is no independent width and height, so we can calculate an average of the horizontal and vertical scales using the `tscale` function.

We can then wrap any properties we want to scale in the appropriate function. For example, our screen margin can use the `tscale` function:

```
readonly property real sizeScreenMargin: tscale(20)
```

Now, not only can you increase the initial size of the window in Style, but your selected properties will automatically scale to the new size.

A really useful module you can add to help with sizing is `QtQuick.Window`. We already added this to `MasterView` in order to access the Window element. There is another object in that module, Screen, which makes available information regarding the user's display. It contains properties for things like the width and height of the screen, and orientation and pixel density, which can be useful if you're working with high DPI displays such as the Microsoft Surface or Macbook. You can use these values in conjunction with your Style properties to do things such as making your window fullscreen, or make it 50% of the screen size and positioning it in the center of the display.

Dashboard

A Dashboard or "home page" is a great place to welcome users and present the current state of play. Daily messages, facts and figures, performance charts, or simply some company branding can all help orient and focus the user. Let's jazz up our Dashboard view a little and demonstrate how to display images to boot.

Grab an image of your choice that has a 1:1 aspect ratio, which means that the width is the same as the height. It's not necessary to be square, it's just simpler to manage the scaling for the purposes of this example. I have picked the **Packt** logo, which is 500 x 500 pixels, and which I have saved as `packt-logo-500x500.jpg`. Save it to `cm/cm-ui/assets` and add it to our `assets.qrc` resources:

```
<file alias="packt-logo-500x500">assets/packt-logo-500x500.jpg</file>
```

Add some new Style properties, leveraging our new scaling capabilities:

```
readonly property color colourDashboardBackground: "#f36f24"
readonly property color colourDashboardFont: "#ffffff"
readonly property int pixelSizeDashboard: tscale(36)
readonly property real sizeDashboardLogo: tscale(500)
```

Then, we can add our image to `DashboardView`:

```
Item {
    Rectangle {
        anchors.fill: parent
        color: Style.colourDashboardBackground
        Image {
            id: logo
            source: "qrc:/assets/packt-logo-500x500"
            anchors.centerIn: parent
```

```
            width: Style.sizeDashboardLogo
            height: Style.sizeDashboardLogo
        }
        Text {
            anchors {
                top: logo.bottom
                horizontalCenter: logo.horizontalCenter
            }
            text: "Client Management System"
            color: Style.colourDashboardFont
            font.pixelSize: Style.pixelSizeDashboard
        }
    }
}
```

Now, when we go to the Dashboard, we can see something a bit more stimulating:

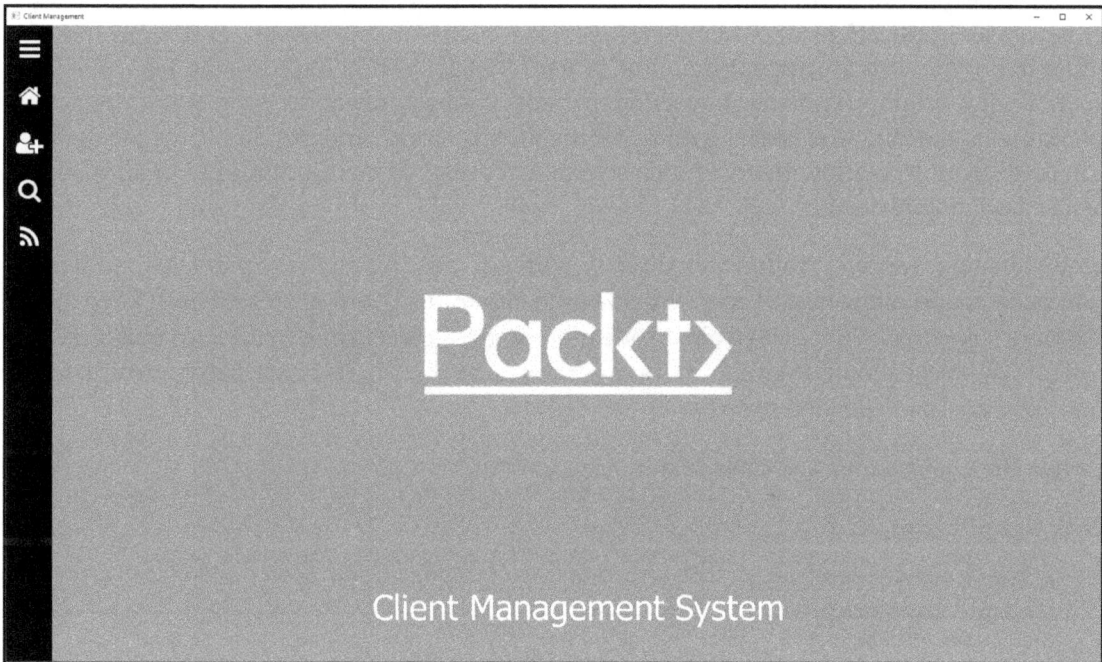

Enumerator selectors

Back in `Chapter 5`, *Data*, we created a Contact model where we implemented a `ContactType` property with an `EnumeratorDecorator`. For the other string-based properties we've worked with in the book, a simple textbox is a fine solution for capturing data, but how can we capture an enumerated value? The user can't be expected to know the underlying integer values of the enumerator, and asking them to type in a string representation of the option they want is asking for trouble. What we really want is a drop-down list that somehow utilizes the `contactTypeMapper` container we added to the class. We'd like to present the string descriptions to the user to pick from but then store the integer value in the `EnumeratorDecorator` object.

Desktop applications generally present drop-down lists in a particular way, with some kind of selector you press that then pops out (or more accurately, drops down!) a scrollable list of options to choose from. However, QML is geared toward not only cross-platform, but cross-device applications, too. Many laptops have touch capable screens, and more and more hybrid devices are appearing in the market that act as both laptops and tablets. As such, it's important to consider how "finger friendly" our application is, even if we're not planning on building the next big thing for the mobile stores, and the classic drop-down list can be difficult to work with on a touch screen. Let's instead use a button-based approach as used on mobile devices.

Unfortunately, we can't really work directly with our existing `std::map` in QML, so we will need to add a few new classes to bridge the gap for us. We'll represent each key/value pair as a `DropDownValue` and hold a collection of these objects in a `DropDown` object. A `DropDown` object should take a `std::map<int, QString>` in its constructor and create the `DropDownValue` collection for us.

Create the `DropDownValue` class first in `cm-lib/source/data`.

`dropdown-value.h`:

```
#ifndef DROPDOWNVALUE_H
#define DROPDOWNVALUE_H
#include <QObject>
#include <cm-lib_global.h>
namespace cm {
namespace data {
class CMLIBSHARED_EXPORT DropDownValue : public QObject
{
    Q_OBJECT
    Q_PROPERTY(int ui_key MEMBER key CONSTANT )
    Q_PROPERTY(QString ui_description MEMBER description CONSTANT)
```

```
public:
    DropDownValue(QObject* parent = nullptr, int key = 0, const QString&
description = "");
    ~DropDownValue();
public:
    int key{0};
    QString description{""};
};
}}
#endif
```

dropdown-value.cpp:

```
#include "dropdown-value.h"
namespace cm {
namespace data {
DropDownValue::DropDownValue(QObject* parent, int _key, const QString&
_description)
        : QObject(parent)
{
    key = _key;
    description = _description;
}
DropDownValue::~DropDownValue()
{
}
}}
```

There's nothing complicated here, it's just a QML friendly wrapper for an integer value and associated string description.

Next, create the DropDown class, again in cm-lib/source/data.

dropdown.h:

```
#ifndef DROPDOWN_H
#define DROPDOWN_H
#include <QObject>
#include <QtQml/QQmlListProperty>
#include <cm-lib_global.h>
#include <data/dropdown-value.h>
namespace cm {
namespace data {
class CMLIBSHARED_EXPORT DropDown : public QObject
{
    Q_OBJECT
    Q_PROPERTY(QQmlListProperty<cm::data::DropDownValue> ui_values READ
ui_values CONSTANT)
```

```
public:
    explicit DropDown(QObject* _parent = nullptr, const std::map<int,
QString>& values = std::map<int, QString>());
    ~DropDown();
public:
    QQmlListProperty<DropDownValue> ui_values();
public slots:
    QString findDescriptionForDropdownValue(int valueKey) const;
private:
    class Implementation;
    QScopedPointer<Implementation> implementation;
};
}}
#endif
```

dropdown.cpp:

```
#include "dropdown.h"

namespace cm {
namespace data {
class DropDown::Implementation
{
public:
    Implementation(DropDown* _dropdown, const std::map<int, QString>&
_values)
        : dropdown(_dropdown)
    {
        for(auto pair : _values) {
            values.append(new DropDownValue(_dropdown, pair.first,
pair.second));
        }
    }
    DropDown* dropdown{nullptr};
    QList<DropDownValue*> values;
};
DropDown::DropDown(QObject* parent, const std::map<int, QString>& values)
    : QObject(parent)
{
    implementation.reset(new DropDown::Implementation(this, values));
}
DropDown::~DropDown()
{
}
QString DropDown::findDescriptionForDropdownValue(int valueKey) const
{
    for (auto value : implementation->values) {
        if (value->key == valueKey) {
```

```
            if(!value->description.isEmpty()) {
                return value->description;
            }
            break;
        }
    }
    return "Select >";
}
QQmlListProperty<DropDownValue> DropDown::ui_values()
{
    return QQmlListProperty<DropDownValue>(this, implementation->values);
}
}}
```

As discussed, we implement a constructor that takes the same kind of `std::map` that we use in our `EnumeratorDecorator` class and create a collection of `DropDownValue` objects based on it. The UI can then access that collection via the `ui_values` property. The other capability we provide for the UI is via the `findDescriptionForDropdownValue` public slot, and this allows the UI to take a selected integer value from an `EnumeratorDecorator` and get the corresponding text description. If there is no current selection (that is, the description is an empty string), then we will return `Select >` to denote to the user that they need to make a selection.

As we will use these new types in QML, we need to register them in `main.cpp`:

```
qmlRegisterType<cm::data::DropDown>("CM", 1, 0, "DropDown");
qmlRegisterType<cm::data::DropDownValue>("CM", 1, 0, "DropDownValue");
```

Add a new `DropDown` property to the Contact named `ui_contactTypeDropDown` and in the constructor, instantiate the member variable with the `contactTypeMapper`. Now, whenever a Contact is presented in the UI, the associated `DropDown` will be available. This can quite easily go into a dedicated component like a drop-down manager instead, if you wanted to reuse drop-downs throughout the application, but for this example, let's avoid the additional complexity.

We will also need to be able to add a new contact object from the UI, so add a new public slot to `Client`:

```
void Client::addContact()
{
    contacts->addEntity(new Contact(this));
    emit contactsChanged();
}
```

With the C++ done, we can move on to the UI implementation.

We will need a couple of components for the dropdown selection. When presenting an `EnumeratorDecorator` property, we want to display the currently selected value, just as we do with our string editor. Visually, it will resemble a button with the associated string description as its label and when pressed, the user will be transitioned to the second component that is essentially a view. This subview will take up the whole of the content frame and present a list of all the available enumerated options, again represented as buttons. When the user makes their selection by pressing one of the buttons, they will be transitioned back to the original view, and their selection will be updated in the original component.

First, we'll create the view the user will transition to, which will list all the available options. To support this, we need a few additional properties in Style:

```
readonly property color colourDataSelectorBackground: "#131313"
readonly property color colourDataControlsBackgroundSelected: "#f36f24"
readonly property color colourDataSelectorFont: "#ffffff"
readonly property int sizeDataControlsRadius: tscale(5)
```

Create `EnumeratorSelectorView.qml` in `cm-ui/components`:

```
import QtQuick 2.9
import QtQuick.Controls 2.2
import CM 1.0
import assets 1.0
Item {
    id: stringSelectorView
    property DropDown dropDown
    property EnumeratorDecorator enumeratorDecorator
    property int selectedValue
    ScrollView {
        id: scrollView
        visible: true
        anchors.fill: parent
        anchors {
            top: parent.bottom
             left: parent.left
             right: parent.right
             bottom: parent.top
             margins: Style.sizeScreenMargin
        }
        Flow {
            flow: Grid.TopToBottom
            spacing: Style.sizeControlSpacing
            height: scrollView.height
            Repeater {
```

```
                        id: repeaterAnswers
                        model: dropDown.ui_values
                        delegate:
                            Rectangle {
                                property bool isSelected: modelData.ui_key.ui_value
=== enumeratorDecorator.ui_value
                                width: Style.widthDataControls
                                height: Style.heightDataControls
                                radius: Style.sizeDataControlsRadius
                                color: isSelected ?
Style.colourDataControlsBackgroundSelected :
Style.colourDataSelectorBackground
                                Text {
                                    anchors {
                                        fill: parent
                                        margins: Style.heightDataControls / 4
                                    }
                                    text: modelData.ui_description
                                    color: Style.colourDataSelectorFont
                                    font.pixelSize: Style.pixelSizeDataControls
                                    verticalAlignment: Qt.AlignVCenter
                                }
                                MouseArea {
                                    anchors.fill: parent
                                    onClicked: {
                                        selectedValue = modelData.ui_key;
                                        contentFrame.pop();
                                    }
                                }
                            }
                    }
                }
            }
        Binding {
            target: enumeratorDecorator
            property: "ui_value"
            value: selectedValue
        }
    }
```

Here, we use a **Repeater** element for the first time. A Repeater instantiates the QML element defined in its delegate property for each item it finds in its model property. We pass it the collection of `DropDownValue` objects as its model and create a delegate inline. The delegate is essentially another button with some selection code. We can create a new custom component and use that for the delegate instead to keep the code cleaner, but we'll skip that here for brevity. The key parts of this component are the `Binding` element that gives us the two-way binding to the supplied `EnumeratorDecorator`, and the `onClicked` event delegate in the `MouseArea`, which performs the update and pops this component off the stack, returning us to whichever view we came from.

Create a new `EnumeratorSelector.qml` in `cm-ui/components`:

```
import QtQuick 2.9
import QtQuick.Controls 2.2
import CM 1.0
import assets 1.0
Item {
    property DropDown dropDown
    property EnumeratorDecorator enumeratorDecorator
    id: enumeratorSelectorRoot
    height: width > textLabel.width + textAnswer.width ?
    Style.heightDataControls : Style.heightDataControls * 2
    Flow {
        anchors.fill: parent
        Rectangle {
            width: Style.widthDataControls
            height: Style.heightDataControls
            Text {
                id: textLabel
                anchors {
                    fill: parent
                    margins: Style.heightDataControls / 4
                }
                text: enumeratorDecorator.ui_label
                color: Style.colourDataControlsFont
                font.pixelSize: Style.pixelSizeDataControls
                verticalAlignment: Qt.AlignVCenter
            }
        }
        Rectangle {
            id: buttonAnswer
            width: Style.widthDataControls
            height: Style.heightDataControls
            radius: Style.sizeDataControlsRadius
            enabled: dropDown ? dropDown.ui_values.length > 0 : false
            color: Style.colourDataSelectorBackground
```

```
        Text {
            id: textAnswer
            anchors {
                fill: parent
                margins: Style.heightDataControls / 4
            }
            text:
dropDown.findDescriptionForDropdownValue(enumeratorDecorator.ui_value)
            color: Style.colourDataSelectorFont
            font.pixelSize: Style.pixelSizeDataControls
            verticalAlignment: Qt.AlignVCenter
        }
        MouseArea {
            anchors.fill: parent
            onClicked:
contentFrame.push("qrc:/components/EnumeratorSelectorView.qml",
 {dropDown: enumeratorSelectorRoot.dropDown,
 enumeratorDecorator: enumeratorSelectorRoot.enumeratorDecorator})
        }
    }
  }
}
```

This component has a lot of similarities to `StringEditorSingleLine` in its layout, but it replaces the Text element with a button representation. We grab the value from the bound `EnumeratorDecorator` and pass that to the slot we created on the `DropDown` class to get the string description for the currently selected value. When the user presses the button, the `onClicked` event of the `MouseArea` performs the same kind of view transition we've seen in `MasterView`, taking the user to the new `EnumeratorSelectorView`.

> We're cheating a bit here in that we are directly referencing the `StackView` in `MasterView` by its `contentFrame` ID. At design time, Qt Creator can't know what `contentFrame` is as it is in a totally different file, so it may flag it as an error, and you certainly won't get auto-completion. At runtime, however, this component will be part of the same QML hierarchy as `MasterView`, so it will be able to find it. This is a risky approach, because if another element in the hierarchy is also called `contentFrame`, then bad things may happen. A safer way to do this is to pass `contentFrame` all the way down through the QML hierarchy from `MasterView` as a `QtObject` property.

When we add or edit a Client, we currently ignore contacts and always have an empty collection. Let's take a look at how we can add objects to a collection and put our shiny new `EnumeratorSelector` to use while we're at it.

Contacts

We will need a handful of new UI components to manage our contacts. We've previously worked with an `AddressEditor` to look after our address details, so we'll continue in that mold and create a `ContactEditor` component. This component will display our collection of contacts, each of which will be represented by a `ContactDelegate`. Upon initially creating a new Client object, there won't be any contacts, so we also need some way for the user to add a new one. We'll enable that with a button press, and we'll create a new component for buttons we can add to a content view. Let's do that first.

To support this new component, as usual, we'll go ahead and add some properties to Style:

```
readonly property real widthFormButton: 240
readonly property real heightFormButton: 60
readonly property color colourFormButtonBackground: "#f36f24"
readonly property color colourFormButtonFont: "#ffffff"
readonly property int pixelSizeFormButtonIcon: 32
readonly property int pixelSizeFormButtonText: 22
readonly property int sizeFormButtonRadius: 5
```

Create `FormButton.qml` in `cm-ui/components`:

```
import QtQuick 2.9
import CM 1.0
import assets 1.0
Item {
    property alias iconCharacter: textIcon.text
    property alias description: textDescription.text
    signal formButtonClicked()
    width: Style.widthFormButton
    height: Style.heightFormButton
    Rectangle {
        id: background
        anchors.fill: parent
        color: Style.colourFormButtonBackground
        radius: Style.sizeFormButtonRadius
        Text {
            id: textIcon
            anchors {
                verticalCenter: parent.verticalCenter
                left: parent.left
                margins: Style.heightFormButton / 4
            }
            font {
                family: Style.fontAwesome
                pixelSize: Style.pixelSizeFormButtonIcon
```

```
                }
                color: Style.colourFormButtonFont
                text: "uf11a"
                horizontalAlignment: Text.AlignHCenter
                verticalAlignment: Text.AlignVCenter
            }
            Text {
                id: textDescription
                anchors {
                    left: textIcon.left
                    bottom: parent.bottom
                    top: parent.top
                    right: parent.right
                }
                font.pixelSize: Style.pixelSizeFormButtonText
                color: Style.colourFormButtonFont
                text: "SET ME!!"
                horizontalAlignment: Text.AlignHCenter
                verticalAlignment: Text.AlignVCenter
            }
            MouseArea {
                anchors.fill: parent
                cursorShape: Qt.PointingHandCursor
                hoverEnabled: true
                onEntered: background.state = "hover"
                onExited: background.state = ""
                onClicked: formButtonClicked()
            }
            states: [
                State {
                    name: "hover"
                    PropertyChanges {
                        target: background
                        color: Qt.darker(Style.colourFormButtonBackground)
                    }
                }
            ]
        }
    }
}
```

Here, we combine aspects of the NavigationButton and CommandButton controls we wrote earlier in the book. The only real difference is that it is intended for more free-form use in the main content frame rather than being constrained to one of the toolbars.

Next, let's add the component we'll use to display/edit a single Contact object. Create `ContactDelegate.qml` in `cm-ui/components`:

```qml
import QtQuick 2.9
import CM 1.0
import assets 1.0
Item {
    property Contact contact
    implicitWidth: flow.implicitWidth
    implicitHeight: flow.implicitHeight + borderBottom.implicitHeight +
Style.sizeItemMargin
    height: width > selectorType.width + textAddress.width +
Style.sizeScreenMargin
            ? selectorType.height + borderBottom.height +
Style.sizeItemMargin
            : selectorType.height + textAddress.height +
Style.sizeScreenMargin + borderBottom.height + Style.sizeItemMargin
    Flow {
        id: flow
        width: parent.width
        spacing: Style.sizeScreenMargin
        EnumeratorSelector {
            id: selectorType
            width: Style.widthDataControls
            dropDown: contact.ui_contactTypeDropDown
            enumeratorDecorator: contact.ui_contactType
        }
        StringEditorSingleLine {
            id: textAddress
            width: Style.widthDataControls
            stringDecorator: contact.ui_address
        }
    }
    Rectangle {
        id: borderBottom
        anchors {
            top: flow.bottom
            left: parent.left
            right: parent.right
            topMargin: Style.sizeItemMargin
        }
        height: 1
        color: Style.colorItemBorder
    }
}
```

This is much the same as the `RssItemDelegate` we added in Chapter 8, *Web Requests*. We add our new `EnumeratorSelector` and bind it to the `ui_contactType` property, using `ui_contactTypeDropDown` to provide the control with the drop-down information it needs.

Create `ContactsEditor.qml` in `cm-ui/components`:

```
import QtQuick 2.9
import CM 1.0
import assets 1.0
Panel {
    property Client client
    id: contactsEditorRoot
    contentComponent:
        Column {
            id: column
            spacing: Style.sizeControlSpacing
            Repeater {
                id: contactsView
                model: client.ui_contacts
                delegate:
                    ContactDelegate {
                        width: contactsEditorRoot.width
                        contact: modelData
                    }
            }
            FormButton {
                iconCharacter: "uf067"
                description: "Add Contact"
                onFormButtonClicked: {
                    client.addContact();
                }
            }
        }
}
```

We've already done all the hard work in our `ContactDelegate` and `FormButton` controls, so this is really short and sweet. We add everything to a `Panel` so that the look and feel will be consistent with the rest of the views. We use another `Repeater` so that we can spin up a `ContactDelegate` for every contact in the collection and immediately after the contacts, we display a button to add a new contact to the list. In order to do this, we call the `addContact()` method we added earlier in this chapter.

Now, we just need to add instances of our `ContactsEditor` to the `CreateClientView`:

```
ContactsEditor {
```

```
        width: scrollView.width
        client: newClient
        headerText: "Contact Details"
    }
```

We can also use the same component in `EditClientView`:

```
ContactsEditor {
    width: scrollView.width
    client: selectedClient
    headerText: "Contact Details"
}
```

That's it. **Build and Run, and you can add and edit contacts to your heart's content:**

Once you save a new client, if you take a look at the database, you will see that the **contacts array has been updated accordingly, as highlighted in the following screenshot:**

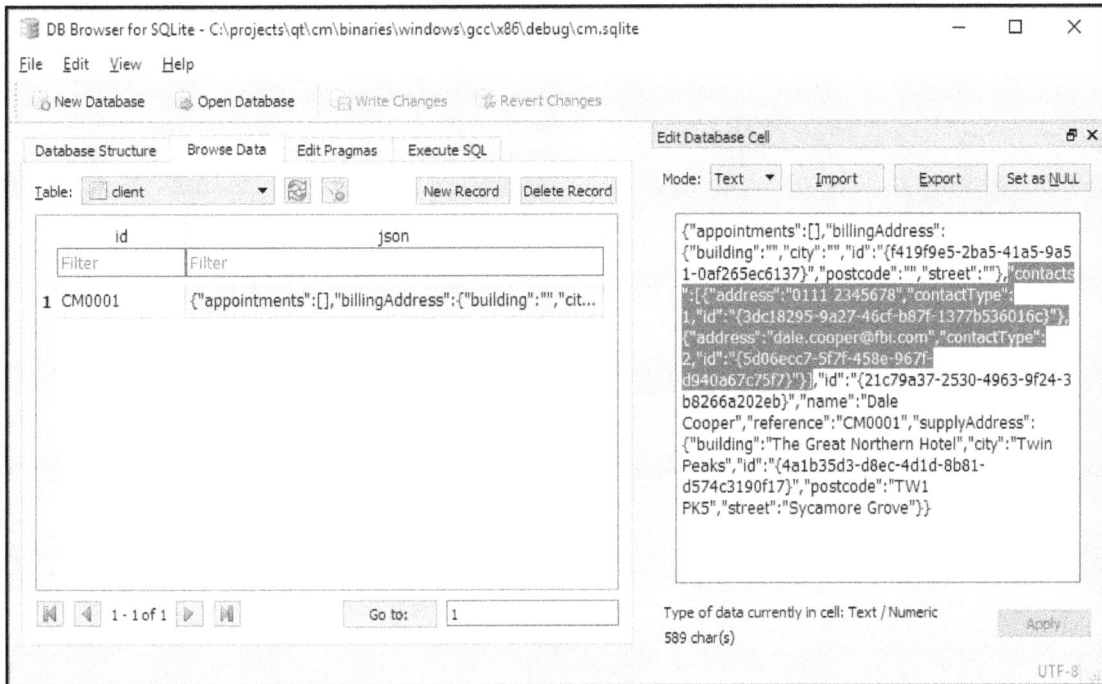

All that's left now is the appointments collection, and we've already covered all the skills you need to tackle that, so we'll leave that as an exercise for the reader and move on to the final topic—deploying our application to our end users.

Deployment preparation

The center piece of our application is the `cm-ui` executable. This is the file that gets launched by the end user and that opens graphical windows and orchestrates all the fancy stuff we've written. When we run the `cm-ui` project in Qt Creator, it opens the executable file for us and everything works perfectly. However, distributing our application to another user is unfortunately more complicated than simply plonking a copy of the executable on their machine and launching it.

Our executable has a variety of dependencies that need to be in place in order for it to run. A prime example of a dependency is our very own cm-lib library. Pretty much all of our business logic is hidden away in there, and without that functionality, our UI can't do much. The implementation details for dependency resolution across the various operating systems are complex and well beyond the scope of this book. However, the fundamental requirements of our application are the same, irrespective of the platform.

There are four categories of dependency that we need to consider and ensure that they are in place on our target user's machine in order for our application to function:

- Item 1: Custom libraries we've written or added to our solution manually. In this case, it is only the cm-lib library that we need to worry about.
- Item 2: The parts of the Qt framework that our application links to, both directly and indirectly. We already know some of these through the modules we've added to our .pro files, for example, the qml and quick modules require the QtQml and QtQuick components.
- Item 3: Any internal dependencies of the Qt framework itself. This includes platform-specific files, resources for the QML subsystem, and third-party libraries such as sqlite or openssl.
- Item 4: Any libraries required by the C++ compiler we have built the application with.

We've already worked extensively with item 1, back in Chapter 2, *Project Structure*, we put a lot of work into controlling exactly where that output goes. We haven't really needed to worry about items 2 and 3, because we have a full installation of the Qt Framework in our development machine and that takes care of everything for us. Similarly, item 4 is dictated by the kit we use, and if we have a compiler available on our machine, it follows that we have the libraries it needs too.

Identifying exactly what we need to copy for our end users (who more than likely don't have Qt or other development tools installed) can be an excruciating exercise. Even once we've done that, packaging everything up into a neat package or installer that is simple for the user to run can be a project in itself. Fortunately, Qt offers us some help in the form of bundled tools.

Linux and macOS X have a concept of application packages, whereby the application executable and all dependencies can be rolled up together into a single file that can then be easily distributed and launched at the click of a button. Windows is a bit more freestyle and if we want to bundle all of our files into a single installable file, we need to do a bit more work, but again, Qt comes to the rescue and comes with the fantastic Qt Installer Framework that simplifies it for us.

Let's take a look at each operating system in turn and produce an application package or installer for each.

OS X

First, build the solution using the kit of your choice in the **Release mode. You already know that if we press the Run button in Qt Creator, our app launches and all is well. However, navigate to the** `cm-ui.app` **file in Finder and try and launch it directly; with this, things aren't quite so rosy:**

The problem here is missing dependencies. We can use **otool** to take a look at what those dependencies are. First, copy the `cm-ui.app` package to a new directory—`cm/installer/osx`.

> This isn't strictly necessary, but I like to keep build and deployment files separate. This way, if we make a code change and rebuild the solution, we will only update the app in the binaries folder, and our deployment files remain untouched.

Next, have a poke around inside the app package and see what we're working with. In Finder, *Ctrl* and click on the `cm-ui.app` we just copied to the installer folder and select **Show Package Contents. The bit we're interested in is the** `Contents/MacOS` **folder. In there, you will find our** `cm-ui` **application executable.**

With that identified, open up a command terminal, navigate to `cm/installer/osx`, and run `otool` on the executable:

```
$ otool -L cm-ui.app/Contents/MacOS/cm-ui
```

You will see an output the same as (or similar to) the following:

```
cm-ui:
libcm-lib.1.dylib (compatibility version 1.0.0, current version 1.0.0)
@rpath/QtQuick.framework/Versions/5/QtQuick (compatibility version 5.9.0,
current version 5.9.1)
@rpath/QtQml.framework/Versions/5/QtQml (compatibility version 5.9.0,
current version 5.9.1)
@rpath/QtNetwork.framework/Versions/5/QtNetwork (compatibility version
5.9.0, current version 5.9.1)
@rpath/QtCore.framework/Versions/5/QtCore (compatibility version 5.9.0,
current version 5.9.1)
/System/Library/Frameworks/DiskArbitration.framework/Versions/A/DiskArbitra
tion (compatibility version 1.0.0, current version 1.0.0)
/System/Library/Frameworks/IOKit.framework/Versions/A/IOKit (compatibility
version 1.0.0, current version 275.0.0)
@rpath/QtGui.framework/Versions/5/QtGui (compatibility version 5.9.0,
current version 5.9.1)
@rpath/QtXml.framework/Versions/5/QtXml (compatibility version 5.9.0,
current version 5.9.1)
/System/Library/Frameworks/OpenGL.framework/Versions/A/OpenGL
(compatibility version 1.0.0, current version 1.0.0)
/System/Library/Frameworks/AGL.framework/Versions/A/AGL (compatibility
version 1.0.0, current version 1.0.0)
/usr/lib/libc++.1.dylib (compatibility version 1.0.0, current version
307.5.0)
/usr/lib/libSystem.B.dylib (compatibility version 1.0.0, current version
1238.50.2)
```

Let's remind ourselves of the dependencies we need to consider and look at how they relate to the output we've just seen:

- Custom libraries we've written or added to our solution manually (cm-lib). This is the libcm-lib.1.dylib reference. The fact that there is no path component suggests that the tool isn't quite sure where this file is located. Should it be in the same folder as the executable itself? Should it be in the standard /usr/lib/ folder? Fortunately, we can specify the location of this file when we package our app.
- The parts of the Qt framework that our application links to. QtQuick, QtQml, and such are all the framework modules we directly reference in our cm-ui code. Some of them are explicitly brought in via the QT variable in our cm-ui.pro file and others are implicitly included using things like QML.

- Any internal dependencies of the Qt framework itself. We don't see those listed earlier, but if we were to run otool against the `QtQuick` module, you would see that it is dependent on `QtQml`, `QtNetwork`, `QtGui`, and `QtCore`. There are also several system level libraries required, such as OpenGL, which we haven't explicitly coded against but are used by Qt.
- Any libraries required by the C++ compiler we have built the application with; `libc++.1.dylib` stands out here.

To bundle all of our dependencies manually, we can copy them all inside the app package and then perform some reconfiguration steps to update the location metadata we saw from otool.

Let's pick one of the framework dependencies—`QtQuick`—and quickly work through what we will have to do to achieve this, and then we'll move on to the really handy tool that does all of this very unpleasant grunt work for us.

First, we will create a `Frameworks` directory where the system will search for the bundled dependencies:

```
$ mkdir cm-ui.app/Contents/Frameworks
```

Next, we will physically copy the referenced file to that new directory. We know where to look for the existing file on our development machine, thanks to the preceding `LC_RPATH` entry, in this case `/Users/<Your Username>/Qt5.9.1/5.9.1/clang_64/lib`:

```
$ cp -R /Users/<Your Username>  /Qt5.9.1 /5.9.1/clang_64 /lib/
QtQuick.framework cm-ui.app/Contents/Frameworks
```

We then need to change the shared library identification name for the copied library file using `install_name_tool`:

```
$ install_name_tool -id @executable_path /../Frameworks /
QtQuick.framework/Versions/5/QtQuick cm-ui.app /Contents /Frameworks /
QtQuick.framework/Versions/5/QtQuick
```

The syntax here is `install_name_tool -id [New name] [Shared library file]`. To get to the library file (not the framework package, which is what we copied), we drill down to `Versions/5/QtQuick`. We set the ID of that binary to where the executable will look to find it, which, in this case, is in the `Frameworks` folder a level up (`../`) from the executable file itself.

Next, we also need to update the executable's list of dependencies to look in the correct place for this new file:

```
$ install_name_tool -change @rpath/QtQuick.framework/Versions/5/QtQuick
@executable_path/../Frameworks/QtQuick.framework/Versions/5/QtQuick cm-
ui.app/Contents/MacOs/cm-ui
```

The syntax here is `install_name_tool -change [old value] [new value] [executable file]`. We want to change the old `@rpath` entry for `QtQuick` to be the new Frameworks path we've just added. Again, we use the `@executable_path` variable so that the dependencies are always located in the same place relative to the executable. Now, the metadata in the executable and the shared library both match each other and relate to the `Frameworks` folder, which we have now added to our app package.

Remember, that's not all, because `QtQuick` itself has dependencies, so we will need to copy and reconfigure all of those files too and then check their dependencies. Once we've exhausted the whole dependency tree for our `cm-ui` executable, we also need to repeat the process for our `cm-lib` library. As you can imagine, this gets tedious very quickly.

Fortunately, the `macdeployqt` Qt Mac Deployment Tool is just what we need here. It scans an executable file for Qt dependencies and copies them across to our app package for us as well as for handling the reconfiguration work. The tool is located in the `bin` folder of the installed kit you have built the application with, for example, `/Qt/5.9.1/5.9.1/clang_64/bin`.

In a command terminal, execute `macdeployqt` as follows (assuming that you are in the `cm/installer/osx` directory):

```
$ <Path to bin>/macdeployqt cm-ui.app -qmldir=<Qt Projects>/cm/cm-ui -
libpath=<Qt Projects>/cm/binaries/osx/clang/x64/release
```

Remember to replace the parameters in angle brackets with the full paths on your system (or add the executable paths to your system PATH variable).

The `qmldir` flag tells the tool where to scan for QML imports and is set to our UI project folder. The `libpath` flag is used to specify where our compiled `cm-lib` file lives.

The output of this operation will be as follows:

```
File exists, skip copy: "cm-
ui.app/Contents/PlugIns/quick/libqtquick2plugin.dylib"
File exists, skip copy: "cm-
ui.app/Contents/PlugIns/quick/libqtquickcontrols2plugin.dylib"
File exists, skip copy: "cm-
ui.app/Contents/PlugIns/quick/libqtquickcontrols2materialstyleplugin.dylib"
File exists, skip copy: "cm-
ui.app/Contents/PlugIns/quick/libqtquickcontrols2universalstyleplugin.dylib
"
File exists, skip copy: "cm-
ui.app/Contents/PlugIns/quick/libwindowplugin.dylib"
File exists, skip copy: "cm-
ui.app/Contents/PlugIns/quick/libqtquicktemplates2plugin.dylib"
File exists, skip copy: "cm-
ui.app/Contents/PlugIns/quick/libqtquickcontrols2materialstyleplugin.dylib"
File exists, skip copy: "cm-
ui.app/Contents/PlugIns/quick/libqtquickcontrols2materialstyleplugin.dylib"
File exists, skip copy: "cm-
ui.app/Contents/PlugIns/quick/libqtquickcontrols2universalstyleplugin.dylib
"
File exists, skip copy: "cm-
ui.app/Contents/PlugIns/quick/libqtquickcontrols2universalstyleplugin.dylib
"
WARNING: Plugin "libqsqlodbc.dylib" uses private API and is not Mac App
store compliant.
WARNING: Plugin "libqsqlpsql.dylib" uses private API and is not Mac App
store compliant.
ERROR: no file at "/opt/local/lib/mysql55/mysql/libmysqlclient.18.dylib"
ERROR: no file at "/usr/local/lib/libpq.5.dylib"
```

Qt is a bit quirky with the SQL module, whereby if you use one SQL driver, it will try and package them all; however, we know that we are only using SQLite and don't need MySQL or PostgreSQL, so we can safely ignore those errors.

Once executed, you should be able to **Show Package Contents again in Finder and see all the dependencies ready and waiting for deployment, as illustrated:**

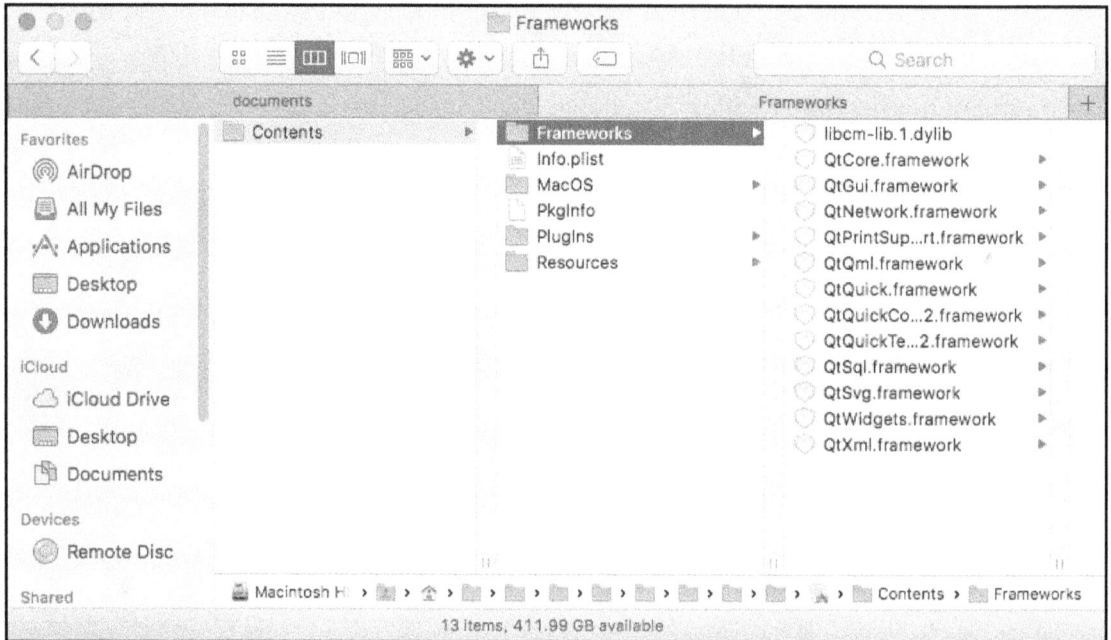

What a huge timesaver! It has created the appropriate file structure and copied all the Qt modules and plugins for us, along with our `cm-lib` shared library. Try and execute the `cm-ui.app` file now, and it should successfully launch the application.

Linux

Linux packaging and deployment is broadly similar to OS X, and we won't cover it in the same level of detail, so at least skim the OS X section first if you haven't already. As with all platforms, the first thing to do is build the solution using the kit of your choice in the **Release** mode in order to generate the binaries.

When building in Release mode for the first time, I received the "cannot find -lGL" error. This was because the dev libraries for OpenGL were not installed on my system. One way of obtaining these libraries is to install FreeGlut:

```
$ sudo apt-get update
$ sudo apt-get install build-essential
$ sudo apt-get install freeglut3-dev
```

Once compiled, copy the cm-ui binary to a new cm/installer/linux directory.

Next, we can take a look at what dependencies our application has. In a command terminal, change to the cm/installer/linux folder and run ldd:

```
$ ldd <Qt Projects>/cm/binaries/linux/gcc/x64/release/cm-ui
```

You will see an output similar to the following:

```
linux-vdso.so.1 => (0x00007ffdeb1c2000)
libcm-lib.so.1 => /usr/lib/libcm-lib.so.1 (0x00007f624243d000)
libQt5Gui.so.5 => /home/nick/Qt/5.9.1/gcc_64/lib/libQt5Gui.so.5
(0x00007f6241c8f000)
libQt5Qml.so.5 => /home/nick/Qt/5.9.1/gcc_64/lib/libQt5Qml.so.5
(0x00007f6241698000)
libQt5Xml.so.5 => /home/nick/Qt/5.9.1/gcc_64/lib/libQt5Xml.so.5
(0x00007f624145e000)
libQt5Core.so.5 => /home/nick/Qt/5.9.1/gcc_64/lib/libQt5Core.so.5
(0x00007f6240d24000)
libstdc++.so.6 => /usr/lib/x86_64-linux-gnu/libstdc++.so.6
(0x00007f62409a1000)
libgcc_s.so.1 => /lib/x86_64-linux-gnu/libgcc_s.so.1 (0x00007f624078b000)
libc.so.6 => /lib/x86_64-linux-gnu/libc.so.6 (0x00007f62403c1000)
libQt5Sql.so.5 => /home/nick/Qt/5.9.1/gcc_64/lib/libQt5Sql.so.5
(0x00007f6240179000)
libQt5Network.so.5 => /home/nick/Qt/5.9.1/gcc_64/lib/libQt5Network.so.5
(0x00007f623fde8000)
libpthread.so.0 => /lib/x86_64-linux-gnu/libpthread.so.0
(0x00007f623fbcb000)
libGL.so.1 => /usr/lib/x86_64-linux-gnu/mesa/libGL.so.1
(0x00007f623f958000)
libz.so.1 => /lib/x86_64-linux-gnu/libz.so.1 (0x00007f623f73e000)
libm.so.6 => /lib/x86_64-linux-gnu/libm.so.6 (0x00007f623f435000)
librt.so.1 => /lib/x86_64-linux-gnu/librt.so.1 (0x00007f623f22c000)
libicui18n.so.56 => /home/nick/Qt/5.9.1/gcc_64/lib/libicui18n.so.56
(0x00007f623ed93000)
libicuuc.so.56 => /home/nick/Qt/5.9.1/gcc_64/lib/libicuuc.so.56
(0x00007f623e9db000)
libicudata.so.56 => /home/nick/Qt/5.9.1/gcc_64/lib/libicudata.so.56
```

```
(0x00007f623cff7000)
libdl.so.2 => /lib/x86_64-linux-gnu/libdl.so.2 (0x00007f623cdf3000)
libgthread-2.0.so.0 => /usr/lib/x86_64-linux-gnu/libgthread-2.0.so.0
(0x00007f623cbf1000)
libglib-2.0.so.0 => /lib/x86_64-linux-gnu/libglib-2.0.so.0
(0x00007f623c8df000)
/lib64/ld-linux-x86-64.so.2 (0x0000562f21a5c000)
libexpat.so.1 => /lib/x86_64-linux-gnu/libexpat.so.1 (0x00007f623c6b6000)
libxcb-dri3.so.0 => /usr/lib/x86_64-linux-gnu/libxcb-dri3.so.0
(0x00007f623c4b2000)
libxcb-present.so.0 => /usr/lib/x86_64-linux-gnu/libxcb-present.so.0
(0x00007f623c2af000)
libxcb-sync.so.1 => /usr/lib/x86_64-linux-gnu/libxcb-sync.so.1
(0x00007f623c0a8000)
libxshmfence.so.1 => /usr/lib/x86_64-linux-gnu/libxshmfence.so.1
(0x00007f623bea4000)
libglapi.so.0 => /usr/lib/x86_64-linux-gnu/libglapi.so.0
(0x00007f623bc75000)
libXext.so.6 => /usr/lib/x86_64-linux-gnu/libXext.so.6 (0x00007f623ba63000)
libXdamage.so.1 => /usr/lib/x86_64-linux-gnu/libXdamage.so.1
(0x00007f623b85f000)
libXfixes.so.3 => /usr/lib/x86_64-linux-gnu/libXfixes.so.3
(0x00007f623b659000)
libX11-xcb.so.1 => /usr/lib/x86_64-linux-gnu/libX11-xcb.so.1
(0x00007f623b457000)
libX11.so.6 => /usr/lib/x86_64-linux-gnu/libX11.so.6 (0x00007f623b11c000)
libxcb-glx.so.0 => /usr/lib/x86_64-linux-gnu/libxcb-glx.so.0
(0x00007f623af03000)
libxcb-dri2.so.0 => /usr/lib/x86_64-linux-gnu/libxcb-dri2.so.0
(0x00007f623acfe000)
libxcb.so.1 => /usr/lib/x86_64-linux-gnu/libxcb.so.1 (0x00007f623aadb000)
libXxf86vm.so.1 => /usr/lib/x86_64-linux-gnu/libXxf86vm.so.1
(0x00007f623a8d5000)
libdrm.so.2 => /usr/lib/x86_64-linux-gnu/libdrm.so.2 (0x00007f623a6c4000)
libpcre.so.3 => /lib/x86_64-linux-gnu/libpcre.so.3 (0x00007f623a453000)
libXau.so.6 => /usr/lib/x86_64-linux-gnu/libXau.so.6 (0x00007f623a24e000)
libXdmcp.so.6 => /usr/lib/x86_64-linux-gnu/libXdmcp.so.6
(0x00007f623a048000)
```

That's some list of dependencies! Crucially, note the dependency on our `cm-lib` library:

```
libcm-lib.so.1 => /usr/lib/libcm-lib.so.1
```

This shows that the executable will look for our library in the `/usr/lib` folder, so let's ensure that it's available there before we move on by copying `libcm-lib.so.1` to `/usr/lib`:

```
$ sudo cp <Qt Projects>/cm/binaries/linux/gcc/x64/release/libcm-lib.so.1
/usr/lib
```

We can already guess what a nightmare managing all these dependencies manually will be, having discussed the OS X process and seen how many dependencies there are, so there must be a tool in our Kit's `bin` folder that does it all for us, right? Well, yes and no. There is no official Qt tool we get out of the box to do this for us like there is for OS X and Windows. Fortunately, a fantastic member of the Qt community `probonopd` has come to the rescue and plugged the gap with `linuxdeployqt`.

You can get a `linuxdeployqt` app image from the releases page of the GitHub project at `https://github.com/probonopd/linuxdeployqt`. Download the file (`linuxdeployqt-continuous-x86_64.AppImage`) and then make it executable:

```
$ chmod a+x <Path to downloaded file>/linuxdeployqt-continuous-
x86_64.AppImage
```

We can then execute it and have it work its dependency-based magic for us. Change the directory to `cm/installer/linux` first:

```
$ <Path to downloaded file>/linuxdeployqt-continuous-x86_64.AppImage cm-ui
-qmldir=<Qt Projects>/cm/cm-ui -appimage
```

The `qmldir` flag tells the tool where to scan for QML imports and is set to our UI project folder. The `appimage` flag is used to get the tool to create an application image file for us, which is a single file with everything bundled inside.

Things may not work perfectly the first time. Your output may look as follows:

```
ERROR: Desktop file missing, creating a default one (you will probably want
to edit it)
ERROR: Icon file missing, creating a default one (you will probably want to
edit it)
ERROR: "/usr/bin/qmake -query" exited with 1 : "qmake: could not exec
'/usr/lib/x86_64-linux-gnu/qt4/bin/qmake': No such file or directoryn"
ERROR: Qt path could not be determined from qmake on the $PATH
ERROR: Make sure you have the correct Qt on your $PATH
ERROR: You can check this with qmake -v
```

The first two errors are just because we haven't provided a desktop file or icon and defaults have been generated for us; we can ignore those. The rest are because `linuxdeployqt` doesn't know where `qmake` is. We can either provide the path as an extra parameter (`-qmake=<PATH>`), or to save us having to do it every time, we can add it to our PATH environment variable:

```
$ export PATH=<Qt Path>/5.9.1/gcc_64/bin/:$PATH
```

We can then check whether qmake can be found by trying to retrieve the version information:

```
$ qmake -v
```

If it is happy, you will see the version information:

```
QMake version 3.1
Using Qt version 5.9.1 in /home/nick/Qt/5.9.1/gcc_64/lib
```

With that fixed, we can now try running the `linuxdeployqt` command again. However, we've fixed one problem, but now experience another:

```
ERROR: Desktop file missing, creating a default one (you will probably want
to edit it)
ERROR: Icon file missing, creating a default one (you will probably want to
edit it)
ERROR: ldd outputLine: "libmysqlclient.so.18 => not found"
ERROR: for binary:
"/home/nick/Qt/5.9.1/gcc_64/plugins/sqldrivers/libqsqlmysql.so"
ERROR: Please ensure that all libraries can be found by ldd. Aborting.
```

Ignore the first two errors again. Now it can't find MySQL drivers, which is annoying, because we aren't even MySQL and it is the same Qt SQL quirk we saw on OS X. As a workaround, let's effectively "hide" the SQL drivers we don't want from the tool by temporarily renaming them:

```
$ cd <Qt Path>/5.9.1/gcc_64/plugins/sqldrivers
$ mv libqsqlmysql.so libqsqlmysql.so_ignore
$ mv libqsqlpsql.so libqsqlpsql.so_ignore
```

Run the `linuxdeployqt` command again. You will get lots of output this time, culminating in a success message, including the following:

```
App name for filename: Application
dest_path: Application-x86_64.AppImage
```

This is telling us that our app image has been named as `Application-x86_64.AppImage`, which it saves to the `Downloads` folder.

Take a look in file manager, and you will see that it has added various files and directories alongside our executable:

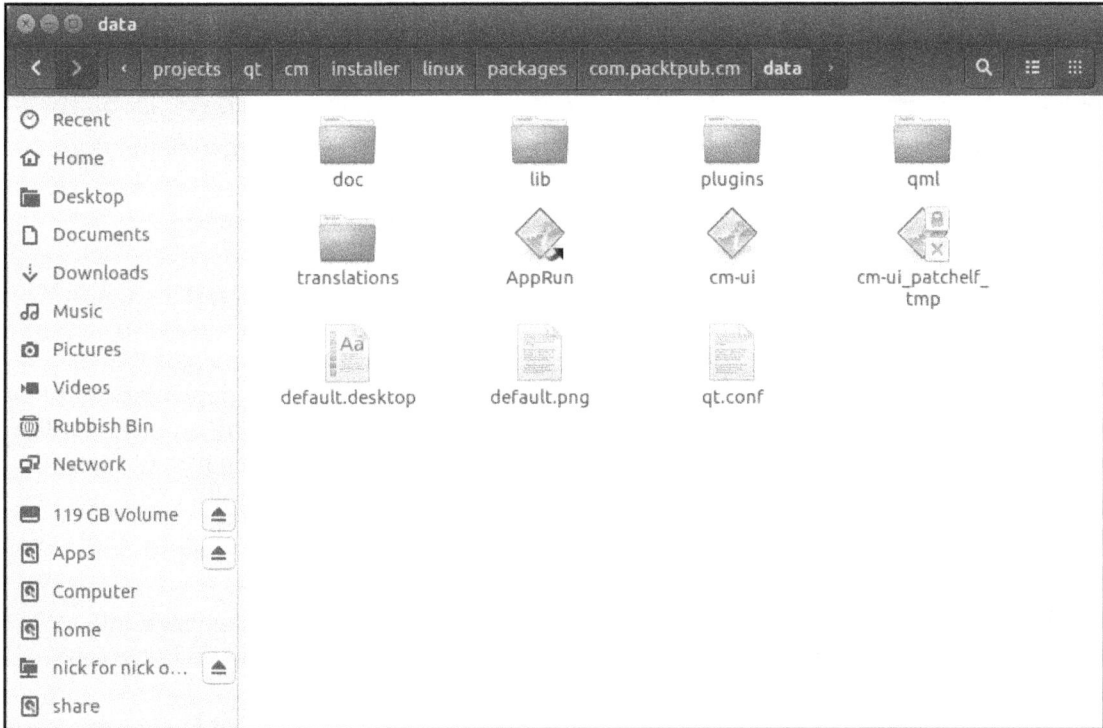

It has also deposited the `Application-x86_64.AppImage` file in the `Downloads` folder that is a single self-contained executable package with all dependencies. However, if you head over to `Downloads` and try and launch the `AppImage`, you may get an error (execute it via a Terminal command to see the error message):

```
QXcbIntegration: Cannot create platform OpenGL context, neither GLX nor EGL
are enabled
```

This appears to be an issue with `linuxdeployqt` missing some dependencies, but for some reason, running the tool a second time magically picks them up. Execute the `linuxdeployqt` command again, and hey presto, the `AppImage` now works correctly.

Windows

First, build the solution using the kit of your choice in the **Release** mode. Once complete, copy the `cm-ui.exe` and `cm-lib.dll` application binaries to a new `cm/installer/windows/packages/com.packtpub.cm/data` directory. This strange directory structure will be explained in the next section—Qt Installer Framework—and we are simply saving ourselves some additional copying later.

Next, let's remind ourselves of the dependencies we need to consider:

- Item 1: Custom libraries we've written or added to our solution manually (`cm-lib`)
- Item 2: The parts of the Qt framework that our application links to
- Item 3: Any internal dependencies of the Qt framework itself
- Item 4: Any libraries required by the C++ compiler we have built the application with

The good news is that item 1 is already done! Windows will look for the dependencies of an executable in the same folder that the executable is in. This is really helpful and by simply copying the DLL to the same folder as the executable, we've already taken care of that dependency. The Qt Installer framework takes all the files from a given folder and deploys them to the target machine in the same place relative to each other, so we know this will be preserved after deployment too.

The bad news is that the remaining steps are a bit of a nightmare to manage manually. We can have a decent first stab at what parts of Qt we need by reviewing the modules we've explicitly added to our `*.pro` files. This will be `qml`, `quick`, and `xml` from `cm-ui` and `sql`, and network and `xml` from `cm-lib` core is also included by default. In File Explorer, navigate to `<Qt Installation Folder>/5.9.1/<Kit>/bin`. In there, you can find all the binaries relating to these modules, for example, `Qt5Qml.dll` for the `qml` module.

We can use the approach that we did for `cm-lib.dll` and simply manually copy each of the Qt DLL files across to the data folder too. This will fulfil item 2 and while deeply tedious, it's fairly straightforward. However, item 3 is a painful exercise that we really don't want to do ourselves.

Fortunately, the `windeployqt` Qt Windows Deployment Tool is just what we need here. It scans an `.exe` file for Qt dependencies and copies them across to our installer folder for us. The tool is located in the `bin` folder of the installed kit you have built the application with, for example, `/Qt/5.9.1/mingw32/bin`.

In a command terminal, execute `windeployqt` as follows:

```
$ <Path to bin>/windeployqt.exe --qmldir <Qt Projects>/cm/cm-ui <Qt
Projects>/cm/installer/windows/packages/com.packtpub.cm/data/cm-ui.exe --
compiler-runtime
```

Remember to replace the parameters in angle brackets with the full paths on your system (or add the executable paths to your system PATH variable).

The `qmldir` flag tells the tool where to scan for QML imports and is set to our UI project folder. After we tell the tool which `.exe` to scan for dependencies, the `compiler-runtime` flag denotes that we want the compiler runtime files too, so it even takes care of item 4 for us as a bonus!

> **TIP**
>
> By default, found dependencies will subsequently be copied to the same folder as the executable being scanned. This is a good reason to copy the compiled binaries to a dedicated installer folder first so that development project output and content for deployment remain separate.

Once executed, you should see a large block of output. Although it's tempting to think "oh, that's done stuff so everything must be ok", it's a good idea to scan through the output, even if you're not sure what it's doing as you can sometimes pick up obvious issues that you can can take action to resolve.

For example, when first deploying a MinGW kit build, I encountered the given line:

```
Warning: Cannot find GCC installation directory. g++.exe must be in the
path.
```

Although the command had executed successfully, and I can see a whole bunch of Qt dependencies in the installer folder, I was actually missing the GCC dependencies. It was a simple fix to follow the instructions and add `<Qt Installation path>/Tools/mingw530_32/bin` to the PATH variable in my system environment variables. After restarting the command terminal and running the `windeployqt` command again, it subsequently completed successfully without the warning, and the GCC files were present as expected in data alongside all the Qt binaries. Without picking up on this quiet little warning, I would have proceeded with some potentially critical missing files.

As you can see, windeployqt is a huge time saver, but unfortunately, it isn't a silver bullet and sometimes misses the required files. Tools like Dependency Walker exist, which can help analyze the dependency tree in detail, but a good starting point is to just manually launch the cm-ui executable from the data folder and see what happens. In our case, it is this:

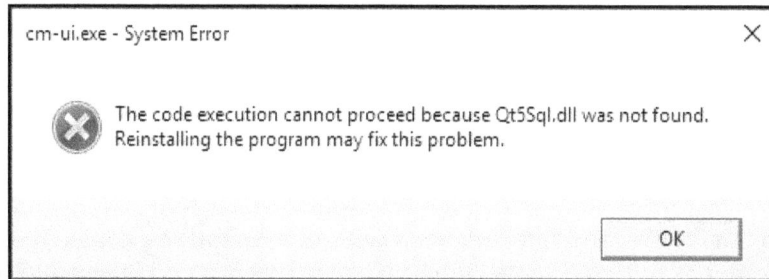

```
cm-ui.exe - System Error                                          ×

    ⊗    The code execution cannot proceed because Qt5Sql.dll was not found.
         Reinstalling the program may fix this problem.


                                                     OK
```

The bad news is that it doesn't work, but the good news is that at least it clearly tells us why it doesn't work—it is missing the Qt5Sql.dll dependency. We know that we do indeed have a dependency there, because we had to add the sql module to our .pro files when we started doing database work. However, wait, we've just executed a command that should pull in all the Qt dependencies for us, right? Right, I don't know why the tool misses out some dependencies that it really should know about, but it does. I don't know if it's a bug, an oversight, or a licensing restriction related to the underlying third-party SQLite implementation, but in any case, the simple solution is that we just need to copy it ourselves.

Head over to <Qt Installation>/5.9.1/<kit>/bin and copy Qt5Sql.dll over to our data folder. Launch the cm-ui.exe again and hurrah, it opens successfully!

> One other thing to look out for apart from missing .dll files from the bin directory is missing files/folders from the plugins directory. You will see in our case that several folders have been copied successfully (bearer, iconengines, and such), but sometimes they don't, and can be very difficult to figure out as you don't get a helpful error message like we did with the missing DLL. I can only recommend three things in that situation: trial, error, and the internet.

So, we now have a folder containing our lovely application binaries and a whole bunch of similarly lovely other files and folders. What now? Well, we can simply copy the folder wholesale onto our users' machines and get them to launch the executable as we did. However, a neater and more professional solution is to bundle up everything into a pretty installation package, and that is where the Qt Installer Framework tool comes in.

Qt Installer framework

Let's edit our Qt installation and grab the Qt Installer framework.

Launch the MaintenanceTool application from your Qt installation directory, and you will be presented with a wizard virtually identical to the one we saw when we first installed Qt. To add Qt Installer Framework to your existing installation, follow these steps:

1. Either log in to your Qt Account or **Skip**
2. Select **Add or remove components and click on Next**
3. On the **Select Components dialog, check Tools > Qt Installer Framework 3.0 and click on Next**
4. Begin the installation by clicking on **Update**

Once complete, you can find the installed tools in `Qt/Tools/QtInstallerFramework/3.0`.

> You can add further modules, kits, and such in exactly the same way. Any components you already have installed will be unaffected unless you actively deselect them.

The Qt Installer Framework requires two specific directories to be present: config and packages. Config is a singular piece of configuration that describes the installer as a whole, whereas you can bundle multiple packages (or components) together in the same installation package. Each component has its own subdirectory within the packages folder, with a data folder containing all the items to be installed for that component and a meta folder where configuration data for the package is held.

In our case, although we have two projects (`cm-lib` and `cm-ui`), it makes no sense to distribute one without the other, so we will aggregate the files together into one package. A common naming convention for packages is `com.<publisher>.<component>`, so we'll name ours `com.packtpub.cm`. We already created the required data folder in the previous section (yay for forward planning!) and `windeployqt` stuffed it full of files for us.

There is no required naming convention here, so feel free to name the package something else if you wish. If we wanted to bundle an additional, optional component with our application, we would do so by simply creating an additional package folder (for example, `com.packtpub.amazingcomponent`) containing the relevant data and meta files, including a separate `package.xml` to configure that component.

Create any missing folders so that you end up with the following folder structure inside `cm/installer/windows`:

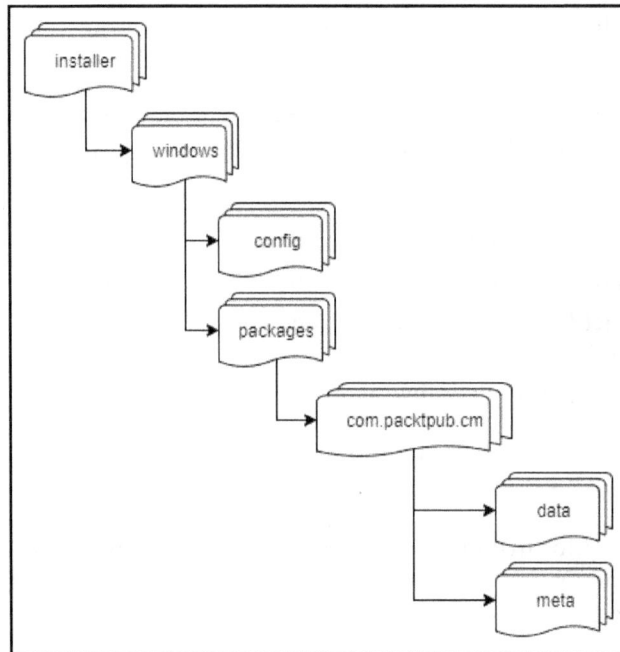

To compliment these folders, we also need to provide two XML configuration files.

Create `config.xml` in the config subfolder:

```
<?xml version="1.0" encoding="UTF-8"?>
<Installer>
    <Name>Client Management</Name>
    <Version>1.0.0</Version>
    <Title>Client Management Application Installer</Title>
    <Publisher>Packt Software Publishing</Publisher>
    <StartMenuDir>Client Management</StartMenuDir>
    <TargetDir>@HomeDir@/ClientManagement</TargetDir>
</Installer>
```

This configuration file customizes the behavior of the installer. The properties we have specified here are as follows:

Property	Purpose
Name	The application name
Version	The application version
Title	The installer name displayed in the title bar
Publisher	The publisher of the software
StartMenuDir	The default program group in the Windows Start menu
TargetDir	The default target directory for the application installation

> You will note strange @ symbols in the `TargetDir` property, and they define a predefined variable `HomeDir` that allows us to dynamically obtain a path to the end user's home directory. You can also access the values of other properties in the same way, for example, `@ProductName@` will return "Client Management". Further information is available at `http://doc.qt.io/qtinstallerframework/scripting.html#predefined-variables`.

Next, create `package.xml` in the `packages/com.packtpub.cm/meta` subfolder:

```xml
<?xml version="1.0" encoding="UTF-8"?>
<Package>
    <DisplayName>Client Management application</DisplayName>
    <Description>Install the Client Management application.</Description>
    <Version>1.0.0</Version>
    <ReleaseDate>2017-10-30</ReleaseDate>
    <Licenses>
        <License name="Fictional Training License Agreement"
file="license.txt" />
    </Licenses>
    <Default>true</Default>
</Package>
```

This file configures the `com.packtpub.cm` package (our Client Management application) with the following properties:

Property	Purpose
`DisplayName`	The name of the component.
`Description`	The text displayed when the component is selected.
`Version`	The version of the component (used to promote component updates).
`ReleaseDate`	The date the component was released.
`Licenses`	A collection of licenses that must be agreed to in order to install the package. The text for the license agreement is obtained from the specified file that must be alongside the configuration file in the meta folder.
`Default`	Boolean flag denoting whether the component is selected by default.

You will also need to create `license.txt` in the meta folder; the content doesn't matter in this case as it's just for demonstration, so write any old nonsense in there.

With all the binaries, dependencies, and configuration in place, we can now run the Qt Framework Installer in a command terminal to generate our installation package. First, change directory to the `cm/installer/windows` folder and then execute `binarycreator`:

```
$ <Qt Installation Path> Tools QtInstallerFramework 3.0 bin
binarycreator.exe -c configconfig.xml -p packages
ClientManagementInstaller.exe
```

The `-c` flag tells the tool where the `config.xml` file resides and `-p` where all the packages are. The final parameter is the name you want to give the resulting installer.

With our application neatly packaged up into a single installer file, `ClientManagementInstaller.exe`, we can now easily distribute it to our end users for installation.

Installation

Upon launching the installer, you will be presented with a welcome dialog, the content of which is derived from our `config.xml` file:

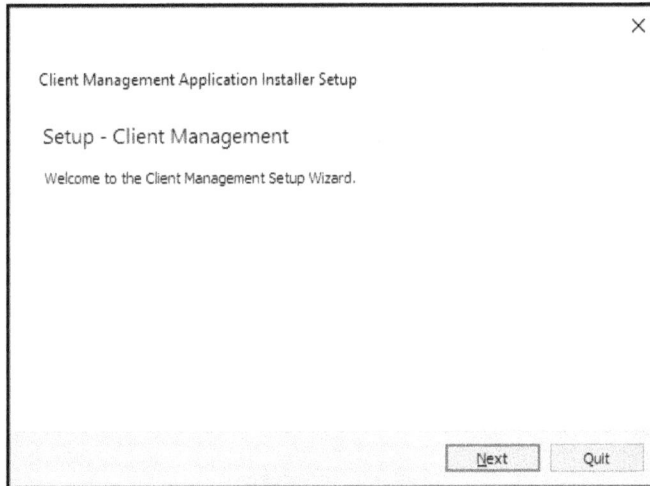

We are then prompted to specify the target directory for the installation and what we expect is that after installation, this folder will contain all the files and folders we pulled together in the data folder:

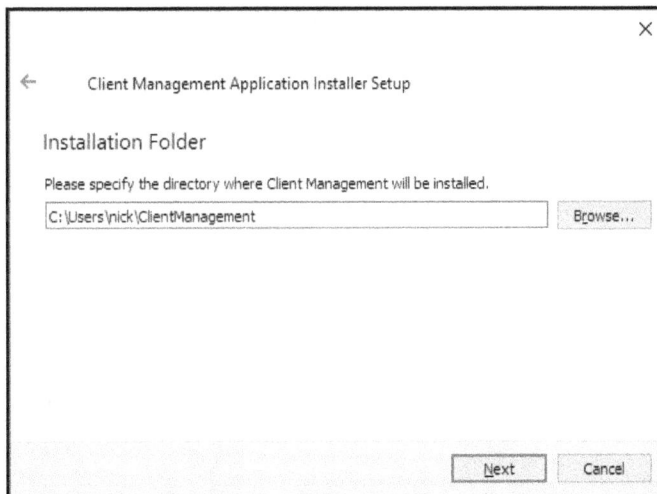

We are then presented with a list of all the components we defined via the packages directory, which in this case is simply the application and dependencies in the `com.packtpub.cm` folder:

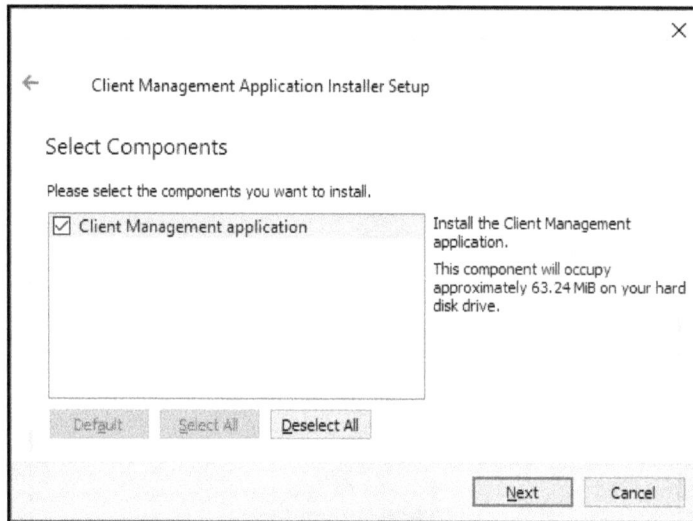

Next, we are presented with any licenses we defined in `packages.xml`, including the license information provided in the text files:

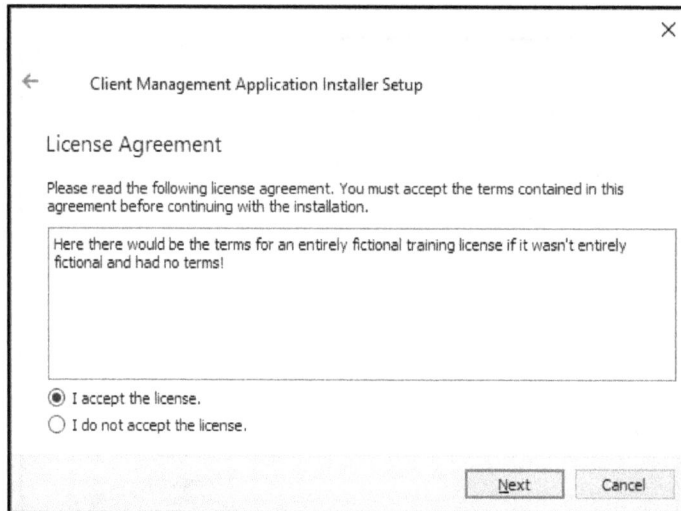

We are then prompted for the **Start Menu shortcuts, with the default provided by** `config.xml:`

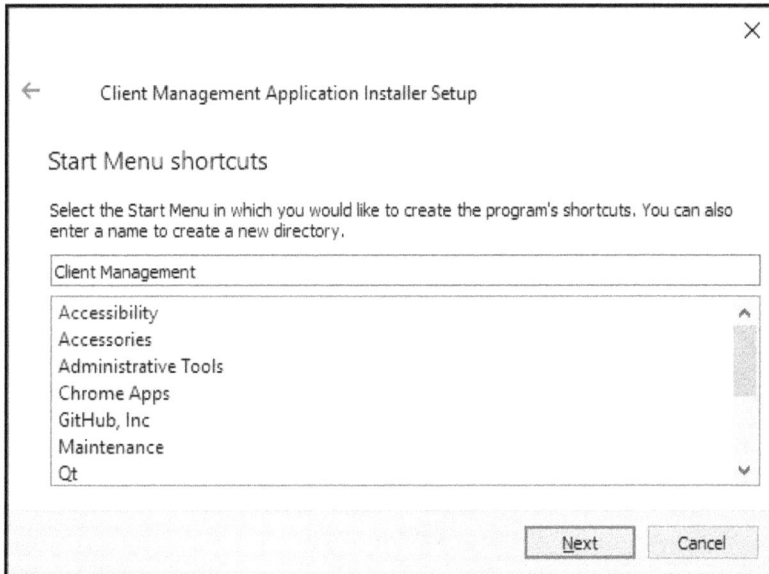

We're ready to install now and are provided with disk usage stats before we confirm:

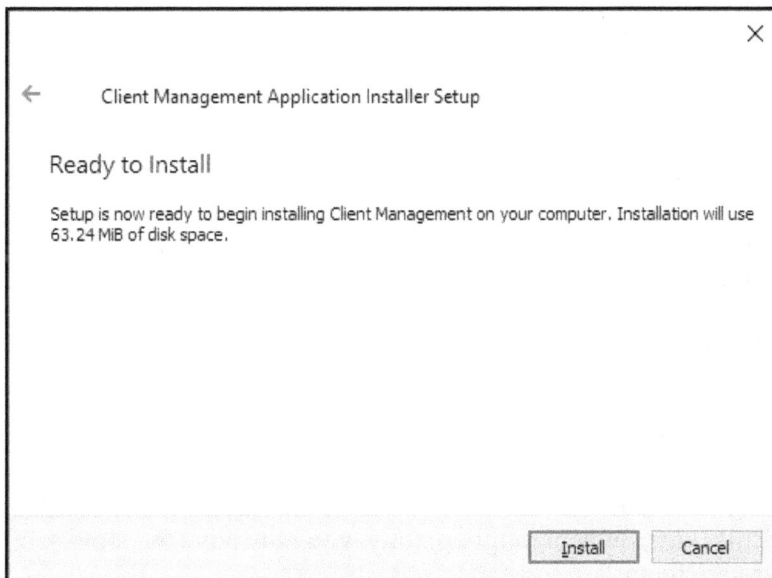

After a brief wait while the installation completes, we are presented with a final confirmation dialog:

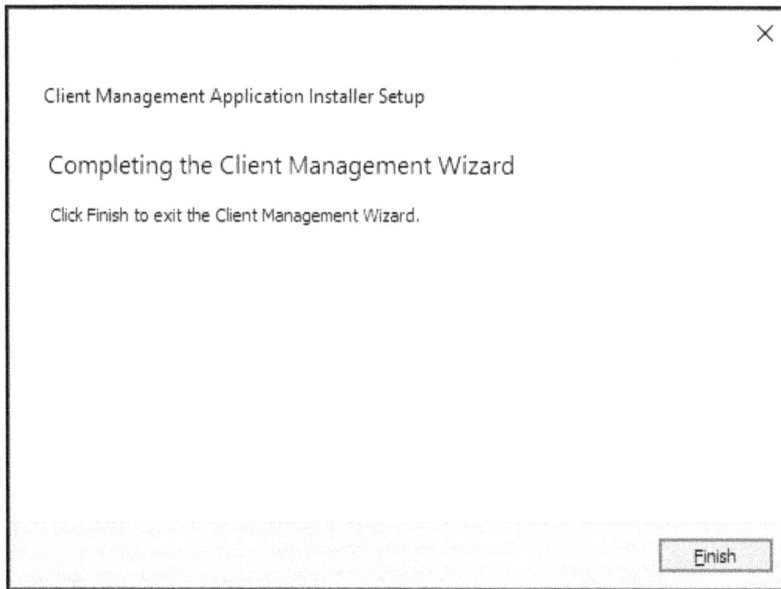

You should see a new `ClientManagement` folder in the target directory containing our installed application!

Summary

In this chapter, we made our application even more testable by introducing our first object factory. They are a really useful layer of abstraction that make unit testing so much easier, and on larger projects, it's common to end up with several factories. We then made our UI even more dynamic by having Style properties that can scale along with the Window. `EnumeratorDecorators` got some love and an editor component of their own, fully finger-friendly to boot. We then put that editor to use and implemented Contact management, showing how collections of objects can easily be viewed and edited.

With our application more fleshed out, we then took a look at how to get our shiny new work of genius into the hands of our end users. Different operating systems each have their own take on things, and you will undoubtedly discover quirks and encounter challenges in your own particular environment, but hopefully, you now have the tools you need to be able to work through them.

That sentiment goes not just for deployment, but for the whole project life cycle. The goal of this book was not to discuss theoretical problems that while interesting, will never come up in your day-to-day role as a developer. The goal was to present solutions to real-world problems. We have developed a functional Line of Business application from start to finish, working through common tasks that you will encounter on a daily basis, whether working on an initiative at work or on a personal project at home.

I hope that some of the approaches detailed in this book prove useful to you and that you go on to enjoy working with Qt as much as I do.

2
Mastering Qt 5

Create stunning cross-platform applications

10
Discovering QMake Secrets

This chapter addresses the issue of creating a cross-platform application that relies on platform-specific code. We will see the impact of qmake on the compilation of your project.

You will learn how to create a system monitoring application that retrieves the average CPU load and the memory used from Windows, Linux, and Mac. For this kind of OS dependent application, architecture is the key to keeping your application reliable and maintainable.

At the end of this chapter, you will be able to create and organize a cross-platform application that uses platform-specific code and displays Qt Charts widgets. Moreover, qmake will not be a mystery anymore.

This chapter covers the following topics:

- Platform-specific code organization
- Design patterns, strategy, and singleton
- Abstract class and pure virtual function
- Qt Charts
- The qmake tool

Designing a cross-platform project

We want to display some visual gauges and chart widgets, so create a new **Qt widgets Application** called ch02-sysinfo. As already discussed earlier, Qt Creator will generate some files for us: main.cpp, MainWindow.h, MainWindow.cpp, and MainWindow.ui.

Before diving into the C++ code, we must think about the software's architecture. This project will handle multiple desktop platforms. Thanks to the combination of C++ and Qt, most of the source code will be common to all targets. However, to retrieve both the CPU and memory usage from the OS (operating system), we will use some platform-specific code.

To successfully achieve this task, we will use two design patterns:

- **Strategy pattern**: This is an interface that describes functionalities (for example, retrieve CPU usage), and specific behaviors (retrieve CPU usage on Windows/Mac OS/Linux) will be performed into subclasses that implement this interface.
- **Singleton pattern**: This pattern guarantees a single instance for a given class. This instance will be easily accessible with a unique access point.

As you can see in the following diagram, the class SysInfo is our interface with the strategy pattern, and is also a singleton. The specific behavior from the strategy pattern is performed in the classes SysInfoWindowsImpl, SysInfoMacImpl, and SysInfoLinuxImpl, subclassing SysInfo:

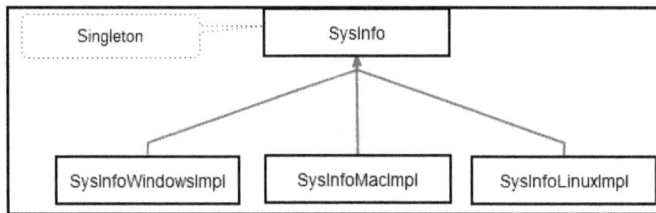

The UI part will only know and use the SysInfo class. The platform-specific implementation class is instantiated by the SysInfo class, and the caller doesn't need to know anything about the SysInfo child classes. As the SysInfo class is a singleton, access will be easier for all widgets.

Let's begin by creating the SysInfo class. On Qt Creator, you can create a new C++ class from the contextual menu, accessible with a right click on the project name in the hierarchy view. Then click on the **Add new** option, or from the menu, go to **File | New file or project | Files and classes**. Then perform the following steps:

1. Go to **C++ Class | Choose**.
2. Set the **Class** name field to SysInfo. As this class does not inherit from another class, we do not need to use the Base class field.
3. Click on **Next**, then **Finish** to generate an empty C++ class.

We will now specify our interface by adding three pure virtual functions:
init(), cpuLoadAverage(), and memoryUsed():

```
// In SysInfo.h
class SysInfo
{
public:
    SysInfo();
    virtual ~SysInfo();

    virtual void init() = 0;
    virtual double cpuLoadAverage() = 0;
    virtual double memoryUsed() = 0;
};

// In SysInfo.cpp
#include "SysInfo.h"

SysInfo::SysInfo()
{
}

SysInfo::~SysInfo()
{
}
```

Each of these functions has specific roles:

- init(): This function allows the derived class to perform any initialization process depending on the OS platform
- cpuLoadAverage(): This function calls some OS-specific code to retrieve the average CPU load and returns it as a percentage value
- memoryUsed(): This function calls some OS-specific code to retrieve the memory used and returns it as a percentage value

The virtual keyword indicates that the function can be overridden in a derived class. The = 0 syntax means that this function is pure virtual, and must be overridden in any concrete derived class. Moreover, this makes SysInfo an abstract class that cannot be instantiated.

We also added an empty virtual destructor. This destructor must be virtual to ensure that any deletion of an instance of a derived class--from a base class pointer--will call the derived class destructor and not only the base class destructor.

Now that our `SysInfo` class is an abstract class and ready to be derived, we will describe three implementations: Windows, Mac OS, and Linux. You can also perform only one implementation if you would rather not use the other two. We will not make any judgment on this. The `SysInfo` class will be transformed into a singleton after adding the implementations.

Adding the Windows implementation

Remember the UML diagram at the beginning of this chapter? The `SysInfoWindowsImpl` class is one of the classes derived from the `SysInfo` class. The main purpose of this class is to encapsulate the Windows-specific code to retrieve CPU and memory usage.

It's time to create the `SysInfoWindowsImpl` class. To do that, you need to perform the following steps:

1. Right click on the `ch02-sysinfo` project name in the hierarchy view.
2. Click on **Add New** | **C++ Class** | **Choose**.
3. Set the **Class name** field to `SysInfoWindowsImpl`.
4. Set the **Base class** field to **<Custom>** and write under the `SysInfo` class.
5. Click on **Next** then **Finish** to generate an empty C++ class.

These generated files are a good starting point, but we must tune them:

```cpp
#include "SysInfo.h"

class SysInfoWindowsImpl : public SysInfo
{
public:
    SysInfoWindowsImpl();

    void init() override;
    double cpuLoadAverage() override;
    double memoryUsed() override;
};
```

The first thing to do is to add the `include` directive to our parent class, `SysInfo`. You can now override virtual functions defined in the base class.

> **Qt Tip** Put your cursor on a derived class name (after the keyword `class`) and press *Alt + Enter* (Windows / Linux) or *Command + Enter* (Mac) to automatically insert virtual functions of the base class.

The `override` keyword comes from C++11. It ensures that the function is declared as virtual in the base class. If the function signature marked as `override` does not match any parent class' `virtual` function, a compile-time error will be displayed.

Retrieving the current memory used on Windows is easy. We will begin with this feature in the `SysInfoWindowsImpl.cpp` file:

```cpp
#include "SysInfoWindowsImpl.h"

#include <windows.h>

SysInfoWindowsImpl::SysInfoWindowsImpl() :
    SysInfo(),
{
}

double SysInfoWindowsImpl::memoryUsed()
{
    MEMORYSTATUSEX memoryStatus;
    memoryStatus.dwLength = sizeof(MEMORYSTATUSEX);
    GlobalMemoryStatusEx(&memoryStatus);
    qulonglong memoryPhysicalUsed =
        memoryStatus.ullTotalPhys - memoryStatus.ullAvailPhys;
    return (double)memoryPhysicalUsed /
        (double)memoryStatus.ullTotalPhys * 100.0;
}
```

Don't forget to include the `windows.h` file so that we can use the Windows API! Actually, this function retrieves the total and the available physical memory. A simple subtraction gives us the amount of memory used. As required by the base class `SysInfo`, this implementation will return the value as a `double` type; for example, the value `23.0` for 23% memory used on a Windows OS.

Retrieving the total memory used is a good start, but we cannot stop now. Our class must also retrieve the CPU load. The Windows API can be messy sometimes. To make our code more readable, we will create two private helper functions. Update your `SysInfoWindowsImpl.h` file to match the following snippet:

```cpp
#include <QtGlobal>
#include <QVector>

#include "SysInfo.h"

typedef struct _FILETIME FILETIME;

class SysInfoWindowsImpl : public SysInfo
{
public:
    SysInfoWindowsImpl();

    void init() override;
    double cpuLoadAverage() override;
    double memoryUsed() override;

private:
    QVector<qulonglong> cpuRawData();
    qulonglong convertFileTime(const FILETIME& filetime) const;

private:
    QVector<qulonglong> mCpuLoadLastValues;
};
```

Let's analyze these changes:

- The `cpuRawData()` is the function that will perform the Windows API call to retrieve system timing information and return values in a generic format. We will retrieve and return three values: the amount of time that the system has spent in idle, in Kernel, and in User mode.
- The `convertFileTime()` function is our second helper. It will convert a Windows `FILETIME` struct syntax to a `qulonglong` type. The `qulonglong` type is a Qt `unsigned long long int`. This type is guaranteed by Qt to be 64-bit on all platforms. You can also use the typedef `quint64`.
- The `mCpuLoadLastValues` is a variable that will store system timing (idle, Kernel, and User) at a given moment.

- Don't forget to include the <QtGlobal> tag to use the qulonglong type, and the <QVector> tag to use the QVector class.
- The syntax typedef struct _FILETIME FILETIME is a kind of forward declaration for FILENAME syntax. As we only use a reference, we can avoid including the <windows.h> tag in our file SysInfoWindowsImpl.h and keep it in the CPP file.

We can now switch to the file SysInfoWindowsImpl.cpp and implement these functions to finish the CPU load average feature on Windows:

```
#include "SysInfoWindowsImpl.h"

#include <windows.h>

SysInfoWindowsImpl::SysInfoWindowsImpl() :
    SysInfo(),
    mCpuLoadLastValues()
{
}

void SysInfoWindowsImpl::init()
{
    mCpuLoadLastValues = cpuRawData();
}
```

When the init() function is called, we store the return value from the cpuRawData() function in our class variable mCpuLoadLastValues. It will be helpful for the cpuLoadAverage() function process.

You may be wondering why we do not perform this task in the initialization list of the constructor. That is because when you call a function from the initialization list, the object is not yet fully constructed! In some circumstances, it may be unsafe because the function can try to access a member variable that has not been constructed yet. However, in this ch02-sysinfo project, the cpuRawData function does not use any member variables, so you are safe, if you really want to do it. Add the cpuRawData() function to the SysInfoWindowsImpl.cpp file:

```
QVector<qulonglong> SysInfoWindowsImpl::cpuRawData()
{
    FILETIME idleTime;
    FILETIME kernelTime;
    FILETIME userTime;

    GetSystemTimes(&idleTime, &kernelTime, &userTime);
```

```
    QVector<qulonglong> rawData;

    rawData.append(convertFileTime(idleTime));
    rawData.append(convertFileTime(kernelTime));
    rawData.append(convertFileTime(userTime));
    return rawData;
}
```

Here we are: the Windows API call to the `GetSystemTimes` function! This function will give us the amount of time that the system has spent idle, and in the Kernel and User modes. Before filling the `QVector` class, we convert each value with our helper `convertFileTime` described in the following code:

```
qulonglong SysInfoWindowsImpl::convertFileTime(const FILETIME& filetime)
const
{
    ULARGE_INTEGER largeInteger;
    largeInteger.LowPart = filetime.dwLowDateTime;
    largeInteger.HighPart = filetime.dwHighDateTime;
    return largeInteger.QuadPart;
}
```

The Windows structure `FILEFTIME` stores 64-bit information on two 32-bit parts (low and high). Our function `convertFileTime` uses the Windows structure `ULARGE_INTEGER` to correctly build a 64-bit value in a single part before returning it as a `qulonglong` type. Last but not least, the `cpuLoadAverage()` implementation:

```
double SysInfoWindowsImpl::cpuLoadAverage()
{
    QVector<qulonglong> firstSample = mCpuLoadLastValues;
    QVector<qulonglong> secondSample = cpuRawData();
    mCpuLoadLastValues = secondSample;

    qulonglong currentIdle = secondSample[0] - firstSample[0];
    qulonglong currentKernel = secondSample[1] - firstSample[1];
    qulonglong currentUser = secondSample[2] - firstSample[2];
    qulonglong currentSystem = currentKernel + currentUser;

    double percent = (currentSystem - currentIdle) * 100.0 /
        currentSystem ;
    return qBound(0.0, percent, 100.0);
}
```

There are three important points to note here:

- Keep in mind that a sample is an absolute amount of time, so subtracting two different samples will give us instantaneous values that can be processed to get the current CPU load.
- The first sample comes from our member variable `mCpuLoadLastValues`, probed the first time by the `init()` function. The second one is retrieved when the `cpuLoadAverage()` function is called. After initializing the samples, the `mCpuLoadLastValues` variable can store the new sample that will be used for the next call.
- The `percent` equation can be a little tricky because the Kernel value retrieved from the Windows API also contains the idle value.

> If you want to learn more about the Windows API, take a look at the MSDN documentation at `https://msdn.microsoft.com/library`.

The final step to finish the Windows implementation is to edit the file `ch02-sysinfo.pro` so that it resembles the following snippet:

```
QT          += core gui
CONFIG      += C++14

greaterThan(QT_MAJOR_VERSION, 4): QT += widgets

TARGET = ch02-sysinfo
TEMPLATE = app

SOURCES += main.cpp
    MainWindow.cpp
    SysInfo.cpp

HEADERS += MainWindow.h
    SysInfo.h

windows {
    SOURCES += SysInfoWindowsImpl.cpp
    HEADERS += SysInfoWindowsImpl.h
}

FORMS       += MainWindow.ui
```

As we did in the ch01-todo project, we also use C++14 with the ch02-sysinfo project. The really new point here is that we removed the files SysInfoWindowsImpl.cpp and SysInfoWindowsImpl.h from the common SOURCES and HEADERS variables. Indeed, we added them into a windows platform scope. When building for other platforms, those files will not be processed by qmake. That is why we can safely include a specific header such as windows.h in the source file SysInfoWindowsImpl.cpp without harming the compilation on other platforms.

Adding the Linux implementation

Let's make the Linux implementation of our ch02-sysinfo project. If you have already done the Windows implementation, it will be a piece of cake! If you have not, you should take a look at it. Some information and tips will not be repeated in this part, such as how to create a SysInfo implementation class, keyboard shortcuts, and details about the SysInfo interface.

Create a new C++ class called SysInfoLinuxImpl that inherits from the SysInfo class, and insert virtual functions from the base class:

```cpp
#include "SysInfo.h"

class SysInfoLinuxImpl : public SysInfo
{
public:
    SysInfoLinuxImpl();

    void init() override;
    double cpuLoadAverage() override;
    double memoryUsed() override;
};
```

We will start by implementing the memoryUsed() function in the file SysInfoLinuxImpl.cpp:

```cpp
#include "SysInfoLinuxImpl.h"

#include <sys/types.h>
#include <sys/sysinfo.h>

SysInfoLinuxImpl::SysInfoLinuxImpl() :
    SysInfo(),
{
}
```

```
double SysInfoLinuxImpl::memoryUsed()
{
    struct sysinfo memInfo;
    sysinfo(&memInfo);

    qulonglong totalMemory = memInfo.totalram;
    totalMemory += memInfo.totalswap;
    totalMemory *= memInfo.mem_unit;

    qulonglong totalMemoryUsed = memInfo.totalram - memInfo.freeram;
    totalMemoryUsed += memInfo.totalswap - memInfo.freeswap;
    totalMemoryUsed *= memInfo.mem_unit;

    double percent = (double)totalMemoryUsed /
        (double)totalMemory * 100.0;
    return qBound(0.0, percent, 100.0);
}
```

This function uses Linux-specific API. After adding the required includes, you can use the Linux `sysinfo()` function that returns information on the overall system statistics. With the total memory and the total memory used, we can easily return the `percent` value. Note that swap memory has been taken into account.

The CPU load feature is a little more complex than the memory feature. Indeed, we will retrieve from Linux the total amount of time the CPU spent performing different kinds of work. That is not exactly what we want. We must return the instantaneous CPU load. A common way to get it is to retrieve two sample values in a short period of time and use the difference to get the instantaneous CPU load:

```
#include <QtGlobal>
#include <QVector>

#include "SysInfo.h"

class SysInfoLinuxImpl : public SysInfo
{
public:
    SysInfoLinuxImpl();

    void init() override;
    double cpuLoadAverage() override;
    double memoryUsed() override;

private:
    QVector<qulonglong> cpuRawData();

private:
```

```
    QVector<qulonglong> mCpuLoadLastValues;
};
```

In this implementation, we will only add one helper function and one member variable:

- The cpuRawData() is a function that will perform the Linux API call to retrieve system timing information and return values in a QVector class of qulonglong type. We retrieve and return four values containing the time the CPU has spent on the following: normal processes in User mode, nice processes in User mode, processes in Kernel mode, and idle.
- The mCpuLoadLastValues is a variable that will store a sample of system timing at a given moment.

Let's go to the SysInfoLinuxImpl.cpp file to update it:

```
#include "SysInfoLinuxImpl.h"

#include <sys/types.h>
#include <sys/sysinfo.h>

#include <QFile>

SysInfoLinuxImpl::SysInfoLinuxImpl()  :
    SysInfo(),
    mCpuLoadLastValues()
{
}

void SysInfoLinuxImpl::init()
{
    mCpuLoadLastValues = cpuRawData();
}
```

As discussed before, the cpuLoadAverage function will need two samples to be able to compute an instantaneous CPU load average. Calling the init() function allows us to set mCpuLoadLastValues for the first time:

```
QVector<qulonglong> SysInfoLinuxImpl::cpuRawData()
{
    QFile file("/proc/stat");
    file.open(QIODevice::ReadOnly);

    QByteArray line = file.readLine();
    file.close();
    qulonglong totalUser = 0, totalUserNice = 0,
        totalSystem = 0, totalIdle = 0;
```

```
std::sscanf(line.data(), "cpu %llu %llu %llu %llu",
    &totalUser, &totalUserNice, &totalSystem,
    &totalIdle);

QVector<qulonglong> rawData;
rawData.append(totalUser);
rawData.append(totalUserNice);
rawData.append(totalSystem);
rawData.append(totalIdle);

return rawData;
}
```

To retrieve the CPU raw information on a Linux system, we chose to parse information available in the /proc/stat file. All we need is available on the first line, so a single readLine() is enough. Even though Qt provides some useful features, sometimes the C standard library functions are simpler. This is the case here; we are using std::sscanf to extract variables from a string. Now let's look at the cpuLoadAvearge() body:

```
double SysInfoLinuxImpl::cpuLoadAverage()
{
    QVector<qulonglong> firstSample = mCpuLoadLastValues;
    QVector<qulonglong> secondSample = cpuRawData();
    mCpuLoadLastValues = secondSample;

    double overall = (secondSample[0] - firstSample[0])
        + (secondSample[1] - firstSample[1])
        + (secondSample[2] - firstSample[2]);

    double total = overall + (secondSample[3] - firstSample[3]);
    double percent = (overall / total) * 100.0;
    return qBound(0.0, percent, 100.0);
}
```

This is where the magic happens. In this last function, we put all the puzzle pieces together. This function uses two samples of the CPU raw data. The first sample comes from our member variable mCpuLoadLastValues, set the first time by the init() function. The second sample is requested by the cpuLoadAverage() function. Then the mCpuLoadLastValues variable will store the new sample that will be used as the first sample on the next cpuLoadAverage() function call.

The `percent` equation should be easy to understand:

- `overall` is equal to user + nice + kernel
- `total` is equal to overall + idle

> **TIP**
>
> You can find more information about `/proc/stat` in the Linux Kernel documentation at `https://www.kernel.org/doc/Documentation/filesystems/proc.txt`.

Like the other implementations, the last thing to do is to edit the `ch02-sysinfo.pro` file like this:

```
QT        += core gui
CONFIG    += C++14

greaterThan(QT_MAJOR_VERSION, 4): QT += widgets

TARGET = ch02-sysinfo
TEMPLATE = app

SOURCES += main.cpp
    MainWindow.cpp
    SysInfo.cpp
    CpuWidget.cpp
    MemoryWidget.cpp
    SysInfoWidget.cpp

HEADERS += MainWindow.h
    SysInfo.h
    CpuWidget.h
    MemoryWidget.h
    SysInfoWidget.h

windows {
    SOURCES += SysInfoWindowsImpl.cpp
    HEADERS += SysInfoWindowsImpl.h
}

linux {
    SOURCES += SysInfoLinuxImpl.cpp
    HEADERS += SysInfoLinuxImpl.h
}

FORMS     += MainWindow.ui
```

With this Linux scope condition in the ch02-sysinfo.pro file, our Linux-specific files will not be processed by the qmake command on other platforms.

Adding the Mac OS implementation

Let's take a look at the Mac implementation of the SysInfo class. Start by creating a new C++ class named SysInfoMacImpl that inherits from the SysInfo class. Override SysInfo virtual functions and you should have a SysInfoMacImpl.h file like this:

```
#include "SysInfo.h"

#include <QtGlobal>
#include <QVector>

class SysInfoMacImpl : public SysInfo
{
public:
    SysInfoMacImpl();

    void init() override;
    double cpuLoadAverage() override;
    double memoryUsed() override;
};
```

The first implementation we will do will be the memoryUsed() function, in the SysInfoMacImpl.cpp file:

```
#include <mach/vm_statistics.h>
#include <mach/mach_types.h>
#include <mach/mach_init.h>
#include <mach/mach_host.h>
#include <mach/vm_map.h>

SysInfoMacImpl::SysInfoMacImpl() :
    SysInfo()
{

}

double SysInfoMacImpl::memoryUsed()
{
    vm_size_t pageSize;
    vm_statistics64_data_t vmStats;

    mach_port_t machPort = mach_host_self();
```

```
        mach_msg_type_number_t count = sizeof(vmStats)
                                      / sizeof(natural_t);
        host_page_size(machPort, &pageSize);

        host_statistics64(machPort,
                        HOST_VM_INFO,
                        (host_info64_t)&vmStats,
                        &count);

        qulonglong freeMemory = (int64_t)vmStats.free_count
                              * (int64_t)pageSize;

        qulonglong totalMemoryUsed = ((int64_t)vmStats.active_count +
                        (int64_t)vmStats.inactive_count +
                        (int64_t)vmStats.wire_count)
                        * (int64_t)pageSize;

        qulonglong totalMemory = freeMemory + totalMemoryUsed;

        double percent = (double)totalMemoryUsed
                      / (double)totalMemory * 100.0;
        return qBound(0.0, percent, 100.0);
    }
```

We start by including the different headers for the Mac OS kernel. Then we initialize `machPort` with the call to the `mach_host_self()` function. A `machPort` is a kind of special connection to the kernel that enables us to request information about the system. We then proceed to prepare other variables so that we can retrieve virtual memory statistics with `host_statistics64()`.

When the `vmStats` class is filled with the information needed, we extract the relevant data: the `freeMemory` and the `totalMemoryUsed`.

Note that Mac OS has a peculiar way of managing its memory: it keeps a lot of memory in cache, ready to be flushed when needed. This implies that our statistics can be misled; we see the memory as used, whereas it was simply kept "just in case".

The percentage calculation is straightforward; we still return a min/max clamped value to avoid any crazy values in our future graph.

Next comes the `cpuLoadAverage()` implementation. The pattern is always the same; take samples at regular intervals and compute the growth on this interval. Therefore, we have to store intermediate values to be able to calculate the difference with the next sample:

```
// In SysInfoMacImpl.h
#include "SysInfo.h"
```

```
#include <QtGlobal>
#include <QVector>

...

private:
    QVector<qulonglong> cpuRawData();

private:
    QVector<qulonglong> mCpuLoadLastValues;
};

// In SysInfoMacImpl.cpp
void SysInfoMacImpl::init()
{
    mCpuLoadLastValues =  cpuRawData();
}

QVector<qulonglong> SysInfoMacImpl::cpuRawData()
{
    host_cpu_load_info_data_t cpuInfo;
    mach_msg_type_number_t cpuCount = HOST_CPU_LOAD_INFO_COUNT;
    QVector<qulonglong> rawData;
    qulonglong totalUser = 0, totalUserNice = 0, totalSystem = 0,
totalIdle = 0;
    host_statistics(mach_host_self(),
                    HOST_CPU_LOAD_INFO,
                    (host_info_t)&cpuInfo,
                    &cpuCount);

    for(unsigned int i = 0; i < cpuCount; i++) {
        unsigned int maxTicks = CPU_STATE_MAX * i;
        totalUser += cpuInfo.cpu_ticks[maxTicks + CPU_STATE_USER];
        totalUserNice += cpuInfo.cpu_ticks[maxTicks
                                            + CPU_STATE_SYSTEM];
        totalSystem += cpuInfo.cpu_ticks[maxTicks
                                            + CPU_STATE_NICE];
        totalIdle += cpuInfo.cpu_ticks[maxTicks + CPU_STATE_IDLE];
    }

    rawData.append(totalUser);
    rawData.append(totalUserNice);
    rawData.append(totalSystem);
    rawData.append(totalIdle);
    return rawData;
}
```

As you can see, the pattern used is strictly equivalent to the Linux implementation. You can even copy-paste the body of the cpuLoadAverage() function from the SysInfoLinuxImpl.cpp file. They do exactly the same thing.

Now, the implementation is different for the cpuRawData() function. We load cpuInfo and cpuCount with host_statistics() and then we loop through each CPU to have the totalUser, totalUserNice, totalSystem, and totalIdle functions filled. Finally, we append all this data to the rawData object before returning it.

The very last part is to compile the SysInfoMacImpl class only on Mac OS. Modify the .pro file to have the following body:

```
...

linux {
    SOURCES += SysInfoLinuxImpl.cpp
    HEADERS += SysInfoLinuxImpl.h
}

macx {
    SOURCES += SysInfoMacImpl.cpp
    HEADERS += SysInfoMacImpl.h
}

FORMS     += MainWindow.ui
```

Transforming SysInfo into a singleton

Promises are made to be kept: we will now transform the SysInfo class into a singleton. C++ offers many ways to implement the singleton design pattern. We will explain one of them here. Open the SysInfo.h file and make the following changes:

```
class SysInfo
{
public:
    static SysInfo& instance();
    virtual ~SysInfo();

    virtual void init() = 0;
    virtual double cpuLoadAverage() = 0;
    virtual double memoryUsed() = 0;

protected:
    explicit SysInfo();
```

```
private:
    SysInfo(const SysInfo& rhs);
    SysInfo& operator=(const SysInfo& rhs);
};
```

The singleton must guarantee that there will be only one instance of the class and that this instance will be easily accessible from a single access point.

So the first thing to do is to change the visibility of the constructor to `protected`. This way, only this class and the child classes will be allowed to call the constructor.

Since only one instance of the object must exist, allowing the copy constructor and the assignment operator is nonsense. One way to solve the problem is to make them `private`.

> **C++ tip** Since C++11, you can define a function as deleted with the syntax
> void `myFunction()` = `delete`. Any use of a deleted function will
> display a compile-time error. It's another way to prevent the use of the
> copy constructor and the assignment operator with a singleton.

The last change is the "unique access point" with a `static` function instance that will return a reference of the `SysInfo` class.

It is now time to commit singleton changes to the `SysInfo.cpp` file:

```cpp
#include <QtGlobal>

#ifdef Q_OS_WIN
    #include "SysInfoWindowsImpl.h"
#elif defined(Q_OS_MAC)
    #include "SysInfoMacImpl.h"
#elif defined(Q_OS_LINUX)
    #include "SysInfoLinuxImpl.h"
#endif

SysInfo& SysInfo::instance()
{
    #ifdef Q_OS_WIN
        static SysInfoWindowsImpl singleton;
    #elif defined(Q_OS_MAC)
        static SysInfoMacImpl singleton;
    #elif defined(Q_OS_LINUX)
        static SysInfoLinuxImpl singleton;
    #endif

    return singleton;
}
```

```
SysInfo::SysInfo()
{
}

SysInfo::~SysInfo()
{
}
```

Here you can see another Qt cross-OS trick. Qt provides some macro `Q_OS_WIN`, `Q_OS_LINUX`, or `Q_OS_MAC`. A Qt OS macro will be defined only on the corresponding OS. By combining these macros with a conditional preprocessor directive`#ifdef`, we can always include and instantiate the correct `SysInfo` implementation on all OSes.

Declaring the `singleton` variable as a static variable in the `instance()` function is a way to make a singleton in C++. We tend to prefer this version because you do not need to worry about the singleton memory management. The compiler will handle the instantiation the first time as well as the destruction. Moreover, since C++11 this method is thread safe.

Exploring Qt Charts

The core part is ready. It's now time to create a UI for this project, and Qt Charts can help us with this task. Qt Charts is a module that provides a set of easy-to-use chart components, such as line chart, area chart, spline chart, pie chart, and so on.

Qt Charts was previously a commercial-only Qt module. Since Qt 5.7, the module is now included in Qt on GPLv3 license for open source users. If you are stuck on Qt 5.6, you can build the module by yourself from sources. More information can be found at `https://github.com/qtproject/qtcharts`.

The aim now is to create two Qt widgets, `CpuWidget` and `MemoryWidget`, to display nice Qt charts of the CPU and the memory used. These two widgets will share a lot of common tasks, so we will first create an abstract class, `SysInfoWidget`:

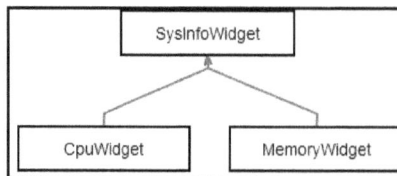

Then the two actual widgets will inherit from the `SysInfoWidget` class and perform their specific tasks.

Create a new C++ class called `SysInfoWidget` with `QWidget` as a base class. Some enhancements must be processed in the `SysInfoWidget.h` file:

```
#include <QWidget>
#include <QTimer>
#include <QtCharts/QChartView>

class SysInfoWidget : public QWidget
{
    Q_OBJECT
public:
    explicit SysInfoWidget(QWidget *parent = 0,
                           int startDelayMs = 500,
                           int updateSeriesDelayMs = 500);

protected:
    QtCharts::QChartView& chartView();

protected slots:
    virtual void updateSeries() = 0;

private:
    QTimer mRefreshTimer;
    QtCharts::QChartView mChartView;
};
```

The `QChartView` is the generic widget that can display many types of chart. This class will handle the layout and display the `QChartView`. A `QTimer` will call the slot function `updateSeries()` regularly. As you can see, this is a pure virtual slot. That is the reason why the `SysInfoWidget` class is abstract. The slot `updateSeries()` will be overridden by child classes to retrieve a system value and define how the chart should be drawn. Note that the parameters `startDelayMs` and `updateSeriesDelayMs` have default values that can be customized by the caller if required.

We can now proceed to the `SysInfoWidget.cpp` file to correctly prepare this `SysInfoWidget` class before creating the child widgets:

```
#include <QVBoxLayout>

using namespace QtCharts;

SysInfoWidget::SysInfoWidget(QWidget *parent,
                             int startDelayMs,
```

```
                                        int updateSeriesDelayMs) :
        QWidget(parent),
        mChartView(this)
    {
        mRefreshTimer.setInterval(updateSeriesDelayMs);
        connect(&mRefreshTimer, &QTimer::timeout,
                this, &SysInfoWidget::updateSeries);
        QTimer::singleShot(startDelayMs,
            [this] { mRefreshTimer.start(); });

        mChartView.setRenderHint(QPainter::Antialiasing);
        mChartView.chart()->legend()->setVisible(false);

        QVBoxLayout* layout = new QVBoxLayout(this);
        layout->addWidget(&mChartView);
        setLayout(layout);
    }

    QChartView& SysInfoWidget::chartView()
    {
        return mChartView;
    }
```

All tasks in the `SysInfoWidget` constructor are common tasks required by the child widgets, `CpuWidget`, and `MemoryWidget`. The first step is the `mRefreshTimer` initialization to define the timer interval and the slot to call whenever a timeout signal is triggered. Then the static function `QTimer::singleShot()` will start the real timer after a delay defined by `startDelayMs`. Here again, Qt combined with lambda functions will give us a powerful code in just a few lines. The next part enables the antialiasing to smooth the chart drawing. We hide the chart's legend to get a minimalist display. The last part handles the layout to display the `QChartView` widget in our `SysInfoWidget` class.

CpuWidget using QCharts

Now that the base class `SysInfoWidget` is ready, let's implement its first child class: `CpuWidget`. We will now use the Qt Charts API to display a good-looking widget. The average CPU load will be displayed in a pie graph with a hole in the center, like a partly eaten donut where the eaten part is the percentage of the CPU used. The first step is to add a new C++ class named `CpuWidget` and make it inherit `SysInfoWidget`:

```
#include "SysInfoWidget.h"

class CpuWidget : public SysInfoWidget
{
```

```
public:
    explicit CpuWidget(QWidget* parent = 0);
};
```

In the constructor, the only parameter needed is a `QWidget* parent`. Since we provided default values for the `startDelayMs` and `updateSeriesDelayMs` variables in `SysInfoWidget` class, we get the best possible behavior; there is no need to remember it when subclassing `SysInfoWidget`, but it is still easy to override it if need be.

The next step is to override the `updateSeries()` function from the `SysInfoWidget` class and start using the Qt Charts API:

```cpp
#include <QtCharts/QpieSeries>

#include "SysInfoWidget.h"

class CpuWidget : public SysInfoWidget
{
    Q_OBJECT
public:
    explicit CpuWidget(QWidget* parent = 0);

protected slots:
    void updateSeries() override;

private:
    QtCharts::QPieSeries* mSeries;
};
```

Since we overrode the `SysInfoWidget::updateSeries()` slot, we have to include the `Q_OBJECT` macro to allow `CPUWidget` to respond to the `SysInfoWidgetmRefreshTimer::timeout()` signal.

We include `QPieSeries` from the Qt Charts module so that we can create a member `QPieSeries*` named `mSeries`. The `QPieSeries` is a subclass of `QAbstractSeries`, which is the base class of all Qt Charts series (`QLineSeries`, `QAreaSeries`, `QPieSeries`, and so on). In Qt Charts, a `QAbstractSeries` subclass holds the data you want to display and defines how it should be drawn, but it does not define where the data should be displayed inside your layout.

We can now proceed to `CpuWidget.cpp` to investigate how we can tell Qt where the drawing takes place:

```
using namespace QtCharts;

CpuWidget::CpuWidget(QWidget* parent) :
    SysInfoWidget(parent),
    mSeries(new QPieSeries(this))
{
    mSeries->setHoleSize(0.35);
    mSeries->append("CPU Load", 30.0);
    mSeries->append("CPU Free", 70.0);

    QChart* chart = chartView().chart();
    chart->addSeries(mSeries);
    chart->setTitle("CPU average load");
}
```

All Qt Charts classes are defined in the `QtCharts` namespace. This is why we start with `using namespace QtCharts`.

First, we initialize `mSeries` in the constructor initializer list. We then proceed to configure it. We carve the donut with `mSeries->setHoleSize(0.35)` and we append two data sets to `mSeries`: a fake `CPU Load` and `Cpu Free`, which are expressed in percentages. The `mSeries` function is now ready to be linked to the class managing its drawing: `QChart`.

The `QChart` class is retrieved from the `SysInfoWidget::chartView()` function. When calling `chart->addSeries(mSeries)`, `chart` takes the ownership of `mSeries` and will draw it according to the series type--in our case, a `QPieSeries`. `QChart` is not a `QWidget`: it is a subclass of `QGraphicsWidget`. `QGraphicsWidget` can be described as a lighter `QWidget` with some differences (its coordinates and geometry are defined with `doubles` or `floats` instead of `integers`, a subset of `QWidget` attributes are supported: custom drag, drop framework, and so on). The `QGraphicsWidget` class is designed to be added in a `QGraphicsScene` class, a high-performance Qt component used to draw hundreds of items on screen at the same time.

In our `SysInfo` application, the `QChart` has to be displayed in a `QVBoxLayout` in `SysInfoWidget`. Here, the `QChartView` class comes in very handy. It lets us add `chart` in a `QWidget` layout.

Up to now, `QPieSeries` has seemed rather abstract. Let's add it to the `MainWindow` file to see how it looks:

```
// In MainWindow.h
```

```
#include "CpuWidget.h"

...

private:
    Ui::MainWindow *ui;
    CpuWidget mCpuWidget;
};

// In MainWindow.cpp
MainWindow::MainWindow(QWidget *parent) :
    QMainWindow(parent),
    ui(new Ui::MainWindow),
    mCpuWidget(this)
{
    ui->setupUi(this);
    SysInfo::instance().init();
    ui->centralWidget->layout()->addWidget(&mCpuWidget);
}
```

We simply declare mCpuWidget in the MainWindow.h file, initialize it, and add it to MainWindow->centralWidget->layout. If you now run the application, you should see something like this:

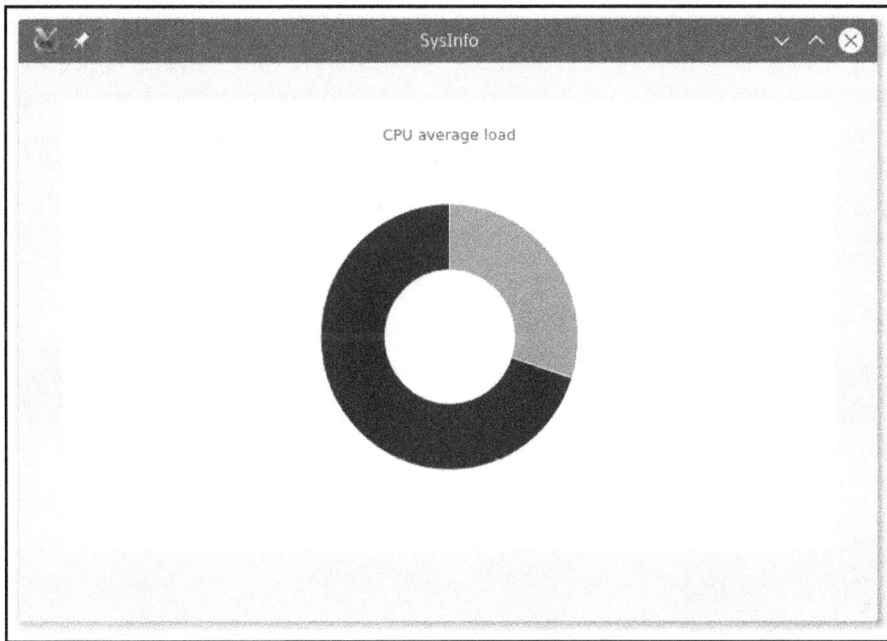

Even though it looks cool, this donut is a bit static and does not reflect the CPU usage. Thanks to the architecture we built with the `SysInfo` and `SysInfoWidget` classes, the remaining part will be implemented swiftly.

Switch back to the `CpuWidget.cpp` file and implement the `updateSeries()` function with the following body:

```
void CpuWidget::updateSeries()
{
    double cpuLoadAverage = SysInfo::instance().cpuLoadAverage();
    mSeries->clear();
    mSeries->append("Load", cpuLoadAverage);
    mSeries->append("Free", 100.0 - cpuLoadAverage);
}
```

First, we get a reference to our `SysInfo` singleton. We then retrieve the current average CPU load in the `cpuLoadAverage` variable. We have to feed this data to our `mSeries`. The `mSeries` object is a `QPieCharts`, which implies that we just want a snapshot of the current CPU average load. Past history is not meaningful with this kind of graph; that's why we clear the `mSeries` data with the `mSeries->clear()` syntax, and append the `cpuLoadAverage` variable and then the free part (`100.0 - cpuLoadAverage`).

The nice thing to note is that, in the `CpuWidget` class, we don't have to worry about refreshing. All the work is done in the `SysInfoWidget` subclass with all the whistles and bells of the `QTimer` class. In a `SysInfoWidget` subclass, we only have to concentrate on the valuable specific code: what data should be displayed and what kind of graph is used to display it. If you look at the whole `CpuWidget` class, it is very short. The next `SysInfoWidget` subclass, `MemoryWidget`, will also be very concise, as well as quick to implement.

Memory using Qcharts

Our second `SysInfoWidget` is a `MemoryWidget` class. This widget will display a history of the data so that we can see how the memory consumption evolves over time. To display this data, we will use a `QLineSeries` class from the Qt Chart module. Create the `MemoryWidget` class and follow the same pattern we used for `CpuWidget`:

```
#include <QtCharts/QLineSeries>

#include "SysInfoWidget.h"

class MemoryWidget : public SysInfoWidget
```

```
{
    Q_OBJECT
public:
    explicit MemoryWidget(QWidget *parent = 0);

protected slots:
    void updateSeries() override;

private:
    QtCharts::QLineSeries* mSeries;
    qint64 mPointPositionX;
};
```

Instead of a being a QPieSeries*, mSeries is a type of QLineSeries* which will be linked to the chart object in a very similar fashion to MemoryWidget.cpp:

```
#include "MemoryWidget.h"
#include <QtCharts/QAreaSeries>

using namespace QtCharts;

const int CHART_X_RANGE_COUNT = 50;
const int CHART_X_RANGE_MAX = CHART_X_RANGE_COUNT - 1;

MemoryWidget::MemoryWidget(QWidget *parent) :
    SysInfoWidget(parent),
    mSeries(new QlineSeries(this)),
    mPointPositionX(0)
{
    QAreaSeries* areaSeries = new QAreaSeries(mSeries);

    QChart* chart = chartView().chart();
    chart->addSeries(areaSeries);
    chart->setTitle("Memory used");
    chart->createDefaultAxes();
    chart->axisX()->setVisible(false);
    chart->axisX()->setRange(0, CHART_X_RANGE_MAX);
    chart->axisY()->setRange(0, 100);
}

void MemoryWidget::updateSeries()
{
}
```

The `mSeries` data is, as usual, initialized in the initializer list. The `mPointPositionX` is an `unsigned long long` (using the Qt notation `qint64`) variable that will track the last X position of our data set. This huge value is used to make sure that `mPointPositionX` never overflows.

We then use an intermediate `areaSeries` that takes ownership of `mSeries` upon its initialization in `QAreaSeries* areaSeries = new QareaSeries(mSeries)`. `areaSeries` is then added to the `chart` object at `chart->addSeries(areaSeries)`. We do not want to display a single line in our `QChart`; instead we want to display an area that represents the used memory percentage. That is why we use an `areaSeries` type. Nonetheless, we will still update the `mSeries` data when adding new points to the dataset in the `updateSeries()` function. The `areaSeries` type will automatically handle them and deliver them to the `chart` object.

After `chart->addSeries(areaSeries)`, we configure the chart display:

- The `chart->createDefaultAxes()` function creates an X and Y axis based on the `areaSeries` type. If we used a 3D series, the `createDefaultAxes()` function would have added a Z axis.
- Hide the X axis tick values with `chart->axisX()->setVisible(false)` (intermediate values displayed at the bottom of the axis). In our `MemoryWidget` class, this information is not relevant.
- To define the number of points we want to display--the size of the display history--we call `chart->axisX()->setRange(0, CHART_X_RANGE_MAX)`. Here we use a constant to make it easier to modify this value afterwards. Seeing the value at the top of the file, we avoid having to skim through `MemoryWidget.cpp`, searching where this value is used to update it.
- `chart->axisY()->setRange(0, 100)` defines the maximum range of the Y axis, which is a percentage, based on the value returned by the `SysInfo::memoryUsed()` function.

The chart is now properly configured. We now have to feed it by filling the `updateSeries()` body:

```
void MemoryWidget::updateSeries()
{
    double memoryUsed = SysInfo::instance().memoryUsed();
    mSeries->append(mPointPositionX++, memoryUsed);
    if (mSeries->count() > CHART_X_RANGE_COUNT) {
        QChart* chart = chartView().chart();
        chart->scroll(chart->plotArea().width()
```

```
                        / CHART_X_RANGE_MAX, 0);
            mSeries->remove(0);
        }
    }
```

We first retrieve the latest memory percentage used and append it to `mSeries` at the *X* coordinate `mPointPositionX` (we post-increment it for the next `updateSeries()` call) and *Y* coordinate `memoryUsed`. As we want to keep a history of `mSeries`, `mSeries->clear()` is never called. However, what will happen when we add more than `CHART_X_RANGE_COUNT` points? The visible "window" on the chart is static and the points will be added outside. This means that we will see the memory usage only for the first `CHART_X_RANGE_MAX` points and then, nothing.

Fortunately, `QChart` provides a function to scroll inside the view to move the visible window. We start to handle this case only when the dataset is bigger than the visible window, meaning `if (mSeries->count() > CHART_X_RANGE_COUNT)`. We then remove the point at the index 0 with `mSeries->remove(0)` to ensure that the widget will not store an infinite dataset. A SysInfo application that monitors the memory usage and has itself a memory leak is a bit sad.

The syntax `chart->scroll(chart->plotArea().width() / CHART_X_RANGE_MAX, 0)` will then scroll to the latest point on the *X* axis and nothing on *Y*. The `chart->scroll(dx, dy)` expects coordinates expressed in our series coordinates. That is the reason why we have to retrieve the `char->plotArea()` divided by `CHART_X_RANGE_MAX`, the *X* axis unit.

We can now add the `MemoryWidget` class in `MainWindow`:

```cpp
// In MainWindow.h
#include "CpuWidget.h"
#include "MemoryWidget.h"

...

private:
    Ui::MainWindow *ui;
    CpuWidget mCpuWidget;
    MemoryWidget mMemoryWidget;
};

// In MainWindow.cpp
MainWindow::MainWindow(QWidget *parent) :
    QMainWindow(parent),
    ui(new Ui::MainWindow),
    mCpuWidget(this),
```

```
        mMemoryWidget(this)
    {
        ui->setupUi(this);
        SysInfo::instance().init();
        ui->centralWidget->layout()->addWidget(&mCpuWidget);
        ui->centralWidget->layout()->addWidget(&mMemoryWidget);
    }
```

Just as we did for `CPUWidget`, add a new member named `mMemoryWidget` to `MainWindow` and add it to the `centralWidget` layout with
the `ui->centralWidget->layout()->addWidget(&mMemoryWidget)` syntax.

Compile, run the application, and wait a few seconds. You should see something close to this:

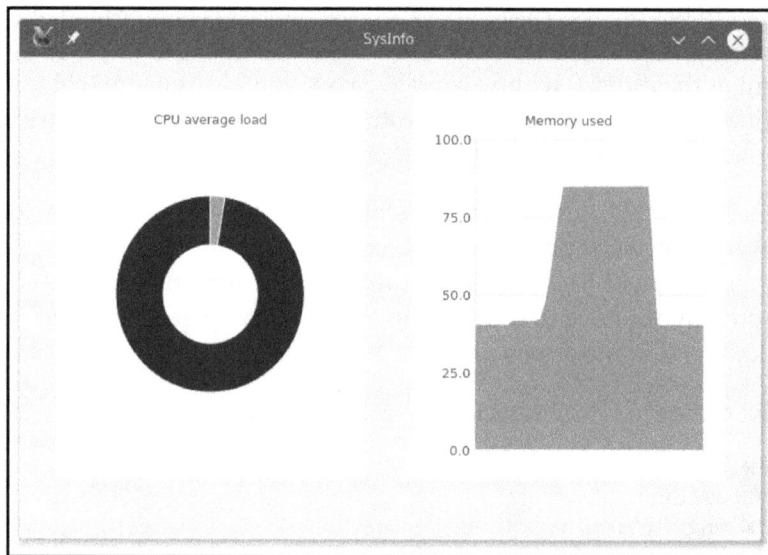

The `MemoryWidget` class works fine, but it looks a bit dull. We can customize it very easily with Qt. The goal is to have a bold line at the top of the memory area and a nice gradient from top to bottom. We just have to modify the `areaSeries` class in
the `MemoryWidget.cpp` file:

```
#include <QtCharts/QAreaSeries>
#include <QLinearGradient>
#include <QPen>

#include "SysInfo.h"
```

```
using namespace QtCharts;

const int CHART_X_RANGE_MAX = 50;
const int COLOR_DARK_BLUE = 0x209fdf;
const int COLOR_LIGHT_BLUE = 0xbfdfef;
const int PEN_WIDTH = 3;

MemoryWidget::MemoryWidget(QWidget *parent) :
    SysInfoWidget(parent),
    mSeries(new QLineSeries(this))
{
    QPen pen(COLOR_DARK_BLUE);
    pen.setWidth(PEN_WIDTH);

    QLinearGradient gradient(QPointF(0, 0), QPointF(0, 1));
    gradient.setColorAt(1.0, COLOR_DARK_BLUE);
    gradient.setColorAt(0.0, COLOR_LIGHT_BLUE);
    gradient.setCoordinateMode(QGradient::ObjectBoundingMode);

    QAreaSeries* areaSeries = new QAreaSeries(mSeries);
    areaSeries->setPen(pen);
    areaSeries->setBrush(gradient);

    QChart* chart = chartView().chart();
    ...
}
```

The QPen pen function is a part of the QPainter API. It is the foundation on which Qt relies to do most of the GUI drawing. This includes the whole QWidget API (QLabel, QPushButton, QLayout, and so on). For the pen, we just have to specify its color and width, and then apply it to the areaSeries class with areaSeries->setPen(pen).

The principle is the same for the gradient. We define the starting point (QPointF(0, 0)) and the final point (QPointF(0, 1)) before specifying the color at each end of the vertical gradient. The QGradient::ObjectBoundingMode parameter defines how the start/final coordinates are mapped to the object. With the QAreaSeries class, we want the gradient coordinates to match the whole QareaSeries class. These coordinates are normalized coordinates, meaning that 0 is the start and 1 is the end of the shape:

- The [0.0] coordinates will point to the top left corner of the QAreaSeries class
- The [1.0] coordinates will point to the bottom left corner of the QAreaSeries class

A last build and run, and the SysInfo application will look like this:

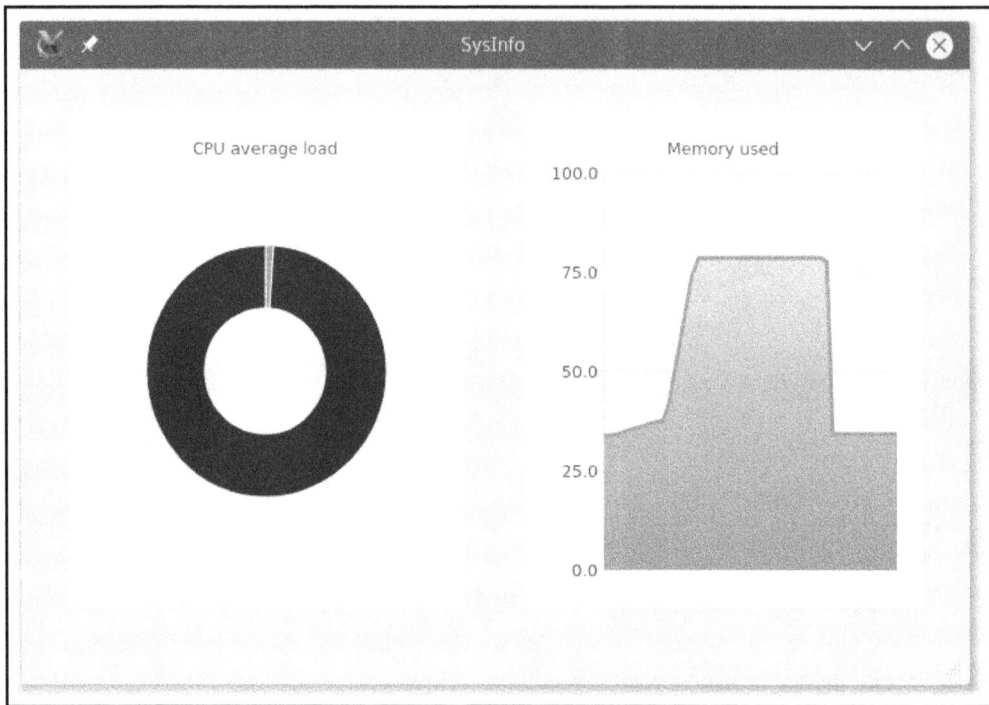

A memory leak or starting a virtual machine is a great way to make your memory go crazy

The SysInfo application is now finished, and we even added some visual polish. You can explore the QGradient classes and the QPainter API if you want to further customize the widget to your taste.

The .pro file in depth

When you click on the **Build** button, what exactly is Qt Creator doing? How does Qt handle the compilation of the different platforms with a single .pro file? What does the Q_OBJECT macro imply exactly? We will dig into each of these questions in the following sections. Our example case will be the SysInfo application we just completed, and we will study what Qt is doing under the hood.

We can start this study by digging into the `.pro` file. It is the main entry point in compiling any Qt project. Basically, a `.pro` file is a qmake project file describing the sources and headers used by the project. It is a platform-agnostic definition of a `Makefile`. First, we can cover the different qmake keywords used in the `ch02-sysinfo` application:

```
#-------------------------------------------------
#
# Project created by QtCreator 2016-03-24T16:25:01
#
#-------------------------------------------------
QT += core gui charts
CONFIG += C++14

greaterThan(QT_MAJOR_VERSION, 4): QT += widgets

TARGET = ch02-sysinfo
TEMPLATE = app
```

Each of these functions has specific roles:

- `#`: This is the prefix needed to comment on a line. Yes, we generated the project on 2016-03-24-crazy, huh?
- `QT`: This is a list of the Qt modules used in the project. In the platform-specific Makefile, each of the values will include the module headers and the corresponding library link.
- `CONFIG`: This is a list of configuration options for the project. Here, we configure the support of C++14 in the Makefile.
- `TARGET`: This is the name of the target output file.
- `TEMPLATE`: This is the project template used when generating the `Makefile`. `app` tells qmake to generate a Makefile targeted for a binary. If you are building a library, use the `lib` value.

In the `ch02-sysinfo` application, we started to use platform-specific compilation rules using the intuitive scope mechanism:

```
windows {
    SOURCES += SysInfoWindowsImpl.cpp
    HEADERS += SysInfoWindowsImpl.h
}
```

If you had to do this with a `Makefile`, you would probably lose some hair before doing it right (being bald is not an excuse). This syntax is simple yet powerful, and is also used for conditional statements. Let's say you wanted to build some files on debug only. You would have written the following:

```
windows {
    SOURCES += SysInfoWindowsImpl.cpp
    HEADERS += SysInfoWindowsImpl.h
    debug {
        SOURCES += DebugClass.cpp
        HEADERS += DebugClass.h
    }
}
```

Nesting the `debug` scope inside `windows` is the equivalent of `if (windows && debug)`. The scoping mechanism is even more flexible; you can have the OR Boolean operator condition with this syntax:

```
windows|unix {
    SOURCES += SysInfoWindowsAndLinux.cpp
}
```

You can even have else if/else statements:

```
windows|unix {
    SOURCES += SysInfoWindowsAndLinux.cpp
} else:macx {
    SOURCES += SysInfoMacImpl.cpp
} else {
    SOURCES += UltimateGenericSources.cpp
}
```

In this code snippet, we also see the use of the += operator. The qmake tool provides a wide range of operators to modify the behavior of variables:

- =: This operator sets the variable to the value. The syntax `SOURCES = SysInfoWindowsImpl.cpp` would have assigned the single`SysInfoWindowsImpl.cpp` value to the `SOURCES` variable.
- +=: This operator adds the value to a list of values. This is what we commonly use in `HEADERS`, `SOURCES`, `CONFIG`, and so on.
- −=: This operator removes the value from the list. You can, for example, add a `DEFINE = DEBUG_FLAG` syntax in the common section and in a platform-specific scope (say a Windows release) remove it with the `DEFINE −= DEBUG_FLAG` syntax.

- *=: This operator adds the value to the list only if it is not already present. The `DEFINE *= DEBUG_FLAG` syntax adds the `DEBUG_FLAG` value only once.

- ~=: This operator replaces any values that match a regular expression with the specified value, `DEFINE ~= s/DEBUG_FLAG/debug`.

You can also define variables in the `.pro` file and reuse them in different places. We can simplify this with the use of the qmake `message()` function:

```
COMPILE_MSG = "Compiling on"

windows {
    SOURCES += SysInfoWindowsImpl.cpp
    HEADERS += SysInfoWindowsImpl.h
    message($$COMPILE_MSG windows)
}

linux {
    SOURCES += SysInfoLinuxImpl.cpp
    HEADERS += SysInfoLinuxImpl.h
    message($$COMPILE_MSG linux)
}

macx {
    SOURCES += SysInfoMacImpl.cpp
    HEADERS += SysInfoMacImpl.h
    message($$COMPILE_MSG mac)
}
```

If you build the project, you will see your platform-specific message each time you build the project in the **General Messages** tab (you can access this tab from **Window | Output Panes | General Messages**). Here, we defined a `COMPILE_MSG` variable and referenced it when calling `message($$COMPILE_MSG windows)`. This offers interesting possibilities when you need to compile external libraries from your `.pro` file. You can then aggregate all the sources in a variable, combine it with the call to a specific compiler, and so on.

> **TIP**
>
> If your scope-specific statement is a single line, you can use the following syntax to describe it:

```
windows:message($$COMPILE_MSG windows)
```

Besides `message()`, there are a few other helpful functions:

- `error(string)`: This function displays the string and exits the compilation immediately.
- `exists(filename)`: This function tests the existence of the `filename`. qmake also provides the `!` operator, which means you can write `!exist(myfile) { ... }`.
- `include(filename)`: This function includes the content of another `.pro` file. It gives you the ability to slice your `.pro` files into more modular components. This will prove very useful when you have multiple `.pro` files for a single big project.

> All the built-in functions are described at `http://doc.qt.io/qt-5/qmake-test-function-reference.html`.

Under the hood of qmake

As we said earlier, qmake is the foundation of the Qt framework compilation system. In Qt Creator, when you click on the **Build** button, qmake is invoked. Let's study what qmake is exactly doing by calling it ourselves on the **CLI** (**Command Line Interface**).

Create a temporary directory where you will store the generated files. We are working on a Linux box, but this is transposable on any OS. We chose `/tmp/sysinfo`. Using the CLI, navigate to this new directory and execute the following command:

```
/path/to/qt/installation/5.7/gcc_64/bin/qmake -makefile -o Makefile
/path/to/sysinfoproject/ch02-sysinfo.pro
```

This command will execute qmake in the `-makefile` mode to generate a Makefile based on your `sysinfo.pro` file. If you skim through the Makefile content, you will see many things we covered earlier in the `.pro` section. The link to Qt modules, headers of different modules, inclusion of the headers and sources files of your project, and so on.

Now, let's build this Makefile by simply typing the `make` command.

This command will generate the binary `ch02-sysinfo` (based on the `TARGET` value of the `.pro` file). If you look at the list of files now present in `/tmp/sysinfo`:

```
$ ls -1
ch02-sysinfo
CpuWidget.o
main.o
MainWindow.o
Makefile
MemoryWidget.o
moc_CpuWidget.cpp
moc_CpuWidget.o
moc_MainWindow.cpp
moc_MainWindow.o
moc_MemoryWidget.cpp
moc_MemoryWidget.o
moc_SysInfoWidget.cpp
moc_SysInfoWidget.o
SysInfoLinuxImpl.o
SysInfo.o
SysInfoWidget.o
ui_MainWindow.h
```

Now this is very interesting, we find all our sources compiled in the usual `.o` extension (`SysInfo.o`, `SysInfoWidget.o`, and so on) but there are also a lot of other files prefixed with `moc_`. Here lies another keystone of the Qt framework: the Meta Object Compiler.

Every time you use the signal/slot system, you have to include the macro `Q_OBJECT` in your header. Each time you emit a signal or receive one in a slot and you did not write any specific code to handle it, Qt took care of it. This is done by generating an intermediate implementation of your class (the `moc_*.cpp` file) containing everything Qt needs to properly handle your signals and slots.

A picture is worth a thousand words. Here is the complete compilation pipeline for a standard qmake project:

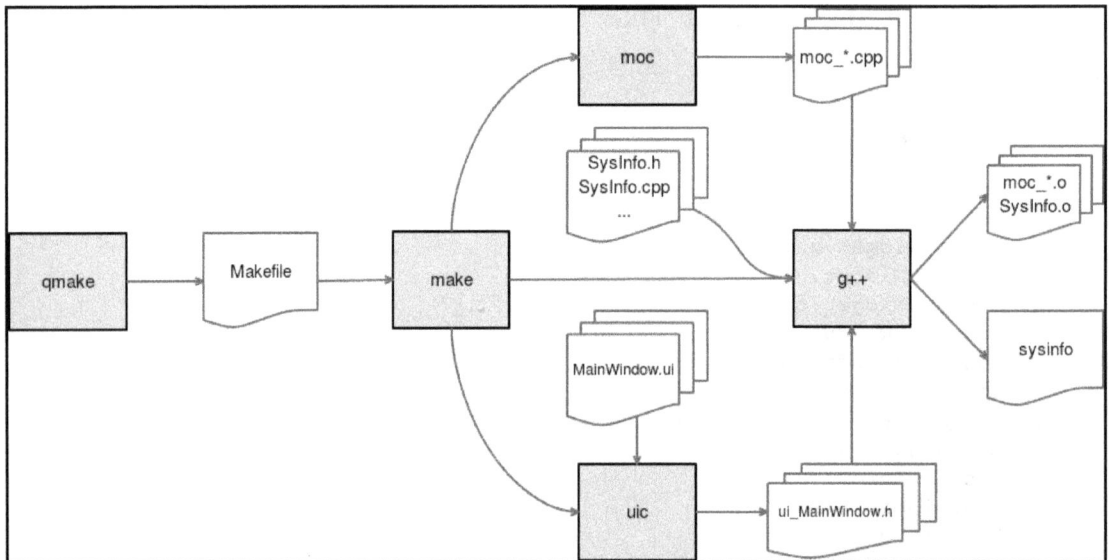

The blue boxes refer to commands and the wavy boxes are documents (sources or final binary). Let's walk through the steps:

1. The qmake command is executed with the project .pro file. It generates a Makefile based on the project file.
2. The make command is executed, which will call other commands to generate intermediate files.
3. The uic command stands for User Interface Compiler. It takes all the .ui files (which are basically an XML description of your interface) and generates the corresponding ui_*.h header that you include in your own .cpp (in our ch02-sysinfo project, it is in MainWindow.cpp).
4. The moc command takes every class containing the Q_OBJECT macro (paired with the superclass QObject) and generates the intermediate moc_*.cpp files, which include everything needed to make the signal/slot framework work.
5. The g++ command is executed, compiling all your sources' files and intermediate moc files into .o files before finally linking everything in the binary ch02-sysinfo.

Note that if you add a `Q_OBJECT` macro after the creation of a class, sometimes the compiler will complain about your signals and slots. To fix this, simply run the `qmake` command from **Build | Run qmake**. You can now see that this stems from the fact that the Makefile has to be regenerated to include the generation of the new intermediate `moc` file.

Generally, source code generation is regarded as bad practice in the developer community. Qt has been criticized on this topic for a long time. We always fear that the machines does some kind of voodoo behind our back. Unfortunately, C++ does not offer any practical way of doing code introspection (namely reflection), and the signal and slots mechanism needs some kind of metadata about your class to resolve your signals and slots. This could have been done partly with the C++ template system, but this solution seemed to Qt to be much less readable, portable, usable, and robust. You also need an excellent compiler support for templates. This cannot be assumed in the wild world of C++ compilers.

The `moc` system is now fully mature. There are some very specific edge cases where it could bring trouble (some have reported problems in very specific situations with Visual Studio), but even so, we think that the gain of this feature largely outweighs the possibly encountered issues. The signal/slot system is a marvel to work with, and if you look at the beginnings of Qt, the system has been present from the very first releases. Adding the functor notation in Qt 5 (which gives a compile time check of the validity of your `connect()`) combined with C++11 `lambas` makes it a real delight.

Beneath Q_OBJECT and signals/slots

The Qt building system should be clearer now. Still, the `Q_OBJECT` macro and the signal/slot/emit keywords are still black boxes. Let's dive into `Q_OBJECT`.

The truth lies in the source code; `Q_OBJECT` is defined in the file `qobjectdefs.h` (in Qt 5.7):

```
#define Q_OBJECT
public:
    // skipped details
    static const QMetaObject staticMetaObject;
    virtual const QMetaObject *metaObject() const;
    virtual void *qt_metacast(const char *);
    virtual int qt_metacall(QMetaObject::Call, int, void **);
    QT_TR_FUNCTIONS
private:
    // skipped details
qt_static_metacall(QObject *, QMetaObject::Call, int, void **);
```

This macro defines some static functions and a `static QMetaObject`. The body of these static functions is implemented in the generated `moc` file. We will not drown you in the gory details of the `QMetaObject` class. The role of this class is to store all the metainformation for the `QObject` subclass. It also maintains a correspondence table between the signals and slots of your class, and to the signals and slots of any connected class. Each signal and each slot is assigned with a unique index:

- The `metaObject()` function returns the `&staticMetaObject` for a normal Qt class and a `dynamicMetaObject` when working with QML objects.
- The `qt_metacast()` function performs a dynamic cast using the name of the class. This function is required because Qt does not rely on standard C++ **RTTI** (**Runtime Type Information**) to retrieve meta data about an object or a class.
- The `qt_metacall()` directly calls an internal signal or slot by its index. Because an index is used rather than a pointer, there is no pointer dereferencing, and the generated switch case can be heavily optimized by the compiler (the compiler can directly include the `jump` instruction to the specific case very early on, avoiding a lot of branch evaluation). Thus, the execution of the signal/slot mechanism is quite fast.

Qt also adds non-standard C++ keywords to manage the signal/slot mechanism, namely `signals`, `slots`, and `emit`. Let's see what is behind each one and see how everything fits inside a `connect()` function.

The `slots` and `signals` keywords are also defined in `qobjectdefs.h`:

```
#      define slots
#      define signals public
```

That is right: `slots` points to nothing and the `signals` keyword is just a placeholder for the `public` keyword. All your `signals`/`slots` are just... functions. The `signals` keyword is forced to be `public` to make sure that your signal functions are visible outside of your class (what is the point of a `private signal` anyway?). The Qt magic is simply the ability to emit a `signal` keyword to any connected `slot` keyword without knowing the detail of the class implementing this `slot`. Everything is done through the `QMetaObject` class implementation in the `moc` file. When a `signal` keyword is emitted, the function `QMetaObject::activate()` is called with the changed value and the signals index.

The last definition to study is `emit`:

```
# define emit
```

So many definitions of nothing, it is almost absurd! The `emit` keyword is completely useless from a code perspective; `moc` plainly ignores it and nothing particular happens with it afterwards. It is merely a hint for the developer to notice he is working with signal/slots rather than plain functions.

To trigger a `slot`, you must connect your `signal` keyword to it using the `QObject::connect()` function. This function creates a new `Connection` instance that is defined in `qobject_p.h`:

```
struct Connection
    {
        QObject *sender;
        QObject *receiver;
        union {
            StaticMetaCallFunction callFunction;
            QtPrivate::QSlotObjectBase *slotObj;
        };
        // The next pointer for the singly-linked ConnectionList
        Connection *nextConnectionList;
        //senders linked list
        Connection *next;
        Connection **prev;
        ...
    };
```

The `Connection` instance stores a pointer to the signal emitter class (`sender`), the slot receiver class (`receiver`), and the indexes of the connected `signal` and `slot` keywords. When a signal is emitted, every connected slot must be called. To be able to do this, every `QObject` has a linked list of `Connection` instances for each of its `signal`, and the same linked list of `Connection` for each of its `slot` keywords.

This pair of linked lists allows Qt to properly walk through each dependent `slot`/`signal` couple to trigger the right functions using the indexes. The same reasoning is used to handle the `receiver` destruction: Qt walks through the double linked list and removes the object from where it was connected.

This walk happens in the famous UI thread, where the whole message loop is processed and every connected signal/slot is triggered according to the possible events (mouse, keyboard, network, and so on). Because the QThread class inherits the QObject, any QThread can use the signal/slot mechanism. Additionally, the signals keyword can be posted to other threads where they will be processed in the receiving threads' event loop.

Summary

In this chapter, we created a cross-platform SysInfo application. We covered the singleton and the strategy pattern to have a neat code organization with platform-specific code. You learned to use the Qt Charts module to display system information in real time. Finally, we took a deep dive into the qmake command to see how Qt implements the signal/slot mechanism, and to see what is hidden behind Qt-specific keywords (emit, signals, and slots).

By now, you should have a clear picture of how Qt works and how you can tackle a cross-platform application. In the next chapter, we will look at how you can split a bigger project in order to keep your sanity as a maintainer. We will study a fundamental pattern in Qt-- the Model/View--and discover how to use a database with Qt.

11
Dividing Your Project and Ruling Your Code

The last chapter delved into qmake to study what lies beneath the signal/slot system and covered a reasonable approach to implementing platform-specific code. This chapter wants to show you how a project can be properly divided to enjoy the maximum leverage from the Qt framework.

To do this, you will create a gallery application that handles albums and pictures. You will be able to create, read, update and delete any album and display the pictures in a grid of thumbnails or in full resolution. Everything will be persisted in a SQL database.

This chapter lays the foundations of the gallery by creating a core library that will be used in the following two chapters: Chapter 12, *Conquering the Desktop UI*, and Chapter 13, *Dominating the Mobile UI*.

This chapter covers the following topics:

- Application/library project separation
- Database interaction with Qt
- Smart pointers with C++14
- Model/View architecture in Qt with an implementation of the model

Designing a maintainable project

The first step in designing a maintainable project is to properly split it in clearly defined modules. A common approach is to separate the engine from the user interface. This separation forces you to reduce coupling between the different parts of your code and make it more modular.

This is exactly the approach we will take with the `gallery` application. The project will be divided into three sub-projects:

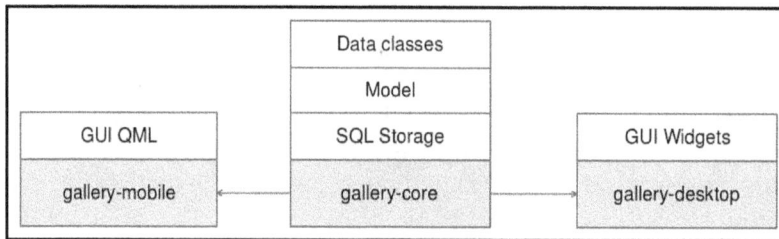

The sub-projects are as follows:

- **gallery-core**: This is a library containing the core of the application logic: the data classes (or business classes), persistent storage (in SQL), and the model that makes the storage available to the UI through a single entry point.
- **gallery-desktop**: This is a Qt widgets application that will depend on the `gallery-core` library to retrieve data and display it to the user. This project will be covered in `Chapter 12`, *Conquering the Desktop UI*.
- **gallery-mobile**: This is a QML application targeted at mobile platforms (Android and iOS). It will also rely on `gallery-core`. This project will be covered in `Chapter 13`, *Dominating the Mobile UI*.

As you can see, each layer has a single responsibility. This principle is applied to both the project structure and the code organization. Throughout these three projects, we will endeavor to live up to the motto of the chapter: "Divide your project and rule your code".

To separate your Qt project this way, we will create a different kind of project, a **Subdirs** project:

1. Click on **File | New File or Project**.
2. In the **Projects** types, select **Other Project | Subdirs Project | Choose**.

3. Name it `ch03-gallery-core` and then click on **Choose**.

4. Select your latest Qt Desktop Kit, and then click on **Next** | **Finish & Add Subproject**.

Here, Qt Creator created the parent project, `ch03-gallery-core`, which will host our three sub-projects (`gallery-core`, `gallery-desktop`, and `gallery-mobile`). The parent project has neither code nor a compilation unit in itself, it is simply a convenient way to group multiple `.pro` projects and express the dependencies between them.

The next step is to create the first `subdir` project, which Qt Creator proposed immediately when you clicked on **Finish & Add Subproject**. We will start with `gallery-core`:

1. Select **Library** in the **Projects** tab.
2. Select **C++ Library**.
3. Choose the **Shared Library** type, and name it `gallery-core`, and click on **Next**.
4. Select the modules, **QtCore**, and **QtSql**, and then click on **Next**.
5. Type **Album** in the **Class name** field, and click on **Next**. Qt Creator will generate the basic skeleton of a library with this class as an example.
6. Check that the project is properly added as a sub-project of `ch03-gallery-core.pro` and click on **Finish**.

Before delving into `gallery-core` code, let's study what Qt Creator just made for us. Open the parent `.pro` file, `ch03-gallery-core.pro`:

```
TEMPLATE = subdirs

SUBDIRS +=
    gallery-core
```

Until now, we used the `TEMPLATE = app` syntax in our `.pro` files. The `subdirs` project template indicates to Qt that it should search for sub-projects to compile. When we added the `gallery-core` project to `ch03-gallery-core.pro`, Qt Creator added it to the `SUBDIRS` variable. As you can see, `SUBDIRS` is a list, so you can add as many sub-projects as you want.

When compiling `ch03-gallery-core.pro`, Qt will scan each `SUBDIRS` value to compile them. We can now switch to `gallery-core.pro`:

```
QT          += sql
QT          -= gui

TARGET = gallery-core
TEMPLATE = lib

DEFINES += GALLERYCORE_LIBRARY
SOURCES += Album.cpp
HEADERS += Album.h
        gallery-core_global.h

unix {
    target.path = /usr/lib
    INSTALLS += target
}
```

Let's see how this works:

- The `QT` has appended the `sql` module and removed the `gui` module. By default, **QtGui** is always included and has to be removed explicitly.
- The `TEMPLATE` value is different, again. We use `lib` to tell qmake to generate a Makefile that will output a shared library named `gallery-core` (as specified by the `TARGET` variable).
- The `DEFINES += GALLERY_CORE_LIBRARY` syntax is a compilation flag that lets the compiler know when it should import or export library symbols. We will come back soon to this notion.
- The `HEADERS` contains our first class `Album.h`, but also another generated header: `gallery-core_global.h`. This file is syntactic sugar provided by Qt to ease the pain of a cross-platform library.
- The `unix { ... }` scope specifies the installation destination of the library. This platform scope is generated because we created the project on Linux. By default it will try to install the library in the system library path (`/usr/lib`).

Please remove the `unix` scope altogether, we don't need to make the library available system-wide.

To have a better understanding of the cross-platform shared object issue, you can open
gallery-core_global.h:

```
#include <QtCore/qglobal.h>

#if defined(GALLERYCORE_LIBRARY)
#  define GALLERYCORESHARED_EXPORT Q_DECL_EXPORT
#else
#  define GALLERYCORESHARED_EXPORT Q_DECL_IMPORT
#endif
```

We encounter again the GALLERYCORE_LIBRARY defined in gallery-core.pro file. Qt
Creator generated a useful piece of code for us: the cross-platform way to handle symbol
visibility in a shared library.

When your application links to a shared library, symbol functions, variables, or classes
must be marked in a special way to be visible by the application using the shared library.
The default visibility of a symbol depends on the platform. Some platforms will hide
symbols by default, other platforms will make them public. Of course, each platform and
compiler has its own macros to express this public/private notion.

To obviate the whole #ifdef windows #else boilerplate code, Qt provides
a Q_DECL_EXPORT (if we are compiling the library) and Q_DECL_IMPORT (if we are
compiling your application using the shared library). Thus, throughout the symbols you
want to mark as public, you just have to use the GALLERYCORESHARED_EXPORT macro.

An example is available in the Album.h file:

```
#ifndef ALBUM_H
#define ALBUM_H

#include "gallery-core_global.h"

class GALLERYCORESHARED_EXPORT Album
{

public:
    Album();
};

#endif // ALBUM_H
```

You include the proper `gallery-core_global.h` file to have access to the macro and you use it just after the `class` keyword. It does not pollute your code too much and is still cross-platform.

> Another possibility is to make a **Statically Linked Library**. This path is interesting if you want fewer dependencies to handle (a single binary is always easier to deploy). There are several downsides:

- Increased compilation time: each time you modify the library, the application will have to be recompiled as well.
- Tighter coupling, multiple applications cannot link to your library. Each one of them must embed it.

Defining data classes

We are building our gallery from the ground up. We will start with the implementation of our data classes to be able to properly write the database layer. The application aims to organize pictures into albums. Hence, the two obvious classes are `Album` and `Picture`. In our example, an album simply has a name. A `Picture` class must belong to an `Album` class and has a file path (the path on your filesystem where the original file is located).

The `Album` class has already been created on project creation. Open the `Album.h` file and update it to include the following implementation:

```
#include <QString>

#include "gallery-core_global.h"

class GALLERYCORESHARED_EXPORT Album
{
public:
    explicit Album(const QString& name = "");

    int id() const;
    void setId(int id);
    QString name() const;
    void setName(const QString& name);

private:
    int mId;
    QString mName;
};
```

As you can see, the `Album` class contains only a `mId` variable (the database ID) and a `mName` variable. In a typical **OOP (Object Oriented Paradigm)** fashion, the `Album` class would have had a `QVector<Picture>mPictures` field. We did not do it on purpose. By decoupling these two objects, we will have more flexibility when we want to load an album without pulling the potential thousands of associated pictures. The other problem in having `mPictures` in the `Album` class is that the developer (you or anybody else) using this code will ask himself: when is `mPictures` loaded? Should I do a partial load of the `Album` and have an incomplete `Album` or should I always load `Album` with every picture in it?

By completely removing the field, the question ceases to exist, and the code is simpler to grasp. The developer knows intuitively that he will have to explicitly load the pictures if he want them; otherwise, he can continue with this simple `Album` class.

The getters and setters are obvious enough; we will let you implement them without showing them to you. We will only take a look at the `Album` class' constructor in `Album.cpp`:

```
Album::Album(const QString& name) :
    mId(-1),
    mName(name)
{
}
```

The `mId` variable is initialized to -1 to be sure that, by default, an invalid id is used, and the `mName` variable is assigned a `name` value.

We can now proceed to the `Picture` class. Create a new C++ class named `Picture` and open `Picture.h` to modify it like so:

```
#include <QUrl>
#include <QString>

#include "gallery-core_global.h"

class GALLERYCORESHARED_EXPORT Picture
{
public:
    Picture(const QString& filePath = "");
    Picture(const QUrl& fileUrl);

    int id() const;
    void setId(int id);

    int albumId() const;
    void setAlbumId(int albumId);
```

```
    QUrl fileUrl() const;
    void setFileUrl(const QUrl& fileUrl);
private:
    int mId;
    int mAlbumId;
    QUrl mFileUrl;
};
```

Do not forget to add the GALLERYCORESHARED_EXPORT macro right before the class keyword to export the class from the library. As a data structure, Picture has a mId variable, belongs to a mAlbumId variable, and has a mUrl value. We use the QUrl type to make path manipulation easier to use depending on the platform (desktop or mobile).

Let's take a look at Picture.cpp:

```
#include "Picture.h"
Picture::Picture(const QString& filePath) :
    Picture(QUrl::fromLocalFile(filePath))
{
}

Picture::Picture(const QUrl& fileUrl) :
    mId(-1),
    mAlbumId(-1),
    mFileUrl(fileUrl)
{
}

QUrl Picture::fileUrl() const
{
    return mFileUrl;
}

void Picture::setFileUrl(const QUrl& fileUrl)
{
    mFileUrl = fileUrl;
}
```

In the first constructor, the static function, QUrl::fromLocalFile, is called to provide a QUrl object to the other constructor, which takes a QUrl parameter.

The ability to call other constructors is a nice addition in C++11.

Storing your data in a database

Now that the data classes are ready, we can proceed to implement the database layer. Qt provides a ready-to-use `sql` module. Various databases are supported in Qt using SQL database drivers. In `gallery-desktop`, we will use the `SQLITE3` driver, which is included in the `sql` module and perfectly fits the use case:

- **A very simple database schema**: No need for complex queries
- **Very few or no concurrent transactions**: No need for a complex transaction model
- **A single-purpose database**: No need to spawn a system service, the database is stored in a single file and does not need to be accessed by multiple applications

The database will be accessed from multiple locations; we need to have a single entry point for it. Create a new C++ class named `DatabaseManager` and modify `DatabaseManager.h` to look like this:

```
#include <QString>

class QSqlDatabase;

const QString DATABASE_FILENAME = "gallery.db";

class DatabaseManager
{
public:
    static DatabaseManager& instance();
    ~DatabaseManager();

protected:
    DatabaseManager(const QString& path = DATABASE_FILENAME);
    DatabaseManager& operator=(const DatabaseManager& rhs);

private:
    QSqlDatabase* mDatabase;
};
```

The first thing to notice is that we implement the singleton pattern in the `DatabaseManager` class, like we did in the *Transforming SysInfo in a singleton* section from `Chapter 10`, *Discovering QMake Secrets*. The `DatabaseManager` class will open the connection in the `mDatabase` field and lend it to other possible classes.

Also, QSqlDatabase is forward-declared and used as a pointer for the mDatabase field. We could have included the QSqlDatabase header, but we would have had a non-desired side-effect: every file, which includes DatabaseManager, must also include QSqlDatabase. Thus, if we ever have some transitive inclusion in our application (which links to the gallery-core library), the application is forced to enable the sql module. As a consequence, the storage layer leaks through the library. The application should not have any knowledge about the storage layer implementation. For all the application cares, it could be in SQL, XML, or anything else; the library is a black box that should honor the contract and persist the data.

Let's switch to DatabaseManager.cpp and open the database connection:

```cpp
#include "DatabaseManager.h"

#include <QSqlDatabase>

DatabaseManager& DatabaseManager::instance()
{
    static DatabaseManager singleton;
    return singleton;
}

DatabaseManager::DatabaseManager(const QString& path)  :
    mDatabase(new QSqlDatabase(QSqlDatabase::addDatabase("QSQLITE")))
{
    mDatabase->setDatabaseName(path);
    mDatabase->open();
}

DatabaseManager::~DatabaseManager()
{
    mDatabase->close();
    delete mDatabase;
}
```

The correct database driver is selected on the mDatabase field initialization with the QSqlDatabase::addDatabase("QSQLITE") function call. The following steps are just a matter of configuring the database name (which is incidentally the file path in SQLITE3) and opening the connection with the mDatabase->open() function. In the DatabaseManager destructor, the connection is closed and the mDatabase pointer is properly deleted.

The database link is now opened; all we have to do is to execute our `Album` and `Picture` queries. Implementing the **CRUD (Create/Read/Update/Delete)** for both our data classes in `DatabaseManager` would quickly push `DatabaseManager.cpp` to be several hundreds of lines long. Add a few more tables and you can already see what a monster `DatabaseManager` would turn into.

For this reason, each of our data classes will have a dedicated database class, responsible for all the database CRUD operations. We will start with the `Album` class; create a new C++ class named `AlbumDao` (data access object) and update `AlbumDao.h`:

```cpp
class QSqlDatabase;

class AlbumDao
{
public:
    AlbumDao(QSqlDatabase& database);
    void init() const;

private:
    QSqlDatabase& mDatabase;
};
```

The `AlbumDao` class's constructor takes a `QSqlDatabase&` parameter. This parameter is the database connection that will be used for all the SQL queries done by the `AlbumDao` class. The `init()` function aims to create the `albums` table and should be called when `mDatabase` is opened.

Let's see the implementation of `AlbumDao.cpp`:

```cpp
#include <QSqlDatabase>
#include <QSqlQuery>

#include "DatabaseManager.h"

AlbumDao::AlbumDao(QSqlDatabase& database) :
    mDatabase(database)
{
}

void AlbumDao::init() const
{
    if (!mDatabase.tables().contains("albums")) {
        QSqlQuery query(mDatabase);
        query.exec("CREATE TABLE albums (id INTEGER PRIMARY KEY
AUTOINCREMENT, name TEXT)");
    }
```

```
    }
```

As usual, the `mDatabase` field is initialized with the database parameter. In the `init()` function, we can see a real SQL request in action. If the table `albums` class does not exist, a `QSqlQuery` query is created that will use the `mDatabase` connection to be executed. If you omit `mDatabase`, the query will use a default anonymous connection.

The `query.exec()` function is the simplest manner of executing a query: you simply pass the `QString` type of your query and it's done. Here we create the `albums` table with the fields matching the data class `Album` (`id` and `name`).

> **TIP**
>
> The `QSqlQuery::exec()` function returns a `bool` value that indicates if the request has been successful. In your production code, always check this value. You can further investigate the error with `QSqlQuery::lastError()`. An example is available in the source code of the chapter in `DatabaseManager::debugQuery()`.

The skeleton of `AlbumDao` class is done. The next step is to link it to the `DatabaseManager` class. Update the `DatabaseManager` class like so:

```cpp
// In DatabaseManager.h
#include "AlbumDao.h"

...

private:
    QSqlDatabase* mDatabase;

public:
    const AlbumDao albumDao;
};

// In DatabaseManager.cpp
DatabaseManager::DatabaseManager(const QString& path) :
    mDatabase(new QSqlDatabase(QSqlDatabase::addDatabase("QSQLITE"))),
    albumDao(*mDatabase)
{
    mDatabase->setDatabaseName(path);
    mDatabase->open();

    albumDao.init();
}
```

The `albumDao` field is declared as a `public const AlbumDao` in
the `DatabaseManager.h` file. This needs some explanation:

- The `public` visibility is to give access to `DatabaseManager` clients to
  the `albumDao` field. The API becomes intuitive enough; if you want to make a
  database operation on an `album`, just
  call `DatabaseManager::instance().albumDao`.
- The `const` keyword is to make sure that nobody can modify `albumDao`. Because
  it is `public`, we cannot guarantee the safety of the object (anybody could modify
  the object). As a side-effect, we force every public function of `AlbumDao` to
  be `const`. This makes sense; after all, the `AlbumDao` field could have been a
  namespace with a bunch of functions. It is more convenient for it to be a class
  because we can keep the reference to the database connection with
  the `mDatabase` field.

In the `DatabaseManager` constructor, the `albumDao` class is initialized with
the `mDatabase` dereferenced pointer. The `albumDao.init()` function is called after the
database connection has opened.

We can now proceed to implement more interesting SQL queries. We can start with the
creation of a new album in the `AlbumDao` class:

```
// In AlbumDao.h
class QSqlDatabase;
class Album;

class AlbumDao
{
public:
    AlbumDao(QSqlDatabase& database);
    void init() const;
    void addAlbum(Album& album) const;
    ...
};

// In AlbumDao.cpp

#include <QSqlDatabase>
#include <QSqlQuery>
#include <QVariant>

...

void AlbumDao::addAlbum(Album& album) const
{
```

```
QSqlQuery query(mDatabase);
query.prepare("INSERT INTO albums (name) VALUES (:name)");
query.bindValue(":name", album.name());
query.exec();
album.setId(query.lastInsertId().toInt());
}
```

The `addAlbum()` function takes an `album` parameter to extract its information and execute the corresponding query. Here, we approach the prepared query notion: the `query.prepare()` function takes a `query` parameter which contains placeholders for parameters provided later. We will provide the `name` parameter with the syntax `:name`. Two syntaxes are supported: Oracle style with a colon-name (for example, `:name`) or ODBC style with a question mark (for example, `?name`).

We then bind the bind `:name` syntax to the value of the `album.name()` function. Because `QSqlQuery::bind()` expects a `QVariant` as a parameter value, we have to add the `include` directive to this class.

In a nutshell, a `QVariant` is a generic data holder that accepts a wide range of primitive types (`char`, `int`, `double`, and so on) and complex types (`QString`, `QByteArray`, `QUrl`, and so on).

When the `query.exec()` function is executed, the bound values are properly replaced. The `prepare()` statement technique makes the code more robust to SQL injection (injecting a hidden request would fail) and more readable.

The execution of the query modifies the state of the object query itself. The `QSqlQuery` query is not simply a SQL query executor, it also contains the state of the active query. We can retrieve information about the query with the `query.lastInsertId()` function, which returns a `QVariant` value containing the ID of the album row we just inserted. This `id` is given to the `album` provided in the `addAlbum()` parameter. Because we modify `album`, we cannot mark the parameter as `const`. Being strict about the `const` correctness of your code is a good hint for a fellow developer, who can deduce that your function might (or not) modify the passed parameter.

The remaining update and delete operations follow strictly the same pattern used for `addAlbum()`. We will just provide the expected function signatures in the next code snippet. Please refer to the source code of the chapter for the complete implementation. However, we need to implement the request to retrieve all the albums in the database. This one deserves a closer look:

```
// In AlbumDao.h
#include <QVector>
```

```
    ...
    void addAlbum(Album& album) const;
    void updateAlbum(const Album& album) const;
    void removeAlbum(int id) const;
    QVector<Album*> albums() const;
    ...
};

// In AlbumDao.cpp
QVector<Album*> AlbumDao::albums() const
{
    QSqlQuery query("SELECT * FROM albums", mDatabase);
    query.exec();
    QVector<Album*> list;
    while(query.next()) {
        Album* album = new Album();
        album->setId(query.value("id").toInt());
        album->setName(query.value("name").toString());
        list.append(album);
    }
    return list;
}
```

The `albums()` function must return a `QVector<Album*>` value. If we take a look at the body of the function, we see yet another property of `QSqlQuery`. To walk through multiple rows for a given request, `query` handles an internal cursor pointing to the current row. We can then proceed to create a `new Album*()` function and fill it with the row data with the `query.value()` statement, which takes a column name parameter and returns a `QVariant` value that is casted to the proper type. This new `album` parameter is appended to the `list` and, finally, this `list` is returned to the caller.

The `PictureDao` class is very similar to the `AlbumDao` class, both in usage and implementation. The main difference is that a picture has a foreign key to an album. The `PictureDao` function must be conditioned by an `albumId` parameter. The following code snippet shows the `PictureDao` header and the `init()` function:

```
// In PictureDao.h
#include <QVector>

class QSqlDatabase;
class Picture;

class PictureDao
{
public:
    explicit PictureDao(QSqlDatabase& database);
```

```
    void init() const;

    void addPictureInAlbum(int albumId, Picture& picture) const;
    void removePicture(int id) const;
    void removePicturesForAlbum(int albumId) const;
    QVector<Picture*> picturesForAlbum(int albumId) const;

private:
    QSqlDatabase& mDatabase;
};

// In PictureDao.cpp
void PictureDao::init() const
{
    if (!mDatabase.tables().contains("pictures")) {
        QSqlQuery query(mDatabase);
        query.exec(QString("CREATE TABLE pictures")
        + " (id INTEGER PRIMARY KEY AUTOINCREMENT, "
        + "album_id INTEGER, "
        + "url TEXT)");
    }
}
```

As you can see, multiple functions take an `albumId` parameter to make the link between the picture and the owning `album` parameter. In the `init()` function, the foreign key is expressed in the `album_id INTEGER` syntax. SQLITE3 does not have a proper foreign key type. It is a very simple database and there is no strict constraint for this type of field; a simple integer is used.

Finally, the `PictureDao` function is added in the `DatabaseManager` class exactly as we did for `albumDao`. One could argue that, if there are a lot of `Dao` classes, adding a `const Dao` member in the `DatabaseManager` class and calling the `init()` function quickly becomes cumbersome.

A possible solution could be to make an abstract `Dao` class, with a pure virtual `init()` function. The `DatabaseManager` class would have a `Dao` registry, which maps each `Dao` to a `QString` key with a `QHash<QString, const Dao> mDaos`. The `init()` function call would then be called in a `for` loop and a `Dao` object would be accessed using the `QString` key. This is outside the scope of this project, but is nevertheless an interesting approach.

Protecting your code with a smart pointer

The code we just described is fully functional, but, it can be strengthened, specifically with the function, `AlbumDao::albums()`. In this function, we iterate through the database rows and create a new `Album` to fill a list. We can zoom in on this specific code section:

```
QVector<Album*> list;
while(query.next()) {
    Album* album = new Album();
    album->setId(query.value("id").toInt());
    album->setName(query.value("name").toString());
    list.append(album);
}
return list;
```

Let's say that the `name` column has been renamed to `title`. If you forget to update `query.value("name")`, you might run into trouble. The Qt framework does not rely on exceptions, but this cannot be said for every API available in the wild. An exception here would cause a memory leak: the `Album* album` function has been allocated on the heap but not released. To handle this, you would have to surround the risky code with a `try catch` statement and deallocate the `album` parameter if an exception has been thrown. Maybe this error should bubble up; hence, your `try catch` statement is only there to handle the potential memory leak. Can you picture the spaghetti code weaving in front of you?

The real issue with pointers is the uncertainty of their ownership. Once it has been allocated, who is the owner of a pointer? Who is responsible for deallocating the object? When you pass a pointer as a parameter, when does the caller retain the ownership or release it to the callee?

Since C++11, a major milestone has been reached in memory management: the smart pointer feature has been stabilized and can greatly improve the safety of your code. The goal is to explicitly indicate the ownership of a pointer through simple template semantics. There are three types of smart pointer:

- The `unique_ptr` pointer indicates that the owner is the only owner of the pointer
- The `shared_ptr` pointer indicates that the pointer's ownership is shared among several clients
- The `weak_ptr` pointer indicates that the pointer does not belong to the client

For now, we will focus on the `unique_ptr` pointer to understand smart pointer mechanics.

A `unique_ptr` pointer is simply a variable allocated on the stack that takes the ownership of the pointer you provide with it. Let's allocate an `Album` with this semantic:

```
#include <memory>
void foo()
{
    Album* albumPointer = new Album();
    std::unique_ptr<Album> album(albumPointer);
    album->setName("Unique Album");
}
```

The whole smart pointer API is available in the `memory` header. When we declared `album` as a `unique_ptr`, we did two things:

- We allocated on the stack a `unique_ptr<Album>`. The `unique_ptr` pointer relies on templates to check at compile time the validity of the pointer type.
- We granted the ownership of `albumPointer` memory to `album`. From this point on, `album` is the owner of the pointer.

This simple line has important ramifications. First and foremost, you do not have to worry anymore about the pointer life cycle. Because a `unique_ptr` pointer is allocated on the stack, it will be destroyed as soon as it goes out of scope. In this example, when we exit `foo()`, `album` will be removed from the stack. The `unique_ptr` implementation will take care of calling the `Album` destructor and deallocating the memory.

Secondly, you explicitly indicate the ownership of your pointer at compile time. Nobody can deallocate the `albumPointer` content if they do not voluntarily fiddle with your `unique_ptr` pointer. Your fellow developers will also know with a single glance who is the owner of your pointer.

Note that, even though `album` is a type of `unique_ptr<Album>`, you can still call `Album` functions (for example, `album->setName()`) using the `->` operator. This is possible thanks to the overload of this operator. The usage of the `unique_ptr` pointer becomes transparent.

Well, this use case is nice, but the purpose of a pointer is to be able to allocate a chunk of memory and share it. Let's say the `foo()` function allocates the `album unique_ptr` pointer and then transfers the ownership to `bar()`. This would look like this:

```
void foo()
{
    std::unique_ptr<Album> album(new Album());
```

```
    bar(std::move(album));
}

void bar(std::unique_ptr<Album> barAlbum)
{
    qDebug() << "Album name" << barAlbum->name();
}
```

Here, we introduce the `std::move()` function: its goal is to transfer the ownership of a `unique_ptr` function. Once `bar(std::move(album))` has been called, `album` becomes invalid. You can test it with a simple `if` statement: `if (album) { ... }`.

From now on, the `bar()` function becomes the owner of the pointer (through `barAlbum`) by allocating a new `unique_ptr` on the stack and it will deallocate the pointer on its exit. You do not have to worry about the cost of a `unique_ptr` pointer, as these objects are very lightweight and it is unlikely that they will affect the performance of your application.

Again, the signature of `bar()` tells the developer that this function expects to take the ownership of the passed `Album`. Trying to pass around `unique_ptr` without the `move()` function will lead to a compile error.

Another thing to note is the different meanings of the . (dot) and the -> (arrow) when working with a `unique_ptr` pointer:

- The -> operator dereferences to the pointer members and lets your call function on your real object
- The . operator gives you access to the `unique_ptr` object functions

The `unique_ptr` pointer provides various functions. Among the most important are:

- The `get()` function returns the raw pointer. The `album.get()` returns an `Album*` value.
- The `release()` function releases the ownership of the pointer and returns the raw pointer. The `album.release()` function returns an `Album*` value.
- The `reset(pointer p = pointer())` function destroys the currently managed pointer and takes ownership of the given parameter. An example would be the `barAlbum.reset()` function, which destroys the currently owned `Album*`. With a parameter, `barAlbum.reset(new Album())` also destroys the owned object and takes the ownership of the provided parameter.

Finally, you can dereference the object with the * operation, meaning *album will return an Album& value. This dereferencing is convenient, but you will see that the more a smart pointer is used, the less you will need it. Most of the time, you will replace a raw pointer with the following syntax:

```
void bar(std::unique_ptr<Album>& barAlbum);
```

Because we pass the unique_ptr by reference, bar() does not take ownership of the pointer and will not try do deallocate it upon its exit. With this, there is no need to use move(album) in foo(); the bar() function will just do operations on the album parameter but will not take its ownership.

Now, let's consider shared_ptr. A shared_ptr pointer keeps a reference counter on a pointer. Each time a shared_ptr pointer references the same object, the counter is incremented; when this shared_ptr pointer goes out of scope, the counter is decremented. When the counter reaches zero, the object is deallocated.

Let's rewrite our foo()/bar() example with a shared_ptr pointer:

```
#include <memory>
void foo()
{
    std::shared_ptr<Album> album(new Album()); // ref counter = 1
    bar(album); // ref counter = 2
} // ref counter = 0

void bar(std::shared_ptr<Album> barAlbum)
{
    qDebug() << "Album name" << barAlbum->name();
} // ref counter = 1
```

As you can see, the syntax is very similar to the unique_ptr pointer. The reference counter is incremented each time a new shared_ptr pointer is allocated and points to the same data, and is decremented on the function exit. You can check the current count by calling the album.use_count() function.

The last smart pointer we will cover is the weak_ptr pointer. As the name suggests, it does not take any ownership or increment the reference counter. When a function specifies a weak_ptr, it indicates to the callers that it is just a client and not an owner of the pointer. If we re implement bar() with a weak_ptr pointer, we get:

```
#include <memory>
void foo()
{
    std::shared_ptr<Album> album(new Album()); // ref counter = 1
```

```
    bar(std::weak_ptr<Album>(album)); // ref counter = 1
} // ref counter = 0

void bar(std::weak_ptr<Album> barAlbum)
{
    qDebug() << "Album name" << barAlbum->name();
} // ref counter = 1
```

If the story stopped here, there would not be any interest in using a `weak_ptr` versus a raw pointer. The `weak_ptr` has a major advantage for the dangling pointer issue. If you are building a cache, you typically do not want to keep strong references to your object. On the other hand, you want to know if the objects are still valid. By using `weak_ptr`, you know when an object has been deallocated. Now, consider the raw pointer approach: your pointer might be invalid but you do not know the state of the memory.

There is another semantic introduced in C++14 that we have to cover: `make_unique`. This keyword aims to replace the `new` keyword and construct a `unique_ptr` object in an exception-safe manner. This is how it is used:

```
unique_ptr<Album> album = make_unique<Album>();
```

The `make_unique` keyword wraps the `new` keyword to make it exception-safe, specifically in this situation:

```
foo(new Album(), new Picture())
```

This code will be executed in the following order:

1. Allocate and construct the `Album` function.
2. Allocate and construct the `Picture` function.
3. Execute the `foo()` function.

If `new Picture()` throws an exception, the memory allocated by `new Album()` will be leaked. This is fixed by using the `make_unique` keyword:

```
foo(make_unique<Album>(), make_unique<Picture>())
```

The `make_unique` keyword returns a `unique_ptr` pointer; the C++ standard committee also provided an equivalent for `shared_ptr` in the form of `make_shared`, which follows the same principle.

All these new C++ semantics try very hard to get rid of `new` and `delete`. Yet, it may be cumbersome to write all the `unique_ptr` and `make_unique` stuff. The `auto` keyword comes to the rescue in our `album` creation:

```
auto album = make_unique<Album>()
```

This is a radical departure from the common C++ syntax. The variable type is deduced, there is no explicit pointer, and the memory is automatically managed. After some time with smart pointers, you will see fewer and fewer raw pointers in your code (and even fewer `delete`, which is such a relief). The remaining raw pointers will simply indicate that a client is using the pointer but does not own it.

Overall, C++11 and C++14 smart pointers are a real step up in C++ code writing. Before them, the bigger the code base, the more insecure we felt about memory management. Our brain is just bad at properly grasping complexity at such a level. Smart pointers simply make you feel safe about what you write. On the other hand, you retain full control of the memory. For performance-critical code, you can always handle the memory yourself. For everything else, smart pointers are an elegant way of explicitly indicating your object's ownership and freeing your mind.

We are now equipped to rewrite the little insecure snippet in the `AlbumDao::albums()` function. Update `AlbumDao::albums()` like so:

```
// In AlbumDao.h
std::unique_ptr<std::vector<std::unique_ptr<Album>>> albums() const;

// In AlbumDao.cpp
unique_ptr<vector<unique_ptr<Album>>> AlbumDao::albums() const
{
    QSqlQuery query("SELECT * FROM albums", mDatabase);
    query.exec();
    unique_ptr<vector<unique_ptr<Album>>> list(new
vector<unique_ptr<Album>>());
    while(query.next()) {
        unique_ptr<Album> album(new Album());
        album->setId(query.value("id").toInt());
        album->setName(query.value("name").toString());
        list->push_back(move(album));
    }
    return list;
}
```

Wow! The signature of the `album()` function has turned into something very peculiar. Smart pointers are supposed to make your life easier, right? Let's break it down to understand a major point of smart pointers with Qt: container behavior.

The initial goal of the rewrite was to secure the creation of `album`. We want the `list` to be the explicit owner of the `album`. This would have changed our `list` type (that is `albums()` return type) to `QVector<unique_ptr<Album>>`. However, when the `list` type is returned, its elements will be copied (remember, we previously defined the return type to `QVector<Album>`). A natural way out of this would be to return a `QVector<unique_ptr<Album>>*` type to retain the uniqueness of our `Album` elements.

Behold, here lies a major pain: the `QVector` class overloads the copy operator. Hence, when the `list` type is returned, the uniqueness of our `unique_ptr` elements cannot be guaranteed by the compiler and it will throw a compile error. This is why we have to resort to a `vector` object coming from the standard library and write the long type: `unique_ptr<vector<unique_ptr<Album>>>`.

> Take a look at the official response for support of the `unique_ptr` pointer in the Qt container. It is clear beyond any possible doubt: `http://lists.qt-project.org/pipermail/interest/2013-July/007776.html`. The short answer is: no, it will never be done. Do not even mention it. Ever.

If we translate this new `albums()` signature into plain English it will read: the `album()` function returns a vector of `Album`. This vector is the owner of the `Album` elements it contains and you will be the owner of the vector.

To finish covering this implementation of `albums()`, you may notice that we did not use the `auto` and `make_unique` keywords for the `list` declaration. Our library will be used on a mobile in *Chapter 13*, *Dominating the Mobile UI*, and C++14 is not yet supported on this platform. Therefore, we have to restrain our code to C++11.

We also encounter the use of the `move` function in the instruction `list->push_back(move(album))`. Until that line, the `album` is "owned" by the `while` scope, the move gives the ownership to the list. At the last instruction, `return list`, we should have written `move(list)`, but C++11 accepts the direct return and will automatically make the `move()` function for us.

What we covered in this section is that the `AlbumDao` class is completely matched in `PictureDao`. Please refer to the source code of the chapter to see the full `PictureDao` class implementation.

Implementing the model

The data is ready to be exposed to potential clients (the applications that will display and edit its content). However, a direct connection between the client and the database will make a very strong coupling. If we decide to switch to another storage type, the view would have to be rewritten, partially at least.

This is where the model comes to our rescue. It is an abstract layer that communicates with the data (our database) and exposes this data to the client in a data-specific, implementation-agnostic form. This approach is a direct offspring of the **MVC** (**Model View Controller**) concept. Let's recapitulate how MVC works:

- The Model manages the data. It is responsible for requesting for the data and updating it.
- The View displays the data to the user.
- The Controller interacts with both the Model and the View. It is responsible for feeding the View with the correct data and sending commands to the Model based on the user interaction received from the View.

This paradigm enables swapping various parts without disturbing the others. Multiple views can display the same data, the data layer can be changed, and the upper parts will not be aware of it.

Qt combines the View and the Controller to form the Model/View architecture. The separation of the storage and the presentation is retained while being simpler to implement than a full MVC approach. To allow editing and view customization, Qt introduces the concept of Delegate, which is connected to both the Model and the View:

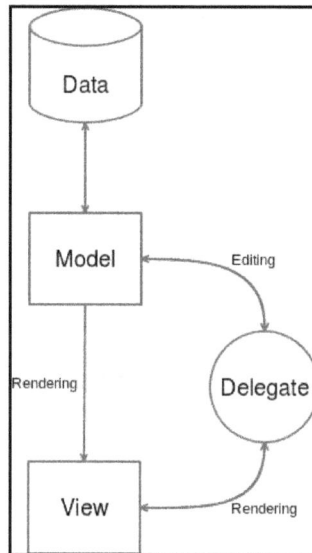

The Qt documentation about Model/View is truly plethoric. It is nevertheless easy to get lost in the details; it feels sometimes a bit overwhelming. We will try to clear things up by implementing the AlbumModel class and seeing how it works.

Qt offers various Model sub-classes that all extend from QAbstractItemModel. Before starting the implementation, we have to carefully choose which base class will be extended. Keep in mind that our data are variations on lists: we will have a list of albums, and each album will have a list of pictures. Let's see what Qt offers us:

- QAbstractItemModel: This class is the most abstract, and therefore, the most complex, to implement. We will have to redefine a lot of functions to properly use it.
- QStringListModel: This class is a model that supplies strings to views. It is too simple. Our model is more complex (we have custom objects).
- QSqlTableModel (or QSqlQueryModel): This class is a very interesting contender. It automatically handles multiple SQL queries. On the other hand, it works only for very simple table schemas. In the pictures table, for example, the album_id foreign key makes it very hard to fit this model. You might save some lines of code, but if feels like trying to shoehorn a round peg into a square hole.
- QAbstractListModel: This class provides a model that offers one-dimensional lists. This fits nicely with our requirements, saves a lot of key strokes, and is still flexible enough.

We will go with the `QabstractListModel` class and create a new C++ class named `AlbumModel`. Update the `AlbumModel.h` file to look like this:

```
#include <QAbstractListModel>
#include <QHash>
#include <vector>
#include <memory>

#include "gallery-core_global.h"
#include "Album.h"
#include "DatabaseManager.h"

class GALLERYCORESHARED_EXPORT AlbumModel : public QAbstractListModel
{
    Q_OBJECT
public:

    enum Roles {
        IdRole = Qt::UserRole + 1,
        NameRole,
    };

    AlbumModel(QObject* parent = 0);

    QModelIndex addAlbum(const Album& album);

    int rowCount(const QModelIndex& parent = QModelIndex()) const override;
    QVariant data(const QModelIndex& index, int role = Qt::DisplayRole)
const override;
    bool setData(const QModelIndex& index, const QVariant& value, int role)
override;
    bool removeRows(int row, int count, const QModelIndex& parent)
override;
    QHash<int, QByteArray> roleNames() const override;

private:
    bool isIndexValid(const QModelIndex& index) const;

private:
    DatabaseManager& mDb;
    std::unique_ptr<std::vector<std::unique_ptr<Album>>> mAlbums;
};
```

The `AlbumModel` class extends the `QAbstractListModel` class and has only two members:

- mDb: This is the link to the database. In the Model/View schema, the model will communicate with the data layer through mDb.

- mAlbums: This acts as a buffer that will avoid hitting the database too much. The type should remind you of what we wrote for AlbumDao::albums() with the smart pointers.

The only specific functions the AlbumModel class has are addAlbum() and isIndexValid(). The rest are overrides of QAbstractListModel functions. We will go through each of these functions to understand how a model works.

First, let's see how the AlbumModel class is constructed in the AlbumModel.cpp file:

```
AlbumModel::AlbumModel(QObject* parent)  :
    QAbstractListModel(parent),
    mDb(DatabaseManager::instance()),
    mAlbums(mDb.albumDao.albums())
{
}
```

The mDb file is initialized with the DatabaseManager singleton address, and, after that, we see the now famous AlbumDao::albums() in action.

The vector type is returned and initializes mAlbums. This syntax make the ownership transfer automatic without any need for an explicit call to the std::move() function. If there are any stored albums in the database, mAlbums is immediately filled with those.

Each time the model interacts with the view (to notify us about changes or to serve data), mAlbums will be used. Because it is in memory only, reading will be very fast. Of course, we have to be careful about maintaining mAlbum coherently with the database state, but everything will stay inside the AlbumModel inner mechanics.

As we said earlier, the model aims to be the central point to interact with the data. Each time the data changes, the model will emit a signal to notify the view; each time the view wants to display data, it will request the model for it. The AlbumModel class overrides everything needed for read and write access. The read functions are:

- rowCount(): This function is used to get the list size
- data(): This function is used to get a specific piece of information about the data to display
- roleNames(): This function is used to indicate to the framework the name for each "role". We will explain in a few paragraphs what a role is

The editing functions are:

- `setData()`: This function is used to update data
- `removeRows()`: This function is used to remove data

We will start with the read part, where the view asks the model for the data.

Because we will display a list of albums, the first thing the view should know is how many items are available. This is done in the `rowCount()` function:

```
int AlbumModel::rowCount(const QModelIndex& parent) const
{
    return mAlbums->size();
}
```

Being our buffer object, using `mAlbums->size()` is perfect. There is no need to query the database, as `mAlbums` is already filled with all the albums of the database. The `rowCount()` function has an unknown parameter: a `const QModelIndex& parent`. Here, it is not used, but we have to explain what lies beneath this type before continuing our journey in the `AlbumModel` class.

The `QModelIndex` class is a central notion of the Model/View framework in Qt. It is a lightweight object used to locate data within a model. We use a simple `QAbstractListModel` class, but Qt is able to handle three representation types:

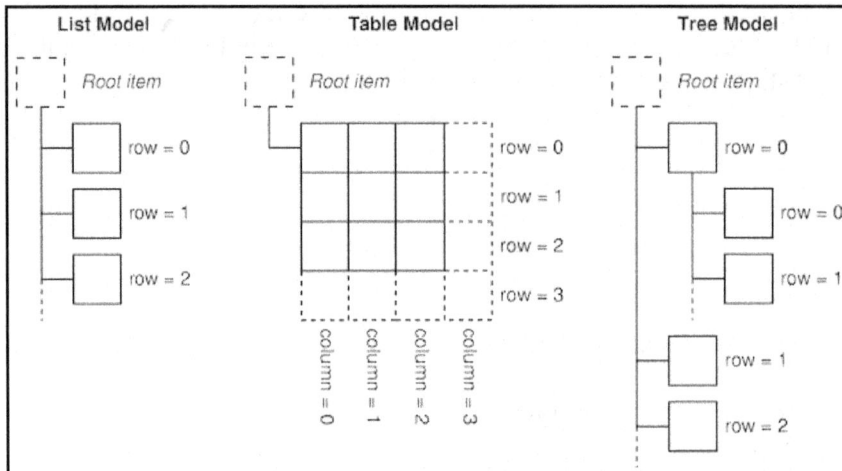

There is no better explanation than an official Qt diagram

Let's now see the models in detail:

- **List Model**: In this model, the data is stored in a one-dimensional array (rows)
- **Table Model**: In this model, the data is stored in a two-dimensional array (rows and columns)
- **Tree Model**: In this model, the data is stored in a hierarchical relationship (parent/children)

To handle all these model types, Qt came up with the QModelIndex class, which is an abstract way of dealing with them. The QModelIndex class has the functions for each of the use cases: row(), column(), and parent()/child(). Each instance of a QModelIndex is meant to be short-lived: the model might be updated and thus the index will become invalid.

The model will produce indexes according to its data type and will provide these indexes to the view. The view will then use them to query back new data to the model without needing to know if an index.row() function corresponds to a database row or a vector index.

We can see the index parameter in action with the implementation of data():

```
QVariant AlbumModel::data(const QModelIndex& index, int role) const
{
    if (!isIndexValid(index)) {
        return QVariant();
    }
    const Album& album = *mAlbums->at(index.row());

    switch (role) {
        case Roles::IdRole:
            return album.id();

        case Roles::NameRole:
        case Qt::DisplayRole:
            return album.name();

        default:
            return QVariant();
    }
}
```

The view will ask for data with two parameters: an index and a role. As we have already covered the index, we can focus on the role responsibility.

When the data is displayed, it will probably be an aggregation of multiple data. For example, displaying the picture will consist of a thumbnail and the picture name. Each one of these data elements needs to be retrieved by the view. The `role` parameter fills this need, it associates each data element to a tag for the view to know what category of data is shown.

Qt provides various default roles (`DisplayRole`, `DecorationRole`, `EditRole`, and so on) and you can define your own if needed. This is what we did in the `AlbumModel.h` file with the `enum Roles`: we added an `IdRole` and a `NameRole`.

The body of the `data()` function is now within our reach! We first test the validity of the `index` with a helper function, `isIndexValid()`. Take a look at the source code of the chapter to see what it does in detail. The view asked for data at a specific `index`: we retrieve the `album` row at the given `index` with `*mAlbums->at(index.row())`.

This returns a `unique_ptr<Album>` value at the `index.row()` index and we dereference it to have an `Album&`. The `const` modifier is interesting here because we are in a read function, and it makes no sense to modify the `album` row. The `const` modifier adds this check at compile time.

The `switch` on the `role` parameter tells us what data category should be returned. The `data()` function returns a `QVariant` value, which is the Awiss Army Knife of types in Qt. We can safely return the `album.id()`, `album.name()`, or a default `QVariant()` if we do not handle the specified role.

The last read function to cover is `roleNames()`:

```
QHash<int, QByteArray> AlbumModel::roleNames() const
{
    QHash<int, QByteArray> roles;
    roles[Roles::IdRole] = "id";
    roles[Roles::NameRole] = "name";
    return roles;
}
```

At this level of abstraction, we do not know what type of view will be used to display our data. If the views are written in QML, they will need some meta-information about the data structure. The `roleNames()` function provides this information so the role names can be accessed via QML. If you are writing for a desktop widget view only, you can safely ignore this function. The library we are currently building will be used for QML; this is why we override this function.

The reading part of the model is now over. The client view has everything it needs to properly query and display the data. We shall now investigate the editing part of AlbumModel.

We will start with the creation of a new album. The view will build a new Album object and pass it to Album::addAlbum() to be properly persisted:

```
QModelIndex AlbumModel::addAlbum(const Album& album)
{
    int rowIndex = rowCount();
    beginInsertRows(QModelIndex(), rowIndex, rowIndex);
    unique_ptr<Album> newAlbum(new Album(album));
    mDb.albumDao.addAlbum(*newAlbum);
    mAlbums->push_back(move(newAlbum));
    endInsertRows();
    return index(rowIndex, 0);
}
```

Indexes are a way to navigate within the model data. This first thing we do is to determinate what will be the index of this new album by getting the mAlbums size with rowCount().

From here, we start to use specific model functions: beginInsertRows() and endInsertRows(). These functions wrap real data modifications. Their purpose is to automatically trigger signals for whoever might be interested:

- beginInsertRows(): This function informs that rows are about to change for the given indexes
- endInsertRows(): This function informs that rows have been changed

The first parameter of the beginInsertRows() function is the parent for this new element. The root for a model is always an empty QModelIndex() constructor. Because we do not handle any hierarchical relationship in AlbumModel, it is safe to always add the new element to the root. The following parameters are the first and last modified indexes. We insert a single element per call, so we provide rowIndex twice. To illustrate the usage of this signal, a view might, for example, display a loading message telling the user "Saving 5 new albums".

For endInsertRows(), the interested view might hide the saving message and display "Save finished".

This may look strange at first, but it enables Qt to handle automatically a lot of signaling for us and in a generic way. You will see very soon how well this works when designing the UI of the application in Chapter 12, *Conquering the Desktop UI.*

The real insertion begins after the beginInsertRows() instruction. We start by creating a copy of the album row with unique_ptr<Album> newAlbum. This object is then inserted in the database with mDb.albumDao.addAlbum(*newAlbum). Do not forget that the AlbumDao::addAlbum() function also modifies the passed album by setting its mId to the last SQLITE3-inserted ID.

Finally, newAlbum is added to mAlbums and its ownership is transferred as well with std::move(). The return gives the index object of this new album, which is simply the row wrapped in a QModelIndex object.

Let's continue the editing functions with setData():

```
bool AlbumModel::setData(const QModelIndex& index, const QVariant& value,
int role)
{
    if (!isIndexValid(index)
            || role != Roles::NameRole) {
        return false;
    }
    Album& album = *mAlbums->at(index.row());
    album.setName(value.toString());
    mDb.albumDao.updateAlbum(album);
    emit dataChanged(index, index);
    return true;
}
```

This function is called when the view wants to update the data. The signature is very similar to data(), with the additional parameter value.

The body also follows the same logic. Here, the album row is an Album&, without the const keyword. The only possible value to edit is the name, which is done on the object and then persisted to the database.

We have to emit ourselves the dataChanged() signal to notify whoever is interested that a row changed for the given indexes (the start index and end index). This powerful mechanism centralizes all the states of the data, enabling possible views (album list and current album detail for example) to be automatically refreshed.

The return of the function simply indicates if the data update was successful. In a production application, you should test the database processing success and return the relevant value.

Finally, the last editing function we will cover is removeRows():

```
bool AlbumModel::removeRows(int row, int count, const QModelIndex& parent)
{
    if (row < 0
            || row >= rowCount()
            || count < 0
            || (row + count) > rowCount()) {
        return false;
    }
    beginRemoveRows(parent, row, row + count - 1);
    int countLeft = count;
    while (countLeft--) {
        const Album& album = *mAlbums->at(row + countLeft);
        mDb.albumDao.removeAlbum(album.id());
    }
    mAlbums->erase(mAlbums->begin() + row,
                   mAlbums->begin() + row + count);
    endRemoveRows();
    return true;
}
```

The function signature should start to look familiar by now. When a view wants to remove rows, it has to provide the starting row, the number of rows to delete, and the parent of the row.

After that, just as we did for addAlbum(), we wrap the effective removal with two functions:

- The beginRemoveRows() function, which expects the parent, the starting index, and the last index
- The endRemoveRows() function, which simply triggers automatic signals in the model framework

The rest of the function is not very hard to follow. We loop on the rows left to delete and, for each one, we delete it from the database and remove it from mAlbums. We simply retrieve the album from our in-memory mAlbums vector and process the real database deletion with mDb.albumDao.removeAlbum(album.id()).

The `AlbumModel` class is now completely covered. You can now create a new C++ class and name it `PictureModel`.

We will not cover the `PictureModel` class in so much detail. The major parts are the same (you simply swap the data class `Album` for `Picture`). There is however one main difference: `PictureModel` always handles pictures for a given album. This design choice illustrates how two models can be linked with only some simple signals.

Here is the updated version of `PictureModel.h`:

```cpp
#include <memory>
#include <vector>

#include <QAbstractListModel>

#include "gallery-core_global.h"
#include "Picture.h"

class Album;
class DatabaseManager;
class AlbumModel;

class GALLERYCORESHARED_EXPORT PictureModel : public QAbstractListModel
{
    Q_OBJECT
public:

    enum PictureRole {
        FilePathRole = Qt::UserRole + 1
    };
    PictureModel(const AlbumModel& albumModel, QObject* parent = 0);

    QModelIndex addPicture(const Picture& picture);

    int rowCount(const QModelIndex& parent = QModelIndex()) const override;
    QVariant data(const QModelIndex& index, int role) const override;
    bool removeRows(int row, int count, const QModelIndex& parent)
override;

    void setAlbumId(int albumId);
    void clearAlbum();

public slots:
    void deletePicturesForAlbum();

private:
    void loadPictures(int albumId);
```

```
    bool isIndexValid(const QModelIndex& index) const;

private:
    DatabaseManager& mDb;
    int mAlbumId;
    std::unique_ptr<std::vector<std::unique_ptr<Picture>>> mPictures;
};
```

The interesting parts are those concerning the album. As you can see, the constructor expects an AlbumModel. This class also stores the current mAlbumId to be able to request the pictures for a given album only. Let's see what the constructor really does:

```
PictureModel::PictureModel(const AlbumModel& albumModel, QObject* parent) :
    QAbstractListModel(parent),
    mDb(DatabaseManager::instance()),
    mAlbumId(-1),
    mPictures(new vector<unique_ptr<Picture>>())
{
    connect(&albumModel, &AlbumModel::rowsRemoved,
            this, &PictureModel::deletePicturesForAlbum);
}
```

As you can see, the albumModel class is used only to connect a signal to our slot deletePicturesForAlbum() which is self-explanatory. This makes sure that the database is always valid: a picture should be deleted if the owning album is deleted. This will be done automatically when AlbumModel emits the rowsRemoved signal.

Now, mPictures is not initialized with all the pictures of the database. Because we chose to restrict PictureModel to work on the pictures for a given album, we do not know at the construction of PictureModel which album to choose. The loading can only be done when the album is selected, in setAlbumId():

```
void PictureModel::setAlbumId(int albumId)
{
    beginResetModel();
    mAlbumId = albumId;
    loadPictures(mAlbumId);
    endResetModel();
}
```

When the album changes, we completely reload `PictureModel`. The reloading phase is wrapped with the `beginResetModel()` and `endResetModel()` functions. They notify any attached views that their state should be reset as well. Any previous data (for example, `QModelIndex`) reported from the model becomes invalid.

The `loadPictures()` function is quite straightforward:

```
void PictureModel::loadPictures(int albumId)
{
    if (albumId <= 0) {
        mPictures.reset(new vector<unique_ptr<Picture>>());
        return;
    }
    mPictures = mDb.pictureDao.picturesForAlbum(albumId);
}
```

By convention, we decided that, if a negative `album id` is provided, we clear the pictures. To do it, we reinitialize `mPictures` with the call `mPictures.reset(new vector<unique_ptr<Picture>>())`. This will call the destructor on the owned vector, which in turn will do the same for the `Picture` elements. We force `mPictures` to always have a valid vector object to avoid any possible null reference (in `PictureModel::rowCount()` for example).

After that, we simply assign the database pictures for the given `albumId` to `mPictures`. Because we work with smart pointers at every level, we do not even see any specific semantics here. Still, `mPicture` is a `unique_ptr<vector<unique_ptr<Picture>>>`. When the = operator is called, the `unique_ptr` pointer overloads it and two things happen:

- The ownership of the right-hand side (the pictures retrieved from the database) is transferred to `mPictures`
- The old content of `mPictures` is automatically deleted

It is effectively the same as calling `mPictures.reset()` and then `mPictures = move(mDb.pictureDao.picturesForAlbum(albumId))`. With the = overload, everything is streamlined and much more pleasant to read.

The `PictureModel` shows you how flexible the model paradigm can be. You can easily adapt it to your own use case without making any strong coupling. After all, the `albumModel` is only used to connect to a single signal; there are no retained references. The remainder of the class is available in the source code of the chapter.

Summary

The chapter was a journey to create a well-defined `gallery-core` library. We studied advanced techniques with `.pro` files to split your project into sub-modules, persisted data in a SQLITE3 database with the help of smart pointers, and finally studied how the Model/View architecture works in Qt.

From now on, a project organization with Qt should hold no terrors for you. The next chapter will continue right where we stopped: the library is ready, now let's make great QWidgets to have a stunning gallery application and look at the other side of the model: the View layer.

Conquering the Desktop UI
12

In the previous chapter, we built the brain of our gallery using Qt models. It is now time to build a desktop application using this engine. This software will use all the features offered by the `gallery-core` library, leading to a completely usable gallery on your computer.

The first task will be to link your project-shared library to this new application. Then you will learn how to create custom widgets, when to use Qt views, and how to synchronize them with the model.

The following topics will be covered in this chapter:

- Linking the application to a project library
- Qt model/view
- Qt resource file
- Promoting custom widgets

Creating a GUI linked to a core shared library

The `gallery-core` shared library is now ready. Let's see how to create the desktop GUI project. We will create a Qt Widgets application sub-project called `gallery-desktop`. Only the first steps differ from a classic Qt Widgets application. Right-click on the main project, and select **ch04-gallery-desktop** | **New subproject** | **Application** | **Qt Widgets Application** | **Choose**.

You will get a nice multi-projects hierarchy like this:

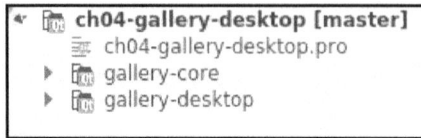

```
▼  ▣ ch04-gallery-desktop [master]
      ▤ ch04-gallery-desktop.pro
   ▶  ▣ gallery-core
   ▶  ▣ gallery-desktop
```

It is now time to link this `gallery-desktop` application to the `gallery-core`. You can edit the file `gallery-desktop.pro` yourself or use the Qt Creator wizard like this: right-click on the project and select **gallery-desktop** | **Add library** | **Internal library** | **gallery-core** | **Next** | **Finish**. Here is the updated `gallery-desktop.pro`:

```
QT       += core gui

TARGET = desktop-gallery
TEMPLATE = app

SOURCES += main.cpp
        MainWindow.cpp

HEADERS  += MainWindow.h

FORMS    += MainWindow.ui

win32:CONFIG(release, debug|release): LIBS += -L$$OUT_PWD/../gallery-
core/release/ -lgallery-core
else:win32:CONFIG(debug, debug|release): LIBS += -L$$OUT_PWD/../gallery-
core/debug/ -lgallery-core
else:unix: LIBS += -L$$OUT_PWD/../gallery-core/ -lgallery-core

INCLUDEPATH += $$PWD/../gallery-core
DEPENDPATH += $$PWD/../gallery-core
```

The `LIBS` variable specifies the libraries to link in this project. The syntax is very simple: you can provide library paths with the `-L` prefix and library names with the `-l` prefix.

```
LIBS += -L<pathToLibrary> -l<libraryName>
```

By default, compiling a Qt project on Windows will create a `debug` and `release` sub-directory. That is why a different `LIBS` edition is created depending on the platform.

Now that the application is linked to the library `gallery-core` and knows where to find it, we must indicate where the library header files are located. That is why we must add the `gallery-core` source path to `INCLUDEPATH` and `DEPENDPATH`.

To complete all those tasks successfully, qmake offers some useful variables:

- `$$OUT_PWD`: The absolute path to the output directory
- `$$PWD`: The absolute path of the current `.pro` file

To ensure that qmake will compile the shared library before the desktop application, we must update the `ch04-gallery-desktop.pro` file according the following snippet:

```
TEMPLATE = subdirs

SUBDIRS +=
    gallery-core
    gallery-desktop

gallery-desktop.depends = gallery-core
```

The `depends` attribute explicitly indicates that `gallery-core` must be built before `gallery-desktop`.

> **TIP**
> Try to always use the `depends` attribute instead of relying on `CONFIG +=` `ordered`, which only specifies a simple list order. The `depends` attribute helps qmake process your projects in parallel, if it can be done.

Instead of rushing into coding blindly, we will take some time to think about the UI architecture. We have a lot of features to implement from the `gallery-core` library. We should split these features into independent QWidgets. The final application will look like this:

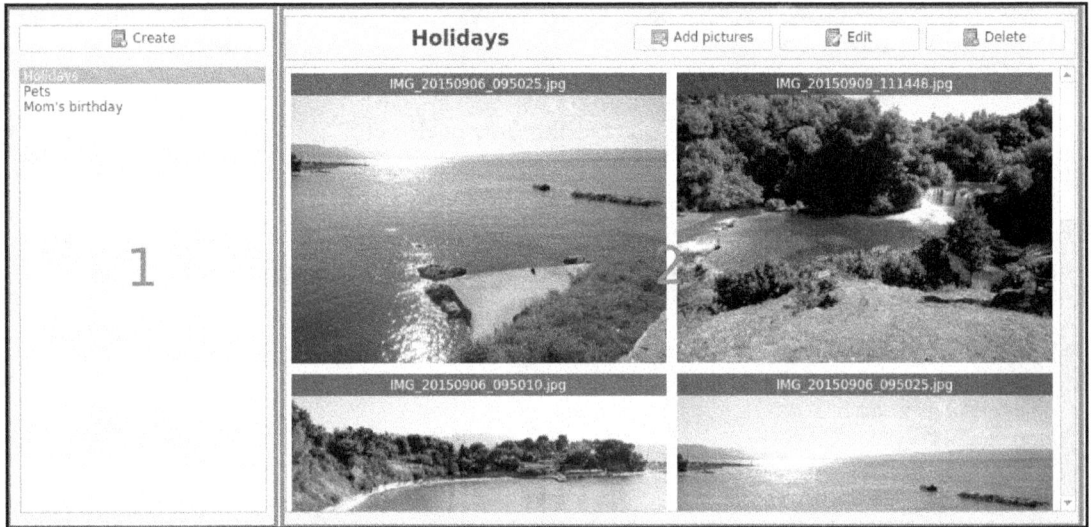

Our future gallery desktop is here!

The exapanded view of a photo will look like this:

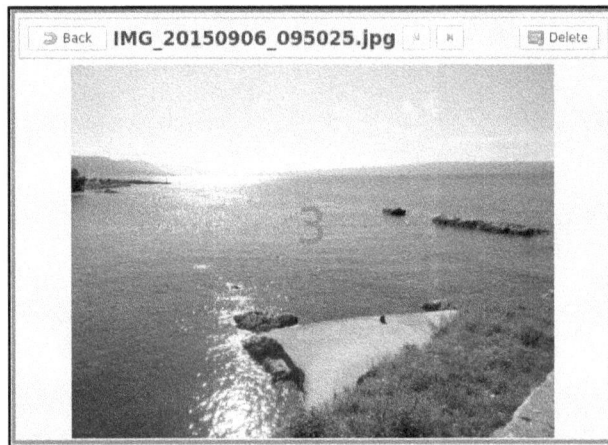

Double-click on a thumbnail to display it in full size.

To sum up the main UI components:

- `AlbumListWidget`: This component lists all existing albums
- `AlbumWidget`: This component shows the selected album and its thumbnails
- `PictureWidget`: This component displays the picture in full size

This is how we will organize it:

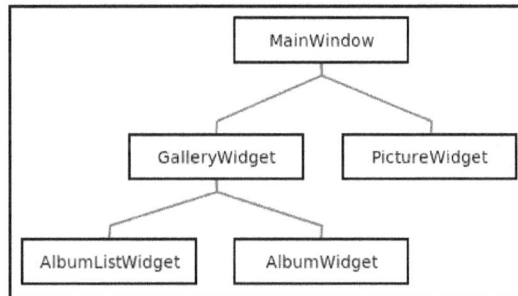

Each widget has a defined role and will handle specific features:

Class name	Features
MainWindow	Handles the switch between the gallery and the current picture
GalleryWidget	• Displays existing albums • Album selection • Album creation
AlbumListWidget	• Displays existing albums • Album selection • Album creation
AlbumWidget	• Displays existing pictures as thumbnails • Adds pictures in the album • Album rename • Album deletion • Picture selection
PictureWidget	• Displays the selected picture • Picture selection • Picture deletion

In the core shared library, we used smart pointers with standard containers (`vector`). Generally, in GUI projects, we tend to only use Qt containers and their powerful parent-child ownership system. This approach seems more appropriate to us. That is why we will rely on Qt containers for the GUI (and won't use smart pointers) in this chapter.

We can now safely begin to create our widgets; all of them are created from **Qt Designer Form Class**. If you have a memory lapse.

Listing your albums with AlbumListWidget

This widget must offer a way to create a new album and display existing ones. Selecting an album must also trigger an event that will be used by other widgets to display the proper data. The `AlbumListWidget` component is the simplest widget in this project using the Qt View mechanism. Take the time to fully understand `AlbumListWidget` before jumping to the next widget.

The following screenshot shows the **Form Editor** view of the file, `AlbumListWidget.ui`:

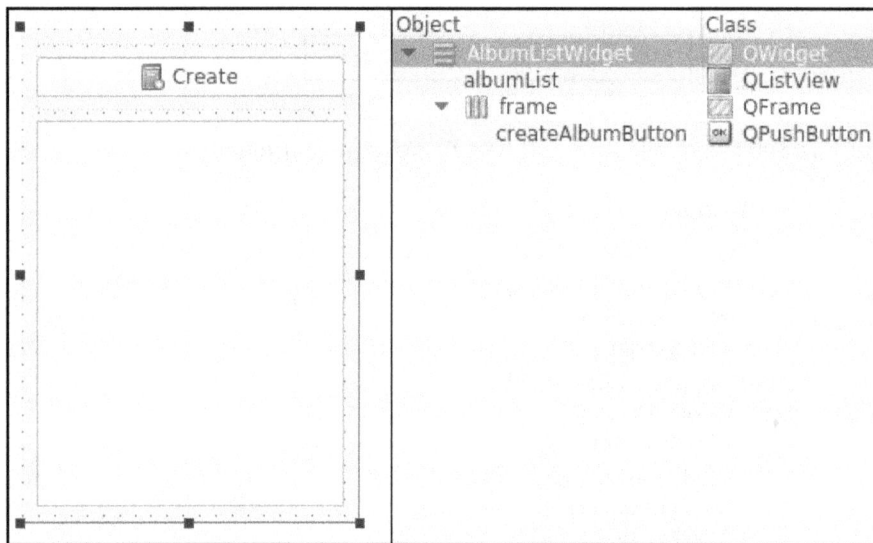

The layout is very simple. The components are described as follows:

- The `AlbumListWidget` component uses a vertical layout to display the **Create** button above the list
- The `frame` component contains an attractive button
- The `createAlbumButton` component handles album creation
- The `albumList` component displays the album list

You should have recognized most of the types used here. Let us take the time to talk about the really new one: QListView. As we already saw in the previous chapter, Qt provides a Model/View architecture. This system relies on specific interfaces that you must implement to provide generic data access via your model classes. That is what we did in the project gallery-core with the AlbumModel and PictureModel classes.

It is now time to deal with the view part. The view is in charge of the presentation of the data. It will also handle user interactions like selection, drag and drop, or item editing. Fortunately, to achieve these tasks, the view is helped by other Qt classes such as QItemSelectionModel, QModelIndex, or QStyledItemDelegate, which we will soon use in this chapter.

We can now enjoy one of the ready-to-use views offered by Qt:

- QListView: This view displays items from a model as a simple list
- QTableView: This view displays items from a model as a two-dimensional table
- QTreeView: This view displays items from a hierarchy of lists

Here, the choice is rather obvious because we want to display a list of album names. But in a more complex situation, a rule of thumb for choosing the proper view is to look for the model type; here we want to add a view for AlbumModel of type QAbstractListModel so the QListView class seems correct.

As you can see in the preceding screenshot, the createAlbumButton object has an icon. You can add one to a QPushButton class by selecting the widget **property: icon** | **Choose resource**. You can now choose a picture from the resource.qrc file.

A **Qt resource** file is a collection of files for embedding binary files in your application. You can store any types of file but we commonly use it to store pictures, sounds, or translation files. To create a resource file, right-click on the project name and then follow **Add New** | **Qt** | **Qt Resource File**. Qt Creator will create a default file, resource.qrc, and add this line in your file gallery-desktop.pro:

```
RESOURCES += resource.qrc
```

The resource file can be mainly displayed in two ways: **Resource Editor** and **Plain Text Editor**. You can choose an editor with by right-clicking on the resource file and selecting **Open With**.

The **Resource Editor** is a visual editor that helps you to easily add and remove files in your resource file, as shown in the following screenshot:

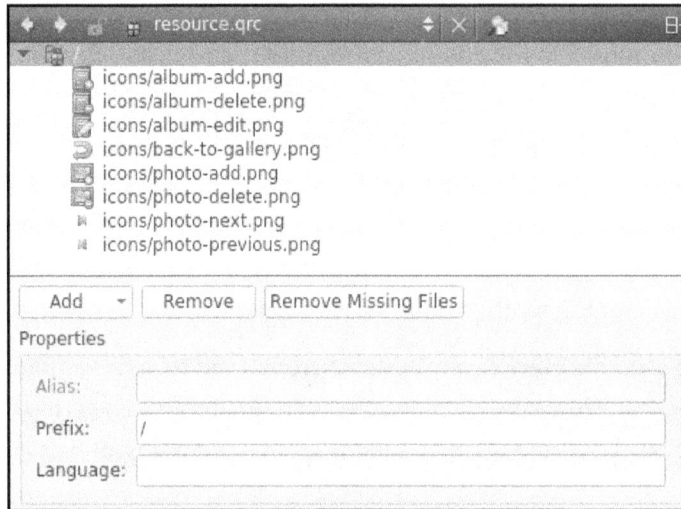

The **Plain Text Editor** will display this XML-based file `resource.qrc` like this:

```
<RCC>
    <qresource prefix="/">
        <file>icons/album-add.png</file>
        <file>icons/album-delete.png</file>
        <file>icons/album-edit.png</file>
        <file>icons/back-to-gallery.png</file>
        <file>icons/photo-add.png</file>
        <file>icons/photo-delete.png</file>
        <file>icons/photo-next.png</file>
        <file>icons/photo-previous.png</file>
    </qresource>
</RCC>
```

At the build time, `qmake` and `rcc` (Qt Resource Compiler) embed your resources into the application binary.

Now that the form part is clear, we can analyze the `AlbumListWidget.h` file:

```
#include <QWidget>
#include <QItemSelectionModel>

namespace Ui {
class AlbumListWidget;
}
```

```
class AlbumModel;

class AlbumListWidget : public QWidget
{
    Q_OBJECT

public:
    explicit AlbumListWidget(QWidget *parent = 0);
    ~AlbumListWidget();

    void setModel(AlbumModel* model);
    void setSelectionModel(QItemSelectionModel* selectionModel);

private slots:
    void createAlbum();

private:
    Ui::AlbumListWidget* ui;
    AlbumModel* mAlbumModel;
};
```

The setModel() and setSelectionModel() functions are the most important lines in this snippet. This widget require two things to work correctly:

- AlbumModel: This is the model class that provides access to data. We already created this class in the gallery-core project.
- QItemSelectionModel: This is a Qt class that handles the selection in a view. By default, views use their own selection model. Sharing the same selection model with different views or widgets will help us to synchronize album selection easily.

This is the main part of AlbumListWidget.cpp:

```
#include "AlbumListWidget.h"
#include "ui_AlbumListWidget.h"

#include <QInputDialog>

#include "AlbumModel.h"

AlbumListWidget::AlbumListWidget(QWidget *parent) :
    QWidget(parent),
    ui(new Ui::AlbumListWidget),
    mAlbumModel(nullptr)
{
    ui->setupUi(this);
```

```
    connect(ui->createAlbumButton, &QPushButton::clicked,
            this, &AlbumListWidget::createAlbum);
}

AlbumListWidget::~AlbumListWidget()
{
    delete ui;
}

void AlbumListWidget::setModel(AlbumModel* model)
{
    mAlbumModel = model;
    ui->albumList->setModel(mAlbumModel);
}

void AlbumListWidget::setSelectionModel(QItemSelectionModel*
selectionModel)
{
    ui->albumList->setSelectionModel(selectionModel);
}
```

The two setters will mainly be used to set the model and the selection model of the
albumList. Our QListView class will then automatically request the model (AlbumModel)
to get the row count and the Qt::DisplayRole (the album's name) for each one of them.

Let's now see the last part of the AlbumListWidget.cpp file that handles the album
creation:

```
void AlbumListWidget::createAlbum()
{
    if (!mAlbumModel) {
        return;
    }

    bool ok;
    QString albumName = QInputDialog::getText(this,
                            "Create a new Album",
                            "Choose an name",
                            QLineEdit::Normal,
                            "New album",
                            &ok);

    if (ok && !albumName.isEmpty()) {
        Album album(albumName);
        QModelIndex createdIndex = mAlbumModel->addAlbum(album);
        ui->albumList->setCurrentIndex(createdIndex);
    }
}
```

We already worked with the `QInputDialog` class. This time we are using it to ask the user to enter an album's name. Then we create an `Album` class with the requested name. This object is just a "data holder;" `addAlbum()` will use it to create and store the real object with a unique ID.

The function `addAlbum()` returns us the `QModelIndex` value corresponding to the created album. From here, we can request the list view to select this new album.

Creating a ThumbnailProxyModel

The future `AlbumWidget` view will display a grid of thumbnails with the pictures attached to the selected `Album`. In Chapter 11, *Dividing Your Project and Ruling Your Code*, we designed the `gallery-core` library to be agnostic of how a picture should be displayed: a `Picture` class contains only a `mUrl` field.

In other words, the generation of the thumbnails has to be done in `gallery-desktop` rather than `gallery-core`. We already have the `PictureModel` class that is responsible for retrieving the `Picture` information, so it would be great to be able to extend its behavior with the thumbnail data.

This is possible in Qt with the use of the `QAbstractProxyModel` class and its subclasses. The goal of this class is to process data from a base `QAbstractItemModel` (sorting, filtering, adding data, and so on) and present it to the view by proxying the original model. To take a database analogy, you can view it as a projection over a table.

The `QAbstractProxyModel` class has two subclasses:

- The `QIdentityProxyModel` subclass proxies its source model without any modification (all the indexes match). This class is suitable if you want to transform the `data()` function.
- The `QSortFilterProxyModel` subclass proxies its source model with the ability to sort and filter the passing data.

The former, QIdentityProxyModel, fits our requirements. The only thing we need to do is to extend the data() function with the thumbnail generation content. Create a new class named ThumbnailProxyModel. Here is the ThumbnailProxyModel.h file:

```
#include <QIdentityProxyModel>
#include <QHash>
#include <QPixmap>

class PictureModel;

class ThumbnailProxyModel : public QIdentityProxyModel
{
public:
    ThumbnailProxyModel(QObject* parent = 0);

    QVariant data(const QModelIndex& index, int role) const override;
    void setSourceModel(QAbstractItemModel* sourceModel) override;
    PictureModel* pictureModel() const;

private:
    void generateThumbnails(const QModelIndex& startIndex, int count);
    void reloadThumbnails();

private:
    QHash<QString, QPixmap*> mThumbnails;

};
```

This class extends QIdentityProxyModel and overrides a couple of functions:

- The data() function to provide the thumbnail data to the client of ThumbnailProxyModel
- The setSourceModel() function to register to signals emitted by sourceModel

The remaining custom functions have the following goals:

- The pictureModel() is a helper function that casts the sourceModel to a PictureModel*
- The generateThumbnails() function takes care of generating the QPixmap thumbnails for a given set of pictures
- The reloadThumbnails() is a helper function that clears the stored thumbnails before calling generateThumbnails()

As you might have guessed, the `mThumbnails` class stores the `QPixmap*` thumbnails using the `filepath` for the key.

We now switch to the `ThumbnailProxyModel.cpp` file and build it from the ground up. Let's focus on `generateThumbnails()`:

```
const unsigned int THUMBNAIL_SIZE = 350;
...
void ThumbnailProxyModel::generateThumbnails(
                                        const QModelIndex& startIndex,
int count)
{
    if (!startIndex.isValid()) {
        return;
    }

    const QAbstractItemModel* model = startIndex.model();
    int lastIndex = startIndex.row() + count;
    for(int row = startIndex.row(); row < lastIndex; row++) {
        QString filepath = model->data(model->index(row, 0),
PictureModel::Roles::FilePathRole).toString();
        QPixmap pixmap(filepath);
        auto thumbnail = new QPixmap(pixmap
                                .scaled(THUMBNAIL_SIZE,
THUMBNAIL_SIZE,
                                            Qt::KeepAspectRatio,
                                            Qt::SmoothTransformation));
        mThumbnails.insert(filepath, thumbnail);
    }
}
```

This function generates the thumbnails for a given range indicated by the parameters (`startIndex` and `count`). For each picture, we retrieve the `filepath` from the original model, using `model->data()`, and we generate a downsized `QPixmap` that is inserted in the `mThumbnails` QHash. Note that we arbitrarily set the thumbnail size using const `THUMBNAIL_SIZE`. The picture is scaled down to this size and respects the aspect ratio of the original picture.

Each time that an album is loaded, we should clear the content of the `mThumbnails` class and load the new pictures. This work is done by the `reloadThumbnails()` function:

```
void ThumbnailProxyModel::reloadThumbnails()
{
    qDeleteAll(mThumbnails);
    mThumbnails.clear();
    generateThumbnails(index(0, 0), rowCount());
```

```
    }
```

In this function, we simply clear the content of `mThumbnails` and call
the `generateThumbnails()` function with parameters indicating that all the thumbnails
should be generated. Let's see when these two functions will be used,
in `setSourceModel()`:

```
void ThumbnailProxyModel::setSourceModel(QAbstractItemModel* sourceModel)
{
    QIdentityProxyModel::setSourceModel(sourceModel);
    if (!sourceModel) {
        return;
    }

    connect(sourceModel, &QAbstractItemModel::modelReset,
                [this] {
        reloadThumbnails();
    });

    connect(sourceModel, &QAbstractItemModel::rowsInserted,
                [this] (const QModelIndex& parent, int first, int last) {
        generateThumbnails(index(first, 0), last - first + 1);
    });
}
```

When the `setSourceModel()` function is called, the `ThumbnailProxyModel` class is
configured to know which base model should be proxied. In this function, we register
lambdas to two signals emitted by the original model:

- The `modelReset` signal is triggered when pictures should be loaded for a given
  album. In this case, we have to completely reload the thumbnails.
- The `rowsInserted` signal is triggered each time new pictures are added. At this
  point, `generateThumbnails` should be called to update `mThumbnails` with
  these newcomers.

Finally, we have to cover the `data()` function:

```
QVariant ThumbnailProxyModel::data(const QModelIndex& index, int role)
const
{
    if (role != Qt::DecorationRole) {
        return QIdentityProxyModel::data(index, role);
    }

    QString filepath = sourceModel()->data(index,
PictureModel::Roles::FilePathRole).toString();
```

```
        return *mThumbnails[filepath];
    }
```

For any role that is not `Qt::DecorationRole`, the parent class `data()` is called. In our case, this triggers the `data()` function from the original model, `PictureModel`. After that, when `data()` must return a thumbnail, the `filepath` of the picture referenced by the `index` is retrieved and used to return the `QPixmap` object of `mThumbnails`. Luckily for us, `QPixmap` can be implicitly cast to `QVariant`, so we do not have anything special to do here.

The last function to cover in the `ThumbnailProxyModel` class is the `pictureModel()` function:

```
    PictureModel* ThumbnailProxyModel::pictureModel() const
    {
        return static_cast<PictureModel*>(sourceModel());
    }
```

Classes that will interact with `ThumbnailProxyModel` will need to call some functions that are specific to `PictureModel` to create or delete pictures. This function is a helper to centralize the cast of the `sourceModel` to `PictureModel*`.

As a side note, we could have tried to generate thumbnails on-the-fly to avoid a possible initial bottleneck during the album loading (and the call to `generateThumbnails()`). However, `data()` is a `const` function, meaning that it cannot modify the `ThumbnailProxyModel` instance. This rules out any way of generating a thumbnail in the `data()` function and storing it in `mThumbnails`.

As you can see, `QIdentityProxyModel`, and more generally `QAbstractProxyModel`, are valuable tools to add behavior to an existing model without breaking it. In our case, this is enforced by design in so far as the `PictureModel` class is defined in `gallery-core` rather than `gallery-desktop`. Modifying `PictureModel` implies modifying `gallery-core` and potentially breaking its behavior for other users of the library. This approach lets us keep things cleanly separated.

Displaying the selected album with AlbumWidget

This widget will display the data of the selected album from `AlbumListWidget`. Some buttons will allow us to interact with this album.

Here is the layout of the `AlbumWidget.ui` file:

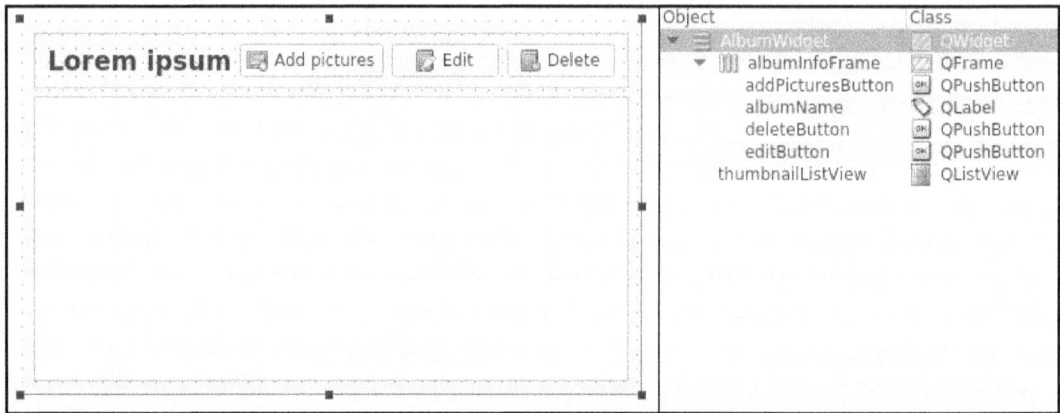

The top frame, `albumInfoFrame`, with a horizontal layout, contains:

- `albumName`: This object displays the album's name (**Lorem ipsum** in the designer)
- `addPicturesButton`: This object allows the user to add pictures selecting files
- `editButton`: This object is used to rename the album
- `deleteButton`: This object is used to delete the album

The bottom element, `thumbnailListView,` is a `QListView`. This list view represents items from `PictureModel`. By default, `QListView` is able to display a picture next to text requesting `Qt::DisplayRole` and `Qt::DecorationRole` from the model.

Take a look at the header `AlbumWidget.h` file:

```
#include <QWidget>
#include <QModelIndex>

namespace Ui {
class AlbumWidget;
}

class AlbumModel;
class PictureModel;
class QItemSelectionModel;
class ThumbnailProxyModel;

class AlbumWidget : public QWidget
{
```

```
    Q_OBJECT

public:
    explicit AlbumWidget(QWidget *parent = 0);
    ~AlbumWidget();

    void setAlbumModel(AlbumModel* albumModel);
    void setAlbumSelectionModel(QItemSelectionModel* albumSelectionModel);
    void setPictureModel(ThumbnailProxyModel* pictureModel);
    void setPictureSelectionModel(QItemSelectionModel* selectionModel);

signals:
    void pictureActivated(const QModelIndex& index);

private slots:
    void deleteAlbum();
    void editAlbum();
    void addPictures();

private:
    void clearUi();
    void loadAlbum(const QModelIndex& albumIndex);

private:
    Ui::AlbumWidget* ui;
    AlbumModel* mAlbumModel;
    QItemSelectionModel* mAlbumSelectionModel;

    ThumbnailProxyModel* mPictureModel;
    QItemSelectionModel* mPictureSelectionModel;
};
```

As this widget needs to deal with `Album` and `Picture` data, this class has `AlbumModel` and `ThumbnailProxyModel` setters. We also want to know and share the model selection with other widgets and views (that is, `AlbumListWidget`). That is why we also have `Album` and `Picture` model selection setters.

The signal `pictureActivated()` will be triggered when the user double-clicks on a thumbnail. We will see later how `MainWindow` will connect to this signal to display the picture at full size.

The private slots, `deleteAlbum()`, `editAlbum()`, and `addPictures()`, will be called when the user clicks on one of these buttons.

Finally, the `loadAlbum()` function will be called to update the UI for a specific album. The `clearUi()` function will be useful to clear all information displayed by this widget UI.

Take a look at the beginning of the implementation in the `AlbumWidget.cpp` file:

```cpp
#include "AlbumWidget.h"
#include "ui_AlbumWidget.h"

#include <QInputDialog>
#include <QFileDialog>

#include "AlbumModel.h"
#include "PictureModel.h"

AlbumWidget::AlbumWidget(QWidget *parent) :
    QWidget(parent),
    ui(new Ui::AlbumWidget),
    mAlbumModel(nullptr),
    mAlbumSelectionModel(nullptr),
    mPictureModel(nullptr),
    mPictureSelectionModel(nullptr)
{
    ui->setupUi(this);
    clearUi();

    ui->thumbnailListView->setSpacing(5);
    ui->thumbnailListView->setResizeMode(QListView::Adjust);
    ui->thumbnailListView->setFlow(QListView::LeftToRight);
    ui->thumbnailListView->setWrapping(true);

    connect(ui->thumbnailListView, &QListView::doubleClicked,
            this, &AlbumWidget::pictureActivated);

    connect(ui->deleteButton, &QPushButton::clicked,
            this, &AlbumWidget::deleteAlbum);

    connect(ui->editButton, &QPushButton::clicked,
            this, &AlbumWidget::editAlbum);

    connect(ui->addPicturesButton, &QPushButton::clicked,
            this, &AlbumWidget::addPictures);
}

AlbumWidget::~AlbumWidget()
{
    delete ui;
}
```

The constructor configures `thumbnailListView`, our `QListView` that will display thumbnails of the current selected album. We set here various parameters:

- `setSpacing()`: In this parameter, by default items are glued to each other. You can add spacing between them.
- `setResizeMode()`: This parameter dynamically lays out items when the view is resized. By default, items keep their original placement even if the view is resized.
- `setFlow()`: This parameter specifies the list direction. Here we want to display items from left to right. By default, the direction is `TopToBottom`.
- `setWrapping()`: This parameter allows an item to wrap when there is not enough space to display it in the visible area. By default, wrapping is not allowed and scrollbars will be displayed.

The end of the constructor performs all the signal connections related to the UI. The first one is a good example of signal relaying. We connect the `QListView::doubleClicked` signal to our class signal, `AlbumWidget::pictureActivated`. Other connections are common; we want to call a specific slot when the user clicks on a button. As always in the **Qt Designer Form Class**, the destructor will delete the member variable `ui`.

Let's see the `AlbumModel` setter implementation:

```
void AlbumWidget::setAlbumModel(AlbumModel* albumModel)
{
    mAlbumModel = albumModel;

    connect(mAlbumModel, &QAbstractItemModel::dataChanged,
        [this] (const QModelIndex &topLeft) {
            if (topLeft == mAlbumSelectionModel->currentIndex()) {
                loadAlbum(topLeft);
            }
    });
}

void AlbumWidget::setAlbumSelectionModel(QItemSelectionModel*
albumSelectionModel)
{
    mAlbumSelectionModel = albumSelectionModel;

    connect(mAlbumSelectionModel,
            &QItemSelectionModel::selectionChanged,
            [this] (const QItemSelection &selected) {
                if (selected.isEmpty()) {
                    clearUi();
```

```
                            return;
                    }
                    loadAlbum(selected.indexes().first());
        });
    }
```

If the selected album's data changed, we need to update the UI with the `loadAlbum()` function. A test is performed to ensure that the updated album is the currently selected one. Notice that the `QAbstractItemModel::dataChanged()` function has three parameters but the lambda slot syntax allows us to omit unused parameters.

Our `AlbumWidget` component must update its UI according to the currently selected album. As we share the same selection model, each time the user selects an album from `AlbumListWidget`, the signal `QItemSelectionModel::selectionChanged` is triggered. In this case, we update the UI by calling the `loadAlbum()` function. As we do not support album multi-selection, we can restrict the process to the first selected element. If the selection is empty, we simply clear the UI.

It is now the turn of the `PictureModel` setter implementation:

```
    void AlbumWidget::setPictureModel(PictureModel* pictureModel)
    {
        mPictureModel = pictureModel;
        ui->thumbnailListView->setModel(mPictureModel);
    }

    void AlbumWidget::setPictureSelectionModel(QItemSelectionModel*
    selectionModel)
    {
        ui->thumbnailListView->setSelectionModel(selectionModel);
    }
```

It is very simple here. We set the model and the selection model of `thumbnailListView`, our `QListView` that will display the selected album's thumbnails. We also keep the picture model to manipulate the data later on.

We can now cover the features one by one. Let's start with album deletion:

```
    void AlbumWidget::deleteAlbum()
    {
        if (mAlbumSelectionModel->selectedIndexes().isEmpty()) {
            return;
        }
        int row = mAlbumSelectionModel->currentIndex().row();
        mAlbumModel->removeRow(row);
```

```
    // Try to select the previous album
    QModelIndex previousModelIndex = mAlbumModel->index(row - 1,
        0);
    if(previousModelIndex.isValid()) {
        mAlbumSelectionModel->setCurrentIndex(previousModelIndex,
            QItemSelectionModel::SelectCurrent);
        return;
    }

    // Try to select the next album
    QModelIndex nextModelIndex = mAlbumModel->index(row, 0);
    if(nextModelIndex.isValid()) {
        mAlbumSelectionModel->setCurrentIndex(nextModelIndex,
            QItemSelectionModel::SelectCurrent);
        return;
    }
}
```

The most important task in the `deleteAlbum()` function is to retrieve the current row index from `mAlbumSelectionModel`. Then, we can request `mAlbumModel` to delete this row. The rest of the function will only try to automatically select the previous or the next album. Once again, as we shared the same selection model, `AlbumListWidget` will automatically update its album selection.

The following snippet shows the album rename feature:

```
void AlbumWidget::editAlbum()
{
    if (mAlbumSelectionModel->selectedIndexes().isEmpty()) {
        return;
    }

    QModelIndex currentAlbumIndex =
        mAlbumSelectionModel->selectedIndexes().first();

    QString oldAlbumName = mAlbumModel->data(currentAlbumIndex,
        AlbumModel::Roles::NameRole).toString();

    bool ok;
    QString newName = QInputDialog::getText(this,
                                            "Album's name",
                                            "Change Album name",
                                            QLineEdit::Normal,
                                            oldAlbumName,
                                            &ok);

    if (ok && !newName.isEmpty()) {
```

```
mAlbumModel->setData(currentAlbumIndex,
                     newName,
                     AlbumModel::Roles::NameRole);
    }
}
```

Here, again the `QInputDialog` class will help us to implement a feature. You should be confident with its behavior now. This function performs three steps:

1. Retrieve the current name from album model.
2. Generate a great input dialog.
3. Request the album model to update the name

As you can see, the generic functions `data()` and `setData()` from the models are very powerful when combined with `ItemDataRole`. As already explained, we do not directly update our UI; this will be automatically performed because `setData()` emits a signal, `dataChanged()`, which `AlbumWidget` handles.

The last feature allows us to add some new picture files in the current album:

```
void AlbumWidget::addPictures()
{
    QStringList filenames =
        QFileDialog::getOpenFileNames(this,
            "Add pictures",
            QDir::homePath(),
            "Picture files (*.jpg *.png)");

    if (!filenames.isEmpty()) {
        QModelIndex lastModelIndex;
        for (auto filename : filenames) {
            Picture picture(filename);
            lastModelIndex =
mPictureModel->pictureModel()->addPicture(picture);
        }
        ui->thumbnailListView->setCurrentIndex(lastModelIndex);
    }
}
```

The QFileDialog class is used here to help the user select several picture files. For each filename, we create a Picture data holder, like we have already seen in this chapter for album creation. Then we can request mPictureModel to add this picture in the current album. Note that, because mPictureModel is a ThumbnailProxyModel class, we have to retrieve the real PictureModel using the helper function, pictureModel(). As the function addPicture() returns us the corresponding QModelIndex, we finally select the most recently added picture in thumbnailListView.

Let's complete AlbumWidget.cpp:

```
void AlbumWidget::clearUi()
{
    ui->albumName->setText("");
    ui->deleteButton->setVisible(false);
    ui->editButton->setVisible(false);
    ui->addPicturesButton->setVisible(false);
}

void AlbumWidget::loadAlbum(const QModelIndex& albumIndex)
{
    mPictureModel->pictureModel()->setAlbumId(mAlbumModel->data(albumIndex,
        AlbumModel::Roles::IdRole).toInt());

    ui->albumName->setText(mAlbumModel->data(albumIndex,
        Qt::DisplayRole).toString());

    ui->deleteButton->setVisible(true);
    ui->editButton->setVisible(true);
    ui->addPicturesButton->setVisible(true);
}
```

The clearUi() function clears the album's name and hides the buttons, while the loadAlbum() function retrieves the Qt::DisplayRole (the album's name) and displays the buttons.

Enhancing thumbnails with PictureDelegate

By default, a `QListView` class will request `Qt::DisplayRole` and `Qt::DecorationRole` to display text and a picture for each item. Thus, we already have a visual result, for free, that looks like this:

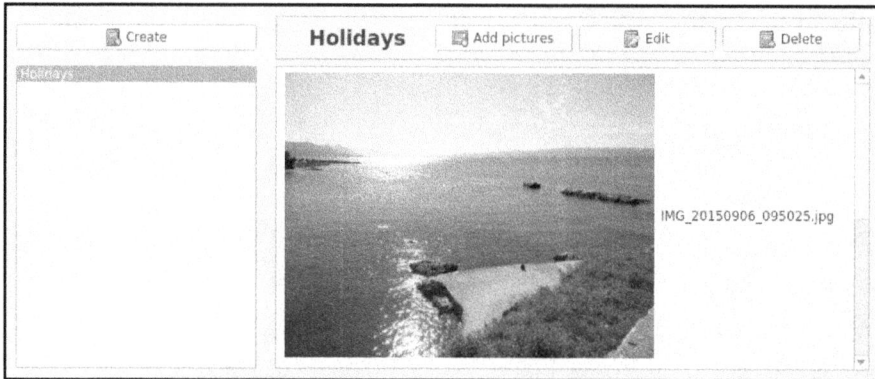

However, our **Gallery** application deserves better thumbnail rendering. Hopefully, we can easily customize it using the view's delegate concept. A `QListView` class provides a default item rendering. We can do our own item rendering by creating a class that inherits `QStyledItemDelegate`. The aim is to paint your dream thumbnails with a name banner like the following screenshot:

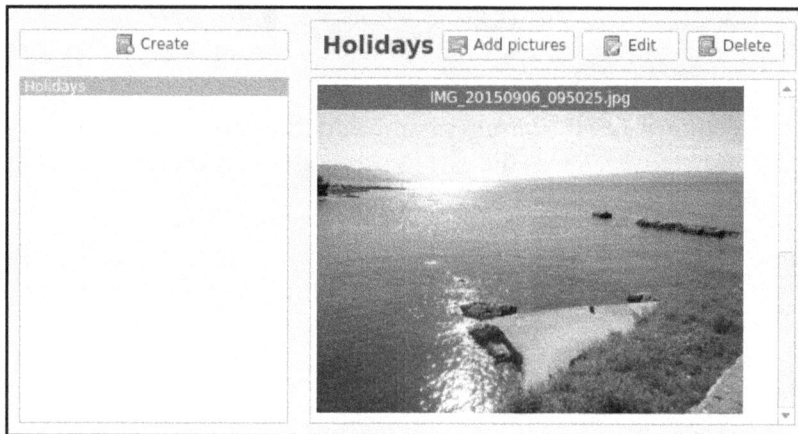

Let's take a look at `PictureDelegate.h`:

```cpp
#include <QStyledItemDelegate>

class PictureDelegate : public QStyledItemDelegate
{
    Q_OBJECT
public:
    PictureDelegate(QObject* parent = 0);

    void paint(QPainter* painter, const QStyleOptionViewItem&
        option, const QModelIndex& index) const override;

    QSize sizeHint(const QStyleOptionViewItem& option,
        const QModelIndex& index) const override;
};
```

That is right, we only have to override two functions. The most important function, `paint()`, will allow us to paint the item like we want. The `sizeHint()` function will be used to specify the item size.

We can now see the painter work in `PictureDelegate.cpp`:

```cpp
#include "PictureDelegate.h"

#include <QPainter>

const unsigned int BANNER_HEIGHT = 20;
const unsigned int BANNER_COLOR = 0x303030;
const unsigned int BANNER_ALPHA = 200;
const unsigned int BANNER_TEXT_COLOR = 0xffffff;
const unsigned int HIGHLIGHT_ALPHA = 100;

PictureDelegate::PictureDelegate(QObject* parent) :
    QStyledItemDelegate(parent)
{
}

void PictureDelegate::paint(QPainter* painter, const QStyleOptionViewItem&
option, const QModelIndex& index) const
{
    painter->save();

    QPixmap pixmap = index.model()->data(index,
        Qt::DecorationRole).value<QPixmap>();
    painter->drawPixmap(option.rect.x(), option.rect.y(), pixmap);

    QRect bannerRect = QRect(option.rect.x(), option.rect.y(),
```

```
        pixmap.width(), BANNER_HEIGHT);
    QColor bannerColor = QColor(BANNER_COLOR);
    bannerColor.setAlpha(BANNER_ALPHA);
    painter->fillRect(bannerRect, bannerColor);

    QString filename = index.model()->data(index,
        Qt::DisplayRole).toString();
    painter->setPen(BANNER_TEXT_COLOR);
    painter->drawText(bannerRect, Qt::AlignCenter, filename);

    if (option.state.testFlag(QStyle::State_Selected)) {
        QColor selectedColor = option.palette.highlight().color();
        selectedColor.setAlpha(HIGHLIGHT_ALPHA);
        painter->fillRect(option.rect, selectedColor);
    }

    painter->restore();
}
```

Each time `QListView` needs to display an item, this delegate's `paint()` function will be called. The paint system can be seen as layers that you paint one on top of each other. The `QPainter` class allows us to paint anything we want: circles, pies, rectangles, text, and so on. The item area can be retrieved with `option.rect()`. Here are the steps:

1. It is easy to break the `painter` state passed in the parameter list, thus we must save the painter state with `painter->save()` before doing anything, to be able to restore it when we have finished our drawing.
2. Retrieve the item thumbnail and draw it with the `QPainter::drawPixmap()` function.
3. Paint a translucent gray banner on top of the thumbnail with the `QPainter::fillRect()` function.
4. Retrieve the item display name and draw it on the banner using the `QPainter::drawText()` function.
5. If the item is selected, we paint a translucent rectangle on the top using the highlight color from the item.
6. We restore the painter state to its original state.

> **TIP**
>
> If you want to draw a more complex item, check the `QPainter` official documentation at doc.qt.io/qt-5/qpainter.html.

This is the `sizeHint()` function's implementation:

```
QSize PictureDelegate::sizeHint(const QStyleOptionViewItem& /*option*/,
const QModelIndex& index) const
{
    const QPixmap& pixmap = index.model()->data(index,
        Qt::DecorationRole).value<QPixmap>();
    return pixmap.size();
}
```

This one is easier. We want the item's size to be equal to the thumbnail size. As we kept the aspect ratio of the thumbnail during its creation in `Picture::setFilePath()`, thumbnails can have a different width and height. Hence, we basically retrieve the thumbnail and return its size.

> When you create an item delegate, avoid directly inheriting the `QItemDelegate` class and instead inherit `QStyledItemDelegate`. This last one supports Qt style sheets, allowing you to easily customize the rendering.

Now that `PictureDelegate` is ready, we can configure our `thumbnailListView` to use it, updating the `AlbumWidget.cpp` file like this:

```
AlbumWidget::AlbumWidget(QWidget *parent) :
    QWidget(parent),
    ui(new Ui::AlbumWidget),
    mAlbumModel(nullptr),
    mAlbumSelectionModel(nullptr),
    mPictureModel(nullptr),
    mPictureSelectionModel(nullptr)
{
    ui->setupUi(this);
    clearUi();

    ui->thumbnailListView->setSpacing(5);
    ui->thumbnailListView->setResizeMode(QListView::Adjust);
    ui->thumbnailListView->setFlow(QListView::LeftToRight);
    ui->thumbnailListView->setWrapping(true);
    ui->thumbnailListView->setItemDelegate(
        new PictureDelegate(this));
    ...
}
```

> **Qt tip** An item delegate can also manage the editing process with the
> `QStyledItemDelegate::createEditor()` function.

Displaying a picture with PictureWidget

This widget will be called to display a picture at its full size. We also add some buttons to go to the previous/next picture or delete the current one.

Let's start to analyze the `PictureWidget.ui` form, here is the design view:

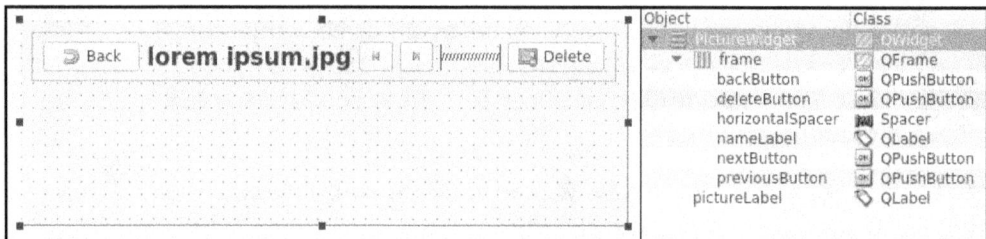

Here are the details:

- `backButton`: This object requests to display the gallery
- `deleteButton`: This object removes the picture from the album
- `nameLabel`: This object displays the picture name
- `nextButton`: This object selects the next picture in the album
- `previousButton`: This object selects the previous picture in the album
- `pictureLabel`: This object displays the picture

We can now take a look at the header `PictureWidget.h`:

```
#include <QWidget>
#include <QItemSelection>

namespace Ui {
class PictureWidget;
}

class PictureModel;
class QItemSelectionModel;
class ThumbnailProxyModel;
```

```
class PictureWidget : public QWidget
{
    Q_OBJECT

public:
    explicit PictureWidget(QWidget *parent = 0);
    ~PictureWidget();
    void setModel(ThumbnailProxyModel* model);
    void setSelectionModel(QItemSelectionModel* selectionModel);

signals:
    void backToGallery();

protected:
    void resizeEvent(QResizeEvent* event) override;

private slots:
    void deletePicture();
    void loadPicture(const QItemSelection& selected);

private:
    void updatePicturePixmap();

private:
    Ui::PictureWidget* ui;
    ThumbnailProxyModel* mModel;
    QItemSelectionModel* mSelectionModel;
    QPixmap mPixmap;
};
```

No surprises here, we have the `ThumbnailProxyModel*` and `QItemSelectionModel*` setters in the `PictureWidget` class. The signal `backToGallery()` is triggered when the user clicks on the `backButton` object. It will be handled by `MainWindow` to display again the gallery. We override `resizeEvent()` to ensure that we always use all the visible area to display the picture. The `deletePicture()` slot will process the deletion when the user clicks on the corresponding button. The `loadPicture()` function will be called to update the UI with the specified picture. Finally, `updatePicturePixmap()` is a helper function to display the picture according to the current widget size.

This widget is really similar to the others. As a result, we will not put the full implementation code of `PictureWidget.cpp` here. You can check the full source code example if needed.

Let's see how this widget is able to always display the picture at its full size in
`PictureWidget.cpp`:

```
void PictureWidget::resizeEvent(QResizeEvent* event)
{
    QWidget::resizeEvent(event);
    updatePicturePixmap();
}

void PictureWidget::updatePicturePixmap()
{
    if (mPixmap.isNull()) {
        return;
    }
    ui->pictureLabel->setPixmap(mPixmap.scaled(ui->pictureLabel->size(),
Qt::KeepAspectRatio));
}
```

So, every time the widget is resized, we call `updatePicturePixmap()`. The `mPixmap`
variable is the full-size picture from `PictureModel`. This function will scale the picture to
the `pictureLabel` size, keeping the aspect ratio. You can freely resize the window and
enjoy your picture with the biggest possible size.

Composing your Gallery app

Alright, we completed `AlbumListWidget`, `AlbumWidget`, and `PictureWidget`. If you
remember correctly, `AlbumListWidget` and `AlbumWidget` are contained in a widget
called `GalleryWidget`.

Let's take a look at the `GalleryWidget.ui` file:

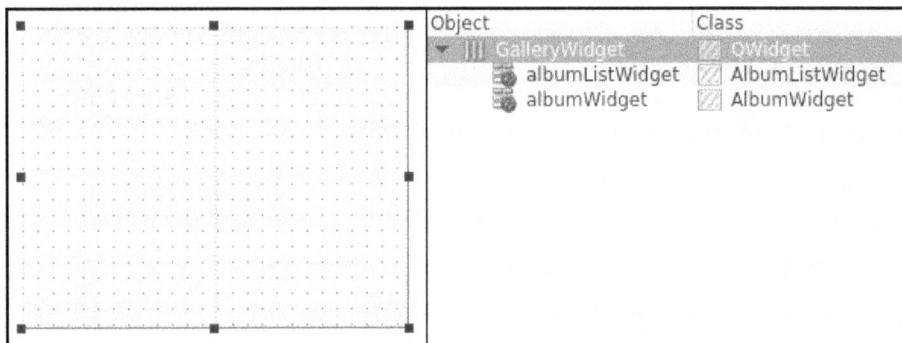

This widget does not contain any standard Qt widgets but only our created widgets. Qt provides two ways to use your own widgets in the Qt designer:

- **Promoting widgets**: This is the fastest and easiest way
- **Creating widget plugin for Qt designer**: This is more powerful but more complex

In this chapter, we will use the first way, which consists of placing a generic `QWidget` as a placeholder and then promoting it to our custom widget class. You can follow these steps to add the `albumListWidget` and the `albumWidget` objects to the `GalleryWidget.ui` file from the Qt designer:

1. Drag and drop a **Widget** from **Containers** to your form.
2. Set the **objectName** (for example, `albumListWidget`) from the **Property Editor**.
3. Select **Promote to...** from the widget contextual menu.
4. Set the promoted class name (for example, `AlbumWidget`).
5. Check that header file is correct (for example, `AlbumWidget.h`).
6. Click on the **Add** button and then click on **Promote**.

If you fail your widget promotion, you can always reverse it with **Demote to QWidget** from the contextual menu.

There is nothing really exciting in the header and implementation of `GalleryWidget`. We only provide setters for the model and model selection of `Album` and `Picture` to forward them to `albumListWidget` and `albumWidget`. This class also relays the signal `pictureActivated` from `albumWidget`. Please check the full source code if needed.

This is the final part of this chapter. We will now analyze `MainWindow`. Nothing is done in `MainWindow.ui` because everything is handled in the code. This is `MainWindow.h`:

```
#include <QMainWindow>
#include <QStackedWidget>

namespace Ui {
class MainWindow;
}

class GalleryWidget;
class PictureWidget;

class MainWindow : public QMainWindow
{
    Q_OBJECT
```

```
public:
    explicit MainWindow(QWidget *parent = 0);
    ~MainWindow();

public slots:
    void displayGallery();
    void displayPicture(const QModelIndex& index);

private:
    Ui::MainWindow *ui;
    GalleryWidget* mGalleryWidget;
    PictureWidget* mPictureWidget;
    QStackedWidget* mStackedWidget;
};
```

The two slots, `displayGallery()` and `displayPicture()`, will be used to switch the display between the gallery (album list with the album and thumbnail) and the picture (full-size). The `QStackedWidget` class can contain various widgets but display only one at a time.

Let's take a look to the beginning of the constructor in the `MainWindow.cpp` file:

```
ui->setupUi(this);

AlbumModel* albumModel = new AlbumModel(this);
QItemSelectionModel* albumSelectionModel =
    new QItemSelectionModel(albumModel, this);
mGalleryWidget->setAlbumModel(albumModel);
mGalleryWidget->setAlbumSelectionModel(albumSelectionModel);
```

First, we initialize the UI by calling `ui->setupUi()`. Then we create `AlbumModel` and its `QItemSelectionModel`. Finally, we call the setters of `GalleryWidget` that will dispatch them to the `AlbumListWidget` and `AlbumWidget` objects.

Continuing our analysis of this constructor:

```
PictureModel* pictureModel = new PictureModel(*albumModel, this);
ThumbnailProxyModel* thumbnailModel = new ThumbnailProxyModel(this);
thumbnailModel->setSourceModel(pictureModel);

QItemSelectionModel* pictureSelectionModel =
    new QItemSelectionModel(pictureModel, this);

mGalleryWidget->setPictureModel(thumbnailModel);
mGalleryWidget->setPictureSelectionModel(pictureSelectionModel);
mPictureWidget->setModel(thumbnailModel);
mPictureWidget->setSelectionModel(pictureSelectionModel);
```

The behavior with `Picture` is close to the previous one with `Album`. But we also share `ThumbnailProxyModel`, which is initialized from `PictureModel`, and its `QItemSelectionModel` with `PictureWidget`.

The constructor now performs the signal/slot connections:

```
connect(mGalleryWidget, &GalleryWidget::pictureActivated,
        this, &MainWindow::displayPicture);

connect(mPictureWidget, &PictureWidget::backToGallery,
        this, &MainWindow::displayGallery);
```

Do you remember the `pictureActivated()` function? This signal is emitted when you double-click on a thumbnail in `albumWidget`. We can now connect it to our `displayPicture` slot, which will switch the display with the picture at its full size. Do not forget to also connect the `backToGallery` signal emitted when the user clicks on the `backButton` from `PictureWidget`. It will switch again to display the gallery.

The last part of the constructor is easy:

```
mStackedWidget->addWidget(mGalleryWidget);
mStackedWidget->addWidget(mPictureWidget);
displayGallery();

setCentralWidget(mStackedWidget);
```

We add our two widgets, `mGalleryWidget` and `mPictureWidget`, to the `mStackedWidget` class. When the application starts, we want to display the gallery, so we call our own slot `displayGallery()`. Finally, we define `mStackedWidget` as the main window's central widget.

To finish this chapter, let's see what happens in these two magic slots that allows to switch the display when the user requests it:

```
void MainWindow::displayGallery()
{
    mStackedWidget->setCurrentWidget(mGalleryWidget);
}

void MainWindow::displayPicture(const QModelIndex& /*index*/)
{
    mStackedWidget->setCurrentWidget(mPictureWidget);
}
```

That seems ridiculously easy. We just request `mStackedWidget` to select the corresponding widget. As `PictureWidget` shares the same selection model with other views, we can even ignore the `index` variable.

Summary

The real separation between data and representation is not always an easy task. Dividing the core and the GUI in two different projects is a good practice. It will force you to design separated layers in your application. At first sight, the Qt model/view system can appear complex. But this chapter taught you how powerful it can be and how easy it is to use. Thanks to the Qt framework, the persistence of data in a database can be done without headaches.

This chapter built on top of the foundations laid with the `gallery-core` library. In the next chapter, we will reuse the same core library and create a mobile UI with Qt Quick in QML.

13
Dominating the Mobile UI

In Chapter 11, *Dividing Your Project and Ruling Your Code*, we created a strong core library to handle a picture gallery. We will now use this gallery-core library to create a mobile application.

We will teach you how to create a Qt Quick project from scratch. You will create custom Qt Quick views with QML. This chapter will also cover how your QML views can communicate with the C++ library.

At the end of this chapter, your gallery application will run on your mobile (Android or iOS) with a dedicated GUI compliant with touch devices. This application will offer the same features as the desktop application.

This chapter covers the following topics:

- Creating a Qt Quick project
- QML
- Qt Quick controls
- Qt for mobile (Android and iOS)
- Calling C++ functions from QML

Starting with Qt Quick and QML

Qt Quick is another way of creating applications with Qt. You can use it to create a complete application in place of Qt Widgets. The Qt Quick module provides transitions, animations, and visual effects. You can also customize graphical effects with shaders. This module is especially efficient at making software for devices using touchscreens. Qt Quick uses a dedicated language: Qt Modeling Language (QML). It is a declarative language; the syntax is close to the JSON (JavaScript Object Notation) syntax. Furthermore, QML also supports JavaScript expressions inline or in a separate file.

Let's begin with a simple example of a Qt Quick application using QML. Create a new file called `main.qml` with this code snippet:

```
import QtQuick 2.5
import QtQuick.Window 2.2

Window {
    visible: true
    width: 640; height: 480

    // A nice red rectangle
    Rectangle {
        width: 200; height: 200
        color: "red"
    }
}
```

Qt 5 provides a nice tool called `qmlscene` to prototype a QML user interface. You can find the binary file in your Qt installation folder, for example: `Qt/5.7/gcc_64/bin/qmlscene`. To load your `main.qml` file, you can run the tool and select the file, or use the CLI with the `.qml` file in an argument: `qmlscene main.qml`. You should see something like this:

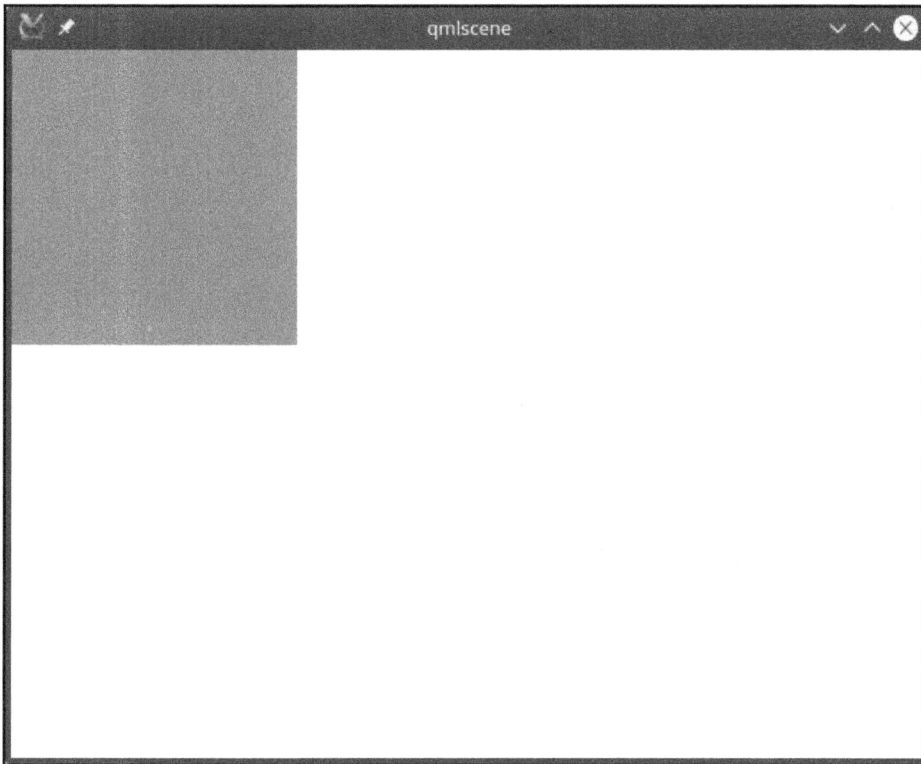

To use a Qt Quick module, you need to import it. The syntax is easy:

```
import <moduleName> <moduleVersion>
```

In this example we import `QtQuick`, which is the common module that will provide basic components (`Rectangle`, `Image`, `Text`) and we also import the `QtQuick.Window` module that will provide the main window application (`Window`).

A QML component can have properties. For example, we set the `width` property of the `Window` class to the value `640`. Here is the generic syntax:

```
<ObjectType> {
    <PropertyName>: <PropertyValue>
}
```

We can now update `main.qml` file with some new rectangles:

```
import QtQuick 2.5
import QtQuick.Window 2.2

Window {
    visible: true
    width: 640; height: 480

    Rectangle {
        width: 200; height: 200
        color: "red"
    }

    Rectangle {
        width: 200; height: 200
        color: "green"
        x: 100; y: 100

        Rectangle {
            width: 50; height: 50
            color: "blue"
            x: 100; y: 100
        }
    }
}
```

Here is the visual result:

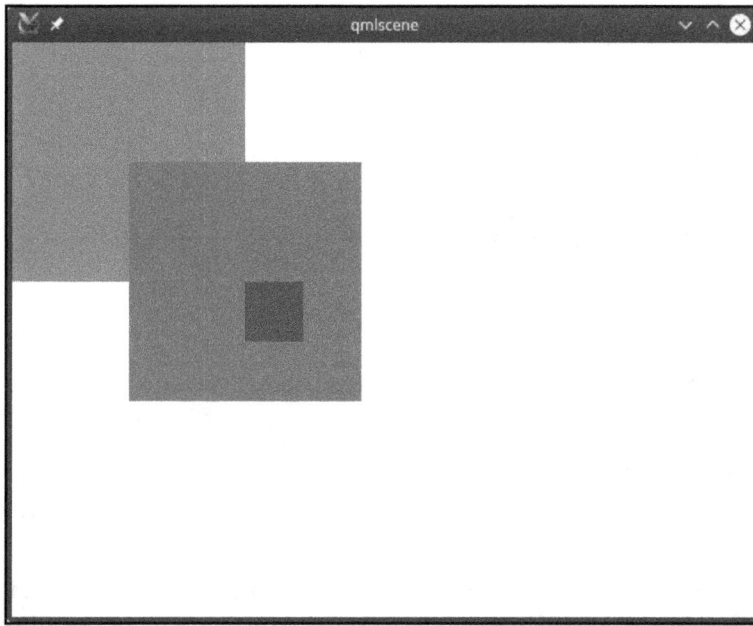

Your QML file describes the UI as a hierarchy of components. The hierarchy below the `Window` element is the following:

- Red `Rectangle`
- Green `Rectangle`
- Blue `Rectangle`

Each nested item will always have its x, y coordinates relative to its parent.

To structure your application, you can build reusable QML components. You can easily create a new component. All QML components must have a single root item. Let's build a new `MyToolbar` component by creating a new file called `MyToolbar.qml`:

```
import QtQuick 2.5

import QtQuick 2.5

Rectangle {
    color: "gray"
    height: 50
```

```
Rectangle {
    id: purpleRectangle
    width: 50; height: parent.height
    color: "purple"
    radius: 10
}

Text {
    anchors.left: purpleRectangle.right
    anchors.right: parent.right
    text: "Dominate the Mobile UI"
    font.pointSize: 30
}
}
```

The gray `Rectangle` element will be our root item used as background. We also created two items:

- A purple `Rectangle` element that can be identified with the ID `purpleRectangle`. The height of this item will be the height of its parent, that is, the gray `Rectangle` element.
- A `Text` item. In this case, we use anchors. It will help us to layout items without using hardcoded coordinates. The left of the `Text` item will be aligned with the right of `purpleRectangle`, and the right of the `Text` item will be aligned with the right of the parent (the gray `Rectangle` element).

> Qt Quick provides a lot of anchors:
> `left`, `horizontalCenter`, `right`, `top`, `verticalCenter`, and `bottom`. You can also use convenience anchors such as `fill` or `centerIn`. For more information on anchors, take a look at `http://doc.qt.io/qt-5/qtquick-positioning-anchors.html`.

You can use `MyToolbar` in your window by updating your `main.qml`:

```
Window {
    ...
    MyToolbar {
        width: parent.width
    }
}
```

We set the width to the parent width. Like this, the toolbar fills the window's width. Here is the result:

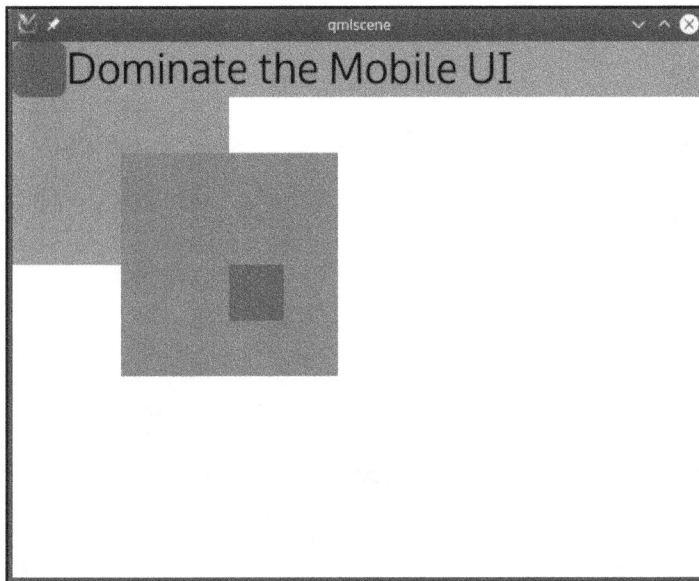

Anchors are great to align specific items, but if you want to layout several items in grid, row, or column fashion, you can use the QtQuick.layouts module. Here is an example of the updated main.qml:

```
import QtQuick 2.5
import QtQuick.Window 2.2
import QtQuick.Layouts 1.3

Window {
    visible: true
    width: 640; height: 480

    MyToolbar {
        id: myToolbar
        width: parent.width
    }

    RowLayout {
        anchors.top: myToolbar.bottom
        anchors.left: parent.left
        anchors.right: parent.right
        anchors.bottom: parent.bottom
```

```
        Rectangle { width: 200; height: 200; color: "red" }
        Rectangle { width: 200; height: 200 color: "green" }
        Rectangle { width: 50; height: 50; color: "blue" }
    }
}
```

You should get something like this:

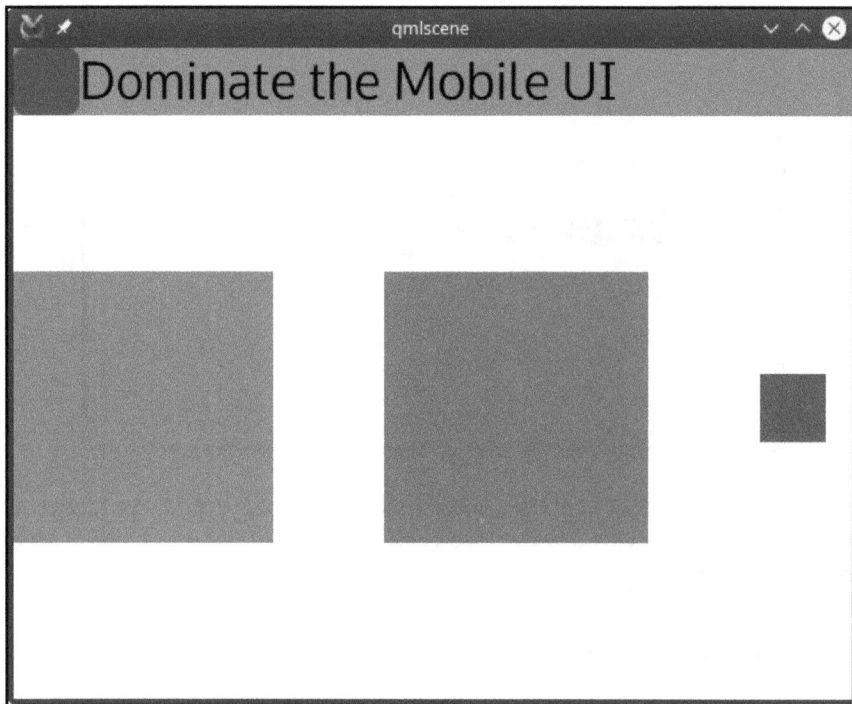

As you can see, we use a `RowLayout` element that fits under the `myToolbar` and to its parent, a `Window` element. This item provides a way to dynamically layout items in a row. Qt Quick also provides other layout items: `GridLayout` and `ColumnLayout`.

Your custom component can also expose custom properties that can be modified outside of the component itself. You can do it by adding the `property` attribute. Please update `MyToolbar.qml`:

```qml
import QtQuick 2.5

Rectangle {

    property color iconColor: "purple"
    property alias title: label.text

    color: "gray"
    height: 50

    Rectangle {
        id: purpleRectangle
        width: 50; height: parent.height
        color: iconColor
        radius: 10
    }

    Text {
        id: label
        anchors.left: purpleRectangle.right
        anchors.right: parent.right
        text: "Dominate the Mobile UI"
        font.pointSize: 30
    }
}
```

The `iconColor` is a really new property that is a fully-fledged variable. We also update the `Rectangle` attribute to use this property as `color`. The `title` property is only an `alias`, you can see it as a pointer to update the `label.text` property.

From outside you can use these attributes with the same syntax; please update the `main.qml` file with the following snippet:

```qml
import QtQuick 2.5
import QtQuick.Window 2.2
import QtQuick.Layouts 1.3

Window {
    visible: true
    width: 640; height: 480

    MyToolbar {
        id: myToolbar
```

```
            width: parent.width

            title: "Dominate Qt Quick"
            iconColor: "yellow"
        }
      ...
    }
```

You should get a nice updated toolbar like this one:

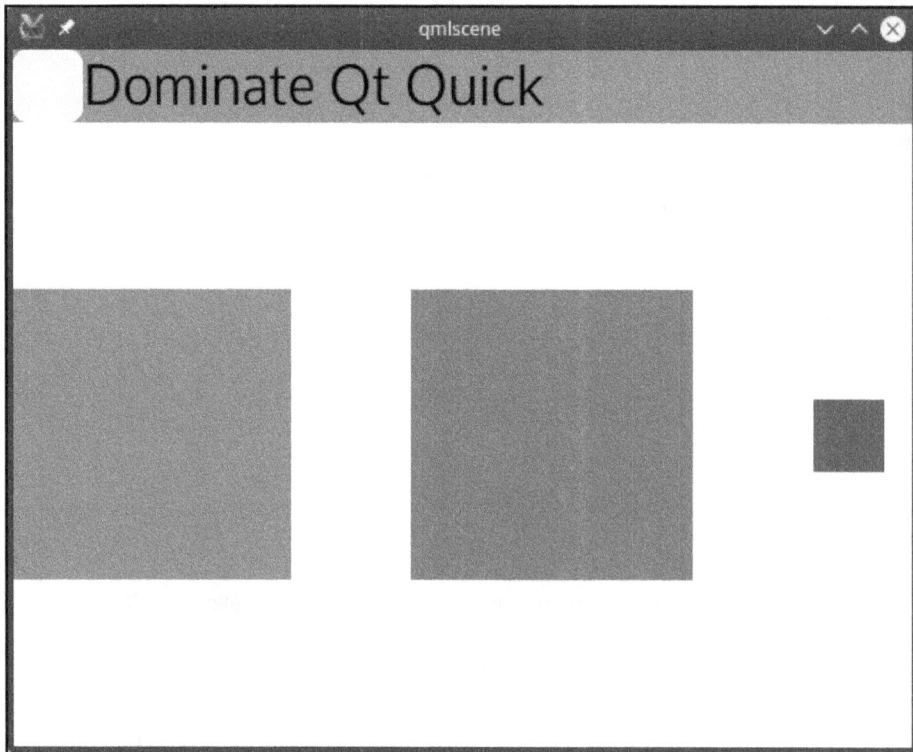

We have covered the basics of QML, now we are going to proceed to mobile application development using QML.

Checking your development environment

To be able to create a Qt application for Android, you must have:

- A device with Android v2.3.3 (API 10) or later
- Android SDK
- Android NDK
- JDK
- Qt Prebuilt Components for Android x86 (from the Qt Maintenance Tool)
- Qt Prebuilt Components for Android ARMv7 (from the Qt Maintenance Tool)

To be able to create a Qt application for iOS, you must have:

- A device with iOS 5.0 or later
- A Mac desktop computer
- Xcode
- Qt for iOS (from Qt Maintenance Tool)

When starting, Qt Creator will detect and create Android and iOS Qt kits. You can check your existing kits from **Tools** I **Options** I **Build & Run** I **Kits**, as shown in the following screenshot:

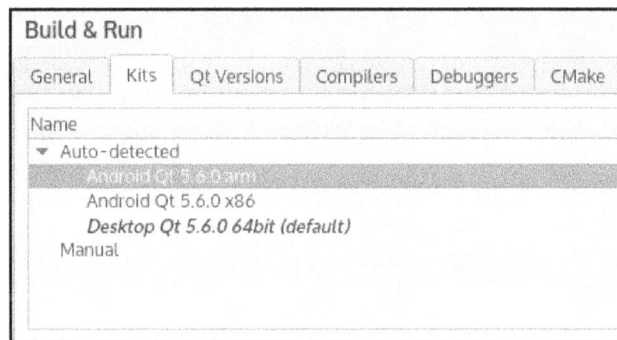

Creating a Qt Quick project

This chapter will follow the same project structure we covered in Chapter 12, *Conquering the Desktop UI*: a parent project ch05-gallery-mobile.pro will host our two subprojects, gallery-core and the new gallery-mobile.

In Qt creator, you can create a Qt Quick subproject from **File** | **New File or Project** | **Application** | **Qt Quick Controls Application** | **Choose**.

The wizard will allow you to customize your project creation:

- Location
    - Choose a project name (gallery-mobile) and a location
- Details
    - Deselect **With ui.qml file**
    - Deselect **Enable native styling**
- Kits
    - Select your desktop kit
    - Select at least one mobile kit
- Summary
    - Be sure to add gallery-mobile as a subproject of ch05-gallery-mobile.pro

Let's take some time to explain why we created our project with these options.

The first thing to analyze is the application template. By default, Qt Quick only provides basic QML components (Rectangle, Image, Text, and so on). Advanced components will be handled by Qt Quick modules. For this project we will use Qt Quick Controls (ApplicationWindow, Button, TextField, and so on). That is why we chose to begin with a **Qt Quick Controls application**. Keep in mind that you can always import and use Qt Quick modules later.

In this chapter, we will not use the Qt Quick Designer. As a consequence, .ui.qml files are not required. Even if the designer can help a lot, it is good to understand and write QML files yourself.

The desktop "native styling" is disabled because this project mainly targets mobile platforms. Moreover, disabling "native styling" avoids heavy dependency on the Qt widgets module.

Finally, we select at least two kits. The first one is our desktop kit. The other kits are the mobile platforms you target. We usually use the following development workflow:

- Fast iterations on desktop
- Check and fix behavior on mobile emulator/simulator
- Real test on the mobile device

Deployment on a real device is generally longer so you can do most development with the desktop kit. The mobile kits will allow you to check your application behavior on a real mobile device or on an emulator (for example with a Qt Android x86 kit).

Let's talk about the files automatically generated by the wizard. Here is the `main.cpp` file:

```
#include <QGuiApplication>
#include <QQmlApplicationEngine>

int main(int argc, char *argv[])
{
    QGuiApplication app(argc, argv);

    QQmlApplicationEngine engine;
    engine.load(QUrl(QStringLiteral("qrc:/main.qml")));

    return app.exec();
}
```

We use here `QGuiApplication` and not `QApplication` because we do not use Qt widgets in this project. Then, we create the QML engine and load `qrc:/mail.qml`. As you may have guessed (with the `qrc:/` prefix), this QML file is in a Qt resource file.

You can open the `qml.qrc` file to find the `main.qml`:

```
import QtQuick 2.5
import QtQuick.Controls 1.4

ApplicationWindow {
    visible: true
    width: 640
    height: 480
    title: qsTr("Hello World")

    menuBar: MenuBar {
        Menu {
            title: qsTr("File")
            MenuItem {
                text: qsTr("&Open")
```

```
                        onTriggered: console.log("Open action triggered");
                    }
                    MenuItem {
                        text: qsTr("Exit")
                        onTriggered: Qt.quit();
                    }
                }
            }

        Label {
            text: qsTr("Hello World")
            anchors.centerIn: parent
        }
    }
```

The first thing to do is to import types used in the file. Notice the module version at the end of each import. The QtQuick module will import basic QML elements (Rectangle, Image, and so on) while the QtQuick.Controls module will import advanced QML elements from the QtQuick Controls submodule (ApplicationWindow, MenuBar, MenuItem, Label, and so on).

Then, we define the root element of type ApplicationWindow. It provides a top-level application window with the following items: MenuBar, ToolBar and StatusBar. The properties visible, width, height, and title of ApplicationWindow are primitive types. The syntax is simple and intelligible.

The menuBar property is more complex. This MenuBar property is composed of a Menu file, itself composed of two MenuItems: Open and Exit. A MenuItem emits a triggered() signal each time it is activated. In this case, the MenuItem file will log a message on the console. The exit MenuItem terminates the application.

Finally, a Label displaying "Hello World" is added in the content area of our ApplicationWindow type. Positioning items with anchors is useful. In our case the label is centered vertically and horizontally in its parent, ApplicationWindow.

Before going ahead, check that this sample runs correctly on your desktop and on your mobile.

Preparing your Qt Quick gallery entry point

First of all, you need to link this project to our `gallery-core` library. We already covered how to link an internal library in `Chapter 12`, *Conquering the Desktop UI*. For more details, refer to it. This is the updated `gallery-mobile.pro` file:

```
TEMPLATE = app

QT += qml quick sql svg

CONFIG += c++11

SOURCES += main.cpp

RESOURCES += gallery.qrc

LIBS += -L$$OUT_PWD/../gallery-core/ -lgallery-core
INCLUDEPATH += $$PWD/../gallery-core
DEPENDPATH += $$PWD/../gallery-core

contains(ANDROID_TARGET_ARCH,x86) {
    ANDROID_EXTRA_LIBS =
        $$[QT_INSTALL_LIBS]/libQt5Sql.so
}
```

Please notice that we made several changes here:

- We added the `sql` module to deploy the dependency on your mobile device
- We added the `svg` module for the button icons
- The `qml.qrc` file has been renamed in `gallery.qrc`
- We linked the `gallery-core` library
- By default, the `sql` shared object (`libQt5Sql.so`) will not be deployed on your Android x86 device. You have to explicitly include it in your `.pro` file.

You can now use classes from the `gallery-core` library in our `gallery-mobile` application. Let's see how to bind C++ models with QML. This is the updated `main.cpp`:

```cpp
#include <QGuiApplication>
#include <QQmlApplicationEngine>
#include <QQmlContext>
#include <QQuickView>

#include "AlbumModel.h"
#include "PictureModel.h"
```

```
int main(int argc, char *argv[])
{
    QGuiApplication app(argc, argv);

    AlbumModel albumModel;
    PictureModel pictureModel(albumModel);

    QQmlApplicationEngine engine;

    QQmlContext* context = engine.rootContext();
    context->setContextProperty("albumModel", &albumModel);
    context->setContextProperty("pictureModel", &pictureModel);

    engine.load(QUrl(QStringLiteral("qrc:/qml/main.qml")));

    return app.exec();
}
```

Our models will be instantiated in C++ and exposed to QML using the root `QQmlContext` object. The `setContextProperty()` function allows us to bind a C++ `QObject` to a QML property. The first argument will be the QML property name. We are only binding a C++ object to a QML property; the context object does not take ownership of this object.

Let's now talk about the mobile application itself. We will define three pages with specific roles:

- `AlbumListPage`
  - Displays existing albums
  - Album creation
  - Album selection

- `AlbumPage`
  - Displays existing pictures as thumbnails
  - Adds pictures in album
  - Album rename
  - Album deletion
  - Picture selection

- `PicturePage`
  - Displays selected picture
  - Picture selection
  - Picture deletion

To handle the navigation, we will use a `StackView` component from Qt Quick Controls. This QML component implements a stack-based navigation. You can push a page when you want to display it. When the user requests to go back, you can pop it. Here is the workflow using a `StackView` component for our gallery mobile application. The page with the solid border is the page currently displayed on screen:

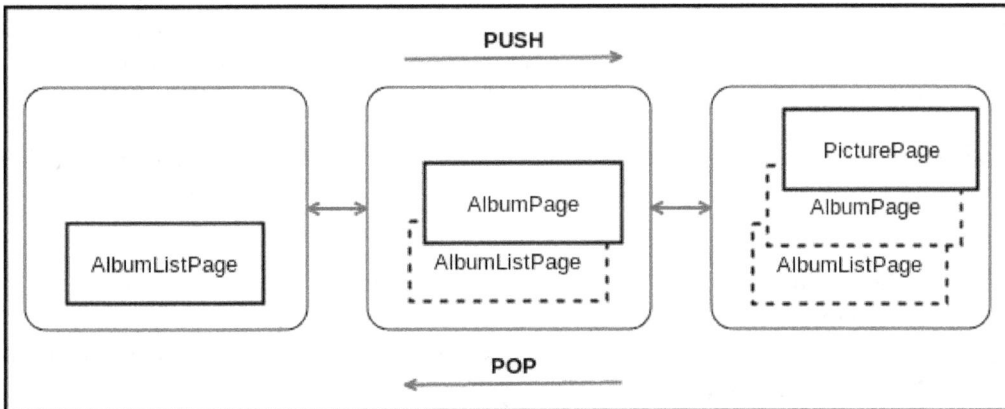

This is the implementation of `main.qml`:

```
import QtQuick 2.6
import QtQuick.Controls 2.0

ApplicationWindow {

    readonly property alias pageStack: stackView

    id: app
    visible: true
    width: 768
    height: 1280

    StackView {
        id: stackView
        anchors.fill: parent
        initialItem: AlbumListPage {}
    }

    onClosing: {
        if (Qt.platform.os == "android") {
            if (stackView.depth > 1) {
                close.accepted = false
                stackView.pop()
```

```
            }
        }
    }
}
```

This main file is really simple. The application is constructed around the `StackView` component. We set the `id` property to allow our `StackView` to be identified and referred to by other QML objects. The `anchors` property will set `stackView` to fill its parent, the `ApplicationWindow` type. Finally, we set the `initialItem` property to a page, `AlbumListPage` that will be implemented soon.

On Android, `onClosing` will be executed each time the user presses the back button. To mimic a native Android application, we will first pop the last stacked page before really closing the application.

At the top of the file, we define a `property alias` for the `stackView`. A `property alias` is a simple reference to another existing property. This alias will be useful to access `stackView` from other QML components. To prevent a QML component to crush the `stackView` we are using the `readonly` keyword. After initialization, the components can access the property but not change its value.

Displaying albums with ListView

Let's make our first page for this mobile application! Create a file in `gallery.qrc` called `AlbumListPage.qml`. Here is the page header implementation:

```
import QtQuick 2.0
import QtQuick.Layouts 1.3

import QtQuick.Controls 2.0

Page {

    header: ToolBar {
        Label {
            Layout.fillWidth: true
            text: "Albums"
            font.pointSize: 30
        }
    }
    ...
}
```

A `Page` is a container control with a header and footer. In this application, we will only use the header item. We assign a `ToolBar` to the `header` property. The height of this toolbar will be handled by Qt and will be adjusted depending on the target platform. In this first simple implementation, we only put a `Label` displaying the text "Albums".

Add a `ListView` element to this page after the `header` initialization:

```
ListView {
    id: albumList
    model: albumModel
    spacing: 5
    anchors.fill: parent

    delegate: Rectangle {
        width: parent.width
        height: 120
        color: "#d0d1d2"

        Text {
            text: name
            font.pointSize: 16
            color: "#000000"
            anchors.verticalCenter: parent.verticalCenter
        }
    }
}
```

The Qt Quick `ListView` is the Qt Widget `QListView` equivalent. It displays a list of items from a provided model. We set the `model` property to value `albumModel`. This refers to the C++ model from `main.cpp` file accessible from QML because we used the `setContextProperty()` function. In Qt Quick, you must provide a delegate to describe how a row will be displayed. In this case, a row will only display the album's name with a `Text` item. Accessing the album's name in QML is easy because our `AlbumModel` model exposes its role list to QML. Let's refresh your memory concerning the overridden `roleNames()` function of `AlbumModel`:

```
QHash<int, QByteArray> AlbumModel::roleNames() const
{
    QHash<int, QByteArray> roles;
    roles[Roles::IdRole] = "id";
    roles[Roles::NameRole] = "name";
    return roles;
}
```

So each time your delegate from Qt Quick uses the `name` role, it will call the `AlbumModel` function `data()` with the correct role integer and return the correct album name string.

To handle the mouse, click on a row and add a `MouseArea` element on the delegate:

```
ListView {
    ...
    delegate: Rectangle {
        ...
        MouseArea {
            anchors.fill: parent
            onClicked: {
                albumList.currentIndex = index
                pictureModel.setAlbumId(id)
                pageStack.push("qrc:/qml/AlbumPage.qml",
                        { albumName: name, albumRowIndex: index })
            }
        }
    }
}
```

The `MouseArea` is an invisible item that can be used with any visible item to handle mouse events. This also applies to a simple touch on a phone touch screen. Here we tell the `MouseArea` element to take the full area of the parent `Rectangle`.

In our case, we only perform tasks on the `clicked` signal. We update the `currentIndex` of the `ListView` with `index`. This `index` is a special role containing the index of the item in the model.

When the user clicks, we will tell `pictureModel` to load the selected album with the `pictureModel.setAlbumId(id)` call. We will see soon how QML can call C++ methods.

Finally, we push `AlbumPage` on `pageStack` property. The `push()` function allows us to set a list of QML properties using a {key: value, ... } syntax. Each property will be copied into the pushed item. Here the `name` and the `index` will be copied in the `albumName` and `albumRowIndex` properties of `AlbumPage`. It is a simple yet powerful way to instantiate a QML page with properties arguments.

From your QML code, you can only call some specific C++ methods:

- Properties (using `Q_PROPERTY`)
- Public slot
- Function decorated as invokable (using `Q_INVOKABLE`)

In this case we will decorate `PictureModel::setAlbumId()` as `Q_INVOKABLE`, please update the `PictureModel.h` file:

```
class GALLERYCORESHARED_EXPORT PictureModel : public QAbstractListModel
{
    Q_OBJECT
public:
    ...
    Q_INVOKABLE void setAlbumId(int albumId);
    ...
};
```

Theming the application with a QML singleton

Styling and theming a QML application can be done in various ways. In this chapter, we will declare a QML singleton with the theme data used by custom components. Moreover, we will also create a custom `Page` component to handle the toolbar and its default item (back button and page's title).

Please create a new `Style.qml` file:

```
pragma Singleton
import QtQuick 2.0

QtObject {
    property color text: "#000000"

    property color windowBackground: "#eff0f1"
    property color toolbarBackground: "#eff0f1"
    property color pageBackground: "#fcfcfc"
    property color buttonBackground: "#d0d1d2"

    property color itemHighlight: "#3daee9"
}
```

We declare a `QtObject` component that will only contain our theme properties. A `QtObject` is a non-visual QML component.

Declaring a singleton type in QML requires two steps. First you need to use the `pragma singleton`, it will indicate the use of a single instance of the component. The second step is to register it. This can be done in C++ or by creating a `qmldir` file. Let's see the second step. Create a new plain-text file called `qmldir`:

```
singleton Style 1.0 Style.qml
```

This simple line will declare a QML `singleton` type named `Style` with the version 1.0 from the file named `Style.qml`.

It is now time to use these theme properties in custom components. Let's see a simple example. Create a new QML file called `ToolBarTheme.qml`:

```
import QtQuick 2.0
import QtQuick.Controls 2.0

import "."

ToolBar {
    background: Rectangle {
        color: Style.toolbarBackground
    }

}
```

This QML object describes a customized `ToolBar`. Here, the `background` element is a simple `Rectangle` with our color. We can easily access our singleton `Style` and its theme property using `Style.toolbarBackground`.

> QML Singletons require an explicit import to load the `qmldir` file. The `import "."` is a workaround for this Qt bug. For more information, please check `https://bugreports.qt.io/browse/QTBUG-34418`.

We will now create a QML file `PageTheme.qml`, with the aim of containing all the code related to the page's toolbar and theme:

```
import QtQuick 2.0

import QtQuick.Layouts 1.3
import Qt.labs.controls 1.0
import QtQuick.Controls 2.0
import "."

Page {
```

```
property alias toolbarButtons: buttonsLoader.sourceComponent
property alias toolbarTitle: titleLabel.text

header: ToolBarTheme {
    RowLayout {
        anchors.fill: parent
        ToolButton {
            background: Image {
                source: "qrc:/res/icons/back.svg"
            }
            onClicked: {
                if (stackView.depth > 1) {
                    stackView.pop()
                }
            }
        }

        Label {
            id: titleLabel
            Layout.fillWidth: true
            color: Style.text
            elide: Text.ElideRight
            font.pointSize: 30
        }

        Loader {
            Layout.alignment: Qt.AlignRight
            id: buttonsLoader
        }
    }
}

Rectangle {
    color: Style.pageBackground
    anchors.fill: parent
}
}
```

This `PageTheme` element will customize the page's header. We use our previously created `ToolBarTheme`. This toolbar only contains a `RowLayout` element to display items horizontally in one row. This layout contains three elements:

- `ToolButton`: This is the "back" that displays an image from `gallery.qrc` and pops the current page if required

- `Label`: This is the element that displays the page title
- `Loader`: This is the element that allows a page to dynamically add specific items in this generic toolbar

The `Loader` element owns a `sourceComponent` property. In this application, this property can be assigned by `PageTheme` pages to add specific buttons. These buttons will be instantiated at runtime.

The `PageTheme` pages also contain a `Rectangle` element that fits the parent and configures the page background color using the `Style.pageBackground`.

Now that our `Style.qml` and `PageTheme.qml` files are ready, we can update the `AlbumListPage.qml` file to use it:

```
import QtQuick 2.6
import QtQuick.Controls 2.0
import "."

PageTheme {

    toolbarTitle: "Albums"

    ListView {
        id: albumList
        model: albumModel
        spacing: 5
        anchors.fill: parent

        delegate: Rectangle {
            width: parent.width
            height: 120
            color: Style.buttonBackground

            Text {
                text: name
                font.pointSize: 16
                color: Style.text
                anchors.verticalCenter: parent.verticalCenter
            }
            ...
        }
    }
}
```

Now that `AlbumListPage` is a `PageTheme` element, we do not manipulate `header` directly. We only need to set the property `toolbarTitle` to display a nice "Albums" text in the toolbar. We can also enjoy nice colors using properties from the `Style` singleton.

By centralizing the theme properties in a single file, you can easily change the look and feel of your application. The source code of the project also contains a dark theme.

Loading a database on mobile

Before continuing the UI implementation, we have to take care of the database deployment on mobile. Spoiler: this will not be fun.

We have to jump back to `DatabaseManager.cpp` in the `gallery-core` project:

```
DatabaseManager& DatabaseManager::instance()
{
    return singleton;
}

DatabaseManager::DatabaseManager(const QString& path) :
    mDatabase(new QSqlDatabase(QSqlDatabase::addDatabase("QSQLITE"))),
    albumDao(*mDatabase),
    pictureDao(*mDatabase)
{
    mDatabase->setDatabaseName(path);
    ...
}
```

Whereas on Desktop, the SQLite3 database is created at the instruction `mDatabase->setDatabaseName()`, on mobile it does not work at all. This is due to the fact that the filesystem is very specific on each mobile platform (Android and iOS). An application has only access to a narrow sandbox where it cannot mess with the rest of the filesystem. All the files inside the application directory must have specific file permissions. If we let SQLite3 create the database file, it will not have the right permission and the OS will block the database from opening.

As a consequence, the database will not be properly created and your data cannot be persisted. When using the native API, this is not a problem since the OS takes care of the proper configuration of the database. Because we are developing with Qt, we do not have easy access to this API (except by using JNI or other black magic). A workaround is to embed a "ready-to-use" database in the application's package and copy it at the right filesystem path with the correct rights.

This database should contain an empty created database without any content. The database is available in the source code of the chapter (you can also generate it from the source code of `Chapter 12`, *Conquering the Desktop UI*). You can add it to the `gallery.qrc` file.

Because our layers are clearly defined, we just have to modify the `DatabaseManager::instance()` implementation to handle this case:

```
DatabaseManager& DatabaseManager::instance()
{
#if defined(Q_OS_ANDROID) || defined(Q_OS_IOS)
    QFile assetDbFile(":/database/" + DATABASE_FILENAME);
    QString destinationDbFile = QStandardPaths::writableLocation(
                        QStandardPaths::AppLocalDataLocation)
            .append("/" + DATABASE_FILENAME);

        if (!QFile::exists(destinationDbFile)) {
            assetDbFile.copy(destinationDbFile);
            Qfile::setPermissions(destinationDbFile,
                        QFile::WriteOwner | QFile::ReadOwner);
        }
    }
    static DatabaseManager singleton(destinationDbFile);
#else
    static DatabaseManager singleton;
#endif
    return singleton;
}
```

We first retrieve the platform-specific path of the application with a nifty Qt class: `QStandardPaths`. This class return paths for multiple types (`AppLocalDataLocation`, `DocumentsLocation`, `PicturesLocation`, and so on). The database should be stored in the application data directory. If the file does not exist, we copy it from our assets.

Finally, the permissions of the file are modified to ensure that the OS does not block the opening of the database (due to permissions not being restrictive enough).

When everything is done, the `DatabaseManager singleton` is instantiated with the correct database file path and the constructor can open this database transparently.

> In the iOS Simulator, the `QStandardPaths::writableLocation()` function will not return the proper path. Since iOS 8, the simulator's storage path on the host has changed and Qt does not reflect this. For more information, please check out `https://bugreports.qt.io/browse/QTCREATORBUG-13655`.

These workarounds were not trivial. This shows the limitations of a cross-platform application on mobile. Each platform has its own very specific way of handling the filesystem and deploying its content. Even if we manage to write platform agnostic code in QML, we still have to deal with differences between the OSes.

Creating a new album from a custom InputDialog

The `AlbumListPage` needs some data to display. The next step is to be able to add a new album. To do this, at some point we will have to call an `AlbumModel` function from QML to add this new album. Before building the UI, we have to make a small modification in `gallery-core`.

The `AlbumModel` function is already available in QML. However, we cannot directly call `AlbumModel::addAlbum(const Album& album)` from the QML code; the QML engine will not recognize the function and will throw an error **TypeError: Property 'addAlbum' of object AlbumModel(...) is not a function**. This can be fixed by simply decorating the desired function with the `Q_INVOKABLE` macro (as we did for `PictureModel::setAlbumId()`).

Nonetheless, there is another issue here: `Album` is a C++ class which is not recognized in QML. If we wanted to have full access to `Album` in QML, it would involve important modifications to the class:

* Force `Album` class to inherit from the `QObject` class.
* Add a `Q_PROPERTY` macro to specify which property of the class should be accessible from QML.
* Add multiple constructors (copy constructor, `QObject* parent`, and so on).
* Force `AlbumModel::addAlbum()` function to take an `Album*` rather than an `Album&`. For complex objects (that is, not primitive types), QML can only handle pointers. This is not a big problem, but using references instead of pointers tends to make the code safer.

These modifications are perfectly reasonable if the class is heavily manipulated in QML. Our use case is very limited: we only want to create a new album. Throughout the application, we will rely on the native Model/View API to display the album data and nothing specific to `Album` will be used.

For all these reasons, we will simply add a wrapper function in `AlbumModel`:

```
// In AlbumModel.h
...
QModelIndex addAlbum(const Album& album);
Q_INVOKABLE void addAlbumFromName(const QString& name);
...

// In AlbumModel.cpp
void AlbumModel::addAlbumFromName(const QString& name)
{
    addAlbum(Album(name));
}
```

The new function `addAlbumFromName()` just wraps the call to `addAlbum()` with the desired album `name` parameter. It can be called from the QML with the `Q_INVOKABLE` macro.

We can now switch back to the UI in the `gallery-mobile` project. We will add this album using a QML `Dialog`. QtQuick provides various default implementations of dialogs:

- `ColorDialog`: This dialog is used to choose a color
- `Dialog`: This dialog is uses the generic dialog with standard buttons (equivalent of a `QDialog`)
- `FileDialog`: This dialog is used to choose a file from the local filesystem
- `FontDialog`: This dialog is used to choose a font
- `MessageDialog`: This dialog is used to display a message

You would have expected to see an `InputDialog` in this list (as we used the `QInputDialog` widget in Chapter 12, *Conquering the Desktop UI*) but Qt Quick does not have it. Create a new **QML File (Qt Quick 2)** and name it `InputDialog.qml`. The content should look like so:

```
import QtQuick 2.6
import QtQuick.Layouts 1.3
import Qt.labs.controls 1.0
import QtQuick.Dialogs 1.2
import QtQuick.Window 2.2
import "."

Dialog {

    property string label: "New item"
    property string hint: ""
    property alias editText : editTextItem
```

```
standardButtons: StandardButton.Ok | StandardButton.Cancel
onVisibleChanged: {
    editTextItem.focus = true
    editTextItem.selectAll()
}
onButtonClicked: {
    Qt.inputMethod.hide();
}
Rectangle {

    implicitWidth: parent.width
    implicitHeight: 100

    ColumnLayout {
        Text {
            id: labelItem
            text: label
            color: Style.text
        }

        TextInput {
            id: editTextItem
            inputMethodHints: Qt.ImhPreferUppercase
            text: hint
            color: Style.text
        }
    }
}
}
```

In this custom `InputDialog`, we take the generic Qt Quick `Dialog` and modify it to contain our `TextInput` item referenced by the ID `editTextItem`. We also added a `labelItem` just above `editTextItem` to describe the expected input. There are several things to note in this dialog.

First, because we want this dialog to be generic, it has to be configurable. The caller should be able to provide parameters to display its specific data. This is done with the three properties at the top of the `Dialog` element:

- `label`: This property configures the displayed text in `labelItem`.
- `hint`: This property is the default text displayed in `editTextItem`.
- `editText`: This property references the "local" `editTextItem` element. This will let the caller retrieve the value when the dialog is closed.

We also configure the `Dialog` element to automatically use the platform buttons to validate or cancel the dialog with `standardButtons: StandardButton.Ok | StandardButton.Cancel` syntax.

Finally, to make the dialog a bit more user-friendly, `editTextItem` has the focus when the `Dialog` element becomes visible and the text is selected. These two steps are done in the `onVisibleChanged()` callback function. When the dialog is hidden (that is, **Ok** or **Cancel** has been clicked), we hide the virtual keyboard with `Qt.InputMethod.hide()`.

The `InputDialog` is ready to be used! Open `AlbumListPage.qml` and modify it like so:

```
PageTheme {

    toolbarTitle: "Albums"
    toolbarButtons: ToolButton {
        background: Image {
            source: "qrc:/res/icons/album-add.svg"
        }
        onClicked: {
            newAlbumDialog.open()
        }
    }

    InputDialog {
        id: newAlbumDialog
        title: "New album"
        label: "Album name:"
        hint: "My Album"

        onAccepted: {
            albumModel.addAlbumFromName(editText.text)
        }
    }
}
```

We add `InputDialog` with the ID `newAlbumDialog` inside `PageTheme` element. We define all our custom properties: `title`, `label`, and `hint`. When the user clicks on the **Ok** button, the `onAccepted()` function is called. Here, it is a simple matter of calling the wrapper function `addAlbumFromName()` in the `AlbumModel` element with the entered text.

This `Dialog` element is not visible by default, we open it by adding a `ToolButton` in `toolbarButtons`. This `ToolButton` will be added at the far right of the header as we specified in the `PageTheme.qml` file. To match mobile standards, we simply use a custom icon inside that button rather than text.

Here you can see that it is possible to reference images stored in the `.qrc` file with the syntax `qrc:/res/icons/album-add.svg`. We use SVG files to have scalable icons, but you are free to use your own icons for the `gallery-mobile` application.

When the user clicks on the `ToolButton`, the `onClicked()` function is called, where we open `newAlbumDialog`. On our reference device, a Nexus 5X, this is how it looks:

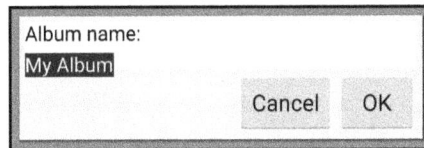

When the user clicks on the **OK** button, the whole Model/View pipeline starts to work. This new album is persisted, the `AlbumModel` element emits the correct signals to notify our `ListView`, `albumList`, to refresh itself. We are starting to leverage the power of our `gallery-core`, which can be used in a desktop application and a mobile application without rewriting a significant portion of the engine code.

Loading images with an ImageProvider

It is now time to display the thumbnails for our freshly persisted album. These thumbnails have to be loaded somehow. Because our application is targeted at mobile devices, we cannot afford to freeze the UI thread while loading thumbnails. We would either hog the CPU or be killed by the OS, neither of which are desirable destinies for `gallery-mobile`. Qt provides a very handy class to handle the image loading: `QQuickImageProvider`.

The `QQuickImageProvider` class provides an interface to load the `QPixmap` class in your QML code in an asynchronous manner. This class automatically spawns threads to load the `QPixmap` class and you simply have to implement the function `requestPixmap()`. There is more to it, `QQuickImageProvider` caches by default the requested pixmap to avoid hitting the data source too much.

Our thumbnails must be loaded from the `PictureModel` element, which gives access to the `fileUrl` of a given `Picture`. Our implementation of rQQuickImageProvider will have to get the `QPixmap` class for a row index in `PicturelModel`. Create a new C++ class named `PictureImageProvider`, and modify `PictureImageProvider.h` like this:

```
#include <QQuickImageProvider>

class PictureModel;
```

```
class PictureImageProvider : public QQuickImageProvider
{
public:

    PictureImageProvider(PictureModel* pictureModel);

    QPixmap requestPixmap(const QString& id, QSize* size,
            const QSize& requestedSize) override;

private:
    PictureModel* mPictureModel;
};
```

A pointer to the `PictureModel` element has to be provided in the constructor to be able to retrieve `fileUrl`. We override `requestPixmap()`, which takes an `id` parameter in its parameters list (the `size` and `requestedSize` can be safely ignored for now). This `id` parameter will be provided in the QML code when we want to load a picture. For a given `Image` in QML, the `PictureImageProvider` class will be called like so:

```
Image { source: "image://pictures/" + index }
```

Let's break it down:

- `image`: This is the scheme for the URL source of the image. This tells Qt to work with an image provider to load the image.
- `pictures`: This is the identifier of the image provider. We will link the `PictureImageProvider` class and this identifier at the initialization of `QmlEngine` in `main.cpp`.
- `index`: This is the ID of the image. Here it is the row index of the picture. This corresponds to the `id` parameter in `requestPixmap()`.

We already know that we want to display a picture in two modes: thumbnail and full resolution. In both cases, a `QQuickImageProvider` class will be used. These two modes have a very similar behavior: they will request `PictureModel` for `fileUrl` and return the loaded `QPixmap`.

There is a pattern here. We can easily encapsulate these two modes in `PictureImageProvider`. The only thing we have to know is when the caller wants a thumbnail or a full resolution `QPixmap`. This can be easily done by making the `id` parameter more explicit.

We are going to implement the `requestPixmap()` function to be able to be called in two ways:

- `images://pictures/<index>/full`: Using this syntax to retrieve the full resolution picture
- `images://pictures/<index>/thumbnail`: Using this syntax to retrieve the thumbnail version of the picture

If the `index` value was 0, these two calls would set the ID to `0/full` or `0/thumbnail` in `requestPixmap()`. Let's see the implementation in `PictureImageProvider.cpp`:

```
#include "PictureModel.h"

PictureImageProvider::PictureImageProvider(PictureModel* pictureModel) :
    QQuickImageProvider(QQuickImageProvider::Pixmap),
    mPictureModel(pictureModel)
{
}

QPixmap PictureImageProvider::requestPixmap(const QString& id, QSize*
/*size*/, const QSize& /*requestedSize*/)
{
    QStringList query = id.split('/');
    if (!mPictureModel || query.size() < 2) {
        return QPixmap();
    }

    int row = query[0].toInt();
    QString pictureSize = query[1];

    QUrl fileUrl = mPictureModel->data(mPictureModel->index(row, 0),
PictureModel::Roles::UrlRole).toUrl();
    return ?? // Patience, the mystery will be soon unraveled
}
```

We start by calling the `QQuickImageProvider` constructor with the `QQuickImageProvider::Pixmap` parameter to configure `QQuickImageProvider` to call `requestPixmap()`. The `QQuickImageProvider` constructor supports various image types (`QImage`, `QPixmap`, `QSGTexture`, `QQuickImageResponse`) and each one has its specific `requestXXX()` function.

In the `requestPixmap()` function, we start by splitting this ID with the / separator. From here, we retrieve the `row` values and the desired `pictureSize`. The `fileUrl` is loaded by simply calling the `mPictureModel::data()` function with the right parameters. We used the exact same call in `Chapter 12`, *Conquering the Desktop UI*.

Great, we know which `fileUrl` should be loaded and what the desired dimension is. However, we have one last thing to handle. Because we manipulate a row and not a database ID, we will have the same request URL for two different pictures, which are in different albums. Remember that `PictureModel` loads a list of pictures for a given `Album`.

We should picture (pun intended) the situation. For an album called `Holidays`, the request URL will be `images://pictures/0/thumbnail` to load the first picture. It will be the same URL for another album `Pets`, which will load the first picture with `images://pictures/0/thumbnail`. As we said earlier, `QQuickImageProvider` automatically generates a cache which will avoid subsequent calls to `requestPixmap()` for the same URL. Thus, we will always serve the same picture, no matter which album is selected.

This constraint forces us to disable the cache in `PictureImageProvider` and to roll out our own cache. This is an interesting thing to do; here is a possible implementation:

```
// In PictureImageProvider.h

#include <QQuickImageProvider>
#include <QCache>

...
public:
    static const QSize THUMBNAIL_SIZE;

    QPixmap requestPixmap(const QString& id, QSize* size, const QSize&
requestedSize) override;

    QPixmap* pictureFromCache(const QString& filepath, const QString&
pictureSize);

private:
    PictureModel* mPictureModel;
    QCache<QString, QPixmap> mPicturesCache;
};

// In PictureImageProvider.cpp
const QString PICTURE_SIZE_FULL = "full";
const QString PICTURE_SIZE_THUMBNAIL = "thumbnail";
const QSize PictureImageProvider::THUMBNAIL_SIZE = QSize(350, 350);

QPixmap PictureImageProvider::requestPixmap(const QString& id, QSize*
/*size*/, const QSize& /*requestedSize*/)
{
    ...
    return *pictureFromCache(fileUrl.toLocalFile(), pictureSize);
```

```
}

QPixmap* PictureImageProvider::pictureFromCache(const QString& filepath,
const QString& pictureSize)
{
    QString key = QStringList{ pictureSize, filepath }
                    .join("-");

        QPixmap* cachePicture = nullptr;
    if (!mPicturesCache.contains(pictureSize)) {
        QPixmap originalPicture(filepath);
        if (pictureSize == PICTURE_SIZE_THUMBNAIL) {
            cachePicture = new QPixmap(originalPicture
                                .scaled(THUMBNAIL_SIZE,
                                    Qt::KeepAspectRatio,
                                    Qt::SmoothTransformation));
        } else if (pictureSize == PICTURE_SIZE_FULL) {
            cachePicture = new QPixmap(originalPicture);
        }
        mPicturesCache.insert(key, cachePicture);
    } else {
        cachePicture = mPicturesCache[pictureSize];
    }

    return cachePicture;
}
```

This new `pictureFromCache()` function aims to store the generated `QPixmap` in `mPicturesCache` and return the proper `QPixmap`. The `mPicturesCache` class relies on a `QCache`; this class lets us store data in a key/value fashion with the possibility to assign a cost for each entry. This cost should roughly map the memory cost of the object (by default, `cost = 1`). When `QCache` is instantiated, it is initialized with a `maxCost` value (by default `100`). When the cost of the sum of all objects' exceeds the `maxCost`, `QCache` starts deleting objects to make room for the new objects, starting with the less recently accessed objects.

In the `pictureFromCache()` function, we first generate a key composed of the `fileUrl` and the `pictureSize` before trying to retrieve the `QPixmap` from the cache. If it is not present, the proper `QPixmap` (scaled to `THUMBNAIL_SIZE` macro if needed) will be generated and stored inside the cache. The `mPicturesCache` class becomes the owner of this `QPixmap`.

The last step to complete the `PictureImageProvider` class is to make it available in the QML context. This is done in `main.cpp`:

```
#include "AlbumModel.h"
#include "PictureModel.h"
#include "PictureImageProvider.h"

int main(int argc, char *argv[])
{
    QGuiApplication app(argc, argv);
    ...

    QQmlContext* context = engine.rootContext();
    context->setContextProperty("thumbnailSize",
PictureImageProvider::THUMBNAIL_SIZE.width());
    context->setContextProperty("albumModel", &albumModel);
    context->setContextProperty("pictureModel", &pictureModel);

    engine.addImageProvider("pictures", new
                        PictureImageProvider(&pictureModel));
    ...
}
```

The `PictureImageProvider` class is added to the QML engine
with `engine.addImageProvider()`. The first argument will be the provider identifier in
QML. Note that the engine takes ownership of the passed `PictureImageProvider`. One
last thing, the `thumbnailSize` parameter is also passed to `engine`, it will constrain the
thumbnails to be displayed with the specified size in the QML code.

Displaying thumbnails in a GridView

The next step is to display these thumbnails. Create a new QML file named
`AlbumPage.qml`:

```
import QtQuick 2.6
import QtQuick.Layouts 1.3
import QtQuick.Controls 2.0
import "."

PageTheme {

    property string albumName
    property int albumRowIndex

    toolbarTitle: albumName
```

```
GridView {
    id: thumbnailList
    model: pictureModel
    anchors.fill: parent
    anchors.leftMargin: 10
    anchors.rightMargin: 10
    cellWidth : thumbnailSize
    cellHeight: thumbnailSize

    delegate: Rectangle {
        width: thumbnailList.cellWidth - 10
        height: thumbnailList.cellHeight - 10
        color: "transparent"

        Image {
            id: thumbnail
            anchors.fill: parent
            fillMode: Image.PreserveAspectFit
            cache: false
            source: "image://pictures/" + index + "/thumbnail"
        }
    }
}
```

This new `PageTheme` element defines two properties: `albumName` and `albumRowIndex`. The `albumName` property is used to update the title in `toolbarTitle`; `albumRowIndex` will be used to interact with `AlbumModel` in order to rename or delete the album from the current page.

To display thumbnails, we rely on a `GridView` element which will layout the thumbnails in a grid of cells. This `thumbnailList` item uses the `pictureModel` to request its data. The delegate is simply a `Rectangle` element with a single `Image` inside. This `Rectangle` element is slightly smaller than the `thumbnailList.cellWidth` or `thumbnailList.cellHeight`. The `GridView` element does not provide a `spacing` property (like `ListView`) for some room between each item. Thus, we simulate it by using a smaller area to display the content.

The `Image` item will try to take all the available space with `anchors.fill: parent` but will still keep the aspect ratio of the provided picture with `fillMode: Image.PreserveAspectFit`. You recognize the `source` attribute where the current delegate `index` is provided to retrieve the thumbnail. Finally, the `cache: false` attribute ensures that the `PictureImageProvider` class will not try to use the native cache.

To display `AlbumPage.qml`, we have to update the `stackView` (located in `main.qml`). Remember that `stackView` has been declared as a property (`pageStack`), it is thus accessible from any QML file.

The `AlbumPage` element will be displayed when the user clicks on the `MouseArea` element for a given `Album` value in `AlbumListPage.qml`.

We will now give the ability to the user to add a new picture. To do this, we will rely on a QtQuick Dialog: `FileDialog`. Here is the updated version of `AlbumPage.qml`:

```
import QtQuick 2.6
import QtQuick.Layouts 1.3
import QtQuick.Controls 2.0
import QtQuick.Dialogs 1.2
import "."

PageTheme {

    property string albumName
    property int albumRowIndex

    toolbarTitle: albumName
    toolbarButtons: RowLayout {
        ToolButton {
            background: Image {
                source: "qrc:/res/icons/photo-add.svg"
            }
            onClicked: {
                dialog.open()
            }
        }
    }

    FileDialog {
        id: dialog
        title: "Open file"
        folder: shortcuts.pictures
        onAccepted: {
            var pictureUrl = dialog.fileUrl
            pictureModel.addPictureFromUrl(pictureUrl)
```

```
            dialog.close()
        }
    }

    GridView {
        ...
    }
}
```

The `FileDialog` element is straightforward to implement. By using the `folder:` `shortcuts.pictures` property, QtQuick will automatically position the `FileDialog` element in the platform-specific pictures directory. Even better, on iOS it will open the native photo application where you can pick your own picture.

When the user validates his picture choice, the path is available in the `onAccepted()` function with the `dialog.fileUrl` field, which we stored in the `pictureUrl` variable. This `pictureUrl` variable is then passed to a new wrapper function of `PictureModel`: `addPictureFromUrl()`. The pattern used is exactly the same as we did for `AlbumModel::addAlbumFromName()`: a `Q_INVOKABLE` wrapper function around `PictureModel::addPicture()`.

The only missing parts of `AlbumPage` are the delete album and rename album features. They follow patterns we already covered. The deletion will be done using a wrapper function in `AlbumModel`, and the rename reuses the `InputDialog` we created for `AlbumListPage.qml`. Please refer to the source code of the chapter to see the implementation for these features. This is how the thumbnails will look on an Android device:

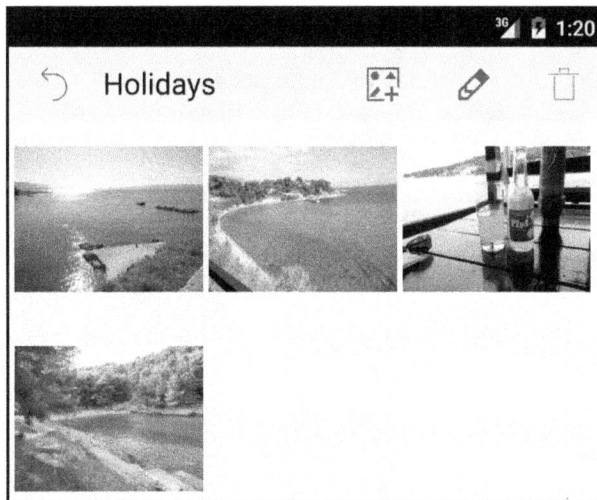

Swiping through full resolution pictures

The last page we have to implement in `gallery-mobile` is the full resolution picture page. In Chapter 12, *Conquering the Desktop UI*, we navigated through the pictures using previous/next buttons. In this chapter, we target the mobile platform. Therefore, the navigation should be done using a touch-based gesture: a fling.

Here is the implementation of this new `PicturePage.qml` file:

```
import QtQuick 2.0
import QtQuick.Layouts 1.3
import QtQuick.Controls 2.0
import "."

PageTheme {

    property string pictureName
    property int pictureIndex

    toolbarTitle: pictureName

    ListView {
        id: pictureListView
        model: pictureModel
        anchors.fill: parent
        spacing: 5
        orientation: Qt.Horizontal
        snapMode: ListView.SnapOneItem
        currentIndex: pictureIndex

        Component.onCompleted: {
            positionViewAtIndex(currentIndex,
                                ListView.SnapPosition)
        }

        delegate: Rectangle {
            property int itemIndex: index
            property string itemName: name

            width: ListView.view.width == 0 ?
                    parent.width : ListView.view.width
            height: pictureListView.height
            color: "transparent"

            Image {
                fillMode: Image.PreserveAspectFit
                cache: false
```

```
            width: parent.width
            height: parent.height
            source: "image://pictures/" + index + "/full"
        }
    }
}
```

We first define two properties, `pictureName` and `pictureIndex`. The current `pictureName` property is displayed in the `toolbarTitle` and `pictureIndex` is used to initialize the correct `currentIndex` in `ListView`, `currentIndex`: `pictureIndex`.

To be able to swipe through the pictures, we again use a `ListView`. Here, each item (a simple `Image` element) will take the full size of its parent. When the component is loaded, even if `currentIndex` is correctly set, the view has to be updated to be positioned at the correct index. This is what we do in `pictureListView` with this:

```
Component.onCompleted: {
    positionViewAtIndex(currentIndex, ListView.SnapPosition)
}
```

This will update the position of the current visible item to `currentIndex`. So far so good. Nonetheless, when a `ListView` is created, the first thing it does is to initialize its delegate. A `ListView` has a `view` property, which is filled with the `delegate` content. That implies that the `ListView.view` (yes, it hurts) does not have any width in `Component.onCompleted()`. As a consequence, the `positionViewAtIndex()` function does... absolutely nothing. To prevent this behavior, we have to provide a default initial width to the delegate with the ternary expression `ListView.view.width == 0 ? parent.width : ListView.view.width`. The view will then have a default width on the first load and the `positionViewAtIndex()` function can happily move until `ListView.view` is properly loaded.

To swipe through each picture, we set the `snapMode` value of the `ListView` to `ListView.SnapOneItem`. Each fling will snap to the next or previous picture without continuing the motion.

The `Image` item of the delegate looks very much like the thumbnail version. The sole difference is the source property, where we request `PictureImageProvider` class with the `full` resolution.

When `PicturePage` opens, the correct `pictureName` property is displayed in the header. However, when the user flings to another picture, the name is not updated. To handle this, we have to detect the motion state. Add the following callbacks in `pictureListView`:

```
onMovementEnded: {
    currentIndex = itemAt(contentX, contentY).itemIndex
}

onCurrentItemChanged: {
    toolbarTitleLabel.text = currentItem.itemName
}
```

The `onMovementEnded()` class is triggered when the motion started by the swipe has ended. In this function, we update the `ListViewcurrentIndex` with the `itemIndex` of the visible item at the `contentX` and `contentY` coordinates.

The second function, `onCurrentItemChanged()`, is called upon the `currentIndex` update. It will simply update the `toolbarTitleLabel.text` with the picture name of the current item.

To display `PicturePage.qml`, the same `MouseArea` pattern is used in the `thumbnailList` delegate of `AlbumPage.qml`:

```
MouseArea {
    anchors.fill: parent
    onClicked: {
        thumbnailList.currentIndex = index
        pageStack.push("qrc:/qml/PicturePage.qml",
    { pictureName: name, pictureIndex: index })
    }
}
```

Again, the `PicturePage.qml` file is pushed on the `pageStack` and the needed parameters (`pictureName` and `pictureIndex`) are provided in the same manner.

Summary

This chapter brings closure to the development of the gallery application. We built a strong foundation with `gallery-core`, created a widget UI with `gallery-desktop`, and finally crafted a QML UI with `gallery-mobile`.

QML enables a very fast approach to UI development. Unfortunately, the technology is still young and rapidly changing. The integration with mobile OSes (Android, iOS) is under heavy development and we hope that it will lead to great mobile applications with Qt. For now, the inherent limits of a mobile cross-platform toolkit are still hard to overcome.

The next chapter will take QML technology to new shores: the development of a snake game running on a Raspberry Pi.

14
Even Qt Deserves a Slice of Raspberry Pi

In the previous chapter, we created a QML UI targeted at Android and iOS. We will continue our journey in the embedded world by discovering how we can deploy a Qt application on a Raspberry Pi. The example project to illustrate this topic will be a snake game using the Qt3D modules. The player will control a snake trying to eat apples to get as big as possible.

In this chapter, you will learn:

- The architecture of the Qt3D modules
- The basic principles of cross-compilation
- How to build your own Qt Creator kit to compile and deploy your game on a Raspberry Pi
- How to handle the differences and limitations of various platforms (desktop, Raspberry Pi)
- The Factory design pattern
- How to write a complete game engine using JavaScript and QML
- The usage of the QML Profiler

Discovering Qt3D

The example project of this chapter will rely on 3D rendering. For this, we will use Qt3D. This part of the framework is divided into various Qt modules that enable the application to have a near-real time simulation of a 3D environment. Built on OpenGL, Qt3D offers a high-level API to describe complex scenes without having to resort to writing low-level OpenGL instructions. Qt3D supports the following basic features:

- 2D and 3D rendering for C++ and Qt Quick
- Meshes
- Materials
- GLSL shaders
- Shadow mapping
- Deferred rendering
- Instance rendering
- Uniform Buffer Object

All these features are implemented in the **ECS** (**entity component system**) architecture. Each mesh, material, or shader that you define is a component. The aggregation of these components makes an entity. If you wanted to draw a 3D red apple, you would need the following components:

- A mesh component, holding the vertices of your apple
- A material component, applying a texture on the mesh or coloring it

These two components will then be regrouped to define the entity Apple. You see here the two parts of the ECS: entities and components. The overall architecture looks like this:

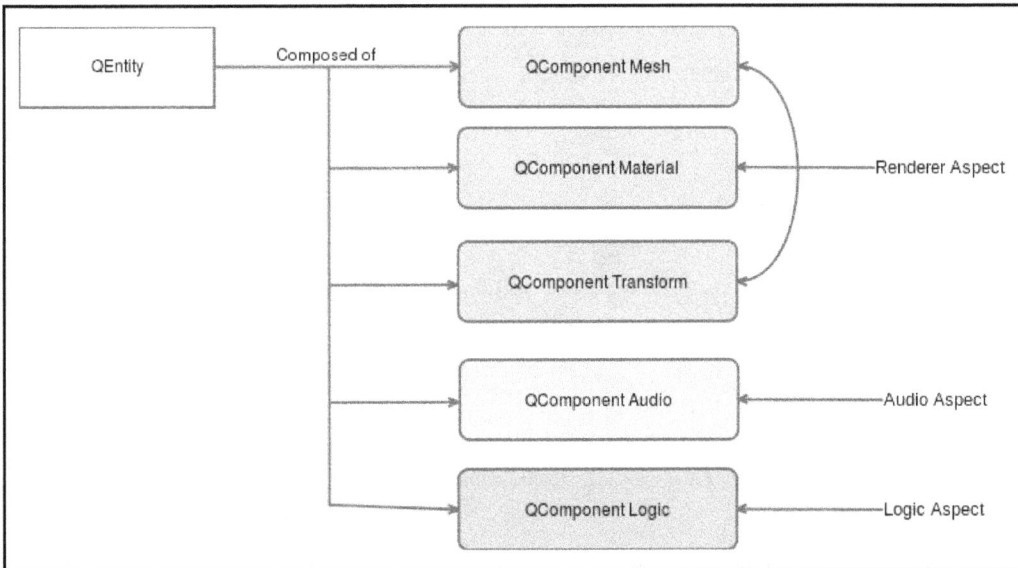

Each of these components can be regrouped in aspects. An aspect is a "slice" of multiple components working on the same part (rendering, audio, logic, and physics). When the graph of all your entities is processed by the Qt3D engine, each layer of aspects is processed sequentially.

The underlying approach is to favor composition over inheritance. In a game, an entity (an apple, a player, an enemy) can have various states during its life cycle: spawning, animating for a given state, dying animation, and so on. Using inheritance to describe these states will lead to a nerve-wracking tree:
`AppleSpawn`, `AppleAnimationShiny`, `AppleDeath`, and so on. It would become quickly unmaintainable. Any modification to a class could have huge impact on many other classes and the number of possible combinations of states would get out of hand. Saying that a state is simply a component for a given entity, gives the flexibility to easily swap components and still keep the entity abstraction; an apple `Entity` element is still an apple, even though it is using the `AnimationShinyComponent` instead of the `AnimationSpawnComponent`.

Let's see how to define a basic `Entity` element in QML. Imagine that this is the apple we have been talking about. The `Apple.qml` file would look like this:

```
import Qt3D.Core 2.0
import Qt3D.Render 2.0
import Qt3D.Extras 2.0
```

```
Entity {

    property alias position: transform.translation
    PhongMaterial {
        id: material
        diffuse: "red"
    }

    SphereMesh {
        id: mesh
    }

    Transform {
        id: transform
    }

    components: [material, mesh, transform]
}
```

In a very few lines, you describe every aspect of the `Entity` element:

- `Entity`: This is the root object of the file; it follows the same QML pattern we studied in Chapter 13, *Dominating the Mobile UI*.
- `PhongMaterial`: This defines how the surface will be rendered. Here, it uses the Phong shading technique to achieve smooth surfaces. It inherits `QMaterial`, which is the base class for all the material classes.
- `CuboidMesh`: This defines what type of mesh will be used. It inherits `QGeometryRenderer`, which also gives the ability to load custom models (exported from 3D modeling software).
- `Transform`: This defines the transformation matrix of the component. It can customize the translation, scale, and position of the `Entity` element.
- `Position`: This is a property to expose `transform.translation` for a given caller/parent. This might quickly become handy if we want to move the apple around.
- `Components`: This is the array containing all the IDs of all the components for the `Entity` element.

If we want to make this `Apple` a child of another `Entity`, it is simply a matter of defining the Apple inside this new `Entity` element. Let's call it `World.qml`:

```
import Qt3D.Core 2.0
import Qt3D.Render 2.0
import Qt3D.Extras 2.0
```

```
Entity {
    id: sceneRoot
     RenderSettings {
        id: frameFraph
        activeFrameGraph: ForwardRenderer {
            clearColor: Qt.rgba(0, 0, 0, 1)
        }
    }

    Apple {
        id: apple
        position: Qt.vector3d(3.0, 0.0, 2.0)
    }

    components: [frameGraph]
}
```

Here, the `World Entity` has no visual representation; we want it to be the root of our 3D scene. It only contains the `Apple` we defined earlier. The *x*, *y*, *z* coordinates of the apple are relative to the parent. When the parent makes a translation, the same translation will be applied to the apple.

This is how the hierarchy of entities/components is defined. If you write your Qt3D code in C++, the same logic applies to the equivalent C++ classes (`QEntity`, `QComponent`, and so on).

Because we decided to use the `World.qml` file as the root of our scene, it has to define how the scene will be rendered. The Qt3D rendering algorithm is data-driven. In other words, there is a clear separation between *what* should be rendered (the tree of entities and components) and *how* it should be rendered.

The *how* relies on a similar tree structure using `framegraph`. In Qt Quick, a single method of rendering is used and it covers the 2D drawing. On the other hand, in 3D, the need for flexible rendering makes it necessary to decouple the rendering techniques.

Consider this example: you play a game where you control your avatar and you encounter a mirror. The same 3D scene must be rendered from multiple viewports. If the rendering technique is fixed, this poses multiple problems: which viewport should be drawn first? Is it possible to parallelize the rendering of the viewports in the GPU? What if we need to make multiple passes for the rendering?

In this code snippet, we use the traditional OpenGL rendering technique with the `ForwardRenderer` tree, where each object is rendered directly on the back buffer, one at a time. Qt3D offers the possibility to choose the renderer (`ForwardRenderer`, `DeferredRenderer`, and so on) and configure how the scene should be rendered.

OpenGL typically uses the double-buffering technique to render its content. The front-buffer is what is displayed on the screen and the back-buffer is where the scene is being rendered. When the back-buffer is ready, the two buffers are swapped.

One last thing to notice at the top of each `Entity` element is that we specified the following:

```
import Qt3D.Core 2.0
import Qt3D.Render 2.0
import Qt3D.Extras 2.0
```

There are only Qt3D modules in the import section. Qt3D classes do not inherit `Item` so cannot be directly mixed with QML components. This inheritance tree of the basic Qt3D building blocks is:

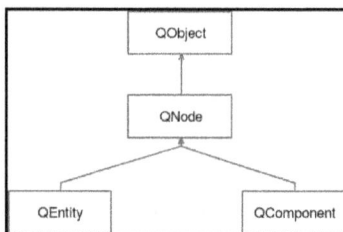

The `QNode` class is the base class of all Qt3D node classes. It relies on the `QObject` class to define the parenting relationship. Each `QNode` class instance also adds a unique `id` variable, which allows it to be recognized from other instances.

Even though `QNode` cannot be mixed with Qt Quick types, they can be added to a `Q3DScene` element (or `Scene3D` in QML), which serves as the canvas for Qt3D content and can be added to a Qt Quick `Item`. Adding `World.qml` to a scene is as simple as this:

```
Rectangle {

    Scene3D {
        id: scene
        anchors.fill: parent
        focus: true
```

```
        World { }
    }
}
```

The `Scene3D` element includes a `World` instance and defines common Qt Quick properties (`anchors`, `focus`).

Configuring Qt for your Raspberry Pi

This project targets a new embedded platform: the Raspberry Pi. Qt officially supports the Raspberry Pi 2, but we got the project running without any trouble on a Raspberry Pi 3. If you do not have one of these devices, it might be nonetheless interesting to read this section to know how the cross-compilation works and how to configure your own kit in Qt Creator. The rest of the chapter will work on a Desktop platform anyway.

Before diving into the Raspberry Pi configuration, let's take a step back to understand our aim. Your computer is probably running on an x86 CPU architecture. This means that every program you run will be executed with the x86 instructions set of your CPU. In Qt Creator, this translates to your available kits. A kit must match your target platform. On startup, Qt Creator searches for available kits in your computer and loads them for you.

In `Chapter 13`, *Dominating the Mobile UI*, we targeted different platforms: Android and iOS. These platforms are running on a different CPU instruction set: ARM. Luckily, the people behind Qt automatically configured for us the necessary nuts and bolts to make it work.

The Raspberry Pi also runs on ARM but it is not ready for Qt by default. We have to prepare it before playing with it in Qt Creator. Note that the following commands are run from a Linux box, but you should be able to run them from Mac or Windows with Cygwin.

> Please follow the complete guide to prepare your Raspberry Pi for Qt at `https://wiki.qt.io/RaspberryPi2EGLFS`, or simply download a precompiled bundle from `http://www.qtrpi.com`.

The complete Raspberry Pi installation guide is outside the scope of the book. It is interesting nonetheless to sum up the main steps:

1. Add development packages to the Raspberry Pi.
2. Retrieve the complete toolchain, including the cross-compiler that will be executed from your machine.

3. Create a `sysroot` folder on your machine that will mirror the necessary directories from the Raspberry Pi.
4. Compile Qt with the cross-compiler in the `sysroot` folder.
5. Synchronize this `sysroot` with the Raspberry Pi.

A `sysroot` is simply a directory containing a minimal filesystem for a given platform. It typically contains the `/usr/lib` and `/usr/include` directories. Having this directory on your machine enables the cross-compiler to properly compile and link the output binary without being executed from the Raspberry Pi.

All these steps are done to avoid compiling anything directly on the Raspberry Pi. Being a low-powered device, the execution of any compilation would take a very, very long time. Compiling Qt on a Raspberry Pi would easily take more than 40 hours. Knowing this, the time spent on configuring the cross-compiler seems much easier to bear.

The `qopenglwidget` example mentioned in the wiki should be properly running before proceeding. Once this has been done, we have to cross-compile a few more Qt modules to have our project running:

- `Qtdeclarative`: This model is used to access Qt Quick
- `qt3d`: This model is used to construct a 3D world
- `qtquickcontrols`: This model is used to include interesting controls (Label)
- `qtquickcontrols2`: This model is used to make some new layouts available

For each of these modules, execute the following commands (from your `~/raspi` directory):

```
git clone git://code.qt.io/qt/<modulename>.git -b 5.7
cd <modulename>
~/raspi/qt5/bin/qmake -r
make
make install
```

> **TIP**
>
> You can speed up the compilation by adding the parameter `-j` (or `--jobs`) to `make`. The `make` command will try to parallelize the compilations jobs over your CPU cores, if you have four cores, use `make -j 4`, eight cores, `make -j 8`, and so on.

When everything has been compiled, synchronize your `sysroot` directory again with:

```
rsync -avz qt5pi pi@IP:/usr/local
```

In the previous command, you must replace the IP with the real Raspberry Pi address.

The Raspberry Pi is ready to execute our Qt code. However, we have to create our own kit in Qt Creator to be able to compile and deploy our program on it. A kit is composed of the following parts:

- A **compiler** that will compile your code using the CPU instruction set of the target platform
- A **debugger** that will know the instruction set of the target platform to properly break and read the memory content
- A **Qt version** compiled for the targeted platform to compile and link your binary to the target platform's shared objects
- A **device** to which Qt Creator can connect to deploy and execute your program

We will start with the compiler. In Qt Creator:

1. Go to **Tools** | **Options** | **Build & Run** | **Compilers**.
2. Click on **Add** | **GCC**.
3. Browse to `~/raspi/tools/arm-bcm2708/gcc-linaro-arm-linux-gnueabihf-raspbian/bin/arm-linux-gnueabihf-g++`.
4. Rename the compiler to `Rpi GCC`.

This strange binary name makes it easier for Qt to parse the **ABI** (**application binary interface**) to find out the platform architecture, file format, and so on. It should look like this:

Now for the debugger. As we said earlier, we are building this project from a Linux box (Ubuntu). Cross-compilation and embedded development tend to be easier on Linux but you should be able to do the same on a Windows or Mac with a few additional steps.

On Ubuntu Linux, just install a multi-architecture `gdb` with the command `sudo apt-get install gdb-multiarch`. In Qt Creator, add this new debugger in the **Debuggers** tab:

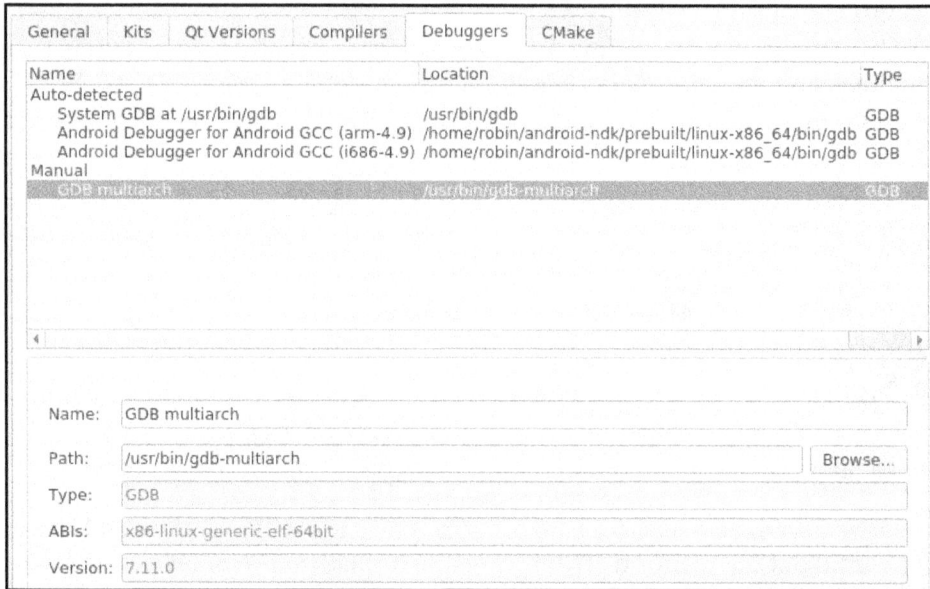

General	Kits	Qt Versions	Compilers	Debuggers	CMake	

Name	Location	Type
Auto-detected		
System GDB at /usr/bin/gdb	/usr/bin/gdb	GDB
Android Debugger for Android GCC (arm-4.9)	/home/robin/android-ndk/prebuilt/linux-x86_64/bin/gdb	GDB
Android Debugger for Android GCC (i686-4.9)	/home/robin/android-ndk/prebuilt/linux-x86_64/bin/gdb	GDB
Manual		
GDB multiarch	/usr/bin/gdb-multiarch	GDB

Name:	GDB multiarch
Path:	/usr/bin/gdb-multiarch
Type:	GDB
ABIs:	x86-linux-generic-elf-64bit
Version:	7.11.0

Next, add the cross-compiled Qt explained on the wiki page in the **Qt Versions** tab. Click on **Add** and browse to `~/raspi/qt5/bin/qmake`. This is the resulting Qt Version:

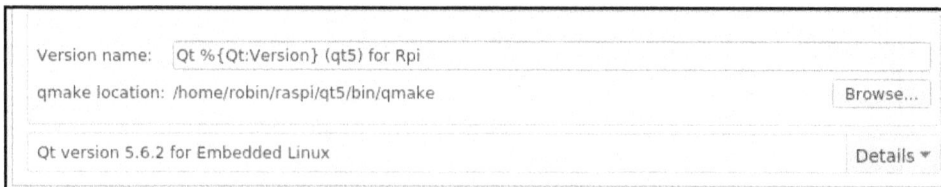

Version name:	Qt %{Qt:Version} (qt5) for Rpi
qmake location:	/home/robin/raspi/qt5/bin/qmake
Qt version 5.6.2 for Embedded Linux	Details ▾

We are almost there! Before building the kit, we simply have to configure Raspberry Pi device access. In **Options** | **Devices**, follow this procedure:

1. Click on **Add..** | **Generic Linux Device** | **Start Wizard**.
2. The name will be Rpi 2 (or 3 if you have one).
3. Enter the IP address of your device (indeed, you have to be connected to your local network!).
4. The default username is **pi**.
5. The default password is "raspberry".
6. Click on **Next** to test the connection to the device.

If everything went well, this is your new device:

Finally, the kit will compose all these parts into a valid Qt Creator platform. Go back to **Build & Run** | **Kits**. From here you simply have to point to each of the parts we built previously. Here is the resulting kit:

General	Kits	Qt Versions	Compilers	Debuggers	CMake

Name
▶ Auto-detected
▼ Manual
   Raspberry PI 2

Name:	Raspberry PI 2
File system name:	
Device type:	Generic Linux Device ▾
Device:	Rpi 2 (default for Generic Linux) ▾
Sysroot:	/home/robin/raspi/sysroot
Compiler:	Rpi GCC ▾
Environment:	No changes to apply.
Debugger:	GDB multiarch ▾
Qt version:	Qt 5.6.2 (qt5) for Rpi ▾
Qt mkspec:	
CMake Tool:	System CMake at /usr/bin/cmake ▾
CMake Generator:	CodeBlocks - Unix Makefiles ▾
CMake Configuration	CMAKE_CXX_COMPILER:STRING=%{Compiler:Executable}; QT_QMAKE_EXECUTABLE...

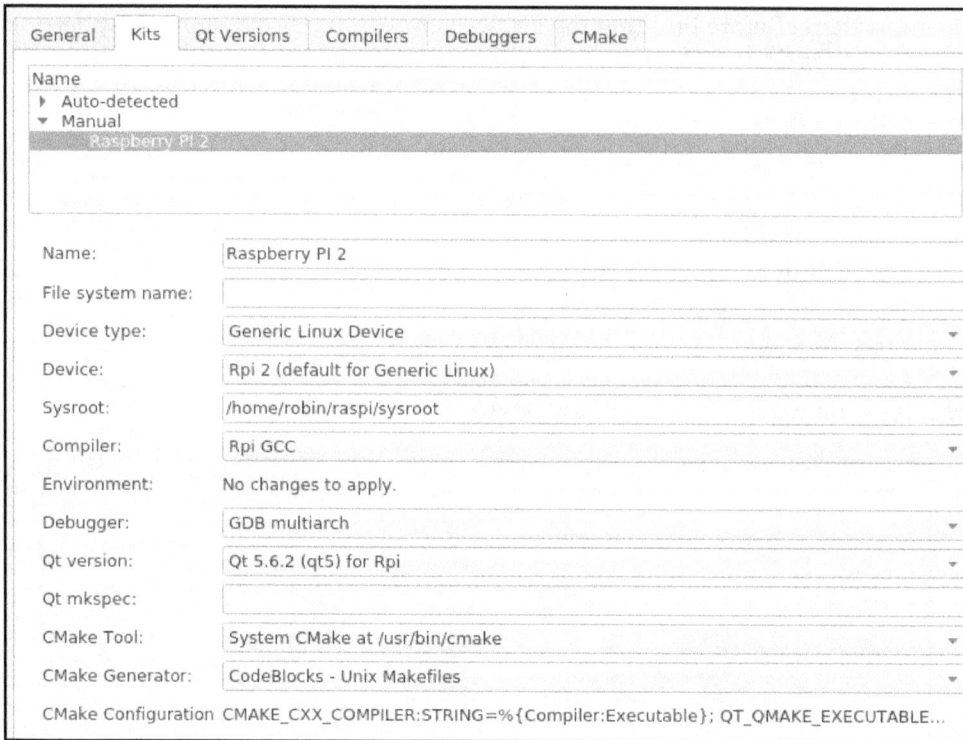

Note that the **Sysroot** filed should point to the `sysroot` folder we previously created at `~/raspi/sysroot`.

> **TIP**
>
> If you click on the button to the right of **Name**, you can choose a custom picture for a kit, such as the Raspberry Pi logo.

Everything is now ready to make an awesome snake game.

Creating an entry point for your Qt3D code

For those who did not play the snake game in their youth, here is a quick reminder of the gameplay:

- You control a snake moving in an empty area
- This area is surrounded by walls

- An apple spawns randomly in the game area
- If the snake eats the apple, it grows and you gain a point. Right after, another apple spawns in the game area
- If the snake touches a wall or a part of its own body, you lose

The goal is to eat as many apples as possible to have the highest score. The longer the snake, the harder it will become to avoid the wall and its own tail. Oh, and the snake goes faster and faster each time it eats an apple. The architecture of the game will be the following:

- All the game items will be defined using Qt3D in QML
- All the game logic will be done in JavaScript, which will communicate with the QML elements

We will keep the 2D feel of the original snake game by placing the camera above the game area but we will spice things up with 3D models and some shaders.

Alright, we spent an awful lot of pages preparing for this moment. It is now time to begin the snake project. Create a new **Qt Quick Controls Application** named `ch06-snake`. In the project details:

1. Select **Qt 5.6** for the **minimal required Qt version** field.
2. Uncheck **With ui.qml file**.
3. Uncheck **Enable native styling**.
4. Click on **Next** and select the following kits:
   - RaspberryPi 2
   - **Desktop**

5. Click on **Next | Finish**.

We have to add the Qt3D modules. Modify `ch06-snake.pro` like this:

```
TEMPLATE = app

QT += qml quick 3dcore 3drender 3dquick 3dinput 3dextras
CONFIG += c++11

SOURCES += main.cpp

RESOURCES +=
    snake.qrc

HEADERS +=
```

```
target.files = ch06-snake
target.path = /home/pi
INSTALLS += target
```

We have to prepare the entry point of the application to have a proper OpenGL context with which Qt3D can work. Open and update `main.cpp` like so:

```cpp
#include <QGuiApplication>
#include <QtGui/QOpenGLContext>
#include <QtQuick/QQuickView>
#include <QtQml/QQmlEngine>

int main(int argc, char *argv[])
{
    QGuiApplication app(argc, argv);

    qputenv("QT3D_GLSL100_WORKAROUND", "");

    QSurfaceFormat format;
    if (QOpenGLContext::openGLModuleType() ==
        QOpenGLContext::LibGL) {
        format.setVersion(3, 2);
        format.setProfile(QSurfaceFormat::CoreProfile);
    }
    format.setDepthBufferSize(24);
    format.setStencilBufferSize(8);

    QQuickView view;
    view.setFormat(format);
    view.setResizeMode(QQuickView::SizeRootObjectToView);
    QObject::connect(view.engine(), &QQmlEngine::quit,
                     &app, &QGuiApplication::quit);
    view.setSource(QUrl("qrc:/main.qml"));
    view.show();

    return app.exec();
}
```

The idea is to configure a `QSurfaceFormat` to properly handle OpenGL and to give it to a custom `QQuickView` view. This `view` will use this format to paint itself.

The `qputenv("QT3D_GLSL100_WORKAROUND", "")` instruction is a workaround related to Qt3D shaders on some embedded Linux devices, such as the Raspberry Pi. It will enable a separate GLSL 1.00 snippet for the lights required by some embedded devices. If you do not use this workaround, you will get a black screen and will not be able to properly run the project on Raspberry Pi.

> The details of the Qt3d lights workaround are here: `https://codereview.` `qt-project.org/#/c/143136/`.

We chose to handle the view using Qt Quick. Another approach would be to create a C++ class that inherits `QMainWindow` and make it the parent of the QML content. This approach can be found in many Qt3D example projects. Both are valid and work. You tend to write more code with the `QMainWindow` approach, but it allows you to create 3D scenes with C++ only.

Note that `view` from the `main.cpp` file tries to load a `main.qml` file. You can see it coming; here is the `main.qml`:

```
import QtQuick 2.6
import QtQuick.Controls 1.4

Item {
    id: mainView

    property int score: 0
    readonly property alias window: mainView

    width: 1280; height: 768
    visible: true

    Keys.onEscapePressed: {
        Qt.quit()
    }

    Rectangle {
        id: hud

        color: "#31363b"
        anchors.left: parent.left
        anchors.right: parent.right
        anchors.top : parent.top
        height: 60

        Label {
            id: snakeSizeText
            anchors.centerIn: parent
            font.pointSize: 25
            color: "white"
            text: "Score: " + score
        }
    }
```

```
        }
    }
```

Here we define the **HUD (heads up display)** at the top of the screen, where the score (the number of apples eaten) will be displayed. Note that we bound the Escape key to the `Qt.quit()` signal. This signal is connected in `main.cpp` to the `QGuiApplication::quit()` signal to quit the application.

The QML context is now ready to welcome Qt3D content. Modify `main.qml` like so:

```
import QtQuick 2.6
import QtQuick.Controls 1.4
import QtQuick.Scene3D 2.0

Item {
    ...

    Rectangle {
        id: hud
        ...
    }

    Scene3D {
        id: scene
        anchors.top: hud.bottom
        anchors.bottom: parent.bottom
        anchors.left: parent.left
        anchors.right: parent.right
        focus: true
        aspects: "input"
    }
}
```

The `Scene3D` element takes all the available space below the `hud` object. It takes the focus of the window to be able to intercept keyboard events. It also enables the input aspect to let the Qt3D engine process keyboard events in its graph traversal.

Setting up the scene

We can now start writing Qt3D code. The first step is to define the root of the scene. Create a new file named `GameArea.qml`:

```
import Qt3D.Core 2.0
import Qt3D.Render 2.0
import Qt3D.Extras 2.0
```

```
Entity {
    id: root

    property alias gameRoot: root

    Camera {
        id: camera
        property real x: 24.5
        property real y: 14.0

        projectionType: CameraLens.PerspectiveProjection
        fieldOfView: 45
        aspectRatio: 16/9
        nearPlane : 0.1
        farPlane : 1000.0
        position: Qt.vector3d( x, y, 33.0 )
        upVector: Qt.vector3d( 0.0, 1.0, 0.0 )
        viewCenter: Qt.vector3d( x, y, 0.0 )
    }



    RenderSettings {
        id: frameFraph
        activeFrameGraph: ForwardRenderer {
            clearColor: Qt.rgba(0, 0, 0, 1)
            camera: camera
        }
    }

    components: [frameFraph]
}
```

The first thing we do is create a camera and position it. Remember that, in OpenGL, the coordinates follow the thumb on your right hand points left!:

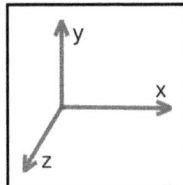

By placing the camera at `Qt.vector3d(x, y, 33)`, we make it come "out of the screen" to be able to express our yet-to-be-created entitiy's coordinates with the simple x, y axis. The `upVector: Qt.vector3d(0.0, 1.0, 0.0)` specifies the up vector of the camera, in our case it is the Y axis. Finally, we point at `Qt.vector(x, y, 0)`, meaning the center of the screen.

The overall goal is to simplify coordinate expression. By positioning the camera this way, placing an object at the coordinate 0, 0 will put it in the bottom-left part of the window, whereas the coordinates 50, 28 mean the top-right part of the window.

We also configure `RenderSettings` with a `ForwardRendered` that defines two properties:

- `clearColor`: This property `Qt.rgba(0, 0, 0, 1)` means that the background will be pitch-black
- `camera`: This property is used to determine the viewport to be rendered

The scene is ready to be rendered, but we need to handle user input, namely the keyboard. To capture keyboard events, modify `GameArea.qml` to look like this:

```
import Qt3D.Core 2.0
import Qt3D.Render 2.0
import Qt3D.Input 2.0

Entity {
    ...
    RenderSettings {
        ...
    }

    KeyboardDevice {
        id: keyboardController
    }

    InputSettings { id: inputSettings }

    KeyboardHandler {
        id: input
        sourceDevice: keyboardController
        focus: true
        onPressed: { }
    }

    components: [frameFraph, input]
}
```

The `KeyboardDevice` element is in charge of dispatching key events to the active `KeyboardHandler`, namely `input`. The `KeyboardHandler` component is attached to the controller and the `onPressed()` function will be called each time a key is pressed. The `KeyboardHandler` is a component; therefore it needs to be added to the list of components for `GameArea`.

The last missing part of `GameArea` is preapring the engine execution (initialization and update):

```
import Qt3D.Core 2.0
import Qt3D.Render 2.0
import Qt3D.Input 2.0
import QtQuick 2.6 as QQ2

Entity {
    id: root

    property alias gameRoot: root
    property alias timerInterval: timer.interval
    property int initialTimeInterval: 80
    property int initialSnakeSize: 5
    property string state: ""
    ...

    KeyboardDevice {
        id: keyboardController
    }

    QQ2.Component.onCompleted: {
        console.log("Start game...");
        timer.start()
    }

    QQ2.Timer {
        id: timer
        interval: initialTimeInterval
        repeat: true
        onTriggered: {}
    }

    components: [frameFraph, input]
}
```

Here we mix Qt Quick elements with Qt3D. Due to possible name collisions, we have to import the module using the alias `QQ2`. We already met `Component.onCompleted` in `Chapter 13`, *Dominating the Mobile UI*. Its job will be to start the game engine and start the `timer` defined right after.

This `timer` variable will repeat every 80 milliseconds (as defined in the `initialTimeInterval` property) and call the engine's `update()` function. This function will be covered when we build the engine code, later in this chapter. The goal is to emulate the original snake game as closely as possible. The whole game logic will be updated at this interval and not at the normal frame refresh interval. After each call to `update()`, the snake will advance. As a result, the snake's movement will not be smooth but rather jerky. This is clearly a design choice we made to have a retro-gaming feeling.

Each time the snake eats an apple, two things happen:

- The `interval` of the timer will be reduced by the engine (accessed by the `timerInterval` property).
- The snake will grow. Its initial size is defined in the `intialSnakeSize` property.

Reducing the timer interval will make the snake advance faster until it becomes very hard to manage its direction.

Assembling your Qt3D entities

We will now proceed to create the building blocks of the game, each in the form of an `Entity` element:

- `Wall`: This represents the limit of where the snake cannot go
- `SnakePart`: This represents a part of the snake's body
- `Apple`: This represents the apple (no way!) spawned at a random location
- `Background`: This represents a good-looking background behind the snake and the apple

Each entity will be placed on a grid handled by the engine and will have a type identifier to make it easier to find. To factorize these properties, let's create a parent QML file named `GameEntity.qml`:

```
import Qt3D.Core 2.0

Entity {
    property int type: 0
```

```
        property vector2d gridPosition: Qt.vector2d(0, 0)
    }
```

This `Entity` element only defines a `type` property and a `gridPosition` property , which will be used by the engine to lay out the content on the grid.

The first item we will build is the `Wall.qml` file:

```
import Qt3D.Core 2.0

GameEntity {
    id: root

    property alias position: transform.translation

    Transform {
        id: transform
    }

    components: [transform]
}
```

As you can see, the `Wall` type does not have any visual representation. Because we target a Raspberry Pi device, we have to be very careful with the CPU/GPU consumption. The game area will be a grid where each cell contains an instance of one of our entities. The snake will be surrounded by `Wall` instances. The Raspberry Pi is much slower than your average computer, to the extent that the game would become unbearably slow if we displayed all the walls.

To address this issue, the walls are invisible. They will be placed outside the visible viewport and the borders of the window will act as the visual limit of the snake. Of course, if you do not target the Raspberry Pi, but rather your computer, it is fine to display the walls and make them look fancier than just nothing.

The next `Entity` element we will implement is `SnakePart.qml`:

```
import Qt3D.Core 2.0
import Qt3D.Render 2.0
import Qt3D.Extras 2.0

GameEntity {
    id: root

    property alias position: transform.translation

    PhongMaterial {
        id: material
```

```
        diffuse: "green"
    }

    CuboidMesh {
        id: mesh
    }

    Transform {
        id: transform
    }

    components: [material, mesh, transform]
}
```

If added to the `GameArea` scene, the `SnakePart` block will display a single green cube. The `SnakePart` block is not the complete snake, rather a part of its body. Remember that the snake grows each time it eats an apple. Growing means adding a new instance of `SnakePart` to a list of `SnakePart`.

Let's proceed with the `Apple.qml`:

```
import Qt3D.Core 2.0
import Qt3D.Render 2.0
import Qt3D.Extras 2.0

GameEntity {
    id: root

    property alias position: transform.translation
    property alias color: material.diffuse

    Transform {
        id: transform
        scale: 0.5
    }

    Mesh {
        id: mesh
        source: "models/apple.obj"
    }

    DiffuseMapMaterial {
        id: material
        diffuse: "qrc:/models/apple-texture.png"
    }

    components: [material, mesh, transform]
```

```
    }
```

This snippet starts with introducing more complex yet easy-to-use features of Qt3D, namely a custom mesh and a texture applied to it. Qt3D supports the Wavefront `obj` format to load custom meshes. Here we added a home-cooked apple to the `.qrc` file of the application and we just have to provide the path to this resource to load it.

The same principle is applied for the `DiffuseMapMaterial` element. We added a custom texture and added it as a source of the component.

As you can see, the `Entity` definition and its components look very much the same. Yet we effortlessly traded a Qt3D `CuboidMesh` with a custom model.

We will push things even further with `Background.qml`:

```
import Qt3D.Core 2.0
import Qt3D.Render 2.0
import Qt3D.Extras 2.0

Entity {
    id: root

    property alias position: transform.translation
    property alias scale3D: transform.scale3D

    MaterialBackground {
        id: material
    }

    CuboidMesh {
        id: mesh
    }

    Transform {
        id: transform
    }

    components: [material, mesh, transform]
}
```

The `Background` block will be displayed behind the snake and the apple. At first sight, this entity looks very much like `SnakePart`. However, `Material` is not a Qt3D class. It is a custom defined `Material` that relies on shaders. Let's see `MaterialBackground.qml`:

```
import Qt3D.Core 2.0
import Qt3D.Render 2.0

Material {
    id: material

    effect: Effect {
        techniques: [
            Technique {
                graphicsApiFilter {
                    api: GraphicsApiFilter.OpenGL
                    majorVersion: 3
                    minorVersion: 2
                }
                renderPasses: RenderPass {
                    shaderProgram: ShaderProgram {
                        vertexShaderCode:
                        loadSource("qrc:/shaders/gl3/grass.vert")
                        fragmentShaderCode:
                        loadSource("qrc:/shaders/gl3/grass.frag")
                    }
                }
            }
        ]
    }
}
```

If you are not familiar with shaders, we can summarize them in the following statement: shaders are computer programs written in a C-style syntax that are executed by the GPU. Data from your logic will be fed by the CPU and made available to the GPU memory where your shaders will run. Here we manipulate two types of shader:

- **Vertex shader**, which is executed on each vertex of the source of your mesh
- **Fragment**, which is executed on each pixel to produce the final rendering

By being executed on the GPU, these shaders utilize the huge parallelization power of the GPU (which is orders-of-magnitude higher than your CPU). It enables modern games to have such stunning visual rendering. Covering shaders and the OpenGL pipeline is beyond the scope of this book (you can fill several bookshelves on this subject alone). We will limit ourselves to showing you how you can use shaders in Qt3D.

> If you want to delve into OpenGL or sharpen your skills with shaders, we recommend the *OpenGL SuperBible*, by Graham Sellers, Richard S Wright Jr., and Nicholas Haemel.

Qt3D supports shaders in a very convenient way. Simply add your shader file to the `.qrc` resource file and load it in the `effect` property of a given `Material`.

In this snippet, we specify that this shader `Technique` should be run only on OpenGL 3.2. This is indicated in the `graphicsApiFilter` block. This version of OpenGL targets your desktop machine. Because the performance gap between your desktop and your Raspberry Pi is very marked, we have the ability to execute different shaders depending on the platform.

Thus, here is the Raspberry Pi-compatible technique:

```
Technique {
    graphicsApiFilter {
        api: GraphicsApiFilter.OpenGLES
        majorVersion: 2
        minorVersion: 0
    }

    renderPasses: RenderPass {
        shaderProgram: ShaderProgram {
            vertexShaderCode:
                loadSource("qrc:/shaders/es2/grass.vert")
            fragmentShaderCode:
                loadSource("qrc:/shaders/es2/grass.frag")
        }
    }
}
```

You just have to add it to the `techniques` property of the `Material`. Note that the targeted OpenGL version is OpenGLES 2.0, which will run fine on your Raspberry Pi and even your iOS/Android phone.

A last thing to cover is how parameters can be passed to shaders. Here is an example:

```
Material {
    id: material

    parameters:  [
        Parameter {
            name: "score"; value: score
        }
```

```
    ]
      ...
  }
```

The `score` variable will be accessible in the shader with this simple section. Please take a look at the source code for the chapter to see the complete content of this `Material` element. We had the fun of writing a shader displaying a moving and glowing wave over a grass texture.

The only fixed element of the game is the background. We can directly add it to `GameArea.qml`:

```
Entity {
    id: root
    ...

    Background {
        position: Qt.vector3d(camera.x, camera.y, 0)
        scale3D: Qt.vector3d(camera.x * 2, camera.y * 2, 0)
    }

    components: [frameFraph, input]
}
```

The `Background` element is positioned to cover the whole visible area behind the snake and the apple. Being defined inside `GameArea`, it will be automatically added to the entity/component tree and will be drawn right away.

Preparing the board game

Even if our game has a 3D representation, we will implement 2D gameplay like the original snake game. Our game items are born, will live, and die in a 2D area. Like chess, this board will be composed of rows and columns. But in our snake game, each square can be:

- An apple
- A snake
- A wall
- Empty

Here is an example of a board representation from the point of view of the engine:

This is a small 10x8 board; even if the size does not matter, you will be able to define a bigger one. Your game, your rules! We have walls (**W**) surrounding the game area. An apple (**A**) is spawned at 7x2. Finally, we have a snake (**S**) beginning at 3x4 and ending at 5x5.

It is time to create our board class. Please create a JS file called `board.js`:

```
function Board(columnCount, rowCount, blockSize) {
    this.columnCount = columnCount;
    this.rowCount = rowCount;
    this.blockSize = blockSize;
    this.maxIndex = columnCount * rowCount;
    this.data = new Array(this.maxIndex);
}
```

This object constructor function required three parameters. The `columnCount` and `rowCount` parameters will help you to choose the board dimension. The last parameter, `blockSize`, is the size of a board square in the OpenGL world. For example, we can set `blockSize` to 10. In this case, the apple in 7x2 on the board we be displayed with x = 70 and y = 20 in the OpenGL world. In this chapter, we will use a `blockSize` of 1, so the board coordinates match OpenGL coordinates.

Let's add some utility functions to `board.js`:

```
Board.prototype.init = function() {
    for (var i = 0; i < this.data.length; i++) {
        this.data[i] = null;
    }
}

Board.prototype.index = function(column, row) {
    return column + (row * this.columnCount);
```

```
    }

    Board.prototype.setData = function(data, column, row) {
        this.data[this.index(column, row)] = data;
    }

    Board.prototype.at = function(column, row) {
        return this.data[this.index(column, row)];
    }
```

Defining a class in JavaScript can be disturbing for a C++ developer. Every JavaScript object has a prototype object to which you can add functions. We are using it to add class methods to `Board`.

Here is a summary of the purpose of each function of the `Board` class:

- `init()`: This function initializes all array values to the `null` value
- `index()`: This function returns the array index from column/row coordinates
- `setData()`: This function assigns the `data` value on the board from column/row coordinates
- `at()`: This function retrieves the `data` value in an array from column/row coordinates

Please note that, in our case, a `null` square means an empty square.

Crafting entities from the factory

Now that we have a board to receive items, we will create the game items factory. The factory is a design pattern that allows us to create an object without exposing the creation logic to the caller. This factory can be seen as a helper class that will handle all the dirty tasks required when you want to create a new game item from JavaScript. Do you remember `GameEntity.qml`? It is the parent class of `Apple.qml`, `Snake.qml`, and `Wall.qml`. The factory will be able to create a specific entity for a given a type and coordinates. We will use the property type to identify an entity kind. Here is the factory pattern schema used in our snake game:

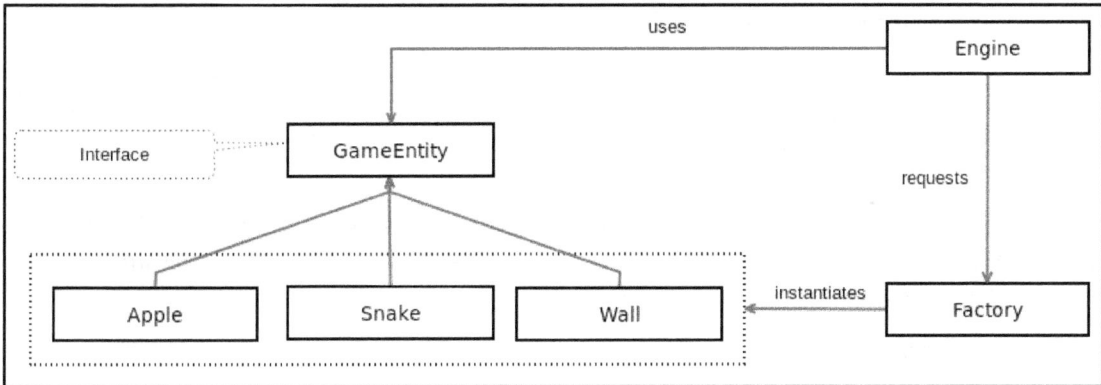

We can now create the `factory.js` file, which begins like this:

```
var SNAKE_TYPE = 1;
var WALL_TYPE  = 2;
var APPLE_TYPE = 3;

var snakeComponent = Qt.createComponent("Snake.qml");
var wallComponent = Qt.createComponent("Wall.qml");
var appleComponent = Qt.createComponent("Apple.qml");
```

First of all, we define all the game entity types. In our case we have apple, snake, and wall types. Then, we create game item components from QML files. These components will be use by the factory to dynamically create new game entities.

We can now add the constructor and a `removeAllEntities()` utility function to remove all instantiated entities:

```
function GameFactory() {

    this.board = null;
    this.parentEntity = null;
    this.entities = [];
}

GameFactory.prototype.removeAllEntities = function() {
    for(var i = 0; i < this.entities.length; i++) {
        this.entities[i].setParent(null);
    }
```

This factory has three member variables:

- A reference to the game `board` described in the previous section
- A reference to the `parentEntity` variable, that is, the game area
- An `entities` array that keeps a reference to created items

The `removeAllEntities()` function will remove the items from their parent (that is, the game area) and create a new empty entities array. This ensures that old entities are deleted by the garbage collector.

Let's add the core function `createGameEnity()` in the factory:

```
GameFactory.prototype.createGameEntity = function(type, column, row) {
    var component;
    switch(type) {
    case SNAKE_TYPE:
        component = snakeComponent;
        break;

    case WALL_TYPE:
        component = wallComponent;
        break;

    case APPLE_TYPE:
        component = appleComponent;
        break;
    }
    var gameEntity = component.createObject(this.parentEntity);
    gameEntity.setParent(this.parentEntity);

    this.board.setData(gameEntity, column, row);
    gameEntity.gridPosition = Qt.vector2d(column, row);
    gameEntity.position.x = column * this.board.blockSize;
    gameEntity.position.y = row * this.board.blockSize;

    this.entities.push(gameEntity);
    return gameEntity;
}
```

As you can see, the caller provides an entity `type` and board coordinates (`column` and `row`). The first part is a switch to select the correct QML component. Once we have the component, we can call `component.createObject()` to create an instance of this component. The parent of this new component will be `this.parentEntity`, in our case, `GameArea`. Then, we can update the board, update the entity position, and add this new entity in the `entities` array.

The last thing to do is to update our QML game entities with the proper factory type. Please open `Apple.qml` and update the file like this:

```
import "factory.js" as Factory

GameEntity {

    id: root
    type: Factory.APPLE_TYPE
    ...
}
```

You can now update `Snake.qml` with the `Factory.SNAKE_TYPE` type and `Wall.qml` with the `Factory.WALL_TYPE` type.

Building a snake engine in JavaScript

It is time to get your hands dirty. Let's see how to create an engine in JavaScript to manage a snake game using our board, our factory, and the power of QML.

Please create a new `engine.js` file with the following snippet:

```
.import "factory.js" as Factory
.import "board.js" as Board

var COLUMN_COUNT = 50;
var ROW_COUNT = 29;
var BLOCK_SIZE = 1;

var factory = new Factory.GameFactory();
var board = new Board.Board(COLUMN_COUNT, ROW_COUNT, BLOCK_SIZE);

var snake = [];
var direction;
```

The first lines are the Qt way to import a JavaScript file from another JavaScript file. Then, we can easily instantiate a `factory` variable and a 50x29 `board` variable. The `snake` array contains all the snake game items instantiated. This array will be useful to move our snake. Finally, the `direction` variable is a 2d vector handling the current snake direction.

This is the first function of our engine:

```
function start() {
    initEngine();

    createSnake();
    createWalls();

    spawnApple();
    gameRoot.state = "PLAY";
}
```

This gives you a summary of what is done when we start the engine:

1. Initialize the engine.
2. Create the initial snake.
3. Create walls surrounding the game area.
4. Spawn the first apple.
5. Switch the GameArea state to PLAY.

Let's begin with the initEngine() function:

```
function initEngine() {
    timer.interval = initialTimeInterval;
    score = 0;

    factory.board = board;
    factory.parentEntity = gameRoot;
    factory.removeAllEntities();

    board.init();
    direction = Qt.vector2d(-1, 0);
}
```

This function initializes and resets all the variables. The first task is to set the GameArea timer interval to its initial value. Each time the snake eats an apple, this interval is reduced, increasing the game speed and thus the snake's movement speed. Logically, we reset the score of the player to 0. Then we initialize the factory, giving the board and gameRoot references. The gameRoot refers to the GameArea; this entity will be the parent of all items instantiated by the factory. Then, we remove all the existing entities from the factory and call the board's init() function to clear the board. Finally, we set a default direction for the snake. The vector -1, 0 means that the snake will begin moving to the left. If you want the snake to start moving up, you can set the vector to 0, 1.

The next function is creating the snake:

```
function createSnake() {
    snake = [];
    var initialPosition = Qt.vector2d(25, 12);
    for (var i = 0; i < initialSnakeSize; i++) {
        snake.push(factory.createGameEntity(Factory.SNAKE_TYPE,
                                initialPosition.x + i,
                                initialPosition.y));
    }
}
```

No big deal here, we reset and initialize the snake array. The first snake item will be created at 25x12. We then proceed to create as many snake items as we need to spawn a snake with the correct initial size. Please note that other snake items will be created to the right of the first item (26x12, 27x12, and so on). You can see how easy it is to call our factory and request a new snake item instance.

Let's add the createWalls() function to engine.js:

```
function createWalls() {
    for (var x = 0; x < board.columnCount; x++) {
        factory.createGameEntity(Factory.WALL_TYPE, x, 0);
        factory.createGameEntity(Factory.WALL_TYPE, x, board.rowCount - 1);
    }
    for (var y = 1; y < board.rowCount - 1; y++) {
        factory.createGameEntity(Factory.WALL_TYPE, 0, y);
        factory.createGameEntity(Factory.WALL_TYPE, board.columnCount - 1,
y);
    }
}
```

The first loop creates the top and bottom walls. The second loop creates the left and right walls. The indexes of the second loop are different from the first one to avoid creating the corners twice.

Let's see now how to implement the spawnApple() function in engine.js:

```
function spawnApple() {
    var isFound = false;
    var position;
    while (!isFound) {
        position = Qt.vector2d(Math.floor(Math.random()
                                * board.columnCount),
                            Math.floor(Math.random()
                                * board.rowCount));
        if (board.at(position.x, position.y) == null) {
```

```
            isFound = true;
        }
    }
    factory.createGameEntity(Factory.APPLE_TYPE, position.x, position.y);

    if (timerInterval > 10) {
        timerInterval -= 2;
    }
}
```

The first step is to find an empty square. The while loop will generate a random board position and check whether a square is empty. As soon as an empty square is found, we request the factory to create an apple entity at this position. Finally, we reduce the `timerInverval` value of `GameArea` to speed up the game.

We will now add some utility functions related to the snake position in `engine.js`:

```
function setPosition(item, column, row) {
    board.setData(item, column, row);
    item.gridPosition = Qt.vector2d(column, row);
    item.position.x = column * board.blockSize;
    item.position.y = row * board.blockSize;
}

function moveSnake(column, row) {
    var last = snake.pop();
    board.setData(null, last.gridPosition.x, last.gridPosition.y);
    setPosition(last, column, row);
    snake.unshift(last);
}
```

The `setPosition()` function handles all the necessary tasks when we want to move a game item. We first assign the game item to the correct board square, then we update the `gridPosition` property (from `GameEntity`) but also the OpenGL `position.x` and `position.y`.

The second function, `moveSnake()`, moves the snake to an adjacent square. Let's dissect all the steps performed by this function:

1. The `snake` is our global array containing all the snake items. The `pop()` method removes and returns the last element that we store in the `last` variable.
2. The `last` variable contains the snake's tail's grid position. We set this board square to `null`; that means an empty square for us.
3. The `last` variable is now put on the adjacent square requested by the caller.
4. The `last` variable is finally inserted at the beginning of the `snake` array.

The next schema illustrates the `moveSnake()` process when a snake is moving on the left. We also name snake items with a letter to visualize how the tail becomes the head, simulating a moving snake:

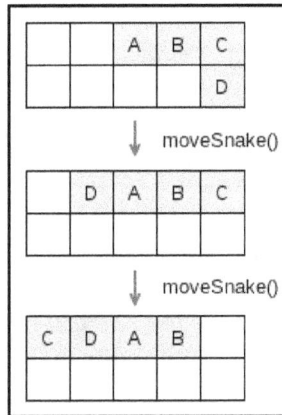

Now that we can move our snake, we must handle key events to move the snake in the correct direction. Please add this new function to `engine.js`:

```
function handleKeyEvent(event) {
    switch(event.key) {
        // restart game
        case Qt.Key_R:
            start();
            break;

        // direction UP
        case Qt.Key_I:
            if (direction != Qt.vector2d(0, -1)) {
                direction = Qt.vector2d(0, 1);
            }
            break;

        // direction RIGHT
        case Qt.Key_L:
            if (direction != Qt.vector2d(-1, 0)) {
                direction = Qt.vector2d(1, 0);
            }
            break;

        // direction DOWN
        case Qt.Key_K:
            if (direction != Qt.vector2d(0, 1)) {
```

```
                    direction = Qt.vector2d(0, -1);
            }
            break;

        // direction LEFT
        case Qt.Key_J:
            if (direction != Qt.vector2d(1, 0)) {
                direction = Qt.vector2d(-1, 0);
            }
            break;
    }
}
```

In this game, we use the I-J-K-L keys to update the snake direction vector. Like the original snake game, you can't reverse your direction. A check is performed to avoid this behavior. Please notice that pressing the R key will call start() and so restart the game. We will see soon how to bind this function with the QML keyboard controller.

Here we are, the last (but not least) function, the update() function of engine.js:

```
function update() {
    if (gameRoot.state == "GAMEOVER") {
        return;
    }

    var headPosition = snake[0].gridPosition;
    var newPosition = Qt.vector2d(headPosition.x + direction.x,
                                  headPosition.y + direction.y);
    var itemOnNewPosition = board.at(newPosition.x,
                                     newPosition.y);

    ...
}
```

This function will be called at regular intervals by QML. As you can see, if the gameRoot (that is GameArea) state variable equals GAMEOVER, this function does nothing and returns immediately. Then, three important steps are performed:

1. Retrieve the grid position of the snake's head in headPosition.
2. Process where the snake goes using the direction vector in newPosition.
3. Put the item where the snake is going in itemOnNewPosition.

The second part of the update() function is the following snippet:

```
function update() {
    ...
    if(itemOnNewPosition == null) {
        moveSnake(newPosition.x, newPosition.y);
        return;
    }

    switch(itemOnNewPosition.type) {
        case Factory.SNAKE_TYPE:
            gameRoot.state = "GAMEOVER";
            break;

        case Factory.WALL_TYPE:
            gameRoot.state = "GAMEOVER";
            break;

        case Factory.APPLE_TYPE:
            itemOnNewPosition.setParent(null);
            board.setData(null, newPosition.x, newPosition.y);
            snake.unshift(factory.createGameEntity(
                    Factory.SNAKE_TYPE,
                    newPosition.x,
                    newPosition.y));
            spawnApple();
            score++;
            break;
    }
}
```

If the snake is going to an empty square (itemOnNewPosition is null), it is alright and we only move the snake to newPosition.

If the square is not empty, we must apply the correct rule depending on the item type. If the next square is a snake part or a wall, we update the state to GAMEOVER. On the other hand, if the next square is an apple, several steps are performed:

1. Detach the apple item from GameArea, setting its parent to null.
2. Remove the apple from the board, setting the board square to null.
3. Grow the snake, creating a snake part at the beginning of the snake array.
4. Spawn a new apple in a random empty square.
5. Increment the score.

Our snake engine is now complete. The last step is to call some engine functions from QML. Please update `GameArea.qml`:

```
...
import "engine.js" as Engine

Entity {
    ...
    QQ2.Component.onCompleted: {
        console.log("Start game...");
        Engine.start();
        timer.start()
    }

    QQ2.Timer {
        id: timer
        interval: initialTimeInterval
        repeat: true
        onTriggered: Engine.update()
    }

    KeyboardInput {
        id: input
        controller: keyboardController
        focus: true
        onPressed: Engine.handleKeyEvent(event)
    }
    ...
}
```

You can already play the game. If you eat an apple, the snake grows and you get one point. When you hit yourself or a wall, the game state switches to GAMEOVER and the game stops. Finally, if you press the R key, the game restarts. The game looks like the next screenshot on to null Raspberry Pi:

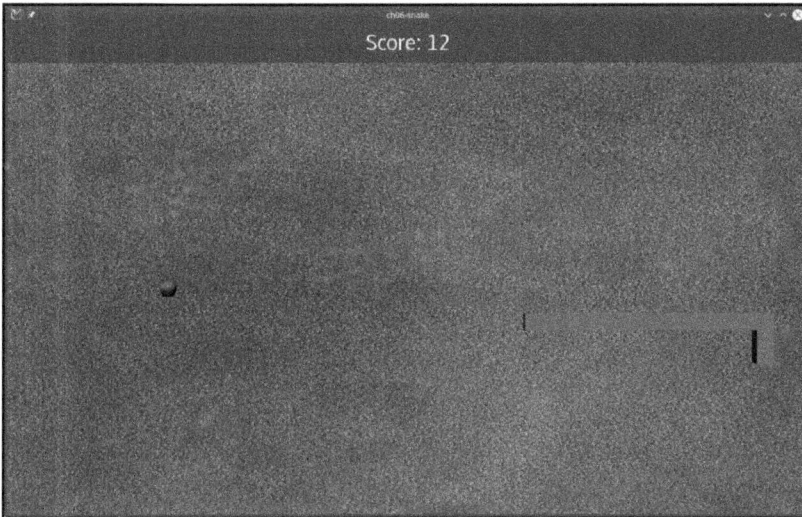

Varying the HUD with QML states

We will now create a "Game Over" HUD, displayed when you lose the game. Create a new file GameOverItem.qml:

```
Item {
    id: root
    anchors.fill: parent

    onVisibleChanged: {
        scoreLabel.text = "Your score: " + score
    }

    Rectangle {
        anchors.fill: parent
        color: "black"
        opacity: 0.75
    }

    Label {
        id: gameOverLabel
        anchors.centerIn: parent
        color: "white"
        font.pointSize: 50
        text: "Game Over"
    }
```

```
Label {
    id: scoreLabel
    width: parent.width
    anchors.top: gameOverLabel.bottom
    horizontalAlignment: "AlignHCenter"
    color: "white"
    font.pointSize: 20
}

Label {
    width: parent.width
    anchors.bottom: parent.bottom
    anchors.bottomMargin: 50
    horizontalAlignment: "AlignHCenter"
    color: "white"
    font.pointSize: 30
    text:"Press R to restart the game"
}
}
```

Let's examine the items of this Game Over screen:

- A black rectangle filling the entire screen with an `opacity` value of 75%. As a consequence, the game area will still be visible at 25% behind the game over screen.
- A `gameOverLabel` label displaying the text "Game Over". This is a traditional video game message but you can edit this label with text such as "Loser!" or "Too bad!".
- A dynamic `scoreLabel` label that will display the final score.
- A label explaining to the player how he can restart the game.

Please notice that, when the visibility of the root item changes, the `scoreLabel` text is updated with the current `score` variable from `main.qml`.

Qt Quick provides an interesting feature related to UI states. You can define several states for an item and describe the behaviors for each state. We will now use this feature and our `GameOverItem` in a new file called `OverlayItem.qml`:

```
Item {
    id: root

    states: [
        State {
            name: "PLAY"
            PropertyChanges { target: root; visible: false }
        },
```

```
    State {
        name: "GAMEOVER"
        PropertyChanges { target: root; visible: true }
        PropertyChanges { target: gameOver; visible: true }
    }
]

GameOverItem {
    id: gameOver
}
}
```

You can see that the `states` element is an `Item` property. By default, the `states` element contains an empty string state. Here we are defining two `State` items named `PLAY` and `GAMEOVER`. We are using the same naming convention as in `engine.js`. Afterwards we can bind property values to a state. In our case, when the state is `GAMEOVER`, we set the visibility to `true` for this `OverlayItem` and its `GameOverItem`. Otherwise, for the state `PLAY`, we hide it.

The overlay HUD and its "Game Over" screen are ready to be used. Please update your `mail.qml` with the following snippet:

```
Item {
    id: mainView
    property int score: 0
    readonly property alias window: mainView
    ...
    OverlayItem {
        id: overlayItem
        anchors.fill: mainView
        visible: false

        Connections {
            target: gameArea
            onStateChanged: {
                overlayItem.state = gameArea.state;
            }
        }
    }
}
```

Our `OverlayItem` element fits the screen and is not visible by default. Like a C++ Qt Widgets signal/slot connection, you can perform a QML connection. The target property contains the item that will send the signal. Then you can use the QML slot syntax:

```
on<PropertyName>Changed
```

In our case, the target is `gameArea`. This item contains the `state` variable, so we can be notified when the state variable is updated using `onStateChanged`. Then, we switch the state of `OverlayItem`. This assignation will trigger all `PropertyChanged` defined in `OverlayItem` element and display or hide our `GameOverItem`.

You can now lose the game and enjoy your Game Over overlay:

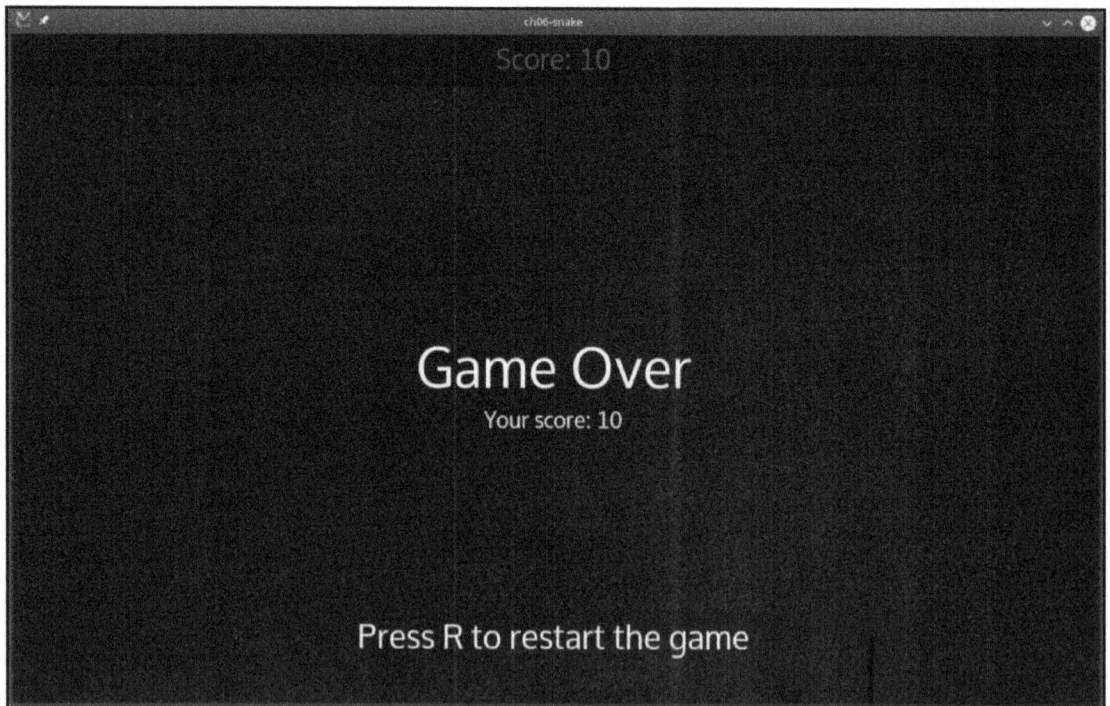

Profiling your QML application

Qt Creator provides a QML profiler to collect useful data on your application during the runtime. You can use it on a desktop and also on a remote target such as our Raspberry Pi. Let's check that your debug build configuration allows QML debugging and profiling. Click on **Projects | Rpi 2 | Build**. Then you can click on **Details** of **qmake** from **Build Steps**. You should also check it for your desktop kit:

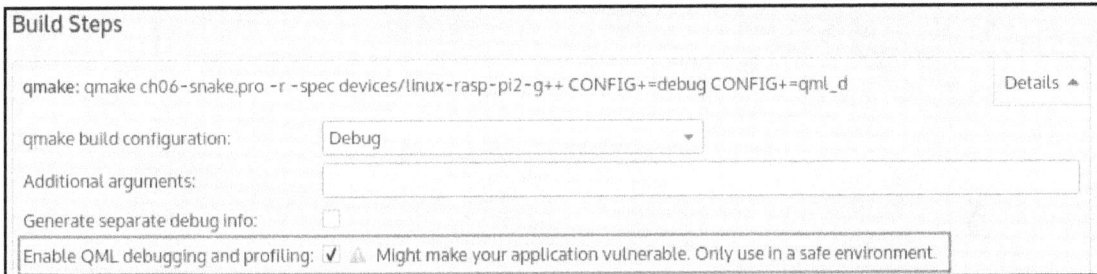

Build Steps		
qmake: qmake ch06-snake.pro -r -spec devices/linux-rasp-pi2-g++ CONFIG+=debug CONFIG+=qml_d		Details ▲
qmake build configuration:	Debug ▼	
Additional arguments:		
Generate separate debug info:	☐	
Enable QML debugging and profiling: ✓ ⚠ Might make your application vulnerable. Only use in a safe environment.		

By default, data is only sent from target to host when you stop profiling. You can flush data periodically: **Tools | Options | Analyser | QML Profiler**.

Keep in mind that flushing data while profiling frees memory on the target device but takes time. Thus, it can affect your profiling result and analysis.

While we are using Qt Creator kits, we can start the QML profiler in the same way for desktops or remote devices. Switch to a kit and click on **Analyze | QML Profiler** to start the QML profiling. If you are profiling an application running on your desktop, Qt Creator starts your software with an argument such as this:

```
-qmljsdebugger=file:/tmp/QtCreator.OU7985
```

If you're profiling an application on a remote device (such as a Raspberry Pi), Qt Creator uses a TCP socket to retrieve data, adding an argument such as this:

```
-qmljsdebugger=port:10000
```

For both targets, the QML profiler will afterwards try to connect to your application. Another way to start the QML profiler on a remote device is to start the application yourself with the -qmljsdebugger argument, for example:

```
./ch06-snake -qmljsdebugger=port:3768
```

Then, you can click on **Analyze | QML Profiler (External)**. Select your remote kit (such as Rpi 2), set the **port** to `3768`, and click on **OK**.

Great, the QML profiler is started, a new toolbar appears. You can play the game for a few seconds and click on the **Stop** button from the QML Profiler toolbar. Then the QML profiler processes data and displays something like this:

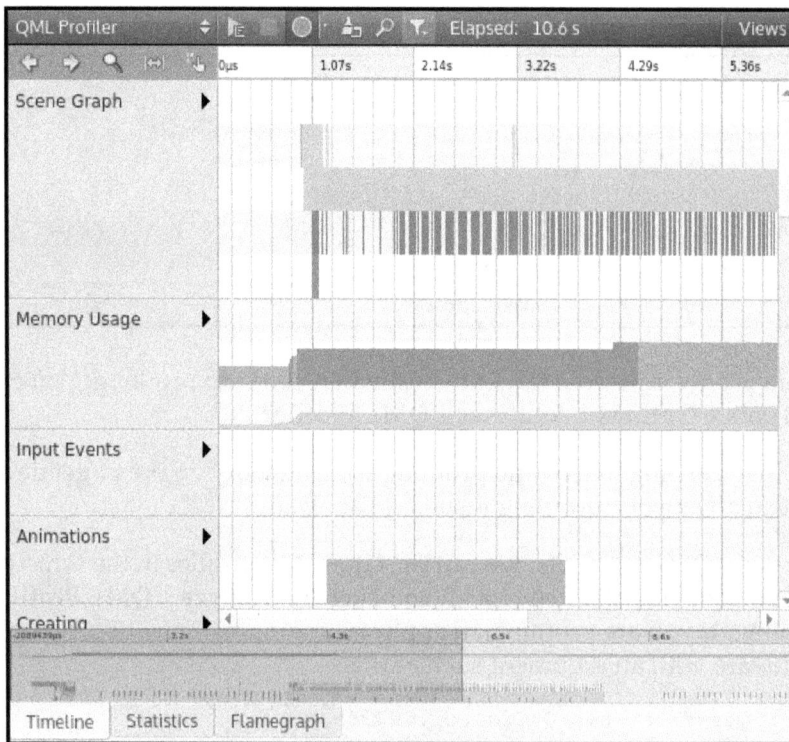

Let's begin analyzing the top buttons from left to right:

1. Start QML profiler.
2. Stop the application and the QML profiler.
3. Enable/disable profiling. You can also select an event to capture.
4. Discard data to clean your profiling session.
5. Search timeline event notes.
6. Hide or show event categories.
7. **Elapsed** indicates the session duration.
8. **Views** hides or shows the **Timeline**, **Statistics**, and **Flamegraph** tabs.

To learn to use the QML profiler, we will take a real case. Restarting the game is a little slow on the Raspberry Pi. Let's find with the QML profiler what requires several seconds to restart the game!

Please follow this operational mode to gather data from the QML profiler:

1. Select the Raspberry Pi kit.
2. Start the QML profiler.
3. Wait for the snake to hit a wall.
4. Press the *R* key to restart the game.
5. Wait for the game to restart and the snake to move again.
6. Stop the QML profiler.

Let's begin our investigation using the **timeline** tab. This view displays a chronological view of events, grouped by event type. The JavaScript row dissects your code and displays useful information. You can click on an item to get some details. Identify in the timeline when you restart the game. The JavaScript row can be read as a call stack, from top to bottom:

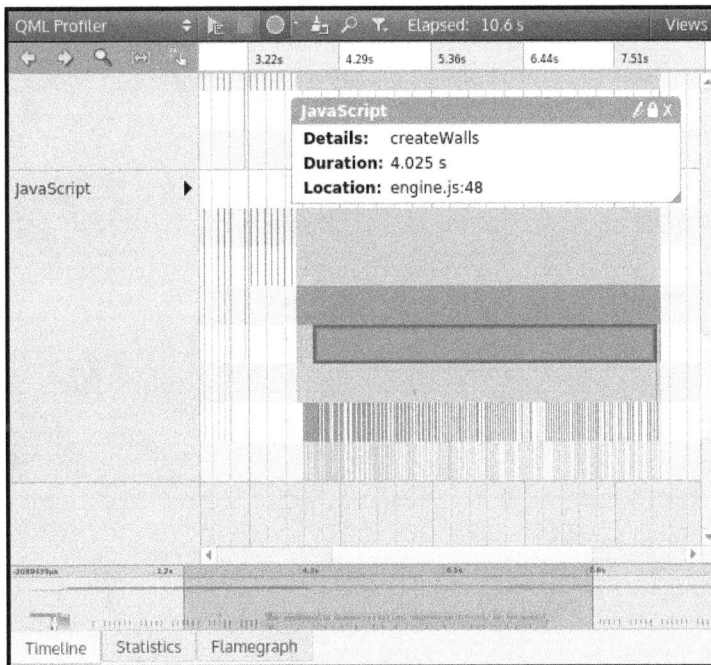

In our case, we restarted the game around 3.5 seconds after the application started. Here is the stack with durations provided by the QML profiler. Here is the stack with durations provided by the QML profiler. Let's track all functions called when we restart the game pressing the R key:

- The onPressed() function from GameArea.qml
- The handleKetEvent() function from engine.js
- The start() function from engine.js at 4.2 seconds
  - initEngine() at 80 ms
  - createSnake() at 120 ms
  - createWalls() at 4.025 seconds!

Here we are, createWalls() takes ~4 seconds on the Raspberry Pi when we restart the game.

Let's switch to the **Statistics** view:

Location	Type	Calls	Time in Percent ▲	Total Time	Self Time in Percent	Self Time
<program>		1	100.00 %	4.912 s	0.00 %	0.001 us
engine.js:14	JavaScript	2	90.61 %	4.451 s	0.01 %	315.937 us
factory.js:16	JavaScript	320	88.70 %	4.357 s	81.29 %	3.993 s
GameArea.qml:62	Signal	1	86.91 %	4.269 s	0.01 %	325.676 us
GameArea.qml:62	JavaScript	1	86.90 %	4.268 s	0.00 %	35.573 us
engine.js:125	JavaScript	1	86.90 %	4.268 s	0.00 %	109.895 us
engine.js:48	JavaScript	2	84.61 %	4.156 s	0.22 %	10.581 ms
main.qml:5	Create	2	6.77 %	332.523 ms	0.01 %	549.685 us
main.qml:37	Create	2	6.06 %	297.657 ms	4.77 %	234.112 ms
GameArea.qml:45	Signal	1	3.73 %	183.407 ms	0.00 %	23.489 us
GameArea.qml:45	JavaScript	1	3.73 %	183.384 ms	0.02 %	935.935 us
engine.js:38	JavaScript	2	3.27 %	160.579 ms	0.02 %	779.110 us

Caller	Caller Description	Total Time ▲	Calls	Callee	Callee Description	Total Time ▲	Calls
engine.js:43	createWalls	4.145 s	308	Wall.qml:4	GameEntity.qml	128.238 ms	308
engine.js:38	createSnake	159.800 ms	10	factory.js:1	%entry	86.241 ms	320
engine.js:59	spawnApple	51.750 ms	2	SnakePart.qml:5	GameEntity.qml	36.024 ms	10
				Wall.qml:15	components: [transf...	22.936 ms	308
				PhongMaterial.qml:57	fragmentShaderCo...	19.038 ms	10
				GameEntity.qml:5	property vector2d g...	17.322 ms	320
				Wall.qml:7	type: Factory.WALL...	10.123 ms	308
				PhongMaterial.qml:51	fragmentShaderCo...	8.922 ms	10
				Apple.qml:5	GameEntity.qml	6.159 ms	2
				board.js:19	Source code not ava...	5.981 ms	320

Timeline   Statistics   Flamegraph

The **Statistics** view displays numbers concerning the call count of an event. An event can be a QML binding, creation, signal triggered, or a JavaScript function. The bottom part shows QML callers and callees.

A caller is the source of a change in a binding. For example, the JS function `createWalls()` is a caller.

A callee is the affected item that a binding triggers. For example, the QML item `Wall.qml` is a callee.

Once again, `createWalls()` requesting many factory item creation seems responsible for the slow restart of the game on Raspberry Pi.

Take a look at the last view of the QML profiler, the **Flamegraph**:

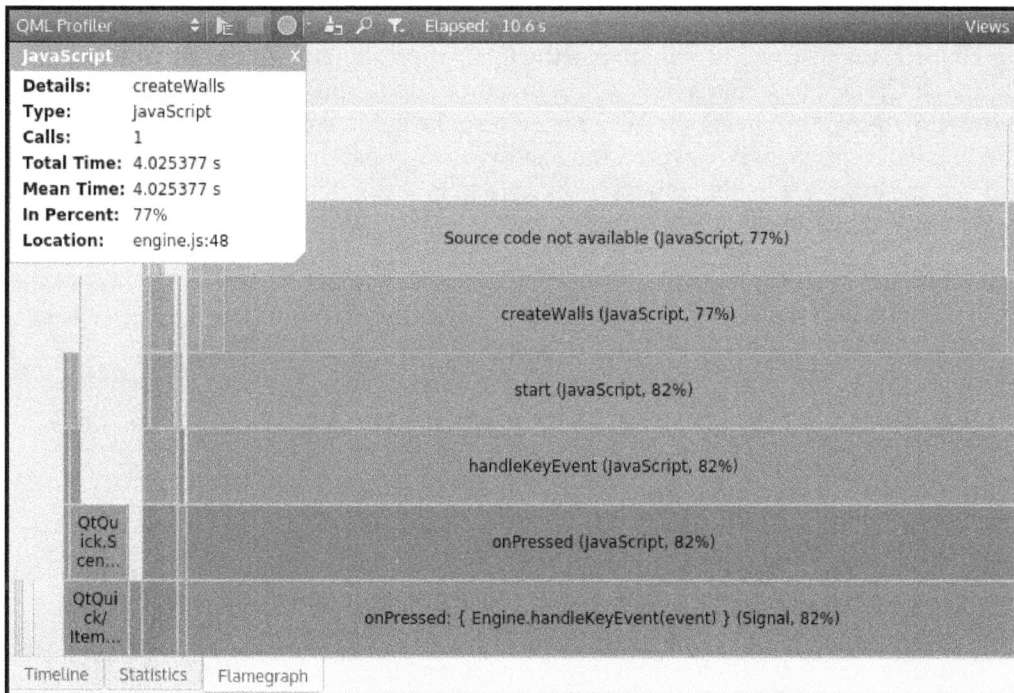

The **Flamegraph** view is a compact summary of your QML and JavaScript code while running the game. You can see the call count and the amount of time relative to the total duration. Like the **Timeline** view, you can see the call stack but from bottom to top!

Again, the profiler indicates `createWalls()` is a heavy function. On a profiling session of 10 seconds with one game restart, 77% of the time is spent in `engine.createWalls()`.

You will now be able to profile a QML application. You can try to edit the code to speed up the restart. Here are some hints:

- Create the walls only once at application startup; do not delete and recreate them on each restart.
- Implement a common design pattern in video games: an object pool of preloaded items. Request a wall when needed, and return the wall to the pool when you do not use it.

Summary

In this chapter, we discovered how to use the Qt3D module. You also learned how to configure Qt Creator to create a new kit for an embedded Linux device. Your Raspberry Pi can now run your Qt applications. We created a snake game using QML views and an engine in JavaScript. We also covered the Factory design pattern to easily create new game items from the engine. Finally, you are now able to investigate the bad behavior of QML software using the powerful QML profiler.

Even if Qt is a powerful framework, sometimes you need to use a third-party library. In the next chapter, we will see how to integrate the OpenCV library into your Qt application.

15
Third-Party Libraries Without a Headache

In previous chapters, we have used our own libraries or the ones provided by Qt. In this chapter, we will learn how to integrate the third-party library OpenCV with a Qt project. This library will give you an impressive image processing toolbox. For each platform, you will learn to use a different specific compiler link configuration.

Qt Designer is a powerful WYSIWYG editor. This is why this chapter will also teach you to build a Qt Designer plugin that can be dragged and dropped from the **Widget Box** to the **Form Editor**, and then configured directly from Qt Creator.

In the example project, the user can load a picture, select a filter from thumbnail previews, and save the result. This application will rely on OpenCV functions for image processing.

This chapter will cover the following topics:

- Prepare a cross-platform project to host a third-party library
- Link with a third party library
- Build a custom `QWidget` class using Qt Designer plugins
- How the OpenCV API can work with Qt
- Create a Qt application that relies on a custom `QWidget` class

Creating your Qt Designer plugin

In Chapter 12, *Conquering the Desktop UI*, we created a custom Qt widget in Qt Designer using the promoting technique. It is now time to learn how to create a custom Qt widget by building a plugin for Qt Designer. Your widget will be available from the **Design mode** in the **Widget Box** alongside other regular Qt widgets. For this project example, we will create a FilterWidget class that processes an input image to apply a filter. The widget will also display the filter name and a dynamic thumbnail of the filtered picture.

This project is composed of two sub-projects:

- filter-plugin-designer: This is a Qt Designer plugin containing FilterWidget class and the image processing code. This plugin is a dynamic library that will be used by the Qt Creator to offer our new FilterWidget in the **Form Editor**.
- image-filter: This is a Qt Widget application using multiple FilterWidget. The user can open an image from their hard disk, select a filter (grayscale, blur, and so on), and save the filtered image.

Our filter-plugin-designer will use the third-party library **OpenCV** (**Open Source Computer Vision**). It is a powerful, cross-platform open source library to manipulate images. Here is an overview schema:

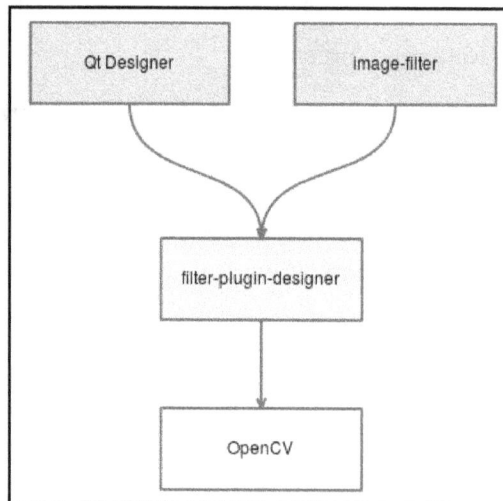

You can see a plugin as a kind of module, which can be easily added to an existing software. A plugin must respect a specific interface to be automatically called by the application. In our case, the Qt Designer is the application that loads Qt plugins. So creating a plugin allows us to enhance the application without the need to modify the Qt Designer source code and recompile it. A plugin is a generally dynamic library (.dll/.so), so it will be loaded at runtime by the application.

Now that you have a clear mind about the Qt Designer plugins, let's build one! First, create a `Subdirs` project called `ch07-image-filter`. Then, you can add a subproject, `filter-plugin-designer`. You can use the **Empty qmake Project** template because we start this project from scratch. Here is the `filter-plugin-designer.pro` file:

```
QT += widgets uiplugin
CONFIG += plugin
CONFIG += c++14
TEMPLATE = lib
DEFINES += FILTERPLUGINDESIGNER_LIBRARY

TARGET = $$qtLibraryTarget($$TARGET)
INSTALLS += target
```

Please note the `uiplugin` and `plugin` keywords for `QT` and `CONFIG`. They are required to create a Qt Designer plugin. We set the `TEMPLATE` keyword to `lib` because we are creating a dynamic library. The define, `FILTERPLUGINDESIGNER_LIBRARY`, will be used by the import/export mechanism of the library. We already covered this topic in `Chapter 11`, *Dividing Your Project and Ruling Your Code*. By default, our `TARGET` is `filter-plugin-designer`; the `$$qtLibraryTarget()` function will update it according to your platform. For example, the suffix "d" (standing for debug) will be appended on Windows. Finally, we append `target` to `INSTALLS`. Right now, this line does nothing, but we will describe a destination path for each platform soon; this way, executing the `make install` command will copy our target library file (.dll/.so) into the correct folder. To automatically perform this task on each compilation, you can add a new build step.

The deploy path is configured, but it will not be done automatically. Open the **Projects** tab and do the following:

1. Open the **Build Settings** | **Build Steps**.
2. Click on **Add Build Step** | **Make**.
3. In the **Make arguments** field, type `install`.

You should get something like this:

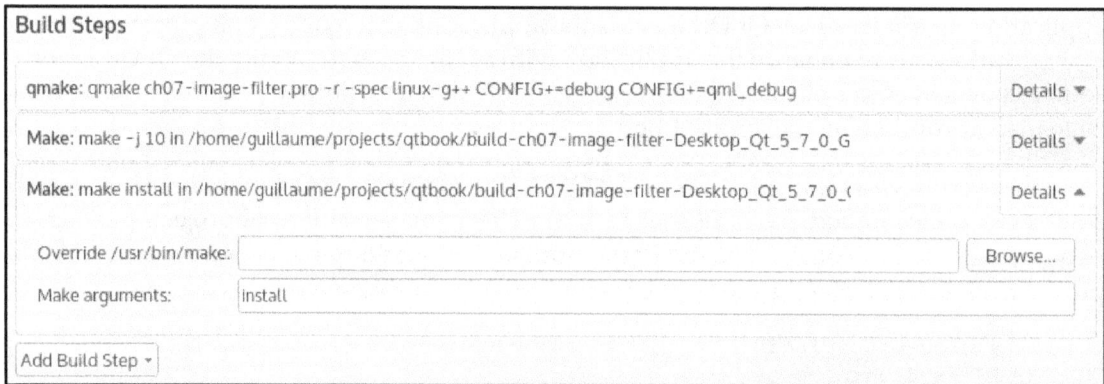

```
Build Steps

  qmake: qmake ch07-image-filter.pro -r -spec linux-g++ CONFIG+=debug CONFIG+=qml_debug          Details ▼

  Make: make -j 10 in /home/guillaume/projects/qtbook/build-ch07-image-filter-Desktop_Qt_5_7_0_G   Details ▼

  Make: make install in /home/guillaume/projects/qtbook/build-ch07-image-filter-Desktop_Qt_5_7_0_(  Details ▲

     Override /usr/bin/make:  [                                                    ]   Browse...

     Make arguments:          [install                                             ]

  Add Build Step ▾
```

Each time you build the project, the `make install` command will be called and it will deploy the library in Qt Creator.

Configuring the project for Windows

Before preparing this project on Windows, let's talk about the available choices when you develop a Qt application on a Windows host. The official Qt website provides multiple binary packages. We are mainly interested in the following:

- Qt for Windows 32-bit (MinGW)
- Qt for Windows 32-bit (VS 2013)

You may already be using one of these versions. The first one comes with a MinGW GCC compiler and the Qt framework. The second only provides the Qt framework and relies on the Microsoft Visual C++ compiler that will be installed with Visual Studio.

Both versions are fine when you want to create a common Qt application for Windows. However, for this chapter, we want to link our `filter-plugin-designer` project with OpenCV libraries. Qt Designer must also be able to dynamically load `filter-plugin-designer`, so we must use a consistent compiler version at all stages.

Please note that Qt Creator on Windows is always based on MSVC, even in the MinGW binary package! So if you create a Qt Designer plugin using a MinGW compiler, your Qt Creator will not be able to load it. OpenCV for Windows provides only MSVC libraries, compile for MSVC11 (which is VS 2012), and MSVC12 (VS 2013).

Here is a summary of the different solutions for building our project example in Windows:

	MinGW GCC	MSVC
OpenCV	Binary not provided Recompilation required	Binary for msvc11 and msvc12 provided
Qt Designer	Binary not provided Recompilation required	Based on msvc12 32-bit

Keep in mind that for open-source software such as Qt Creator and OpenCV you can always try to compile them from a source with a different compiler. So, if you absolutely want to use a MinGW compiler, you must recompile OpenCV and Qt Creator from sources. Otherwise, we suggest that you use Qt for Windows 32-bit (VS 2013) as explained shortly. Here are the steps to prepare your development environment:

1. Download and install Visual Studio Community Edition.
2. Download and install Qt for Windows 32-bit (VS 2013).
3. Download and extract OpenCV for Windows (for example: C:libopencv).
4. Create a new OPENCV_HOME: C:libopencvbuildx86vc12 environment variable.
5. Append to your system Path: C:libopencvbuildx86vc12bin environment variable.

The OPENCV_HOME directory will be used in our .pro file. We also add an OpenCV libraries folder to the Path directory to easily resolve the dependencies at runtime.

You can now add the following snippet to the filter-plugin-designer.pro file:

```
windows {
target.path = $$(QTDIR)/../../Tools/QtCreator/bin/plugins/designer

debug:target_lib.files = $$OUT_PWD/debug/$${TARGET}.lib
release:target_lib.files = $$OUT_PWD/release/$${TARGET}.lib
target_lib.path = $$(QTDIR)/../../Tools/QtCreator/bin/plugins/designer
    INSTALLS += target_lib

    INCLUDEPATH += $$(OPENCV_HOME)/../../include
    LIBS += -L$$(OPENCV_HOME)/lib
        -lopencv_core2413
        -lopencv_imgproc2413
}
```

The `target` path is set to the Qt Creator plugin folder. We also create a `target_lib` library to copy the `.lib` file generated by MSVC when we make a dynamic library (`.dll`). We add the OpenCV headers folder to the `INCLUDEPATH` to easily include them in our code. Finally, we update `LIBS` variable to link our plugin with the OpenCV modules (`core` and `imgproc`) from the OpenCV `lib` folder.

Please note that the standalone Qt Designer application and the Qt Creator are different software. Both programs use a different plugin path. In our case, we only used the form editor from the Qt Creator, so we are targeting the Qt Creator plugin path.

Just as we appended `target` and `target_lib` to `INSTALLS`, both `.dll` and `.lib` files will be copied in the Qt Creator plugin path on a `make install` command. Qt Creator only requires the `.dll` file to load the plugin at runtime. The `.lib` file is only used to resolve the links with `filter-plugin-designer` when building our `image-filter` application. For simplicity, we are using the same directory.

Configuring the project for Linux

OpenCV binaries are certainly available in official software repositories. Depending on your distribution and your package manager, you can install it with commands such as the following:

```
apt-get install libopencv
yum install opencv
```

When OpenCV is installed on your Linux, you can add this snippet to the `filter-plugin-designer.pro` file:

```
linux {
target.path = $$(QTDIR)/../../Tools/QtCreator/lib/Qt/plugins/designer/

    CONFIG += link_pkgconfig
    PKGCONFIG += opencv
}
```

This time we do not use the LIBS variable but PKGCONFIG, which relies on pkg-config. It is a helper tool that will insert the correct options into the compile command line. In our case, we will request pkg-config to link our project with OpenCV.

> You can list all the libs managed by pkg-config with the pkg-config --list-all command.

Configuring the project for Mac

The first step in making the project work on Mac OS is to install OpenCV. Fortunately, this is very easy using the brew command. If you develop on Mac OS and do not use it already, you should download it right now. In a nutshell, brew is an alternate package manager that gives you access to many packages (for developers and non-developers) that are not available on the Mac App Store.

> You can download and install brew from http://brew.sh/.

In a terminal, simply type the following command:

```
brew install opencv
```

This will download, compile, and install OpenCV on your machine. At the time of writing, the latest OpenCV version available on brew was version 2.4.13. Once this is done, open filter-plugin-designer.pro and add the following block:

```
macx {
target.path = "$$(QTDIR)/../../QtCreator.app/Contents/PlugIns/designer/"
target_lib.files = $$OUT_PWD/lib$${TARGET}.dylib
target_lib.path =
"$$(QTDIR)/../../QtCreator.app/Contents/PlugIns/designer/"
    INSTALLS += target_lib

    INCLUDEPATH += /usr/local/Cellar/opencv/2.4.13/include/

    LIBS += -L/usr/local/lib
        -lopencv_core
        -lopencv_imgproc
}
```

We add OpenCV headers and link the path with INCLUDEPATH and LIBS variables. The target definition and INSTALLS are used to automatically deploy the output shared object to the Qt Creator application plugins directory.

The last thing we have to do is to add an environment variable to let the Qt Creator know where it will find the library that will link it to the final application. In the **Projects** tab, go through the following steps:

1. Open the **Details** window in **Build Environment**.
2. Click on the **Add** Button.
3. Type DYLD_LIBRARY_PATH in the <VARIABLE> field.
4. Type the path of the build directory in <VALUE> (you can copy and paste it from the section **General** | **Build directory**).

Implementing your OpenCV filters

Now that your development environment is ready, we can begin the fun part! We will implement three filters using OpenCV:

- FilterOriginal: This filter does nothing and returns the same picture (lazy!)
- FilterGrayscale: This filter converts a picture from color to grayscale
- FilterBlur: This filter smoothes the picture

The parent class of all these filters is Filter. Here is this abstract class:

```
//Filter.h
class Filter
{
public:
 Filter();
 virtual ~Filter();

 virtual QImage process(const QImage& image) = 0;
};

//Filter.cpp
Filter::Filter() {}
Filter::~Filter() {}
```

As you can see, process() is a pure abstract method. All filters will implement a specific behavior with this function. Let's begin with the simple FilterOriginal class. Here is FilterOriginal.h:

```
class FilterOriginal : public Filter
{
public:
 FilterOriginal();
 ~FilterOriginal();

 QImage process(const QImage& image) override;
};
```

This class inherits Filter and we override the process() function. The implementation is also really simple. Fill FilterOriginal.cpp with the following:

```
FilterOriginal::FilterOriginal() :
 Filter()
{
}

FilterOriginal::~FilterOriginal()
{
}

QImage FilterOriginal::process(const QImage& image)
{
 return image;
}
```

No modification is performed; we return the same picture. Now that the filter structure is clear, we can create FilterGrayscale. The .h/.cpp files are close to FilterOriginalFilter, so let's jump to the process() function of FilterGrayscale.cpp:

QImage FilterGrayscale::process(const QImage& image)

```
{
    // QImage => cv::mat
    cv::Mat tmp(image.height(),
                image.width(),
                CV_8UC4,
                (uchar*)image.bits(),
                image.bytesPerLine());
    cv::Mat resultMat;
    cv::cvtColor(tmp, resultMat, CV_BGR2GRAY);
    // cv::mat => QImage
```

```
QImage resultImage((const uchar *) resultMat.data,
                   resultMat.cols,
                   resultMat.rows,
                   resultMat.step,
                   QImage::Format_Grayscale8);
    return resultImage.copy();
}
```

In the Qt framework, we use the `QImage` class to manipulate pictures. In the OpenCV world, we use the `Mat` class, so the first step is to create a correct `Mat` object from the `QImage` source. OpenCV and Qt both handle many image formats. An image format describes the data bytes organization with information such as the following:

- `Channel count`: A grayscale picture only needs one channel (white intensity), while a color picture requires three channels (red, green, and blue). You will even need four channels to handle the opacity (alpha) pixel information.
- `Bit depth`: The number of bits used to store a pixel color.
- `Channel order`: The most common orders are RGB and BGR. Alpha can be placed before or after the color information.

For example, the OpenCV image format, `CV_8UC4`, means four channels of unsigned 8-bit, which is the perfect fit for an alpha color picture. In our case, we are using a compatible Qt and OpenCV image format to convert our `QImage` in `Mat`. Here is a little summary:

Qt		OpenCV	
Order	QImage	Order	cv::Mat
BGRX	Format_RGB32	BGRA	CV_8UC4
BGRA	Format_ARGB32		
RGBA	Format_RGBA8888		
RGB	Format_RGB888	BGR	CV_8UC3
Gray	Format_Grayscale8	Gray	CV_8UC1

Please note that some `QImage` class formats also depend on your platform endianness. The preceding table is for a little endian system. For OpenCV, the order is always the same: `BGRA`. It is not required in our project example, but you can swap blue and red channels as follows:

```
// with OpenCV
cv::cvtColor(mat, mat, CV_BGR2RGB);

// with Qt
QImage swapped = image.rgbSwapped();
```

OpenCV `Mat` and Qt `QImage` classes perform shallow construction/copy by default. This means that only metadata is really copied; the pixel data is shared. To create a deep copy of a picture, you must call the `copy()` function:

```
// with OpenCV
mat.clone();

// with Qt
image.copy();
```

We created a `Mat` class called `tmp` from the `QImage` class. Note that `tmp` is not a deep copy of `image`; they share the same data pointer. Then, we can call the OpenCV function to convert the picture from color to grayscale using `cv::cvtColor()`. Finally, we create a `QImage` class from the grayscale `resultMat` element. In that case too, `resultMat` and `resultImage` share the same data pointer. Once we're done, we return a deep copy of `resultImage`.

It is now time to implement the last filter. Here is the `process()` function of `FilterBlur.cpp`:

```
QImage FilterBlur::process(const QImage& image)
{
    // QImage => cv::mat
    cv::Mat tmp(image.height(),
                image.width(),
                CV_8UC4,
                (uchar*)image.bits(),
                image.bytesPerLine());
    int blur = 17;
    cv::Mat resultMat;
    cv::GaussianBlur(tmp,
                     resultMat,
                     cv::Size(blur, blur),
                     0.0,
                     0.0);
    // cv::mat => QImage
    QImage resultImage((const uchar *) resultMat.data,
                       resultMat.cols,
                       resultMat.rows,
                       resultMat.step,
                       QImage::Format_RGB32);
    return resultImage.copy();
}
```

The conversion from `QImage` to `Mat` is the same. The processing differs because we use the `cv::GaussianBlur()` OpenCV function to smooth the picture. The `blur` is the kernel size used by the Gaussian blur. You can increase this value to get a softer picture, but only use an odd and positive number. Finally, we convert the `Mat` to `QImage` and return a deep copy to the caller.

Designing the UI with FilterWidget

Fine. Our filter classes are implemented, and we can now create our custom widget. This widget will take in input, a source, and a thumbnail picture. Then the thumbnail is immediately processed to display a preview of the filter. If the user clicks on the widget, it will process the source picture and trigger a signal with the filtered picture. Keep in mind that this widget will later be dragged and dropped in the **Form Editor** of Qt Creator. That's why we will provide properties with getters and setters to select a filter from Qt Creator. Please create a new widget called `FilterWidget` using the **Qt Designer Form Class** template. The `FilterWidget.ui` is really simple:

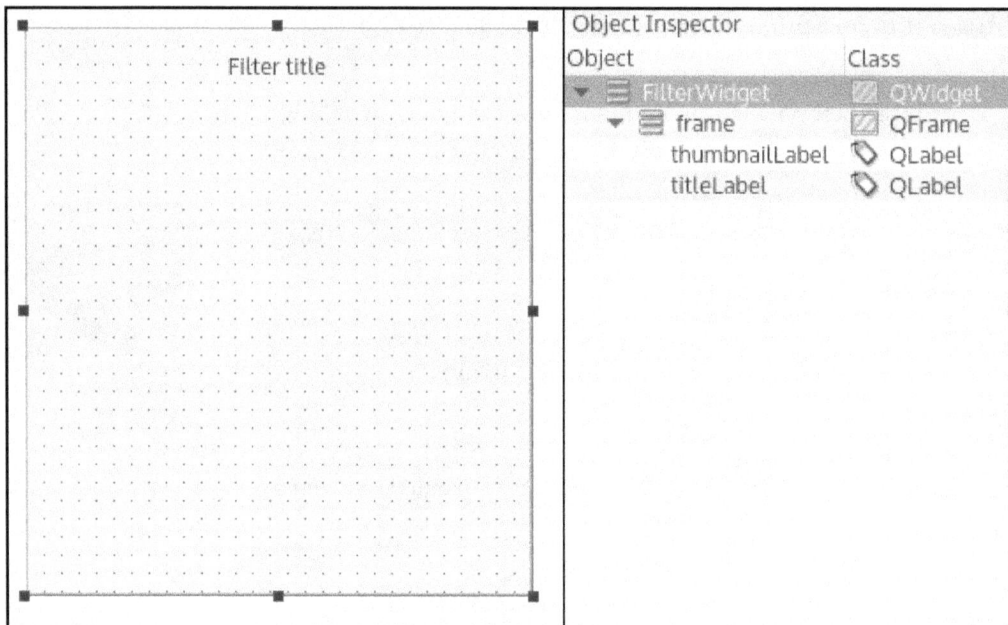

The `titleLabel` is a `QLabel` on top of the `QWidget`. Below, `thumbnailLabel` will display the filtered picture thumbnail. Let's switch to `FilterWidget.h`:

```
class FILTERPLUGINDESIGNERSHARED_EXPORT FilterWidget : public QWidget
{
    Q_OBJECT
    Q_ENUMS(FilterType)
    Q_PROPERTY(QString title READ title WRITE setTitle)
    Q_PROPERTY(FilterType filterType READ filterType WRITE setFilterType)
public:
    enum FilterType { Original, Blur, Grayscale };
    explicit FilterWidget(QWidget *parent = 0);
    ~FilterWidget();
    void process();
    void setSourcePicture(const QImage& sourcePicture);
    void updateThumbnail(const QImage& sourceThumbnail);
    QString title() const;
    FilterType filterType() const;
public slots:
    void setTitle(const QString& tile);
    void setFilterType(FilterType filterType);
signals:
    void pictureProcessed(const QImage& picture);
protected:
    void mousePressEvent(QMouseEvent*) override;
private:
    Ui::FilterWidget *ui;
    std::unique_ptr<Filter> mFilter;
    FilterType mFilterType;
    QImage mDefaultSourcePicture;
    QImage mSourcePicture;
    QImage mSourceThumbnail;
    QImage mFilteredPicture;
    QImage mFilteredThumbnail;
};
```

The top part defines all the available filter types with the `enumFilterType`. We also use the Qtproperty system to expose the widget title and the current filter type to the **Property Editor** of Qt Creator. The syntax is like this:

```
Q_PROPERTY(<type><name> READ <getter> WRITE <setter>)
```

Please note that exposing an enumeration requires it to be registered using the `Q_ENUM()` macro, so the **Property Editor** will display a combo box that allows you to choose the filter type from Qt Creator.

The middle part lists all functions, slots, and signals. The most notable is the `process()` function that will use the current filter to modify the source picture.
The `pictureProcessed()` signal will notify the application with the filtered picture.

The bottom part lists the picture and thumbnail `QImage` variables used in this class. In both cases, we handle both source and filtered pictures. The default source picture is an embedded picture in the plugin. This allows you to display a default preview when no thumbnail has been provided. The `mFilter` variable is a smart pointer to the current `Filter` class.

Let's switch to the implementation with `FilterWidget.cpp`:

```
FilterWidget::FilterWidget(QWidget *parent) :
    QWidget(parent),
    ui(new Ui::FilterWidget),
    mFilterType(Original),
    mDefaultSourcePicture(":/lenna.jpg"),
    mSourcePicture(),
    mSourceThumbnail(mDefaultSourcePicture.scaled(QSize(256, 256),
                    Qt::KeepAspectRatio,
                    Qt::SmoothTransformation)),
    mFilteredPicture(),
    mFilteredThumbnail()
{
    ui->setupUi(this);
    setFilterType(Original);
}
FilterWidget::~FilterWidget()
{
    delete ui;
}
```

Here are the constructor and the destructor. Please note that the default source picture loads an embedded picture of the gorgeous Lenna often used in image processing literature. The picture is in the resource file, `filter-plugin-designer.qrc`.
The `mSourceThumbnail` function is initialized with a scaled picture of Lenna. The constructor calls the `setFilterType()` function to initialize an `Original` filter by default. Here is the core `process()` function:

```
voidFilterWidget::process()
{
    mFilteredPicture = mFilter->process(mSourcePicture);
    emitpictureProcessed(mFilteredPicture);
}
```

The process() function is powerful, but really simple. We call process() of the current filter to update our filtered picture from the current source picture. Then we trigger the pictureProcessed() signal with the filtered picture. We can now add our QImage setters:

```
voidFilterWidget::setSourcePicture(constQImage&sourcePicture)
{
    mSourcePicture = sourcePicture;
}

voidFilterWidget::updateThumbnail(constQImage&sourceThumbnail)
{
    mSourceThumbnail = sourceThumbnail;
    mFilteredThumbnail = mFilter->process(mSourceThumbnail);
    QPixmappixmap = QPixmap::fromImage(mFilteredThumbnail);
    ui->thumbnailLabel->setPixmap(pixmap);
}
```

The setSourcePicture() function is a simple setter called by the application with a new source picture. The updateThumbnail() method will filter the new source thumbnail and display it. Let's add the setters used by Q_PROPERTY:

```
voidFilterWidget::setTitle(constQString& tile)
{
    ui->titleLabel->setText(tile);
}

voidFilterWidget::setFilterType(FilterWidget::FilterTypefilterType)
{
    if (filterType == mFilterType&&mFilter) {
        return;
    }
    mFilterType = filterType;

    switch (filterType) {
        case Original:
            mFilter = make_unique<FilterOriginal>();
            break;

        case Blur:
            mFilter = make_unique<FilterBlur>();
            break;

        case Grayscale:
            mFilter = make_unique<FilterGrayscale>();
            break;
```

```
        default:
            break;
    }

    updateThumbnail(mSourceThumbnail);
}
```

The `setTitle()` function is a simple setter used to customize the widget title. Let's talk about the `setFilterType()` function. As you can see, this function does not just update the current filter type, `mFilterType`. Depending on the type, the corresponding filter will be created. Do you remember the smart pointer from `Chapter 11`, *Dividing Your Project and Ruling Your Code*? Here we are using a `unique_ptr` pointer for the `mFilter` variable, so we can use `make_unique` instead of a `new` raw. The `FilterWidget` class takes the ownership of the `Filter` class, and we do not need to worry about the memory management. Upon the `make_unique` instruction, the old owned pointer (if there is any) will be automatically deleted.

Finally, we call the `updateThumbnail()` function to display a filtered thumbnail corresponding to the selected filter type. Here are the getters and the mouse event handler:

```
QStringFilterWidget::title() const
{
    returnui->titleLabel->text();
}

FilterWidget::FilterTypeFilterWidget::filterType() const
{
    returnmFilterType;
}

voidFilterWidget::mousePressEvent(QMouseEvent*)
{
    process();
}
```

The `title()` and `filterType()` functions are getters used by the Qt Property System. We override the `mousePressEvent()` function to call our `process()` function each time the user clicks on the widget.

Exposing your plugin to Qt Designer

The `FilterWidget` class is completed and ready to be used. We now have to register `FilterWidget` with the Qt Designer plugin system. This glue code is made using a child class of `QDesignerCustomWidgetInterface`.

Create a new C++ class named `FilterPluginDesigner` and update `FilterPluginDesigner.h` like so:

```
#include <QtUiPlugin/QDesignerCustomWidgetInterface>

class  FilterPluginDesigner : public QObject, public
QDesignerCustomWidgetInterface
{
    Q_OBJECT
    Q_PLUGIN_METADATA(IID
        "org.masteringqt.imagefilter.FilterWidgetPluginInterface")
    Q_INTERFACES(QDesignerCustomWidgetInterface)
public:
    FilterPluginDesigner(QObject* parent = 0);
};
```

The `FilterPlugin` class inherits from two classes:

- The `QObject` class, to rely on the Qt parenting system
- The `QDesignerCustomWidgetInterface` class to properly expose the `FilterWidget` information to the plugin system

The `QDesignerCustomWidgetInterface` class brings two new macros:

- The `Q_PLUGIN_METADATA()` macro annotates the class to indicate a unique name for our filter to the meta-object system
- The `Q_INTERFACES()` macro tells the meta-object system which interface the current class has implemented

Qt Designer is now able to detect our plugin. We now have to provide information about the plugin itself. Update `FilterPluginDesigner.h`:

```
class FilterPluginDesigner : public QObject, public
QDesignerCustomWidgetInterface
{
    ...
    FilterPluginDesigner(QObject* parent = 0);

    QStringname() const override;
    QStringgroup() const override;
    QStringtoolTip() const override;
    QStringwhatsThis() const override;
    QStringincludeFile() const override;
    QIconicon() const override;
    boolisContainer() const override;
    QWidget* createWidget(QWidget* parent) override;
    boolisInitialized() const override;
    void initialize(QDesignerFormEditorInterface* core) override;

private:
    boolmInitialized;
};
```

This is much less overwhelming than it looks. The body of each one of these functions usually takes a single line. Here is the implementation of the most straightforward functions:

```
QStringFilterPluginDesigner::name() const
{
    return "FilterWidget";
}

QStringFilterPluginDesigner::group() const
{
    return "Mastering Qt5";
}

QStringFilterPluginDesigner::toolTip() const
{
    return "A filtered picture";
}

QStringFilterPluginDesigner::whatsThis() const
{
    return "The filter widget applies an image effect";
}
```

```
QIconFilterPluginDesigner::icon() const
{
    returnQIcon(":/icon.jpg");
}

boolFilterPluginDesigner::isContainer() const
{
    return false;
}
```

As you can see, there isn't much to say about these functions. Most of them will simply return a `QString` value that will be displayed on the appropriate spot in the Qt Designer UI. We will focus only on the most interesting ones. Let's start with `includeFile()`:

```
QStringFilterPluginDesigner::includeFile() const
{
    return "FilterWidget.h";
}
```

This function will be called by `uic` (**User Interface Compiler**) to generate the header corresponding to a `.ui` file. Continuing with `createWidget()`:

```
QWidget* FilterPluginDesigner::createWidget(QWidget* parent)
{
    return new FilterWidget(parent);
}
```

This function makes the bridge between Qt Designer and `FilterWidget`. When you add the `FilterWidget` class in a `.ui` file, Qt Designer will call the `createWidget()` function to have an instance of the `FilterWidget` class and display its content. It also provides the `parent` element to which `FilterWidget` will be attached.

Let's finish with `initialize()`:

```
voidFilterPluginDesigner::initialize(QDesignerFormEditorInterface*)
{
    if (mInitialized)
        return;

    mInitialized = true;
}
```

Nothing much is done in this function. However, the `QDesignerFormEditorInterface*` parameter is worth some explanation. This pointer, provided by Qt Designer, gives access to a few of Qt Designer's components via functions:

- `actionEditor()`: This function is the action editor (bottom panel of the designer)
- `formWindowManager()`: This function is the interface that enables you to create a new form window
- `objectInspector()`: This function is the hierarchical representation of your layout (top right panel of the designer)
- `propertyEditor()`: This function is the list of all the editable properties of the currently selected widget (bottom right panel of the designer)
- `topLevel()`: This function is the top-level widget of the designer

If your widget plugin needs to intervene in any of these areas, this function is the entry point to customize the behavior of Qt Designer.

Using your Qt Designer plugin

Our custom plugin is now finished. Because we added a custom `Build` command to automatically deploy the filter-widget library, it should be visible in Qt Designer. The deploy path we specified is inside the Qt Creator directory. Qt Creator integrates Qt Designer via a plugin that displays the UI inside Qt Creator.

When Qt Creator starts, it will try to load every library available in its specific paths. This means that you have to restart Qt Creator each time you modify the plugin (if you want to see the result of your modifications in the designer).

To see the plugin in action, we now have to create the application project of the chapter. Create a **Qt Widgets Application** sub-project in the `ch07-image-filter` project named `image-filter`. In the wizard, let it generate the form, `MainWindow.ui`.

To properly use the plugin, just link the `filter-plugin-designer` library in `image-filter.pro` like so:

```
QT          += core gui

greaterThan(QT_MAJOR_VERSION, 4): QT += widgets

TARGET = image-filter
TEMPLATE = app

INCLUDEPATH += ../filter-plugin-designer

win32 {
    LIBS += -L$$(QTDIR)/../../Tools/QtCreator/bin/plugins/designer -
lfilter-plugin-designer
}

macx {
    LIBS += -L$$(QTDIR)/../../"QtCreator.app"/Contents/PlugIns/designer/ -
lfilter-plugin-designer
}

linux {
    LIBS += -L$$(QTDIR)/../../Tools/QtCreator/lib/Qt/plugins/designer/ -
lfilter-plugin-designer
}

SOURCES += main.cpp
        MainWindow.cpp

HEADERS   += MainWindow.h

FORMS     += MainWindow.ui
```

To have access to the headers of `filter-plugin-designer`, we simply add it to the `INCLUDEPATH` directory. Finally, the linker is instructed to link to the library we deployed in Qt Creator. This ensures that the same library is used by Qt Designer and by our application.

Open the `MainWindow.ui` file and scroll to the bottom of the **Widget box**. Lo and behold, you should see this:

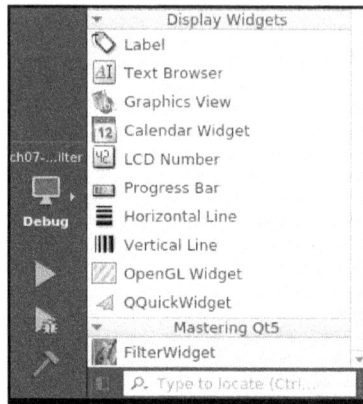

The `FilterWidget` plugin appears under the Mastering Qt5 section. It even displays the famous Lenna as a preview icon. If you do not see the `FilterWidget` plugin, then restart Qt Creator and make sure that the plugin is properly loaded. To check this (in the **Design** tab), go to **Tools | Form Editor | About Qt Designer Plugins**. This is what it should display:

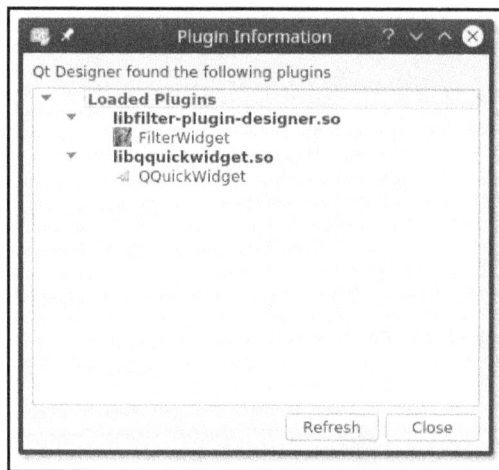

If the `FilterWidget` plugin does not appear in this list, you should check the Qt Creator plugin directory content (the path is stated in `image-filter.pro`).

Building the image-filter application

We can proceed to build the UI of the application. The idea is to open a picture from the filesystem and apply to it the various filters we developed in the `filter-designer-plugin` project. If you want to keep the result, you can save the resulting image.

We will start by designing the UI. Modify `MainWindow.ui` to look like this:

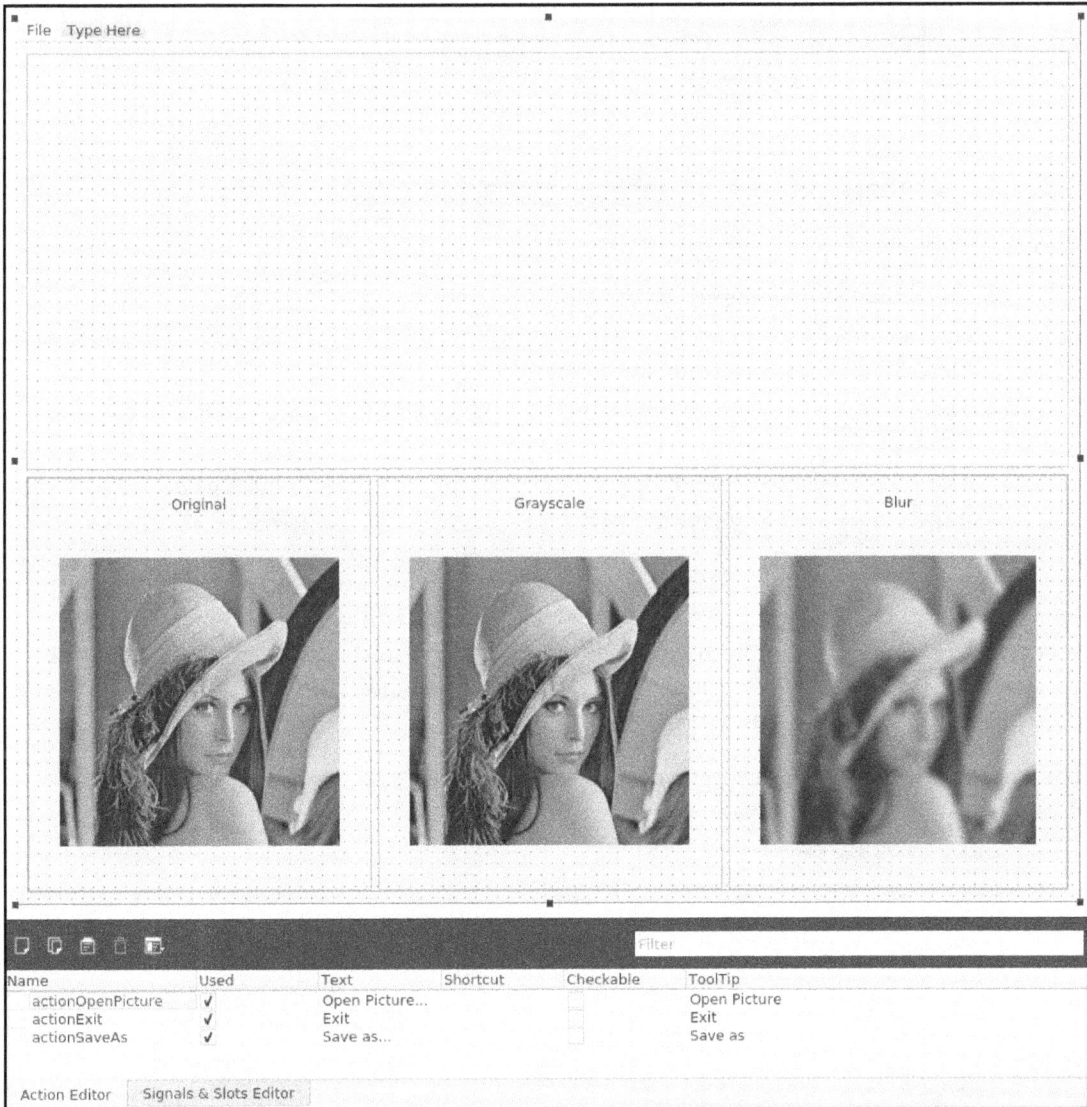

Here is the Object Inspector content to help you build this layout:

Object	Class
▼ MainWindow	QMainWindow
▼ ≣ centralWidget	QWidget
▼ ▯▯ filtersLayout	QHBoxLayout
filterWidgetBlur	FilterWidget
filterWidgetGrayscale	FilterWidget
filterWidgetOriginal	FilterWidget
▼ ≣ pictureFrame	QFrame
pictureLabel	QLabel
▼ menuBar	QMenuBar
▼ menuFile	QMenu
actionOpenPicture	QAction
actionSaveAs	QAction
actionExit	QAction

There are three elements of this UI:

- The menuFile element, which contains three possible actions: actionOpenPicture, actionExit, and actionSaveAs. You can see the details of these actions in the Action Editor window.
- The pictureLabel element, which will display the loaded picture in the empty top part.
- The filtersLayout element, which contains the three instances of our FilterWidget class in the bottom part.

As you add a FilterWidget class in filtersLayout, you can see that you can customize the title and the filterType in the **Property Editor** window. The preview will be automatically updated with the selected filter applied to our default picture. A dynamic preview like this is simply awesome, and you can foresee that your custom Qt Designer widgets can become quite powerful.

Let's implement the logic of our application. Update MainWindow.h like so:

```
#include <QMainWindow>
#include <QImage>
#include <QVector>

namespaceUi {
classMainWindow;
}

classFilterWidget;
```

```
classMainWindow : public QMainWindow
{
    Q_OBJECT

public:
    explicitMainWindow(QWidget *parent = 0);
    ~MainWindow();

    voidloadPicture();

private slots:
    voiddisplayPicture(constQImage& picture);

private:
    voidinitFilters();
    voidupdatePicturePixmap();

private:
    Ui::MainWindow *ui;
    QImagemSourcePicture;
    QImagemSourceThumbnail;
    QPixmapmCurrentPixmap;
    FilterWidget* mCurrentFilter;
    QVector<FilterWidget*>mFilters;
};
```

Here are some elements that we have to explain:

- mSourcePicture: This element is the loaded picture.
- mSourceThumbnail: This element is the generated thumbnail from mSourcePicture. To avoid wasting CPU cycles, mSourcePicture will be resized only once, and each of the FilterWidget instances will process this thumbnail rather than the full-resolution picture.
- mCurrentPixmap: This element is the currently displayed QPixmap in the pictureLabel widget.
- mCurrentFilter: This element is the currently applied filter. Each time the user clicks on a different FilterWidget, this pointer will be updated.
- mFilters: This element is a QVector of the FilterWidget class that we added to MainWindow.ui. It is only a helper, introduced to easily apply the same instructions to each FilterWidget class.

Now for the functions, we will limit ourselves to a broad overview. The details will be covered when we look at the implementation of each function:

- `loadPicture()`: This function triggers the whole pipeline. It will be called when the user clicks on `actionOpenPicture`.
- `initFilters()`: This function is in charge of initializing `mFilters`.
- `displayPicture()`: This function is the slot called by `mCurrentWidget::pictureProcessed()` to display the filtered picture.
- `updatePicturePixmap()`: This function handles the display of `mCurrentPixmap` inside `pictureLabel`.

Let's look at the `MainWindow` class's constructor implementation in `MainWindow.cpp`:

```
#include <QFileDialog>
#include <QPixmap>
#include <QDir>

#include "FilterWidget.h"

MainWindow::MainWindow(QWidget *parent) :
    QMainWindow(parent),
    ui(new Ui::MainWindow),
    mSourcePicture(),
    mSourceThumbnail(),
    mCurrentPixmap(),
    mCurrentFilter(nullptr),
    mFilters()
{
    ui->setupUi(this);
    ui->pictureLabel->setMinimumSize(1, 1);

    connect(ui->actionOpenPicture, &QAction::triggered,
        this, &MainWindow::loadPicture);
    connect(ui->actionExit, &QAction::triggered,
        this, &QMainWindow::close);
    initFilters();
}
```

We connect the `actionOpenPicture::triggered()` signal to our yet-to-be-implemented `loadPicture()` function. The `actionExit` is straightforward; it is simply connected to the `QMainWindow::close()` slot. Finally, `initFilter()` is called. Let's see its body:

```
voidMainWindow::initFilters()
{
```

```
    mFilters.push_back(ui->filterWidgetOriginal);
    mFilters.push_back(ui->filterWidgetBlur);
    mFilters.push_back(ui->filterWidgetGrayscale);

    for (inti = 0; i<mFilters.size(); ++i) {
        connect(mFilters[i], &FilterWidget::pictureProcessed,
                this, &MainWindow::displayPicture);
    }
    mCurrentFilter = mFilters[0];
}
```

Each `FilterWidget` instance is added to `mFilters`. We then proceed to connect the `pictureProcessed()` signal to the `MainWindow::displayPicture` instruction and `mCurrentFilter` is initialized to the original filter.

The class is now ready to load some pictures! This is the implementation of `loadPicture()`:

```
voidMainWindow::loadPicture()
{
    QString filename = QFileDialog::getOpenFileName(this,
                        "Open Picture",
                        QDir::homePath(),
                tr("Images (*.png *.jpg)"));
    if (filename.isEmpty()) {
        return;
    }
    mSourcePicture = QImage(filename);
    mSourceThumbnail = mSourcePicture.scaled(QSize(256, 256),
                        Qt::KeepAspectRatio,
Qt::SmoothTransformation);
    for (inti = 0; i<mFilters.size(); ++i) {
        mFilters[i]->setSourcePicture(mSourcePicture);
        mFilters[i]->updateThumbnail(mSourceThumbnail);
    }

    mCurrentFilter->process();
}
```

The `mSourcePicture` method is loaded using a `QFileDialog`, and `mSourceThumbnail` is generated from this input. Every `FilterWidget` class is updated with this new data and the `mCurrentFilter` element is triggered by calling its `process()` function.

When `FilterWidget::process()` is finished, it emits the `pictureProcessed()` signal, which is connected to our `displayPicture()` slot. Let's switch to this function:

```
voidMainWindow::displayPicture(constQImage& picture)
{
mCurrentPixmap = QPixmap::fromImage(picture);
updatePicturePixmap();
}
```

Nothing very fancy here: `mCurrentPixmap` is updated from the given picture and the `updatePicturePixmap()` function is in charge of updating the `pictureLabel` element. Here is the implementation of `updatePicturePixmap()`:

```
voidMainWindow::updatePicturePixmap()
{
    if (mCurrentPixmap.isNull()) {
        return;
    }
    ui->pictureLabel->setPixmap(
                mCurrentPixmap.scaled(ui->pictureLabel->size(),
                Qt::KeepAspectRatio,
                    Qt::SmoothTransformation));
}
```

This function simply creates a scaled version of `mCurrentPixmap` that fits inside `pictureLabel`.

The whole picture loading/filter processing is completed. If you run the application you should be able to load and modify your pictures. However, if you resize the window, you will see that the `pictureLabel` element does not scale very well.

To address this issue, we have to regenerate the scaled version of `mCurrentPixmap` each time the window is resized. Update `MainWindow` like so:

```
// In MainWindow.h
classMainWindow : public QMainWindow
{
    ...
    voidloadPicture();

protected:
    voidresizeEvent(QResizeEvent* event) override;
    ...
};

// In MainWindow.cpp
voidMainWindow::resizeEvent(QResizeEvent* /*event*/)
```

```
{
    updatePicturePixmap();
}
```

Here, the separation of `mCurrentPixmap` and the `pictureLabel` element's pixmap makes sense. Because we always generate the scaled version from the full-resolution `mCurrentPixmap`, we are sure that the resulting pixmap will look good.

The image-filter application would not be complete without the ability to save your filtered picture. This will not take much effort. Here is the updated version of `MainWindow.h`:

```
classMainWindow : public QMainWindow
{
    ...

private slots:
    voiddisplayPicture(constQImage& picture);
    voidsaveAsPicture();
    ...

private:
    Ui::MainWindow *ui;
    QImagemSourcePicture;
    QImagemSourceThumbnail;
    QImage&mFilteredPicture;
    ...
};
```

Here, we simply added a `saveAsPicture()` function that will take the `mFilteredPicture` element and save it to a file. The implementation in `MainWindow.cpp` should not blow your mind:

```
// In MainWindow.cpp
MainWindow::MainWindow(QWidget *parent) :
    QMainWindow(parent),
    ui(new Ui::MainWindow),
    mSourcePicture(),
    mSourceThumbnail(),
    mFilteredPicture(mSourcePicture),
    ...
{
    ui->setupUi(this);
    ui->actionSaveAs->setEnabled(false);
    ui->pictureLabel->setMinimumSize(1, 1);

    connect(ui->actionOpenPicture, &QAction::triggered,
            this, &MainWindow::loadPicture);
```

```
        connect(ui->actionSaveAs, &QAction::triggered,
                this, &MainWindow::saveAsPicture);
    ...
}

voidMainWindow::loadPicture()
{
    ...
    if (filename.isEmpty()) {
        return;
    }
    ui->actionSaveAs->setEnabled(true);
    ...
}

voidMainWindow::displayPicture(constQImage& picture)
{
    mFilteredPicture = picture;
    mCurrentPixmap = QPixmap::fromImage(picture);
    updatePicturePixmap();
}

voidMainWindow::saveAsPicture()
{
    QString filename = QFileDialog::getSaveFileName(this,
            "Save Picture",
            QDir::homePath(),
            tr("Images (*.png *.jpg)"));
    if (filename.isEmpty()) {
        return;
    }
    mFilteredPicture.save(filename);
}
```

The code snippet is long, but not very complex. The actionSaveAs function is enabled
only when a picture is loaded. When the picture has been processed, mFilteredPicture is
updated with the given picture. Because it is a reference, it costs absolutely nothing to store
this filtered picture.

Finally, the saveAsPicture() function asks the user for a path and saves it using
the QImage API, which tries to deduce the picture type based on the file extension.

Summary

In this chapter, you learned how to integrate a third-party library with each desktop OS (Windows, Linux, and Mac). We chose the OpenCV library, which has been included in a custom Qt Designer plugin, and which can display a live preview of your image processing result in Qt Designer. We created an image filtering application that can open pictures, apply filters to them, and save the result on your machine.

We had a good look at how you can integrate third-party libraries and how to make a Qt Designer plugin. In the next chapter, we will push things forward by making the `image-filter` application ready to load filter plugins that could be implemented by third-party developers. To make things even cooler, we will cover the Qt animation framework to make the `image-filter` more spectacular.

Animations - Its Alive, Alive!

16

In the previous chapter, you learned how to create a custom Qt Designer plugin. This chapter will push things further and teach you how to create a distributable Software Development Kit (SDK) to third-party developers, how the plugin system works with Qt, and how to make your application more attractive using fancy animations.

The example project will be a reimplementation of the project from Chapter 15, *Third-Party Libraries Without a Headache*. You will build the same image processing application, but with the ability to import the filters from plugins.

This chapter will teach you how to do the following:

- Create an SDK using the Qt Plugin system
- Implement custom plugins using the SDK
- Factorize build tasks using .pri
- Dynamically load plugins in your final application
- Understand the Qt Animation framework
- Use simple, sequential, and parallel animations
- Apply custom effects using QPropertyAnimation and QGraphics effects

Preparing an SDK

Before diving into the code, we have to take a moment to reflect on how we are going to structure it. This chapter has two goals:

- Cover the Qt Plugin system in more depth
- Study and integrate the Qt Animation Framework

The first part of the chapter will focus on the plugin system. What we aim to do is provide a way to build plugins that can be integrated in our application to third-party developers. These plugins should be dynamically loaded. The application will be a direct offspring of the example project from Chapter 15, *Third-Party Libraries Without a Headache*. The features will be exactly the same, except it will be using this new plugin system and will have fancy animations.

The structure of the project will be as follows:

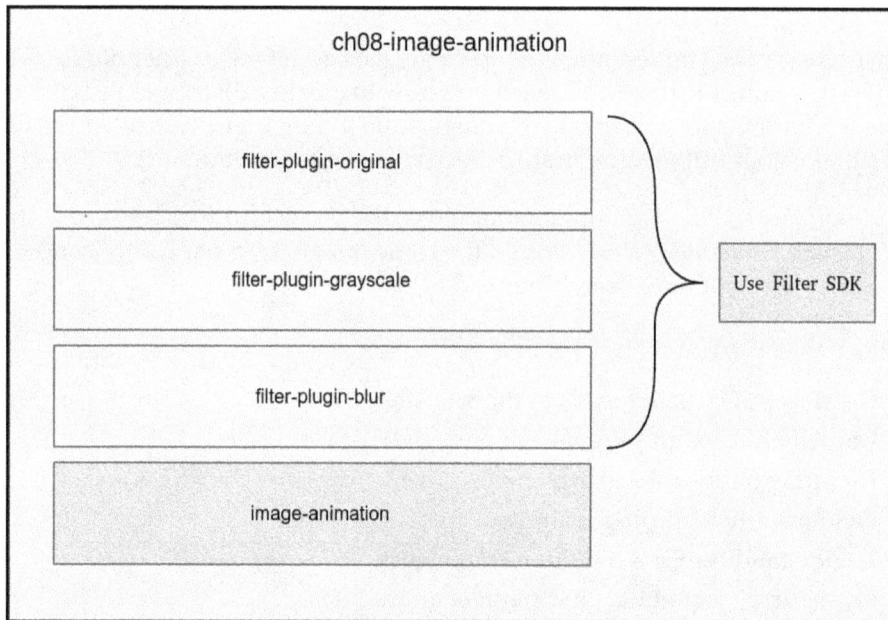

The parent project is ch08-image-animation, which is composed of the following:

- filter-plugin-original: A library project, which is the implementation of the original filter
- filter-plugin-grayscale: A library project, which is the implementation of the grayscale filter
- filter-plugin-blur: A library project, which is the implementation of the blur filter
- image-animation: A Qt Widgets application, which will load the plugins needed to display them and make it possible to apply each one to a loaded picture

We will develop each one of these plugins, but keep in mind that they might have been created by a third-party developer. To achieve this openness, an SDK will be available for each plugin. This SDK relies on the Qt Plugin system.

It is crucial to think about what should be handled by the plugin. Our application is an image processing piece of software. We chose to limit the responsibility of the plugin to the picture processing part, but this is definitely a design choice.

Another approach could have been to let the plugin developer provide its own UI to configure the plugin (for example, to vary the intensity of the blur). In this chapter, we have kept it simple by focusing only on the plugin development itself. It is really up to you and how you want to design your application. By opening up the range of what the plugin can do, you also increase the burden for the plugin developer. There is always a trade-off; giving more choice tends to increase the complexity. It is a well-known fact that we developers are a bunch of lazy people. At least, we want to be lazy while the computer is working for us.

We will start by building the SDK that will be deployed in each plugin. Execute the following steps:

1. Create a **Subdirs project** named `ch08-image-animation` (do not add a sub-project at the end of the wizard).
2. In your filesystem explorer, open the `ch08-image-animation` directory and create an `sdk` directory.
3. Inside `sdk`, create an empty `Filter.h` file.

Our SDK will consist of a single file, `Filter.h`, the interface (or header) that should be implemented with each plugin. Each plugin is responsible for returning the modified picture according to its desired features. Because this SDK is not linked to any particular project, we will simply display it in Qt Creator under the special folder **Other files**. To do so, update `ch08-image-animation.pro`:

```
TEMPLATE = subdirs

CONFIG += c++14

OTHER_FILES += \
        sdk/Filter.h
```

After ch08-image-animation.pro has been parsed by Qt Creator, you should see the following in the **Projects** tab:

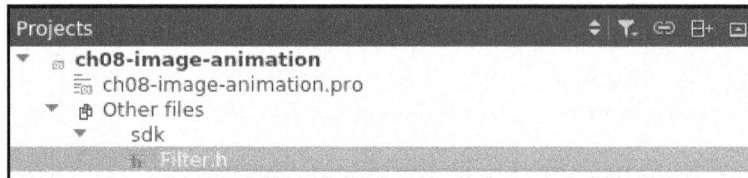

The Filter.h file is available at the parent project level. As a result, it will be easier to factorize the SDK plumbing code between our various plugins. Let's implement Filter.h:

```
#include <QImage>

class Filter
{
public:
    virtual ~Filter() {}
    virtual QString name() const = 0;
    virtual QImage process(const QImage& image) = 0;
};

#define Filter_iid "org.masteringqt.imageanimation.filters.Filter"
Q_DECLARE_INTERFACE(Filter, Filter_iid)
```

Let's break down this interface: a Filter subclass must provide a name by implementing name() and returning a processed image when implementing process(). As you can see, Filter.h is indeed very close to the version seen in Chapter 15, *Third-Party Libraries Without a Headache*.

However, the really new stuff comes right after the class definition:

```
#define Filter_iid "org.masteringqt.imageanimation.filters.Filter"
Q_DECLARE_INTERFACE(Filter, Filter_iid)
```

The Filter_iid is a unique identifier to let Qt know the interface name. This will be enforced on the implementer side, which will also have to state this identifier.

> **TIP**
>
> For a real-world use case, you should add a version number to this unique identifier. This will let you properly handle the versioning of your SDK and the attached plugins.

The Q_DECLARE_INTERFACE macro associates the class to the given identifier. It will give Qt the ability to check that the loaded plugin can be safely casted to the Filter type.

> **TIP**
>
> In production code, it is safer to declare your interfaces inside a namespace. You never know the code environment in which your SDK will be deployed. This, way, you avoid potential name collision. If you do declare in a namespace, make sure that the Q_DECLARE_INTERFACE macro is outside the namespace scope.

Creating your plugins

The SDK was painless to create. We can now proceed to create our first plugin. We already know that all our plugins will include the SDK we just completed. Fortunately, this can be easily factorized in a .pri file (PRoject Include). A .pri file behaves exactly like a .pro file; the only difference is that it is intended to be included inside .pro files.

In the ch08-image-animation directory, create a file named plugins-common.pri that contains the following code:

```
INCLUDEPATH += $$PWD/sdk
DEPENDPATH += $$PWD/sdk
```

This file will be included in each .pro plugin. It aims to tell the compiler where it can find the headers of the SDK and where to look to resolve dependencies between headers and sources. This will enhance the modification detection and properly compile the sources when needed.

To see this file in the project, we have to add it to the OTHER_FILES macro in ch08-image-animation.pro:

```
OTHER_FILES +=
            sdk/Filter.h
            plugins-common.pri
```

The most straightforward plugin to build is filter-plugin-original as it does not perform any specific processing on the image. Let's create this plugin with the following steps:

1. Create a new **Subproject** in ch08-image-animation.
2. Select **Library | C++ Library | Choose...**.

3. Choose a **Shared Library**, name it `filter-plugin-original`, and then click on **Next**.
4. Select **QtCore** and go to **QtWidgets** | **Next**.
5. Name the created class `FilterOriginal` and click on **Next**.
6. Add it as a **subproject** to `ch08-image-animation` then click on **Finish**.

Qt Creator creates a lot of boilerplate code for us, but in this case, we do not need it. Update `filter-plugin-original.pro` like so:

```
QT        += core widgets

TARGET = $$qtLibraryTarget(filter-plugin-original)
TEMPLATE = lib
CONFIG += plugin

SOURCES +=
    FilterOriginal.cpp

HEADERS +=
    FilterOriginal.h

include(../plugins-common.pri)
```

We start by specifying that the `TARGET` should be properly named according to the OS convention with `$$qtLibraryTarget()`. The `CONFIG` property adds the `plugin` directive, which tells the generated `Makefile` to include the necessary instructions to compile a dll/so/dylib (pick your OS).

We removed the unnecessary `DEFINES` and `FilterOriginal_global.h`. Nothing specific to the plugin should be exposed to the caller, and therefore, there is no need to handle the symbol export.

We can now proceed to `FilterOriginal.h`:

```
#include <QObject>

#include <Filter.h>

class FilterOriginal : public QObject, Filter
{
    Q_OBJECT
    Q_PLUGIN_METADATA(IID "org.masteringqt.imageanimation.filters.Filter")
    Q_INTERFACES(Filter)

public:
```

```
    FilterOriginal(QObject* parent = 0);
    ~FilterOriginal();

    QString name() const override;
    QImage process(const QImage& image) override;
};
```

The `FilterOriginal` class must first inherit `QObject`; when the plugin will be loaded, it will first be a `QObject` class before being casted to the real type, `Filter`.

The `Q_PLUGIN_METADATA` macro is stated to export the proper implemented interface identifier to Qt. It annotates the class to let the Qt metasystem know about it. We meet the unique identifier we defined in `Filter.h` again.

The `Q_INTERFACES` macro tells the Qt metaobject system which interface the class implements.

Finally, the `FilterOriginal.cpp` barely deserves to be printed:

```
FilterOriginal::FilterOriginal(QObject* parent) :
    QObject(parent)
{
}

FilterOriginal::~FilterOriginal()
{
}

QString FilterOriginal::name() const
{
    return "Original";
}

QImage FilterOriginal::process(const QImage& image)
{
    return image;
}
```

As you can see, its implementation is a no-op. The only thing we added to the version from `Chapter 15`, *Third-Party Libraries Without a Headache*, is the `name()` function, which returns `Original`.

We will now implement the grayscale filter. As we did in `Chapter 15`, *Third-Party Libraries Without a Headache*, we will rely on the OpenCV library to process the picture. The same can be said for the following plugin, the blur.

Since these two projects have their own .pro file, you can already foresee that the OpenCV linking will be the same. This is a perfect use-case for a .pri file.

Inside the ch08-image-animation directory, create a new file called plugins-common-opencv.pri. Do not forget to add it to OTHER_FILES in ch08-image-animation.pro:

```
OTHER_FILES +=
            sdk/Filter.h
            plugins-common.pri
            plugins-common-opencv.pri
```

Here is the content of plugins-common-opencv.pri:

```
windows {
    INCLUDEPATH += $$(OPENCV_HOME)/../../include
    LIBS += -L$$(OPENCV_HOME)/lib
        -lopencv_core2413
        -lopencv_imgproc2413
}

linux {
    CONFIG += link_pkgconfig
    PKGCONFIG += opencv
}

macx {
    INCLUDEPATH += /usr/local/Cellar/opencv/2.4.13/include/

    LIBS += -L/usr/local/lib
        -lopencv_core
        -lopencv_imgproc
}
```

The content of plugins-common-opencv.pri is a direct copy of what we made in Chapter 15, *Third-Party Libraries Without a Headache*.

All the plumbing is now ready; we can now go ahead with the filter-plugin-grayscale project. As with filter-plugin-original, we will build it the following way:

1. Create a **C++ Library Subproject** of ch08-image-animation with the **Shared Library** type.
2. Create a class named FilterGrayscale.
3. In the **Required Modules**, select **QtCore** and **QWidgets**.

Here is the updated version of `filter-plugin-grayscale.pro`:

```
QT          += core widgets

TARGET = $$qtLibraryTarget(filter-plugin-grayscale)
TEMPLATE = lib
CONFIG += plugin

SOURCES +=
    FilterGrayscale.cpp

HEADERS +=
    FilterGrayscale.h

include(../plugins-common.pri)
include(../plugins-common-opencv.pri)
```

The content is very much like `filter-plugin-original.pro`. We only added `plugins-common-opencv.pri` to let our plugin link with OpenCV.

As for `FilterGrayscale`, the header is exactly like `FilterOriginal.h`. Here are the relevant pieces on `FilterGrayscale.cpp`:

```
#include <opencv/cv.h>

// Constructor & Destructor here
...

QString FilterOriginal::name() const
{
    return "Grayscale";
}

QImage FilterOriginal::process(const QImage& image)
{
    // QImage => cv::mat
    cv::Mat tmp(image.height(),
                image.width(),
                CV_8UC4,
                (uchar*)image.bits(),
                image.bytesPerLine());

    cv::Mat resultMat;
    cv::cvtColor(tmp, resultMat, CV_BGR2GRAY);

    // cv::mat => QImage
    QImage resultImage((const uchar *) resultMat.data,
                        resultMat.cols,
```

```
                         resultMat.rows,
                         resultMat.step,
                         QImage::Format_Grayscale8);
        return resultImage.copy();
    }
```

The inclusion of `plugins-common-opencv.pri` lets us properly include the `cv.h` header.

The last plugin we will implement is the blur plugin. Once again, create a **C++ Library Subproject** and create the `FilterBlur` class. The project structure and the content of the `.pro` file are the same. Here is `FilterBlur.cpp`:

```cpp
QString FilterOriginal::name() const
{
    return "Blur";
}

QImage FilterOriginal::process(const QImage& image)
{
    // QImage => cv::mat
    cv::Mat tmp(image.height(),
                image.width(),
                CV_8UC4,
                (uchar*)image.bits(),
                image.bytesPerLine());

    int blur = 17;
    cv::Mat resultMat;
    cv::GaussianBlur(tmp,
                resultMat,
                cv::Size(blur, blur),
                0.0,
                0.0);

    // cv::mat => QImage
    QImage resultImage((const uchar *) resultMat.data,
                resultMat.cols,
                resultMat.rows,
                resultMat.step,
                QImage::Format_RGB32);
    return resultImage.copy();
}
```

The amount of blur is hard-coded at `17`. In a production application, it could have been compelling to make this amount variable from the application.

> **TIP**
>
> If you want to push the project further, try to include a layout in the SDK that contains a way to configure the plugin properties.

Loading your plugins dynamically

We will now deal with the application loading these plugins:

1. Create a new **Subproject** inside `ch08-image-animation`.
2. Select the type **Qt Widgets Application**.
3. Name it `image-animation` and accept the default **Class Information settings**.

We have a few last things to do in the `.pro` files. First, `image-animation` will try to load the plugins from somewhere in its output directory. Because each filter plugin project is independent, its output directory is separated from `image-animation`. Thus, each time you modify a plugin, you will have to copy yourself the compiled shared library inside the proper `image-animation` directory. This works to make it available to the `image-animation` application, but we are lazy developers, right?

We can automate this by updating `plugins-common-pri` like so:

```
INCLUDEPATH += $$PWD/sdk
DEPENDPATH += $$PWD/sdk

windows {
    CONFIG(debug, debug|release) {
        target_install_path = $$OUT_PWD/../image-animation/debug/plugins/
    } else {
        target_install_path = $$OUT_PWD/../image-animation/release/plugins/
    }

} else {
    target_install_path = $$OUT_PWD/../image-animation/plugins/
}

# Check Qt file 'spec_post.prf' for more information about
'$$QMAKE_MKDIR_CMD'
createPluginsDir.path = $$target_install_path
createPluginsDir.commands = $$QMAKE_MKDIR_CMD $$createPluginsDir.path
```

```
INSTALLS += createPluginsDir

target.path = $$target_install_path
INSTALLS += target
```

In a nutshell, the output library is deployed in the output `image-animation/plugins` directory. Windows has a different output project structure; that is why we have to have a platform-specific section.

Even better, the `plugins` directory is automatically created with the instruction `createPluginsDir.commands = $$QMAKE_MKDIR_CMD $$createPluginsDir.path`. Instead of using a system command (`mkdir`), we have to use the special `$$QMAKE_MKDIR_CMD` command. Qt will then replace it with the correct shell command (depending on your OS) to create the directory only if it does not already exist. Do not forget to add the `make install` build step to execute this task!

The last thing to do in the `.pro` files concerns `image-animation`. The application will manipulate `Filter` instances. As a consequence, it needs to access the SDK. Add the following to `image-animation.pro`:

```
INCLUDEPATH += $$PWD/../sdk
DEPENDPATH += $$PWD/../sdk
```

Fasten your seatbelt. We will now load our freshly baked plugins. In `image-animation`, create a new class named `FilterLoader`. Here is the `FilterLoader.h` content:

```cpp
#include <memory>
#include <vector>

#include <Filter.h>

class FilterLoader
{

public:
    FilterLoader();
    void loadFilters();

    const std::vector<std::unique_ptr<Filter>>& filters() const;

private:
    std::vector<std::unique_ptr<Filter>> mFilters;
};
```

This class is responsible for loading the plugins. Once again, we rely on C++11 smart pointers with `unique_ptr` to explicate the ownership of the `Filter` instances. The `FilterLoader` class will be the owner with `mFilters` and provides a getter to the `vector` with `filters()`.

Note that `filter()` returns a `const&` to the `vector`. This semantic brings two benefits:

- The reference makes sure that the `vector` is not copied. Without it, the compiler would have barked something like "`FilterLoader` is not the owner anymore of `mFilters` content!" at us. Of course, because it deals with C++ templates, the compiler error would have looked rather like an astounding insult to the English language.
- The `const` keyword makes sure that the `vector` type cannot be modified by callers.

Now we can create the `FilterLoader.cpp`: file:

```
#include "FilterLoader.h"

#include <QApplication>
#include <QDir>
#include <QPluginLoader>

FilterLoader::FilterLoader() :
    mFilters()
{
}

void FilterLoader::loadFilters()
{
    QDir pluginsDir(QApplication::applicationDirPath());
#ifdef Q_OS_MAC
    pluginsDir.cdUp();
    pluginsDir.cdUp();
    pluginsDir.cdUp();
#endif
    pluginsDir.cd("plugins");

    for(QString fileName: pluginsDir.entryList(QDir::Files)) {
        QPluginLoader pluginLoader(
                pluginsDir.absoluteFilePath(fileName));
        QObject* plugin = pluginLoader.instance();
        if (plugin) {
            mFilters.push_back(std::unique_ptr<Filter>(
                    qobject_cast<Filter*>(plugin)
            ));
```

```
        }
    }
}

const std::vector<std::unique_ptr<Filter>>& FilterLoader::filters() const
{
    return mFilters;
}
```

The meat of the class lies in `loadFilter()`. We start by moving in the `plugins` directory with `pluginsDir`, located in the output directory of `image-animation`. A special case is handled for the Mac platform: `QApplication::applicationDirPath()` returns a path inside the bundle of the generated application. The only way to get out is to climb our way up three times with the `cdUp()` instruction.

For each `fileName` in this directory, we try to load a `QPluginLoader` loader. A `QPluginLoader` provides access to a Qt plugin. It is the cross-platform way to load a shared library. Moreover, the `QPluginLoader` loader has the following benefits:

- It checks that the plugin is linked with the same version of Qt as the host application
- It simplifies the loading of the plugin by providing direct access to the plugin via `instance()` rather than relying on C functions

We then proceed to try to load the plugin using `pluginLoader.instance()`. This will try to load the root component of the plugin. In our case, the root component is either `FilerOriginal`, `FilterGrayscale`, or `FilterBlur`. This function always returns a `QObject*`; if the plugin could not be loaded, it returns 0. This is the reason why we inherited the `QObject` class in our custom plugins.

The call to `instance()` implicitly tries to load the plugin. Once this has been done, the `QPluginLoader` does not handle the memory of the `plugin`. From here, we cast the plugin to `Filter*` using `qobject_cast()`.

The `qobject_cast()` function behaves similarly to the standard C++ `dynamic_cast()`; the difference is that it does not require **RTTI (runtime type information)**.

Last but not least, the `Filter*` casted `plugin` is wrapped inside a `unique_ptr` and added to `mFilters` vector.

Using the plugins inside the application

Now that the plugins are properly loaded, they have to be reachable from the UI of the application. To do so, we are going to take some inspiration (shameless stealing) from the FilterWidget class of Chapter 15, *Third-Party Libraries Without a Headache*.

Create a new Qt Designer **Form Class** using the **Widget** template named FilterWidget. The FilterWidget.ui file is exactly the same as the one completed in Chapter 15, *Third-Party Libraries Without a Headache*.

Create the FilterWidget.h file like this:

```cpp
#include <QWidget>
#include <QImage>

namespace Ui {
class FilterWidget;
}

class Filter;

class FilterWidget : public QWidget
{
    Q_OBJECT

public:
    explicit FilterWidget(Filter& filter, QWidget *parent = 0);
    ~FilterWidget();

    void process();

    void setSourcePicture(const QImage& sourcePicture);
    void setSourceThumbnail(const QImage& sourceThumbnail);
    void updateThumbnail();

    QString title() const;

signals:
    void pictureProcessed(const QImage& picture);

protected:
    void mousePressEvent(QMouseEvent*) override;

private:
    Ui::FilterWidget *ui;
    Filter& mFilter;
```

```
        QImage mDefaultSourcePicture;
        QImage mSourcePicture;
        QImage mSourceThumbnail;

        QImage mFilteredPicture;
        QImage mFilteredThumbnail;
};
```

Overall, we trimmed everything concerning the Qt Designer plugin and simply passed the `mFilter` value by reference to the constructor. The `FilterWidget` class is not the owner of the `Filter` anymore; it is rather the client that calls it. Remember that the owner of `Filter` (aka the plugin) is `FilterLoader`.

The other modification is the new `setThumbnail()` function. It should be called in place of the old `updateThumbnail()`. The new `updateThumbnail()` now only performs the thumbnail processing and does not touch the source thumbnail. This division is done to prepare the work for the coming animation section. The thumbnail update will be done only once the animation has been finished.

Please refer to the source code of the chapter to see `FilterWidget.cpp`.

All the low layers have been completed. The next step is to fill `MainWindow`. Once again, it follows the same pattern we covered in Chapter 15, *Third-Party Libraries Without a Headache*. The sole difference with `MainWindow.ui` is that `filtersLayout` is empty. Obviously, the plugin is loaded dynamically, so we have nothing to put inside it at compile time.

Let's cover `MainWindow.h`:

```
#include <QMainWindow>
#include <QImage>
#include <QVector>

#include "FilterLoader.h"

namespace Ui {
class MainWindow;
}

class FilterWidget;

class MainWindow : public QMainWindow
```

```
{
    Q_OBJECT

public:
    explicit MainWindow(QWidget *parent = 0);
    ~MainWindow();

    void loadPicture();

protected:
    void resizeEvent(QResizeEvent* event) override;

private slots:
    void displayPicture(const QImage& picture);
    void saveAsPicture();

private:
    void initFilters();
    void updatePicturePixmap();

private:
    Ui::MainWindow *ui;
    QImage mSourcePicture;
    QImage mSourceThumbnail;
    QImage& mFilteredPicture;
    QPixmap mCurrentPixmap;

    FilterLoader mFilterLoader;
    FilterWidget* mCurrentFilter;
    QVector<FilterWidget*> mFilters;
};
```

The only notable thing is the addition of `mFilterLoader` as a member variable. In `MainWindow.cpp`, we will focus on the changes only:

```
void MainWindow::initFilters()
{
    mFilterLoader.loadFilters();

    auto& filters = mFilterLoader.filters();
    for(auto& filter : filters) {
        FilterWidget* filterWidget = new FilterWidget(*filter);
        ui->filtersLayout->addWidget(filterWidget);
        connect(filterWidget, &FilterWidget::pictureProcessed,
                this, &MainWindow::displayPicture);
        mFilters.append(filterWidget);
    }
```

```
        if (mFilters.length() > 0) {
            mCurrentFilter = mFilters[0];
        }
    }
```

The `initFilters()` function does not load the filters from the `ui` content. Rather, it starts by calling the `mFilterLoader.loadFilters()` function to dynamically load the plugins from the `plugins` directory.

After that, an `auto&` filter is assigned with `mFilterLoader.filters()`. Note that it is much more readable to use `auto` keyword. The real type is `std::vector<std::unique_ptr<Filter>>&`, which looks more like a cryptic incantation than a simple object type.

For each of these filters, we create a `FilterWidget*` and pass it the reference of the `filter`. Here, `filter` is effectively a `unique_ptr`. The people behind C++11 wisely modified the dereferencing operator, making it transparent to the new `FilterWidget(*filter)`. The combination of the `auto` keyword and the overload of the `->` operator, or the dereference operator, makes the use of new C++ features much more enjoyable.

Look at the for loop. For each `filter` we do the following tasks:

1. Create a `FilterWidget` template.
2. Add the `FilterWidget` template to the `filtersLayout` children.
3. Connect the `FilterWidget::pictureProcessed` signal to the `MainWindow::displayPicture` slot.
4. Add the new `FilterWidget` template to the `QVectormFilters`.

In the end, the first `FilterWidget` is selected.

The only other modification to `MainWindow.cpp` is the implementation of `loadPicture()`:

```
void MainWindow::loadPicture()
{
    ...
    for (int i = 0; i <mFilters.size(); ++i) {
        mFilters[i]->setSourcePicture(mSourcePicture);
        mFilters[i]->setSourceThumbnail(mSourceThumbnail);
```

```
        mFilters[i]->updateThumbnail();
    }
    mCurrentFilter->process();
}
```

The updateThumbnail() function has been split into two functions, and here is where it is used.

The application can now be tested. You should be able to execute it and see the dynamic plugins loaded and displaying the processed default Lenna picture.

Discovering the Animation Framework

Your application works like a charm. It is now time to look at how we can make it jump and move, or, in a word, live. The Qt Animation Framework can be used to create and start animations of Qt properties. The property value will be smoothly interpolated by an internal global timer handle by Qt. You can animate anything as long as it is a Qt property. You can even create a property for your own object using Q_PROPERTY. If you forgot about Q_PROPERTY, please refer to Chapter 15, *Third-Party Libraries Without a Headache*.

Three main classes are provided to build animations:

- QPropertyAnimation: This class animates one Qt property animation
- QParallelAnimationGroup: This class animates multiple animations in parallel (all the animations start together)
- QSequentialAnimationGroup: This class animates multiple animations in sequence (the animations run one by one in a defined order)

All those classes inherit QAbstractAnimation. Here is a diagram from the official Qt documentation:

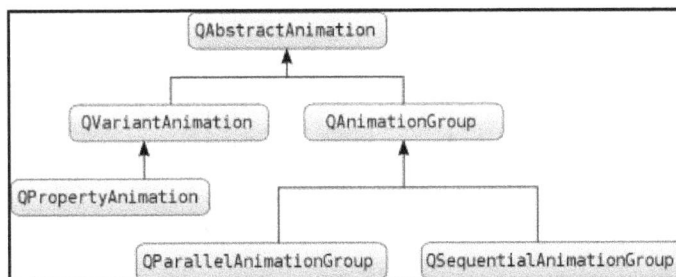

Please notice that `QAbstractAnimation`, `QVariantAnimation`, and `QAnimationGroup` are abstract classes. Here is a simple example of a Qt animation:

```
QLabel label;
QPropertyAnimation animation;

animation.setTargetObject(&label);
animation.setPropertyName("geometry");
animation.setDuration(4000);
animation.setStartValue(QRect(0, 0, 150, 50));
animation.setEndValue(QRect(300, 200, 150, 50));
animation.start();
```

The preceding snippet moves a `QLabel` label from the 0 x 0 position to 300 x 200 in four seconds. The first thing to do is to define the target object and its property. In our case, the target object is `label` and we want to animate the property called `geometry`. Then, we set the animation duration in milliseconds: `4000` milliseconds for four seconds. Finally, we can decide the start and end values of the `geometry` property, which is a `QRect`, defined like this:

```
QRect(x, y, width, height)
```

The `label` object starts with the 0 x 0 position and ends with 300 x 200. In this example, the size is fixed (150 x 50), but you can also animate the width and the height if you want.

Finally, we call the `start()` function to begin the animation. In four seconds, the animation smoothly moves the label from the 0 x 0 position to 300 x 200. By default, the animation uses a linear interpolation to provide intermediate values, so, after two seconds, the `label` will be at the 150 x 100 position. The linear interpolation of the value looks like the following schema:

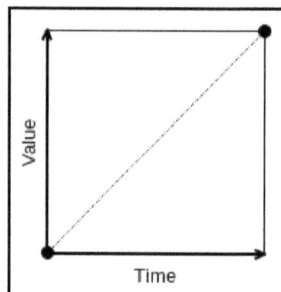

In our case, the `label` object will move with a constant speed from the start to the end position. An easing function is a mathematical function that describes the evolution of a value over time. The easing curve is the visual representation of the mathematical function. The default linear interpolation is a good start, but Qt provides plenty of easing curves to control the speed behavior of your animation. Here is the updated example:

```
QLabel label;
QPropertyAnimation animation(&label, "geometry");
animation.setDuration(4000);
animation.setStartValue(QRect(0, 0, 150, 50));
animation.setEndValue(QRect(300, 200, 150, 50));
animation.setEasingCurve(QEasingCurve::InCirc);
animation.start();
```

You can set the target object and the property name directly using the `QPropertyAnimation` constructor. As a result, we removed the `setTargetObject()` and `setPropertyName()` functions. After that, we use `setEasingCurve()` to specify a curve for this animation. The `InCirc` looks like the following:

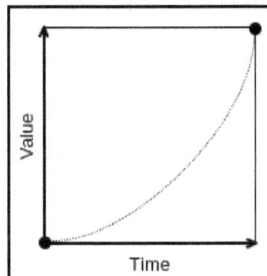

With this easing curve, the label starts to move really slowly but accelerates progressively during the animation.

Another way is to define the intermediate key steps yourself, using the `setKeyValueAt()` function. Let's update our example:

```
QLabel label;
QPropertyAnimation animation(&label, "geometry");
animation.setDuration(4000);
animation.setKeyValueAt(0, QRect(0, 0, 150, 50));
animation.setKeyValueAt(0.25, QRect(225, 112.5, 150, 50));
animation.setKeyValueAt(1, QRect(300, 200, 150, 50));
animation.start();
```

We are now setting key frames using `setKeyValueAt()`. The first argument is the time step in the range 0 to 1. In our case, step 1 means four seconds. The key frames at step 0 and step 1 provide the same positions as the start/end positions of the first example. As you can see, we also add a key frame at step 0.25 (that's one second for us) with the position 225 x 112.5. The next schema illustrates this:

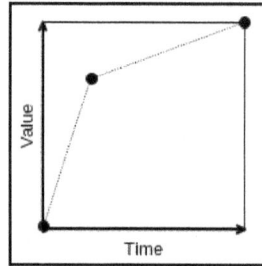

You can clearly distinguish the three key frames created with `setKeyValueAt()`. In our example, our `label` will quickly reach the 225 x 112.5 position in one second. Then the label will slowly move to the 300 x 200 position during the remaining three seconds.

If you have more than one `QPropertyAnimation` object, you can use groups to create more complex sequences. Let's see an example:

```
QPropertyAnimation animation1(&label1, "geometry");
QPropertyAnimation animation2(&label2, "geometry");
...
QSequentialAnimationGroup animationGroup;
animationGroup.addAnimation(&anim1);
animationGroup.addAnimation(&anim2);
animationGroup.start();
```

In this example, we are using a `QSequentialAnimationGroup` to run animations one by one. The first thing to do is to add animations to `animationGroup`. Then, when we call `start()` on our animation group, `animation1` is `launched`. When `animation1` is finished, `animationGroup` runs `animation2`. A `QSequentialAnimationGroup` is finished when the last animation of the list ends. The next schema depicts this behavior:

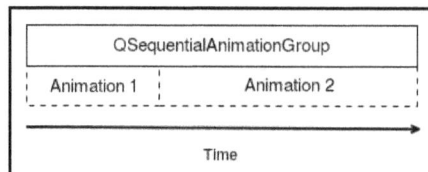

The second animation group, `QParallelAnimationGroup`, is initialized and started in the same way as `QSequentialAnimationGroup`. But the behavior is different: it starts all the animations in parallel, waiting for the longest animation to end. Here is an illustration of this:

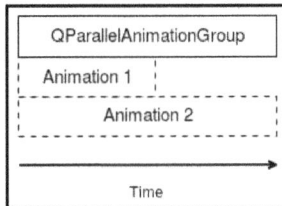

Keep in mind that an animation group is itself an animation (it inherits `QAbstractAnimation`). As a consequence, you can add animation groups to other animation groups to create a very complex animation sequence!

Making your thumbnails jump

Let's apply what we learned about the Qt Animation Framework to our project. Each time the user clicks on a filter thumbnail, we want to poke it. All modifications will be done on the `FilterWidget` class. Let's start with `FilterWidget.h`:

```
#include <QPropertyAnimation>

class FilterWidget : public QWidget
{
    Q_OBJECT

public:
    explicit FilterWidget(Filter& filter, QWidget *parent = 0);
    ~FilterWidget();
    ...

private:
    void initAnimations();
    void startSelectionAnimation();

private:
    ...
    QPropertyAnimation mSelectionAnimation;
};
```

The first function, `initAnimations()`, initializes the animations used by `FilterWidget`. The second function, `startSelectionAnimation()`, performs tasks required to start this animation correctly. As you can see, we are also declaring a `QPropertyAnimation` class, as covered in the previous section.

We can now update `FilterWidget.cpp`. Let's update the constructor:

```
FilterWidget::FilterWidget(Filter& filter, QWidget *parent) :
    QWidget(parent),
    ...
    mSelectionAnimation()
{
    ...
    initAnimations();
    updateThumbnail();
}
```

We initialize our `QPropertyAnimation` called `mSelectionAnimation`. The constructor also calls `initAnimations()`. Here is its implementation:

```
void FilterWidget::initAnimations()
{
    mSelectionAnimation.setTargetObject(ui->thumbnailLabel);
    mSelectionAnimation.setPropertyName("geometry");
    mSelectionAnimation.setDuration(200);
}
```

You should be familiar with these animation initialization steps now. The target object is the `thumbnailLabel` displaying the filter plugin preview. The property name to animate is `geometry`, because we want to update the position of this `QLabel`. Finally, we set the animation duration to 200 ms. Like jokes, keep it short and sweet.

Update the existing mouse event handler like this:

```
void FilterWidget::mousePressEvent(QMouseEvent*)
{
    process();
    startSelectionAnimation();
}
```

Each time the user clicks on the thumbnail, the selection animation moving the thumbnail will be called. We can now add this most important function like this:

```
void FilterWidget::startSelectionAnimation()
{
    if (mSelectionAnimation.state() ==
        QAbstractAnimation::Stopped) {
```

```
        QRect currentGeometry = ui->thumbnailLabel->geometry();
        QRect targetGeometry = ui->thumbnailLabel->geometry();
        targetGeometry.setY(targetGeometry.y() - 50.0);

        mSelectionAnimation.setKeyValueAt(0, currentGeometry);
        mSelectionAnimation.setKeyValueAt(0.3, targetGeometry);
        mSelectionAnimation.setKeyValueAt(1, currentGeometry);
        mSelectionAnimation.start();
    }
}
```

The first thing to do is to retrieve the current geometry of thumbnailLabel called currentGeometry. Then, we create a targetGeometry object with the same x, width, and height values. We only reduce the y position by 50, so the target position is always above the current position.

After that, we define our key frames:

- **At step 0**, the value is the current position.
- **At step 0.3** (60 ms, because the total duration is 200 ms), the value is the target position.
- **At step 1** (the end of the animation), we bring it to back the original position. The thumbnail will quickly reach the target position, then slowly fall down to its original position.

These key frames must be initialized before each animation starts. Because the layout is dynamic, the position (and so the geometry) could have been updated when the user resizes the main window.

Please note that we are preventing the animation from starting again if the current state is not stopped. Without this precaution, the thumbnail could move to the top again and again if the user clicks like a mad man on the widget.

You can now test your application and click on a filter effect. The filter thumbnail will jump to respond to your click!

Fading the picture in

When the user opens a picture, we want to fade in the image by playing with its opacity. The classes QLabel or QWidget do not provide an opacity property. However, we can add a visual effect to any QWidget using a QGraphicsEffect. For this animation, we will use QGraphicsOpacityEffect to provide an opacity property.

Here is a schema to describe the role of each one:

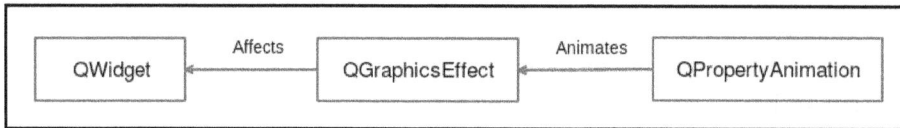

In our case, the QWidget class is our QLabel and the QGraphicsEffect class is QGraphicsOpacityEffect. Qt provides the Graphics Effect system to alter the rendering of a QWidget class. The abstract class QGraphicsEffect has a pure virtual method draw() that is implemented by each graphics effect.

We can now update the MainWindow.h according to the next snippet:

```
#include <QPropertyAnimation>
#include <QGraphicsOpacityEffect>

class MainWindow : public QMainWindow
{
    ...
private:
    ...
    void initAnimations();
private:
    ...
    QPropertyAnimation mLoadPictureAnimation;
    QGraphicsOpacityEffect mPictureOpacityEffect;
};
```

The initAnimations() private function is in charge of all the animation initializations. The mLoadPictureAnimation member variable performs the fade-in animation on the loaded picture. Finally, we declare mPictureOpacityEffect, the mandatory QGraphicsOpacityEffect.

Let's switch to the implementation part with the `MainWindow.cpp` constructor:

```
MainWindow::MainWindow(QWidget *parent) :
    QMainWindow(parent),
    ...
    mLoadPictureAnimation(),
    mPictureOpacityEffect()
{
    ...
    initFilters();
    initAnimations();
}
```

No surprises here. We use the initializer list to construct our two new member variables. The `MainWindow` constructor also calls `initAnimations()`.

Let's look at how this animation is initialized:

```
void MainWindow::initAnimations()
{
    ui->pictureLabel->setGraphicsEffect(&mPictureOpacityEffect);
    mLoadPictureAnimation.setTargetObject(&mPictureOpacityEffect);
    mLoadPictureAnimation.setPropertyName("opacity");
    mLoadPictureAnimation.setDuration(500);
    mLoadPictureAnimation.setStartValue(0);
    mLoadPictureAnimation.setEndValue(1);
    mLoadPictureAnimation.setEasingCurve(QEasingCurve::InCubic);
}
```

The first thing to do is to link our `QGraphicsOpacityEffect` with our `QLabel`. This can be easily done by calling the `setGraphicsEffect()` function on `pictureLabel`.

Now we can set our animation up. In this case, `mLoadPictureAnimation` targets `mPictureOpacityEffect` and will affect its property named `opacity`. The animation duration is 500 milliseconds. Next, we set the opacity value when the animation starts and ends:

- At the beginning, the picture is completely transparent (`opacity` value is 0)
- At the end, the picture is fully visible (`opacity` value is 1)

For this animation, we use the easing curve `InCubic`. This curve looks like this:

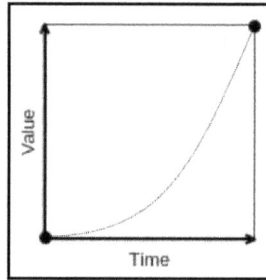

Feel free to try other curves to find the one that looks the best for you.

> You can get the list of all easing curves with a visual preview here: `http:/`
> `/doc.qt.io/qt-5/qeasingcurve.html`

The last step is to start the animation at the right place:

```
void MainWindow::loadPicture()
{
    ...
    mCurrentFilter->process();
    mLoadPictureAnimation.start();
}
```

You can now start your application and load a picture. You should see your picture fade in over 500 milliseconds!

Flashing the thumbnail in a sequence

For this last animation, we want to display a blue flash on each filter preview when the thumbnail is updated. We do not want to flash all previews at the same time, but in a sequence, one by one. This feature will be achieved in two parts:

- Create a color animation in `FilterWidget` to display a blue flash
- Build a sequential animation group in `MainWindow` containing all `FilterWidget` color animations

Let's start to add the color animation. Update `FilterWidget.h` as shown in the following snippet:

```
#include <QGraphicsColorizeEffect>

class FilterWidget : public QWidget
{
    Q_OBJECT

public:
    explicit FilterWidget(Filter& filter, QWidget *parent = 0);
    ~FilterWidget();
    ...
    QPropertyAnimation* colorAnimation();

private:
    ...
    QPropertyAnimation mSelectionAnimation;
    QPropertyAnimation* mColorAnimation;
    QGraphicsColorizeEffect mColorEffect;
};
```

This time we do not want to affect the opacity, but rather colorize the thumbnail in blue. Thus, we use another Qt standard effect: `QGraphicsColorizeEffect`. We also declare a new `QPropertyAnimation` named `mColorAnimation` and its corresponding getter, `colorAnimation()`. We declare `mColorAnimation` as a pointer because the ownership will be taken by the animation group of `MainWindow`. This topic will be covered soon.

Let's update the constructor in `FilterWidget.cpp`:

```
FilterWidget::FilterWidget(Filter& filter, QWidget *parent) :
    QWidget(parent),
    ...
    mColorAnimation(new QPropertyAnimation()),
    mColorEffect()
{
    ...
}
```

We just have to construct our two new member variables, `mColorAnimation` and `mColorEffect`. Let's look at the amazing complexity of the getter:

```
QPropertyAnimation* FilterWidget::colorAnimation()
{
    return mColorAnimation;
}
```

It was a lie: we always try to write comprehensive code!

Now that the preliminaries are done, we can initialize the color animation by updating the `initAnimations()` function like this:

```
void FilterWidget::initAnimations()
{
    ...
    mColorEffect.setColor(QColor(0, 150, 150));
    mColorEffect.setStrength(0.0);
    ui->thumbnailLabel->setGraphicsEffect(&mColorEffect);

    mColorAnimation->setTargetObject(&mColorEffect);
    mColorAnimation->setPropertyName("strength");
    mColorAnimation->setDuration(200);
    mColorAnimation->setStartValue(1.0);
    mColorAnimation->setEndValue(0.0);
}
```

The first part sets the color filter up. Here, we chose a kind of turquoise color for the flash effect. The colorize effect is handled by its `strength` property. By default, the value is `1.0`, so, we set it to `0.0` to keep it from affecting our default thumbnail of Lenna. Finally, we link the `thumbnailLabel` with this `mColorEffect` calling `setGraphicsEffect()`.

The second part is the color animation preparation. This animation targets the color effect and its property, named `strength`. This is a short flash; `200` milliseconds is enough:

- We want to start with a full strength effect, so we put the start value at `1.0`
- During the animation, the colorize effect will decrease until it reaches `0.0`

The default linear interpolation is fine here, so we do not use any easing curve.

Here we are. The color effect/animation is initialized and we provided a
`colorAnimation()` getter. We can now begin the second part of this feature,
Updating `MainWindow.h`:

```
#include <QSequentialAnimationGroup>

class MainWindow : public QMainWindow
{
    Q_OBJECT
    ...

private:
    ...
    QSequentialAnimationGroup mFiltersGroupAnimation;
};
```

We declare a `QSequentialAnimationGroup` class to trigger, one by one,
all `FilterWidget` color animations displaying the blue flash. Let's update the constructor
in `MainWindow.cpp`:

```
MainWindow::MainWindow(QWidget *parent) :
    QMainWindow(parent),
    ...
    mFiltersGroupAnimation()
{
    ...
}
```

A new member variable means a new construction in the initializer list: that is the rule!

We can now update `initAnimations()` to prepare our animation group:

```
void MainWindow::initAnimations()
{
    ...
    for (FilterWidget* filterWidget : mFilters) {
        mFiltersGroupAnimation.addAnimation(
            filterWidget->colorAnimation());
    }
}
```

Do you remember that an animation group is only an animation container? As a consequence, we iterate on every `FilterWidget` to get its color animation and fill our `mFiltersGroupAnimation` calling `addAnimation()`. Thanks to C++11's range-based for loop, it is really readable. Keep in mind that when you add an animation to an animation group, the group takes ownership of this animation.

Our animation group is ready. We can now start it:

```
void MainWindow::loadPicture()
{
    ...
    mCurrentFilter->process();
    mLoadPictureAnimation.start();
    mFiltersGroupAnimation.start();
}
```

Start your application and open a picture. You can see that all filter thumbnails will flash one by one from left to right. This is what we intended, but it's still not perfect because all the thumbnails are already updated before the flashes. We have this behavior because the `loadPicture()` function actually sets and updates all thumbnails, and then finally starts the sequential animation group. Here is a schema illustrating the current behavior:

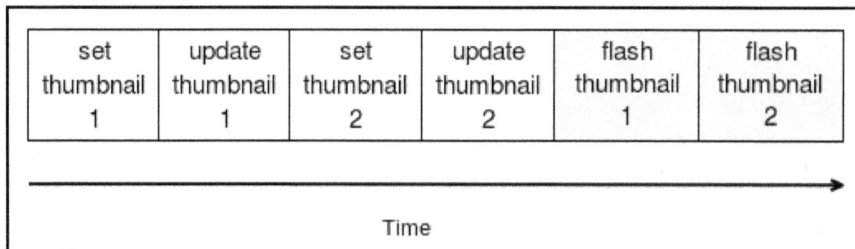

set thumbnail 1	update thumbnail 1	set thumbnail 2	update thumbnail 2	flash thumbnail 1	flash thumbnail 2

Time →

The schema only describes the behavior for two thumbnails, but the principle is the same with three thumbnails. Here is the targeted behavior:

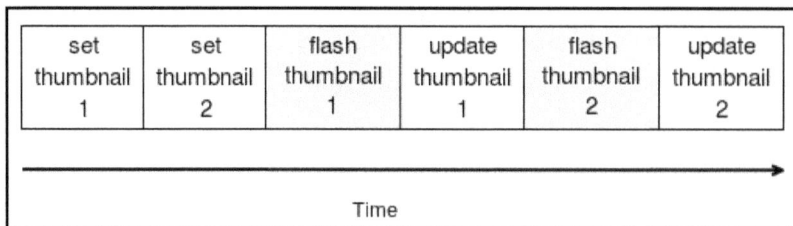

set thumbnail 1	set thumbnail 2	flash thumbnail 1	update thumbnail 1	flash thumbnail 2	update thumbnail 2

Time →

We must only update the thumbnail when the flash animation is over. Fortunately, QPropertyAnimation emits the finished signal when the animation is over, so we only have to make a few changes. Update loadPicture() function from MainWindow.cpp:

```
void MainWindow::loadPicture()
{
    ...
    for (int i = 0; i <mFilters.size(); ++i) {
        mFilters[i]->setSourcePicture(mSourcePicture);
        mFilters[i]->setSourceThumbnail(mSourceThumbnail);
        //mFilters[i]->updateThumbnail();
    }
    ...
}
```

As you can see, we kept the set and only removed the update thumbnail when a new picture is opened by the user. At this stage, all FilterWidget instances have the correct thumbnail, but they don't display it. Let's fix this by updating FilterWidget.cpp:

```
void FilterWidget::initAnimations()
{
    ...
    mColorAnimation->setTargetObject(&mColorEffect);
    mColorAnimation->setPropertyName("strength");
    mColorAnimation->setDuration(200);
    mColorAnimation->setStartValue(1.0);
    mColorAnimation->setEndValue(0.0);
    connect(mColorAnimation, &QPropertyAnimation::finished, [this]
    {
        updateThumbnail();
    });
}
```

We connect a lambda function to the finished signal of the color animation. This lambda simply updates the thumbnail. You can now start your application again and load a picture. You should see that we not only animate the sequential blue flash, but also the thumbnail update.

Summary

In this chapter, you defined a `Filter` interface in your own SDK. Your filters are now plugins. You know how to create and load a new plugin, so your application is now modular and can be easily extended. We have also enhanced the application with the Qt Animation Framework. You know how to animate the position, the color, and the opacity of any `QWidget`, using `QGraphicsEffect` if necessary. We created a sequential animation that starts three animations one by one with `QSequentialAnimationGroup`.

In the next chapter, we will talk about a big subject: threading. The Qt framework can help you build a robust and reliable multithreading application. To illustrate the chapter, we will create a Mandelbrot fractal generator using threadpools.

17
Keeping Your Sanity with Multithreading

In previous chapters, we managed to always write code without ever relying on threads. It is time to face the beast and truly understand how threading works in Qt. In this chapter, you will develop a multithreaded application that displays a Mandelbrot fractal. It is a heavy computational process that will bring tears to your CPU cores.

In the example project, the user can see the Mandelbrot fractal, zoom in the picture, and pan around to discover the magic of fractals.

The chapter covers the following topics:

* Deep understanding of the `QThread` framework
* Overview of all the available threading technologies in Qt
* Using a `QThreadPool` class to dispatch jobs and aggregate the results
* How to synchronize threads and minimize sharing states
* Low-level drawing to optimize the performances
* Common threading pitfalls and challenges

Discovering QThread

Qt provides a sophisticated threading system. We assume you already know threading basics and the associated issues (deadlocks, threads synchronization, resource sharing, and so on) and we will focus on how Qt implements it.

The QThread is the central class of the Qt threading system. A QThread instance manages one thread of execution within the program.

You can subclass QThread to override the run() function, which will be executed in the QThread framework. Here is how you can create and start a QThread:

```
QThread thread;
thread.start();
```

The start() function calling will automatically call the run() function of the thread and emit the started() signal. Only at this point will the new thread of execution be created. When run() is completed, the thread object will emit the finished() signal.

This brings us to a fundamental aspect of QThread: it works seamlessly with the signal/slot mechanism. Qt is an event-driven framework, where a main event loop (or the GUI loop) processes events (user input, graphical, and so on) to refresh the UI.

Each QThread comes with its own event loop that can process events outside the main loop. If not overridden, run() calls the QThread::exec() function, which starts the thread object's event loop. You can also override QThread and call yourself exec(), like so:

```
class Thread : public QThread
{
Q_OBJECT
protected:
    void run()
    {
      Object* myObject = new Object();
        connect(myObject, &Object::started,
                this, &Thread::doWork);
        exec();
    }

private slots:
    void doWork();
};
```

The started() signal will be processed by the Thread event loop only upon the exec() call. It will block and wait until QThread::exit() is called.

A crucial thing to note is that a thread event loop delivers events for all `QObjects` that are living in that thread. This includes all objects created in that thread or moved to that thread. This is referred to as the thread affinity of an object. Let's see an example:

```
class Thread : public QThread
{
    Thread() :
        mObject(new QObject())
    {
    }
private :
    QObject* myObject;
};

// Somewhere in MainWindow
Thread thread;
thread.start();
```

In this snippet, `myObject` is constructed in `Thread` class's constructor, which is created in turn in `MainWindow`. At this point, `thread` is living in the GUI thread. Hence, `myObject` is also living in the GUI thread.

> An object created before a `QCoreApplication` object has no thread affinity. As a consequence, no event will be dispatched to it.

It is great to be able to handle signals and slots in our own `QThread`, but how can we control signals across multiple threads? A classic example is a long-running process that is executed in a separate thread that has to notify the UI to update some state:

```
class Thread : public QThread
{
    Q_OBJECT
    void run() {
        // long running operation
        emit result("I <3 threads");
    }
signals:
    void result(QString data);
};
```

```
// Somewhere in MainWindow
Thread* thread = new Thread(this);
connect(thread, &Thread::result, this, &MainWindow::handleResult);
connect(thread, &Thread::finished, thread, &QObject::deleteLater);
thread->start();
```

Intuitively, we assume that the first `connect` sends the signal across multiple threads (to have results available in `MainWindow::handleResult`), whereas the second `connect` should work on thread's event loop only.

Fortunately, this is the case due to a default argument in the `connect()` function signature: the connection type. Let's see the complete signature:

```
QObject::connect(
    const QObject *sender, const char *signal,
    const QObject *receiver, const char *method,
    Qt::ConnectionType type = Qt::AutoConnection)
```

The `type` keyword takes `Qt::AutoConnection` as a default value. Let's review the possible values of the `Qt::ConectionType` enum as the official Qt documentation states:

- `Qt::AutoConnection`: If the receiver lives in the thread that emits the signal, `Qt::DirectConnection` is used. Otherwise, `Qt::QueuedConnection` is used. The connection type is determined when the signal is emitted.
- `Qt::DirectConnection`: This slot is invoked immediately when the signal is emitted. The slot is executed in the signaling thread.
- `Qt::QueuedConnection`: This slot is invoked when control returns to the event loop of the receiver's thread. The slot is executed in the receiver's thread.
- `Qt::BlockingQueuedConnection`: This is the same as `Qt::QueuedConnection`, except that the signaling thread blocks until the slot returns. This connection must not be used if the receiver lives in the signaling thread, or else the application will deadlock.
- `Qt::UniqueConnection`: This is a flag that can be combined with any one of the previous connection types, using a bitwise OR. When `Qt::UniqueConnection` is set, `QObject::connect()` will fail if the connection already exists (that is, if the same signal is already connected to the same slot for the same pair of objects).

When using `Qt::AutoConnection`, the final `ConnectionType` is resolved only when the signal is effectively emitted. If you look again at our example, at the first `connect()`:

```
connect(thread, &Thread::result,
        this, &MainWindow::handleResult);
```

When `result()` is emitted, Qt will look at the `handleResult()` thread affinity, which is different from the thread affinity of the `result()` signal. The `thread` object is living in `MainWindow` (remember that it has been created in `MainWindow`), but the `result()` signal has been emitted in the `run()` function, which is running in a different thread of execution. As a result, a `Qt::QueuedConnection` slot will be used.

We can now take a look at the second `connect()`:

```
connect(thread, &Thread::finished, thread, &QObject::deleteLater);
```

Here, `deleteLater()` and `finished()` live in the same thread; therefore, a `Qt::DirectConnection` slot will be used.

It is crucial that you understand that Qt does not care about the emitting object thread affinity, it looks only at the signal "context of execution".

Loaded with this knowledge, we can take another look at our first `QThread` class example to have a full understanding of this system:

```
class Thread : public QThread
{
Q_OBJECT
protected:
    void run()
    {
        Object* myObject = new Object();
        connect(myObject, &Object::started,
                this, &Thread::doWork);
        exec();
    }

private slots:
    void doWork();
};
```

When the `Object::started()` function is emitted, a `Qt::QueuedConnection` slot will be used. This is where your brain freezes. The `Thread::doWork()` function lives in another thread than `Object::started()`, which has been created in `run()`. If Thread has been instantiated in the UI thread, this is where `doWork()` would have belonged.

This system is powerful, but complex. To make things simpler, Qt favors the worker model. It splits the threading plumbing from the real processing. Here is an example:

```
class Worker : public QObject
{
    Q_OBJECT
```

```
public slots:
    void doWork()
    {
        emit result("workers are the best");
    }

signals:
    void result(QString data);
};

// Somewhere in MainWindow
QThread* thread = new Thread(this);
Worker* worker = new Worker();
worker->moveToThread(thread);

connect(thread, &QThread::finished,
        worker, &QObject::deleteLater);
connect(this, &MainWindow::startWork,
        worker, &Worker::doWork);
connect(worker, &Worker::resultReady,
        this, handleResult);

thread->start();

// later on, to stop the thread
thread->quit();
thread->wait();
```

We start by creating a Worker class that has:

- A doWork() slot that will have the content of our old QThread::run()
- A result() signal that will emit the resulting data

Next in the MainWindow class, we create a simple thread object and an instance of Worker. The worker->moveToThread(thread) is where the magic happens. It changes the affinity of the worker object. The worker now lives in the thread object.

You can only push an object from your current thread to another thread. Conversely, you cannot pull an object that lives in another thread. You cannot change the thread affinity of an object if the object does not live in your thread. Once thread->start() is executed, we cannot call worker->moveToThread(this) unless we are doing it from this new thread.

After that, we do three `connect()`:

1. We handle the `worker` life cycle by reaping it when the thread is finished. This signal will use a `Qt::DirectConnection`.
2. We start the `Worker::doWork()` upon a possible UI event. This signal will use a `Qt::QueuedConnection`.
3. We process the resulting data in the UI thread with `handleResult()`. This signal will use a `Qt::QueuedConnection`.

To sum up, `QThread` can be either subclassed or used in conjunction with a `worker` class. Generally, the worker approach is favored because it separates more cleanly the threading affinity plumbing from the actual operation you want to execute in parallel.

Flying over Qt multithreading technologies

Built upon `QThread`, several threading technologies are available in Qt. First, to synchronize threads, the usual approach is to use a mutual exclusion (mutex) to have a mutual exclusion for a given resource. Qt provides it by means of the `QMutex` class. Its usage is straightforward:

```
QMutex mutex;
int number = 1;

mutex.lock();
number *= 2;
mutex.unlock();
```

From the `mutex.lock()` instruction, any other thread trying to lock the `mutex` will wait until `mutex.unlock()` has been called.

The locking/unlocking mechanism is error-prone in complex code. You can easily forget to unlock a mutex in a specific exit condition, causing a deadlock. To simplify this situation, Qt provides a `QMutexLocker` that should be used where the `QMutex` needs to be locked:

```
QMutex mutex;
QMutexLocker locker(&mutex);

int number = 1;
number *= 2;
if (overlyComplicatedCondition) {
    return;
} else if (notSoSimple) {
    return;
```

```
    }
```

The `mutex` is locked when the `locker` object is created and will be unlocked when the `locker` object is destroyed; for example, when it goes out of scope. This is the case for every condition we stated where the `return` statement appears. It makes the code simpler and more readable.

You may need to create and destroy threads frequently, as managing `QThread` instances by hand can become cumbersome. For this, you can use the `QThreadPool` class, which manages a pool of reusable `QThreads`.

To execute code within threads managed by a `QThreadPool` class, you will use a pattern very close to the worker we covered earlier. The main difference is that the processing class has to extend the `QRunnable` class. Here is how it looks:

```cpp
class Job : public QRunnable
{
    void run()
    {
        // long running operation
    }
}

Job* job = new Job();
QThreadPool::globalInstance()->start(job);
```

Just override the `run()` function and ask `QThreadPool` to execute your job in a separate thread. The `QThreadPool::globalInstance()` is a static helper function that gives you access to an application global instance. You can create your own `QThreadPool` if you need to have finer control over the `QThreadPool` life cycle.

Note that the `QThreadPool::start()` function takes the ownership of `job` and will automatically delete it when `run()` finishes. Watch out, this does not change the thread affinity like `QObject::moveToThread()` does with workers! A `QRunnable` class cannot be reused, it has to be a freshly baked instance.

If you fire up several jobs, `QThreadPool` automatically allocates the ideal number of threads based on the core count of your CPU. The maximum number of threads that the `QThreadPool` class can start can be retrieved with `QThreadPool::maxThreadCount()`.

> **TIP**
>
> If you need to manage threads by hand, but you want to base it on the number of cores of your CPU, you can use the handy static function, `QThreadPool::idealThreadCount()`.

Another approach to multi-threaded development is available with the Qt Concurrent framework. It is a higher-level API that avoids the use of mutexes/lock/wait conditions and promotes the distribution of the processing among CPU cores.

Qt Concurrent relies on the `QFuture` class to execute a function and expects a result later on:

```
void longRunningFunction();
QFuture<void> future = QtConcurrent::run(longRunningFunction);
```

The `longRunningFunction()` function will be executed in a separated thread obtained from the default `QThreadPool` class.

To pass parameters to a `QFuture` class and retrieve the result of the operation, use the following code:

```
QImage processGrayscale(QImage& image);
QImage lenna;

QFuture<QImage> future = QtConcurrent::run(processGrayscale,
    lenna);

QImage grayscaleLenna = future.result();
```

Here we pass `lenna` as a parameter to the `processGrayscale()` function. Because we want a `QImage` as a result, we declare the `QFuture` class with the template type, `QImage`. After that, `future.result()` blocks the current thread and waits for the operation to be completed to return the final `QImage`.

To avoid blocking, `QFutureWatcher` comes to the rescue:

```
QFutureWatcher<QImage> watcher;
connect(&watcher, &QFutureWatcher::finished,
        this, &QObject::handleGrayscale);

QImage processGrayscale(QImage& image);
QImage lenna;
QFuture<QImage> future = QtConcurrent::run(processImage, lenna);
watcher.setFuture(future);
```

We start by declaring a QFutureWatcher class with the template argument matching the one used for QFuture. Then simply connect the QFutureWatcher::finished signal to the slot you want to be called when the operation has been completed.

The last step is to tell the watcher object to watch the future object with watcher.setFuture(future). This statement looks almost like it comes from a science-fiction movie.

Qt Concurrent also provides a MapReduce and FilterReduce implementation. The MapReduce is a programming model that basically does two things:

- Maps or distributes the processing of the dataset among multiple cores of the CPU
- Reduces or aggregates the results to provide it to the caller

This technique was first promoted by Google to be able to process huge datasets within a cluster of CPUs.

Here is an example of a simple map operation:

```
QList images = ...;

QImage processGrayscale(QImage& image);
QFuture<void> future = QtConcurrent::mapped(
                                    images, processGrayscale);
```

Instead of QtConcurrent::run(), we use the mapped function that takes a list and the function to apply to each element in a different thread each time. The images list is modified in place, so there is no need to declare QFuture with a template type.

The operation can be made to block by using QtConcurrent::blockingMapped() instead of QtConcurrent::mapped().

Finally, a MapReduce operation looks like this:

```
QList images = ...;

QImage processGrayscale(QImage& image);
void combineImage(QImage& finalImage, const QImage& inputImage);

QFuture<void> future = QtConcurrent::mappedReduced(
                                        images,
                                        processGrayscale,
                                        combineImage);
```

Here we added a `combineImage()` function that will be called for each result returned by the map function, `processGrayscale()`. It will merge the intermediate data, `inputImage`, into the `finalImage`. This function is called only once at a time per thread, so there is no need to use a mutex to lock the result variable.

The `FilterReduce` follows exactly the same pattern; the filter function simply allows you to filter the input list instead of transforming it.

Architecting the Mandelbrot project

The example project of this chapter is the multi-threaded calculation of a Mandelbrot fractal. The user will see the fractal and will be able to pan and zoom in that window.

Before diving into the code, we have to have a broad understanding of a fractal and how we are going to achieve its calculation.

The Mandelbrot fractal is a numerical set that works with complex numbers (a + bi). Each pixel is associated with a value calculated through iterations. If this iterated value diverges towards infinity then the pixel is out of the Mandelbrot set. If not, then the pixel is inside the Mandelbrot set. A visual representation of the Mandelbrot fractal looks like this:

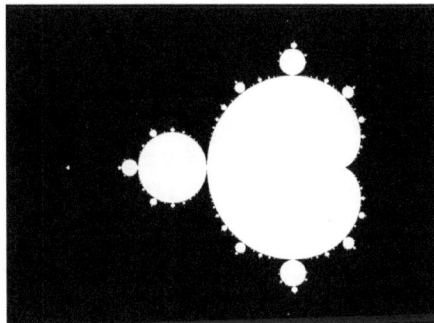

Every black pixel in this image tends to diverge to an infinite value, whereas white pixels are bounded to a finite value. The white pixels belong to the Mandelbrot set.

What makes it interesting from a multi-threaded perspective, is that to determine if the pixel belongs or not to the Mandelbrot set, we have to iterate on a formula to be able to hypothesize its divergence or not. The more iterations we perform, the safer we are in claiming "yes, this pixel is in the Mandelbrot set, it is a white pixel".

Even more fun, we can take any value in the graphical plot and always apply the Mandelbrot formula to deduce if the pixel should be black or white. As a consequence, you can zoom endlessly inside the graphics of your fractal. There are only two main limitations:

- The power of your CPU hinders the picture generation speed.
- The floating number precision of your CPU architecture limits the zoom. If you keep zooming, you will get visual artifacts because the scale factor can only handle 15 to 17 significant digits.

The architecture of the application has to be carefully designed. Because we are working with threads, it is very easy to cause deadlock, starve threads, or even worse, freeze the UI.

We really want to maximize the use of the CPU. To do so, we will execute as many threads as possible on each core. Each thread will be responsible for calculating a part of the Mandelbrot set before giving back its result.

The architecture of the application is as follows:

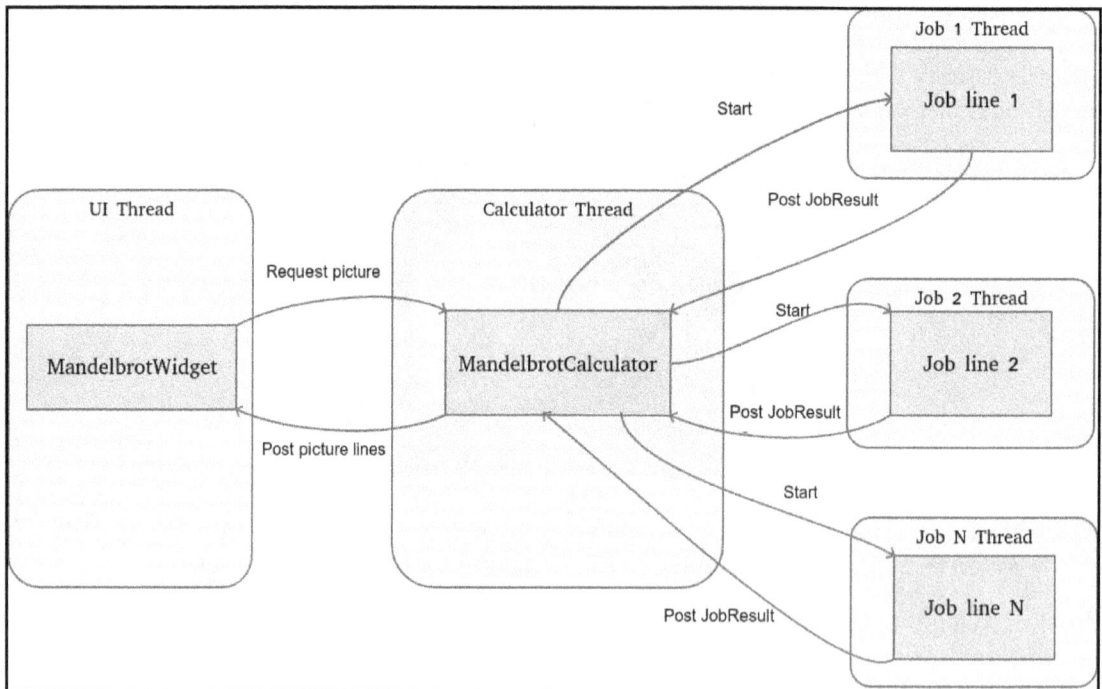

The application is divided into three parts:

- `MandelbrotWidget`: This requests a picture to display. It handles the drawing and the user interaction. This object lives in the UI thread.
- `MandelbrotCalculator`: This handles the picture requests and aggregates the resulting `JobResults` before sending it back to `MandelbrotWidget`. This object lives in its own thread.
- `Job`: This calculates a part of the final picture before transmitting the result back to `MandelbrotCalculator`. Each job lives in its own thread.

The `MandelbrotCalculator` thread will use a `QThreadPool` class to dispatch jobs in their own thread. This will scale perfectly according to your CPU cores. Each job will calculate a single line of the final picture before sending it back to `MandelbrotCalculator` through a `JobResult` object.

The `MandelbrotCalculator` thread is really the orchestrator of the calculation. Consider a user that zooms in the picture before the calculation is complete; `MandelbrotWidget` will request a new picture to `MandelbrotCalculator`, which in turn has to cancel all the current jobs before dispatching new jobs.

We will add a last constraint to this project: it has to be mutex free. Mutexes are very convenient tools, but they force threads to wait for each other and are error-prone. To do this, we will rely on multiple concepts and technologies provided by Qt: multi-threaded signal/slots, implicit sharing, and so on.

By minimizing the sharing state between our threads, we will be able to let them execute as fast as they possibly can. That is why we are here, to burn some CPU cores, right?

Now that the broad picture is clearer, we can start the implementation. Create a new **Qt Widget Application** project named `ch09-mandelbrot-threadpool`. Remember to add the `CONFIG += c++14` to the `.pro` file.

Defining a Job class with QRunnable

Let's dive into the project's core. To speed up the Mandelbrot picture generation, we will split the whole computation into multiple jobs. A `Job` is a request of a task. Depending on your CPU architecture, several jobs will be executed simultaneously. A `Job` class produces a `JobResult` function containing result values. In our project, a `Job` class generates values for one line of the complete picture. For example, an image resolution of 800 x 600 requires 600 jobs, each one generating 800 values.

Please create a C++ header file called `JobResult.h`:

```cpp
#include <QSize>
#include <QVector>
#include <QPointF>

struct JobResult
{
    JobResult(int valueCount = 1) :
        areaSize(0, 0),
        pixelPositionY(0),
        moveOffset(0, 0),
        scaleFactor(0.0),
        values(valueCount)
    {
    }

    QSize areaSize;
    int pixelPositionY;
    QPointF moveOffset;
    double scaleFactor;

    QVector<int> values;
};
```

This structure contains two parts:

- Input data (`areaSize`, `pixelPositionY`, ...)
- Result `values` generated by a `Job` class

We can now create the `Job` class itself. Create a C++ class `Job` using the next snippet of `Job.h` for the content:

```cpp
#include <QObject>
#include <QRunnable>

#include "JobResult.h"
class Job : public QObject, public QRunnable
{
    Q_OBJECT
public:
    Job(QObject *parent = 0);
    void run() override;
};
```

This `Job` class is a `QRunnable`, so we can override `run()` to implement the Mandelbrot picture algorithm. As you can see, `Job` also inherits from `QObject`, allowing us to use the signal/slot feature of Qt. The algorithm requires some input data. Update your `Job.h` like this:

```cpp
#include <QObject>
#include <QRunnable>
#include <QPointF>
#include <QSize>
#include <QAtomicInteger>
class Job : public QObject, public QRunnable
{
    Q_OBJECT
public:
    Job(QObject *parent = 0);
    void run() override;

    void setPixelPositionY(int value);
    void setMoveOffset(const QPointF& value);
    void setScaleFactor(double value);
    void setAreaSize(const QSize& value);
    void setIterationMax(int value);

private:
    int mPixelPositionY;
    QPointF mMoveOffset;
    double mScaleFactor;
    QSize mAreaSize;
    int mIterationMax;
};
```

Let's talk about these variables:

- The `mPixelPositionY` variable is the picture height index. Because each `Job` generates data only for one picture line, we need this information.
- The `mMoveOffset` variable is the Mandelbrot origin offset. The user can pan the picture, so the origin will not always be (0, 0).
- The `mScaleFactor` variable is the Mandelbrot scale value. The user can also zoom into the picture.
- The `mAreaSize` variable is the final picture size in a pixel.
- The `mIterationMax` variable is the count of iterations allowed to determine the Mandelbrot result for one pixel.

We can now add a signal, `jobCompleted()`, and the abort feature to `Job.h`:

```cpp
#include <QObject>
#include <QRunnable>
#include <QPointF>
#include <QSize>
#include <QAtomicInteger>

#include "JobResult.h"

class Job : public QObject, public QRunnable
{
    Q_OBJECT
public:
    ...
signals:
    void jobCompleted(JobResult jobResult);

public slots:
    void abort();

private:
    QAtomicInteger<bool> mAbort;
    ...
};
```

The `jobCompleted()` signal will be emitted when the algorithm is over. The `jobResult` parameter contains result values. The `abort()` slot will allow us to stop the job updating the `mIsAbort` flag value. Notice that `mAbort` is not a classic `bool`, but a `QAtomicInteger<bool>`. This Qt cross-platform type allows us to perform atomic operations without interruption. You could use a mutex or another synchronization mechanism to do the job, but using an atomic variable is a fast way to safely update and access a variable from different threads.

It is time to switch to the implementation part with `Job.cpp`. Here is the `Job` class's constructor:

```cpp
#include "Job.h"

Job::Job(QObject* parent) :
    QObject(parent),
    mAbort(false),
    mPixelPositionY(0),
    mMoveOffset(0.0, 0.0),
    mScaleFactor(0.0),
    mAreaSize(0, 0),
    mIterationMax(1)
```

```
{
}
```

This is a classic initialization; do not forget to call the `QObject` constructor.

We can now implement the `run()` function:

```
void Job::run()
{
    JobResult jobResult(mAreaSize.width());
    jobResult.areaSize = mAreaSize;
    jobResult.pixelPositionY = mPixelPositionY;
    jobResult.moveOffset = mMoveOffset;
    jobResult.scaleFactor = mScaleFactor;
    ...
}
```

In this first part, we initialize a `JobResult` variable. The width of the area size is used to construct `JobResult::values` as a `QVector` with the correct initial size. Other input data is copied from `Job` to `JobResult` to let the receiver of `JobResult` get the result with the context input data.

Then we can update the `run()` function with the Mandelbrot algorithm:

```
void Job::run()
{
    ...
    double imageHalfWidth = mAreaSize.width() / 2.0;
    double imageHalfHeight = mAreaSize.height() / 2.0;
    for (int imageX = 0; imageX < mAreaSize.width(); ++imageX) {
        int iteration = 0;
        double x0 = (imageX - imageHalfWidth)
                * mScaleFactor + mMoveOffset.x();
        double y0 = (mPixelPositionY - imageHalfHeight)
                * mScaleFactor - mMoveOffset.y();
        double x = 0.0;
        double y = 0.0;
        do {
            if (mAbort.load()) {
                return;
            }

            double nextX = (x * x) - (y * y) + x0;
            y = 2.0 * x * y + y0;
            x = nextX;
            iteration++;
```

```
    } while(iteration < mIterationMax
           && (x * x) + (y * y) < 4.0);

    jobResult.values[imageX] = iteration;
}

emit jobCompleted(jobResult);
}
```

The Mandelbrot algorithm itself is beyond the scope of this book. But you have to understand the main purpose of this `run()` function. Let's break it down:

- The for loop iterates over all x positions of pixels over one line
- The pixel position is converted into complex plane coordinates
- If the trial count exceeds the maximum authorized iteration, the algorithm ends with `iteration` to the `mIterationMax` value
- If the Mandelbrot check condition is true, the algorithm ends with `iteration < mIterationMax`
- In any case, for each pixel, the iteration count is stored in `values` of `JobResult`
- Finally, the `jobCompleted()` signal is emitted with result values of this algorithm
- We perform an atomic read with `mAbort.load()`; notice that if the return value is `true`, the algorithm is aborted and nothing is emitted

The last function is the `abort()` slot:

```
void Job::abort()
{
    mAbort.store(true);
}
```

This method performs an atomic write of the value, `true`. The atomic mechanism ensures that we can call `abort()` from multiple threads without disrupting the `mAbort` read in the `run()` function.

In our case, `run()` lives in the thread affected by the `QThreadPool` (we will cover it soon), while the `abort()` slot will be called in the `MandelbrotCalculator` thread context.

You might want to secure the operations on mAbort with a QMutex. However, keep in mind that locking and unlocking a mutex can become a costly operation if you do it often. Using a QAtomicInteger class here presents only the advantages: the access to mAbort is thread-safe and we avoid an expensive lock.

The end of the Job implementation only contains setter functions. Please refer to the complete source code if you have any doubt.

Using QThreadPool in MandelbrotCalculator

Now that our Job class is ready to be used, we need to create a class to manage the jobs. Please create a new class, MandelbrotCalculator. Let's see what we need in the file, MandelbrotCalculator.h:

```cpp
#include <QObject>
#include <QSize>
#include <QPointF>
#include <QElapsedTimer>
#include <QList>

#include "JobResult.h"

class Job;

class MandelbrotCalculator : public QObject
{
    Q_OBJECT
public:
    explicit MandelbrotCalculator(QObject *parent = 0);
    void init(QSize imageSize);

private:
    QPointF mMoveOffset;
    double mScaleFactor;
    QSize mAreaSize;
    int mIterationMax;
    int mReceivedJobResults;
    QList<JobResult> mJobResults;
    QElapsedTimer mTimer;
};
```

We have already discussed `mMoveOffset`, `mScaleFactor`, `mAreaSize`, and `mIterationMax` in the previous section. We also have some new variables:

- The `mReceivedJobResults` variable is the count of the `JobResult` received, which was sent by the jobs
- The `mJobResults` variable is a list that contains received `JobResult`
- The `mTimer` variable calculates the elapsed time to run all jobs for a requested picture

Now that you get a better picture of all member variables, we can add the signals, slots, and private methods. Update your `MandelbrotCalculator.h` file:

```
...
class MandelbrotCalculator : public QObject
{
    Q_OBJECT
public:
    explicit MandelbrotCalculator(QObject *parent = 0);
    void init(QSize imageSize);

signals:
    void pictureLinesGenerated(QList<JobResult> jobResults);
    void abortAllJobs();

public slots:
    void generatePicture(QSize areaSize, QPointF moveOffset,
                         double scaleFactor, int iterationMax);
    void process(JobResult jobResult);

private:
    Job* createJob(int pixelPositionY);
    void clearJobs();

private:
    ...
};
```

Here are the roles of these:

- `generatePicture()`: This slot is used by the caller to request a new Mandelbrot picture. This function prepares and starts jobs.
- `process()`: This slot handles results generated by the jobs.
- `pictureLinesGenerated()`: This signal is regularly triggered to dispatch results.
- `abortAllJobs()`: This signal is used to abort all active jobs.

- createJob(): This is a helper function to create and configure a new job.
- clearJobs(): This slot removes queued jobs and aborts active jobs.

The header file is completed and we can now perform the implementation. Here is the beginning of the MandelbrotCalculator.cpp implementation:

```
#include <QDebug>
#include <QThreadPool>

#include "Job.h"

const int JOB_RESULT_THRESHOLD = 10;

MandelbrotCalculator::MandelbrotCalculator(QObject *parent)
    : QObject(parent),
      mMoveOffset(0.0, 0.0),
      mScaleFactor(0.005),
      mAreaSize(0, 0),
      mIterationMax(10),
      mReceivedJobResults(0),
      mJobResults(),
      mTimer()
{
}
```

As always, we are using the initializer list with default values for our member variables. The role of JOB_RESULT_THRESHOLD will be covered soon. Here is the generatePicture() slot:

```
void MandelbrotCalculator::generatePicture(QSize areaSize, QPointF
moveOffset, double scaleFactor, int iterationMax)
{
    if (areaSize.isEmpty()) {
        return;
    }

    mTimer.start();
    clearJobs();

    mAreaSize = areaSize;
    mMoveOffset = moveOffset;
    mScaleFactor = scaleFactor;
    mIterationMax = iterationMax;

    for(int pixelPositionY = 0;
        pixelPositionY < mAreaSize.height(); pixelPositionY++) {
        QThreadPool::globalInstance()->
```

```
                    start(createJob(pixelPositionY));
        }
    }
```

If the `areaSize` dimension is 0x0, we have nothing to do. If the request is valid, we can start `mTimer` to track the whole generation duration. Each new picture generation will first cancel existing jobs by calling `clearJobs()`. Then we set our member variables with the ones provided. Finally, we create a new `Job` class for each vertical picture line. The `createJob()` function that returns a `Job*` value will be covered soon.

The `QThreadPool::globalInstance()` is a static function that gives us the optimal global thread pool depending on the core count of our CPU. Even if we call `start()` for all the `Job` classes, only the firsts starts immediately. Others are added to the pool queue waiting for an available thread.

Let's see now how a `Job` class is created with the `createJob()` function:

```cpp
Job* MandelbrotCalculator::createJob(int pixelPositionY)
{
    Job* job = new Job();

    job->setPixelPositionY(pixelPositionY);
    job->setMoveOffset(mMoveOffset);
    job->setScaleFactor(mScaleFactor);
    job->setAreaSize(mAreaSize);
    job->setIterationMax(mIterationMax);

    connect(this, &MandelbrotCalculator::abortAllJobs,
            job, &Job::abort);

    connect(job, &Job::jobCompleted,
            this, &MandelbrotCalculator::process);

    return job;
}
```

As you can see, the jobs are allocated on the heap. This operation takes some time in the `MandelbrotCalculator` thread. But the results are worth it; the overhead is being compensated by the multi-threading system. Notice that when we call `QThreadPool::start()`, the thread pool takes ownership of the `job`. As a consequence, it will be deleted by the thread pool when `Job::run()` ends. We set the input data of the `Job` class required by the Mandelbrot algorithm.

Then two connections are performed:

- Emitting our `abortAllJobs()` signal will call the `abort()` slot of all jobs
- Our `process()` slot is executed each time a `Job` completes its task

Finally, the `Job` pointer is returned to the caller, in our case, the `generatePicture()` slot.

The last helper function is `clearJobs()`. Add it to your `MandelbrotCalculator.cpp`:

```
void MandelbrotCalculator::clearJobs()
{
    mReceivedJobResults = 0;
    emit abortAllJobs();
    QThreadPool::globalInstance()->clear();
}
```

The counter of received job results is reset. We emit our signal to abort all active jobs. Finally, we remove queued jobs waiting for an available thread in the thread pool.

The last function of this class is `process()`, and is maybe the most important function. Update your code with the following snippet:

```
void MandelbrotCalculator::process(JobResult jobResult)
{
    if (jobResult.areaSize != mAreaSize ||
            jobResult.moveOffset != mMoveOffset ||
            jobResult.scaleFactor != mScaleFactor) {
        return;
    }

    mReceivedJobResults++;
    mJobResults.append(jobResult);

    if (mJobResults.size() >= JOB_RESULT_THRESHOLD ||
            mReceivedJobResults == mAreaSize.height()) {
        emit pictureLinesGenerated(mJobResults);
        mJobResults.clear();
    }

    if (mReceivedJobResults == mAreaSize.height()) {
        qDebug() << "Generated in " << mTimer.elapsed() << " ms";
    }
}
```

This slot will be called each time a job completes its task. The first thing to check is that the current JobResult is still valid with the current input data. When a new picture is requested, we clear the jobs queue and abort the active jobs. However, if an old JobResult is still sent to this process() slot, we must ignore it.

After that, we can increment the mReceivedJobResults counter and append this JobResult to our member queue, mJobResults. The calculator waits to get JOB_RESULT_THRESHOLD (that is, 10) results before dispatching them by emitting the pictureLinesGenerated() signal. You can try to tweak this value with caution:

- A lower value, for example 1, will dispatch each line of data to the widget as soon as the calculator gets it. But the widget will be slower than the calculator to handle each line. Moreover, you will flood the widget event loop.
- A higher value relieves the widget event loop. But the user will wait longer before seeing something happening. A continuous partial frame update gives a better user experience.

Also notice that when the event is dispatched, the QList class with the job result is sent by copy. But Qt performs implicit sharing with QList, so we only send a shallow copy not a costly deep copy. Then we clear the current QList of the calculator.

Finally, if the processed JobResult is the last one in the area, we display a debug message with the elapsed time since the user call, generatePicture().

Qt tip You can set the thread count used by the QThreadPool class with setMaxThreadCount(x) where x is the thread count.

Displaying the fractal with MandelbrotWidget

Here we are, the Mandelbrot algorithm is done and the multi-threading system is ready to compute complex fractals over all your CPU cores. We can now create the widget that will convert all JobResult to display a pretty picture. Create a new C++ class called MandelbrotWidget. For this widget, we will handle the painting ourselves.

Thus, we do not need any `.ui` Qt Designer Form file. Let's begin with the `MandelbrotWidget.h` file:

```cpp
#include <memory>

#include <QWidget>
#include <QPoint>
#include <QThread>
#include <QList>

#include "MandelbrotCalculator.h"

class QResizeEvent;

class MandelbrotWidget : public QWidget
{
    Q_OBJECT

public:
    explicit MandelbrotWidget(QWidget *parent = 0);
    ~MandelbrotWidget();

private:
    MandelbrotCalculator mMandelbrotCalculator;
    QThread mThreadCalculator;
    double mScaleFactor;
    QPoint mLastMouseMovePosition;
    QPointF mMoveOffset;
    QSize mAreaSize;
    int mIterationMax;
    std::unique_ptr<QImage> mImage;
};
```

You should recognize some known variable names such as `mScaleFactor`, `mMoveOffset`, `mAreaSize`, or `mIterationMax`. We have already covered them in the `JobResult` and `Job` implementation. Here are the real new ones:

- The `mMandelbrotCalculator` variable is our multi-threaded `Job` manager. The widget will do requests to it and wait for results.
- The `mThreadCalculator` variable allows the Mandelbrot calculator to run in its own thread.
- The `mLastMouseMovePosition` variable is used by the widget to handle user events for the pan feature.
- The `mImage` variable is the current picture displayed by the widget. It is a `unique_ptr` pointer, so `MandelbrotWidget` is the owner of `mImage`.

We can now add the functions. Update your code like this:

```
class MandelbrotWidget : public QWidget
{
...
public slots:
    void processJobResults(QList<JobResult> jobResults);

signals:
    void requestPicture(QSize areaSize, QPointF moveOffset, double
scaleFactor, int iterationMax);

protected:
    void paintEvent(QPaintEvent*) override;
    void resizeEvent(QResizeEvent* event) override;
    void wheelEvent(QWheelEvent* event) override;
    void mousePressEvent(QMouseEvent* event) override;
    void mouseMoveEvent(QMouseEvent* event) override;

private:
    QRgb generateColorFromIteration(int iteration);

private:
    ...
};
```

Before we dive into the implementation, let's talk about these functions:

- The `processJobResults()` function will handle the `JobResult` list dispatched by `MandelbrotCalculator`.
- The `requestPicture()` signal is emitted each time the user changes the input data (offset, scale, or area size).
- The `paintEvent()` function draws the widget with the current `mImage`.
- The `resizeEvent()` function resizes the Mandelbrot area size when the user resizes the window.
- The `wheelEvent()` function handles the user mouse wheel event to apply a scale factor.
- The `mousePressEvent()` function and `mouseMoveEvent()` retrieve user mouse events to move the Mandelbrot picture.
- The `generateColorFromIteration()` is a helper function to colorize the Mandelbrot picture. The iteration value by pixel is converted into a color value.

We can now implement the `MandelbrotWidget` class. Here is the beginning of the `MandelbrotWidget.cpp` file:

```cpp
#include "MandelbrotWidget.h"

#include <QResizeEvent>
#include <QImage>
#include <QPainter>
#include <QtMath>

const int ITERATION_MAX = 4000;
const double DEFAULT_SCALE = 0.005;
const double DEFAULT_OFFSET_X = -0.74364390249094747;
const double DEFAULT_OFFSET_Y = 0.13182589977450967;

MandelbrotWidget::MandelbrotWidget(QWidget *parent) :
    QWidget(parent),
    mMandelbrotCalculator(),
    mThreadCalculator(this),
    mScaleFactor(DEFAULT_SCALE),
    mLastMouseMovePosition(),
    mMoveOffset(DEFAULT_OFFSET_X, DEFAULT_OFFSET_Y),
    mAreaSize(),
    mIterationMax(ITERATION_MAX)
{
    mMandelbrotCalculator.moveToThread(&mThreadCalculator);

    connect(this, &MandelbrotWidget::requestPicture,
        &mMandelbrotCalculator,
        &MandelbrotCalculator::generatePicture);

    connect(&mMandelbrotCalculator,
        &MandelbrotCalculator::pictureLinesGenerated,
        this, &MandelbrotWidget::processJobResults);

    mThreadCalculator.start();
}
```

At the top of the snippet, we set some constant default values. Feel free to tweak these values if you want a different view when you start the application. The first thing the constructor does is to change the thread affinity of the `mMandelbrotCalculator` class. In this way, processing performed by the calculator (creating and starting jobs, aggregating job results, and clearing jobs) does not disturb the UI thread. Then we perform connections with the signal and slot of `MandelbrotCalculator`. Because the widget and the calculator have a different thread affinity, the connection will be automatically a `Qt::QueuedConnection` slot.

Finally, we can start the thread of `mThreadCalculator`. We can now add the destructor:

```
MandelbrotWidget::~MandelbrotWidget()
{
    mThreadCalculator.quit();
    mThreadCalculator.wait(1000);
    if (!mThreadCalculator.isFinished()) {
        mThreadCalculator.terminate();
    }
}
```

We need to request the calculator thread to quit. When the calculator thread event loop handles our request, the thread will return a code 0. We wait 1,000 ms for the thread to end. We can continue this implementation with all the cases that request a new picture. Here is the `resizeEvent()` slot:

```
void MandelbrotWidget::resizeEvent(QResizeEvent* event)
{
    mAreaSize = event->size();

    mImage = std::make_unique<QImage>(mAreaSize,
        QImage::Format_RGB32);
    mImage->fill(Qt::black);

    emit requestPicture(mAreaSize, mMoveOffset, mScaleFactor,
        mIterationMax);
}
```

We update `mAreaSize` with the new widget size. Then, a new black `QImage` is created with the correct dimensions. Finally, we request a picture computation to `MandelbrotCalculator`. Let's see how the mouse wheel is handled:

```
void MandelbrotWidget::wheelEvent(QWheelEvent* event)
{
    int delta = event->delta();
    mScaleFactor *= qPow(0.75, delta / 120.0);
    emit requestPicture(mAreaSize, mMoveOffset, mScaleFactor,
        mIterationMax);
}
```

The mouse wheel value can be retrieved from `QWheelEvent::delta()`. We use a power function to apply a coherent value on `mScaleFactor` and we request an updated picture. We can now implement the pan feature:

```
void MandelbrotWidget::mousePressEvent(QMouseEvent* event)
{
    if (event->buttons() & Qt::LeftButton) {
        mLastMouseMovePosition = event->pos();
    }
}
```

The first function stores the mouse position where the user begins the move gesture. Then the next function will use `mLastMouseMovePosition` to create an offset:

```
void MandelbrotWidget::mouseMoveEvent(QMouseEvent* event)
{
    if (event->buttons() & Qt::LeftButton) {
        QPointF offset = event->pos() - mLastMouseMovePosition;
        mLastMouseMovePosition = event->pos();
        offset.setY(-offset.y());
        mMoveOffset += offset * mScaleFactor;
        emit requestPicture(mAreaSize, mMoveOffset, mScaleFactor,
            mIterationMax);
    }
}
```

The difference between the new and the old mouse position gives us the pan offset. Notice that we invert a y-axis value because the mouse event is in a top-left referential, whereas the Mandelbrot algorithm relies on a bottom-left referential. Finally, we request a picture with updated input values. We covered all the user events that emit a `requestPicture()` signal. Let's see now how we handle `JobResult` dispatched by `MandelbrotCalculator`:

```
void MandelbrotWidget::processJobResults(QList<JobResult> jobResults)
{
    int yMin = height();
    int yMax = 0;

    for(JobResult& jobResult : jobResults) {

        if (mImage->size() != jobResult.areaSize) {
            continue;
        }

        int y = jobResult.pixelPositionY;
        QRgb* scanLine =
            reinterpret_cast<QRgb*>(mImage->scanLine(y));
```

```
            for (int x = 0; x < mAreaSize.width(); ++x) {
                scanLine[x] =
                    generateColorFromIteration(jobResult.values[x]);
            }

            if (y < yMin) {
                yMin = y;
            }

            if (y > yMax) {
                yMax = y;
            }
        }

    repaint(0, yMin,
            width(), yMax);
}
```

The calculator sends us a `QList` of `JobResult`. For each one, we need to check if the concerned area size is still valid. We directly update the pixel colors of `mImage`. The `scanLine()` function returns a pointer on the pixel data. It is a fast way to update a `QImage` pixel color. The `JobResult` function contains the iteration count, and our helper function, `generateColorFromIteration()`, returns a RGB value depending on the iteration value. A complete repaint of the widget is not necessary, because we only update several lines of the `QImage`. Thus, we repaint only the updated region.

Here is how we convert an iteration value in an RGB value:

```
QRgb MandelbrotWidget::generateColorFromIteration(int iteration)
{
    if (iteration == mIterationMax) {
        return qRgb(50, 50, 255);
    }

    return qRgb(0, 0, (255.0 * iteration / mIterationMax));
}
```

Colorizing a Mandelbrot is an art on its own. We implement here a simple linear interpolation on the blue channel. A nice Mandelbrot picture depends on the maximum iteration per pixel and its color technique. Feel free to enhance it like you want!

Here we are, the last but not least function, `paintEvent()`:

```
void MandelbrotWidget::paintEvent(QPaintEvent* event)
{
    QPainter painter(this);
    painter.save();

    QRect imageRect = event->region().boundingRect();
    painter.drawImage(imageRect, *mImage, imageRect);

    painter.setPen(Qt::white);

    painter.drawText(10, 20, QString("Size: %1 x %2")
        .arg(mImage->width())
        .arg(mImage->height()));

    painter.drawText(10, 35, QString("Offset: %1 x %2")
        .arg(mMoveOffset.x())
        .arg(mMoveOffset.y()));

    painter.drawText(10, 50, QString("Scale: %1")
        .arg(mScaleFactor));

    painter.drawText(10, 65, QString("Max iteration: %1")
        .arg(ITERATION_MAX));

    painter.restore();
}
```

We must override this function because we handle the widget drawing by ourselves. The first thing to do is to draw the updated region of the image. The `QPaintEvent` object contains the region that needs to be updated. The `QPainter` class makes the drawing easy. Finally, we draw some information texts of the current input data in white. You now have a complete overview of the progressive picture display line by line. Let's sum up the workflow of this feature:

1. Each `Job::run()` generates a `JobResult` object.
2. The `MandelbrotCalculator::process()` signal aggregates the `JobResult` object and dispatches them by groups (by default, 10).
3. The `MandelbrotWidget::processJobResults()` signal updates only concerned lines of the picture and requests a partial repaint of the widget.
4. The `MandelbrotWidget::paintEvent()` signal only redraws the picture with the new values.

This feature causes a little overhead, but the user experience is smoother. Indeed, the application reacts quickly to the user events: the first lines are updated almost immediately. The user does not have to wait for the full picture generation to see something happening.

The widget is ready; do not forget to add it to `MainWindow`. Promoting a custom widget should be an easy task for you now. If you have any doubt, check `Chapter 12`, *Conquering the Desktop UI*, or the complete source code of this chapter. You should now be able to display and navigate into your multi-threaded Mandelbrot set!

If you start the application, you should see something like this:

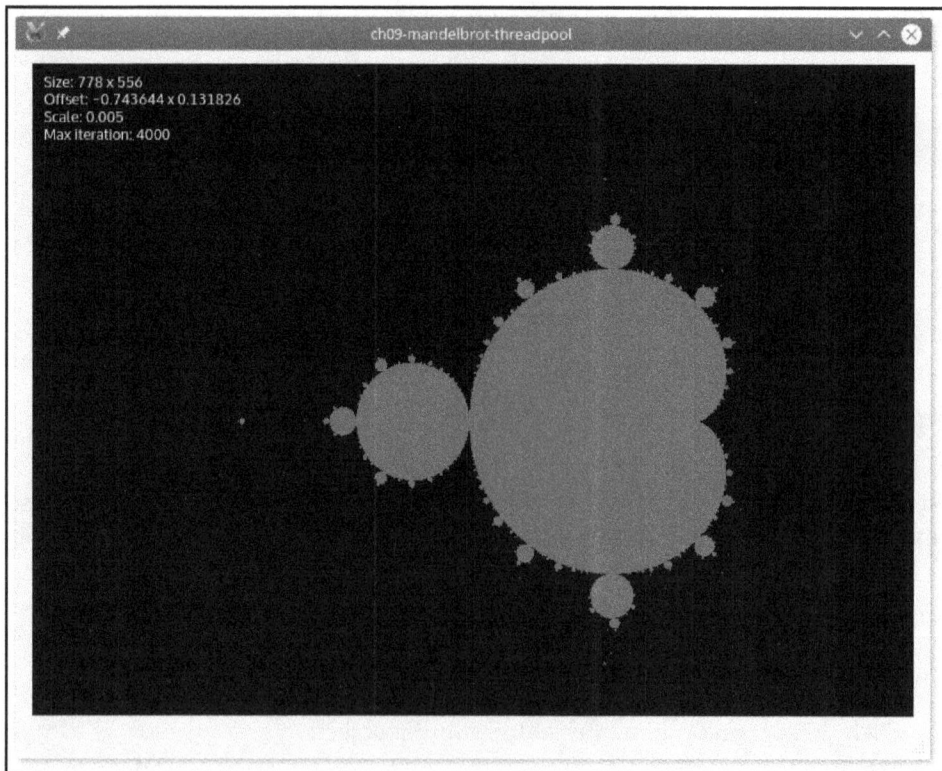

Try to zoom now and pan into the Mandelbrot set. You should find some funny places like this one:

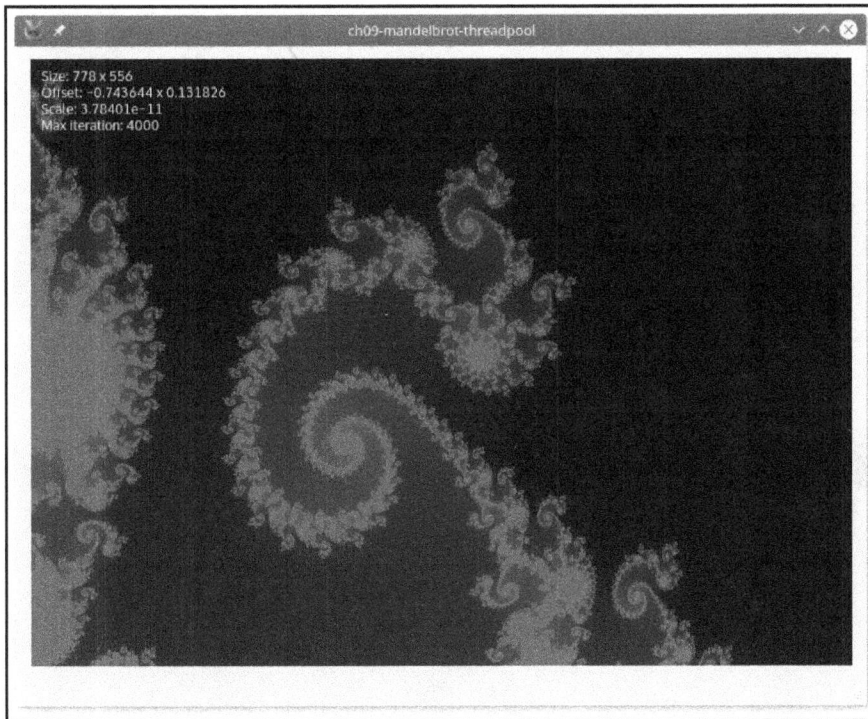

Summary

You discovered how a `QThread` class works and learned how to efficiently use tools provided by Qt to create a powerful multi-threaded application. Your Mandelbrot application is able to use all cores of your CPU to compute a picture quickly.

Creating a multi-threaded application presents a lot of pitfalls (deadlock, event loop flood, orphan threads, overhead, and so on). The application architecture is important. If you are able to isolate the heavy code that you want to parallelize, everything should go well. Nevertheless, the user experience is of primary importance; you will sometimes have to accept a little overhead if your application gives the user a smoother feeling.

In the next chapter, we will see several ways to implement an IPC (Inter-Process Communication) between applications. The project example will enhance your current Mandelbrot application with a TCP/IP socket system. So the Mandelbrot generator will compute pictures over several CPU cores from multiple computers!

18
Need IPC? Get Your Minions to Work

In the previous chapter, you learned how to send information across threads of the same process. In this chapter, you will discover how to share data between threads of different processes. We will even share information between applications running on different physical computers. We will enhance the Mandelbrot generator application from Chapter 17, *Keeping Your Sanity with Multithreading*. The Mandelbrot application will now only display results processed by the worker programs. These minions have only one mission: compute the tasks as fast as possible and return a result to your main application.

Here are the topics covered in this chapter:

- How two applications can communicate together
- Creating a multithreaded TCP server
- Reading and writing on a TCP socket
- Other IPC techniques like QSharedMemory, QProcess, and Qt D-Bus
- Network serialization using QDataStream
- Computer clustering
- Inter-process communication techniques

An **IPC (inter-process communication)** is a communication between two or more processes. They can be instances of the same or a different application. The Qt framework provides multiple modules to help you implement a communication between your applications. Most of these modules are cross-platform. Let's talk about the IPC tools provided by Qt.

The first tools are the TCP/IP sockets. They provide a bidirectional data exchange over a network. Therefore, you can use them to talk with processes on different computers. Moreover, the `loopback` interface allows you to communicate with processes running on the same computer. All the required classes are inside the `QtNetwork` module. This technique relies on a client-server architecture. Here is an example of the server part:

```
QTcpServer* tcpServer = new QTcpServer(this);
tcpServer->listen(QHostAddress::Any, 5000);

connect(tcpServer, &QTcpServer::newConnection, [tcpServer] {
    QTcpSocket *tcpSocket = tcpServer->nextPendingConnection();
    QByteArray response = QString("Hello").toLatin1();
    tcpSocket->write(response);
    tcpSocket->disconnectFromHost();
    qDebug() << "Send response and close the socket";
});
```

The first step is to instantiate a `QTcpServer` class. It deals with the new incoming TCP connections. Then, we call the `listen()` function. You can provide a network interface and specify the port on which the server must listen for incoming connections. In this example, we listen on all network addresses (for example, `127.0.0.1`, `192.168.1.4`, and so on) on the port `5000`. When a client establishes a connection with this server, the `QTcpServer::newConnection()` signal is triggered. Let's break together this lambda slot:

1. We retrieve the `QTcpSocket` class related to this new connection with a client.
2. A `QByteArray` response is prepared with the ASCII message "Hello". Forget the lack of originality.
3. The message is sent to the client through the socket.
4. Finally, we close the socket. So the client, on this side, will be disconnected.

> **TIP**
>
> You can test a `QTcpServer` class with a telnet tool like Putty on Windows or the `telnet` command on Linux and Mac OS.

The following snippet is the client part:

```
QTcpSocket *tcpSocket = new QTcpSocket(this);
tcpSocket->connectToHost("127.0.0.1", 5000);

connect(tcpSocket, &QTcpSocket::connected, [tcpSocket] {
    qDebug() << "connected";
});
```

```
connect(tcpSocket, &QTcpSocket::readRead, [tcpSocket] {
    qDebug() << QString::fromLatin1(tcpSocket->readAll());
});
connect(tcpSocket, &QTcpSocket::disconnected, [tcpSocket] {
    qDebug() << "disconnected";
});
```

The client also uses a `QTcpSocket` class to communicate. It turns out that the connection is initiated by the client, therefore we need to call the `connectToHost()` function with the server address and port. This class provides a lot of useful signals such as `connected()` and `disconnected()` that indicate the connection status. The `readRead()` signal is emitted when new data is available for reading. The `readAll()` function returns `QByteArray` with all the available data. In our case, we know that the server sends an ASCII message to its client. Thus, we can convert this byte array in a `QString` and display it.

For this example, the server writes in the TCP socket and the client reads in it. But this communication is bidirectional, so the client can also write data and the server can read it. Try to send data from the client and display it in the server. Notice that you need to keep the communication alive by removing the `disconnectFromHost()` call in the server part.

The Qt framework provides a helper class, `QDataStream`, to easily send a complex object and handle the package fragmentation. This notion will be covered later with the project example of this chapter.

Let's talk about the second IPC technique: **shared memory**. By default, different processes do not use the same memory space. The `QSharedMemory` class provides a cross-platform method to create and use a shared memory across multiple processes. Nevertheless, the processes must run on the same computer. A shared memory is identified by a key. All the processes must use the same key to share the same shared memory segment. The first process will create the shared memory segment and put data in it:

```
QString sharedMessage("Hello");
QByteArray sharedData = sharedMessage.toLatin1();

QSharedMemory* sharedMemory = new QSharedMemory(
    "sharedMemoryKey", this);
sharedMemory->create(sharedMessage.size());

sharedMemory->lock();

memcpy(sharedMemory->data(),
       sharedData.data(),
       sharedData.size());
```

```
sharedMemory->unlock();
```

Let's analyze all the steps together:

1. Once again, we want to share the `QString` "Hello" converted in a `QByteArray` class.
2. A `QSharedMemory` class is initialized with the key, `sharedMemoryKey`. This same key should be used by the second process.
3. The first process creates the shared memory segment with a specific size in bytes. The creation also attaches the process to the shared memory segment.
4. You should now be confident with the lock/unlock system. The `QSharedMemory` class uses semaphore to protect the shared access. You must lock it before manipulating the shared memory.
5. A classical `memcpy()` function is used to copy data from the `QByteArray` class to the `QSharedMemory` class.
6. Finally, we can unlock the shared memory.

Destroying a `QShareMemory` class will call the `detach()` function that detaches the process from the shared memory segment. If this process was the last one attached, `detach()` also destroys the shared memory segment. While an attached `QShareMemory` is alive, the shared memory segment is available for other processes. The next snippet describes how a second segment can access the shared memory:

```
QSharedMemory* sharedMemory = new QSharedMemory(
    "sharedMemoryKey", this);
sharedMemory->attach();

sharedMemory->lock();

QByteArray sharedData(sharedMemory->size(), '');

memcpy(sharedData.data(),
       sharedMemory->data(),
       sharedMemory->size());
sharedMemory->unlock();

QString sharedMessage = QString::fromLatin1(sharedData);
qDebug() << sharedMessage;

sharedMemory->detach();
```

Here are the key steps:

1. As with the first process, this second process initializes a `QShareMemory` class with the key, `sharedMemoryKey`.
2. Then we attach the process to the shared memory segment with the `attach()` function.
3. We must lock the `QShareMemory` class before accessing it.
4. We initialize a `QByteArray` with the null character, , with the size of the shared memory.
5. The `memcpy()` function copies the data from the `QShareMemory` to the `QByteArray`.
6. We can convert the `QByteArray` in a `QString` and display our message.
7. The last step is to call the `detach()` function to detach the process from the shared memory segment.

Please notice that `create()` and `attach()` functions specify by default a `QShareMemory::ReadWrite` access. You can also use the `QShareMemory::ReadOnly` access.

> You can use the classes, `QBuffer` and `QDataStream` to serialize a complex object in or from a bytes array.

Another IPC way is to use the `QProcess` class. The main process starts an external application as a child process. The communication is done using the standard input and output devices. Let's create a `hello` console application relying on the standard input and output channels:

```
QTextStream out(stdout);
QTextStream in(stdin);

out << QString("Please enter your name:n");
out.flush();

QString name = in.readLine();

out << "Hello " << name << "n";
return 0;
```

We use the `QTextStream` class to easily work with the standards streams, `stdout` and `stdin`. The application prints the message `Please enter your name:`. Then we wait while the user types his name by calling the `readLine()` function. Finally, the program displays the message `Hello` and the user `name`. If you start yourself this console application, you must type your name on the keyboard to see the final hello message with your name.

The following snippet runs and communicates with the `hello` application. Furthermore, we can programmatically control the child `hello` application:

```
QProcess* childProcess = new QProcess(this);

connect(childProcess,
    &QProcess::readyReadStandardOutput, [childProcess] {
        qDebug().noquote() << "[*]" << childProcess->readAll();
});

connect(childProcess, &QProcess::started, [childProcess] {
    childProcess->write("Sophien");
});

childProcess->start("/path/to/hello");
```

Here are all the steps performed by this main application:

1. We initialize a `QProcess` object that can start an external application.
2. The child process displays messages on the console and so writes in the standard output. Then, the `readyReadStandardOutput()` signal is sent. In this case, we print the message as debug text with the prefix `[*]` to identify that it comes from the child process.
3. As soon as the child process is started, the `started()` signal is sent. In our case, we write in the child standard input the name `Sophie` (Lenna will be jealous!).
4. All is ready, we can start the `QProcess` class with the path to the `hello` console application.

If you start the main application you should get this result in its console:

```
[*] Please enter your name:
[*] Hello Sophie
```

Mission completed! The main application is a wrapper for the `hello` application. We receive all messages from the child process and we can send it some information like a specific name.

The `QProcess::start()` function also accepts a second variable: the command line arguments for the child process.

The last IPC mechanism that we will cover together is the **D-Bus protocol**. Currently, the Qt D-Bus module is officially supported only on Linux. If you need to use it on Windows, you will have to compile it from Qt sources. It can be seen as a unified protocol for IPC and **RPC (remote procedure calling)**. Many forms of communication are possible, such as:

- One-to-one
- One-to-many
- Many-to-many

The best thing about Qt D-Bus is that you can even use the signal/slot mechanism across the bus. A signal emitted from one application can be connected to a slot from another application. Linux desktop environments like KDE and GNOME use the D-Bus. That implies that you can (also) control your desktop with D-Bus.

Here are the main concepts of D-Bus:

- `Bus`: This is used in many-to-many communication. D-Bus defines two buses: the **system bus** and the **session bus**.
- `Service name`: This is the identifier of a service on a bus.
- `Message`: This is a message sent by one application. If a bus is used, the message contains the destination.

A Qt D-Bus Viewer tool can be found in your Qt installation folder (for example, `/Qt/5.7/gcc_64/bin/qdbusviewer`). All objects and messages from all services of the system and the session bus are displayed. Try to invoke exposed methods and retrieve a result.

Now that you have messed about with your Linux D-Bus services, it is time to create your own! At first, we will create a simple `HelloService` object:

```
//HelloService.h
class HelloService : public QObject
{
    Q_OBJECT

public slots:
    QString sayHello(const QString &name);
};
```

```
//HelloService.cpp
QString HelloService::sayHello(const QString& name)
{
    qDebug().noquote() << name << " is here!";
    return QString("Hello %1!").arg(name);;
}
```

No big deal here, the only function is a public slot that requires a `name`, displays who is here, and returns a hello message. In the following snippet, the main application registers a new D-Bus service and the `HelloService` object:

```
HelloService helloService;
QString serviceName("org.masteringqt.QtDBus.HelloService");

QDBusConnection::sessionBus().registerService(serviceName);
QDBusConnection::sessionBus().registerObject("/",
    &helloService, QDBusConnection::ExportAllSlots);
```

The main application initializes an `HelloService` object. Then, we register a new service named `org.masteringqt.QtDBus.HelloService` on the session bus. Finally, we register the `HelloService` object, exposing all its slots. Notice the simple object path / used for this example. The service application part is finished. Here is the client application calling the `HelloService` object:

```
QString serviceName("org.masteringqt.QtDBus.HelloService");
QDBusInterface serviceInterface(serviceName, "/");
QDBusReply<QString> response = serviceInterface.call(
    "sayHello", "Lenna");
qDebug().noquote() << response;
```

Let's analyze the client part step by step:

1. We initialize a `QDBusInterface` object with the same service name and path as the service application.
2. We call the remote method, `sayHello()` on `HelloService`, with the parameter `Lenna` (Wait, where is Sophie!?).
3. The response is stored in a `QDBusReply` object. In our case, type `QString`.
4. Finally, we display the message generated by the `HelloService` object.

If you start the service application and then the client application, you should get this console output:

```
//service application output
Lenna is here!
```

```
//client application output
Hello Lenna!
```

Use the `QDBusViewer` tool to find your D-Bus service. Select the **Session Bus** tab. Choose your service in the list. Then you can select the method `sayHello`. A right-click on it allows you to call the method. An input popup will ask you to fill the method parameter that is a name in our example. The following screenshot shows you what it looks like (it seems that Sophie is here):

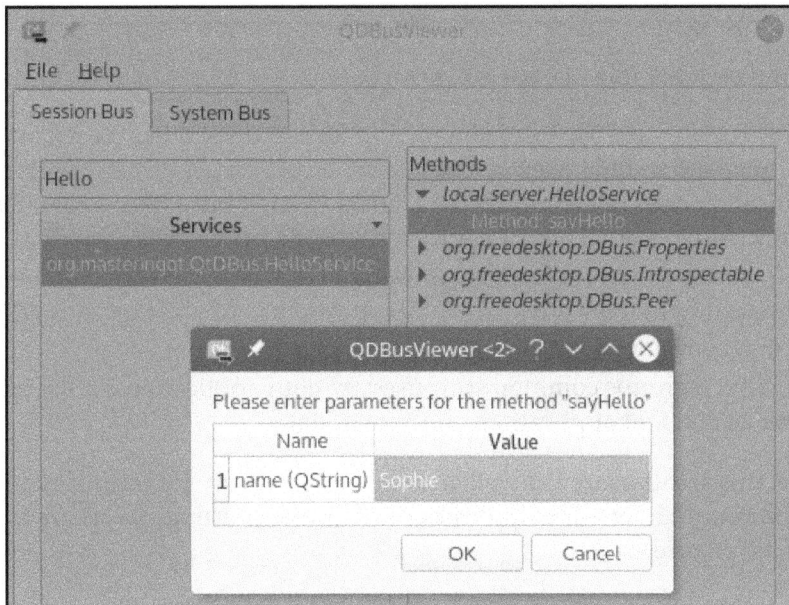

Architecturing an IPC project

The Mandelbrot picture generator from `Chapter 17`, *Keeping Your Sanity with Multithreading*, uses all cores of your computer to speed up the computing. This time, we want to use all the cores of all your computers! The first thing to do is to choose an appropriated IPC technique. For this project example, we want to establish communication between several clients acting as workers to a server running the main application. The TCP/IP sockets allows a one-to-many communication. Moreover, this IPC method is not bounded to a single computer and can operate through a network on multiple computers. This project example uses sockets by implementing a multi-threaded TCP server.

The next diagram describes the architecture:

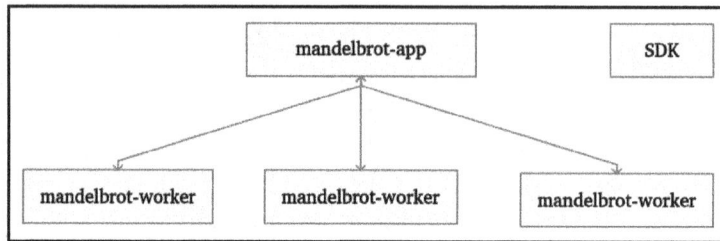

Let's talk about the global role of each actor:

- `mandelbrot-app`: This is the main application displaying the Mandelbrot picture and handling user mouse events. However, in this chapter, the application does not compute the algorithm itself but rather generates requests to connected workers. Then, it aggregates results provided by workers.
- `mandelbrot-worker`: Here is our minion! A worker is a standalone program. It is connecting to the `mandelbrot-app` through a TCP socket. A worker receives a request, computes a job, and sends back a result.
- `SDK`: This regroups common stuff used by both applications. If the SDK changes, all the dependent applications must be updated.

As you can see, this architecture fits well with the one-to-many communication required by this project. The `mandelbrot-app` application can use one or many workers to generate the same Mandelbrot picture.

Now that you get the big picture, let's look in detail at each module. You can see all of the classes in the SDK in the following diagram:

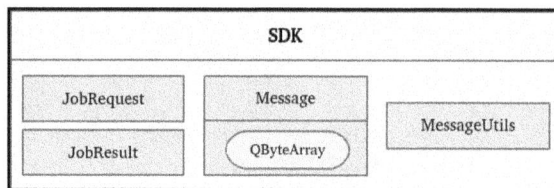

An SDK is essential when you have several modules (applications, libraries, and so on) that communicate together or need to perform the same actions. You can give the SDK to a third-party developer without compromising your main source code. In our project, mandelbrot-app and mandelbrot-worker communicate together by exchanging Message. The message structure must be known by both entities. A Message class contains a type and a raw data of the type, QByteArray. Depending on the message type, the raw data can be empty or can contain an object. In this project, a message data can be a JobRequest or a JobResult. The mandelbrot-app sends a JobRequest to mandelbrot-worker. Then, the worker returns JobResult to the main application. Finally, MessageUtils contains functions used by the main application and the workers to send and retrieve a Message.

We can now talk about the mandelbrot-worker in more detail. The next diagram describes it:

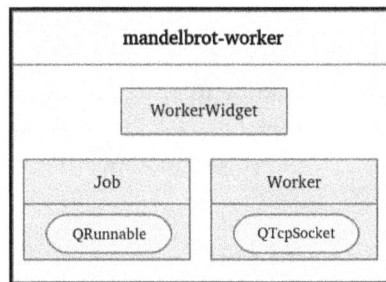

The mandelbrot-worker program is able to use all the CPU cores of a machine. The socket mechanism allows us to run it on multiple physical machines at the same time. The WorkerWidget class displays the status of the Worker object. The Worker object handles the communication with mandelbrot-app using a QTcpSocket. A Job is a QRunnable class that computes a task. Here is the workflow of this software:

1. Send a register Message to mandelbrot-app application.
2. Receive some JobRequest from mandelbrot-app and create several Job instances to complete all tasks.
3. Each Job is running in a dedicated thread and will generate a JobResult.
4. Send JobResult to mandelbrot-app.
5. On exit, send an unregister Message to mandelbrot-app.

It is now time to talk about the `mandelbrot-app` architecture. Look at the next diagram:

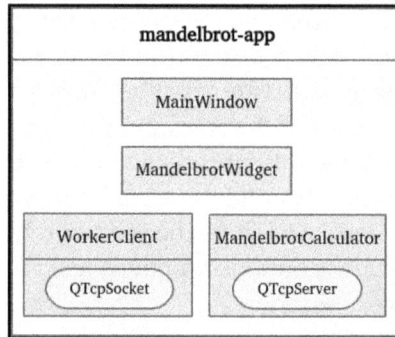

This is the main application. You can launch it on a computer with a weak CPU and the real heavy work is done by workers running the `mandelbrot-worker` software. The GUI `MainWindow` and `MandelbrotWidget` objects are the same as those in Chapter 17, *Keeping Your Sanity with Multithreading*. The `MandelbrotCalculator` class is a little different in this project, because it does not run any `QRunnable` itself. It is a TCP server that handles all registered workers and dispatches tasks to those tasks. Each `mandelbrot-worker` is managed by a `WorkerClient` object instance with a dedicated `QTcpSocket`. Here is the workflow for `mandelbrot-app`:

1. Run a TCP server on a specific port.
2. Receive a register `Message` and create a `WorkerClient` object for each registered worker.
3. When `MandelbrotWidget` requests a picture generation, `MandelbrotCalculator` creates the `JobRequest` object required to compute the full Mandelbrot picture.
4. The `JobRequest` objects are sent to the workers.
5. Receive and aggregate `JobResult` from the `mandelbrot-worker`.
6. Transmit `JobResult` to the `MandelbrotWidget` object that displays the picture.
7. If an unregister `Message` is received from a worker, the `WorkerClient` object is released and this worker will not be used for picture generation anymore.

You should now get a complete overview of this project architecture. We can begin the implementation of this project. Create a **Subdirs** project called `ch10-mandelbrot-ipc`. As you might guess, we now create two sub-projects: `mandelbrot-app` and `mandelbrot-worker`.

The implementation in the subsequent sections follows the architecture presentation order:

1. SDK.
2. `mandelbrot-worker`.
3. `mandelbrot-app`.

The implementation is a step up in complexity. Do not hesitate to take a break and come back to this section to keep the overall architecture clear.

Laying down the foundations with an SDK

The first step is to implement the classes that will be shared between our application and the workers. To do so, we are going to rely on a custom SDK. If you need to refresh your memory about this technique, take a look at `Chapter 16`, *Animations-- It's Alive, Alive!*.

As a reminder, here is the diagram describing the SDK:

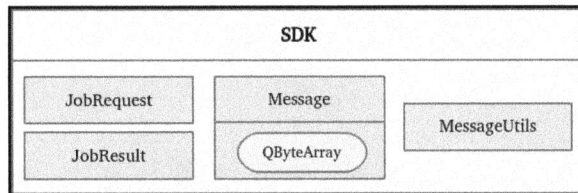

Let's describe the job of each of these components:

- The `Message` component encapsulates a piece of information that is exchanged between the application and the worker
- The `JobRequest` component contains the necessary information to dispatch a proper job to a worker
- The `JobResult` component contains the result of the Mandelbrot set calculation for a given line
- The `MessageUtils` component contains helper functions to serialize/deserialize data across the TCP socket

All these files have to be accessible from each side of our IPC mechanism (application and worker). Note that the SDK will contain only header files. We did it on purpose to simplify the SDK usage.

Let's start with `Message` implementation in the `sdk` directory. Create a `Message.h` file with the following content:

```
#include <QByteArray>

struct Message {

    enum class Type {
        WORKER_REGISTER,
        WORKER_UNREGISTER,
        ALL_JOBS_ABORT,
        JOB_REQUEST,
        JOB_RESULT,
    };

    Message(const Type type = Type::WORKER_REGISTER,
            const QByteArray& data = QByteArray()) :
        type(type),
        data(data)
    {
    }

    ~Message() {}

    Type type;
    QByteArray data;
};
```

The first thing to note is the `enum class Type` which details all the possible message types:

- `WORKER_REGISTER`: This is the message sent by the worker when it first connects to the application. The content of the message is only the number of cores of the worker's CPU. We will see soon why this is useful.
- `WORKER_UNREGISTER`: This is the message sent by the worker when it is disconnected. This lets the application know that it should remove this worker from its list and stop sending any messages to it.
- `ALL_JOBS_ABORT`: This is the message sent by the application each time a picture generation is canceled. The worker is then responsible for canceling all its current local threads.
- `JOB_REQUEST`: This is the message sent by the application to calculate a specific line of the desired picture.
- `JOB_RESULT`: This is the message sent by the worker with the calculated result from the `JOB_REQUEST` inputs.

A quick word about the `enum` class type, which is a C++11 addition. It is a safer version of enum (some might say that it is enum as it should have been from the beginning):

- The scope of the values is local. In this example, you can only reference an `enum` value with the syntax `Message::Type::WORKER_REGISTER`; no more `Message::WORKER_REGISTER` shortcuts. The good thing about this restriction is that you do not need to prefix `enum` values with a `MESSAGE_TYPE_` to be sure that the name does not conflict with anything else.
- There is no implicit conversion to `int`. The `enum` class acts like a real type, to cast an `enum` class to `int`, you have to write `static_cast<int>(` `Message::Type::WORKER_REGISTER)`.
- There is no forward declaration. You can specify that an `enum class` is a char type (with the syntax `enum class Test : char { ... }`), but the compiler will not be able to deduce the `enum` class size with a forward declaration. Therefore, it has been simply forbidden.

We tend to use the `enum` class whenever possible, meaning when it does not clash with Qt `enum` usage.

As you can see, a message has only two members:

- `type`: This is the message type we just described
- `data`: This is an opaque type that contains the piece of information to be transmitted

We chose to make `data` very generic to place the responsibility of serializing/deserializing on the `Message` callers. Based on the message `type`, they should know how to read or write the message content.

By using this approach, we avoid a tangled class hierarchy with `MessageRegister`, `MessageUnregister`, and so on. Adding a new `Message type` is simply adding a value in the `Type` enum class and doing the proper serialization/deserialization in `data` (which you have to do anyway).

To see the file in Qt Creator, do not forget to add the `Message.h` in `ch10-mandelbrot-ipc.pro` file:

```
OTHER_FILES +=
sdk/Message.h
```

The next header we will look at is `JobRequest.h`:

```
#include <QSize>
#include <QPointF>

struct JobRequest
{
    int pixelPositionY;
    QPointF moveOffset;
    double scaleFactor;
    QSize areaSize;
    int iterationMax;
};

Q_DECLARE_METATYPE(JobRequest)

// In ch10-mandelbrot-ipc
OTHER_FILES +=
    sdk/Message.h
    sdk/JobRequest.h
```

This `struct` element contains all the necessary data for the worker to calculate a line of the target Mandelbrot picture. Because the application and the worker(s) will live in different memory spaces (or even different physical machines), the parameters to calculate the Mandelbrot set have to be transmitted somehow. This is the purpose of `JobRequest`. The meaning of each field is the same as `JobResult` from Chapter 17, *Keeping Your Sanity with Multithreading*.

Note the presence of the `Q_DECLARE_METATYPE(JobRequest)` macro. This macro is used to let the Qt meta-object system know about `JobRequest`. This is needed to be able to use the class in conjunction with `QVariant`. We will not use `QVariant` directly, but rather through the use of `QDataStream` which relies on `QVariant`.

Speaking of `JobResult`, here is the new `JobResult.h`:

```
#include <QSize>
#include <QVector>
#include <QPointF>

struct JobResult
{
    JobResult(int valueCount = 1) :
        areaSize(0, 0),
        pixelPositionY(0),
        moveOffset(0, 0),
        scaleFactor(0.0),
```

```
            values(valueCount)
        {
        }

        QSize areaSize;
        int pixelPositionY;
        QPointF moveOffset;
        double scaleFactor;

        QVector<int> values;
    };

    Q_DECLARE_METATYPE(JobResult)

    // In ch10-mandelbrot-ipc
    OTHER_FILES +=
        sdk/Message.h
        sdk/JobRequest.h
        sdk/JobResult.h
```

The new version is a shameless copy-paste (with the small Q_DECLARE_METATYPE addition) of the project example of Chapter 17, *Keeping Your Sanity with Multithreading*.

Working with QDataStream and QTcpSocket

The missing piece of the SDK is MesssageUtils. It deserves a dedicated section because it covers two major topics: serialization and QDataStream transactions.

We will start with the serialization. We already know that Message stores only an opaque QByteArray data member. As a consequence, the desired data has to be serialized as a QByteArray before being passed to Message.

If we take the example of a JobRequest object, it is not directly sent. We first put in in a generic Message object with the appropriate Message type. The following diagram summarizes the sequence of actions to be done:

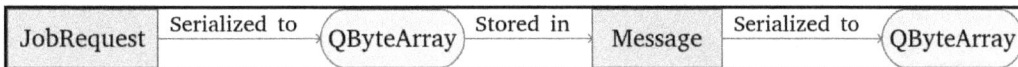

JobRequest	Serialized to	QByteArray	Stored in	Message	Serialized to	QByteArray

The JobRequest object is first serialized to a QByteArray class; it is then passed to a Message instance which is in turn serialized to a final QByteArray. The deserialization process is the exact mirror of this sequence (from right to left).

Serializing data brings a lot of questions. How can we do it in a generic fashion? How do we handle the possible endianness of the CPU architecture? How do we specify the length of the data to be able to deserialize it properly?

Once again, the Qt folks did a great job and provided us a great tool to deal with these issues: QDataStream.

The QDataStream class enables you to serialize binary data to any QIODevice (QAbstractSocket, QProcess, QFileDevice, QSerialPort, and so on). The great advantage of QDataStream is that it encodes the information in a platform-agnostic format. You do not have to worry about the byte order, the operating system, or the CPU.

The QDataStream class implements the serialization of C++ primitive types and several Qt type (QBrush, QColor, QString, and so on). Here is an example of a basic write:

```
QFile file("myfile");
file.open(QIODevice::WriteOnly);
QDataStream out(&file);
out << QString("QDataStream saved my day");
out << (qint32)42;
```

As you can see, QDataStream relies on the overload of the << operator to write data. To read information, open the file with the correct mode and read with the >> operator.

Back to our case; we want to serialize custom classes, like JobRequest. To do so, we have to overload the << operator for JobRequest. The signature of the function will be like so:

```
QDataStream& operator<<(QDataStream& out,
                        const JobRequest& jobRequest)
```

What we write have here is that we want to overload the out << jobRequest operator call with our custom version. By doing so, we intend to fill the out object with the content of jobRequest. Because QDataStream already supports the serialization of primitive types, all we have to do is serialize them.

Here is the updated version of JobRequest.h:

```
#include <QSize>
#include <QPointF>
#include <QDataStream>

struct JobRequest
{
    ...
};
```

```
inline QDataStream& operator<<(QDataStream& out,
                               const JobRequest& jobRequest)
{
    out << jobRequest.pixelPositionY
        << jobRequest.moveOffset
        << jobRequest.scaleFactor
        << jobRequest.areaSize
        << jobRequest.iterationMax;
    return out;
}

inline QDataStream& operator>>(QDataStream& in,
                               JobRequest& jobRequest)
{
    in >> jobRequest.pixelPositionY;
    in >> jobRequest.moveOffset;
    in >> jobRequest.scaleFactor;
    in >> jobRequest.areaSize;
    in >> jobRequest.iterationMax;
    return in;
}
```

We include `QDataStream` and overload the << very easily. The returned `out` will be updated with the platform-agnostic content of the passed `jobRequest`. The >> operator overload follows the same pattern: we fill the `jobRequest` parameter with the content of the `in` variable. Behind the scenes, `QDataStream` stores the variable size in the serialized data to be able to read it afterwards.

Be careful to serialize and deserialize the members in the same order. If you do not pay attention to this, you might encounter very peculiar values in `JobRequest`.

The `JobResult` operators overload follows the same pattern, and it does not deserve to be included in the chapter. Look at the source code of the project if you have any doubt about its implementation.

On the other hand, `Message` operator overload needs to be covered:

```
#include <QByteArray>
#include <QDataStream>

#include <QByteArray>
#include <QDataStream>

struct Message {
    ...
};
```

```
inline QDataStream &operator<<(QDataStream &out, const Message &message)
{
    out <<   static_cast<qint8>(message.type)
        << message.data;
    return out;
}

inline QDataStream &operator>>(QDataStream &in, Message &message)
{
    qint8 type;
    in >> type;
    in >> message.data;

    message.type = static_cast<Message::Type>(type);
    return in;
}
```

Because the Message::Type enum class signal does not have an implicit conversion to int, we need to explicitly convert it to be able to serialize it. We know that there will not be more than 255 message types, therefore we can safely cast it to a qint8 type.

The same story applies to the reading part. We start by declaring a qint8 type variable that will be filled with in >> type, and then, the type variable is casted to a Message::Type in message.

Our SDK classes are ready to be serialized and deserialized. Let's see it in action in MessageUtils with the serialization of a message and its writing to a QTcpSocket class.

Always in the sdk directory, create a MessageUtils.h header with the following content:

```
#include <QByteArray>
#include <QTcpSocket>
#include <QDataStream>

#include "Message.h"

namespace MessageUtils {

inline void sendMessage(QTcpSocket& socket,
                        Message::Type messageType,
                        QByteArray& data,
                        bool forceFlush = false)
{
    Message message(messageType, data);

    QByteArray byteArray;
    QDataStream stream(&byteArray, QIODevice::WriteOnly);
```

```
        stream << message;
        socket.write(byteArray);
        if (forceFlush) {
            socket.flush();
        }
    }
}
```

There is no need to instantiate a MessageUtils class, as it does not hold any state. Here we used a MessageUtils namespace to simply protect our function against any name collision.

The meat of the snippet lies in sendMessage(). Let's look at the parameters:

- socket: This is the QTcpSocket class in which the message will be sent. It is the responsibility of the caller to ensure that it is properly opened.
- messageType: This is the type of the message to be sent.
- data: This is the serialized data to be included in the message. It is a QByteArray class, meaning that the caller already serialized its custom class or data.
- forceFlush: This is a flag to force the socket to flush upon the message shipment. The OS keeps socket buffers that wait to be filled before being sent across the wire. Some messages need to be delivered immediately, like an abort all jobs message.

In the function itself, we start by creating a message with the passed parameters. Then, a QByteArray class is created. This byteArray will be the receptacle of the serialized data.

As a matter of fact, byteArray is passed in the constructor of the QDataStream stream, which is opened in the QIODevice::WriteOnly mode. It means that the stream will output its data to the byteArray.

After that, the message is elegantly serialized to stream with stream << message and the modified byteArray is written to the socket with socket.write(byteArray).

Finally, if the forceFlush flag is set to true, the socket is flushed with socket.flush().

Some messages will not have any payload associated. For this reason, we add a small helper function for this purpose:

```
inline void sendMessage(QTcpSocket& socket,
                        Message::Type messageType,
                        bool forceFlush = false) {
    QByteArray data;
    sendMessage(socket, messageType, data, forceFlush);
```

```
}
```

Now that the `sendMessage()` is done, let's turn to the `readMessages()`. Because we are working in IPC and more specifically with sockets, interesting issues arise when we want to read and parse messages.

When something is ready to be read in the socket, a signal will notify us. But how do we know how much to read? In the case of a `WORKER_DISCONNECT` message, there is no payload. On the other hand, a `JOB_RESULT` message can be very heavy. Even worse, several `JOB_RESULT` messages can line up in the socket, waiting to be read.

To make things more difficult, we have to acknowledge the fact that we are working with the network. Packets can be lost, retransmitted, incomplete or whatever. Sure, TCP ensures that we eventually get all of the information, but it can be delayed.

If we had to do it ourselves, it would have implied a custom message header, with a payload size and a footer for each message.

A feature introduced in Qt 5.7 comes to the rescue: `QDataStream` transaction. The idea is the following: when you start reading on a `QIODevice` class, you already know how much you have to read (based on the size of the object you want to fill). However, you might not get all the data in a single read.

If the read is not complete, `QDataStream` stores what was already read in a temporary buffer and restores it upon the next read. The next read will contain what was already loaded plus the content of the new read. You can see it as a checkpoint in the read stream that can be loaded later.

This process can be repeated until data is read. The official documentation provides a simple enough example:

```
in.startTransaction();
qint8 messageType;
QByteArray messageData;
in >> messageType >> messageData;

if (!in.commitTransaction())
    return;
```

In the `QDataStream` class in which we want to read, `in.startTransaction()` marks the checkpoint in the stream. It will then try to read `messageType` and `messageData` atomically. If it cannot do it, `in.commitTransaction()` returns `false` and the read data is copied in an internal buffer.

Upon the next call to this code (more data to read), `in.startTransaction()` will restore the preceding buffer and try to finish the atomic read.

In our `readMessages()` situation, we can receive several messages at once. This is why the code is a bit more complex. Here is the updated version of `MessageUtils`:

```
#include <memory>
#include <vector>
#include <QByteArray>
#include <QTcpSocket>
#include <QDataStream>

#include "Message.h"

...

inline std::unique_ptr<std::vector<std::unique_ptr<Message>>>
readMessages(QDataStream& stream)
{
    auto messages =
std::make_unique<std::vector<std::unique_ptr<Message>>>();
    bool commitTransaction = true;
    while (commitTransaction
                    && stream.device()->bytesAvailable() > 0) {
        stream.startTransaction();
        auto message = std::make_unique<Message>();
        stream >> *message;
        commitTransaction = stream.commitTransaction();
        if (commitTransaction) {
            messages->push_back(std::move(message));
        }
    }
    return messages;
}

}
```

In the function, the parameter is only a `QDataStream`. We assume that the caller linked the stream with the socket with `stream.setDevice(socket)`.

Because we do not know the length of the content to be read, we prepare ourselves to read several messages. To explicitly indicate ownership and avoid any memory leaks, we return a vector<unique_ptr<Message>>. This vector has to be a unique_ptr pointer to be able to allocate it on the heap and avoid any copy during the return of the function.

In the function itself, we start by declaring the vector. After that, a while loop is executed. The two conditions to stay in the loop are:

- commitTransaction == true: This an atomic read in the stream that has been performed; a complete message has been read
- stream.device().bytesAvailable() > 0: This states that there is still data to read in the stream

In the while loop, we start by marking the stream with stream.startTransaction(). After that, we try to perform an atomic read of a *message signal and see the result with stream.commitTransaction(). If it succeeded, the new message is added to the messages vector. This is repeated until we read all the content of the stream with the bytesAvailable() > 0 test.

Let's study a use case to understand what will happen. Consider that we receive multiple messages in readMessages():

- The stream object will try to read it into message.
- The commitTransaction variable will be set to true and the first message will be added to messages.
- If there are still bytes to read in the stream, repeat from step one. Otherwise, exit the loop.

To sum up, working with sockets raises its own set of questions. On one hand, it is a very powerful IPC mechanism with a lot of flexibility. On the other hand, it brings a lot of complexity due the nature of the network itself. Luckily, Qt (and moreover Qt 5.7) brings great classes to help us.

Keep in mind that we tolerate the QDataStream serialization and transactions overhead because it fits well to our need. If you are working on a constrained embedded platform, you might not have so much liberty about serializing overhead and buffer copies. However, you will still have to rebuild messages by hand for incoming bytes.

Interacting with sockets in the worker

Now that the SDK is completed, we can turn to the worker. The project is complex enough; we can refresh our memory with the `mandelbrot-worker` architecture:

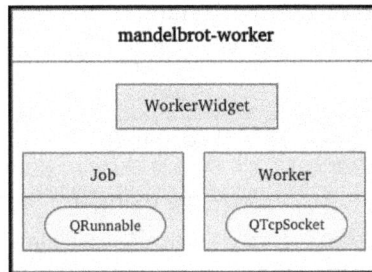

We will start by implementing the `Job` class. Inside the `mandelbrot-worker` project, create a new C++ class named `Job`. Here is the `Job.h` content:

```cpp
#include <QObject>
#include <QRunnable>
#include <QAtomicInteger>

#include "JobRequest.h"
#include "JobResult.h"

class Job : public QObject, public QRunnable
{
    Q_OBJECT
public:
    explicit Job(const JobRequest& jobRequest,
                 QObject *parent = 0);
    void run() override;

signals:
    void jobCompleted(JobResult jobResult);

public slots:
    void abort();

private:
    QAtomicInteger<bool> mAbort;
    JobRequest mJobRequest;
};
```

If you remember the Job class from Chapter 17, *Keeping Your Sanity with Multithreading*, this header should ring a bell. The only difference is that the parameters of the job (area size, scale factor, and so on) are extracted from the JobRequest object rather than stored directly as member variables.

As you can see, the JobRequest object is provided in the constructor of Job. We will not cover Job.cpp, as it is very much like the version of it in Chapter 17, *Keeping Your Sanity with Multithreading*.

We now proceed to the Worker class. This class has the following roles:

- It interacts with the mandelbrot-app using a QTcpSocket class
- It dispatches JobRequests to a QThreadPool class, aggregates the results, and sends them back to mandelbrot-app application through the QTcpSocket class

We will start by studying the interaction with the QTcpSocket class. Create a new class named Worker with the following header:

```
#include <QObject>
#include <QTcpSocket>
#include <QDataStream>

#include "Message.h"
#include "JobResult.h"

class Worker : public QObject
{
    Q_OBJECT
public:
    Worker(QObject* parent = 0);
    ~Worker();

private:
    void sendRegister();

private:
    QTcpSocket mSocket;
};
```

The `Worker` class is the owner of `mSocket`. The first thing we will implement is the connection with `mandelbrot-app`. Here is the constructor of `Worker` in `Worker.cpp`:

```
#include "Worker.h"

#include <QThread>
#include <QDebug>
#include <QHostAddress>

#include "JobRequest.h"
#include "MessageUtils.h"

Worker::Worker(QObject* parent) :
    QObject(parent),
    mSocket(this)
{
    connect(&mSocket, &QTcpSocket::connected, [this] {
        qDebug() << "Connected";
        sendRegister();
    });
    connect(&mSocket, &QTcpSocket::disconnected, [] {
        qDebug() << "Disconnected";
    });

    mSocket.connectToHost(QHostAddress::LocalHost, 5000);
}
```

The constructor initializes `mSocket` with `this` as the parent and it then proceeds to connecting the relevant `mSocket` signals to lambdas:

- `QTcpSocket::connected`: When the socket is connected, it will send its register message. We will soon cover this function
- `QTcpSocket::disconnected`: When the socket is disconnected, it simply prints a message in the console

Finally, `mSocket` tries to connect on the `localhost` on the port `5000`. In the code example, we assume that you execute the worker and the application on the same machine. Feel free to change this value if you run the worker and the application on different machines.

The body of `sendRegister()` function looks like this:

```
void Worker::sendRegister()
{
    QByteArray data;
    QDataStream out(&data, QIODevice::WriteOnly);
    out << QThread::idealThreadCount();
```

```
        MessageUtils::sendMessage(mSocket,
                                  Message::Type::WORKER_REGISTER,
                                  data);
    }
```

A `QByteArray` class is filled with the `idealThreadCount` function of the worker's machine. After that, we call `MessageUtils::sendMessage` to serialize the message and send it through our `mSocket`.

Once the worker is registered, it will start to receive job requests, process them, and send job results back. Here is the updated `Worker.h`:

```
class Worker : public QObject
{
    ...
signals:
    void abortAllJobs();

private slots:
    void readMessages();

private:
    void handleJobRequest(Message& message);
    void handleAllJobsAbort(Message& message);
    void sendRegister();
    void sendJobResult(JobResult jobResult);
    void sendUnregister();
    Job* createJob(const JobRequest& jobRequest);

private:
    QTcpSocket mSocket;
    QDataStream mSocketReader;
    int mReceivedJobsCounter;
    int mSentJobsCounter;
};
```

Let's review the role of each one of these new members:

- `mSocketReader`: This is the `QDataStream` class through which we will read `mSocket` content. It will be passed as a parameter to our `MessageUtils::readMessages()` function.
- `mReceivedJobsCounter`: This is incremented each time a new `JobRequest` is received from `mandelbrot-app`.
- `mSentJobsCounter`: This is incremented each time a new `JobResult` is sent to `mandelbrot-app`.

Now for the new functions:

- `abortAllJobs()`: This is a signal emitted when the `Worker` class receives the appropriate message.
- `readMessages()`: This is the slot called each time there is something to read in `mTcpSocket`. It parses the messages and, for each message type, it will call the corresponding function.
- `handleJobRequest()`: This function creates and dispatches a `Job` class according to the `JobRequest` object contained in the message parameter.
- `handleAllJobsAbort()`: This function cancels all the current jobs and clear the thread queue.
- `sendJobResult()`: This function sends the `JobResult` object to `mandelbrot-app`.
- `sendUnregister()`: This function sends the unregister message to `mandelbrot-app`.
- `createJob()`: This is a helper function to create and properly connect the signals of a new `Job`.

The header is now complete. We can proceed to the updated constructor in `Worker.cpp`:

```
Worker::Worker(QObject* parent)  :
    QObject(parent),
    mSocket(this),
    mSocketReader(&mSocket),
    mReceivedJobsCounter(0),
    mSentJobsCounter(0)
{

    ...

    connect(&mSocket, &QTcpSocket::readyRead,
            this, &Worker::readMessages);

    mSocket.connectToHost(QHostAddress::LocalHost, 5000);
}
```

The `QDataStream mSocketReader` variable is initialized with the address of `mSocket`. This means that it will read its content from the `QIODevice` class. After that, we add the new connect to the `QTcpSocket` signal, `readyRead()`. Each time that data is available to read on the socket, our slot, `readMessages()`, will be called.

Here is the implementation of readMessages():

```
void Worker::readMessages()
{
    auto messages = MessageUtils::readMessages(mSocketReader);
    for(auto& message : *messages) {
        switch (message->type) {
            case Message::Type::JOB_REQUEST:
                handleJobRequest(*message);
                break;
            case Message::Type::ALL_JOBS_ABORT:
                handleAllJobsAbort(*message);
                break;
            default:
                break;
        }
    }
}
```

The messages are parsed with the MessageUtils::readMessages() function. Note the use of C++11 semantics with auto, which elegantly hides the smart pointers syntax and still handles the memory for us.

For each parsed message, it is handled in the switch case. Let's review handleJobRequest():

```
void Worker::handleJobRequest(Message& message)
{
    QDataStream in(&message.data, QIODevice::ReadOnly);
    QList<JobRequest> requests;
    in >> requests;

    mReceivedJobsCounter += requests.size();
    for(const JobRequest& jobRequest : requests) {
        QThreadPool::globalInstance()
                ->start(createJob(jobRequest));
    }
}
```

In this function, the message object is already deserialized. However, message.data still needs to be deserialized. To achieve this, we create a QDataStream in a variable that will read from message.data.

From here, we parse the requests QList. Because QList already overrides the >> operator, it works in cascade and calls our JobRequest >> operator overload. Deserializing data has never been so easy!

After that, we increment mReceivedJobsCounter and start processing these JobRequests. For each one, we create a Job class and dispatch it to the global QThreadPool class. If you have a doubt about QThreadPool, get back to Chapter 17, *Keeping Your Sanity with Multithreading*.

The createJob() function is straightforward to implement:

```
Job* Worker::createJob(const JobRequest& jobRequest)
{
    Job* job = new Job(jobRequest);
    connect(this, &Worker::abortAllJobs,
            job, &Job::abort);
    connect(job, &Job::jobCompleted,
            this, &Worker::sendJobResult);
    return job;
}
```

A new Job class is created and its signals are properly connected.
When Worker::abortAllJobs is emitted, every running Job should be canceled with the Job::abort slot.

The second signal, Job::jobCompleted is emitted when the Job class has finished calculating its values. Let's see the connected slot, sendJobResult():

```
void Worker::sendJobResult(JobResult jobResult)
{
    mSentJobsCounter++;
    QByteArray data;
    QDataStream out(&data, QIODevice::WriteOnly);
    out << jobResult;
    MessageUtils::sendMessage(mSocket,
                              Message::Type::JOB_RESULT,
                              data);
}
```

We first increment the mSentJobsCounter and then serialize the JobResult to a QByteArray data which is passed to MessageUtils::sendMessage().

We completed the tour of the `JobRequest` handling and the following `JobResult` shipment. We still have to cover `handleAllJobsAbort()`, which is called from `readMessages()`:

```
void Worker::handleAllJobsAbort(Message& /*message*/)
{
    emit abortAllJobs();
    QThreadPool::globalInstance()->clear();
    mReceivedJobsCounter = 0;
    mSentJobsCounter = 0;
}
```

The `abortAllJobs()` signal is emitted first to tell all the running jobs to cancel their process. After that, the `QThreadPool` class is cleared and the counters are reset.

The last piece of `Worker` is the `sendUnregister()`, which is called in the `Worker` destructor:

```
Worker::~Worker()
{
    sendUnregister();
}

void Worker::sendUnregister()
{
    MessageUtils::sendMessage(mSocket,
                              Message::Type::WORKER_UNREGISTER,
                              true);
}
```

The `sendUnregister()` function just calls `sendMessage` without any data to serialize. Note that it passes the `forceFlush` flag to `true` to make sure that the socket is flushed and that `mandelbrot-app` application will receive the message as fast as possible.

The `Worker` instance will be managed by a widget which will display the progress of the current calculation. Create a new class named `WorkerWidget` and update `WorkerWidget.h`, like so:

```
#include <QWidget>
#include <QThread>
#include <QProgressBar>
#include <QTimer>

#include "Worker.h"

class WorkerWidget : public QWidget
```

```
{
    Q_OBJECT
public:
    explicit WorkerWidget(QWidget *parent = 0);
    ~WorkerWidget();

private:
    QProgressBar mStatus;
    Worker mWorker;
    QThread mWorkerThread;
    QTimer mRefreshTimer;
};
```

The members of `WorkerWidget` are:

- `mStatus`: The `QProgressBar` that will display the percentage of processed `JobRequests`
- `mWorker`: The `Worker` instance owned and started by `WorkerWidget`
- `mWorkerThread`: The `QThread` class in which `mWorker` will be executed
- `mRefreshTimer`: The `QTimer` class that will periodically poll `mWorker` to know the process advancement

We can proceed to `WorkerWidget.cpp`:

```
#include "WorkerWidget.h"

#include <QVBoxLayout>

WorkerWidget::WorkerWidget(QWidget *parent) :
    QWidget(parent),
    mStatus(this),
    mWorker(),
    mWorkerThread(this),
    mRefreshTimer()
{
    QVBoxLayout* layout = new QVBoxLayout(this);
    layout->addWidget(&mStatus);

    mWorker.moveToThread(&mWorkerThread);

    connect(&mRefreshTimer, &QTimer::timeout, [this] {
        mStatus.setMaximum(mWorker.receivedJobsCounter());
        mStatus.setValue(mWorker.sentJobCounter());
    });

    mWorkerThread.start();
```

```
        mRefreshTimer.start(100);
    }

    WorkerWidget::~WorkerWidget()
    {
        mWorkerThread.quit();
        mWorkerThread.wait(1000);
    }
```

First, the `mStatus` variable is added to the `WorkerWidget` layout. Then the `mWorker` thread affinity is moved to `mWorkerThread` and `mRefreshTimer` is configured to poll `mWorker` and update `mStatus` data.

Finally, `mWorkerThread` is started, triggering the `mWorker` process. The `mRefreshTimer` object is also started with an interval of 100 milliseconds between each timeout.

The last thing to cover in `mandelbrot-worker` is the `main.cpp`:

```cpp
#include <QApplication>

#include "JobResult.h"

#include "WorkerWidget.h"

int main(int argc, char *argv[])
{
    qRegisterMetaType<JobResult>();

    QApplication a(argc, argv);
    WorkerWidget workerWidget;

    workerWidget.show();
    return a.exec();
}
```

We start by registering `JobResult` with `qRegisterMetaType` because it is used in the signal/slot mechanism. After that, we instantiate a `WorkerWidget` layout and display it.

Interacting with sockets from the application

The next project to complete is `mandelbrot-app`. It will contain the `QTcpServer` that will interact with the workers and the picture drawing of the Mandelbrot set. As a reminder, the diagram of the `mandelbrot-app` architecture is shown here:

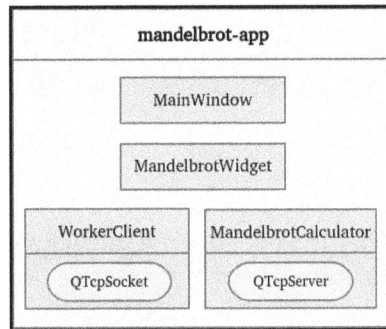

We will build this application from the ground up. Let's start with the class responsible for maintaining the connection with a specific `Worker`: `WorkerClient`. This class will live in its specific `QThread` and will interact with a `Worker` class using the same `QTcpSocket`/`QDataStream` mechanism we covered in the last section.

In `mandelbrot-app`, create a new C++ class named `WorkerClient` and update `WorkerClient.h` like so:

```
#include <QTcpSocket>
#include <QList>
#include <QDataStream>

#include "JobRequest.h"
#include "JobResult.h"
#include "Message.h"

class WorkerClient : public QObject
{
    Q_OBJECT
public:
    WorkerClient(int socketDescriptor);

private:
    int mSocketDescriptor;
    int mCpuCoreCount;
    QTcpSocket mSocket;
    QDataStream mSocketReader;
```

```
};

Q_DECLARE_METATYPE(WorkerClient*)
```

It looks very similar to `Worker`. Yet it may behave differently from a life cycle point of view. Each time a new `Worker` connects to our `QTcpServer`, a new `WorkerClient` will be spawned with an associated `QThread`. The `WorkerClient` object will take the responsibility of interacting with the `Worker` class through the `mSocket`.

If the `Worker` disconnects, the `WorkerClient` object will be deleted and removed from the `QTcpServer` class.

Let's review the content of this header, starting with the members:

- `mSocketDescriptor`: This is the unique integer assigned by the system to interact with the socket. `stdin`, `stdout`, and `stderr` are also descriptors that point to specific streams in your application. For a given socket, the value will be retrieved in `QTcpServer`. More on this later on.
- `mCpuCoreCount`: This is the CPU core count for the connected `Worker`. This field will be initialized when the `Worker` sends the `WORKER_REGISTER` message.
- `mSocket`: This is the `QTcpSocket` used to interact with the `Worker` class.
- `mSocketReader`: This has the same role it had in `Worker` - it reads `mSocket` content.

Now we can add the functions to `WorkerClient.h`:

```cpp
class WorkerClient : public QObject
{
    Q_OBJECT
public:
    WorkerClient(int socketDescriptor);
    int cpuCoreCount() const;

signals:
    void unregistered(WorkerClient* workerClient);
    void jobCompleted(WorkerClient* workerClient,
                    JobResult jobResult);
    void sendJobRequests(QList<JobRequest> requests);

public slots:
    void start();
    void abortJob();

private slots:
    void readMessages();
```

```
    void doSendJobRequests(QList<JobRequest> requests);

private:
    void handleWorkerRegistered(Message& message);
    void handleWorkerUnregistered(Message& message);
    void handleJobResult(Message& message);

    ...
};
```

Let's see what each function does:

- `WorkerClient()`: This function expects a `socketDescriptor` as a parameter. As a consequence, a `WorkerClient` function cannot be initialized without a valid socket.
- `cpuCoreCount()`: This function is a simple getter to let the owner of `WorkerClient` know how many cores the `Worker` has.

The class has three signals:

- `unregister()`: This is the signal sent by `WorkerClient` when it has received the `WORKER_UNREGISTER` message.
- `jobCompleted()`: This is the signal sent by `WorkerClient` when it has received the `JOB_RESULT` message. It will pass by copying the deserialized `JobResult`.
- `sendJobRequests()`: This is emitted from the owner of `WorkerClient` to pass `JobRequests` in a queued connection to the proper slot: `doSendJobRequests()`.

Here are the details of the slots:

- `start()`: This slot is called when `WorkerClient` can start its process. Typically, it will be connected to the `start` signal of the `QThread` associated with the `WorkerClient`.
- `abortJob()`: This slot triggers the shipment of the `ALL_JOBS_ABORT` message to the `Worker`.
- `readMessages()`: This slot is called each time there is something to read in the socket.
- `doSendJobRequests()`: This slot is the real slot that triggers the shipment of the `JobRequests` to the `Worker`.

And finally, here are the details of the private functions:

- `handleWorkerRegistered()`: This function processes the `WORKER_REGISTER` message and initializes `mCpuCoreCount`
- `handleWorkerUnregistered()`: This function processes the `WORKER_UNREGISTER` message and emits the `unregistered()` signal
- `handleJobResult()`: This function processes the `JOB_RESULT` message and dispatches the content through the `jobCompleted()` signal

The implementation in `WorkerClient.cpp` should be quite familiar. Here is the constructor:

```
#include "MessageUtils.h"

WorkerClient::WorkerClient(int socketDescriptor) :
    QObject(),
    mSocketDescriptor(socketDescriptor),
    mSocket(this),
    mSocketReader(&mSocket)
{
    connect(this, &WorkerClient::sendJobRequests,
            this, &WorkerClient::doSendJobRequests);
}
```

The fields are initialized in the initialization list and the `sendJobRequests` signal is connected to the private slot, `doSendJobRequests`. This trick is used to still have a queued connection across threads while avoiding multiple functions declarations.

We will proceed with the `start()` function:

```
void WorkerClient::start()
{
    connect(&mSocket, &QTcpSocket::readyRead,
            this, &WorkerClient::readMessages);
    mSocket.setSocketDescriptor(mSocketDescriptor);
}
```

This is very short indeed. It first connects the `readyRead()` signal from the socket to our `readMessages()` slot. After that, `mSocket` is properly configured with `mSocketDescriptor`.

The connect has to be done in start() because it should be executed in the QThread class associated with our WorkerClient. By doing so, we know that the connect will be a direct connection and that mSocket will not have to queue signals to interact with WorkerClient.

Note that at the end of the function, the associated QThread is not terminated. On the contrary, it is executing its event loop with QThread::exec(). The QThread class will continue to run its event loop until someone calls QThread::exit().

The only purpose of the start() function is to do the mSocket connect work in the right thread affinity. After that, we rely solely on the Qt signal/slot mechanism to process data. There is no need for a busy while loop.

The readMessages() class is waiting for us; let's see it:

```
void WorkerClient::readMessages()
{
    auto messages = MessageUtils::readMessages(mSocketReader);
    for(auto& message : *messages) {
        switch (message->type) {
            case Message::Type::WORKER_REGISTER:
                handleWorkerRegistered(*message);
                break;
            case Message::Type::WORKER_UNREGISTER:
                handleWorkerUnregistered(*message);
                break;
            case Message::Type::JOB_RESULT:
                handleJobResult(*message);
                break;
            default:
                break;
        }
    }
}
```

No surprises here. It's exactly like we did for Worker. The Messages are deserialized using MessageUtils::readMessages() and, for each message type, the appropriate function is called.

Here is the content of each of these functions, starting with `handleWorkerRegistered()`:

```
void WorkerClient::handleWorkerRegistered(Message& message)
{
    QDataStream in(&message.data, QIODevice::ReadOnly);
    in >> mCpuCoreCount;
}
```

For the `WORKER_REGISTER` message, `Worker` only serialized an `int` in `message.data`, so we can initialize `mCpuCoreCount` on the spot with `in >> mCpuCoreCount`.

Now the body of `handleWorkerUnregistered()`:

```
void WorkerClient::handleWorkerUnregistered(Message& /*message*/)
{
    emit unregistered(this);
}
```

It is a relay to send the `unregistered()` signal, which will be picked up by the owner of `WorkerClient`.

The last "read" function is `handleJobResult()`:

```
void WorkerClient::handleJobResult(Message& message)
{
    QDataStream in(&message.data, QIODevice::ReadOnly);
    JobResult jobResult;
    in >> jobResult;
    emit jobCompleted(this, jobResult);
}
```

This is deceptively short. It only deserializes the `jobResult` component from `message.data` and emits the `jobCompleted()` signal.

The "write-to-socket" functions are `abortJob()` and `doSendJobRequest()`:

```
void WorkerClient::abortJob()
{
    MessageUtils::sendMessage(mSocket,
                               Message::Type::ALL_JOBS_ABORT,
                               true);
}

void WorkerClient::doSendJobRequests(QList<JobRequest> requests)
{
    QByteArray data;
    QDataStream stream(&data, QIODevice::WriteOnly);
```

```
stream << requests;

MessageUtils::sendMessage(mSocket,
                          Message::Type::JOB_REQUEST,
                          data);
}
```

The abortJob() function sends the ALL_JOBS_ABORT message with the forceFlush flag set to true and doSendJobRequests() serializes the requests to stream before sending them using MessageUtils::sendMessage().

Building your own QTcpServer

Everything is ready to read and write in our sockets. We still need a server to orchestrate all these instances. To do so, we will develop a modified version of the MandelbrotCalculator class, which was covered in Chapter 17, *Keeping Your Sanity with Multithreading*.

The idea is to respect the same interface, in order to have MandelbrotWidget oblivious to the fact that the Mandelbrot picture generation is deported on different processes/machines.

The main difference between the old MandelbrotCalculator and the new one is that we replaced the QThreadPool class by a QTcpServer. The MandelbrotCalculator class now only has the responsibility to dispatch JobRequests to Workers and aggregate the result, but it never interacts anymore with a QThreadPool class.

Create a new C++ class named MandelbrotCalculator.cpp and update MandelbrotCalculator.h to match this:

```
#include <memory>
#include <vector>

#include <QTcpServer>
#include <QList>
#include <QThread>
#include <QMap>
#include <QElapsedTimer>

#include "WorkerClient.h"
#include "JobResult.h"
#include "JobRequest.h"

class MandelbrotCalculator : public QTcpServer
```

```
{
    Q_OBJECT
public:
    MandelbrotCalculator(QObject* parent = 0);
    ~MandelbrotCalculator();

signals:
    void pictureLinesGenerated(QList<JobResult> jobResults);
    void abortAllJobs();

public slots:
    void generatePicture(QSize areaSize, QPointF moveOffset,
                         double scaleFactor, int iterationMax);

private slots:
    void process(WorkerClient* workerClient, JobResult jobResult);
    void removeWorkerClient(WorkerClient* workerClient);

protected:
    void incomingConnection(qintptr socketDescriptor) override;

private:
    std::unique_ptr<JobRequest> createJobRequest(
                                                int pixelPositionY);
    void sendJobRequests(WorkerClient& client,
                         int jobRequestCount = 1);
    void clearJobs();

private:
    QPointF mMoveOffset;
    double mScaleFactor;
    QSize mAreaSize;
    int mIterationMax;
    int mReceivedJobResults;
    QList<JobResult> mJobResults;
    QMap<WorkerClient*, QThread*> mWorkerClients;
    std::vector<std::unique_ptr<JobRequest>> mJobRequests;
    QElapsedTimer mTimer;
};
```

The modified (or new) data is highlighted. First, note that the class now inherits from `QTcpServer` rather than `QObject`. The `MandelbrotCalculator` class is now a `QTcpServer` and is able to accept and manage connections. Before digging into this topic, we can review the new members:

- `mWorkerClients`: This is a `QMap` that stores the pair `WorkerClient` and `QThread`. Each time a `WorkerClient` is created, an associated `QThread` is also spawned and both of them are stored in `mWorkerClients`.
- `mJobRequests`: This is the list of `JobRequests` for the current picture. Each time a picture generation is requested, the full list of `JobRequest` is generated, ready to be dispatched to `WorkerClients` (that is, to the `Worker` on the other side of the socket).

And the functions are:

- `process()`: This function is a slightly modified version of the one seen in Chapter 17, *Keeping Your Sanity with Multithreading*. It not only aggregates `JobResults` before sending them with the `pictureLinesGenerated()` signal, but also dispatches `JobRequest` to the passed `WorkerClient` to keep them busy.
- `removeWorkerClient()`: This function removes and deletes the given `WorkerClient` from `mWorkerClients`.
- `incomingConnection()`: This function is an overloaded function from `QTcpServer`. It is called each time a new client tries to connect to `MandelbrotCalculator`.
- `createJobRequest()`: This is a helper function that creates a `JobRequest` that is added to `mJobRequests`.
- `sendJobRequests()`: This function is responsible for sending a list of `JobRequests` to the specified `WorkerClient`.

Let's turn to `MandelbrotCalculator.cpp` with the constructor:

```cpp
#include <QDebug>
#include <QThread>

using namespace std;

const int JOB_RESULT_THRESHOLD = 10;

MandelbrotCalculator::MandelbrotCalculator(QObject* parent) :
    QTcpServer(parent),
    mMoveOffset(),
```

```
            mScaleFactor(),
            mAreaSize(),
            mIterationMax(),
            mReceivedJobResults(0),
            mWorkerClients(),
            mJobRequests(),
            mTimer()
    {
        listen(QHostAddress::Any, 5000);
    }
```

This is the common initialization list with the `listen()` instruction in the body. Because we are subclassing `QTcpServer`, we can call listen on ourselves. Note that `QHostAddress::Any` works either for IPv4 and IPv6.

Let's see the overloaded function, `incomingConnection()`:

```
    void MandelbrotCalculator::incomingConnection(
                                        qintptr socketDescriptor)
    {
        qDebug() << "Connected workerClient";
        QThread* thread = new QThread(this);
        WorkerClient* client = new WorkerClient(socketDescriptor);
        int workerClientsCount = mWorkerClients.keys().size();
        mWorkerClients.insert(client, thread);
        client->moveToThread(thread);

        connect(this, &MandelbrotCalculator::abortAllJobs,
                client, &WorkerClient::abortJob);

        connect(client, &WorkerClient::unregistered,
                this, &MandelbrotCalculator::removeWorkerClient);
        connect(client, &WorkerClient::jobCompleted,
                this, &MandelbrotCalculator::process);

        connect(thread, &QThread::started,
                client, &WorkerClient::start);
        thread->start();

        if(workerClientsCount == 0 &&
            mWorkerClients.size() == 1) {
            generatePicture(mAreaSize, mMoveOffset,
                        mScaleFactor, mIterationMax);
        }
    }
```

Once `listen()` has been called, each time someone connects to our ip/port pair, `incomingConnection()` will be triggered with `socketDescriptor` passed as a parameter.

> You can test this on your machine connection with a simple `telnet 127.0.0.1 5000` command. You should see the `Connected workerClient` log in `mandelbrot-app`.

We start by creating a `QThread` class and a `WorkerClient`. This pair is immediately inserted in the `mWorkerClients` map and `client` thread affinity is changed to `thread`.

After that, we do all the connects to manage the `client` (`abortJob`, `unregister`, and `jobCompleted`). We continue with the `QThread::started()` signal, which is connected to the `WorkerClient::start()` slot and finally, `thread` is started.

The last part of the function is used to trigger a picture generation upon the first `client` connection. If we did not do this, the screen would have remained black until we panned or zoomed.

We have covered the `WorkerClient` creation; let's finish its life cycle with its destruction with `removeWorkerClient()`:

```
void MandelbrotCalculator::removeWorkerClient(WorkerClient* workerClient)
{
    qDebug() << "Removing workerClient";
    QThread* thread = mWorkerClients.take(workerClient);
    thread->quit();
    thread->wait(1000);
    delete thread;
    delete workerClient;
}
```

The `workerClient`/`thread` pair is removed from `mWorkerClients` and cleanly deleted. Note that this function can be called from the `WorkerClient::unregistered` signal or in the `MandelbrotCalculator` destructor:

```
MandelbrotCalculator::~MandelbrotCalculator()
{
    while (!mWorkerClients.empty()) {
        removeWorkerClient(mWorkerClients.firstKey());
    }
}
```

When `MandelbrotCalculator` is deleted, `mWorkerClients` has to be properly emptied. The iterator style `while` loop does a good job of calling `removeWorkerClient()`.

In this new version of `MandelbrotCalculator`, `generatePicture()` does not have exactly the same behavior:

```
void MandelbrotCalculator::generatePicture(
                            QSize areaSize, QPointF moveOffset,
                            double scaleFactor, int iterationMax)
{
    // sanity check & members initization
    ...

    for(int pixelPositionY = mAreaSize.height() - 1;
        pixelPositionY >= 0; pixelPositionY--) {
        mJobRequests.push_back(move(
                            createJobRequest(pixelPositionY)));
    }

    for(WorkerClient* client : mWorkerClients.keys()) {
        sendJobRequests(*client, client->cpuCoreCount() * 2);
    }
}
```

The beginning is the same. However, the end is quite different. Rather than creating `Jobs` and giving them to a `QThreadPool`, `MandelbrotCalculator` now:

- Creates `JobRequests` to generate the whole picture. Note that they are created in reverse order. We will soon see why.
- Dispatches a number of `JobRequests` to each `WorkerClient` it owns.

The second point deserves a strong emphasis. If we want to maximize the speed of our system, we have to use multiple workers, each one having multiple cores to process multiple jobs at the same time.

Even though a `Worker` class can process multiple jobs at the same time, it can only send us `JobResults` one by one (through `WorkerClient::jobCompleted`). Each time we process a `JobResult` object from a `WorkerClient`, we will dispatch a single `JobRequest` to it.

Assume that the `Worker` class has eight cores. If we send `JobRequests` one by one, the `Worker` will always have seven cores idle. We are here to heat up your CPUs, not to let them drink mojitos on the beach!

To mitigate this, the first batch of `JobResults` we send to a worker has to be higher than its `coreCount()`. By doing so, we ensure that is always has a queue of `JobRequests` to process until we generate the whole picture. This is why we send `client->cpuCoreCount() * two` initial `JobRequests`. If you play with this value, you will see that:

- If `jobCount < cpuCoreCount()`, some cores of your `Worker` will be idle and you will not leverage the full power of its CPU
- If `jobCount > cpuCoreCount()` by too much, you might overload the queue of one your `Workers`

Remember that this system is flexible enough to have multiple workers. If you have a RaspberryPI and an x86 with 16 cores, the RaspberryPI will lag behind the x86 CPU. By giving too much initial `JobRequests`, the RaspberryPI will hinder the whole picture generation while the x86 CPU has already finished all its jobs.

Let's cover the remaining functions of `MandelbrotCalculator`, starting with `createJobRequest()`:

```
std::unique_ptr<JobRequest> MandelbrotCalculator::createJobRequest(int
pixelPositionY)
{
    auto jobRequest = make_unique<JobRequest>();
    jobRequest->pixelPositionY = pixelPositionY;
    jobRequest->moveOffset = mMoveOffset;
    jobRequest->scaleFactor = mScaleFactor;
    jobRequest->areaSize = mAreaSize;
    jobRequest->iterationMax = mIterationMax;
    return jobRequest;
}
```

This is a simple creation of a `jobRequest` with the member fields of `MandelbrotCalculator`. Again, we use `unique_ptr` to explicitly indicate the ownership of `jobRequest` and avoid any memory leaks.

Next, with `sendJobRequests()`:

```
void MandelbrotCalculator::sendJobRequests(WorkerClient& client, int
jobRequestCount)
{
    QList<JobRequest> listJobRequest;
    for (int i = 0; i < jobRequestCount; ++i) {
        if (mJobRequests.empty()) {
            break;
        }
```

```
        auto jobRequest = move(mJobRequests.back());
        mJobRequests.pop_back();
        listJobRequest.append(*jobRequest);
    }

    if (!listJobRequest.empty()) {
        emit client.sendJobRequests(listJobRequest);
    }
}
```

Because we can send multiple `JobRequest`s at the same time, we loop on `jobRequestCount` by taking the last `jobRequest` of `mJobRequests` and adding it to `listJobRequest`. This is the reason for which we had to fill `mJobRequests` in the reverse order.

Finally, the `client.sendJobRequests()` signal is emitted, which in turns triggers the `WorkerClient::doSendJobRequests()` slot.

We are now going to see the modified version of `process()`:

```
void MandelbrotCalculator::process(WorkerClient* workerClient,
                                   JobResult jobResult)
{
    // Sanity check and JobResult aggregation

    if (mReceivedJobResults < mAreaSize.height()) {
        sendJobRequests(*workerClient);
    } else {
        qDebug() << "Generated in" << mTimer.elapsed() << "ms";
    }
}
```

In this version, we pass `workerClient` as a parameter. This is used at the end of the function, to be able to dispatch a new `JobRequest` to the given `workerClient`.

Finally, the updated version of `abortAllJobs()`:

```
void MandelbrotCalculator::clearJobs()
{
    mReceivedJobResults = 0;
    mJobRequests.clear();
    emit abortAllJobs();
}
```

This simply cleared `mJobRequests` instead of emptying `QThreadPool`.

The `MandelbrotCalculator` class is completed! You can copy and paste `MandelBrotWidget` and `MainWindow` (`.ui` file included) from Chapter 17, *Keeping Your Sanity with Multithreading*. We designed it to be plug and play, without knowing who generates the picture: a local `QThreadPool` with `QRunnable` or minions through an IPC mechanism.

There is only a tiny difference in `main.cpp`:

```cpp
#include <QApplication>
#include <QList>

#include "JobRequest.h"
#include "JobResult.h"
#include "WorkerClient.h"

int main(int argc, char *argv[])
{
    qRegisterMetaType<QList<JobRequest>>();
    qRegisterMetaType<QList<JobResult>>();
    qRegisterMetaType<WorkerClient*>();

    QApplication a(argc, argv);
    MainWindow w;
    w.show();

    return a.exec();
}
```

You can now launch `mandelbrot-app` and after that, the one or many `mandelbrot-worker` programs that will connect to the application. It should automatically trigger a picture generation. The Mandelbrot picture generation is now working across multiple processes! Because we chose to use sockets, you can start the application and the workers on different physical machines.

Using IPv6, you may very easily test the app/worker connection in different locations. If you do not have a high-speed Internet connection, you will see how the network hinders the picture generation.

You may want to take some time to deploy the application on multiple machines and see how this cluster works together. During our tests, we ramped up our cluster up to 18 cores with very heterogeneous machines (PC, laptop, Macbook, and so on).

Summary

IPC is a fundamental mechanism in computer science. In this chapter, you learned the various techniques offered by Qt to do IPC and how to create an application that uses sockets to interact, send, and receive commands. You took the original `mandelbrot-threadpool` application to the next level by enabling it to generate pictures on a cluster of machines.

Adding IPC on top of a multi-threaded application brings some issues. You have many more possible bottlenecks, chances of leaking memory, and have an inefficient calculation. Qt provides multiple mechanisms to do IPC. In Qt 5.7, the addition of transactions makes the serialization/deserialization part much easier.

In the next chapter, you will discover the Qt Multimedia framework and how to save and load an C++ object from a file. The project example will be a virtual drum machine. You will be able to save and load your tracks.

Having Fun with Serialization

19

The previous chapter was a firework of threads, sockets, and workers. We hope that your minions have been working hard. In this chapter, we will turn our attention to the serialization with Qt. You will learn how to serialize data in multiple formats with a flexible system. The example project will be a virtual drum machine, in which you can compose you own drum beat, record it, play it, save it, and load it back. Your drum beat will be probably so awesome that you will want to share it: you will now be able to do it in various formats.

This chapter will cover the following topics:

- How to architecture an application that plays and records sounds
- The `QVariant` class and its inner mechanics
- A flexible serialization system
- JSON serialization
- XML serialization
- Binary serialization
- The Qt Multimedia framework
- Drag and drop handling with Qt
- Triggering a button from your keyboard

Architecting the drum machine project

As usual, before diving into the code, let's study the structure of the project. The aim of the project is to be able to:

- Play and record a sound track from a drum machine
- Save this track to a file and load it to play it back

To play a sound, we will lay out four big buttons that will play a specific drum sound upon click (or a keyboard event): a kick, a snare, a hi-hat, and a cymbal crash. These sounds will be `.wav` files loaded by the application. The user will be able to record his sequence of sounds and replay it.

For the serialization part, we do not only want to save the track to a single file format, we would rather do three:

- **JSON (JavaScript Object Notation)**
- **XML (eXtensible Markup Language)**
- **Binary**

Not only is it more fun to cover three formats, but it also gives us the opportunity to understand the advantages and limitations of each one, and how it fits within the Qt framework. The architecture we are going to implement will try to be flexible to handle future evolutions. You never know how a project can evolve!

The classes' organization looks like this:

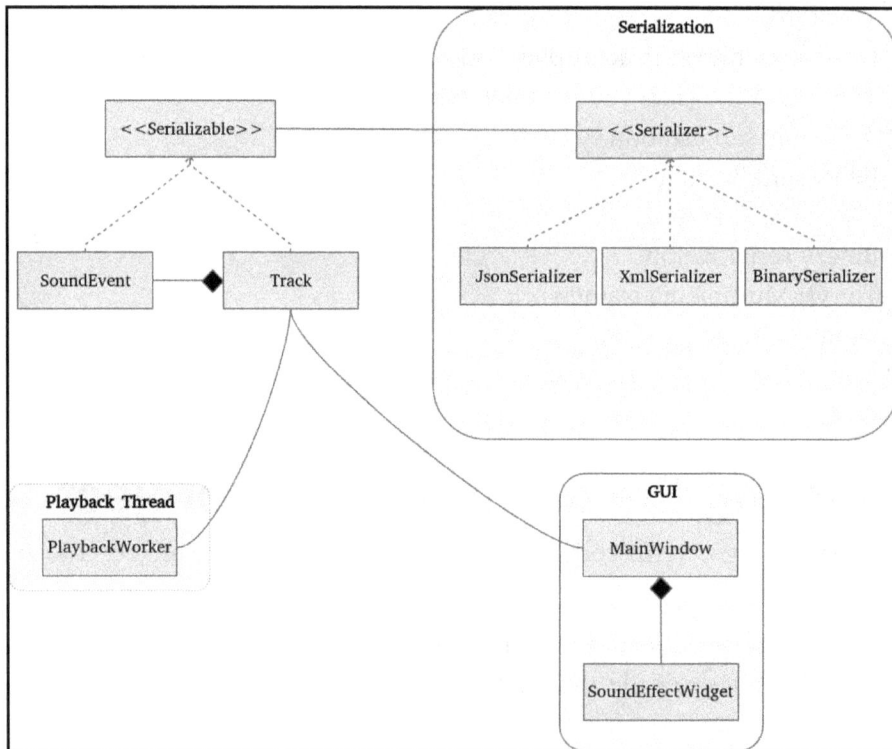

Let's review the role of these classes:

- The SoundEvent class is the basic building block of a track. It is a simple class containing timestamp (when the sound has been played) and soundId variables (what sound has been played).
- The Track class contains a list of SoundEvents, a duration and a state (playing, recording, stopped). Each time the user plays a sound, a SoundEvent class is created and added to the Track class.
- The PlaybackWorker class is a worker class that runs in a different thread. It is responsible of looping through the Track class's soundEvents and triggering the proper sound when its timestamp has been reached.
- The Serializable class is an interface that must be implemented by each class that wants to be serialized (in our case: SoundEvent and Track).
- The Serializer class is an interface that must be implemented by each format-specific implementation class.
- The JsonSerializer, XmlSerializer, and BinarySerializer are the sub-classes of Serializer class that do the format-specific job to serialize/deserialize a Serializable instance.
- The SoundEffectWidget class is the widget that holds the information to play a single sound. It displays the button for one of our four sounds. It also owns a QSoundEffect class that sends the sound to the audio card.
- The MainWindow class holds everything together. It owns the Track class, spawns the PlaybackWorker thread, and triggers the serialization/deserialization.

The output format should be easily swapped. To achieve this, we will rely on a modified version of the bridge design pattern that will allow Serializable and Serializer classes to evolve independently.

The whole project revolves around this notion of independence between modules. It goes to the extent that a sound can be replaced on the spot during a playback. Let's say that you listen to your incredible beat, and you want to try another snare sound. You will be able to replace it with a simple drag and drop of a .wav file on the SoundEffectWidget class holding the snare sound.

Creating a drum track

Let's buckle up and do this project! Create a new **Qt Widgets Application** project named ch11-drum-machine. As usual, add the CONFIG += c++14 in ch11-drum-machine.pro.

Now create a new C++ class named SoundEvent. Here is SoundEvent.h stripped from its functions:

```
#include <QtGlobal>

class SoundEvent
{

public:
    SoundEvent(qint64 timestamp = 0, int soundId = 0);
    ~SoundEvent();

    qint64 timestamp;
    int soundId;
};
```

This class contains only two public members:

- timestamp: A qint64 (long long type) that contains the current time of the SoundEvent in milliseconds since the beginning of the track
- soundId: The ID of the sound that has been played

In recording mode, each time the user plays a sound, a SoundEvent is created with the appropriate data. The SoundEvent.cpp file is so boring that we will not inflict it on you.

The next class to build is Track. Again, create the new C++ class. Let's review Track.h with its members only:

```
#include <QObject>
#include <QVector>
#include <QElapsedTimer>

#include "SoundEvent.h"

class Track : public QObject
{
    Q_OBJECT
public:
    enum class State {
        STOPPED,
```

```
        PLAYING,
        RECORDING,
    };

    explicit Track(QObject *parent = 0);
    ~Track();

private:
    qint64 mDuration;
        std::vector<std::unique_ptr<SoundEvent>> mSoundEvents;
    QElapsedTimer mTimer;
    State mState;
    State mPreviousState;
};
```

We can now go into detail about them:

- mDuration: This variable holds the duration of the Track class. This member is reset to 0 when a recording is started and updated when the recording is stopped.
- mSoundEvents: This variable is the list of SoundEvents for the given Track. As the unique_ptr semantic states it, Track is the owner of the sound events.
- mTimer: This variable is started each time Track is played or recorded.
- mState: This variable is the current State of Track class, which can have three possible values: STOPPED, PLAYING, RECORDING.
- mPreviousState: This variable is the previous State of Track. This is useful when you want to know which action to do on a new STOPPEDState. We will have to stop the playback if mPreviousState is in the PLAYING state.

The Track class is the pivot of the business logic of the project. It holds mState, which is the state of the whole application. Its content will be read during a playback of your awesome musical performance and also be serialized to a file.

Let's enrich Track.h with functions:

```
class Track : public QObject
{
    Q_OBJECT
public:
    ...
    qint64 duration() const;
    State state() const;
    State previousState() const;
    qint64 elapsedTime() const;
    const std::vector<std::unique_ptr<SoundEvent>>& soundEvents() const;
```

```
signals:
    void stateChanged(State state);

public slots:
    void play();
    void record();
    void stop();
    void addSoundEvent(int soundEventId);

private:
    void clear();
    void setState(State state);

private:
    ...
};
```

We will skip the simple getters and concentrate on the important functions:

- `elapsedTime()`: This function returns the value of the `mTimer.elapsed()`.
- `soundEvents()`: This function is a little more complicated getter. The `Track` class is the owner of `mSoundEvents` content and we really want to enforce it. For this, the getter returns a `const &` to `mSoundEvents`.
- `stateChanged()`: This function is emitted when the `mState` value is updated. The new `State` is passed as a parameter.
- `play()`: This function is a slot that starts to play the `Track`. This play is purely logical, the real playback will be triggered by `PlaybackWorker`.
- `record()`: This function is a slot that starts the recording state of `Track`.
- `stop()`: This function is a slot that stops the current start or record state.
- `addSoundEvent()`: This function creates a new `SoundEvent` with the given `soundId` and adds it to `mSoundEvents`.
- `clear()`: This function resets the content of `Track`: it clears `mSoundEvents` and sets `mDuration` to 0.
- `setState()`: This function is a private helper function that updates `mState`, `mPreviousState` and emits the `stateChanged()` signal.

Now that the header has been covered, we can study the interesting parts of `Track.cpp`:

```
void Track::play()
{
    setState(State::PLAYING);
    mTimer.start();
}
```

Calling `Track.play()` simply updates the state to `PLAYING` and starts `mTimer`. The `Track` class does not hold anything related to the Qt Multimedia API; it is limited to an evolved data holder (as it also manages a state).

Now for `record()`, which brings a lot of surprises:

```
void Track::record()
{
    clearSoundEvents();
    setState(State::RECORDING);
    mTimer.start();
}
```

It starts by clearing the data, sets the state to `RECORDING`, and also starts `mTimer`. Now consider `stop()`, which is a slight variation:

```
void Track::stop()
{
    if (mState == State::RECORDING) {
        mDuration = mTimer.elapsed();
    }
    setState(State::STOPPED);
}
```

If we are stopping in the `RECORDING` state, `mDuration` is updated. Nothing very fancy here. We saw three times the `setState()` call without seeing its body:

```
void Track::setState(Track::State state)
{
    mPreviousState = mState;
    mState = state;
    emit stateChanged(mState);
}
```

The current value of `mState` is stored in `mPreviousState` before being updated. Finally, `stateChanged()` is emitted with the new value.

The state system of `Track` is completely covered. The last missing part is the `SoundEvents` interactions. We can start with the `addSoundEvent()` snippet:

```
void Track::addSoundEvent(int soundEventId)
{
    if (mState != State::RECORDING) {
        return;
    }
    mSoundEvents.push_back(make_unique<SoundEvent>(
                                mTimer.elapsed(),
                                soundEventId));
}
```

A `soundEvent` is created only if we are in the `RECORDING` state. After that, a `SoundEvent` is added to `mSoundEvents` with the current elapsed time of `mTimer` and the passed `soundEventId`.

Now for the `clear()` function:

```
void Track::clear()
{
    mSoundEvents.clear();
    mDuration = 0;
}
```

Because we use `unique_ptr<SoundEvent>` in `mSoundEvents`, the `mSoundEvents.clear()` function is enough to empty the vector and also delete each `SoundEvent`. This is one less thing you have to worry with smart pointers.

The `SoundEvent` and `Track` are the base classes that hold the information about your future beat. We are going to see the class responsible for reading this data to play it: `PlaybackWorker`.

Create a new C++ class and update `PlaybackWorker.h` like so:

```
#include <QObject>
#include <QAtomicInteger>

class Track;

class PlaybackWorker : public QObject
{
    Q_OBJECT
public:
    explicit PlaybackWorker(const Track& track, QObject *parent = 0);
```

```
signals:
    void playSound(int soundId);
    void trackFinished();

public slots:
    void play();
    void stop();

private:
    const Track& mTrack;
    QAtomicInteger<bool> mIsPlaying;
};
```

The `PlaybackWorker` class will be running in a different thread. If your memory needs to be refreshed, go back to `Chapter 17`, *Keeping Your Sanity with Multithreading*. Its role is to iterate through the `Track` class's content to trigger the sounds. Let's break down this header:

- `mTrack`: This function is the reference to the `Track` class on which `PlaybackWorker` is working. It is passed in the constructor as a `const` reference. With this information, you already know that `PlaybackWorker` cannot modify `mTrack` in any way.

- `mIsPlaying`: This function is a flag used to be able to stop the worker from another thread. It is a `QAtomicInteger` to guarantee an atomic access to the variable.

- `playSound()`: This function is emitted by `PlaybackWorker` each time a sound needs to be played.

- `trackFinished()`: This function is emitted when the playback has been played until the end. If it has been stopped along the way, this signal will not be emitted.

- `play()`: This function is the main function of `PlaybackWorker`. In it, `mTrack` content will be queried to trigger sounds.

- `stop()`: This function is the function that updates the `mIsPlaying` flag and causes `play()` to exit its loop.

The meat of the class lies in the `play()` function:

```
void PlaybackWorker::play()
{
    mIsPlaying.store(true);
    QElapsedTimer timer;
    size_t soundEventIndex = 0;
    const auto& soundEvents = mTrack.soundEvents();
```

```
        timer.start();
        while(timer.elapsed() <= mTrack.duration()
              && mIsPlaying.load()) {
            if (soundEventIndex < soundEvents.size()) {
                const auto& soundEvent =
                                    soundEvents.at(soundEventIndex);

                if (timer.elapsed() >= soundEvent->timestamp) {
                    emit playSound(soundEvent->soundId);
                    soundEventIndex++;
                }
            }
            QThread::msleep(1);
        }

        if (soundEventIndex >= soundEvents.size()) {
            emit trackFinished();
        }
    }
```

The first thing that `play()` function does is to prepare its reading: `mIsPlaying` is set to `true`, a `QElapsedTimer` class is declared, and a `soundEventIndex` is initialized. Each time `timer.elapsed()` is called, we will know if a sound should be played.

To know which sound should be played, `soundEventIndex` will be used to know where we are in the `soundEvents` vector.

Right after that, the `timer` object is started and we enter in the `while` loop. This `while` loop has two conditions to continue:

- `timer.elapsed() <= mTrack.duration()`: This condition states that we did not finish playing the track
- `mIsPlaying.load()`: This condition returns **true**: nobody asked `PlaybackWorker` to stop

Intuitively, you might have added the `soundEventIndex < soundEvents.size()` condition in the `while` condition. By doing so, you would have exited `PlaybackWorker` as soon as the last sound has been played. Technically, it works, but that would not have respected what the user recorded.

Consider a user that created a complex beat (do not underestimate what you can do with four sounds!) and decided on a long pause of 5 seconds at the end of the song. When he clicks on the stop button, the time display indicates 00:55 (for 55 seconds). However, when he plays back his performance, the last sound finishes at 00:50. The playback stops at 00:50 and the program does not respect what he recorded.

For this reason, the `soundEventIndex < size()` test is moved inside the `while` loop and is used only as a fuse for the `soundEvents` read through.

Inside this condition, we retrieve the reference to the current `soundEvent`. We then compare the elapsed time against the `timestamp` of the `soundEvent`. If `timer.elapsed()` is greater or equal to `soundEvent->timestamp`, the signal `playSound()` is emitted with the `soundId`.

This is only a request to play a sound. The `PlaybackWorker` class limits itself to read through `soundEvents` and trigger a `playSound()` at the proper moment. The real sound will be handled later on, with the `SoundEffectWidget` class.

At each iteration in the `while` loop, a `QThread::msleep(1)` is done to avoid a busy loop. We minimize the sleep because we want the playback to be as faithful as possible to the original score. The longer the sleep, the more discrepancy we may encounter in the playback timing.

Finally, if the whole `soundEvents` has been processed, the `trackFinished` signal is emitted.

Making your objects serializable with QVariant

Now that we implemented the logic in our business classes, we have to think about what we are going to serialize and how we are going to do it. The user interacts with a `Track` class that contains all the data to be recorded and played back.

Starting from here, we can assume that the object to be serialized is `Track`, which in turn should somehow bring along its `mSoundEvents` containing a list of `SoundEvent` instances. To achieve this, we will rely heavily on the `QVariant` class.

You might have worked with QVariant before. It is a generic placeholder for any primitive type (char, int, double, and so on) but also complex types (QString, QDate, QPoint, and many more).

> The complete list of QVariant supported types is available at http://doc.qt.io/qt-5/qmetatype.html#Type-enum.

A simple example of QVariant is:

```
QVariant variant(21);

int answer = variant.toInt() * 2;

qDebug() << "what is the meaning of the universe,
            life and everything?"
         << answer;
```

We store 21 in variant. From here, we can ask for variant to have a copy of the value casted to our desired type. Here we want an int value, so we call variant.toInt(). There are a lot of conversions already available with the variant.toX() syntax.

We can take a very quick peek at what happens behind the curtain in QVariant. How does it store all we feed it? The answer lies in the C++ type union. The QVariant class is a kind of super union.

A union is a special class type that can hold only one of its non-static data members at a time. A short snippet should illustrate this:

```
union Sound
{
    int duration;
    char code;
};

Sound s = 10;
qDebug() << "Sound duration:" << s.duration;
// output= Sound duration: 10

s.code = 'K';
qDebug() << "Sound code:" << s.code;
// output= Sound code: K
```

First, a union class is declared like a struct. By default, all the members are public. The specificity of the union is that it takes only the largest member size in memory. Here, Sound will take only as much as the int duration space in memory.

Because union takes only this specific space, every member variable shares the same memory space. Therefore, only one member is available at a time, unless you want to have undefined behaviors.

When using the Sound snippet, we start by initializing with the value 10 (by default the first member is initialized). From here, s.duration is accessible but s.code is considered undefined.

Once we assign a value to s.code, s.duration becomes undefined and s.code is now accessible.

The union class makes the memory usage very efficient. In QVariant, when you store a value, it is stored in a private union:

```
union Data
{
    char c;
    uchar uc;
    short s;
    signed char sc;
    ushort us;
    ...
    qulonglong ull;
    QObject *o;
    void *ptr;
    PrivateShared *shared;
} data;
```

Note the list of primitive types and at the end the complex types, QObject* and void*.

Besides Data, a QMetaType object is initialized to know the type of the stored object. The combination of union and QMetaType lets QVariant know which Data member it should use to cast the value and give it back to the caller.

Now that you know what a union is and how QVariant uses it, you might ask: why make a QVariant class at all? A simple union would not have been enough?

The answer is no. It is not enough because a `union` class cannot have members that do not have a default constructor. It drastically reduces the number of classes you can put in a `union`. Qt folks wanted to include many classes that did not have a default constructor in `union`. To mitigate this, `QVariant` was born.

What makes `QVariant` very interesting is that it is possible to store custom types. If we wanted to convert `SoundEvent` class to a `QVariant` class, we would have added the following in `SoundEvent.h`:

```
class SoundEvent
{
    . . .
};
Q_DECLARE_METATYPE(SoundEvent);
```

We already used `Q_DECLARE_METATYPE` macro in `Chapter 18`, *Need IPC? Get Your Minions to Work*. This macro effectively registers `SoundEvent` to the `QMetaType` register, making it available for `QVariant`. Because `QDataStream` relies on `QVariant`, we had to use this macro in the last chapter.

Now to convert back and forth with a `QVariant`:

```
SoundEvent soundEvent(4365, 0);
QVariant stored;
stored.setValue(soundEvent);

SoundEvent newEvent = stored.value<SoundEvent>();
qDebug() << newEvent.timestamp;
```

As you can guess, the output of this snippet is `4365`, the original `timestamp` stored in `soundEvent`.

This approach would have been perfect if we wanted to do only binary serialization. Data can be easily written and read from. However, we want to output our `Track` and `SoundEvents` to standard formats: JSON and XML.

There is a major issue with the `Q_DECLARE_METATYPE`/`QVariant` combo: it does not store any key for the fields of the serialized class. We can already foresee that the JSON object of a `SoundEvent` class will look like this:

```
{
    "timestamp": 4365,
    "soundId": 0
}
```

There is no way the QVariant class could know that we want a timestamp key. It will only store the raw binary data. The same principle applies for the XML counterpart.

For this reason, we are going to use a variation of a QVariant with a QVariantMap. The QVariantMap class is only a typedef on QMap<QString, QVariant>. This map will be used to store the key names of the fields and the value in the QVariant class. In turn, these keys will be used by the JSON and XML serialization system to output a pretty file.

Because we aim to have a flexible serialization system, we have to be able to serialize and deserialize this QVariantMap in multiple formats. To achieve this, we will define an interface that gives the ability for a class to serialize/deserialize its content in a QVariantMap.

This QVariantMap will be used as an intermediate format, agnostic of the final JSON, XML, or binary.

Create a C++ header named Serializer.h. Here is the content:

```
#include <QVariant>

class Serializable {
public:
    virtual ~Serializable() {}
    virtual QVariant toVariant() const = 0;
    virtual void fromVariant(const QVariant& variant) = 0;
};
```

By implementing this abstract base class, a class will be Serializable. There are only two virtual pure functions:

- The toVariant() function, in which the class must return a QVariant (or, more precisely a QVariantMap, which can be casted to a QVariant thanks to the QMetaType system)
- The fromVariant() function, in which the class must initialize its members from the variant passed as a parameter

By doing so, we give the responsibility to the final class to load and save its content. After all, who knows better SoundEvent than SoundEvent itself?

Let's see Serializable in action with SoundEvent. Update SoundEvent.h like this:

```
#include "Serializable.h"

class SoundEvent : public Serializable
{
    SoundEvent(qint64 timestamp = 0, int soundId = 0);
    ~SoundEvent();

    QVariant toVariant() const override;
    void fromVariant(const QVariant& variant) override;

    ...
};
```

The SoundEvent class is now Serializable. Let's do the real work in SoundEvent.cpp:

```
QVariant SoundEvent::toVariant() const
{
    QVariantMap map;
    map.insert("timestamp", timestamp);
    map.insert("soundId", soundId);
    return map;
}

void SoundEvent::fromVariant(const QVariant& variant)
{
    QVariantMap map = variant.toMap();
    timestamp = map.value("timestamp").toLongLong();
    soundId = map.value("soundId").toInt();
}
```

In toVariant(), we simply declare a QVariantMap that gets filled with timestamp and soundId.

On the other side, in fromVariant(), we convert variant to a QVariantMap and retrieve its content with the same keys we used in toVariant(). It is as simple as that!

The next class that have to be `Serializable` is `Track`. After making `Track` inherit from `Serializable`, update `Track.cpp`:

```
QVariant Track::toVariant() const
{
    QVariantMap map;
    map.insert("duration", mDuration);

    QVariantList list;
    for (const auto& soundEvent : mSoundEvents) {
        list.append(soundEvent->toVariant());
    }
    map.insert("soundEvents", list);

    return map;
}
```

The principle is the same, although a bit more complex. The `mDuration` variable is stored in `map` object as we have seen for `SoundEvent`. For `mSoundEvents`, we have to generate a list of `QVariant` (a `QVariantList`) where each item is the converted `QVariant` version of a `soundEvent` key.

To do so, we simply loop over `mSoundEvents` and fill `list` with the `soundEvent->toVariant()` result we covered a few paragraphs before.

Now for `fromVariant()`:

```
void Track::fromVariant(const QVariant& variant)
{
    QVariantMap map = variant.toMap();
    mDuration = map.value("duration").toLongLong();

    QVariantList list = map.value("soundEvents").toList();
    for(const QVariant& data : list) {
        auto soundEvent = make_unique<SoundEvent>();
        soundEvent->fromVariant(data);
        mSoundEvents.push_back(move(soundEvent));
    }
}
```

Here, for each element of the key `soundEvents`, we create a new `SoundEvent`, load it with the content of `data`, and finally add it to the vector `mSoundEvents`.

Serializing objects in JSON format

The Track and SoundEvent classes can now be converted to a common Qt format QVariant. We now need to write a Track (and its SoundEvent objects) class in a file with a text or a binary format. This example project allows you to handle all the formats. It will allow you to switch the saved file format in one line. So where to put the specific format code? That is the million dollar question! Here is a primary approach:

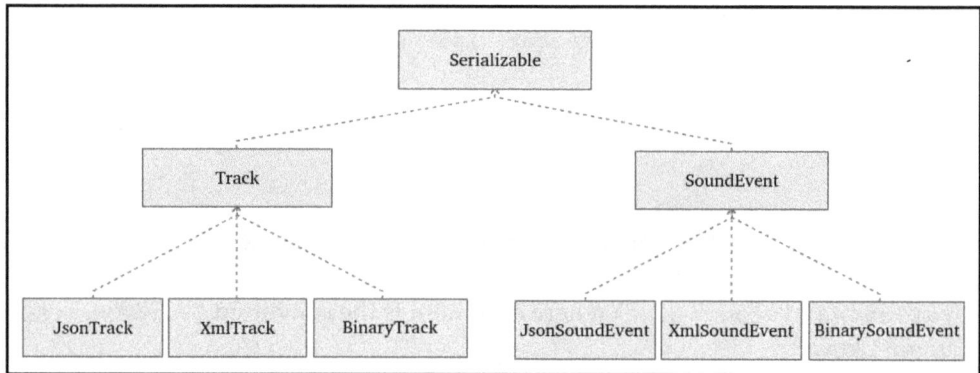

In this proposition, the specific file format serialization code is inside a dedicated child class. Well, it works but what would the hierarchy look like if we add two new file formats? Moreover, each time we add a new object to serialize, we have to create all these children classes to handle the different serialization file formats. This massive inheritance tree can quickly become a sticky mess. The code will be unmaintainable. You do not want to do that. So, here is where the bridge pattern can be a good solution:

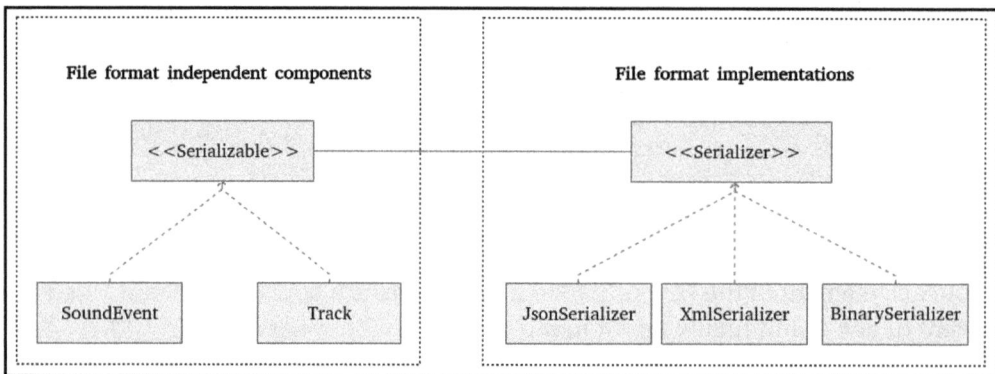

In a bridge pattern, we decouple the classes in two inheritance hierarchies:

- The components independent from the file format. The SoundEvent and Track objects do not care about JSON, XML, or a binary format.
- The file format implementations. The JsonSerializer, XmlSerializer and BinarySerializer handle a generic format, Serializable, not a specific component such as SoundEvent or Track.

Notice that in a classic bridge pattern, an abstraction (Serializable) should contains an implementor (Serializer) variable. The caller only deals with the abstraction. However in this project example, MainWindow has the ownership of Serializable and also of Serializer. This is a personal choice to use the power of design pattern while keeping uncoupled functional classes.

The architecture of Serializable and Serializer is clear. The Serializable class is already implemented so you can now create a new C++ header file called Serializer.h:

```cpp
#include <QString>

#include "Serializable.h"

class Serializer
{
public:
    virtual ~Serializer() {}

    virtual void save(const Serializable& serializable,
        const QString& filepath,
        const QString& rootName = "") = 0;
    virtual void load(Serializable& serializable,
        const QString& filepath) = 0;
};
```

The Serializer class is an interface, an abstract class with only pure virtual functions and no data. Let's talk about the save() function:

- This function saves Serializable to a file on the hard disk drive.
- The Serializable class is const and cannot be modified by this function.
- The filepath function indicates the destination file to create.

- Some `Serializer` implementations can use the `rootName` variable. For example, if we request to save a `Track` object, the `rootName` variable could be the string `track`. This is the label used to write the root element. The XML implementation requires this information.

The `load()` function is also easy to understand:

- This function loads data from a file to fill a `Serializable` class
- The `Serializable` class will be updated by this function
- The `filepath` function indicates which file to read

The interface `Serializer` is ready and waits for some implementations! Let's start with JSON. Create a C++ class, `JsonSerializer`. Here is the header for `JsonSerializer.h`:

```
#include "Serializer.h"

class JsonSerializer : public Serializer
{
public:
    JsonSerializer();

    void save(const Serializable& serializable,
        const QString& filepath,
        const QString& rootName) override;
    void load(Serializable& serializable,
        const QString& filepath) override;
};
```

No difficulties here; we have to provide an implementation of `save()` and `load()`. Here is the `save()` implementation:

```
void JsonSerializer::save(const Serializable& serializable,
    const QString& filepath, const QString& /*rootName*/)
{
    QJsonDocument doc =
        QJsonDocument::fromVariant(serializable.toVariant());
    QFile file(filepath);
    file.open(QFile::WriteOnly);
    file.write(doc.toJson());
    file.close();
}
```

The Qt framework provides a nice way to read and write a JSON file with the
QJsonDocument class. We can create a QJsonDocument class from a QVariant class.
Notice that the QVariant accepted by QJsonDocument must be
a QVariantMap, QVariantList, or QStringList. No worries, the toVariant() function
of Track class and SoundEvent generates a QVariantMap. Then, we can create a QFile
file with the destination filepath. The QJsonDocument::toJson() function converts it
to a UTF-8 encoded text representation. We write this result to the QFile file and close the
file.

> The QJsonDocument::toJson() function can produce an Indented or
> a Compact JSON format. By default, the format
> is QJsonDocument::Indented.

The load() implementation is also short:

```
void JsonSerializer::load(Serializable& serializable,
    const QString& filepath)
{
    QFile file(filepath);
    file.open(QFile::ReadOnly);
    QJsonDocument doc = QJsonDocument::fromJson(file.readAll());
    file.close();
    serializable.fromVariant(doc.toVariant());
}
```

We open a QFile with the source filepath. We read all the data
with QFile::readAll(). Then we can create a QJsonDocument class with
the QJsonDocument::fromJson() function. Finally, we can fill our
destination Serializable with the QJsonDocument converted to a QVariant class.
Notice that the QJsonDocument::toVariant() function can return QVariantList or
a QVariantMap depending the nature of the JSON document.

Here is an example of a Track class saved with this JsonSerializer:

```
{
    "duration": 6205,
    "soundEvents": [
        {
            "soundId": 0,
            "timestamp": 2689
        },
        {
            "soundId": 2,
            "timestamp": 2690
```

```
        },
        {
            "soundId": 2,
            "timestamp": 3067
        }
    ]
}
```

The root element is a JSON object, represented by a map with two keys:

- Duration: This is a simple integer value
- soundEvents: This is an array of objects. Each object is a map with the following keys:

- soundId: This is an integer
- timestamp: This is also an integer

Serializing objects in XML format

The JSON serialization was a direct representation of the C++ objects and Qt already provides all we need. However, the serialization of a C++ object can be done with various representations in an XML format. So we have to write the XML <-> QVariant conversion ourselves. We have decided to use the following XML representation:

```
<[name]> type="[type]">[data]</[name]>
```

For example, the soundId type gives this XML representation:

```
<soundId type="int">2</soundId>
```

Create a C++ class XmlSerializer that also inherits from Serializer. Let's begin with the save() function, here is XmlSerializer.h:

```cpp
#include <QXmlStreamWriter>
#include <QXmlStreamReader>

#include "Serializer.h"

class XmlSerializer : public Serializer
{
public:
    XmlSerializer();

    void save(const Serializable& serializable,
```

```
        const QString& filepath,
        const QString& rootName) override;
};
```

Now we can see the `save()` implementation in `XmlSerializer.cpp`:

```cpp
void XmlSerializer::save(const Serializable& serializable, const QString&
filepath, const QString& rootName)
{
    QFile file(filepath);
    file.open(QFile::WriteOnly);
    QXmlStreamWriter stream(&file);
    stream.setAutoFormatting(true);
    stream.writeStartDocument();
    writeVariantToStream(rootName, serializable.toVariant(),
        stream);
    stream.writeEndDocument();
    file.close();
}
```

We create a `QFile` file with the `filepath` destination. We construct a `QXmlStreamWriter` object that writes in the `QFile`. By default, the writer will produce a compact XML; you can generate a pretty XML with the `QXmlStreamWriter::setAutoFormatting()` function. The `QXmlStreamWriter::writeStartDocument()` function writes the XML version and the encoding. We write our `QVariant` in the XML stream with our `writeVariantToStream()` function. Finally, we end the document and close the `QFile`. As already explained, writing a `QVariant` to an XML stream depends on how you want to represent the data. So we have to write the conversion function. Please update your class with `writeVariantToStream()` like this:

```cpp
//XmlSerializer.h
private:
    void writeVariantToStream(const QString& nodeName,
        const QVariant& variant, QXmlStreamWriter& stream);

//XmlSerializer.cpp
void XmlSerializer::writeVariantToStream(const QString& nodeName,
    const QVariant& variant, QXmlStreamWriter& stream)
{
    stream.writeStartElement(nodeName);
    stream.writeAttribute("type", variant.typeName());

    switch (variant.type()) {
        case QMetaType::QVariantList:
            writeVariantListToStream(variant, stream);
            break;
```

```
        case QMetaType::QVariantMap:
            writeVariantMapToStream(variant, stream);
            break;
        default:
            writeVariantValueToStream(variant, stream);
            break;
    }

    stream.writeEndElement();
}
```

This `writeVariantToStream()` function is a generic entry point. It will be called each time we want to put a `QVariant` in the XML stream. The `QVariant` class could be a list, a map, or data. So we apply a specific treatment if the `QVariant` is a container (`QVariantList` or `QVariantMap`). All the other cases are considered to be a data value. Here are the steps of this function:

1. Start a new XML element with the `writeStartElement()` function. The `nodeName` will be used to create the XML tag. For example, `<soundId`.

2. Write an XML attribute called `type` in the current element. We use the name of the type stored in the `QVariant`. For example, `<soundId type="int"`.

3. Depending on the `QVariant` data type, we call one of our XML serialization functions. For example, `<soundId type="int">2`.

4. Finally, we end the current XML element with `writeEndElement()`:

    - The final result is: `<soundId type="int">2</soundId>`
    - In this function, we call three helper functions that we will create now. The easiest one is `writeVariantValueToStream()`. Please update your `XmlSerializer` class with:

```
//XmlSerializer.h
void writeVariantValueToStream(const QVariant& variant,
    QXmlStreamWriter& stream);

//XmlSerializer.cpp
void XmlSerializer::writeVariantValueToStream(
    const QVariant& variant, QXmlStreamWriter& stream)
{
    stream.writeCharacters(variant.toString());
}
```

If the `QVariant` is a simple type, we retrieve its `QString` representation. Then we use `QXmlStreamWriter::writeCharacters()` to write this `QString` in the XML stream.

The second helper function is `writeVariantListToStream()`. Here is its implementation:

```
//XmlSerializer.h
private:
    void writeVariantListToStream(const QVariant& variant,
        QXmlStreamWriter& stream);

//XmlSerializer.cpp
void XmlSerializer::writeVariantListToStream(
    const QVariant& variant, QXmlStreamWriter& stream)
{
    QVariantList list = variant.toList();

    for(const QVariant& element : list) {
        writeVariantToStream("item", element, stream);
    }
}
```

At this step, we already know that the `QVariant` is a `QVariantList`. We call `QVariant::toList()` to retrieve the list. Then we iterate over all elements of the list and call our generic entry point, `writeVariantToStream()`. Notice that we retrieve the elements from a list so we do not have an element name. But the tag name does not matter for a list item serialization, so insert the arbitrary label `item`.

The last write helper function is `writeVariantMapToStream()`:

```
//XmlSerializer.h
private:
    void writeVariantMapToStream(const QVariant& variant,
        QXmlStreamWriter& stream);

//XmlSerializer.cpp
void XmlSerializer::writeVariantMapToStream(
    const QVariant& variant, QXmlStreamWriter& stream)
{
    QVariantMap map = variant.toMap();
    QMapIterator<QString, QVariant> i(map);

    while (i.hasNext()) {
        i.next();
        writeVariantToStream(i.key(), i.value(), stream);
    }
}
```

The `QVariant` is a container but a `QVariantMap` this time. We call `writeVariantToStream()` for each element found. The tag name is important because this is a map. We use the map key from `QMapIterator::key()` as the node name.

The saving part is over. We can now implement the loading part. Its architecture follows the same spirit as the saving functions. Let's begin with the `load()` function:

```cpp
//XmlSerializer.h
public:
    void load(Serializable& serializable,
        const QString& filepath) override;

//XmlSerializer.cpp
void XmlSerializer::load(Serializable& serializable,
    const QString& filepath)
{
    QFile file(filepath);
    file.open(QFile::ReadOnly);
    QXmlStreamReader stream(&file);
    stream.readNextStartElement();
    serializable.fromVariant(readVariantFromStream(stream));
}
```

The first thing to do is to create a `QFile` with the source `filepath`. We construct a `QXmlStreamReader` with the `QFile`. The `QXmlStreamReader::readNextStartElement()` function reads until the next start element in the XML stream. Then we can use our read helper function, `readVariantFromStream()`, to create a `QVariant` class from an XML stream. Finally, we can use our `Serializable::fromVariant()` to fill the destination `serializable`. Let's implement the helper function, `readVariantFromStream()`:

```cpp
//XmlSerializer.h
private:
    QVariant readVariantFromStream(QXmlStreamReader& stream);

//XmlSerializer.cpp
QVariant XmlSerializer::readVariantFromStream(QXmlStreamReader& stream)
{
    QXmlStreamAttributes attributes = stream.attributes();
    QString typeString = attributes.value("type").toString();

    QVariant variant;
    switch (QVariant::nameToType(
            typeString.toStdString().c_str())) {
        case QMetaType::QVariantList:
            variant = readVariantListFromStream(stream);
```

```
            break;
        case QMetaType::QVariantMap:
            variant = readVariantMapFromStream(stream);
            break;
        default:
            variant = readVariantValueFromStream(stream);
            break;
    }

    return variant;
}
```

The role of this function is to create a QVariant. Firstly, we retrieve the "type" from the XML attributes. In our case, we have only one attribute to handle. Then, depending on the type, we will call one of our three read helper functions. Let's implement the readVariantValueFromStream() function:

```
//XmlSerializer.h
private:
    QVariant readVariantValueFromStream(QXmlStreamReader& stream);

//XmlSerializer.cpp
QVariant XmlSerializer::readVariantValueFromStream(
    QXmlStreamReader& stream)
{
    QXmlStreamAttributes attributes = stream.attributes();
    QString typeString = attributes.value("type").toString();
    QString dataString = stream.readElementText();

    QVariant variant(dataString);
    variant.convert(QVariant::nameToType(
        typeString.toStdString().c_str()));
    return variant;
}
```

This function create a QVariant with its data depending on the type. Like the previous function, we retrieve the type from the XML attribute. We also read the data as a text with the QXmlStreamReader::readElementText() function. A QVariant class is created with this QString data. At this step, the QVariant type is a QString. So we use the QVariant::convert() function to convert the QVariant to the real type (int, qlonglong, and so on).

The second read helper function is `readVariantListFromStream()`:

```
//XmlSerializer.h
private:
    QVariant readVariantListFromStream(QXmlStreamReader& stream);

//XmlSerializer.cpp
QVariant XmlSerializer::readVariantListFromStream(QXmlStreamReader& stream)
{
    QVariantList list;
    while(stream.readNextStartElement()) {
        list.append(readVariantFromStream(stream));
    }
    return list;
}
```

We know that the stream element contains an array. So, this function creates and returns a `QVariantList`. The `QXmlStreamReader::readNextStartElement()` function reads until the next start element and returns `true` if a start element is found within the current element. We call the entry-point function, `readVariantFromStream()`, for each element. Finally, we return the `QVariantList`.

The last helper function to cover is `readVariantMapFromStream()`. Update your file with the following snippet:

```
//XmlSerializer.h
private:
    QVariant readVariantMapFromStream(QXmlStreamReader& stream);

//XmlSerializer.cpp
QVariant XmlSerializer::readVariantMapFromStream(
    QXmlStreamReader& stream)
{
    QVariantMap map;
    while(stream.readNextStartElement()) {
        map.insert(stream.name().toString(),
                    readVariantFromStream(stream));
    }
    return map;
}
```

This function sounds like the `readVariantListFromStream()`. This time we have to create a `QVariantMap`. The key used for inserting a new item is the element name. We retrieve the name with the `QXmlStreamReader::name()` function.

A `Track` class serialized with the `XmlSerializer` looks like this:

```
<?xml version="1.0" encoding="UTF-8"?>
<track type="QVariantMap">
    <duration type="qlonglong">6205</duration>
    <soundEvents type="QVariantList">
        <item type="QVariantMap">
            <soundId type="int">0</soundId>
            <timestamp type="qlonglong">2689</timestamp>
        </item>
        <item type="QVariantMap">
            <soundId type="int">2</soundId>
            <timestamp type="qlonglong">2690</timestamp>
        </item>
        <item type="QVariantMap">
            <soundId type="int">2</soundId>
            <timestamp type="qlonglong">3067</timestamp>
        </item>
    </soundEvents>
</track>
```

Serializing objects in binary format

The XML serialization is fully functional! We can now switch to the last type of serialization covered in this chapter.

The binary serialization is easier because Qt provides a direct way to do it. Please create a `BinarySerializer` class that inherits from `Serializer`. The header is common, we have only the override functions, `save()` and `load()`. Here is the implementation of the `save()` function:

```
void BinarySerializer::save(const Serializable& serializable,
    const QString& filepath, const QString& /*rootName*/)
{
    QFile file(filepath);
    file.open(QFile::WriteOnly);
    QDataStream dataStream(&file);
    dataStream << serializable.toVariant();
    file.close();
}
```

We hope you recognized the `QDataStream` class used in Chapter 18, *Need IPC? Get Your Minions to Work*. This time we use this class to serialize binary data in a destination `QFile`. A `QDataStream` class accepts a `QVariant` class with the << operator. Notice that the `rootName` variable is not used in the binary serializer.

Here is the `load()` function:

```
void BinarySerializer::load(Serializable& serializable, const QString&
filepath)
{
    QFile file(filepath);
    file.open(QFile::ReadOnly);
    QDataStream dataStream(&file);
    QVariant variant;
    dataStream >> variant;
    serializable.fromVariant(variant);
    file.close();
}
```

Thanks to the `QVariant` and the `QDataStream` mechanism, the task is easy. We open the `QFile` with the source `filepath`. We construct a `QDatastream` class with this `QFile`. Then, we use the >> operator to read the root `QVariant`. Finally, we fill the source `Serializable` with our `Serializable::fromVariant()` function.

Do not worry, we will not include an example of a `Track` class serialized with the `BinarySerializer` class.

The serialization part is completed. The GUI part of this example project has been covered many times during the previous chapters of this book. The following sections will only cover specific features used in our `MainWindow` and `SoundEffectWidget` classes. Check the source code if you need the complete C++ classes.

Playing low latency sounds with QSoundEffect

The project application `ch11-drum-machine` displays four `SoundEffectWidget` widgets: `kickWidget`, `snareWidget`, `hihatWidget`, and `crashWidget`.

Each `SoundEffectWidget` widget displays a `QLabel` and a `QPushButton`. The label displays the sound name. If the button is clicked, a sound is played.

The Qt Multimedia module provides two main ways to play an audio file:

- QMediaPlayer: This file can play songs, movies, and Internet radio with various input formats
- QSoundEffect: This file can play low-latency .wav files

This project example is a virtual drum machine, so we are using a QSoundEffect object. The first step to use a QSoundEffect is to update your .pro file like this:

```
QT       += core gui multimedia
```

Then you can initialize the sound. Here is an example:

```
QUrl urlKick("qrc:/sounds/kick.wav");
QUrl urlBetterKick = QUrl::fromLocalFile("/home/better-kick.wav");

QSoundEffect soundEffect;
QSoundEffect.setSource(urlBetterKick);
```

The first step is to create a valid QUrl for your sound file. The urlKick is initialized from a .qrc resources file path, while urlBetterKick is created from a local file path. Then we can create QSoundEffect and set the URL sound to play with the QSoundEffect::setSource() function.

Now that we have a QSoundEffect object initialized, we can play the sound with the following code snippet:

```
soundEffect.setVolume(1.0f);
soundEffect.play();
```

Triggering a QButton with your keyboard

Let's explore the public slot, triggerPlayButton(), in the SoundEffectWidget class:

```
//SoundEffectWidget.h
class SoundEffectWidget : public QWidget
{
...
public slots:
    void triggerPlayButton();
    ...

private:
    QPushButton* mPlayButton;
```

```
        . . .
};

//SoundEffectWidget.cpp
void SoundEffectWidget::triggerPlayButton()
{
    mPlayButton->animateClick();
}
```

This widget has a QPushButton called mPlayButton. The triggerPlayButton() slot calls the QPushButton::animateClick() function, which simulates a click on the button over 100 ms by default. All signals will be sent as a real click does. The button really appears to be down. If you do not want the animation you can call QPushButton::click().

Let's see now how to trigger this slot with a key. Each SoundEffectWidget has a Qt:Key:

```
//SoundEffectWidget.h
class SoundEffectWidget : public QWidget
{
...
public:
    Qt::Key triggerKey() const;
    void setTriggerKey(const Qt::Key& triggerKey);
};

//SoundEffectWidget.cpp
Qt::Key SoundEffectWidget::triggerKey() const
{
    return mTriggerKey;
}

void SoundEffectWidget::setTriggerKey(const Qt::Key& triggerKey)
{
    mTriggerKey = triggerKey;
}
```

The SoundEffectWidget class provides a getter and a setter to get and set the member variable, mTriggerKey.

The MainWindow class initializes the keys of its four SoundEffectWidget like this:

```
ui->kickWidget->setTriggerKey(Qt::Key_H);
ui->snareWidget->setTriggerKey(Qt::Key_J);
ui->hihatWidget->setTriggerKey(Qt::Key_K);
ui->crashWidget->setTriggerKey(Qt::Key_L);
```

By default, the `QObject::eventFilter()` function is not called. To enable it and intercept these events, we need to install an event filter on the `MainWindow`:

```
installEventFilter(this);
```

So each time the `MainWindow` receives an event, the `MainWindow::eventFilter()` function is called.

Here is the `MainWindow.h` header:

```
class MainWindow : public QMainWindow
{
    Q_OBJECT
public:
    ...
    bool eventFilter(QObject* watched, QEvent* event) override;

private:
    QVector<SoundEffectWidget*> mSoundEffectWidgets;
    ...
};
```

The `MainWindow` class has a `QVector` with the four `SoundEffectWidgets`
(`kickWidget`, `snareWidget`, `hihatWidget`, and `crashWidget`). Let's see the implementation in `MainWindow.cpp`:

```
bool MainWindow::eventFilter(QObject* watched, QEvent* event)
{
    if (event->type() == QEvent::KeyPress) {
        QKeyEvent* keyEvent = static_cast<QKeyEvent*>(event);
        for(SoundEffectWidget* widget : mSoundEffectWidgets) {
            if (keyEvent->key() == widget->triggerKey()) {
                widget->triggerPlayButton();
                return true;
            }
        }
    }
    return QObject::eventFilter(watched, event);
}
```

The first thing to do is to check that the QEvent class is a KeyPress type. We do not care about other event types. If the event type is correct, we proceed to the following steps:

1. Cast the QEvent class to QKeyEvent.
2. Then we search if the pressed key belongs to the SoundEffectWidget class.
3. If a SoundEffectWidget class corresponds to the key, we call our SoundEffectWidget::triggerPlayButton() function and we return true to indicate that we consumed the event and it must not be propagated to others classes.
4. Otherwise, we call the QObject class implementation of eventFilter().

Bringing PlaybackWorker to life

The user can play a sound live with a mouse click or a keyboard key. But when he records an awesome beat, the application must be able to play it again with the PlaybackWorker class. Let's see how MainWindow uses this worker. Here is the MainWindow.h related to the PlaybackWorker class:

```
class MainWindow : public QMainWindow
{
...
private slots:
    void playSoundEffect(int soundId);
    void clearPlayback();
    void stopPlayback();
    ...

private:
    void startPlayback();
    ...

private:
    PlaybackWorker* mPlaybackWorker;
    QThread* mPlaybackThread;
    ...
};
```

As you can see, MainWindow has PlaybackWorker and a QThread member variables. Let's see the implementation of startPlayback():

```
void MainWindow::startPlayback()
{
    clearPlayback();

    mPlaybackThread = new QThread();

    mPlaybackWorker = new PlaybackWorker(mTrack);
    mPlaybackWorker->moveToThread(mPlaybackThread);

    connect(mPlaybackThread, &QThread::started,
            mPlaybackWorker, &PlaybackWorker::play);
    connect(mPlaybackThread, &QThread::finished,
            mPlaybackWorker, &QObject::deleteLater);

    connect(mPlaybackWorker, &PlaybackWorker::playSound,
            this, &MainWindow::playSoundEffect);

    connect(mPlaybackWorker, &PlaybackWorker::trackFinished,
            &mTrack, &Track::stop);

    mPlaybackThread->start(QThread::HighPriority);
}
```

Let's analyze all the steps:

1. We clear the current playback with the clearPlayback() function, which will be covered soon.
2. The new QThread and PlaybackWorker are constructed. The current track is given to the worker at this moment. As usual, the worker is then moved to its dedicated thread.
3. We want to play the track as soon as possible. So, when the QThread emits the started() signal, the PlaybackWorker::play() slot is called.
4. We do not want to worry about the PlaybackWorker memory. So when the QThread is over and it has sent the finished() signal, we call the QObject::deleteLater() slot, which schedules the worker for deletion.
5. When the PlaybackWorker class needs to play a sound, the playSound() signal is emitted and our MainWindow:playSoundEffect() slot is called.

6. The last connect covers when the `PlaybackWorker` class finishes playing the whole track. A `trackFinished()` signal is emitted and we call the `Track::Stop()` slot.

7. Finally, the thread is started with a high priority. Notice that some operating systems (for example, Linux) do not support thread priorities.

We can now see the `stopPlayback()` body:

```
void MainWindow::stopPlayback()
{
    mPlaybackWorker->stop();
    clearPlayback();
}
```

We call the `stop()` function of the `PlaybackWorker` from our thread. Because we use a `QAtomicInteger` in `stop()`, the function is thread-safe and can be directly called. Finally, we call our helper function, `clearPlayback()`. This is the second time that we use `clearPlayback()`, so let's implement it:

```
void MainWindow::clearPlayback()
{
    if (mPlaybackThread) {
        mPlaybackThread->quit();
        mPlaybackThread->wait(1000);
        mPlaybackThread = nullptr;
        mPlaybackWorker = nullptr;
    }
}
```

No surprises here. If the thread is valid, we ask the thread to exit and wait 1 second. Then, we set the thread and the worker to `nullptr`.

The `PlaybackWorker::PlaySound` signal is connected to `MainWindow::playSoundEffect()`. Here is the implementation:

```
void MainWindow::playSoundEffect(int soundId)
{
    mSoundEffectWidgets[soundId]->triggerPlayButton();
}
```

This slot retrieves the `SoundEffectWidget` class corresponding to the `soundId`. Then, we call the `triggerPlayButton()`, the same method that is called when you press the trigger key on your keyboard.

So, when you click on the button, press a key, or when the `PlaybackWorker` class requests to play a sound, the `QPushButton` of `SoundEffectWidget` emits the signal, `clicked()`. This signal is connected to our `SoundEffectWidget::play()` slot. The next snippet describes this slot:

```
void SoundEffectWidget::play()
{
    mSoundEffect.play();
    emit soundPlayed(mId);
}
```

Nothing fancy here. We call the `play()` function on the `QSoundEffect` already covered. Finally, we emit the `soundPlayed()` signal that is used by `Track` to add a new `SoundEvent` if we are in the `RECORDING` state.

Accepting mouse drag and drop events

In this project example, if you drag and drop a `.wav` file on a `SoundEffectWidget`, you can change the sound played. The constructor of `SoundEffectWidget` performs a specific task to allow drag and drop:

```
setAcceptDrops(true);
```

We can now override the drag and drop callbacks. Let's start with the `dragEnterEvent()` function:

```
//SoundEffectWidget.h
class SoundEffectWidget : public QWidget
{
...
protected:
    void dragEnterEvent(QDragEnterEvent* event) override;
...
};

//SoundEffectWidget.cpp
void SoundEffectWidget::dragEnterEvent(QDragEnterEvent* event)
{
    if (event->mimeData()->hasFormat("text/uri-list")) {
        event->acceptProposedAction();
    }
}
```

The `dragEnterEvent()` function is called each time the user drags an object on the widget. In our case, we only want to allow drag and drop on files that are of the MIME type: `"text/uri-list"` (a list of URIs, which can be `file://`, `http://`, and so on). In this case, though we can call the `QDragEnterEvent::acceptProposedAction()` function to notify that we accept this object for a drag and drop.

We can now add a second function, `dropEvent()`:

```
//SoundEffectWidget.h
class SoundEffectWidget : public QWidget
{
...
protected:
    void dropEvent(QDropEvent* event) override;
...
};

//SoundEffectWidget.cpp
void SoundEffectWidget::dropEvent(QDropEvent* event)
{
    const QMimeData* mimeData = event->mimeData();
    if (!mimeData->hasUrls()) {
        return;
    }
    const QUrl url = mimeData->urls().first();
    QMimeType mime = QMimeDatabase().mimeTypeForUrl(url);
    if (mime.inherits("audio/wav")) {
        loadSound(url);
    }
}
```

The first step is a sanity check. If the event does not have a URL, we do nothing. The `QMimeData::hasUrls()` function returns `true` only with the MIME type: `"text/uri-text"`. Notice that a user can drag and drop multiple files at once. In our case, we only handle the first URL. You can check that the file is a `.wav` file with its MIME type. If the MIME type is `"audio/wav"`, we call the `loadSound()` function, which updates the sound assigned to this `SoundEffectWidget`.

The following screenshot show the complete application for ch11-drum-machine:

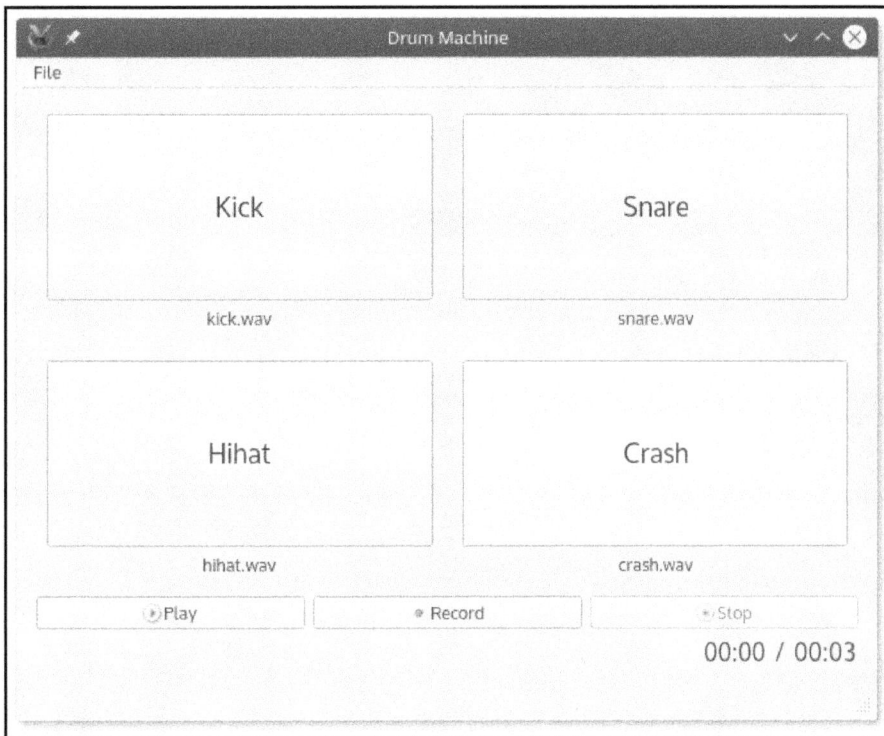

Summary

Serialization is a good way to make your data persistent when you close your application. In this chapter, you learned to make your C++ objects serializable with QVariant. You created a flexible serialization structure with the Bridge pattern. You saved an object in a different text format such as JSON or XML and also in a binary format.

You also learned to use the Qt Multimedia module to play some sound effects. These sounds can be triggered by a mouse click or by a keyboard key. You implemented a friendly user interaction, allowing you to load a new sound with a file drag and drop.

In the next chapter, we will discover the QTest framework and how you can organize your project so it has a clean application/test separation.

20
You Shall (Not) Pass with QTest

In the previous chapter, we created a drum machine software with some serialization feature. In this chapter, we will write the unit tests for this application. To achieve this goal, we will use Qt Test, a dedicated test module for Qt applications.

The example project is a test application using CLI commands to execute and generate a test report. We will cover different types of tests including datasets, GUI, signals, and benchmarking.

This chapter will cover the following topics:

- Qt Test framework
- Project layout for unit tests
- Personalize your test execution
- Write tests with datasets
- Benchmark your code
- Simulating GUI events
- Perform signal introspection with the `QSignalSpy` class

Discovering Qt Test

The Qt framework provides Qt Test, a complete API to create your unit tests in C++. A test executes the code of your application and performs verification on it. Usually, a test compares a variable with an expected value. If the variable does not match the specific value, the test fails. If you wish to go further, you can benchmark your code and get the time/CPU tick/events required by your code. Clicking over and over on a GUI to test it can quickly become boring. Qt Test offers you the possibility to simulate keyboard entries and mouse events on your widgets to completely check your software.

In our case, we want to create a unit test program named `drum-machine-test`. This console application will check the code of our famous drum machine from the previous chapter. Create a `subdirs` project called `ch12-drum-machine-test` with the following topology:

- `drum-machine:`
    - `drum-machine.pro`
- `drum-machine-test:`
    - `drum-machine-test.pro`
- `ch12-drum-machine-test.pro`
- `drum-machine-src.pri`

The `drum-machine` and `drum-machine-test` projects share the same source code. So all common files are put in a project include file: `drum-machine-src.pri`. Here is the updated `drum-machine.pro`:

```
QT += core gui multimedia widgets
CONFIG += c++14

TARGET = drum-machine
TEMPLATE = app

include(../drum-machine-src.pri)

SOURCES += main.cpp
```

As you can see, we only perform a refactoring task; the project drum-machine is not affected by the drum-machine-test application. You can now create the `drum-machine-test.pro` file like this:

```
QT += core gui multimedia widgets testlib
CONFIG += c++14 console
```

```
TARGET = drum-machine-test
TEMPLATE = app

include(../drum-machine-src.pri)

DRUM_MACHINE_PATH = ../drum-machine
INCLUDEPATH += $$DRUM_MACHINE_PATH
DEPENDPATH += $$DRUM_MACHINE_PATH

SOURCES += main.cpp
```

The first thing to notice is that we need to enable the `testlib` module. Then even if we are creating a console application, we want to perform a test on the GUI so the modules (`gui`, `multimedia`, and `widgets`) used by the primary application are also required here. Finally, we include the project include file with all application files (sources, headers, forms, and resources). The `drum-machine-test` application will also contain new source files, so we must correctly set the `INCLUDEPATH` and `DEPENDPATH` variables to the source files folder.

Qt Test is easy to use and relies on some simple assumptions:

- A test case is a `QObject` class
- A private slot is a test function
- A test case can contain several test functions

Notice that the private slots with the following names are not test functions, but special functions automatically called to initialize and clean up your test:

- `initTestCase()`: This function is called before the first test function
- `init()`: This function is called before each test function
- `cleanup()`: This function is called after each test function
- `cleanupTestCase()`: This function is called after the last test function

Alright, we are ready to write our first test case in the `drum-machine-test` application. The serialization of the `drum-machine` object is an important part. A bad modification on the save feature can easily break the load feature. It can produce no errors at compile time, but it can lead to an unusable application. That is why tests are important. The first thing is to validate the serialization/deserialization process. Create a new C++ class, `DummySerializable`. Here is the header file:

```
#include "Serializable.h"

class DummySerializable : public Serializable
{
```

```
public:
    DummySerializable();

    QVariant toVariant() const override;
    void fromVariant(const QVariant& variant) override;

    int myInt = 0;
    double myDouble = 0.0;
    QString myString = "";
    bool myBool = false;
};
```

It is a simple class implementing our `Serializable` interface created in `Chapter 19`, *Having Fun with Serialization*. This class will be helpful to validate the lower layer in our serialization process. As you can see, the class contains some variables with various types to ensure a complete functioning serialization. Let's see the file, `DummySerializable.cpp`:

```
#include "DummySerializable.h"

DummySerializable::DummySerializable() :
    Serializable()
{
}

QVariant DummySerializable::toVariant() const
{
    QVariantMap map;
    map.insert("myInt", myInt);
    map.insert("myDouble", myDouble);
    map.insert("myString", myString);
    map.insert("myBool", myBool);
    return map;
}

void DummySerializable::fromVariant(const QVariant& variant)
{
    QVariantMap map = variant.toMap();
    myInt = map.value("myInt").toInt();
    myDouble = map.value("myDouble").toDouble();
    myString = map.value("myString").toString();
    myBool = map.value("myBool").toBool();
}
```

No surprise here; we perform our operation with a `QVariantMap`, as already performed in the previous chapter. Our dummy class is ready; create a new C++ class, `TestJsonSerializer`, with the following header:

```cpp
#include <QtTest/QTest>

#include "JsonSerializer.h"

class TestJsonSerializer : public QObject
{
    Q_OBJECT

public:
    TestJsonSerializer(QObject* parent = nullptr);

private slots:
    void cleanup();
    void saveDummy();
    void loadDummy();

private:
    QString loadFileContent();

private:
    JsonSerializer mSerializer;
};
```

Here we are, our first test case! This test case performs verifications on our class, `JsonSerializer`. You can see two test functions, `saveDummy()` and `loadDummy()`. The `cleanup()` slot is the special Qt Test slot that we covered earlier, which is executed after each test function. We can now write the implementation in `TestJsonSerializer.cpp`:

```cpp
#include "DummySerializable.h"

const QString FILENAME = "test.json";
const QString DUMMY_FILE_CONTENT = "{n    "myBool": true,n    "myDouble":
5.2,n    "myInt": 1,n    "myString": "hello"n}n";

TestJsonSerializer::TestJsonSerializer(QObject* parent) :
    QObject(parent),
    mSerializer()
{
}
```

Two constants are created here:

- FILENAME: This is the filename used to test the save and load the data
- DUMMY_FILE_CONTENT: This is the referential file content used by the test functions, saveDummy() and loadDummy()

Let's implement the test function, saveDummy():

```
void TestJsonSerializer::saveDummy()
{
    DummySerializable dummy;
    dummy.myInt = 1;
    dummy.myDouble = 5.2;
    dummy.myString = "hello";
    dummy.myBool = true;

    mSerializer.save(dummy, FILENAME);

    QString data = loadFileContent();
    QVERIFY(data == DUMMY_FILE_CONTENT);
}
```

The first step is to instantiate a DummySerializable class with some fixed values. So, we call the function to test, JsonSerializer::save(), that will serialize our dummy object in the test.json file. Then, we call a helper function, loadFileContent(), to get the text contained in the test.json file. Finally, we use a Qt Test macro, QVERIFY(), to perform the verification that the text saved by the JSON serializer is the same as the expected value in DUMMY_FILE_CONTENT. If data equals the correct value, the test function succeeds. Here is the log output:

```
PASS    : TestJsonSerializer::saveDummy()
```

If the data is different than the expected value, the test fails and an error is displayed in the console log:

```
FAIL!   : TestJsonSerializer::saveDummy()
'data == DUMMY_FILE_CONTENT' returned FALSE. ()
Loc: [../../ch12-drum-machine-test/drum-machine-
test/TestJsonSerializer.cpp(31)]
```

Let's briefly see the helper function, loadFileContent():

```
QString TestJsonSerializer::loadFileContent()
{
    QFile file(FILENAME);
    file.open(QFile::ReadOnly);
```

```
        QString content = file.readAll();
        file.close();
        return content;
    }
```

No big deal here. We open the file, test.json, read all the text content, and return the corresponding QString.

The macro, QVERIFY(), is great to check a Boolean value, but Qt Test provides a better macro when you want to compare data to an expected value. Let's discover QCOMPARE() with the test function, loadDummy():

```
    void TestJsonSerializer::loadDummy()
    {
        QFile file(FILENAME);
        file.open(QFile::WriteOnly | QIODevice::Text);
        QTextStream out(&file);
        out << DUMMY_FILE_CONTENT;
        file.close();

        DummySerializable dummy;
        mSerializer.load(dummy, FILENAME);

        QCOMPARE(dummy.myInt, 1);
        QCOMPARE(dummy.myDouble, 5.2);
        QCOMPARE(dummy.myString, QString("hello"));
        QCOMPARE(dummy.myBool, true);
    }
```

The first part creates a test.json file, with a referential content. Then we create an empty DymmySerializable and call the function to test Serializable::load(). Finally, we use the Qt Test macro, QCOMPARE(). The syntax is simple:

```
    QCOMPARE(actual_value, expected_value);
```

We can now test each field of the dummy loaded from JSON. The test function, loadDummmy(), will only succeed if all QCOMPARE() calls succeed. An error with a QCOMPARE() is much more detailed:

```
    FAIL!   : TestJsonSerializer::loadDummy() Compared values are not the same
       Actual    (dummy.myInt): 0
       Expected (1)            : 1
    Loc: [../../ch12-drum-machine-test/drum-machine-
    test/TestJsonSerializer.cpp(45)]
```

Each time a test function is executed, the special `cleanup()` slot is called. Let's update your file, `TestJsonSerializable.cpp`, like this:

```
void TestJsonSerializer::cleanup()
{
    QFile(FILENAME).remove();
}
```

This is a simple security that will remove the `test.json` file after each test function and prevent the save and load tests from colliding.

Executing your tests

We wrote a test case, `TestJsonSerializer`, with some test functions. We need a `main()` function in our `drum-machine-test` application. We will explore three possibilities:

- The `QTEST_MAIN()` function
- Write our own simple `main()` function
- Write our own enhanced `main()` supporting multiple test classes

The `QTest` module provides an interesting macro, `QTEST_MAIN()`. This macro generates a complete `main()` function for your application. This generated method runs all the test functions of your test case. To use it, add the following snippet at the end of the `TestJsonSerializer.cpp` file:

```
QTEST_MAIN(TestJsonSerializer)
```

Moreover, if you declare and implement your test class only in the `.cpp` file (without a header file), you need to include the generated moc file after the `QTEST_MAIN` macro:

```
QTEST_MAIN(TestJsonSerializer)
#include "testjsonserializer"
```

If you use the `QTEST_MAIN()` macro, do not forget to remove the existing `main.cpp`. Otherwise, you will have two `main()` functions and a compilation error will happen.

You can now try to run your drum-machine-test application and look at the application output. You should see something similar to this:

```
$ ./drum-machine-test
********* Start testing of TestJsonSerializer *********
Config: Using QtTest library 5.7.0, Qt 5.7.0 (x86_64-little_endian-lp64
shared (dynamic) release build; by GCC 4.9.1 20140922 (Red Hat 4.9.1-10))
```

```
PASS    : TestJsonSerializer::initTestCase()
PASS    : TestJsonSerializer::saveDummy()
PASS    : TestJsonSerializer::loadDummy()
PASS    : TestJsonSerializer::cleanupTestCase()
Totals: 4 passed, 0 failed, 0 skipped, 0 blacklisted, 1ms
********* Finished testing of TestJsonSerializer *********
```

Our test functions, `saveDummy()` and `loadDummy()`, are executed in the declaration order. Both succeed with the PASS status. The generated test application handles some options. Commonly, you can display the help menu executing this command:

$ ./drum-machine-test -help

Let's see some cool features. We can execute only one function with the name. The following command only executes the `saveDummy` test function:

$ ./drum-machine-test saveDummy

You can also execute several test functions separating their names with a space.

The QTest application provides log detail options:

- `-silent` for silent. Only displays fatal errors and summary messages.
- `-v1` for verbose. Shows the test function entered information.
- `-v2` for extended verbose. Shows each QCOMPARE() and QVERIFY().
- `-vs` for verbose signal. Shows the emitted signal and the connected slot.

For example, we can display details of the execution of `loadDummy` with the following command:

```
$ ./drum-machine-test -v2 loadDummy
********* Start testing of TestJsonSerializer *********
Config: Using QtTest library 5.7.0, Qt 5.7.0 (x86_64-little_endian-lp64
shared (dynamic) release build; by GCC 4.9.1 20140922 (Red Hat 4.9.1-10))
    INFO    : TestJsonSerializer::initTestCase() entering
    PASS    : TestJsonSerializer::initTestCase()
    INFO    : TestJsonSerializer::loadDummy() entering
    INFO    : TestJsonSerializer::loadDummy() QCOMPARE(dummy.myInt, 1)
       Loc: [../../ch12-drum-machine-test/drum-machine-
test/TestJsonSerializer.cpp(45)]
    INFO    : TestJsonSerializer::loadDummy() QCOMPARE(dummy.myDouble, 5.2)
       Loc: [../../ch12-drum-machine-test/drum-machine-
test/TestJsonSerializer.cpp(46)]
    INFO    : TestJsonSerializer::loadDummy() QCOMPARE(dummy.myString,
QString("hello"))
       Loc: [../../ch12-drum-machine-test/drum-machine-
```

```
test/TestJsonSerializer.cpp(47)]
    INFO   : TestJsonSerializer::loadDummy() QCOMPARE(dummy.myBool, true)
       Loc: [../../ch12-drum-machine-test/drum-machine-
test/TestJsonSerializer.cpp(48)]
    PASS   : TestJsonSerializer::loadDummy()
    INFO   : TestJsonSerializer::cleanupTestCase() entering
    PASS   : TestJsonSerializer::cleanupTestCase()
    Totals: 3 passed, 0 failed, 0 skipped, 0 blacklisted, 1ms
    ********* Finished testing of TestJsonSerializer *********
```

Another great feature is the logging output format. You can create a test report file with various formats (.txt, .xml, .csv, and so on). The syntax requires a filename and a file format separated by a comma:

```
$ ./drum-machine-test -o <filename>,<format>
```

In the following example, we create an XML report named test-report.xml:

```
$ ./drum-machine-test -o test-report.xml,xml
```

Notice that some log level affects only the plain text output. Moreover, the CSV format can be used only with the test macro QBENCHMARK, which is covered later in this chapter.

If you want to customize the generated test application, you can write the main() function. Remove the QTEST_MAIN macro in TestJsonSerializer.cpp. Then create a main.cpp like this:

```cpp
#include "TestJsonSerializer.h"

int main(int argc, char *argv[])
{
    TestJsonSerializer test;
    QStringList arguments = QCoreApplication::arguments();
    return QTest::qExec(&test, arguments);
}
```

In this case, we are using the static function, QTest::qExec(), to start a TestJsonSerializer test. Do not forget to provide the command-line arguments to enjoy the QTest CLI options.

If you wrote your test functions in different test classes, you would have created one application by a test class. If you keep one test class by test application you can even use the QTEST_MAIN macro to generate the main functions.

Sometimes you want to create only one test application to handle all your test classes. In this case, you have multiple test classes in the same application, so you cannot use the QTEST_MAIN macro because you do not want to generate several main functions for each test class.

Let's see a simple way to call all your test classes in a unique application:

```
int main(int argc, char *argv[])
{
    int status = 0;
    TestFoo testFoo;
    TestBar testBar;
    status |= QTest::qExec(&testFoo);
    status |= QTest::qExec(&testBar);
    return status;
}
```

In this simple custom main() function, we are executing the TestFoo and TestBar tests. But we are losing the CLI options. Indeed, executing the QTest::qExec() function with command-line arguments more than once will lead to errors and bad behaviors. For example, if you want to execute only one specific test function from TestBar. The execution of TestFoo will not find the test function, display an error message, and stop the application.

Here is a workaround to handle several test classes in a unique application. We will create a new CLI option, -select, to our test application. This option allows you to select a specific test class to execute. Here is a syntax example:

$ ./drum-machine-test -select foo fooTestFunction

The -select option, if used, must be at the beginning of the command followed by the test class name (foo in this example). Then, we can optionally add Qt Test options. To achieve this goal, we will create an enhanced main() function that parses the new select option and execute the corresponding test class.

We will create our enhanced main() function together:

```
QApplication app(argc, argv);
QStringList arguments = QCoreApplication::arguments();

map<QString, unique_ptr<QObject>> tests;
tests.emplace("jsonserializer",
    make_unique<TestJsonSerializer>());
tests.emplace("foo", make_unique<TestFoo>());
tests.emplace("bar", make_unique<TestBar>());
```

The `QApplication` will be required later by our other GUI test cases. We retrieve the command line arguments for later use. The `std::map` template named `tests` contains the smart pointers of the test classes and a `QString` label is used as a key. Notice that we are using the `map::emplace()` function that does not copy the source to the map, but creates it in place. Using the `map::insert()` function leads to an error due to the illegal copy of a smart pointer. Another syntax that could be used with a `std::map` template and a `make_unique` is:

```
tests["bar"] = make_unique<TestBar>();
```

We can now parse the command line arguments:

```
if (arguments.size() >= 3 && arguments[1] == "-select") {
    QString testName = arguments[2];
    auto iter = tests.begin();
    while(iter != tests.end()) {
        if (iter->first != testName) {
            iter = tests.erase(iter);
        } else {
            ++iter;
        }
    }
    arguments.removeOne("-select");
    arguments.removeOne(testName);
}
```

If the `-select` option is used, this snippet performs two important tasks:

- Removes from the map `tests`, the test classes that do not match the test name
- Removes the arguments from the `-select` option and the `testName` variable to provide cleaned arguments to the `QTest::qExec()` function

We can now add the final step to execute the test classes:

```
int status = 0;
for(auto& test : tests) {
    status |= QTest::qExec(test.second.get(), arguments);
}

return status;
```

Without the `-select` option, all the test classes will be performed. If we use the `-select` option with a test class name, only this one will be executed.

Writing factorized tests with datasets

We will now turn our attention to testing the `Track` class. We will focus specifically on the different states a `Track` class can have: `STOPPED`, `PLAYING`, and `RECORDING`. For each one of these states, we want to make sure that adding `SoundEvents` works only if we are in the proper state (`RECORDING`).

To do so, we could write the following test functions:

- `testAddSoundEvent()`: This function puts the `Track` in the `STOPPED` state, calls `track.addSoundEvent(0)`, and checks `track.soundEvents().size == 0`
- `testAddSoundEvent()`: This function puts the `Track` in the `PLAYING` state, calls `track.addSoundEvent(0)`, and checks `track.soundEvents().size == 0`
- `testAddSoundEvent()`: This function puts the `Track` in the `RECORDING` state, calls `track.addSoundEvent(0)`, and checks `track.soundEvents().size == 1`

As you can see, the logic is the same, we simply change the inputs and the desired outputs. To factorize this, Qt Test provides another module: datasets.

A dataset can be seen as a two-dimensional table where each row is a test, and the columns are the inputs and expected outputs. For our `Track` state test, it would look like this:

index	name	input (Track::State)	result (soundEvents count)
0	STOPPED	State::STOPPED	0
1	PLAYING	State::PLAYING	0
2	RECORDING	State::RECORDING	1

With this approach, you write a single `addSoundEvent()` test function and Qt Test takes care of iterating over this table and comparing the result. Right now, it seems like magic. Let's implement it!

Create a new C++ class named `TestTrack`, following the same pattern used for the `TestJsonSerializer` class (inherits `QObject`, includes `QTest`). Update `TestTrack.h` like so:

```
class TestTrack : public QObject
{
    Q_OBJECT
public:
    explicit TestTrack(QObject *parent = 0);

private slots:
    void addSoundEvent_data();
    void addSoundEvent();
};
```

Here we added two functions:

- `addSoundEvent_data()`: This is the function that fills the dataset for the real test
- `addSoundEvent()`: This is the function that executes the test

As you can see, the function that fills the dataset for a given `xxx()` function must be named `xxx_data()`. Let's see the implementation of `addSoundEvent_data()`:

```
void TestTrack::addSoundEvent_data()
{
    QTest::addColumn<int>("trackState");
    QTest::addColumn<int>("soundEventCount");

    QTest::newRow("STOPPED")
            << static_cast<int>(Track::State::STOPPED)
            << 0;
    QTest::newRow("PLAYING")
            << static_cast<int>(Track::State::PLAYING)
            << 0;
    QTest::newRow("RECORDING")
            << static_cast<int>(Track::State::RECORDING)
            << 1;
}
```

As you can see, a dataset is constructed like a table. We start by defining the structure of the table with the `trackState` and `soundEventCount` columns. Note that `QTest::addColumn` relies on templating to know the type of the variable (`int` in both cases).

After that, a row is appended to the table with the QTest::newRow() function, with the name of the test passed as a parameter. The QTest::newRow syntax supports the << operator, making it very easy to pack all the data for a given row.

Note that each row added to the dataset corresponds to an execution of the addSoundEvent() function in which the data of the row will be available.

We can now turn our attention to addSoundEvent():

```
void TestTrack::addSoundEvent()
{
    QFETCH(int, trackState);
    QFETCH(int, soundEventCount);

    Track track;
    switch (static_cast<Track::State>(trackState)) {
        case Track::State::STOPPED:
            track.stop();
            break;
        case Track::State::PLAYING:
            track.play();
            break;
        case Track::State::RECORDING:
            track.record();
            break;
        default:
            break;
    }

    track.addSoundEvent(0);
    track.stop();

    QCOMPARE(track.soundEvents().size(),
            static_cast<size_t>(soundEventCount));
}
```

Because addSoundEvent() is executed by QTest and is fed with the dataset data, we can safely access the current row of the dataset like we would do with a cursor on a database. The QFETCH(int, trackState) is a helpful macro that does two things:

- Declares an int variable named trackState
- Fetches the current column index data of the dataset and stores its content in trackState

The same principle is applied to `soundEventCount`. Now that we have our desired track state and the expected sound events count, we can proceed to the real test:

1. Put the track in the proper state according to `trackState`. Remember that the `Track::setState()` function is private, because the `Track` keyword handles the `trackState` variable alone, based on the caller instruction (`stop()`, `play()`, `record()`).
2. Try to add a `SoundEvent` to track.
3. Stop the track.
4. Compare the number of `SoundEvents` in track to what is expected in `soundEventCount`.

Do not forget to add the `TestTrack` class in `main.cpp`:

```
#include "TestJsonSerializer.h"
#include "TestTrack.h"

. . .

int main(int argc, char *argv[])
{
    . . .
    map<QString, unique_ptr<QObject>> tests;
    tests.emplace("jsonserializer",
                  make_unique<TestJsonSerializer>());
    tests.emplace("track",
                  make_unique<TestTrack>());
    . . .
}
```

You can now run the tests and see the three tests of `addSoundEvent()` output their result in the console:

```
PASS   : TestTrack::addSoundEvent(STOPPED)
PASS   : TestTrack::addSoundEvent(PLAYING)
PASS   : TestTrack::addSoundEvent(RECORDING)
```

Datasets make the writing of tests less dull, by factorizing variations of data for a single test.

You can also run a single test for a specific entry of a dataset using the command line:

```
$ ./drum-machine-test <testfunction>:<dataset entry>
```

Let's say we want to execute the test function `addSoundEvent()` from `TestTrack` with only the `RECORDING` state. Here is the command line to run:

```
$ ./drum-machine-test -select track addSoundEvent:RECORDING
```

Benchmarking your code

Qt Test also provides a very easy to use semantic to benchmark the execution speed of your code. To see it in action, we will benchmark the time it takes to save a `Track` in the JSON format. Depending on the track length (the number of `SoundEvent`s), the serialization should take more or less time.

Of course, it is more interesting to benchmark this feature with different track lengths and see if the time saving is linear. Datasets come to the rescue! It is not only useful to run the same function with expected inputs and outputs, but also to run the same function with different parameters.

We will start by creating the dataset function in `TestJsonSerializer`:

```cpp
class TestJsonSerializer : public QObject
{
    ...

private slots:
    void cleanup();
    void saveDummy();
    void loadDummy();

    void saveTrack_data();
    ...
};

void TestJsonSerializer::saveTrack_data()
{
    QTest::addColumn<int>("soundEventCount");

    QTest::newRow("1") << 1;
    QTest::newRow("100") << 100;
    QTest::newRow("1000") << 1000;
}
```

The `saveTrack_data()` function simply stores the number of `SoundEvent` to be added to a `Track` class before it is saved. The `"1"`, `"100"`, and `"1000"` strings are here to have a clear label in the test execution output. These strings will be displayed in each execution of `saveTrack()`. Feel free to tweak these numbers!

Now for the real test with the benchmark call:

```
class TestJsonSerializer : public QObject
{
    ...
    void saveTrack_data();
    void saveTrack();
    ...
};

void TestJsonSerializer::saveTrack()
{
    QFETCH(int, soundEventCount);
    Track track;
    track.record();
    for (int i = 0; i < soundEventCount; ++i) {
        track.addSoundEvent(i % 4);
    }
    track.stop();

    QBENCHMARK {
        mSerializer.save(track, FILENAME);
    }
}
```

The `saveTrack()` function starts by fetching the `soundEventCount` column from its dataset. After that, it adds the correct number of `soundEvent` (with the proper `record()` state!) and finally benchmarks the serialization in the JSON format.

You can see that the benchmark itself is simply a macro that looks like this:

```
QBENCHMARK {
    // instructions to benchmark
}
```

The instructions enclosed in the `QBENCHMARK` macro will be measured automatically. If you execute the test with the updated `TestJsonSerializer` class, you should see an output similar to this:

```
PASS   : TestJsonSerializer::saveTrack(1)
RESULT : TestJsonSerializer::saveTrack():"1":
     0.041 msecs per iteration (total: 84, iterations: 2048)
```

```
PASS    : TestJsonSerializer::saveTrack(100)
RESULT  : TestJsonSerializer::saveTrack():"100":
     0.23 msecs per iteration (total: 59, iterations: 256)
PASS    : TestJsonSerializer::saveTrack(1000)
RESULT  : TestJsonSerializer::saveTrack():"1000":
     2.0 msecs per iteration (total: 66, iterations: 32)
```

As you can see, the QBENCHMARK macro makes Qt Test output very interesting data. To save a Track class with a single SoundEvent, it took 0.041 milliseconds. Qt Test repeated this test 2048 times and it took a total of 84 milliseconds.

The power of the QBENCHMARK macro starts to be visible in the following test. Here, the saveTrack() function tried to save a Track class with 100 SoundEvents. It took 0.23 milliseconds to do it and it repeated the instruction 256 times. This shows you that the Qt Test benchmark automatically adjusts the number of iterations based on the average time a single iteration takes.

The QBENCHMARK macro has this behavior because a metric tends to be more accurate if it is repeated multiple times (to avoid possible external noise).

> **TIP**
> If you want your test to be benchmarked without multiple iterations, use QBENCHMARK_ONCE.

If you execute the test using the command line, you can provide additional metrics to QBENCHMARK. Here is the table recapitulating the available options:

Name	Command-line argument	Availability
Walltime	(default)	All platforms
CPU tick counter	-tickcounter	Windows, OS X, Linux, many UNIX-like systems.
Event Counter	-eventcounter	All platforms
Valgrind Callgrind	-callgrind	Linux (if installed)
Linux Perf	-perf	Linux

Each one of these options will replace the selected backend used to measure the execution time of the benchmarked code. For example, if you run `drum-machine-test` with the `-tickcounter` argument:

```
$ ./drum-machine-test -tickcounter
...
RESULT : TestJsonSerializer::saveTrack():"1":
     88,062 CPU cycles per iteration (total: 88,062, iterations: 1)
PASS   : TestJsonSerializer::saveTrack(100)
RESULT : TestJsonSerializer::saveTrack():"100":
     868,706 CPU cycles per iteration (total: 868,706, iterations: 1)
PASS   : TestJsonSerializer::saveTrack(1000)
RESULT : TestJsonSerializer::saveTrack():"1000":
     7,839,871 CPU cycles per iteration (total: 7,839,871, iterations: 1)
...
```

You can see that the wall time, measured in milliseconds, has been replaced by the number of CPU cycles completed for each iteration.

Another interesting option is `-eventcounter`, which measures the numbers that were received by the event loop before they are sent to their corresponding target. This could be an interesting way of checking that your code emits the proper number of signals.

Testing your GUI

It is now time to see how you can test your GUI using the Qt Test API. The `QTest` class offers several functions to simulate keys and mouse events.

To demonstrate it, we will stay with the notion of testing a `Track` state, but on an upper level. Rather than testing the `Track` state itself, we will check that the UI state of the `drum-machine` application is properly updated when the `Track` state is changed. Namely, the control buttons (play, stop, record) should be in a specific state when a recording is started.

Start by creating a `TestGui` class in the `drum-machine-test` project. Do not forget to add the `TestGui` class in the `tests` map of `main.cpp`. As usual, make it inherit `QObject` and update `TestGui.h` like so:

```
#include <QTest>

#include "MainWindow.h"

class TestGui : public QObject
{
```

```
    Q_OBJECT
public:
    TestGui(QObject* parent = 0);

private:
    MainWindow mMainWindow;
};
```

In this header, we have a member, `mMainWindow`, which is an instance of the `MainWindow` keyword from the `drum-machine` project. Throughout the tests of `TestGui`, a single `MainWindow` will be used, in which we will inject events and check how it reacts.

Let's switch to the `TestGui` constructor:

```
#include <QtTest/QtTest>

TestGui::TestGui(QObject* parent) :
    QObject(parent),
    mMainWindow()
{
    QTestEventLoop::instance().enterLoop(1);
}
```

The constructor initializes the `mMainWindow` variable. Notice that `mMainWindow` is never shown (using `mMainWindow.show()`). We do not need to display it, we solely want to test its states.

Here, we use a rather obscure function call (`QTestEventLoop` is not documented at all) to force the event loop to be started after 1 second.

The reason why we have to do this lies in the `QSoundEffect` class. The `QSoundEffect` class is initialized when the `QSoundEffect::setSource()` function is called (in `MainWindow`, this is done at the initialization of the `SoundEffectWidgets`). If we omit the explicit `enterLoop()` call, the `drum-machine-test` execution will crash with a segmentation fault.

It seems that the event loop has to be explicitly entered to let the `QSoundEffect` class properly complete its initialization. We found this undocumented workaround by studying the Qt unit tests of the `QSoundEffect` class.

Now for the real GUI test! To test the control buttons, update `TestGui`:

```
// In TestGui.h
class TestGui : public QObject
{
    ...
```

```
    private slots:
        void controlButtonState();
        ...
    };

    // In TestGui.cpp
    #include <QtTest/QtTest>
    #include <QPushButton>
    ...
    void TestGui::controlButtonState()
    {
        QPushButton* stopButton =
            mMainWindow.findChild<QPushButton*>("stopButton");
        QPushButton* playButton =
            mMainWindow.findChild<QPushButton*>("playButton");
        QPushButton* recordButton =
            mMainWindow.findChild<QPushButton*>("recordButton");

        QTest::mouseClick(recordButton, Qt::LeftButton);

        QCOMPARE(stopButton->isEnabled(), true);
        QCOMPARE(playButton->isEnabled(), false);
        QCOMPARE(recordButton->isEnabled(), false);
    }
```

In the `controlButtonState()` function, we start by retrieving our buttons by using the handy `mMainWindow.findChild()` function. This function is available in `QObject`, and the passed name corresponds to the `objectName` variable we used for each button in Qt Designer when we created `MainWindow.ui`.

Once we retrieve all the buttons, we inject a mouse click event using the `QTest::mouseClick()` function. It takes a `QWidget*` parameter as a target and the button that should be clicked. You can even pass keyboard modifiers (control, shift, and so on) and a possible click delay in milliseconds.

Once the `recordButton` has been clicked, we test the states of all the control buttons to make sure that they are in the desired enabled state.

> This function can be easily extended to test all the states (`PLAYING`, `STOPPED`, `RECORDING`) with a dataset where the input is the desired state and the outputs are the expected buttons states.

The `QTest` class offers many useful functions to inject events, including:

- `keyEvent()`: This function is used to simulate a key event
- `keyPress()`: This function is used to simulate a key press event
- `keyRelease()`: This function is used to simulate a key release event
- `mouseClick()`: This function is used to simulate a key click event
- `mouseDClick()`: This function is used to simulate a mouse double click event
- `mouseMove()`: This function is used to simulate a mouse move event

Spying on your application with QSignalSpy

The last part we will cover in the Qt Test framework is the ability to spy on signals with `QSignalSpy`. This class allows you to do introspection of the emitted signal of any `QObject`.

Let's see it in action with `SoundEffectWidget`. We will test that when the `SoundEffectWidget::play()` function is called, the `soundPlayed` signal is emitted with the correct `soundId` parameter.

Here is the `playSound()` function of `TestGui`:

```
#include <QTest>

#include "MainWindow.h"

// In TestGui.h
class TestGui : public QObject
{
    ...
    void controlButtonState();
    void playSound();
    ...
};

// In TestGui.cpp
#include <QPushButton>
#include <QtTest/QtTest>
#include "SoundEffectWidget.h"
...
void TestGui::playSound()
{
    SoundEffectWidget widget;
    QSignalSpy spy(&widget, &SoundEffectWidget::soundPlayed);
```

```
        widget.setId(2);
        widget.play();

        QCOMPARE(spy.count(), 1);
        QList<QVariant> arguments = spy.takeFirst();
        QCOMPARE(arguments.at(0).toInt(), 2);
    }
```

We start by initializing a `SoundEffectWidget` widget and a `QSignalSpy` class. The `spy` class's constructor takes the pointer to the object to spy and the pointer to the member function of the signal to be watched. Here, we want to check the `SoundEffectWidget::soundPlayed()` signal.

Right after, `widget` is configured with an arbitrary `soundId` (2) and `widget.play()` is called. This is where it gets interesting: `spy` stores the signal's emitted parameters in a `QVariantList`. Each time `soundPlayed()` is emitted, a new `QVariantList` is created in `spy`, which contains the emitted parameters.

The first step is to check that the signal is emitted only once, by comparing `spy.count()` to 1. Just after that, we store the parameters of this signal in `arguments` and check that it has the value 2, the initial `soundId` that `widget` was configured with.

As you can see, `QSignalSpy` is simple to use; you can create as many as you need for each signal you want to spy on.

Summary

The Qt Test module gracefully helps us to easily create a test application. You learned to organize your project with a standalone test application. You are able to compare and verify a specific value in your simple tests. For your complex tests, you could use the datasets. You implemented a simple benchmark, recording the time or the CPU ticks required to execute a function. You have simulated GUI events and spy Qt signals to ensure that your application works well.

Your application is created and your unit tests indicates a PASS status. In the next chapter, we will learn how to deploy your application.

21
All Packed and Ready to Deploy

In the previous chapter, you learned to create a robust application with unit tests. The final step for an application is packaging. The Qt framework enables you to develop cross-platform applications but packaging is really a platform-specific task. Moreover, when your application is ready to be shipped, you need a one-step procedure to generate and pack your application.

In this chapter, we will reuse the gallery application (both on desktop and mobile platforms) to learn the steps required to package a Qt application. There are many ways to prepare the packaging of an application. In this chapter, we want to package the gallery application, from Chapter 12, *Conquering the Desktop UI*, and Chapter 13, *Dominating the Mobile UI*, on the supported platforms (Windows, Linux, Mac, Android, and iOS).

Here are the topics covered in this chapter:

- Packaging a Qt application on Windows
- Packaging a Qt application on Linux
- Packaging a Qt application on Mac
- Packaging a Qt application on Android
- Packaging a Qt application on iOS

Packaging your application

You will create, for each platform, a dedicated script to perform all the tasks required to build a standalone application. Depending on the OS type, the packaged application will be `gallery-desktop` or `gallery-mobile`. Because the whole gallery project has to be compiled, it also has to include `gallery-core`. Therefore, we will create a parent project with `gallery-core`, `gallery-desktop`, and `gallery-mobile`.

For each platform, we will prepare the project to be packaged and create a specific script. All the scripts follow the same workflow:

1. Set the input and output directories.
2. Create Makefiles with `qmake`.
3. Build the project.
4. Regroup only the necessary files in the output directory.
5. Package the application with platform-specific tasks.
6. Store the packed application in the output directory.

These scripts could run on a developer computer or on a continuous integration server running software such as Jenkins as long as the packaging computer OS matches the script target OS (except for the mobile platforms). In other words, you need to run the Windows script on a computer that runs Windows to be able to package a Qt application for Windows.

Technically, you can perform cross-compilation (given the appropriate toolchain and libraries), but this is beyond the scope of this book. It is easy to cross-compile for a RaspberryPI when you are on Linux, but the same cannot be said when you want to compile for MacOS and you are on Windows.

> From Linux, you can cross-compile Qt for Windows with tools such as MXE at `http://mxe.cc/`.

Create a new subdir project named `ch13-gallery-packaging` with the following hierarchy:

- `ch13-gallery-packaging`:

    - `gallery-core`
    - `gallery-desktop`
    - `gallery-mobile`

Even if you are now an expert on Qt subdirs projects, here is the `ch13-gallery-packaging.pro` file:

```
TEMPLATE = subdirs

SUBDIRS +=
    gallery-core
    gallery-desktop
    gallery-mobile

gallery-desktop.depends = gallery-core
gallery-mobile.depends = gallery-core
```

You are now ready to work through any of the following sections, depending on the platform you are targeting.

Packaging for Windows

To package a standalone application on Windows, you need to provide all the dependencies of your executable. The `gallery-core.dll` file, the Qt libraries (for example, `Qt5Core.dll`), and compiler-specific libraries (for example, `libstdc++-6.dll`) are some examples of dependencies required by our executable. If you forget to provide a library, an error will be displayed when you run the `gallery-desktop.exe` program.

> On Windows, you can use the utility Dependency Walker (`depends`). It will give you a list of all libraries required by your application. You can download it here: `www.dependencywalker.com`.

For this section, we will create a script to build the project via the command line interface. Then we will use the Qt tool `windeployqt` to gather all dependencies required by our application. This example is for a MinGW compiler but you can easily adapt it for a MSVC compiler.

Here is a list of required files and folders gathered by `winqtdeploy`, to properly run `gallery-desktop` on Windows:

- `iconengines:`
  - `qsvgicon.dll`
- `imageformats:`
  - `qjpeg.dll`
  - `qwbmp.dll`
  - `...`
- `Platforms:`
  - `qwindows.dll`
- `translations:`
  - `qt_en.qm`
  - `qt_fr.qm`
  - `...`
- `D3Dcompiler_47.dll`
- `gallery-core.dll`
- `gallery-desktop.exe`
- `libEGL.dll`
- `libgcc_s_dw2-1.dll`
- `libGLESV2.dll`
- `libstdc++-6.dll`
- `libwinpthread-1.dll`
- `opengl32sw.dll`
- `Qt5Core.dll`
- `Qt5Gui.dll`
- `Qt5Svg.dll`
- `Qt5Widgets.dll`

Check that your environment variables are correctly set:

Name	Example
QTDIR	C:\Qt\5.7\mingw49_32
MINGWROOT	C:\Qt\Tools\mingw492_32

Create a file, `package-windows.bat`, in the `scripts` directory:

```
@ECHO off

set DIST_DIR=distdesktop-windows
set BUILD_DIR=build
set OUT_DIR=gallery

mkdir %DIST_DIR% && pushd %DIST_DIR%
mkdir %BUILD_DIR% %OUT_DIR%

pushd %BUILD_DIR%
%QTDIR%binqmake.exe ^
  -spec win32-g++ ^
  "CONFIG += release" ^
  ......ch13-gallery-packaging.pro

%MINGWROOT%binmingw32-make.exe qmake_all

pushd gallery-core
%MINGWROOT%binmingw32-make.exe && popd

pushd gallery-desktop
%MINGWROOT%binmingw32-make.exe && popd

popd
copy %BUILD_DIR%gallery-corereleasegallery-core.dll %OUT_DIR%
copy %BUILD_DIR%gallery-desktopreleasegallery-desktop.exe %OUT_DIR%
%QTDIR%binwindeployqt %OUT_DIR%gallery-desktop.exe %OUT_DIR%gallery-
core.dll

popd
```

Let's talk about the steps performed:

1. Set the main path variables. The output directory is `DIST_DIR`. All files are generated in the `dist/desktop-windows/build` directory.
2. Create all directories and launch `dist/desktop-windows/build`.

3. Execute `qmake` in release mode for the Win32 platform to generate the parent project `Makefile`. The spec `win32-g++` is for the MinGW compiler. You should use the spec `win32-msvc` if you want to use the MSVC compiler.

4. Run the `mingw32-make qmake_all` command to generate the sub-project Makefiles. With an MSVC compiler you must replace `mingw32-make` with `nmake` or `jom`.

5. Perform the `mingw32-make` commands to build each required sub-project.

6. Copy the generated files, `gallery-desktop.exe` and `gallery-core.dll`, into the `gallery` directory.

7. Call the Qt tool, `windeployqt`, on both files and copy all required dependencies (for example, `Qt5Core.dll`, `Qt5Sql.dll`, `libstdc++-6.dll`, `qwindows.dll`, and so on).

Packaging for Linux with a distribution package

Packaging an application for a Linux distribution is a bumpy road. Because each distribution can have its own packaging format (`.deb`, `.rpm`, and so on), the first question to answer is: which distribution do you wish to target? Covering every major packaging format would take several chapters. Even detailing a single distribution could be unfair (you wanted to package for RHEL? Too bad, we only covered Arch Linux!). After all, from a Qt application developer perspective, what you want is to ship your product to your users, you do not (yet) aim to become an official Debian repository maintainer.

Having all this in mind, we decided to focus on a tool that packages the application for you for each distribution. That is right, you do not need to learn the internals of Debian or Red Hat! We will still explain the common principles in the packaging systems without excessive detail.

For our purpose, we will demonstrate how a packaging can be done using the `.deb` format on an Ubuntu machine, but as you will see it can be easily updated to generate a `.rpm`.

The tool we are going to use is named `fpm` (**eFfing Package Management**).

> The `fpm` tool is available at `https://github.com/jordansissel/fpm`.

The `fpm` tool is a Ruby application that aims to do exactly what we need: take care of the distribution-specific details and generate the final package. First, take the time to install `fpm` on your machine and make sure that it is working.

In a nutshell, a Linux package is a file format that contains all the files you want to deploy with a lot of metadata. It can contain description of the content, a changelog, a license file, the list of dependencies, checksums, pre- and post-installation triggers, and much, much more.

> If you want to learn how to package a Debian binary by hand, go to
> `http://tldp.org/HOWTO/html_single/Debian-Binary-Package-Building-HOWTO/`.

In our case, we still have to do some project preparation to let `fpm` do its job. The files we want to deploy have to match the target filesystem. Here is how the deployment should look:

- `gallery-desktop`: This binary should be deployed in `/usr/bin`
- `libgallery-core.so`: This should be deployed in `/usr/lib`

To achieve this, we are going to organize our outputs in `dist/desktop-linux` like so:

- The `build` directory will contain the compiled project (it is our release shadow build)
- The `root` directory will contain the to-be-packaged files, meaning the binary and library files in the proper hierarchy (`usr/bin` and `usr/lib`)

To generate the root directories, we will rely on Qt and the power of the `.pro` files. When compiling a Qt project, the target files are already tracked. All we have to do is to add an additional install target for `gallery-core` and `gallery-desktop`.

Add the following scope in `gallery-core/gallery-core.pro`:

```
linux {
    target.path = $$_PRO_FILE_PWD_/../dist/desktop-linux/root/usr/lib/
    INSTALLS += target
}
```

Here we define a new `target.path` that is going to deploy the `DISTFILES` (the `.so` files) to our desired root tree. Note the use of `$$_PRO_FILE_PWD_`, which points to the directory where the current `.pro` file is stored.

Almost the same procedure is carried out in `gallery-desktop/gallery-desktop.pro`:

```
linux {
    target.path = $$_PRO_FILE_PWD_/../dist/desktop-linux/root/usr/bin/
    INSTALLS += target
}
```

With these lines, when we call make install, the files are going to be deployed in `dist/desktop-linux/root/....`

Now that the project configuration is completed, we can switch to the packaging script. We will cover the script in two parts:

- Project compilation and `root` preparation
- The `.deb` package generation with `fpm`

First, check that your environment variables are correctly set:

Name	Example
QTDIR	$HOME/qt/5.7/gcc_64

Create `scripts/package-linux-deb.sh` with the following content:

```
#!/bin/bash

DIST_DIR=dist/desktop-linux
BUILD_DIR=build
ROOT_DIR=root

BIN_DIR=$ROOT_DIR/usr/bin
LIB_DIR=$ROOT_DIR/usr/lib

mkdir -p $DIST_DIR && cd $DIST_DIR
mkdir -p $BIN_DIR $LIB_DIR $BUILD_DIR

pushd $BUILD_DIR
$QTDIR/bin/qmake
    -spec linux-g++
    "CONFIG += release"
    ../../../ch13-gallery-packaging.pro

make qmake_all
pushd gallery-core && make && make install ; popd
pushd gallery-desktop && make && make install ; popd
popd
```

Let's break this down:

1. Set the main path variables. The output directory is DIST_DIR. All files are generated in the dist/desktop-linux/build folder.
2. Create all the directories and launch dist/desktop-linux/build.
3. Execute qmake in release mode for the Linux platform to generate the parent project Makefile.
4. Run the make qmake_all command to generate the sub-projects Makefiles.
5. Perform the make commands to build each required sub-project.
6. Use the make install command to deploy the binary and the libraries to the dist/desktop-linux/root directory.

If you execute scripts/package-linux-deb.sh, the final file tree in dist/desktop-linux looks like this:

- build/
    - gallery-core/*.o
    - gallery-desktop/*.p
    - Makefile
- root/
    - usr/bin/gallery-desktop
    - usr/lib/libgallery-core.so

Everything is now ready for fpm to work. The final part of scripts/package-linux-deb.sh contains this:

```
fpm --input-type dir
    --output-type deb
    --force
    --name gallery-desktop
    --version 1.0.0
    --vendor "Mastering Qt 5"
    --description "A Qt gallery application to organize and manage your
pictures in albums"
    --depends qt5-default
    --depends libsqlite3-dev
    --chdir $ROOT_DIR
    --package gallery-desktop_VERSION_ARCH.deb
```

Most of the arguments are explicit enough. We will focus on the most important ones:

- `--input-type`: This argument refers to what `fpm` will work with. It can take `deb`, `rpm`, `gem`, `dir` and so on and repackage it to another format. Here we use the `dir` option to tell `fpm` to use a directory tree as the input source.
- `--output-type`: This argument refers to the desired output type. Take a look at the official documentation to see how many platforms are supported.
- `--name`: This is the name given to the package (if you want to uninstall it, you write `apt-get remove gallery-desktop`).
- `--depends`: This argument refers to a library package dependency of the project. You can add as many dependencies as you want. In our case, we only depend on `qt5 -default` and `sqlite3-dev`. This option is very important so be sure that the application will be able to run on the target platform. You can specify the version of the dependency with `--depends library >= 1.2.3`.
- `--chdir`: This argument refers to the base directory from which `fpm` will run. We set it to `dist/desktop-linux/root`, where our file tree is ready to be loaded!
- `--package`: This argument is the name of the final package. The `VERSION` and `ARCH` are placeholders that are automatically filled based on your system.

The rest of the options are purely informative; you can specify a changelog, a license file, and much more. Just by changing the `--output-type` `deb` to `rpm`, the package format is properly updated. The `fpm` tool also provides specific package format options, letting you have fine control over what is generated.

If you now execute `scripts/package-linux-deb.sh`, you should get a new `dist/desktop-linux/gallery-desktop_1.0.0_amd64.deb` file. Try to install it with the commands:

```
sudo dpkg -i  dist/desktop-linux/gallery-desktop_1.0.0_amd64.deb
sudo apt-get install -f
```

The first command deploys the package in your system. You should now have the files `/usr/bin/gallery-desktop` and `/usr/lib/libgallery-core.so`.

However, because we installed the package using the `dpkg` command, the dependencies are not automatically installed. This would be done if the package was provided by a Debian repository (thus, installing the package with `apt-get install gallery-desktop`). The missing dependencies are still "marked" and `apt-get install -f` does their installation.

You can now start `gallery-desktop` from anywhere in your system with the command, `gallery-desktop`. When we wrote this chapter in 2016, if you execute it on a "fresh" Ubuntu, you might run into the following issue:

```
$ gallery-desktop
gallery-desktop: /usr/lib/x86_64-linux-gnu/libQt5Core.so.5: version
`Qt_5.7' not found (required by gallery-desktop)
gallery-desktop: /usr/lib/x86_64-linux-gnu/libQt5Core.so.5: version
`Qt_5' not found (required by gallery-desktop)
...
gallery-desktop: /usr/lib/x86_64-linux-gnu/libQt5Core.so.5: version
`Qt_5' not found (required by /usr/lib/libgallery-core.so.1)
```

What happened? We installed the dependencies with `apt-get install -f`! We encounter here a major pain point in Linux package management. The dependencies we specify in our `.deb` could refer to a specific version of Qt, but the reality is that we depend on the package version maintained by the upstream. In other words, each time a new version of Qt is released, the distribution maintainers (Ubuntu, Fedora, and so on) have to repackage it to make it available in the official repository. This can be a long process and the maintainers have a huge number of packages to port!

To be confident about what we are stating, let's view the library dependencies of `gallery-desktop` with an `ldd` command:

```
$ ldd /usr/bin/gallery-desktop
        libgallery-core.so.1 => /usr/lib/libgallery-core.so.1
(0x00007f8110775000)
        libQt5Widgets.so.5 => /usr/lib/x86_64-linux-gnu/libQt5Widgets.so.5
(0x00007f81100e8000)
        libQt5Gui.so.5 => /usr/lib/x86_64-linux-gnu/libQt5Gui.so.5
(0x00007f810fb9f000)
        libQt5Core.so.5 => /usr/lib/x86_64-linux-gnu/libQt5Core.so.5
(0x00007f810f6c9000)
        ...
        libXext.so.6 => /usr/lib/x86_64-linux-gnu/libXext.so.6
(0x00007f810966e000)
```

As you can see, `libgallery-core.so` is correctly resolved in `/usr/lib` and the Qt dependencies too in `/usr/lib/x86_64-linux-gnu`. But what version of Qt is used? The answer lies in the details of the libraries:

```
$ ll /usr/lib/x86_64-linux-gnu/libQt5Core.*
-rw-r--r-- 1 root root    1014 may     2 15:37 libQt5Core.prl
lrwxrwxrwx 1 root root      19 may     2 15:39 libQt5Core.so ->
libQt5Core.so.5.5.1
lrwxrwxrwx 1 root root      19 may     2 15:39 libQt5Core.so.5 ->
```

```
libQt5Core.so.5.5.1
    lrwxrwxrwx 1 root root        19 may    2 15:39 libQt5Core.so.5.5 ->
libQt5Core.so.5.5.1
    -rw-r--r-- 1 root root 5052920 may    2 15:41 libQt5Core.so.5.5.1
```

The `libQt5Core.so` file is a soft link to `libQt5Core.so.5.5.1`, meaning that the system version of Qt is 5.5.1, whereas `gallery-desktop` relies on Qt 5.7. You can configure your system to have the system Qt pointing to your Qt installation (done with the Qt installer). However, it is highly improbable that your customer will install Qt by hand just to have `gallery-desktop` running.

Even worse, for an older version of your distribution, the packages are usually not updated at all after some time. Just try to install a Qt 5.7 Debian package on Ubuntu 14.04 to understand how complicated things become. We did not even mention incompatible dependencies. If we rely on a specific version of `libsqlite3-dev` and another application needs another one, things will get ugly, and only one can survive.

A Linux package has many advantages if you want it to be available on an official repository or if you have specific needs. Using official repositories is a common way of installing an application on Linux and your users will not be disoriented. If you can restrict your Qt version to the one deployed on the Linux distribution that may be a fine solution.

Unfortunately, it also brings major headaches: you need to support multiple distributions, handle the dependencies without breaking the system, and make sure that your application has old enough dependencies, and so on.

Do not worry, everything is not lost; smart people are already resolving this issue on Linux with self-contained packages. As a matter of fact, we are going to cover a self-contained package.

Packaging for Linux with AppImage

On Windows or Mac, an application is self-sufficient: it contains all the dependencies it needs to be executed. On the one hand, this creates more file duplication, and on the other hand it simplifies packaging for the developer.

Based on this premise, efforts have been made to have the same pattern on Linux (as opposed to a repository/distribution-specific package). Today, several solutions offer a self-contained package on Linux. We suggest you study one of these solutions: AppImage. This particular tool is gaining traction in the Linux community. There is a growing number of developers relying on AppImage to package and deploy their application.

AppImage is a file format that contains an application with all its libraries included. You download a single AppImage file, execute it, and you are done: the application is running. Behind the scenes, an AppImage is an ISO file on steroids, mounted on-the-fly when you execute it. The AppImage file itself is read-only and can also run in a sandbox such as Firejail (a SUID sandbox program that reduces the risk of security breaches by restricting the running environment of applications).

> More information on AppImage is available at http://appimage.org/.

To package gallery-desktop into an AppImage, there are two major steps:

1. Gather all the dependencies of gallery-desktop.
2. Package gallery-desktop and its dependencies in the AppImage format.

Fortunately, this whole process can be done by using a nifty tool: linuxdeployqt. It started as a hobby project and became the official way to package a Qt application in the AppImage documentation.

> Get linuxdeployqt from https://github.com/probonopd/linuxdeployqt/.

The script we are going to write now assumes that the binary linuxdeployqt is available in your $PATH variable. Check that your environment variables are correctly set:

Name	Example
QTDIR	$HOME/qt/5.7/gcc_64

Create scripts/package-linux-appimage.sh and update it like so:

```bash
#!/bin/bash

DIST_DIR=dist/desktop-linux
BUILD_DIR=build

mkdir -p $DIST_DIR && cd $DIST_DIR
mkdir -p $BUILD_DIR

pushd $BUILD_DIR
```

```
$QTDIR/bin/qmake
    -spec linux-g++
    "CONFIG += release"
    ../../../ch13-gallery-packaging.pro
make qmake_all
pushd gallery-core && make ; popd
pushd gallery-desktop && make ; popd
popd

export QT_PLUGIN_PATH=$QTDIR/plugins/
export LD_LIBRARY_PATH=$QTDIR/lib:$(pwd)/build/gallery-core

linuxdeployqt
    build/gallery-desktop/gallery-desktop
    -appimage

mv build/gallery-desktop.AppImage .
```

The first part is the compilation of the project:

1. Set the main path variables. The output directory is DIST_DIR. All files are generated in the dist/desktop-linux/build folder.
2. Create all the directories and go in dist/desktop-linux/build.
3. Execute qmake in release mode for the Linux platform to generate the parent project Makefile.
4. Run the make qmake_all command to generate the sub-project Makefiles.
5. Perform the make commands to build each required sub-project.

The second part of the script concerns linuxdeployqt. We first have to export some paths to let linuxdeployqt properly find all the dependencies of gallery-desktop (Qt libraries and the gallery-core library).

After that, we execute linuxdeployqt by specifying the source binary to work with and the target file type (AppImage). The resulting file is a single gallery-desktop.AppImage ready to be launched on the user's computer without any Qt package installed!

Packaging for Mac OS X

On OS X, applications are built and run from a bundle: a single directory that contains the application binary and all its dependencies. In the Finder, these bundles are viewed as .app special directories.

When running `gallery-desktop` from Qt Creator, the application is already bundled in a `.app` file. Because we are using a custom library, `gallery-core`, this `gallery-desktop.app` does not contain all the dependencies and Qt Creator handles it for us.

What we aim to create is a script that completely packages `gallery-desktop` (`gallery-core` included) in a `.dmg` file, a Mac OS X disk image file that is mounted upon execution and lets the user install the application with ease.

To achieve this, Qt provides the `macdeployqt` tool, which gathers the dependencies and creates the `.dmg` file.

First, check that your environment variables are correctly set:

Name	Example
QTDIR	$HOME/Qt/5.7/clang_64

Create the `scripts/package-macosx.sh` file with the following content:

```bash
#!/bin/bash

DIST_DIR=dist/desktop-macosx
BUILD_DIR=build

mkdir -p $DIST_DIR && cd $DIST_DIR
mkdir -p $BUILD_DIR

pushd $BUILD_DIR
$QTDIR/bin/qmake
  -spec macx-clang
  "CONFIG += release x86_64"
  ../../../ch13-gallery-packaging.pro
make qmake_all
pushd gallery-core && make ; popd
pushd gallery-desktop && make ; popd

cp gallery-core/*.dylib
    gallery-desktop/gallery-desktop.app/Contents/Frameworks/

install_name_tool -change
  libgallery-core.1.dylib
  @rpath/libgallery-core.1.dylib
  gallery-desktop/gallery-desktop.app/Contents/MacOS/gallery-desktop
popd

$QTDIR/bin/macdeployqt
```

```
build/gallery-desktop/gallery-desktop.app
-dmg
```

```
mv build/gallery-desktop/gallery-desktop.dmg .
```

We can split the script in two. The first part prepares the application for `macdeployqt`:

1. Set the main path variables. The output directory is `DIST_DIR`. All files are generated in the `dist/desktop-macosx/build` folder.
2. Create all the directories and go in `dist/desktop-macosx/build`.
3. Execute `qmake` in release mode for the Mac OS X platform to generate the parent project `Makefile`.
4. Run the `make qmake_all` command to generate the sub-projects Makefiles.
5. Perform the `make` commands to build each required sub-project.

The following part includes the `gallery-core` library in the generated `gallery-desktop.app`. If we do not execute the `cp` command stated in the script and everything that comes after it, we might be quite surprised by the `gallery-desktop` binary content. Let's take a look at it by executing the following command:

```
$ otool -L dist/desktop-macosx/build/gallery-desktop/gallery-desktop.app/Contents/MacOS/gallery-desktop
    dist/desktop-macosx/build/gallery-desktop/gallery-desktop.app/Contents/MacOS/gallery-desktop:
        libgallery-core.1.dylib (compatibility version 1.0.0, current version 1.0.0)
        @rpath/QtWidgets.framework/Versions/5/QtWidgets (compatibility version 5.7.0, current version 5.7.0)
        ...
        /usr/lib/libSystem.B.dylib (compatibility version 1.0.0, current version 1226.10.1)
```

As you can see, `libgallery-core.1.dylib` is resolved in the local path but not in the special dependencies path as is done for `QtWidget` with `@rpath` (namely `Contents/Frameworks/`). To mitigate this, `package-macosx.sh` copies the `.dylib` file in `gallery-desktop.app/Contents/Frameworks/` and regenerates the dependencies index of the binary with `install_name_tool`.

Finally, in `package-macosx.sh`, `macdeployqt` is called with the updated `gallery-deskop.app` and the target `dmg` format. The resulting `gallery-desktop.dmg` can be deployed on your user computer.

Packaging for Android

The aim of this section is to generate a standalone APK file for the `gallery-mobile` application. Packaging and deploying an application for Android require multiple steps:

1. Configure the Android build details.
2. Generate a keystore and a certificate.
3. Customize the Android manifest from a template.
4. Create a script to automate the packaging.

You can do most of the tasks directly from Qt Creator. Under the hood, the Qt tool, `androiddeployqt`, is called to generate the APK file. Go to **Projects** | **Android for armeabi-v7a** | **Build Steps**. You should see a special build step: **Build Android APK**. The details look like the following screenshot:

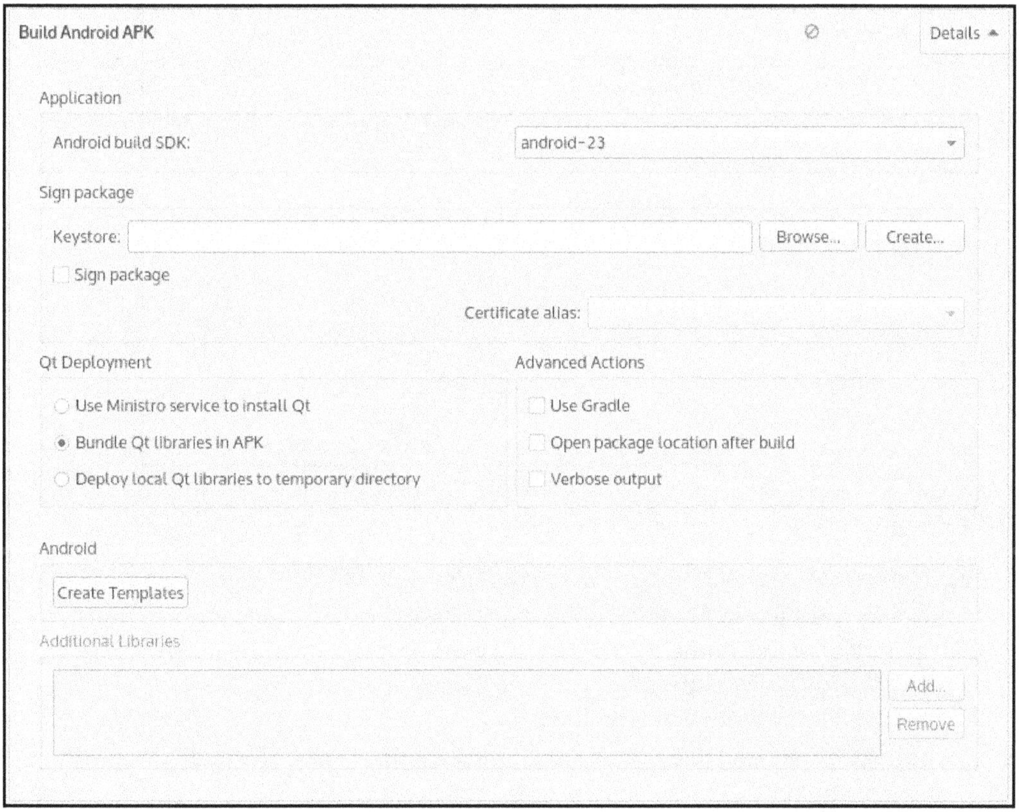

The first thing to do is to select which Android API level you want to use to generate the **Application**. In our case, we selected **android-23** for the Android API Level 23. Try to always build your application with the latest SDK version available.

To publish your application on the Play Store, you must sign the package. To be able to update an application, the signature of the current version and the new version must be the same. This procedure is a protection to make sure that any future versions of the application were really created by you. The first time you should create a keystore, the next time you can reuse it with the **Browse...** button. For now, click on the **Create...** button on the **Sign package** | **Keystore** line. You will get the following popup:

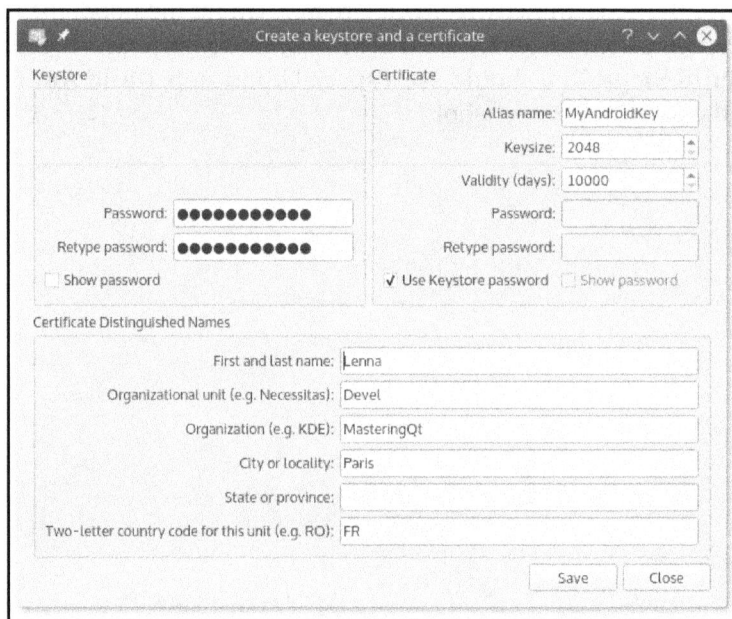

Follow these steps to generate a new keystore:

1. The keystore must be protected by a password. Do not forget it or you will not be able to use this keystore for a future release.
2. Specify an **Alias name** for the certificate. The default values for **Keysize** and **Validity(days)** are fine. You can specify a different password for the certificate or use the keystore one.
3. In the **Certificate Distinguished Names** group, enter information about you and your company.
4. Save the keystore file in a safe place.
5. Enter the keystore password to validate its selection for the deployment.

The next part concerns **Qt deployment**. Indeed, your application needs some Qt libraries. Qt supports three kinds of deployment:

- Create a minimal APK relying on **Ministro** for the Qt dependencies. Ministro is an Android application that can be downloaded from the Play Store. It acts as a Qt shared libraries installer/provider for all Qt applications on Android.
- Create a standalone **bundle** APK that embeds Qt libraries.
- Create an APK that relies on the fact that the Qt libraries are in a specific directory. The libraries are copied into a **temporary directory** during the first deployment.

During the developing and debugging phase, you should select the **temporary directory** way to reduce the packaging time. For a deployment, you can use the **Ministro** or the **bundle** option. In our case, we chose the standalone bundle to generate a complete APK.

The **Advanced actions** pane offers three options:

- **Use Gradle**: This option generates Gradle wrappers and a script, useful if you plan to customize the Java part in an IDE such as Android Studio
- **Open package location after build**: This option opens the directory with the packages generated by `androiddeployqt`
- **Verbose Output**: This option displays additional information about the `androiddeployqt` processing

The Android build details and signing options are finished. We can now customize the Android manifest. Click on **Create Templates**, select the `gallery-mobile.pro` file, and click on **Finish**. The wizard creates for you an `android` sub-directory with several files; for example, `AndroidManifest.xml`. The `gallery-mobile.pro` file has to be updated automatically with these files. However, do not forget to add the `android` scope like the following snippet:

```
TEMPLATE = app
...
android {
    contains(ANDROID_TARGET_ARCH,x86) {
        ANDROID_EXTRA_LIBS =
            $$[QT_INSTALL_LIBS]/libQt5Sql.so
    }

    DISTFILES +=
        android/AndroidManifest.xml
        android/gradle/wrapper/gradle-wrapper.jar
```

```
        android/gradlew
        android/res/values/libs.xml
        android/build.gradle
        android/gradle/wrapper/gradle-wrapper.properties
        android/gradlew.bat

    ANDROID_PACKAGE_SOURCE_DIR = $$PWD/android
}
```

You can now edit the `AndroidManifest.xml` file. Qt Creator provides a dedicated editor. You can also edit it with a plain text editor with caution. You can open it from the hierarchical project view: **gallery-mobile** I **Other files** I **android**.

Here is our Android manifest in Qt Creator:

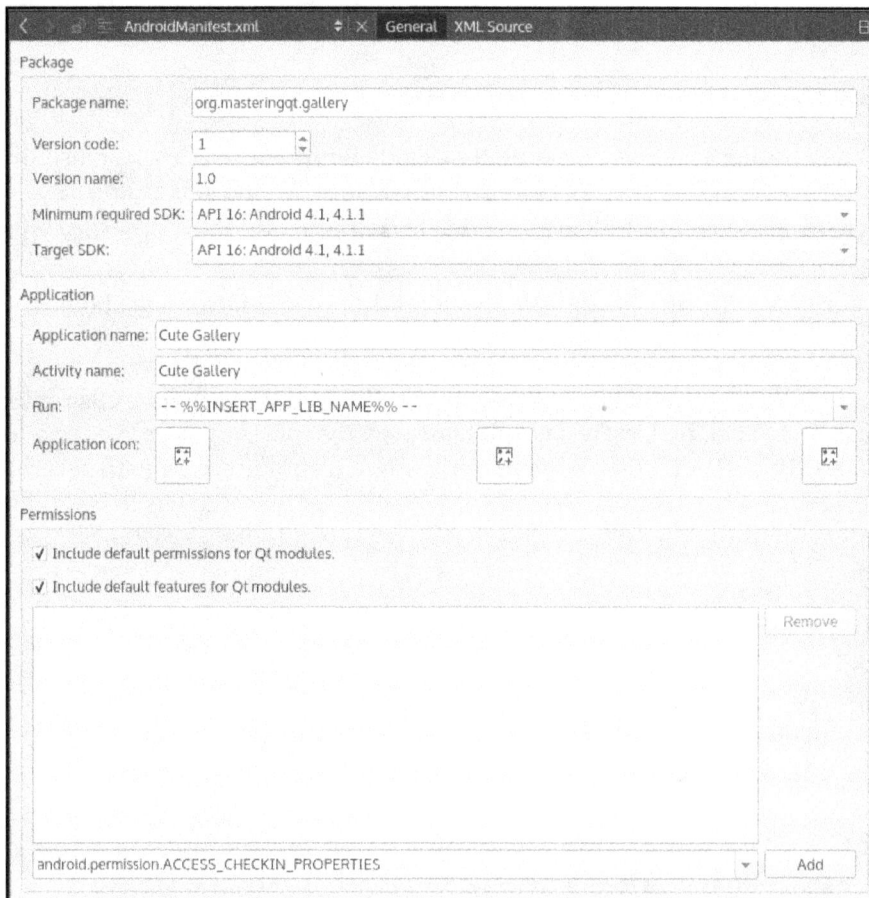

Here are the most important steps:

1. Replace the default **Package name** with yours.
2. The **Version code** is an integer that must be increased for each official release.
3. The **Version name** is the displayed version for users.
4. Select the **Minimum required SDK**. Users with an older version will not be able to install your application.
5. Select the SDK that will be used to compile your application with the **Target SDK.**
6. Change the application and activity name.
7. Select an **Application icon** depending on the screen DPI (Dots per Inch). From left to right: the low, medium, and high DPI icon.
8. Finally, if required by your application, you can add some Android permissions.

You can already build and deploy your signed application from Qt Creator. You should see the new application name and icon on your Android phone or emulator. However, we will now create a script to easily generate and package the signed APK from the command line.

Several environment variables are required by the Android and Qt tools but also for the script itself. Here is a summary with an example:

Name	Example
QTROOT	$HOME/qt/5.7
QTDIR_ANDROID	$QTROOT/android_armv7
JAVA_HOME	/usr/lib/jvm/java-8-openjdk-amd64
ANT_ROOT	/opt/apache-ant
ANDROID_SDK_ROOT	$HOME/android-sdk
ANDROID_NDK_ROOT	$HOME/android-ndk

This example is a bash script but feel free to adapt it to a `.bat` file if you are on Windows. Create a `package-android.sh` file in the `scripts` directory:

```
#!/bin/bash

DIST_DIR=dist/mobile-android
BUILD_DIR=build
APK_DIR=apk
KEYSTORE_PATH="$(pwd)/scripts/android-data"
ANDROID_BUILD_PATH="$(pwd)/$DIST_DIR/$BUILD_DIR/android-build"

mkdir -p $DIST_DIR && cd $DIST_DIR
mkdir -p $APK_DIR $BUILD_DIR
```

```
pushd $BUILD_DIR
$QTDIR_ANDROID/bin/qmake
    -spec android-g++
    "CONFIG += release"
    ../../../ch13-gallery-packaging.pro
make qmake_all
pushd gallery-core && make ; popd
pushd gallery-mobile && make ; popd
pushd gallery-mobile && make INSTALL_ROOT=$ANDROID_BUILD_PATH install ;
popd

$QTDIR_ANDROID/bin/androiddeployqt
    --input ./gallery-mobile/android-libgallery-mobile.so-deployment-
settings.json
    --output $ANDROID_BUILD_PATH
    --deployment bundled
    --android-platform android-23
    --jdk $JAVA_HOME
    --ant $ANT_ROOT/ant
    --sign $KEYSTORE_PATH/android.keystore myandroidkey
    --storepass 'masteringqt'
cp $ANDROID_BUILD_PATH/bin/QtApp-release-signed.apk ../apk/cute-gallery.apk
popd
```

Let's analyze this script together:

1. Set the main path variables. The output directory is DIST_DIR. All files are generated in the dist/mobile-android/build directory. The final signed APK is copied in the dist/mobile-android/apk directory.

2. Create all the directories and go in dist/mobile-android/build.

3. Execute qmake in release mode for the Android platform to generate the parent project Makefile.

4. Run the make qmake_all command to generate the sub-project Makefiles.

5. Perform the make commands to build each required sub-project.

6. Run the make install command on the gallery-mobile directory specifying the INSTALL_ROOT to copy all binaries and files required by the APK generation.

The final part of the script calls the `androiddeployqt` binary, a Qt tool to generate the APK. Take a look at the following options:

- The `--deployment` option used here is `bundled` like the mode we used in Qt Creator.
- The `--sign` option requires two parameters: the URL to the keystore file and the alias to the key for the certificate.
- The `--storepass` option is used to specify the keystore password. In our case the password is "masteringqt".

Finally, the generated signed APK is copied to the `dist/mobile-android/apk` directory with the name `cute-gallery.apk`.

Packaging for iOS

Packaging a Qt application for iOS relies on XCode. When you build and run gallery-mobile from Qt Creator, XCode will be called under the hood. In the end, an `.xcodeproj` file is generated and passed to XCode.

Knowing this, the packaging part will be fairly limited: the only thing than can be automated is the generation of the `.xcodeproj`.

First, check that your environment variables are correctly set:

Name	Example
QTDIR_IOS	$HOME/Qt/5.7/ios

Create `scripts/package-ios.sh` and add this snippet to it:

```bash
#!/bin/bash

DIST_DIR=dist/mobile-ios
BUILD_DIR=build

mkdir -p $DIST_DIR && cd $DIST_DIR
mkdir -p $BIN_DIR $LIB_DIR $BUILD_DIR

pushd $BUILD_DIR
$QTDIR_IOS/bin/qmake
  -spec macx-ios-clang
  "CONFIG += release iphoneos device"
  ../../../ch13-gallery-packaging.pro
```

```
make qmake_all
pushd gallery-core && make ; popd
pushd gallery-mobile && make ; popd

popd
```

The script performs the following steps:

1. Set the main path variables. The output directory is `DIST_DIR`. All files are generated in the `dist/mobile-ios/build` folder.
2. Create all the directories and go in `dist/mobile-ios/build`.
3. Execute `qmake` in release mode for the iPhone device (as opposed to the iPhone simulator) platform to generate the parent project `Makefile`.
4. Run the `make qmake_all` command to generate the sub-project Makefiles.
5. Perform the `make` command to build each required sub-projects.

Once this script has been executed, `dist/mobile-ios/build/gallery-mobile/gallery-mobile.xcodeproj` is ready to be opened in XCode. The remaining steps are entirely done in XCode:

1. Open `gallery-mobile.xcodeproj` in XCode.
2. Compile the application for an iOS device.
3. Follow the Apple procedure to distribute your application (through the App Store or as a standalone file).

After that, `gallery-mobile` will be ready for your users!

Summary

Even if your application runs well on your computer, your development environment can affect this behavior. Its packaging must be correct to run your application on the user's hardware. You learned the steps required to package an application before deploying it. Some platforms required specific tasks that must be followed carefully. You can now bake a standalone package if your application is running a unique script.

The next chapter describes some tricks that can be useful for developing applications with Qt. You will learn some tips concerning Qt Creator.

Qt Hat Tips and Tricks

22

The previous chapter taught you how to package a Qt application on all the major desktop and mobile platforms. This was the final step before shipping your application to your users. This chapter gathers some tips and tricks that will help you to develop your Qt applications with more ease.

This chapter covers the following topics:

- Qt Creator tips - Useful keyboard shortcuts, session management, and more
- Examining the memory with Qt Creator
- Generating random numbers
- Silencing unused variables and compiler warnings
- How to easily log an object's content to `QDebug`
- Customizing `QDebug` formatting
- Saving logs to a file
- Creating a friendly command-line interface
- Sending `HTTPGET` and `POST` requests

Managing your workspace with sessions

It is common for a commercial product to be composed of several Qt projects. We regularly encountered this practice in this book-for example, an application composed of a core project and a GUI project. The Qt subdirs project is a nice way of handling inter-dependent projects within the same application.

However, when your product grows up, you'll want to open some unrelated projects in Qt Creator. In this case, you should use a **session**. A session is a complete snapshot of your workspace in Qt Creator. You can easily create a new session from **File | Session Manager | New**. Do not forget to switch to the new session. For example, you can create a session "Mastering Qt5" and load all project examples in a common workspace.

The sessions are useful when you need to quickly switch between two different workspaces. The following items in Qt Creator will be automatically saved in the session:

* Opened projects of the hierarchical view
* Editor's windows (including the splits)
* Debug breakpoints and expressions views
* Bookmarks

You can change to a different session with **File | Session Manager** or by using the **Welcome** tab. A session can be destroyed without any impact on your projects.

Searching with the Locator

Another way to improve your productivity with Qt Creator is to use keyboard shortcuts. Qt Creator provides a lot of great keyboard shortcuts. Here is our selection:

Action	Shortcut
Comment / uncomment	Ctrl + /
Autocomplete	Ctrl + Space
View help of symbol under cursor	F1
Follow symbol under cursor	F2
Switch between header / source file	F4
Switch between function declaration and definition	Shift + F2
Switch between form / source file	Shift + F4
Rename symbol under cursor	Ctrl + Shift + R
Find usages of symbol under cursor	Ctrl + Shift + U
Select the kit	Ctrl + T
Build current project	Ctrl + B
Start / continue debugging	F5
Debugging : step over	F10
Debugging : step into	F11
Debugging : step out	Shift + F11
Run	Ctrl + R
Open next file from Open Documents	Ctrl + Tab
Open previous file from Open Documents	Ctrl + Shift + Tab
Toggle the left sidebar	Atl + 0
Toggle Issues pane	Alt + 1
Activate Locator	Ctrl + K
Auto indent the selection	Ctrl + I
Go to the line	Ctrl + L
Toggle fullscreen	Ctrl + Shift + F11
Remove current split editor	Ctrl + E, 0
Split editor horizontally	Ctrl + E, 2
Split editor vertically	Ctrl + E, 3

One of our favorites is the Locator. Press *Ctrl + K* to activate it. Then you can enjoy several features:

- Enter a filename (you can even use a partial entry) and press *Enter* to open this file. If the Locator suggests multiple files, you can use the arrows up and down to navigate.
- Prefix your search by . (a dot followed by a space) to search C++ symbols in the current document. For example, on the `Task.cpp` file of the first chapter, try to use the Locator with . `set` and press *Enter* to go to the `Task::setName()` function.
- Enter `l` (*L* followed by a space) to go to a specific line. For example, "l 37" will bring us to line 37 of the current file

The Locator provides plenty of features; take a look when you press *Ctrl + K* the next time!

Increasing the compilation speed

You can speed up the compilation on a multicore computer. By default, when you build your project with Qt Creator, you only use one job (and, therefore, one core). But `make` supports the compilation with multiple jobs. You can use the `make -j N` option to allow N jobs at once. Do not forget to update your packaging scripts!

If you build your project from Qt Creator, you can set this option from **Projects** | **Build Steps** | **Make**. Click on **Details**, then, in the **Make arguments** field, put the value `-j 8` to allow eight jobs during the compilation, as shown in the following screenshot:

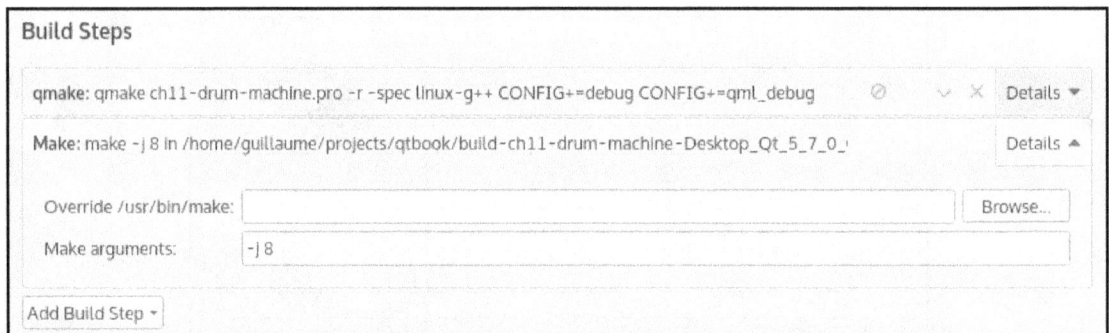

Examining the memory with Qt Creator

For this section, we will use the following code snippet:

```
bool boolean = true;
int integer = 5;
char character = 'A';
int* integerPointer = &integer;

qDebug() << "boolean is:" << boolean;
qDebug() << "integer is:" << integer;
qDebug() << "character is:" << character;
qDebug() << "integerPointer is:" << integerPointer;
qDebug() << "*integerPointer is:" << *integerPointer;
qDebug() << "done!";
```

We declared three primitive types: boolean, integer, and character. We also added a integerPointer pointer that refers to the integer variable. Put a breakpoint at the last line and start the debugging. On the Debug pane, you should have the **Locals and Expressions** view. You can easily add/remove it from **Window** | **Views** | **Locals and Expressions**. Here is a screenshot of it:

Locals and Expressions					
Name	Value				Type
boolean	true				bool
character	'A'	65		0x41	char
integer	5				int
integerPointer	5				int

You can see that all our local variables are displayed with their values. The character line even displays three formats (ASCII, integer, and hexadecimal) of the letter '**A**'. You may also notice that the integerPointer line displays the automatically dereferenced value, not the pointer address. You can disable it with a right-click on the background of the **Locals and Expressions** window and then select **Dereference Pointers automatically**. You can see the pointer address and the dereferenced value appearing as shown in the following screenshot:

Locals and Expressions					
Name	Value				Type
boolean	true				bool
character	'A'	65		0x41	char
integer	5				int
▼ integerPointer	0x7ffe601153ac				int *
*integerPointer	5				int

The console output displays the following information:

```
boolean is: true
integer is: 5
character is: A
integerPointer is: 0x7ffe601153ac
*integerPointer is: 5
```

You can see that we retrieve the same information in the console output. The **Locals and Expressions** view helps you to save time. You can display a lot of information without logging it with a qDebug() function.

Qt Creator provides a useful memory editor. You can open it with a right-click on a variable name in the **Locals and Expressions** window, and then select **Open Memory Editor** | **Open Memory Editor at Object's Address**.

Within the memory editor, look at the value of the `boolean` variable:

```
0000:7ffe:6011:5390 30 55 11 60 fe 7f 00 00 58 4d 40 00 00 00 00 00  0U·`····XM@·····
0000:7ffe:6011:53a0 20 54 11 60 fe 7f 00 00 20 54 01 41 05 00 00 00   T·`···· T A····
0000:7ffe:6011:53b0 30 3a 18 02 00 00 00 00 ac 53 11 60 fe 7f 00 00  0:·······S·`····
```

A hexadecimal editor appears with three parts (from the left to the right):

- The memory address of the data
- The hexadecimal representation of the data
- The ASCII representation of the data

The selection in the hexadecimal representation corresponds to the variable. We can confirm that the `boolean` variable is represented in memory by 1 byte. Because the value is `true`, the memory representation is **0x01**.

Let's examine the `character` memory with the **Memory Editor** tool:

```
0000:7ffe:6011:5390 30 55 11 60 fe 7f 00 00 58 4d 40 00 00 00 00 00  0U·`····XM@·····
0000:7ffe:6011:53a0 20 54 11 60 fe 7f 00 00 20 54 01 41 05 00 00 00   T·`···· T·A····
0000:7ffe:6011:53b0 30 3a 18 02 00 00 00 00 ac 53 11 60 fe 7f 00 00  0:·······S·`····
```

The character is also stored in memory with 1 byte. The hexadecimal representation is **0x41**. The character is encoded with the well-known ASCII format. Note that, on the right-hand side, the ASCII representation displays the '**A**'.

Here is the **Memory Editor** location of the `integer` variable:

```
0000:7ffe:6011:5390 30 55 11 60 fe 7f 00 00 58 4d 40 00 00 00 00 00  0U·`····XM@·····
0000:7ffe:6011:53a0 20 54 11 60 fe 7f 00 00 20 54 01 41 05 00 00 00   T·`···· T·A···
0000:7ffe:6011:53b0 30 3a 18 02 00 00 00 00 ac 53 11 60 fe 7f 00 00  0:·······S·`····
```

There are two interesting facts to note. The integer is stored on 4 bytes. The value **05** is stored in hexadecimal as **05 00 00 00**. The byte order depends on the endianness of your processor. We are using an Intel CPU that is Little-Endian. Another CPU architecture with a Big-Endian memory storage will display the variable as **00 00 00 05**.

Before we continue to dive into the memory of our application, look at the last three screenshots closely. You might notice that, in this case, the three variables are contiguous in the stack memory. This behavior is not guaranteed depending on the implementation of your OS.

Try to open the memory editor on the integerPointer variable. The context menu offers you two different ways:

- The **Open Memory Editor at Object's Address** option dereferences the pointer and brings you directly to the pointed value. You get the same result as the integer memory view.
- The **Open Memory Editor at Pointer's Address** option displays the raw pointer data, which is a memory address to where it is pointing.

Here is the **Memory Editor** tool showing the pointer's address of integerPointer:

```
0000:7ffe:6011:53a0 20 54 11 60 fe 7f 00 00 20 54 01 41 05 00 00 00  T.`.... T.A....
0000:7ffe:6011:53b0 30 3a 18 02 00 00 00 00 ac 53 11 60 fe 7f 00 00  0:......S....
0000:7ffe:6011:53c0 02 00 00 00 66 00 00 00 10 9e 40 00 00 00 00 00  ....f.....@.....
```

We are on a 64-bit OS, so our pointer is stored on 8 bytes. The data of this pointer is the hexadecimal value ac 53 11 60 fe 7f 00 00. This is the Little-Endian representation of the memory address 0x7ffe601153ac displayed by the **Locals and Expressions** and by our console output.

We display the memory, but we can also change it. Follow these steps:

1. Remove the current breakpoint and add a new one on the first qDebug() line.
2. Restart the debugging and look at the **Locals and Expressions**. If you double-click a variable's value, you can edit it. Note that the **Memory Editor** window immediately updates its representation.
3. In our case, we set boolean value to false, character to 68 (that is 'D') and integer to 9. When you are confident with your changes, continue the debugging.

Here is the final console output reflecting our modifications:

```
boolean is: false
integer is: 9
character is: D
integerPointer is: 0x7fff849203dc
*integerPointer is: 9
done!
```

The **Memory Editor** is a powerful tool: You can display and change your variable's value, at runtime, without changing your source code and recompiling your application.

Generating random numbers

Generating real random numbers is quite a difficult task for a computer. Commonly, we are using only a **pseudo-random number generation** (**PRNG**). The Qt framework provides the function qrand(), a thread-safe version of std::rand(). This function returns an integer between 0 and RAND_MAX (defined in stdlib.h). The following code shows two pseudo-random numbers:

```
qDebug() << "first number is" << qrand() % 10;
qDebug() << "second number is" << qrand() % 10;
```

We are using a modulo operator to get a value between 0 and 9. Try to run your application several times. The numbers are always the same, in our case, 3 then 7. That is because each time we call qrand(), we retrieve the next number of the pseudo-random sequence, but the sequence is always the same! Fortunately, we can use qsrand() to initialize the PRNG with a seed. A seed is an unsigned integer that is used to generate a sequence. Try the next snippet:

```
qsrand(3);
qDebug() << "first number is" << qrand() % 10;
qDebug() << "second number is" << qrand() % 10;
```

In this example, we are using the seed 3, and we get a different value from qrand()--on our computer it is 5 and 4. Great, but if you run this application several times, you will always have this sequence. One way of generating a different sequence each time you run your application is to use a different seed on each run. Run the following code snippet:

```
qsrand(QDateTime::currentDateTime().toTime_t());
qDebug() << "first number is" << qrand() % 10;
qDebug() << "second number is" << qrand() % 10;
```

As you can see, we are now initializing the PRNG with the epoch time from QDateTime. You can try to run your application multiple times to see that we get different numbers each time! However, this solution is not recommended for cryptography. In this case, you should use a stronger random number engine.

Silencing unused variable warnings

If your compiler is configured to output its warnings, you will probably sometimes see this kind of log:

```
warning: unused parameter 'myVariable' [-Wunused-parameter]
```

This is a safety warning to tell the developer to keep their code clean and avoid dead variables. It is a good practice to try to minimize this kind of warning. However, sometimes you have no choice: You override an existing function and you do not use all the parameters. You now face a conundrum: On the one hand you can silence the warning for your whole application, and on the other hand, you can let these safety warnings pile up in your compile output. There must be a better option.

Indeed, you can silence the warning for your function only. There are two ways of doing this:

- Using the C/C++ syntax
- Using a Qt macro

Let's say you override myFunction(QString name, QString myVariable) and you do not use myVariable. Using the C/C++ syntax, you just have to implement myFunction() like so:

```
void myFunction(QString name, QString /*myVariable*/)
```

By commenting the variable's name, myVariable, in the function signature, you ensure that you will not (that is, cannot) use the variable in the function body. The compiler will also interpret it like this and will not output any warning.

Qt also provides a way of marking unused variables with the Q_UNUSED macro. Let's see it in action:

```
void myFunction(QString name, QString myVariable)
{
    Q_UNUSED(myVariable)
    ...
}
```

Simply pass myVariable to Q_UNUSED and it will remove the warning from the compiler output. Behind the curtain, Q_UNUSED does not do anything magical with the variable:

```
#define Q_UNUSED(x) (void)x;
```

It is a simple trick to fool the compiler; it sees myVariable "used", but nothing is done with it.

Logging custom objects to QDebug

When you are debugging complex objects, it is nice to output their current members' value to qDebug(). In other languages (such as Java), you may have encountered the toString() method or equivalent, which is very convenient.

Sure, you could add a function void toString() to each object you want to log in order to write code with the following syntax:

```
qDebug() << "Object content:" << myObject.toString()
```

There must be a more natural way of doing this in C++. Moreover, Qt already provides this kind of feature:

```
QDate today = QDate::currentDate();
qDebug() << today;
// Output: QDate("2016-10-03")
```

To achieve this, we will rely on a C++ operator overload. This will look very similar to what we did with QDataStream operators in Chapter 18, *Need IPC? Get Your Minions to Work*.

Consider a struct Person:

```
struct Person {
    QString name;
    int age;
};
```

To add the ability to properly output to QDebug, you just have to override the << operator between QDebug and Person like so:

```
#include <QDebug>

struct Person {
    ...
};

QDebug operator<<(QDebug debug, const Person& person)
{
    QDebugStateSaver saver(debug);
    debug.nospace() << "("
                    << "name: " << person.name << ", "
                    << "age: " << person.age
                    << ")";
    return debug;
}
```

The `QDebugStateSaver` is a convenience class to save the settings of `QDebug` and restore them automatically upon destruction. It is good practice to always use it to be sure that you do not break `QDebug` in an << operator overload.

The rest of the function is the usual way of using `QDebug` and finally returning the modified `debug` variable. You can now use `Person` like this:

```
Person person = { "Lenna", 64 };
qDebug() << "Person info" << person;
```

No need for a `toString()` function; simply use the person object. For those of you who wondered, yes, `Lenna` is really `64` at the time of wrting (2016).

Improving log messages

Qt offers multiple ways of doing this. A good compromise between the result and its complexity is to combine the Qt log type with a custom message pattern.

Qt defines five log types, from the least to the most critical level:

- `qDebug()`: This is used to write custom debug messages
- `qInfo()`: This is used to write informational messages
- `qWarning()`: This is used to write warnings and recoverable errors in your applications
- `qCrtitical()`: This is used to write critical error messages and report system errors
- `qFatal()`: This is used to write a last message before automatically existing

Try to always use the most appropriate one!

By default, the message pattern is configured to only display your message without any extra data, but you can customize the pattern to display more information. This pattern can be changed at runtime by setting the `QT_MESSAGE_PATTERN` environment variable. You can also call the `qSetMessagePattern` function from your software to change the pattern. The pattern is just a string with some placeholders.

These are the most common placeholders you can use:

- `%{appname}`: This is your application name
- `%{file}`: This is the path to the source file
- `%{function}`: This is the function name
- `%{line}`: This is a line in the source file
- `%{message}`: This is an original message
- `%{type}`: This is the Qt log type ("debug", "info", "warning", "critical" or "fatal")
- `%{time [format]}`: This is the system time when the message occurred

An easy way to use it is to edit your `main.cpp` file like this:

```
#include <QApplication>
#include <QDebug>
...
int main(int argc, char *argv[])
{
    qSetMessagePattern("[%{time yyyy-MM-dd hh:mm:ss}] [%{type}]
        %{function} %{message}");
    qInfo() << "Application starting...";

    QApplication a(argc, argv);
    ...
    return a.exec();
}
```

You should get something like this in your application output:

```
[2016-10-03 10:22:40] [info] qMain Application starting...
```

Try to play around with the Qt log types and the custom message pattern until you find a useful pattern for you.

> **TIP**
> For more complex applications, you can use the `QLoggingCategory` class to define categories of logging. Visit `http://doc.qt.io/qt-5/qloggingcategory.html` for more information on this.

Saving your logs to a file

A common need for a developer is to have logs. In some situations, you cannot have access to the console output, or you have to study the application state afterwards. In both cases, the log has to be outputted to a file.

Qt provides a practical way of redirecting your logs (qDebug, qInfo, qWarning, and so on) to any device that is convenient for you: QtMessageHandler. To use it, you have to register a function that will save the logs to the desired output.

For example, in your main.cpp, add the following function:

```cpp
#include <QFile>
#include <QTextStream>

void messageHander(QtMsgType type,
                   const QMessageLogContext& context,
                   const QString& message) {
    QString levelText;
    switch (type) {
        case QtDebugMsg:
            levelText = "Debug";
            break;
        case QtInfoMsg:
            levelText = "Info";
            break;
        case QtWarningMsg:
            levelText = "Warning";
            break;
        case QtCriticalMsg:
            levelText = "Critical";
            break;
        case QtFatalMsg:
            levelText = "Fatal";
            break;
    }
    QString text = QString("[%1] %2")
                        .arg(levelText)
                        .arg(message);
    QFile file("app.log");
    file.open(QIODevice::WriteOnly | QIODevice::Append);
    QTextStream textStream(&file);
    textStream << text << endl;
}
```

The signature of the function must be respected to be properly called by Qt. Let's review the parameters:

- `QtMsgType type`: This is an `enum` that describes the function that generated the message (`qDebug()`, `qInfo()`, `qWarning()`, and so on)
- `QMessageLogContext& context`: This contains additional information about the log message (source file where the log was produced, name of the function, line number, and so on)
- `const QString& message`: This is the actual message that was logged

The body of the function formats the log message before appending it to a file named `app.log`. You can easily add features in this function by adding a rotating log file, sending the logs through the network, or anything else.

The last missing part is the registration of `messageHandler()`, which is done in the `main()` function:

```
int main(int argc, char *argv[])
{
    QCoreApplication a(argc, argv);
    qInstallMessageHandler(messageHander);
    ...
}
```

The call to the `qInstallMessageHander()` function is enough to reroute all the log messages to `app.log`. Once this is done, the logs will no longer be displayed in the console output and will be appended to `app.log` only.

> **TIP**
>
> If you need to unregister your custom message handler function, call `qInstallMessageHandler(0)`.

Generating a command-line interface

The command-line interface can be a wonderful way to start your application with some specific options. The Qt framework provides an easy way to define your options with the `QCommandLineParser` class. You can provide a short (for example, `-t`) or a long (for example, `--test`) option name. The application version and help menu is automatically generated. You can easily retrieve in your code if an option is set or not. An option can take a value and you can define a default value.

For example, we can create a CLI to configure the log files. We want to define three options:

- The -debug command, if set, enables the log file writing
- The -f or --file command to define where to write the logs
- The -l or --level <level> command to specify the minimum log level

Look at the following snippet:

```
QCoreApplication app(argc, argv);

QCoreApplication::setApplicationName("ch14-hat-tips");
QCoreApplication::setApplicationVersion("1.0.0");

QCommandLineParser parser;
parser.setApplicationDescription("CLI helper");
parser.addHelpOption();
parser.addVersionOption();

parser.addOptions({
    {"debug",
        "Enable the debug mode."},

    {{"f", "file"},
        "Write the logs into <file>.",
        "logfile"},

    {{"l", "level"},
        "Restrict the logs to level <level>. Default is 'fatal'.",
        "level",
        "fatal"},
});

parser.process(app);

qDebug() << "debug mode:" << parser.isSet("debug");
qDebug() << "file:" << parser.value("file");
qDebug() << "level:" << parser.value("level");
```

Let's talk about each step:

1. The first part uses the functions from QCoreApplication to set the application name and version. This information will be used by the --version option.
2. Instantiate a QCommandLineParser class. Then we instruct it to automatically add the help (-h or --help) and version (-v or --version) options.
3. Add our options with the QCommandLineParser::addOptions() function.

4. Request the `QCommandLineParser` class to process the command-line arguments.

5. Retrieve and use the options.

Here are the parameters to create an option:

- `optionName`: By using this parameter, you can use a single or multiple names
- `description`: In this parameter, the description of the option is displayed in the help menu
- `valueName` (Optional): This shows the value name if your option expects one
- `defaultValue` (Optional): This shows the default value of the option

You can retrieve and use the option using `QCommandLineParser::isSet()`, which returns true if the option was set by the user. If your option requires a value, you can retrieve it with `QCommandLineParser::value()`.

Here is the display of the generated help menu:

```
$ ./ch14-hat-tips --help
Usage: ./ch14-hat-tips [options]
Helper of the command-line interface

Options:
  -h, --help              Displays this help.
  -v, --version           Displays version information.
  --debug                 Enable the debug mode.
  -f, --file <logfile>    Write the logs into <file>.
  -l, --level <level>     Restrict the logs to level <level>. Default is
'fatal'.
```

Finally, the following snippet displays the CLI in use:

```
$ ./ch14-hat-tips --debug -f log.txt --level info
debug mode:   true
file:   "log.txt"
level:   "info"
```

Sending and receiving HTTP data

Requesting information to an HTTP server is a common task. Here again, the Qt folks prepared some useful classes to make it easy. To achieve this, we will rely on three classes:

- QNetworkAccessManager: This class allows your application to send requests and receive replies
- QNetworkRequest: This class holds the request to be sent with all the information (headers, URL, data, and so on)
- QNetworkReply: This class contains the result of a QNetworkRequest class with the headers and the data

The QNetworkAccessManager class is the pivot point of the whole Qt HTTP API. It is built around a single QNetworkAccessManager object that holds the configuration of the client, proxy settings, cache information, and much more. This class is designed to be asynchronous, so you do not need to worry about blocking your current thread.

Let's see it in action in a custom HttpRequest class. First, the header:

```
#include <QObject>
#include <QNetworkAccessManager>
#include <QNetworkReply>

class HttpRequest : public QObject
{
    Q_OBJECT
public:
    HttpRequest(QObject* parent = 0);

    void executeGet();

private slots:
    void replyFinished(QNetworkReply* reply);

private:
    QNetworkAccessManager mAccessManager;
};
```

The QNetworkAccessManager class works with the signal/slot mechanism, so HttpRequest inherits from QObject and uses the Q_OBJECT macro. We declare the following functions and member:

- executeGet(): This is used to trigger an HTTP GET request
- replyFinished(): This is the slot called when the GET request has completed
- mAccessManager: This is the object that will be used for all our asynchronous requests

Let's turn our attention to the constructor of the `HttpRequest` class in the `HttpRequest.cpp`:

```
HttpRequest::HttpRequest(QObject* parent) :
    QObject(parent),
    mAccessManager()
{
    connect(&mAccessManager, &QNetworkAccessManager::finished,
            this, &HttpRequest::replyFinished);
}
```

In the body of the constructor, we connect the `finished()` signal from `mAccessManager` to our `replyFinished()` slot. This implies that every request sent through `mAccessManager` will trigger this slot.

Enough with the preparation; let's see the request and reply in action:

```
// Request
void HttpRequest::executeGet()
{
    QNetworkRequest request(QUrl("http://httpbin.org/ip"));
    mAccessManager.get(QNetworkRequest(request));
}

// Response
void HttpRequest::replyFinished(QNetworkReply* reply)
{
    int statusCode =
reply->attribute(QNetworkRequest::HttpStatusCodeAttribute).toInt();
    qDebug() << "Reponse network error" << reply->error();
    qDebug() << "Reponse HTTP status code" << statusCode;
    qDebug() << "Reply content:" << reply->readAll();
    reply->deleteLater();
}
```

The `HTTP GET` request is processed using `mAccessManager.get()`. The `QNetworkAccessManager` class provides the function for other HTTP verbs (`head()`, `post()`, `put()`, `delete()`, and so on). It expects a `QNetworkRequest` access, which takes a URL in its constructor. This is the simplest form of an HTTP request.

Note that we did our request using the URL `http://httpbin.org/ip`, which will respond to the emitter's IP address in the JSON format:

```
{
  "origin": "1.2.3.4"
}
```

This website is a practical developer resource, where you can send your test requests and have useful information sent back to you. It avoids having to launch a custom web server to only test a few requests. This website is an open-source project freely hosted by Runscope. Of course, you can replace the request URL with anything you wish.

> Take a look at `http://httpbin.org/` to see all the supported request types.

After the `executeGet()` function is completed, the `mAccessManager` object executes the request in a separate thread and calls our slot, `replyFinished()`, with the resulting `QNetworkReply*` object. In this code snippet, you can see how to retrieve the HTTP status code and check if any network error happened, as well as how to get the body of the response with `reply->readAll()`.

The `QNetworkReply` class inherits from `QIODevice`, and therefore, you can read it all at once with `readAll()`, or by chunks with a loop on `read()`. This lets you adapt the reading to your needs using a familiar `QIODevice` API.

Note that you are the owner of the `QNetworkReply*` object. You should not delete it by hand (your application might crash if you do so); instead, it's better to use the `reply->deleteLater()` function, which will let the Qt event loop pick the appropriate moment to delete this object.

Now let's see a more complex example of `QNetworkReply` with an `HTTP POST` method. There are times where you will need to keep track of the `QNetworkReply` class and have a more fine-grained control over its life cycle.

Here is the implementation of an `HTTP POST` method that also relies on `HttpRequest::mAccessManager`:

```
void HttpRequest::executePost()
{
    QNetworkRequest request(QUrl("http://httpbin.org/post"));
    request.setHeader(QNetworkRequest::ContentTypeHeader,
                      "application/x-www-form-urlencoded");
    QUrlQuery urlQuery;
    urlQuery.addQueryItem("book", "Mastering Qt 5");

    QUrl params;
    params.setQuery(urlQuery);

    QNetworkReply* reply = mAccessManager.post(
```

```
                                   request, params.toEncoded());
        connect(reply, &QNetworkReply::readyRead,
            [reply] () {
            qDebug() << "Ready to read from reply";
        });
        connect(reply, &QNetworkReply::sslErrors,
                [this] (QList<QSslError> errors) {
            qWarning() << "SSL errors" << errors;
        });
    }
```

We start by creating a `QNetworkRequest` class with a custom header: `Content-Type` is now `application/x-www-form-urlencoded` to respect the HTTP RFC. After that, a URL form is built, ready to be sent with the request. You can add as many items as you wish to the `urlQuery` object.

The next part gets interesting. When executing `mAccessManager.post()` with the request and the URL encoded form, the `QNetworkReply*` object is immediately returned to us. From here, we use some lambdas slots connected directly to reply rather than using `mAccessManage` slots. This lets you have precise control over what happens for each reply.

Note that the `QNetworkReploy::readyRead` signal comes from the `QIODevice` API and that it does not pass the `QNetworkReply*` object in the parameter. It is your job to store the reply in a member field somewhere or retrieve the emitter of the signal.

Finally, this code snippet does not undo our preceding slot, `replyFinished()`, which is connected to `mAccessManager`. If you execute this code, you will have the following output sequence:

```
Ready to read from reply
Reponse network error QNetworkReply::NetworkError(NoError)
Reponse HTTP status code 200
```

The lambda connected to the `QNetworkReply::readyRead` signal is first called, and after that, the `HttpRequest::replyFinished` signal is called.

The last feature we will cover on the Qt HTTP stack is synchronous requests. If you happen to need to manage the request threading yourself, the default asynchronous work mode of `QNetworkAccessManager` can get in your way. To circumvent this, you can use a custom `QEventLoop`:

```
void HttpRequest::executeBlockingGet()
{
    QNetworkAccessManager localManager;
```

```
QEventLoop eventLoop;
QObject::connect(
    &localManager, &QNetworkAccessManager::finished,
    &eventLoop, &QEventLoop::quit);

QNetworkRequest request(
            QUrl("http://httpbin.org/user-agent"));
request.setHeader(QNetworkRequest::UserAgentHeader,
                    "MasteringQt5Browser 1.0");

QNetworkReply* reply = localManager.get(request);
eventLoop.exec();

qDebug() << "Blocking GET result:" << reply->readAll();
reply->deleteLater();
}
```

In this function, we declare another `QNetworkAccessManager` that will not interfere with the one declared in `HttpRequest`. Right after, a `QEventLoop` object is declared and connected to `localManager`. When `QNetworkAccessManager` emits the `finished()` signal, `eventLoop` will quit and the calling function will resume.

The `request` is built as usual, the `reply` object is retrieved, and the function becomes blocked with the call to `eventLoop.exec()`. The function is blocked until `localManager` has emitted its finished signal. In other words, the request is still done asynchronously; the sole difference is that the function is blocked until the request is completed.

Finally, the `reply` object can be safely read and deleted at the end of the function. This `QEventLoop` trick can be used any time a synchronous wait for a Qt signal is needed; use it wisely to avoid blocking the UI thread!

Summary

In this chapter, you learned some tips that complete your Qt knowledge. You should now have the ability to use Qt Creator with ease and efficiency. The `QDebug` format should not hold any secrets now, and you can now save your logs to a file without even blinking. You can create a good-looking CLI interface, debug the memory of any program without shaking, and execute an HTTP request with confidence.

We sincerely hope that you had as much fun reading this book as we did writing it. In our opinion, Qt is a great framework, and it covers many areas that deserve to be deepened with a book (or several books!). We hope you keep coding C++ Qt code with fun and pleasure by building efficient and beautifully crafted applications.

3
Qt 5 Projects

Develop cross-platform applications with modern UIs using the powerful Qt framework

23
Writing Acceptance Tests and Building a Visual Prototype

Qt (pronounced like the English adjective *cute*) is just that, incredibly cute.

If you start working with Qt extensively, you will hardly find another piece of software that tickles your imagination and creativity while catering for your professional needs as much as Qt does. It's got it all. As a professional, you will certainly value its more than 20 years of maturity, solid release cycle, and backward compatibility promises. As a hobbyist, you will fall for its cutting-edge features. In both cases, you will appreciate its smooth and powerful graphic capabilities, extensive collection of general purpose programming libraries, unrivaled cross-platform support, great all-around tooling, good documentation, and thriving community. Furthermore, you will treasure its concise syntax with the QML and JavaScript languages, and its horsepower and expressiveness with the C++ language, as well as its language bindings for Python, Go, and more.

Given its magnificence, you will be tempted to just jump into coding and learn things as you go along. I know how it goes; I went through it, and now I am here, and I probably have something to say about it. Do I regret having taken the hard route? Well, yes and no. Yes, because it took me a few complete app remakes to get things reasonably right; no, because, of course, I learned a lot along the way. At least, I learned exactly (and this is still an ongoing process) what *not* to do with the many facilities that Qt has to offer.

On the other hand, you have this book in front of you; it probably means that you didn't want to begin this journey all by yourself, right? Maybe you did, and you soon realized that you needed a travel mate. Well, here I am, your new travel mate. Where shall we start from? I can see you now; you are all excited. However, before we jump in, let us first look at the larger picture.

You won't be able to dwell in the *house* you are trying to build if you don't first sit down to do your planning and research before laying the very first brick. You can take care of how the mirror in the bathroom will look later on. You just need to start with the most important thing, and that is a high-level plan that provides you with an overview about what you want to build.

Don't come to me with an idea, come to me with a plan

One summer, I had the pleasure to be mentored by a guy called Shai. From what I gathered, Shai was probably a serial entrepreneur, certainly an investor, and most definitely an excellent trainer.

One of the things I learned from him during the brief summer school, which he was leading, is that you have to drink plenty of water for your body to function properly and your ideas to flow.

Another thing that I learned from him is that in entrepreneurship, just as in software development, plans are far superior to ideas. Having a good idea is essential, but it is not enough. You need a plan. This is what he used to say to soon-to-be entrepreneurs who went to him to present their shiny, groundbreaking ideas:

> *"Don't come to me with an idea. Come to me with a plan."*

Exploration is one thing, learning to achieve expertise is another. While exploring, you taste a bit of this and a bit of that, without a clear purpose or plan — that is, without a blueprint. Exploration is good and necessary, but it has its limits. If you want to just explore what Qt does, there is plenty of very good material covering that:

- Other Qt-related Packt titles (`https://www.packtpub.com/all?search=qt`)
- The official Qt documentation (`http://doc.qt.io/`)
- Examples and tutorials included in Qt Creator (Qt's official IDE) (`http://doc.qt.io/qt-5.9/qtexamplesandtutorials.html`)
- Tutorial videos and webinars available from many core Qt contributors
- User-contributed material of all kinds

I'll give you specific pointers to many of these resources wherever needed. I also covered many of these in the Preface.

In this book, I will follow a strong goal, project, and scenario-based approach, showing you how to apply current best practices of software development by leveraging what Qt has to offer. I'll provide you with some ready-made plans in the hope that you will come up with even better ones for your own projects, be it a hobby project or a business-related endeavor. We will use an outside-in approach, starting from clear functional goals all the way inwards to implementation details. Enough said! Let's get started with the first project.

In this chapter, we will lay the foundations for a simple to-do list-like application by dealing with its intended goals, main scenarios and `usecases`, and UI prototyping. This will give you a good introduction to how you can perform **Behavior-Driven Development** (**BDD**) with the `QtTest` framework, Qt's object model, introspection features and signals/slots, an overview of available Qt rendering frameworks, and UI prototyping with Qt Creator's Quick Designer.

The problem — what's in my fridge?

If you are an out-of-town student, and even if you are not, you may know all too well the sensation of desolation that often surfaces when you open the fridge and find empty shelves. Look! A lonely slice of cheese is greeting you and asking for your companionship. Oh, and that thing nearby probably used to be an apple a few months back. Dammit! You were working on your much-beloved personal project and completely forgot to buy groceries, and now the shops are closed, or are too far away to bother going.

The solution — an app idea

No problem, right? If you are lucky, there is yet another cheap pizza waiting for you in the deep freeze, otherwise you will be once again eating some cheap takeaway.

Wrong! If this becomes the normal solution, in a few years' time, your liver will curse you in ways you cannot even imagine. The real solution is this: don't be lazy, take good care of yourself. Remember Shai? Besides drinking plenty of water, you should also eat stuff that is good for your body (at the entrepreneurship camp, apart from great catering, next to the water bottles, there was a pile of apples, and both the water bottles and the apples were freely accessible all day long).

How could you start implementing this sensible advice? One good thing to do would be to keep track of your food resources and intervene before it's too late. Of course, you could do that with just a pencil and paper, but you are a nerd, right? You need an app, and a cute one! Well, here you go; finally, your personal project will contribute to your health rather than taking its share from it.

The plan — start from user stories

OK, we need an app. Let's start building the **user interface (UI)**.

But what if we wanted the same application to have a graphical UI and at the same time leave the door open to add a console-based UI, or even a voice interface in the future? We need a way to specify our app's functional requirements before describing how it will look, or how it will be delivered to our users. Also, it would be very useful if we could verify that those requirements are actually met *within the code*. Even better, in an automatic fashion, by means of what are usually labeled as *acceptance tests*, using procedures that verify that all or most of our app's usage scenarios are actually working as expected. We can achieve that by starting from user stories.

Writing features and scenarios

Behavior-**Driven Development** (**BDD**) is a way of developing software that encourages starting from user stories (or *features*) and then moving on from those to system implementation. According to Dan North, one of BDD's initiators, a feature is a description of a requirement and its business benefit, and a set of criteria by which we all agree that it is "done". The main goal of BDD is for project stakeholders (customers, business people, project managers, developers, and people who work in quality assurance) to share common expectations about a feature. The description of how a feature should behave in a specific context of preconditions and outcomes is called a *scenario*. All scenarios outlined for a specific feature constitute its acceptance criteria: if the feature behaves as expected in all scenarios, it can be considered as done. For a clear and synthetic introduction to BDD take a look at `https://dannorth.net/whats-in-a-story/`.

BDD is now a widespread approach, and some standards exist to make it easier for stakeholders to share the description of scenarios and their verification. *Gherkin* (`https://github.com/cucumber/cucumber/wiki/Gherkin`) is such a standard: a human-readable language, which can also be used by a software system to link usage expectations to system instructions by means of acceptance tests, which strictly follow the structure of scenarios.

The following is what a Gherkin feature specification (a user story outlined as a set of scenarios) looks like:

```
Feature: Check available groceries
    I want to check available groceries in my fridge
    to know when to buy them before I run out of them

    Scenario: One or more grocery items available
        Given there is a list of available grocery items
        And one or more grocery items are actually available
        When I check available groceries
        Then I am given the list of available grocery items
        And the grocery items are ordered by name, ascending

    Scenario: No grocery items available
        Given there is a list of available grocery items
        And no grocery items are actually available
        When I check available groceries
        Then I am informed that no grocery items are available
        And I am told to go buy some more
```

The `Check available groceries` feature, which encapsulates assumptions and expected outcomes relative to a specific user action, is analyzed in two scenarios, which show how the outcomes vary depending on different assumptions (`one or more grocery items are available` **versus** `no grocery items are available`).

I guess you can figure out the basic structure of a scenario in its commonest form: one or more `Given` clauses describing preconditions, one or more `When` clauses describing user-initiated or system-initiated actions, and one or more `Then` clauses describing expected outcomes.

Specifying the behavior of your application in terms of feature scenarios has many benefits, as follows:

- The specification can be understood even by nontechnical people (in the case of *What's in my fridge*, this means that your family members can offer their expertise in taking care of home food provisions to help you sketch out the most important features for the app).

- There are quite a few libraries around that can help you link the specification to the actual code and can then run the gherkin feature file and check whether the preconditions, actions, and expected outcomes (collectively known as *steps*) are actually implemented by the system (these constitute the *acceptance tests* for a feature).

- You need, either individually or as a group of stakeholders, to actually sit down and write the acceptance criteria for a feature in full before writing any code that relates to it. By doing so, you often find out early on about any inconsistencies and corner cases you would have otherwise ignored.

Does Qt provide off-the-shelf support for gherkin-style feature descriptions and for writing automated acceptance tests? Currently, it doesn't. Is there any way to implement this very sensible approach to software development in Qt projects? Yes, there is.

I know of at least the following ways:

- You can download and build the `cucumber-cpp` (`https://github.com/cucumber/cucumber-cpp`) project, which also contains a Qt driver, and try and link it to your project. I haven't tested this way yet, but if you are braver than I, you could give it a go.

- You can buy a (admittedly, not cheap) license for `Froglogic Squish` (`https://www.froglogic.com/squish/editions/qt-gui-test-automation/`), a professional grade solution for many types of application testing, including BDD, which fully supports Qt.

- You can write your acceptance tests with the Qt Test framework and give them a Gherkin-style structure. This is the approach I currently use in my projects, and in the next section I will show you a couple of ways to achieve this.

So, now that we have written our first feature, with as many as two scenarios, we are ready to dive into code, right?

Not really. How would you add grocery items to the list? How about removing them from the list when you take them out of the fridge? We'll first need to write those two other features at least, if we want to have a *minimum viable product*.

If you haven't done it yet, now is the time to download Qt for Application Development distribution and install it.
There are a few options available, in terms of *licensing* (commercial, GPL, and LGPLv3), supported *host* (macOS, Windows, and Linux), *target* platforms (several available) and *installation mode* (online versus offline). Regarding licensing, take your time to make an informed choice, and ask a lawyer in case of doubt. For more information, take a look at the Qt Project's licensing page at `http://doc.qt.io/qt-5/licensing.html`.

To download Qt with the online installer for your host platform, go to `http://www.qt.io/download`, choose one of the available options, and follow the installation instructions.

The projects contained in this book are based on Version 5.9, which is a **Long Term Support** (**LTS**) version. For a smooth ride, you are encouraged to use the latest available bugfix release of version 5.9. If you are adventurous enough, you could also install a later version. The book's projects *should* still work with any later 5.x version, but please understand that they haven't been tested for that, so your mileage may vary.

Implementing scenarios as acceptance tests

As I mentioned in the preceding section, the standard Qt distribution does not give off-the-shelf support for BDD. However, it does provide a rich testing framework (Qt Test), which can be leveraged to implement most kinds of tests, from unit tests to acceptance tests. In the coming sections, we will implement our first acceptance test with Qt Test. First, however, let us spend a few words on project organization and introduce the two main programming languages currently used in the Qt world: C++ and QML.

Our project structure

Throughout the book, all online documentation links will point to Version 5.9 for consistency. If you want or need to access the latest version of a document, you can just remove the minor version from the URL, as follows: `http://doc.qt.io/qt-5.9/qobject.html` > `http://doc.qt.io/qt-5/qobject.html`. Similarly, a later minor version can be accessed by changing the minor version in the URL: `http://doc.qt.io/qt-5.10/qobject.html`

This book uses the *Qt Creator* IDE for project development, together with the QMake build and project organization system. Both tools are included in the default precompiled Qt distributions. I will give you hints on how to carry out project-specific operations with both Qt Creator and QMake. For further details on how to operate them, you can look at other specific Packt titles, as well as the official Qt documentation for Qt Creator (`http://doc.qt.io/qtcreator/`) and QMake (`http://doc.qt.io/qt-5.9/qmake-manual.html`).

> Both Qt Creator and Qt support other build and project organization systems beyond QMake. The most widespread are *Qbs* (pronounced as *cubes*, which is part of the Qt Project, `http://doc.qt.io/qbs/`) and *CMake* (`http://doc.qt.io/qtcreator/creator-project-cmake.html`). The deep integration with Qt Creator makes QMake the best choice to get started. You can take a look at using the other systems if your workflow benefits from it. CMake is often used for larger projects, and is sometimes preferred by C++ programmers who are already familiar with it. Qbs might replace QMake as the default build system for the Qt project in future versions of Qt.

The QMake build system provides a way to organize projects into subprojects. Each project structure is described in a `.pro` file. It is good practice to keep the test suites in separate subprojects (also called **test harnesses**), which can be run independently of the app's client code. If you look at a file like `part1-whats_in_my_fridge.pro` file in folder `part1-whats_in_my_fridge`, at the beginning of the file you'll see the following statements:

```
# part1-whats_in_my_fridge.pro
TEMPLATE = subdirs

SUBDIRS += usecases
```

The preceding statements just say *this QMake project has child projects, and the first of these is called* `usecases`. If a folder called `usecases` that contains a `usecases.pro` file is found, a node representing the subproject will appear in Qt Creator's **Projects** pane.

> Qt Creator provides several kinds of *project templates*. These templates create most or some of the project's boilerplate code for you. To achieve a structure, such as the one described earlier, from scratch, you will need to first create a `SUBDIRS` project (**New file** or **Project...** > **Other Project** > **Subdirs Project**) called `qt5projects`, then click on **Finish & Add Subproject** and add another `SUBDIRS` project called `part1-whats_in_my_fridge`, and then in turn add to it a `SUBDIRS` project called `usecases`.

At this point, we face our first, fairly important, technological decision.

QML and C++ — when to use each of them

Many Qt modules are offered with two different APIs; one for QML and one for C++. While I can take for granted that you know enough about the C++ language and how to work with it, the same may not be true for QML, which is a language that was born in and is mostly used within the Qt world.

You may hear sooner or later that QML is the language used for building modern UIs with Qt. Although that is certainly true, this often implies to many that QML is only good for implementing UIs. That's not the case, although you should always carefully think what kind of API (C++ or QML) is best suited for the project or the component at hand.

QML is a declarative language, which, on one hand, supports JavaScript expressions and features (such as garbage collection), and, on the other hand, allows us to use Qt objects defined in C++ in both a declarative and an imperative way by taking care of most data conversions between C++ and JavaScript. Another of QML's strengths is that it can be extended from C++ to create new visual and non-visual object types. For more details about the QML language, you can read the documentation of the `QtQml` module (`http://doc.qt.io/qt-5.9/qtqml-index.html`), which provides QML-related functionality to Qt.

The following is a brief comparison of the most remarkable differences between the two languages:

C++

- Compiled
- Imperative syntax
- APIs available for most Qt modules
- Integration with other C++ modules
- Power of expression
- Richer debugging information
- No property bindings
- Less overhead

QML

- Interpreted with optional compilation
- Declarative + imperative syntax
- APIs available for selected Qt modules
- Integration with existing JavaScript code
- Conciseness of expression
- Limited debugging information
- Property bindings
- Garbage collected
- Extensible from C++

We'll touch upon some of these differences later on.

So, depending on the nature of the project at hand, and of the specific aspect you are working on, you will want to pick one over the other, knowing that some minimal C++ boilerplate code is required for Qt applications to run as executables.

When deciding what language to write a specific application layer in, the availability of relevant Qt APIs for that language is a key factor that influences our choice. At the time of writing, for example, there is no public C++ API for most *Qt Quick* UI components, and, conversely, there is no QML API for most *Qt Widgets* UI components. Although it is always possible to write interface code to pass data between C++ and QML, you should always consider whether it is strategic and affordable to do so.

If your Qt application has an evident structure and distinct layers (that is, if it is well organized), it is sometimes possible to swap a specific application layer or a single component written in QML with one written in C++, and vice versa, provided the needed Qt APIs are available in both languages. QML has some more constraints, as it requires you to instantiate a `QQmlEngine` C++ object in order to be used, and thread-based programming is supported in QML code in a limited way.

There are Qt developers, especially on mobile platforms, who write their applications almost entirely in QML, and developers who just use it for writing Qt Quick UIs, some of them only because there is no C++ API available for the Qt Quick module yet. Sometimes, taking a side for one approach over the other causes almost-religious wars in the community. After you have written a few applications, you'll find where the sweet spot lies for you and your team, also taking into account your specific project constraints (deadlines, target device, developer language skills, and so on). However, as I am here to help you, I will give you all the advice I can about this matter.

A typical Qt-based application has all of its visual appearance defined in QML and all or most of its functional building blocks defined in C++. This allows you on the one hand to make rapid UI changes and explore new UI concepts, and, on the other, to build the UI on a solid foundation. Besides the technology advantages and disadvantages, you will also experience that developers using QML think more like front-end developers and lean towards UI design, while those mostly using Qt's C++ APIs think more like backend developers and lean more towards system functionality, and they are also aware of memory and performance issues. This mix makes Qt great for creating high-performance UI applications.

If you can afford to write all your non-UI components in C++, then go for it. It is definitely a more solid choice and gives you a potential performance edge. However, writing good C++ can be hard and time-consuming. In projects where I already know that I'll be using QML for the UI, I often sketch most of the other application layers in QML and then fully develop some of them in C++ later on, wherever performance or other considerations require it. It's a personal and project-dictated choice, and I reserve the right to change my mind in the future. So, I ask you not to go shouting around that I was the one responsible for instilling bad practices in you.

To give you a taster of how it feels to write Qt components in QML as opposed to C++, I'll show you now how you could express your use case tests both in C++ and QML/JS.

Writing the first acceptance tests in C++

The QtTest framework (http://doc.qt.io/qt-5.9/qttest-index.html, and, in overview, http://doc.qt.io/qt-5.9/qtest-overview.html) is a collection of C++ classes and QML types that provides many tools for writing effective test cases for Qt applications. To create a test case with the C++ API, you should subclass a QObject, and add a method for each test (each method/test corresponding to a BDD scenario).

> **TIP**
> Qt Creator provides specific templates to generate projects for both single test cases (the **Qt Unit Test** template) and complete test suites (the **Auto Test Project** template, which shows up after enabling the **AutoTest** plugin from the **About Plugins...** menu entry).

For learning's sake, we'll configure our C++ acceptance tests project from scratch by adding the needed subprojects to the usecases project, and then make the first test fail. We'll make the test pass in the next chapter by implementing the relevant code.

Creating the first C++ test case

At this level of analysis, we may consider a test case as the representation in code of all scenarios that pertain to a certain feature. Each test, in turn, represents a specific scenario. The term use case comes from Alistair Cockburn's classic *Writing Effective Use Cases*. In our context, you can consider a use case as the system-level description of a feature, a set of instructions that have as an outcome the user story's success or failure, depending on the given preconditions (the current system state).

As we started our feature enumeration by working on `check available groceries`, we will begin adding tests for that.

Each test case requires its own subproject to be run as an executable. This means that we will subclass `QObject` into a class that we could call `Usecases_check_available_groceries`.

> Incorporating `Usecases_` as a prefix will make it much easier to run the tests with Qt Creator's plugins, such as AutoTest, which scans for all test cases available within a certain project and allows them to be run selectively without switching the build target. In fact, until Qt Creator's version 4.5, AutoTest did not group test cases by folder or subproject, so using a common prefix is the only way to group test cases of the same kind together. In Qt Creator 4.6, AutoTest does provide folder-based test grouping.

We should by now have a `subdirs` project called `usecases`, which contains nothing except an empty `usecases.pro` file, which, in turn, contains a `TEMPLATE = subdirs` directive.

> Ensure that you don't confuse QMake templates with Qt Creator's templates. QMake templates help you specify whether QMake should build an executable (`app`), a library (`lib`), or nothing (`subdirs`) with the current project. Qt Creator templates, on the contrary, are just collections of boilerplate code and project configuration wizards. You can learn more about the kinds of projects available for QMake at `http://doc.qt.io/qt-5.9/qmake-common-projects.html` and on how to create your own Qt Creator's template wizards at `http://doc.qt.io/qtcreator/creator-project-wizards-json.html`.

We will now add a **Qt Unit Test** project for our first test case as a subproject of `usecases`, which we will call `check_available_groceries`. Because we are using Qt Creator's **Qt Unit Test** template wizard, we can specify the name of the first test (which we will call `one_or_more_grocery_items_available`) in the wizard's mask. Here are the values I put in for this test case.

As they differ from the defaults, you may want to take a look at them. Note how the
Requires QApplication box is also checked:

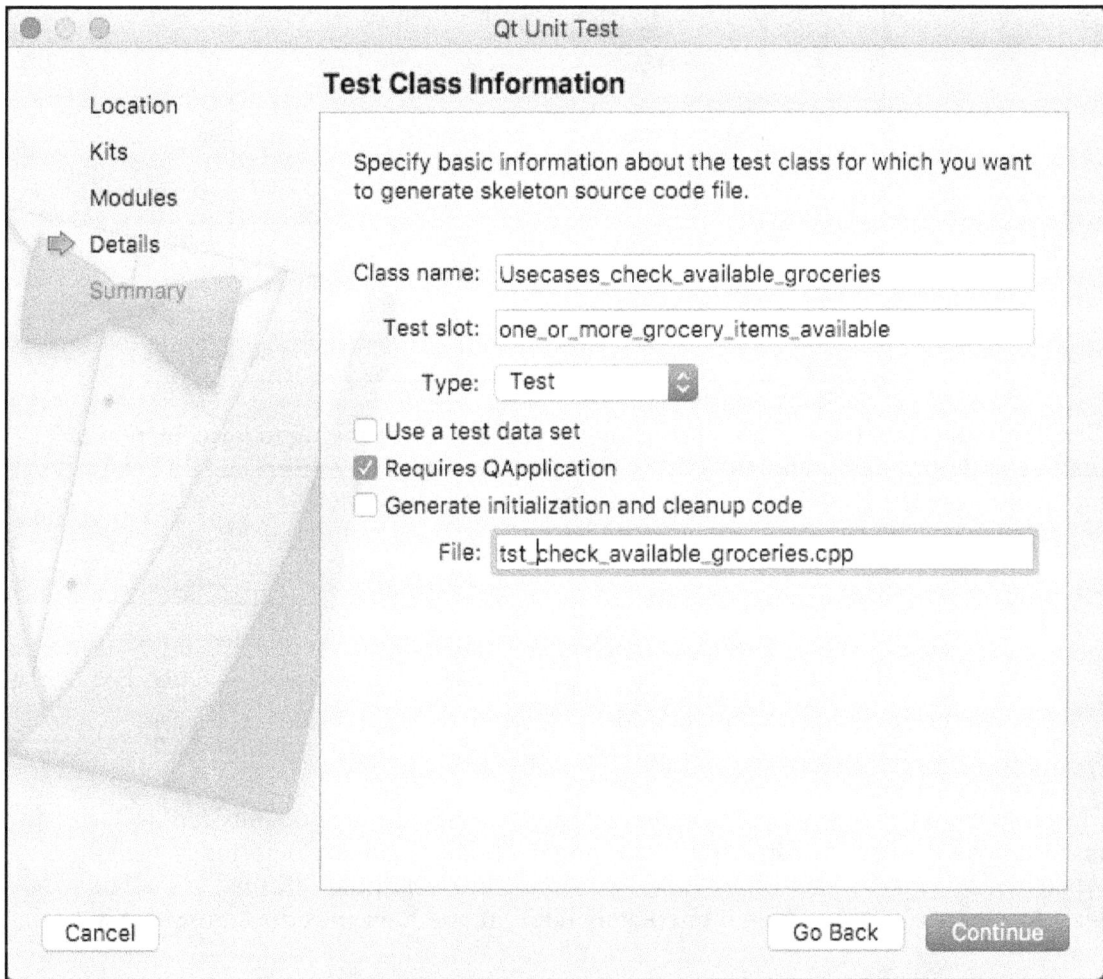

> Qt Creator's wizard will present you with a list of Qt modules to include
> in the test case's QMake project. You don't need to select any of them for
> the time being.

If everything goes as planned, you should end up with a project structure as follows:

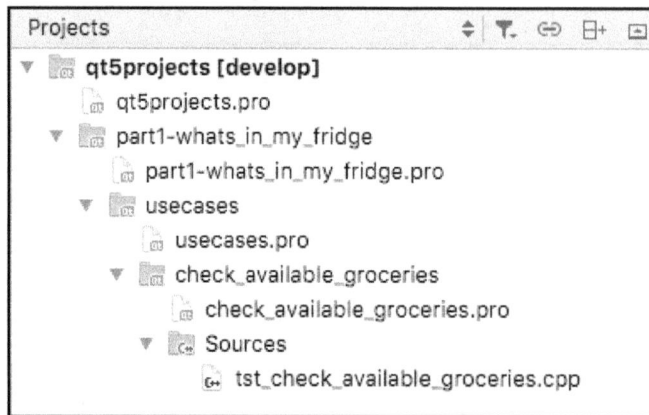

Generally speaking, the practice of starting with tests before moving to implementations is called **test-driven-development (TDD)**. TDD is a common way to translate BDD features into working code. The TDD development process goes as follows:

1. Write a failing test
2. Run all tests you have written so far, and see the new test failing
3. Write the minimum amount of functionality to make the new test pass
4. Run all tests you have written so far and see them all passing — if not, go back to
5. (If needed) refactor the code that you wrote to make the new test pass
6. Move to a new test and repeat the procedure

TDD is there to give you as a developer confidence about the functionality that is deemed important for the system you are creating, and confidence about refactoring as well. In fact, when you make a change to your code, by running the test under scrutiny, and all other tests of your test suite, you can immediately notice if you have introduced unintended side effects.

If you now click on the big bold **Run** button in Qt Creator, you should see output as follows in Qt Creator's **Application Output** pane:

```
********* Start testing of Usecases_check_available_groceries *********
Config: Using QtTest library 5.9.3, Qt 5.9.3 (x86_64-little-endian-lp64
shared (dynamic) release build; by Clang 7.0.2 (clang-700.1.81) (Apple))
PASS   : Usecases_check_available_groceries::initTestCase()
PASS   :
Usecases_check_available_groceries::one_or_more_grocery_items_available()
PASS   : Usecases_check_available_groceries::cleanupTestCase()
```

```
Totals: 3 passed, 0 failed, 0 skipped, 0 blacklisted, 1ms
********* Finished testing of Usecases_check_available_groceries *********
```

Wonderful! Our first use case test is passing—but, wait a minute, it shouldn't be passing, we haven't written a single line of code to make it pass yet.

This is indeed an unfortunate default choice for the template. If you take a look at the implementation of `one_or_more_grocery_items_available()` in `tst_check_available_groceries.cpp`, you'll note the following statement:

```
QVERIFY2(true, "Failure");
```

The `QVERIFY2` macro checks the truth value of the first argument, and, in case it is false, it prints the message contained in the second argument. To make the test fail, as a placeholder, you just need to change the first value to `false`, and perhaps change the message to something more informative, such as `"not implemented"`:

```
QVERIFY2(false, "not implemented");
```

Alternatively, you can change it as follows:

```
QFAIL("not implemented");
```

Congratulations! Your test does nothing interesting! Don't worry, we will deal with that in the next section.

Now, take your time and start inspecting the contents of the implementation file, `tst_check_available_groceries.cpp`. If this is your first encounter with a source file based on some Qt classes, you will note a few unusual things:

- A `Q_OBJECT` macro at the beginning of the class.
- A `Q_SLOTS` macro after the private access keyword.
- A top-level `QTEST_MAIN(Usecases_check_available_groceries)` macro.
- A top-level `#include "tst_check_available_groceries.moc"`.

The last two points are mostly specific to `QtTest`; the former provides a default main function to call in order to run the test, and the latter explicitly includes the meta-code file generated by Qt. When a class is defined in a header file, as is customary in application and library code, there is no need to include that file explicitly.

Conversely, you will often encounter the first two macros in many kinds of Qt classes. The macros augment the class definition with, respectively, Qt's *object model* capabilities and the *signals & slots* communication system.

Some of the most notable features brought by the Qt object model are as follows:

- Introspection through the *meta-object system*
- The *parent-child* relationship between objects (which also defines a common pattern of memory management in Qt)
- Support for *properties* (intended as groups of accessor methods)
- Support for the *signals & slots* communication system

Most of these features, which we will encounter again and again, are activated by including the `Q_OBJECT` macro in classes that inherit from the `QObject` class.

Slots are normal class methods, with the added benefit that they can be invoked automatically whenever another method (a *signal*), from an object of either a different class or the same class (including the same object instance), is called. In other words, a slot subscribes to a specific signal and runs whenever the signal is triggered. For a test case, marking the test functions as slots makes it possible to use them within a test harness so that the tests are run automatically by the system.

This is the right time to start familiarizing yourself with Qt's object model (`http://doc.qt.io/qt-5.9/object.html`) and the signals and slots communication system (`http://doc.qt.io/qt-5.9/signalsandslots.html`). Please do it before moving forward! We will have many chances to discuss some aspects of these when they come into play, but a solid understanding of the basics will help you along the way.

Now that the armature of our first test case is in place, we can start writing the first acceptance test.

Adding the first C++ test

Let us recall the first scenario that we came up with:

```
Scenario: One or more grocery items available
    Given there is a list of available grocery items
    And one or more grocery items are actually available
    When I check available groceries
    Then I am given the list of available grocery items
    And the grocery items are ordered by name, ascending
```

Our first test will need to make sure that this scenario can be completed using our implementation. To do this in an efficient manner, we will have to simulate a few things, including the initiation of the user action (I check available groceries), as well as the precondition and outcome data. We want to use mock data rather than making database or web service calls so that we can write our tests focusing on business logic rather than low-level system details and run our test suites multiple times without experiencing unneeded latencies. To make sure that our database or web service calls work as intended, we will later encapsulate those aspects into dedicated classes that can be tested independently.

By implementing the one_or_more_grocery_items_available() test, we are obliged to start thinking about the entities (or business objects) that are needed by our application. We'll perhaps want to model a user, certainly a grocery item, as well as a collection of such items. The details of those entities, especially the method and properties that allow entities to interact with the context they live in (their API), will gradually surface while we keep adding features and scenarios.

From the preceding scenario description, we reckon that we will have to implement a few steps (Given-And-When-Then-And) for the test to pass. We thus revisit the first test and make it fail four times rather than one, by adding a comment for each step that we need to implement:

```
void
Usecases_check_available_groceries::one_or_more_grocery_items_available()
{
    // Given there is a list of available grocery items
    QFAIL("not implemented");
    // And one or more grocery items are actually available
    QFAIL("not implemented");
    // When I check available groceries
    QFAIL("not implemented");
    // Then I am given the list of available grocery items
    QFAIL("not implemented");
    // And the grocery items are ordered by name, ascending
    QFAIL("not implemented");
}
```

This way, we can make sure that we are fulfilling each scenario step, as each QFAIL statement needs to be substituted with some form of verification that will have to pass, instead of failing.

Let's start with the first step.

Given there is a list of available grocery items

First of all, we should make sure that a list of available grocery items exists. Here is a way of expressing it:

```
auto groceryItems = new entities::GroceryItems(this);
QVERIFY(groceryItems);
```

Of course you shouldn't expect this snippet to compile; we have not defined the relevant classes yet; we are just calling their interfaces! Let's look at the snippet line by line. We first create an object representing a collection of `GroceryItems`. To keep our code well structured, we decide that objects of this kind (business objects or `entities`, as we have called them) will be grouped under the entities namespace:

```
auto groceryItems = new entities::GroceryItems(this);
```

The parameter passed to the constructor (`this`) represents the *parent* of that object. As already mentioned, the parent/child relationship in Qt, among other things, plays an important role in memory management: When the parent object (the `QObject`-based test case) gets destroyed, the child will be destroyed too, without the need for explicit deletion.

Then, we are using the `QVERIFY` macro (similar to the already-encountered `QVERIFY2` macro, but without the option to print a custom message) to make sure the object to which `groceryItems` is pointing has been created:

```
QVERIFY(groceryItems);
```

And (given) one or more grocery items are actually available

This means that somewhere in our system, either locally or remotely, there are one or more objects that represent the actual grocery items currently available in the fridge. For convenience, these data *repositories* should be distinct from the business objects (the `entities`) that interact in our application. Repositories should just act as an abstraction to fetch the data from specific storage implementations (databases, files, the web... maybe even a sensor in the fridge?) while keeping the business logic of the entities untouched. For example, it would be very convenient if I could retrieve a list of grocery items in exactly the same way without caring whether they are stored in a local database, in memory, or on the web.

So, whatever the backend of the repository in the final app will be (local JSON file, web-service, SQL database, serialized binary), for the time being we just need to define and then create a dummy object which, upon request, returns the count of available grocery items. We assume that, for this particular scenario to be fulfilled, that count should be greater than zero. The API for the verification of such an object could look like this:

```
auto groceryItemsRepoDummy = new
repositories::GroceryItemsRepoDummy(groceryItems);
groceryItems->setRepository(groceryItemsRepoDummy);
QVERIFY(groceryItemsRepoDummy->count() > 0);
```

Let us take a look at the above code line by line. First, we want to instantiate the dummy data repository and give it the `groceryItems` entity as a parent. This way, when we destroy the entity, we will also destroy the repository that is feeding the data to it:

```
auto groceryItemsRepoDummy = new
repositories::GroceryItemsRepoDummy(groceryItems);
```

Also, we want to connect the dummy repository to the corresponding entity, to make sure this is the repository used by the entity to fetch the data:

```
groceryItems->setRepository(groceryItemsRepoDummy);
```

Finally, we want to verify the precondition, that is to say make sure that the repository contains at least one object.

```
QVERIFY(groceryItemsRepoDummy->count() > 0);
```

When I check available groceries

After having checked that the app's initial state for our particular scenario is satisfied, we want to simulate a user-initiated action to trigger the use case.

As always, there are many ways we can implement this. For example, we could create a `CheckAvailableGroceries` class and call some action method (for example, `run()`) to trigger the logic manipulations that will ultimately result in the `Then` steps (the scenario outcomes) being fulfilled. Another way is to create a collection of all possible system actions (both user- and system-initiated) in a file, and make use of Qt's signals and slots communication system to fire the actions and handle them in a listening class instance. Alternatively, we could implement the use case actions as pure functions. Here, we choose to model the use case as a class and implement a `run()` method.

Here is the implementation of this step:

```
auto checkAvailableGroceries = new
usecases::CheckAvailableGroceries(groceryItems, this);
QSignalSpy checkAvailableGroceriesSuccess(checkAvailableGroceries,
&usecases::CheckAvailableGroceries::success);
checkAvailableGroceries->run();
QTRY_COMPARE_WITH_TIMEOUT(checkAvailableGroceriesSuccess.count(), 1, 1000);
```

Let's go through the step definition line by line again.

In the first line, we are creating an instance of the use case object, which will encapsulate all the logic operations that we perform over entities, as well as govern their interactions, when more than one entity is involved. `this` has the same meaning that it had in the constructor of `entities::GroceryItems`. Notice also how we are passing a pointer to the `groceryItems` instance as the first argument:

```
auto checkAvailableGroceries = new
usecases::CheckAvailableGroceries(groceryItems, this);
```

Then, we are constructing an instance of another important class that comes with the `QtTest` framework: `QSignalSpy`. A signal spy makes it possible to listen for a Qt signal within a test:

```
QSignalSpy checkAvailableGroceriesSuccess(checkAvailableGroceries,
&usecases::CheckAvailableGroceries::success);
```

By being able to wait for a signal to fire before continuing the program flow, we have a convenient means of implementing asynchronous programming techniques, which are very useful if we want to avoid to block the UI whenever a result takes time to be computed. With the preceding line, we are expressing the following:

- The `checkAvailableGroceries` will have a signal called `success`
- We set up a `QSignalSpy` called `checkAvailableGroceriesSuccess` that should inform us once the system action `checkAvailableGroceries` has been carried out successfully (that is, in practice, when we decide that it's meaningful to emit the `success` signal because all our use case-related business logic has completed)

Next, we start our use case action by invoking the `run` method:

```
checkAvailableGroceries->run();
```

Finally, this is how we are making sure that the `success` signal has been fired once (at least and at most) within a given timeout (1,000 msecs):

```
QTRY_COMPARE_WITH_TIMEOUT(checkAvailableGroceriesSuccess.count(), 1, 1000);
```

> **TIP**
>
> `QCOMPARE` (as well as the asynchronous versions `QTRY_COMPARE` and `QTRY_COMPARE_WITH_TIMEOUT`) is preferable to `QVERIFY` whenever you can check for equality, as `QtTest` will provide you with both the actual and expected values in the test diagnostics. `QVERIFY` is needed when you are checking for inequality, or other kinds of relationships (such as *greater than* and *less than*).

Then I am given the list of available grocery items

After the use case is completed, we expect a couple of outcomes. The first of these is that the data stored in the repository is loaded into the `groceryItems` entity and made accessible through a list. The entity, or some other application layer (such as a presentation layer), will then be responsible for making the data available to a UI, which will take care of showing it somehow (a print statement, a spoken enumeration, or, in our case, a list view in the UI). To verify this, we can make sure that the count of the items that the `groceryItems` list delivers corresponds to the number of objects stored in the repository.

> Here we are taking for granted that the count of objects in the repository and the count of items in the `groceryItems` list coincide. The addition of other features, such as a search feature, may require us to revise this assumption.

Thus, we could verify that the first `Then` step is met with the following check:

```
QCOMPARE(groceryItems->list().count(), groceryItemsDummy->count());
```

And (then) the grocery items are ordered by name, ascending

In this last step, we are checking that the grocery items are returned in ascending order by their name. This seemingly simple statement actually tells us a bit more about what we should include in our `groceryItems` entity:

- A method that checks whether the grocery items are ordered by name in ascending order
- A field for each grocery item that defines its *name* (which could just be a string)
- A definition of *ascending order* for the name field

For now, we just need to name the first method. Let's call it `isSortedBy`:

```
QVERIFY(groceryItems->isSortedBy("name","ASC"));
```

In the method implementation, we will be able to leverage algorithms and iterators provided by either Qt or some other library to perform the check efficiently.

> The correctness of the `isSortedBy` method should not be taken for granted. In a complete project, you should add a unit test at the entity level to make sure the method behaves properly. Alternatively, and perhaps even better, the sorting check should be taken out of the entity's API and performed in the acceptance test itself with a utility function.

A huge step for humanity

Congratulations! Our first acceptance test has been written. Here is the entire test:

```
void
Usecases_check_available_groceries::test_one_or_more_grocery_items_availabl
e()
{
    // Given there is a list of available grocery items
    auto groceryItems = new entities::GroceryItems(this);
    QVERIFY(groceryItems);
    // And one or more grocery items are actually available
    auto groceryItemsRepoDummy = new
repositories::GroceryItemsRepoDummy(groceryItems);
    groceryItems->setRepository(groceryItemsRepoDummy);
    QVERIFY(groceryItemsRepoDummy->count() > 0);
    // When I check available groceries
    auto checkAvailableGroceries = new
usecases::CheckAvailableGroceries(groceryItems, this);
    QSignalSpy checkAvailableGroceriesSuccess(checkAvailableGroceries,
&usecases::CheckAvailableGroceries::success);
```

```
    checkAvailableGroceries->run();
    QTRY_COMPARE_WITH_TIMEOUT(checkAvailableGroceriesSuccess.count(), 1,
1000);
    // Then I am given the list of available grocery items
    QCOMPARE(groceryItems->list().count(), groceryItemsRepoDummy->count());
    // And the grocery items are ordered by name, ascending
    QVERIFY(groceryItems->isSortedBy("name","ASC"));
}
```

> In this test we are not dealing with the destruction of objects created on the heap, because for now this is the only test running, after which the test application quits. In the next chapters we will see a few Qt strategies to deal with this issue.

Sure enough, as we go along, we will come up with better checks for each of the steps, but this test should suffice to give us enough confidence about this first scenario and continue to build the rest of the implementation. Also, when implementing our components, we will need to add a few lines of code to make things work properly.

However, not only does the test still certainly fail, it also does not even compile. Be patient, we'll make it compile (and pass!) in the next chapter.

After all this hard work, you deserve some fun. In short we'll be turning our attention to prototyping the UI. Yay! but first, I'll give you a glimpse about how the same test could be written in QML.

Writing usecase tests in QML

As we previously mentioned, a use case test, such as the one we have just written in C++, could also be written in QML, a declarative language with support for imperative JavaScript expressions.

A short QML primer

Here is what a simple QML document looks like:

```
import QtQml 2.2

QtObject {
    id: myQmlObject
    readonly property real myNumber: {
        return Math.random() + 1
    }
    property int myNumber2: myNumber + 1
    property var myChildObject: QtObject {}
    signal done(string message)
    onDone: {
        print(message);
        doSomething();
    }
    function doSomething() {
        print("hello again!");
    }
    Component.onCompleted: {
        console.log("Hello World! %1 %2".arg(myNumber).arg(myNumber2))
        done("I'm done!")
    }
}
```

Yes, it's got curly braces and colons, but it's not JSON. If you run this document, you'll see nothing but a couple of print statements:

```
qml: Hello World! 1.88728 2

qml: I'm done!
qml: Hello again!
```

> You can run this snippet in Qt Creator by creating a new QML document (**New File or Project... > Qt > QML File (Qt Quick 2)**), replacing the generated code with the snippet, and running `qmlscene` (**Tools > External > QtQuick > QtQuick 2 Preview (qmlscene)**). The same can be achieved from the command line by looking for `qmlscene` in the Qt distribution's bin folder for your host platform.
>
> Alternatively, create a new Qt Quick UI Prototype (**New File or Project... > Other Project > Qt Quick UI Prototype**), paste the contents into the newly created QML file, save it, and hit the **Run** button in Qt Creator.

Take a moment to go through the document and recall the documentation for the `QtQml` module, which, following my recommendations, you should have read already. The object does nothing interesting really, apart from highlighting a few QML-specific constructs that you will encounter again and again:

- `import QtQml 2.2`: An `import` statement which exposes a few QML types (such as `QtObject`).
- `QtObject {...}`: A QML object definition. Every QML document requires one, and only one, root component.
- `id: myQmlObject` : An `id` that identifies the QML object uniquely within the document.
- `readonly property real myNumber`: A property declaration. The property evaluates to the result of a JavaScript expression, which is cast to a `real`. The property is `readonly`; it cannot be re-assigned.
- `property int myNumber2: myNumber + 1`: A property that is bound to the value of another property (`myNumber`). This means that every time `myNumber` changes, `myNumber2` will also change automatically without the need to use setters and getters. This mechanism is called *property binding*. It is one of QML's most powerful features (see `http://doc.qt.io/qt-5.9/qtqml-syntax-objectattributes.html#property-attributes`).
- `property var myChildObject: QtObject {}`: We are creating a pointer to another `QtObject` instance. The child instance will follow the parent-child memory management that we already encountered in C++, with the addition that objects owned by QML to which there are no pointers will be garbage collected at some point.
- `signal done(string message)`: A `signal` declaration.
- `onDone:{...}`: A signal handler expression. The signal handler (a slot) is created automatically from the preceding signal declaration. As you can notice, an `on` prefix is added to the signal name in capitals.
- `function doSomething()`: A JavaScript member function of the QML object that we call in the `onDone` signal handler.
- `Component.onCompleted`: This is a built-in signal handler that is called as soon as the QML object is complet, useful to perform post-creation initialization operations.
- `console.log`, `print`: Some of the functions accessible in QML's global scope.

This is lots of information, and it is only intended to give you a bit more information about what comes in the next section. Once again, please familiarize yourself with the Qt documentation if any of the preceding points do not make much sense. And, please also read the docs even if you think they all make sense! That said, we'll have a chance to encounter each of these constructs again and again.

Expressing the first acceptance test in QML

Now that you know a bit more about the structure of QML, here is what the same functional test that we wrote in C++ could look like in QML:

```
import QtTest 1.0

TestCase {
    name: "Usecases_check_available_groceries"

    function test_one_or_more_grocery_items_available() {
        // Given there is a list of available grocery items
        var groceryItems =
createTemporaryObject(groceryItemsComponent,this);
        verify(groceryItems);
        // Given one or more grocery items are available
        var groceryItemsRepoDummy =
createTemporaryObject(groceryItemsRepoDummyComponent, groceryItems);
        groceryItems.repo = groceryItemsRepoDummy;
        verify(groceryItemsRepoDummy.count > 0);
        // When I check available groceries
        var checkAvailableGroceries =
createTemporaryObject(CheckAvailableGroceriesComponent, this);
        checkAvailableGroceries.run();
        checkAvailableGroceriesSuccess.wait();
        tryCompare(checkAvailableGroceriesSuccess.count, 1);
        // Then I am given the list of available grocery items
        compare(groceryItems.list.count, groceryItemsDummy.count);
        // And the grocery items are ordered by type, ascending
        verify(groceryItems.isSortedBy("type","ASC"));
    }
}
```

The QML + JavaScript syntax is a bit different, but you should easily notice that there is almost a one-to-one correspondence between the two APIs. Someone may tell you that C++ is always the language of choice if you are not working on the UI layer. That makes sense when you mainly think about bare performance and, possibly, maintainability in the long term. However, if you also consider a developer's skillset and development time, there may be situations where writing good QML + JS could be a compromise, especially in the prototyping phase. That said, Qt's C++ APIs together with recent C++ language features also make for a very concise way of expression. So, when implementing logic layers, whenever possible, C++ is preferred.

Note that the QML example above is not intended to be run, but only to show you how the QML and C++ APIs compare, as it lacks several object definitions.

Building a visual prototype

What we have seen so far is all nice and useful, but probably not exciting — unless you are an application architecture dude like me, that is.

It's likely you have come to Qt because of its rendering capabilities, not so much for its general programming facilities. Yet, I hope that by now you have come to appreciate the non-rendering capabilities of Qt as well.

Now that we have spent a little brain power on laying down our first use case and its main scenario, we can consider a UI that will serve the use case well. Right, serve. The UI is there to serve a purpose, that is, enable a user to carry out some task (check out what's left in the fridge). While we are at it, we should also add the other two `usecases` that we deemed essential for a minimum viable product:

- Add a grocery item to the list
- Remove a grocery item from the list

Let's do it straight away — by now we know the rules of the game:

```
Feature: Add grocery item
    Scenario: Item can be added
        Given I am given a list of available groceries
        When I add a grocery item with name X
        Then the grocery item with name X is contained in the list
        And the groceries are ordered by name, ascending

Feature: Remove grocery item
    Scenario: Item can be removed
        Given I am given a list of available groceries
```

```
And the grocery item with name X is contained in the list
When I remove the grocery item with name X
Then the grocery item with name X is not contained in the list
And the groceries are ordered by name, ascending
```

In the previous feature scenarios, we are assuming that our system only supports one item per name (for example, bananas). An extension to this could be to add the quantity for each item, or, alternatively, support more than one item with the same name (in which chase, we would need to add an attribute other than the name that identifies each item uniquely).

We have lazily limited ourselves to two very simple scenarios, and also to the optimistic path (what if something goes wrong while we are adding/removing the item?), but it will suffice for now. Fleshing out these examples is, as usual, left to your good will. A few suggestions will be left as an exercise at the end of this chapter.

So, we have a minimal specification for our little app, where a user can add, remove, and check available grocery items. Let's sketch a simple and clean UI to serve these `usecases` well.

Deciding upon the UI technology

A past Qt webinar was so entitled: *The Curse of Choice: An overview of GUI technologies in Qt* (`https://www.qt.io/event/the-curse-of-choice-an-overview-of-gui-technologies-in-qt/`). In its description, you could find a list like this:

QWidgets, QPainter, QGraphicsView, Qt Quick 1, Qt Quick 2, Qt Quick Controls 1 and 2, QWindow, OpenGL, Vulkan, Direct3D.

And that's not all; you could also find the following mentioned too: **Qt3D, Qt Canvas 3D, QtQuick Canvas**.

All these elements refer somehow to graphics, so it is therefore legitimate to ask what is available in Qt for creating graphical UI, and what should be used when.

As always, the answer is *it depends*. While the choice is wide, if the focus is on `usecases` and context, it is not so hard to choose the right graphics framework from the ones that Qt provides.

So, let's start with our `What's in my fridge?` application and answer a couple of questions to make the decision easier and motivated.

What kind of visual metaphors should our application use?

A first split is between 2D and 3D UIs. Do we aim for a classic 2D interface or do we want to actually recreate a fridge in 3D and fill it with banana models? If the latter is the case, then *Qt 3D* is probably a better choice than **Qt Canvas 3D**. It is newer, it's got almost feature-pare QML and C++ APIs, and it is much more powerful. Also, Qt 3D is soon going to support virtual reality systems, and it has many more features beyond UI. We will explore it in Part II. *Qt Canvas 3D*, on the other hand, supports a port of the `three.js` 3D JavaScript framework, and may thus still be a valid option if you already have some code written in that JS library (see `http://blog.qt.io/blog/2015/06/05/porting-three-js-code-to-canvas3d/`).

If we go for a 2D interface, we may as well go for classic UI controls, as found on desktop, mobile, and embedded, or just come up with something completely different, more similar to a video game UI. Also, in this case there is plenty of choice: both *Qt Widgets* and *Qt Quick Controls 2* provide classic UI controls out of the box, while **QPainter**, **QGraphicsView**, and **Qt Quick 2** are choices which give more freedom, each one with its own limitations and benefits. For example, because of QML and OpenGL, *Qt Quick 2* provides a very powerful animation framework.

Let's say for now that for our app we want a classic 2D UI with standard controls. That's probably what an average user would expect in the first place.

What kind of devices should our application run on?

We could run the fridge application on our desktop, on our mobile phone, or even on an embedded device that we glue to the fridge's door. Depending on the intended deployment device, we will pick one framework over another. *Qt Widgets* were born in the desktop era, and still serve the desktop context primarily. They provide a rich set of controls and layouts, with a C++ API. However, they are not particularly suited for devices with touch input. In this case, *Qt Quick 2* is more suitable, as it was developed with touch devices in mind. It also provides a rich set of controls via the *Qt Quick Controls 2* module: a recent module which was designed for devices having limited resources (for example, embedded) in mind. *Qt Quick Controls 2* are also well supported on desktop. They do not provide, however, native look and feel on all platforms out of the box, and lack (at the time of writing) some widely used controls like tables and treeviews, although these should be added fairly soon.

There are also third parties providing additional control libraries, both for Qt Quick and Qt Widgets. These are available as open source projects as well as commercial offerings. Among the former, *QWT* is a set of *Qt Widgets* for scientific applications (`http://qwt.sourceforge.net/`); among the latter, the *V-Play* framework based on *Qt Quick 2* provides a rich set of controls and functional plugins particularly suited for mobile platforms (`https://v-play.net/apps/`).

That said, creating your own custom *Qt Widgets* and *Qt Quick* components is very doable, but it requires a bit of experience.

Should a non-coding designer implement the UI?

This is also an important consideration before deciding upon one framework. Both Qt Widgets and Qt Quick are supported by dedicated visual editors that ship with Qt Creator: **Designer** and **Qt Quick Designer**. These fully fledged visual editors output clean markup files, also known as *forms* (XML for the Qt Widgets - `.ui` file extension, QML for the Qt Quick - `.ui.qml` file extension) without requiring any coding. The same facilities are not yet fully available for other frameworks, such as Qt 3D, although that's in the plans.

Why limit yourself to one?

Lastly, you should consider that Qt provides many integration options for all its graphic frameworks. This means that, in the same application, and even in the same UI, you could potentially mix Qt Quick controls, Qt 3D components, and Qt Widgets controls. We will see an example of this kind later on. Whether this makes sense is again a matter of taking a good look at the usage context and at the available technologies.

Also, if you find a clean way of structuring your application, as I am advocating here, you should be able to swap the UI layer later in the project without suffering too much, just a bit.

Our initial choice

As you may have guessed, for the fridge project we will be using a UI based on **Qt Quick Controls 2** and **Qt Quick 2**. This will give us the option to go from desktop to embedded seamlessly by providing a good user experience on each platform. Also, the current public Qt Quick API is QML only, which will give us a way to get more familiar with the language and its advantages.

Prototyping with Qt Quick Designer

Not too many Qt developers are huge fans of Qt Quick Designer. Indeed, in the past it was usually easier and quicker to write QML code by hand, perhaps with the aid of a live preview tool, because Designer's functionality was limited with respect to coding, and also because stability was not one of Designer's virtues. Recently, however, the Qt Company seems to have invested a good amount of resources in the tool, and the fruits of this overhaul can already be appreciated in current versions of Qt Creator.

Using the Designer represents a good alternative to writing UIs completely in code when non-programmers are allocated this task, or when the project in question does not require the development of custom components.

Creating the UI subproject

We start by adding a new subproject to the `part1-whats_in_my_fridge` project. To do this, as before, right click on the project and click **New Subproject...**:

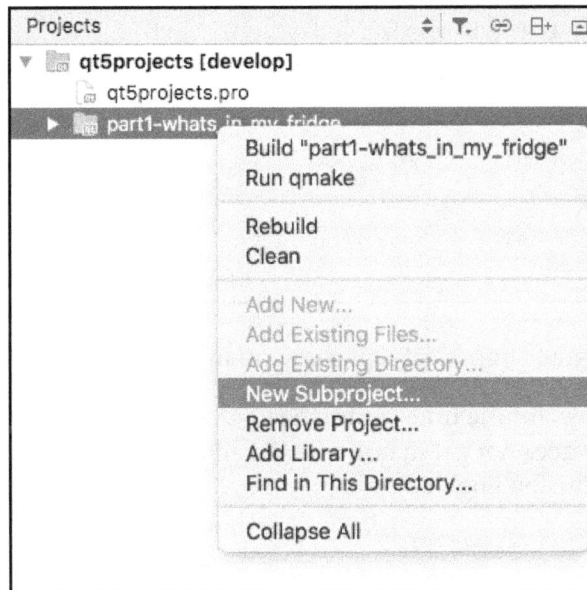

We will start off from a **Qt Quick Application - Empty** template and call the subproject `gui` (*graphical* UI). Let us leave all other wizard options unaltered. When Qt Creator prompts for a kit, if you have several options, select the one starting with **Desktop....**

A *kit* consists of a set of values that define one environment, such as a device, compiler, and the Qt version. For more information about this important Qt Creator concept, see `http://doc.qt.io/qtcreator/creator-configuring-projects.html`.

If all goes well, you should see a summary page like the following at the end of the wizard:

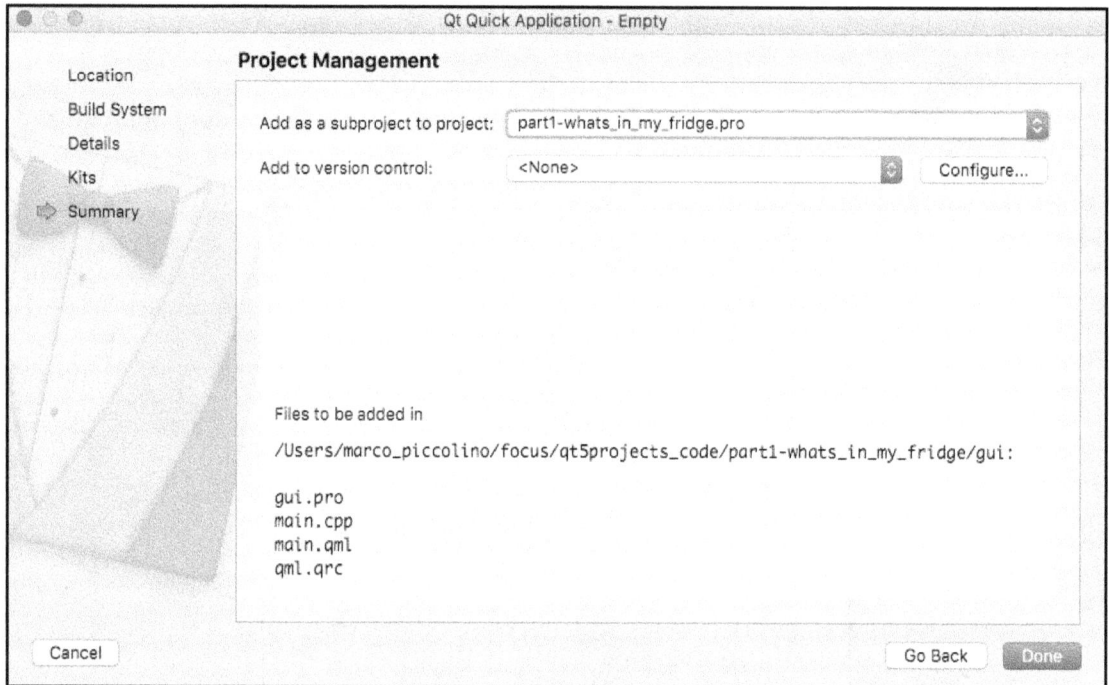

By clicking **Finish**, the `gui` subproject will show up in the project tree.

Next, we want to disable, for the time being, the `usecases` subproject, so that the fact that it does not compile yet does not get in our way. To achieve this, it's enough to comment with a `#` the project inclusion line in `part1-whats_in_my_fridge.pro`:

```
# part1-whats_in_my_fridge.pro
TEMPLATE = subdirs

SUBDIRS +=
#    usecases
    gui
```

The next thing we should do is to add a QML file an its corresponding UI form to file `qml.qrc`. To do so, right click on `qml.qrc` in the project tree and then click on **Add New...** :

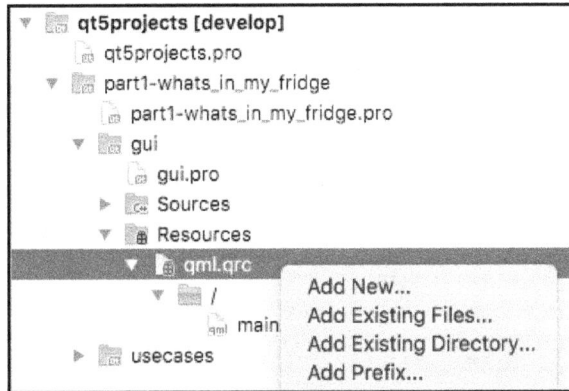

The QML component should be called `Page1`. The corresponding UI file will automatically be called `Page1Form.qml`:

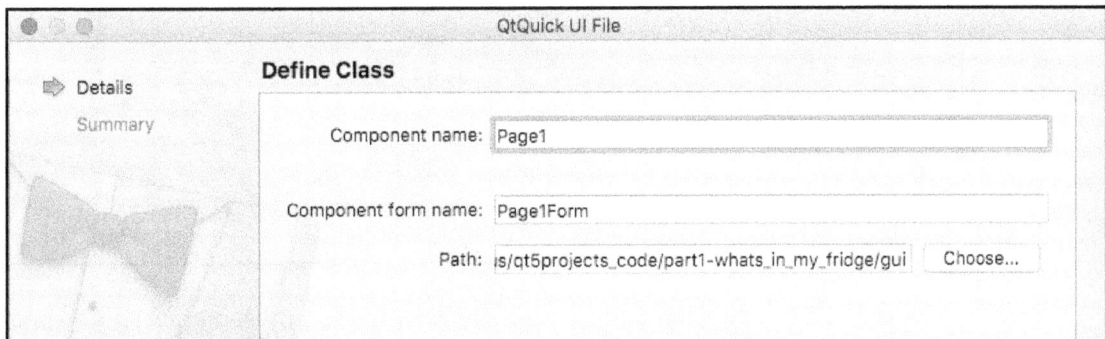

Once the file creation wizard has completed, in the project tree we want to click on `Page1Form.ui.qml`. By doing this, Qt Creator will recognize the `.ui.qml` extension and take us automatically to the *Design* mode.

By default, the design mode offers a visual representation of the form we are working on. Starting with Qt Creator 4.3, we can get the code representation (**Text Editor**) of the same form in parallel. To do this, we click on the tiny vertical split icon at the bottom right of the main form area:

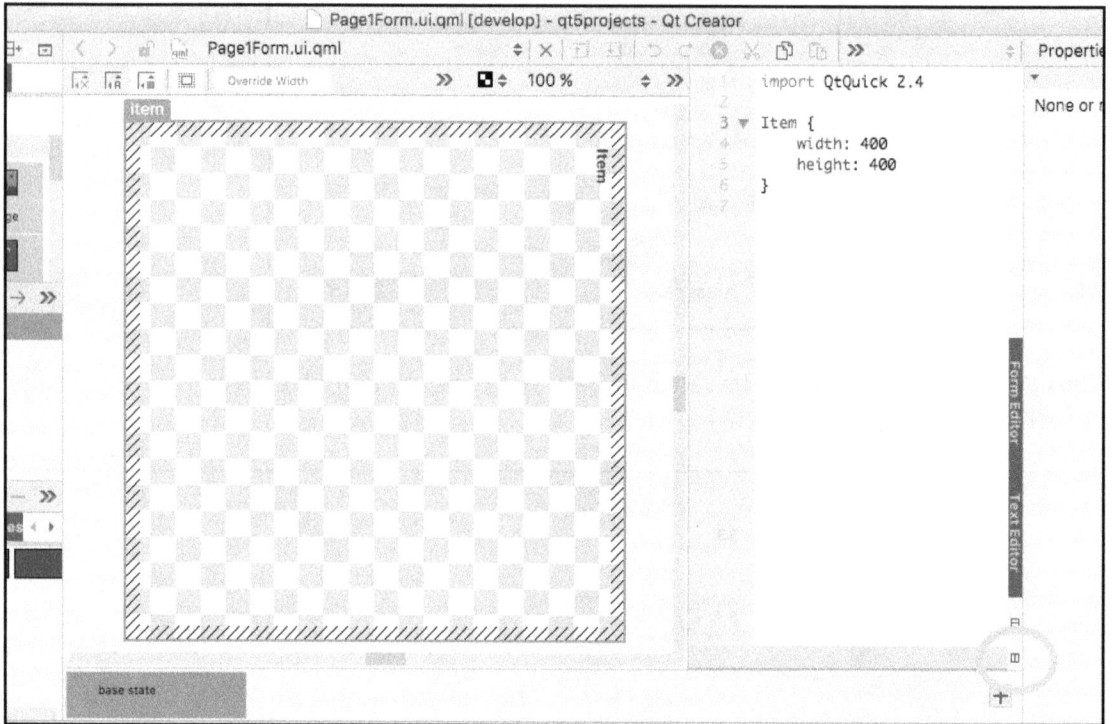

By activating the **Text Editor**, you can understand how the visual representation corresponds to the structure of the QML document.

Laying out the UI components required by the scenarios

Going back to our scenarios, we need:

1. A way to represent the list of available grocery items
2. A way to add new grocery items by their name
3. A way to remove existing grocery items that are no longer in the fridge

We first add `Page1` to `main.qml`, and make changes, until we get the following:

```
// gui/main.qml

import QtQuick 2.9
import QtQuick.Controls 2.2
import QtQuick.Layouts 1.3

ApplicationWindow {
    visible: true
    width: 320
    height: 480
    title: "What's in my fridge?"

    Page1 {
        anchors.fill: parent
    }
}
```

> **TIP**
> The width and height of 320x340 has been chosen as it is the minimum resolution of some mobile devices still present on the market, and thus serves as a minimal area for which you should make sure the UI is functional, if you decide to also target these smaller screens. Feel free to increase it if you have other requirements.

Check available groceries

We open again `Page1Form.ui.qml` in the Designer. By browsing the components available by default in Qt Quick Designer (the *QML Types* tab on the top left), we will find a few that we may think are suitable for representing a list. Yet, if we perform a keyword lookup for a *list* in the search field at the top of **QML Types**, we'll only see one result: **List View**. A quick look at Qt's documentation (`http://doc.qt.io/qt-5.9/qml-qtquick-listview.html`) will tell us what `ListView` is useful for, and whether it can be useful to us. It turns out it is. The `ListView` is capable of showing data dynamically from a model, updating itself every time the model changes. On top of that, `ListView` provides scroll support for touch interactions, in case the height of our grocery items list exceeds the available vertical screen estate.

It's a deal! If we drag the `ListView` component into the Form Editor, we will see both the canvas and the Text Editor change at once as follows:

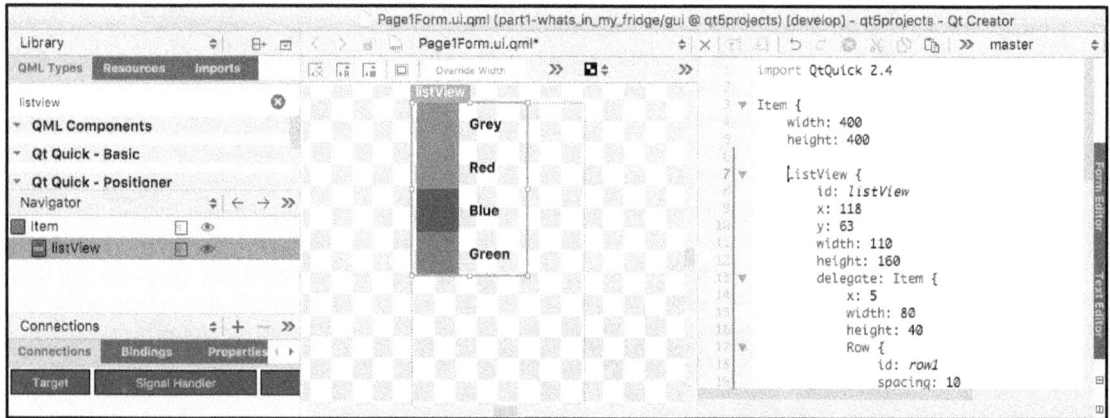

Let us examine the code that has been generated:

```
ListView {
    id: listView
    x: 118
    y: 63
    width: 110
    height: 160
    delegate: Item {
        x: 5
        width: 80
        height: 40
        Row {
            id: row1
            Rectangle {
                width: 40
                height: 40
                color: colorCode
            }
            Text {
                text: name
                anchors.verticalCenter: parent.verticalCenter
                font.bold: true
            }
            spacing: 10
        }
    }
    model: ListModel {
        ListElement {
```

```
                name: "Grey"
                colorCode: "grey"
            }
            ...
        }
    }
```

A few properties of the `ListView` QML type should be self-explanatory, while others certainly require a bit of explanation. `model` is the data model that feeds data into the view. Ultimately, it will be our `groceryItems.getList()`. For the time being, we can adapt the simple QML model called `ListModel` to generate some mock data. Each grocery item will be a `ListElement`. Instead of the `name` and `colorCode` fields of the example, we are only interested in a `name` field (go back to our scenarios and you'll remember why). Thus, in the text editor, we can modify the `ListModel` as follows:

```
ListModel {
    ListElement {
        name: "Bananas"
    }
    ListElement {
        name: "Orange Juice"
    }
    ListElement {
        name: "Grapes"
    }
    ListElement {
        name: "Eggs"
    }
}
```

A bit further down in `ListView`'s definition we find the `delegate` property. The `delegate` is the visual representation of each list element (or record) contained in the model. Besides describing the visual appearance of the `delegate`, the code describes how the attributes of each list element should be displayed. In the default delegate that Designer provides, `name` shows up as a text label (it is bound to the `text` property of a `Text` QML type), while `colorCode` defines the background color (the `color` property) of a `Rectangle`.

Since we just want to display the type of our grocery item, we can change the `delegate` from the default types to the convenient `ItemDelegate` control type. In order to have the `ItemDelegate` available in Designer, we should first import the `QtQuick.Controls 2` module that exposes it:

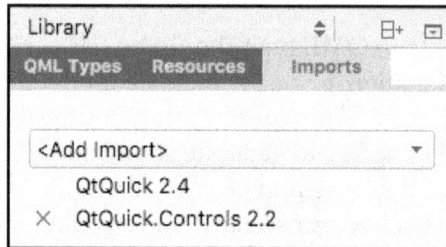

Once we have added the import, we switch to the **Text Editor** and change the `delegate`'s type and properties as follows:

```
delegate: ItemDelegate {
        width: parent.width
        text: modelData.name || model.name
        font.bold: true
    }
```

the `modelData.name || model.name` JS expression allows us to use the same delegate with both proper Qt data models and simpler, JS-array like models. For historical reasons, JS models can be accessed through the `modelData` context property, while Qt models require the use of the `model` property.

If we now refresh the Form Editor (click on the small counter-clockwise arrow button **Reset view** at the top right of the editor), we shall see our list view containing the grocery items:

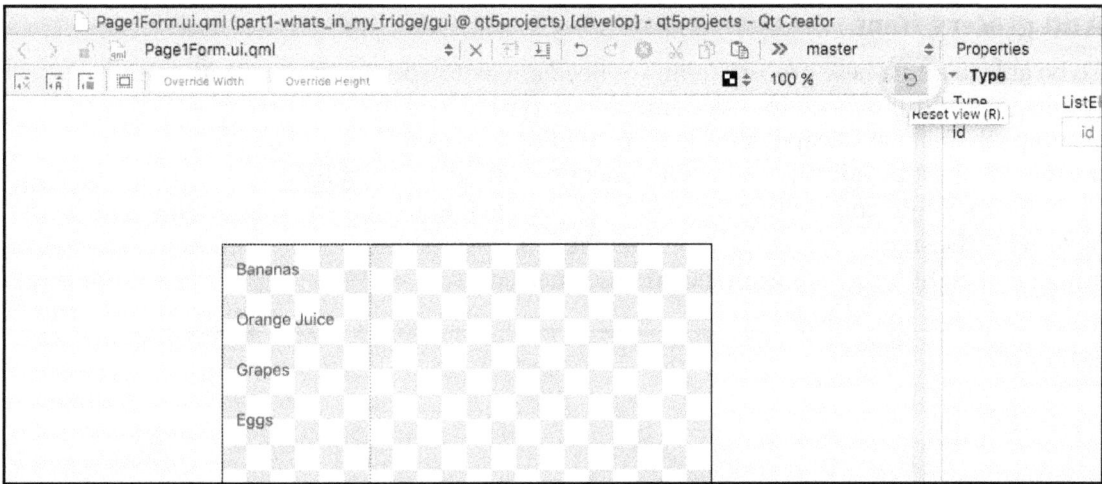

Let us now have the list view occupy all available space. Instead of using absolute width and height values, we can tell the list view to occupy all available space by going to the **Layout** tab on the right (**Properties** pane) and selecting **Anchors** on all four sides to fill `ListView`'s parent (the `Item`). Now the list fills all of the available space:

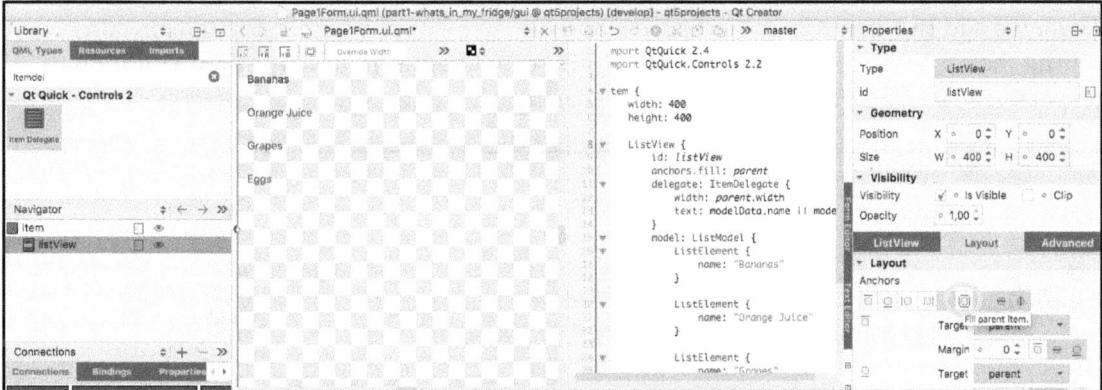

If you now push the Run button (green arrow) in Qt Creator, you should be able to run the application and see the list view. By dragging the mouse on to the list view, and then up and down, you'll see the list sliding and coming back. Fancy, huh?

Add grocery item

To be able to add a new grocery item, we need a way to specify its type, and a way to confirm the addition once we have entered the type. There are of course many ways to accomplish this. Let's keep it simple by providing an input field and a submission button. We start by adding a `Row` component to contain our text field and button, anchor it to the bottom, left, and right of the root `Item`, by also removing any margin that may have been set by Designer. we set the `Row`'s height to a reasonable amount, such as `64`, which is a sufficient height for a toolbar that contains touch controls.

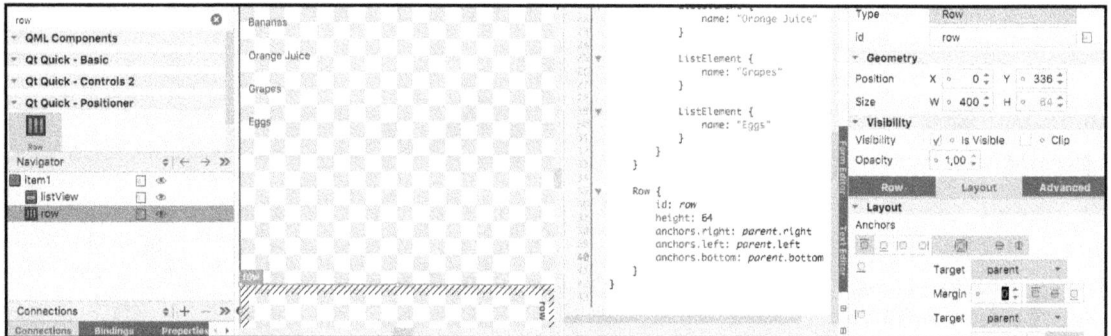

Then, we add two controls, a `TextField` and a `Button` as children to the `Row`, by also setting their `placeholderText` and `text` property to **enter item name** and **Add item**, respectively, and give a left margin and a spacing of 8 to the `Row`:

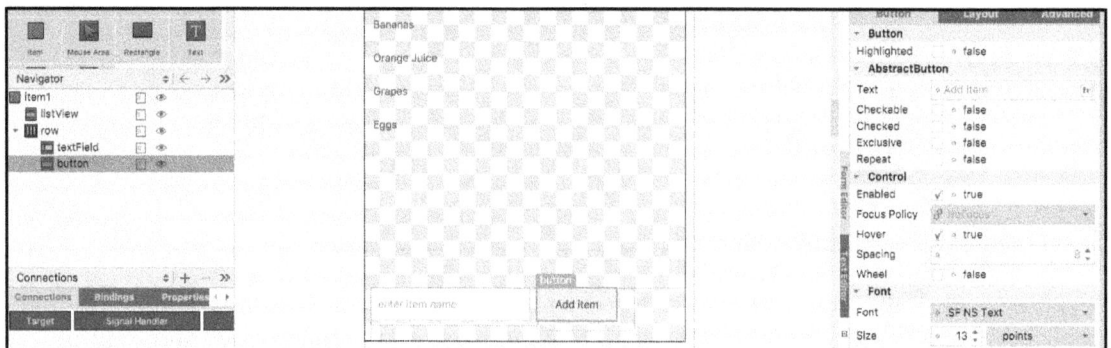

If you are looking for the `placeholderText` property in the **Properties** pane, you won't find it, as it is not exposed. You can however just add it to the `TextField` from the Text Editor, as seen in the preceding screenshot. This is one more reason to inspect a component's description and API thoroughly in the docs before starting to use it.

> If you want to quickly access the documentation for a component in Qt Creator, click on the component's type in the Text Editor and press *F1*.

If you now press the **Run** button, you will see the row with the text field and button at the bottom of the page. Clicking on either the `TextField` will bring the focus to it, while clicking on the `Button` will display a visual effect.

Remove grocery item

Removing a grocery item can also be achieved in several ways: for example, long press on a `delegate`, swipe, and so on.

We will take a more visual way and simply add an "X" button to each `delegate`. Because the `delegate` is part of the `ListItem`, we will need to make any modifications through the Text Editor, as follows:

```
delegate: ItemDelegate {
        width: parent.width
        text: modelData.name || model.name
        font.bold: true
        Button {
            width: height
            height: parent.height
            text: "X"
            anchors.right: parent.right
        }
    }
```

From a visual point of view, we have everything that is needed to cover our first usecases. Congratulations! Of course, as we haven't tied any logic to the button and item presses, nothing will happen. Run the completed UI again and check it out.

Taking it further

Here are a few suggestions if you feel confident enough to expand upon the minimal use case scenarios and UI we have outlined in this chapter.

- The Gherkin feature Check available groceries also contains a scenario for when no grocery items are available (No grocery items available). In such an event, we may want our use case to return a message which indicates this fact. Try and implement the test function for this second scenario.
- Try and refine Check available groceries by extending its requirements in terms of preconditions and/or expected outcomes. For example, we may want to display the number of available pieces for each grocery item next to the type. If this is the case, we'd also want to be able to increase/decrease the number of available pieces.
- We have written scenarios for Add grocery item and Remove grocery item, but haven't written any test cases for them. Create a new subproject for each test case and add a test for the main scenario.
- Come up with a different layout for a list of grocery items. For example, there is a GridView component that supports dynamic models much like ListView does.
- Add a background to the row that contains the TextField and the Button. You can use a Rectangle for that purpose, as it was done for the list view delegate example.
- Add a header which displays the name of the application. You could use a ToolBar (which is provided by the Qt Quick Controls 2 module) or a Rectangle, for example, with a Text or a Label inside.

Summary

In this chapter, we showed how careful planning by means of BDD and upfront testing with `QtTest` can help you shape an application by focusing on its features rather than on the technical details of file I/O and UI.

We also discussed the relative merits and usage contexts for the various UI technologies offered by Qt.

We finally created a prototype for the UI of our application with Qt Quick and Qt Quick Controls 2, by leveraging Qt Creator's Quick Designer.

In the next chapter we will implement the `usecases` and test them in a complete scenario by creating a simple command line application, and in the following one we will mount the UI on to the application logic and refine it.

24
Defining a Solid and Testable App Core

We have started our journey into application development with Qt by providing a clear map of what we want to achieve by means of scenarios, acceptance tests, and usecases. In turn, transforming scenarios into usecases has revealed the most important business object we need for our What's in my fridge? app: *a list of* grocery items. usecases have also outlined some of the *characteristics* of the grocery items business object; for example, it must be countable, and each list item should have a name that can be used to refer to, sort, add, and remove it from the list.

In this chapter, we will implement first the check available groceries usecase object, and then the grocery items business object (entity), plus any related object that is needed; for example, we will also need to implement the object (a repository) to retrieve the data and populate the list. By carrying out these activities, we will discover some of Qt's fundamental idioms and data structures.

We will also discover a possible way to keep our business logic separated from external agencies, such as databases or web APIs, so that we can concentrate on application logic without committing too deeply to specific Qt and non-Qt technologies, and keep our test suites fast to run.

Finally, we will create a small command-line application which will carry out the usecase when we type in the proper action.

After all this work, in the next chapter, we will be able to add a UI on top of the application's logic and have a simple modular and scalable UI app that we can deploy to our device of choice.

Prepare to sweat. Test-driven development and BDD may seem daunting at first, but you'll come to appreciate their fruits as long as you progress.

Implementing the first usecase

Our first `usecase` extracted from a scenario was `check available groceries`. We now want to define the class that represents the `usecase`. In order to do that, we look at the object's API that we consume in the `test_one_or_more_grocery_items_available()` test:

```
// tst_check_available_groceries.cpp
...
// When I check available groceries
auto checkAvailableGroceries = new
usecases::CheckAvailableGroceries(groceryItems, this);
QSignalSpy checkAvailableGroceriesSuccess(checkAvailableGroceries,
&usecases::CheckAvailableGroceries::success);
checkAvailableGroceries->run();
QTRY_COMPARE_WITH_TIMEOUT(checkAvailableGroceriesSuccess.count(), 1, 1000);
...
```

Here is the API we are consuming:

- A constructor (`CheckAvailableGroceries(groceryItems, this)`) for the `usecase`, which takes as arguments a pointer to any involved business objects (entities), that is `groceryItems`, and a pointer to the `usecase`'s parent object (for memory management purposes)
- A `run` method which triggers the `usecase`
- A `success` signal, which is emitted if the `usecase` completes successfully

So much for the API. As to the implementation, by looking at preconditions and expected outcomes, we notice that the `usecase` will have to make modifications to the `groceryItems` object so that, once the `usecase` is successful, the list of grocery items' count becomes greater than zero and matches the number of grocery items available in the storage backend, or repository (`groceryItemsRepoDummy`). This is the reason why we pass a pointer to `groceryItems` in the `usecase`'s constructor. Furthermore, the `usecase` will instruct the grocery items list to be sorted in ascending order by `name`.

The preconditions are:

```
QVERIFY(groceryItemsRepoDummy->count() > 0);
```

The expected outcomes are:

```
QCOMPARE(groceryItems->list().count(), groceryItemsRepoDummy->count());
...
QVERIFY(groceryItems->isSortedBy("name","ASC"));
```

Creating the usecase class

Let's start implementing the CheckAvailableGroceries usecase class. Remember from Chapter 23, *Writing Acceptance Tests and Building a Visual Prototype*, that in the *Creating the first C++ test case* section, we already created the check_available_groceries subproject, with an autogenerated check_available_groceries.pro. We will now need to create a file for the usecase classes, so that we can include them as a module in whatever client project requires them. To this purpose, in a QMake project, we can use a .pri file, or project include file.

> QMake's .pri files are just convenience files that can be included in .pro files to keep sources and resources modular and organized, and to separate the source files from other resources (for example, the test suites). They can contain most of what goes into a .pro file. Qt Creator recognizes them, although it does not provide any special facility for their creation or inclusion into .pro files. Thus, you should usually create them as empty files and add them manually to the .pro files.

We create a new empty file with Qt Creator (**New File or Project... > General > Empty File**) called check_available_groceries.pri, and add it manually to the check_available_groceries.pro file by means of the include() directive:

```
# check_available_groceries.pro
...
include(check_available_groceries.pri)
```

We then create a new C++ class in the `check_available_groceries` subproject, which inherits from `QObject`:

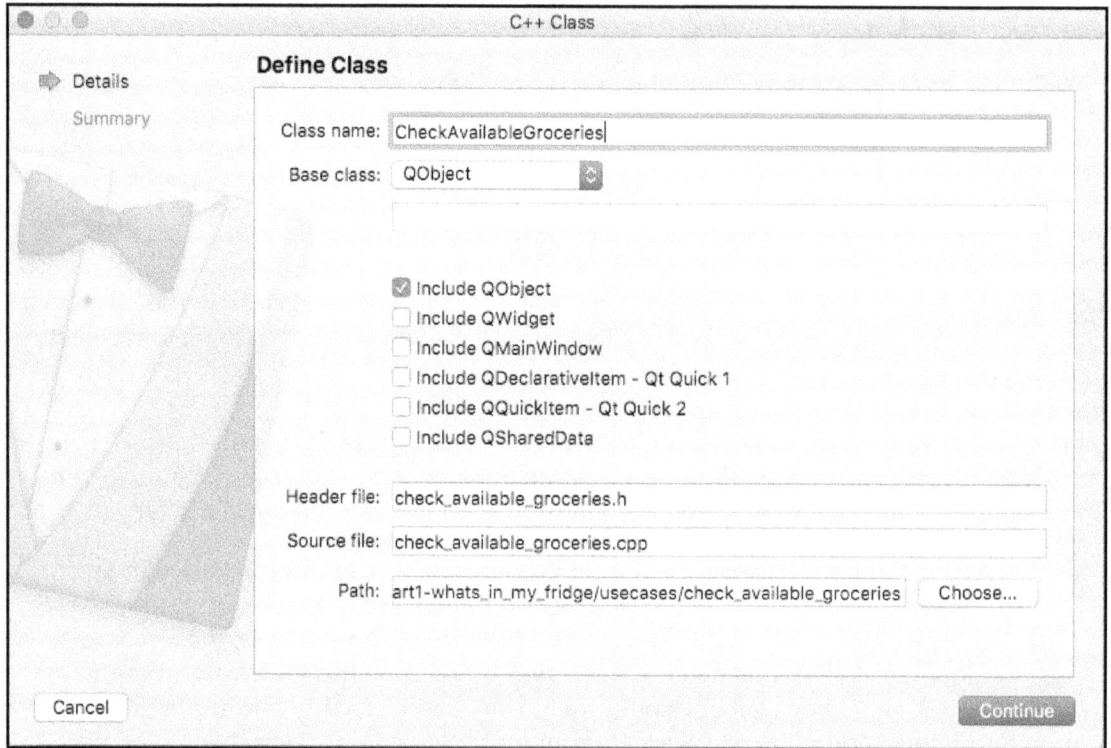

> ⓘ I have manually modified the header and source filenames in the form by inserting underscores to make them more readable.

Then, if Qt Creator does not allow you to select `check_available_groceries.pri` as the project file to which the headers and sources should be added, you can add them manually after the wizard has finished:

```
# check_available_groceries.pri
HEADERS +=
    $$PWD/check_available_groceries.h

SOURCES +=
    $$PWD/check_available_groceries.cpp
```

Remember that all relative paths referenced in a `.pri` file are resolved as relative to the enclosing `.pro` file, not to the `.pri` file itself. This means that if the `.pri` file is in a different folder from the `.pro` file, you might get confused. QMake's `$$PWD` variable makes it easy to describe all paths relative to the project's work directory, thus reducing ambiguity (`http://doc.qt.io/qt-5/qmake-variable-reference.html#pwd`).

If all goes well, the header and source files of the newly-created class should now show up in Qt Creator's **Projects** pane.

Anatomy of a QObject-derived class

The header file `check_available_groceries.h`, being a `QObject`-derived class, has the following default contents:

```
#ifndef CHECK_AVAILABLE_GROCERIES_H
#define CHECK_AVAILABLE_GROCERIES_H

#include <QObject>

class CheckAvailableGroceries : public QObject
{
    Q_OBJECT
public:
    explicit CheckAvailableGroceries(QObject *parent = nullptr);

signals:

public slots:
};

#endif // CHECKAVAILABLEGROCERIES_H
```

Besides what is customary in a C++ class definition, you might notice a few novel, Qt-specific elements. This is what they are for:

- `#include <QObject>`: Qt generally follows the rule of one class per file. So you can expect to be able to include a file corresponding to the class that you want to derive from. The `Q` prefix is common to all Qt-defined types. If you want to have a bird's-eye view on all classes that Qt provides, take a look here (hint: there are a lot of them!): `http://doc.qt.io/qt-5.9/classes.html`.

- Q_OBJECT: As seen in `Chapter 23`, *Writing Acceptance Tests and Building a Visual Prototype*, adding this macro is required to make Qt work its magic. Signals and slots, properties, and, in general, all introspection capabilities of `QObject`-derived classes are activated by adding this macro to the private section of the `QObject`-derived class.

- `explicit`: Classes which extend `QObject` declare an explicit constructor with a parent, to avoid using the one provided by default by C++. Additionally, the `Q_OBJECT` macro ensures that the copy constructor and assignment operator are made private, and disables them. This is because each `QObject` has an *identity* (for example, it might be referred to by an `objectName`, and it appears within a specific parent-child relationship, which also affects its lifetime). For more information on this topic, refer to `http://doc.qt.io/qt-5.9/object.html#identity-vs-value`.

- `signals`: This section is reserved for the declaration of methods that will act as signals that can be emitted. More on these later.

- `public slots`: This section is reserved for the declaration of methods that will act as slots that can be connected to signals and react to them. Slots can also be marked `private`, in which case they can be invoked by client code in a signal/slot connection, but not directly as methods. More on slots later.

> If you haven't already done so, this is a good time to visit `http://doc.qt.io/qt-5.9/object.html`, where the Qt object model is explained, with pointers to related key concepts.

Describing the usecase flow with signals and slots

In order to implement our `usecase`, as we have seen, we need a way to tell the `groceryItems` entity to load the list of available items and to sort them in ascending order based on their *name*. Only then can we declare the `usecase` as successful.

The standard way of accomplishing this would be to invoke some method of groceryItems to retrieve and sort the items, and then get back a return value, perhaps a boolean indicating whether the method was successful. In a completely synchronous setting this could work OK, but often we might need part of this task to happen asynchronously (as we, for example, want to retrieve the grocery items from a web server without blocking the application's UI). Also, for more complex usecases, success might be given by a fairly complicated sequence of business object operations and interactions, and keeping track of all return value combinations might complicate the code.

One way to mitigate these issues is to use callbacks, which, however, do not scale well, as they tend to make code hard to follow. Instead, Qt's native way is to use *signals* and *slots*.

Signals and slots is one of the two main communication models that Qt implements (the other model being that of events, which is mostly used to handle user input). It is widely used as it allows a high level of decoupling among application components, as well as application layers. It can be regarded as an instance of the *observer* pattern: an object emits signals (with or without argument payloads), and a registered method of either the same object or a different object (of the same type or a different one) reacts to the signal, optionally making use of the attached payload.

So, turning back to our usecase, we might want groceryItems to emit a signal once it's done loading and sorting the items, and have the usecase class connect to that signal with a slot, to either do something else or, in this simple case, emit a success signal.

So, assuming that we want to name groceryItems' public method retrieveAll(), here is what our usecase class definition in its simplest form might look like:

```
namespace entities {
  class GroceryItems;
}

namespace usecases {
class CheckAvailableGroceries : public QObject
{
  Q_OBJECT
public:
  explicit CheckAvailableGroceries(entities::GroceryItems* groceryItems,
QObject *parent = nullptr);
  void run();

signals:
  void failure(QString message);
  void success(QString message);

private slots:
```

```
    void onGroceryItemsAllRetrieved();
    void onGroceryItemsAllNotRetrieved();
};
}
```

We already know the `run` method, which triggers the `usecase` and gives a pointer to the entity whose state we want to alter.

The `success` and `failure` signals are very simple; we just declare them, and specify a `QString` argument, as we want to carry a message with details about success, or the cause of the failure. Of course, we might also opt for more complex data structures, as we will see in later examples.

> `QString` is Qt's string type. You will encounter this type very often. Among other things, it provides out-of-the-box support for UTF-8, many useful methods for string manipulation, and the `implicit sharing` mechanism, common across Qt value types, which performs a deep copy of a string only when it is written to, thus providing efficient memory usage. See `http://doc.qt.io/qt-5.9/qstring.html`.

What's more interesting is the two private slots: `onGroceryItemsAllRetrieved` and `onGroceryItemsAllNotRetrieved`. We want these to be invoked as soon as `groceryItems` is finished doing its data retrieval and sorting, the former in case of success, and the latter in case something goes wrong. These two slots, which are private because there is no reason to expose them to the outside world, will need to be connected to the corresponding signals emitted by `groceryItems`.

But how is the connection between a signal and a corresponding slot set up?

That happens via `QObject`'s *connection* method, which is available both as static and non-static, depending on the usage scenario. In our case, as we have access to `groceryItems` in the `usecase`'s constructor, the connection will be established in the constructor's definition from `check_available_groceries.cpp`:

```
CheckAvailableGroceries::CheckAvailableGroceries(entities::GroceryItems
*groceryItems, QObject *parent)
    : QObject(parent),
      m_groceryItems(groceryItems)
{

    connect(groceryItems, &entities::GroceryItems::allRetrieved,
            this, &CheckAvailableGroceries::onGroceryItemsAllRetrieved);
    connect(groceryItems , &entities::GroceryItems::allNotRetrieved,
            this, &CheckAvailableGroceries::onGroceryItemsAllNotRetrieved);
}
```

This flavor of the `connect` method accepts five arguments:

- A pointer to the object emitting the signal (the *sender*).
- A reference to the signal method.
- A pointer to the object consuming the signal (the *receiver*).
- A reference to the slot (or to a plain `QObject` method) consuming the signal.
- A type of connection (optional); for example, `Qt::UniqueConnection` would ensure that there is only one such connection at any given time. This is not required in this case, as the connection is not expected to be created more than once.

The method returns a handle to the connection, which can be used to disconnect at a later point if it is ever needed.

> For more details about all variants of `connect`, including an older macro-based version which is still to be found in much Qt code, take a look at `QObject`'s documentation: `http://doc.qt.io/qt-5.9/qobject.html`.

In the first case, we connect `groceryItem`'s `allRetrieved` signal to the `usecase`'s `onGroceryItemsAllRetrieved` slot. Similarly, in the second case, we connect `allNotRetrieved` to `onGroceryItemsAllNotRetrieved`.

After establishing the connection, we invoke `groceryItems`'s `retrieveAll` method and wait for either signal to be emitted.

Once either signal is emitted by `groceryItems`, if nothing else needs to be done, the `usecase` will emit a success or failure signal with a message, as it is done here:

```
void CheckAvailableGroceries::onGroceryItemsAllRetrieved() {
    emit success("CHECK_AVAILABLE_GROCERIES__SUCCESS");
}

void CheckAvailableGroceries::onGroceryItemsAllNotRetrieved() {
    emit failure("CHECK_AVAILABLE_GROCERIES__FAILURE");
}
```

The `emit` macro keyword is optional; it is just used for clarity to show that the method we are invoking is a signal.

Since the `usecase` is interacting with a business object of type `entities::GroceryItems`, to compile and run the `usecase` we will have to implement that object first.

From usecases to business objects

To write the `usecase` test `test_one_or_more_grocery_items_available()`, we had to define some of the `entities::GroceryItems` business object's API, namely a `list` method returning the list of items (which in turn should expose a `count` method), an `isSortedBy` method checking that the list is sorted according to a specific field and direction, and a `setRepository` method defining a store, or repository, from where the data should be fetched.

In addition, by implementing the `usecase` class, we also figured out we would need a `retrieveAll` method to retrieve the data from the repository into the list, as well as two signals (`allRetrieved` and `allNotRetrieved`) to notify the `usecase` and any other interested party of the completed task.

Let us now create a class to represent such an object. It will live in a new `entities` subproject of `part1-whats_in_my_fridge`:

```
# part1-whats_in_my_fridge.pro
TEMPLATE = subdirs
SUBDIRS +=
    usecases
    # gui
    entities
```

After creating the `entities subdirs` project and adding an `entities.pri` file as done before for `check_available_groceries`, we will create a new `GroceryItems` C++ class, which derives from `QObject`, and add it to `entities.pri`.

According to the `GroceryItem`'s API as we have explored it so far, here is what the public part of the class definition should look like:

```
#ifndef GROCERY_ITEMS_H
#define GROCERY_ITEMS_H

#include <QObject>
```

```
#include <QVariantList>

namespace repositories {
class GroceryItemsRepo;
}

namespace entities {
class GroceryItems : public QObject
{
    Q_OBJECT

public:
    explicit GroceryItems(QObject *parent = nullptr);
    ~GroceryItems();
    bool isSortedBy(const QString& field, const QString& direction) const;
    void setRepository(repositories::GroceryItemsRepo* repository);
    void retrieveAll();
    QVariantList list() const;

signals:
    void allRetrieved(QString message);
    void allNotRetrieved(QString message);

private:
...
};
}

#endif // GROCERY_ITEMS_H
```

All Qt idioms and data structures encountered here should already make sense to you, except perhaps for the list's type, `QVariantList`, which is a `typedef` for `QList<QVariant>`. `QList` is one of the available Qt containers. You can find out all about its properties and methods at `http://doc.qt.io/qt-5.9/qlist.html`. Now, let's take a closer look at `QVariant`.

Introducing the almighty QVariant

Besides `QObject`, another type which makes Qt code so powerful is `QVariant`, a type which *acts like a union for the most common Qt data types* (`http://doc.qt.io/qt-5.9/qvariant.html`).

`QVariant`'s usefulness derives from the fact that it represents an abstraction over several Qt and C++ built-in data types, and allows conversion between them. Thanks to its various constructors, `QVariant` stores both a value and a specific type (`QString`, `int`, and so on). The value can be retrieved (by copy) by invoking one of the built-in methods (`toString`, `toInt`), and the stored type via the `typeName` method. Conversion between types happens via the `convert` and `canConvert` methods.

`QVariant` plays a crucial role in supporting Qt's property system (the system which also underlies the QML properties seen in `Chapter 23`, *Writing Acceptance Tests and Building a Visual Prototype*) and in building bridges between C++'s strong typing and weakly-typed languages (JavaScript, QML, and SQL). In particular, `QVariant` makes it possible to pass data between C++ and QML/JS pretty seamlessly.

In the preceding example, we have chosen `QList<QVariant>` (that is `QVariantList`) as the type of `GroceryItems` list, as this kind of data structure will be automatically converted into an array of JavaScript objects when used in QML, and is also automatically supported by several QML model-based view components. In many cases, however, you might want to choose a more powerful (but more complex) data model, as we will see in the coming chapters.

In turn, each `QVariant` will be a wrapper of a dictionary-like object, where we can keep pairs of field names and field values (one of these being the grocery item's name: banana, apple, and so on; another one being, for example, quantity: 0,1,2). More on this in the next section.

Implementing the GroceryItems entity

As described in `Chapter 23`, *Writing Acceptance Tests and Building a Visual Prototype*, keeping data retrieval separate from business logic is very often a reasonable choice, which makes it possible to swap several kinds of backends (SQL, web service, and so on) without having to change the business rules. Additionally, using a lightweight, fake data backend (a so-called *test double*) in tests makes them run fast.

For these reasons, while writing the test for the `usecase`, we introduced a data repository object that would both function as a data feed for the `GroceryItems` entity (`groceryItems->setRepository(groceryItemsRepoDummy)`) and give an oracle against which we could check if all data was loaded (`QCOMPARE(groceryItems->list().count(), groceryItemsRepoDummy->count())`).

Thus, when implementing the `GroceryItems` entity, we'll want the `retrieveAll` method to call into the repository and have it return all grocery items records, wherever they come from, and whatever technology is needed to get them:

```
// grocery_items.cpp
...
void GroceryItems::retrieveAll()
{
    if (m_repository) {
        m_repository->retrieveAllRecords();
    }
}
```

Once again, instead of returning the data synchronously, we will leverage signals and slots, by listening for an `allRecordsRetrieved` signal from the repository:

```
void GroceryItems::setRepository(repositories::GroceryItemsRepo
*repository)
{
    m_repository = repository;
    connect(m_repository,
&repositories::GroceryItemsRepo::allRecordsRetrieved,
            this, &GroceryItems::onAllRecordsRetrieved,
            Qt::UniqueConnection);
}
```

The repository's `allRecordsRetrieved` signal will also have a payload (an argument): a `QVariantList` of records, which will be consumed and processed by the `onAllRecordsRetrieved` slot. As you can notice, the argument does not show up in the `connect`. However, by including it in both signal and slot's signatures, it will be automatically passed along and be available in the slot.

> Production code would require us to also deal with the disconnection of any repository that has been previously connected to the entity. For more information, visit http://doc.qt.io/qt-5.9/qobject.html#disconnect.

After the list of records is passed (by value) from the repository to the entity, we can further sort it and add it to the list. Here is an overly-simplified implementation of the two steps of sorting and assignment:

Remember that, as already described for QString, also for QList, the implicit sharing mechanism ensures that a deep copy of the list is only performed when it diverges from the original (for example, upon write). For this reason, passing many Qt types by value is relatively efficient.

```
void GroceryItems::onAllRecordsRetrieved(QVariantList records)
{
    m_list = records;
    sortBy("name","ASC");
    emit listChanged();

    emit allRetrieved("ENTITIES_GROCERY_ITEMS__ALL_RETRIEVED");
}
```

For the time being, you can ignore the listChanged signal. The sortBy method is implemented as follows:

```
void GroceryItems::sortBy(const QString &field, const QString &direction)
{
    if (field == "name" && direction == "ASC") {
        std::sort(m_list.begin(), m_list.end(), [](const QVariant &v1,
const QVariant &v2) {
            return v1.toMap().value("name") < v2.toMap().value("name");
        });
        m_isSortedByNameAsc = true;
    }
}
```

We define a C++11 lambda function (https://isocpp.org/wiki/faq/cpp11-language#lambda) to use in C++ Standard Library's sort algorithm, and then run the said algorithm on m_list which, as you shall recall, is a QList of QVariant.

Qt used to have (and still has, albeit they are now deprecated) its own algorithms collection (for example, qSort). As you can see, however, many kinds of Qt containers work perfectly well with the Standard Library's algorithms.

We also define the comparison expression which determines which of any two elements of the list should be considered as the lesser one:

```
return v1.toMap().value("name") < v2.toMap().value("name")
```

As explained in the previous section, `QVariant` is just a convenient wrapper for other data types. In this specific case, we said that we would like to have a dictionary-like structure for each grocery item, so that we can add a few fields to it, one of them being `name`, which we need for the current `usecase`. Such a structure is provided by Qt in the form of a `QMap`, a container class which stores key-value pairs (`http://doc.qt.io/qt-5.9/qmap.html`). In the comparison expression, you can see how the `QMap` is returned from the `QVariant` with the `toMap` method, and the value of the `name` key compared with the corresponding value of another item. Since the value of `name` is a `QString`, we are actually performing an alphabetic string comparison.

To consider the sorting as done, as a convenience, we change the value of an `m_isSortedByNameAsc` flag to `true`. This is not a robust strategy, but it is enough for our simple example. After the sorting, we emit the `allRetrieved` signal with a message.

To fulfill the requirements of the `CheckAvailableItems usecase`, we still need to implement the `isSortedBy` method, which is part of `GroceryItems`' API. Again, as an over-simplification, we just return the value of the `m_isSortedByNameAsc` flag that we defined previously if the arguments to `isSortedBy` are the `name` and `ASC` character sequences, respectively:

```
bool GroceryItems::isSortedBy(const QString &field, const QString
&direction) const {
    if (field == "name" && direction == "ASC") {
        return isSortedByNameAsc;
    } else {
        return false;
    }
}
```

Here is the complete implementation of `GroceryItems` to cover the usecase, `CheckAvailableItems`:

```
// grocery_items.cpp
#include <algorithm>
#include <QVariant>
#include "grocery_items.h"
#include "../repositories/grocery_items_repo.h"

namespace entities {

GroceryItems::GroceryItems(QObject *parent)
    : QObject(parent),
      m_list(QVariantList()),
      m_repository(nullptr)
{}
```

```
GroceryItems::~GroceryItems()
{}

void GroceryItems::sortBy(const QString &field, const QString &direction)
{
    if (field == "name" && direction == "ASC") {
        std::sort(m_list.begin(), m_list.end(), [](const QVariant &v1,
const QVariant &v2) {
            return v1.toMap().value("name") < v2.toMap().value("name");
        });
        m_isSortedByNameAsc = true;
    }
}

bool GroceryItems::isSortedBy(const QString &field, const QString
&direction) const {
    if (field == "name" && direction=="ASC") {
        return m_isSortedByNameAsc;
    } else {
        return false;
    }
}

void GroceryItems::setRepository(repositories::GroceryItemsRepo
*repository)
{
    m_repository = repository;
    connect(m_repository,
&repositories::GroceryItemsRepo::allRecordsRetrieved,
            this, &GroceryItems::onAllRecordsRetrieved,
            Qt::UniqueConnection);
}

void GroceryItems::retrieveAll()
{
    if (m_repository) {
        m_repository->retrieveAllRecords();
    }
}

QVariantList GroceryItems::list() const
{
    return m_list;
}

void GroceryItems::onAllRecordsRetrieved(const QVariantList& records)
{
    m_list = records;
```

```
    sortBy("name","ASC");
    emit listChanged();
    emit allRetrieved("ENTITIES_GROCERY_ITEMS__ALL_RETRIEVED");
  }
}
```

As this entity requires a data repository of type `repositories::GroceryItemsRepo`, we will now see how to implement that so that we can finally put it all together.

Implementing a fake data repository

We already stressed several times the importance of keeping data retrieval separated from business logic. We now turn our attention to the data retrieval component (the repository) and build a fake implementation that we can use in our acceptance tests without having to access databases, files, or web resources.

In order to do so, we create a new `subdirs` project called `repositories`, as well as the corresponding `repositories.pri` file to keep source files separated from test harnesses and other kinds of resources:

```
# part1-whats_in_my_fridge.pro
TEMPLATE = subdirs

SUBDIRS +=
    usecases
    # gui
    entities
    repositories
```

Once we are done with it, since we'd typically want to have not only a *fake* repository, but also one or more *useful* repositories, before creating our `repositories::GroceryItemsRepoDummy` class, we shall first create a common abstract interface that we can refer to in client code, independently of the specific implementation. That class is `repositories::GroceryItemsRepo`, a header-only, pure virtual class which we already included in the implementation of `entities::GroceryItems` as `grocery_items_repo.h`.

> **TIP**
>
> Even when creating a header-only Qt-based class, it's better to use Qt Creator's C++ Class template and then remove the auto-created source file, rather than using the C++ Header File template, which does nothing more than creating a file which only contains an `#ifndef` preprocessor directive.

The abstract class definition includes all APIs that we want the derived repository classes to implement:

```cpp
#ifndef GROCERY_ITEMS_REPO_H
#define GROCERY_ITEMS_REPO_H

#include <QObject>
#include <QVariantList>

namespace repositories {
class GroceryItemsRepo : public QObject
{
    Q_OBJECT
protected:
    explicit GroceryItemsRepo(QObject *parent = nullptr) : QObject(parent)
{}
public:
    virtual int count() const = 0;
    virtual void retrieveAllRecords() = 0;
signals:
    void allRecordsRetrieved(QVariantList records);
};
}

#endif // GROCERY_ITEMS_REPO_H
```

The previous code listing should contain no big surprises, provided you already know what a pure virtual function is (if not, check out `https://isocpp.org/wiki/faq/virtual-functions#pure-virtual`); we find a `count` method, a `retrieveAllRecords` method, and an `allRecordsRetrieved` signal with a `QVariantList` payload.

> **TIP**
>
> If you wanted to make it explicit that this class is an abstract interface, you could call it `AbstractGroceryItemsRepo` instead.

Next, we provide the dummy implementation class which extends `GroceryItemsRepo`. We will create a new `QObject`-based class with a header file `grocery_items_repo_dummy.h` and class name `GroceryItemsRepoDummy`. Given it is a simple fake, we keep method implementations in the header file.

First we start with the `count` method. In the fake implementation, we just return a predefined integer value:

```
// grocery_items_repo_dummy.h
...
int count() const { return 3; }
...
```

Then, we return a `QVariantList` of item records when calling `retrieveAllRecords`. We do that by first creating an empty `QVariantList`, and then manually appending three `QVariantMap` structures representing each one a different item, each containing a `name` key-value pair:

```
void retrieveAllRecords() {
    QVariantList recordsArray;
    recordsArray.push_back(QVariantMap{{"name", "bananas"}});
    recordsArray.push_back(QVariantMap{{"name", "apples"}});
    recordsArray.push_back(QVariantMap{{"name", "cheese"}});
    emit allRecordsRetrieved(recordsArray);
}
```

> In this case, we have used `push_back` instead of `append`, which we used in the implementation of `entities::GroceryItems`. Both methods achieve the same result. `push_back` conforms to STL-style naming, in case you ever need it for consistency or habit.

So much for the dummy grocery items repository. Here is the full code:

```
// grocery_items_repo_dummy.h
#ifndef GROCERY_ITEMS_REPO_DUMMY_H
#define GROCERY_ITEMS_REPO_DUMMY_H

#include <QObject>
#include <QVariantList>
#include "grocery_items_repo.h"

namespace repositories {
class GroceryItemsDummy : public GroceryItemsRepo
{
    Q_OBJECT
public:
```

```
    explicit GroceryItemsDummy(QObject *parent = nullptr)
        :GroceryItemsRepo(parent){}
    int count() const { return 3; }
    void retrieveAllRecords() {
        QVariantList recordsArray;
        recordsArray.push_back(QVariantMap{{"name", "bananas"}});
        recordsArray.push_back(QVariantMap{{"name", "apples"}});
        recordsArray.push_back(QVariantMap{{"name", "cheese"}});
        emit allRecordsRetrieved(recordsArray);
    }
};
}

#endif // GROCERY_ITEMS_REPO_DUMMY_H
```

Making the first usecase test pass

We have implemented the usecase CheckAvailableGroceries, together with the
required entity and repository: GroceryItems and GroceryItemsRepoDummy. For
the test_one_or_more_grocery_items_available() test to pass, we need to do one
more thing: import the relevant .pri files in check_available_groceries.pro:

```
# check_available_groceries.pro
...

TARGET = tst_check_available_groceries
CONFIG  += console
CONFIG  -= app_bundle

TEMPLATE = app

include(../../entities/entities.pri)
include(../../repositories/repositories.pri)
include(check_available_groceries.pri)

...
```

And make sure that the relevant headers are imported
into tst_check_available_groceries.cpp:

```
#include "../check_available_groceries.h"
#include "../../entities/grocery_items.h"
#include "../../repositories/grocery_items_dummy.h"
```

That's it. We hit the **Run** button or press *Ctrl + R* (*command + R* on a Mac) and we shall now see the first test pass:

```
********* Start testing of Usecases_check_available_groceries *********
Config: Using QtTest library 5.9.3, Qt 5.9.3 (x86_64-little-endian-lp64
shared (dynamic) release build; by Clang 7.0.2 (clang-700.1.81) (Apple))
PASS : Usecases_check_available_groceries::initTestCase()
PASS :
Usecases_check_available_groceries::test_one_or_more_grocery_items_availabl
e()
PASS : Usecases_check_available_groceries::cleanupTestCase()
Totals: 3 passed, 0 failed, 0 skipped, 0 blacklisted, 4ms
********* Finished testing of Usecases_check_available_groceries *********
```

> **TIP**
>
> If you have build errors or a failing test, make sure you have added all the necessary method implementations and member variables to the classes. If in doubt, as always, check the provided code project.

Using the AutoTest plugin

If you enable Qt Creator's **AutoTest** plugin, you will be able to enjoy a better output for your passing (and failing) tests.

To enable the plugin, click on the **About Plugins...** menu item, search for **AutoTest,** and tick the corresponding checkbox:

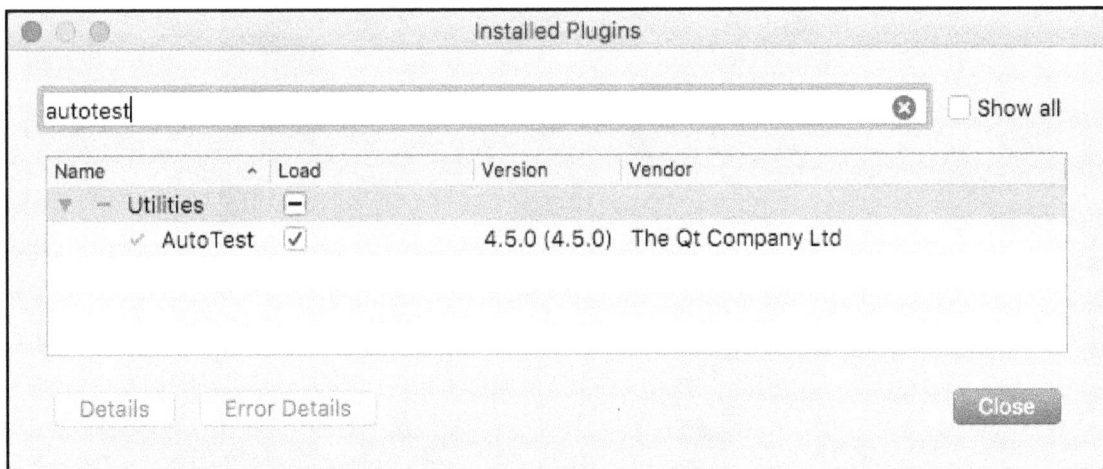

Then, click on the **Split** icon in the **Projects** pane and select the **Tests** menu entry:

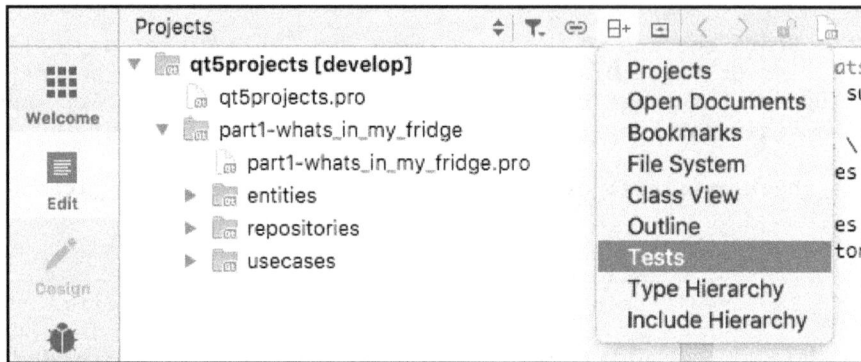

The **Tests** pane will appear underneath **Projects**, showing available test cases grouped by test framework. If you expand the QtTest node, you can check out our implemented test case and test:

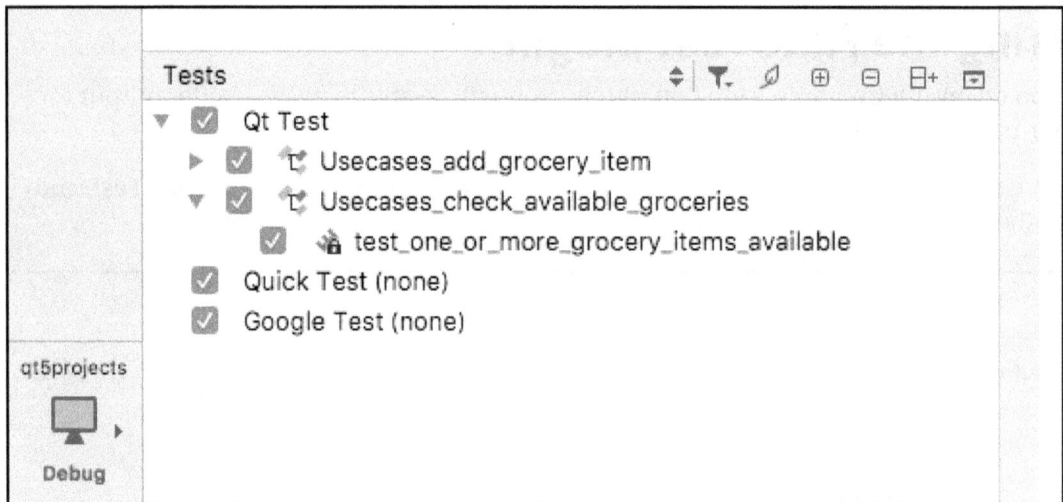

From this interface, when more test cases and tests will be added, you will be able to selectively disable some of them and only run the selected ones.

Tests can be run by switching to Qt Creator's **Test Results** pane and clicking the small green play button:

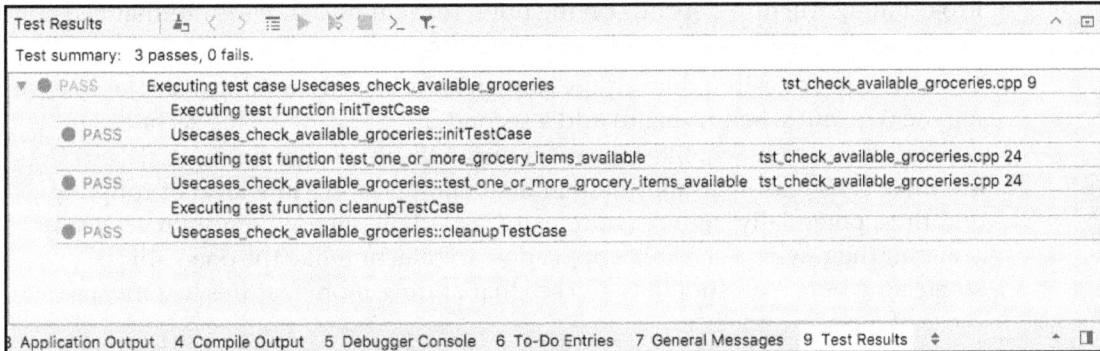

If you want to run only the selected subset of tests, you should use the small green play button with checkboxes, which is located next to it, instead.

> **TIP**
>
> When you have several subprojects and many test cases and tests, being able to selectively run only some of them with **AutoTest** will be a great time saver. Until recently tests were not grouped per subproject, but this feature is now available starting with Qt Creator 4.6.

Wait a second!

I can hear you now. You might be saying: "We have developed all these classes and all this project infrastructure just to get a single printed line on the screen: `PASS : Usecases_check_available_groceries::test_one_or_more_grocery_items_avai lable()`. I could have easily achieved the same results by only writing a single class, maybe two. Also, I thought this was a book about graphical user interfaces!"

If this is your line of reasoning, that's fine, it does makes sense. However, here are a few points you should consider:

- Project infrastructure depends on the build tool, and QMake's is not that bad either–you need a few files, but statements are pretty concise.
- You could have easily achieved the same results by only writing a single class, or maybe two, but when trying to add a second usecase, or even a second scenario, your code will likely grow in unpredictable ways. Qt's signals and slots are there for a reason, as they help in maintaining a very low level of coupling and thus, potentially, reduce complexity, especially when the system grows. If you pair them with a sensible application architecture like the one I am suggesting here, you should easily see that adding more features just means more of the same, mostly.
- By now you should have understood that Qt is not *just* about graphical user interfaces. It is a full-featured general programming framework that just happens to be particularly strong on graphics. This said, you could of course choose to develop some application layers with vanilla C++ or the Standard Library, if you so fancy. That is completely fine, as long as you are ready to deal with a few type conversions, and potentially different memory management strategies.

The interesting thing is, with this approach, we could reap the fruit of our labor (that is, deploy a working application) without the need to attach a graphical UI on top of the business logic. Let's add a simple *textual* user interface instead!

Adding a textual user interface

Dividing an application into clear layers brings a few advantages. One of these is being able to swap user interfaces, another one is being able to swap data repositories. We will now add a textual user interface to run our first usecase. Yes, Qt has got ample provisions also for textual input/output.

Setting up the console application project

We start by creating a new subproject called textual user interface (`tui`). For this subproject, we use Qt Creator's **Qt Console Application** template:

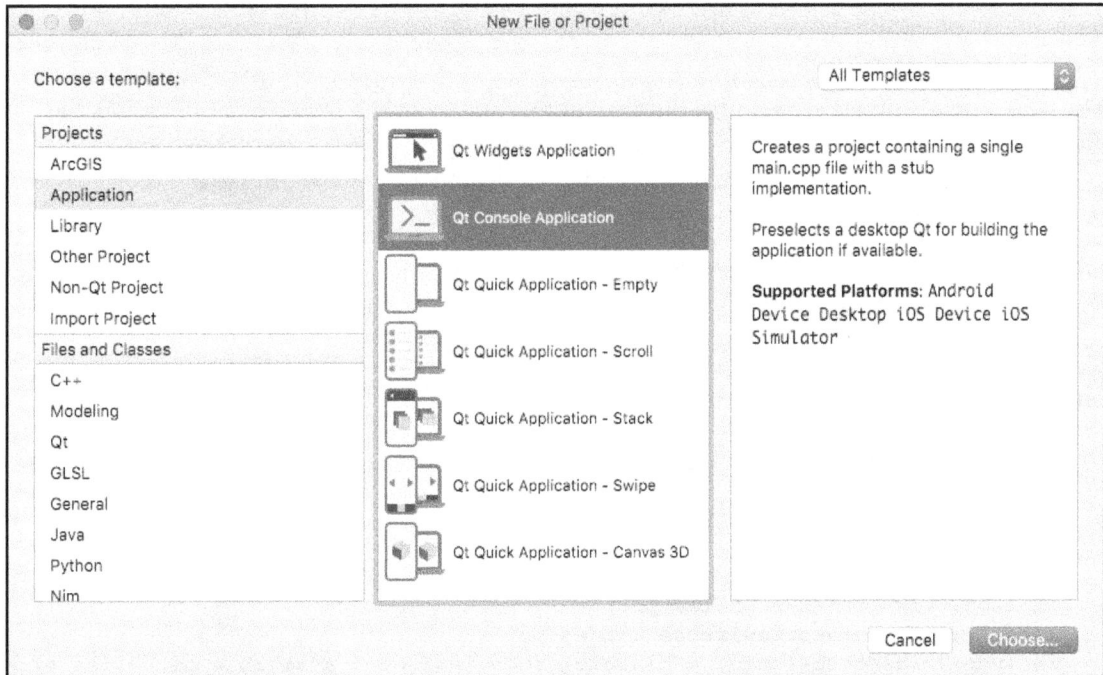

In `part1-whats_in_my_fridge` we should thus get the following project structure:

```
# part1-whats_in_my_fridge.pro
TEMPLATE = subdirs

SUBDIRS +=
    usecases
    entities
    repositories
    #gui
    tui
```

Looking into the `tui` subproject, we will find the `tui.pro` file, and a generated `main.cpp`.

The `.pro` file has got a bunch of qmake directives. Among these, we can see:

```
# tui.pro
QT -= gui
...
CONFIG += console
CONFIG -= app_bundle
...
```

The `QT -= gui` directive excludes the Qt Gui module from the resulting application. Qt Gui provides the basic graphic capabilities and data types to a Qt project (`http://doc.qt.io/qt-5.9/qtgui-module.html`). It is included as a dependency by QMake by default, but it is thus not needed for our console application.

`CONFIG += console` tells qmake that we want to be able to use a console for input-output, so it will be opened automatically for us when we run the program.

`CONFIG -= app_bundle` is macOS-specific, and avoids generating an app bundle, outputting a simple executable instead.

In order to be able to use our newly-created components, we need to include their `.pri` in `tui.pro`:

```
# tui.pro
...
include(../entities/entities.pri)
include(../repositories/repositories.pri)
include(../usecases/check_available_groceries/check_available_groceries.pri
)
...
```

Writing the textual application

Once we are done with project setup, we can turn our attention to `main.cpp`. This minimal, autogenerated file contains the following:

```
#include <QCoreApplication>

int main(int argc, char *argv[])
{
    QCoreApplication a(argc, argv);
    return a.exec();
}
```

There is an `include`, plus a `main` function with two short instructions: the first one creates a `QCoreApplication` instance on the stack, and the second one calls its `exec` method.

QCoreApplication's many responsibilities

`QCoreApplication` (`http://doc.qt.io/qt-5.9/qcoreapplication.html`) is a `QObject`-derived class which is used in non-UI Qt applications to achieve quite a few things:

- It handles the application's event loop, which for non-UI applications is important whenever you need timers for processing, and other kinds of interaction with the operating system, mostly disk or network I/O. The event loop is started by the `exec` function.
- It stores and retrieves any application properties via accessor methods (name, version, organization, organization domain, and so on).
- It provides support for localization by managing installed translation files and providing string translation methods.
- It gives access to application-related executable and library paths.
- It can serve as a parent for `QObject`s, which are usually created on the heap, by providing them with automatic deletion upon application exit.
- It takes command-line arguments as parameters and provides automatic conversion of these into Qt data types for easy manipulation.

> **TIP**
>
> In this simple example, we won't need the event loop, mostly because we stubbed the repository and do not yet use a server connection, which would require asynchronous network I/O.

Creating the business objects

We first remove the `a.exec` call, as we won't need any event loop.

Then, we create the `usecase`, `entity`, and repository, and pass a reference to the application instance `a` as the parent:

```
// tui/main.cpp
...
auto groceryItems = new entities::GroceryItems(&a);
auto groceryItemsRepoDummy = new repositories::GroceryItemsRepoDummy(&a);
```

```
auto checkAvailableGroceries = new
usecases::CheckAvailableGroceries(groceryItems, &a);
...
```

We still need to tell the entity to use the repository as a data source:

```
// tui/main.cpp
...
groceryItems->setRepository(groceryItemsDummyRepo);
...
```

Defining application output upon success

What should happen if, after instructing the application to run the usecase, this ends successfully?

Let's say we want to print the list of grocery items, each item displaying its name. We achieve this by:

1. Creating an object that handles text output
2. Creating a slot that writes the list to the text output
3. Connecting the usecase's success signal to the slot

For the text output object, we use the convenient QTextStream (http://doc.qt.io/qt-5. 9/qtextstream.html) class and connect it with the console's stdout device:

```
// tui/main.cpp
...
QTextStream cout(stdout);
...
```

For the slot, we can make use of a C++11 lambda, which can be defined directly as the third argument to connect:

```
// tui/main.cpp
...
QObject::connect(checkAvailableGroceries,
&usecases::CheckAvailableGroceries::success,
                    [&cout, groceryItems](QString message) {
    cout << message << endl;
    QVariantList::const_iterator i;
    for (auto item : groceryItems->list())
          cout << item.toMap().value("name").toString() << endl;
  });
...
```

There are a few interesting things going on in this snippet. First, as mentioned, we see how to use a lambda instead of an object's slot. Also, we see a static version of `QObject::connect` at work.

Further on, we notice how a `QTextStream` supports the `<<` operator for output concatenation, by providing support for many Qt data types. Here we are printing the `usecase`'s success message:

```
cout << message << endl;
```

Then, we loop through the `QVariantList` with a C++11 range-based `for`.

> Qt containers also support Standard Library-style iterators and Java-style iterators. The choice is up to you. For more information, visit `http://doc.qt.io/qt-5.9/containers.html`.

We finally print the value of each grocery item's name field:

```
cout << item.toMap().value("name").toString() << endl;
```

Collecting and acting upon user input

After having defined what happens upon `usecase` success, we need to handle user input.

We want the user to type in an action name (`check available groceries`). If the name is correct, we trigger the `usecase` and exit; otherwise, we print an `Action not supported` message and exit.

We first display the action prompt to the user:

```
(cout << "Enter action: ").flush();
```

> The `flush` method displays the text without the need to append an `endl`.

We then create another `QTextStream` and bind it to `stdin`:

```
QTextStream cin(stdin);
```

Further, we wait for user input and save it to a `QString` called `action`:

```
QString action(cin.readLine());
```

The `readLine` is triggered as soon as the user presses the **Return** key.

Finally, check the string, and trigger the `usecase` if the string corresponds to `check available groceries`:

```
if (action == "check available groceries") {
        checkAvailableGroceries->run(groceryItems);
        a.exit(0);
    } else {
        cout << "Action not supported" << endl;
        a.exit(1);
    }
```

> **TIP**
> For command-line arguments, check out the `QCommandLineParser` class: `http://doc.qt.io/qt-5.9/qcommandlineparser.html`

That's it. Here is the whole console application:

```
// tui/main.cpp
#include <QCoreApplication>
#include <QTextStream>

#include "../entities/grocery_items.h"
#include "../repositories/grocery_items_repo_dummy.h"
#include
"../usecases/check_available_groceries/check_available_groceries.h"

int main(int argc, char *argv[])
{
    QCoreApplication a(argc, argv);

    auto groceryItems = new entities::GroceryItems(&a);
    auto groceryItemsRepoDummy = new
repositories::GroceryItemsRepoDummy(&a);
    auto checkAvailableGroceries = new
usecases::CheckAvailableGroceries(groceryItems, &a);

    groceryItems->setRepository(groceryItemsRepoDummy);

    QTextStream cout(stdout);
```

```
    QObject::connect(checkAvailableGroceries,
&usecases::CheckAvailableGroceries::success,
                    [&cout, groceryItems](QString message) {
        cout << message << endl;
        for (auto item : groceryItems->list())
            cout << item.toMap().value("name").toString() << endl;
    });

    (cout << "Enter action: ").flush();

    QTextStream cin(stdin);
    QString action(cin.readLine());

    if (action == "check available groceries") {
        checkAvailableGroceries->run();
        a.exit(0);
    } else {
        cout << "Action not supported" << endl;
        a.exit(1);
    }
}
```

Running the console app

To run the application, you first need to make sure that the `tui` subproject is Qt Creator's current target:

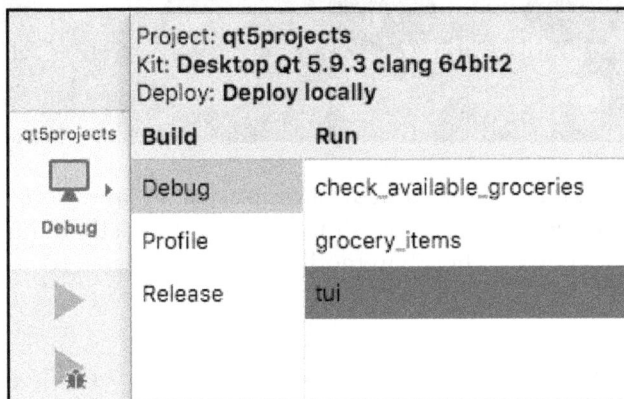

Project: qt5projects Kit: **Desktop Qt 5.9.3 clang 64bit2** Deploy: **Deploy locally**		
qt5projects	**Build**	**Run**
	Debug	check_available_groceries
Debug	Profile	grocery_items
	Release	tui

Then, you can press the big green play button and, if all goes well, a console should show up prompting you for input:

If the string you entered matches the predefined one, you'll see the following output:

In terms of functionality, it is a pretty dull application, but by now you should grasp that adding functionality to it should be pretty straightforward, mostly requiring you to just add new classes and methods, rather than modify existing ones.

About unit testing

If you still think that we have written a whole lot of code for such a simple app, let me reveal to you a little secret: *we have taken a lot of shortcuts.*

Yes! In fact, we have limited our testing to `usecases` (functional tests), yet we should have written unit tests for the single business objects, by writing dedicated test harnesses for the `entities` project (and also for `repositories`, as soon as we add a real data backend), to make sure that each component behaves well in isolation. This is left as an exercise for you. Just follow what we have done for the `usecases` (and read the docs!).

Also, we have avoided handling all cases where things could go wrong (for example, in fetching data). We will look into some of these in the next chapter. But you can work on it now on your own, if you so will.

Summary

In this chapter, we have created a full (yet limited in terms of functionality) application core by combining together a `usecase`, a business object or entity, and a fake data repository. To achieve these results, we have taken advantage of many Qt data structures and idioms along the way: signals and slots, `QObject`, `QString`, `QVariant`, `QList`, and `QMap`, just to name the most relevant ones.

Further on, we have developed a very rudimentary textual interface to provide a delivery mechanism to our app. By doing so, we have explored some of the properties of `QCoreApplication` and `QTextStream`.

Your patience will be rewarded in the next chapter, where we will be doing something more exciting by adding a nice UI to our application core, and implementing the two remaining `usecases` (add and remove grocery items) to make the application useful in the real world. Ahead!

25
Wiring User Interaction and Delivering the Final App

In this chapter, we will sketch the implementation of the two remaining usecases of Chapter 23, *Writing Acceptance Tests and Building a Visual Prototype*, so that the app reaches the minimal set of functionalities that will make it (almost) useful in the real world.

Further on, we will add the already-designed **Qt Quick UI** on top of the use case logic implemented in the previous chapter, and show how easy it is to mount this (or any other) UI layer without altering the underlying logic at all.

Finally, we will discuss some guidelines about platform-specific resources and workflows to deploy the app to a few different desktop (Windows and macOS) and mobile (Android and iOS) platforms.

Completing the app's core functionality

In the last chapter, we implemented the main scenario for a single feature: check available groceries. In order to have an app with minimal functionality, at least two other features, and the respective usecases need to be added: add grocery item and remove grocery item.

From an architecture perspective, adding these usecases is pretty straightforward; there are no new business objects (entities) involved; we just need to manipulate the GroceryItems entity by extending its API with the relevant methods, and implement them.

To add each new use case, we add a **New Subproject...** to the `usecases` project, with Qt Creator's **Qt Unit Test** template:

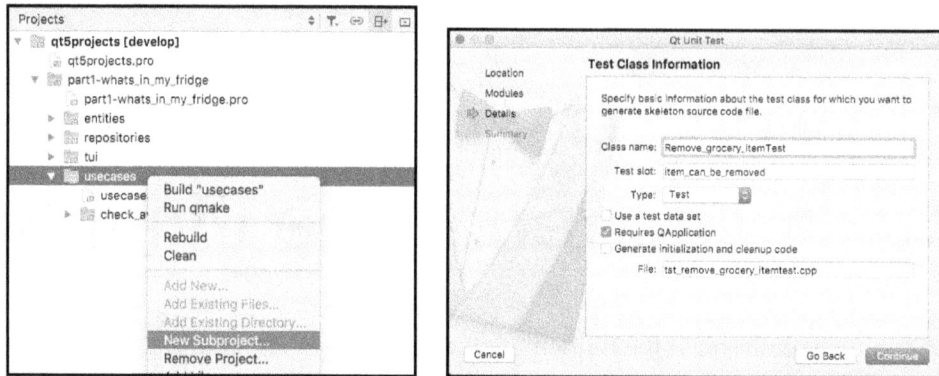

Once the stub source file for the use case test has been created, we modify the first test slot by adding the steps we are going to implement. We have outlined these steps already in `Chapter 23`, *Writing Acceptance Tests and Building a Visual Prototype*, as a premise to building the visual prototype. Here is an example for `add grocery item`:

```cpp
// tst_add_grocery_item.cpp
#include <QString>
#include <QtTest>

class Usecases_add_grocery_item : public QObject
{
    Q_OBJECT

public:
    Usecases_add_grocery_item();

private Q_SLOTS:
    void item_can_be_added();
};

Usecases_add_grocery_item::Usecases_add_grocery_item()
{
}

void Usecases_add_grocery_item::item_can_be_added()
{
    // Given I am given a list of available groceries
    QFAIL("not implemented");
    // When I add a grocery item with name X
```

```
    QFAIL("not implemented");
    // Then the grocery item with name X is contained in the list
    QFAIL("not implemented");
    // And the groceries are ordered by name, ascending
    QFAIL("not implemented");
}

QTEST_MAIN(Usecases_add_grocery_item)

#include "tst_add_grocery_item.moc"
```

Adding a grocery item

Let's now briefly go through the outlined steps for add grocery item to see what implications there are for our APIs.

Defining the precondition step

This is nothing less than the outcome of our first use case, checkAvailableGroceries. We will thus run that use case as a precondition for this one, and just check that the run is successful, as follows:

```
...
void Usecases_add_grocery_item::test_item_can_be_added()
{
    // Given I am given a list of available groceries
    auto checkAvailableGroceries = new
usecases::CheckAvailableGroceries(groceryItems, this);
    QSignalSpy checkAvailableGroceriesSuccess(checkAvailableGroceries,
&usecases::CheckAvailableGroceries::success);
    checkAvailableGroceries->run();
    QTRY_COMPARE_WITH_TIMEOUT(checkAvailableGroceriesSuccess.count(), 1,
1000);
    delete checkAvailableGroceries;
    ...
}
```

Before doing that, though, we need to create the business object and repository. Since these might be needed in more than one scenario test, we can make use of two special methods provided by the QtTest framework, init() and cleanup(), which are automatically run on each test execution.

Test init and cleanup

The QtTest framework provides special functionality, according to which, if two slots called init and cleanup are added to the test case class, they are invoked automatically, respectively, before and after every test method of the test case class.

For example, if we want to create an instance of the GroceryItems entity before each test and make sure it is destroyed after the test has finished, we can do the following:

```cpp
// tst_add_grocery_item.cpp
...
class Usecases_add_grocery_item : public QObject
{
...

private Q_SLOTS:
    void init();
    void cleanup();
private:
    entities::GroceryItems* m_groceryItems;
...

void Usecases_add_grocery_item::init()
{
    qDebug() &lt;&lt; "init";
    m_groceryItems = new entities::GroceryItems(this);
    auto groceryItemsRepoDummy = new
repositories::GroceryItemsRepoDummy(groceryItems);
    m_groceryItems->setRepository(groceryItemsRepoDummy);
}

void Usecases_add_grocery_item::cleanup()
{
    qDebug() &lt;&lt; "cleanup";
    delete m_groceryItems;
}
```

The `qDebug()` macro is a construct that you will find quite often in Qt code. By default, it prints a debug message to the standard output and, as you can see from the preceding code, supports the streaming operators and several C++ and Qt data types. If it is not available, it can be imported with `#include &lt;QDebug>`.

The two methods will be called before and after
`Usecases_add_grocery_item::test_item_can_be_added()` (and any other test method we decide to add later), respectively.

Similarly, a `QtTest` harness can automatically invoke the `initTestCase()` and `cleanupTestCase()` methods, the former once after the test case class has been created, and the latter before it is destroyed, thus once per test case. You just need to add slot declarations and implementations as we have done previously for `init()` and `cleanup()`.

Defining the usecase action step

This step will implement the call to the use case. Following what was done for `CheckAvailableItems`, we could call a `run` method by passing in any other necessary argument. In this case, we need to specify the name of the grocery item, as that will be the attribute which is unique for every grocery item. Thus, a possible API for this step could look like this:

```
usecases::AddGroceryItem::run(const QString& name)
```

And here is a test call:

```
...
void Usecases_add_grocery_item::test_item_can_be_added()
{
    ...
    // When I add a grocery item with name X
    auto addGroceryItem = new usecases::AddGroceryItem(m_groceryItems,
this);
    QSignalSpy addGroceryItemSuccess(addGroceryItem,
&usecases::AddGroceryItem::success);
    addGroceryItem->run("avocados");
    QTRY_COMPARE_WITH_TIMEOUT(addGroceryItemSuccess.count(), 1, 1000);
    delete addGroceryItem;
```

```
    ...
}
...
```

Defining the first outcome step

In this step, we need to check that the `entities::GroceryItems` list actually contains an item with the name "X", that is, the name that was passed as an argument to the use case in the previous step. To implement this step, we can just add a simple wrapper method to `entities::GroceryItems`, which calls into the list's available search mechanisms (for example, `QList`'s `contains` or `indexOf`). We can call such a method, `contains`:

```
...
void Usecases_add_grocery_item::test_item_can_be_added()
{
    ...
    // Then the grocery item with name X is contained in the list
    QVERIFY(m_groceryItems->contains("name", "avocados"));
    ...
}
...
```

Defining the second outcome step

This step requires calling into the already implemented method, `isSortedBy(const QString& field, const QString& direction) const`:

```
...
void Usecases_add_grocery_item::test_item_can_be_added()
{
    ...
    // And the groceries are ordered by name, ascending
    QVERIFY(m_groceryItems->isSortedBy("name", "ASC"));
}
...
```

> As already mentioned, you might prefer to test the sorting by writing an external utility function that works on the list, rather than calling the `isSortedBy` method.

use case implementation

Going through the preceding use case steps should provide us with enough hints about the course of the use case and entity implementations, including:

- Adding an item to the list by its name
- Allowing us to check whether it is in the list or not
- Allowing us to check the list is still ordered alphabetically by name

To achieve this, we first need to implement the API for `usecases::AddGroceryItem`, and then extend `entities::GroceryItems`.

The use case's structure will be very similar to that of `usecases::CheckAvailableGroceries`:

```cpp
// add_grocery_item.h
#ifndef ADD_GROCERY_ITEM_H
#define ADD_GROCERY_ITEM_H

#include <QObject>

namespace entities {
    class GroceryItems;
}
namespace usecases {
class AddGroceryItem : public QObject
{
    Q_OBJECT
public:
    explicit AddGroceryItem(entities::GroceryItems* groceryItems, QObject
*parent = nullptr);
    void run(const QString& type);

signals:
    void failure(QString message);
    void success(QString message);

private slots:
    void onGroceryItemCreated();
    void onGroceryItemNotCreated();

private:
    entities::GroceryItems* m_groceryItems;
```

```
};
}


#endif // ADD_GROCERY_ITEM_H
```

The constructor passes a pointer to the `groceryItems` entity and connects the relevant signals, while the `run` method triggers the creation of a new entry in `groceryItems`:

```cpp
// add_grocery_item.cpp
#include "add_grocery_item.h"
#include "../entities/grocery_items.h"

namespace usecases {

AddGroceryItem::AddGroceryItem(entities::GroceryItems *groceryItems,
QObject *parent)
    : QObject(parent),
      m_groceryItems(groceryItems)
{
    connect(m_groceryItems, &entities::GroceryItems::created,
            this, &AddGroceryItem::onGroceryItemCreated);
    connect(m_groceryItems , &entities::GroceryItems::notCreated,
            this, &AddGroceryItem::onGroceryItemNotCreated);
}

void AddGroceryItem::run(const QString& name)
{
    m_groceryItems->create(name);
}
```

Once the entry has been created (we'll see how in a bit), the use case signals a success; otherwise, it signals a failure:

```cpp
// add_grocery_item.cpp
...
void AddGroceryItem::onGroceryItemCreated() {
    emit success("ADD_GROCERY_ITEM__SUCCESS");
}

void AddGroceryItem::onGroceryItemNotCreated() {
    emit failure("ADD_GROCERY_ITEM__FAILURE");
}
```

Again, this use case is fairly simple. Had more entities been involved in it besides `GroceryItems`, the `create` entity action would have been followed by some other actions before declaring the use case as successfully complete.

Implementing the GroceryItems entity

The `create` method of `entity::GroceryItems` must ensure that:

- The new item is added to the list
- The list is sorted

> In a real setting, the creation should also trigger that the new item is persisted as a record in whatever data repository happens to be in use and, possibly, that the data is fetched again from the repository to make sure synchronization has happened. For the time being, we will focus on the item addition and list sorting steps.

Having already implemented the `sortBy` method, to implement the `create` method, we can just flag `isSortedByNameAsc` as `false`, add a new record to the list, and resort the list:

```cpp
// grocery_items.cpp
...
void GroceryItems::create(const QString& name)
{
    isSortedByNameAsc = false;
    m_list.append(QVariantMap{{"name", name}});
    sortBy("name","ASC");
    emit listChanged();
    emit created("ENTITIES_GROCERY_ITEMS__CREATED");
}
...
```

After this is done, we will emit two new signals, `listChanged()` and `created(QString)` (make sure you add them to the class definition first). We will learn more about `listChanged` in the *Exposing groceryItems' list to QML* section. The `created` signal is there to inform the use case that the creation step is complete.

Finally, we add the implementation for `contains`:

```
// grocery_items.cpp
...
bool GroceryItems::contains(const QString &field, const QString &value)
const
{
    return m_list.contains(QVariantMap{{field, value}});
}
...
```

> **TIP**
>
> The implementation of `m_list.contains` will only work if the `QVariantMap` is only made of a single field-value map. When adding other fields to the map, you will have to come up with a more elaborate solution.

After having extended the `GroceryItems` entity this way, our second `usecase` should pass.

Removing a grocery item

The `RemoveGroceryItem` use case is pretty simple too — we mostly need to remove an item from the `entities::GroceryItems` list, and check that the item isn't there anymore (leaving aside, again, data persistence considerations).

We give here a possible API, leaving the implementation to the reader:

```
void Usecases_remove_grocery_item::item_can_be_removed()
{
    // Given I am given a list of available groceries
    auto checkAvailableGroceries = new
usecases::CheckAvailableGroceries(groceryItems, this);
    QSignalSpy checkAvailableGroceriesSuccess(checkAvailableGroceries,
&usecases::CheckAvailableGroceries::success);
    checkAvailableGroceries->run();
    QTRY_COMPARE_WITH_TIMEOUT(checkAvailableGroceriesSuccess.count(), 1,
1000);
    delete checkAvailableGroceries;
    // And the grocery item of name X is contained in the list
    QVERIFY(m_groceryItems->contains("name","bananas"));
    // When I remove the grocery item with name X
    auto removeGroceryItem = new
usecases::RemoveGroceryItem(m_groceryItems, this);
    QSignalSpy removeGroceryItemSuccess(removeGroceryItem,
&usecases::RemoveGroceryItem::success);
```

```
removeGroceryItem->run(m_groceryItems, "bananas");
QTRY_COMPARE_WITH_TIMEOUT(removeGroceryItemSuccess.count(), 1, 1000);
delete removeGroceryItem;
// Then the grocery item with name X is not contained in the list
QVERIFY(! m_groceryItems->contains("name","bananas"));
// And the groceries are ordered by type, ascending
QVERIFY(m_groceryItems->isSortedBy("name", "ASC"));
}
```

Adding a fridge

To truly understand the usefulness of separating usecases from entities, we might also want to add another entity, the *fridge*. In usecases like add/remove grocery item, we could change the fridge's status (empty/non-empty) whenever an item is added/removed. To achieve this, we will add entities::Fridge to our system, and call the update of its isEmpty method when a grocery item has been added/removed, and before returning the success/failure of the respective use case.

> Try adding entities::Fridge as described, and augment usecases::AddGroceryItem and usecases::RemoveGroceryItem accordingly. In the use case tests, you will likely need to add a few scenarios to take into consideration what happens to the fridge (and the groceries list) when no items are in the list, as opposed to when one or more items are in it (for example, try adding the test method Usecases_check_available_groceries::test_no_grocery_items _available).

Connecting visual input/output and usecases

Now that we have a minimal set of testable use case scenarios which give us the basic functionality that we need, we can wire these to the UI prototype developed in Chapter 23, *Writing Acceptance Tests and Building a Visual Prototype*.

The QMake project structure that we have devised helps us keep the layers clearly separated, thus preventing strong coupling between the UI and the logic layers.

Setting up the client application

In Chapter 23, *Writing Acceptance Tests and Building a Visual Prototype*, we chose to provide our client application with a Qt Quick UI and created a prototype, UI-only, runnable application with the help of Qt Creator's Quick Designer. We will now get back to that project and write the little glue code we need to connect the UI to the business logic, similar to what we did in Chapter 24, *Defining a Solid and Testable App Core*, for the Textual User Interface.

As a first step, we need to re-enable the gui subproject by removing the # symbol, if necessary:

```
part1-whats_in_my_fridge.pro                                    ⇕  ✕                              Line: 6, Col: 11      ⊟⁺
1  # part1-whats_in_my_fridge.pro
2  TEMPLATE = subdirs
3
4  SUBDIRS += \
5      usecases \
6  #    gui \
7      entities \
8      repositories \
9      tui
```

> **TIP**
>
> In what follows, we will write the glue code to create a Qt Quick UI-based client within the gui subproject, to keep project complexity at bay. In a real-world project, I would usually keep the gui subproject for UI components only, and create a separate application project for the client. From the client project, I would then import usecases, entities, repositories, and also UI components.

Then, in gui.pro, we import all the logic layers:

```
# gui.pro
...
include(../entities/entities.pri)
include(../repositories/repositories.pri)
include(../usecases/check_available_groceries/check_available_groceries.pri
)
include(../usecases/add_grocery_item/add_grocery_item.pri)
...
```

Finally, in gui/main.cpp, we create our logic components, pretty much as we did for the TUI in Chapter 24, *Defining a Solid and Testable App Core*:

```
// gui/main.cpp
#include <QGuiApplication>
#include <QQmlApplicationEngine>
```

```
#include "../entities/grocery_items.h"
#include
"../usecases/check_available_groceries/check_available_groceries.h"
#include "../usecases/add_grocery_item/add_grocery_item.h"
#include "../repositories/grocery_items_repo_dummy.h"

int main(int argc, char *argv[])
{
    QCoreApplication::setAttribute(Qt::AA_EnableHighDpiScaling);
    QGuiApplication app(argc, argv);

    auto groceryItems = new entities::GroceryItems(&app);
    auto groceryItemsRepoDummy = new repositories::GroceryItemsDummy(&app);
    groceryItems->setRepository(groceryItemsRepoDummy);
    auto checkAvailableGroceries = new
usecases::CheckAvailableGroceries(groceryItems, &app);
    auto addGroceryItem = new usecases::AddGroceryItem(groceryItems, &app);

    QQmlApplicationEngine engine;
    engine.load(QUrl(QLatin1String("qrc:/main.qml")));
    if (engine.rootObjects().isEmpty())
        return -1;

    return app.exec();
}
```

Finally, we need to expose the logic layers to QML so that usecases can be triggered by UI actions, and the outcomes displayed back in the UI.

Exposing C++ objects to QML

There are two main paths to expose C++ code to QML: we can either expose already instantiated C++ objects to a QML engine's context or, alternatively, register C++ classes as QML types, and then create object instances on the QML side.

Each of the two techniques has got its advantages and usage scenarios. Broadly speaking, we'd want to pass C++ object instances to QML if we wanted some C++ application layer to be in control of the object's lifetime; conversely, we would wrap a C++ class as a QML type if we wanted some QML layer run by the QML/JS engine to be in charge of the object's lifetime.

> Despite the general rules outlined earlier, it is still possible to set the ownership of an object's lifetime (C++ vs. QML/JS) explicitly. For more information, visit: `http://doc.qt.io/qt-5.9/qqmlengine.html#setObjectOwnership`.

For our fridge inventory application, as we have developed all our logic layers in C++, we will use the first technique. We'll see examples of the second in later projects.

QML engines and contexts

Any QML component requires an environment where it should be instantiated. Such an environment is the sum of a `QQmlContext` (`http://doc.qt.io/qt-5.9/qqmlcontext.html`), which is responsible for exposing data to the QML component, and a `QQmlEngine` (`http://doc.qt.io/qt-5.9/qqmlengine.html`), which is responsible for instantiating the component and managing a hierarchy of `QQmlContexts`. The `QQmlContext` manages property bindings and contextual properties like the C++ object instances we want to expose to the QML UI.

Looking at GUI's `main.cpp`, you'll see that Qt Creator's application template created these two lines of code for us:

```
QQmlApplicationEngine engine;
engine.load(QUrl(QLatin1String("qrc:/main.qml")));
```

In the first line, a `QQmlApplicationEngine` is created, and in the second line, a QML document (`main.qml`) is loaded into it, and a QML component hierarchy is created. The `QQmlApplicationEngine` is a specialization of `QQmlEngine` which offers a few additional features commonly used in Qt QML applications (`http://doc.qt.io/qt-5.9/qqmlapplicationengine.html`), such as multi-language support.

Exposing object instances via context properties

By default, a QML engine automatically provides a root context, which can be accessed by calling the engine's `rootContext()` method. To expose our business objects to QML, we can thus get this default context and set a property onto the context for each object via the context's `setContextProperty` method:

```
// gui/main.cpp
...
#include &lt;QQmlContext>
...

QQmlApplicationEngine engine;

engine.rootContext()->setContextProperty("groceryItems", groceryItems);
engine.rootContext()->setContextProperty("checkAvailableGroceries",
checkAvailableGroceries);
engine.rootContext()->setContextProperty("addGroceryItem", addGroceryItem);
...
```

> The name of the context property (the first argument to `setContextProperty`) is arbitrary. We have chosen to keep it the same as the one of the variable associated to the object's pointer as there was no specific reason to do otherwise. An alternative could be to prefix the property names with their logic layer (for example, `entities_groceryItems`)

Once this is done, the context property names will be available in `main.qml` along with all its child QML items, and they will refer to our C++ object instances. This means the context property will be globally accessible from anywhere in the QML tree.

Triggering usecases from the UI

Moving to the UI code, we would want the `usecases` to be triggered when specific user-generated or system-generated events happen. Specifically, in the following UI, we would like to:

- Trigger `usecases::CheckAvailableGroceries::run` as soon as the page which displays the list of grocery items appears, so that we see a full list instead of an empty one
- Trigger `usecases::AddGroceryItem::run` whenever the user enters an item type in the text field and presses the **Add item** button

- Trigger `usecases::RemoveGroceryItem::run` whenever the user presses the **X** button next to a list entry:

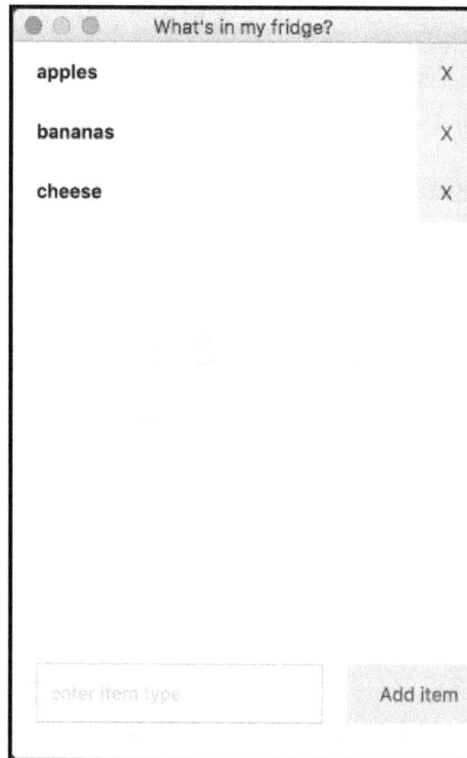

We have already exposed the use case instances from C++ to QML, so we could think that just invoking something like `checkAvailableGroceries.run()` somewhere in one of the QML documents would be enough. So let's try, and see what happens.

Triggering usecases::CheckAvailabeGroceries::run

We have seen briefly in Chapter 23, *Writing Acceptance Tests and Building a Visual Prototype*, that `Component.onCompleted` is a built-in signal handler, which is called as soon as the instantiation of a QML object is completed. Thus, it looks like a good entry point in order to trigger `checkAvailableGroceries.run()`.

In the `gui` subproject, we then open `Page1.qml` which was automatically created by Qt Creator's project template with the following content:

```
// Page1.qml
import Qt Quick 2.7

Page1Form {
}
```

The root component of this document is a QML object of type `Page1Form`. And `Page1Form.ui.qml` is nothing but the QML UI document that we prototyped in Qt Quick Designer. `Page1.qml` represents the application layer where our business logic and UI get in contact. It represents what in some architectural models is known as a *view controller*. Let's add the following line to it:

```
// Page1.qml
import Qt Quick 2.7

Page1Form {
    Component.onCompleted: checkAvailableGroceries.run()
}
```

With this statement, we are saying: as soon as `Page1`, which is a component of type `Page1Form`, is instantiated, trigger the method `run` from the use case object `checkAvailableProperties`.

If we now selected the **gui** subproject as the active run configuration in Qt Creator's lower left corner, and pressed the big green play button to run the project, we would encounter the following error:

```
TypeError: Property 'run' of object
usecases::CheckAvailableGroceries(0x7fd119d09300) is not a function
```

The error is due to the fact that it is not enough to expose a C++ object via a context property for its methods to be invoked from QML; we also need to mark all methods that we intend to invoke with the `Q_INVOKABLE` macro (http://doc.qt.io/qt-5.9/qobject.html#Q_INVOKABLE). This macro registers the method with Qt's Meta-Object system.

Let's then open `check_available_groceries.h` and modify it as follows:

```
// check_available_groceries.h
...
class CheckAvailableGroceries : public QObject
{
    Q_OBJECT
public:
```

```
        explicit CheckAvailableGroceries(entities::GroceryItems* groceryItems,
    QObject *parent = nullptr);
        Q_INVOKABLE void run();
    ...
```

By running the `gui` subproject again, the previous error notice should now disappear.

Triggering usecases::AddGroceryItem::run

The use case add grocery item should be triggered when the **Add item** button is pressed or clicked. We thus need a signal and a signal handler for a button press event. By looking at the documentation for the Qt Quick Controls 2 `Button` (`https://doc.qt.io/qt-5.9/qml-qtquick-controls2-button.html`), we discover that it provides a `clicked` signal, with the respective `onClicked` signal handler.

But how can we get hold of the button element in `Page1`? The **Add item** button is a child of `Page1Form`, and as such it cannot be referenced directly from outside `Page1Form`; that is, the button is not part of `Page1Form`'s API. For cases like this, QML provides *property aliases* (`http://doc.qt.io/qt-5/qtqml-syntax-objectattributes.html#property-aliases`).

A property alias is a reference to an object, or an object's property. The target of the referencing should be specified in the same instruction where the property alias is defined. In our present case, we shall do two things:

1. Provide the **Add item** button with an `id`, so that we can reference it from within `Page1Form`.
2. Create a property alias in `Page1Form`'s root `Item` to expose the button to the outside world.

To specify the `id` property for the button, we open `Page1Form` in Qt Creator's **Design** mode, and from the **Text Editor** pane (consult `Chapter 23`, *Writing Acceptance Tests and Building*, a Visual Prototype to be reminded on how to activate it), we add the following line to it (it's the last `Button` occurrence in the page, the one within the `Row`):

```
// Page1Form.ui.qml
...
TextField {
    id: textField
    placeholderText: "enter item type"
}

Button {
```

```
    id: addItemButton
    text: qsTr("Add item")
}
...
```

Then, still in `Page1Form`, we add the alias to the button in the root `Item`:

```
// Page1Form.ui.qml
import Qt Quick 2.9
import Qt Quick.Controls 2.2
import Qt Quick.Layouts 1.3

Item {
    id: item1
    property alias addItemButton: addItemButton
...
```

> Both operations (adding the `id` and adding the `alias`) can be also performed from Designer's **Form Editor**, rather than from its **Text Editor**. The `id` can be easily added from the **Properties** pane on the screen's right-hand side, while the alias is a bit trickier to spot: it can be toggled from the **Navigator** pane on the left-hand side.

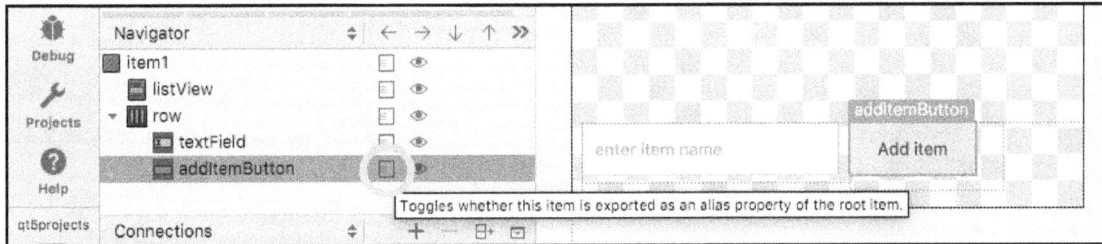

Having exposed `addItemButton` through the alias, we can now reference its `onClicked` handler in `Page1`:

```
// Page1.qml
import Qt Quick 2.7

Page1Form {
    addItemButton.onClicked: console.log("add item")
    Component.onCompleted: checkAvailableGroceries.run()
}
```

For the add grocery item use case to be performed from the UI, we still need to collect the input text from the user. QML properties come to the rescue: by looking at `TextField`'s documentation (`http://doc.qt.io/qt-5.9/qml-qtquick-controls-textfield.html`), we notice that user input is available in the `text` property. Hence, we will just have to pass the contents of `text` to the use case `run` function.

We first add an `id` and another `alias` for the text field in `Page1Form`:

```
// Page1Form.ui.qml
...
Item {
    id: item1
    property alias listView: listView
    property alias addItemField: addItemField
    ...
    TextField {
        id: addItemField
        placeholderText: "enter item name"
    }
...
```

Now that `addItemField` is accessible from the outside, we can access its text property from `Page1`:

```
// Page1.qml
...
Page1Form {
    addItemButton.onClicked: addGroceryItem.run(addItemField.text)
    Component.onCompleted: checkAvailableGroceries.run()
}
```

> We could have exposed the `TextField`'s `text` property directly as well:
>
> ```
> property alias addItemFieldText: addItemField.text.
> ```
>
> Such an approach would create a deeper coupling between `Page1Form` and `TextField`, but also more encapsulation. This kind of choice ultimately boils down to the degree of modularity that is needed for your UI.

Triggering usecases::RemoveGroceryItem::run

To enable the `remove grocery item` use case in the UI, we cannot proceed as we have done for `add grocery item`, which is by creating an alias for the remove item (X) button: there are many such buttons, and their number is not known in advance and varies — thus we cannot assign an `id` to each of them and expose it as an alias. We will have to resort to a proxy object which, whenever an X button is clicked, emits a custom signal with a type argument. By listening to this second signal, we will then trigger the use case.

As the list delegate is an integral part of `ListView`, we will add the custom signal to the `ListView`, and expose `ListView` via an alias:

```
// Page1Form.ui.qml
...
Item {
    id: item1
    property alias groceriesListView: groceriesListView
...
    ListView {
        id: groceriesListView

        signal itemRemoved(string itemName)
...
```

Finally, we will trigger the `itemRemoved` signal whenever the "X" button is clicked. We can do this in the Designer with a `Connections` object:

```
// Page1Form.ui.qml
...
delegate: ItemDelegate {
            width: parent.width
            text: modelData.name || model.name
            font.bold: true
            Button {
                id: removeItemButton
                width: height
                height: parent.height
                text: "X"
                anchors.right: parent.right
                Connections {
                    target: removeItemButton
                    onClicked: groceriesListView.itemRemoved(modelData.name
|| model.name)
```

```
                    }
                }
            }
    . . .
```

> **TIP**
>
> While the Designer has a UI pane called **Connections** to add the preceding code, the created snippet is placed by the Designer under the root `Item` object (at the end of the QML document) rather than in the `Button`. This will generate an error when you run the program, since the `Button` is part of a delegate which does not exist yet when the signal connection is established. Thus, it is better to add the snippet manually in the Designer's **Text Editor**.

Finally, the remove grocery item use case (provided you implemented it as required!) can be triggered by adding the following to `Page1`:

```
// Page1.qml
...
Page1Form {
    addItemButton.onClicked: addGroceryItem.run(addItemField.text)
    groceriesListView.onItemRemoved: removeGroceryItem.run(itemName)
    Component.onCompleted: checkAvailableGroceries.run()
}
```

Here we go! All `usecases` have been wired to the UI. Moreover, the wiring has been delegated to a single QML document, `Page1.qml`, which gives us a clear and synthetic overview of all the `usecases` that can be triggered from that page.

Showing usecase outcomes in the UI

There is still one bit missing before we can appreciate the fruit of our labor: how shall we display the outcomes of our `usecases`? We know that the only entity involved so far is `GroceryItems`, which wraps a list. We exposed this entity from C++ to QML via a context property as `groceryItems`. We now want to use this list as the data model for `groceriesListView`. Then, if all goes well, running our use cases will produce changes in `groceriesListView`: and its items will be listed (use case `CheckAvailableGroceries`), added (use case `AddGroceryItem`), or removed (use case `RemoveGroceryItem`).

Displaying the contents of the `groceryItems` list in `groceriesListView` requires two steps:

1. Exposing the list to QML.
2. Binding `groceriesListView`'s `model` property to the exposed list.

Exposing the groceryItems list to QML

We have already exposed the `GroceryItems` entity from C++ to QML via the `groceryItems` context property. However, if we want to get access from QML to the `GroceryItem` list and take advantage of the power of property bindings, so that the UI updates automatically whenever the list changes, we need to expose the list as a property of `GroceryItems`. For this to happen, we get back to `grocery_items.h` and add the property, as follows:

```
...
class GroceryItems : public QObject
{
    Q_OBJECT
    Q_PROPERTY(QVariantList list READ list NOTIFY listChanged)
```

With this macro, we are creating a property called `list` of type `QVariantList`. This property makes use of the following methods and signals when we `read` the property; we are in fact calling the `list()` method, and expect to get a `QVariantList`. When the `listChanged()` signal is emitted, the property notifies whoever is bound to the signal that the list has changed. We could also expose *writable* properties, which will require us to define what method needs to be called upon by property assignment. For more details about this macro, visit the already mentioned: `http://doc.qt.io/qt-5.9/properties.html`.

Now that we have exposed the list as a property, we will be able to refer to it from QML as `groceryItems.list`.

Binding groceriesListView.model to groceryItems.list

Binding the `ListView` model to the list is then just a one-liner in `Page1.qml`:

```
// Page1.qml
...
Page1Form {
    addItemButton.onClicked: addGroceryItem.run(addItemField.text)
    groceriesListView.model: groceryItems.list
    groceriesListView.onItemRemoved: removeGroceryItem.run(itemType)
    Component.onCompleted: checkAvailableGroceries.run()
}
```

The list is initially assigned to the `model` property. Every time the `listChanged` signal is emitted, the model value is updated form the list value. This happens to the already introduced property binding mechanism: upon update, there is no need to poll data.

Trying out the usecases from the UI

We can now select the `gui` subproject and run it from Qt Creator as usual. When the app launches, upon completion of the page, we should see the list of groceries populated.

More interestingly, if we enter a new item type in the text field and press **Add item**, we should see that the item is added to the list using the correct sorting (alphabetical order, ascending).

Similarly, if you implemented `remove grocery item` and press on the X for an item, the item will disappear from the list.

How awesome is that?

Improving the UI

The UI we have developed as a prototype is enough to support the intended `usecases`; however, it certainly lacks several essential usability features. Among these, we should, for example, remove the user's text input when the use case succeeds. Thanks to the power of QML and to our clean application architecture, this is easily done, as follows:

```
// Page1.qml
...
Page1Form {
    ...
    Connections {
        target: addGroceryItem
        onSuccess: addItemField.text = ""
    }
}
```

> **TIP**
>
> Take some time and explore other ways to improve the Qt Quick UI by making it more user-friendly. Have someone else do a test-run of your app to give you feedback. Keep in mind that you will only be able to properly assess some aspects once your app runs on the intended target platform (for example, a smartphone).

Deploying the app

Basic Qt application deployment is fairly straightforward, especially with the help of QMake and Qt Creator. While QMake takes care of generating the necessary project files for the different target platforms and compile systems, Qt Creator provides many default settings which streamline the whole deployment process.

In many cases, Qt allows us to cross-compile a project for a target platform which is different from the platform of the host machine, where the project was developed. However, not all Qt host versions can cross-compile for all Qt target versions. For example, if you are developing with Qt under Windows, you typically won't be able to generate binary code for, say, macOS or iOS. You will be able, however, to generate binary code for Android. So, make sure your development tools are the right ones to compile for your intended target platforms. For more information about supported host and target platforms, and related requirements, take a look at `https://doc.qt.io/qt-5.9/supported-platforms-and-configurations.html`.

The best way to learn more about the compilation steps for a specific target platforms is to watch Qt Creator and QMake generate the necessary files in the application's build target folder.

The target folder can be checked and manually modified as follows: you need to switch Qt Creator's mode to **Projects**, make sure that the **kit** for your target platform under **Build&Run** is selected (there will be one or more kits available depending on what Qt platforms are installed on your system), and then, under the **Build** menu item, check (or modify) the path contained in the **Build directory** input field:

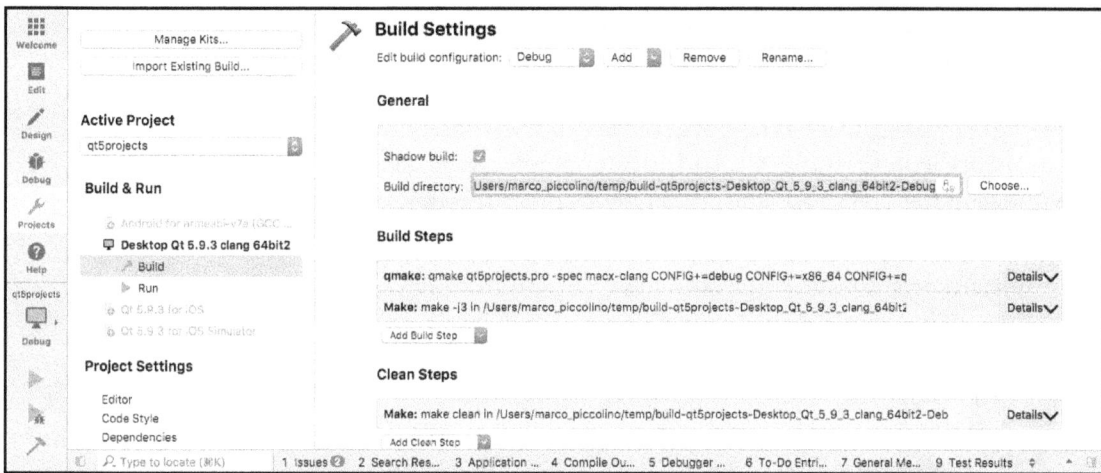

If, like in our case, more sub-projects are available, sub-project directories will be created underneath this main directory. For more details about available build settings with Qt Creator, check out: `http://doc.qt.io/qtcreator/creator-build-settings.html`.

Deploying the app to macOS

Deploying to macOS is typically only possible from a macOS host machine. Qt Creator takes care of most hassles for you, including packaging the needed Qt libraries into the target application bundle and compiling the executable from an Xcode project or Unix makefiles.

The application bundle is the default output setting for QMake and Qt Creator. If you want to obtain a target executable only, you just need to add the following line to your `.pro` file (for the Qt Quick UI app, this is `gui.pro`):

```
CONFIG   -= app_bundle
```

As you might remember, this instruction was generated for us by Qt Creator for the use case tests `.pro` files.

If you create an app bundle, you can easily specify a custom icon file for it. You just need to grab a `.png` icon and convert it to an `.icns` icon resource. There are several free online and offline tools that can operate the conversion. Once you have the `.icns` file, you can put it somewhere in the project folder, and reference it in the `.pro` file with the `ICON` variable. To add a custom icon for our QML UI fridge app, we can create a `macos` subfolder in `gui`, copy the icon file there, and add the following to `gui.pro`:

```
macx {
    ICON = macos/fridge.icns
}
```

> **TIP**
>
> The `macx` braces in the previous snippet are not mandatory. They are telling QMake to consider the following instruction only for the OSX/macOS platform. It's just a way to achieve better code organization in our project.

For the nitty-gritty details about macOS deployment, check out: `http://doc.qt.io/qt-5.9/osx-deployment.html`. The command-line tool that Qt Creator calls for deployment is called `macdeployqt`. Submitting an app to Apple's App Store will require additional steps and a greater effort from your side.

> **TIP**
>
> For troubleshooting, hit the usual Qt information sources, especially the Forums and the Qt Interest mailing list (`http://lists.qt-project.org/mailman/listinfo/interest`).

Deploying the app to Windows

You would typically want to deploy an app to Windows by using a Qt Windows host. However, it is in fact possible to build a Qt app for Windows on a Linux box. This second path is less documented and also depends on the compiler toolchain you have chosen (Mingw versus MSVC), but there are reports of success; you just need to hit your search engine for that.

Windows applications are, by default, deployed with shared libraries, although like on many other platforms, static builds are also available.

Depending on the Qt for Windows version you have chosen (Universal Windows Platform/WinRT versus Windows), two main output types are possible: a Windows Runtime sandbox (MSVC environment only, see: `http://doc.qt.io/qt-5.9/winrt-support.html`) or an installation tree for Windows desktop applications.

Specifying an application icon is pretty easy. You just need to create an `.ico` file from any icon image you might want (for example, a PNG - free online and offline tools are available for this task) and reference it from the project's `.pro` file. To add a custom icon for our qml GUI fridge app, we can create a `win` subfolder in `gui`, copy the icon file there, and add the following to `gui.pro`:

```
win {
    RC_ICONS = win/fridge.ico
}
```

> **TIP**
>
> The `win` braces in the previous snippet are not mandatory. They are telling QMake to consider the following instruction only for the Windows platform. It's just a way to achieve better code organization in our project.

For more details about Windows deployment, check out: `http://doc.qt.io/qt-5.9/windows-deployment.html`. The command-line tool that Qt Creator calls for deployment is called `windeployqt`. Submitting an app to the Windows Store will require additional steps and a greater effort from your side.

> **TIP**
>
> For troubleshooting, hit the usual Qt information sources, including the specific `#qt-winrt` IRC channel on Freenode.

Deploying the app to Android

Cross-compiling for Android is well-supported on many host platforms, including Linux, Windows, and macOS. Besides Qt for Android, on your host machine, you will need both Android's SDK and NDK. Especially for NDK, you should make sure you install a version that is supported by Qt for Android, as the used NDK gets updated less frequently than the SDK. For Qt 5.9, the recommended version is 10e. For complete requirements, take a look at `http://doc.qt.io/qt-5.9/androidgs.html`. An introductory video about Qt on Android is available at `http://bit.ly/QtAndroidIntro`, and one covering more advanced topics is available at `https://www.kdab.com/all-about-qt-on-android/`.

While the Android requirements page still lists Apache ANT, the currently supported and recommended build system is in fact Gradle. Qt Creator disabled the option to use ANT starting with Qt Creator 4.4.

The simplest deployment scenario amounts to activating one of the available Android kits from Qt Creator's **Projects** > **Build & Run** view (armeabi-v7a or x86, depending on your target devices—just click on the menu entry to activate it) and connecting a deployable Android device:

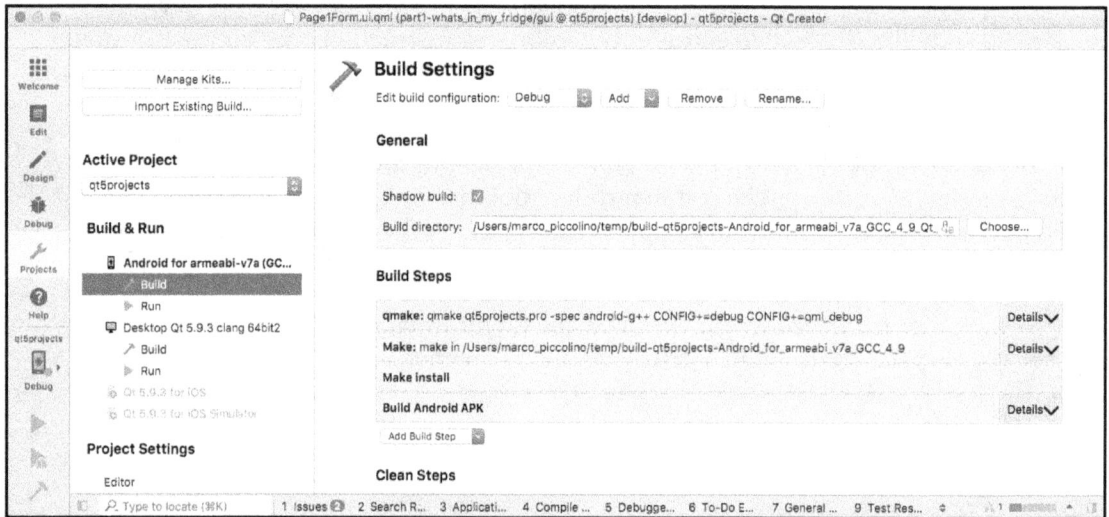

The device to be deployed to can be selected from a UI panel when the application is run with the Android kit selected:

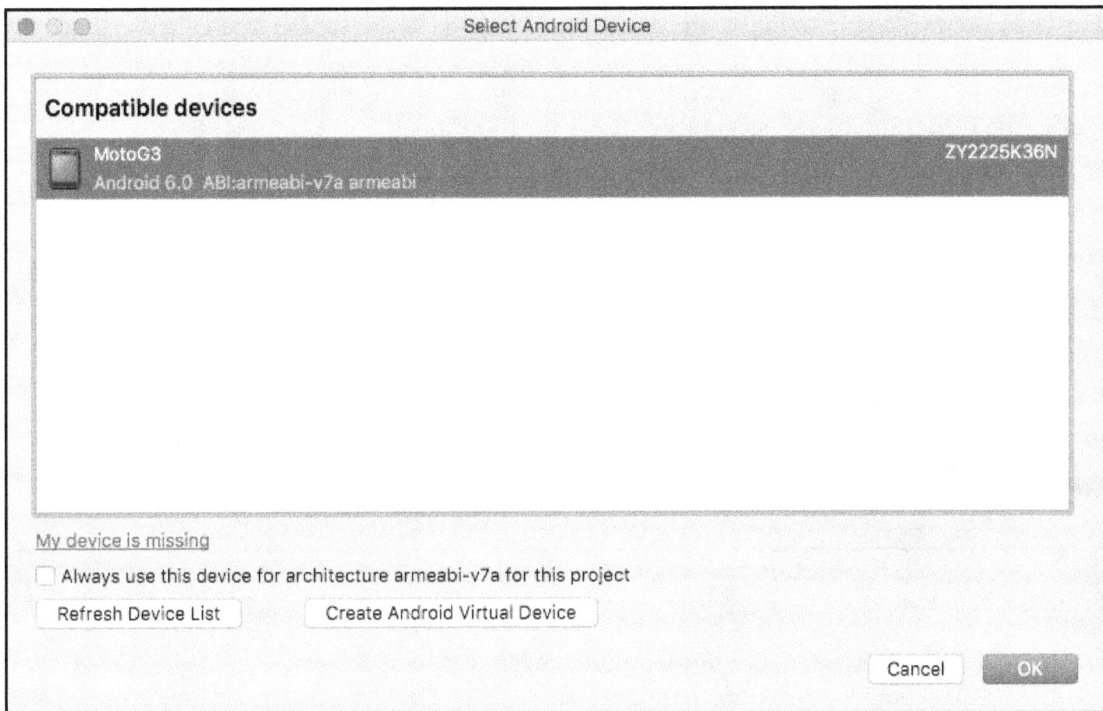

For the device to show up in the target devices list, it should be first enabled as a development device. Please refer to Android's or your device's official documentation for further details. If a device is not available, you can create a virtual device through the **Create Android Virtual Device** button above.

If the environment is properly set up, the application package will be compiled, pushed to the device, and run.

The simplest way to add a launcher icon for the package requires you to create Android template files for your project (**Projects** > **Build & Run** > **Android...** > **Build** > **Build Settings** > **Create Templates**), open the newly created `AndroidManifest.xml` in GUI mode (the **General** tab) and select icon PNGs for the available resolutions:

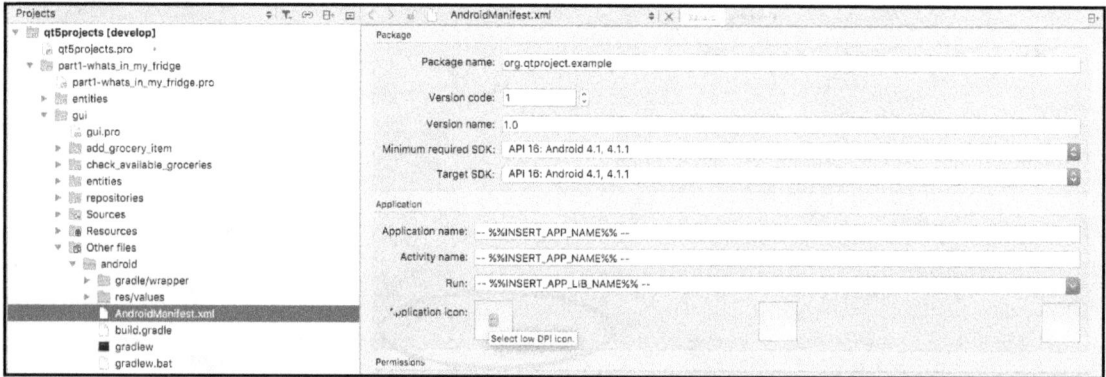

From the same view, it is also possible to specify a custom Android package name.

For more details about Android deployment, check out: `http://doc.qt.io/qtcreator/creator-deploying-android.html` and: `http://doc.qt.io/qt-5.9/deployment-android.html`. The command-line tool that Qt Creator calls for deployment is called `androiddeployqt`. Submitting an app to Google App Store will require additional steps and a greater effort from your side.

> For troubleshooting, hit the usual Qt information channels, including the specific `#necessitas` IRC channel on Freenode, the `#android` channel on the QtMob Slack chat (`http://slackin.qtmob.org`), the Android blog on KDAB's website (`https://www.kdab.com/category/blogs/android/`), and the Qt for the Android development mailing list (`http://lists.qt-project.org/mailman/listinfo/android-development`).

Deploying the app to iOS

Cross-compiling for iOS is typically supported only on a macOS host platform. As is the case for macOS development, you will need a recent version of XCode. For detailed requirements and getting started instructions, take a look at: `http://doc.qt.io/qt-5.9/ios-support.html`. An introductory video about Qt on iOS is available at: `http://bit.ly/QtIOSIntro`. As the iOS toolchain is quite often subject to changes, make sure that the version of Xcode you use is already supported by your Qt distribution.

Before deploying your app to an iOS device, you need to at least set up a development team in Xcode and generate a provisioning profile.

Once you have made sure your iOS deployment environment is set up properly, you should activate one of the available iOS kits in Qt Creator's **Projects** > **Build & Run** pane, and select a development team from the **Build** > **Build Settings** pane:

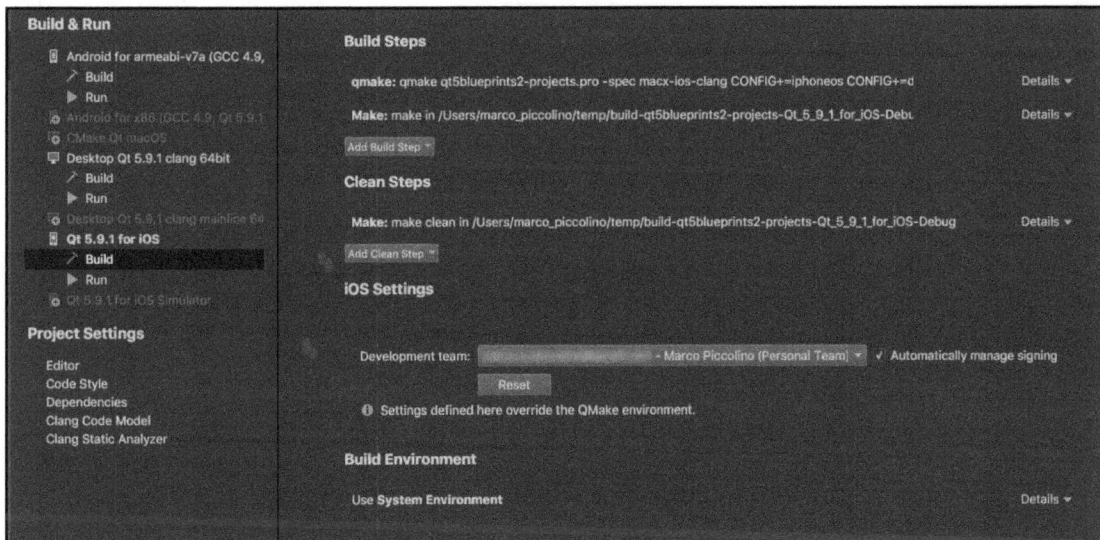

The next thing you will need to do is create a provisioning profile for your app.

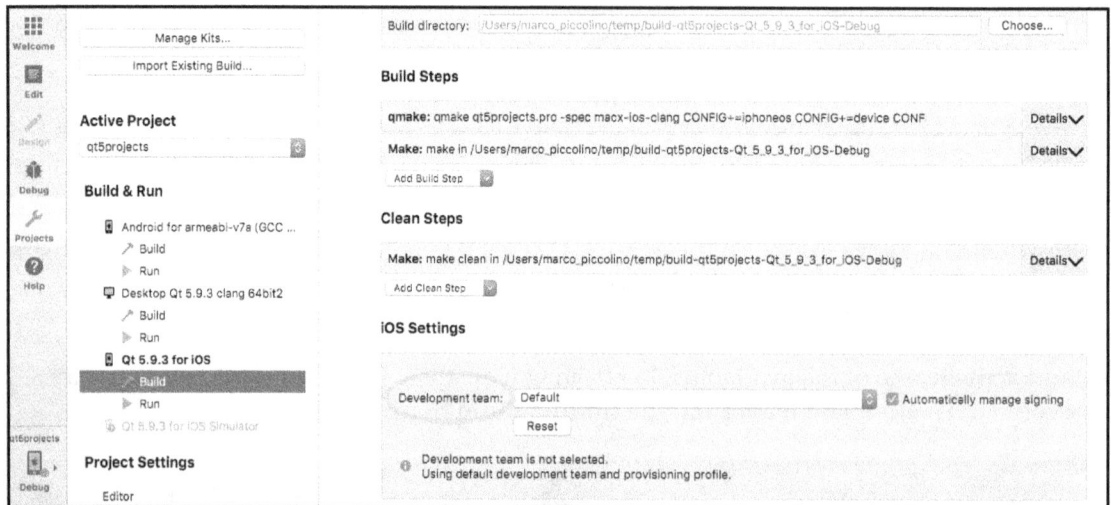

If you don't have a paid Apple Developer account, and thus you selected a **Personal Team**, there is currently no way to do this from within Qt Creator. Thus, instead of running your app from Qt Creator, you will need to run it from Xcode.

To run your app from Xcode, just build it (for example, click on the hammer icon in Qt Creator's bottom left corner) so that QMake is called, and the Xcode project generated. After the Xcode project has been generated, you should launch Xcode and open the generated Xcode project (navigate to the iOS build directory that is set in Qt Creator's **Projects** pane and open the .xcodeproj file; for example gui.xcodeproj). Once the project is open in Xcode, you can customize the app's bundle identifier, and hit Xcode's **Build and Run** button. The app will be deployed to the active device.

> You might need to perform an online verification of the package from your iOS device before being able to launch it. Please refer to Apple's documentation for further instructions.

If, conversely, you have already set up an active development team on your machine, Qt Creator is able to figure out things on its own. Just select **Default** in the **Development team:** selection widget from the previous image, and make sure the **Automatically manage signing** checkbox is checked.

To deploy the application to a connected iOS device from within Qt Creator, you will need to check that at least one device has been detected by Qt Creator. If this is the case, the phone icon with Apple's logo on the bottom left of the GUI will be superimposed with a green badge. Otherwise, you'll see a red badge. You can select the device manually from the **Device:** selection widget at the top of the kit selection popup:

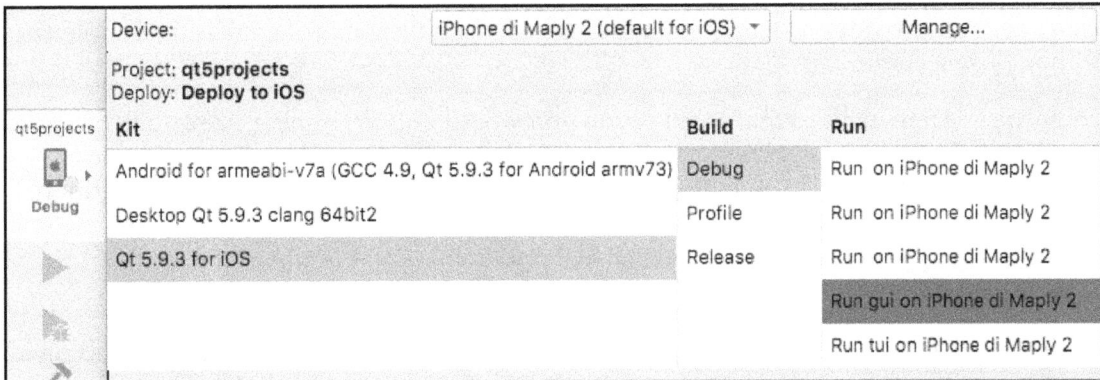

	Device:	iPhone di Maply 2 (default for iOS) ▾	Manage...
	Project: **qt5projects** Deploy: **Deploy to iOS**		
qt5projects	**Kit**	**Build**	**Run**
[icon] ▸	Android for armeabi-v7a (GCC 4.9, Qt 5.9.3 for Android armv73)	Debug	Run on iPhone di Maply 2
Debug	Desktop Qt 5.9.3 clang 64bit2	Profile	Run on iPhone di Maply 2
▷	Qt 5.9.3 for iOS	Release	Run on iPhone di Maply 2
			Run gui on iPhone di Maply 2
↗			Run tui on iPhone di Maply 2

If you want to add a custom launcher icon in your app package, the process is a bit more involved than for other platforms, as it requires the creation of a custom `Info.plist` file. Please refer to: `http://doc.qt.io/qt-5/platform-notes-ios.html` for a how-to.

> For troubleshooting, hit the usual Qt information channels, including the specific `#qt-ios` IRC channel on Freenode, and the `#ios` channel on the QtMob Slack chat (`http://slackin.qtmob.org`).

Deploying the app to Linux

Since there are many Linux distributions where Qt is supported, you are encouraged to find specific instructions for your distribution to learn what is the best strategy for your specific usage scenario.

You can start here: `http://doc.qt.io/qt-5.9/linux-deployment.html`.

Summary

In this chapter, we completed the necessary steps to add a few essential `usecases`, create a Qt Quick-based UI client, and deploy it to various operating systems and device types. Our app shows a nice multi-layer organization where entities, `usecases`, data interfaces (repositories), and the UI are clearly separated and communicate in a predictable manner. This approach provides us with a solid base to create applications of increasing complexity without losing control.

There are still a few things that a real-world app would require: among these, data persistence. In fact, in the current version of *What's in my fridge?*, data is just stored in memory and is thus erased on every app launch. However, you could use the blueprint of `GroceryItemsRepo` and `GroceryItemsRepoDummy` to implement your own persistence layer; for example, with the help of the Qt SQL module (`https://doc.qt.io/qt-5.9/qtsql-index.html`).

In the next chapter, we will get familiar with Qt's amazing graphic capabilities, including a more in-depth look at Qt Quick and **Quick Controls 2**, and get to know Qt 3D and Qt Widgets, as well as many other useful Qt components, by creating a useful set of simple apps for comic creators.

So, take a good break, get something nice from your fridge, and then get ready for the next adventure!

26
Learning About Laying Out Components by Making a Page Layout Tool

In this chapter, we will create a simple application to make it easier for comic creators to prototype page layouts. We will first uncover the power of the Qt Quick framework by building a UI that makes extensive use of different, dynamic item positioning methods.

Further on, we will explore the QML camera API from the Qt Multimedia module, and discover how easy it is to integrate imaging input into our application.

Finally, we will also see how to load images from the filesystem into the UI. Here is a preview of the final result:

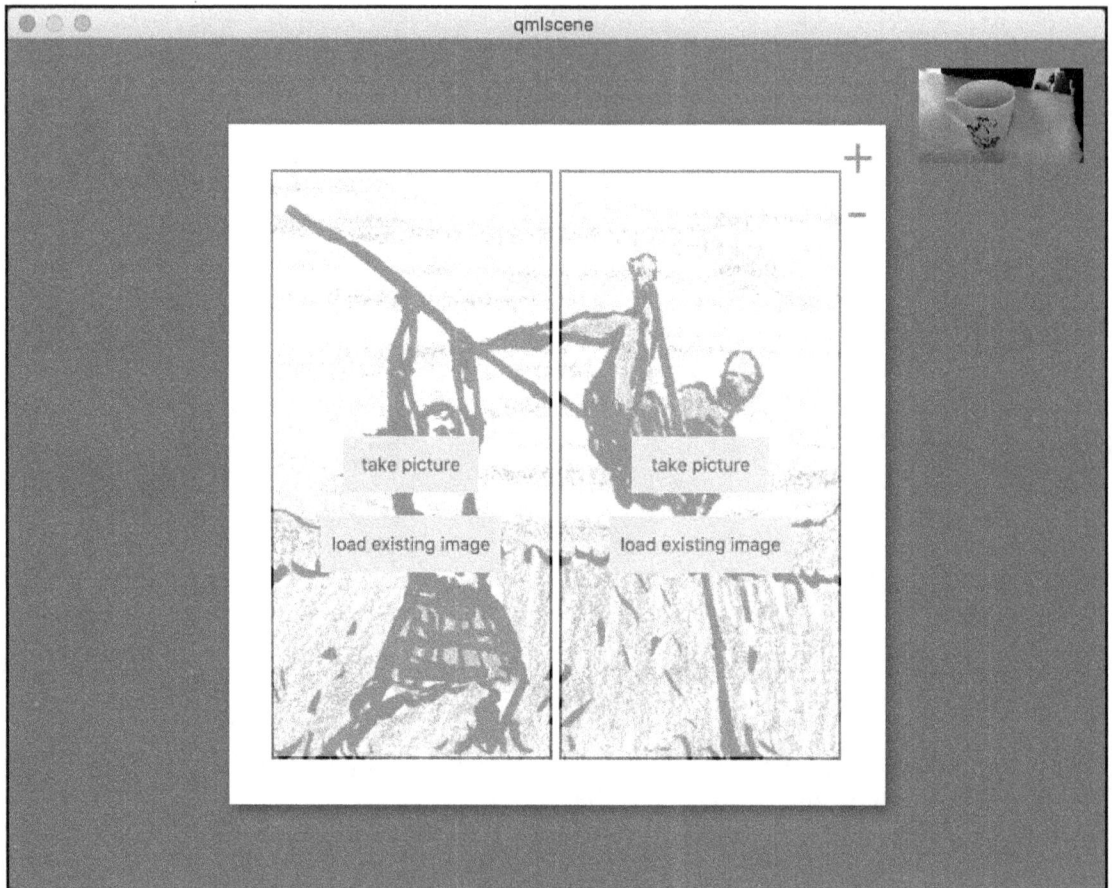

A tool to prototype page layouts quickly

Independent comic creators (or visual storytellers, as some of them prefer to be called) have it pretty tough.

Many of them do not have the option to exert their craft as a profession, and thus create and self-publish their comics during their spare time. Having to squeeze their comic creation activity into usually very limited time slots, which compete with family needs, work, and their other daily duties, they desperately need to optimize their workflow. Furthermore, for those publishing their work as regularly-updated web comics, time pressure is a constant. While various digital drawing and painting tools exist to support the comic production stage, other steps of the comic creation process are not well-covered yet.

Wanting to improve the workflow on independent comic creators, I once asked the following in a forum:

> *"Do you feel as a self-publishing comic creator, you have all the tools you need? If not, which areas are you struggling with the most, and do you think having a specialized tool would make your life easier?"*

To this, one of them, S.L., answered:

> *"For me, the thumbnail stage is the worst. Mainly because you have to take into account the word bubbles in order to lay the page out in a way that makes sense and you can actually tell if it is working or not. And moving around hundreds of layers or constantly changing drawings are both headaches. I've honestly never found a way that totally works for me."*

Thumbnailing is the stage in which small, low-fidelity versions of comic panels and pages are created, in order to work out what compositions and panel arrangements work best. As S.L. pointed out, most of the tools used by digital comic creators are not optimized for this kind of workflow.

Our task will be to create an app for a hypothetical `cutecomics` suite which assists creators in the process of laying out pages and panels. The app will be called `cutecomics` *Panels* and will initially support the following `usecases`:

- Adding panels to a page
- Removing panels from a page
- Taking a picture and loading it into a panel
- Loading an existing picture into a panel

Before diving into the features, we will first perform the initial setup for our code base and app.

Initial setup

There is no need to spend much time on application organization issues; the application architecture model we have provided from `Chapter 23`, *Writing Acceptance Tests and Building a Visual Prototype*, to `Chapter 25`, *Wiring User Interaction and Delivering the Final App*, is general enough to be applicable also in this case, and that's precisely its beauty.

Since the application we will be developing in this chapter and the applications we will be developing in the next two chapters will be part of the same fictitious application suite (cutecomics), we will certainly share some entities, and perhaps other components, between applications.

Creating sub-projects

Go ahead and create all the needed sub-projects in Qt Creator. We could envision the following code base structure:

```
# part2-cute_comics.pro
TEMPLATE = subdirs

SUBDIRS +=
    cutecomics/entities
    cutecomics/usecases
    cutecomics/gui
    ccpanels
```

The main sub-project will be called part2-cute_comics.pro, and should be generated from a **Subdirs Project** template. Its first three sub-projects (entities, usecases, and gui) should also be generated from a **Subdirs Project** template, while the last one (ccpanels, short for cutecomics Panels) should be generated from a **Qt Quick Application** template.

Then, to each of the first three sub-projects, create and manually add a .pri file of the same name; for example:

```
# entities.pro
TEMPLATE = subdirs

include(entities.pri)
```

Like for the What's in my fridge? app (see *Part I*), creating pris (which QMake project includes) allows us to include all our application layers as bundles of sources and resources into the final executable project, by also keeping them well-organized.

In Chapter 23, *Writing Acceptance Tests and Building a Visual Prototype*, we created a visual prototype of the fridge application with one of Qt Creator's visual tools, the **Qt Quick Designer**. For the current app, in order to understand QML and Qt Quick deeper, we are going to write our UI prototype by hand rather than using a visual editor. I hope that at the end of this process, you will find out how pleasing it is to write QML code, provided you have an efficient workflow, and you structure your code properly.

Previewing QML code

Being an interpreted language, QML code allows rapid prototyping. Qt Creator offers a few facilities to assist with the process. Also, a few extra tools exist which allow live previews of your file.

> At the time of writing, QmlLive (`https://doc.qt.io/QtQmlLive/index.html`) has been included into Qt's official repositories—the source code can be downloaded from there (`http://code.qt.io/cgit/qt-apps/qmllive.git`). It is possible that at some point, this very useful tool will also be incorporated into Qt Creator. Other tools which offer live coding are Terrarium (`http://www.terrariumapp.com/`) and DQML (`https://github.com/CrimsonAS/dqml`).

One tool that I find particularly useful is the `qmlscene` command-line tool, which is part of the Qt distribution. It can be accessed in Qt Creator from **Tools** > **External** > **Qt Quick** > **QtQuick 2 Preview (qmlscene)**.
The menu shortcut in Qt Creator is set up to take the current active editor file as input — so, if you run it, it will display the file you are currently editing. If you plan to use the tool frequently, as I do recommend, you might want to create a keyboard shortcut for it. This can be done under **Environment** > **Keyboard** in Qt Creator's **Options** (or **Preferences**, depending on your platform) menu.

Creating a QML module

In what follows, we will develop our QML components in the `gui` sub-project, and then import these into our `ccpanels` application project as a *QML module*. A QML module is a bundle of QML documents that share a namespace. It exposes a list of QML and JS files as types and resources, with specific version numbers. For introductory information about QML modules, check out: `http://doc.qt.io/qt-5.9/qtqml-modules-topic.html`.

Defining a QML module requires the presence of a `qmldir` file in the folder containing the types to be exposed. We go ahead and create this file in the `gui` folder by making use of Qt Creator's **Empty File** template (**New File or Project > Files and Classes > General > Empty File**). We then add it to `gui.pri` (Qt Creator should prompt you about this in the wizard) as follows:

```
# gui.pri
DISTFILES +=
    $$PWD/qmldir
```

This instruction marks the `qmldir` file as being part of the distribution, and makes it show up in Qt Creator's project tree.

Creating a Qt Resource Collection

The next thing we will want to do in our `gui` sub-project is to create a Qt Resource Collection file (`.qrc`), an XML file that indexes a group of application resources and makes them accessible through the powerful *Qt resource system*.

The Qt resource system (`http://doc.qt.io/qt-5.9/resources.html`) allows you to store resources in binary format, either within the main application executable or in separate files, and makes them accessible via a custom resource location scheme (`:/` or `qrc:/`). Clear advantages of this approach are easier deployment, speed of access, and maximum portability (no need to deal with platform-specific filesystem differences to load resources!). Take a look at the preceding link to have a better grasp of what this very widespread Qt technology can achieve. The resource system is the right choice for many kinds of resources (QML files, images, translation files, and so on) — pretty much everything except for your C++ headers and sources, which are compiled into the executable directly.

We are going to create a `gui.qrc` in the `gui` sub-project (**New File or Project > Qt > Qt Resource File**). Instead of having Qt Creator add the file to `gui.pro` in the wizard, we will add it manually to `gui.pri`, as follows:

```
# gui.pri
RESOURCES += $$PWD/gui.qrc
```

Once this is done, the project infrastructure, and specifically the UI sub-project, should show up as follows in Qt Creator's **Projects** pane:

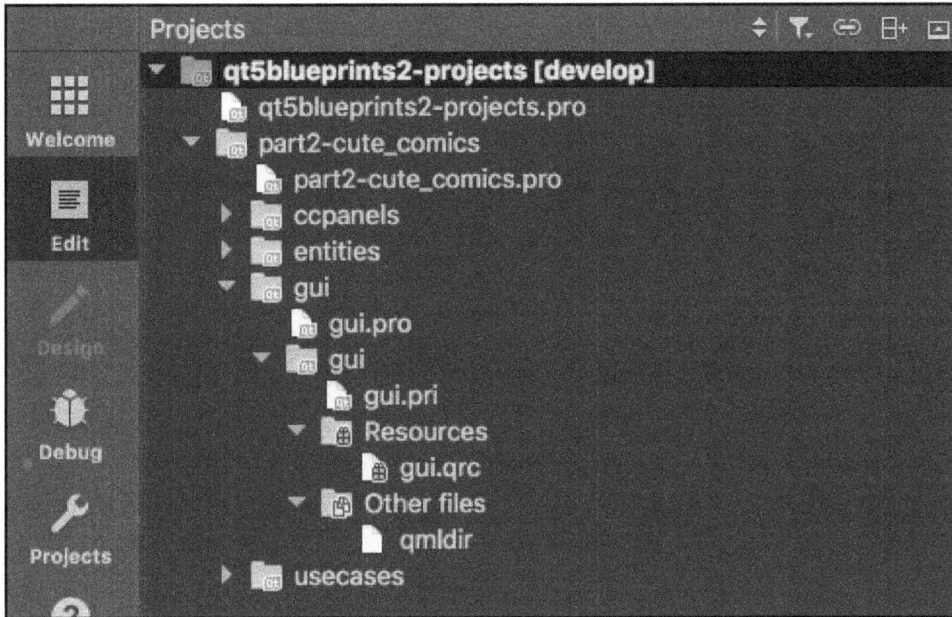

Back to scenarios

Now that we have a bit of project infrastructure in place, before diving into other application layers, we should start from feature scenarios. As you know by now, in order to have a solid and testable application, we could create a **Qt Unit Test** sub-project for each use case (or *feature*, in BDD terminology), and write a few tests corresponding to different scenarios. Let's start with an example for the first use case before moving to the UI.

Adding a panel to the page

In what follows, we are going to use the concepts of *panel* and *page*. These are *entities*, or business objects from the comics domain. Since visual components with the same or similar names but different meanings are available (for example, from the **Qt Quick Controls 2** module (`Page` and `Pane`)), make sure you don't confuse them. I will use domain-specific names when implementing the entities' UI counterparts (`ComicPage` and `ComicPanel`).

The first entity we want to model is the *page*. We might need a page to be part of a complex higher-level entity (for example, a comic book, a chapter, or a sequence), but let's keep things simple for now, and pretend the page is our top-level entity, and that the page we will be adding panels to is already created. What should we assume and expect from adding a *panel* to the page?

```
Given there is a page
And the page has no panels
And the page has size 480 x 480 px
When I add a panel to the page
Then the page has one panel
And the panel fills up the whole page
```

> In this book, we are not dealing with resolution independence concerns, and thus use pixels instead of `dp` (resolution-independent pixels). If you want to know more about Qt's resolution independence capabilities and other scalability-related issues, take a look at `http://doc.qt.io/qt-5.9/` `scalability.html`.

More interestingly, what will happen when we add another panel? Here is a possible scenario:

```
Given there is a page
And the page has one panel
And the page has size 480 x 480 px
When I add a panel to the page
Then the page has two panels
And the first panel fills the left half of the page
And the second panel fills the right half of the page
```

Finally, what will happen when we add a third panel to the page? Here is what we might want in a simple setting:

```
Given there is a page
And the page has two panels
And the page has size 480 x 480 px
When I add a panel to the page
Then the page has three panels
And the first panel fills the left third of the page
And the second panel fills the central third of the page
And the third panel fills the right third of the page
```

You could of course come up with more elaborate layouts; feel free to do so.

Implementing usecases and entities

This can be expressed in code in many ways. Here is one:

> **TIP**
> Try and come up with your own API for the entities and `usecases` involved in this scenario before looking at the suggested one! Also, remember that since we are only implementing one test, the code does not contain special provisions for deallocating the objects at the end of the test. If you add more tests, you will have to take care of this aspect too.

```
void Usecases_add_panel_to_page::test_no_panels()
{
    // Given there is a page
    auto page = new entities::Page(this);
    QVERIFY(page);
    // And the page has no panels
    QCOMPARE(page->panels().count(), 0);
    // And the page has size 480 x 480 px
    page->setSize(QSize(480,480));
    QCOMPARE(page->size(),QSize(480,480));
    // When I add a panel to the page
    auto addPanelToPage = new usecases::AddPanelToPage(this, page);
    QSignalSpy addPanelToPageSuccess(addPanelToPage, SIGNAL(success()));
    addPanelToPage->run();
    QTRY_COMPARE_WITH_TIMEOUT(addPanelToPageSuccess.count(), 1, 1000);
    // Then the page has one panel
    QCOMPARE(page->panels().count(), 1);
    // And the panel fills up the whole page
    QCOMPARE(page->panels().at(0).size(), page->size());
}
```

If you have (as you should have done!) worked through Chapter 23, *Writing Acceptance Tests and Building a Visual Prototype,* to Chapter 25, *Wiring User Interaction and Delivering the Final App* of *Part I,* there should be no big surprises in the way the test is written. You might rework some of the API details as you implement the involved objects.

From the preceding test, we single out the entities we need: a `Page` entity, and likely a separate `Panel` entity, of which we will create an instance in the use case implementation. We will then let `Page` manage a collection of `Panels` (in a real-world example, we might want to keep the two entities more independent).

Before moving to the UI, as an exercise to corroborate what you have learned in *Part I*, you should try and implement the use case and the entities to have the preceding test (or the corresponding version you came up with) pass. You will find my implementation in the code repository.

Now, implementing each use case and entity is what you would want to do in a real-world scenario. For example at some point, you might need to change your UI from Qt Quick to HTML5, or pass information about pages and panels over the internet; having the logic core well-separated will make the transition from one delivery technology to another very easy. But developing the use case and entity layers requires time, and this chapter focuses on the Qt Quick UI. For this reason, in what follows, we will just focus on the UI layer, and mock `usecases` and entities in the QML client. The good news is that we can still use our feature scenario specification exactly as it is, and verify it visually rather than programmatically:

```
Given there is a page
And the page has no panels
And the page has size 480 x 480 px
When I add a panel to the page
Then the page has one panel
And the panel fills up the whole page
```

Designing and implementing the UI for the usecase

So, we are taking a shortcut and jumping straight to the UI layer. We still want to make sure that our use case is satisfied, and we will verify it by looking at the UI and interacting with it.

Looking at our use case, the page is a given entity, so we will just create its visual counterpart as an already given instance, place it on top of a table surface, and give it a bit of shadow, to show that it is actually a page and not a window, or a simple rectangle.

We start off by creating a new `.qml` file in the `gui` folder, which will contain the table surface. Let's call it `TableSurface.qml`. Qt Creator provides a specific template wizard for QML files, you can find it under **Files and Classes** > **Qt** > **QML File (Qt Quick 2)**.

If you open a file in Qt Creator's editor by clicking on it from the **Projects** pane, when you open the **New File or Project...** wizard, you will get the path of the currently open file as the destination path for the new file. That will save you some extra typing and directory browsing.

When adding the new file, Qt Creator will figure out that `gui.qrc` is present in the folder, and ask you whether you want to add `TableSurface.qml` to that file as a resource, as follows:

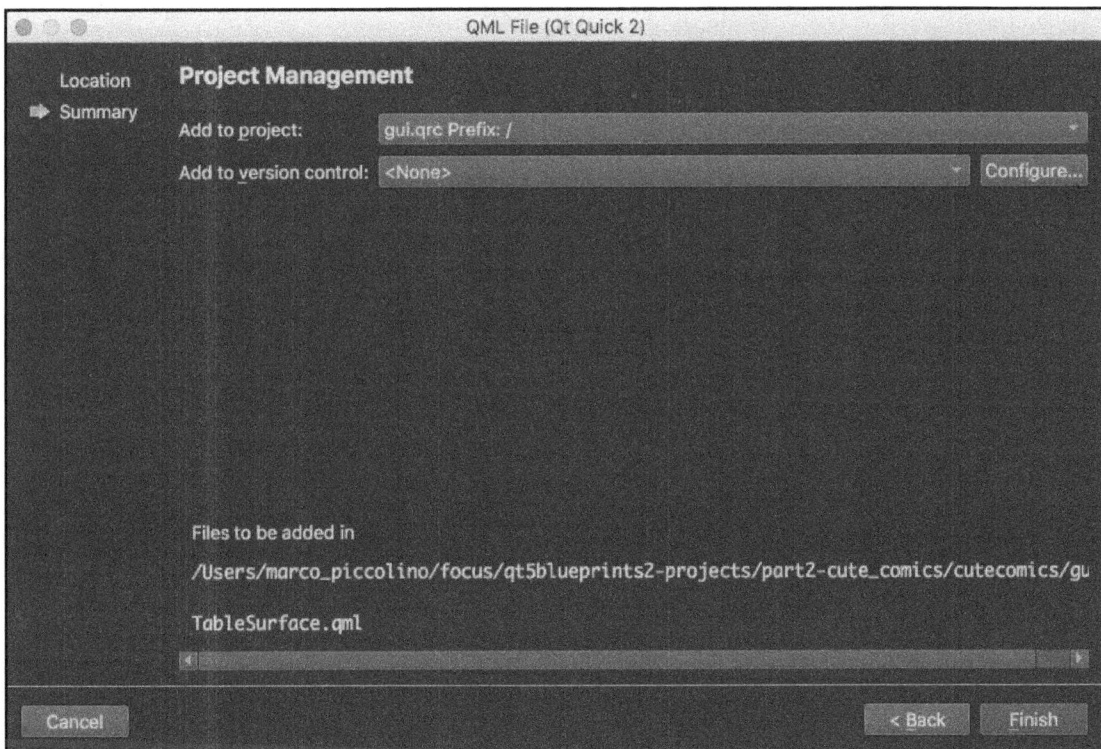

If, for some reason, this does not happen, you can right click on `gui.qrc` in the **Projects** pane and select **Add Existing files...**

A QML file whose name begins with an **upper case** letter is automatically recognized by Qt as a new QML type, and will be available for import in other files as such. On the contrary, notice, for example, how the `main.qml` entry point of a Qt Quick application starts with a lower case letter.

Now, let's open the `TableSurface.qml` file and take a look at its default content:

```
// TableSurface.qml
import QtQuick 2.0

Item {

}
```

As already explained, the `import` line makes the Qt Quick module type definitions exposed as version `2.0`, available in the current document.

> Between minor versions of QML modules, there might be some API and implementation changes. For APIs, these are typically only incremental changes and thus do not break existing code.
> Knowing what version of a QML module to import is not always easy, since at present, there seems to be no regularly updated and easily accessible reference in the docs which contain this information. As a rule of thumb, though, for Qt Quick the latest available minor version corresponds to Qt's minor version (for example, Qt 5.9 -> Qt Quick 2.9). This linkage is enforced starting with Qt 5.11.
> For other QML modules, Qt Creator's autocompletion is helpful in figuring things out, but not always reliable. Trial and error is sometimes the most effective option, together with peeking into the `qmldir` file of the QML module in your Qt distribution.

We can run `qmlscene` through the keyboard shortcut we set up previously. You should see an empty window popping up. The dimensions of the window are not calculated from the `Item` object's configuration; they are just `qmlscene`'s default window value.

`Item` (http://doc.qt.io/qt-5.9/qml-qtquick-item.html) is the base type in Qt Quick's type hierarchy. It is a *visual* (it has a geometry, a position, and so on) but not a *visible* type.

> Take some time to read `Item`'s description in the docs, and check out all the properties it exposes: this object has no fancy appearance, but it builds the foundation block for most other Qt Quick types—knowing it in depth will give you a very good understanding of most other Qt Quick types.

Instead, we want our table surface to be visible, have a color, and possibly a size. We start by giving the table surface a name (`id`) and a size, as follows:

```
// TableSurface.qml
import QtQuick 2.9

Item {
    id: tableSurface
    width: 800
    height: 600
}
```

If you save and fire `qmlscene` again, you should see a bigger window. The `Item` now has an explicit size, and `qmlscene` took it into account. The `id` is not required, but as we saw in Chapter 25, *Wiring User Interaction and Delivering the Final App*, it plays a big role when defining property bindings between objects which have no direct parent-child relationship.

`Item` does not support any visual cues. If we want to give a color to the table surface, we should use a visual object, such as a `Rectangle`. We create the `Rectangle` as a child to `TableSurface`, provide its `color`, and, instead of giving it an explicit size, we configure it to fill its parent's size via the `anchors` grouped property:

> A grouped property is a bundle of logically-related properties. For more information, visit: `http://doc.qt.io/qt-5.9/qtqml-syntax-objectattributes.html#grouped-properties`

```
// TableSurface.qml
...
Item {
    id: tableSurface
    width: 800
    height: 600
    Rectangle {
        anchors.fill: parent
        color: "dimgray"
    }
}
```

TIP

color is one of the so-called QML basic types provided by the Qt Quick module. These are domain-specific additions to the basic types provided by the Qt Qml module. It supports SVG-named colors (dimgray), HEX (A) RGB values, and more. Knowing all the basic QML types is essential to write optimal code. You can learn more about them here: http://doc. qt.io/qt-5.9/qtqml-typesystem-basictypes.html.

If you save and fire qmlscene again, you will now see a gray rectangle filling up the whole window.

TIP

Defining the Rectangle as the root object of TableSurface could also have been an option, and spared the creation of the extra Item. However, having an Item as the root object gives better encapsulation, as Rectangle has a richer and more specific API which won't be exposed to the outside world. Also, this choice requires no API changes if, for example, we ever want to substitute the Rectangle with another type of object, such as an Image.

The anchors positioning model

Anchoring is one of the positioning models available in QML. It is used to specify relative positioning between visual items, and, from a computational perspective, it represents a very efficient model. However, it is only applicable between items which have either a parent-child relationship, or a sibling-sibling relationship.

Common anchoring options include anchors.left, anchors.right, anchors.top, and anchors.bottom—these properties can be bound to the left, right, top, and bottom properties of parent and sibling objects. These objects can be referenced via their object ids or, in case of a parent, via the parent property, which is available in all Item-derived types. anchors.fill, which we used in the preceding example, is a convenience option that sets the four aforementioned properties at once, and takes an id or the parent property as value. anchors.centerIn is also available. Similarly to fill, it takes parent or an id as values. We will see a few more anchoring properties in the upcoming code sample. For a very clear and exhaustive treatment of the anchoring model, visit: http:// doc.qt.io/qt-5.9/qtquick-positioning-anchors.html.

Adding the page

We now create a separate QML document for the `ComicPage` UI component:

```
// ComicPage.qml
import QtQuick 2.9

Item {
    id: page
    width: 480
    height: width

    Rectangle {
        anchors.fill: parent
    }
}
```

Nothing new here, except for the fact that we decide the `ComicPage` to be square-shaped by default, and thus make its `height` reflect its `width`. We also do not specify the color of the `Rectangle`, as we are content with its default value, `"#ffffff"`. Firing qmlscene will show a non-exciting white square.

Now that the `ComicPage` is there, we can stack it on top of the `TableSurface`. Let's first create a `CCPanels.qml` document that we will use for testing purposes to combine our components:

```
// CCPanels.qml
import QtQuick 2.9

TableSurface {
    ComicPage { }
}
```

By opening `CCPanels.qml` with `qmlscene`, we'll see both the table surface and the page:

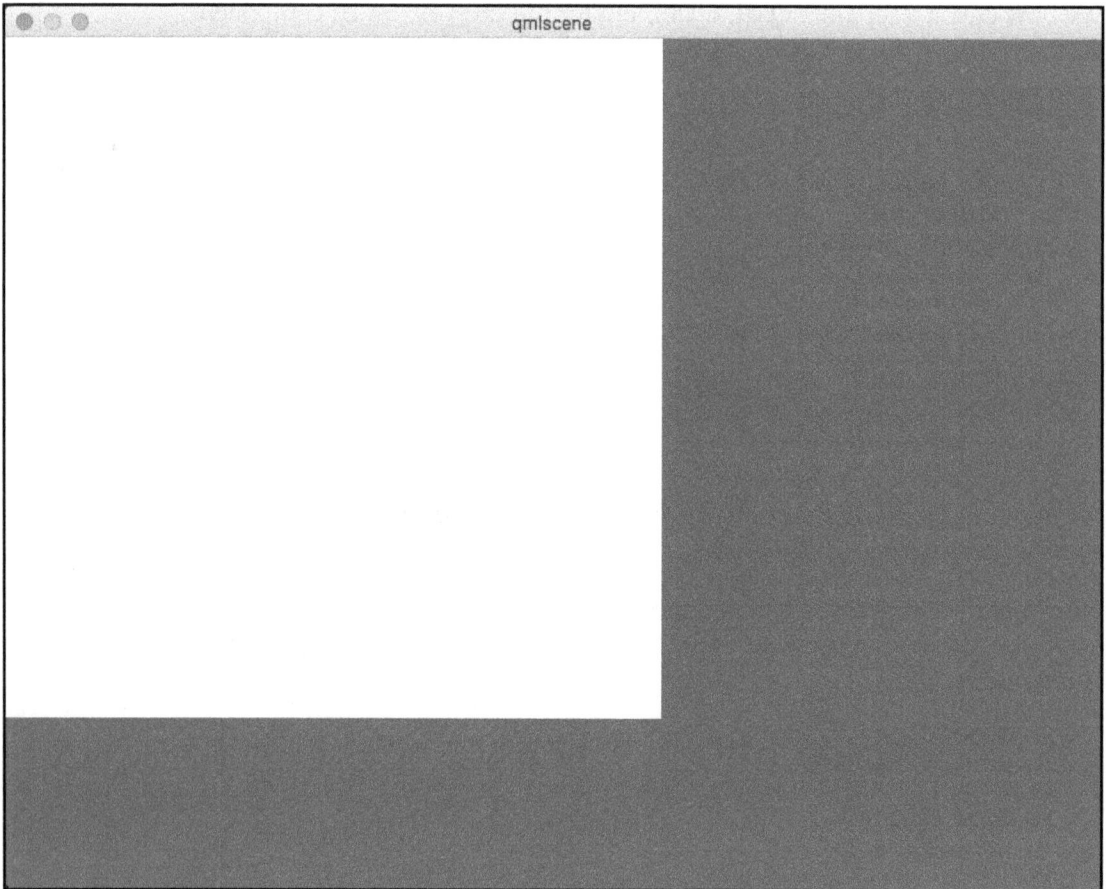

We would probably want the page to be centered in the surface. We can achieve this with the already introduced `anchors.centerIn` property:

```
// CCPanels.qml
...
TableSurface {
    ComicPage {
        anchors.centerIn: parent
    }
}
```

As a QML programmer, one of your major duties is to recognize what properties are inherent to the object that you want to create, and what are instead meaningful only when you consider the context the object lives in. The `anchors.centerIn` property from the preceding example could have been defined in `ComicPage.qml`, but that does not seem a very sensible choice, as we might want the `ComicPage` to be placed differently in another context (for example, a book). In this specific case, the choice is made easier by the fact that `ComicPage` in isolation has no meaningful `parent`.

One thing we shall do for our `ComicPage` to look like a real page is to give it a bit of depth by means of a `DropShadow` object:

```
// ComicPage.qml
import QtQuick 2.9
import QtGraphicalEffects 1.0

Item {
    ...
    Rectangle {
        id: pageFace
        anchors.fill: parent
    }
    DropShadow {
        source:pageFace
        anchors.fill: source
        horizontalOffset: 3
        verticalOffset: 3
        radius: 8.0
        color: "#80000000"
    }
}
```

The `DropShadow` object, one of many effects provided by a separate Qt Graphical Effects module (http://doc.qt.io/qt-5.9/qtgraphicaleffects-index.html), requires a `source` object to get its geometry, and the setting of a few more properties (check the documentation to see what other properties are available). Its `color` value is expressed here as an ARGB HEX value (alpha 0x80 + black).

If you now preview `CCPanels` again, you'll see the page with a nice shadow beneath.

We might also want our page to have a margin by defining a drawing surface:

```
// ComicPage.qml
...
```

```
Item {
    id: page
    ...
    Item {
        id: drawingSurface
        anchors.fill: parent
        anchors.margins: 32
    }
}
```

The drawing surface's border won't be visible; we might instead want to draw borders for each single `panel`. As you can see, by combining `anchors.fill` and `anchors.margins`, we can have an item whose size equals the size of the filled object minus the size of the borders. Besides `anchors.margins`, `anchors.leftMargin`, `anchors.rightMargin`, `anchors.topMargin`, and `anchors.bottomMargin` are also available.

To enable the addition of a comic panel, we also need an affordance, that is, an interactive element which makes it clear that panels can be added through it. This element, which will be part of the comic page, can be named `panelAdder`. It will be a simple button located on the top-right corner of the page, with a "+" sign on it. To implement it, we could use an off-the-shelf **Qt Quick Controls 2** `Button`. For learning purposes, however, let's see how it can be done with Qt Quick types alone:

```
// ComicPage.qml
...
Item {
    id: page
    ...
    Item {
        id: drawingSurface
        anchors.fill: parent
        anchors.margins: 32
    }
    Item {
        id: panelAdder
        width: 40
        height: width
        anchors.right: parent.right
        opacity: 0.5
        Text {
            text: "+"
            anchors.centerIn: parent
            font.pixelSize: 40
        }
        MouseArea {
            anchors.fill: parent
```

```
            }
        }
    }
```

The `Item` itself only shows a new property, `opacity`, which controls the `opacity` of an `Item` and all its children. We don't want the button to obfuscate any content that might be present underneath. We have already encountered the `Text` element in Chapter 23, *Writing Acceptance Tests and Building a Visual Prototype*. What is new here is the `MouseArea`, a non-visual type which provides interaction capabilities, exposing, for example, the `pressed` and `clicked` signals, just like a `Button` does. By placing it on top of the `Text` element, and having it fill the size of the containing `panelAdder`, we are making the whole `Item` interactive.

> Being a button, a self-contained and possibly reusable component, in a real-world project it would be better placed into a separate document. I will show you how to achieve that in a later section. Whenever possible, however, you are encouraged to use off-the-shelf controls, such as **Qt Quick Controls 2** `Button`.

Previewing `CCPanels`, you should now see a page with shadow, and a "+" symbol in the top-right corner:

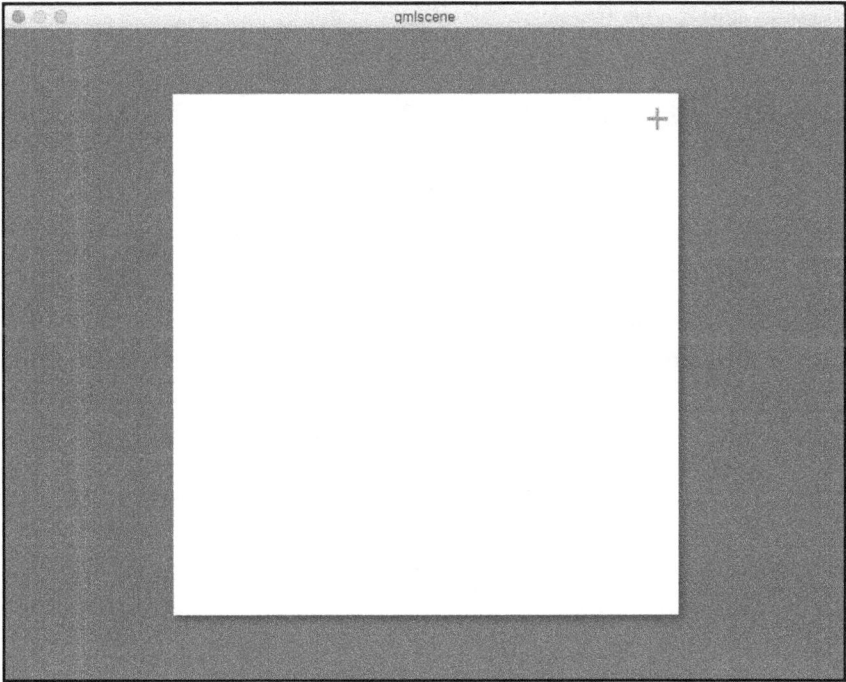

The first iteration of the visual page is, from a graphic point of view, complete. We can now focus on the comic panels.

Creating the comic panels

Given a page with no panels, our first use case scenario expects that, after the panel's addition action has completed successfully, the page will contain one panel, and the panel will fill up the whole page. We shall thus represent the preconditions and expected outcomes of this change in the UI.

Given what you already know, you might think about fulfilling these requirements in the UI by perhaps intervening on the `anchors` properties of the comic panel. This could work out well for the first use case scenario (from 0 to 1 panels). However, if you look at the second (from 1 to 2 panels), as we have sketched it out, you might realize that the anchoring model might give origin to unnecessary complexity. When looking also at the third use-case scenario (from 2 to 3 panels), you should foresee that the anchoring model would be hardly capable of expressing the setup we need. For this reason, we might better ask ourselves in advance whether Qt provides an alternative, more flexible positioning system to cope with these requirements.

It turns out that a more elaborate positioning system exists. The module which exposes this system is called *Qt Quick Layouts*.

The Qt Quick Layouts system

The Qt Quick Layouts system (`http://doc.qt.io/qt-5.9/qtquicklayouts-index.html`) is a more recent introduction among the QML options for positioning items. It provides a few QML types that can modify and calculate the size of their children items based on the available space and given constraints.

It currently ships four container types: `ColumnLayout`, `GridLayout`, `RowLayout`, and `StackLayout`. Besides providing these types, the module also exposes a few so-called attached properties (`http://doc.qt.io/qt-5.9/qtqml-syntax-objectattributes.html#attached-properties-and-attached-signal-handlers`), which extend the capabilities of children items. One of the most important things to remember regarding layouts is that the sizing behavior of their children should be defined via the children's `Layout.preferredWidth` and `Layout.preferredHeight` attached properties (or other compatible options), rather than `width` and `height`.

By using layouts, we can have our comic panels fill up all available page space, independently of their number.

Managing comic panels with a grid layout

Among the types provided by the Qt Quick Layouts module, the GridLayout is the one which allows us to place its children in a grid arrangement, by defining the columns and/or rows of the desired grid, and a few additional properties. We go ahead and create a GridLayout object in our drawingSurface:

```
// ComicPage.qml
...
import QtQuick.Layouts 1.3

Item {
    id: page
    ...
    Item {
        id: drawingSurface
        anchors.fill: parent
        anchors.margins: 32
        GridLayout {
            id: panelsGrid
            anchors.fill: parent
            rows: 1
            columns: 0
        }
    }
}
```

The layout fills the drawingSurface and has, initially, no columns and one row. Remember that, in our use-case scenarios, we wanted the added panels to grow from left to right, so we just need one row for now.

Creating new panels dynamically with a repeater

In our feature scenarios, we are adding up to three panels to the page. We have two basic options regarding panel creation. We can treat each panel as an object with a well-defined identity, and add each one individually, or rather prefer a model-view based approach as we did in Chapter 23, *Writing Acceptance Tests and Building a Visual Prototype*, when we used ListView.

This second approach means that we won't have to treat each panel addition as a special case—we can just add an element to an underlying data model (a JavaScript array, a `QList`, and so on), and see the visual representation of the panels collection grow accordingly. We will look at this second approach, as it is more elegant and forward-thinking (at some point, we might want to add maybe 10 or 12 panels!).

`ListView` is quite a powerful item, providing scrolling, interaction, and much more, perhaps too much for what we need to do here. QML provides a much simpler non-visual type, `Repeater` (http://doc.qt.io/qt-5.9/qml-qtquick-repeater.html), which exposes `model` and `delegate` properties (pretty much as `ListView` does), and creates replicas of the QML component specified as a `delegate`, based on the model's characteristics. The repeated objects will become children of the `Repeater` parent item. Here is how we add the `Repeater` to the `GridLayout`:

```
// ComicPage.qml
...
Item {
    id: page
    ...
    Item {
        id: drawingSurface
        anchors.fill: parent
        anchors.margins: 32
        GridLayout {
            id: panelsGrid
            anchors.fill: parent
            rows: 1
            columns: panelsRepeater.count
            Repeater {
                id: panelsRepeater
                model: 0
            }
        }
    }
}
```

The model can be just an integer (which represents the number of `delegate` replicas we want), a JS array, or a model-compatible Qt type, such as `QList` or `QStandardItemModel` (http://doc.qt.io/qt-5.9/qstandarditemmodel.html). You can notice how we now compute the number of `panelsGrid` columns based on the repeater's `count` property, that is, the number of `delegate` replicas generated by the repeater.

Defining the comic panel

To keep things clean, we won't define our panel within the page, but rather define a separate component, and use property aliases to pass it as the `delegate` of the repeater. We go ahead and create a `ComicPanel.qml` file with this content:

```
// ComicPanel.qml
import QtQuick 2.9

Item {
    width: 100
    height: 100
    Rectangle {
        anchors.fill: parent
        border.color: "#000"
        border.width: 2
        opacity: 0.5
    }
}
```

We have given the panel an arbitrary size to make it visible in isolation. The `GridLayout` will take care to modify its appearance via the attached properties, as we will see shortly.

> **TIP**
>
> In this case, make sure you don't have one dimension of the root `Item` rely on the other via property binding (for example, `width: height`), as this might confuse the layout system when performing its calculations.

To use the `ComicPanel` in the page, we expose the `Repeater`:

```
// ComicPage.qml
...
Item {
    id: page

    property alias panelsRepeater: panelsRepeater
    ...
}
```

> **TIP**
>
> Another option would be to expose the repeater's `delegate` and `model` directly.

We finally add the panel `delegate` to the scene, by making use of the `Layout.fillWidth` and `Layout.fillHeight` attached properties to fill up all available space in the grid:

```
// CCPanels.qml
import QtQuick 2.0
import QtQuick.Layouts 1.3
import "."

TableSurface {
    ComicPage {
        anchors.centerIn: parent
        panelsRepeater.delegate: ComicPanel {
            Layout.fillWidth: true
            Layout.fillHeight: true
        }
    }
}
```

If you want to check out what a bunch of panels will look like in the repeater, you just need to add one line to the scene:

```
// CCPanels.qml
...
TableSurface {
    ComicPage {
        anchors.centerIn: parent
        panelsRepeater.delegate: ComicPanel {
            Layout.fillWidth: true
            Layout.fillHeight: true
        }
        panelsRepeater.model: 3 // or any other number
    }
}
```

Can you explain what is going on here? Try and change the number and see if the layout behaves as expected. Here is what you should see:

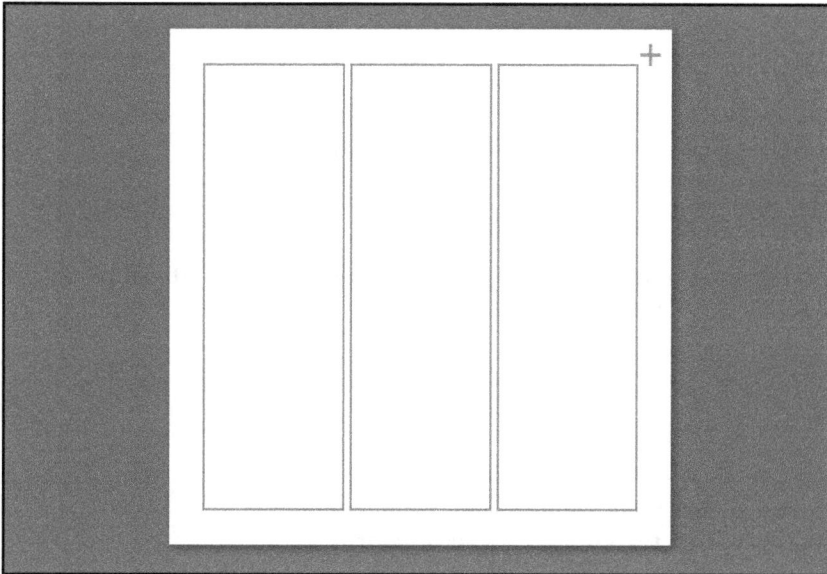

Simulating the usecase action

Instead of having to change the model from code, as we did in the last line of the scene, we want the panels number to increase when pressing the "+" button. Let's do a little refactoring and extract `panelAdder` as a standalone component into a separate `PanelButton` document, so that we can expose the `clicked` signal of its `MouseArea` in a clean way:

```
// PanelButton.qml
import QtQuick 2.0

Item {
    signal clicked()
    width: 40
    height: width
    anchors.right: parent.right
    opacity: 0.5
    Text {
        text: "+"
        anchors.centerIn: parent
        font.pixelSize: 40
```

```
    }
    MouseArea {
        onClicked: parent.clicked()
        anchors.fill: parent
    }
}
```

> Unlike properties, signals cannot be aliased, hence the need to "repeat" the signal from the inner object to the outer one.

We can then expose `panelAdder` at the `ComicPage` level, so that it can be accessed from `CCPanels`:

```
// ComicPage.qml
...
Item {
    id: page

    property alias panelsRepeater: panelsRepeater
    property alias panelAdder: panelAdder
    ...
    PanelButton {
        id: panelAdder
        anchors.right: parent.right
    }
}
```

We are now ready to fulfil the first use case from a visual point of view. Here is how:

```
// CCPanels.qml
...
TableSurface {
    ListModel {
        id: panelsEntity
    }

    ComicPage {
        id: page
        anchors.centerIn: parent
        panelsRepeater.delegate: ComicPanel {
            Layout.fillWidth: true
            Layout.fillHeight: true
        }
        panelsRepeater.model: panelsEntity
        panelAdder.onClicked:
```

```
panelsEntity.append({"pid":panelsEntity.count})
    }
}
```

We fake our panel's entity with a simple `ListModel`, and create a panel ID (`pid`) attribute for each new panel entity instance. If you wanted to display the `pid` (or any other model field), you could extend `ComicPanel`, as follows:

```
// ComicPanel.qml
...
Item {
    property alias displayText: textItem.text
    ...
    Rectangle {
        ...
    }
    Text {
        id: textItem
        anchors.centerIn: parent
    }
}
```

Then, in `CCPanels`:

```
// CCPanels.qml
...
TableSurface {
    ...
    ComicPage {
        id: page
        anchors.centerIn: parent
        panelsRepeater.delegate: ComicPanel {
            displayText: pid || 0
        }
        ...
    }
}
```

And here is the final result:

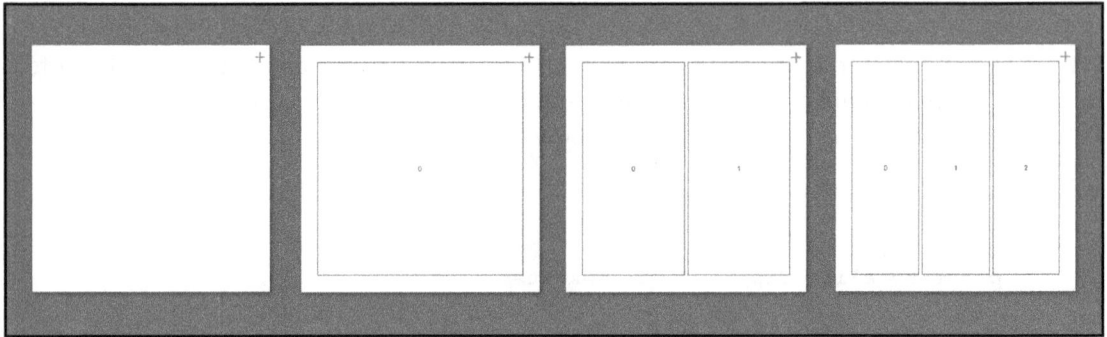

Removing a panel from the page

Given what we have done with the previous use case, from a visual point of view, supporting *remove panel from page* amounts to two activities:

- Adding an affordance to the page to trigger the use case (a minus button)
- Removing an item from the panel's data model

Thanks to the power of Qt Quick, both tasks are pretty trivial. For the first one, we reuse the already created `PanelButton` by exposing its text property:

```
// PanelButton.qml
...
Item {
    signal clicked()
    property alias text: textItem.text
    ...
    Text {
        id: textItem
        ...
    }
    ...
}
```

Then, we add the instance below `panelAdder` and expose it:

```
// ComicPage.qml
...
Item {
    id: page
```

```
    . . .
    property alias panelAdder: panelAdder
    property alias panelRemover: panelRemover
    . . .
    PanelButton {
        id: panelAdder
        anchors.right: parent.right
        text: "+"
    }
    PanelButton {
        id: panelRemover
        anchors.top: panelAdder.bottom
        anchors.right: parent.right
        text: "-"
    }
}
```

Finally, we connect the button click to the item removal in the fake panel's entity:

```
// CCPanels.qml
. . .
TableSurface {
    ListModel {
        id: panelsEntity
    }

    ComicPage {
        id: page
        . . .
        panelAdder.onClicked:
panelsEntity.append({"pid":panelsEntity.count})
        panelRemover.onClicked: if (panelsEntity.count > 0) {
panelsEntity.remove(panelsEntity.count-1);
                                }
    }
}
```

Well, that's it!

> If you want to improve on this solution, you might want to also
> implement use case tests for this use case, use a C++ data model instead of
> the fake `ListModel`, and set up the wiring between C++ and QML. Go
> back to Chapters 23, *Writing Acceptance Tests and Building a Visual
> Prototype*, to Chapter 25, *Wiring User Interaction and Delivering the Final
> App*, for a refresher on how you could do that.

Taking a picture and loading it into a panel

Now, what if we could have those panels show us something interesting instead of being blank? How about a picture of a doodle from the camera? Many comic creators still like to draw with pencil and paper, so this looks like a worthy feature. Let's sketch a use-case scenario and go ahead:

```
Given there is a page
And the page has one or more panels
And I select one panel
When I add a camera picture to the selected panel
Then the picture shows up in the selected panel
```

Here is the road map: we will first enhance our `ComicPanel` implementation to support clicking and images, then add a camera preview to our scene, and finally add the behavior to show the captured image in the selected panel when the panel is clicked.

To show the image in the panel, we use an `Image` item type (http://doc.qt.io/qt-5.9/qml-qtquick-image.html). It exposes a `source` property, which is typically a local or remote URL, and supports many image formats:

```
// ComicPanel.qml
import QtQuick 2.9

Item {
    id: panel
    property alias imageSource: image.source
    ...
    Image {
        id: image
        anchors.fill: parent
        fillMode: Image.PreserveAspectCrop
    }
    Rectangle {
        ...
    }
    ...
}
```

Then, in `CCPanels`:

```
// CCPanels.qml
...
TableSurface {
    ...
    ComicPage {
```

```
            id: page
            anchors.centerIn: parent
            panelsRepeater.delegate: ComicPanel {
                displayText: pid || 0
                imageSource: pictureSource || ""
            }
            ...
        }
    }
```

The `pictureSource` is the attribute that we will use in our data model to store the URL of the captured image, while `fillMode` is an important property of `Image` which controls the way the source image is displayed with respect to the size of the image item. For example, in this case, we want the image item to fill the available panel space, but don't want the source image to be deformed, and thus we select the enum mode `Image.PreserveAspectCrop`. Check out `Image`'s documentation to know about other available fill modes.

Also, we add a `MouseArea` to `ComicPanel` and expose the `clicked` signal:

```
// ComicPanel.qml
import QtQuick 2.9

Item {
    id: panel
    signal clicked()
    ...
    Text {
        id: textItem
        anchors.centerIn: parent
    }
    MouseArea {
        anchors.fill: parent
        onClicked: panel.clicked()
    }
}
```

The rest of the necessary code will be added to the scene. I would not consider this a production-ready option, but you will be able to refactor it if you develop this project further. For now, let's just prototype it. To capture the picture, we will use the Camera QML type, and to show a preview of it, we will use the VideoOutput QML type, both from the rich Qt Multimedia module.

Qt Multimedia (http://doc.qt.io/qt-5.9/multimediaoverview.html) is a cross-platform solution for interfacing with media sources (both video and audio) and exposes both a QML and a (currently richer) C++ API. It is a vast collection of QML types and C++ classes—take the time to check out the document linked earlier, which provides common recipes for different multimedia needs.

Here are Camera and VideoOutput added to CCPanels.qml:

```
// CCPanels.qml
...
TableSurface {
    ...
    ComicPage {
        ...
    }

    Camera {
        id: camera
    }

    VideoOutput {
        source: camera
        width: 120
        height: 75
        anchors.right: parent.right
        anchors.top: parent.top
        anchors.margins: 16
    }
}
```

The Camera is not a visual object, while the VideoOutput is.

Now that all necessary objects are in place, we can add the logic:

```
// CCPanels.qml
...
TableSurface {
    ListModel {
        id: panelsEntity
        property int currentIndex: -1
    }
```

```
ComicPage {
    id: page
    ...
    panelsRepeater.delegate: ComicPanel {
        displayText: pid || 0
        imageSource: pictureSource || ""
        Layout.fillWidth: true
        Layout.fillHeight: true
        onClicked: {
            panelsEntity.currentIndex = index;
            camera.imageCapture.capture();
        }
    }
    panelsRepeater.model: panelsEntity
    panelAdder.onClicked:
panelsEntity.append({"pid":panelsEntity.count,"pictureSource":""})
    ...
}

Camera {
    id: camera
    imageCapture {
        onImageCaptured:
panelsEntity.get(panelsEntity.currentIndex).pictureSource = preview
    }
}
...
```

By setting `panelsEntity.currentIndex` to the delegate's `index`, we are keeping track of the currently selected (clicked) panel. After doing that, we tell the `Camera` object to capture an image via its `imageCapture` member object. We also add an empty `pictureSource` attribute to any element that we append to `panelsEntity`. Finally, we describe what should happen once the image has been captured. The image is available as `preview`, which is a temporary URL to the image data.

Here is the result, and it also works for any further panels that you add (however, do not overdo it; we haven't dealt with any memory concerns in this prototype!):

Pretty impressive for the little code we had to add!

Loading an existing picture into a panel

Another useful feature would be to be able to choose an existing image (for example, from the local filesystem) instead of taking a camera picture:

```
Given there is a page
And the page has one or more panels
And I select one panel
When I add an existing picture to the selected panel
Then the picture shows up in the selected panel
```

Also, in this case, supporting the use case does not require much extra work. We start by adding two Button instances from **Qt Quick Controls 2** to the panel, instead of the MouseArea, and creating two separate signals (cameraClicked and existingClicked), rather than the single clicked:

```
// ComicPanel.qml
import QtQuick 2.9
import QtQuick.Controls 2.2

Item {
    id: panel
    signal cameraClicked()
    signal existingClicked()
    ...
    Text {
        anchors.horizontalCenter: parent.horizontalCenter
    }
    Button {
        id: cameraButton
        anchors.centerIn: parent
        text: "take picture"
        onClicked: panel.cameraClicked()
    }
    Button {
        id: existingButton
        anchors.top: cameraButton.bottom
        anchors.margins: 16
        anchors.horizontalCenter: cameraButton.horizontalCenter
        text: "load existing picture"
        onClicked: panel.existingClicked()
    }
}
```

Then, in the scene, we add a FileDialog object from QtQuick.Dialogs, and handle the two cameraClicked and existingClicked signals differently:

> Starting with Qt 5.7, a new module is being worked on, called Qt.labs.platform 1.0. This module contains overhauled platform-specific dialogs. However, as it seems, it cannot be used with qmlscene. Consider using it in your projects instead of QtQuick.Dialogs.

```
// CCPanels.qml
...
import QtQuick.Dialogs 1.2
```

```
TableSurface {
    ...
    ComicPage {
        id: page
        anchors.centerIn: parent
        panelsRepeater.delegate: ComicPanel {
            ...
            onCameraClicked: {
                panelsEntity.currentIndex = index;
                camera.imageCapture.capture();
            }
            onExistingClicked: {
                panelsEntity.currentIndex = index;
                fileDialog.open();
            }
        }
        ...
    }
    Camera {
        ...
    }
    VideoOutput {
        ...
    }
    FileDialog {
        id: fileDialog
        folder: shortcuts.home
        nameFilters: [ "Image files (*.jpg *.png)"]
        onAccepted:
panelsEntity.get(panelsEntity.currentIndex).pictureSource =
Qt.resolvedUrl(fileUrl)
    }
}
```

This was also pretty easy, wasn't it?

Now that the UI prototype is in place, you could extend the application by either adding more features, or consolidating the existing code to make it more maintainable. The first thing you could do is add the UI code to the ccpanels Qt Quick application project. Also, as already suggested, you could flesh out usecases and entities into single components, and add tests for them.

Summary

In this chapter, we have learned how easy it is to create captivating and feature-rich user interfaces, by getting to know many types exposed by the Qt Quick and Qt Quick Controls 2 modules.

We also learned how to include multimedia and file I/O functionality in QML, thanks to simple QML APIs for the Qt Multimedia and Qt Quick Dialogs modules. By leveraging these tools, being productive and having well-written code are no distant goals.

Take some time to refine the code you created, by refactoring it and trying to package it as a self-standing application.

In the next chapter, we will add another dimension and get to know another powerful Qt module: Qt 3D. Brace yourself!

27
Creating a Scene Composer to Explore 3D Capabilities

In the previous chapter, we hopefully made life a bit easier for independent comic creators by giving them a prototype for easily experimenting with page layouts. In this chapter, we enter the panel-creation stage, by crafting a small tool for quickly putting together 3D shape composition.

We will have a chance to deepen our knowledge and understanding of QML, by looking at more elaborate examples of property bindings, JS functions, and by learning how to expose a named QML module.

We will get to know Qt 3D, a feature-rich module for 3D rendering and nearly real-time simulations, which provides equally powerful C++ and QML APIs.

We will also discover how to integrate a 3D scene into a Qt Quick application, and overlay 2D controls to modify the contents of the scene.

Finally, we will learn how to easily export the contents of the scene to an image file.

Arranging 3D elements in a composition

I'm pretty confident that, by looking at a comic page, you are able to tell whether it is easy to read and understand or not, and I don't mean just the text, but also the images. Among other things (including the way the sequence of individual panels is laid out), it is composition that makes a single panel easily readable.

Composition is the art and science of placing elements into a scene (characters, props, scenery, speech bubbles, and so on) so that their storytelling effect is maximized. It requires thinking about empty spaces and blocked-out areas, lighting, contrast, size, balance, color value, and much more.

Just like panel placement (and interaction with it), it is an essential part of the thumbnailing stage, and comic artists spend a good deal of time working on this aspect.

Once again, we are here to make their lives easier, by devising a simple tool to quickly throw around a few shapes and explore their interactions. Given the limited space, the tool as implemented here will not be extremely useful, but by the end of the chapter, you should have sufficient knowledge to extend it as you see fit.

The implemented tool will look something like the following:

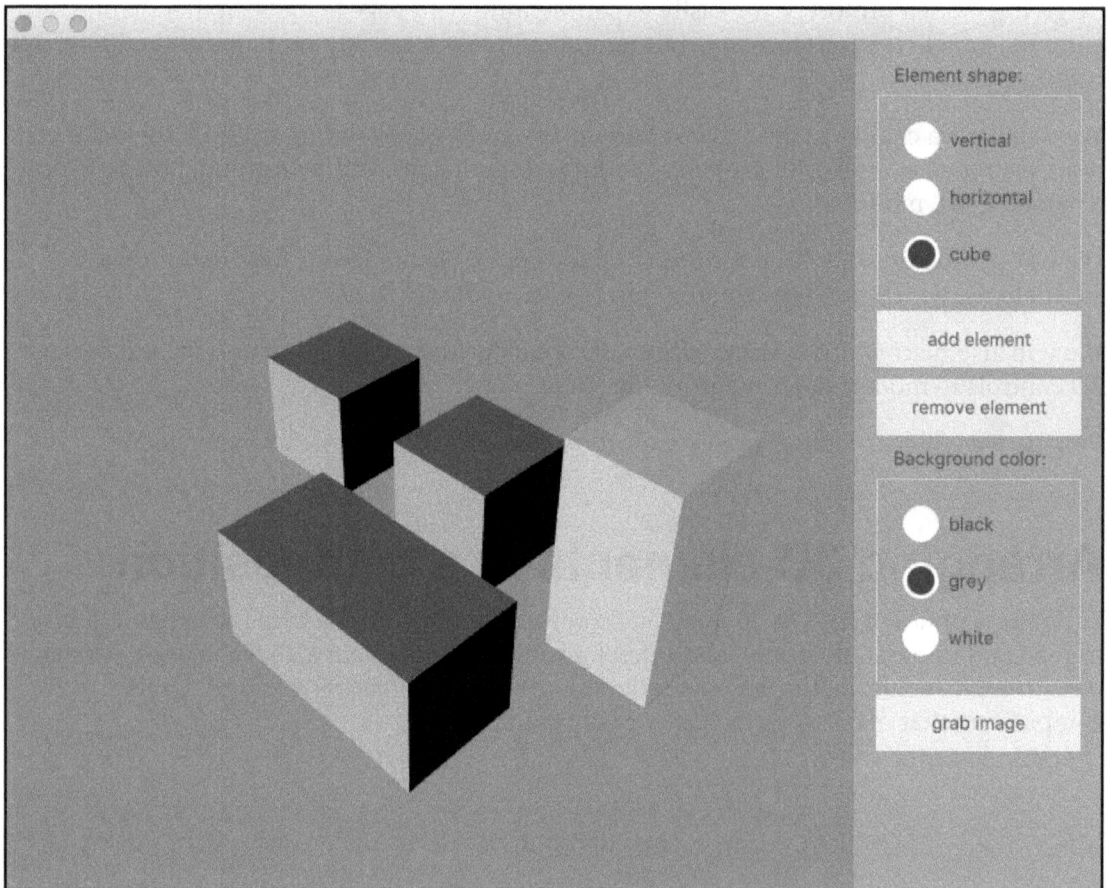

As you can see, the user can specify a 3D shape type to the element upon its creation (for example, a cube, a vertically extended cuboid, a horizontally extended cuboid), as well as switching the color for the scene's background at any time. An image of the current composition can be obtained by clicking on a dedicated button, which will open up a file selector to pick the destination file path. With an input device like a mouse, the user can control the position and zoom of the camera, as well as select and move the elements around. A selected element can be removed from the composition via a dedicated button.

Defining feature scenarios

As usual, we specify the intended behavior of our application by sketching the main scenarios for each of the features that we want to support. Due to space and time constraints, however, we will not implement all use-case and entity tests here, just sketching entities and `usecases` without an automatic verification of their functioning, focusing on the UI instead. Yet, you should try to equally care for all aspects. Feel free to refer back to Part I and to the previous chapter if you don't know where to start.

Adding elements to a composition

First of all, we want our users to be able to add a few 3D *elements* to what we call a composition.

Here, the 3D elements will just be simple shapes, but nothing prevents us from extending the notion to more elaborate 3D models to be imported from tools like Blender (`https://www.blender.org/`).

We can check automatically that the addition was successful as follows:

```
Feature: Add element to composition

    Scenario: Zero to one elements
        Given there is a composition with zero elements in it
        When I add element "A" to the composition
        Then the composition contains exactly one element
        And the new contained element is "A"

    Scenario: One to two elements
        Given there is a composition with element "A" in it
        When I add element "B" to the composition
        Then the composition contains exactly two elements
        And the new contained element is "B"
```

If we don't implement formal use case tests, we will have to visually check that the element was indeed added to the scene, and that its visual cues reflect the ones we chose when creating it. Alternatively, for debugging purposes, we could also display the element's ID on top of the element's shape.

Removing elements from a composition

We want our users to be able to change their mind and remove elements from the composition to their heart's desire. To achieve this, we need a mechanism to select an already existing element and destroy it. Here is the feature specification:

```
Feature: Remove element from composition

    Scenario: One to zero elements
        Given there is a composition with one element in it
        And the element is "A"
        When I select element "A" from the composition
        And I remove the selected element from the composition
        Then the composition contains zero elements

    Scenario: One to two elements
        Given there is a composition with two elements in it
        And one element is "A"
        And one element is "B"
        When I select element "A" from the composition
        And I remove the selected element from the composition
        Then the composition contains one element
        And the contained element is "B"
```

With the second scenario, we are making sure that we are not eliminating all or random elements, but rather the element we intended to.

Saving a composition as an image

A feature our users will certainly want is a way to save the result of their experimentation to use as the basis for further creation steps. We will thus give them the option to save a composition as an image to disk:

```
Feature: Save composition to image

    Scenario: Success
        Given there is a composition
        When I save the composition to image
```

```
        And I specify a save location
        And the save is successful
        Then I am told that the save was successful
        And I can find the image in the specified location

    Scenario: Failure
        Given there is a composition
        When I save the composition to image
        And I specify a save location
        And the save is not successful
        Then I am told that the save was not successful
```

Again, this feature specification is very trivial. Ideally, we would want to at least check the error type and give actionable feedback to the user.

> In the prototype, we will provide a bit more functionality to our users than what was described in the preceding usecases. We won't write, however, any usecases for these secondary features. After the early prototyping phase, these other usecases should be also written down and tested automatically.

Defining entities and their visual counterparts

From the usecases outlined, it looks like we will need *at least* two entities: A Composition and an Element. To define both of these, we will take advantage of Qt 3D's APIs and focus on the visual counterparts of both entities, always keeping in mind that a full application would require a neat separation between the logic entity layer and the visual layer.

Introducing Qt 3D

In Chapter 23, *Writing Acceptance Tests and Building a Visual Prototype*, we discussed how many options Qt provides when it comes to UI technologies. Its 3D offering, which had provided the QML and JS-focused **Qt Canvas 3D** module since release 5.5, now also includes the extremely powerful Qt 3D framework (https://doc.qt.io/qt-5/qt3d-overview.html).

In fact, Qt 3D is not *just* a 3D package; it is a generic framework for near-real-time simulations that does not only include rendering; it encompasses physics, audio, logic, and much more. The good news is that as well as being so powerful, Qt 3D makes it easy to implement simple solutions, while also making it possible to implement more complex ones.

The three core concepts around which Qt 3D revolves are entities, components, and aspects. Qt 3D is, in fact, an **entity component system** (**ECS**). An ECS is a way of conceptualizing an object-oriented system by leveraging composition, as opposed to inheritance, as the main mechanism that defines behavior. In Qt 3D's ECS, an entity (https://doc.qt.io/qt-5.9/qt3dcore-qentity.html) is an abstract type which aggregates one or more components. Each component (https://doc.qt.io/qt-5.9/qt3dcore-qcomponent.html), in turn, is responsible for describing a group of related characteristics. For example, a component might describe an entity's shape, another component might describe its material, a further component its position, and yet another component a sound that the entity should emit, and so on.

Different Qt 3D *aspects* will then be responsible for processing one or more components and integrating their information into some sort of output. For example, shape (mesh), material (surface appearance), and position (transform) will be processed by the rendering aspect to produce data for rendering the object in a 3D space.

It is not hard to see how this approach makes for a flexible and extensible framework, since components of the same kind can be switched very easily (for example, from cube to sphere), and with more effort new, arbitrary aspects can be implemented. Currently implemented aspects include rendering, input, animation, and logic, and more (for example, 3D audio) will likely be added in coming Qt versions.

Qt 3D has got a lot going on behind the scenes; for example, the code that runs the various aspects is heavily threaded, but the nice thing is that all these complexities are mostly hidden behind two clear declarative (QML) and imperative (C++) APIs.

Let's now see how we can leverage Qt 3D to implement the visual representation of the entities involved in our usecases. As we have learned by reasoning about the usecases, we should model at least an Element entity and a Composition entity.

Qt 3D entities are not quite the same as the entities (business logic units) that we devised in the previous chapters. Among other things, they provide a specific API based on composition, as discussed in the previous section. For this very same reason, a Qt 3D entity (QEntity) knows about, or at least references, the visual and non-visual components associated to it. Since in this chapter we are not going to work on a separate entity layer, we will consider a Qt 3D entity as a bundle made of a business object and its visual representation. Keep it in mind while reading the next sections!

Comparing C++ and QML APIs

Qt 3D is one of the few Qt sub-frameworks that provides C++ and QML APIs that are almost on-par, at least as long as you don't need to extend its behavior by, for example, implementing custom aspects.

In what follows, we will use the QML API, since QML should not be the most familiar beast for you just yet, and also because it allows rapid prototyping by writing substantially less code. Of course, these advantages come with a certain performance cost. You can explore both APIs by looking at the respective documentation (https://doc.qt.io/qt-5.9/qt3d-cpp.html, https://doc.qt.io/qt-5.9/qt3d-core-qmlmodule.html), as well as the parallel examples accessible from QtCreator (**Welcome** > **Examples**, then filter by qt3d).

Previewing Qt 3D entities in QML

The qmlscene tool that we used in the last chapter can also be used here to quickly visualize our Qt 3D QML code as soon as we write it. In order to achieve this, you just need a little boilerplate code. Just create a file called Preview3D.qml in the gui subfolder and fill it in with the following code:

```
// Preview3D.qml
import QtQuick.Scene3D 2.0
import Qt3D.Core 2.0
import Qt3D.Render 2.0
import Qt3D.Extras 2.0

Scene3D {
    id: scene3d
    Entity {
        id: sceneRoot
```

```
    Element {}

    Camera {
        id: camera
        projectionType: CameraLens.PerspectiveProjection
        fieldOfView: 45
        nearPlane : 0.1
        farPlane : 1000.0
        position: Qt.vector3d( 5.0, 5.0, 5.0 )
        upVector: Qt.vector3d( 0.0, 1.0, 0.0 )
        viewCenter: Qt.vector3d( 0.0, 0.0, 0.0 )
    }

    components: [
        RenderSettings {
            activeFrameGraph: ForwardRenderer {
                id: rendered
                camera: camera
            }
        }
    ]
    }
}
```

You will then be able to open the file with **qmlscene** (either via the command line or via Qt Creator, as shown in Chapter 26, *Learning About Laying Out Components by Making a Page Layout Tool*) by just substituting Element with the type that you want to preview. You can also change its size by changing the width and height properties of the root object (Scene3D). We will look at the contents of this file in more detail when implementing the Composition entity.

The Element entity

The Element entity represents a 3D object that we place within a composition. In our business domain (comics creation), it could stand for a character, a prop, a speech bubble, and so on. In order for the entity to show up within the composition, we should give it at least a mesh (3D shape), a material, and a position. Furthermore, we should make it also selectable so that we can move it around or remove it. Let's implement each of these capabilities with Qt 3D.

We start by creating an `Element` QML file in `gui` and defining its root type as a Qt 3D entity:

```
// Element.qml
import Qt3D.Core 2.9

Entity {
    id: element
}
```

Running the example in `Preview3D` won't yield any results, as the entity has no visual components attached to it yet. In order to be able to see a 3D representation of the entity, we will need to add a mesh, a material, and a position to it.

Adding visual components to the element

Adding a visual representation for the element entity is achieved as follows:

```
// Element.qml
import Qt3D.Core 2.9
import Qt3D.Extras 2.9
import Qt3D.Render 2.9

Entity {
    id: element

    CuboidMesh {
        id: cuboid
    }
    PhongMaterial {
        id: phongMaterial
    }
    Transform {
        id: transform
    }
    components: [cuboid, phongMaterial, transform]
}
```

We added a `CuboidMesh` and a `PhongMaterial`, both provided by `Qt3D.Extras` (https:/
/doc.qt.io/qt-5.9/qt3d-core-qmlmodule.html#qt-3d-extras-module), as well as a
`Transform`, provided by `Qt3D.Core` (https://doc.qt.io/qt-5.9/qt3d-core-qmlmodule.
html#qt-3d-core-module), so that we will be able to move the shape around later on. While
we have defined these objects as children to `Entity`, this is not a requirement. What makes
them become components of the `element` entity is the way their `ids` are referred to in
its components property.

> Feel free to check out the documentation for `Qt3D.Extras` to know what
> kind of meshes, materials, and so on are available off the shelf.

If you now add Element as a child of `Preview3D` and open `Preview3D.qml` with
qmlscene, you should see a nice little greyish cube on a white background:

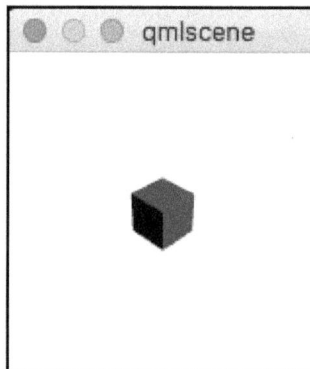

Varying the properties of the mesh

From the tool's screenshot at the beginning of the chapter, you can see how we want to
allow our users to choose from three different shape variations: a cube, a vertical cuboid,
and a horizontal cuboid. Thus, we will want to expose a property of our element to control
this parameter, and check out the documentation of `CuboidMesh` (https://doc.qt.io/qt-
5.9/qml-qt3d-extras-cuboidmesh.html) to see which properties govern the meshes size.
As it turns out, these are `xExtent`, `yExtent`, and `zExtent`.

All of these have a default value of 1. Thus, we will set to 2 either the *x* (horizontal cuboid) or the *y* extent (vertical cuboid), depending on the value of the element's shape property:

```
// Element.qml
import Qt3D.Core 2.9
import Qt3D.Extras 2.9

Entity {
    id: element
    property string shape: ""

    CuboidMesh {
        id: cuboid
        yExtent: shape === "vertical" ? 2 : 1
        xExtent: shape === "horizontal" ? 2 : 1
    }
    ...
}
```

If you now set the value of the element's shape property in Preview3D to either horizontal or vertical, you should see the change reflected in the shape. Every other value will yield a cube.

> **TIP**
>
> Starting with Qt 5.10, you can now declare enumerations in QML. That would be a good option for expressing the horizontal/vertical/cube alternatives. For more info: http://doc.qt. io/qt-5.10/qtqml-syntax-objectattributes.html#enumeration-attributes.

Changing the element's position

Another property that we want to expose is the position of the element, so that later on, we can move it around with the mouse, and also place it into a random location when we add it to the composition, so that it does not overlap with previously added elements. We can achieve this by creating an alias to the translation property of the Transform component:

```
// Element.qml
import Qt3D.Core 2.9
import Qt3D.Extras 2.9

Entity {
    id: element
    property string shape: ""
    property alias translation: transform.translation
```

```
    ...
    Transform {
        id: transform
    }
    ...
}
```

> The type of `translation` is `vector3d`, which is a QML basic type
> (`http://doc.qt.io/qt-5/qml-vector3d.html`) that represents a vector in
> three dimensions.

We can now move the element around in 3D space by assigning different values for *x*, *y*,
and *z* with a `vector3d` to its `translation` property. You can experiment with it
from `Preview3D`.

Selecting an element

Looking back at the tool's screenshot and description at the beginning of this chapter, we
will also recall that we might want to be able to select an element, to either move it around
with the mouse input or delete it. We thus add a `selected` Boolean property to the
element's API, and change the element's material color from black to red to signify that the
element is selected, by changing the material's `ambient` color property (`https://doc.qt.
io/qt-5.9/qml-qt3d-extras-phongmaterial.html`), which provides a color overlay:

```
import Qt3D.Core 2.9
import Qt3D.Extras 2.9

Entity {
    id: element
    property bool selected
    ...
    PhongMaterial {
        id: phongMaterial
        ambient: selected ? Qt.rgba(255,0,0,1)  : Qt.rgba(0,0,0,0)
    }
    ...
}
```

If we now set the element's `selected` property to `true` in the preview, it will turn from black to red.

Dealing with user input

Yet, how should we interact with the object to select it and move it around via a mouse click, or any other input? To handle input, we need to augment the element entity with an extra component; the `ObjectPicker` component (https://doc.qt.io/qt-5.9/qml-qt3d-render-objectpicker.html) from the `Qt3D.Render` module (https://doc.qt.io/qt-5.9/qt3d-core-qmlmodule.html#qt-3d-render-module):

```
import Qt3D.Core 2.9
import Qt3D.Extras 2.9
import Qt3D.Render 2.9

Entity {
    id: element
    property bool selected
    property vector3d translation: Qt.vector3d(0,0,0)
    property string shape: ""

    ...
    Transform {
        id: transform
        translation: element.translation
    }
    ObjectPicker {
        id: picker
        onMoved: {
            element.translation = Qt.vector3d(
                        pick.worldIntersection.x,
                        element.translation.y,
                        pick.worldIntersection.z
                        )
        }
        onClicked: {
            selected = !selected;
        }
        dragEnabled: selected
    }

    components: [cuboid, phongMaterial, transform, picker]
}
```

In the preceding code snippet, we defined the `ObjectPicker` as a child to the entity, and added its `id` to the list of entity components. We also added a behavior to two of the signal handlers exposed by `ObjectPicker` as a result of input interaction with it: `onMoved` and `onClicked`. The latter is pretty straightforward; when the `ObjectPicker` is clicked, invert the value of the element's `selected` property.

> **TIP**
>
> Always remember that from a JS context, in a QML document, you have direct access to the properties in the local object's context (`ObjectPicker`, in this case) and in the root object's context (`Entity`), if these are not shadowed by local properties of the same name. This is why, in this specific case, writing `element.selected` or simply `selected` achieves the same result.

When listening to the `onMoved` signal, we want to modify the element's `translation` property. Here is how we are doing it. The `onMoved` signal handler gives access to a `pick` event object (QML type `PickEvent`), which, among other things, contains a representation of the `ObjectPicker` in our 3D world's coordinate system (`pick.worldIntersection`) in the form of a `vector3d`. As in this specific case, we only want our meshes to move along the x and z axes, while keeping their y axis fixed; we calculate the new entity translation by keeping the original y, and using the x and z from the object picker as it moves across the 3D world. We also enable dragging only when the entity is selected, via `dragEnabled: selected`.

To test the interaction features of `Element`, we need to augment `Preview3D` as follows:

```
import QtQuick.Scene3D 2.0
import Qt3D.Core 2.0
import Qt3D.Render 2.0
import Qt3D.Extras 2.0
import Qt3D.Input 2.0
Scene3D {
    id: scene3d
    aspects: ['input','logic']
    Entity {
        id: sceneRoot
        Element {}

        Camera {
            id: camera
            projectionType: CameraLens.PerspectiveProjection
            fieldOfView: 45
            nearPlane : 0.1
            farPlane : 1000.0
            position: Qt.vector3d( 5.0, 5.0, 5.0 )
```

```
        upVector: Qt.vector3d( 0.0, 1.0, 0.0 )
        viewCenter: Qt.vector3d( 0.0, 0.0, 0.0 )
    }

    FirstPersonCameraController {
        id: cameraController
        camera: camera
    }

    components: [
        RenderSettings {
            activeFrameGraph: ForwardRenderer {
                id: rendered
                camera: camera
            }
        },
        InputSettings { }
    ]
    }
}
```

We will explain the meaning of these sub-components in short when dealing with the Composition entity.

Keeping track of the currently selected element

To wrap up the `Element` API, remember from the `usecases` that we will need to keep track of the selected element's identity in the composition to just destroy the one we intended to. We can do that by defining an `Element` identity in its `objectName` property, which is already part of the `QObject` API. This is not a robust technique (`objectNames` are not guaranteed to be unique), but it will do for now. So, when the object is either selected or deselected, we cast its `objectName` to the outside world by means of two new signals, `wasSelected` and `wasDeselected`:

```
import Qt3D.Core 2.9
import Qt3D.Extras 2.9
import Qt3D.Render 2.9

Entity {
    id: element
    signal wasSelected(string objectName)
    signal wasDeselected(string objectName)
    property bool selected
    ...
    ObjectPicker {
```

```
        id: picker
        ...
        onClicked: {
            selected = !selected;
            if (selected) wasSelected(element.objectName)
            else wasDeselected(element.objectName);
        }
    ...
}
```

Our element should now have a sufficient API to support all `usecases` that we want to address. As usual, in production code, you can (and you should) make sure of that by writing and implementing the relevant use case tests. Let's now create the Composition entity that will group our elements together.

The Composition entity

By looking back at our `usecases`, we might notice that the composition's main responsibilities from a logical point of view are as follows:

- Expose a list of elements that are contained in it
- Keep track of the selected element's `id` so that it can be removed from the composition when the user requires it

Furthermore, as we are not clearly separating the business entity from its visual representation, we will also define a few properties regarding the composition's look, the 3D scene representation, and input handling. Not very clean indeed, but hey, we are still prototyping!

Composition will be a Qt 3D entity containing a few more *entities*: a camera, a `cameraController`, and a group of `Elements`. It will also have a few components, comprising render settings, input settings, and lights.

Having the composition reference a list of entities

Let's first create the `Composition.qml` document and add a child entity called `elements` to it, which will group all elements that we want to add to the composition. We will also add a `selectedElement` string property, which will hold the `objectName` of the currently selected element:

```
// Composition.qml
import Qt3D.Core 2.0

Entity {
    id: composition
    property alias elements: elements
    property string selectedElement
    Entity {
        id: elements
    }
}
```

Previewing the composition

Since the composition will take the place of the `sceneRoot` in `Preview3D.qml`, you can update `Preview3D` as follows:

```
// Preview3D.qml
import QtQuick.Scene3D 2.0
import QtQml 2.2
Scene3D {
    id: scene3d
    aspects: ['input','logic']
    Component {
        id: elementC
        Element {}
    }

    Composition {
        id: composition
    }
    Component.onCompleted: {
        elementC.createObject(composition.elements);
    }
}
```

As you can see, besides substituting the `sceneRoot` entity with the Composition entity, we also added a `Component` object, as well as a JavaScript call to the `Component.onCompleted` signal handler, that you should already know from the QML primer given in `Chapter 23`, *Writing Acceptance Tests and Building a Visual Prototype*. The `Component` type is exposed by the Qt QML module. Let's have a closer look at what we are trying to achieve by using this idiom.

Adding elements to the composition

The most common way of using QML is declaratively. You have seen many examples of this right now; object declarations and simple property bindings work this way. There are times, however, where a dynamic approach is either preferred or required. Qt provides a few APIs for the dynamic creation of QML objects from JavaScript. We see an example of this in the preceding code snippet, by calling the `createObject` method of a `Component` type.

But what is a QML `Component` (`http://doc.qt.io/qt-5.9/qml-qtqml-component.html`)? It is an inline type definition; instead of using a `.qml` file to create our object from, we make the wanted component definition (`Element`, in the preceding example) available from within our current QML document, so that we can create instances of `Element` whenever we need.

And how do we create a type instance from a specific component? By using the `createObject` method. We will have to specify the parent which, for *visual* types, will typically be both an owning parent and a visual parent at once. In the preceding example, the `onCompleted` signal handler is called as soon as the `Scene3D` item is completed, and a new element is added as a child to `composition.elements`, the entity that we defined earlier.

Components are used in several occasions in QML code, even in declarative contexts. For example, when you specify a `delegate` in a `ListView`, as we did in `Chapter 23`, *Writing Acceptance Tests and Building a Visual Prototype*, and `Chapter 25`, *Wiring User Interaction and Delivering the Final App*, the delegate is a `Component`, instances of which will be created and destroyed as needed.

Besides using the `Component` type, you can also instantiate QML types from QML documents and inline QML code snippets. The `Component` method is, however, generally preferred, as it is more portable. For further details about these three techniques, consult:

```
http://doc.qt.io/qt-5.9/qtqml-javascript-dynamicobjectcreation.html.
```

Adding camera and interaction to the composition

Before being able to preview what the element looks like within the composition, we need to add a few more entities and components to it.

The first thing that we want to add is a Camera (https://doc.qt.io/qt-5/qml-qt3d-render-camera.html), which is an `Entity` exposed by the `Qt3D.Render` module. The Camera takes in a few parameters, mostly regarding the position, direction, and properties of the lens, the details of which can be learned by checking the docs. The positional parameters take a `vector3d`. Let's place the Camera on the front top right corner with respect to the elements by giving relatively high positive values to `position`:

```qml
import Qt3D.Core 2.0
import Qt3D.Render 2.0
import Qt3D.Extras 2.0

Entity {
    id: composition
    property alias elements: elements
    property string selectedElement

    Camera {
        id: camera
        projectionType: CameraLens.PerspectiveProjection
        fieldOfView: 45
        nearPlane : 0.1
        farPlane : 1000.0
        position: Qt.vector3d( 5.0, 5.0, 5.0 )
        upVector: Qt.vector3d( 0.0, 1.0, 0.0 )
        viewCenter: Qt.vector3d( 0.0, 0.0, 0.0 )
    }
    components: [
        RenderSettings {
            activeFrameGraph: ForwardRenderer {
                id: rendered
                camera: camera
            }
        }
    ]
```

```
    . . .
}
```

To be able to render the composition entity and all its children, we shall add a `RenderSettings` component to it, and use a predefined `ForwardRenderer` (https://doc.qt.io/qt-5.9/qml-qt3d-extras-forwardrenderer.html) to perform this job, which is provided by `Qt3D.Extras`. Since we have added the Camera entity, previewing composition with `Preview3D` will now work.

We also want the user to be able to move the Camera about. This can be achieved quite easily by adding a `FirstPersonCameraController` (https://doc.qt.io/qt-5.9/qml-qt3d-extras-firstpersoncameracontroller.html) from `Qt3D.Extras`. However, we want the Camera movements to be disabled selectively, for example when we are interacting with the elements in the scene. We will thus expose a `moveCamera` Boolean property in the `Composition` API. Finally, to have Qt 3D handle user input and control the Camera, we need to add an `InputSettings` component (https://doc.qt.io/qt-5.9/qml-qt3d-input-inputsettings.html), provided by `Qt3D.Input`, to Composition:

```qml
// Composition.qml
import Qt3D.Core 2.0
import Qt3D.Render 2.0
import Qt3D.Input 2.0
import Qt3D.Extras 2.0

Entity {
    id: composition
    property alias elements: elements
    property string selectedElement
    property bool moveCamera: true

    Camera {
        id: camera
        ...
    }

    FirstPersonCameraController {
        id: cameraController
        enabled: moveCamera
        camera: camera
    }

    components: [
        RenderSettings {
            activeFrameGraph: ForwardRenderer {
                id: rendered
                camera: camera
```

```
        }
    },
    InputSettings { }
]
    ...
}
```

You should now be able to move the camera around in `Preview3D`.

Adding custom lighting and changing the background color

We can also add a custom light source to the composition. There are a few types of light sources, exposed by the `Qt3D.Render` module: `DirectionalLight`, `PointLight`, and `SpotLight`. We will choose a `DirectionalLight` (`https://doc.qt.io/qt-5.9/qml-qt3d-render-directionallight.html`). In Qt 3D, lights are not entities but components. We should thus add it as a component to the composition.

Finally, we want to be able to change the composition's background color from the GUI. To do so, we expose the `clearColor` property of `ForwardRenderer` as part of the Composition API:

```
// Composition.qml
import Qt3D.Core 2.0
import Qt3D.Render 2.0
import Qt3D.Input 2.0
import Qt3D.Extras 2.0

Entity {
    id: composition
    property alias elements: elements
    property string selectedElement
    property string backgroundColor: "white"
    property bool moveCamera: true

    ...

    components: [
        RenderSettings {
            activeFrameGraph: ForwardRenderer {
                id: rendered
                camera: camera
                clearColor: composition.backgroundColor
            }
        },
```

```
        InputSettings { },
        DirectionalLight {
            worldDirection: Qt.vector3d( 0, -2.0, -5.0 )
            color: "#fff"
            intensity: 1
        }
    ]


    . . .

}
```

Previewing the Composition, we will now be able to see the custom lighting and modify the Camera point of view and zoom (by default, you can use the mouse wheel to zoom):

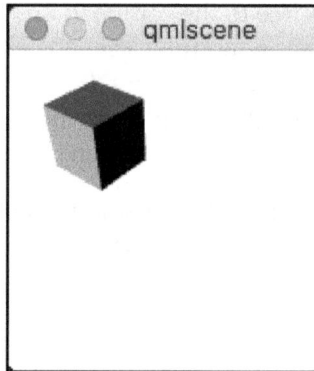

Creating the client application

Now that our 3D entities are complete, we just need to create the 2D UI controls and implement the logic for the usecases. Before doing that, however, we go back to what we started in Chapter 25, *Wiring User Interaction and Delivering the Final App*, by learning how to expose our UI components as a QML module to our cccomposer client application.

Exporting QML components in a namespaced module

In Chapter 25, *Wiring User Interaction and Delivering the Final App*, when dealing with the initial setup for the Cute Comics project, we learned how to create a qmldir file to expose a QML module, and later on we added both the qmldir file and the TableSurface QML document to the gui.qrc resource file. It is now time to expose the UI components that we created for the Cute Comics Composer project through the QML module, so that we can use them in our client application by importing them, without needing to care whether the components live on the filesystem or as embedded resources. We thus open the qmldir file and add references to our gui components:

```
// gui/qmldir
module cutecomics.gui

Composition 1.0 Composition.qml
Element 1.0 Element.qml
```

We are creating a QML module called cutecomics.gui, and flagging two QML types as belonging to the module, by also giving them a name (which in this case, is the same as the file name) and a version. By doing this, we will be able to import our components into a client application with the following statement:

```
import cutecomics.gui 1.0
```

In order for that to work, however, one more thing is left to be done — have Qt look for the module in the right location. An easy way to do this is to change the prefix of the QRC file that contains both the qmldir and the type definitions from its current value (/) to the following: /qt-project.org/imports/cutecomics/gui.

This can be achieved in Qt Creator by right clicking on the `gui.qrc` child node (the `/`) and selecting **Change Prefix...**:

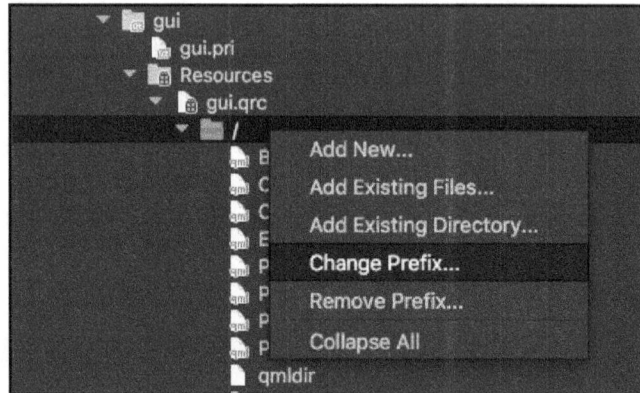

`qt-project.org/imports` is a default prefix which is automatically searched by Qt when locating resources.

If we also want the exposed QML module's types to be correctly highlighted in Qt Creator, we should add the following line to `part2-cute_comics.pro`:

```
QML_IMPORT_PATH += $$PWD
```

Setting up the client application

We can now create a client application. The project will be named `cccomposer`. It will be a sub-project of `part2-cute_comics.pro`. We can use a **Qt Quick Application** template from Qt Creator. Once we have added the sub-project, we should end up with a `cccomposer.pro` file and a `main.qml` file, among other things. To include our UI module, we shall add the following to `cccomposer.pro`:

```
# cccomposer.pro
include(../cutecomics/gui/gui.pri)
```

Once this is done, we will be able to `import` the QML module in `main.qml` with the `import cutecomics.gui 1.0` directive.

To show Composition in the client app, we will set up a QML Window (http://doc.qt.io/qt-5.9/qml-qtquick-window-window.html) and create a Scene3D to contain it, as follows:

```
// cccomposer/main.qml
import QtQuick 2.0
import cutecomics.gui 1.0
import QtQuick.Window 2.3
import QtQuick.Scene3D 2.0

Window {
    visible: true
    width: 800
    height: 600

    Scene3D {
        id: scene
        anchors.top: parent.top
        anchors.bottom: parent.bottom
        anchors.left: parent.left
        anchors.right: parent.right
        aspects: ['logic','input']
        Composition {
            id: composition
        }
    }
}
```

> We did not use the more convenient anchors.fill: parent to lay out Scene3D, as we will want to anchor it to the left of the 2D controls in the next step.

By running the cccomposer application, you should see an empty window, as we haven't added any elements to the composition yet. However, there should be no errors.

Creating the 2D controls

Take a look back at the screenshot at the beginning of this chapter. We want to provide the following controls for our user to interact with the 3D scene and perform the planned usecases:

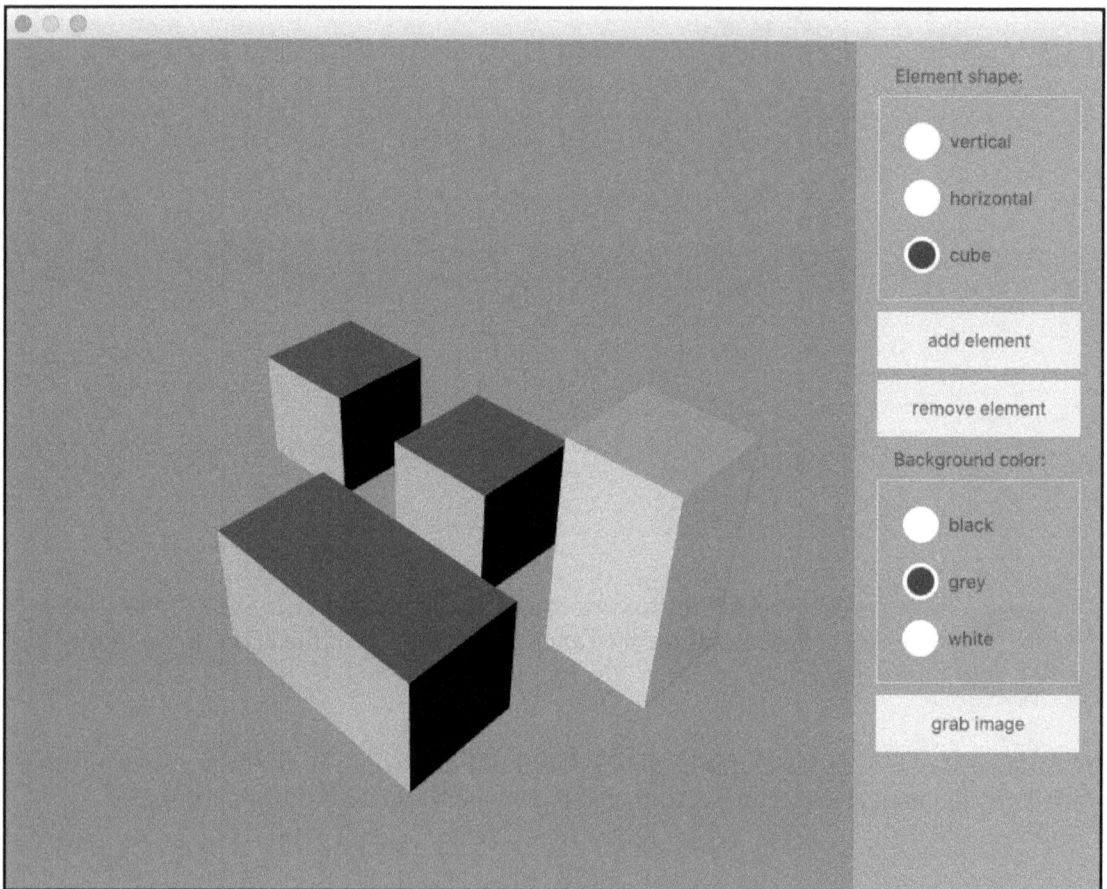

Adding the controls menu and the element creation options

All of these controls are provided by default by the Qt Quick Controls 2 module. We create a simple grey `Rectangle` to contain the controls, a `Column` positioner to display them vertically, and then add the checkboxes to choose the element's shape and the **add element** and **remove element** buttons, as follows:

```qml
// cccomposer/main.qml
import QtQuick 2.0
import cutecomics.gui 1.0
import QtQuick.Window 2.3
import QtQuick.Scene3D 2.0
import QtQuick.Controls 2.2

Window {
    visible: true
    width: 800
    height: 600

    Scene3D {
        anchors.top: parent.top
        anchors.bottom: parent.bottom
        anchors.left: parent.left
        anchors.right: menu.left
        ...
    }
    Rectangle {
        id: menu
        width: 160
        color: "#999"
        anchors.right: parent.right
        anchors.top: parent.top
        anchors.bottom: parent.bottom
        Column {
            anchors.margins: 16
            anchors.fill: parent
            spacing: 8

            GroupBox {
                id: shapeSelector
                title: "Element shape:"
                width: parent.width
                readonly property string shape:
                    shapeGroup.checkedButton.objectName
                ButtonGroup {
                    id: shapeGroup
```

```
                    buttons: shapeButtons.children
                }
                Column {
                    id: shapeButtons
                    RadioButton {
                        id: verticalButton
                        objectName: "vertical"
                        text: "vertical"
                        checked: true
                    }
                    RadioButton {
                        id: horizontalButton
                        objectName: "horizontal"
                        text: "horizontal"
                    }
                    RadioButton {
                        id: cubeButton
                        objectName: "cube"
                        text: "cube"
                    }
                }
            }
            Button {
                text: "add element"
                width: parent.width
            }
            Button {
                text: "remove element"
                width: parent.width
            }
        }
    }
}
```

Column (http://doc.qt.io/qt-5.9/qml-qtquick-column.html) is one of the available Qt
Quick positioner types. These are less powerful than the QtQuick.Layouts that we saw in
Chapter 25, *Wiring User Interaction and Delivering the Final App*, but also simpler to use in
certain scenarios like the preceding one, where no specific responsive or dynamic
behavior is required. You can learn more about available positioners, including Row, Grid,
and Flow in this very-well written primer: http://doc.qt.io/qt-5.9/qtquick-
positioning-layouts.html.

GroupBox (`https://doc.qt.io/qt-5.9/qml-qtquick-controls2-groupbox.html`) just provides visual grouping and a title label for a group of controls, while ButtonGroup (`https://doc.qt.io/qt-5.9/qml-qtquick-controls2-buttongroup.html`) provides the logical grouping, exposing a reference to the currently checked button via the `checkedButton` property. The rest of the code should already be familiar to you. Here is what the top part of the application should look like after these additions:

As you can see, the **remove element** button is not disabled yet — we will bind its `enabled` property to some logic states.

Adding the Background color selector and the grab image button

Adding the **Background color** selector and the **grab image** button is just more of the same:

```
// cccomposer/main.qml
...

Window {
    ...
    Rectangle {
        ...
        Button {
            text: "remove element"
            anchors.horizontalCenter: parent.horizontalCenter
        }
        GroupBox {
```

```
                        id: backgroundSelector
                        title: "Background color:"
                        width: parent.width
                        readonly property string backgroundColor:
                            backgroundGroup.checkedButton.objectName
                        ButtonGroup {
                            id: backgroundGroup
                            buttons: backgroundButtons.children
                        }
                        Column {
                            id: backgroundButtons
                            RadioButton {
                                id: blackButton
                                objectName: "black"
                                text: "black"
                            }
                            RadioButton {
                                id: greyButton
                                objectName: "grey"
                                text: "grey"
                                checked: true
                            }
                            RadioButton {
                                id: whiteButton
                                objectName: "white"
                                text: "white"
                            }
                        }
                    }
                    Button {
                        text: "grab image"
                        anchors.horizontalCenter: parent.horizontalCenter
                    }
                }
            }
        }
    }
```

We can now simply switch the composition color at any time by adding the following line to Composition:

```
Composition {
    id: composition
    backgroundColor: backgroundSelector.backgroundColor
}
```

With these additions, the GUI of our tool is almost complete. Let's add the missing logic to it then.

Prototyping the usecases in JavaScript

As we already mentioned, since we consider this to be a prototype, we won't be implementing the usecases fully, with automated tests and all the bells and whistles; we will just add a few QtObjects to main.qml that will encapsulate our usecases and entities. Feel free to improve on this aspect by providing the necessary refactoring.

Adding the elements business object

The first thing that we might want to do is create an elements business object to encapsulate operations on a collection of Element entities. We implement it as a simple QtObject, by adding:

- A list property to keep reference to the elements that we have added to the composition
- A selectedElement string to keep track of the objectName for the currently selected Element
- A counter integer to generate unique, progressive objectNames for the entities
- A factory property of type Component to reference the QML Component in charge of generating Element instances:

```
// cccomposer/main.qml
...

Window {
    ...
    QtObject {
        id: elements
        property int counter: 0
        property string selectedElement
        property var list: []
        readonly property Component factory: Component {
            Element {}
        }
    }
    Scene3D {
        ...
        Composition {
            id: composition
```

```
                moveCamera: elements.selectedElement === ""
        }
    }
    Rectangle {
    ...
            Button {
                text: "remove element"
                enabled: elements.selectedElement !== ""
                anchors.horizontalCenter: parent.horizontalCenter
            }
    ...
}
```

Now that we have the `elements.selectedElement` property, we can bind the `enabled` state of the **remove element** button to it; when no element is selected, the button will be disabled. Also, we can disable camera movement in the composition whenever an element is selected.

Adding the usecases

Along the same lines, we can add another `QtObject` to encapsulate the `usecases`, which will be implemented as JavaScript methods of this object:

```
// cccomposer/main.qml
...

Window {
    ...
    QtObject {
        id: elements
        ...
    }

    QtObject {
        id: usecases

        function addElementToComposition(shape) {}

        function removeElementFromComposition() {}

        function saveCompositionToImage() {}
    }
    ...
}
```

Now that we have methods for the `usecases`, we can wire these to the previously created buttons:

```
// cccomposer/main.qml
...

            Button {
                text: "add element"
                anchors.horizontalCenter: parent.horizontalCenter
                onClicked: {
                    usecases.addElementToComposition(shapeSelector.shape);
                }
            }
            Button {
                text: "remove element"
                anchors.horizontalCenter: parent.horizontalCenter
                onClicked: {
                    usecases.removeElementFromComposition();
                }
            }
            ...
            Button {
                text: "grab image"
                anchors.horizontalCenter: parent.horizontalCenter
                onClicked: {
                    usecases.saveCompositionToImage();
                }
            }
    ...
```

Implementing add element to Composition

To add an element to the Composition, we:

- Increase the `elements.counter` to be able to generate a unique object name for the new element
- Instantiate the `Element` QML component as a child of the elements entity, by passing a few creation parameters to the `createObject` call; the shape we get from the GUI option selected by the user, and the initial translation by a vector of random numbers:

```
// cccomposer/main.qml
...
function addElementToComposition(shape) {
    elements.counter += 1;
```

```
        var element = elements.factory.createObject(
                composition.elements,
                {
                    shape: shape,
                    objectName: "element"+elements.counter,
                    translation: Qt.vector3d(
                            Math.random()*3, 0.0, Math.random()*3)
                });
        elements.list.push(element);
}
...
```

If you now run the application and click on `add element`, you should see cuboids with the selected shape appear at random locations.

Implementing remove element from composition

To remove an `element` from a Composition, we can loop over the list of existing `elements`, and destroy it if its `objectName` corresponds to the value of `elements.selectedElement`:

```
// cccomposer/main.qml
...
function removeElementFromComposition() {
    for (var i=0; i < elements.list.length; ++i) {
        if (elements.list[i].objectName === elements.selectedElement) {
            elements.list[i].destroy();
            elements.selectedElement = "";
            break;
        }
    }
}
...
```

For this to work, however, we must ensure that `elements.selectedElement` is filled with the `objectName` of the last `Element` that was selected by the user. This can be achieved by notifying the `elements` business object whenever an element instance was selected, via a signal-slot connection to be established when the `element` is created and added to the composition:

```
// cccomposer/main.qml
...
QtObject {
    id: usecases
```

```
        function addElementToComposition() {
            ...
            element.wasSelected.connect(elements.onSelected);
            element.wasDeselected.connect(elements.onDeselected);
            elements.list.push(element);
            elements.counter += 1;
        }
    }
    ...
```

And:

```
    // cccomposer/main.qml
    ...
    QtObject {
        id: elements
        ...
        function onSelected(objectName) {
            selectedElement = objectName;
            list.forEach(function(element) {
                if (element.objectName !== selectedElement) {
                    element.selected = false;
                }
            });
        }
        function onDeselected(objectName) {
            selectedElement = "";
        }
    }
    ...
```

As you can see, the signal-slot connection can also be established in JavaScript imperatively, by calling the connect() method of a signal and passing the intended slot function as its argument.

> Alternatively, the connection could be set up declaratively in factory by adding to Element the signal handlers onWasSelected: elements.onSelected(objectName), and onWasDeselected: elements.onDeselected(objectName)

By running the application, a user will now be able to add and remove elements from the composition.

Implementing save composition to an image

Saving a composition to an image is straightforward. If we look at the QQuickItem's API (http://doc.qt.io/qt-5.9/qquickitem.html), from which both Item and Scene3D derive, we can notice how it exposes a grabToImage method. In turn, this method returns a pointer to a QQuickItemGrabResult object (http://doc.qt.io/qt-5.9/qquickitemgrabresult.html) which exposes a saveToFile method. Since grabToImage works asynchronously, the grab result should be accessed in a callback function, which can be passed as an argument to grabToImage, as in the following example:

```
item.grabToImage(function(image) {
    image.saveTofile();
});
```

To save the image, we will thus just have to call grabToImage for the Scene3D, ask the user where to save the file, and then inform the user about success/failure.

For the file selection, we can use FileDialog from the Qt.labs.platform module (https://doc.qt.io/qt-5.9/qml-qt-labs-platform-filedialog.html). Finally, we can give feedback to the user by implementing a simple snackbar to be displayed with a timeout. We thus add the following objects to main.qml:

```
// cccomposer/main.qml
import QtQuick 2.0
import cutecomics.gui 1.0
import QtQuick.Window 2.3
import QtQuick.Controls 2.2
import QtQuick.Scene3D 2.0
import Qt.labs.platform 1.0

Window {
    ...
    FileDialog {
        id: fileDialog
        fileMode : FileDialog.SaveFile
        folder:
StandardPaths.writableLocation(StandardPaths.DocumentsLocation)
    }

    Rectangle {
        id: snackbar
        visible: false
        width: 180
        height: 40
        color: "#333"
        anchors.horizontalCenter: parent.horizontalCenter
```

```
            anchors.bottom: parent.bottom
            anchors.bottomMargin: 16
            Text {
                id: snackbarText
                color: "white"
                anchors.centerIn: parent
            }
            Timer {
                id: snackbarTimer
                interval: 2000
                onTriggered: parent.visible = false
            }
        }
    }
}
```

Implement the `saveCompositionToImage` use case as follows:

```
// cccomposer/main.qml
...
function saveCompositionToImage() {
    fileDialog.open();
}
...
FileDialog {
    id: fileDialog
    fileMode : FileDialog.SaveFile
    folder: StandardPaths.writableLocation(StandardPaths.DocumentsLocation)
    onAccepted: {
        scene.grabToImage(function(image) {
            var saved = image.saveToFile((fileDialog.file+"")
                                    .replace('file://', ''));
            snackbarText.text = saved ? "image saved" : "something went
wrong :(";
            snackbar.visible = true;
            snackbarTimer.start();
        });
    }
}
...
```

Take your time to work out what happens in the preceding code, especially how the
visibility of `fileDialog` and `snackbar` are controlled, and the data is passed around.
Admittedly, this is not the most readable implementation one could think of, but for this
prototype, we are just content if it works as it should.

The `Timer` object (`http://doc.qt.io/qt-5.9/qml-qtqml-timer.html`), a QML wrapper for `QTimer`, is a very useful component to implement any kind of time-based logic, since functions like `delay()` and `setTimeout()`, which you might be familiar with, are not available in QML's JavaScript engine.

With these final steps, when a user presses the **grab image** button and chooses a file name with the `.png` file extension, the file will be saved in the intended location:

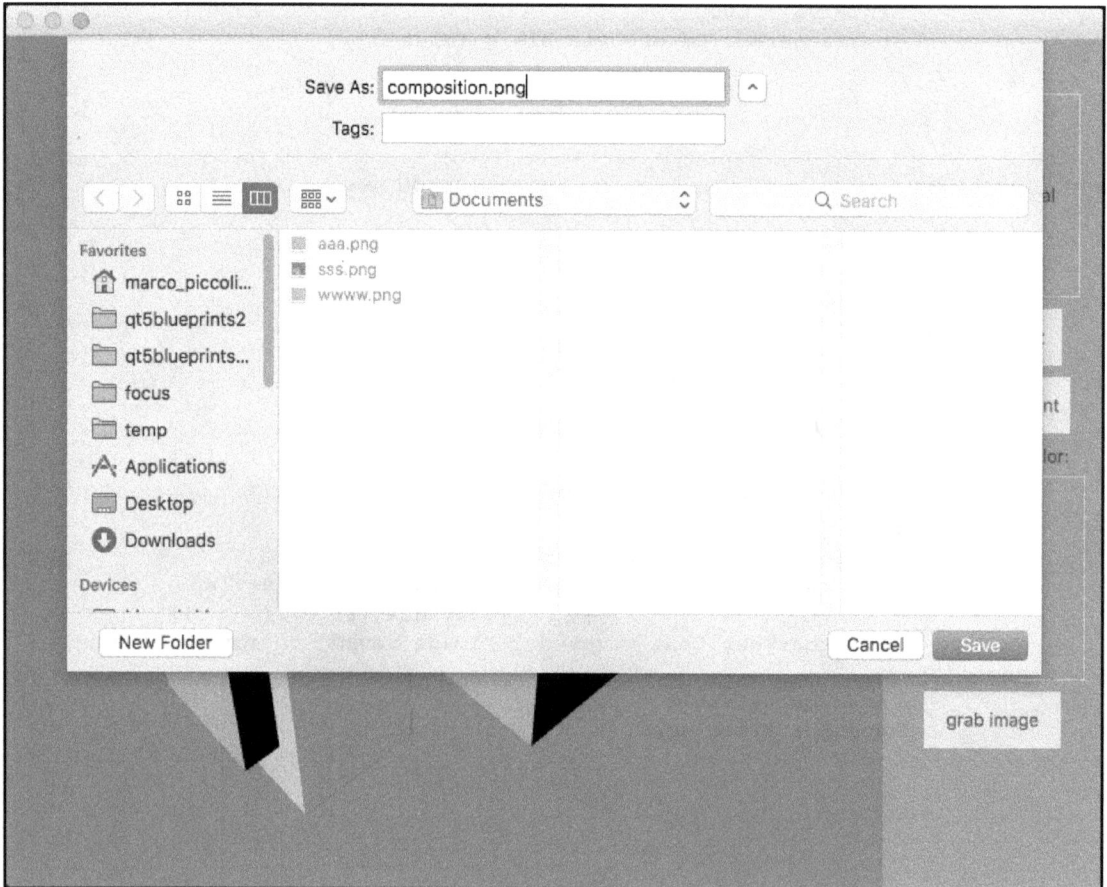

With this, our intended `usecases` are complete.

Going further

We have just touched upon Qt 3D's power. Feel free to further explore it to your heart's content. For example, you could try and recreate the tool by using C++ only, or maybe add more usecases, interactions, and GUI options. Qt's extensive documentation and the many tutorials that are available online about Qt 3D should help you further. Give it a go!

Summary

In this chapter, we have created a useful tool that enables comic creators to quickly sketch element composition. By doing so, we learned the basics and usage of the Qt 3D framework to easily create 3D-enabled applications.

We have focused on Qt 3D's QML APIs, which are a good solution for prototyping and relatively lightweight applications.

We have also learned more about QML syntax and useful QML types; for example, creating and exposing a QML module.

Finally, we have learned how to grab an image from any type that extends the QQuickItem class, including Item and Scene3D.

In the next chapter, we will prototype another useful tool to help comic creators be more efficient in writing dialogue. By doing so, we will introduce the Qt Widgets module, as well as many other useful Qt classes.

28
Building an Entity-Aware Text Editor for Writing Dialogue

In the previous chapters, we provided independent comic creators with two pretty useful tools to address the scene composition stage (thumbnailing) and the page layout stage. In this chapter, we will build an app for creating simple comic scripts, which contain scene descriptions and character dialogue. The app will be a specialized text editor whose contents can be modified by either typing in or selecting predefined entities (the comic's characters) from a list.

By developing this app, we will get to know Qt Widgets, a set of mature, C++ only, desktop-oriented UI components that cover a wide range of needs. We will also learn how to create widget-based UIs with Qt Designer, similar to what we have already seen for Qt Quick, and how to apply CSS-like styling to single widgets.

We will discover how to create more complex and extensible data models with full support for Qt's model/view paradigm.

We will finally take a look at how to process text documents with regular expressions to produce syntax-highlighted text, write them to disk, and export PDFs.

Writing comic scripts efficiently

Before tackling the visual stages of comic creation, an independent comic creator usually drafts a description of the various scenes and dialogue therein in written form since editing text is usually less time-consuming than editing images. The product of this work is the comic's *script*. The script is then used as a guide by the same person or a different artist to lay contents out visually.

The default option for writing a script is to use a regular document editor. However, the scripting process contains repetitive actions and references to various entities, such as scenes, panels, environments, and character names in dialogue. It would be nice for comic creators not to have to write the repetitive parts, but rather select them as needed from lists of existing entities, and instead focus on the creative aspects, such as dialogue lines and scene descriptions.

In this chapter, we will prototype an app that tackles one of these automations; we will allow creators to define a list of characters once and then insert the character names in the script's dialogue by simply double-clicking on a character's name from a list.

Furthermore, we will provide automatic syntax highlighting for the script by formatting character names in the text with a different font weight and color so that they stand out clearly. We will also allow our users to save the script as a text file and export it as a PDF to preserve the formatting.

The UI of our application will look as shown in the following screenshot:

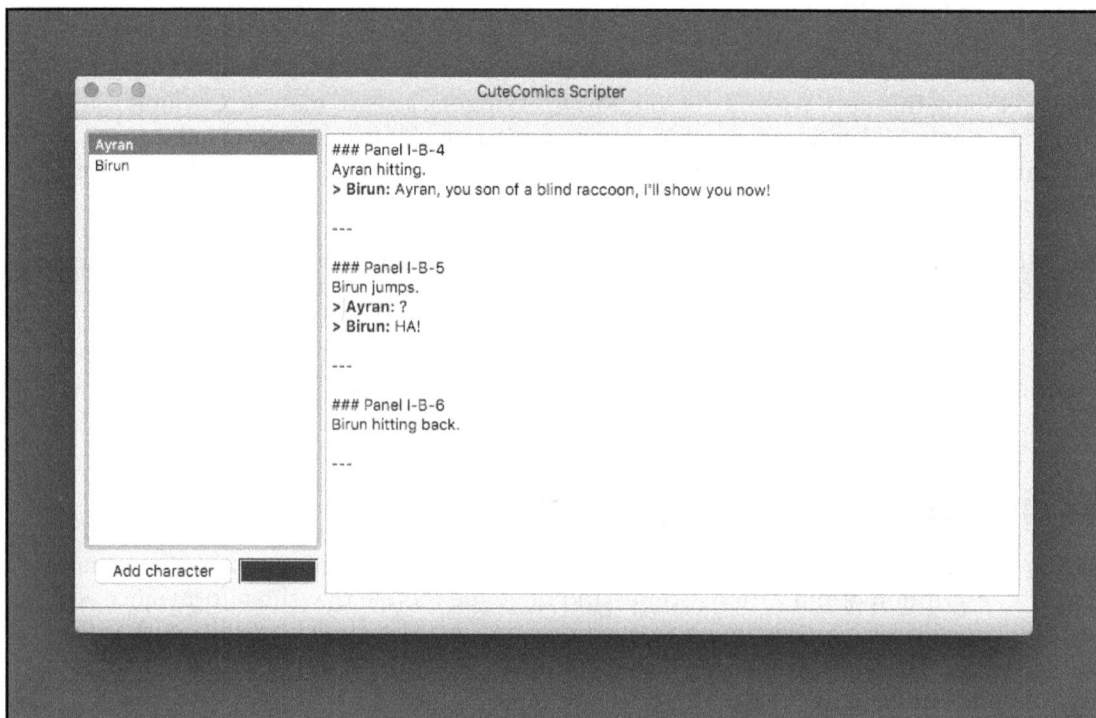

In the preceding screenshot, note how dialogue lines show the character's name in bold (and a different color) from the surrounding text.

Before diving into code, let's define the main use cases for this application so that we have a clear route ahead.

Defining use cases

Two fundamental use cases that we would want to support are adding new characters to the characters list and inserting a character's name into the script:

```
Feature: Add character to characters list

    Scenario: No characters in characters list
        Given there are no characters in the characters list
        When I add a character with name "X" to the characters list
        Then there is a character with name "X" in the characters list

Feature: Insert character name into script

    Scenario: No character names in script
        Given there is at least one character with name "X" in the
characters list
        And there are no character names in the script
        When I insert character name "X" into the script
        Then a character name "X" appears in the script
```

Besides these, we will also support the following use cases that are not detailed here since they are pretty straightforward and common:

- Saving script to a text file
- Exporting script as a PDF

Before diving into the design and implementation of the UI and use cases, let's set up the minimal project structure we will require.

Setting up the project

We will name this product `Cute Comics Scripter`. Since this will be a prototype, most of the code for use cases and UI will reside in the client application, while any entities we might need will be added to the already existing `entities` subproject, as we might want to reuse one or more entities in other applications. As usual, feel free to impose a more sustainable structure to your project by better separating the use cases and other components if you plan on extending it beyond what is shown in this chapter.

The client application will be based on the **Qt Widgets Application** template of Qt Creator. Let's go ahead and create a new project—`ccscripter`—as a subproject of `part2-cute_comics.pro`:

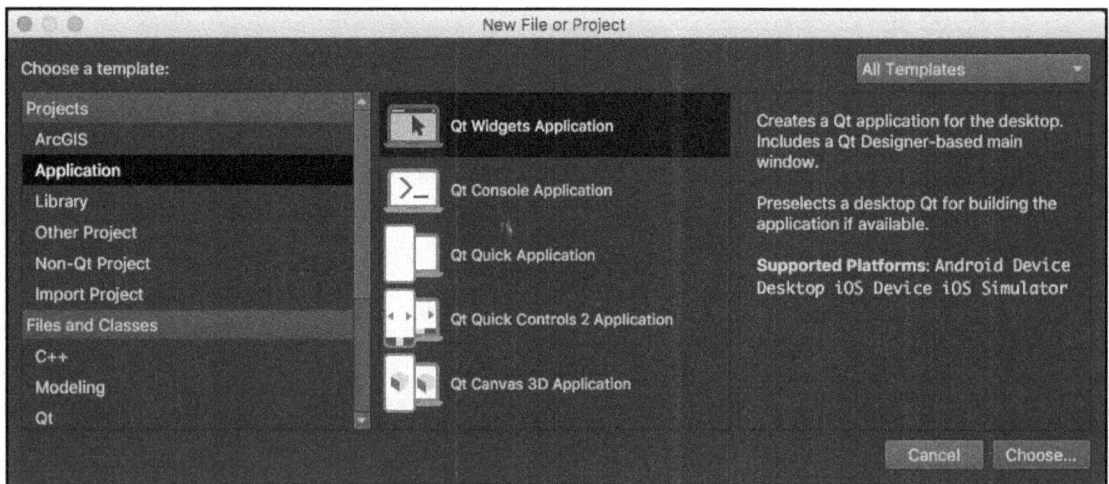

We can leave the names for the files to be created as suggested by Qt Creator.

The newly created project will have, in addition to the customary C++ source files, a new section called **Form**, which contains a file named `mainwindow.ui`. This is a UI form file encoded in XML which contains the form layout information generated by creating the UI visually with Qt Widgets Designer. In fact, double-clicking on the `.ui` file will open Qt Creator's **Design** mode.

Another thing we should do now is to include the already created `entities.pri` into `ccscripter.pro` so that we can use the entities library in the client app. We can achieve this by adding the following line to `ccscripter.pro`:

```
# ccscripter.pro
...
include(../cutecomics/entities/entities.pri)
```

The basic project structure for `Cute Comics Scripter` is now in place. We'll be adding any further files we might need in the coming sections.

Prototyping the UI

As described at length in `Chapter 23`, *Writing Acceptance Tests and Building a Visual Prototype*, under *Deciding upon the UI technology*, many factors come into play when choosing the right Qt UI technology. Although Qt Quick with its QML interface is by now a very powerful technology, many applications that even now target desktop environments are still build with the Qt Widgets framework.

Introducing Qt Widgets

Qt Widgets (`http://doc.qt.io/qt-5.9/qtwidgets-index.html`) is a very mature framework, which provides an impressive range of controls and related components that can seamlessly integrate with the native look and feel of most desktop operating systems, while also supporting custom styling. They represent a viable solution for applications that are mostly oriented to classical desktop applications with standard input devices (mouse and keyboard), since their support for touch gestures on some platforms is extremely limited.

Qt Widgets also represents a viable solution to implement specific components, such as efficient table views, that might not be already readily available in Qt Quick Controls. The `QQuickWidget` class makes it possible to include Qt Quick-based components into Widgets-based UIs.

Currently, Qt Widgets only provides a C++ API. Additionally, it allows you to encode a partial UI called a *form* using the Qt Widgets Designer (`http://doc.qt.io/qtcreator/ creator-using-qt-designer.html`). UI forms are converted to C++ objects either at compile time with the `uic` command (`http://doc.qt.io/qt-5.9/uic.html`) or at runtime via the UI Tools module (`http://doc.qt.io/qt-5.9/qtuitools-module.html`). Both tools are fully integrated in Qt Creator and mostly transparent to the application developer.

Being derived from `QObject`, widgets also have the concept of a parent-child relationship. For widgets, this relationship does not only have implications for memory management, but is also used to build visual hierarchies. A widget that is parented to another widget will be also displayed in it—a widget without parents automatically becomes a window. Additionally, a child widget's geometry is relative to that of the parent.

For a detailed handling of widgets, take a look at `http://doc.qt.io/qt-5.9/qwidget. html#details`.

> In this book, we won't be showing how to use the C++ API for creating QtWidgets interfaces. Yet, it is one of the first APIs provided by Qt, and you might even prefer it over using Qt Designer. As a rule of thumb, the C++ API is recommended for UIs which are complex either in terms of number of controls or interaction patterns, as it provides more flexibility. For a tutorial on how to get started, take a look at `http://doc.qt.io/qt-5.9/widgets-tutorial.html`.

Using Qt Widgets Designer

We can prototype a functional graphical user interface built around widgets with Qt Widgets Designer.

Qt Widgets Designer (or simply *Qt Designer*—not to be confused with the *QtQuick Designer* we already know from `Chapter 23`, *Writing Acceptance Tests and Building a Visual Prototype*) is a component of Qt Creator, which is loaded automatically whenever a `.ui` form file is selected. If you open the `mainwindow.ui` file created by the template, you will note something like the following screenshot:

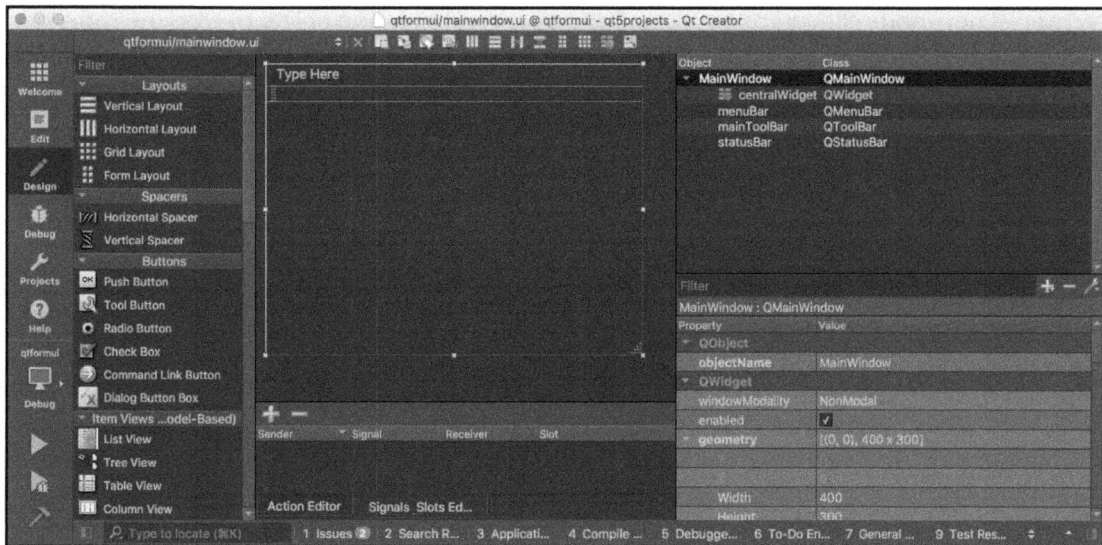

As you can see in the preceding screenshot, the layout of this tool is quite similar to the one provided by QtQuick Designer (refer to `Chapter 23`, *Writing Acceptance Tests and Building a Visual Prototype*). On the left, we will find a collection of widgets that can be dragged into the main canvas at the center, whereas on the right, we can see an object tree at the top and object properties at the bottom.

The form already contains a few components, which are typically needed in a classic desktop application: a window (the root), a root widget to be used as a parent for all other widgets, a menu bar, a toolbar, and a status bar. To create the UI for `Cute Comics Scripter`, we will just have to drag the right widgets into the canvas and configure some of their properties.

Adding the main layout

The first thing that we want to do is to define the main layout for our window, which will contain the characters list and other controls on the left and the text editor on the right. We can lay out the widgets into two columns with a **Horizontal Layout** (http://doc.qt.io/qt-5.9/qhboxlayout.html). We will thus drag the **Horizontal Layout** component into the canvas. A new node called `horizontalLayout` is created in the object tree on the right side of the window, as a child to `centralWidget`. To have the layout take up all available space in the window, we need to right-click on `MainWindow` and select **Lay Out... > Lay Out in a grid**. In the canvas, we will see that the red rectangle representing the child layout now spans the whole window. If we resize the window manually by clicking on its bottom-right corner and drag the mouse, the layout is also resized:

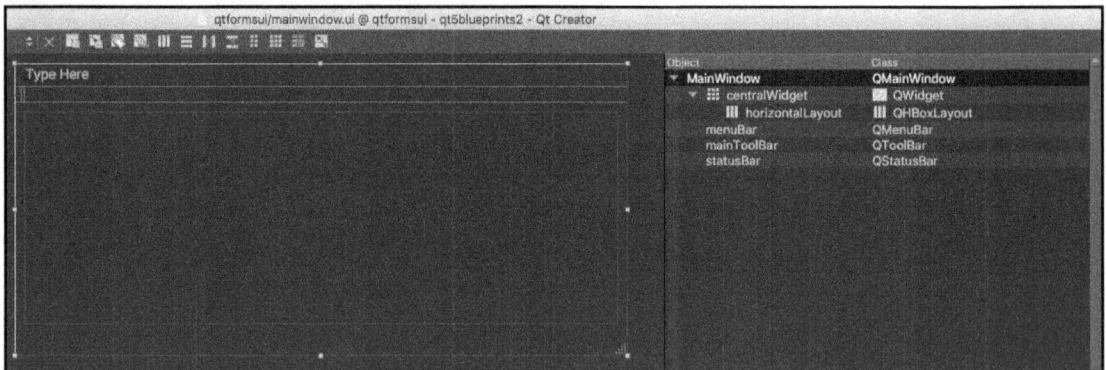

Adding the left column and the text editor

We can now add the children to the main layout. The left child will be another layout, this time, a vertical one, which will contain both the character's list and the widgets to add a new character; the right child will be the text editor. You can see the intended arrangement in the picture at the beginning of the chapter. We will drop a **Text Edit** (http://doc.qt.io/qt-5.9/qtextedit.html) widget and then a **Vertical Layout** (http://doc.qt.io/qt-5.9/qvboxlayout.html) into `horizontalLayout`.

> **TIP**
>
> While adding and removing widgets and layout components, keep in mind that in case anything goes wrong, a full undo stack is available in Qt Creator.

The next thing we want do is to have the vertical layout take up the first fourth of the available window space, and the text edit the remaining three fourths. We can achieve this by selecting `horizontalLayout` in the objects tree and modifying the value of its `layoutStretch` property to `1,3` (one-fourth and three-fourths). Once this is done, we can compile and launch the application. You should get a result similar to this, with the text edit occupying the right-hand side of the window:

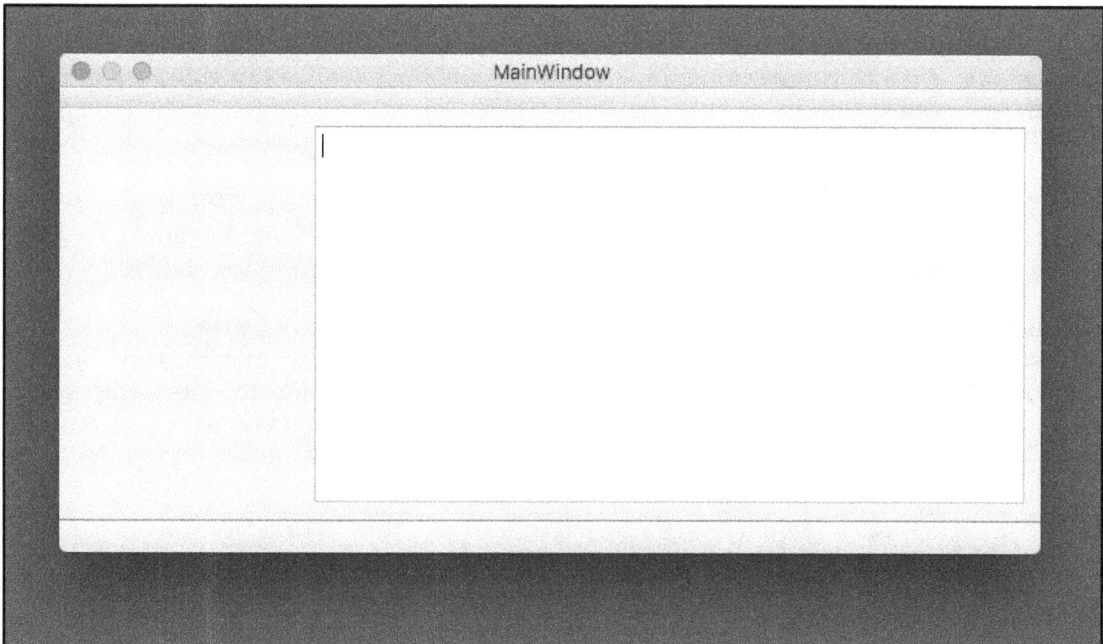

> You can learn more about managing layouts at `http://doc.qt.io/qt-5.9/layout.html`.

`QTextEdit` is a rich text editor, which allows us to apply different font styles to the comic script text document. Since it will be an important element we want to make reference to from C++ once we add the logic layer, we will change its `objectName` property (which, as you might remember, is a `QObject` property) to `scriptEditor`. To change `objectName` we will click on the text edit in the object tree and modify the corresponding property field. The change shows up in the object tree as well.

Adding the List View, button, and line edit

What we want for our app is a list of characters to show up in the top part of the left column and a horizontal sequence of a button as well as a line edit to be displayed underneath it. Thus, we first add a new horizontal layout and then a **List View** (http://doc.qt.io/qt-5.9/qlistview.html) widget as children to the vertical layout we created before.

> If you find it hard to drag a child component into a parent layout in the canvas, you can drag the component onto the parent layout's node in the object tree.

QListView corresponds in the widgets world to the ListView Qt Quick component we made use of in the previous chapters; it is a component based on the model/view paradigm, which automatically gets updated whenever a change is made to its source data model.

We also add a **Push Button** and a **Line Edit** as children to the newly created horizontal layout. If they are inverted in their positions, you can select one of them in the canvas and change their order. The obtained UI structure will look something like the following screenshot—the object names might have a number added to them if you have added and removed more than one instance:

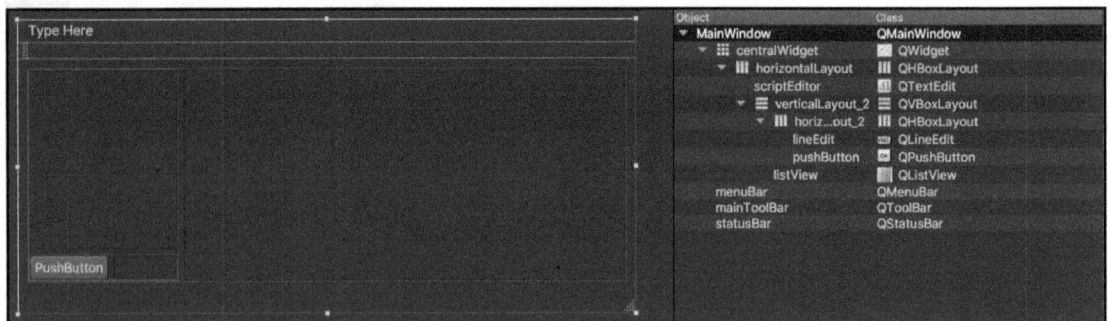

We will also want to rename a few components to better reference them when we add the logic.

1. We will first select the **PushButton**, and change its objectName to addCharacterButton. While we are at it, we will also change its text property (scroll down or filter the properties table to find it) to add character.

2. We then change the object name of the line edit to `addCharacterInput` and the name of the list view to `charactersListView`. Once this is done, the main UI elements for our app will be in place.
3. The last change we will do for now to the UI is to change the `windowTitle` property of `MainWindow` to `Cute Comics Scripter`.

Implementing the characters entity

By looking at our first use case (`Add character to characters list`), we will note that an entity representing a list of characters is involved. Our characters entity needs a few methods: at least one to add an item to the list, and one to retrieve the items in the list. We will thus keep things simple and implement the entity *as a list*, without additional members. The list is quite simple, requiring only a character's name to be used for the use cases here.

Introducing QAbstractItemModel and QAbstractListModel

The first option would be to implement the list with a simple `QList` of `QStrings` or `QVariants`, as we did in `Chapter 24`, *Defining a Solid and Testable App Core*. However, Qt provides more powerful data structures that make it easier to implement the model/view paradigm. All these models derive from `QAbstractItemModel`, provide automatic means of updating the views that rely on them, and can conveniently represent relatively complex data structures, such as trees and tables. A useful starting point for implementing custom data models of a certain complexity is the flexible `QStandardItemModel`. When the model can be represented as a list, `QAbstractListModel` (http://doc.qt.io/qt-5.9/qabstractlistmodel.html) is a simpler starting point, and it is what we will be using now.

When we take a look at the documentation of `QAbstractListModel`, we will know that if we want to implement this data model that provides us with all features of Qt rich data models, including automatic updates of views and the possibility to use convenient filters and sorters such as `QSortFilterProxyModel` (http://doc.qt.io/qt-5.9/ qsortfilterproxymodel.html), we will just need to override the following two methods: `rowCount`, which returns the number of rows (items) in the model, and `data`, which returns the data currently available in the model. The data itself can be stored within the model using a simple data structure, such as the already encountered `QStringList`.

> If your model is used within QML and requires roles other than the default ones provided by the `roleNames()` method of `QAbstractListModel`, you must override this method as well. This won't be the case here. For more information, take a look at http://doc. qt.io/qt-5.9/qabstractitemmodel.html#roleNames. For an off-the-shelf solution which implements `QAbstractListModel` for `QStringList`-like data, you can also take a look at http://doc.qt.io/qt-5.9/ qstringlistmodel.html.

Creating the characters entity

We will now go ahead and create a new entity called `Characters` to be added to `entities.pri`. Since this entity will be a subclass of a `QAbstractListModel`, we can use one of Qt Creator's file templates to create it. We will open `entities.pri` and use Qt Creator's **New File or Project...** menu. In the template selector, we will choose the **Qt Item Model** template under the **Qt** submenu. We'll want to define the following options in the wizard, ensuring that **QAbstractListModel** is selected as the base class:

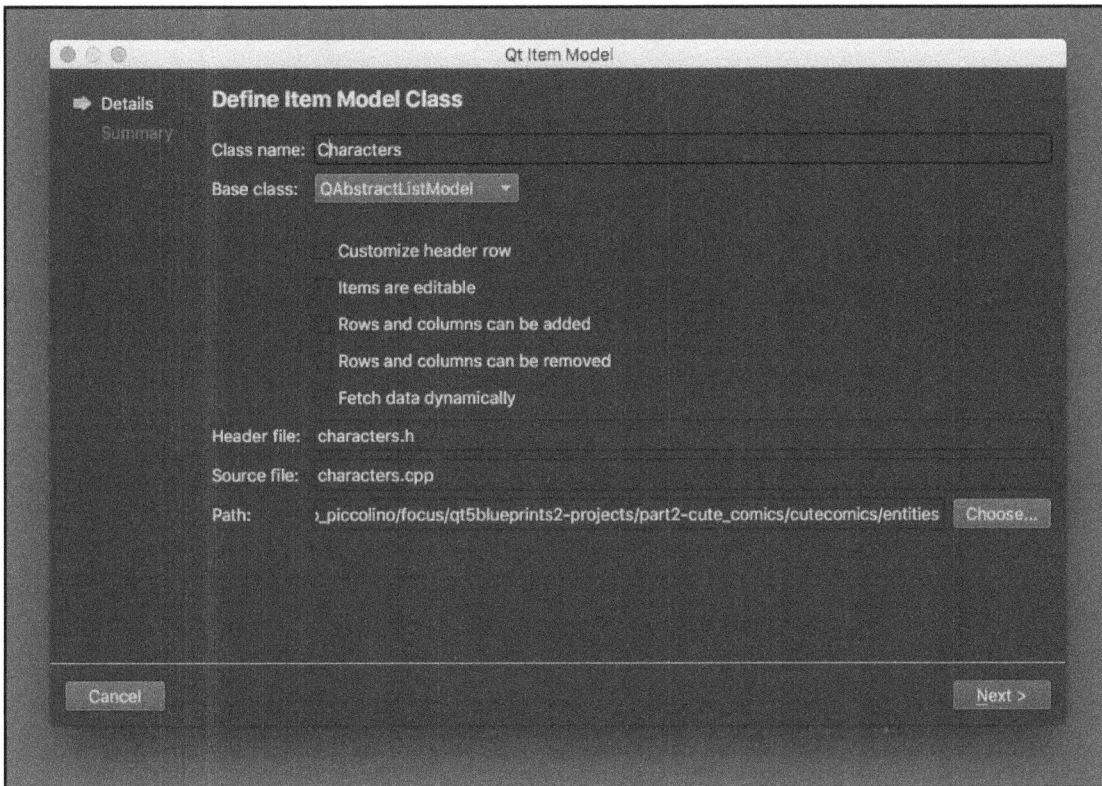

Then, in the **Project Managemen**t step, choose `entities.pri` as the project to be added to.

The newly created header stub will look like this:

```cpp
// characters.h

#ifndef CHARACTERS_H
#define CHARACTERS_H

#include <QAbstractListModel>

class Characters : public QAbstractListModel
{
    Q_OBJECT

public:
    explicit Characters(QObject *parent = nullptr);

    // Basic functionality:
    int rowCount(const QModelIndex &parent = QModelIndex()) const override;
```

```
     QVariant data(const QModelIndex &index, int role = Qt::DisplayRole)
const override;

private:
};


#endif // CHARACTERS_H
```

As you can note in the preceding code, the declarations for the `rowCount` and `data` methods to be overridden are added automatically, and so are their definition stubs.

Take a look at the first `rowCount` and note how it requires a data structure of the `QModelIndex` type as an argument. A `QModelIndex` (http://doc.qt.io/qt-5.9/qmodelindex.html) encapsulates information about the position of a specific item within a model. In the case of our list, an item's `index` is simply defined by its `row()` component. However, when representing 2D data structures, or hierarchical structures, the `column()` and `parent()` methods will return essential data about the location of an item within the model, hence the need to use this more complex structure instead of a simple integer. In the case of `rowCount`, the `QModelIndex` argument is the index of the parent item of the current model, which in our case will be invalid as we are dealing with a simple, nonhierarchical list model made of only columns.

Before implementing the two methods, we will need to place `Characters` into the `entities` namespace and add a member variable to store the model's items in memory. We will modify the header file as follows:

```
// characters.h

#ifndef CHARACTERS_H
#define CHARACTERS_H

#include <QAbstractListModel>

namespace entities {
class Characters : public QAbstractListModel
{
    Q_OBJECT

public:
    ...
private:
    QStringList m_list;
};
}

#endif // CHARACTERS_H
```

Once this is done, we can implement `rowCount` by calling into the already familiar `count` method of `QList`:

```cpp
// characters.cpp

#include "characters.h"

using namespace entities;

...

int Characters::rowCount(const QModelIndex &parent) const
{
    ...
    if (parent.isValid()) // items in a list have no parent node
        return 0;

    return m_list.count();
}
```

Similarly, we will implement the model's data method by returning the item in `QStringList` at the specified row index with the `at` method of `QList`:

```cpp
// characters.cpp

QVariant Characters::data(const QModelIndex &index, int role) const
{
    if (!index.isValid())
        return QVariant();

    if (role == Qt::DisplayRole && index.column() == 0)
        return m_list.at(index.row());
    return QVariant();
}
```

What have we done here? What is a *role*? When creating a derived model of QAbstractItemModel, each item in the model should have a set of data elements associated with it, each with its own *role*. The roles are used by a view to indicate to the model which type of data it needs for specific purposes. For example, when providing a view that comprises editable fields, we might want the same data to look differently in the **Display** mode from the **Edit** mode. Thus, we could return different data representations for Qt::DisplayRole and Qt::EditRole. In our case, we return the string as a display role, which is the default role requested by models. For more information about available built-in roles, refer to http://doc.qt.io/qt-5.9/qt.html#ItemDataRole-enum.

This is enough to transform a simple QStringList into a full-featured Qt data model.

For a deeper understanding of the model/view paradigm and all subtleties associated to the handling of QAbstractItemModel-derived models, you should go through the comprehensive overview available at http://doc.qt.io/qt-5.9/model-view-programming.html.

Nowadays, there are some simpler models available, provided by third parties, which hide some of the complexity away when you just need list-like models. For an example, refer to http://gitlab.unique-conception.org/qt-qml-tricks/qt-qml-models.

Adding a character to the characters model

Now that we have made our Characters entity model/view aware, we will still need a utility method to add a new character to it. This method will be called add and will take the character's name as an argument.

We will add its declaration to characters.h:

```
// characters.h

#ifndef CHARACTERS_H
...
class Characters : public QAbstractListModel
{
...
public:
    ...
    void add(const QString& name);
...
```

```
}
...
```

Then, we will provide its implementation in `characters.cpp`:

```cpp
// characters.cpp
...
void Characters::add(const QString &name)
{
    if (! m_list.contains(name)) {
        beginInsertRows(QModelIndex(), m_list.count(), m_list.count());
        m_list.append(name);
        endInsertRows();
    }
}
...
```

Besides the `push_back` method of `QList` (which is equivalent to `append`, just with a C++ Standard Library naming), you can note two extra method calls: `beginInsertRows` and `endInsertRows`. These need to be called whenever the internal data structure of the model is being modified, so that the view is notified about the changes to reflect them in the user interface. The first argument is the `index` of the parent model (which does not exist in this case, hence the empty `QModelIndex` instance), whereas the second and third arguments specify the row numbers that the newly inserted rows will take after insertion. Since we are pushing just one item at a time at the back of the list, these correspond to the length of the list (that is, the `index` of the current last item, plus one).

Note how the item addition is carried out only if an item with the same name is not already in the list:

```cpp
if (! m_list.contains(name))
```

If we wanted to add a remove function (which we will not be using in this example), we could do it as follows, by calling the corresponding `beginRemoveRows` and `endRemoveRows` functions. The former takes the parent model `index`, plus the first and last row numbers to be removed, which, being only one item, obviously coincide:

```cpp
// characters.cpp
...
void Characters::remove(const QString &name)
{
    int index = m_list.indexOf(name);
    if (index > -1) {
        beginRemoveRows(QModelIndex(), index, index);
        m_list.removeAt(index);
        endRemoveRows();
```

```
        }
    }
    ...
```

Now that we have an API to add new `characters` to the `characters` list, let's connect this to the UI and write a simple use case implementation for it. For the sake of simplicity, the use cases will be implemented directly in the client application's `main` via C++ lambda functions, and they will have direct access to the UI. This is not, however, something we would want to do for anything more than a prototype. Refer back to Chapters 1-3 for a sounder application architecture.

Let's open `main.cpp` in Qt Creator. First, we will need to get hold of the widgets that should be involved in the use case. We can query the widgets by making sure that the `ui` member of the generated `MainWindow` class is public:

```
// mainwindow.h
...
public:
    explicit MainWindow(QWidget *parent = 0);
    ~MainWindow();
    Ui::MainWindow *ui;
};

#endif // MAINWINDOW_H
```

We can then use the object names as members of `ui` tol get pointers to `charactersListView`, `addCharacterButton`, and `addCharacterInput`:

```
// ccscripter/main.cpp

#include "mainwindow.h"
#include <QApplication>
#include <QListView>
#include <QPushButton>
#include <QLineEdit>
#include "ui_mainwindow.h"

int main(int argc, char *argv[])
{
    QApplication a(argc, argv);

    MainWindow w;
    auto charactersListView = w.ui->charactersListView;
    auto addCharacterButton = w.ui->addCharacterButton;
    auto addCharacterInput = w.ui->addCharacterInput;
    ...
}
```

Then, we will need to create an instance of the `Characters` entity and set it as the model for `charactersListView`; we will do it as follows:

```
// ccscripter/main.cpp
...
#include "../cutecomics/entities/characters.h"

int main(int argc, char *argv[])
{
    QApplication a(argc, argv);

    MainWindow w;
    auto charactersListView = w.ui->charactersListView;
    ...

    auto characters = new entities::Characters(&a);
    if (charactersListView) {
        charactersListView->setModel(characters);
    }
...
}
```

Once this is done, we can respond to the user when they click on the **Add character** button by adding a new item to the character's list with a connection on the `clicked` signal of the button and taking the character's name from `addCharacterInput`:

```
// ccscripter/main.cpp
...
if (addCharacterButton && addCharacterInput) {
    QObject::connect(addCharacterButton, &QPushButton::clicked,
[characters, addCharacterInput]() {
        if (! addCharacterInput->text().isEmpty()) {
            characters->add(addCharacterInput->text());
            addCharacterInput->clear();
        }
    });
}
...
```

> For alternative ways of reacting to UI signals in designer, including taking advantage of built-in `on_*` signal handlers as it is done in QML, check out `http://doc.qt.io/qt-5.9/designer-using-a-ui-file.html`

We will now verify that the input text is not empty, add a new character with the input as its name, and then clear the input widget. This is enough to have our first use case working. Run the application and try adding a character; it should show up in the character's list view on the left:

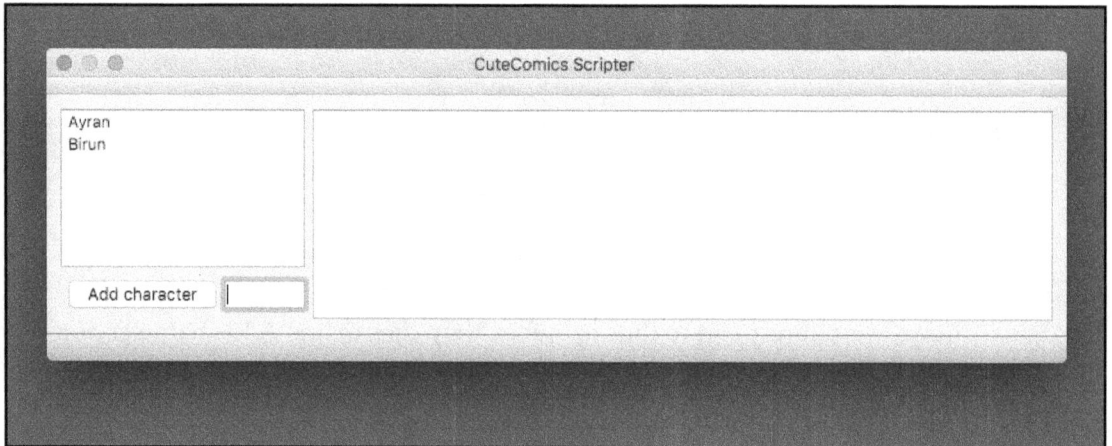

At this point, you could also write a use case for removing a character from the list and implement it.

Inserting a character's name into the dialogue script

Once a character's name is in the list, we will want our user to insert it into the list as a dialogue opener by just double-clicking on the character's name.

To retrieve a single item at a specified index from `Characters`, we can use the already implemented `data` method. In order to do so, we will first need a pointer to the `scriptEditor` widget:

```
// ccscripter/main.cpp
...
auto scriptEditor = w.ui->scriptEditor;
...
```

Implementing the use case is then as simple as the following:

```
// ccscripter/main.cpp
...
if (charactersListView && scriptEditor) {
    QObject::connect(charactersListView, &QListView::doubleClicked,
[characters, scriptEditor](QModelIndex index) {
        scriptEditor->append(QString("> %1:
").arg(characters->data(index).toString()));
    });
}
...
```

The `scriptEditor`, which is a `QTextEdit` widget, has an `append` function that puts a string at the end of the currently held text document as a new paragraph (that is, it also inserts a new line). We will format the string using the `arg` function of `QString` (http://doc.qt.io/qt-5.9/qstring.html#arg): `%1` is the placeholder for the string, which is provided as the first argument to `arg`.

> The `arg` function is overloaded and can take up to nine input string arguments. Alternatively, calls to arg with a single argument can be concatenated.

In this case, we have decorated the character's name in the editor by enclosing it between > and :. Run the application and check whether it works, as follows:

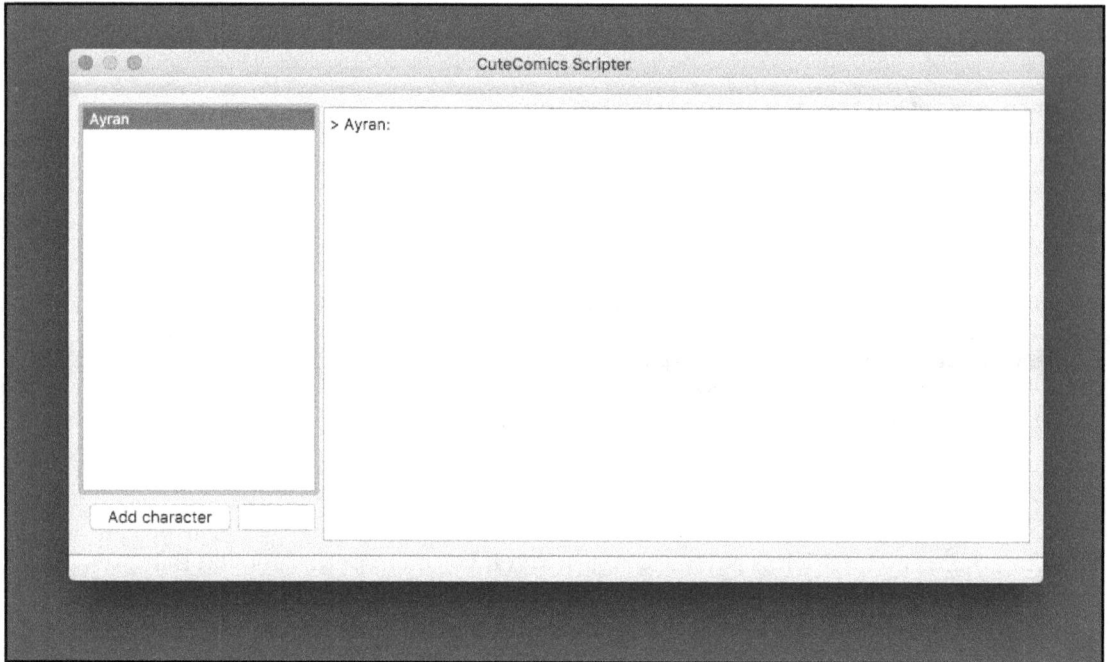

Auto-highlighting a character name

A nice addition to improve the readability of the comic script would be to provide auto-highlighting for the character names. It turns out that Qt exposes a `QSyntaxHighlighter` (`http://doc.qt.io/qt-5.9/qsyntaxhighlighter.html`) component, which just does this. It can be attached to a `QTextDocument` (`http://doc.qt.io/qt-5.9/qtextdocument.html`), such as the default text document, which is embedded in our `QTextEdit` script editor.

A full tutorial to implement a custom syntax highlighter is available at `http://doc.qt.io/qt-5.9/qtwidgets-richtext-syntaxhighlighter-example.html`.

We will make use of a regular expression to find any sequence of type > *character name*: and display it as bold, blue text. To achieve this, the first thing we will need to do is to subclass `QSyntaxHighlighter`; to do so, we will create a new C++ class in our client application called `ScriptHighlighter`. We can provide `QSyntaxHighlighter` as a base class in Qt Creator's wizard. As the example linked earlier informs us, in order to use a custom syntax highlighter, we will need to reimplement the `highlightBlock` method. `scripthighlighter.h` will thus look as follows:

```cpp
// scripthighlighter.h

#ifndef SCRIPTHIGHLIGHTER_H
#define SCRIPTHIGHLIGHTER_H

#include <QObject>
#include <QSyntaxHighlighter>

class ScriptHighlighter : public QSyntaxHighlighter
{
    Q_OBJECT
public:
    explicit ScriptHighlighter(QTextDocument *parent = nullptr);
protected:
    void highlightBlock(const QString& text) override;
};

#endif // SCRIPTHIGHLIGHTER_H
```

We also need some member variables to store the regular expressions and text formats that we will apply to the text. We will implement these as a vector of highlight rules that associate a regular expression to a text format. While we are only concerned with the character names in dialogue openings in this example, this will give us a chance to extend the formatting to other text patterns as well. The following are the data structures added to `scripthighlighter.h`:

```cpp
// scripthighlighter.h

#ifndef SCRIPTHIGHLIGHTER_H
#define SCRIPTHIGHLIGHTER_H

#include <QObject>
#include <QSyntaxHighlighter>
#include <QRegularExpression>
#include <QTextCharFormat>

class ScriptHighlighter : public QSyntaxHighlighter
{
    {
```

```
    . . .

private:
    struct HighlightingRule
    {
        QRegularExpression pattern;
        QTextCharFormat format;
    };
    QVector<HighlightingRule> highlightingRules;

    QTextCharFormat characterFormat;
    . . .
```

When constructing the highlighter in `scripthighlighter.cpp`, we will initialize the highlighting rules with the regular expression values and text formats:

```
// scripthighlighter.cpp

ScriptHighlighter::ScriptHighlighter(QTextDocument *parent) :
QSyntaxHighlighter(parent)
{
    HighlightingRule rule;

    characterFormat.setFontWeight(QFont::Bold);
    characterFormat.setForeground(Qt::darkBlue);

    rule.format = characterFormat;
    rule.pattern = QRegularExpression("> \w+:");

    highlightingRules.append(rule);
}
```

For more details about how regular expressions are supported in Qt, take a look at `http://doc.qt.io/qt-5.9/qregularexpression.html`. In this example, we replaced the character name with a sequence of one or more (+) word-like characters (\w).

We will now need to implement the `highlightBlock` method that will be called automatically whenever the content of the text document is updated:

```cpp
// scripthighlighter.cpp
...
void ScriptHighlighter::highlightBlock(const QString &text)
{
    for (auto rule : qAsConst(highlightingRules)) {
        QRegularExpressionMatchIterator matchIterator =
rule.pattern.globalMatch(text);
        while (matchIterator.hasNext()) {
            QRegularExpressionMatch match = matchIterator.next();
            setFormat(match.capturedStart(), match.capturedLength(),
rule.format);
        }
    }
}
```

We will loop over the rules (just one, in our case), match the regular expression (`rule.pattern`) in the text document, and make all found matches in the text document available via an iterator. We will then loop over the matches by applying the custom formatting to the corresponding segment of the text document (identified by `capturedStart` and `capturedLength`).

> The qAsConst macro ensures that a non-const implicitly shared container is not accidentally detached. For more information, refer to http://doc. qt.io/qt-5.9/qtglobal.html#qAsConst

To link the highlighter to the text document in the `scriptEditor`, we will need to add the following code to `main.cpp`:

```cpp
// ccscripter/main.cpp
...
#include "scripthighlighter.h"
...
if (scriptEditor) {
    new ScriptHighlighter(scriptEditor->document());
}
```

That is all that is needed to enable the highlighting of character names at the beginning of dialogue in the editor, as shown in the following screenshot:

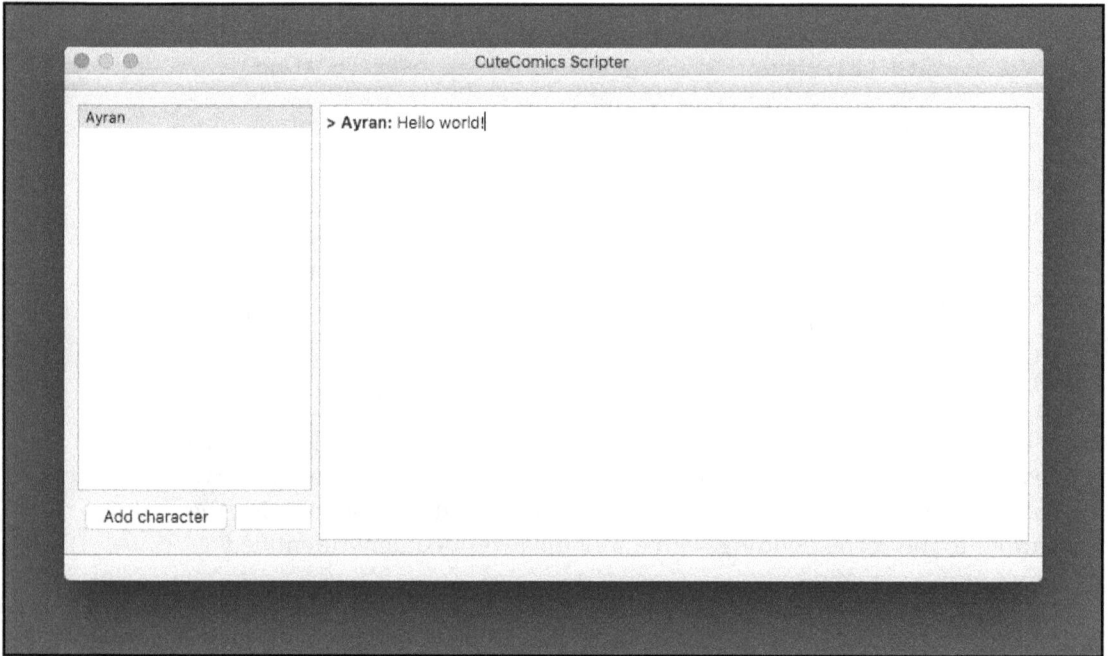

Saving the comic script

Now that our `scriptEditor` has minimal functionality, we want the user to be able to save their work. We will add this option as a menu entry, using a `QAction` (`http://doc.qt.io/qt-5.9/qaction.html`), which is an implementation of the *command* pattern. It provides an abstraction for a similar action that could be invoked via the UI from several entry points, such as a menu entry, toolbar icon, and keyboard shortcut.

To add the menu entry, we will open `mainwindow.ui` again and select the element in the canvas at the top-left corner with the **Type Here** label. We then edit this text and rename it as **File**. A popup with a couple of menu entries will appear, where we will modify the first one (**Type Here**), call it **Save as...**, and press *Enter*:

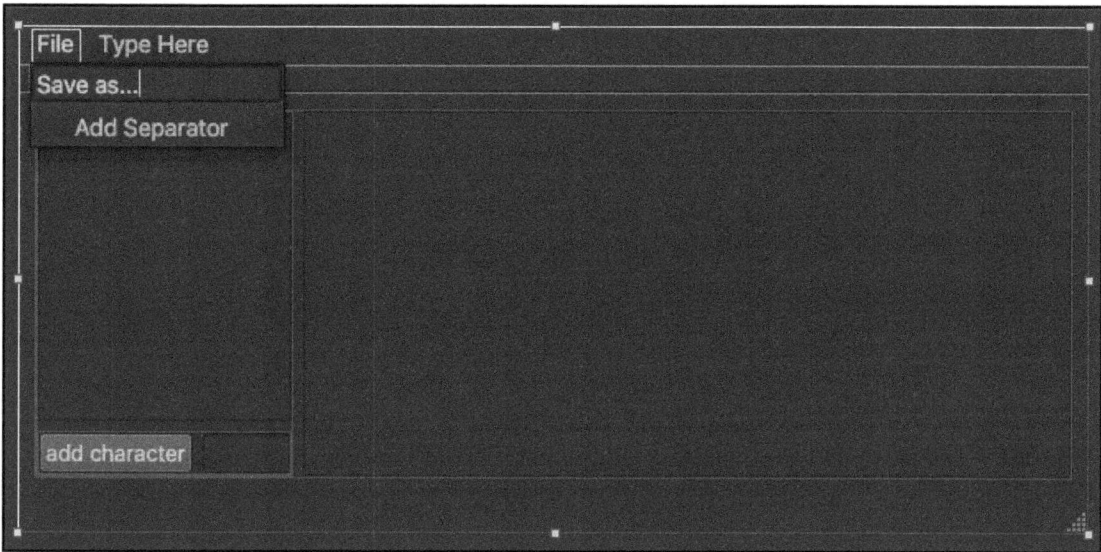

If we now look at the object hierarchy in Qt Designer, we will note a new node of the QMenu type with its object name as menuFile, and a child node of the QAction type with its object name as actionSave_as. We might want to change the latter to actionSaveAs. If you now run the application, you will see the menu and the menu entry appearing. Depending on your platform, the menu will show up at the top of the application window (for example, on Windows) or in the OS toolbar at the top of the screen (for example, macOS).

Now that we've got a clickable menu entry, we can get hold of it and add the use case to file save main.cpp; in order to do so, we will first create a pointer to the QAction:

```cpp
// ccscripter/main.cpp
...
#include <QAction>
...
auto actionSaveAs =  w.ui->aactionSaveAs;
```

Once this is done, we can run the use case file save by listening to the triggered signal of QAction:

```cpp
// ccscripter/main.cpp
...
if (actionSaveAs && scriptEditor) {
    QObject::connect(actionSaveAs, &QAction::triggered, [scriptEditor]() {
        QString fileName = QFileDialog::getSaveFileName();
        if (!fileName.isEmpty()) {
```

```
QFile file(fileName);

if (!file.open(QIODevice::WriteOnly)) {
    QMessageBox::information(0, "Unable to open file",
file.errorString());
        return;
    }
    QDataStream out(&file);
    out << scriptEditor->toPlainText();
}
    });
}
...
```

`QFileDialog::getSaveFileName()` creates a temporary file dialog, which returns a string with the destination file path of the file we want to save the document to. Once we have a destination file path, we will create a `QFile` (http://doc.qt.io/qt-5.9/qfile. html) that points to that path. We will try to open the `QFile`, which is a subclass of `QIODevice`, in write mode. If that fails, we will create a message box and return; otherwise, we create a `QDataStream` that points to the file and write the content of `scriptEditor` to it as plain text. Since the file object goes out of scope, it will be closed automatically.

You can now run the application, write some text in the editor, and save the file to a location of your choice. The contents of the editor should be found in the **Saved file**:

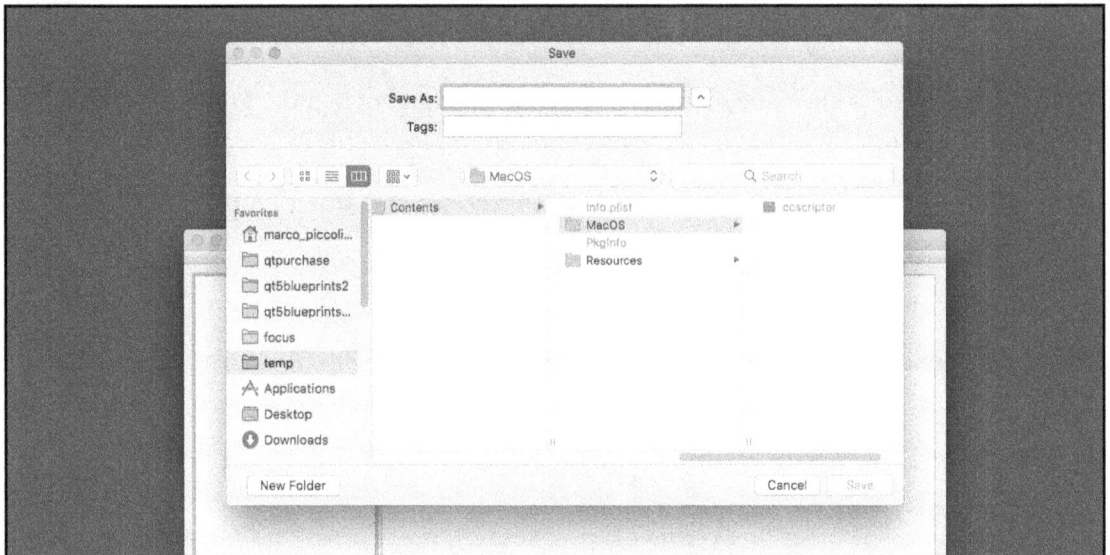

Exporting the comic script to PDF

What if we also gave a means to our user to export the comic script as a PDF to preserve the nice formatting?

It turns out that this can be done fairly easily with Qt's `printsupport` module. To enable this functionality, we will need to add the `printsupport` module to `ccscripter.pro`:

```
# ccscripter.pro

QT += core gui
QT += printsupport
```

Once this is done, we can add a new `QAction` to the **File** `QMenu` in `mainwindow.ui`, change the action's name object name to `actionExportPdf`, and point to it in `main.cpp`:

```
// ccscripter/main.cpp
...
auto actionExportPdf =  w.ui->actionExportPdf;
...
```

Performing the PDF export can be done via the following steps:

1. Choose a destination file path with a `QFileDialog`, as we have done for the text file save
2. Ensure that the filename ends with the `.pdf` extension and append it if it's missing
3. Create a `QPrinter` object (`http://doc.qt.io/qt-5.9/qprinter.html`), which will be in charge of painting the contents that we want to print and forwarding them to a printer
4. Configure the `QPrinter` object to print to a PDF device with a desired resolution, paper size, and font
5. Print the text document by passing a reference to the `QPrinter` object to it

As you will see, once again, the powerful Qt APIs make the task fairly trivial, abstracting away most of the details of this process. Here is the implementation of the preceding steps that we should add to `main.cpp`:

```
// ccscripter/main.cpp
...
if (actionExportPdf && scriptEditor) {
    QObject::connect(actionExportPdf, &QAction::triggered, [scriptEditor]()
{
        QString fileName = QFileDialog::getSaveFileName();
        if (!fileName.isEmpty()) {
            if (QFileInfo(fileName).suffix().isEmpty())
                fileName.append(".pdf");

            QPrinter printer(QPrinter::PrinterResolution);
            printer.setOutputFormat(QPrinter::PdfFormat);
            printer.setPaperSize(QPrinter::A4);
            printer.setOutputFileName(fileName);
            printer.setFontEmbeddingEnabled(true);

            auto doc = scriptEditor->document();
            doc->print(&printer);
        }
    });
}
...
```

As you can see in the preceding code, to `print` to PDF, it is enough to set the output format and output filename of the `QPrinter` instance. Also, the text document provides a convenient `print` method, which takes a reference to the configured printer.

If you now run the application, write it into the text editor and export it as a PDF, you should find a PDF file at the destination that you specified in the file dialog. The file should look similar to the following screenshot:

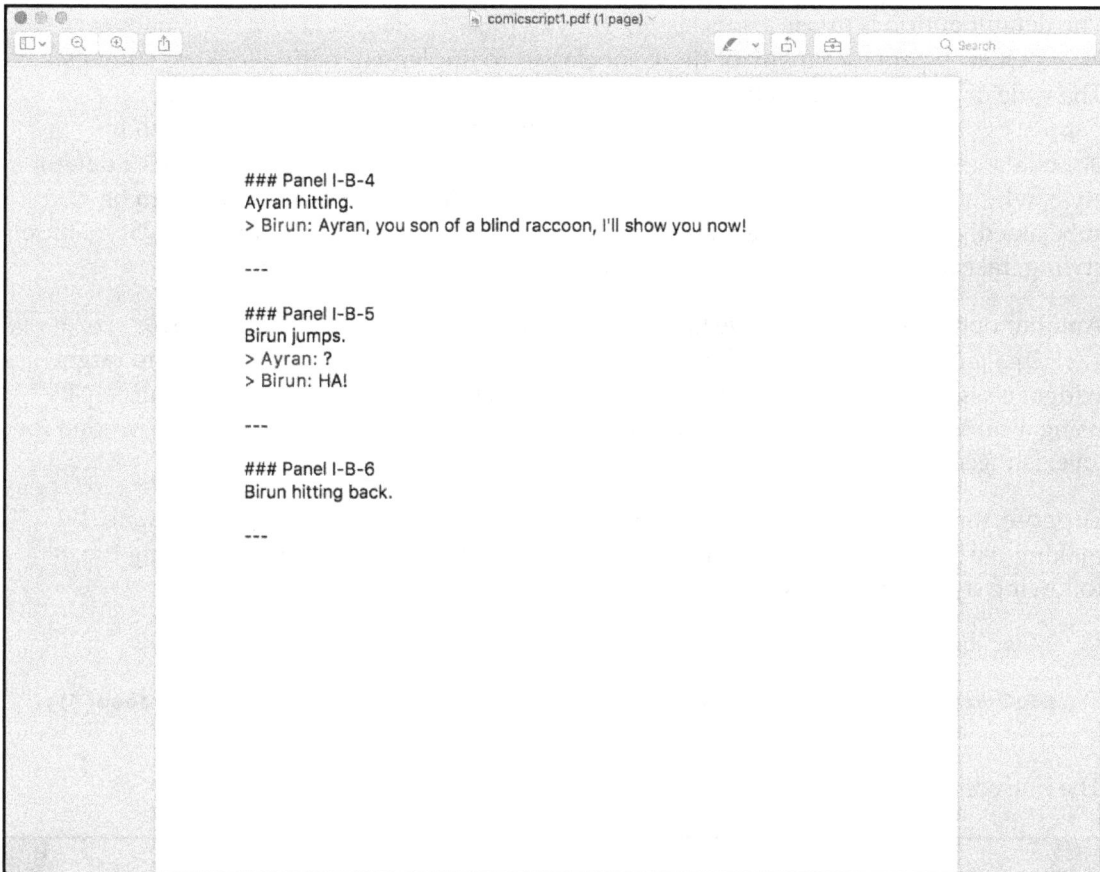

As simple as that.

Styling the UI

The UI that we created sports a very standard and OS-specific look. We and our customers might be content with that, or maybe not.

Qt Widgets offer a few different options to implement custom styling of an application's look & feel.

The default option is to use a subclass of `QStyle` (`http://doc.qt.io/qt-5.9/qstyle.html`). Qt itself provides many of these subclasses to implement native-looking widgets. The style of an entire application can be set explicitly and programmatically via `QApplication::setStyle()`. Styles can also be set for individual widgets with the `QWidget::setStyle()` method. When no style is selected explicitly, Qt applies a default style, which is generally dependent on the target OS platform. Existing styles can be subclassed, and completely new stiles can be created. For a complete guide on QStyle-based styling, take a look at `http://doc.qt.io/qt-5.9/style-reference.html`.

Another option available to style Qt Widgets is to use stylesheets (`http://doc.qt.io/qt-5.9/stylesheet-syntax.html`). This approach allows us to use CSS-like selectors to target widget classes and specific widget instances, and define their properties declaratively by using a subset of CSS. This choice is a viable option when only some tweaks are needed for an existing style.

Suppose, for example, that we wanted to alter the look of our `addCharacterInput`, by making the background dark and the text light. This could be achieved by adding the following stylesheet syntax to `main.cpp`:

```
// ccscripter/main.cpp
...
addCharacterInput->setStyleSheet("background-color: #333; color: #eee;");
...
```

The line edit field will now appear dark with a white text:

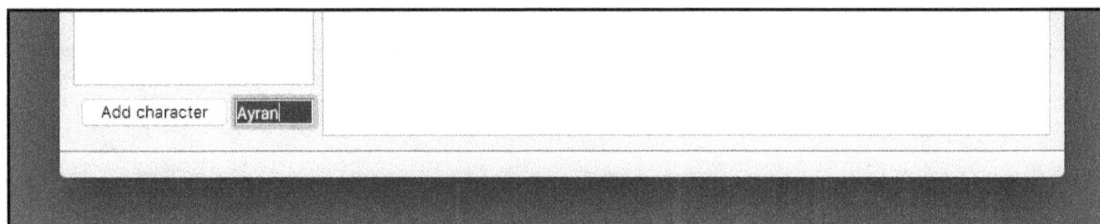

You can use this very approach to customize all widgets in the UI.

The selectors are quite powerful, and also allow us to target specific class types of children widgets by setting the stylesheet of the parent widget. For a comprehensive coverage of what is possible with the selectors, take a look at `http://doc.qt.io/qt-5.9/stylesheet-reference.html`.

Summary

We have created an enhanced comic script editor that has knowledge about character entities, that can be inserted into the text from a list view. The editor also has a custom highlighting for character names, and this can be easily extended to other text patterns that our customers might be interested in.

By implementing the characters list, we encountered the `QAbstractItemModel` class and the derived `QAbstractListModel` class. The former is the base class for all advanced data models in Qt that power the model/view paradigm.

We also created a UI based on Qt Widgets, a rich set of visual components that represents a good option for developing classic desktop applications. You might have also noticed how many Qt Widgets have a direct Qt Quick counterpart, and that many of their APIs are similar (for example, think about the `clicked` signal in `Button` and `QPushButton`).

We saw that, thanks to Qt Creator's Designer it is possible and convenient to develop moderately complex UIs visually, by having a direct feedback about the UI's appearance.

Further on, we introduced regular expressions and showed how they can be leverage to perform syntax highlighting in text documents thanks to the `QSyntaxHighlighter` class.

We also managed to easily save the contents of a rich text document to both a text file with `QDataStream`, and a PDF by means of the `QPrinter` class.

We finally introduced `QStyle`, and saw how the look & feel of a widgets-based UI can be easily tweaked with stylesheets.

Here we are! In the last three chapters, we managed to create three different prototypes of tools that should assist independent comic creators throughout various phases of their work. All of these could be expanded and enriched with ease by leveraging the application architecture principles introduced in Chapters 23, *Writing Acceptance Tests and Building a Visual Prototype* to Chapter 25, *Wiring User Interaction and Delivering the Final App*.

In the next chapters, we will devote our attention to industrial customers, and see how Qt provides components and complete frameworks to tackle the issues of data creation, wireless transport, and visualization in a powerful and unified manner. Get ready!

29
Sending Sensor Readings to a Device with a Non-UI App

In Part I, we explored Qt's cross-platform application development capabilities by implementing a simple grocery list-type application with a Qt Quick interface.

In Part II, we focused on Qt's further graphics capabilities by developing a set of tools for independent comic creators, which gave us the opportunity to get familiar with Qt 3D and Qt Widgets.

In this part, we will continue our journey by looking at some of Qt's connectivity offerings, and we will also get to know a few more frameworks for creating rich graphical user interfaces, specifically the Qt Charts framework (in `Chapter 30`, *Building a Mobile Dashboard to Display Real-Time Sensor Data*) and the Qt Web Engine framework (in `Chapter 31`, *Running a Web Service and an HTML5 Dashboard*).

As usual, we will look at Qt's APIs in action with an eye for good application architectures.

Outline

By now, terms like **Internet of Things (IoT)** and Industry 4.0 represent a consistent segment of IT applications. While these terms are used in many contexts as buzzwords, the concepts behind them have been circulating in IT for decades; connectivity, embedded systems, machine-to-machine communication, remote sensing, remote monitoring, and so on are all concepts that are central to the life and operations of many industry segments.

While Qt started out as a library devoted to UI, as you have already seen, it was able to outgrow that limited field of application to provide a full set of libraries and tools that go well beyond graphics, allowing developers like you to create full-stack systems on many different types of hardware. C++ means a potential for efficiency and power. Combined with Qt's extensive APIs, this technology stack represents an appealing choice for many usage scenarios.

In this and the following chapters, we are going to develop a suite called Cute Measures. It will provide an IoT application ecosystem for businesses that want to gather sensor data of various natures, aggregate them, transmit them over different types of channels (for example, Bluetooth, HTTP, and so on), and build rich visualizations of the data on various platforms.

The examples we'll be working on, as usual, will be fairly simple and focus on core concepts while giving you the opportunity to expand them on your own.

In this chapter, we will be creating a prototype of the first application required in our remote monitoring software stack; a non-UI application that collects data from one or more sensors and makes them available through a connection. Specifically, we will be looking at how to implement a classic Bluetooth connection. But this will be just a detail, and you could easily substitute the Bluetooth transmission module with some other technology without touching other application layers.

The `usecases` and entities that we will be developing for the first application will be re-usable in the applications we'll see in the following chapters.

Setting up the project

We will first create a new `subdirs` project called `part3-cute_measures` and add it as a subproject of `qt5projects.pro`. Next, we will create `subdirs` projects for our `usecases` and `entities`. Each subproject of `usecases` and `entities`, in turn, will be a **Qt Unit Test** project template, including both the entity or use case header and source files, and a test class to make sure each component works as intended.

Additionally, for this project, we will also want to have a `channels` subproject, where we will be hosting and testing components related to data transmission that encapsulate specific technologies, such as Bluetooth.

For the broadcasting application, we will create a **Qt Console Application** project and call it `cmbroadcast`.

The project outline should, then, look like the following:

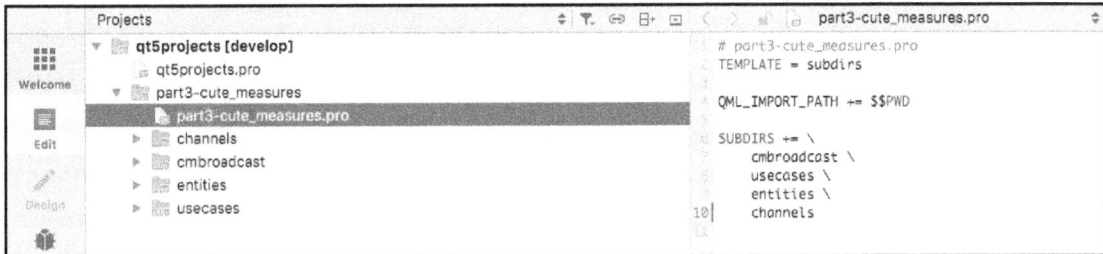

I'll give you indications on how to name the single component subprojects in the coming sections.

Publishing sensor readings

To start with, our data transmission application will only deal with one major feature — a broadcaster publishes some sensor readings, and these are made available to clients via a Bluetooth connection.

Here is the use case scenario:

```
Feature: broadcaster publishes sensor readings
    Background:
        Given there is a broadcaster
        And there is a sensor
        And the broadcaster connects to the sensor

    Scenario: sensor emits one reading
        Given the sensor emits a reading
        When the broadcaster publishes the sensor readings
        Then the corresponding published reading coincides with the sensor
reading
```

We are, as usual, setting up some preconditions, performing an action (the broadcaster publishes the sensor reading), and defining one or more expected outcomes. As you can see, some of these preconditions can be also be cast in terms of additional usecases. For example, the broadcaster connects to the sensor step could be a separate use case. The sensor emits a reading step could also be cast as a separate use case if we wanted the sensor readings to be a fully-fledged entity rather than simply a piece of data. Also, as we would like some of the preconditions to be checked for more than one scenario, we have put those under the Background section. A Background describes a set of preconditions to be carried out and checked for all scenarios of a given feature (see: https:/ /github.com/cucumber/cucumber/wiki/Background).

Setting up the use case project

To manage and maintain our usecase, we will create a new subproject with the template **Qt Unit Test** and name it uc_broadcaster_publishes_sensor_readings (where uc means usecase). The test class will be called Uc_broadcaster_publishes_sensor_readings. As already explained, we should also create a corresponding .pri file where we list the usecases header and source files, along with any other additional resource that we might want to bundle for import into the unit test suite and other programs.

Implementing the background steps

Here is how the background steps could be implemented by writing a Qt Test: these steps can be run in the init() private slot. As you might remember, in a Qt Test harness, all private slots are tests, and the init() slot gets invoked by the test harness before the execution of each test, and is thus very suitable for implementing the execution of any background steps:

```
// tst_uc_broadcaster_publishes_sensor_readings.cpp
...
void Uc_broadcaster_publishes_sensor_readings::init()
{
    // Given there is a broadcaster
    // And there is a sensor
    // And the broadcaster connects to the sensor
}
```

First, we need to create a `Broadcaster` instance and a `Sensor` instance. Both will be entities. Since these will need to be accessed from both the `init` method and the test method, a pointer to these entity instances should be stored in the test class. To ensure object destruction and avoid memory leaks, we could take advantage of `QObject` and its automatic memory management by parenting the allocated entities to the test class. However, we want our object instances to be destroyed and recreated for each test, while the test class lives longer than that, so using the parent-child relationship for memory management is not useful in this case. Instead, we will take care of deleting the object instances in the `cleanup` slot, which is invoked automatically after each test:

> In the Cute Measures project, we will adopt a slightly different coding style from Cute Comics. For example, as already shown, `usecase` classes and projects will be prepended with the `uc` prefix. Also, private class members will start with an underscore (_) rather than the `m_` prefix. This is to show that you can adopt whatever style you prefer for your application project, as long as your code is internally consistent.

```
void Uc_broadcaster_publishes_sensor_reading::init()
{
    // Given there is a broadcaster
    _broadcaster = new entities::Broadcaster;
    QVERIFY(_broadcaster);
    // And there is a sensor
    _sensor = new entities::Sensor("mockSensor1");
    QVERIFY(_sensor);
    // And the broadcaster connects to the sensor
}
void Uc_broadcaster_publishes_sensor_reading::cleanup()
{
    delete _broadcaster; _broadcaster = nullptr;
    delete _sensor; _sensor = nullptr;
}
```

> Qt provides a range of smart pointers for easier memory management. Some of these are counterparts of the C++ standard library smart pointers, while others have Qt-specific semantics. For a list of the available types and their differences, take a look at `http://doc.qt.io/qt-5.9/qsharedpointer.html#other-pointer-classes`.

Once the `broadcaster` and `sensor` have been created, we need to somehow connect them, so that the broadcaster knows when one (or more) sensor provides a reading. Since we are dealing with the interaction of two different entities, we might want to cast this interaction as a `usecase`, `broadcaster connects to sensor`. We create a header and source file for the `usecase`. You can decide whether to put them in a separate subproject together with their own test suite or keep things simpler and test all `usecases` with the same test class. The latter choice is not recommended if you want to develop the project further, but that's your call:

```cpp
void Uc_broadcaster_publishes_sensor_reading::init()
{
    // Given there is a broadcaster
    ...
    // And the broadcaster connects to the sensor
    QVERIFY(usecases::broadcaster_connects_to_sensor(*_broadcaster,
*_sensor));
}
```

As you can see, here we have taken a different route from previous `usecase` implementations, by implementing the `usecase` as a free function rather than a class method. If you think about it, `usecases` do not need to store data for longer than needed for the `usecase` to succeed or fail, so opting for free functions seems indeed a reasonable choice. Also, instead of waiting for an asynchronous signal to emit as we did in other cases, we just wait for the function to return and verify the truth of its return value. This is just to show you that reasoning based on `usecase` applies equally well to different programming paradigms.

In the header file for `broadcaster_connects_to_sensor`, we forward declare the entities involved in the interaction. In the implementation, we simply connect a signal from the Sensor (`emitReading`) to a slot in the Broadcaster (`publishReadings`):

```cpp
// broadcaster_connects_to_sensor.h
#ifndef BRODCASTER_CONNECTS_TO_SENSOR_H
#define BRODCASTER_CONNECTS_TO_SENSOR_H

namespace entities {
class Broadcaster;
class Sensor;
}

namespace usecases {
bool broadcaster_connects_to_sensor(const entities::Broadcaster&
broadcaster, const entities::Sensor& sensor);
}
```

```
#endif // BRODCASTER_CONNECTS_TO_SENSOR_H
#include <QObject>

#include "../../entities/entity_sensor/sensor.h"
#include "../../entities/entity_broadcaster/broadcaster.h"

#include "brodcaster_connects_to_sensor.h"

bool usecases::broadcaster_connects_to_sensor(const entities::Broadcaster&
broadcaster, const entities::Sensor& sensor) {
    return QObject::connect(
                &sensor, &entities::Sensor::emitReading,
                &broadcaster, &entities::Broadcaster::publishReadings,
                Qt::UniqueConnection);
}
```

As you can appreciate, the implementation contains include statements to the entity header files that we have not yet created. We'll do that in the following sections.

Once we have taken care of running the background steps and cleaning up, we can focus on the main usecase, broadcaster publishes sensor readings:

```
void Uc_broadcaster_publishes_sensor_reading::test_sensor_emits_single()
{
    // And the sensor emits a reading
    // When the broadcaster publishes the sensor readings
    // Then the corresponding published reading coincides with the sensor
reading
}
```

We choose to call the test test_sensor_emits_single because later on, we might want to check what happens when many Sensor readings are emitted one after the other, and see if the broadcaster can keep up with them.

For this project, we decide that Sensor readings is a simple data structure, a map of key-value pairs. As we have seen before, Qt provides QMap<KeyType, ValueType>, together with some pre-baked type definitions, like QVariantMap. Alternatively, if we want our type to be strings only, we could use a QMap<QString, QString>. The map will contain the following key-value pairs:

- A sensor_id to identify the Sensor that sent the data
- A timestamp
- A value containing the actual reading data

This could of course be extended as needed — for example, it could also include the unit of measure information.

For the timestamp, we choose a number encoding, the milliseconds since unix epoch, a standard choice when performance is required. Time values like these can be manipulated by using QDateTime (http://doc.qt.io/qt-5.9/qdatetime.html), a powerful component that contains static and non-static functions and data structures for date-time manipulations. Among these, QDateTime::currentMSecsSinceEpoch() provides the current milliseconds-since-epoch value.

To provide the reading to the outside world, we take advantage of signals and slots:

```
void Uc_broadcaster_publishes_sensor_reading::test_sensor_emits_single()
{
    // And the sensor emits a reading
    QSignalSpy sensorEmitReading(_sensor,
SIGNAL(emitReading(QVariantMap)));
    _sensor->emitReading(QVariantMap({
                {"sensor_id", _sensor->identifier()},
                 {"timestamp", QDateTime::currentMSecsSinceEpoch()},
                   {"value", 1.5}
                                      }));
    QCOMPARE(sensorEmitReading.count(), 1);
    // When the broadcaster publishes the sensor readings
    ...
}
```

Finally, we can have the usecase run and check its outcome:

```
void Uc_broadcaster_publishes_sensor_reading::test_sensor_emits_single()
{
    // And the sensor emits a reading
    ...
    // When the broadcaster publishes the sensor readings
    bool published_reading_coincides_with_sensor_readings =
            usecases::broadcaster_publishes_sensor_readings(*_broadcaster,
*_sensor);
    // Then the corresponding published reading coincides with the sensor
reading
    QVERIFY(published_reading_coincides_with_sensor_reading);
}
```

Also, in this case, the `usecase` is implemented as a function with a Boolean return value that indicates whether the `usecases` seems to have succeeded or not.

We create the interface for the `usecase` in the header:

```
// broadcaster_publishes_sensor_readings.h
#ifndef BROADCASTER_PUBLISHES_SENSOR_READINGS_H
#define BROADCASTER_PUBLISHES_SENSOR_READINGS_H

namespace entities {
class Sensor;
class Broadcaster;
}

namespace usecases {

bool broadcaster_publishes_sensor_readings(entities::Broadcaster&
broadcaster, entities::Sensor& sensor);
}

#endif // BROADCASTER_PUBLISHES_SENSOR_READINGS_H
```

And implement it in the source file:

```
// broadcaster_publishes_sensor_reading.cpp
#include <QtGlobal>

#include "../../entities/entity_broadcaster/broadcaster.h"
#include "../../entities/entity_sensor/sensor.h"

#include "broadcaster_publishes_sensor_reading.h"

bool usecases::broadcaster_publishes_sensor_reading(entities::Broadcaster&
broadcaster, entities::Sensor& sensor) {
    quint64 broadcasterTimestamp =
broadcaster.lastPublishedReadings().at(0).value("timestamp").toUInt();
    quint64 sensorTimeStamp =
sensor.lastReading().value("timestamp").toUInt();
    return broadcasterTimestamp > 0
            && sensorTimeStamp > 0
            && broadcasterTimestamp == sensorTimeStamp;
}
```

Since we have connected the `Broadcaster` to the `Sensor` in the previous use case, in the implementation, we just need to make sure that the last reading emitted by the `Sensor` corresponds to the last reading temporarily cached by the `Broadcaster`. To make things slightly more interesting, we assume that the `Broadcaster` can store the last reading of more than one `Sensor` in a list. However, we will leave the implementation of the functionality required to deal with more than one `Sensor` at once to you.

To make sure that things are working as intended, we compare the `timestamp` of the last reading emitted by the `Sensor` to the `timestamp` of the last reading published by the `Broadcaster`, and also check that both `timestamp` values are non-zero. To correctly compare `timestamp` values, we make use of `quint64`, a type definition for `unsigned long long int` (and `unsigned __int64` on Windows) that is provided alongside many other utilities by the `QtGlobal` header file (`http://doc.qt.io/qt-5.9/qtglobal.html`).

Now that a way to check that our use case works as intended is laid out, we have to implement the involved entities.

Defining the sensor entity

We will define an entity called `Sensor`, which will act as a general-purpose sensor. Behind the scenes, the way that the sensor gathers the data could be very different and make use of various kinds of technologies and physical sensors. Among these, one obvious method for implementing a sensor that gathers real data from a physical sensor is using the Qt Sensors module.

Introducing Qt Sensors

Qt Sensors (`http://doc.qt.io/qt-5.9/qtsensors-index.html`) is a module that makes it easy for application developers to access sensor information in a cross-platform way. It provides classes for both C++ and QML, and supports out-of-the-box different kinds of sensors on a few platforms. Its architecture is based on the separation between front-end and back-end classes. While front-end classes are dedicated to application developers, back-end classes allow hardware and library developers to create wrappers for new sensors or new platforms.

The sensor data is exposed conveniently via the QSensorReading (http://doc.qt.io/qt-5.9/qsensorreading.html) class' specific subclasses, such as QAccelerometerReading (http://doc.qt.io/qt-5.9/qaccelerometerreading.html). Another way of accessing the data is via the specialized subclasses in QSensor, and their available properties and methods.

> It must be noted that not all sensor types are supported on all platforms. Specific sensor-platform support is documented at http://doc.qt.io/qt-5.9/compatmap.html, so make sure you take a look at it before deciding to use Qt Sensors for a specific sensor-platform combination.

A detailed introduction about the design principles behind Qt Sensors is provided at http://doc.qt.io/qt-5.9/qtsensors-cpp.html.

Since it would be hard to make use of a sensor type that works on a few different platforms, in this project, we will just confine ourselves to implementing the entity. The actual sensor device feeding the data could be cast as a repository (as we have shown in previous chapters) that extends a QSensor subclass, so that the logic governing its consumption stays independent.

> If you ever want to try implementing your own custom sensor based on QSensor, you can take a look at the following example: http://doc.qt.io/qt-5.9/qtsensors-grue-example.html.

Modeling the sensor abstraction

To model the sensor abstraction, we create a project of type **Qt Unit Test** and add it as a subproject of entities.pro. The test class could be named entity_sensor. We won't be adding specific unit tests for the entity, but just check that it is working as intended within the use case. Feel free to add unit tests for the API that we'll be adding as an exercise.

By looking at use case `broadcaster connects to sensor` and `broadcaster publishes sensor reading`, we notice we need the following API:

- An `emitReading(QVariantMap)` signal
- A `QVariantMap lastReading` method to retrieve the last reading emitted for comparison purposes
- A `QString identifier` method to retrieve the sensor's identifier

Also, we'll probably want to modify the sensor's constructor to accept an identifier string as the first argument.

To bootstrap the header and source, you can start from a `QObject` template in Qt Creator. Here is the header file that describes the API:

```
#ifndef SENSOR_H
#define SENSOR_H

#include <QObject>
#include <QString>
#include <QVariantMap>

namespace entities {
class Sensor : public QObject
{
    Q_OBJECT
public:
    explicit Sensor(const QString& identifier, QObject *parent = nullptr);
    QVariantMap lastReading() const;
    QString identifier() const;
signals:
    void emitReading(QVariantMap sensorReading);
};
}

#endif // SENSOR_H
```

We will also want to declare in the header any members and private methods that we need in order to store and process data:

```
#ifndef SENSOR_H
#define SENSOR_H
...

namespace entities {
class Sensor : public QObject
{
```

```
    Q_OBJECT
public:
    ...
private slots:
    void _onEmitReading(QVariantMap sensorReading);
private:
    QVariantMap _lastReading;
    QString _identifier;
};
}

#endif // SENSOR_H
```

Finally, we implement the methods in `sensor.cpp`, which contains the definitions:

```
#include "sensor.h"
#include <QDateTime>

entities::Sensor::Sensor(const QString& identifier, QObject *parent) :
QObject(parent)
{
    _identifier = identifier;
    connect(this,&Sensor::emitReading,
            this,&Sensor::_onEmitReading);
}

QVariantMap entities::Sensor::lastReading() const {
    return _lastReading;
}

QString entities::Sensor::identifier() const
{
    return _identifier;
}

void entities::Sensor::_onEmitReading(QVariantMap sensorReading)
{
    QDateTime timestamp;
timestamp.setMSecsSinceEpoch(sensorReading.value("timestamp").toUInt());
    if (timestamp.isValid()) {
        _lastReading = sensorReading;
    }
}
```

As you can see, in the implementation of the private `_onEmitReading` slot, we create a `QDateTime` object on the stack and use it to convert the unsigned long-long integer representing the date as a timestamp to a proper date-time object, by means of the `setMSecsSinceEpoch` method. We decide to store the last reading only if the `timestamp` is valid, by invoking `QDateTime::isValid`.

Implementing the Broadcaster entity

The Broadcaster entity is responsible for collecting sensor readings from one or more sensors and for *publishing* them, that is, processing them or filtering them out as needed, and making them available to the outside world for either local or remote consumption.

There are several ways in which the sensor readings gathering might be implemented. In the current scenario, we have limited ourselves to a simple Qt signal/slot connection, where the signal is fired by a sensor and the processing happens in the broadcaster's slot. Of course, this might not always be the best option; you might prefer some sort of polling mechanism, which might be a responsibility of the broadcaster, or of a dedicated component, and be part of the business logic or relegated to a more external layer.

By looking at the implemented use case, we can see that the broadcaster should support the following API:

- A `QList<QVariantMap> lastPublishedReadings()` method to retrieve the last stored reading
- A `publishReadings(QVariantMap)` slot to process a received sensor reading
- A `readingsPublished(QList<QVariantMap>)` signal, to notify any further component once that a list of sensor readings has been processed and published

We will also add already a private member variable to the header, to store the last published readings:

```
#ifndef BROADCASTER_H
#define BROADCASTER_H

#include <QObject>
#include <QList>
#include <QVariantMap>

namespace entities {
class Broadcaster : public QObject
{
    Q_OBJECT
```

```
public:
    explicit Broadcaster(QObject *parent = nullptr);
    QList<QVariantMap> lastPublishedReadings() const;
signals:
    void readingsPublished(QList<QVariantMap> readings);
public slots:
    void publishReadings(QVariantMap sensorReading);

private:
    QList<QVariantMap> _lastPublishedReadings;
};
}

#endif // BROADCASTER_H
```

The implementation of `lastPublishedReadings` is trivial:

```
QList<QVariantMap> entities::Broadcaster::lastPublishedReadings() const {
    return _lastPublishedReadings;
}
```

In the `publishReadings` slot, we clear the list of previously stored sensor readings with the `clear` method which `QList` provides, and then append the newly arrived reading. After doing this, we emit the `readingsPublished` signal, containing the value of the readings as a payload:

```
void entities::Broadcaster::publishReadings(QVariantMap sensorReading) {
    _lastPublishedReadings.clear();
    _lastPublishedReadings.append(sensorReading);
    emit readingsPublished(_lastPublishedReadings);
}
```

> As long as there is only one type of `sensorReading`, there is not much point in having `_lastPublishedReadings` as a list. In fact, as you can see, we clear the list each time. When you add more types of `sensorReading`, however, you could implement more complex logics that collect the various types of sensor readings, and emit the `readingsPublished` signal only when all types of sensor readings within a specific timestamp have been collected.

Now that both the `Sensor` and `Broadcaster` entities are implemented, we can add them to the previously specified use case tests in the usual ways, run the tests, and see if they pass.

Adding the broadcaster Bluetooth channel

We could easily have added the code to perform the broadcasting of sensor information over a Bluetooth channel in the `Broadcaster` component, but we should know by now that such an option would not help the maintainability of our applications. First of all, like every technology, Bluetooth is subject to refinements of various sorts, as we will discuss shortly. In the second instance, we might decide that Bluetooth is not the most suitable transport channel to expose the sensor data to remote devices, and might opt instead for a Wi-Fi connection, or some other technology. In both cases, we would not want technology-related details to pollute our business logic. Hence, there is need for a separate component that we might call `BroadcasterChannel`, of which a `broadcaster` BT Channel is a concrete implementation.

Being that this is a component that involves connectivity and calls to remote devices, we certainly want to test it in isolation to make sure it works as expected. We probably want to also have a test double (a *dummy*, as we called it in Part I), if our architecture involves this kind of component for use with entities and `usecases`.

Setting up the channel project

The `BroadcasterChannel` project will be another **Qt Unit Test** subproject. To distinguish the `Channel` from the `entity_broadcaster`, we will name the QMake project `channel_broadcaster`. The test harness source file will be called `tst_broadcaster_bt.cpp`, as in this case, we want to test the Bluetooth implementation of the `broadcasterChannel`. The test class will be named `Test_Channel_broadcasterBt`.

We will also add `channel_broadcaster.pri` to the project, where we will be adding the necessary Qt dependencies and header and source files.

Defining the BroadcasterChannel API

We want to define a common API for all broadcaster channels that we might want to implement, be it Bluetooth, Wi-Fi, or any other technology. To do so, we will have to define at least:

- A way to connect a `Channel` to an Broadcaster entity, so that the channel can listen to any changes in the entity to behave accordingly — for example, when the entity emits a `readingsPublished` signal
- A way to implement the behavior — for example, by means of a slot

We will call the first `connectToBroadcaster`, and the second `sendReadings(QList<QVariantMap>)`.

Since we are dealing with devices that rely on system APIs, we will also want to check that instances are instantiated and initialized correctly, and the same for their destruction. For this reason, we start by creating a test that makes sure that the `Channel` component is initialized correctly:

```
#include <QString>
#include <QtTest>

#include "broadcaster_bt.h"

class Test_channel_broadcasterBt : public QObject
{
    Q_OBJECT

public:
    Test_channel_broadcasterBt();

private Q_SLOTS:
    void init();
    void cleanup();
    void test_connectToBroadcaster();
private:
    channels::BroadcasterBt* _broadcaster_bt;
};

Test_channel_broadcasterBt::Test_channel_broadcasterBt()
{
}

void Test_channel_broadcasterBt::init()
{
    _broadcaster_bt = new channels::BroadcasterBt(this);
```

```
    QVERIFY(_broadcaster_bt->init());
}

void Test_channel_broadcasterBt::cleanup()
{
    delete _broadcaster_bt;
}

QTEST_APPLESS_MAIN(Test_channel_broadcasterBt)

#include "tst_broadcaster_bt.moc"
```

To have the test pass, we will now implement the `init()` method of `BroadcasterBt` (do not confuse it with the `init()` method of the test class). This gives us the opportunity to introduce the Qt Bluetooth module.

Introducing the Qt Bluetooth module

The Qt Bluetooth module (`http://doc.qt.io/qt-5.9/qtbluetooth-overview.html`) provides Bluetooth functionality to Qt-based applications. It supports a few different scenarios, such as retrieving information about the local and remote Bluetooth adapters, device discovery, pushing files to remote devices via OBEX, and establishing connections between devices.

Besides classes based on classic Bluetooth APIs, recent Qt versions have added support for Bluetooth **Low Energy** (**LE**) or Bluetooth 4.0, a technology that makes it possible to exploit Bluetooth connections to peripherals with low power consumption, making it ideal for applications in the field of wearable and IoT. While classic BT classes have the `QBluetooth` prefix, the newer LE API classes begin with `QLowEnergy`. Bluetooth components are available through a C++ API (`http://doc.qt.io/qt-5.9/qtbluetooth-module.html`), and some also in QML (`http://doc.qt.io/qt-5.9/qtbluetooth-qmlmodule.html`).

Bluetooth LE would represent a suitable choice for connecting, for example, a `sensor` with a `broadcaster`. It's still limited support on desktop devices, however, and the very limited support of Bluetooth LE in *peripheral* mode on mobile devices, makes the classical model with a server/client architecture a better choice for our prototype. The best option for our scenario seems thus to be providing a RFCOMM server that allows incoming connections from clients using a **Serial Port Profile** (**SPP**).

> If you get hold of a device that supports Bluetooth LE in the peripheral mode, you could try implementing a Bluetooth LE backend for the `BroadcasterChannel`, and deploy the `cmbroadcast` application on the device.

To add the Qt Bluetooth module to a qmake project, you should use the following directive:

```
QT += bluetooth
```

We can add it to `channel_broadcaster.pri` to make sure it gets added to each project where the `BroadcasterChannel` module is included.

Creating the channel base and derived classes

Before implementing the Bluetooth flavor of the channel initialization method, we need to create the abstract base class that will provide method signatures for all broadcast channel implementations. We create a class named `BroadcasterChannel`, with the header file `broadcaster_channel.h` and source `broadcaster_channel.cpp`, to provide a little functionality common to all specialized class implementations.

In the header file, we define the `init` method as a `virtual` function, and the constructor as `protected`, as it will only be invoked by concrete subclasses of this abstract class:

```
#ifndef BROADCASTER_CHANNEL_H
#define BROADCASTER_CHANNEL_H

#include <QObject>
#include <QList>
#include <QVariantMap>

namespace channels {
class BroadcasterChannel : public QObject
{
    Q_OBJECT
protected:
    BroadcasterChannel(QObject *parent = nullptr) : QObject(parent) {}
public:
    virtual bool init() = 0;
};
}

#endif // BROADCASTER_CHANNEL_H
```

> If you want to follow the conventions used in Qt's own code, you can
> mark the class as abstract by prefixing with `Abstract` or postfixing it
> with `Base`.

Then, we create a subclass called `BroadcasterBt` with the files `broadcaster_bt.h` and
`broadcaster_bt.cpp`. Here is the header file, which declares the override to the `init`
method:

```
#ifndef BROADCASTER_BT_H
#define BROADCASTER_BT_H

#include "broadcaster_channel.h"

namespace channels {
class BroadcasterBt : public BroadcasterChannel
{
    Q_OBJECT
public:
    explicit BroadcasterBt(QObject* parent = nullptr);
    bool init() override;
};
}

#endif // BROADCASTER_BT_H
```

Implementing the channel initialization method

It is now time to implement the BT channel initialization method and get to know a few Qt
Bluetooth classes.

To do that, we need to ask ourselves, what does the initialization of the Bluetooth
connection involve? Remember that we want to create an RFCOMM server; the
initialization would then likely include the creation of the server, and the exposure of a
discoverable service that Bluetooth clients can connect to. Here is a list of steps required to
achieve this result:

1. Identify the local adapter and create a server that listens to it
2. Provide information about the service ID
3. Provide information about the service's textual descriptors

4. Provide information about service's discoverability for remote devices

5. Provide information about the protocol we intend to use for communication

6. Register the service with the local Bluetooth adapter

Given this sequence of steps, we want our initialization to succeed if all are completed successfully, or fail otherwise. We choose to implement each step as a `private` method with a Boolean return value, check on the return value of each step, and have the `init` method succeed if all return values are `true`. Here is a possible implementation:

```
bool channels::BroadcasterBt::init() {
    qDebug() << Q_FUNC_INFO;
    if (!_listenToAdapter()) return false;
    if (!_provideServiceId()) return false;
    if (!_provideServiceTraits()) return false;
    if (!_provideServiceDiscoverability()) return false;
    if (!_provideProtocolDescriptorList()) return false;
    if (!_registerService()) return false;
    return true;
}
```

As you can see, for debugging purposes, at the beginning of the method implementation, we are printing to standard output the fully qualified name of the method whenever it is invoked, thanks to the `Q_FUNC_INFO` macro and the `qDebug()` function (which is available by including the `QDebug` class).

Of course, the `private` methods should also be added to the header file:

```
#ifndef BROADCASTER_BT_H
#define BROADCASTER_BT_H
...
namespace channels {
class BroadcasterBt : public BroadcasterChannel
{
    Q_OBJECT
public:
    explicit BroadcasterBt(QObject* parent = nullptr);
    bool init() override;

private:
    bool _listenToAdapter();
    bool _provideProtocolDescriptorList();
    bool _provideServiceId();
    bool _provideServiceDiscoverability();
    bool _provideServiceTraits();
    bool _registerService();
```

```
};
}

#endif // BROADCASTER_BT_H
```

Making the server listen to the adapter

The first step involves a few operations:

- Getting hold of the Bluetooth adapter's address
- Creating a local device instance from the adapter
- Making the device instance discoverable
- Creating a Bluetooth server based on the RFCOMM protocol
- Having the server listen to the adapter's address

We will also save a pointer to the server instance and the local adapter address in our channels instance, so that we can refer to them during the various initialization steps:

```
#ifndef BROADCASTER_BT_H
#define BROADCASTER_BT_H
...
namespace channels {
class BroadcasterBt : public BroadcasterChannel
{
    Q_OBJECT
public:
    explicit BroadcasterBt(QObject* parent = nullptr);
    bool init() override;

private:
    QBluetoothServer* _server;
    QBluetoothAddress _localAdapter;
    ...
};
}

#endif // BROADCASTER_BT_H
```

Making the server listen to the adapter is then expressed with the available Qt `Bluetooth` classes as follows:

```
bool channels::BroadcasterBt::_listenToAdapter()
{
    qDebug() << Q_FUNC_INFO;
    _localAdapter = QBluetoothLocalDevice::allDevices().value(0).address();
    QBluetoothLocalDevice localDevice(_localAdapter);
    localDevice.setHostMode(QBluetoothLocalDevice::HostDiscoverable);
    _server = new QBluetoothServer(QBluetoothServiceInfo::RfcommProtocol,
this);
    bool success = _server->listen(_localAdapter);
    qDebug() << (success ? "listening: " : "not listening: ") <<
localDevice.name();
    return success;
}
```

We first invoke the `QBluetoothLocalDevice::allDevices()` static method and save the address of the first available device in the member variable `_localAdapter` of type `QBluetoothAddress`. Then, we create a temporary instance of a `QBluetoothLocalDevice` class, that we immediately use to set the host mode to `HostDiscoverable`. After this is done, we create an instance of a `QBluetoothServer` on the heap, and specify in its constructor that communications will be based on the RFCOMM protocol. Finally, we have the server listen to the local adapter's address to monitor available connections, and return `true` if the listening happened successfully.

Providing information about the service ID

The next thing we will do is to create an instance of `QBluetoothServiceInfo` (http://doc.qt.io/qt-5.9/qbluetoothserviceinfo.html), which will act as a proxy class to provide information about the service we are going to register on the local adapter. Since we'll be accessing the class in more than one step, we add it as a `private` member:

```
#ifndef BROADCASTER_BT_H
#define BROADCASTER_BT_H
...
namespace channels {
class BroadcasterBt : public BroadcasterChannel
{
    Q_OBJECT
    ...
private:
    QBluetoothServer* _server;
    QBluetoothAddress _localAdapter;
```

```
        QBluetoothServiceInfo _serviceInfo;
        ...
    };
    }

    #endif // BROADCASTER_BT_H
```

First we need to define the service's UUID so that it can be used during service discovery by a client to uniquely identify the service that we are advertising. For reasons that we will explain later on, we use the same UUID provided by the btchat Qt example (http://doc. qt.io/qt-5.9/qtbluetooth-btchat-example.html), which you can also check out for more information about the upcoming steps. We add the following at the top of broadcaster_bt.cpp:

```
    ...

    #include "broadcaster_bt.h"

    namespace channels {
    static const QLatin1String
    serviceUuid("e8e10f95-1a70-4b27-9ccf-02010264e9c8");
    }
```

Once the service UUID is defined, we can add the information to _serviceInfo as follows:

```
    bool channels::BroadcasterBt::_provideServiceId()
    {
        qDebug() << Q_FUNC_INFO;
        QBluetoothServiceInfo::Sequence classId;
        classId <<
    QVariant::fromValue(QBluetoothUuid(QBluetoothUuid::SerialPort));
    _serviceInfo.setAttribute(QBluetoothServiceInfo::BluetoothProfileDescriptor
    List, classId);
        classId.prepend(QVariant::fromValue(QBluetoothUuid(serviceUuid)));
        _serviceInfo.setAttribute(QBluetoothServiceInfo::ServiceClassIds,
    classId);
        _serviceInfo.setServiceUuid(QBluetoothUuid(serviceUuid));
        return _serviceInfo.isValid();
    }
```

We are first adding the SPP to the `Bluetooth Profile Descriptor List` attribute, and then adding the service ID to the `ServiceClassIds` attribute. Both attributes need to be set for the service discovery to happen successfully. As you can see, the generation of the values takes advantage of `QBluetoothServiceInfo::Sequence`, which stores Bluetooth attributes, supports the stream operator to make manipulation easier, and supports `QVariant` by operating all necessary type conversions automatically.

As we have no easy way to check that each of these operations completed successfully, we check 's validity of `_serviceInfo` at the end of each step. If we come up with a checking policy later on, we can implement it here.

Providing information about the service's textual descriptors

After having set service UUID information, we provide human-readable information (`ServiceName`, `ServiceDescription`, `ServiceProvider`) for identifying the origin and purpose of the provided service:

```
bool channels::BroadcasterBt::_provideServiceTraits()
{
    qDebug() << Q_FUNC_INFO;
    _serviceInfo.setAttribute(QBluetoothServiceInfo::ServiceName, "CM BT
Broadcaster Channel");
    _serviceInfo.setAttribute(QBluetoothServiceInfo::ServiceDescription,
"Cute Measures bluetooth broadcaster channel for sensor readings");
    _serviceInfo.setAttribute(QBluetoothServiceInfo::ServiceProvider, "Cute
Measures");
    return _serviceInfo.isValid();
}
```

Providing information about service discoverability

To make the service discoverable by remote devices, we need to add the `PublicBrowseGroup` UUID to the `BrowseGroupList` attribute. This is done as follows:

```
bool channels::BroadcasterBt::_provideServiceDiscoverability()
{
    qDebug() << Q_FUNC_INFO;
    QBluetoothServiceInfo::Sequence publicBrowse;
    publicBrowse <<
QVariant::fromValue(QBluetoothUuid(QBluetoothUuid::PublicBrowseGroup));
    _serviceInfo.setAttribute(QBluetoothServiceInfo::BrowseGroupList,
publicBrowse);
```

```
    return _serviceInfo.isValid();
}
```

Providing information about the transport protocol

The next thing that is required is to provide information about the transport protocol, which is stored in the `ProtocolDescriptorList` attribute. The protocol is based on RFCOMM, which in turn is based on L2CAP. Thus, we just create a new `QBluetoothServiceInfo::Sequence` and append the required attributes:

```
bool channels::BroadcasterBt::_provideProtocolDescriptorList()
{
    qDebug() << Q_FUNC_INFO;
    QBluetoothServiceInfo::Sequence protocolDescriptorList;
    QBluetoothServiceInfo::Sequence protocol;
    protocol << QVariant::fromValue(QBluetoothUuid(QBluetoothUuid::L2cap));
    protocolDescriptorList.append(QVariant::fromValue(protocol));
    protocol.clear();
    protocol << QVariant::fromValue(QBluetoothUuid(QBluetoothUuid::Rfcomm))
            << QVariant::fromValue(quint8(_server->serverPort()));
    protocolDescriptorList.append(QVariant::fromValue(protocol));
_serviceInfo.setAttribute(QBluetoothServiceInfo::ProtocolDescriptorList,
protocolDescriptorList);
    return _serviceInfo.isComplete();
}
```

As we should have provided all necessary information required by `_serviceInfo`, we check it with the `isComplete` method.

Registering the service with the adapter

After all the setting up, the service can finally be registered with the adapter.

> Keep in mind that if you ever need to change any attribute in the service info, you will have to re-register the service.

This is done by calling the `registerService` method of the `QBluetoothServiceInfo` instance:

```
bool channels::BroadcasterBt::_registerService()
{
    qDebug() << Q_FUNC_INFO;
    bool success = _serviceInfo.registerService(_localAdapter);
    if (success) qDebug()
            << "registered service" << _serviceInfo.serviceName()
            << "on adapter" << _localAdapter.toString();
    return success;
}
```

If the service was registered successfully, we will print a message with qDebug, showing the service name and the adapter's address.

Now that the `init` method is fully implemented, we can verify it as the precondition for further tests to run. If your machine has a Bluetooth adapter and it is turned on, everything should be working. If you want to turn the adapter on automatically, you can do so with the `QBluetoothLocalDevice::powerOn()` non-static method, provided you have the right privileges.

Now, we will implement the test where the `BroadcasterBt` channel is connected to an `entity_Broadcaster`, and have a chance to run the initialization code as a pre-condition.

Connecting the broadcaster channel to the Broadcaster entity

We add a test to the BT channel's test suite to verify that a Bluetooth channel connects successfully to a `broadcaster_entity`:

```
void Channel_broadcasterBt::test_connectToBroadcaster()
{
    auto broadcaster_entity = new entities::Broadcaster();
    QVERIFY(_broadcaster_bt->connectToBroadcaster(broadcaster_entity));
    delete broadcaster_entity;
}
```

Since for our purposes `connectToBroadcaster` will be the same, independent of the underlying technological stack, we add it to the `BroadcasterChannel` base class:

```
#ifndef BROADCASTER_CHANNEL_H
#define BROADCASTER_CHANNEL_H
...

namespace entities {
class Broadcaster;
}

namespace channels {
class BroadcasterChannel : public QObject
{
    ...
public:
    virtual bool init() = 0;
    bool connectToBroadcaster(entities::Broadcaster* broadcaster);
};
}

#endif // BROADCASTER_CHANNEL_H
```

The implementation is a `QObject` connection:

```
#include <QDebug>
#include "broadcaster_channel.h"
#include "../../entities/entity_broadcaster/broadcaster.h"

bool
channels::BroadcasterChannel::connectToBroadcaster(entities::Broadcaster*
broadcaster)
{
    qDebug() << Q_FUNC_INFO;
    return connect(broadcaster, &entities::Broadcaster::readingsPublished,
            this, &BroadcasterChannel::sendReadings);
}
```

If you now run the test, you should see something along the following lines:

```
********* Start testing of Channel_broadcasterBt *********
Config: Using QtTest library 5.9.2, Qt 5.9.2 (x86_64-little_endian-lp64 shared (dynamic) release build; by Clang 7.0.2 (clang-700.1.81) (Apple))
PASS   : Channel_broadcasterBt::initTestCase()
QDEBUG : Channel_broadcasterBt::test_connectToBroadcaster() channels::BroadcasterBt::BroadcasterBt(QObject *)
QDEBUG : Channel_broadcasterBt::test_connectToBroadcaster() virtual bool channels::BroadcasterBt::init()
QDEBUG : Channel_broadcasterBt::test_connectToBroadcaster() bool channels::BroadcasterBt::_listenToAdapter()
QDEBUG : Channel_broadcasterBt::test_connectToBroadcaster() listening:  "Marco's MacBook Air"
QDEBUG : Channel_broadcasterBt::test_connectToBroadcaster() bool channels::BroadcasterBt::_provideServiceId()
QDEBUG : Channel_broadcasterBt::test_connectToBroadcaster() bool channels::BroadcasterBt::_provideServiceTraits()
QDEBUG : Channel_broadcasterBt::test_connectToBroadcaster() bool channels::BroadcasterBt::_provideServiceDiscoverability()
QDEBUG : Channel_broadcasterBt::test_connectToBroadcaster() bool channels::BroadcasterBt::_provideProtocolDescriptorList()
QDEBUG : Channel_broadcasterBt::test_connectToBroadcaster() bool channels::BroadcasterBt::_registerService()
QDEBUG : Channel_broadcasterBt::test_connectToBroadcaster() registered service "CM BT Broadcaster Channel" on adapter "2C:F0:EE:20:2E:E5"
QDEBUG : Channel_broadcasterBt::test_connectToBroadcaster() bool channels::BroadcasterChannel::connectToBroadcaster(entities::Broadcaster *)
QDEBUG : Channel_broadcasterBt::test_connectToBroadcaster() virtual channels::BroadcasterBt::~BroadcasterBt()
PASS   : Channel_broadcasterBt::test_connectToBroadcaster()
PASS   : Channel_broadcasterBt::cleanupTestCase()
```

Gluing components into the CM Broadcast console app

Now that we have all necessary entities and `usecases`, and the Bluetooth broadcaster channel is in place, we can start putting it all together in the CM Broadcast console app. We will need to:

- Instantiate a Bluetooth `BroadcasterChannel`
- Instantiate the Broadcaster entity
- Connect the `BroadcasterChannel` to the Broadcaster entity
- Instantiate the Sensor entity
- Instantiate the `usecases`
- Emit `Sensor::emitReading`

Additionally, we will also test that the Bluetooth service is being advertised to remote devices by installing an existing Qt example app onto a mobile device or another PC. In the following chapter, we will substitute the example app with our own mobile client.

Including and instantiating the components

First, we import into cmbroadcast.pro all the components that we have developed by including all of the QMake project's include files that we should have already created:

```
# cmbroadcast.pro
...
include(../entities/entities.pri)
include(../usecases/uc_broadcaster_publishes_sensor_readings/uc_broadcaster
_publishes_sensor_readings.pri)
include(../usecases/uc_broadcaster_connects_to_sensor/uc_broadcaster_connec
ts_to_sensor.pri)
include(../channels/channel_broadcaster/channel_broadcaster.pri)
```

Then, we start instantiating the components in main.cpp. We begin with the Broadcaster entity and BroadcasterBt channel. If the Bluetooth channel is initialized correctly, we connect it to the entity_broadcaster:

```
#include <QCoreApplication>
#include "../channels/channel_broadcaster/broadcaster_bt.h"
#include "../entities/entity_broadcaster/broadcaster.h"

int main(int argc, char *argv[])
{
    QCoreApplication app(argc, argv);

    auto broadcasterBt = new channels::BroadcasterBt(&app);
    auto broadcaster = new entities::Broadcaster(&app);

    if (broadcasterBt->init()) {
        broadcasterBt->connectToBroadcaster(broadcaster);
    }
    return app.exec();
}
```

Then, we instantiate the Sensor entity, and connect it to the Broadcaster entity with the corresponding usecase:

```
#include <QCoreApplication>
#include "../channels/channel_broadcaster/broadcaster_bt.h"
#include "../entities/entity_broadcaster/broadcaster.h"
#include "../entities/entity_sensor/sensor.h"
#include
"../usecases/uc_broadcaster_connects_to_sensor/brodcaster_connects_to_senso
r.h"

int main(int argc, char *argv[])
```

```
{
    QCoreApplication app(argc, argv);

    auto broadcasterBt = new channels::BroadcasterBt(&app);
    auto broadcaster = new entities::Broadcaster(&app);

    if (broadcasterBt->init()) {
        broadcasterBt->connectToBroadcaster(broadcaster);
    }

    auto sensor = new entities::Sensor("mockSensor1", &app);

    usecases::broadcaster_connects_to_sensor(*broadcaster, *sensor);

    return a.exec();
}
```

Finally, we have the `sensor` emit a reading and the `broadcaster` publish it. Since the Bluetooth channel is connected to the `broadcaster` and has been correctly initialized when the `broadcaster` publishes the sensor readings, these will be available over the Bluetooth channel to any connected remote devices:

```
#include <QCoreApplication>
#include <QDateTime>
#include <QtMath>
...
#include
"../usecases/uc_broadcaster_publishes_sensor_readings/broadcaster_publishes
_sensor_readings.h"

int main(int argc, char *argv[])
{
    QCoreApplication app(argc, argv);
    ...
    usecases::broadcaster_connects_to_sensor(*broadcaster, *sensor);
    sensor->emitReading(
                QVariantMap({{"sensor_id", sensor->identifier()},
                             {"timestamp",
QDateTime::currentMSecsSinceEpoch()},
                             {"value",
qSin(QDateTime::currentMSecsSinceEpoch())}
                            }));
    qDebug() <<
      (usecases::broadcaster_publishes_sensor_readings(*broadcaster,
*sensor)
                ? "readings published"
                : "readings not published");
```

```
        return app.exec();
}
```

> Since the `broadcaster_publishes_sensor_readings` use case
> establishes a signal/slot connection, it just needs to be run once explicitly,
> while the connection will be triggered every time the `emitReading` signal
> is emitted.

If you run the application, you will notice that it terminates right after the last use case is run. This happens because we have a console application and we don't have any instruction that triggers the event loop. One solution to this is to start a `QTimer`, which will activate Qt's event loop, and exit the program only when the timer's timeout is triggered. To achieve this, we use the `singleShot` static method in `QTimer` , which takes the timer's interval in milliseconds, with an object instance and a slot to be called once the timer is triggered:

```
// cmbroadcast/main.cpp
...
#include <QTimer>

int main(int argc, char *argv[])
{
    QCoreApplication app(argc, argv);
    QTimer::singleShot(600000, &app, SLOT(quit()));
    ...
}
```

Testing the service discovery

Since we haven't implemented any Bluetooth client yet, we need a way to make sure that the service is available to remote devices, and is being advertised by the local Bluetooth adapter.

We can achieve this by using a ready-made client, and having it search for our service. Qt provides a **Bluetooth Chat Example** (`http://doc.qt.io/qt-5.9/qtbluetooth-btchat-example.html`) that can be used for this purpose. The example should already be available in your Qt distribution, and be accessible via Qt Creator's **Examples** tab in the **Welcome** mode:

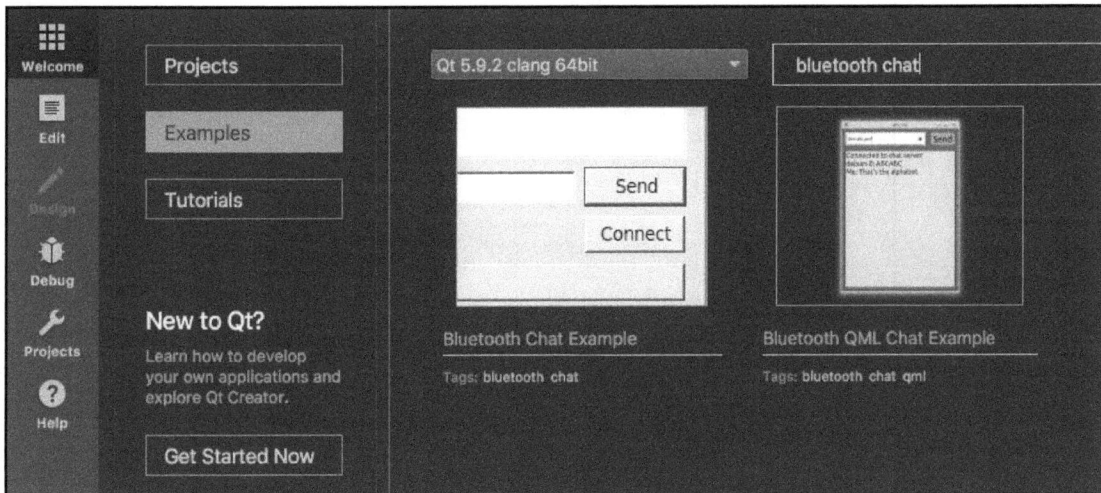

Both Qt Widgets and a QML Example are available. While both work, the Widgets example (titled **Bluetooth Chat Example**) is preferable as it provides a more flexible way of connecting the **Bluetooth Chat** client to our server. The qmake example project that will be opened when clicking on the example is called btchat.

To test the connection, you'll have to deploy the example to another device that has a Bluetooth adapter, such as an Android device or another PC. Before trying our console server application, however, you should run the btchat example on both your host device and the client device by following the example's instructions, and make sure that you are able to establish a connection between one of the two machines acting as the chat server, and the other acting as the client. Both client and server are contained in the btchat application.

Here is the desktop host on macOS, to which an Android client has connected:

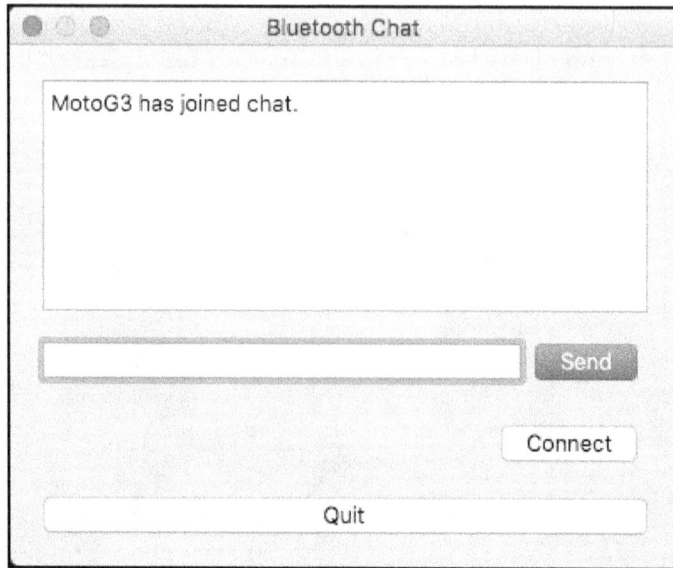

> If you have trouble connecting your device to the host because the device was not found, first try pairing the device and host with the tools provided by their operating systems and repeat the procedure until it works. If that doesn't help either, seek assistance on Qt's IRC channels or the forums. Connectivity is often an ugly beast!

If the connection procedure between two btchat instances worked, you can now try and close the instance on your host and launch `cmbroadcast` instead. As you might remember, I instructed you to using a specific Service UUID for the `BroadcasterBt` channel's service. That is the service ID that the btchat client is looking for, and so the service discovery still works. So, when connecting to the `cmbroadcast` server with a btchat client, once the connection has been established, you'll still see the message **[your host's name] has joined chat.** in the chat client's message area. If this happens, it means the service is correctly advertised to remote Bluetooth clients. In the following chapter, we'll make something interesting with it.

Summary

In this chapter, we started working on an application ecosystem for transmitting and consuming sensor measures.

We have seen how to implement a sensor entity and briefly introduced the Qt Sensors module.

We have also developed a Bluetooth channel component that implements a server-client connection with the RFCOMM protocol, which emulates serial communication by publishing a Bluetooth service and connecting to it from an example client.

In thefollowing chapter, we will build our own Bluetooth client, transmit some fake sensor data, and come up with interesting visualizations by getting to know the Qt Charts module.

Stay with me, as your patience will be rewarded!

30
Building a Mobile Dashboard to Display Real-Time Sensor Data

In the previous chapter, we built and deployed a server application to broadcast data coming from one or more sensors to the outside world via a classic Bluetooth connection. We tested the application by connecting to it by means of the standard **Qt Bluetooth Chat** example.

In this chapter, we will create an ad-hoc UI application, a dashboard, to display the sensor data in real time on a chart, by taking advantage of the Bluetooth connection. The chart will be shown with the help of the QtCharts module. The application will be compatible with mobile usage. Here is what the chart visualization will look like:

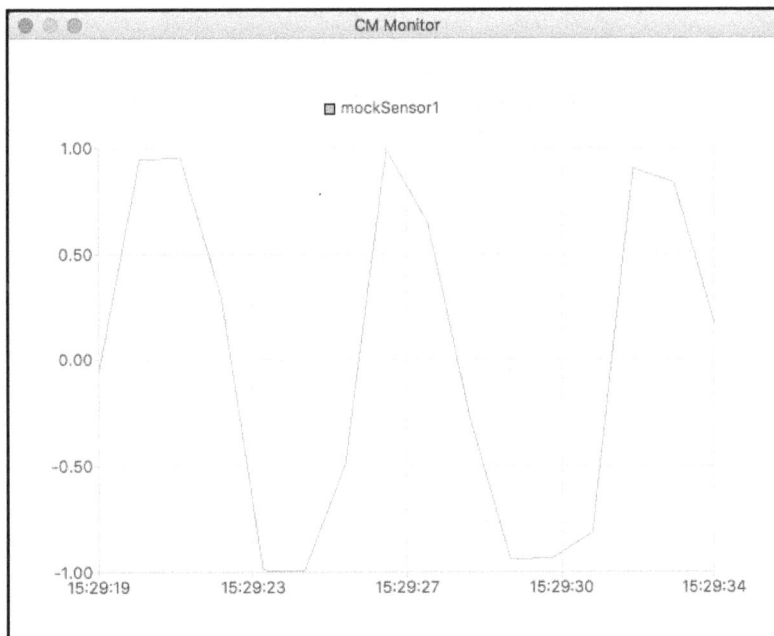

We will also show how to provide multi-language support to our users with the help of the `QTranslator` class, and the `lupdate`, `lrelease`, and **Qt Linguist** tools.

Overview

After having built a little non-UI application that broadcasts sensor readings over a Bluetooth connection (or any other connection, as long as the proper Broadcaster Channel component is implemented), it is now time to turn to something aesthetically more pleasing: a nice visualization of the sensor data with (nearly) real-time updates.

This application should help the business customers of Cute Measures to monitor the status of their systems whenever they are in the immediate surroundings (within tens of meters) of a broadcaster instance. We don't want, however, to be constrained by the limits of Bluetooth, so the component that deals with fetching the data from the BT connection will have to be easily replaceable with any other technology that might fit better, such as Wi-Fi (which we will deal with in the next chapter), MQTT (which is supported by the Qt MQTT module, starting with Qt 5.10: `http://doc.qt.io/QtMQTT/index.html`), or Remote Objects (available in Qt 5.9 as a Technical Preview: `https://doc.qt.io/qt-5.9/qtremoteobjects-index.html`).

We will keep things simple and start with one of the simplest chart visualizations, the line series. You are, however, encouraged to expand the application to offer a few more options to our users.

Besides chart visualizations, another important aspect we will touch upon is how to deal with multi-language support for the user interface, which Qt has been providing out of the box for a very long time. As we will see, there are a few options available that we should consider based on the intended `usecases`.

To keep things concise, we won't implement `usecases` for this example. However, as usual, you are warmly encouraged to do it in your own time, especially if you plan on further implementing the application. What we will do instead is sketch out the main scenarios for our application. Here they are:

```
Feature: inspect sensor readings over time

    Scenario: waiting for readings
        Given that no readings are available yet
        When I inspect sensor readings
        I should be told that the system is waiting for readings

    Scenario: readings available
        Given that some readings are available
        When I inspect sensor readings
        I should be given sensor readings for the last 15 seconds
```

Before diving into the components that will support these use case scenarios, let's deal with project setup.

Project setup

For this prototype, we will limit ourselves to a couple of key components to get going: a `ReceiverBt` channel component to fetch the readings data, and a Qt Quick UI client application where we will also define the UI components.

Setting up the CM Monitor project

We want to add a new subproject to `part3-cute_measures.pro` called `cmmonitor`. The Cute Measures Monitor will be a **Qt Quick Application**, so we thus choose the appropriate template in Qt Creator:

Starting with version 4.5, Qt Creator provides more than one template for **Qt Quick Application**. If you are using this QT version, which might be included by default in the latest bugfix releases of Qt 5.9, and in subsequent Qt versions, choose the **Qt Quick Application - Empty** template, as shown in the following screenshot. In previous Qt Creator versions, pick the **Qt Quick Application** template.

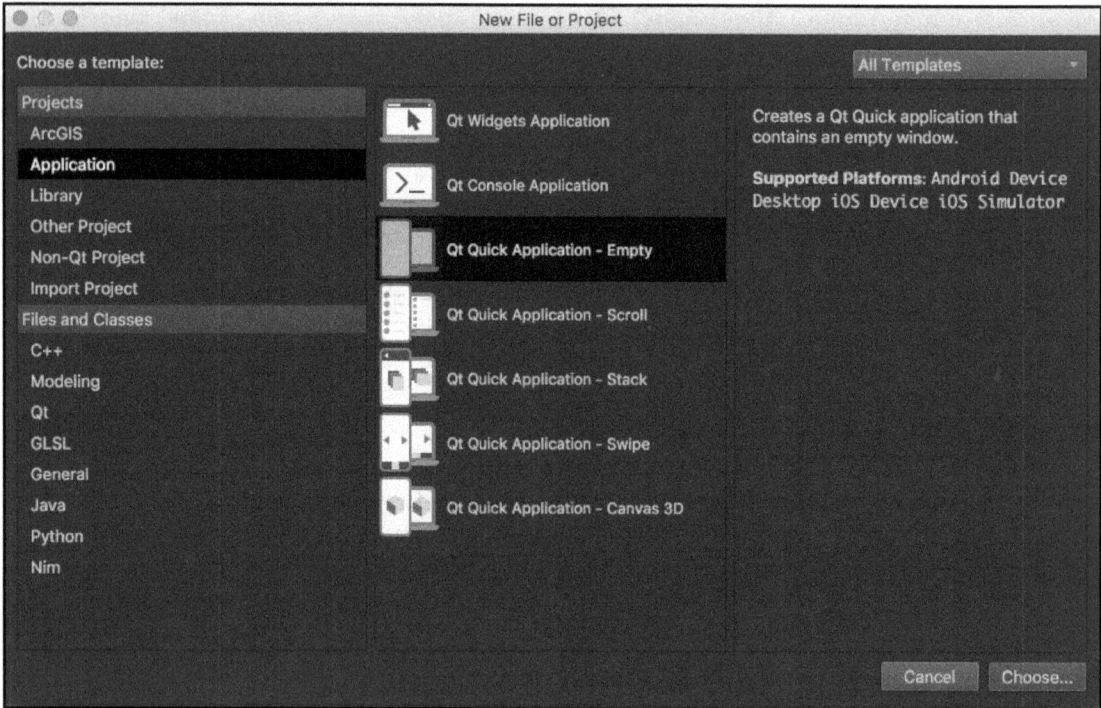

Now, since we are going to use `QtCharts`, we will have to change the setup of the bootstrapped `main.cpp` slightly. Instead of the default `QGuiApplication` object, applications that make use of `QtCharts` require the use of the `QApplication` object. `QApplication` (http://doc.qt.io/qt-5.9/qguiapplication.html) is a subclass of `QGuiApplication` (http://doc.qt.io/qt-5.9/qapplication.html), which is specialized for dealing with Qt Widgets. In fact, `QtCharts` still depend on the Qt Widgets module, despite also having a QML interface (in addition to a C++ one). We will thus have to make two changes to our project:

1. Instantiate a `QApplication`

2. Add the `widgets` module to `cmmmonitor.pro`, so that all necessary classes will be included by QMake during the build process:

```cpp
// main.cpp
#include <QApplication>
#include <QQmlApplicationEngine>

int main(int argc, char *argv[])
{
    QCoreApplication::setAttribute(Qt::AA_EnableHighDpiScaling);

    QApplication app(argc, argv);
    QQmlApplicationEngine engine;
    ...
}
```

While we are at it, we will also add the `charts` module to `cmmonitor`:

```
// cmmonitor.pro
QT += quick widgets charts
```

Creating the Bluetooth Receiver channel project

To be able to test and include the Bluetooth Receiver channel component with ease, we will create a dedicated subproject of type **Qt Unit Test** for it under the previously created `channels` project, and name it `channel_receiver`. The test file will be called `tst_channel_receiver.cpp`, and the test class, `Test_channel_receiver`. We won't show how to implement tests for the Bluetooth Receiver channel — make sure you do add a few tests to ensure that its public methods behave properly. We will also add a `channel_receiver.pri` file, so that we can import all our source files and resources and dependencies easily into client projects such as `cmmonitor`.

As we did in the previous chapter, we want to create a base class for the Receiver channel, which is the same for all technology-dependent implementations (Bluetooth, Wi-Fi, MQTT , and so on). It will provide a few virtual methods, and a few methods that are shared across all implementations, and it will not declare any private member. The class will be called `ReceiverChannel`. As usual, we can create it via a **C++ Class** template and add it to `channel_receiver.pri`.

If we now think about the `ReceiverChannel` class, it should do the following:

- Receive and process the readings in whatever format they were provided
- Make them available to other components (for example, a `Receiver` entity for further logical processing) in a convenient format

The first task will be performed by a slot called `receiveReadings`, whose implementation will be technology-specific, while for the second a signal will be enough. We will call the signal `readingsProcessed`, and make the readings available as a `QVariantList`, or `QList` of `QVariant`. This format seems the most convenient because:

- It provides automatic type marshalling between C++ and QML
- `QVariant` can transparently wrap `QVariantMap`, which is what we used in the previous chapter to represent a reading

Additionally, if we wanted to be able to connect the channel to an entity to perform any further business logic beyond simple data format conversion, we could also add a `connectToReceiver(entities::Receiver*)` method.

Given this, here is the header file for `ReceiverChannel`:

```
// receiver_channel.h
#ifndef RECEIVER_CHANNEL_H
#define RECEIVER_CHANNEL_H

#include <QObject>
#include <QVariantList>

namespace entities {
class Receiver;
}

namespace channels {
class ReceiverChannel : public QObject
{
    Q_OBJECT
protected:
    ReceiverChannel(QObject *parent = nullptr) : QObject(parent) {}
public:
    bool connectToReceiver(entities::Receiver* receiver) {}
public slots:
    virtual void receiveReadings() = 0;
signals:
    void readingsProcessed(QVariantList readings);
};
}
```

```
#endif // RECEIVER_CHANNEL_H
```

Once `ReceiverChannel` is there, we can add the Bluetooth-specific implementation by means of the `ReceiverBt` subclass:

```cpp
// receiver_bt.h
#ifndef RECEIVER_BT_H
#define RECEIVER_BT_H

#include <QObject>

#include "receiver_channel.h"

namespace channels {
class ReceiverBt : public ReceiverChannel
{
    Q_OBJECT
public:
    explicit ReceiverBt(QObject* parent = nullptr);
    ~ReceiverBt();
public slots:
    void receiveReadings() override;
};
}

#endif // RECEIVER_BT_H
```

We also add the stubs for the implementations by adding debugging information for when a method is entered with `QDebug` and the `Q_FUNC_INFO` macro:

```cpp
// receiver_bt.cpp
#include <QDebug>

#include "receiver_bt.h"

channels::ReceiverBt::ReceiverBt(QObject* parent)
    : ReceiverChannel(parent)
{
    qDebug() << Q_FUNC_INFO;
}

channels::ReceiverBt::~ReceiverBt()
{
    qDebug() << Q_FUNC_INFO;
}

void channels::ReceiverBt::receiveReadings()
{
```

```
    qDebug() << Q_FUNC_INFO;
}
```

Finally, we need to add the `bluetooth` module to `channel_receiver.pro`:

```
// channel_receiver.pro
QT += bluetooth
...
```

After setting up these files, the subproject will have the following structure:

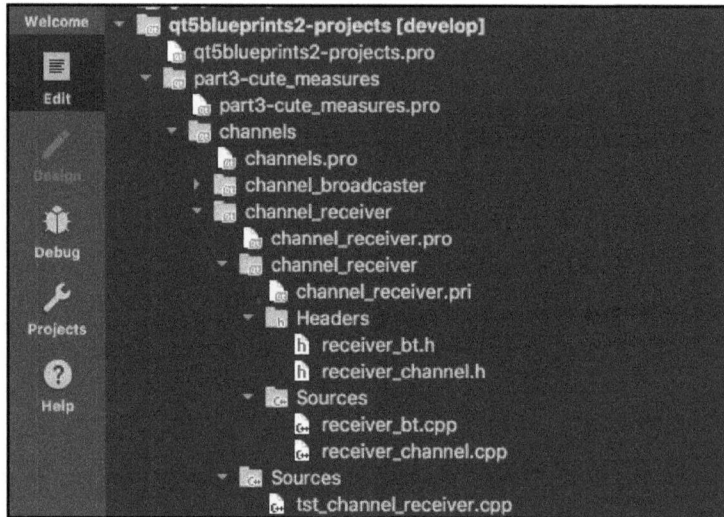

Implementing the Bluetooth Receiver channel

Implementing the Bluetooth Receiver channel consists of:

1. Implementing the `init` method
2. Implementing the `receiveReadings` slot and emitting the `readingsProcessed` signal once it's done

Implementing the init method

In order to initialize the Receiver channel, we need to launch a service discovery agent on the local adapter's address, and once the service has been found, connect to it by opening a socket. Since we don't know when the service discovery agent will find the readings broadcast service, we will use a slot for the second step.

First, we will need a pointer to the service discovery agent instance so that we can stop it once the service has been found:

```
// receiver_bt.h
#ifndef RECEIVER_BT_H
#define RECEIVER_BT_H
...

class QBluetoothServiceDiscoveryAgent;

namespace channels {
class ReceiverBt : public ReceiverChannel
{
    Q_OBJECT
public:
    ...
private:
    QBluetoothServiceDiscoveryAgent* _discoveryAgent;
};
}

#endif // RECEIVER_BT_H
```

Here is how the service discovery is implemented:

```
// receiver_bt.cpp
...
#include <QBluetoothServiceDiscoveryAgent>
#include <QBluetoothLocalDevice>
...
static const QLatin1String
serviceUuid("e8e10f95-1a70-4b27-9ccf-02010264e9c8");
...
void channels::ReceiverBt::init()
{
    qDebug() << Q_FUNC_INFO;
    auto localAdapter =
QBluetoothLocalDevice::allDevices().value(0).address();
    _discoveryAgent = new QBluetoothServiceDiscoveryAgent(localAdapter,
this);
    connect(_discoveryAgent,
```

```
&QBluetoothServiceDiscoveryAgent::serviceDiscovered,
            this, &channels::ReceiverBt::_connectService);
    _discoveryAgent->setUuidFilter(QBluetoothUuid(serviceUuid));
    _discoveryAgent->start(QBluetoothServiceDiscoveryAgent::FullDiscovery);
}
```

> **TIP**
> For the sake of conciseness, the preceding code does not deal with the case where no local adapter is found. To improve on this, you should have the init method return a Boolean and deal with this case.

The discovery agent is an instance of QBluetoothServiceDiscoveryAgent (http://doc. qt.io/qt-5.9/qbluetoothservicediscoveryagent.html). It starts scanning for available services on the given local adapter. To make sure we find only the service we want to connect to, we use the setUuidFilter method and specify the serviceUuid as a static const. This allows us to connect to the service as soon as it is discovered, without having to perform any further checks.

> The serviceUuid provided here is still the one from Qt's **Bluetooth Chat Example** that we used for the Broadcaster in Chapter 29, *Sending Sensor Readings to a Device with a Non-UI App*. You can either use this device or a new one.

The discovery agent provides a convenient signal, serviceDiscovered, which is emitted once a service is discovered, and exposes a QBluetoothServiceInfo object. Hence, we create a private _connectToService slot to open the socket on the service. We declare the method and the pointer to the socket object (http://doc.qt.io/qt-5.9/ qbluetoothsocket.html) in the header file:

```
// receiver_bt.h
#ifndef RECEIVER_BT_H
#define RECEIVER_BT_H
...
class QBluetoothServiceDiscoveryAgent;
class QBluetoothSocket;
class QBluetoothServiceInfo;

namespace channels {
class ReceiverBt : public ReceiverChannel
{
    Q_OBJECT
public:
    ...
private slots:
    void _connectService(const QBluetoothServiceInfo &serviceInfo);
```

```
    private:
        QBluetoothServiceDiscoveryAgent* _discoveryAgent;
        QBluetoothSocket* _socket;
    };
    }


    #endif // RECEIVER_BT_H
```

Then we implement the _connectService slot:

```
    // receiver_bt.cpp
    ...
    #include <QBluetoothSocket>
    #include <QBluetoothServiceInfo>
    ...
    void channels::ReceiverBt::_connectService(const QBluetoothServiceInfo
    &serviceInfo)
    {
        qDebug() << Q_FUNC_INFO;
        _discoveryAgent->stop();
        qDebug() << "connecting to service" << serviceInfo.serviceName();
        _socket = new QBluetoothSocket(QBluetoothServiceInfo::RfcommProtocol,
    this);
        connect(_socket, &QBluetoothSocket::readyRead, this,
    &ReceiverBt::receiveReadings);
        connect(_socket, &QBluetoothSocket::connected, []{
            qDebug() << "socket connected";
        });
        _socket->connectToService(serviceInfo, QIODevice::ReadOnly);
    }
```

The QBluetoothSocket inherits from QIODevice (http://doc.qt.io/qt-5.9/qiodevice.
html), which provides a shared API for many kinds of data I/O mechanism (including
QBuffer, QFileDevice, and QNetworkReply). QIODevice provides the readyRead
signal, which is emitted once every time new data is available for reading from the device's
current read channel. In QBluetoothSocket, this happens when a write is performed on
the peer device's socket. Hence, we set up a connection between readyRead and the
receiveReadings slot, which we are going to implement now.

Implementing the receiveReadings method

In the `receiveReadings` method, our goal is to transform a `QByteArray` containing JSON text (see `Chapter 29`, *Sending Sensor Readings to a Device with a Non-UI App*, on how we encoded it) into a `QVariantList` of sensor readings that can be handled automatically by QML. Here is how we do it:

```
void channels::ReceiverBt::receiveReadings()
{
    qDebug() << Q_FUNC_INFO;
    if (!_socket)
        return;
    QByteArray readingsLine = _socket->readLine();
    QJsonDocument readingsDoc = QJsonDocument::fromJson(readingsLine);
    QJsonArray readingsArray = readingsDoc.array();
    QVariantList readings;
    for (int i=0; i<readingsArray.count(); ++i) {
        readings.append(readingsArray.at(i).toObject().toVariantMap());
    }
    emit readingsProcessed(readings);
}
```

> **TIP**
> Production code would require you to perform a few checks about the byte data that you are marshalling first to JSON and then to `QVariantList`.

The `QByteArray` with the JSON data is obtained by calling `readLine`, which is implemented in the socket and returns the last message written by the peer onto the socket. The `QByteArray`-encoded JSON can be converted into a `QJsonDocument` object (the same object we used for JSON encoding) thanks to the static `fromJson` method. Since we know that the root value is an array, we return the document as a `QJsonArray` with the array method, and create an empty `QVariantList`. For each of the JSON values contained in the array, we make sure they are each interpreted as a `QJsonObject`, convert them to a `QVariantMap` with `toVariantMap`, and append the map to `QVariantList`. As you can see, `QVariantList` can handle both `QVariant` and `QVariantMap` items seamlessly.

Every time that the `readyRead` signal is emitted by the socket, if there are no impediments, the `readingsProcessed` signal will be emitted by the `ReceiverBt` channel.

Having the broadcaster emit readings at regular intervals

In the previous chapter, in `cmbroadcast`'s `main.cpp`, we only called `Sensor::emitReading` once. Since we now need a time series to be displayed on the chart, we are going to improve on that. We will be emitting a reading every second by using a `QTimer` instance, and have the emitted values follow a sinusoidal shape as a function of time by means of the `qSin` macro. Furthermore, we will start this regular broadcasting as soon as a receiver connects to the broadcaster. Here is how:

```cpp
// cmbroadcast/main.cpp
...
#include <QtMath>

int main(int argc, char *argv[])
{
    QCoreApplication app(argc, argv);
    ...
    QTimer sensorTimer;
    sensorTimer.setInterval(1000);
    QObject::connect(&sensorTimer, &QTimer::timeout, [&sensor] {
        sensor->emitReading(
                    QVariantMap({
                      {"sensor_id", sensor->identifier()},
                      {"timestamp", QDateTime::currentMSecsSinceEpoch()},
                      {"value", qSin(QDateTime::currentMSecsSinceEpoch())}
                    }));
    });
    QObject::connect(broadcasterBt,
&channels::BroadcasterBt::clientConnected,                [&sensorTimer] {
            sensorTimer.start();
        }
    );

    return app.exec();
}
```

Checking the broadcaster-receiver communication

To check that the data arrives over the Bluetooth channel, we can fire the `cmbroadcast` application created in the previous chapter on one of our Bluetooth devices, fire the `cmmonitor` application on the other Bluetooth device, and use `qDebug()` to monitor initialization and any incoming readings data. To do that, we first need to create an instance of `ReceiverBt` in `main.cpp`, and initialize it:

```cpp
#include <QApplication>
#include <QQmlApplicationEngine>

#include "../channels/channel_receiver/receiver_bt.h"

int main(int argc, char *argv[])
{
    QCoreApplication::setAttribute(Qt::AA_EnableHighDpiScaling);

    QApplication app(argc, argv);

    auto receiverChannel = new channels::ReceiverBt(&app);

    receiverChannel->init();

    ...
}
```

We can then set up a `QObject::connection` between `ReceiverBt`'s relevant signals and a Lambda function where we print the signal's payload with `qDebug`—you should know how to do that by now!

> After invoking the `init` method, the service discovery and connection to the remote socket can take up to 10-20 seconds. Just monitor the information on Qt Creator's **Application Output** pane, and print more if necessary. Keep in mind that we made `cmbroadcast` run for 5 minutes before quitting.

Implementing the readings chart

Now that we have data exposed by the Receiver channel, we can implement the first data visualization of our dashboard, the readings chart. We create a new QML file called `ReadingsChart.qml` and add it to `qml.qrc` in the `cmmonitor` project.

Introducing QtCharts

As already hinted, Qt provides an easy way to incorporate several kinds of charts by means of the `QtCharts` module (`https://doc.qt.io/qt-5.9/qtcharts-index.html`). A very good overview about available chart types and basic API usage is available at `https://doc.qt.io/qt-5.9/qtcharts-overview.html`. Some of the available data series representations include Line Series, Area Series, Bar Series, Pie Series, BoxPlot Series, and Candlestick Series. All of these need to be added to a `ChartView` (`QChartView`) object, which also handles the axes, titles, and legends. A specialized chart view exists for Polar charts, `PolarChartView` (`QPolarChart`).

Originally available only through a C++ API, the module is now also accessible from QML with a dedicated declarative API. Yet, as we mentioned before, for QML applications it still depends on the Qt Widgets module because of `QApplication`. The `QtCharts` module is added to a project with the `QT += charts` QMake directive.

Adding a line series to the chart view

We agreed that a reasonable visualization for the near-sinusoidal data produced by the mock sensor and transmitted via the broadcaster is a line series, where subsequent data points are linearly interpolated. You can choose an alternative visualization if you prefer. The `LineSeries` QML type (`https://doc.qt.io/qt-5.9/qml-qtcharts-lineseries.html`) should be contained in a `ChartView` type (`https://doc.qt.io/qt-5.9/qml-qtcharts-chartview.html`):

```
// ReadingsChart.qml
import QtQuick 2.9
import QtCharts 2.2

ChartView {
    id: chartView
    LineSeries {
```

```
            id: lineSeries
    }
}
```

By previewing the QML document with **qmlscene**, you'll get an empty *X/Y* chart with a default grid and legend color:

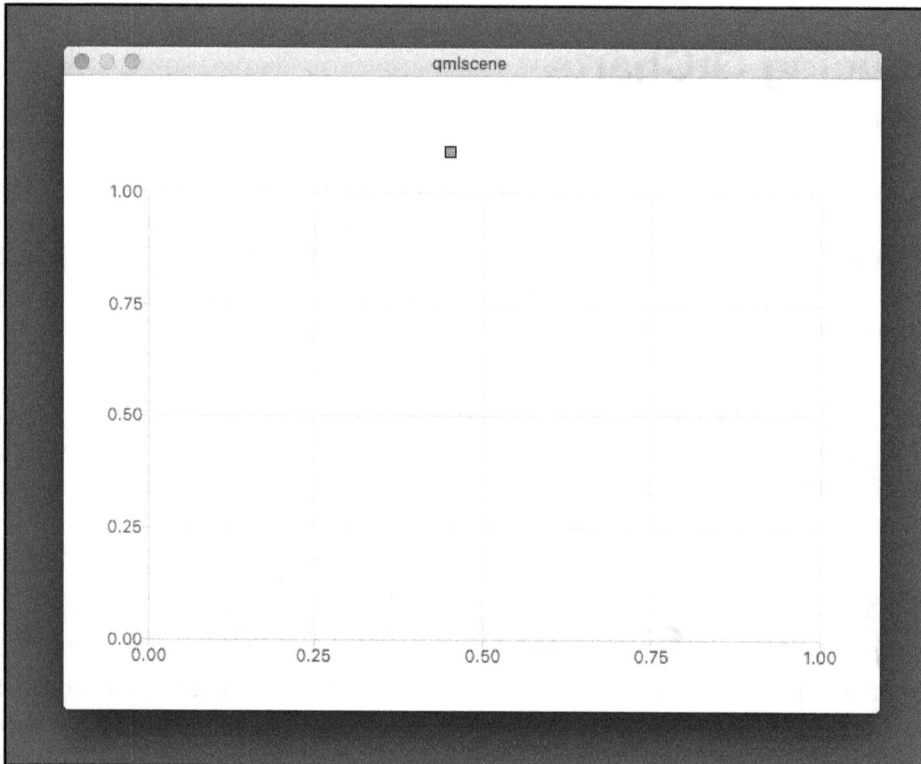

What should we display on the *X* and *Y* axes? By looking at our usecases, we decide that the *X* axis will display a window of 15 seconds, where the maximum value is the timestamp of the last sensor reading available (or the current time in case there is no reading available), while the *Y* axis will represent the actual sin value, which is comprised between -1 and 1. To have the axes represent these two kinds of data, we need two different types: DateTimeAxis (https://doc.qt.io/qt-5.9/qml-qtcharts-datetimeaxis.html) and ValueAxis (https://doc.qt.io/qt-5.9/qml-qtcharts-valueaxis.html).

As the name suggests, the former is capable of making sense of `QDateTime` objects and JavaScript `Date` objects, by also providing easy formatting options. The format can be specified by passing a string to the `format` property, and the max and min values of the series (the current time, and the time 15 seconds ago, respectively) can be set by creating JS `Date` objects and binding them to the `max` and `min` properties.

On the other hand, `ValueAxis` is suited for numeric values, both integers and reals. We can have `LineSeries` use `DateTimeAxis` and `ValueAxis` by setting the `axisX` and `axisY` properties, as follows:

```
// ReadingsChart.qml
import QtQuick 2.9
import QtCharts 2.2

ChartView {
    id: chartView
    ...
    DateTimeAxis {
        id: valueAxisX
        format: "H:mm:ss"
        min: new Date(Date.now() - 15000) // 15 secs
        max: new Date(Date.now())
    }
    ValueAxis{
        id: valueAxisY
        max: 1
        min: -1
    }
    LineSeries {
        id: lineSeries
        axisX: valueAxisX
        axisY: valueAxisY
    }
}
```

We can pass a name for the line series to be displayed in the chart's legend, and customize the line's color:

```
...
LineSeries {
    id: lineSeries
    axisX: valueAxisX
    axisY: valueAxisY
    name: "mockSensor1"
```

```
        color: "orange"
    }
    ...
```

To fulfill the first use case scenario in a simple manner, we will add `Text` to be shown while the chart is empty:

```
import QtQuick 2.9
import QtCharts 2.2

ChartView {
    id: chartView
    ...
    Text {
        id: emptyText
        anchors.centerIn: parent
        text: "waiting for data..."
    }
}
```

Finally, to have the empty chart always display the current time as the max value, we add a timer and have it set the *X* axis values every second:

```
import QtQuick 2.9
import QtCharts 2.2

ChartView {
    ...
    Text {
        id: emptyText
        ...
    }
    Timer {
        id: axisTimer
        running: true
        repeat: true
        interval: 1000
        onTriggered: {
            valueAxisX.min = new Date(Date.now() - 15000);
            valueAxisX.max = new Date(Date.now());
        }
    }
}
```

If you now preview the `ReadingsChart` in `qmlscene`, you should see the following, with the time values on the *X* axis updating every second:

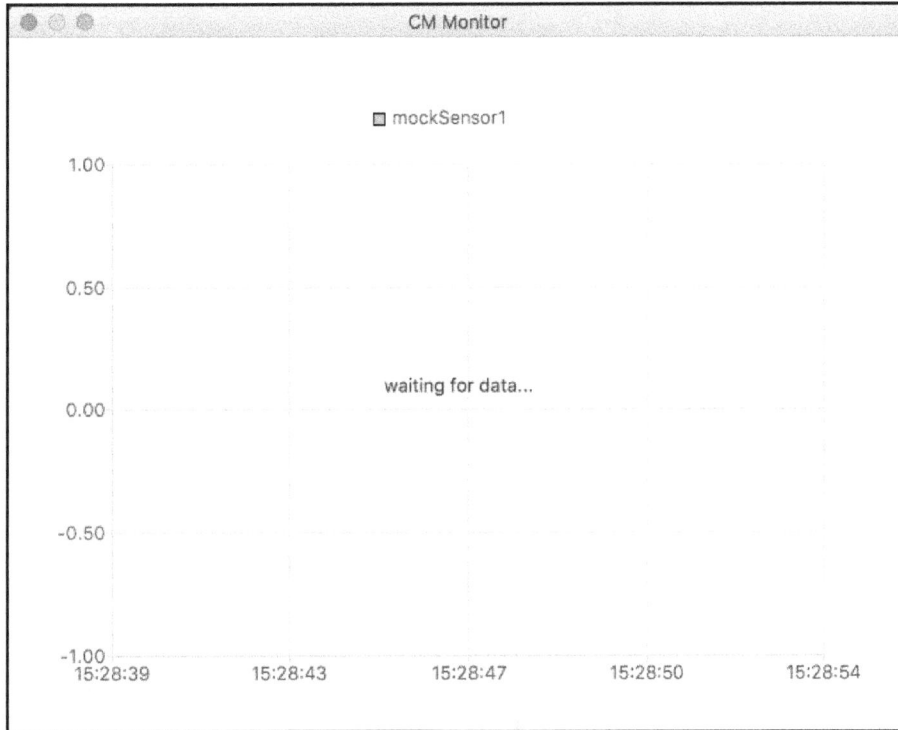

Wiring the receiverChannel to the chart

To wire the `receiverChannel` to the chart, we need to:

1. Expose the `receiverChannel` instance to QML
2. Connect to the `readingsPublished` signal and update the chart every time the signal is emitted

The first operation is done in `main.cpp` with the help of `QQmlContext`'s `setContextProperty` method. We already encountered this technique in Chapter 25, *Wiring User Interaction and Delivering the Final App*:

```
#include <QApplication>
#include <QQmlApplicationEngine>
#include <QQmlContext>

#include "../channels/channel_receiver/receiver_bt.h"

int main(int argc, char *argv[])
{
    ...
    QQmlApplicationEngine engine;
    engine.rootContext()->setContextProperty("receiverChannel", receiverChannel)
;
    engine.load(QUrl(QStringLiteral("qrc:/main.qml")));
    if (engine.rootObjects().isEmpty())
        return -1;

    return app.exec();
}
```

To connect the `receiverChannel` instance to the `ReadingsChart`, we will instantiate the latter in `main.qml` and make use of a `Connections` object:

```
// main.qml
import QtQuick 2.9
import QtQuick.Window 2.2

Window {
    visible: true
    width: 640
    height: 480
    title: "CM Monitor"

    ReadingsChart {
        id: readingsChart
        anchors.fill: parent
        Connections {
            target: receiverChannel
            onReadingsProcessed: {
            }
        }
    }
}
```

How shall we update the chart when `onReadingsProcessed` is emitted? Here is the plan:

1. Stop `axisTimer`, as we will update the X axis based on the timestamp coming from the readings payload

2. Hide `emptyText`

3. Set `valueAxisX.max` to the reading's timestamp

4. Set `valueAxisX.min` to the reading's timestamp minus `15` seconds.

5. Append the timestamp and value of the sensor reading to `lineSeries`

To do all of this, we create a JavaScript function called `plot` in `ReadingsChart`:

```
// ReadingsChart.qml
import QtQuick 2.9
import QtCharts 2.2

ChartView {
    id: chartView
    width: 640
    height: 480
    function plot(readings) {
        if (readings[0]) {
            readingsChart.axisTimer.stop();
            readingsChart.emptyText.visible = false;
            readingsChart.valueAxisX.min =
                new Date(readings[0].timestamp - 15000);
            readingsChart.valueAxisX.max =
                new Date(readings[0].timestamp);
            readingsChart.lineSeries.append(
                new Date(readings[0].timestamp), readings[0].value);

        }
    }
    ...
}
```

> **TIP**
> As already mentioned in the previous chapter, we are broadcasting and consuming only one sensor reading (the one indexed at 0), but you could add more and have them display in time series of different kinds.

Once this is done, we can implement `Connections.onReadingsProcessed` by just calling `plot`:

```
// main.qml
import QtQuick 2.9
import QtQuick.Window 2.2

Window {
    ...
    ReadingsChart {
        id: readingsChart
        anchors.fill: parent
        Connections {
            target: receiverChannel
            onReadingsProcessed: {
                readingsChart.plot(readings);
            }
        }
    }
}
```

If you now launch `cmbroadcast` and `cmmonitor` on two different devices with an active Bluetooth adapter, you will see the data flowing in as soon as the connection is established. Pretty neat, huh?

Adding internationalization support

Besides being strong on graphics, Qt also shines when it comes to internationalization and multi-language support. Qt has out-of-the-box provisions to:

- Display `Dates`, currencies, and other kinds of values according to predefined locales (combinations of country codes and languages)
- Select a predefined locale at startup based on platform information and render string translations and formats accordingly
- Switch between locales at runtime, with automatic updates of UI elements where text is marked as translatable
- Install new locales and make them available to the application
- Support specific language features, such as left-to-right and right-to-left writing

Beyond this, Qt also provides tools for multi-language content authoring (**Qt Linguist**) and resource generation (`lupdate` and `lrelease`). An overview of all the internationalization capabilities of Qt is to be found at `http://doc.qt.io/qt-5.9/internationalization.html`, where you will also find links to Qt Quick-specific documentation.

We will show by means of a simple example how to add multi-language support to the `cmmonitor` application.

Marking strings for translation

The first thing that Qt's tools need to know to provide translations is what strings need to be translated. This is mostly achieved by surrounding each `QString` with `QObject`'s `tr` function (in C++) or the `qsTr` function (in QML). When you need to translate strings in other contexts, a few more options are available. You can check them all out at `http://doc.qt.io/qt-5.9/i18n-source-translation.html`.

If, for example, we wanted to translate the Window title of `cmmonitor`, we should do the following:

```
// main.qml
import QtQuick 2.9
import QtQuick.Window 2.2

Window {
    visible: true
    width: 640
    height: 480
    title: qsTr("CM Monitor")
    ...
}
```

With the `qsTr` approach, Qt uses the concept of a developer English translation. The developers write an invalidated English string in the code (`"CM Monitor"` in this case), and this wording is used as an identifier key for the translation, together with the derived context (the document it appears in), to differentiate between identical key strings.

Once this is done, the string can be picked up by a tool called `lupdate`, which will generate an XML translation file that includes the string for one or more languages.

Generating the XML translation files

Since translation files do not exist yet, we should tell `lupdate` to create them for us the first time we run the tool. To do so, we can add the following to `cmmonitor.pro`:

```
// cmmonitor.pro
...
TRANSLATIONS =
    cmmonitor_en_US.ts
    cmmonitor_it_IT.ts

OTHER_FILES += $${TRANSLATIONS}
```

`TRANSLATIONS` is a special QMake directive that is used by `lupdate` on the first and subsequent runs to identify the output translation files and supported locales. On the first run of `lupdate`, the tool scans the filenames and identifies any known locale suffixes (`en_US` and `it_IT`, in the example). The rest of the filename is arbitrary, while the `.ts` suffix identifies XML translation files. The `OTHER_FILES` directive serves only the purpose of showing the `TS` files in the project structure.

> **TIP**
>
> In the example, I have used US English and Italian, my mother tongue. You are welcome to use any language you prefer. Keep in mind that the locales correspond to standards ISO 639-1 for the language part (https://en.wikipedia.org/wiki/List_of_ISO_639-1_codes) and ISO 3166 alpha-2 for the country part (https://en.wikipedia.org/wiki/ISO_3166-1_alpha-2).

Once you have added the references to the `TS` files to `cmmonitor.pro`, you can run `lupdate`. The tool can be easily run from Qt Creator's **Tools** > **External** > **Linguist** menu:

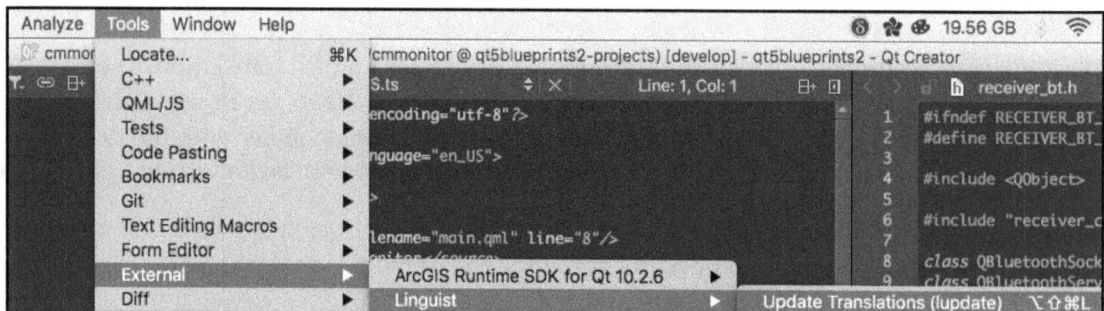

You can also set up a keyboard shortcut for this command, as you can see I have done in the preceding screenshot. As usual, shortcuts can be set from Qt Creator's **Preferences/Options** menu.

Running `lupdate`, you'll see in the **General Messages** pane information about the tool creating the `TS` files.

If the process was successful, you will see the newly created files in the project tree. You might need to modify and save the `.pro` file for this to happen. You will then be able to open one of the two files, which only diverge in the `language` XML attribute. Here is, for example, the content of `cmmonitor_en_US.ts`:

```
<?xml version="1.0" encoding="utf-8"?>
<!DOCTYPE TS>
<TS version="2.1" language="en_US">
<context>
    <name>main</name>
    <message>
        <location filename="main.qml" line="8"/>
        <source>CM Monitor</source>
        <translation type="unfinished"></translation>
    </message>
</context>
</TS>
```

After the `XML` version and `DOCTYPE` information, you can see the `TS` root element, and the `context` child element. One `TS` element can have more than one `context` child. If no `context` is specified, translation messages will be added to the `main` context. This will be enough for our purposes. Each message is composed from three elements:

- `location`: This identifies the source file and line number of the string to be translated
- `source`: This provides the placeholder string
- `translation`: Providing the translation for the source in the specified language
- `unfinished`: As you can see, since the translation hasn't been specified yet, it is marked as `unfinished`

Translating a string

To implement the translation, we could just provide a value between the `translation` opening and closing tags, and remove the `type="unfinished"` attribute. However, there is a less error-prone, and potentially more efficient way of doing it: **Qt Linguist**.

Qt Linguist is a UI tool that is shipped with the Qt distribution. Its purpose is to make it easy also for non-programmers to work on UI translations. You can open the `TS` file in **Qt Linguist** by right clicking on it in the **Projects** pane, and selecting **Open with... > Qt Linguist**. If you open the `cmmonitor_en_US.ts` file, you should see the following:

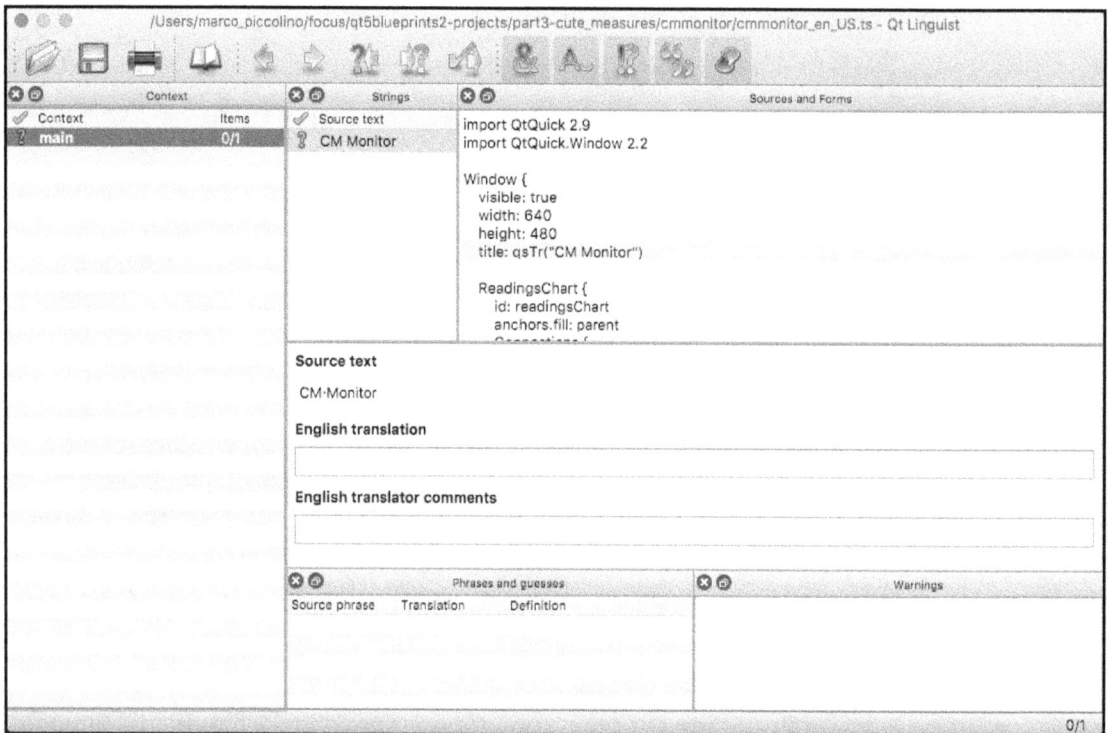

As you can see, it provides information about the context, source file, and source text, and allows to specify both a translation and translator's comments. Once you enter a translation, you can mark it as complet by clicking on the question mark next to the **Source text**:

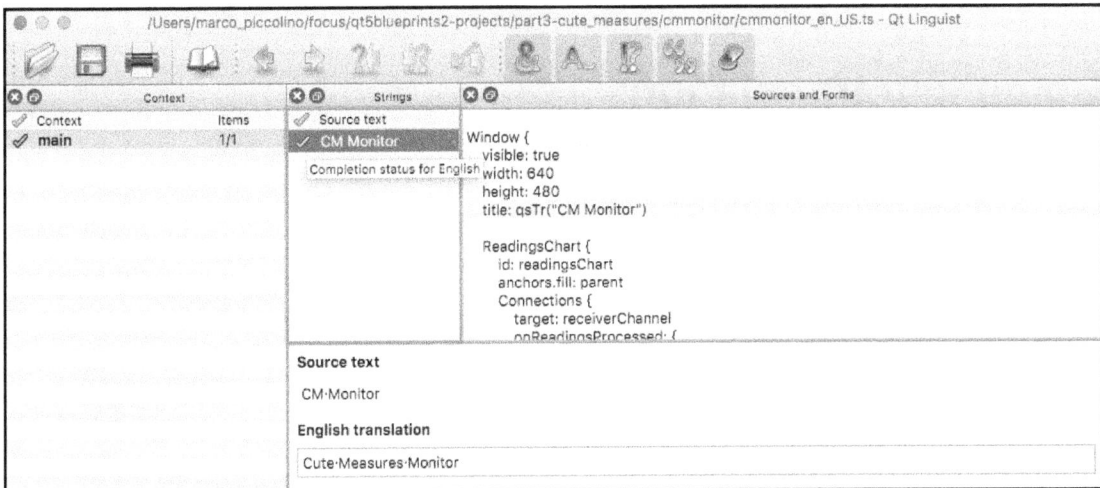

If you then save the file, you will see that the TS file has changed and now contains the translation:

```
<?xml version="1.0" encoding="utf-8"?>
<!DOCTYPE TS>
<TS version="2.1" language="en_US">
<context>
    <name>main</name>
    <message>
        <location filename="main.qml" line="8"/>
        <source>CM Monitor</source>
        <translation>Cute Measures Monitor</translation>
    </message>
</context>
</TS>
```

> **Qt Linguist** also allows you to select multiple language files at once, and is capable of showing translation for different languages that correspond to the same source text next to each other.

The second language file can be translated in the same way.

You can find more information about all aspects of **Qt Linguist** at `http://doc.qt.io/qt-5.9/qtlinguist-index.html`.

Compiling translations

Now that the source translation files are ready, we need to compile them and ship them with the program. To compile the files, you need to run the `lrelease` tool. You'll find it under Qt Creator's **Tools** > **External** > **Qt Linguist** menu, next to `lupdate`.

> **TIP**
>
> Because of a limitation of the `lrelease` tool, it won't work out of the box with `.pro` files contained in subprojects, like in the case of `cmmonitor`. You can circumvent this limitation by opening `cmmonitor` as an independent project in Qt Creator, instead of having it as a subproject of `qt5blueprints2-projects`.

If you run `lrelease`, it should create two files named `cmmonitor_en_US.qm` and `cmmonitor_it_IT.qm` in the same folder where the `TS` files are. Check the **General Messages** pane for any issues. There are several ways to ship these with the program. The simplest is to include them in a `.qrc` file. For simplicity, you can use the already existing `qml.qrc`; however, I would recommend you create a new file, for example, `translations.qrc`, and add the files there.

Once we have added the binary translation files to the application, we just need to load them with the `QTranslator` class.

Loading translations

`QTranslator` (`http://doc.qt.io/qt-5.9/qtranslator.html`) provides the ability to load and apply binary translation files. To do that, you need to create an instance of `QTranslator`, have the app instance install the translator, and load a translation file. Here is how it can be implemented in `main.cpp`:

```
#include <QApplication>
#include <QQmlApplicationEngine>
#include <QQmlContext>
#include <QTranslator>
...
int main(int argc, char *argv[])
{
```

```
    . . .
    QApplication app(argc, argv);
    QTranslator translator;
    app.installTranslator(&translator);
    translator.load(QString(":/cmmonitor_%1.qm").arg(QLocale().name()));
    . . .
}
```

The last line simply loads the file corresponding to the name (the `language_country` sequence) of the current locale. You could also call the following overload instead: `translator.load(QLocale(), ":/cmmonitor", "_")`.

If your locale is set to `en_US`, when you run the program you should see the translated window title. If you want to change locale before loading the file, you can use:

```
QLocale::setDefault(QLocale("it_IT"));
```

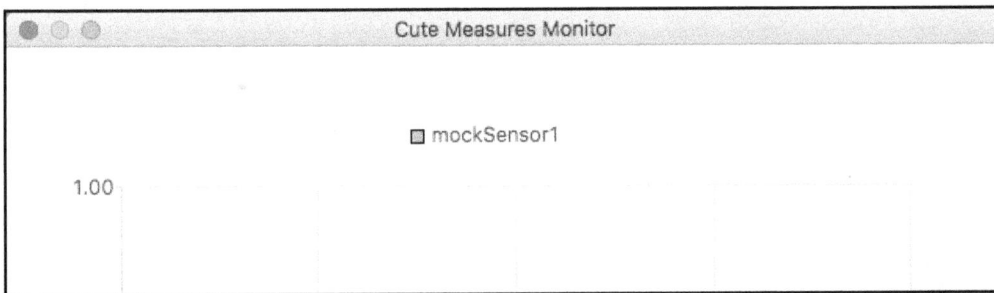

With signals and slots, by changing the default locale as a response to user input, you will be able to also change the UI's translation on the fly.

Summary

We have created a client application that displays on a chart sensor readings data coming over a Bluetooth channel in near real time.

We have also learned how to provide translations for UI strings in QML applications with **Qt Linguist** and `QTranslator`.

In the next chapter, we will broaden again our knowledge of the Qt UI and data technologies by developing an alternative, desktop-oriented dashboard application that will sport an HTML5 UI and receive data over a network connection.

31
Running a Web Service and an HTML5 Dashboard

In the preceding chapter, we implemented a simple monitoring client, discussed how to receive data over a Bluetooth connection, and displayed the data in a chart as a time series with the help of the Qt Charts module.

However, what if we wanted to enable the monitoring client to connect to a remote broadcaster? In such a scenario, a short-range connection such as Bluetooth would not help at all, and we would need to rely on a different technology, such as an HTTP server or other kinds of TCP-based connection. Furthermore, we might have other project constraints; for example, we might not have the time or budget to create an ad hoc QML dashboard like the one we developed in the preceding chapter, and might need instead to display the sensor data in a way that can be reused in other contexts, for example, on a website. Well, Qt has us covered for both occurrences.

In this chapter, we will expose fake sensor data over an HTTP server via a REST web service, thanks to the third-party QHttp library. We will access the service from our client with the Qt Network module and develop an alternative solution to the QML UI from the preceding chapter, which uses Qt WebEngine to display web content instead. We will leverage one of the existing JavaScript chart libraries to display the data to ensure that the same HTML5 UI could be served to a standard web browser in future. In doing all of this, we will reuse several components developed in the preceding chapter.

Overview

In the preceding chapter, we helped Cute Measures put in place its sensor-broadcasting system using a Bluetooth connection. The Bluetooth channel is convenient in scenarios where low latency is critical, and where the client device consuming the sensor data is within a few meters from the emitting device. This scenario is, however, just one of the many possible ones, and Cute Measures also wants to cater for distributed systems, where the device producing sensor data is not necessarily on the same site as the one consuming them. For this reason, Cute Measures now entrusts us with the task of providing an HTTP connectivity between a broadcaster and a receiver, relying on a classic REST-based, client-server model where the receiver regularly issues a request to the broadcaster for new data.

We haven't come to the challenge unprepared, having taken care in the previous chapter to properly encapsulate the communication channel beyond a generic API that should be fairly transparent to the consuming application, with possibly a few tweaks required by the generalization.

Another new requirement is developing the UI for displaying the sensor data using HTML5 and JS technologies so that the very same UI code can also be used to display sensor data in the browser. This is a sensible requirement in many scenarios, which allows for code reuse. Another advantage of such an approach is that it enables the delegation of UI development to frontend web developers, who can leverage their existing HTML5, JS, and web framework skills. Granted, in contexts where hardware resources are constrained, an HTML5 UI might not be the best option.

To meet the new requirements, we will perform the following things:

- Implementing a `BroadcasterChannel` that wraps an HTTP server
- Implementing a `ReceiverChannel` that can perform HTTP requests
- Adding the new channels to the `cmbroadcast` and `cmmonitor` applications
- Implementing an HTML5-based dashboard showing a sensor chart
- Adding the dashboard to `cmmonitor`

Creating a BroadcasterChannel based on HTTP

In `Chapter 30`, *Building a Mobile Dashboard to Display Real-Time Sensor Data*, we designed and implemented a communication channel for the `Broadcaster` entity. This `BroadcasterChannel` is responsible for wiring sensor readings over a connection. While we implemented a version of the channel based on the classic Bluetooth, we wisely decided to consider this choice an implementation detail by assigning the role of an interface to `BroadcasterChannel` and subclassing the specific classic Bluetooth implementation as `BroadcasterBt`. This choice provides us with several benefits, as follows:

- The reuse of common functionality across implementations (for example, the `connectToBroadcaster` method)
- A transparent API for client code to be invoked
- The option to implement, and rely on, test doubles instead of actual device calls for use case and entity tests

We will now reap some of these benefits, and, in particular, the second point mentioned in the preceding list of benefits. First, however, we should spend a few words on Qt Networking support so that we can make an informed choice for our HTTP server implementation.

Networking support in Qt

Networking is one of the many areas where the Qt offering is overwhelmingly rich in options and in constant expansion. A good overview of the current offering can be found at `http://doc.qt.io/qt-5.9/qtnetwork-programming.html`. Most core networking functionalities are provided by the Qt Network module. Besides the classes that revolve around `QNetworkAccessManager`, which exposes the client functionality for HTTP, HTTPS, and other common protocols (we will talk more about it when implementing `ReceiverChannel` in the coming sections), Qt provides classes for TCP- and UDP-level socket communication, network proxies, bearer management, SSL, and much more. You can take a look at the aforementioned document for more information. One useful feature is that many of these classes extend `QIODevice`, thus providing a unified API for managing data streams across various channels.

Besides these, the separate Qt Network Authorization module is now available at `https://doc.qt.io/qt-5.9/qtnetworkauth-index.html` (as a technical preview, and officially starting with 5.10, with support for OAuth 1 and OAuth 2 clients).

Furthermore, the `QtWebEngine` module (which we will be discussing more in the next sections) also provides access to Chromium's networking APIs.

Yet, the Qt Project currently lacks the offering of an HTTP server, which we require for our use case. Luckily, there are several third parties built on Qt that provide this functionality. Among these, we will be choosing the QHttp library, mainly developed by Amir Zamani and provided under the permissive MIT license. This will also give us a chance to take a look at how we can compile QMake library projects and link the resulting libraries in QMake app projects.

Compiling and linking the QHttp library

Besides being popular and well designed, the QHttp library also has the advantage of leveraging QMake as the out-of-the-box build system. This means that we will be able to compile it without needing to rely on external tools, such as CMake.

> To make things easier for you, we will choose version 2.1 of the library since it requires C++11, just like Qt does. This ensures that the compiler that you have been using so far for the other projects will be enough. Feel free to use one of the subsequent versions, which require C++14, if you so wish.

As we will be using the library to implement the server component of our HTTP `BroadcasterChannel`, we will add the resulting library to the previously created `channel_broadcaster` project. First, however, we will need to compile the library. We can grab the source code at `https://github.com/azadkuh/qhttp/releases/tag/version-2.1`.

We will need to extract the `.zip` or `.tar.gz` archive and move the resulting folder to the `3rdparty/qhttp` folder under `channel_broadcaster`. The `qhttp` folder should contain the `src` and `examples` subfolders, plus other project files. Once the source files are in place, we will need to fetch QHttp's dependencies, which, for version 2.1, amount to `http-parser` (`https://github.com/joyent/http-parser`), an HTTP parser written in C.

If you are on a Unix system with `git`, you can grab `http-parser` by simply running the `update-dependencies.sh` shell script under the `qhttp` folder. On other systems such as Windows, you should manually download the source code of `http-parser` and place it in the `3rdparty/http-parser` subfolder under the `qhttp` folder. Having fetched this dependency either way, we can now compile QHttp as a static library.

> Since QHttp is not regularly built on Windows, on this platform, you'll need to comment two lines in the source code that prevent it from compiling with MSVC. These are the lines starting with `warning`. They can be found in `qhttpfwd.hpp`, line 172, and `qhttpabstracts.cpp`, line 9. Go ahead and comment these lines before proceeding with compilation.

To compile QHttp easily, we will just need to open the `qhttp.pro` file in Qt Creator and issue the **Build** command for any of the available example projects. Alternatively, compilation can be done from the command line by following `README.md` of QHttp. If the compilation process ends successfully, the `qhttp` folder will contain a new subfolder called `xbin`, which in turn will contain the library file, which is called `libqhttp.a` on Unix systems and `qhttp.lib` on Windows.

> On Windows, if you chose to compile by selecting a target from Qt Creator, you might encounter a few errors/warnings during compilation. You should not worry about these, as they are only related to the example code, which we won't be using. The important thing is that at the end of the compilation, you can locate the `qhttp.lib` library file under the `xbin` folder.

`qhttp.pro` is an example of QMake's `library` template. To know more about how to compile static and shared library projects with QMake and the various options it provides, take a look at `https://wiki.qt.io/How_to_create_a_library_with_Qt_and_use_it_in_an_application`.

Now that we have obtained a library file, we will need to reference it in the `channel_broadcaster` project.

Adding the QHttp library to the channel broadcaster project

In `Chapter 29`, *Sending Sensor Readings to a Device with a Non-UI App*, we chose to place all configuration related to the `channel_broadcaster` subproject in the `channel_broadcaster.pri` QMake project include. This allowed us to easily include the `channel_broadcaster` component in our client applications. For the very same reason, we will now add the QHttp library dependency to the same file so that when the component's sources are compiled, the library is properly linked. This process amounts to the following steps:

- Adding the path containing the QHttp header files to QMake's INCLUDEPATH variable
- Ensuring that the library binary file is copied to the `deployment` folder
- Ensuring that the library is properly linked

Adding the path containing library headers is a one-liner. We open `channel_broadcaster.pri` and add the following code:

```
# channel_broadcaster.pri
QT += bluetooth

HEADERS += \
    $$PWD/broadcaster_bt.h \
    $$PWD/broadcaster_channel.h

SOURCES += \
    $$PWD/broadcaster_bt.cpp \
    $$PWD/broadcaster_channel.cpp

INCLUDEPATH += $$PWD/3rdparty/qhttp/src
```

Next, we will need to ensure that the already-compiled library binary is copied over to the destination folder. One way of doing this would be to add the library project as a subproject to our project tree and have the `channel_broadcaster` subproject depend on it. In fact, QMake provides the `depends` instruction for expressing subproject dependencies (for example, `broadcaster_channel.depends = qhttp`). This strategy, however, does not scale well when we need to link other libraries that are not built with QMake, and, by default, it also retriggers linking of the library's object files, which is usually a waste of time. Thus, we will just copy the previously produced library binary to the `deployment` folder.

To do so, we will add a few QMake instructions to `channel_broadcaster.pri`, which will invoke system commands to copy the library file:

```
# channel_broadcaster.pri
...

INCLUDEPATH += $$PWD/3rdparty/qhttp/src

QHTTP_SOURCE_DIR = $$PWD/3rdparty/qhttp/xbin
QHTTP_TARGET_DIR = $$OUT_PWD

unix {
    LIBFILE = $$QHTTP_SOURCE_DIR/libqhttp.a
    QMAKE_PRE_LINK += $$quote(cp $$LIBFILE $$QHTTP_TARGET_DIR)
}

win32 {
    LIBFILE = $$QHTTP_SOURCE_DIR/qhttp.lib
    LIBFILE ~= s,/,\,g
    TARGET_DIR ~= s,/,\,g
    QMAKE_PRE_LINK += $$quote(cmd /c copy /y $$LIBFILE $$QHTTP_TARGET_DIR)
}
```

Although the syntax might be new, the spirit of the code should be fairly self-evident. We reference a source and a destination directory using existing QMake variables ($$PWD and $$OUT_PWD), define platform-specific library filenames, by also substituting forward slashes with backslashes on Windows, and then tell QMake to carry out the file copy before the linking stage (QMAKE_PRE_LINK).

Finally, we will need to link the QHttp library in the client project. This is again a one-liner to be added at the end of `channel_broadcaster.pri`, as follows:

```
# channel_broadcaster.pri
...

LIBS += -L$$TARGET_DIR -lqhttp
```

This is a special QMake directive, which provides a cross-platform way to inform the compiler of the directory and the file to be included for static linking. It works as long as platform-specific naming conventions are followed.

Before proceeding with compilation, you must be aware that on Windows there is a limit to the length of paths for file inclusion. You have probably encountered such a limit if you have seen a message like the following: `dependent [very long file name] does not exist.`
If you hit such a limit, try and choose a short path for the build directory of the active kit (in Qt Creator: **Projects** > **Build** > **Build directory**).

If all went well, when you build the `channel_broadcaster` target, it should not complain about any library-related errors. Since this is a fairly involved step, if you need any assistance, hit the forums, IRC, and Stack Overflow.

Implementing the HTTP BroadcasterChannel

Now that we have an HTTP server library in our project, we can use it to create an HTTP-based `BroadcasterChannel` that sends sensor data over HTTP.

In the usual way, we create a new class called `channels::BroadcasterHttp` that inherits from `channels::BrodcasterChannel`, just like `channels::BroadcasterBt` did. The following is the API that we will want to provide specific implementations for:

```cpp
// broadcaster_http.h
#ifndef BROADCASTER_HTTP_H
#define BROADCASTER_HTTP_H

#include "broadcaster_channel.h"

namespace channels {
class BroadcasterHttp : public BroadcasterChannel
{
public:
    explicit BroadcasterHttp(QObject* parent = nullptr);
    bool init() override;
public slots:
    void sendReadings(QList<QVariantMap> readings) override;
};
}

#endif // BROADCASTER_HTTP_H
```

In the `init` method, we will instantiate and start the HTTP server and define how to serve the readings data when there is an incoming client request. We will also take a look at how to exploit the `sendReadings` slot, which is invoked any time the `Broadcaster` entity emits the `readingsPublished` signal (refer to the implementation of `connectToBroadcaster` in `broadcaster_channel.cpp` from `Chapter 29`, *Sending Sensor Readings to a Device with a Non-UI App*).

The QHttp library provides a class named `QHttpServer`. The server needs to be instantiated and is initialized by calling its `listen` method with `QHostAddress` (http:// doc.qt.io/qt-5.9/qhostaddress.html) and a port number as arguments. Once this is done, one of the available ways to provide a response for clients to consume is to listen to the `newRequest` signal, which exposes pointers to a `QHttpRequest` and a `QHttpResponse` as arguments. The response is sent to the HTTP endpoint by calling `QHttpResponse::end(const QByteArray&)`.

In our case, we will need to get hold of the most recent sensor readings and return these as the argument to the `end` method. One way of doing this would be to cache the latest readings whenever they arrive (that is, whenever the `sendReadings` slot is called) and then serve them whenever the `newRequest` signal is fired. The later step can be implemented with a lambda function. The following is the implementation for `init` and `sendReadings` in `broadcaster_http.cpp`:

```
// broadcaster_http.cpp
#include "broadcaster_http.h"

#include <QHostAddress>
#include <QJsonArray>
#include <QJsonObject>
#include <QJsonDocument>

#include "../../entities/entity_broadcaster/broadcaster.h"

#include "qhttpserver.hpp"
#include "qhttpserverconnection.hpp"
#include "qhttpserverrequest.hpp"
#include "qhttpserverresponse.hpp"


using namespace qhttp::server;

namespace entities {
    class Broadcaster;
}
```

```
channels::BroadcasterHttp::BroadcasterHttp(QObject* parent)
    : BroadcasterChannel(parent),
      _server(nullptr)
{
}

bool channels::BroadcasterHttp::init()
{
    bool initialised = false;
    _server = new QHttpServer(this);
    if (_server) {
        initialised = _server->listen(QHostAddress::Any, 8081);
        connect(_server,&QHttpServer::newRequest, [=](QHttpRequest*,
QHttpResponse* response){
            QJsonArray readingsJson;
            for (int i=0;i<_lastReadings.count();++i) {
readingsJson.append(QJsonObject::fromVariantMap(_lastReadings.at(0)));
            }
            QByteArray message =
QJsonDocument(readingsJson).toJson(QJsonDocument::Compact);
            response->end(message);
        });
    }
    return initialised;
}

void channels::BroadcasterHttp::sendReadings(QList<QVariantMap> readings)
{
    _lastReadings = readings;
}
```

In the `sendReadings` slot, we will just cache the latest available readings. The `init` method, on the other hand, consists of the following steps:

1. Create a `QHttpServer` instance
2. Have the server listen to external connections with `QHostAddress::Any`
3. Connect the `newRequest` signal with a `callback` function, exposing the request and response objects
4. Return data as JSON text in the response's end method

Of course, this is the bare minimum for our prototype; in a production system, we would also need to tackle error handling, authorization, request checking, concurrency, and more. The conversion from `QList<QVariantMap>` to JSON text is the same as previously done for the `BroadcasterBt` channel. To compile the code, we will first need to declare our private members in the header file:

```
// broadcaster_http.h
#ifndef BROADCASTER_HTTP_H
#define BROADCASTER_HTTP_H

#include "broadcaster_channel.h"

namespace qhttp { namespace server {
class QHttpServer;
}}

namespace channels {
class BroadcasterHttp : public BroadcasterChannel
{
...

private:
    qhttp::server::QHttpServer* _server;
    QList<QVariantMap> _lastReadings;
};
}

#endif // BROADCASTER_HTTP_H
```

You can test the HTTP `BroadcasterChannel` by changing the content of `main.cpp` of `cmbroadcast`:

```
// cmbroadcast/main.cpp
...

// #include "../channels/channel_broadcaster/broadcaster_bt.h"
#include "../channels/channel_broadcaster/broadcaster_http.h"
...

int main(int argc, char *argv[])
{
    QCoreApplication a(argc, argv);
    QTimer::singleShot(600000, &a, SLOT(quit()));

    // auto broadcasterBt = new channels::BroadcasterBt(&a);
    auto broadcasterHttp = new channels::BroadcasterHttp(&a);
    auto broadcaster = new entities::Broadcaster(&a);
```

```
// if (broadcasterBt->init()) {
// broadcasterBt->connectToBroadcaster(broadcaster);
// }
if (broadcasterHttp->init()) {
    broadcasterHttp->connectToBroadcaster(broadcaster);
}

auto sensor = new entities::Sensor("mockSensor1", &a);
...
return a.exec();
}
```

> **TIP**
>
> If you want to add more `BroadcasterChannel` that support different technologies, you might consider setting up a `BroadcasterChannel` factory, which returns a `BroadcasterChannel` instance of the right kind, given some input parameters.

As you can see, given that the API for both Bluetooth and HTTP channel classes is the same, the changes in the client are transparent. You can now run `cmbroadcast` and point a web browser to `http://localhost:8081`. You should see the sensor readings in the JSON format. The readings change if you issue a new request by reloading the page. As for the Bluetooth version, `cmbroadcast` will remain active for five minutes before quitting.

Making an HTTP ReceiverChannel implementation

Now that the HTTP `BroadcasterChannel` is in place, we will need to implement the corresponding HTTP `rceiverChannel`. As hinted in the preceding section, this can be achieved using an out-of-the-box Qt functionality, thanks to the Qt Network module (`http://doc.qt.io/qt-5.9/qtnetwork-index.html`), and, specifically, the `QNetworkAccessManager` class (`http://doc.qt.io/qt-5.9/qnetworkaccessmanager.html`) and related classes.

By instantiating QNetworkAccessManager, we can use its methods to perform get, post, and many other types of asynchronous request. Many of these methods take an object of the QNetworkRequest type (http://doc.qt.io/qt-5.9/qnetworkrequest.html) as an argument. A QNetworkRequest can be constructed, for example, from a URL. Once a reply is obtained from the server, QNetworkAccessManager emits the finished signal, which makes an argument of the QNetworkReply type (http://doc.qt.io/qt-5.9/qnetworkreply.html) that is accessible for further processing of any data, HTTP response codes, or errors. Internally, the network APIs use threads so that the asynchronous calls are non-blocking.

> The Qt Network module APIs are very rich and allow you to configure many characteristics of the network access manager, handle SSL connection errors, and do much more. Ensure that you take your time to explore the documentation and the examples available in your Qt distribution and accessible from Qt Creator.

Subclassing the ReceiverChannel

Just like we did for BroadcasterChannel, we will implement the abstract ReceiverChannel API that we have already created for the Bluetooth implementation in Chapter 30, *Building a Mobile Dashboard to Display Real-Time Sensor Data*. To do so, we will add a ReceiverHttp class to the already existing channel_receiver.pri file. The following is the header file containing the class, which extends ReceiverChannel:

```
// receiver_http.h
#ifndef RECEIVER_HTTP_H
#define RECEIVER_HTTP_H

#include <QObject>

#include "receiver_channel.h"

namespace channels {
class ReceiverHttp : public ReceiverChannel
{
    Q_OBJECT
public:
    explicit ReceiverHttp(QObject *parent = nullptr);
    ~ReceiverHttp();
    Q_INVOKABLE void init() override;
public slots:
    void receiveReadings() override;
};
```

```
}

#endif // RECEIVER_HTTP_H
```

We will need to figure out what happens when we create and initialize the `ReceiverHttp` object and what happens when the `receiveReadings` slot gets called.

> **TIP**
>
> As usual, feel free to proceed in a test-driven manner by adding tests where `init` and `receiveReadings` get called by checking their preconditions and predicting their outcomes. For brevity, we'll skip those.

On the other hand, from the bidirectional communication of the Bluetooth channel, where the client peer listens to the server and the server sends messages, HTTP requires the client to issue a request to the server, which returns a reply that the client can consume and process. Thus, we will have to issue a request at regular intervals, get a response containing the sensor data, and so on. We will keep things minimal; however, you should consider putting in place a *Keep-Alive* strategy to have multiple requests and responses leveraging a single TCP connection. QHttp has got example code for that, which you can refer to at https://github.com/azadkuh/qhttp/tree/master/example/keep-alive.

Implementing the constructor and init method

Upon creation and initialization of the HTTP Receiver, we should perform the following things:

1. Instantiate a network access manager to perform HTTP requests
2. Set up a timer to perform requests at regular intervals
3. Connect the timer's timeout with the issuing of an HTTP request
4. Connect the network access manager's finished signal, containing the reply, to the `receiveReadings` slot
5. Start the timer

We decided to put the first four steps of the preceding list in the class constructor, and start the timer in the `init` method. The choice, of course, is up to you, depending on your specific requirements. The constructor for `ReceiverHttp` will thus look as follows:

```cpp
// receiver_http.cpp
#include "receiver_http.h"
#include <QNetworkAccessManager>

namespace channels {
```

```
static const QUrl broadcasterHttpUrl("http://127.0.0.1:8081");
}

channels::ReceiverHttp::ReceiverHttp(QObject *parent) :
ReceiverChannel(parent)
{
    qDebug() << Q_FUNC_INFO;
    _timer.setInterval(1000);
    _nam = new QNetworkAccessManager(this);
    connect(_nam, &QNetworkAccessManager::finished, this,
&ReceiverHttp::_replyFinished);
    connect(&_timer, &QTimer::timeout, this,
&ReceiverHttp::receiveReadings);
}
```

The timer and network access manager, as well as the
private _replyFinished method, also need to be added to the header:

```
// receiver_http.h
#ifndef RECEIVER_HTTP_H
#define RECEIVER_HTTP_H

#include <QObject>
#include <QTimer>

QT_FORWARD_DECLARE_CLASS(QNetworkAccessManager);
QT_FORWARD_DECLARE_CLASS(QNetworkReply);

#include "receiver_channel.h"

namespace channels {
class ReceiverHttp : public ReceiverChannel
{
    Q_OBJECT
public:
    ...

private:
    QTimer _timer;
    QNetworkAccessManager* _nam;

    void _replyFinished(QNetworkReply* reply);
};
}

#endif // RECEIVER_HTTP_H
```

The preceding code also makes use of the `QT_FORWARD_DECLARE_CLASS` macro, which can be used instead of plain C++ forward declarations to account for custom namespaces for the Qt framework. In this case, using the macro or the plain forward declaration does not make a difference.

As agreed, when the `init` method is called, the `Receiver` will start performing HTTP requests. By virtue of the signal/slot connection between the timer's timeout and the `receiveReadings` slot (where the request will be issued), we just need to start the timer to make this happen:

```
void channels::ReceiverHttp::init()
{
    _timer.start();
}
```

Performing the HTTP request and consuming the response

The HTTP request is issued in the `receiveReadings` slot. Being an asynchronous request, we will have to consume the reply in the `_replyFinished` slot after issuing the request. Another thing we might want to do is extract the address of the HTTP server to be called from the method implementations and define it in a static constant at the top of the file instead. This will make it easier to change it whenever we want to:

```
// receiver_http.cpp
#include "receiver_http.h"
#include <QVariantList>
#include <QNetworkAccessManager>
#include <QNetworkReply>

namespace channels {
static const QUrl broadcasterHttpUrl("http://127.0.0.1:8081");
}

...

void channels::ReceiverHttp::receiveReadings()
{
    if (_nam) _nam->get(QNetworkRequest(channels::broadcasterHttpUrl));
}
```

As you can see in the preceding code, in this example, we will run the server and client on the same machine, and thus use the localhost's URL as the `Broadcaster` URL. Now that we have defined when to trigger the request, we will need to describe what will happen once a response is returned. Just as in the case of the Bluetooth implementation, this will amount to turning the `QByteArray` containing JSON text into a `QVariantList` for easy consumption in QML and elsewhere. All this is done in the private `_replyFinished` slot:

```
void channels::ReceiverHttp::_replyFinished(QNetworkReply *reply)
{
    QByteArray readingsBytes = reply->readAll();
    QJsonDocument readingsDoc = QJsonDocument::fromJson(readingsBytes);
    QJsonArray readingsArray = readingsDoc.array();
    QVariantList readings;
    for (int i=0; i<readingsArray.count(); ++i) {
        readings.append(readingsArray.at(i).toObject().toVariantMap());
    }
    emit readingsProcessed(readings);
    reply->deleteLater();
}
```

For the `QByteArray` -> JSON -> `QVariantList` conversion, we used the same classes that we used for the Bluetooth `ReceiverChannel` (which in itself could be a hint to refactor the code to be part of a utility function). At the end of the function, we called `QObject::deleteLater` since the `QNetworkReply` instance has no parent, and thus wouldn't be automatically deallocated. `deleteLater` does not immediately perform deletion, but only after making sure that all events relating to the object have been vacated. The `readingsProcessed` signal can then be listened to from attached clients, for example, in QML.

Given the work done in the previous chapters, adding the HTTP `ReceiverChannel` to the `cmmonitor` app is very easy:

```
#include <QApplication>
#include <QQmlApplicationEngine>
#include <QQmlContext>
#include <QTranslator>

// #include "../channels/channel_receiver/receiver_bt.h"
#include "../channels/channel_receiver/receiver_http.h"

int main(int argc, char *argv[])
{
    QApplication app(argc, argv);

    ...
```

```
    // auto receiverChannel = new channels::ReceiverBt(&app);
    auto receiverChannel = new channels::ReceiverHttp(&app);
    QQmlApplicationEngine engine;
engine.rootContext()->setContextProperty("receiverChannel",receiverChannel)
;
    engine.load(QUrl(QStringLiteral("qrc:/main.qml")));
    if (engine.rootObjects().isEmpty())
        return -1;

    receiverChannel->init();

    return app.exec();
}
```

Implementing an HTML5 UI

Now that our data I/O over HTTP is set, we can move to the next requirement, which is to put an HTML5-based UI on top of it. The goal is twofold:

- Reuse existing libraries and skills from the world of web development.
- Make it easier to move the UI to a website if it will ever be needed. You'll also appreciate, for a case like this, how small the effort required by Qt is.

Browser technologies in Qt: WebEngine, WebView, and WebKit

When it comes to web browser technology, Qt's offering is manyfold, as it needs to cater for a vast range of differing requirements. The key feature of it all is, however, easy integration with other Qt modules.

The most solid web browser offering is the Qt WebEngine set of modules (http://doc.qt.io/qt-5.9/qtwebengine-index.html), which provides a Qt wrapper around the Chromium web engine. Qt WebEngine was developed especially for those operating systems that do not ship a web browser that is tightly coupled with the OS, thus, especially, desktop operating systems. For this reason, Qt WebEngine is available on Windows, macOS, and Linux. You typically need to select the Qt WebEngine component explicitly when installing Qt.

The component is divided into three different modules: QtWebEngineCore, QtWebEngine, and QtWebEngineWidgets. Whereas the first provides a common functionality, the second is dedicated to QML integration, and the third to Widgets integration.

An alternative technology, available on platforms that provide a native browser (like mobile platforms typically do) is Qt WebView (http://doc.qt.io/qt-5.9/qtwebview-qmlmodule.html), a more lightweight option with a much-reduced API with respect to what Qt WebEngine provides.

Finally, recently, the Qt WebKit project was significantly updated and is now available on most platforms where Qt runs. While it is currently not shipped with Qt distributions and follows an independent versioning scheme, it is regularly packaged for the major platforms and might represent a good alternative if you require a full-featured web browser on desktop and mobile platforms at once. For more information, including release and pre-release packages for a few platforms, take a look at https://github.com/annulen/webkit.

For our prototype, we will use QtWebEngine.

Adding WebEngineView to cmmonitor

We will create a WebEngineView QML component in cmmonitor, with the goal of having an HTML5 graph underneath the QML graph. In this way, we will be able to see that they are consuming the very same sensor data that is coming over the HTTP channel, despite the two very different UI technologies.

To add QtWebEngine to cmmonitor, after having installed the module for your intended target platform, you'll need to add it to cmmonitor.pro:

```
# cmmonitor.pro
QT += quick charts webengine
...
```

Then, in main.cpp, you will have to initialize webengine before being able to use it in the QML engine. This is achieved by calling the QtWebEngine::initialize() static method:

```
// cmmonitor/main.cpp
#include <QApplication>
#include <QQmlApplicationEngine>
#include <QQmlContext>
#include <QTranslator>
#include <qtwebengineglobal.h>

#include "../channels/channel_receiver/receiver_bt.h"
```

```
#include "../channels/channel_receiver/receiver_http.h"

int main(int argc, char *argv[])
{
    ...
    QtWebEngine::initialize();
    QQmlApplicationEngine engine;
    ...
}
```

Once this is done, we can add the `WebEngineView` component to `main.qml`:

```
// cmmonitor/main.qml
import QtQuick 2.9
import QtQuick.Window 2.2
import QtWebEngine 1.5

Window {
    visible: true
    width: 600
    height: 960
    title: qsTr("CM Monitor")

    ReadingsChart {
        id: readingsChart
        width: parent.width
        height: parent.height / 2
        ...
    }

    WebEngineView {
        id: readingsChartJS
        anchors.top: readingsChart.bottom
        width: parent.width
        height: parent.height / 2
    }
}
```

Our `WebEngineView`, however, is empty. You can test whether the component is working by pointing its `url` property to an arbitrary URL address, provided your machine is connected to the internet. You should see the target web page appear underneath the `readingsChart` component.

Our HTML5 chart component will leave in a local web page. We will call the page
ReadingsChartJS.html and add it to qml.qrc as a resource.

> **TIP**
>
> To create the web page in Qt Creator, you can right-click on qml.qrc,
> select **Add New...**, and use the **General > Empty File** template.

Once the page has been added, we can set it as the webengine view's URL:

```
// cmmonitor/main.qml
import QtQuick 2.9
import QtQuick.Window 2.2
import QtWebEngine 1.5

Window {
    ...

    WebEngineView {
        id: readingsChartJS
        anchors.top: readingsChart.bottom
        width: parent.width
        height: parent.height / 2
        url: "qrc:///ReadingsChartJS.html"
        webChannel: defaultWebChannel
    }
}
```

Now add some basic HTML to ReadingsChartJS.html to ensure that it is showing up
when running cmmonitor.

Data transport between app and browser with WebChannel

One piece of the puzzle is still missing, that is, how do we interact, within a standard web
page, with objects that might have been created on the C++ or QML side?

A dedicated Qt module — `QtWebChannel` — comes to the rescue (http://doc.qt.io/qt-5.9/qtwebchannel-index.html). The concept is simple; you register with the `WebChannel` any objects that you want to have available in your client JavaScript environment. Once this is done, these objects will be accessible from the JavaScript code, including their signals, properties, and so on. In our case, we want the HTTP `receiverChannel` instance implemented in the previous sections to be available in the HTML page.

`QtWebChannel` provides communication between a JavaScript client (including a remote browser, a Qt WebEngine view, or a QML environment) and a C++ or QML server. It does so by leveraging the web technology known as web sockets. The client just needs to have support for web sockets and load the `qwebchannel.js` JavaScript library. The server also needs to implement a custom transport based on Qt WebSockets (http://doc.qt.io/qt-5.9/qtwebsockets-index.html) if this is not already provided.

Luckily, `QtWebEngine` provides out-of-the-box support for `QtWebChannel`, and the transport layer between the two is already implemented and ready to use. To add it to the `cmmonitor` project, a couple of steps are required. First, we will add the module to `cmmonitor.pro`:

```
# cmmonitor.pro
QT += quick charts webengine webchannel
...
```

Then, we'll have to create a `QQmlWebChannel` instance and expose it to the QML engine:

> If the objects you want to expose to the web browser are implemented in QML, you could use the QML `WebChannel` type instead.

```
// cmmonitor/main.cpp
...
#include <QtWebChannel>

...

int main(int argc, char *argv[])
{
    ...
    auto receiverChannel = new channels::ReceiverHttp(&app);
    QtWebEngine::initialize();
    qRegisterMetaType<QQmlWebChannel*>();
    auto defaultWebChannel = new QQmlWebChannel(&app);
    defaultWebChannel->registerObject(QStringLiteral("receiverChannel"),
receiverChannel);
```

```
    QQmlApplicationEngine engine;
engine.rootContext()->setContextProperty("receiverChannel", receiverChannel)
;
engine.rootContext()->setContextProperty("defaultWebChannel",defaultWebChan
nel);
    engine.load(QUrl(QStringLiteral("qrc:/main.qml")));
    ...
}
```

Now, the `receiverChannel` object is registered on `defaultWebChannel`, with
the `receiverChannel` ID. Once this is done, we should tell the `WebEngineView` QML
component to make use of `defaultWebChannel`. This is achieved by simply setting the
`webChannel` property, as follows:

```
// cmmonitor/main.qml
import QtQuick 2.9
import QtQuick.Window 2.2
import QtWebEngine 1.5

Window {
    ...

    WebEngineView {
        id: readingsChartJS
        anchors.top: readingsChart.bottom
        width: parent.width
        height: parent.height / 2
        url: "qrc:///ReadingsChartJS.html"
        webChannel: defaultWebChannel
    }
}
```

There we go! At this stage, we can focus on the HTML side and `import` the
`qwebchannel.js` client. The library does not need to be bundled explicitly with our
application; it is enough that it is included by pointing at the specific QRC path
`qrc:///qtwebchannel/qwebchannel.js`:

```
<!--ReadingsChartJS.html-->
<html>
    <head>
        <title>ReadingsChartJS</title>
        <script src ="qrc:///qtwebchannel/qwebchannel.js"></script>
    </head>
...
```

Once the JS library is included, we can create an instance of the QWebChannel object, where we define a transport object to be used for server-client communication and a callback to be invoked once the QWebChannel has been properly initialized. Since WebEngineView supports out-of-the-box a pre-implemented transport object called qt.webChannelTransport, we will use that one. To know how to implement custom transport objects, you can take a look at http://doc.qt.io/qt-5.9/qtwebchannel-javascript.html. In the callback function, we can reference the receiverChannel instance and add any code that should be executed, for example, in response to the readingsProcessed signal being emitted:

```html
<!--ReadingsChartJS.html-->
<html>
    <head>
...
    </head>
    <body>
...
        <script>
        new QWebChannel(qt.webChannelTransport, function(channel) {
            window.receiverChannel = channel.objects.receiverChannel;

            receiverChannel.readingsProcessed.connect(function() {
            // call charting functions
            });
        });
        </script>
    </body>
</html>
```

We shortened the reference to receiverChannel by making it globally accessible and added a callback function to the readingsProcessed signal with the connect method. We can now add an HTML5 chart to the document and update it every time readingsProcessed is fired.

Adding an HTML5 time series

We should now decide upon a charting library based on HTML5 and JavaScript to use. Although there are many options available, `Chart.js` (`http://www.chartjs.org/`) is ideal because of its permissive MIT license and relatively simple APIs. Starting from the QML graph example of `Chapter 30`, *Building a Mobile Dashboard to Display Real-Time Sensor Data*, we will re-implement it with `Chart.js`. I won't go into the details of the re-implementation since this is out of scope for this title — you can check out the `Chart.js` documentation and samples to get the specifics. Besides `Chart.js`, we'll be using `Moment.js`, which fully integrates with the charting library for the easy handling of dates and times. The following is the code that produces a chart similar in appearance to the QML one we created in `Chapter 30`, *Building a Mobile Dashboard to Display Real-Time Sensor Data*. The main difference is only that for brevity's sake, the HTML5 version does not implement the seconds running when there is no incoming data:

```
<!--ReadingsChartJS.html-->
<html>
...
    <body>
        <div style="position:relative;">
            <canvas id="my-chart" width=2 height=1></canvas>
        </div>
        <script>
            var date = moment(Date.now()-15000);
            var chartLabels = [date];
            var chartData = [null];
            var i = 0;
            while (i < 15) {
                    date = date.clone().add(1, 'seconds');
                    chartLabels.push(date);
                    chartData.push(null);
                    ++i;
            }
            var ctx = document.getElementById('my-chart').getContext('2d');
            var chart = new Chart(ctx, {
                type: 'line',
                data: {
                    labels: chartLabels,
                    datasets: [{
                        label: 'mockSensor1',
                        data: chartData,
                        type: 'line',
                        borderColor: 'orange',
                        backgroundColor: 'rgba(0,0,0,0)'
                    }]
                },
```

```
                options: {
                    elements: {
                        line: {
                            tension: 0,
                            fill: false
                        }
                    },
                    scales: {
                        xAxes: [{
                            type: 'time',
                            distribution: 'series',
                            ticks: {
                                source: 'labels'
                            },
                            time: {
                                unit: 'second',
                                displayFormats: {
                                    second: 'H:mm:ss'
                                }
                            }
                        }]
                    }
                }
            });
            function addData(chart, label, data) {
                chart.data.labels.push(label);
                chart.data.datasets.forEach((dataset) => {
                    dataset.data.push(data);
                });
                chart.update();
            }
            function removeData(chart) {
                chart.data.labels.shift();
                chart.data.datasets.forEach((dataset) => {
                    dataset.data.shift();
                });
                chart.update();
            }

            new QWebChannel(qt.webChannelTransport, function(channel) {
                ...
            });
        </script>
    </body>
</html>
```

As you can note in the preceding code, `Chart.js` uses canvas to perform the painting. The `Chart` instance requires a canvas context and a nested configuration object to be specified, where the data, labels, and visual aspects of the chart are defined. The following is how the empty JS line chart should look like:

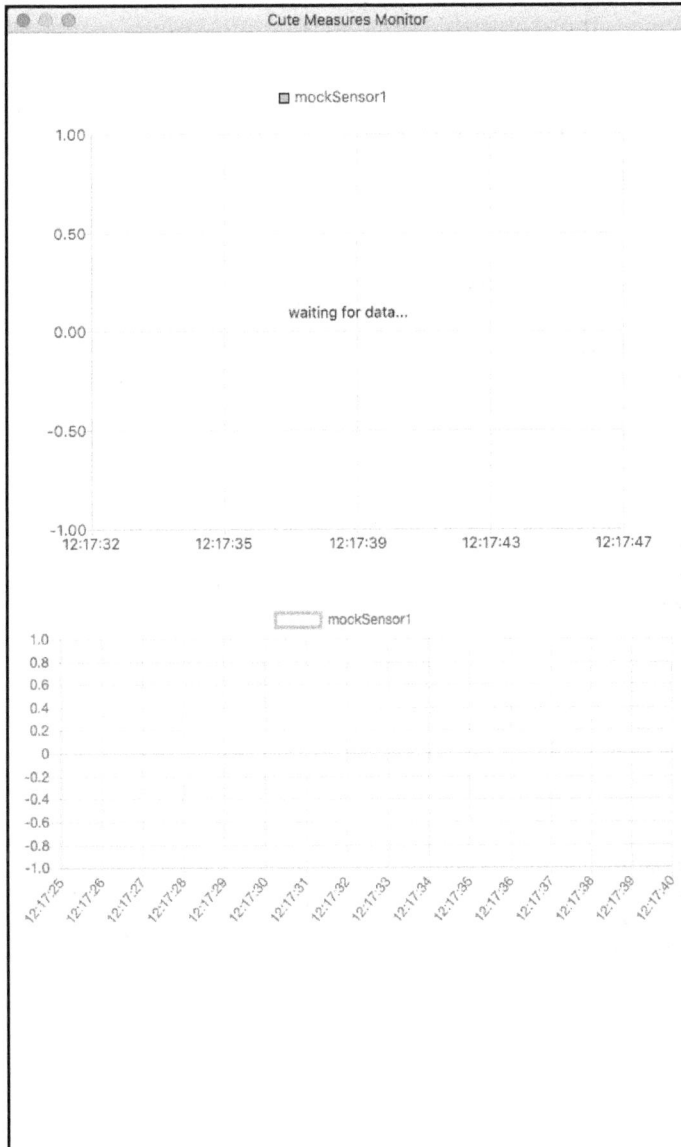

Given how the API of `Chart.js` works, to update the chart with the sensor data, we will need to add two methods, one that removes the first point in the dataset (we'll call it `removeData`) and one that adds a new point at the end of the dataset (let's call it `addData`), and then call the `update` function to refresh the drawing. We will be invoking these two methods in the `callback` function that is triggered every time `readingsProcessed` is fired. In `QtWebChannel`, the arguments of `readingsProcessed` can be accessed through the `arguments` variable. Here is the updated code:

```
<!--ReadingsChartJS.html-->
...
var chart = new Chart(ctx, {
    ...
});

function addData(chart, label, data) {
    chart.data.labels.push(label);
    chart.data.datasets.forEach((dataset) => {
        dataset.data.push(data);
    });
    chart.update();
}

function removeData(chart) {
    chart.data.labels.shift();
    chart.data.datasets.forEach((dataset) => {
        dataset.data.shift();
    });
    chart.update();
}

new QWebChannel(qt.webChannelTransport, function(channel) {
    window.receiverChannel = channel.objects.receiverChannel;

    receiverChannel.readingsProcessed.connect(function() {
        if (arguments[0][0]) {
            removeData(chart);
            addData(chart, arguments[0][0]["timestamp"],
arguments[0][0]["value"]);
        }
    });
});
</script>
</html>
```

Note how the `QVariantList` returned by `readingsProcessed` is automatically converted to a `JavaScript` object (`arguments[0]`), as it happens in QML.

If you now run `cmmonitor`, you should not see the chart updating since `cmbroadcast` is not running. However, when you first run `cmbroadcast` (which should be running the HTTP `BroadcasterChannel` as shown in the previous sections) and then run `cmmonitor`, you'll see both the QML chart and the HTML5 chart updating as shown in the screenshot, possibly at slightly different speeds:

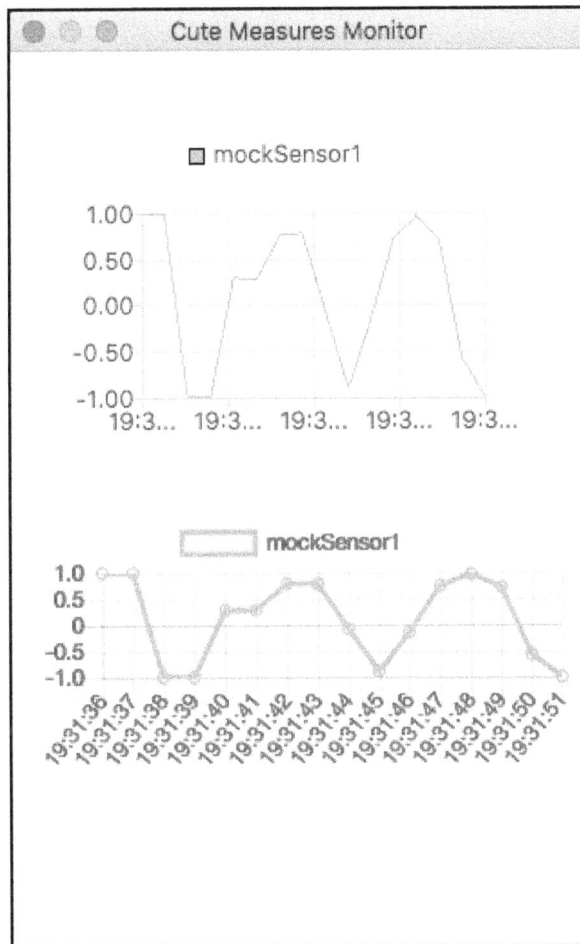

The style of the two components is still a little different, feel free to tweak either of them so that they become more similar.

Summary

In this chapter, we built upon the work we did in Chapters 7, *Sendinging Sensor Readings to a Device with a Non-UI App,* and Chapter 30, *Building a Mobile Dashboard to Display Real-Time Sensor Data,* by augmenting our sensor dashboard application with two core features:

- Support for the HTTP channel to sensor data transmission
- Use of web technology to create an alternative charting UI

By doing this, we engaged with several new Qt modules and APIs — Qt Network, QtWebEngine, and QtWebChannel — and also made good use of the third-party QHttp project.

This chapter has shown you how Qt, while still not being a viable choice for implementing UIs in the browser (but things are changing, see Appendix *Additional and Upcoming Qt Features* for that), has got a firm foot in the web world, and you can take advantage of it to cover many different requirements.

32
Additional and Upcoming Qt Features

By now, you should have a grasp of Qt's features and API's extent. Given the limited breadth of this book, I did not have a chance to introduce you to all the currently available and upcoming Qt APIs. I chose only those APIs that seemed the most relevant because of either their widespread usage or their novelty. In this section, I will briefly introduce you to other current Qt APIs that you may need for your daily work, and to the new and upcoming Qt features beyond what is provided by Qt 5.9 **Long Term Support** (**LTS**).

For an overview of all the modules available for each version, check out `https://doc.qt.io/qt-5.9/qtmodules.html`, substituting the appropriate minor version. Alongside general-purpose modules, you will find all sorts of specialty modules, which are either mostly interesting for specific kinds of applications, or only supported on a limited number of platforms.

Also, keep in mind that there are other Packt titles and third-party resources that provide coverage and sample projects for some of the technologies mentioned in the coming sections.

Additional Qt features in 5.9 LTS

Among the technologies we mentioned, the **Qt SQL** module (`https://doc.qt.io/qt-5.9/qtsql-index.html`) is most likely something you will deal with, or at least consider, when looking for a persistence mechanism or connecting with already-existing databases. It provides drivers for different database technologies. A list is available on `http://doc.qt.io/qt-5.9/sql-driver.html`. Qt Quick also provides an integrated **local storage** mechanism, similar to what you find in modern web browsers, based on SQLite; for more details on Qt Quick, refer to `http://doc.qt.io/qt-5.9/qtquick-localstorage-qmlmodule.html`.

Another, more lightweight, option to consider when in need of persisting data is the **QSettings** class (`http://doc.qt.io/qt-5.9/qsettings.html`—also available in QML), which provides file-based, platform-specific backends. It is often a valid choice to retain local configuration settings specified by the user.

Qt also provides first-class **multithreading** facilities. These are available through a few different APIs, which cater for both low-level and high-level control. Qt Concurrent (`https://doc.qt.io/qt-5.9/qtconcurrent-index.html`) provides a high-level API, whereas a few Qt Core classes can be used for more fine-grained control. For a complete overview and comparison, check out `http://doc.qt.io/qt-5.9/threads-technologies.html`.

When planning your application architecture or specific components, you may find it helpful to conceptualize some aspects in terms of **Finite State Machines** (**FSMs**). Qt provides APIs for FSMs in C++ and QML/JS; check out more details on these at `http://doc.qt.io/qt-5.9/statemachine-api.html`. Starting with Qt 5.8, it also supports **SCXML**-based FSM specifications, which can be parsed to generate the corresponding C++ or QML/JS code; check out more details on these at `https://doc.qt.io/qt-5.9/qtscxml-index.html`.

The Qt Positioning and **Qt Location** modules (`https://doc.qt.io/qt-5.9/qtlocation-index.html`) provide a set of classes for both retrieving and manipulating position data and other geographic entities and for displaying map data, with an emphasis on QML integration.

To write dynamic UIs, another technology worth exploring is **Qt Quick's animations and transitions** (`http://doc.qt.io/qt-5.9/qtquick-statesanimations-animations.html`). Thanks to the power of QML property bindings and the OpenGL backend, you will be able to create more complex animations of shape, color, and many other kinds of properties in no time. A very good introduction to what can be achieved with Qt Quick animations is provided by the QML Book at `https://qmlbook.github.io/en/ch05/index.html#animations`.

Qt Quick Controls 2 also supports a *styling* mechanism (`https://doc.qt.io/qt-5.9/qtquickcontrols2-styles.html`) that helps you achieve platform-dependent or completely customized looks easily.

Besides these features, there are also a few technicalities we didn't have time to explore in the book, including how to provide extension capabilities to your applications by creating plugins (`http://doc.qt.io/qt-5.9/plugins-howto.html`) and a few more. As usual, the official Qt documentation is your best friend.

New and upcoming Qt features

Although Qt 5.9 LTS focused on consolidating existing features and bugfixes by providing a solid and up-to-date development platform, subsequent Qt versions make it possible to take advantage of a cutting-edge functionality. Recently, the expanding markets of **In-Vehicle Infotainment** (**IVI**) and digital cockpits, industrial automation, and the **Internet of Things** (**IoT**) have steered many areas of development. Beyond the already-existing generic offering for application development and embedded devices, developers, and businesses have now access to specific commercial feature bundles for their industry of choice, including Qt for **Automotive** (`https://www.qt.io/qt-in-automotive`) and Qt for **Automation** (`https://www.qt.io/qt-in-automation/`).

Among the most notable recent additions to the Qt distribution are a couple of enhancements on the UI side. **Qt Quick Controls 2** now provides a style called *Imagine* with out-of-the-box support for Controls graphic assets (http://doc.qt.io/qt-5/qtquickcontrols2-imagine.html). This feature makes it really easy to export assets for use in Qt Quick UIs from design programs, such as the Adobe Suite or Sketch. Another enhancement in the Qt Quick world is the ability to define arbitrary shapes simply using QML types (refer to https://doc.qt.io/qt-5/qtquick-shapes-example.html). When it comes to multitouch interaction and gestures, the Qt Quick Pointer Handlers (http://doc.qt.io/qt-5/qtquickhandlers-index.html) promise great improvements over previously available solutions. The addition of the Qt 3D Studio graphical tool and runtime makes it easier to create and embed 3D content, with support for the Qt 3D module being added. A new platform plugin makes it possible to stream graphics content in a browser via WebGL (http://blog.qt.io/blog/2017/07/07/qt-webgl-streaming-merged/), and a web assembly platform plugin is also in the works.

In terms of connectivity and I/O, Qt **MQTT** (http://doc.qt.io/QtMQTT/index.html) and Qt Remote Objects (a package for high-level interprocess communication available at https://doc.qt.io/qt-5/qtremoteobjects-index.html, already in 5.9 as a technical preview) provide further options particularly suited for embedded distributed applications.

Finally, the Qt Speech module (https://doc.qt.io/qt-5/qtspeech-index.html, currently in technical preview) will provide a common frontend for open source and commercial text-to-speech (TTS) and speech-to-text (STT or ASR) solutions. TTS support is already available for some backends on selected platforms.

Ensure that you check out the official blog of The Qt Company (http://blog.qt.io) to keep up to date with the new features.

Bibliography

This Learning Path combines some of the best that Packt has to offer in one complete, curated package. It includes content from the following Packt products:

- *Learn Qt 5*, Nicholas Sherriff
- *Mastering QT 5*, Guillaume Lazar, Robin Penea
- *Qt 5 Projects*, Marco Piccolino

Index

Runtime Type Information (RTTI) 366

www.ingramcontent.com/pod-product-compliance
Lightning Source LLC
Chambersburg PA
CBHW081206220326
41598CB00037B/6689